Whitman Encyclopedia of Obsolete Paper Money

Whitman Encyclopedia of Obsolete Paper Money

Notes Issued by United States Banks, 1782–1866

Q. David Bowers

States, districts, and territories covered in this series, in order:

Connecticut, Maine, New Hampshire, Massachusetts, Rhode Island, Vermont, Florida, Georgia, South Carolina, North Carolina, Alabama, Arkansas, Kentucky, Louisiana, Mississippi, Tennessee, Texas, Delaware, District of Columbia, Maryland, Virginia, New Jersey, Pennsylvania, New York, Illinois, Indiana, Michigan, Ohio, Iowa, Kansas, Minnesota, Missouri, Nebraska, Utah, and Wisconsin

Also see volume 1, *An Introduction for Collectors and Historians.*

For news (or announcements) and more information, refer to www.Whitman.com.

Volume 3

New England Region, Part 2

Massachusetts, Book 1

From Abbington to Greenfield

Edited by C. John Ferreri

Whitman Publishing, LLC
PUBLISHING SINCE 1934
www.whitman.com

WHITMAN ENCYCLOPEDIA OF OBSOLETE PAPER MONEY

NOTES ISSUED BY UNITED STATES BANKS, 1782–1866

VOLUME 3: NEW ENGLAND REGION, PART 2

MASSACHUSETTS, BOOK 1

Whitman Publishing, LLC
PUBLISHING SINCE 1934
www.whitman.com

3101 Clairmont Road • Suite G • Atlanta, GA 30329

ISBN: 0794842925
Printed in China

If you have new information about any banks or notes listed in this volume, contact Whitman Publishing, Attn: Obsolete Paper Money, 3101 Clairmont Road, Suite G, Atlanta, GA 30329.

OCG™ COLLECTING GUIDE

WHITMAN®

Contents

Foreword

by Anne E. Bentley, Curator, Massachusetts Historical Society

Prolific author Q. David Bowers's latest project, the *Whitman Encyclopedia of Obsolete Paper Money,* truly embodies the very definition of the word *encyclopedia:* a book, or set of books, covering all branches of knowledge or all aspects of one subject—in this case, the wonderfully decorative and colorful currency issued by American banks from 1782 to 1866.

As a fledgling numismatist back in the early 1980s, facing the task of re-cataloging the obsolete currency in the collections of the Massachusetts Historical Society, my first reference was David C. Wismer's *The Obsolete Bank Notes of New England,* a descriptive catalog that served its purpose . . . just. In 1988 I welcomed James A. Haxby's four-volume set, the *Standard Catalog of United States Obsolete Bank Notes, 1782–1866,* with its miniature half-tone reproductions and new numbering system. It was a terrific step forward in reference works on the subject.

Then Dave Bowers and Whitman Publishing joined forces in 2006 to produce *Obsolete Paper Money Issued by Banks in the United States 1782–1866,* which gave us an impressively comprehensive overview of the banking and paper-money history of that period—along with illustrations that spoiled me forever for anything less than digital, high-resolution imagery as a reference tool.

Now, I am delighted to have been asked to play a role in a new and eagerly awaited series, the *Whitman Encyclopedia of Obsolete Paper Money.*

Massachusetts issued her first paper notes in 1690 to pay soldiers involved in the failed Phips Expedition to take Quebec. From that time to the institution of a federal currency, Massachusetts was an enthusiastic partner in the production and circulation of paper notes of all descriptions—the better to support her very active role as a center of commerce, especially during the early 19th century. In this time period the banking system was ripe for exploitation by greedy and unscrupulous characters. The sheer volume of Massachusetts obsolete bank notes stamped "counterfeit" or "spurious" bears witness to that fact. Even Newburyport native Jacob Perkins, with his Patent Stereotype Steel Plate, couldn't stem the tide of fraudulent issues. The Panic of 1837 saw many of the larger banks in the state fail during the ensuing depression that lasted until 1844, leaving us with the notes that we collect so enthusiastically today.

The Massachusetts Historical Society's obsolete section of paper currency spans from Connecticut to Tennessee, with the larger sections pertaining to Massachusetts and New York. I confess that the wonderfully engraved vignettes provide our chief purpose in using them as illustrations in exhibitions and online features. From village greens to portraits to whaling scenes, these exquisite miniature views are fascinating to examine, detailed, and sometimes puzzling. For example, why did the Harvard Bank choose to place an engraved copy of the portrait that the Historical Society commissioned of our benefactor Thomas Dowse on its 1861 $1 note? He was neither an officer of the bank nor an elected official—yet there he is, seated in the library he donated to us in 1856.

As you examine these pages with their vivid illustrations, you'll find a host of interesting stories about the banks, their notes, and the era they represent. This encyclopedic series is designed not just for specialists and collectors of paper currency, but also for all who enjoy learning more about various aspects of our nation's financial history, as well as for those of us who are entrusted with the cataloging and care of such material. Gentle Reader, you hold in your hands a treasure trove of information and images to enjoy at your leisure. Now if you'll excuse me, I'm off to add the Whitman numbers to our catalog records. . . .

—Boston, Massachusetts

Credits and Acknowledgements

For global and general credits for the *Whitman Encyclopedia of Obsolete Paper Money,* see volume 1. For volume 3's study of Massachusetts, specific credit goes to:

American Bank Note Co.; American Numismatic Association; American Numismatic Society; Irene Axelrod; Georgia Barnhill; Anne E. Bentley; Steve Blum; Wynn Bowers; Karen Bridges; Mark Carter; Ashley Clark; Rich Deming; Thomas Denly; Richard Doty; C. John Ferreri; Jeffrey M. Feuerman; Roberta French; Bruce Hagen; James A. Haxby; Heritage Auctions; Danielle Hill; Wayne Homren; Peter Huntoon; Christine Karstedt; Michael Keane; Kevin Lafond; Littleton Coin Co.; Massachusetts Historical Society; Don Munro; Eric P. Newman; Steve Noyes; Gary Parietti; Phillips Library at the Peabody-Essex Museum; Michael Rocco; Smithsonian Institution; Stack's Bowers Galleries; David M. Sundman; John and Nancy Wilson.

Valuations editors for volume 3: C. John Ferreri, Bruce Hagen, John Rowe, and Peter Treglia.

Image Credits

AAS	American Antiquarian Society, Worcester, Massachusetts
ABNCo	American Bank Note Co. Archives
ANS	American Numismatic Society, New York City, New York
BC	Bob Casper
CC	Caine Collection
CJF	C. John Ferreri Collection
HA	Heritage Auction Archives
HS	Hugh Shull Collection
HSPA	Historical Society of Pennsylvania, Philadelphia, Pennsylvania
JF	Jeffrey M. Feuerman Collection
MC	Mark Carter Collection
MHS	Massachusetts Historical Society, Boston, Massachusetts
MK	Michael Keane Collection
MR	Michael Rocco Collection
NJW	Nancy and John Wilson Collection
PEM	Peabody-Essex Museum, Salem, Massachusetts
QDB	Q. David Bowers Archives
RD	Rich Deming Collection
RMS	R.M. Smythe Collection
SBG	Stack's Bowers Galleries
SI	Smithsonian Institution, National Numismatic Collection
SN	Steve Noyes Collection
TD	Tom Denly Archives

How to Use This Book

When considering the purchase or sale of a note, two main considerations are grade and price. Beyond that, there are other aspects that are important in study and set one note apart from another. In certain aspects the study of notes is different from that of coins. Notes that are spurious (not official) can have significant value, as can counterfeits of standard notes. In some instances, a note in Extremely Fine-40 (EF-40) grade can be more valuable than an Uncirculated or unused note.

This guide explains the different aspects of typical bank listings in this book—covering the state of Massachusetts. Volume 1 of this series contains a thoroughly detailed study of the entire field of obsolete state bank notes issued from 1782 to 1866, including a glossary of bank-note engravers, information on how currency was designed, printed, and distributed, and much more. If read even casually, Volume 1 will set you on your way to becoming an expert. In the meantime, "How to Use This Book" will explain the current listings in the volume at hand.

Types of Notes

There are several classes of collectible notes in this series. Their status affects their collectability and desirability.

Valid Issues

Valid issues are notes that were printed from plates made by skilled engravers and produced by bank-note companies or other authorized sources. In their time, they were paid out at face value by banks. Such bills were often later redeemed for face value and replaced by new issues. If a bank failed and its notes could not be redeemed, today its notes are still considered to be valid issues by collectors. Valid notes form the main focus of collecting obsolete currency.

A valid issue from the North River Banking Co., New York.

Non-Valid Issues

These exist in several categories:

Counterfeit notes: Illegally issued notes from false plates that imitated genuine bills. They are collectible as "fillers" in some instances but generally sell for low prices. They are collectible mainly as curiosities.

Note counterfeited to be passed as an issue from the Bank of Cumberland, Maine.

Raised notes: It was a common deceptive practice to raise the value of a low-denomination note to a higher one by chemically removing the counters (as they are called) or denomination ornaments and altering them to read as a higher value. Such notes have nominal values as collectibles today.

Original note of the Merchants & Manufacturers Bank.

Raised note.

Altered notes: Notes that were valid or spurious when first printed but then fell into the hands of criminals who altered them. When a bank failed, its notes became worthless and could not be redeemed for face value. There was a market for such, often at 2 percent or 3 percent of face value. Criminals bought them and, by the use of chemicals, removed certain information such as the town, state, and sometimes even the name of the bank. New information was then printed in the blank spaces. As an example, quantities of worthless $10 notes of the Egg Harbor Bank, Egg Harbor, New Jersey, were altered to appear as $10 notes of the active and strong Valley Bank, Hillsborough, New Hampshire. Altered notes are collectible, but their values are considerably less than the genuine.

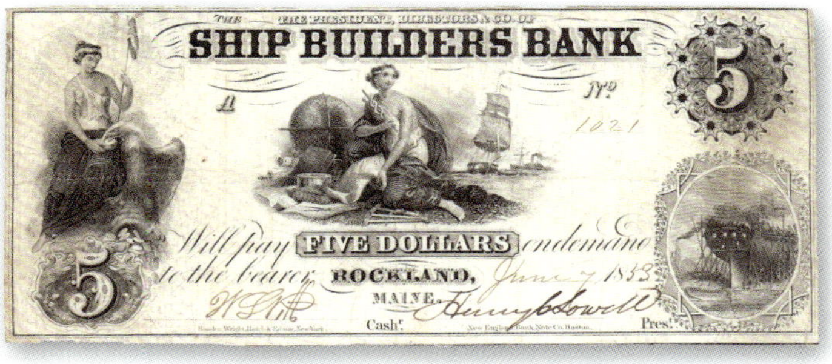

Original note of the Ship Builders Bank.

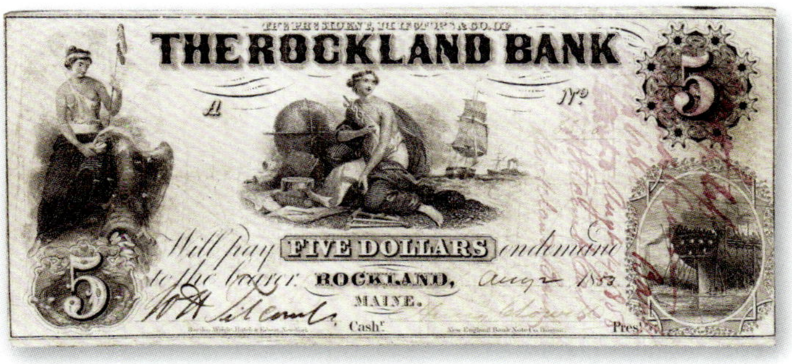

Altered note.

Spurious Issues

Spurious issues are notes from established engravers and printers that were delivered to banks that never opened their doors or to fraudsters who issued notes bearing the names of banks that never existed. Often these have fascinating stories. These are a basic part of collecting and in many instances are valued for as much as, or higher than, valid issues.

In this text Spurious issues are located in one of two places—under Valid Issues if the bank as a whole never opened or was fraudulently run, but the notes were genuinely printed, or under Non-Valid issues if notes from a genuine bank were taken into the hands of fraudsters and illegally distributed in a similar fashion to other Non-Valid notes such as counterfeits and altered notes.

Spurious note from a non-existent bank in a non-existent town. Fraudsters intended to alter it to represent the BOSTON bank of the same name.

Signed and Issued Notes

Banks typically received notes from the printer in sheets, most often a four-subject sheet bearing one to four denominations. Certain features needed to be added once the notes were received. Law cases affirmed that a bill was monetized only after the cashier affixed his signature. It was standard practice in small banks for the cashier to prepare the sheets in advance and then sign them only when the sheets were cut apart and ready to be issued. These features were added to prepare a note for distribution:

Date: Each note needed to bear a year, month, and day of when it was issued. Some notes had printed dates, such as *Jany 1st, 1854*, and did not require hand entry. Sometimes these referred to the charter date or were an annual date. It was not unusual for a note to be issued later than the date shown. Accordingly, if a note with a printed date of *Jany 1st, 1854*, was signed by cashier John Doe, who was named to that office on May 6, 1856, this was not an extraordinary situation. Many other notes had the number partially printed, such as 18__ or 185_, with the remainder to be inked in.

Partially printed date with the remainder inked in by hand.

Serial number: Serial numbers were usually added by hand in ink. Some notes had the same serial number twice on a note. The combination of the serial number, the date, and the plate letter defines a note as one of a kind.

To cut down on the work involved, serial-number sequences were often started anew when the date changed. This kept the numbers low. Unlike the situation for federal paper money, it is not unusual for an obsolete note to have a serial number below 100. Very few were higher than four digits. Sometimes colored ink was used for serial numbers. Certain notes of larger banks have the serial numbers printed by machine, but these are unusual.

Printed serial number.

President's signature: The primary duty of the president was to conduct meetings of the board of directors and the annual meeting of stockholders. Many directors lived at a distance from the bank and visited it infrequently. Accordingly, it was the custom of the president to sign large quantities of notes far in advance. The president of a small bank usually received a nominal salary, say $100 or $200 per year, or none at all.

Cashier's signature on the left. President's signature on the right.

Cashier's signature: The cashier was the person in charge. Often, for small banks, he was the only employee. It was not unusual for banks in small villages to be kept in the house of the cashier or, if the bank had its own building, for the cashier and his family to live on the premises. Security systems usually consisted only of locks and bolts. The cashier could keep watch at all times, including when the bank was closed.

The cashier was the highest-paid person, often $1,000 per year, more or less. The cashier opened the bank and closed it, kept the books, and took charge of money receipts and payments. Loans were usually arranged with another person on hand, such as one or two directors. Loans were given on "discount days," usually one or two days a week. This made it easier for one or more directors to attend. The discount day schedule was published in local papers. When the cashier affixed his signature to a note, it was officially monetized. That way, if notes were stolen but lacked the signature, the bank could simply declare them to be worthless.

Cashier's signature *D. Holmes*.

Notes in Circulation

Most bills circulated at face value locally or regionally. A $10 bill issued in New Haven, Connecticut, by a sound bank would be received at par with a slight discount for handling in Providence, Boston, or New York City. In Pittsburgh, Richmond, or another distant place, it would be taken in at a discount. Many earned extra profits by selling notes at a discount to brokers or runners who put them into circulation in distant places. The Hillsborough Bank of Amherst, New Hampshire, shipped bundles of notes to Marietta, Ohio, where they were placed into circulation easily. Storekeepers would buy them at a discount. The recipients would spend them, as would others. Hardly anyone went back to New Hampshire to exchange them for coins. Brokers in New York City handled large quantities of discounted notes.

Printed bank-note reporters and counterfeit detectors, as they were called, were published in many forms. These usually told of new counterfeits as well as of banks that had failed or were in financial difficulty. Long lists were presented by state, town, and bank, rating the notes and stating the discount from par at which banks and merchants should be valued.

Grading of Notes

There are no hard and fast rules for grading obsolete currency. Interpretations can vary, sometimes widely. Most old-time dealers and experienced auction houses tend to be more conservative than many who list in Internet sales or who are otherwise not part of the profession. A "Fine" note to one dealer may be another's "Very Fine." Similar to the situation for coins, grading has become looser over the years. A bill bought in the 1960s as Fine will easily be Very Fine today. Years ago, a bill with even a slight trace of a fold or crease was automatically excluded from the Uncirculated category. Today, bills described as such can have these traces, and, perhaps, one without such traces would be given a loftier designation such as Choice Uncirculated or Gem Uncirculated. And so it goes. The methodology is not as consistent or as well developed as is the grading of coins. Two commercial grading services are prominent in grading notes. PCGS Currency, once a part of the Professional Coin Grading Service but now independently owned, and PMG (Paper Money Grading), a division of the Numismatic Guaranty Corporation, have found wide acceptance in the marketplace. As of today they have published no standards, but they seem to more or less follow the guidelines given below.

These categories reflect the author's observations of current grading methods by many dealers and collectors. Beginning in the early 21st century, numbers have been attached to grades by some sellers based on the American Numismatic Association Grading Standards for United States Coins. However, as bills were printed, not minted, the term "Mint State" is not used for paper money.

Grading System

Choice or Gem Uncirculated

Unc-63 and 64 (Choice), Unc-65 (Gem).

A crisp, bright bill with no evidence of creases, folds, or stains. Tom Denly commented in 2004: "I consider centering to be a most important part of grade. For instance, a poorly centered note possibly cut into the design can never be called Gem or even Choice, no matter how nice it otherwise is." Most notes in this category are remainders.

Uncirculated

Unc-60.

A new, never circulated bill, but perhaps with slight evidences of a fold, a crease, or smudges from handling (presumably by bank officers). If part of the margin is trimmed away, this should be mentioned, but often is not. Most notes in this category are remainders.

About Uncirculated

AU-53, 55, and 58.

A bright, attractive note, with some creases, folds, or light discoloration, but with only slight evidences of use in commerce or, in the case of remainders, numismatic or bank handling. If signed and issued for circulation, this is a top-of-the-line grade in great demand.

Extremely Fine

EF-40 and 45.

Bright and attractive but with some slight stains or discoloration, perhaps with a pinhole or two or some small defect. Overall excellent appearance. A bill in this grade saw limited service in circulation.

Very Fine

VF-20 and 30.

This is a widely used grade for a "nice" note, worn but with nice features. Such a bill may be somewhat faded, but the printing and vignettes will be clear and with an attractive overall appearance. There may be an edge chip or two or perhaps a tiny piece off of a corner (but not into the printed part of the note). As most bank tellers and users were right-handed, the right side of a note usually has some discoloration from everyday handling.

Fine

Fine-12.

A note with even more wear, often limp or flimsy from extended use in commerce, but with all printed areas intact and most of them sharply defined. May be stained or discolored in areas.

Very Good

VG-8.

Well circulated, usually with some problems, tears, perhaps a small piece missing from the border, etc. Flimsy and often faded or discolored.

Good

G-4.

Extensively circulated and with evidence of such, including small tears, perhaps edge pieces missing, areas of the printing and vignettes indistinct, and, often, old writing on the face of the note.

Poor, Fair, and About Good

Poor-1, Fair-2, AG-3.

Notes that have been in circulation for a very long time, now with ragged edges or pieces missing and often with significant areas of the note faded or otherwise indiscernible. A filler note. There are quite a few very early bills from the late 18th and early 19th century for which these grades may represent the finest known.

Grade as a Determinant of Value

Remainder notes: Surprise! In the field of bank notes, a well-worn example is often worth more than an Uncirculated bill of the same variety! However, the explanation is simple: most Uncirculated bills are remainders that were never distributed. Most have no officers' signatures. Years after certain banks closed, large quantities of their unissued notes became available. In most instances, a nice Very Fine bill of the same denomination and design, signed and serially numbered, is worth more. Remainder notes of this kind are designated as Unc-Rem. A signed and dated Uncirculated note is designated as Unc-S&D.

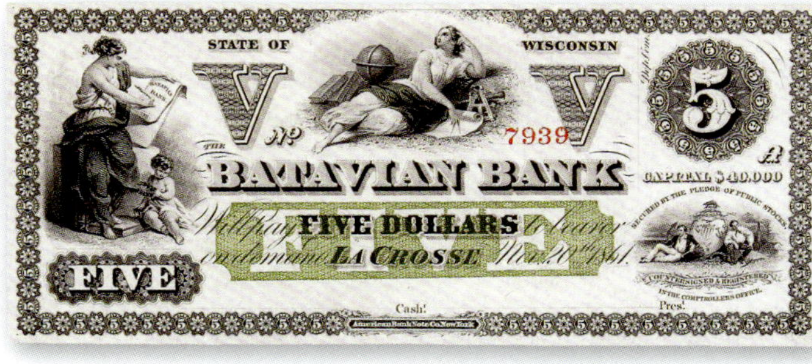

An Uncirculated remainder note.

Circulated notes: Among signed and numbered notes, higher-grade examples are more desirable than those in lower levels of preservation. In all instances, an About Uncirculated bill is worth more than an Extremely Fine one, and an EF is worth more than a Very Fine, and on down the line. Among the most desirable of circulated notes are those that are serially numbered, dated, and signed in ink by the cashier and president and which are in a high grade today.

A signed, dated, circulated note.

Cancelled notes: When worn notes were redeemed to be exchanged for others, banks often destroyed them. In many instances, however, they were saved but "canceled" to prevent them from being placed into circulation again. Several small, circular punch holes will either not affect the value of a note or will affect it only slightly, unless uncancelled notes are readily available. Large holes, notches cut out from the border, signatures cut off, and other cancellations that are unattractive are viewed negatively, as are stamped overprints, such as the common WORTHLESS and COUNTERFEIT.

A note cancelled to prevent further circulation.

Proof notes: Proof notes are special printings on special paper or light card stock, are usually found Uncirculated, and can be very valuable, if they are contemporary (made in the 19th century). Modern Proof reprints are worth varying lesser amounts. Beware of scanned or photographic modern copies.

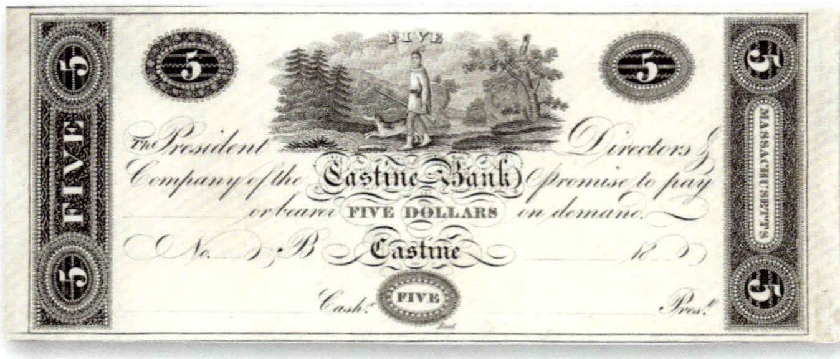

A Proof note, without signatures, printed on special stock.

Valuation of Notes

Explanation of Values

Values assigned to notes in given grades have been compiled by consulting with dealers and collectors and by studying listed prices and auction results. Unlike coins, which often have values determined by "bid" prices and, for some such as gold, trade on close margins, the valuation of paper currency is much more subjective. In a way, the pricing can be compared to that in the fields of tokens and medals.

Many notes are infrequently traded. This is especially true for rare early issues. Sometimes, years can elapse between offerings. In such instances the values here are "educated guesses." Actual sale results such as an offering at auction may differ widely. For that reason values in this book should be considered as estimates compiled at the time of publication. Although the future is unknown, in past decades the price trends have been upward. Many notes valued at $100 a decade ago may be valued at $125 to $175 or more now. Few if any valid-issue notes have decreased in value. When contemplating a purchase or sale it is recommended that you check with experts and other sources for current values.

Even for common remainder notes and for certain common circulated bills in a given grade, prices can vary in the same time frame. One note might be priced at $200, another at $175, and a third at $250. It may be worthwhile to say that the same variations are seen in many other collectibles markets—such as Currier & Ives prints, postcards, colonial coins, ancient coins, antique furniture, tokens and medals, and more. The point here is that federal coins of the past 200 years are often quite common, trade frequently, and have bid and ask prices—a situation not comparable to other collectible specialties as mentioned.

To aid in current valuation we recommend subscribing to publications about paper money and checking auction and sale listings, often available on the Internet.

If a long-sought rarity is offered, many if not most experienced dealers and collectors will "reach" for it. A rarity listed for $1,000 may be a good buy for $2,000 if it is the only one to be offered in recent years.

With some experience, you will get a grasp for pricing—just as collectors of tokens, medals, prints, and other things have. What starts as being esoteric will in time become familiar.

Factors Affecting Values

Grade or condition: Among notes that were signed, numbered, dated, and placed into circulation, the higher the grade, the more valuable the note is. Uncirculated notes or remainders can be worth less than a circulated signed note.

Location: Notes of certain states or territories can be worth a premium. Western notes of a given rarity, such as from Utah, Kansas Terrritory, or Arkansas can be worth more than notes from New York, Pennsylvania, or New Jersey.

Rarity: In a given series, a rare note is worth more a common one.

Demand and popularity: Notes of certain towns and states can be worth more if there are more collectors desiring to buy them. Notes from Florida are more widely collected than are those of Vermont. Accordingly, a note of a given rarity can be worth more if from Florida. Such popularity may change over a period of time. If two or three well-financed buyers each seek to build a collection of a state, there will be great competition for rarities, and prices will be much higher than if this competition were not present. In addition, the publication of a new reference work on a particular state or category can serve to increase the number of people desiring such notes.

Denomination: Within a given rarity, an unusual denomination such as $4, $6, $7, $8, or $9 will be worth more than a $1, $2, $3, $5, $10, or $20 (these being the most often seen). On their own, $3 notes have always attracted a following; once common in circulation, the denomination is considered unusual today. It has not been used since the federal government began issuing notes in quantity in 1861, despite being very popular with state-chartered banks. $50 and $100 notes are scarce for most banks, and with relatively few exceptions, $500 and $1,000 notes are great rarities.

Vignette topic: The illustration or vignette of a note can add value. A Connecticut note showing Iranistan, the palatial home of P.T. Barnum, or "the Battle of the Frogs" is worth more than one showing a train or buildings. Notes showing Santa Claus are extremely popular and often sell for much more than what a comparable-rarity bill of a miscellaneous subject might command.

"Battle of the Frogs."

Santa Claus at upper left.

Proofs: Proof notes printed on special paper and intended as samples or for reference are usually found in Uncirculated preservation and will sell for many multiples of the price of common remainder notes.

Market and economic trends: The general market for obsolete paper money has been quite strong in recent decades. However, it was rather quiet before then. Market strength is based on the number of buyers at a given time and how much money they have to spend.

Imaging of Notes

Given their age and extensive circulation, obsolete bank notes are sometimes found with a high level of wear and tear. Within this encyclopedia, some images have been digitally enhanced to mitigate the effects of rust, water damage, stains, age, circulation wear, color fading, and other environmental stresses. Where necessary, they have been conceptually restored to more closely resemble their original form in an attempt to aid collectors and historians in identifying and analyzing the various issues, vignettes, engravings, and styles of the bank notes.

Printed Features of Note Designs

A typical note includes these printed features:

Name of bank: The name of the bank is usually the most prominently printed figure and can be found either high on the center of the note face or in a position about half way down. New Haven Bank, Derby Bank, Cochituate Bank, Bank of Commerce, Warner Bank, and Butchers and Drovers Bank are examples. Such titles often reflect the location of the bank, an industry such as farming or manufacturing, a geographical feature such as an ocean or river, or a proper name from history. Among the latter there are banks named Franklin, Washington, Lafayette, and Indian names such as Amoskeag, Oneida, Quinnipiack, and Mohawk. At any given time there was only one bank of a certain name in operation in a given state.

Location of bank: Every note gives the town and state. The town often appears near the bank name or is sometimes tagged on to it, such as the Tradesmens Bank of New Haven. The name of the state often appears away from the town name, perhaps in the field of the note or at a border.

Denomination: This is the face value of a note. The most popular values were $1, $2, $3, $5, and $10 among the lower denominations and were made in the largest quantities. $20, $50, and S100 values were made in smaller quantities. Only a few banks issued $500 or $1,000 notes. There are also fractional notes such as 25¢, 50¢, and 75¢ in existence, issued by banks as part of a series that included higher denominations. The more times a denomination was printed on a note, the harder it was to alter by raising. Many notes have the denomination given dozens of times in micro-letters in addition to larger digits. Odd-value notes such as $1.25, $1.50, $1.75, $4, and $6 to $9 were issued by a few banks.

Scattered small notes denominated in cents were sometimes issued, usually but not always privately, in times of economic distress and are called scrip. Scrip notes were usually made by local printers. They are not studied herein.

Denomination counters: While the denominations of many notes, especially early ones, were lettered or in script, most bills after about 1810 had the value as a number surrounded with an oval, circle, or fancy engraving. These are referred to as counters. Volume 1 gives many examples.

Main vignette: Most notes have a large vignette at the center or to one side extending to the center. These are often scenic in nature—a seated figure, laborers at work, a train and cars, capitols and commercial buildings, figures from mythology, seascapes, and more. After 1820 vignettes became increasingly ornate.

Other vignettes: Most notes also had two or more smaller vignettes. Portraits of people ranging from well-known, such as a national president, to obscure, such as a bank president, were popular. Others show standing or seated figures, people in various activities, etc. Medallion vignettes reproduce medals, cameos, or plaques by means of a medal-ruling machine.

Ornaments and borders: Various geometric figures and engraved ornaments add to the complexity of many notes, as do ornamental borders.

Seals and arms: State arms, seals stating that a note was backed by securities or liens on real estate, etc., were added to many notes.

The state arms of Connecticut can be seen in the upper left corner.

Plate letter: It was common practice to assign a letter such as A, B, or C to the face of a note. A sheet of four notes might include, as an example, $1-$1-$1-$2. The three $1 notes would bear letters A, B, and C, and the $2 note would start again with A.

Engraver's imprint: The name of the bank-note printing company was nearly always stated in the face, usually in tiny letters at the bottom border but sometimes elsewhere. On some occasions ornamental vignettes were signed in micro-letters by engravers.

Place of redemption: While most bank notes could be redeemed over the counter of the banks that issued them, some others gave distant places where they could be redeemed, as at an office in another state, often in New York City. Such notes were frequently of questionable value.

Time of redemption: Most notes could be redeemed on demand, but many had a printed inscription stating that they could be redeemed only at a specified time later than the date on the note—six months, a year, or some other interval. Later-payment bills are called post notes, a term printed on some of them. Confederate States of America notes were redeemable two years after a peace treaty was signed with the United States, which, of course, never happened.

Overprints: Many notes, especially those after the 1820s, have overprints in color. These often give the denomination, such as ONE, FIVE, or TWENTY. Some later notes have grillwork, the denomination in micro-printing, or other features added in panels of color printing. On some the entire face can be overprinted in color.

Backs of notes: With only scattered exceptions, the backs of notes have not been discussed in reference books or auction catalogs. Hence, there are many notes listed in this book that have ornate backs not described.

Security features: Security features to deter counterfeiting or altering are seen on many notes. The most common is the "Canada green" or "Patent Green Tint" used on notes of Rawdon, Wright, Hatch & Edson in 1857 and by the American Bank Note Co. from 1858 onward. This color was said to deter copying by photographic means. Jacob Perkins's Patented Stereotype Steel Plate (PSSP) used micro-lettering to deter counterfeiting.

Other information: Ruled spaces and lettering were provided to indicate where the bank officers should sign and where the serial number should be placed. Various inscriptions, monograms, and other elements were sometimes added.

Listings of Notes

There are various elements to each bank and note in this book. Not every note will have the same or all of these characteristics. For ease of communication, description, and inventory, "Whitman numbers" have been assigned to the various notes.

Town / Town information: The name of and a brief historical sketch of the city or town in which the bank was located.

Bank name: The name of the bank. This is usually the name as imprinted on notes. Often on a note "The" will be the preface. "And" in a bank title is used in bank charters and is used here, as in Farmers and Merchants Bank. However, some notes and many numismatic listings use an ampersand (&) instead. It is numismatic practice to drop punctuation, to use Citizens instead of Citizens', for example. On some notes the name of the town is added to the title, such as the Farmers Bank of River City or the Farmers Bank in River City. Some notes of a given bank have such suffixes and others do not. They are not used here unless they are a main part of the title as boldly printed on a note, such as Smithville Bank of Commerce or Greenville Grocers Bank.

Date of operation: Years of existence, from the bank's charter date until it ceased operations, such as 1851–1865. Sometimes a bank did not begin operations until a year or two after it was chartered.

History: A synopsis of the history of the bank during its note-issuing period. Often much additional information can be found in historical texts or on the Internet and makes an interesting pursuit.

Numismatic commentary: Comments on the bank, the notes' overall availability, and more. In this volume C. John Ferreri was among those who assisted with this content.

Note listing: Divided into sections by Valid Issues (genuine notes from functioning banks), Issues (spurious notes from non-functioning or fraudulent banks), and Non-Valid Issues (notes from genuine banks that were later counterfeited, raised, made spurious by fraudsters, altered, etc.). The sample listing below is from the Abington Bank, Abington, Massachusetts:

$1 • **W-MA-010-001-G010a** TD

Overprint: Red ONE. ***Engraver:*** Rawdon, Wright, Hatch & Edson / New England Bank Note Co. ***Comments:*** H-Unlisted. Similar to W-MA-010-001-G010. Oct. __, 185_. 1850s.

Rarity: URS-1
G $1,000

$1: Denomination of the note shown.

W-MA-010-001-G010a

W: Whitman number. This number is a sortable code unique to each bank and note.

MA: Abbreviation for the state under study.

010: Numerical designation for the Abington Bank, Abington. Other banks have different numbers.

001: The denomination in dollars.

G010a: G indicates a good or valid note. Other categories are indicated thus: C (counterfeit); R (raised); S (spurious); N (not-attributed); A (altered). 010a is the specific note shown. Notes are listed in a bank-series by increments of 10 in order of denomination—a "porous" system so new discoveries can be added if needed. Terminal letters following the numerical designation, in this example "a," indicate variations of a note: a series of different colored overprints, tints, payees, etc., all on the same design of note. Thus the first type of a note will have no letter, the second an "a," the third a "b," the fourth a "c," and so on as necessary.

TD: Photographic image of an actual note in a collection, museum, or other location. Each photograph shown identifies its original source, when known, by an abbreviation at the upper right-hand corner of the image. A list of these creditors can be found at the front of the volume.

Vignette description: Primarily divided into Left, Center, Bottom center, and Right, these describe what is seen on the face of the note. Other descriptors include Overprint, Tint, Back, Payee, Engraver, and Comments, which includes other details about the note. For notes that are not illustrated, descriptions are given—based on information, when available, from contemporary bank-note reporters, counterfeit detectors, and other listings. Some are partial or may even prove to be inaccurate if an actual note is discovered. PSSP refers to a note of the Patent Stereotype Steel Plate by Jacob Perkins or his successor, the New England Bank Note Co. (see volume 1 for details). Illustrated notes will not have the primary descriptions included.

Rarity and Value: Estimate of the number of notes in existence today and the typical market value of a note at the time of publication. The figure indicates the center of a range. As an example, $400 suggests a range of about $350 to $450. Included as available.

Rarity (URS) Ratings

The Universal Rarity Scale

The Universal Rarity Scale uses a simple geometric progression of numbers by doubling the preceding value for each successive "rank": 1, 2, 4, 8, 16, 32, etc. (see the rightmost of each number pair), with the higher numbers rounded off for simplicity. Introduced in 1993, this has been widely used in various publications since that time. It is not copyrighted.

URS-1 = 1 known, unique
URS-2 = 2 known
URS-3 = 3 or 4
URS-4 = 5 to 8
URS-5 = 9 to 16
URS-6 = 17 to 32
URS-7 = 33 to 64
URS-8 = 65 to 124
URS-9 = 125 to 249
URS-10 = 250 to 499
URS-11 = 500 to 999
URS-12 = 1,000 to 1,999
URS-13 = 2,000 to 3,999
URS-14 = 4,000 to 7,999

Population Estimates

Drawing from authoritative catalogs, input from dealers and collectors, and other sources, rarity estimates have been given for many notes. In the past there have been many instances in which additional examples of previously rare notes have been found or new information has been learned. This will continue to be the case. Accordingly, some notes may become more plentiful than now listed. Many estates and other holdings with notes have not as of yet been examined or surveyed. To paraphrase an old comment, if Jones was not seen at a football game, he still might have been there.

Factors Affecting Present-Day Rarity

Some obsolete notes are very common. Others are so rare that only one or two exist. In some cases, a note may have been described in a bank-note reporter or other early reference, but no physical examples are known to exist. Such notes are assigned a Rarity listing of *None known.* Still others are so intangible that a guess has not been made as to their rarity; these are given a dash (—) as their Rarity listing.

If a bank was well-run and had no difficulties, its notes were usually redeemed at par. Sometimes these were burned—as mandated for banks in the state of Maine. There are many Maine notes that were once in circulation by the thousand but for which few are known today. In other states, notes were burned or were canceled at the option of the directors. In many instances quantities of canceled notes were saved, and later generations of collectors and dealers obtained them.

Many banks failed or otherwise could not redeem their notes. Spurious banks did not redeem any currency. Bills of such banks can be very common today. Quantities of unissued remainder notes, often as original sheets, exist for some banks. With increasing demand, many of the sheets have been cut apart. Notes of certain banks are extremely common as Uncirculated remainders, but signed and issued notes are rare and much more valuable. Original sheets can be collected as a specialty and are listed in this book. However, as they are not convenient to display and as the four notes to a sheet have been worth more individually in the past, most have been cut apart, as noted.

Learning More

Collecting obsolete bank notes can be a fascinating pursuit. Scarce and rare bills can often be obtained for fractions of the cost of comparably rare coins. With modest financial means it is often possible to build a first-class collection of notes from a particular area or with a particular theme.

As you have read to this point, you know that notes can be complex—and to an enthusiast, wonderfully so. Your enjoyment can be enriched by learning more. Whitman Publishing offers three key volumes that are guaranteed to please:

Volume 1 of the *Whitman Encyclopedia of Obsolete Paper Money* series is an in-depth study of obsolete paper money, how it was conceived, created, and distributed. Chapters go into great detail concerning engravers, vignettes, counterfeiting, and more. It is probably correct to say that if you spend a few evenings with your copy, you will be well on your way to becoming an expert. This book is a companion to the volume you are now holding and has been designed to complement it with much additional information.

Obsolete Paper Money Issued by Banks in the United States 1782–1866, published in 2006, is another essential volume on your way to becoming an expert and smart buyer.

The third book in the Whitman suite is *100 Greatest American Currency Notes*, a "for fun" volume that includes many different types of paper money with many obsolete bills featured.

Bank Note Reporter, issued monthly by Krause Publications, is filled with news and offerings. *Paper Money*, the journal of the Society of Paper Money Collectors, has much valuable information and many research articles.

The Professional Currency Dealers Association (PCDA) has dozens of members and opens the door to buying notes. It is strongly recommended that unless you are aware of special qualifications, you avoid buying notes on the Internet or other non-professional sources without an iron-clad money-back guarantee.

Obsolete notes are meant to be enjoyed. With some study of historical books and newspapers on the Internet or in a library, a single note can be your passport to a lot of ownership pleasure.

1

The Obsolete Bank Notes of Massachusetts

State Banking in Massachusetts

The Colonial Era

The Massachusetts Bay Colony, which incorporated much of what is now New England, was a pioneer in the American monetary system. The Massachusetts General Court authorized the first coinage of our country in 1652. From that year until the early 1780s, various silver denominations were struck at a mint in Boston. Perhaps the most familiar of these to numismatists are the Pine Tree shillings.

There seem to have been banks, or at least projected banks, in Massachusetts during the early days, according to scattered accounts. In 1688 John Blackwell was granted the privilege of erecting and managing a bank of credit. He was also permitted to issue bills on the security of real and personal estate. However, no such bills are known today.[1]

The first paper money issued by an American colony consisted of notes authorized December 10, 1690, by the Massachusetts Bay Colony. Before that time there were other types of money in use, ranging from corn to musket balls and cows to furs. Wampum beads used in trade with Indians (Native Americans) had assigned values as well. Silver and gold coins from Europe and the Spanish-controlled colonies in Central and South America facilitated commerce. The colony also issued many of its own notes in various series during the 18th century, including bills from plates engraved by Paul Revere.

In 1740 a large number of Boston merchants and others banded together to create the Land Bank, which seems to have issued £120,000 in bills and to have arranged dozens of mortgages, among other banking activities. The royal governor frowned on the action and warned citizens not to accept the currency. This was to no avail, and the court and other papers from that point up to 1760 show that many transactions occurred.[2]

Early State-Chartered Banks

This state had an early entry into American banking: the Massachusetts Bank was chartered on February 7, 1784, the backers having been inspired by the success of the Bank of North America in Philadelphia, which had been chartered on March 8, 1782, two months after it had actually commenced business. The Massachusetts Bank was thus the second banking institution to be established in the United States. Business began on July 5, 1784, by which time $253,500 of the authorized $300,000 capital had been paid in. Shares were priced at $500, a very large figure at the time, to restrict wide ownership by the general public. The Manufactory House, a building that had been used for other purposes, was purchased for $4,000 and became the bank's headquarters. It was well situated with 125 feet fronting on Common (now Tremont) Street. The bank issued bills in denominations of $1.50, $2.50, $3.50, $4.50, $6, $7, $8, $9, $15, $25, $30, $35, and $40. Certain of the denominations were familiar to the public, as some of the Continental Currency notes, by then nearly worthless, had similar imprints.

In 1791 Congress chartered the Bank of the United States. Headquartered in Philadelphia, it was to have branches in the larger cities, including Boston. The Boston branch opened in 1792 with offices on State Street. The cashier drew a salary of $1,600 per year. Notes printed in Philadelphia—which were of a common design that was used for all branches—were issued by the Boston office. These are extreme rarities today. Among the directors was Joseph Barrell, who in 1787 had been a backer of the famous voyages of the *Columbia* and *Lady Washington*, which sailed out of Boston Harbor to the Pacific. Commemorative medals were issued for the occasion.

The next Massachusetts state charter was for the Union Bank, Boston, which was granted in 1792 with $1,200,000 in capital to be paid in specie (gold or silver coins). The state took $400,000 worth and named it as the official depository for its funds. The bank was required to loan funds to the state in an amount up to $100,000 at an interest rate not to exceed 5 percent. In the same year the state mandated that no bank could issue bills with a face value of less than $5. This law was the first of many regulations over the years designed to promote the use of coins for small transactions.

That same year, the new Philadelphia Mint of 1792 had yet to strike any coins for circulation, Continental Currency bills were in disrepute, and most commercial transactions were conducted in gold and silver coins, especially of Spanish-American and European countries. Newspapers published lists of "prices current" giving exchange values for the foreign coins.

In 1795 two more banks were incorporated. The Nantucket Bank, located on an island off the coast famed for its whaling industry, was chartered for $100,000. On June 20 of that year, someone with false keys entered the bank and made off with "a considerable sum of money in dollars, crowns, and some gold." A reward of $1,000 was posted.[3] In 1796 two men were arrested in Philadelphia, implicated in the burglary, and put in jail. One escaped soon afterward. They said they had buried the money on a nearby island and later dug it up, but none was recovered. The crime was a sensation and widely reported. The loss was placed at about $10,000—a fortune in those times.

The Merrimac Bank in Newburyport, a busy maritime trading center, had a capital authorized to be at least $70,000 but not more than $150,000. This bank remained important for decades afterward. By special exception, both this bank and the Nantucket Bank were permitted to issue bills as low as $2.

Bills of this early era were issued from hand-engraved copper plates and were rather crude in their design compared to later issues. They were easily counterfeited by making false plates or by hand-drawing with pen and ink. Typical of many newspaper notices on this subject is this from the *Hampshire Gazette*, published in Northampton, Massachusetts, on October 18, 1797:

A Caution

> The public are cautioned against counterfeit five dollar bills of the Massachusetts Bank, dated January the 1st, 1795; two of which have been exhibited to the directors of said bank, and are so badly executed as to must render their detection easy to anyone in the smallest degree conversant with bank bills. The paper is thin and ordinary, even as to suffer the ink to soak through and cause an appearance on the back very different from the true bills; while the general face and complexion of them must excite instant apprehension and lead directly to the discovery of the forgery. . . .
>
> Ten dollar counterfeit bills of the Union Bank have also been discovered and brought to that bank. They appear to be executed by the same engraver as those of the Massachusetts Bank and were found in the hands of the same person. The description of the false bills of the Massachusetts Bank applies in almost every particular to the false bills of the Union Bank. Those of the Union Bank which have been detected are of the date October 1, 1792. . . .

Banking in the Early 19th Century

In the early years of the new century, other banks were chartered. By June 1805, there were 16 authorized banks in business in the state with a combined capital of $5,760,000 (of which $5,460,000 had been paid in). Banks were allowed to issue paper money amounting to double their paid-in capital.

The Embargo Act of 1807, later remembered by many historians as one of the greatest mistakes of the Jefferson administration, restricted maritime commerce. At the time American vessels were being intercepted by British and some French ships; their sailors were captured and their cargos summarily stolen. As a result, the act forbade ships from engaging in anything other than coastal trade. This decision wreaked hardship on all coastal areas and on New England in particular. Along with the ensuing Non-Intercourse Act, the Embargo Act forced the failure of many New England banks, among which was the Nantucket Bank earlier mentioned.

Meanwhile, many coins disappeared from circulation and went into the hands of hoarders. Many small-denomination bills, some legitimate, others not, flooded the channels of commerce. Counterfeiting became endemic. In 1809 the discounts on legitimate bank notes in terms of coins ranged from 10 percent to 50 percent or more in Boston. On January 1, 1810, the state Legislature enacted a law providing a penalty of 2 percent per month, payable by banks to holders of their bills, if they failed to redeem the notes promptly in coins. As a general rule, this and other regulations regarding currency over the years were loosely enforced. In 1811 a rechartering of most banks in the state reduced the amount of notes a bank could issue to 150 percent of its capital.

Jacob Perkins

In Newburyport, Jacob Perkins, a skilled engraver and artisan, entered the bank-note printing business at the turn of the century. By 1803 he had devised a method of engraving on soft steel and then hardening it, a method which permitted plates to produce many more impressions than the copper versions then in wide use. He also devised a transfer press whereby engravings could be reproduced, a process known as siderography. Later, he made a cylinder die in circular form, patented in 1813, which was a great improvement in siderography.

In the *Newburyport Herald*, March 8, 1805, an advertisement by Perkins included this:

Stereotype Plates for Banks

> The patentee of the Stereotype Plates for the impression of bank bills informs the public that he has constantly on hand ready-made plates (the name of the bank and town excepted), and will be happy to supply banks on the shortest notice. His terms are reasonable and uniform, the plates well executed, and he has the authority of many eminent artists, as well as the sanction of experience, to say that bills impressed from these plates cannot be counterfeited. No attempts of the kind have ever yet been made, tho' it has been adopted and is now used by sixteen banks in New England.
>
> Encouraged by the success of his principle, and the increasing demand for his plates, he has at a great expense improved his former invention by adding beauty to security. He has formed a steel plate of sixty-four dies, impressed by the same dies now used for copperplates, neatly fitted and keyed together in a strong iron frame. The name of the bank and town and the denomination of the bill are removed and substituted at pleasure.
>
> The standing parts of the plates are elegantly engraved by Mr. James Akin. When completed there will be from six to seven hundred days' work in the plate, and being

> well hardened, it will, without injury, print more paper than will be used by the United States. It is now nearly finished, and any orders addressed to him at Newburyport will be punctually honored.
>
> *Jacob Perkins*

No patent for the above has been located. Seemingly, by this time Perkins was involved in multiple businesses. James Akin, the engraver of what would be billed as the Perkins Patent Stereotype Steel Plate, had recently moved from Salem to Newburyport, where he would remain until about 1808.

The basic Perkins bank-note innovation consisted of a plate of rectangular shape on which a design was impressed, the design being more ornate than used earlier. Although there were variations, a popular early motif consisted of an approximately elliptical ("watermelon" shaped) border composed of lettering for the denomination and floral decorations, outside of which the denomination was given as a number in each of the four corners. Within the ellipse was standard lettering, often a plate letter (sometimes designated as Check Plate A, etc.), and a place for the number, payee, date, and signatures of the bank officers.

Rectangular openings in the plate provided spaces where steel slugs could be inserted with the bank name, town, and state. By switching the slugs, notes could be made for many different banks. Later versions had large areas on the face of the note filled with tiny repeated letters indicating the denomination, in italic type, such as *Five Dollars Five Dollars Five Dollars*, etc.

In 1806 Perkins addressed a memorial to the Massachusetts General Court suggesting that the state mandate use of his plates to deter counterfeiting. The idea met with a warm reception, and although it was not enacted into law at the time, much favorable publicity resulted.

In 1808 Jacob's brother Abraham, a storekeeper in Newburyport, relinquished that trade and joined in the bank-note engraving and printing business. Soon, a small three-story brick factory was erected on land behind Jacob's home on Fruit Street.[4]

In 1809 the Massachusetts Banking Act was passed, mandating use, beginning in July, of the Perkins plate for denominations from $1 to $5. The $5 denomination was to have the Perkins check plate on the back. The use of this extra security was optional for other denominations. In actual practice, some $5 notes were made with this feature, but many were not. Higher denominations were made as well. This type of note is known as a Patent Stereotype Steel Plate bill, abbreviated as PSSP.

Many New England banks used PSSP notes, with Connecticut being an exception. The most distant bank was in Detroit.

Perkins filled orders for all comers, it seems, including from bank officers who ordered quantities of currency far in excess of the amounts permitted by their charters. The Berkshire Bank of Pittsfield and the Northampton Bank, both controlled by the scheming Andrew Dexter Jr. (of the Farmers Exchange Bank of Gloucester, Rhode Island, infamy), were good customers of Perkins. These two banks failed: upon examination, one bank was found to have about $30 in its vaults and the other absolutely nothing.

Despite a lot of publicity to the contrary, the PSSP notes proved to be a boon to counterfeiters, who made up their own plates with slugs to be inserted, creating false notes for multiple banks.

Effects of the War of 1812

The despised Embargo Act and the Non-Intercourse Act continued to cause hardships for all New England ports and, consequently, the banks in port towns. British (and to a lesser extent French) interference with American shipping, now on a reduced scale due to restrictions, reached a breaking point. On June 18, 1814, Congress declared war against Great Britain. For most citizens in New England, economic matters went from bad to worse.

For the next three years, the War of 1812, as it became known, saw many military engagements, including naval battles fought in the Atlantic Ocean, Lake Champlain, and Lake Erie. For many Americans this was a war that few wanted. It was felt that the maritime problems with England had been blown far out of proportion and that other means could have been used to settle them.

Countless gold coins were exported despite the blockade of American ports at various times by British ships.[5] Certain banking interests were charged with aiding the enemy by making coins available to them under various subterfuges, including shipments to Canada, which was prohibited, as it was considered trade with "the contiguous British provinces."

Niles' Weekly Register, February 5, 1814, included this:

> The *Albany Argus* says, "Such has been the demand for specie in this city, for the Canada market, and for the banks, that ten percent premium has been paid for it in exchange for paper."
>
> We are satisfied that mighty efforts will be made to supply the enemy with this needful article; but would hope the vigilance of our officer may render the commerce too hazardous. British government bills are at a great discount in Canada, as, indeed, they are in all parts of Europe and America, and the bait is tempting.

A related article in the same issue reported:

> A quantity of specie, about $140,000, was boxed up in New-York some days ago and forwarded for Boston, ostensibly for the "New-England Bank." Mr. Gelston, collector of the port of New-York, seized it, under a clause of the embargo law, had it brought back and deposited in the Manhattan Bank. When the collector shall be satisfied that the money was really destined for Boston, he will, doubtless restore it.
>
> In the meantime the stockholders of the New-England Bank have petitioned the Legislature of Massachusetts to demand of the president of the United States the restitution of the money illegally seized by the collector of the port of New York, and the punishment of the offender. . . .

In the summer of 1814, British troops fought on land in Maryland and continued to Washington, where the Capitol, Executive Mansion (White House), and other buildings were burned. The troops boarded their ships and headed to Baltimore, where a bombardment of Fort McHenry ensued (inspiring "The Star Spangled Banner"). The effort was not a success, and the ships headed back to England. The war was over, and in December a peace treaty was signed. News traveled slowly, and on January 8, 1815, General Andrew Jackson was successful against British forces in the Battle of New Orleans. The combatants were not aware that the conflict had officially ended.

During the war the various Massachusetts banks were under pressure to redeem their notes in coins, which was nearly always done. Unlike the situation elsewhere in America, none suspended payments, mainly because of the penalty to be levied if this was done. In 1814 there were 21 banks in operation in the state.

Later in the Decade

It was thought that peace and the removal of shipping restrictions would bring a revival of the economy. This did not happen, and many banks across America were in trouble. Coins disappeared into the hands of hoarders, resulting in a flood of fractional bills issued by banks, usually printed in haste at a local or regional shop.

In August 1816, the Dedham Bank, Massachusetts, issued a large quantity of bills payable at par at the Middletown Bank in the Connecticut town of the same name. Bills could be exchanged for coins at the Dedham facility but only at a 1 percent discount. This idea, as strange as it may seem, was widely practiced by various American banks over a long period of years. The Massachusetts Legislature effectively put an end to the practice in December by passing a law prohibiting distant places being used as redemption centers unless the bills were also exchanged at the bank's home office at the same rate.

Coins remained scarce. As bills had to be redeemed promptly in coins by law, the banks issued a relatively low amount of currency. In June 1816, the capital of banks in the state was $11,475,000, but only $2,134,690 in bills was in circulation, a tiny fraction of the 150 percent of capital that was legally authorized.[6]

These strict rules resulted in great strength among Massachusetts banks in comparison to the situation in nearly all other states, most of which were dotted with bank failures. The numismatic result is that bills of Massachusetts banks of this decade range from scarce to rare as a class, while those of failed banks in other states are common.

In 1816 Congress chartered the second Bank of the United States for a period of 20 years, at which time the charter might be extended. In July of that year, subscription offices to raise $28,000,000 in capital were opened in various cities, including Boston. The Boston branch opened on January 1, 1817, and began giving loans on February 10 to those who had revenue bonds as collateral. The general public was accommodated beginning on February 20. President William Gray drew a salary of $1,500 per year, and cashier Samuel Frothingham received $3,000. The Boston branch offered paper money of a common design used by other branches and printed in Philadelphia. Today these notes are extremely rare.

The Suffolk Bank System

Boston was the focal point of banking in New England. Bills from the other states—Maine, New Hampshire, Vermont, Rhode Island, and Connecticut—were actively traded there at a discount from their value in the towns and cities of issue. New York City was another trading venue for New England notes at even deeper discounts.

In April 1824, the Suffolk Bank in Boston proposed setting up a clearing house for New England bills. A committee met with other Boston banks in a successful effort to gain their cooperation. A letter of proposal stated:

> Of the whole incorporated banking capital of New England, amounting to less than twenty millions of dollars, the eleven banks in this city possess ten million one hundred and fifty thousand. That estimating the circulation of the country banks at only seventy-five percent, of their capital, which they believe to be a moderate computation, these banks furnish seven million five hundred thousand dollars of the circulating medium, while the banks in the city with a capital equal to all the rest, keep in what may be fairly termed permanent circulation only three hundred thousand dollars.

The Suffolk Bank stated that in the space of three months it had received for exchange nearly $1,000,000 in notes from "country banks" (the term used for banks that were not in large cities or were distant from Boston). These were received at a discount and then given to agents who would travel over sometimes difficult roads to redeem the bills in coins at the offices of the issuing banks. This was a profitable enterprise for the Suffolk Bank.

If other banks would sign up with Suffolk, there would be a great economy in transporting and redeeming the bills. Six Boston banks did this and set up a fund of $300,000 to implement it. Bills received by the other banks were sent to Suffolk under an agreement perfected on May 24, 1824.

This news caused great consternation among distant banks, as the longer their bills could remain in circulation, the more money a bank could use for other purposes such as loans. It was common practice to ship notes in bulk, discounted, to distant banks, with the expectation that it would be a long time until they were presented for redemption. As an example, the Hillsborough Bank in Amherst, New Hampshire, made a point to ship large quantities of its bills to the Marietta Bank in distant Ohio, hoping that few would be returned.

The Suffolk Bank system, as it was known, was eventually viewed with favor by most New England banks, once they realized that having a clearing house in Boston that received its bills at only a small discount was a boon to their business. Most banks joined the system, placing deposits of $2,000 or more (depending upon capital and volume of notes) with the Suffolk Bank to make it possible to redeem their bills near face value. Banks shipped bundles of miscellaneous bills to Boston at frequent intervals and were immediately credited with the proceeds.[7]

The Suffolk Bank system was unique in America at the time and facilitated the public's acceptance of bills from distant banks and gave the notes a greater exchange value. Whenever a shipment of notes contained a counterfeit, the Suffolk Bank prominently stamped it as such and returned it to the bank that sent it. This policy had the benefit of forcing bank tellers to be alert in order to detect fraudulent bills.

Elsewhere on the Banking Scene

The American monetary system underwent several crises in the late 1810s and early 1820s, mainly due to variations in agriculture, commerce, and international trade. In 1820 the international value of gold bullion rose, and it cost more than face value to mint the two gold coin denominations then in use—the $2.50 quarter eagle and the $5 half eagle. From 1821 until the authorized weight of gold coins was reduced by the Act of June 28, 1834, no such coins were seen in circulation. Production continued at the Philadelphia Mint on behalf of depositors who valued the coins at their intrinsic worth and used them in international trade. If a $5 gold coin cost $5.05 to mint, it was of no consequence, as it was valued at the increased amount when it was received in another country.

As a result of this, the largest circulating federal coins in the United States from 1821 to 1834 were half dollars. In addition, various silver and gold coins of Spanish-American and European countries were legal tender at various assigned values.

By January 1, 1825, 49 banks had been chartered in Massachusetts with a total authorized capital of $20,800,000. Six of these had failed, and three others never opened for business. In operation were 40 banks with a combined authorized capital of $14,305,000, of which $13,300,000 was said to have been paid in.

From 1824 to 1829 there were only seven new banks chartered in the state. Although Massachusetts had strict laws on the books, enforcement was casual at best. Capital was to be paid in gold or silver coins (specie) but was often in the form of promissory notes from stockholders. There was no system of audit or verification.

This laxness changed with the Banking Law of February 28, 1829, which would apply to all future charters as well as to any existing bank extending its charter or changing its capital. Under the new regulations, banks were to have at least 50 percent of their capital paid in verifiable specie before they could commence business. Specie included any legal-tender gold or silver coins, American or foreign. No loans could be made to shareholders unless their stock subscriptions had been paid in full. Total loans secured by pledging shares of the bank's own stock could not exceed 50 percent of the paid-in capital. Currency could be circulated to the extent of 125 percent of paid-in capital. By this time most Massachusetts banks had been extremely conservative in this regard, in the aggregate issuing only a small fraction of the bills they could have paid out.

Under state law, banks continued to use only Patent Stereotype Steel Plate (PSSP) notes printed in Newburyport. Jacob Perkins had left Massachusetts in the early 1810s and had gone to Philadelphia, then on to London. The business was conducted by his brother along with staff engravers and printers.

The Farmers Bank of Belchertown

In 1825 the Farmers Bank of Belchertown, Massachusetts, was chartered by the Legislature. The authorized capital was $100,000. Its bills were printed by Perkins and were well received in commerce. At first they typically traded at a 2 percent discount from face value in places other than its home town. After it joined the Suffolk Bank system, the discount was only 1/2 of 1%. In New York City they could be exchanged at a discount ranging from 3/4 of 1% to 1%. This was the typical rate for nearly all Massachusetts banks. The following from the *Evening Post* in New York City was reprinted from the *Journal of Commerce*:

Another Bank Failure

News was received yesterday that the Farmers Bank at Belchertown has stopped payment. We were apprised of the circumstances which led to this result, but it may be sufficient to state in general that the bank having received the paper of certain gentlemen (still supposed to be responsible) to a large amount, was unable to realize the money when it was need, and was thus compelled to yield to the pressure of circumstances.

One of the principal merchants of Northampton (8 miles from Belchertown) tells us that he should be happy to purchase a quantity of the notes at 75 cents on the dollar. He is confident only that all the bills will eventually be redeemed, but also a considerable percentage paid on the stock.—*Journal of Commerce.*

An investigation held by state authorities in January 1830 revealed that the bank was insolvent by early 1829, but this was disguised by paying a three percent dividend on the stock. Rather than loaning money, the directors of the bank had borrowed large sums from local and regional people. In January 1830, the hard assets consisted of $1.25 in specie! The cashier, Theodore D. Lyman, stated that $27,822.90 in bills was in circulation, but the actual figure is unknown and was probably much larger. Perkins had a history of supplying huge quantities of unrecorded notes to fraudulent banks, no questions asked.[8]

In March 1830, the editor of the *Belchertown Sentinel* advertised that he had $2,500 in such bills "for sale at a great discount for cash" or "to be exchanged for real estate in Belchertown or its vicinity."

As was true of other worthless notes, the bills of the Farmers Bank continued to be bought and sold by exchange houses and brokers, particularly in New York City. These were bought by crooks who would peddle them in small amounts to merchants and others who either were not aware of their nature or who simply took in bills regardless of quality and then paid them out again to other customers.

The Jacksonian Era

The decade of the 1830s was very tumultuous. Andrew Jackson, who was inaugurated as president on March 4, 1829, was strongly challenged by his opponents under different party designations, including Whigs beginning in 1833. The Indian Removal Act of 1830 ejected Cherokees and other Native Americans from their traditional tribal lands in the Carolinas and forced them to relocate in the Midwest. Thousands died, especially on the infamous "Trail of Tears."

The second Bank of the United States, chartered in 1816, was called "The Monster" by many, especially those in the banking community who resented that its currency traded at par everywhere in America, including at its many branches, while bills of state-chartered banks were exchanged at a discount. Jackson took a stand against the bank, and it seemed that its future would be in doubt when its charter came up for renewal or extension in 1836. To settle the matter, certain of Jackson's adversaries, including Daniel Webster and Henry Clay, had Congress pass legislation in 1832 to authorize the renewal far in advance. Although it passed both houses, Jackson vetoed it. The fate of the Bank of the United States was sealed, and for the next several years certain operations were wound down, including the Boston office. Amid much criticism, federal deposits were moved to "pet banks" selected by the administration. In 1836 the remaining branches closed their doors. Jackson's actions were lampooned by dozens of cartoons. He was unpopular with much of the "establishment," including educators and moneyed interests, but was loved by the general public.

In the meantime, during the early 1830s, the economy was robust in most of America, including in Massachusetts where the benefits of restrictive tariffs in 1828 decreased imports and spurred manufacturing, such as in the many mills in the state. In 1832 the New England Bank Note Co. was formed in Boston and assumed the business conducted by the Perkins interests in Newburyport. The PSSP notes continued to be made for all Massachusetts banks as mandated by law and for any banks in other states that desired them.

Steam power came into increasing use in factories, and railroads were a growth industry as construction of new canals faded. In contrast, there was a chill in the commerce of Eastern cities that seemed to have no cure. In January 1834, a mass meeting of merchants was held in Boston, after which a petition was sent to Congress urging the prompt restoration of deposits to the Bank of the United States.

On the frontier—the land west of Pennsylvania—the government opened up millions of acres of land to settlers, who could buy acreage cheaply, usually paying for it in various bank bills or promissory notes. While much land was bought by settlers who planned to operate farms or set up residences in towns, speculators were the dominant force in the market. Deeds changed hands at ever-increasing prices. This brought great prosperity to the Midwest, mainly to the speculators. To stop the cycle, on July 11, 1836, President Jackson issued the Specie Circular, a document stating that henceforth federal lands had to be paid for in gold and silver coins.

Despite generally good times, the mercantile interests in some larger cities including Boston and New York saw a softening of business. On the other hand, the closing of the Bank of the United States spurred the chartering of many new banks by various state legislatures. Most citizens felt secure. In November 1836, Martin Van Buren, Jackson's vice president, was elected president on the Democratic ticket.

During 1836, as stated in a memorial of the Boston Chamber of Commerce to the Legislature in January 1837, the mercantile community was "subjected to a pressure in their financial operations unexampled in its severity and duration." For more than a year the rate of interest "ranged from twelve to thirty-six percent per annum." The memorialists believed the chief cause was to be found in the operation of the usury laws and recommended their total or partial repeal. "It is well known," said the memorial, "that they are publicly and generally evaded by circuitous transactions through agents; the difficulty of obtaining money has been thereby increased, and the price of it enhanced." "Many of our capitalists, from an unwillingness to evade these laws, have sent large sums to other states, particularly New York, where the legal rate of interest is higher. Large amounts have thus been withdrawn when most needed."[9] It was hardly to be expected that such a memorial would be heeded.

Uncertainty prevailed. With speculators no longer on the scene, the business atmosphere in the Midwest was one of insecurity. Unrest increased in cities as employment declined while prices rose. New York City in particular was distressed. In December 1835, a huge conflagration leveled much of the financial district: nearly 700 buildings were destroyed, and many businesses were wiped out. The premises of Rawdon, Wright, Hatch & Edson, America's leading bank-note printer, located in the Merchants Exchange, was a total loss. The next year was unsettled in the city. In early 1837 business and employment worsened while prices of commodities rose. Barrels of flour that had once sold for $7 and had already risen in price up to $12 jumped to $20. Bread, an essential of life, became unaffordable to many. Rumors spread, meetings were held, and speakers encouraged action. On February 10, a crowd assembled in Chatham Square and marched to storm the premises of Eli Hart & Co. and S.H. Herrick & Co., flour dealers who were accused of hoarding and driving up prices. Quantities of warehoused flour and wheat were destroyed.

Hard Times

On March 4, 1837, Martin Van Buren was inaugurated as president. Jackson left Washington and headed for The Hermitage, his plantation near Nashville, Tennessee. He left behind an era that, for the most part, was prosperous. In the same month, the prices of many stocks on Wall Street fell. Holders of paper money became increasingly concerned with the news of bankruptcies, increased unemployment, and generally unsettled conditions; they redeemed many bills for gold and silver coins.

In Massachusetts the Legislature set about investigating several new banks that had been chartered in 1836 but whose operations seemed questionable: the Chelsea, Kilby, Middling Interest, and Lafayette banks. The bank cashiers must have presented documents that satisfied the examiners, for all were allowed to continue business. However, each of these banks closed its doors in the next few years with losses to the holders of their currency. The Chelsea Bank folded on April 12, 1837, with just $36.71 in cash available to redeem over $110,000 of its bills![10] This caused great concern in Boston, and many business activities were curtailed.

Officially inaugurating what became known as the Hard Times era, New York City banks suspended specie payments on May 10, 1837. The next day, Boston bankers met in Faneuil Hall and reluctantly agreed to do the same thing. On May 12, the suspension took effect. Almost immediately, gold and silver coins became worth a premium of 10 to 13 percent. To facilitate trade, many merchants and others issued copper tokens with advertising or political messages. Most were the size of a copper cent and traded for that value but cost just $6 to $7 per 1,000 wholesale. Paper scrip notes were also issued in abundance. Massachusetts law prohibited banks from issuing bills for less than $1. In 1837 the state enacted a penalty of $50 per note for any individual issuing fractional bills. To facilitate making change, this spawned such unusual denominations as $1.25, $1.50, and $1.75. Terry, Pelton & Co., relatively new on the

Boston bank-note printing scene, produced many of these in addition to the output of the New England Bank Note Co.

On September 1, 1837, the *New York Journal of Commerce* ran this:

> Banks have been more freely incorporated in Massachusetts than in any other state, if we except Rhode Island. Charters have been given so freely that the necessity of getting them was but a form, for they have been granted whenever asked under circumstances which gave any tolerable warrant for the grant. Charters have been granted until chartered monopolies have been brought upon the ground of free trade; for the charters are so numerous that anybody can have one.
>
> The business has in fact been overdone, and free trade will probably cause a considerable number of the charters to be given up, and the capitals divided. So there will be charters to be had gratis. We know that a considerable number of the Massachusetts banks are seriously considering the question of winding up their affairs. . . .

The large and important Lafayette Bank folded in July 1837. The legislature appointed a special committee to investigate the affairs of this bank. A report issued on January 6, 1838, related that very little of the stated $150,000 in capital was ever paid in. $124,558.50 worth of bills were reported to have been circulated in addition to unstated amounts not recorded. False reports had been filed, the books of the bank "had been in disarray since the beginning of business," and at the time of collapse, the officers of the bank were trying to work out a currency distribution scheme with a New York City bank.[11] In July the Franklin Bank also collapsed.

On January 11, 1838, the Commonwealth Bank of Boston failed. With outstanding paper money and other liabilities worth $915,946, this was the greatest loss to the public to date in the state's history. To make matters worse, the Commonwealth Bank was a "pet bank" that the Treasury Department had designated as a depository for federal funds. Contemporary accounts laid part of the problem to the recent death of bank president John K. Simpson, who was heavily indebted to the institution. Simpson, in collusion with the cashier, had issued $120,000 in bills for which no record had been kept and had secretly reissued $40,000 in notes that were stated to have been burned.[12] On January 16, the Middlesex Bank of Cambridge closed up. Many others experienced difficulties. In 1837 the Legislature revoked the charters of three banks, followed by 10 more in 1838, but this did not stop the flood of worthless notes. The prime supplier was the New England Bank Note Co., successor to the Perkins interests, which accepted orders for bills and never asked questions. In 1838 the Board of Bank Commissioners was established to audit and analyze the financial documents of banks in the state.

In 1838 many Massachusetts banks began to redeem their smaller bills (up to $3) in coin. The City Bank of Lowell was chartered at $75,000 and immediately set about ordering quantities of bills from the New England Bank Note Co. Soon, banking authorities learned that it had borrowed on short term some specie from Boston and had IOUs for the rest of its capital, and there were no assets at all. In July 1838, an injunction was issued forbidding it to open. That same month the Roxbury Bank, a phony operation run by swindlers in New York City, was enjoined from continuing. However, this did not deter its owners from passing out a further $50,000 or so of bills, including some of the popular $1.25, $1.50, and $1.75 denominations. By August 1838, nearly all banks in Massachusetts had resumed exchanging coins for their paper money.

From 1837 to 1844, the latter year seeing the resumption of strong economic conditions in America, 32 Massachusetts banks failed or forfeited their charters, a sorry showing among New England states. These defunct institutions included five of the 15 incorporated in 1831, two of the 16 chartered in 1832, six of the 14 new banks of 1833, and 11 of the 32 incorporated in 1836. During this time only two new banks were chartered—the Cabot in Springfield (1837) and the Fishermens Bank, Provincetown (1839). Neither ever went into operation. Bills from these failed banks form a sizeable proportion of the collectible notes in numismatic hands today. In 1844 there were 103 active banks in the state, a reduction from the number a decade earlier.

Recovery

After the Hard Times era there was not much interest in forming new banks. Noted by historian Dudley P. Bailey Jr.:

> For the five years 1845–49, little new capital was asked for or authorized for banking purposes. Twenty-five new banks were incorporated with $3,300,000 of capital. Of these 25 banks, three, the Hampshire and Franklin, of Amherst, the Bank of Barre, and the Cape Cod Bank, of Provincetown, with $300,000 of capital, never went into operation.[13]

The Legislature mandated that all banks chartered before 1849 had to apply for new charters in 1851, at which time their affairs could be studied. At that time, of the 115 banks involved, all but the Manufacturers Bank of Georgetown (which was first located in Rowley and then in 1838 moved to nearby Georgetown) continued in business. This bank was solvent, liquidated its affairs, and returned a profit to its shareholders.

In 1851 the Free Banking Law was passed, permitting any group of 50 or more stockholders to set up a bank with capital to be at least $100,000 and no more than $1,000,000. Half the capital had to be paid in before the bank could commence business. Bills could be issued, backed in part with securities posted with the state, totaling no less than $50,000 or no more than 25 percent of the face value, whichever amount was larger. In 1852 the number of people needed to form a bank was reduced to just 10.

Unlike the situation in many other states, in Massachusetts the new law elicited no interest from investors. It was not until the Bank of the Metropolis, Boston, opened in November 1858 that an institution was organized under its provisions. It folded in November 1863. No more than half a dozen other banks were founded under the law.[14]

By the early 1850s, the state of Massachusetts had on its books a long list of banking rules and regulations dating back many years, including these:

> No bill or note can be issued by or on account of any bank, at any other place than its banking-house.
>
> No bank is allowed to pay out from its own counter any other bills than its own.
>
> All bills are to be issued in the name of the president, directors, and company of the bank issuing them, and to be signed by the president and cashier of the bank; but all bills signed by either the president or cashier, in circulation through the agency or neglect of any officer of the bank, must be redeemed by the corporation.
>
> Banks are liable to pay to any bona fide holder the original amount of any of their bills which may have been altered to a larger amount in the course of circulation, notwithstanding the alteration.
>
> Banks may issue bills under five dollars to the amount of one quarter part of their capital actually paid in; but no bank can issue bills of a less denomination than one dollar, under a penalty of one hundred dollars for each offense.
>
> The amount of bills issued by a bank must not at any time exceed its capital actually paid in more than twenty-five per cent.
>
> If the officers of any bank refuse or delay payment in gold or silver money of any note or bill of the bank, presented for payment in their usual hours of business, the bank will be liable to pay to the holder, as damages, at the rate of 24% a year during such delay or refusal.

As might be imagined, many rules were overlooked in practice or were not enforced. By this time the state had racked up the worst banking record by far in the Northeast in terms of problems, mainly due to there being more banks to supervise.

At the same time, 110 banks in New England conducted the Association of Banks for the Suppression of Counterfeiting to track down the passers of false bills and, among other challenges, persuade the Massachusetts Legislature to outlaw use of the easily counterfeited PSSP bills. *Banker's Magazine*, February 1852, told of a curious situation:

> **Counterfeiting**
>
> A singular development has taken place in regard to the special agency in Boston, for the detection of counterfeiters. An association of the banks has, for some years, appropriated quite a liberal sum annually for the suppression of counterfeiting. The Legislature of Massachusetts granted last year the sum of $2,500, annually for five years, in aid of this object.
>
> The special agent appointed by the banks to discover the source or sources of counterfeiting, has himself been detected in engraving and printing spurious notes. He has been in the habit of buying the spurious plates from professional counterfeiters, and selling them to the Banking Association, with a view to the plates being destroyed. Sufficient evidence is brought forward to show that the agent has deceived his employers, and has contributed very largely to the numerous counterfeits that have been afloat within a year or two past. The name of this person is William W. Wilson, who is charged with counterfeiting on the Merchants' Bank, Boston, and the Tradesman's Bank, Chelsea, and having in his possession dies and bank plates for that purpose.
>
> His case came up in the Police Court on Tuesday, 18th January, per assignment. A fifth complaint was entered against him, charging the same offences of the Housatonic Bank, after which the examination upon the previous complaint proceeded. The government produced about a dozen witnesses. Police officer Galen Holmes and Constable Wm. K. Jones detailed the circumstances of the arrest, and what implements, counterfeit bills, &c., were seized; and Mr. Pelton, an engraver, testified concerning certain bank plates and dies made by him, which passed into Wilson's possession. and by the use of which, it is alleged by the prosecution, he counterfeited bank bills.

Other News of the 1850s

In the meantime, during the 1850s there were scattered failures, the most prominent of which was the Cochituate Bank of Boston in 1854, for which the bank president had made poor investments in the South and West. Thousands of worthless notes were preserved, much to the delight of a later generation of numismatists. Several subsequent failures prompted the Legislature to revise banking laws that permitted secrecy, requiring banks to publish weekly figures of condition if located in Boston and monthly if elsewhere.

In April 1855, "some few" banks in the state omitted their quarterly dividends, as they were short of funds. The culprit proved to be unwise or slow-paying investments in the distant Midwest, where speculation in lands and businesses was active again. Such banks did little in the way of loans locally and were viewed by some to be in violation of their chartered purpose.[15] Loaning funds outside of the state in order to gain high rates of interest had been practiced by other banks for a long time.

The Panic of 1857 was precipitated by the failure of the Ohio Life Insurance and Trust Co. branch office in New York City, which handled many bank transfers and loans. Concern spread, and other banks, brokerage offices, and businesses in the financial district became distressed. "Runs" on banks took place, and a shortage of coins forced all but one bank in New York City (the Chemical Bank) to suspend specie payments on October 13. The next day all Boston banks stopped paying out coins. The malaise spread to other institutions. In Massachusetts, only one bank failed, the Western Bank of Springfield, which was closed by injunction on October 6 in the face of long-standing problems unrelated to the panic.

Banks nationwide scaled down their operations, uncertain if this was to be a repetition of the Hard Times era of the 1830s. Faced with diminished business, most of the leading bank-note printers consolidated and formed the American Bank Note Co. in March 1858. Its ABNCo. monogram was added to printing plates of the founding partners when new bills were ordered by past clients.

In 1858 there was a big fight between proponents of the Suffolk Bank system and the perceived upstart Bank of Mutual Redemption, which had been chartered in 1855 but did not begin business until three years later. The latter drew much business from banks outside of Boston. In the city of Boston, the leading banks banded together to deny the Bank of Mutual Redemption membership in the Clearing House Association. Not long after, the Suffolk Bank stated that as of November 30 it would no longer do business with "country banks," these being small institutions. By April 1859, the Bank of Mutual Redemption had 143 banks as members, about half of the institutions in New England.

The *Boston Advertiser*, August 25, 1859, told of a burglary of the house that belonged to the president of an unnamed bank, in which 200 sheets of bank bills awaiting his signature were stolen. Apparently this was far from being an isolated occurrence, as Thompson & Brothers, exchange brokers in New York City, reported that thousands of genuine notes from various banks with forged signatures had turned up in Wall Street.[16]

After the Panic of 1857, only a few new banks were formed in Massachusetts. By 1862 there were 183 of them in operation, just 10 more than at the onset of the financial crisis. After the Civil War commenced in 1861, the banks of the state continued business as normal with no problems of significance. Statewide, the banks had a surplus of $5,902,598 and held specie in their vaults to the amount of $8,877,193.[17] Both the Confederacy and the Union had a share of military victories. By December, with the war in progress and no clear conclusion in sight, many citizens began to hoard coins. By late in the month gold coins were no longer being paid out at par by banks.

After Legal Tender Notes were authorized in March 1862, these not redeemable in gold or silver coins, public concern increased. By late spring silver coins were no longer available at par, and in the second week of July one-cent pieces, with little intrinsic value, disappeared as well. Although the Massachusetts banks no longer redeemed their notes in specie, all were financially sound. Business from the summer of 1862 through 1863 was conducted by various monetary substitutes, including Postage Currency notes issued by the Treasury Department, ordinary postage stamps, which were given legal-tender status, encased postage stamps, bronze and brass cent-size tokens, and paper scrip.

Federal cents returned to circulation in 1864, but silver coins did not appear until 1876 and gold until late 1878. In 1863 the National Banking Act allowed the directors of state-chartered banks in sound condition to apply for a charter to become a National Banking Association. The state banks were dissolved and their businesses assumed by new National Banks, often with similar names. The October 1865 report of the Bank Commissioners stated that beginning with the Safety Fund Bank in 1863, 178 state-chartered banks had evolved into National Banks. Four had surrendered their charters and discontinued business. The sole exception remaining under state charter was the North Bridgewater Bank.

Notes of state banks were redeemed by their successors for a period of several years. The government enacted a law stating that after July 1, 1866, there would be a tax of 10 percent on any transactions involving state-bank notes. This tax effectively ended their circulation, although redemptions continued. Thus concluded the era of currency issued by state-chartered banks.

Most redeemed notes were burned. Others were punch canceled. Some of the latter survived to enter numismatic circles years later.

Numismatic Comments

The state of Massachusetts offers a vast panorama of obsolete bank bills ranging from prior to 1800 up to 1866. In addition to banks located in what is today considered Massachusetts, several banks that existed in the Maine District of Massachusetts, in towns such as Castine, Hallowell, and Portland, have Massachusetts imprints. After Maine became a state on March 15, 1820, banks doing business there adopted Maine addresses. Accordingly, currency issued before March 1820 is of interest to specialists in Maine as well as in Massachusetts.

Study of the Amherst Bank, Amherst, revealed that it was preceded by the formerly unknown Sunderland Bank, Sunderland, a short distance away. In 1831 the bank changed its name and moved to Amherst. Today, no bills of the Sunderland Bank have been located. In 1862 there was a boundary line adjustment in Fall River with the result that two banks that had been in Rhode Island previously were now located in Massachusetts without moving. The history of a bank can be endlessly fascinating!

As noted above, in 1809 the state mandated that all banks use PSSP notes printed by Perkins in Newburyport. This gave the currency a uniform appearance for many years afterward, in contrast to the varied motifs used by banks in other states. It became the case that the Perkins system was easy to counterfeit, causing many problems. In 1829 the Farmers Bank of Belchertown exploded (to use a popular word of the time for fraudulent banks being exposed and failing) with the result that countless tens of thousands of dollars in bills remained in circulation with no possibility of being redeemed. Today, these bills are the earliest of the state that are very common in numismatic hands.

In 1832 the Perkins business was merged into the New England Bank Note Co. in Boston, after which the PSSP notes carry that imprint. By the late 1830s, other companies were making currency for Massachusetts banks, most notably the short-lived Terry, Pelton & Co. with offices in Boston and in Providence, Rhode Island.

The Hard Times of the late 1830s caused other banks to fail, some simply because of economic conditions, others through fraud. From this point forward currency of failed banks is easily obtained by collectors today. Many of such surviving bills are in higher grades such as Fine, Very Fine, and Extremely Fine. From the 1850s through the 1860s, bills became much more varied in appearance as different firms began supplying currency, using ornate vignettes not different in concept from those used in other Eastern states at the time. Most later bills have colored overprints giving the denominations.

In 1854 the Cochituate Bank of Boston collapsed, leaving being a large quantity of bills—easily enough found today. In contrast, of the nearly 300 state-chartered banks in Massachusetts that were in operation from the late 18th century through the 1860s, 80 percent or more redeemed and destroyed their paper money. This widescale destruction is much different from the scenario for many banks of other states, where in many instances redeemed bills were canceled but kept on hand and later fell into the hands of numismatists. The unusual result is that today the signed and issued bills of the vast majority of Massachusetts banks are those that somehow were saved by chance and are in lower grades. In some instances the finest known bills exist in grades such as About Good and Good.

Some very early bills survive only as tattered paper. As noted, bills of failed banks are usually available in grades of Fine to Extremely Fine.

It is frustrating to read the accounts of many banks issuing bills of denominations from $1 to $100 or more, only to realize that not a single example is known of many varieties that were once circulated by the thousands. Among the New England states, Massachusetts differs from the other five in this regard.

Proof impressions are known for many varieties, most of which came on the market beginning with the dispersal of the long-stored American Bank Note Co. archives in Christie's memorable sales of 1990 and 1991, followed by other distributions. These offerings brought to light many designs unknown to earlier generations of numismatists. Proofs appear with regularity in auctions and always draw enthusiastic competition.

This volume covers the cities of Abington through Greenfield. For Hallowell through Yarmouth, see volume 4.

Abington, Massachusetts

Established in 1668 by European settlers, the lands that comprised the town of Abington in the early days included the current towns of Bridgewater, Rockland, Whitman, and sections of Hanover. In 1694 the town was given its present name, and in 1712 it was incorporated. Later, in 1874 and 1875, Rockland and Whitman were incorporated as separate towns.

In this high-quality lumbering region, saw mills producing quantities of timber were in operation by 1698. In 1765 earthenware manufacturing became another source of revenue after a natural resource of clay was located. John Henry Benner, a German craftsman, moved around 1760 to Abington, where he lived and worked until the 1790s. Known as "Bennerware," the pottery he produced during this time is recognized as being of the finest quality. During the 19th century, boots and shoes were manufactured as the town's primary industry, providing nearly half of the footwear for the Union Army in the Civil War.

The casting of meeting-hall bells, cannons, and railroad tracks also took place here. Jesse Reed invented a machine that produced the rails, and from 1820 to 1865, several factories in Abington took part in their manufacture.

Abington Bank

1850–1865

W-MA-010

History: The Abington Bank was incorporated in 1850 with an initial authorized capital of $100,000. By June 1855, it had increased to $150,000, where it remained throughout the bank's existence.

In 1852 Asaph Dunbar became the president of the Abington Bank. He had once been a shoe manufacturer. In 1857 circulating bills amounted to $87,329, specie totaled $6,702.46, and real estate was valued at $5,988.16.[18] According to the *Annual Report of the Bank Commissioners*, by 1860 the circulation had increased to $98,522, deposits were valued at $45,351.16, loans totaled $275,713.19, real estate was worth $5,988.16, and profits equaled $26,468.88. March of that same year saw a circulation of $5 bills and higher at $67,200. Smaller denominations made up $20,129 of the total circulation. The *Annual Report of the Secretary of the Treasury on the Condition of Banks* stated on January 3, 1863, that circulation had dropped to $87,665.

In July 1866, the Abington Bank closed after the shareholders formed the Abington National Bank with a capital of $150,000, limited to $500,000. Notes of the state-chartered bank continued to be redeemed for several years after that time.

Numismatic Commentary: Finding a valid note from the Abington Bank is one of the greatest challenges of Massachusetts numismatics. The one collectible issue with this bank's imprint is the altered $5, which will show up only occasionally. The finder of a genuine Abington Bank note should cherish it.

This first-listed bank sets the tone for *many* Massachusetts institutions that issued large quantities of paper money but later burned the notes after they were redeemed. In countless instances for this state, what was once common is now very rare.

Valid Issues

$1 • W-MA-010-001-G010

Left: Train / ONE. ***Center:*** 1. ***Bottom center:*** State arms. ***Right:*** ONE over 1 / Three cherubs holding cornucopias, Liberty holding flag in clouds. ***Engraver:*** Rawdon, Wright, Hatch & Edson / New England Bank Note Co. ***Comments:*** H-MA-10-G2. 18__. 1850s.

Rarity: —

$1 • W-MA-010-001-G010a

TD

Overprint: Red ONE. ***Engraver:*** Rawdon, Wright, Hatch & Edson / New England Bank Note Co. ***Comments:*** H-Unlisted. Similar to W-MA-010-001-G010. Oct. __, 185_. 1850s.

Rarity: URS-1
G $1,000

$2 • W-MA-010-002-G020

Left: Two men fishing, Three cows, Men plowing, Train / 2. ***Center:*** 2. ***Bottom center:*** Female portrait. ***Right:*** 2 / State arms. ***Engraver:*** Rawdon, Wright, Hatch & Edson / New England Bank Note Co. ***Comments:*** H-MA-10-G4. 18__. 1850s.

Rarity: —

Collectors and Researchers:

If you have new information about any banks or notes listed in this volume, contact Whitman Publishing,
Attn: Obsolete Paper Money,
3101 Clairmont Road, Suite G, Atlanta, GA 30329.

$2 • W-MA-010-002-G020a JF

Overprint: Red TWO. ***Engraver:*** Rawdon, Wright, Hatch & Edson / New England Bank Note Co. ***Comments:*** H-Unlisted. Similar to W-MA-010-002-G020. Oct. __, 185_. 1850s.

Rarity: URS-1
F $1,500

$3 • W-MA-010-003-G030

Left: State arms flanked by two women / THREE. ***Center:*** Cherub. ***Bottom center:*** Gears and bales. ***Right:*** THREE / Woman seated on bale, right hand on die bearing 3 / THREE. ***Comments:*** H-MA-10-G6. 18__. 1850s.

Rarity: URS-2
F $1,000

$5 • W-MA-010-005-G040

Left: Woman flying in clouds with arm around eagle / 5. ***Center:*** Ceres kneeling in large V. ***Bottom center:*** Gears and bale. ***Right:*** FIVE / Woman standing with arm on 5. ***Comments:*** H-MA-10-G8. 18__. 1850s.

Rarity: URS-3
F $750

$10 • W-MA-010-010-G050

Left: Woman seated holding key, Eagle and safe nearby, Ship / 10. ***Center:*** X. ***Right:*** TEN / Portrait of John Adams. ***Comments:*** H-MA-10-G10. 18__. 1850s.

Rarity: URS-2
F $750

$20 • W-MA-010-020-G060

Left: 20 / Minerva standing with spear. ***Center:*** Woman seated between 2 and 0. ***Right:*** 20 / Woman reclining on cornucopia / 20. ***Engraver:*** Rawdon, Wright, Hatch & Edson. ***Comments:*** H-MA-10-G12. 18__. 1850s–1860s.

Rarity: URS-1
F $1,500

$50 • W-MA-010-050-G070

Left: 50 / Minerva standing by column. ***Center:*** Ceres and Vulcan flanking cornucopia. ***Right:*** 50 / Cherub in sailboat / 50. ***Engraver:*** Rawdon, Wright, Hatch & Edson. ***Comments:*** H-MA-10-G14. 18__. 1850s.

Rarity: —

$100 • W-MA-010-100-G080

Left: 100 / Vulcan seated with sledge and anchor. ***Center:*** Train on bridge, Eagle on limb, Canal locks / C. ***Bottom center:*** 100. ***Right:*** 100 / Ceres standing, Cornucopia. ***Engraver:*** Rawdon, Wright, Hatch & Edson. ***Comments:*** H-MA-10-G16. 18__. 1850s.

Rarity: —

Non-Valid Issues

$5 • W-MA-010-005-S010 SI, TD

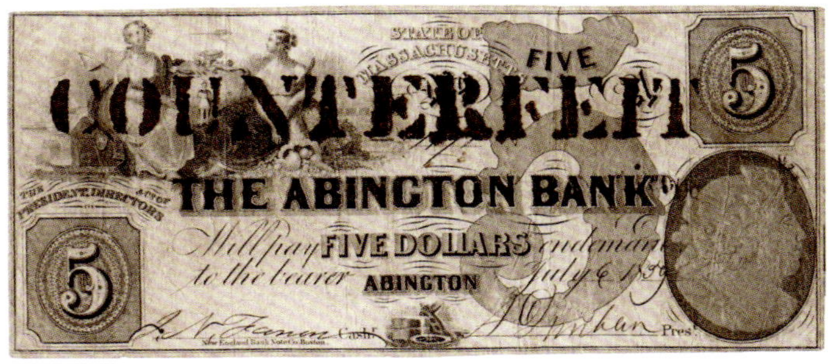

Engraver: New England Bank Note Co. ***Comments:*** H-MA-10-S5. July __, 18__. 1850s.

Rarity: URS-7
F $75; **VF** $135

$5 • W-MA-010-005-S010a TD

Overprint: Red FIVE. ***Engraver:*** New England Bank Note Co. ***Comments:*** H-Unlisted. Similar to W-MA-010-005-S010. July __, 18__. 1850s.

Rarity: URS-3
VF $1,200

$5 • W-MA-010-005-A010

Left: 5 / Tools, Woman seated on rocks, Shield bearing scene. ***Center:*** Ceres standing, Liberty seated. ***Right:*** 5 / Portrait of Zachary Taylor. ***Comments:*** H-MA-10-A5. Altered from $5 Merchants Bank, Fort Leavenworth, Kansas. 18__. 1850s.

Rarity: —

$10 • W-MA-010-010-R010

Comments: H-MA-10-R5. Raised from W-MA-010-002-G020. 18__. 1850s.

Rarity: —

$20 • W-MA-010-020-R020

Comments: H-MA-10-R10. Raised from W-MA-010-001-G010. 18__. 1850s.

Rarity: —

$20 • W-MA-010-020-R030

Comments: H-MA-10-R15. Raised from W-MA-010-002-G020. 18__. 1850s.

Rarity: —

$100 • W-MA-010-100-C080

Engraver: Rawdon, Wright, Hatch & Edson. ***Comments:*** H-MA-10-C16. Counterfeit of W-MA-010-100-G080. 18__. 1850s.

Rarity: —

Adams, Massachusetts

Originally settled in 1737, the land that would become Adams was purchased by Nathan Jones in 1762 when it was still known as East Hoosac. It was incorporated in 1778. Named in honor of Samuel Adams, a signer of the Declaration of Independence and later governor of the province (today a popular beer bears his name), the farmland was mostly divided into lots along the Hoosic River. Later that river would turn water power into mills for woolen, cotton, lumber, and plastic products. Water power provided the opportunity to build a variety of mills.

Early settlers during the 1760s were made up by a group of Quakers from Smithfield, Rhode Island, and other areas. The population declined during the early 1800s as farmers left for better land. The War of 1812 created a boom in the textile industry when the Embargo and Non-Intercourse acts made British textiles no longer available. Susan B. Anthony, a champion of women's rights, was born in Adams in 1820.

See also Adams South Village, North Adams, and South Adams, Massachusetts.

Adams Bank

1831–1865

W-MA-025

History: The Adams Bank was chartered in June 1831 with an authorized capital of $100,000. In 1837 the capital was increased to $200,000. On November 2, 1839, the circulation of bills $5 and higher in value was $39,930, and circulation of smaller-denomination bills was $13,942. By 1840 the Adams Bank was using a North Adams address.

In 1845 the capital was reduced to $100,000, and by 1851 it was $150,000. By that time the circulation of higher-denomination bills had increased to $83,520; the circulation of bills valued less than $5 had decreased to $12,110.

Capital was increased to $300,000 in 1856. In 1857 it was $350,000. Bills in circulation were listed at $193,248, specie was $7,080.54, and real estate was valued at $8,815. In October 1849, circulation was at $83,510. On January 3, 1863, it was reported at $339,697.

On May 4, 1865, the bank was succeeded by the Adams National Bank of North Adams.

See also listing under North Adams, W-MA-2510.

Adams South Village, Massachusetts

Adams South Village was the name assigned to a district in Adams, Massachusetts. It was a center for several mills and factories. The Adams South Village Cotton Manufacture Company was established in 1814, and the population of Adams increased to 4,000 between 1820 and 1835 as a result of this and other newly built mills.

See also Adams, North Adams, and South Adams, Massachusetts.

Farmers and Mechanics Bank

1836–1837

W-MA-040

History: The Farmers and Mechanics Bank was incorporated on April 1, 1836, with an authorized capital of $100,000 to be paid in within a year. An additional act extended the original time limit six months further. Finally, on September 30, 1837, the full capital stock was said to have been paid in. An inspection revealed only $50,000 on hand. However, even that claim was a fraud, as specie had been borrowed from a New York operator who took it away after the audit, leaving just $2,000 in the vault. The president of the bank denied knowledge of the caper. The proper amount of money could not be raised, and the bank was turned over to others who claimed to have provided funds. Circulation at the time was estimated to be $16,011 but may have been much more in the absence of records. The bank was closed by injunction, although in actuality it never operated in a legal manner.

See also listing under South Adams, W-MA-3020.

Numismatic Commentary: Collectors will find notes dated at Adams South Village as well as South Adams. However, notes from South Adams are the rarest by far. With notes from this bank, numismatists will find issues with odd denominations, which are always a welcome addition to a collection.

Valid Issues

$1 • W-MA-040-001-G010

QDB

Engraver: PSSP / New England Bank Note Co. ***Comments:*** H-MA-15-G4. 18__. 1830s.

Rarity: URS-6

G $125; **F** $200; **EF** $350

$1.25 • W-MA-040-001.25-G020

Left: 1 25/100, Factories, 1 25/100. ***Center:*** Ships. ***Right:*** 1 25/100, Eagle. ***Engraver:*** New England Bank Note Co. ***Comments:*** H-MA-15-G8. 18__. 1830s.

Rarity: URS-3

F $500

$1.50 • W-MA-040-001.50-G030

Left: 1 Doll. 50 Cts. vertically. ***Center:*** Eagle on rock in ocean, $1 50/100. ***Right:*** 1 50/100, Justice. ***Engraver:*** New England Bank Note Co. ***Comments:*** H-MA-15-G10. 18__. 1830s.

Rarity: URS-3

F $500

$1.75 • W-MA-040-001.75-G040
Left: $1.75 Cts., 1 75/100. ***Center:*** Three sailing ships. ***Right:*** $1.75 Cts., 1 75/100. ***Engraver:*** New England Bank Note Co. ***Comments:*** H-MA-15-G12. 18__. 1830s.

Rarity: URS-3
F $500

$2 • W-MA-040-002-G050
Left: 2 / TWO. ***Center:*** Man standing / TWO. ***Right:*** 2 / TWO. ***Engraver:*** New England Bank Note Co. ***Comments:*** H-MA-15-G16. 18__. 1830s.

Rarity: —

$5 • W-MA-040-005-G060
Left: 5 / Boy with arm raised / FIVE. ***Center:*** Man holding shield bearing 5 / V. ***Right:*** 5 / Woman seated / FIVE. ***Engraver:*** PSSP / New England Bank Note Co. ***Comments:*** H-MA-15-G24. 18__. 1830s.

Rarity: URS-5
VG $300

$10 • W-MA-040-010-G070
Left: 10 / Farmer sowing / TEN. ***Center:*** Mercury standing with 10, Merchandise, Factories and ship, Canal scene / TEN. ***Right:*** 10 / Ship / TEN. ***Engraver:*** PSSP / New England Bank Note Co. ***Comments:*** H-MA-15-G28. 18__. 1830s.

Rarity: —

$20 • W-MA-040-020-G080
Left: Steamboat / XX / Primitive train. ***Center:*** Three women seated with eagle, pole and cap, shield, scales and book / 20 / TWENTY. ***Right:*** XX / Milkmaid holding pail. ***Engraver:*** New England Bank Note Co. ***Comments:*** H-MA-15-G34. 18__. 1830s.

Rarity: —

$50 • W-MA-040-050-G090
Left: 50 / Steamboat and schooner. ***Center:*** Farmyard scene, Load of hay bearing two men, Man with rake and pail. ***Right:*** L / Justice kneeling. ***Engraver:*** New England Bank Note Co. ***Comments:*** H-MA-15-G38. 18__. 1830s.

Rarity: —

$100 • W-MA-040-100-G100
Engraver: Unverified, but likely New England Bank Note Co. ***Comments:*** H-MA-15-G42. No description available. 18__. 1830s.

Rarity: *None known*

AMHERST, MASSACHUSETTS

The first record of Amherst dates to 1658, when a deed of purchase was transacted between John Pynchon and three Indians known as Umpanchla, Quonquont, and Chickwalopp. The area was sold in exchange for "two Hundred fatham of Wampam & Twenty fatham, and one large Coate at Eight fatham wch Chickwollop set of, of trusts, besides severall small giftes [*sic*]."[19]

The first English settlers arrived in 1727. Originally a part of Hadley, Amherst gained precinct status in 1734. It was later granted township in 1759 and named after Jeffrey Amherst, who was a hero of the French and Indian War. According to legend, Amherst singlehandedly took Canada for the British, banishing the French from North America. Hat making and brick manufacturing were among the early industries of the area. In 1821 Amherst College was founded, and the Massachusetts Agricultural School, the precursor to the University of Massachusetts, was established there in 1863.

Amherst Bank
1831–1845
W-MA-050

History: The Amherst Bank was originally the Sunderland Bank, W-MA-2880, located in a town of that name a short distance from Amherst. No notes with that imprint or location are known to exist. On June 13, 1831, an act was approved for the Sunderland Bank to relocate to Amherst and be renamed the Amherst Bank. The old bills would continue to be honored and the board of directors was to stay the same. The capital was $100,000, and Nathaniel Root became the first president of the Amherst Bank, accompanied by Luther Root as cashier, both continuing from the Sunderland Bank where they had held the same offices since that bank's founding in 1825.

In December 1835 and January 1836, Lucius Boltwood, president, took a quantity of bank-note sheets already signed by the cashier to the West, in order to pass the bills. The other directors had no knowledge of this action, and when the activities came to light he was removed from his position and succeeded by Solomon Pitkin. During 1837 the bank was plagued by counterfeit $5 bills in circulation.

On July 10, 1838, the bank was visited and examined by the commissioners, and a statement of the condition was declared by the cashier, Luther Root. All was found to agree; even some odd bookkeeping, although unorthodox, aroused no suspicions. However, it was discovered in October that same year that the cashier had been loaning funds from the bank to an associate who had subsequently failed to repay the loans. This was reported by the *Hampshire Gazette*:

> After it had laid in this situation so long that the cashier was unwilling to let the directors know about it—and after Clapp's sureties on the note had become very importunate to have it taken up, Clapp persuaded the cashier to allow him to take away the old note, and leave his own note alone in its stead for a few days, promising him that it should be punctually paid. When the time came round, Clapp told him he had been disappointed and could not meet it—and further, that unless he could raise several hundred dollars more immediately, he must fail, and thus the debt he already owed would be lost. Root then consented to loan him more money on his note for ten days. It is evident that the cashier was now entirely in the power of Clapp, who by threatening an exposure, could and did extort money from him, whenever he wished it, until about a year ago, when the aggregate loans amounted to about the sum above stated.[20]

The bank was expected to suffer no loss, regardless, as the security gathered from the cashier was sufficient in making up the difference, which totaled about $19,500. The cashier was removed from his position. This fraud led the commissioners to be more strict in their investigations toward other banks.[21]

On November 2, 1839, the capital of the Amherst Bank was $100,000 and its circulation $44,586. That same year 26 counterfeiters in a gang in Canada were arrested and jailed, and a quantity of notes of the Amherst Bank was discovered. By 1842 the bank had surrendered its charter.

Numismatic Commentary: All issues from the Amherst Bank are printed from PSSP plates. They are numerous enough that a collector will have the opportunity to obtain many of the available denominations. This is due to many notes becoming worthless and unredeemable in their time.

Valid Issues

$1 • W-MA-050-001-G010

Left: Narrow lathework panel bearing MASSACHUSETTS vertically. ***Center:*** 1 / 1 / Flower garlands and gridwork segments surrounding ONE / 1 / 1. ***Right:*** ONE, D, ONE vertically. ***Engraver:*** PSSP. ***Comments:*** H-MA-20-G2. 18__. 1830s.

Rarity: —

$2 • W-MA-050-002-G020

Left: MASSACHUSETTS vertically. ***Center:*** 2 / 2 / Flower garlands and gridwork segments / 2 / 2. ***Right:*** Five TWOs vertically. ***Engraver:*** PSSP. ***Comments:*** H-MA-20-G8. Similar to W-MA-050-002-C020. 18__. 1830s.

Rarity: URS-7
F $350

$3 • W-MA-050-003-G030

Left: Narrow lathework panel bearing MASSACHUSETTS vertically. ***Center:*** 3 / 3 / Flower garlands and gridwork segments surrounding THREE / 3 / 3. ***Right:*** THREE vertically. ***Engraver:*** PSSP. ***Comments:*** H-MA-20-G14. 18__. 1830s.

Rarity: URS-4
F $500

$5 • W-MA-050-005-G040

Left: Lathework chain bearing MASSACHUSETTS / 5 / 5. ***Center:*** Flower garlands and gridwork segments surrounding FIVE DOLLARS. ***Right:*** 5 / 5 vertically. ***Engraver:*** PSSP. ***Comments:*** H-MA-20-G18. 18__. 1820s.

Rarity: —

$5 • W-MA-050-005-G050

Left: Lathework chain bearing MASSACHUSETTS / 5 / 5. ***Center:*** White boxes flanking FIVE DOLLARS. ***Right:*** 5 / 5 vertically. ***Engraver:*** PSSP. ***Comments:*** H-MA-20-G20. 18__. 1830s.

Rarity: —

$10 • W-MA-050-010-G060

Left: Lathework chain bearing MASSACHUSETTS / 10 / 10 vertically. ***Center:*** White boxes flanking MASSACHUSETTS. ***Right:*** 10 / 10 vertically. ***Engraver:*** PSSP. ***Comments:*** H-MA-20-G24. 18__. 1820s.

Rarity: URS-3
F $1,000

$10 • W-MA-050-010-G070

Left: Lathework chain bearing MASSACHUSETTS / 10 / 10 vertically. ***Center:*** White boxes flanking TEN DOLLARS. ***Right:*** 10 / 10 vertically. ***Engraver:*** PSSP. ***Comments:*** H-MA-20-G26. 18__. 1830s.

Rarity: —

$20 • W-MA-050-020-G080

Left: Lathework chain bearing MASSACHUSETTS / 20 / 20 vertically. ***Center:*** Flower garlands and gridwork segments. ***Right:*** 20 / 20 vertically. ***Engraver:*** PSSP. ***Comments:*** H-MA-20-G30. 18__. 1830s.

Rarity: —

$50 • W-MA-050-050-G090

Left: Lathework chain bearing MASSACHUSETTS / 50 / 50 vertically. ***Center:*** Flower garlands and gridwork segments. ***Right:*** 50 / 50 vertically. ***Engraver:*** PSSP. ***Comments:*** H-MA-20-G34. 18__. 1830s.

Rarity: —

$100 • W-MA-050-100-G100

Left: Lathework chain bearing MASSACHUSETTS / 100 / 100 vertically. ***Center:*** Flower garlands and gridwork segments. ***Right:*** 100 / 100 vertically. ***Engraver:*** PSSP. ***Comments:*** H-MA-20-G38. 18__. 1830s.

Rarity: —

Non-Valid Issues

$1 • W-MA-050-001-C010

Engraver: PSSP. ***Comments:*** H-MA-20-C2. Counterfeit of W-MA-050-001-G010. 18__. 1835.

Rarity: —

$2 • W-MA-050-002-C020

HA

Engraver: PSSP. ***Comments:*** H-MA-20-C8. Counterfeit of W-MA-050-002-G020. 18__. 1830s.

Rarity: URS-7
F $100; **VF** $175

$5 • W-MA-050-005-C050

SI

Engraver: PSSP. ***Comments:*** H-MA-20-C20. Counterfeit of W-MA-050-005-G050. 18__. 1830s.

Rarity: URS-7
F $100; **VF** $150

$10 • W-MA-050-010-C060

CJF

Engraver: PSSP. ***Comments:*** H-MA-20-C24. Counterfeit of W-MA-050-010-G060. 18__. Circa 1840.

Rarity: URS-5
F $150

Andover, Massachusetts

In 1634 the General Court of Massachusetts set aside the land around Lake Cochichewick to be used as a plantation. Part of this land included areas which are now Andover, North Andover, and South Lawrence. The first settlement in Andover of permanent nature was established by John Woodbridge in 1641.

In May 1646, the area was incorporated as an official town, named after Andover, England, which was the birthplace of some of the settlers. In 1778 Samuel Phillips Jr. began a school for boys in a remodeled carpenter's shop, and today Phillips Academy is one of the premier private schools in the nation. Mills were built to process corn and wood, and in 1775 a powder mill produced gunpowder for the Continental Army. Textile mills were important through the 1780s and later. By 1835 there were six mill districts in existence: Sutton Mills and Stevens Mills on the Cochichewick River, and Ballardvale, Abbot Village, Marland Mills, and Frye Village adjacent to the Shawsheen River.

In 1854 the town was divided into political halves, with Andover representing the west and south and North Andover representing the north.

Andover Bank

1826–1865

W-MA-060

History: The Andover Bank was chartered on March 4, 1826, with a starting capital of $100,000. The founding directors were elected on March 26, 1826, and were listed as: Samuel Farrar, Mark Newman, Amos Abbot, Francis Kidder, Stephen Abbot, Joseph Kittredge, Hobart Clark, Amos Spaulding, and Nathaniel Stephens. Subsequently, Samuel Farrar was elected president and Amos Blanchard cashier.

By 1837 the capital had increased by $100,000; in 1851 it was $275,000. November 1839 showed the capital at $300,000 and circulation at $51,084. By November 1845, the capital was reduced again to $250,000, where it remained constant throughout the bank's existence. Circulation ranged from $80,260 to $139,249 between 1849 and 1863. Deposits in 1851 were $14,025.11; loans $356,161.90; real estate $5,000; and specie $6,850.19. Specie in 1857 was $10,359.74, and real estate was valued at $5,000.

According to the *Annual Report of the Commissioner of Banks*, in 1858 loans totaled $361,592.83; real estate $5,000; deposits $41,428.38; profits $22,344.47; and specie $7,709.96.

In October 1864, counterfeit $5 bills appeared. A year later, on April 3, 1865, the stockholders voted to apply to form a National Banking association. The Andover Bank closed and was replaced by the Andover National Bank in May 1865.

Numismatic Commentary: There are many more non-valid notes available from this bank than there are valid or genuine examples. Some of the genuine issues will show a portrait of Samuel Farrar, the treasurer of the renowned Phillips Academy in Andover during its early years.

As of 2003 there was one $500-$1,000 face plate remaining in the American Bank Note Co. archives.

Valid Issues

$1 • W-MA-060-001-G010

Left: Narrow panel of lathework circle segments. ***Center:*** 1 / 1 / Flower garlands and gridwork segments / 1 / 1. ***Right:*** Narrow panel of lathework circle segments. ***Engraver:*** PSSP. ***Comments:*** H-MA-25-G2. 18__. 1820s–1830s.

Rarity: —

$1 • W-MA-060-001-G020

Left: ONE / D / ONE vertically. ***Right:*** ONE / D / ONE vertically. ***Engraver:*** PSSP. ***Comments:*** H-MA-25-G4. Similar to W-MA-060-001-G010. 18__. 1830s.

Rarity: —

$1 • W-MA-060-001-G030

Left: 1 / Minerva standing with 1 / 1. ***Center:*** ONE / Plow, Commerce seated with caduceus and cornucopia, Ships / ONE. ***Right:*** 1 / Eagle / 1. ***Engraver:*** PSSP / New England Bank Note Co. ***Comments:*** H-MA-25-G8. 18__. 1830s.

Rarity: —

$1 • W-MA-060-001-G040

CJF

Back: Black Check Plate. ***Engraver:*** PSSP / New England Bank Note Co. ***Comments:*** H-MA-25-G12. 18__. 1830s–1840s.

Rarity: URS-2
F $300

$1 • W-MA-060-001-G050

Left: 1 / Justice. ***Center:*** Train. ***Bottom center:*** Eagle. ***Right:*** 1 / Portrait of Samuel Farrar. ***Engraver:*** Toppan, Carpenter, Casilear & Co. ***Comments:*** H-MA-25-G16. 18__. 1850s.

Rarity: URS-3
F $500

$1 • W-MA-060-001-G050a

CJF

Overprint: Red ONE. ***Engraver:*** Toppan, Carpenter, Casilear & Co. ***Comments:*** H-Unlisted. Similar to W-MA-060-001-G050. Oct. 1, 18__. 1850s.

Rarity: URS-3
F $1,500

$2 • W-MA-060-002-G060

Left: Narrow panel of lathework circle segments. ***Center:*** 2 / 2 / Flower garlands and gridwork segments / 2 / 2. ***Engraver:*** PSSP. ***Comments:*** H-MA-25-G20. 18__. 1820s–1830s.

Rarity: URS-2
F $2,000

$2 • W-MA-060-002-G070

Left: Five TWOs vertically. ***Right:*** Five TWOs vertically. ***Engraver:*** PSSP. ***Comments:*** H-MA-25-G22. Similar to W-MA-060-002-G060. 18__. 1830s.

Rarity: URS-2
F $2,000

$2 • W-MA-060-002-G080

Left: 2 / Hebe watering eagle / 2. ***Center:*** 2 / Plow, Commerce seated on shore, Cornucopia / 2. ***Right:*** 2 / Justice standing / 2. ***Engraver:*** PSSP. ***Comments:*** H-MA-25-G24. 18__. 1830s.

Rarity: URS-2
F $2,000

$2 • W-MA-060-002-G090

Left: 2 / Cornucopia, Woman standing with staff / TWO. ***Center:*** TWO / Machinery and merchandise flanking Ceres seated holding sickle and rake, Factories and harbor / Panel outlining white TWO. ***Right:*** 2 / Woman wearing hat, Trees / TWO. ***Back:*** Black Check Plate. ***Engraver:*** PSSP / New England Bank Note Co. ***Comments:*** H-MA-25-G28. 18__. 1830s–1840s.

Rarity: URS-2
F $2,000

$2 • W-MA-060-002-G100

Left: TWO / Liberty. ***Center:*** Three women. ***Bottom center:*** Portrait of Indian man. ***Right:*** Portrait of Samuel Farrar. ***Engraver:*** Unverified, but likely Toppan, Carpenter & Co. ***Comments:*** H-MA-25-G32. 18__. 1850s.

Rarity: URS-2
F $2,000

$2 • W-MA-060-002-G110

JF

Engraver: New England Bank Note Co. ***Comments:*** H-Unlisted. 18__. 1850s.

Rarity: URS-3
F $1,250

$3 • W-MA-060-003-G120

Left: Narrow panel of lathework circle segments. ***Center:*** 3 / 3 / Flower garlands and gridwork segments / 3 / 3. ***Right:*** Narrow panel of lathework circle segments. ***Engraver:*** PSSP. ***Comments:*** H-MA-25-G36. 18__. 1820s–1830s.

Rarity: URS-2
F $2,000

$3 • W-MA-060-003-G130

Left: THREE vertically. ***Right:*** THREE vertically. ***Engraver:*** PSSP. ***Comments:*** H-MA-25-G38. Similar to W-MA-060-003-G120. 18__. 1830s.

Rarity: URS-2
F $2,000

$3 • W-MA-060-003-G140

Left: 3 / Eagle on rock / 3. ***Center:*** 3 / Plow, Commerce seated with caduceus and cornucopia, Ships / 3 / Panel bearing THREE. ***Right:*** 3 / Woman standing with cornucopia / 3. ***Engraver:*** PSSP. ***Comments:*** H-MA-25-G40. 18__. 1830s.

Rarity: URS-2
F $2,000

$3 • W-MA-060-003-G150

Left: THREE / Beehive and foliage / THREE. ***Center:*** Machinery and merchandise flanking Ceres seated holding sickle and rake, Factories and harbor / THREE / Panel outlining white THREE. ***Right:*** 3 on THREE / Two reapers / 3 on THREE. ***Back:*** Black Check Plate. ***Engraver:*** PSSP / New England Bank Note Co. ***Comments:*** H-MA-25-G44. 18__. 1830s–1840s.

Rarity: URS-2
F $2,000

$3 • W-MA-060-003-G160

Left: 3 / State arms. ***Center:*** Three women seated. ***Bottom center:*** Cog wheels. ***Right:*** 3 / Portrait of Samuel Farrar. ***Engraver:*** Unverified, but likely Toppan, Carpenter & Co. ***Comments:*** H-MA-25-G48. 18__. 1850s.

Rarity: URS-2
F $2,000

$5 • W-MA-060-005-G170

Left: Lathework chain bearing MASSACHUSETTS / 5 / 5. ***Center:*** Alternating flower garlands and gridwork segments. ***Right:*** 5 / 5. ***Engraver:*** PSSP. ***Comments:*** H-MA-25-G52. 18__. 1820s.

Rarity: URS-2
F $1,250

$5 • W-MA-060-005-G170a

Engraver: PSSP. ***Comments:*** H-MA-25-G54. Similar to W-MA-060-005-G170 but with zigzag ruled lines. 18__. 1820s–1830s.

Rarity: URS-2
F $1,250

$5 • W-MA-060-005-G170b

Engraver: PSSP. ***Comments:*** H-MA-25-G56. Similar to W-MA-060-005-G170 but with spiral lathework lines. 18__. 1830s.

Rarity: URS-2
F $1,250

$5 • W-MA-060-005-G180

Left: Panel bearing FIVE / Plenty and Minerva seated / V. ***Center:*** FIVE, Allegorical woman seated, FIVE / Panel of microletters. ***Right:*** 5 / Eagle / 5. ***Back:*** Check Plate. ***Engraver:*** PSSP. ***Comments:*** H-MA-25-G58. 18__. 1830s.

Rarity: URS-2
F $1,250

$5 • W-MA-060-005-G190

Left: 5 / Blacksmith at anvil / FIVE. ***Center:*** Mercury standing with 5, Cornucopia and merchandise, Factories / V / Panel outlining white FIVE. ***Right:*** 5 / Ceres kneeling / FIVE. ***Back:*** Black Check Plate. ***Engraver:*** PSSP / New England Bank Note Co. ***Comments:*** H-MA-25-G60. 18__. 1830s–1840s.

Rarity: URS-2
F $1,250

$5 • W-MA-060-005-G200

Left: Three women / FIVE. ***Center:*** Eagle and shield. ***Bottom center:*** Portrait of girl. ***Right:*** 5 / Portrait of Samuel Farrar. ***Engraver:*** Unverified, but likely Toppan, Carpenter & Co. ***Comments:*** H-MA-25-G64. 18__. 1850s.

Rarity: URS-2
F $1,250

$10 • W-MA-060-010-G210

Left: Lathework chain bearing MASSACHUSETTS / 10 / 10 vertically. ***Center:*** Alternating flower garlands and gridwork segments. ***Right:*** 10 / 10 vertically. ***Engraver:*** PSSP. ***Comments:*** H-MA-25-G68. 18__. 1820s.

Rarity: URS-2
F $1,500

$10 • W-MA-060-010-G210a

Engraver: PSSP. ***Comments:*** H-MA-25-G70. Similar to W-MA-060-010-G210 but with zigzag ruled lines. 18__. 1820s–1830s.

Rarity: URS-2
F $1,500

$10 • W-MA-060-010-G210b

Engraver: PSSP. ***Comments:*** H-MA-25-G72. Similar to W-MA-060-010-G210 but with spiral lathework lines. 18__. 1830s.

Rarity: URS-2
F $1,500

$10 • W-MA-060-010-G220

Left: Panel bearing TEN / Manhattan and spilling water jug / TEN. ***Center:*** TEN / Ceres seated / TEN / Panel of microletters. ***Right:*** Panel bearing 10 / Portrait of Indian / 10. ***Back:*** Check Plate. ***Engraver:*** PSSP. ***Comments:*** H-MA-25-G74. 18__. 1830s.

Rarity: URS-2
F $1,500

$10 • W-MA-060-010-G230

Left: 10 / Farmer sowing / TEN. ***Center:*** Mercury standing with 10, Merchandise, Factories and ship / Canal scene / Panel outlining white TEN. ***Right:*** 10 / Ship / TEN. ***Back:*** Black Check Plate. ***Engraver:*** PSSP / New England Bank Note Co. ***Comments:*** H-MA-25-G76. 18__. 1830s–1840s.

Rarity: —

$10 • W-MA-060-010-G240

Left: 10 / Portrait of Samuel Farrar. ***Center:*** Angel in clouds blowing trumpet, Globe, Eagle and flags. ***Bottom center:*** Tools and merchandise. ***Right:*** 10 / Justice. ***Engraver:*** Unverified, but likely Toppan, Carpenter & Co. ***Comments:*** H-MA-25-G80. 18__. 1850s.

Rarity: —

$20 • W-MA-060-020-G250

Left: Lathework chain bearing MASSACHUSETTS / 20 / 20 vertically. ***Center:*** Alternating flower garlands and gridwork segments. ***Right:*** 20 / 20 vertically. ***Engraver:*** PSSP. ***Comments:*** H-MA-25-G84. 18__. 1820s–1830s.

Rarity: —

$20 • W-MA-060-020-G260

Left: Steamboat / XX / Train. ***Center:*** Three women seated with eagle, pole and cap, shield, scales and book / 20 / Panel outlining white TWENTY. ***Right:*** XX / Milkmaid standing with pail. ***Back:*** Black Check Plate. ***Engraver:*** PSSP / New England Bank Note Co. ***Comments:*** H-MA-25-G88. 18__. 1830s–1840s.

Rarity: —

$20 • W-MA-060-020-G270

Left: 20 / Portrait of Samuel Farrar. ***Center:*** Woman seated with child, Four reapers resting, Men loading hay. ***Right:*** 20 / Indian woman as Liberty. ***Engraver:*** Toppan, Carpenter, Casilear & Co. ***Comments:*** H-MA-25-G90. 18__. 1850s.

Rarity: —

$20 • W-MA-060-020-G270a

JF

Overprint: Red TWENTY. ***Engraver:*** Toppan, Carpenter, Casilear & Co. ***Comments:*** H-Unlisted. Similar to W-MA-060-020-G270. Proof. Oct. 1, 18__. 1850s.

Rarity: URS-2
Proof $3,000

$50 • W-MA-060-050-G280

Left: Lathework chain bearing MASSACHUSETTS / 50 / 50 vertically. ***Center:*** Alternating flower garlands and gridwork segments. ***Right:*** 50 / 50 vertically. ***Engraver:*** PSSP. ***Comments:*** H-MA-25-G94. 18__. 1820s–1830s.

Rarity: —

$50 • W-MA-060-050-G290

Engraver: Unverified, but likely New England Bank Note Co. ***Comments:*** H-MA-25-G98. No description available. 18__. 1830s–1840s.

Rarity: *None known*

$50 • W-MA-060-050-G300

Left: Woman holding sheaf and shading eyes with hand / 50. ***Center:*** Landing of Christopher Columbus. ***Right:*** 50 / Male portrait. ***Engraver:*** Unverified, but likely Toppan, Carpenter & Co. ***Comments:*** H-MA-25-G100. 18__. 1850s.

Rarity: —

$100 • W-MA-060-100-G310

Left: Lathework chain bearing MASSACHUSETTS / 100 / 100 vertically. ***Center:*** Alternating flower garlands and gridwork segments. ***Right:*** 100 / 100 vertically. ***Engraver:*** PSSP. ***Comments:*** H-MA-25-G104. 18__. 1820s–1830s.

Rarity: —

$100 • W-MA-060-100-G320

Engraver: Unverified, but likely New England Bank Note Co. ***Comments:*** H-MA-25-G108. No description available. 18__. 1830s–1840s.

Rarity: *None known*

$100 • W-MA-060-100-G330

Left: Woman seated with shield, Eagle and flags / 100. ***Center:*** Female portrait. ***Right:*** 100 / Female portrait. ***Engraver:*** Unverified, but likely Toppan, Carpenter & Co. ***Comments:*** H-MA-25-G110. 18__. 1850s.

Rarity: —

$500 • W-MA-060-500-G340

Engraver: Unverified, but likely New England Bank Note Co. ***Comments:*** H-MA-25-G114. No description available. 18__. 1830s–1840s.

Rarity: *None known*

$500 • W-MA-060-500-G350

Left: 500 / Female portrait. ***Center:*** Eagle. ***Right:*** 500 / Three women seated / 500. ***Overprint:*** Red D. ***Engraver:*** Toppan, Carpenter, Casilear & Co. ***Comments:*** H-MA-25-G116a. 18__. 1850s–1860s.

Rarity: URS-3
Proof $5,000
Selected auction price: Stack's Bowers Galleries, August 2014, Lot 2050, Proof $5,875

$1,000 • W-MA-060-1000-G360

CC

Engraver: Toppan, Carpenter, Casilear & Co. ***Comments:*** H-Unlisted. Proof. 18__. 1850s–1860s.

Rarity: URS-2
Proof $3,200

$1,000 • W-MA-060-1000-G360a

Left: M / Ship, Two women with bales, Train and canal locks / 1000. ***Right:*** 1000 / ONE THOUSAND / 1000. ***Overprint:*** Red M. ***Engraver:*** Toppan, Carpenter, Casilear & Co. ***Comments:*** H-MA-25-G118a. Similar to W-MA-060-1000-G360. 18__. 1850s–1860s.

Rarity: URS-2
Proof $5,000
Selected auction price: Stack's Bowers Galleries, August 2014, Lot 2051, Proof $4,406

Non-Valid Issues

$1 • W-MA-060-001-A010

Left: ONE on die vertically. ***Center:*** Man on horse overseeing cotton harvest / Indian stalking two deer. ***Bottom center:*** Sleeping dog. ***Right:*** 1 / Female portrait. ***Overprint:*** Red ONE. ***Engraver:*** Bald, Cousland & Co. / Baldwin, Bald & Cousland. ***Comments:*** H-MA-25-A5. Altered from $1 Southern Bank of Georgia, Bainbridge, Georgia. 18__. 1860s.

Rarity: —

$2 • W-MA-060-002-A020

SI

Overprint: Red TWO. ***Engraver:*** Bald, Cousland & Co. / Baldwin, Bald & Cousland. ***Comments:*** H-MA-25-A10. Altered from $2 Southern Bank of Georgia, Bainbridge, Georgia. 18__. 1860s.

Rarity: URS-6
VG $100; **F** $125

$2 • W-MA-060-002-A030

Left: 2 / Farmer plowing with black and white horses. ***Center:*** Two men loading wagon with sheaves, Three men cradling and binding. ***Right:*** 2 / Two floating cherubs with caduceus and sheaf. ***Tint:*** Red-brown 2s and TWO DOLLARS. ***Engraver:*** Danforth, Wright & Co. ***Comments:*** H-MA-25-A15. Altered from $2 Southern Bank of Georgia, Bainbridge, Georgia. March 1, 1958.

Rarity: —

$3 • W-MA-060-003-S010

NJW

Comments: H-MA-25-S5. Oct. 1, 18__. 1850s.

Rarity: URS-4
F $200

$3 • W-MA-060-003-S020

NJW

Engraver: New England Bank Note Co. ***Comments:*** H-MA-25-S10. Jan. 1, 1856.

Rarity: URS-5
F $175

$3 • W-MA-060-003-S030

NJW

Engraver: New England Bank Note Co. ***Comments:*** H-Unlisted. Jan. 1, 1856. 1850s.

Rarity: URS-5
F $200

$3 • W-MA-060-003-A040

Left: 3 / Portrait of Benjamin Franklin. ***Center:*** Woman seated / 3 on shield. ***Right:*** 3 / Woman seated. ***Engraver:*** Danforth, Wright & Co. ***Comments:*** H-MA-25-A20. Altered from $3 Columbus Bank, Washington, D.C. 18__. 1860s.

Rarity: URS-6
VG $75; **F** $125

$10 • W-MA-060-010-N010

Center: Harbor scene and ships. ***Back:*** Plain. ***Engraver:*** New England Bank Note Co. ***Comments:*** H-MA-25-N5. Genuine note has Check Plate. 18__. 1840s.

Rarity: —

$10 • W-MA-060-010-A050

SN

Overprint: Red TEN. ***Engraver:*** Bald, Cousland & Co. / Baldwin, Bald & Cousland. ***Comments:*** H-MA-25-A25. Altered from $10 Southern Bank of Georgia, Bainbridge, Georgia. 18__. 1860s.

Rarity: URS-6
VG $100

$20 • W-MA-060-020-A060

Left: Woman floating in clouds holding U.S. shield and flowers above head / XX. ***Center:*** XX / Slain deer / Indian man with headdress reclining. ***Right:*** 20 / Portrait of George Washington. ***Engraver:*** Rawdon, Wright, Hatch & Edson. ***Comments:*** H-MA-25-A30. Altered from $20 of the fraudulent New England Bank, Fairmount, Maine. Oct. 1, 1857.

Rarity: —

Essex Bank

1836–1847

W-MA-070

History: Chartered on April 1, 1836, with $100,000 capital, the Essex Bank was incorporated in the Andover North Parish. In May 1836, the directors were elected and listed as: Dr. Joseph Kittredge, Gayton P. Osgood, Nathaniel Stevens, John Tenny, Nathaniel Swift, George Hodges, William Johnson, James Stevens 2nd, and N.W. Hazen. The bank opened for business on July 1, 1836, with William Stevens as cashier. In November 1839, the Essex Bank's capital was $100,000, and its circulation was $46,753. On March 25, 1845, the Legislature passed an act to close its business, allowing extra time for a period of two years after December 1, 1845, to accomplish this.[22]

See also listing under North Andover, W-MA-2520.

Numismatic Commentary: All notes bear the New England Bank Note Co. imprint. As indicated below, they are non-collectible.

Valid Issues

$1 • W-MA-070-001-G010

Comments: H-MA-30-G3. No description available. 18__. 1830s–1840s.

Rarity: *None known*

$2 • W-MA-070-002-G020

Comments: H-MA-30-G6. No description available. 18__. 1830s–1840s.

Rarity: *None known*

$3 • W-MA-070-003-G030

Comments: H-MA-30-G9. No description available. 18__. 1830s–1840s.

Rarity: *None known*

$5 • W-MA-070-005-G040

Comments: H-MA-30-G12. No description available. 18__. 1830s–1840s.

Rarity: *None known*

$10 • W-MA-070-010-G050

Comments: H-MA-30-G15. No description available. 18__. 1830s–1840s.

Rarity: *None known*

$20 • W-MA-070-020-G060

Comments: H-MA-30-G18. No description available. 18__. 1830s–1840s.

Rarity: *None known*

$50 • W-MA-070-050-G070

Comments: H-MA-30-G21. No description available. 18__. 1830s–1840s.

Rarity: *None known*

$100 • W-MA-070-100-G080

Comments: H-MA-30-G24. No description available. 18__. 1830s–1840s.

Rarity: *None known*

$500 • W-MA-070-500-G090

Comments: H-MA-30-G27. No description available. 18__. 1830s–1840s.

Rarity: *None known*

Athol, Massachusetts

The area known as Athol, which means "pleasant place" in Scots Gaelic, was settled under the original name of Pequoiag in September 1735. Incorporated in 1762, the town then became Athol after the ancestral home of the founder, John Murray, who was from Blair Atholl in Scotland.

Agriculture and hunting were the primary industries early on, and by 1791 there were four grist mills, six saw mills, and a fulling mill. In 1811 the Athol Cotton Factory was built. Through the 1800s, further industries such as textile, leather, wood, and metal were developed in Athol.

By the 1840s the railroads had generated so much growth that the train lines had to be extended, and industries, homes, and stores developed all along the river valley, making Athol the center of commerce and activity in that area.

Millers River Bank

1854–1865

W-MA-080

History: In April 1854, the *Banker's Magazine* reported that a bill had been passed to establish the Miller's River Bank with a starting capital of $100,000. Circulation was $120,890, real estate was valued at $3,000, and specie totaled $6,492.32.

The capital stock was increased in 1857 to $150,000. Circulation was listed at $117,581, specie was $19,215, and real estate was valued at $3,000. Circulation hovered around $138,000 from 1858 to 1863. Specie ranged from $16,528.88 to $138,704 during the same period.

In 1864 the stockholders voted to form the Millers River National Bank, which was chartered on December 15 of that year. It assumed the assets and liabilities of the state-chartered bank, which wound down its operations.

Numismatic Commentary: Enough lower denomination notes from this bank have come to light in the last two decades that it is now possible to hope to find an example. However, they are still among some of the hardest Massachusetts notes to find.

As of 2003 there was a $1 tint, $2 tint, $3 tint, $5 tint, $5 tint, $10 tint, and $50 tint plates remaining at the American Bank Note Co. archives.

Valid Issues

$1 • W-MA-080-001-G010

Left: Woman seated on ground, Woman scattering flowers. ***Right:*** 1 / ONE / 1. ***Engraver:*** Danforth, Wright & Co. ***Comments:*** H-MA-35-G2. 18__. 1850s.

Rarity: URS-3

VF $1,000

$1 • W-MA-080-001-G010a

CJF

Overprint: Red 1. ***Engraver:*** Danforth, Wright & Co. ***Comments:*** H-Unlisted. Similar to W-MA-080-001-G010. 18__. 1850s.

Rarity: URS-2

F $1,500; **VF** $2,000; **Proof** $4,000

$1 • W-MA-080-001-G010b

CJF

Tint: Red. ***Engraver:*** Danforth, Wright & Co. ***Comments:*** H-MA-35-G2a. Similar to W-MA-080-001-G010. January 12, 18__. 1860s.

Rarity: URS-3

VF $1,000; **Proof** $4,000

$2 • W-MA-080-002-G020

Left: 2 / TWO / River, trees, Train on bridge. ***Center:*** Two lathework ovals. ***Right:*** 2 / Indian woman and child. ***Engraver:*** Danforth, Wright & Co. ***Comments:*** H-MA-35-G4. 18__. 1850s.

Rarity: URS-2

F $1,000

$2 • W-MA-080-002-G020a

RMS

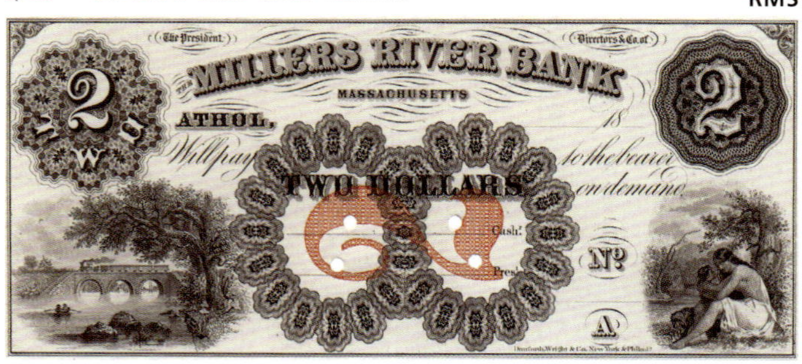

Overprint: Red lazy 2. ***Engraver:*** Danforth, Wright & Co. ***Comments:*** H-Unlisted. Similar to W-MA-080-002-G020. 18__. 1850s.

Rarity: URS-2

Proof $3,000

Selected auction price: Stack's Bowers Galleries, August 2014, Lot 2052, Proof $5,581

$2 • W-MA-080-002-G020b

CJF

Tint: Red. ***Engraver:*** Danforth, Wright & Co. ***Comments:*** H-MA-35-G4a. Similar to W-MA-080-002-G020. January 12, 18__. 1860s.

Rarity: URS-2
Proof $3,500

$3 • W-MA-080-003-G030

Left: 3 / Woman, man, two children, Sheep and grain. ***Center:*** Lathework triangle. ***Right:*** 3 / THREE / 3. ***Engraver:*** Danforth, Wright & Co. ***Comments:*** H-MA-35-G6. 18__. 1850s.

Rarity: URS-2
F $1,500; **Proof** $7,000
Selected auction price: Heritage, April 2011, Lot 15223, Choice Fine $1,265

$3 • W-MA-080-003-G030a

RMS

Overprint: Red 3. ***Engraver:*** Danforth, Wright & Co. ***Comments:*** H-Unlisted. Similar to W-MA-080-003-G030. 18__. 1850s.

Rarity: URS-1
Proof $6,500

$3 • W-MA-080-003-G030b

CC

Tint: Red. ***Engraver:*** Danforth, Wright & Co. / ABNCo. monogram. ***Comments:*** H-MA-35-G6a. Similar to W-MA-080-003-G030. January 12, 18__. 1860s.

Rarity: URS-2
EF $2,900

$5 • W-MA-080-005-G040

Left: V / FIVE, 5, FIVE. ***Center:*** Man shoeing horse in blacksmith's shop. ***Engraver:*** Danforth, Wright & Co. ***Comments:*** H-MA-35-G8. 18__. 1850s.

Rarity: —

$5 • W-MA-080-005-G040a

RMS

Overprint: Red 5. ***Engraver:*** Danforth, Wright & Co. ***Comments:*** H-Unlisted. Similar to W-MA-080-005-G040. 18__. 1850s.

Rarity: URS-2
Proof $3,000
Selected auction price: Stack's Bowers Galleries, August 2014, Lot 2053, Proof $4,993

$5 • W-MA-080-005-G040b

Tint: Red and five-pointed star with 5. ***Engraver:*** Danforth, Wright & Co. ***Comments:*** H-MA-35-G8a. Similar to W-MA-080-005-G040. 18__. 1860s.

Rarity: —

$10 • W-MA-080-010-G050

CC

Engraver: Unverified, but likely Danforth, Wright & Co. ***Comments:*** H-MA-35-G10. 18__. 1850s.

Rarity: URS-1
Proof $3,500

$10 • W-MA-080-010-G050a

Left: Lathework shield containing bank officer names. ***Center:*** Woman seated with scroll, Woman with elbow on shield bearing ship and plow. ***Right:*** 10 / Portrait of George Washington. ***Tint:*** Red. ***Engraver:*** Unverified, but likely Danforth, Wright & Co. ***Comments:*** H-MA-35-G10a. Similar to W-MA-080-010-G050. 18__. 1860s.

Rarity: —

$20 • W-MA-080-020-G060

JF

Engraver: Danforth, Wright & Co. ***Comments:*** H-MA-35-G12. Proof. 18__. 1850s.

Rarity: URS-1
Proof $4,000

$50 • W-MA-080-050-G070

Left: FIFTY / Five women seated in clouds. ***Center:*** L on die. ***Right:*** 50 / Eagle on limb. ***Engraver:*** Danforth, Wright & Co. ***Comments:*** H-MA-35-G14. 18__. 1850s.

Rarity: URS-1
Proof $6,500

$50 • W-MA-080-050-G070a

Tint: Ochre. ***Engraver:*** Danforth, Wright & Co. ***Comments:*** H-MA-35-G14a. Similar to W-MA-080-050-G070. 18__.

Rarity: —

Uncut Sheets

$1-$2-$3 • W-MA-080-001.002.003-US010

JF

Tint(s): Red. ***Engraver:*** Danforth, Wright & Co. ***Comments:*** H-MA-35-G2a, G4a, G6a. Partial sheet. January 12, 18__. 1860s.

Rarity: URS-1
Proof $14,000

$1-$2-$3-$5 • W-MA-080-001.002.003.005-US020

RMS

Overprint(s): Red. ***Engraver:*** Danforth, Wright & Co. ***Comments:*** All unlisted in Haxby. 18__. 1850s.

Rarity: URS-1
Proof $18,000

Non-Valid Issues

$1 • W-MA-080-001-A010

Left: ONE / Woman / ONE. ***Center:*** 1 / Train / 1. ***Right:*** ONE / Woman standing. ***Engraver:*** W.L. Ormsby. ***Comments:*** H-MA-35-A5. Altered from $1 Potomac River Bank, Georgetown, D.C. 18__. 1850s.

Rarity: URS-6
VG $200

$2 • W-MA-080-002-A020

CJF

Engraver: W.L. Ormsby. ***Comments:*** H-MA-35-A10. Altered from $2 Potomac River Bank, Georgetown, D.C. 185_. 1850s.

Rarity: URS-5
F $125

$3 • W-MA-080-003-A030

Left: THREE / Woman seated with scroll and pen / THREE. ***Center:*** Train, Woman in clouds with shield and eagle. ***Right:*** THREE / Laureate woman standing with legs crossed, Shield bearing 3. ***Engraver:*** W.L. Ormsby. ***Comments:*** H-MA-35-A15. Altered from $3 Potomac River Bank, Georgetown, D.C. 18__. 1850s.

Rarity: —

$5 • W-MA-080-005-A040

Left: FIVE / Laureate woman standing with legs crossed, Shield bearing 5. ***Center:*** Woman in clouds with shield and eagle / 5. ***Bottom center:*** Train. ***Right:*** FIVE / Woman standing with pole and cap, Cornucopia and sheaf. ***Engraver:*** W.L. Ormsby. ***Comments:*** H-MA-35-A20. Altered from $5 Potomac River Bank, Georgetown, D.C. 18__. 1850s.

Rarity: URS-5
F $125

$10 • W-MA-080-010-C050

Engraver: Danforth, Wright & Co. ***Comments:*** H-MA-35-C10. Counterfeit of W-MA-080-010-G050 or G050a. 18__. 1850s.

Rarity: URS-5
F $125

$10 • W-MA-080-010-S010

CC

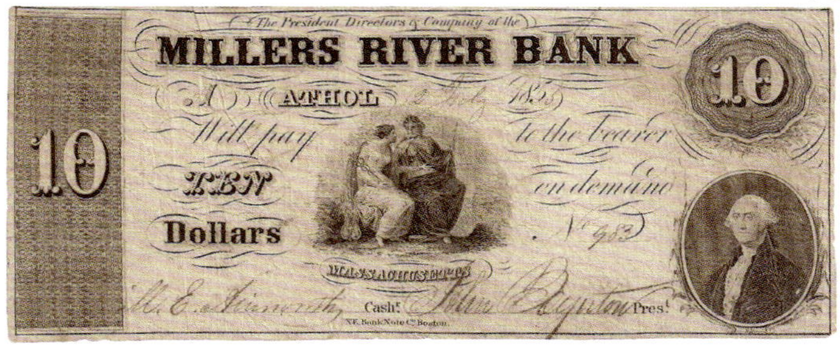

Engraver: New England Bank Note Co. ***Comments:*** H-Unlisted. 185_. 1850s.

Rarity: URS-2
VF $600

$10 • W-MA-080-010-N010

Center: Two women seated, Ship. ***Comments:*** H-MA-35-N5. 18__. 1850s.

Rarity: URS-5
F $100

ATTLEBOROUGH, MASSACHUSETTS

Originally part of Rehoboth, the town of Attleborough was incorporated in 1694. This included Cumberland, Rhode Island, until 1747, and also the town of North Attleborough until 1887. The "ugh" was dropped when the city re-incorporated in 1914, although North Attleborough kept it. Both were named after a British town.

A brass-working forge was set up in 1780 by a Frenchman in North Attleborough. This brought in the button and jewelry industries. Attleborough was called "The Jewelry Capital of the World" for a time.

Attleborough Bank
1836–1865
W-MA-090

History: The Attleborough Bank was chartered on April 1, 1836, with Jacob Bolkcom, Jonathan Bliss, Richard Robinson, and others as incorporators. The charter was to be extended to October 1, 1851. The first board of directors was comprised of N.W. Sanford, Jonathan Bliss, Bacob Bolkcom, Samuel Carpenter, Willard Blackington, Capron Peck, Herbert M. Draper, William Otis, Richard Robinson, Samuel B. Scheck, and Laban M. Wheaton.

How to Read the Whitman Numbering System

$1 • W-MA-010-001-G010a

Denomination: Value of the note shown.

W: Whitman number. This number is a sortable code unique to each bank and note.

MA: Abbreviation for the state under study.

010: Numerical designation specific to each bank.

001: The denomination in dollars.

G010a: G indicates a good or valid note. Other categories are indicated thus: C (counterfeit); R (raised); S (spurious); N (not-attributed); A (altered). Numbers are assigned starting with 010, 020, et seq. Terminal letters following the number indicate variations of a note: a series of different colored overprints, tints, payees, etc., all on the same design of note. For more information, see the "How to Use This Book" section at the front of the volume, page xiv.

The original office was located in East Attleborough, but by 1858 it had moved to North Attleborough. In November 1839, the Attleborough Bank had a capital of $100,000. This remained constant throughout the bank's existence. Circulation ranged from $21,555 in 1849 to $58,275 in 1845.

Samuel Carpenter was president of the bank from 1848 until 1852, when he resigned. Laban M. Wheaton was elected in his place. E. Fuller was cashier from 1848 until 1855, when H.N. Richardson held that position. E. Ira Richards became president in 1857 with W.D. Cotton as cashier. In December 1863, Homer M. Daggett became cashier.

Figures for 1857 were thus: bills in circulation $40,384; bills in the vault $1,876.85; specie $1,980.82; real estate $7,500.

The Attleborough Bank dissolved in 1865, and in its stead the directors opened the Attleborough National Bank, which assumed its assets and liabilities.

Numismatic Commentary: The Attleborough Bank is another of the hardest Massachusetts banks to collect. Non-valid issues may be the only ones available to collectors. Genuine notes are extremely hard to locate as nearly all were redeemed and burned.

Valid Issues

$1 • W-MA-090-001-G010

Comments: H-MA-40-G2. No description available. 18__. 1830s.

Rarity: *None known*

$1 • W-MA-090-001-G020

CJF

Engraver: New England Bank Note Co. ***Comments:*** H-MA-40-G4. 18__. 1830s–1840s.

Rarity: URS-3
F $800

$1 • W-MA-090-001-G020a

Left: Train / 1. ***Center:*** 1. ***Right:*** 1 / Man on horseback, Two cattle / ONE. ***Overprint:*** Red ONE. ***Engraver:*** New England Bank Note Co. ***Comments:*** H-MA-40-G4a. Similar to W-MA-090-001-G020. 18__. 1850s.

Rarity: —

$2 • W-MA-090-002-G030

Comments: H-MA-40-G8. No description available. 18__. 1830s.

Rarity: *None known*

$2 • W-MA-090-002-G040

Left: Plow, Men with cart of hay, Man on horseback, Man with scythe, Dog, Cattle / 2. ***Center:*** 2. ***Right:*** 2 / Female portrait / TWO. ***Engraver:*** New England Bank Note Co. ***Comments:*** H-MA-40-G10. 18__. 1830s–1850s.

Rarity: URS-2
Proof $2,500

$2 • W-MA-090-002-G040a

CJF

Overprint: Red TWO. ***Engraver:*** New England Bank Note Co. ***Comments:*** H-MA-40-G10a. Similar to W-MA-090-002-G040. 18__. 1850s.

Rarity: URS-3
F $1,000

$3 • W-MA-090-003-G050

Comments: H-MA-40-G12. No description available. 18__. 1830s.

Rarity: *None known*

$3 • W-MA-090-003-G060

Left: Woman standing with sheaf, Reapers and house / 3. ***Center:*** Medallion 3. ***Right:*** 3 / Eagle / THREE. ***Engraver:*** New England Bank Note Co. ***Comments:*** H-MA-40-G14. 18__. 1830s–1850s.

Rarity: —

$3 • W-MA-090-003-G060a

Overprint: Red THREE. ***Engraver:*** New England Bank Note Co. ***Comments:*** H-MA-40-G14a. Similar to W-MA-090-003-G060. 18__. 1850s.

Rarity: —

$5 • W-MA-090-005-G070

Comments: H-MA-40-G18. No description available. 18__. 1830s–1840s.

Rarity: *None known*

$5 • W-MA-090-005-G080

Left: 5 / Farmer seated with scythe and hat / 5. ***Center:*** Medallion head / Two women and three cherubs with 5. ***Right:*** 5 / Man picking corn. ***Engraver:*** Rawdon, Wright & Hatch. ***Comments:*** H-MA-40-G20. 18__. 1840s–1850s.

Rarity: URS-3
F $1,000

$5 • W-MA-090-005-G080a

Overprint: Red. ***Engraver:*** Rawdon, Wright & Hatch. ***Comments:*** H-MA-40-G20a. Similar to W-MA-090-005-G080. 18__. 1850s.

Rarity: URS-3
F $1,000

$10 • W-MA-090-010-G090

Comments: H-MA-40-G22. No description available. 18__. 1830s–1840s.

Rarity: *None known*

$10 • W-MA-090-010-G100

Left: 10 / Portrait of John Quincy Adams. ***Center:*** Woman floating in clouds with shield and eagle. ***Bottom center:*** Man shearing sheep. ***Right:*** 10 / Man cradling grain. ***Engraver:*** Rawdon, Wright & Hatch. ***Comments:*** H-MA-40-G24. 18__. 1840s–1850s.

Rarity: URS-3
F $1,000

$10 • W-MA-090-010-G100a
Overprint: Red TEN. ***Engraver:*** Rawdon, Wright & Hatch. ***Comments:*** H-MA-40-G24a. Similar to W-MA-090-010-G100. 18__. 1850s.

Rarity: URS-3
F $1,000

$20 • W-MA-090-020-G110
Left: Train. ***Center:*** Beehive / Blacksmith shoeing horse, Man and horse. ***Right:*** Woman. ***Engraver:*** New England Bank Note Co. ***Comments:*** H-MA-40-G26. 18__. 1830s–1840s.

Rarity: URS-3
F $1,500

$20 • W-MA-090-020-G120
Left: 20 / Eagle / XX. ***Center:*** Two women seated flanking shield bearing plow, surmounted by eagle / Factory, train, and farmer. ***Bottom center:*** Dog. ***Right:*** 20 / Male portrait / XX. ***Engraver:*** Rawdon, Wright & Hatch. ***Comments:*** H-MA-40-G28. 18__. 1840s.

Rarity: URS-3
F $1,500

$20 • W-MA-090-020-G120a
Overprint: Red. ***Engraver:*** Rawdon, Wright & Hatch. ***Comments:*** H-MA-40-G28a. Similar to W-MA-090-020-G120. 18__. 1850s–1860s.

Rarity: URS-3
F $1,500

$50 • W-MA-090-050-G130
Left: 50 / Female portrait / 50. ***Center:*** Figure with arms extended, flanked by two cherubs, being carried by eagle. ***Bottom center:*** State arms. ***Right:*** 50 / Woman seated / 50. ***Engraver:*** Unverified, but likely Rawdon, Wright, Hatch & Edson. ***Comments:*** H-MA-40-G32. 18__. 1840s–1860s.

Rarity: —

$100 • W-MA-090-100-G140
Left: Woman seated. ***Center:*** 100 / Woman and man flanking cornucopia / 100. ***Bottom center:*** Deer. ***Right:*** Reaper with sickle and grain. ***Engraver:*** Unverified, but likely Rawdon, Wright, Hatch & Edson. ***Comments:*** H-MA-40-G36. 18__. 1840s–1860s.

Rarity: —

NON-VALID ISSUES

$1 • W-MA-090-001-N010
Center: Train, steamboat. ***Right:*** Portrait. ***Comments:*** H-MA-40-N5.

Rarity: —

$2 • W-MA-090-002-A010
Left: 2 / Female portrait. ***Center:*** Covered wagon pulled by four horses, Man riding horse. ***Right:*** 2 / Portrait of Thomas Jefferson. ***Tint:*** Brown-orange lathework outlining white TWO. ***Engraver:*** Bald, Cousland & Co. ***Comments:*** H-MA-40-A5. Altered from $2 Pioneer Association, Lafayette, Indiana. 18__. 1850s.

Rarity: —

$5 • W-MA-090-005-S010

CJF

Engraver: Toppan, Carpenter & Co. ***Comments:*** H-MA-40-S10. 18__. 1840s.

Rarity: URS-6
F $100

$5 • W-MA-090-005-A020
Left: Indian standing with rifle / 5. ***Center:*** V / Man and woman standing, Train on wharf, Men in boat. ***Bottom center:*** Royal crest. ***Right:*** Minerva standing with staff. ***Engraver:*** Unverified, but likely Hufty & Spencer. ***Comments:*** H-MA-40-A10. Altered from $5 Bank of Lower Canada, Quebec, Canada. 18__. 1830s.

Rarity: —

$10 • W-MA-090-010-C100a

CJF

Overprint: Red TEN. ***Engraver:*** Rawdon, Wright, & Hatch. ***Comments:*** H-MA-40-C24a. Counterfeit of W-MA-090-010-G100a. 18__. 1860s.

Rarity: URS-6
F $100

$10 • W-MA-090-010-N020
Left: X / X. ***Center:*** Woman seated, Ship. ***Right:*** TEN. ***Comments:*** H-MA-40-N10. 18__. 1840s.

Rarity: —

$20 • W-MA-090-020-C110
Engraver: New England Bank Note Co. ***Comments:*** H-MA-40-C26. Counterfeit of W-MA-090-020-G110. 18__. 1840s.

Rarity: —

AUGUSTA, MASSACHUSETTS

Augusta, today in the state of Maine, was in the Maine District of Massachusetts until March 1820. The city is situated on both sides of the Kennebec River. It became the shire town of Kennebec County in 1799 and in 1831 was named as the capital. The first bridge across the Kennebec was constructed in 1797 at a cost of $28,000 but deteriorated over time and was rebuilt in 1808. The second bridge burned in 1827 but was immediately rebuilt at a cost of $13,000. Augusta was incorporated as a town in 1797 and a city in 1849. On February 20, 1797, the northern part of Hallowell was separated and incorporated as Harrington, but on June 9, 1798, the name was changed to Augusta. In the mid-19th century, a dam 15 feet high and about 600 feet wide was built above Augusta and served to power several different saw mills, a flour mill, machine shops, and a cotton factory with 10,000 spindles. The main business was the processing of lumber. An iron foundry, two shovel factories, and an organ-building enterprise were also important. In the late 1850s a modest ship-building industry turned out about two ships per year.

See also Augusta, Maine.

Augusta Bank

1814–1820 • 1820–1864

W-MA-100 • W-ME-050

History: The Augusta Bank was incorporated on August 28, 1814.[23] The original charter was set to expire on October 31, 1831, but was renewed on a timely basis. The authorized capital was $100,000. Word spread, great profits were envisioned, and investors oversubscribed the stock in a rush. By October 1845, circulation had grown to $83,743. Circulation of the bank in 1846 was $81,795. In January 1849, the bank was broken into and about $29,500 was stolen by a pair of brothers. However, most of the money was recovered upon discovery of one of the burglars. The other burglar was apprehended and sentenced to prison. Using the same ingenuity that fueled the success of the robbery, he forged his own key to escape and was never heard of again.

In 1864 the bank closed. In 1866 bills remaining in circulation totaled $3,648, reduced to $3,102 in 1867. The bills of the bank continued to be redeemed over the counter at the First National Bank of Augusta until its obligation to do so expired after March 1, 1868, per an act of the legislature. Records of the bank stated that over a period of years currency totaling $168,665 had been received from the engravers.

See also listing under Maine.

Numismatic Commentary: This bank formed in 1820 before Maine became a state and was still a part of Massachusetts called the Maine District. As nearly all bills of the Augusta Bank were redeemed, very few exist today. After statehood, the Augusta Bank continued using the PSSP notes, even into the 1860s, by which time nearly all other Maine banks had long since adopted scenic bills. Later notes have the ABNCo. monogram after the company's founding in 1858.

VALID ISSUES

Notes With Massachusetts Address

$1 • W-MA-100-001-G010

Left: 1 / 1. ***Center:*** ONE DOLLAR, Text. ***Right:*** 1 / 1. ***Engraver:*** PSSP. ***Comments:*** H-MA-45-G2, Wait-Unlisted. 1810s.

Rarity: —

$2 • W-MA-100-002-G020

Engraver: PSSP. ***Comments:*** H-MA-45-G8, Wait-Unlisted. Similar to W-MA-100-001-G010 but with different denomination. 1810s.

Rarity: —

$3 • W-MA-100-003-G030

Engraver: PSSP. ***Comments:*** H-MA-45-G10, Wait-Unlisted. Similar to W-MA-100-001-G010 but with different denomination. 1810s.

Rarity: —

$5 • W-MA-100-005-G040

Left: MASSACHUSETTS vertically / 5, Plate letter, 5. ***Center:*** FIVE DOLLARS, Text. ***Right:*** 5, Plate letter, 5. ***Engraver:*** PSSP. ***Comments:*** H-MA-45-G12, Wait-Unlisted. 1810s.

Rarity: —

$10 • W-MA-100-010-G050

Left: State arms / 10, Plate letter, 10. ***Center:*** TEN DOLLARS, Text. ***Right:*** 10, Plate letter, 10. ***Engraver:*** PSSP. ***Comments:*** H-MA-45-G14, Wait-Unlisted. 1810s.

Rarity: —
VF $300

$20 • W-MA-100-020-G060

Engraver: PSSP. ***Comments:*** H-MA-45-G16, Wait-Unlisted. Similar to W-MA-100-010-G050 but with different denomination. 1810s.

Rarity: —

$50 • W-MA-100-050-G070

Left: MASSACHUSETTS vertically / 50, Plate letter, 50. ***Center:*** FIFTY DOLLARS, Text. ***Right:*** 50, Plate letter, 50. ***Engraver:*** PSSP. ***Comments:*** H-MA-45-G18, Wait-Unlisted. 1810s.

Rarity: —

$100 • W-MA-100-100-G080

Engraver: PSSP. ***Comments:*** H-MA-45-G20, Wait-Unlisted. Similar to W-MA-100-010-G050 but with different denomination. 1810s.

Rarity: —

Notes With Maine Address

$1 • W-ME-050-001-G010

Left: ONE, D, ONE vertically. ***Center:*** 1 / 1 / AUGUSTA BANK, Text / 1 / 1. ***Right:*** ONE, D, ONE vertically. ***Payee:*** C. Dole. ***Engraver:*** PSSP. ***Comments:*** H-ME-15-G2, Wait-1. Printed black or red-brown with or without Stereotype Steel Check Plate back. 1820s.

Rarity: —

$1 • W-ME-050-001-G020 QDB

Engraver: PSSP. ***Comments:*** H-ME-15-G6, Wait-Unlisted. 18__. 1840s.

Rarity: URS-2
EF $2,500

$1 • W-ME-050-001-G020a

Left: ONE, D, ONE vertically. ***Center:*** 1 / 1 / MAINE, Text / 1 / 1. ***Right:*** ONE, D, ONE vertically. ***Engraver:*** PSSP. ***Comments:*** H-ME-15-G6a, Wait-Unlisted. Similar to W-ME-050-001-G020. Printed red-brown. 1840s–1850s.

Rarity: —

$1 • W-ME-050-001-G020b QDB

Back: Brown Stereotype Steel Check Plate. ***Engraver:*** PSSP. ***Comments:*** H-ME-15-G6b, Wait-Unlisted. Similar to W-ME-050-001-G020. 18__. 1850s.

Rarity: URS-2
EF $2,500

$1 • W-ME-050-001-G020c

Engraver: PSSP / ABNCo. monogram. ***Comments:*** H-ME-15-G6c, Wait-Unlisted. Similar to W-ME-050-001-G020. Issued after March 1858.

Rarity: URS-3
EF $400

$2 • W-ME-050-002-G030

Left: Five TWOs vertically. ***Center:*** 2 / 2 / MAINE, Text / 2 / 2. ***Right:*** Five TWOs vertically. ***Engraver:*** PSSP. ***Comments:*** H-ME-15-G8, Wait-Unlisted. Printed in red-brown and likely in black. 1820s.

Rarity: —

$2 • W-ME-050-002-G040

Engraver: PSSP. ***Comments:*** H-ME-15-G12, Wait-Unlisted. Similar to W-ME-050-002-G030. Printed in black. 1830s–1840s.

Rarity: URS-4
F $250; **VF** $400; **EF** $1,000

$2 • W-ME-050-002-G040a

Engraver: PSSP. ***Comments:*** H-ME-15-G12a, Wait-Unlisted. Similar to W-ME-050-002-G030. Printed in red-brown. 1840s–1850s.

Rarity: URS-4
F $250; **VF** $400; **EF** $1,000

$2 • W-ME-050-002-G040b QDB, QDB

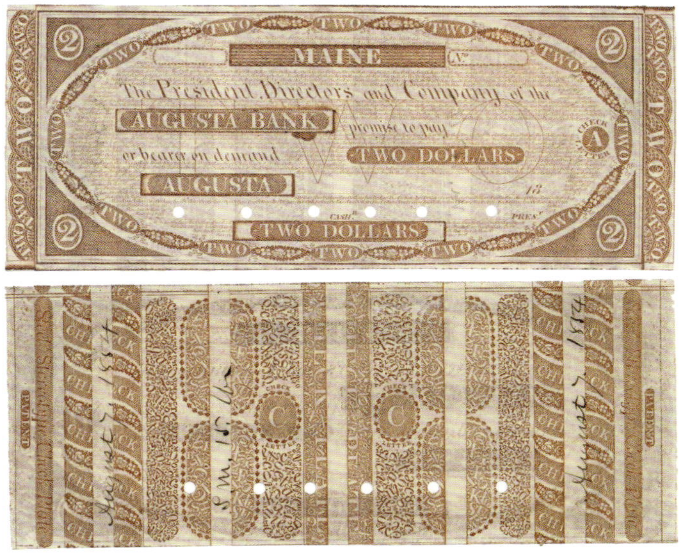

Back: Brown Stereotype Steel Check Plate. ***Engraver:*** PSSP. ***Comments:*** H-ME-15-G12b, Wait-Unlisted. Similar to W-ME-050-002-G030. 18__. 1850s.

Rarity: URS-3
F $500; **VF** $1,000; **EF** $2,500

$2 • W-ME-050-002-G040c QDB, QDB

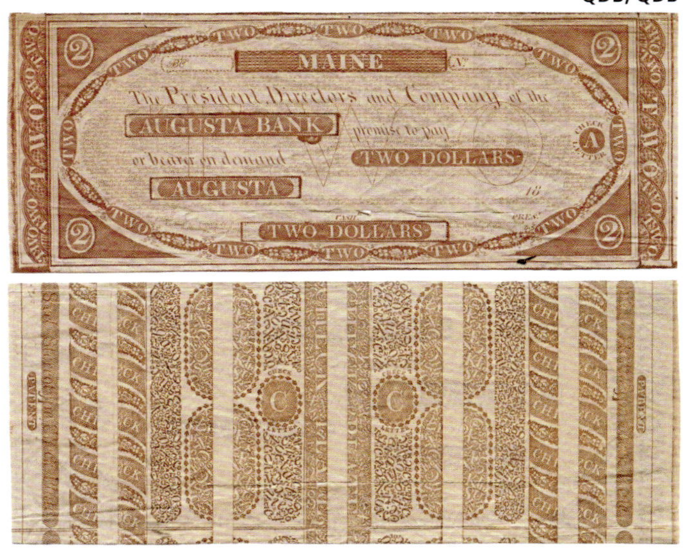

Back: Brown Stereotype Steel Check Plate. ***Engraver:*** PSSP / ABNCo. monogram. ***Comments:*** H-ME-15-G12c, Wait-Unlisted. Similar to W-ME-050-002-G030. 18__. Issued after March 1858.

Rarity: URS-4
EF $1,250

$3 • W-ME-050-003-G050

Left: THREE vertically. ***Center:*** 3 / 3 / MAINE, Text / 3 / 3. ***Right:*** THREE vertically. ***Back:*** Inked notation August 7, 1854, "S.M. 15 lb". ***Engraver:*** PSSP. ***Comments:*** H-ME-15-G14, Wait-Unlisted. Printed in red-brown and likely in black. 1820s.

Rarity: —

$3 • W-ME-050-003-G060

Engraver: PSSP. ***Comments:*** H-ME-15-G18, Wait-Unlisted. Similar to W-ME-050-003-G050. Printed in black. 1830s–1840s.

Rarity: URS-2
EF $1,000

Collectors and Researchers:

If you have new information about any banks or notes listed in this volume, contact Whitman Publishing, Attn: Obsolete Paper Money, 3101 Clairmont Road, Suite G, Atlanta, GA 30329.

$3 • W-ME-050-003-G060a

Engraver: PSSP. ***Comments:*** H-ME-15-G18a, Wait-Unlisted. Similar to W-ME-050-003-G060. Printed in red-brown. 1840s–1850s.

Rarity: URS-2
EF $1,000

$3 • W-ME-050-003-G060b

QDB, QDB

Back: Brown Stereotype Steel Check Plate. ***Engraver:*** PSSP. ***Comments:*** H-ME-15-G18b, Wait-Unlisted. Similar to W-ME-050-003-G060. 18__. 1850s.

Rarity: URS-2
VF $2,000

$3 • W-ME-050-003-G060c

Engraver: PSSP / ABNCo. monogram. ***Comments:*** H-ME-15-G18c, Wait-Unlisted. Similar to W-ME-050-003-G060. Issued after March 1858. 1860s.

Rarity: —
VF $400

$5 • W-ME-050-005-G070

SBG

Back: Brown Stereotype Steel Check Plate. ***Engraver:*** PSSP. ***Comments:*** H-ME-15-G26a, Wait-Unlisted. Printed in black. 18__. 1830s.

Rarity: URS-2
VF $2,000

$5 • W-ME-050-005-G070a

Left: STATE OF MAINE vertically / 5 / Liberty seated with pole and shield / 5. ***Center:*** FIVE DOLLARS / Text. ***Right:*** 5 / Indian portrait / 5. ***Back:*** Brown Stereotype Steel Check Plate. ***Engraver:*** PSSP. ***Comments:*** H-Unlisted, Wait-Unlisted. Similar to W-ME-050-005-G070. Style of the 1820s without illustrative vignettes.

Rarity: —

$5 • W-ME-050-005-G070b

Engraver: PSSP. ***Comments:*** H-ME-15-G26b, Wait-Unlisted. Similar to W-ME-050-005-G070. Printed in red-brown. 1840s–1850s.

Rarity: URS-2
VF $1,000

$10 • W-ME-050-010-G080

Center: TEN DOLLARS / AUGUSTA BANK. ***Engraver:*** PSSP. ***Comments:*** H-ME-15-G28, Wait-Unlisted. Style of the 1820s without illustrative vignettes. 1820s.

Rarity: —

$10 • W-ME-050-010-G090

Left: STATE OF MAINE vertically / 10 / Woman standing with rudder / 10. ***Center:*** TEN DOLLARS, Text. ***Right:*** 10 / Indian portrait / 10. ***Back:*** Black Stereotype Steel Check Plate. ***Engraver:*** PSSP. ***Comments:*** H-ME-15-G30a, Wait-Unlisted. Style of the 1820s without illustrative vignettes. 1830s.

Rarity: —

$10 • W-ME-050-010-G090a

QDB

Back: Brown Stereotype Steel Check Plate. ***Engraver:*** PSSP. ***Comments:*** H-ME-15-G30b, Wait-Unlisted. Similar to W-ME-050-010-G090. Printed red-brown. 18__. 1840s–1850s.

Rarity: URS-3
G $150; **F** $250; **Proof** $2,000

$20 • W-ME-050-020-G100

Center: TWENTY DOLLARS / AUGUSTA. ***Engraver:*** PSSP. ***Comments:*** H-Unlisted, Wait-Unlisted.

Rarity: —

$20 • W-ME-050-020-G110

Left: MAINE vertically / 20, Plate letter, 20. ***Center:*** TWENTY / Text. ***Right:*** 20, Plate letter, 20. ***Engraver:*** PSSP. ***Comments:*** H-Unlisted, Wait-Unlisted.

Rarity: —

$20 • W-ME-050-020-G110a

QDB

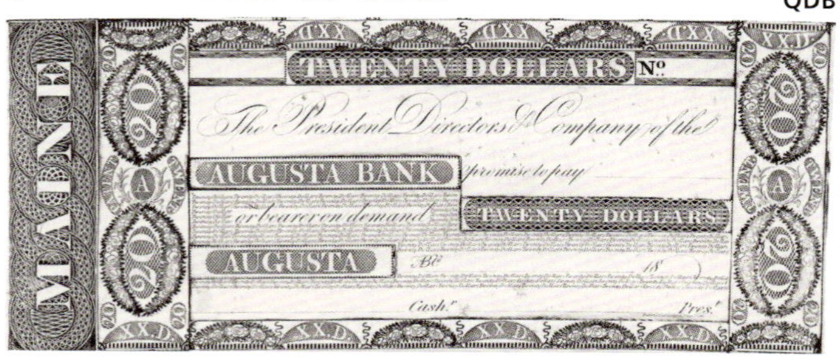

Engraver: PSSP / ABNCo. monogram. ***Comments:*** H-Unlisted, Wait-Unlisted. Similar to W-ME-050-020-G110. 18__. Issued after March 1858.

Rarity: URS-1
Proof $2,900

$50 • W-ME-050-050-G120

Left: MAINE vertically / 50, Plate letter, 50. ***Center:*** FIFTY / Text. ***Right:*** 50, Plate letter, 50. ***Engraver:*** PSSP. ***Comments:*** H-Unlisted, Wait-Unlisted.

Rarity: —

$50 • W-ME-050-050-G120a

Engraver: PSSP. ***Comments:*** H-Unlisted, Wait-Unlisted. Similar to W-ME-050-050-G120.

Rarity: —

$50 • W-ME-050-050-G120b

QDB

Engraver: PSSP / ABNCo. monogram. ***Comments:*** H-Unlisted, Wait-Unlisted. Similar to W-ME-050-050-G120. 18__. Issued after March 1858.

Rarity: URS-1
Proof $2,900

$100 • W-ME-050-100-G130

Left: MAINE vertically / 100, Plate letter, 100. ***Center:*** ONE HUNDRED / Text. ***Right:*** 100, Plate letter, 100. ***Engraver:*** PSSP. ***Comments:*** H-Unlisted, Wait-Unlisted.

Rarity: —

$100 • W-ME-050-100-G130a

Engraver: PSSP. ***Comments:*** H-Unlisted, Wait-Unlisted. Similar to W-ME-050-100-G130.

Rarity: —

$100 • W-ME-050-100-G130b

QDB

Engraver: PSSP / ABNCo. monogram. ***Comments:*** H-Unlisted, Wait-Unlisted. Similar to W-ME-050-100-G130. 18__. Issued after March 1858.

Rarity: URS-1
Proof $2,500

NON-VALID ISSUES

$1 • W-ME-050-001-C020

QDB

Engraver: PSSP. ***Comments:*** H-Unlisted, Wait-Unlisted. Counterfeit of W-ME-050-001-G020. 18__. 1840s.

Rarity: URS-6
VG $75

$1 • W-ME-050-001-N010

Payee: M. Crady (Letter E). ***Comments:*** H-Unlisted, Wait-2. Imitation of PSSP. Jan. 1, 1842.

Rarity: —

$1 • W-ME-050-001-N020

Payee: W. Craig (Letter E). ***Comments:*** H-Unlisted, Wait-3. Imitation of PSSP. Various dates.

Rarity: —

$3 • W-ME-050-003-N030

Comments: H-Unlisted, Wait-6. Imitation of PSSP. Watermelon note.

Rarity: —

$10 • W-ME-050-010-N040

Center: Woman reclining / Male portrait. ***Comments:*** H-Unlisted, Wait-9.

Rarity: —

$10 • W-ME-050-010-N050

Center: Wagon and team. ***Comments:*** H-Unlisted, Wait-10.

Rarity: —

$100 • W-ME-050-100-N060

Center: Liberty and Justice seated with pole and scales. ***Comments:*** H-Unlisted, Wait-11.

Rarity: —

Kennebec Bank

1812–1820 • 1820–1826

W-MA-110 • W-ME-090

History: The Kennebec Bank in Augusta was located in the Maine District of Massachusetts until March 1820, when Maine achieved statehood. The bank was incorporated on June 23, 1812, with an authorized capital of $100,000. Trade had been in a slump since the Embargo Act of 1807 initiated a depression in the maritime trade. The repeal of such in 1809 and the failure of Congress to renew the charter of the Bank of the United States stimulated the growth of local banking the country over. By 1812 the conditions had improved and trade was flourishing. The Kennebec Bank became the first with an Augusta address. In reality it was a *Hallowell* bank, as most stockholders and principals were located in the town not far distant. It could not be chartered in Hallowell, as the second Hallowell and Augusta Bank was chartered on the same date. There were not enough citizens in Hallowell to permit two banks there.[24]

In 1816 the Legislature responded to a petition and allowed the Kennebec Bank to move to Hallowell. Henceforth, its paper money bore the address of Hallowell, Massachusetts. See W-MA-1825 for continuation. See also listing under Maine.

Numismatic Commentary: Both Abner Reed and Jacob Perkins supplied bank notes to this bank. The notes most available to collectors today are the Perkins type issues. Most are found in mid to lower grades, which applies to the Perkins issues of most Maine banks. PSSP notes in better than VF grades are somewhat hard to locate.

Valid Issues

Notes With Massachusetts Address

$1 • W-MA-110-001-G010

Left: 1 / 1. ***Center:*** Flower garlands, ONE. ***Right:*** 1 / 1. ***Engraver:*** PSSP. ***Comments:*** H-MA-50-G2, Wait-Unlisted. 1810s.

Rarity: —

$2 • W-MA-110-002-G020

Engraver: PSSP. ***Comments:*** H-MA-50-G8, Wait-Unlisted. Similar to W-MA-110-001-G010 but with different denomination. 1810s.

Rarity: —

$3 • W-MA-110-003-G030

Engraver: PSSP. ***Comments:*** H-MA-50-G10, Wait-Unlisted. Similar to W-MA-110-001-G010 but with different denomination. 1810s.

Rarity: —

$5 • W-MA-110-005-G040

QDB, CJF

Engraver: PSSP. ***Comments:*** H-MA-50-G12, Wait-Unlisted. 18__. 1810s.

Rarity: URS-3
G $150; **F** $300; **VF** $400

$10 • W-MA-110-010-G050

Left: State arms / 10, Plate letter, 10. ***Center:*** TEN. ***Right:*** 10, Plate letter, 10. ***Engraver:*** PSSP. ***Comments:*** H-MA-50-G14, Wait-Unlisted. 1810s.

Rarity: —

$20 • W-MA-110-020-G060

Left: State arms / 20, Plate letter, 20. ***Right:*** 20, Plate letter, 20. ***Engraver:*** PSSP. ***Comments:*** H-MA-50-G16, Wait-Unlisted. 1810s.

Rarity: —

$50 • W-MA-110-050-G070

Left: State arms / 50, Plate letter, 50. ***Right:*** 50, Plate letter, 50. ***Engraver:*** PSSP. ***Comments:*** H-MA-50-G18, Wait-Unlisted. 1810s.

Rarity: —

$100 • W-MA-110-100-G080

Left: State arms / 100, Plate letter, 100. ***Right:*** 100, Plate letter, 100. ***Engraver:*** PSSP. ***Comments:*** H-MA-50-G20, Wait-Unlisted. 1810s.

Rarity: —

Notes With Maine Address

$1 • W-ME-090-001-G010

Left: 1 / 1. ***Center:*** Watermelon design. ***Right:*** 1 / 1. ***Engraver:*** PSSP. ***Comments:*** H-Unlisted, Wait-42.

Rarity: —

$5 • W-ME-090-005-G020

Left: State arms. ***Center:*** Watermelon design. ***Right:*** 5 / 5. ***Back:*** Stereotype Steel Check Plate. ***Engraver:*** PSSP. ***Comments:*** H-Unlisted, Wait-43.

Rarity: —

$10 • W-ME-090-010-G030

Left: State arms. ***Center:*** Watermelon design. ***Right:*** 10, Plate letter, 10. ***Engraver:*** PSSP. ***Comments:*** H-Unlisted, Wait-44.

Rarity: —

Bangor, Massachusetts

Bangor is situated on the Kenduskeag River and was important as a port of entry for international maritime commerce. It was first known as the Kenduskeag Plantation, incorporated on February 25, 1791. Prior to March 1820, it was located in the Maine District of Massachusetts. When Maine joined the Union, the city became located in a new state. Bangor was incorporated as a city in 1834.

Prime businesses included shipbuilding and lumber. The Panic of 1837 hit Bangor in a disastrous way, causing almost all business to come to a standstill. An act of the U.S. Congress provided funds to help with rebuilding the economy.

In 1848 Bangor became an official port of entry for maritime shipments. In 1849 steamships began to service the Penobscot River at Bangor. In 1855 lumber boards to the extent of about 3 billion feet were produced.

Bangor Bank

1814–1820 • 1820–1831

W-MA-120 • W-ME-110

History: In 1814 the Bangor Bank was one of four banks organized in the Maine District of Massachusetts, capitalized for $100,000.[25] Chartered on February 26, 1814, the institution did not go into operation as the directors were unable to raise the required capital. The charter expired. On June 17, 1817, the charter was revived, and the bank was organized on September 15 of that year. In January 1820, the *Report of the Maine District Banks to the Commonwealth of Massachusetts* gave the paid-in capital as $100,000 and the bills in circulation as $187,693. As was true of other banks, the "paid-in capital" consisted in part of money borrowed by stockholders from the bank, pledging stock certificates as collateral—a circular arrangement. This was legal at the time.

On October 29, robbers got as far as the vault door of the bank but found that it was an obstacle too difficult to master with the tools at hand. The cashier, Mr. Wilkins, lay in wait for them on their second attempt, but the robbers did not try again.

In July 1822, the Bangor Bank failed, and on October 1, 1831, the charter expired by limitation. After the failure, the bank continued to issue bills, much to the consternation of state officials. See also listing under Maine.

Numismatic Commentary: Notes of the Bangor Bank are essentially uncollectible today.

VALID ISSUES

Notes With Massachusetts Address

$1 • W-MA-120-001-G010

Left: 1 / 1. ***Center:*** Flower garlands, ONE. ***Right:*** 1 / 1. ***Engraver:*** PSSP. ***Comments:*** H-MA-55-G2, Wait-Unlisted. 1810s.

Rarity: —

$2 • W-MA-120-002-G020

Engraver: PSSP. ***Comments:*** H-MA-55-G4, Wait-Unlisted. Similar to W-MA-120-001-G010 but with different denomination. 1810s.

Rarity: —

$3 • W-MA-120-003-G030

Engraver: PSSP. ***Comments:*** H-MA-55-G6, Wait-Unlisted. Similar to W-MA-120-001-G010 but with different denomination. 1810s.

Rarity: —

$5 • W-MA-120-005-G040

Left: MASSACHUSETTS / 5, Plate letter, 5. ***Right:*** 5, Plate letter, 5. ***Engraver:*** PSSP. ***Comments:*** H-MA-55-G8, Wait-Unlisted. 1810s.

Rarity: —

$10 • W-MA-120-010-G050

Left: MASSACHUSETTS / 10, Plate letter, 10. ***Center:*** TEN DOLLARS, Text. ***Right:*** 10, Plate letter, 10. ***Engraver:*** PSSP. ***Comments:*** H-MA-55-G10, Wait-Unlisted. 1810s.

Rarity: —

$20 • W-MA-120-020-G060

Left: State arms / 20, Plate letter, 20. ***Right:*** 20, Plate letter, 20. ***Engraver:*** PSSP. ***Comments:*** H-MA-55-G12, Wait-Unlisted. 1810s.

Rarity: —

$50 • W-MA-120-050-G070

Left: State arms / 50, Plate letter, 50. ***Right:*** 50, Plate letter, 50. ***Engraver:*** PSSP. ***Comments:*** H-MA-55-G14, Wait-Unlisted. 1810s.

Rarity: —

$100 • W-MA-120-100-G080

Left: State arms / 100, Plate letter, 100. ***Right:*** 100, Plate letter, 100. ***Engraver:*** PSSP. ***Comments:*** H-MA-55-G16, Wait-Unlisted. 1810s.

Rarity: —

Notes With Maine Address

$1 • W-ME-110-001-G010

Left: 1. ***Center:*** Garlands bearing ONE, ONE. ***Right:*** 1. ***Engraver:*** PSSP. ***Comments:*** H-ME-45-G2, Wait-Unlisted. 1820s.

Rarity: —

$2 • W-ME-110-002-G020

Left: 2. ***Center:*** Garlands bearing TWO, TWO. ***Right:*** 2. ***Engraver:*** PSSP. ***Comments:*** H-ME-45-G6, Wait-Unlisted. 1820s.

Rarity: —

$3 • W-ME-110-003-G030

Left: 3. ***Center:*** Garlands bearing THREE, THREE. ***Right:*** 3. ***Engraver:*** PSSP. ***Comments:*** H-ME-45-G10, Wait-Unlisted. 1820s.

Rarity: —

$5 • W-ME-110-005-G040

Left: MAINE vertically / 5, Plate letter, 5. ***Center:*** FIVE DOLLARS, Text. ***Right:*** 5, Plate letter, 5. ***Engraver:*** PSSP. ***Comments:*** H-ME-45-G14, Wait-Unlisted. 1820s.

Rarity: —

$10 • W-ME-110-010-G050

Left: MAINE vertically / 10, Plate letter, 10 vertically. ***Center:*** TEN DOLLARS, Text. ***Right:*** 10, Plate letter, 10. ***Engraver:*** PSSP. ***Comments:*** H-ME-45-G18, Wait-Unlisted. 1820s.

Rarity: —

$20 • W-ME-110-020-G060

Left: MAINE vertically / 20, Plate letter, 20. ***Center:*** TWENTY DOLLARS, Text. ***Right:*** 20, Plate letter, 20 vertically. ***Engraver:*** PSSP. ***Comments:*** H-ME-45-G22, Wait-Unlisted. 1820s.

Rarity: —

BARRE, MASSACHUSETTS

Originally known as the Northwest District of Rutland, Barre was first settled in 1720 and incorporated as the Rutland District in 1753. On June 17, 1774, the name changed again to Hutchinson, after Thomas Hutchinson, who was the colonial governor of Massachusetts. On November 7, 1776, the name of Barre was taken in honor of Isaac Barré.

The land is surrounded by rivers and falls that lend themselves as useful sources of power, but the town was also known for its dairy products. A cotton factory, a straw hat factory, a machine shop, a foundry, a planning mill, and a saw mill were located there. Textiles, gunpowder, and wood products were also profitable businesses until the 20th century. The town is made up of several villages, including Barre, Barre Plains, Smithville—the former two being post offices—South Barre, Heald's Village, and Mill Village.

Barre Bank
1849
W-MA-130

History: In 1849 the following was reported: "New Banks Established in Massachusetts. The Barre Bank, at Barre, chartered, but not yet in operation."[26] There is no record that the bank ever opened. Notes with this imprint have not been seen, but there is the possibility some were made in anticipation of the bank's opening.

Barry, Massachusetts

Barry was a non-existent town in Massachusetts that appeared on altered notes of other banks. It is most likely a misspelling of Barre, Massachusetts.

Farmers Bank of Sandstone
1830s
W-MA-140

History: A non-existent bank represented only by notes altered from those of other banks. The *American Masonic Register* reported this in 1841:

> A man is in the city putting off bills on this bank. The bills of some of the banks of Massachusetts, and are dated at Barry. There is, however, no such bank at the East; but there was once such a bank in Michigan; which broke long ago.[27]

Issues

$1 • W-MA-140-001-A010

Left: 1 / Woman wearing bonnet, standing by pail / ONE. ***Center:*** Machinery and merchandise flanking Ceres seated holding sickle and rake, Factories and harbor / ONE. ***Right:*** 1 / Ship / ONE. ***Engraver:*** New England Bank Note Co. ***Comments:*** H-MA-60-A5. Altered from $1 Farmers Bank of Sandstone, Barry, Michigan. 18__. 1830s.

Rarity: —

$2 • W-MA-140-002-A020

Left: 2 / Cornucopia, Woman standing with staff / TWO. ***Center:*** TWO / Machinery and merchandise flanking Ceres seated holding sickle and rake, Factories and harbor. ***Engraver:*** New England Bank Note Co. ***Comments:*** H-MA-60-A10. Altered from $2 Farmers Bank of Sandstone, Barry, Michigan. 18__. 1830s.

Rarity: —

$3 • W-MA-140-003-A030

Left: THREE / Beehive and foliage / THREE. ***Center:*** Machinery and merchandise flanking Ceres seated holding sickle and rake, Factories and harbor / THREE. ***Right:*** 3 on THREE / Two reapers / 3 on THREE. ***Engraver:*** New England Bank Note Co. ***Comments:*** H-MA-60-A15. Altered from $3 Farmers Bank of Sandstone, Barry, Michigan. 18__. 1830s.

Rarity: —

$5 • W-MA-140-005-A040

Left: 5 / Blacksmith at anvil / FIVE. ***Center:*** Mercury standing with 5, Cornucopia and merchandise, Factories and ship / V. ***Right:*** 5 / Ceres kneeling / FIVE. ***Engraver:*** New England Bank Note Co. ***Comments:*** H-MA-60-A20. Altered from $5 Farmers Bank of Sandstone, Barry, Michigan. 18__. 1830s.

Rarity: —

$10 • W-MA-140-010-A050

Left: 10 / Farmer sowing / TEN. ***Center:*** Mercury standing with 10, Merchandise, Factories and ship / Canal scene. ***Right:*** 10 / Ship / TEN. ***Engraver:*** New England Bank Note Co. ***Comments:*** H-MA-60-A25. Altered from $10 Farmers Bank of Sandstone, Barry, Michigan. 18__. 1830s.

Rarity: —

Bath, Massachusetts

Bath was located in the Maine District of Massachusetts until Maine achieved statehood in March 1820. It is the capital of Sagadahoc County and is situated on the west bank of the Kennebec River, about 12 miles from the sea. The community was settled in the 1660s and incorporated on February 17, 1781. Early activities were primarily shipbuilding and lumbering. Planks and boards for building ships were exported to Europe and elsewhere. In 1847 Bath was chartered as a city, and in 1854 it became the county seat. By 1858 and 1859 the shipbuilding industry had dwindled. Bath had a good harbor, deep enough for the largest ships in the 1850s. When the Panic of 1857 hit, many people left Bath to seek opportunities in the West. Later, shipbuilding revived, and in time Bath became a very important location of shipbuilding for the U.S. Navy, which it remains today.

See also Bath, Maine.

Bath Bank {1st}
1812–1820 • 1820–1831
W-MA-150 • W-ME-360

History: The Bath Bank was chartered on June 23, 1812, in the district of Maine (then a part of Massachusetts) by the Massachusetts General Court.[28] The capital was authorized at $100,000. This was an era of optimism, as the dreaded Embargo Act of 1807 and related legislation that had impaired commerce in New England coastal areas had been repealed, and the maritime trade was strong. In 1812 20 new banks were chartered by Massachusetts, of which six were in the Maine district.

In 1824 the bank commissioners reported that 80 percent of the capital of the Bath Bank was loaned on pledges of its own stock, an undesirable situation as it prevented these funds from being available for general commercial loans.[29] The charter of the bank expired in 1831 and was not renewed. See also listing under Maine.

Numismatic Commentary: Issues from the Bath Bank with the Maine address are not known to exist today with the exception of one unsigned remainder, leaving speculation that there could still be an uncut sheet somewhere to be discovered.

VALID ISSUES

Notes With Massachusetts Address

$1 • W-MA-150-001-G010

Left: 1 / 1. ***Center:*** Flower garlands, ONE. ***Right:*** 1 / 1. ***Engraver:*** PSSP. ***Comments:*** H-MA-65-G2, Wait-Unlisted. 1810s.

Rarity: URS-3
Unc-Rem $750

$2 • W-MA-150-002-G020

Engraver: PSSP. ***Comments:*** H-MA-65-G8, Wait-Unlisted. Similar to W-MA-150-001-G010 but with different denomination. 1810s.

Rarity: —

$3 • W-MA-150-003-G030

Engraver: PSSP. ***Comments:*** H-MA-65-G10, Wait-Unlisted. Similar to W-MA-150-001-G010 but with different denomination. 1810s.

Rarity: —

$5 • W-MA-150-005-G040

Left: MASSACHUSETTS across / 5, Plate letter, 5. ***Center:*** Flower garlands, FIVE. ***Right:*** 5, Plate letter, 5. ***Engraver:*** PSSP. ***Comments:*** H-MA-65-G12, Wait-Unlisted. 1810s.

Rarity: —

$10 • W-MA-150-010-G050

CC, CC

Engraver: PSSP. ***Comments:*** H-MA-65-G14, Wait-Unlisted. 18__. 1810s.

Rarity: URS-6
VF $200

$20 • W-MA-150-020-G060

Left: MASSACHUSETTS across / 20, Plate letter, 20. ***Center:*** Flower garlands, TWENTY. ***Right:*** 20, Plate letter, 20. ***Engraver:*** PSSP. ***Comments:*** H-MA-65-G16, Wait-Unlisted. 1810s.

Rarity: —

$50 • W-MA-150-050-G070

Left: MASSACHUSETTS across / 50, Plate letter, 50. ***Center:*** Flower garlands, FIFTY. ***Right:*** 50, Plate letter, 50. ***Engraver:*** PSSP. ***Comments:*** H-MA-65-G18, Wait-Unlisted. 1810s.

Rarity: —

$100 • W-MA-150-100-G080

Left: MASSACHUSETTS across / 100, Plate letter, 100. ***Center:*** Flower garlands, ONE HUNDRED. ***Right:*** 100, Plate letter, 100. ***Engraver:*** PSSP. ***Comments:*** H-MA-65-G20, Wait-Unlisted. 1810s.

Rarity: —

Notes With Maine Address

$1 • W-ME-360-001-G010

CJF

Engraver: PSSP. ***Comments:*** H-ME-145-G2, Wait-1. 18__. 1820s.

Rarity: URS-4
F $500

$2 • W-ME-360-002-G020

Center: Flower garlands bearing TWO, TWO. ***Engraver:*** PSSP. ***Comments:*** H-ME-145-G4, Wait-Unlisted. 1820s.

Rarity: —

$3 • W-ME-360-003-G030

Left: 3 / 3. ***Center:*** Flower garlands bearing THREE, THREE. ***Right:*** 3 / 3. ***Engraver:*** PSSP. ***Comments:*** H-ME-145-G6, Wait-Unlisted. 1820s.

Rarity: —

$5 • W-ME-360-005-G040

Left: MAINE vertically / 5, Plate letter, 5. ***Center:*** FIVE DOLLARS, Text. ***Right:*** 5, Plate letter, 5. ***Engraver:*** PSSP. ***Comments:*** H-ME-145-G10, Wait-Unlisted. 1820s.

Rarity: —

$10 • W-ME-360-010-G050

Left: MAINE vertically / 10, Plate letter, 10 / State arms. ***Center:*** TEN DOLLARS, Text. ***Right:*** 10, Plate letter, 10. ***Engraver:*** PSSP. ***Comments:*** H-ME-145-G14, Wait-2. 1820s.

Rarity: —

$10 • W-ME-360-020-G060

Left: MAINE vertically / 20, Plate letter, 20. ***Center:*** TWENTY DOLLARS, Text. ***Right:*** 20, Plate letter, 20. ***Engraver:*** PSSP. ***Comments:*** H-ME-145-G18. 1820s.

Rarity: —

Lincoln Bank
1813–1820 • 1820–1865
W-MA-160 • W-ME-400

History: The Lincoln Bank in Bath was incorporated on June 16, 1813, with a capital of $100,000. This was paid in by January 1820.[30] Circulation of the bank was $32,573 in 1820 and $52,582 in 1838. By October 1845, it had increased to $98,132. Real estate was valued at $3,000 in 1838.

The Lincoln Bank's charter was set to expire on October 31, 1831. On January 27, 1865, it was succeeded by the Lincoln National Bank of Bath. In 1867 circulation was reported to be $23, bills destroyed $295,103, bills in the bank upon examination, September 8, 1867, $2,374. See also listing under Maine.

Numismatic Commentary: This bank was one of Maine's longest-lived banks, and bank notes are still available in today's marketplace. Collectors should be able to find both early and later issues.

Valid Issues
Notes With Massachusetts Address

$1 • W-MA-160-001-G010
Left: 1 / 1. ***Center:*** MASSACHUSETTS, Text. ***Right:*** 1 / 1. ***Engraver:*** PSSP. ***Comments:*** H-MA-70-G2, Wait-Unlisted. 1810s.
Rarity: URS-2
F $1,500

$2 • W-MA-160-002-G020
Left: 2 / 2. ***Center:*** Flower garlands, TWO. ***Right:*** 2 / 2. ***Engraver:*** PSSP. ***Comments:*** H-MA-70-G8, Wait-Unlisted. 1810s.
Rarity: —

$3 • W-MA-160-003-G030
Engraver: PSSP. ***Comments:*** H-MA-70-G10, Wait-Unlisted. Similar to W-MA-160-002-G020 but with different denomination. 1810s.
Rarity: —

$5 • W-MA-160-005-G040
Left: MASSACHUSETTS across / 5, Plate letter, 5. ***Center:*** FIVE DOLLARS, Text. ***Right:*** 5, Plate letter, 5. ***Engraver:*** PSSP. ***Comments:*** H-MA-70-G12, Wait-Unlisted. 1810s.
Rarity: —

$10 • W-MA-160-010-G050
Engraver: PSSP. ***Comments:*** H-MA-70-G14, Wait-Unlisted. Similar to W-MA-160-005-G040 but with different denomination. 1810s.
Rarity: —

$20 • W-MA-160-020-G060
Engraver: PSSP. ***Comments:*** H-MA-70-G16, Wait-Unlisted. Similar to W-MA-160-005-G040 but with different denomination. 1810s.
Rarity: —

$50 • W-MA-160-050-G070
Engraver: PSSP. ***Comments:*** H-MA-70-G18, Wait-Unlisted. Similar to W-MA-160-005-G040 but with different denomination. 1810s.
Rarity: —

$100 • W-MA-160-100-G080
Engraver: PSSP. ***Comments:*** H-MA-70-G20, Wait-Unlisted. Similar to W-MA-160-005-G040 but with different denomination. 1810s.
Rarity: —

Notes With Maine Address

$1 • W-ME-400-001-G010
Engraver: Unverified, but likely PSSP. ***Comments:*** H-ME-160-G4, Wait-Unlisted. No description available. 1820s.
Rarity: *None known*

$1 • W-ME-400-001-G020
Engraver: Unverified, but likely PSSP. ***Comments:*** H-ME-160-G8, Wait-Unlisted. No description available. 1830s.
Rarity: *None known*

$1 • W-ME-400-001-G030
CJF

Engraver: New England Bank Note Co. ***Comments:*** H-ME-160-G12, Wait-43. 18__. 1840s–1850s.
Rarity: URS-3
F $2,000

$2 • W-ME-400-002-G040
Engraver: Unverified, but likely New England Bank Note Co. ***Comments:*** H-ME-160-G16, Wait-Unlisted. No description available. 1820s.
Rarity: *None known*

$2 • W-ME-400-002-G050
Left: Farmer plowing with two horses, Men sowing, Train / 2. ***Center:*** Girl on 2. ***Right:*** 2 / Woman leaning on barrel. ***Engraver:*** New England Bank Note Co. ***Comments:*** H-ME-160-G24, Wait-44. 1840s–1850s.
Rarity: —

$3 • W-ME-400-003-G060
Engraver: Unverified, but likely PSSP. ***Comments:*** H-ME-160-G28, Wait-Unlisted. No description available. 1820s.
Rarity: *None known*

$3 • W-ME-400-003-G070
Left: Ships at sea / 3. ***Center:*** 3. ***Right:*** 3 / Ship / THREE. ***Engraver:*** New England Bank Note Co. ***Comments:*** H-ME-160-G36, Wait-45. 1840s–1850s.
Rarity: —

$5 • W-ME-400-005-G080
Engraver: Unverified, but likely PSSP. ***Comments:*** H-ME-160-G40, Wait-Unlisted. No description available. 1820s.
Rarity: *None known*

$5 • W-ME-400-005-G090

CJF

Engraver: PSSP. ***Comments:*** H-ME-160-G44, Wait-Unlisted. 18__. 1830s.

Rarity: URS-5
F $150

$5 • W-ME-400-005-G100

Left: 5 / Blacksmith at anvil / FIVE. ***Center:*** Mercury standing with 5, Cornucopia and merchandise, Factories and ship / V. ***Right:*** 5 / Ceres kneeling / FIVE. ***Engraver:*** New England Bank Note Co. / PSSP. ***Comments:*** H-ME-160-G48, Wait-Unlisted. 1830s.

Rarity: —

$5 • W-ME-400-005-G110

Comments: H-ME-160-G52, Wait-Unlisted. No description available. 1830s–1840s.

Rarity: *None known*

$5 • W-ME-400-005-G120

Left: Four ships at sea / 5. ***Center:*** Woman and cherub in V. ***Right:*** 5 / Girl with basket of flowers. ***Engraver:*** New England Bank Note Co. ***Comments:*** H-ME-160-G56, Wait-46. 1840s–1850s.

Rarity: —

$10 • W-ME-400-010-G130

Engraver: Unverified, but likely PSSP. ***Comments:*** H-ME-160-G60, Wait-Unlisted. No description available. 1820s.

Rarity: *None known*

$10 • W-ME-400-010-G140

Engraver: PSSP. ***Comments:*** H-ME-160-G64, Wait-Unlisted. Similar to W-ME-400-001-G030 but with different denomination. 1830s.

Rarity: —

$10 • W-ME-400-010-G150

Left: 10 / Farmer sowing / TEN. ***Center:*** Mercury standing with 10, Merchandise, factories, and ship / Canal scene. ***Right:*** 10 / Ship / TEN. ***Engraver:*** New England Bank Note Co. ***Comments:*** H-ME-160-G68, Wait-Unlisted. 1830s.

Rarity: —

$10 • W-ME-400-010-G160

Comments: H-ME-160-G72, Wait-Unlisted. No description available. 1830s–1840s.

Rarity: *None known*

$10 • W-ME-400-010-G170

CJF

Engraver: New England Bank Note Co. ***Comments:*** H-ME-160-G76, Wait-51. 18__. 1840s.

Rarity: URS-1
Proof $2,000

$20 • W-ME-400-020-G180

Comments: H-ME-160-G80, Wait-Unlisted. No description available. 1820s–1830s.

Rarity: *None known*

$20 • W-ME-400-020-G190

Left: XX / Steamboat. ***Center:*** Wharf scene, Train, house, steamboat. ***Right:*** TWENTY on 20 / Sailing ship. ***Engraver:*** New England Bank Note Co. ***Comments:*** H-ME-160-G84, Wait-53. 1840s–1850s.

Rarity: —

$50 • W-ME-400-050-G200

Comments: H-ME-160-G88, Wait-Unlisted. No description available. 1820s–1830s.

Rarity: *None known*

$50 • W-ME-400-050-G210

Left: 50 / Steamboat, Sailing ship. ***Center:*** Farm house and buildings, Load of hay, Two men, Man with rake and pail / 50. ***Right:*** L / Justice kneeling. ***Engraver:*** New England Bank Note Co. ***Comments:*** H-ME-160-G92, Wait-54. 1840s–1850s.

Rarity: —

$100 • W-ME-400-100-G220

Comments: H-ME-160-G96, Wait-Unlisted. No description available. 1820s–1830s.

Rarity: *None known*

$100 • W-ME-400-100-G230

Left: 100 / Eagle / 100. ***Center:*** C / Neptune in cart drawn by three horses / 100. ***Right:*** C / Portrait of George Washington / C. ***Engraver:*** New England Bank Note Co. ***Comments:*** H-ME-160-G100, Wait-55. 1840s–1850s.

Rarity: —

Non-Valid Issues

$5 • W-ME-400-005-N010

Comments: H-Unlisted, Wait-47. No description available.

Rarity: *None known*

$5 • W-ME-400-005-N020

Comments: H-Unlisted, Wait-48. No description available.

Rarity: *None known*

$5 • W-ME-400-005-N030

Comments: H-Unlisted, Wait-49. No description available.

Rarity: *None known*

$10 • W-ME-400-010-N040

Comments: H-Unlisted, Wait-52. Imitation of W-ME-400-005-N030.

Rarity: *None known*

Belchertown, Massachusetts

Initially inhabited by the Nipmuc Indians, the land that became Belchertown was sold to Connecticut locals in 1716. Jonathan Belcher acquired some of the land, and Belchertown was settled in 1731 and incorporated on June 30, 1761. Later, in 1816, part of Belchertown merged with Greenwich, Massachusetts, to become Enfield, Massachusetts.

The first railroad in the area ran from Amherst to Palmer and was known as the Belchertown & Amherst Railroad. The land provided good hunting grounds and pastureland, accommodating cattle and sheep and also providing pine trees for the early industry of candlewood and turpentine. The poor soil made farming difficult, leading to a commercial preeminence of lumbering, the planting of orchards, and the raising of cattle, sheep, and hogs. There were also many river-powered saw mills, grist mills, plaster mills, cider mills, and turning mills. Carriage shops in Belchertown earned national fame.

Farmers Bank

1825–1830

W-MA-175

History: The Farmers Bank was the first bank to open in Belchertown and flourished for about five years. The initial capital was $100,000. However, the bank was fraudulently operated. On August 29, 1829, *Niles' Weekly Register* reported that "the bank at Belchertown, Mass. has stopped payment." The bank failed that same year.[31]

In the inaugural issue of *Bicknell's Counterfeit Detector,* July 31, 1830, the Farmers Bank of Belchertown was included on the "List of Broken Banks." On October 11, the same source reported: "it is said that the dies were lately discovered in New Hampshire, for altering Belchertown Bank bills to those of the Globe and American Bank, Boston." The bank's charter was repealed.

Numismatic Commentary: All examples from this bank are of the PSSP type. The notes are not especially rare. Each denomination is available on both white and pink paper. This phenomenon is only rarely encountered and offers an interesting twist to collecting. The pink paper varieties seem to be the older of the two issues by perhaps a year.

Valid Issues

$1 • W-MA-175-001-G010

Left: Lathework panel. ***Center:*** 1 / ONE / 1 / Oval of flower garlands and gridwork segments / 1 / ONE / 1. ***Right:*** Lathework panel. ***Engraver:*** PSSP. ***Comments:*** H-MA-75-G2. 18__. 1820s.

Rarity: URS-7

VG $32; **F** $75; **VF** $125; **EF** $250

$1 • W-MA-175-001-G010a

QDB

Engraver: PSSP. ***Comments:*** H-MA-75-G4. Similar to W-MA-175-001-G010. 18__. 1820s.

Rarity: URS-7

VG $32; **F** $75; **VF** $125; **EF** $250

$2 • W-MA-175-002-G020

CC

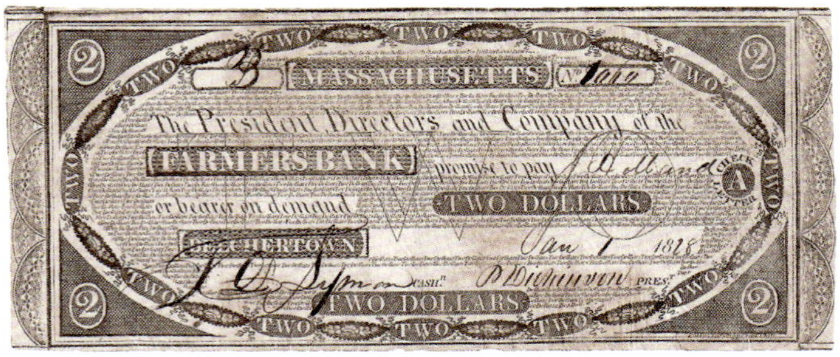

Engraver: PSSP. ***Comments:*** H-MA-75-G6. Similar to W-MA-175-001-G010 but with different denomination. 18__. 1820s.

Rarity: URS-6

F $75; **VF** $125; **EF** $250

$2 • W-MA-175-002-G020a

Engraver: PSSP. ***Comments:*** H-MA-75-G8. Similar to W-MA-175-001-G010 but with different denomination. 18__. 1820s.

Rarity: URS-6

F $75; **VF** $125; **EF** $250

$3 • W-MA-175-003-G030

CC

Engraver: PSSP. ***Comments:*** H-MA-75-G10. Similar to W-MA-175-001-G010 but with different denomination. 18__. 1820s.

Rarity: URS-6

VG $30; **F** $100; **VF** $150; **EF** $250

$3 • W-MA-175-003-G030a

Engraver: PSSP. ***Comments:*** H-MA-75-G12. Similar to W-MA-175-001-G010 but with different denomination. 18__. 1820s.

Rarity: URS-6

F $100; **VF** $150; **EF** $250

$5 • W-MA-175-005-G040

Left: MASSACHUSETTS vertically / 5 / 5. ***Center:*** FIVE DOLLARS. ***Right:*** 5 / 5. ***Engraver:*** PSSP. ***Comments:*** H-MA-75-G14. Printed on pink paper. 18__. 1820s.

Rarity: URS-6
F $75; **VF** $150

$5 • W-MA-175-005-G040a

CJF

Engraver: PSSP. ***Comments:*** H-MA-75-G14a. Similar to W-MA-175-005-G040. Printed on white paper. 18__. 1820s.

Rarity: URS-6
F $75; **VF** $125; **EF** $250

$10 • W-MA-175-010-G050

Engraver: PSSP. ***Comments:*** H-MA-75-G16. Similar to W-MA-175-005-G040 but with different denomination. Printed on pink paper. 18__. 1820s.

Rarity: URS-4
F $150

$10 • W-MA-175-010-G050a

CJF

Engraver: PSSP. ***Comments:*** H-MA-75-G16a. Similar to W-MA-175-010-G050. Printed on white paper. 18__. 1820s.

Rarity: URS-4
F $150

Beverly, Massachusetts

Named after Beverley in Yorkshire, England, the town of Beverly was split from the rest of the Naumkeag Territory and incorporated in 1668 due to religious disagreements. Part of the town was annexed in 1857 to create Danvers. In 1894 the town was officially incorporated as a city.

Beverly became known to historians as the "birthplace of the American Industrial Revolution" after the first cotton mill was established there in 1787. The various villages in Beverly consist of Goat Hill, Fish Flake Hill, Downtown, Gloucester Crossing, Ryal Side, The Cove, Motserrat, Beverly Farms, Pride's Crossing, North Beverly, and Centerville.

In 1765 the population was 2,164; by 1800 it had increased to 3,881; 1830 saw 4,073; and 1850 saw 5,376. Between 1835 and 1845, many immigrants from Ireland, Italy, Sweden, and Russia settled here.

Bass River Bank
1854–1859
W-MA-190

History: "A bill has been passed to establish this as a new bank," reported the *Banker's Magazine* of April 1854. The bank commenced operations on October 2, 1854. It had an authorized capital of $100,000, which remained a constant value through at least 1857. In 1858 the following figures were given in the *Annual Report of the Commissioner of Banks*: circulation $66,008; specie $3,319.36; real estate $5,527.48.

On August 8, 1859, the Board of Commissioners examined the bank and reported that it was in "very satisfactory condition," despite an unexplained deficiency of $17,000 and some past irregularities. This optimistic report was premature. In reality, the bank was in serious trouble. By October the bank had been closed by injunction and ceased business. Receivers and liquidators stepped in to salvage what they could, and the bills became worthless.

Numismatic Commentary: Notes from this bank are moderately available today. Some have a nice vignette showing the approach to Beverly from the bridge connecting Salem. All of its genuine issues were engraved by the combined efforts of Rawdon, Wright, Hatch & Edson and the New England Bank Note Co. At least one error note is known to exist: a $1 denomination with a "TWO" overprint.

Valid Issues

$1 • W-MA-190-001-G010

Left: ONE / Man reclining on bales / 1. ***Center:*** View of Beverly. ***Bottom center:*** Man plowing with two horses. ***Right:*** 1 / Steamboat / ONE. ***Overprint:*** Red ONE. ***Engraver:*** Rawdon, Wright, Hatch & Edson / New England Bank Note Co. ***Comments:*** H-MA-80-G2a. Oct. 2, 185_. 1850s.

Rarity: URS-2
F $150; **EF** $375; **Unc-Rem** $500

$1 • W-MA-190-001-G010a

CJF

Overprint: Red ONE. ***Engraver:*** Rawdon, Wright, Hatch & Edson / New England Bank Note Co. ***Comments:*** H-Unlisted. Similar to W-MA-190-001-G010 but with different date. April 2, 185_. 1850s.

Rarity: URS-6
VG $300

$1 • W-MA-190-001-G010b

CJF

Overprint: Grey TWO. ***Engraver:*** Rawdon, Wright, Hatch & Edson / New England Bank Note Co. ***Comments:*** H-Unlisted. Error overprint. Similar to W-MA-190-001-G010 but with different date. April 2, 185_. 1850s.

Rarity: URS-3

Proof $1,500

$2 • W-MA-190-002-G020

QDB

Overprint: Red TWO. ***Engraver:*** Rawdon, Wright, Hatch & Edson / New England Bank Note Co. ***Comments:*** H-MA-80-G4a. Oct. 2, 185_. 1850s.

Rarity: URS-4

VG $200; **F** $250; **EF** $375

$3 • W-MA-190-003-G030

Left: 3 / Female portrait / 3. ***Center:*** View of Beverly. ***Right:*** 3 / Mechanic, Sailor, and Farmer in and around 3. ***Overprint:*** Red THREE. ***Engraver:*** Rawdon, Wright, Hatch & Edson / New England Bank Note Co. ***Comments:*** H-MA-80-G6a. Oct. 2, 185_. 1850s.

Rarity: URS-4

VG $250; **F** $300; **EF** $375

$3 • W-MA-190-003-G030a

CC

Overprint: Red THREE. ***Engraver:*** Rawdon, Wright, Hatch & Edson / New England Bank Note Co. ***Comments:*** H-Unlisted. Similar to W-MA-190-003-G030 but with different date. April 2, 185_. 1850s.

Rarity: URS-5

F $400

$5 • W-MA-190-005-G040

QDB

Overprint: Red FIVE. ***Engraver:*** Rawdon, Wright, Hatch & Edson / New England Bank Note Co. ***Comments:*** H-MA-80-G8a. Oct. 2, 185_. 1850s.

Rarity: URS-5

VG $200; **F** $350; **EF** $425

$10 • W-MA-190-010-G050

CJF

Overprint: Red X. ***Engraver:*** Rawdon, Wright, Hatch & Edson / New England Bank Note Co. ***Comments:*** H-MA-80-G10a. Oct. 2, 185_. 1850s.

Rarity: URS-4

F $600; **VF** $500; **EF** $750

$20 • W-MA-190-020-G060

Left: TWENTY / 20 / TWENTY vertically. ***Center:*** Woman with train and steamship. ***Right:*** 20 / XX. ***Overprint:*** Red. ***Engraver:*** Rawdon, Wright, Hatch & Edson / New England Bank Note Co. ***Comments:*** H-MA-80-G12a. Oct. 2, 185_. 1850s.

Rarity: —

$50 • W-MA-190-050-G070

Left: 50 / Woman. ***Center:*** Shipping scene. ***Right:*** 50 / Sailor with chart. ***Overprint:*** Red. ***Engraver:*** Rawdon, Wright, Hatch & Edson / New England Bank Note Co. ***Comments:*** H-MA-80-G14a. Oct. 2, 185_. 1850s.

Rarity: —

$100 • W-MA-190-100-G080

Left: 100 / Ships / 100. ***Center:*** Wheels and bales. ***Right:*** C / Woman churning. ***Overprint:*** Red. ***Engraver:*** Rawdon, Wright, Hatch & Edson / New England Bank Note Co. ***Comments:*** H-MA-80-G16a. Oct. 2, 185_. 1850s.

Rarity: —

Non-Valid Issues

$1 • W-MA-190-001-A010

CJF

Engraver: W.L. Ormsby. ***Comments:*** H-MA-80-A5. Altered from $1 Potomac River Bank, Georgetown, D.C. 185_. 1850s.

Rarity: URS-5

F $100

$2 • W-MA-190-002-A020

CC

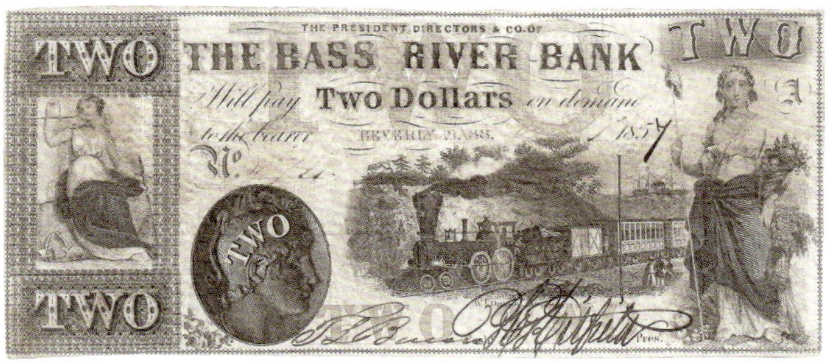

Engraver: W.L. Ormsby. ***Comments:*** H-MA-80-A10. Altered from $2 Potomac River Bank, Georgetown, D.C. 185_. 1850s.

Rarity: URS-5

VF $275

$3 • W-MA-190-003-A030

QDB

Engraver: W.L. Ormsby. ***Comments:*** H-MA-80-A15. Altered from $3 Potomac River Bank, Georgetown, D.C. 185_. 1850s.

Rarity: URS-5

VG $95

Beverly Bank {1st}

1802–1812

W-MA-200

History: On June 23, 1802, an act was passed to incorporate the Beverly Bank for a period of ten years. The founding directors were Captain Joseph Lee, Nathan Dane, Moses Brown, Captain Benjamin Lovett Jr., Captain John Derby, Thomas Stevens, and Israel Thorndike. Thorndike became president, accompanied by Josiah Gould as cashier. The first annual meeting of the stockholders was held on the first Monday of October 1802. The starting capital was to not exceed $160,000 or fall below $80,000 in specie, divided into shares of $100 apiece, and was to be paid in on or before October of the same year.

In April 1804, counterfeit $30 bills of the Beverly Bank were found. Four men were arrested on April 4 in New Boston, New Hampshire, who were found to be carrying plates of the counterfeit notes, as well as plates for fraudulent bills for the Union Bank, Boston, and the Essex Bank, Salem. The men were sent to jail. Nevertheless, $3 and $6 counterfeit bills were in circulation in 1811.

On June 23, 1812, the Beverly Bank was succeeded by the second bank of that name, W-MA-210.

Numismatic Commentary: This is a very hard bank to collect. On occasion collectors will find an early example of a Perkins type note or perhaps a PSSP type note.

Valid Issues

$1 • W-MA-200-001-G010

Center: 1 / 1 / Black oval bearing white flower buds / 1 / 1. ***Engraver:*** PSSP. ***Comments:*** H-MA-85-G6. 18__. 1800s.

Rarity: —

$1 • W-MA-200-001-G020

Center: 1 / 1 / Flower garlands and gridwork segments / 1 / 1. ***Engraver:*** PSSP. ***Comments:*** H-MA-85-G8. 18__. 1807–1809.

Rarity: —

$2 • W-MA-200-002-G030

Center: 2 / 2 / Black oval bearing white flower buds / 2 / 2. ***Engraver:*** PSSP. ***Comments:*** H-MA-85-G14. 18__. 1800s.

Rarity: —

$2 • W-MA-200-002-G040

Center: 2 / 2 / Flower garlands and gridwork segments / 2 / 2. ***Engraver:*** PSSP. ***Comments:*** H-MA-85-G16. 18__. 1807–1809.

Rarity: —

$3 • W-MA-200-003-G050

Center: 3 / 3 / Flower garlands and gridwork segments / 3 / 3. ***Engraver:*** PSSP. ***Comments:*** H-MA-85-G22. 18__. 1800s.

Rarity: URS-4

F $200

$3 • W-MA-200-003-G060

Center: 3 / 3 / Flower garlands and gridwork segments / 3 / 3. ***Engraver:*** PSSP. ***Comments:*** H-MA-85-G24. 18__. 1807–1809.

Rarity: —

$5 • W-MA-200-005-G070

Left: Gridwork panel bearing MASSACHUSETTS / 5 / 5. ***Center:*** Alternating flower garlands and gridwork segments. ***Right:*** 5 / 5. ***Engraver:*** PSSP. ***Comments:*** H-MA-85-G30. 18__. 1806 and 1807.

Rarity: —

$5 • W-MA-200-005-G070a

Center: Rose-covered FIVE. ***Engraver:*** PSSP. ***Comments:*** H-MA-85-G32. Similar to W-MA-200-005-G070. 18__. 1808 and 1809.

Rarity: —

$8 • **W-MA-200-008-G080**

Center: Alternating flower garlands and gridwork segments. ***Engraver:*** PSSP. ***Comments:*** H-Unlisted. 1800s–1810s.

Rarity: URS-2
F $750
Selected auction price: Heritage,
April–May 2011, Lot 15224, F $632

$10 • **W-MA-200-010-G090**

Left: Gridwork panel bearing MASSACHUSETTS / 10 / 10 vertically. ***Center:*** Alternating flower garlands and gridwork segments. ***Right:*** 10 / 10 vertically. ***Engraver:*** PSSP. ***Comments:*** H-MA-85-G38. 18__. 1806 and 1807.

Rarity: —

$10 • **W-MA-200-010-G090a**

Center: Rose-covered TEN. ***Engraver:*** PSSP. ***Comments:*** H-MA-85-G40. Similar to W-MA-200-010-G090. 18__. 1808 and 1809.

Rarity: —

$20 • **W-MA-200-020-G100**

Left: Gridwork panel bearing MASSACHUSETTS / 20 / 20 vertically. ***Center:*** Alternating flower garlands and gridwork segments. ***Right:*** 20 / 20 vertically. ***Engraver:*** PSSP. ***Comments:*** H-MA-85-G46. 18__. 1806–1809.

Rarity: —

Non-Valid Issues

$3 • **W-MA-200-003-C050**

CJF

Engraver: Perkins. ***Comments:*** H-MA-85-C22. Counterfeit W-MA-200-003-G050. 18__. 1800s.

Rarity: URS-5
F $150

Beverly Bank {2nd}

1812–1865

W-MA-210

History: The second Beverly Bank was incorporated on June 23, 1812. Capital was stated as $160,000 in 1814; it was later increased to $185,000 in 1837. By 1839 it had dropped to $125,000 and remained there until 1864. Circulation ranged from $57,946 in November 1839 to $101,725 in 1863. In 1856 bills of this bank and other New England states held in the vault amounted to $4,489, and specie totaled $11,155.74.

The Beverly National Bank was chartered on April 1, 1865, and succeeded the interests of the state bank. Nearly all of the older currency was redeemed or burned.

Numismatic Commentary: Collectors may have to settle for a spurious issue from this bank to fill the gaps. Although many varieties were issued, very few exist today.

Valid Issues

$1 • **W-MA-210-001-G010**

Center: 1 / 1 / Flower garlands and gridwork segments / ONE / 1 / 1. ***Engraver:*** PSSP. ***Comments:*** H-MA-86-G2. 18__. 1810s–1820s.

Rarity: —

$1 • **W-MA-210-001-G010a**

Left: Narrow panel of lathework circle segments. ***Right:*** Narrow panel of lathework circle segments. ***Engraver:*** PSSP. ***Comments:*** H-MA-86-G4. Similar to W-MA-210-001-G010. 18__. 1820s.

Rarity: —

$1 • **W-MA-210-001-G010b**

Left: Narrow panel of lathework circle segments. ***Right:*** Narrow panel of lathework circle segments. ***Engraver:*** PSSP. ***Comments:*** H-MA-86-G6. Similar to W-MA-210-001-G010. 18__. 1820s–1830s.

Rarity: —

$1 • **W-MA-210-001-G010c**

Left: ONE / D / ONE vertically. ***Right:*** ONE / D / ONE vertically. ***Engraver:*** PSSP. ***Comments:*** H-MA-86-G8. Similar to W-MA-210-001-G010. 18__. 1830s.

Rarity: —

How to Read the Whitman Numbering System

$1 • **W-MA-010-001-G010a**

Denomination: Value of the note shown.

W: Whitman number. This number is a sortable code unique to each bank and note.

MA: Abbreviation for the state under study.

010: Numerical designation specific to each bank.

001: The denomination in dollars.

G010a: G indicates a good or valid note. Other categories are indicated thus: C (counterfeit); R (raised); S (spurious); N (not-attributed); A (altered). Numbers are assigned starting with 010, 020, et seq. Terminal letters following the number indicate variations of a note: a series of different colored overprints, tints, payees, etc., all on the same design of note. For more information, see the "How to Use This Book" section at the front of the volume, page xiv.

$1 • **W-MA-210-001-G020**

Left: 1 / Woman wearing bonnet, standing by pail / ONE. ***Center:*** Machinery and merchandise flanking Ceres seated holding sickle and rake, Factories and harbor / Panel outlining white ONE. ***Right:*** 1 / Ship / ONE. ***Engraver:*** PSSP / New England Bank Note Co. ***Comments:*** H-MA-86-G12. 18__. 1830s–1840s.

Rarity: —

$1 • **W-MA-210-001-G030**

Left: Commerce seated with rudder, leaning on barrel / 1. ***Center:*** 1 bearing "Presentation of the Declaration of Independence". ***Right:*** 1 / Woman standing with elbow on fence, apron full of grain. ***Engraver:*** New England Bank Note Co. ***Comments:*** H-MA-86-G14. 18__. 1840s–1850s.

Rarity: —

$1 • **W-MA-210-001-G040**

Left: Woman holding distaff, resting arm on 1 / ONE / Cherub holding die bearing 1. ***Center:*** Harbor view, Ship. ***Right:*** 1 / Woman seated on ground with arms around 1. ***Engraver:*** Rawdon, Wright, Hatch & Edson / New England Bank Note Co. ***Comments:*** H-MA-86-G16. 18__. 1850s.

Rarity: —

$1 • **W-MA-210-001-G040a**

Overprint: Red. ***Engraver:*** Rawdon, Wright, Hatch & Edson / New England Bank Note Co. ***Comments:*** H-MA-86-G16a. Similar to W-MA-210-001-G040. 18__. 1850s.

Rarity: —

$1 • **W-MA-210-001-G040b**

Overprint: Red. ***Engraver:*** Rawdon, Wright, Hatch & Edson / New England Bank Note Co. / ABNCo. monogram. ***Comments:*** H-MA-86-G16b. Similar to W-MA-210-001-G040 but with additional engraver imprint. 18__. 1850s–1860s.

Rarity: —

$2 • **W-MA-210-002-G050**

Center: 2 / 2 / Flower garlands and gridwork segments / TWO / 2 / 2. ***Engraver:*** PSSP. ***Comments:*** H-MA-86-G20. 18__. 1810s–1820s.

Rarity: —

$2 • **W-MA-210-002-G050a**

Left: Narrow panel of lathework circle segments. ***Right:*** Narrow panel of lathework circle segments. ***Engraver:*** PSSP. ***Comments:*** H-MA-86-G22. Similar to W-MA-210-002-G050. 18__. 1820s.

Rarity: —

$2 • **W-MA-210-002-G050b**

Left: Narrow panel of lathework circle segments. ***Right:*** Narrow panel of lathework circle segments. ***Engraver:*** PSSP. ***Comments:*** H-MA-86-G24. Similar to W-MA-210-002-G050. 18__. 1820s–1830s.

Rarity: —

$2 • **W-MA-210-002-G050c**

Left: Five TWOs vertically. ***Right:*** Five TWOs vertically. ***Engraver:*** PSSP. ***Comments:*** H-MA-86-G26. Similar to W-MA-210-002-G050. 18__. 1830s.

Rarity: —

$2 • **W-MA-210-002-G060**

Left: 2 / Cornucopia, Woman standing with staff / TWO. ***Center:*** TWO / Machinery and merchandise flanking Ceres seated holding sickle and rake, Factories and harbor / Panel outlining white TWO. ***Right:*** 2 / Woman wearing hat, Trees / TWO. ***Engraver:*** PSSP / New England Bank Note Co. ***Comments:*** H-MA-86-G30. 18__. 1830s–1840s.

Rarity: —

$2 • **W-MA-210-002-G070**

Left: 2. ***Center:*** Men driving sheep into stream, 2 bearing "Presentation of the Declaration of Independence". ***Right:*** TWO / Woman seated with wreath of flowers / TWO. ***Engraver:*** New England Bank Note Co. ***Comments:*** H-MA-86-G32. 18__. 1840s–1850s.

Rarity: —

$2 • **W-MA-210-002-G080**

Left: 2 / 2. ***Center:*** Liberty draped in flag, Bale and eagle, Ships. ***Right:*** 2 / Women seated flanking fruit. ***Engraver:*** Rawdon, Wright, Hatch & Edson / New England Bank Note Co. ***Comments:*** H-MA-86-G34. 18__. 1850s.

Rarity: —

$2 • **W-MA-210-002-G080a**

Overprint: Red. ***Engraver:*** Rawdon, Wright, Hatch & Edson / New England Bank Note Co. ***Comments:*** H-MA-86-G34a. Similar to W-MA-210-002-G080. 18__. 1850s.

Rarity: —

$2 • **W-MA-210-002-G080b**

Overprint: Red. ***Engraver:*** Rawdon, Wright, Hatch & Edson / New England Bank Note Co. / ABNCo. monogram. ***Comments:*** H-MA-86-G34b. Similar to W-MA-210-002-G080 but with additional engraver imprint. 18__. 1850s–1860s.

Rarity: —

$3 • **W-MA-210-003-G090**

Center: 3 / 3 / Flower garlands and gridwork segments / 3 / 3. ***Engraver:*** PSSP. ***Comments:*** H-MA-86-G38. 18__. 1810s–1820s.

Rarity: —

$3 • **W-MA-210-003-G090a**

Left: Narrow panel of lathework circle segments. ***Right:*** Narrow panel of lathework circle segments. ***Engraver:*** PSSP. ***Comments:*** H-MA-86-G40. Similar to W-MA-210-003-G090. 18__. 1820s.

Rarity: —

$3 • **W-MA-210-003-G090b**

Left: Narrow panel of lathework circle segments. ***Right:*** Narrow panel of lathework circle segments. ***Engraver:*** PSSP. ***Comments:*** H-MA-86-G42. Similar to W-MA-210-003-G090. 18__. 1820s–1830s.

Rarity: —

$3 • **W-MA-210-003-G090c**

Left: THREE vertically. ***Right:*** THREE vertically. ***Engraver:*** PSSP. ***Comments:*** H-MA-86-G44. Similar to W-MA-210-003-G090. 18__. 1830s.

Rarity: —

$3 • W-MA-210-003-G100

Left: THREE / Beehive and foliage / THREE. ***Center:*** Machinery and merchandise flanking Ceres seated holding sickle and rake, Factories and harbor / Panel outlining white THREE. ***Right:*** 3 on THREE / Two reapers / 3 on THREE. ***Engraver:*** PSSP / New England Bank Note Co. ***Comments:*** H-MA-86-G48. 18__. 1830s–1840s.

Rarity: —

$3 • W-MA-210-003-G110

Left: Barnyard scene, Man on horse, Boy and cattle / 3. ***Center:*** 3. ***Right:*** 3 on THREE / Woman with flowers on shoulder / THREE. ***Engraver:*** New England Bank Note Co. ***Comments:*** H-MA-86-G50. 18__. 1840s–1850s.

Rarity: —

$3 • W-MA-210-003-G120

Left: Three women seated with distaff, sextant, staff, and sickle / 3. ***Center:*** Portrait of Daniel Webster. ***Right:*** 3 / Sailing ship. ***Engraver:*** Rawdon, Wright, Hatch & Edson / New England Bank Note Co. ***Comments:*** H-MA-86-G52. 18__. 1850s.

Rarity: —

$3 • W-MA-210-003-G120a

Overprint: Red. ***Engraver:*** Rawdon, Wright, Hatch & Edson / New England Bank Note Co. ***Comments:*** H-MA-86-G52a. Similar to W-MA-210-003-G120. 18__. 1850s.

Rarity: —

$3 • W-MA-210-003-G120b

Overprint: Red. ***Engraver:*** Rawdon, Wright, Hatch & Edson / New England Bank Note Co. / ABNCo. monogram. ***Comments:*** H-MA-86-G52b. Similar to W-MA-210-003-G120 but with additional engraver imprint. 18__. 1850s–1860s.

Rarity: —

$5 • W-MA-210-005-G130

Left: Lathework panel bearing MASSACHUSETTS / 5 / 5. ***Center:*** Alternating flower garlands and gridwork segments. ***Right:*** 5 / 5. ***Engraver:*** PSSP. ***Comments:*** H-MA-86-G56. 18__. 1810s–1820s.

Rarity: —

$5 • W-MA-210-005-G130a

Engraver: PSSP. ***Comments:*** H-MA-86-G58. Similar to W-MA-210-005-G130 but with white boxes flanking the top. 18__. 1820s.

Rarity: —

$5 • W-MA-210-005-G130b

Engraver: PSSP. ***Comments:*** H-MA-86-G60. Similar to W-MA-210-005-G130 but with zigzag ruled lines. 18__. 1820s–1830s.

Rarity: —

$5 • W-MA-210-005-G130c

Engraver: PSSP. ***Comments:*** H-MA-86-G62. Similar to W-MA-210-005-G130 but with spiral lathework lines. 18__. 1830s.

Rarity: —

$5 • W-MA-210-005-G140

Left: 5 / Blacksmith at anvil / 5. ***Center:*** Mercury standing with 5, Cornucopia and merchandise, Factories and ship / V / Panel outlining white FIVE. ***Right:*** 5 / Ceres kneeling / FIVE. ***Engraver:*** PSSP / New England Bank Note Co. ***Comments:*** H-MA-86-G66. 18__. 1830s–1840s.

Rarity: —

$5 • W-MA-210-005-G150

Left: FIVE / Sailor hoisting flag. ***Center:*** Three women seated around 5. ***Right:*** 5 / Portrait of George Washington. ***Engraver:*** Rawdon, Wright, Hatch & Edson / New England Bank Note Co. ***Comments:*** H-MA-86-G70. 18__. 1850s.

Rarity: —

$5 • W-MA-210-005-G150a

Overprint: Red. ***Engraver:*** Rawdon, Wright, Hatch & Edson / New England Bank Note Co. ***Comments:*** H-MA-86-G70a. Similar to W-MA-210-005-G150. 18__. 1850s.

Rarity: —

$5 • W-MA-210-005-G150b

Overprint: Red. ***Engraver:*** Rawdon, Wright, Hatch & Edson / New England Bank Note Co. / ABNCo. monogram. ***Comments:*** H-MA-86-G70b. Similar to W-MA-210-005-G150 but with additional engraver imprint. 18__. 1850s–1860s.

Rarity: —

$10 • W-MA-210-010-G160

Left: Lathework panel bearing MASSACHUSETTS / 10 / 10 vertically. ***Center:*** Alternating flower garlands and gridwork segments / TEN. ***Right:*** 10 / 10 vertically. ***Engraver:*** PSSP. ***Comments:*** H-MA-86-G74. 18__. 1810s–1820s.

Rarity: —

$10 • W-MA-210-010-G160a

Engraver: PSSP. ***Comments:*** H-MA-86-G76. Similar to W-MA-210-010-G160 but with white boxes flanking the top. 18__. 1820s.

Rarity: —

$10 • W-MA-210-010-G160b

Engraver: PSSP. ***Comments:*** H-MA-86-G78. Similar to W-MA-210-010-G160 but with zigzag ruled lines. 18__. 1820s–1830s.

Rarity: —

$10 • W-MA-210-010-G160c

Engraver: PSSP. ***Comments:*** H-MA-86-G80. Similar to W-MA-210-010-G160 but with spiral lathework lines. 18__. 1830s.

Rarity: —

$10 • W-MA-210-010-G170

Left: 10 / Farmer sowing / TEN. ***Center:*** Mercury standing with right hand on 10, Merchandise, Factories and ship / Canal scene / Panel outlining white TEN. ***Right:*** 10 / Ship / TEN. ***Engraver:*** New England Bank Note Co. ***Comments:*** H-MA-86-G84. 18__. 1830s–1840s.

Rarity: —

$10 • W-MA-210-010-G180

Left: Train / Mechanic seated with tools / Building / TEN. ***Center:*** X. ***Right:*** 10 / Reaper standing with sheaf on knee. ***Engraver:*** New England Bank Note Co. ***Comments:*** H-MA-86-G86. 18__. 1840s–1850s.

Rarity: —

$10 • W-MA-210-010-G190

Left: 10 / Woman seated, Barrel, Ships. ***Center:*** TEN. ***Right:*** X / Cherub with shield bearing 10. ***Engraver:*** Rawdon, Wright, Hatch & Edson / New England Bank Note Co. ***Comments:*** H-MA-86-G88. July 1, 18__. 1850s.

Rarity: —

$10 • W-MA-210-010-G190a

Overprint: Red TEN. ***Engraver:*** Rawdon, Wright, Hatch & Edson / New England Bank Note Co. ***Comments:*** H-MA-86-G88a. Similar to W-MA-210-010-G190. July 1, 18__. 1850s.

Rarity: —

$10 • W-MA-210-010-G190b

CJF

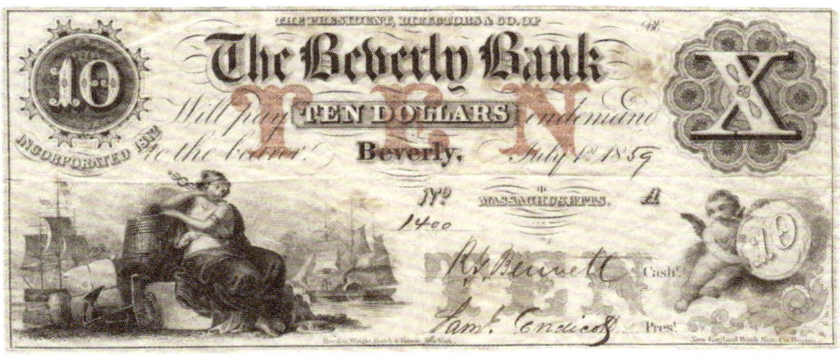

Overprint: Red TEN. ***Engraver:*** Rawdon, Wright, Hatch & Edson / New England Bank Note Co. / ABNCo. monogram. ***Comments:*** H-MA-86-G88b. Similar to W-MA-210-010-G190 but with additional engraver imprint. July 1, 18__. 1850s–1860s.

Rarity: URS-3
F $750

$20 • W-MA-210-020-G200

Left: Panel bearing state arms / 20 / 20 vertically. ***Center:*** Alternating flower garlands and gridwork segments. ***Right:*** 20 / 20 vertically. ***Engraver:*** PSSP. ***Comments:*** H-MA-86-G92. 18__. 1810s–1820s.

Rarity: —

$20 • W-MA-210-020-G200a

Left: Lathework chain bearing MASSACHUSETTS vertically. ***Right:*** Lathework chain bearing MASSACHUSETTS vertically. ***Engraver:*** PSSP. ***Comments:*** H-MA-86-G94. Similar to W-MA-210-020-G200. 18__. 1820s–1830s.

Rarity: —

$20 • W-MA-210-020-G210

Left: Steamboat / XX / Train. ***Center:*** Three women seated with eagle, pole and cap, shield, scales, and book / 20 / Panel outlining white TWENTY. ***Right:*** XX / Milkmaid standing with pail. ***Engraver:*** New England Bank Note Co. ***Comments:*** H-MA-86-G98. 18__. 1840s.

Rarity: —

$20 • W-MA-210-020-G220

Left: 20 / Woman seated with book and opening chest. ***Center:*** XX / Eagle on rock / XX. ***Right:*** 20 / Ship in harbor. ***Engraver:*** New England Bank Note Co. ***Comments:*** H-MA-86-G100. 18__. 1840s–1850s.

Rarity: —

$20 • W-MA-210-020-G230

Left: 20 / Fowl. ***Center:*** Cattle in stream, Girl and boy on bank. ***Right:*** 20 / Woman with sheaf. ***Tint:*** Green. ***Engraver:*** Unverified, but likely American Bank Note Co. ***Comments:*** H-MA-86-G102a. 18__. 1860s.

Rarity: —

$50 • W-MA-210-050-G240

Left: Panel bearing state arms / 50 / 50 vertically. ***Center:*** Alternating flower garlands and gridwork segments. ***Right:*** 50 / 50 vertically. ***Engraver:*** PSSP. ***Comments:*** H-MA-86-G106. 18__. 1810s–1820s.

Rarity: —

$50 • W-MA-210-050-G240a

Left: Lathework chain bearing MASSACHUSETTS vertically. ***Right:*** Lathework chain bearing MASSACHUSETTS vertically. ***Engraver:*** PSSP. ***Comments:*** H-MA-86-G108. Similar to W-MA-210-050-G240. 18__. 1820s–1830s.

Rarity: —

$50 • W-MA-210-050-G250

Left: FIFTY / Woman standing with wreath and flowers / FIFTY. ***Center:*** 50 / Man restraining prancing horse / 50. ***Right:*** FIFTY / Woman standing with cornucopia / FIFTY. ***Engraver:*** New England Bank Note Co. ***Comments:*** H-MA-86-G112. 18__. 1840s–1850s.

Rarity: —

$50 • W-MA-210-050-G260

Left: Farmer seated with grain, Sailor leaning on capstan, Boy and dog. ***Right:*** 50 / Dog and strongbox. ***Tint:*** Green 50s. ***Engraver:*** Unverified, but likely American Bank Note Co. ***Comments:*** H-MA-86-G114a. 18__. 1860s.

Rarity: —

$100 • W-MA-210-100-G270

Left: Panel bearing state arms / 100 / 100 vertically. ***Center:*** Alternating flower garlands and gridwork segments. ***Right:*** 100 / 100 vertically. ***Engraver:*** PSSP. ***Comments:*** H-MA-86-G118. 18__. 1810s–1820s.

Rarity: —

$100 • W-MA-210-100-G270a

Left: Lathework chain bearing MASSACHUSETTS vertically. ***Right:*** Lathework chain bearing MASSACHUSETTS vertically. ***Engraver:*** PSSP. ***Comments:*** H-MA-86-G120. Similar to W-MA-210-100-G270. 18__. 1820s–1830s.

Rarity: —

$100 • W-MA-210-100-G280

Left: ONE HUNDRED on 100 / Portrait of William Henry Harrison. ***Center:*** Wharf scene, Men loading wagon with barrels. ***Right:*** ONE HUNDRED on 100 / Portrait of Christopher Columbus. ***Engraver:*** New England Bank Note Co. ***Comments:*** H-MA-86-G124. 18__. 1840s–1850s.

Rarity: —

$100 • W-MA-210-100-G290

Left: 100 / Woman holding wreath above state arms. ***Center:*** Portrait of George Washington. ***Right:*** 100 / Woman reclining with globe and sextant. ***Tint:*** Green C C. ***Engraver:*** Unverified, but likely American Bank Note Co. ***Comments:*** H-MA-86-G126a. 18__. 1860s.

Rarity: —

$500 • W-MA-210-500-G300

Left: 500 / 500 / 500. ***Center:*** 500 / Woman seated with shield bearing D, Fasces, cornucopia, lyre, and sheaf on ground / 500. ***Right:*** 500 / D / 500. ***Engraver:*** PSSP / New England Bank Note Co. ***Comments:*** H-MA-86-G130. 18__. 1830s–1840s.

Rarity: —

$1,000 • W-MA-210-1000-G310

Left: THOUSAND vertically. ***Center:*** 1000 / Woman standing with legs crossed, right hand on lyre, Cornucopia / 1000. ***Right:*** 1000 / M / 1000. ***Engraver:*** New England Bank Note Co. ***Comments:*** H-MA-86-G134. 18__. 1830s–1840s.

Rarity: —

Non-Valid Issues

$1 • W-MA-210-001-A010

Left: 1 / State arms / ONE. ***Center:*** Ship, Three allegorical women reclining around shield surmounted by eagle. ***Right:*** 1 / Dog, Two farmers walking. ***Engraver:*** Danforth, Wright & Co. ***Comments:*** H-MA-86-A5. Altered from $1 Bank of Washtenaw, Washtenaw, Michigan series. 1850s.

Rarity: —

$1 • W-MA-210-001-A020

Left: Woman standing with apron full of flowers / ONE vertically. ***Center:*** Two reapers, Reaper seated by cradle, Hay wagon / 1. ***Right:*** ONE / Indian standing on cliff. ***Overprint:*** Red ONE. ***Engraver:*** New England Bank Note Co. / Rawdon, Wright, Hatch & Edson. ***Comments:*** H-MA-86-A10. Altered from $1 Waubeek Bank, De Soto, Nebraska. 1857.

Rarity: —

$3 • W-MA-210-003-S010

CC

Overprint: Red overall outlining white 3 / 3 / THREE and dies outlining 3s. ***Comments:*** H-MA-86-S5. Sept. 10, 18__. 1850s.

Rarity: URS-5
VG $300

$3 • W-MA-210-003-S010a

CJF

Overprint: Brown overall and 3 / 3 / THREE. ***Comments:*** H-MA-86-S5a. Similar to W-MA-210-003-S010. Sept. 10, 18__. 1850s.

Rarity: URS-4
VG $350

$3 • W-MA-210-003-A030

PEM

Tint: Red-brown panel outlining white THREE. ***Engraver:*** American Bank Note Co. ***Comments:*** H-MA-86-N5. Altered note. July 4, 1861.

Rarity: URS-3
VG $100

$5 • W-MA-210-005-A040

Left: FIVE / Portrait of Benjamin Franklin / V. ***Center:*** 5 / Agricultural implements, Two allegorical women standing and one seated, Ship. ***Bottom center:*** Anchor and implements. ***Right:*** V / Portrait of Marquis de Lafayette / FIVE. ***Engraver:*** Terry, Pelton & Co. ***Comments:*** H-MA-86-A15. Altered from W-MA-2860-005-G110, or from notes of other failed banks using the same plate. 18__. 1830s.

Rarity: —

Beverly Bank of Beverly

1850s

W-MA-220

History: A non-existent bank represented only by notes altered from those of other banks. The notes were intended to pass for those of the Beverly Bank, 2nd, W-MA-210.

Issues

$1 • W-MA-220-001-A010

Left: ONE on die vertically. ***Center:*** Man on horseback overseeing cotton harvest / Indian stalking two deer. ***Right:*** 1 / Female portrait. ***Overprint:*** Red ONE. ***Engraver:*** Bald, Cousland & Co. / Baldwin, Bald & Cousland. ***Comments:*** H-MA-87-A5. Altered from $1 Southern Bank of Georgia, Bainbridge, Georgia. 18__. 1860s.

Rarity: —

$1 • W-MA-220-001-A020

CC

Tint: Red-brown dies outlining white 1s and panel outlining white ONE DOLLAR. ***Engraver:*** Danforth, Wright & Co. ***Comments:*** H-MA-87-A10. Altered from $1 Southern Bank of Georgia, Bainbridge, Georgia. March 1, 1858.

Rarity: URS-6
F $100

$2 • W-MA-220-002-A030

SI

Overprint: Red TWO. ***Engraver:*** Bald, Cousland & Co. / Baldwin, Bald & Cousland. ***Comments:*** H-MA-87-A15. Altered from $2 Southern Bank of Georgia, Bainbridge, Georgia. 18__. 1860s.

Rarity: URS-5

G $50

Blackstone, Massachusetts

The first inhabitants of Blackstone were the Nipmuc Indians. Named after William Blaxton, who was the first settler in Boston and Rhode Island, the town was officially incorporated in 1845. The town eventually became a part of Mendon, Massachusetts, and later part of the area divided to become Millville, Massachusetts.

The Mill and Blackstone rivers provided for a cotton mill, a worsted mill, a textile mill, a rubber factory, and a woolen mill. Manufacturing villages were set up on these rivers, including Millville, Blackstone, Waterford, Upper Canada, and Lower Canada.

From the late 1850s until the early 20th century, feudal rivalry between French and Irish immigrants caused great unrest in the area, evoking an unascertained number of skirmishes and deaths.

Worcester County Bank

1850–1865

W-MA-230

History: The Worcester County Bank was incorporated in May 1849. It commenced business on July 1, 1850, with an authorized capital of $100,000. In 1851 Henry S. Mansfield Jr. became president with Alex Ballou as cashier. The cashier position changed yet again in 1852 to be held by Moses Farnum. Mansfield and Farnum served as officers together until 1864.

On May 3, 1865, the Worcester National Bank of Blackstone was chartered and succeeded the interests of the state bank.

Numismatic Commentary: One of the counterfeit notes listed for this bank, a $5 note, is a fine imitation, right down to the ABNCo. monogram. This imitation will probably be the easiest example out of all the notes of this bank to obtain and can be used as a filler until and if a genuine note is found.

Valid Issues

$1 • W-MA-230-001-G010

Left: Commerce seated with rudder, learning on barrel / 1. ***Center:*** 1 bearing "Presentation of the Declaration of Independence". ***Right:*** 1 / Woman standing with elbow on fence, apron full of grain. ***Engraver:*** New England Bank Note Co. ***Comments:*** H-MA-90-G2. 18__. 1850s.

Rarity: —

$1 • W-MA-230-001-G020

Left: Portrait of Daniel Webster. ***Center:*** Mechanic seated with hammer / Factories and river. ***Right:*** 1 / Indian woman seated. ***Engraver:*** Rawdon, Wright, Hatch & Edson / New England Bank Note Co. ***Comments:*** H-MA-90-G4. Jan. 1, 1850.

Rarity: —

$1 • W-MA-230-001-G020a

CJF

Overprint: Green ONE. ***Engraver:*** American Bank Note Co. ***Comments:*** H-MA-90-G4c. Similar to W-MA-230-001-G020 but with different engraver imprint. Jan. 1, 18__. 1860s.

Rarity: URS-4

F $400

$2 • W-MA-230-002-G030

Left: Men driving sheep into stream / 2. ***Center:*** 2 bearing "Presentation of the Declaration of Independence". ***Right:*** TWO / Woman seated with wreath of flowers / TWO. ***Engraver:*** New England Bank Note Co. ***Comments:*** H-MA-90-G6. 18__. 1850s.

Rarity: —

$2 • W-MA-230-002-G040

Left: 2 / Woman seated. ***Center:*** Indian woman holding wreath over bust of George Washington, Woman standing with shield and bale, Ship. ***Right:*** 2 / Portrait of George Washington. ***Engraver:*** Rawdon, Wright, Hatch & Edson / New England Bank Note Co. ***Comments:*** H-MA-90-G8. Jan. 1, 18__. 1850s.

Rarity: —

$2 • W-MA-230-002-G040a

Overprint: Green TWO. ***Engraver:*** Rawdon, Wright, Hatch & Edson / New England Bank Note Co. / ABNCo. monogram. ***Comments:*** H-MA-90-G8c. Similar to W-MA-230-002-G040 but with additional engraver imprint. Jan. 1, 18__. 1850s.

Rarity: —

$3 • W-MA-230-003-G050

Left: Barnyard scene, Man on horse, Boy and cattle / 3. ***Center:*** 3. ***Right:*** 3 on THREE / Woman with flowers on shoulder / THREE. ***Engraver:*** New England Bank Note Co. ***Comments:*** H-MA-90-G10. Beware of spurious note resembling the genuine. 18__. 1850s.

Rarity: —

$5 • W-MA-230-005-G060

Left: Eagle on shield and anchor, Factories and ships / FIVE. ***Center:*** Woman with cornucopia and cherub in V. ***Right:*** 5 / Girl with ringlets holding basket. ***Engraver:*** New England Bank Note Co. ***Comments:*** H-MA-90-G12. 18__. 1850s.

Rarity: —

$5 • **W-MA-230-005-G070**

Left: 5 / Train. ***Center:*** Woman reclining, Train, Women with cattle. ***Right:*** 5 / Shield. ***Engraver:*** Rawdon, Wright, Hatch & Edson / New England Bank Note Co. ***Comments:*** H-MA-90-G14. 18__. 1850s.

Rarity: —

$5 • **W-MA-230-005-G070a**

Engraver: Rawdon, Wright, Hatch & Edson / New England Bank Note Co. / ABNCo. monogram. ***Comments:*** H-MA-90-G14b. Similar to W-MA-230-005-G070 but with additional engraver imprint. 18__. 1860s.

Rarity: —

$5 • **W-MA-230-005-G070b**

JF

Overprint: Green FIVE. ***Engraver:*** American Bank Note Co. ***Comments:*** H-Unlisted. Similar to W-MA-230-005-G070 but with different engraver imprint. Jan. 1, 18__. 1860s.

Rarity: —
F $1,000

$10 • **W-MA-230-010-G080**

Left: Train, Mechanic seated with tools, Building / TEN. ***Center:*** X. ***Right:*** 10 / Reaper standing with sheaf on knee. ***Engraver:*** New England Bank Note Co. ***Comments:*** H-MA-90-G16. 18__. 1850s.

Rarity: —

$10 • **W-MA-230-010-G090**

Left: X / Indian woman. ***Center:*** Agriculture, Commerce, and Industry. ***Right:*** 10 / Cherub and dolphin. ***Engraver:*** Rawdon, Wright, Hatch & Edson / New England Bank Note Co. ***Comments:*** H-MA-90-G18. 18__. 1850s.

Rarity: —

$10 • **W-MA-230-010-G090a**

Engraver: Rawdon, Wright, Hatch & Edson / New England Bank Note Co. / ABNCo. monogram. ***Comments:*** H-MA-90-G18b. Similar to W-MA-230-010-G090 but with additional engraver imprint. 18__. 1860s.

Rarity: —

$20 • **W-MA-230-020-G100**

Left: 20 / Minerva standing with spear. ***Center:*** Woman seated between 2 and 0. ***Right:*** 20 / Woman reclining on cornucopia / 20. ***Engraver:*** Rawdon, Wright, Hatch & Edson. ***Comments:*** H-MA-90-G20. 18__. 1850s.

Rarity: —

$20 • **W-MA-230-020-G110**

CC

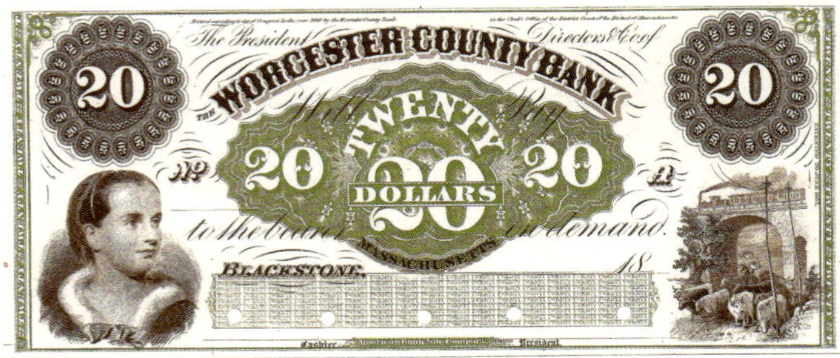

Tint: Green. ***Engraver:*** American Bank Note Co. ***Comments:*** H-MA-90-G22a. Proof. 18__. 1850s–1860s.

Rarity: URS-3
Proof $2,250

$20 • **W-MA-230-020-G120**

Left: Woman with eagle / 20. ***Center:*** Female portrait. ***Right:*** 20 / Portrait of Benjamin Franklin. ***Tint:*** Red XX on 20 on TWENTY. ***Engraver:*** Unverified, but likely American Bank Note Co. ***Comments:*** H-MA-90-G24a. 18__. 1860s.

Rarity: —

$50 • **W-MA-230-050-G130**

Left: 50 / Minerva standing by column. ***Center:*** Ceres and Vulcan flanking cornucopia. ***Right:*** 50 / Cherub in sailboat / 50. ***Engraver:*** Rawdon, Wright, Hatch & Edson. ***Comments:*** H-MA-90-G26. 18__. 1850s.

Rarity: —

$50 • **W-MA-230-050-G140**

Left: FIFTY / Sheaves and fruit / 50. ***Center:*** 50 / Three women seated with eagle, pole and cap, shield, scales and book. ***Right:*** FIFTY across 50 / Train, Vulcan seated with tools. ***Engraver:*** New England Bank Note Co. ***Comments:*** H-MA-90-G28. 18__. 1850s.

Rarity: —

$50 • **W-MA-230-050-G150**

CC

Tint: Green. ***Engraver:*** American Bank Note Co. ***Comments:*** H-MA-90-G30a. Proof. 18__. 1860s.

Rarity: URS-3
Proof $2,250

$100 • **W-MA-230-100-G160**

Left: 100 / Vulcan seated with sledge and anchor. ***Center:*** Train on bridge, Eagle on limb, Canal locks / C. ***Bottom center:*** 100. ***Right:*** 100 / Ceres seated, Cornucopia. ***Engraver:*** Rawdon, Wright, Hatch & Edson. ***Comments:*** H-MA-90-G32. 18__. 1850s.

Rarity: —

$100 • W-MA-230-100-G170

Left: C / Men with fishing boat at shore / 100. ***Center:*** Cornucopia, Eagle perched on bale, Sheaf / 100. ***Right:*** 100 / Ceres / 100. ***Engraver:*** New England Bank Note Co. ***Comments:*** H-MA-90-G34. 18__. 1850s.

Rarity: —

$100 • W-MA-230-100-G180

CC

Tint: Green die bearing 100, C, and HUNDRED DOLLARS. ***Engraver:*** American Bank Note Co. ***Comments:*** H-MA-90-G36. Proof. 186_. 1860s.

Rarity: URS-3
Proof $2,500

Non-Valid Issues

$3 • W-MA-230-003-S010

CC

Engraver: New England Bank Note Co. ***Comments:*** H-MA-90-S5. Spurious design imitating a rough verbal description of a genuine note. March 1, 185_. 1850s.

Rarity: URS-7
VG $100; **F** $125

$3 • W-MA-230-003-A010

Left: 3 / Portrait of Benjamin Franklin. ***Center:*** Woman reclining with strongbox / Shield bearing 3 / Produce. ***Right:*** 3 / Indian woman seated under tree. ***Engraver:*** Danforth, Bald & Co. ***Comments:*** H-MA-90-A5. Altered from $3 Columbia Bank, Washington, D.C. 18__. 1850s.

Rarity: —

$3 • W-MA-230-003-A020

Left: 3 / Portrait of Daniel Webster. ***Center:*** Ceres and Liberty seated flanking U.S. shield surmounted by eagle. ***Right:*** THREE across 3 / Female portrait. ***Overprint:*** Red THREE. ***Engraver:*** Rawdon, Wright, Hatch & Edson / New England Bank Note Co. ***Comments:*** H-MA-90-A10. Altered from $3 Waubeek Bank, De Soto, Nebraska. 18__. 1857.

Rarity: —

$5 • W-MA-230-005-C070a

CJF

Engraver: Rawdon, Wright, Hatch & Edson / New England Bank Note Co. / ABNCo. monogram. ***Comments:*** H-MA-90-C14b. Counterfeit of W-MA-230-005-G070a. 18__. 1860s.

Rarity: URS-8
F $75; **VF** $85; **EF** $150

$5 • W-MA-230-005-S020

CJF

Comments: H-MA-90-N5. Spurious note. 18__. 1850s.

Rarity: URS-7
VF $100; **EF** $150

Boston, Massachusetts

The capital of Massachusetts and also the largest city in the state, Boston was originally called Trimountaine by the first European settlers to discover the peninsula. The name comes from the three hills located on the land, one of which is called Beacon Hill and is still a well-known feature today.

A direct result of the Cambridge Agreement in 1628, the area that became Boston was inhabited in a search for good resources by the immigrating Puritans led by John Winthrop. It was named after Boston in the county of Lincolnshire, England. Harvard College, the first in America, was founded here in 1636. Until 1780 commerce was slow, but by 1800 the seaport and diverse town had grown to an international hub of trade, including the exportation of rum, fish, salt, and tobacco. During that time the population more than doubled. The British naval blockade of the American Revolution shut down the economy, but matters revived after the British left. Boston was officially chartered as a city in 1822.

William Lloyd Garrison's abolitionist newsletter the *Liberator* saw its 1831 inception in Boston, making the area the heart of the abolitionist cause. During the 19th century, Boston also became a haven for Irish immigrants, particularly those fleeing the potato famine that ravaged Ireland from 1845 to 1849.

From 1631 to 1890 the city's land tripled in size due to the filling and draining of marshes and much of Boston Harbor. This was the largest of such land reclamations taking place in the 19th century. In 1872 a great fire wiped out almost 65 acres of the city, a conflagration which destroyed 776 buildings, totaling $60 million in damage. But from the ashes rose innovation, and workers used the burnt rubble to extend the waterfront in even further land reclamations downtown. Between 1804 and 1912, the towns of South Boston, East Boston, Roxbury, Dorchester, Brighton, West Roxbury, Charlestown, and Hyde Park were annexed into Boston proper.

Following the suspension of specie payments by New York City banks on May 10, 1837, Boston banks followed suit the very next day. The Panic of 1837, as it was called, had lingering effects into the early 1840s and resulted in the failure of several banks.

Boston was the home of the Suffolk Bank System, which cleared currency transactions from the 1820s into the 1850s, at which time the Bank of Mutual Redemption took over most of the business. In 1853 *Banker's Magazine* reported that a convention of delegates was held at Tremont Bank, Boston, in an attempt to organize a Banker's Association to suppress and control the rampant activities of counterfeiting. Any bank in Massachusetts was welcome to join by paying an assessment of $5 for every $100,000 in capital.[32] In 1857 *Banker's Magazine* also gave an account for the organization of the Boston Clearing House, which commenced business on March 29, 1856. The 35 banks in the city joined the institution, representing a combined capital of $31,900,000.[33]

See also East Boston and South Boston, Massachusetts.

American Bank
1824–1838
W-MA-240

History: The American Bank was incorporated on February 20, 1824, and was located on State Street in the financial district of Boston. Its capital was $750,000 in 1829. This value had decreased to $500,000 by 1832. It remained at this figure through 1841.

The following was reported in *Bicknell's Counterfeit Detector* on September 27, 1830:

> Counterfeit five dollar notes, purporting to be of the American Bank, Boston, from Perkins's patent steel plate, have just made their appearance, signed I.S. Wright, Cashier, and Geo. Odiorne, president, letter L. payable to B. West, and dated May 1, 1824. The plate is genuine and probably altered from a bankrupt bank bill. The signatures are well executed, but the filling up bad.

In October of the same year, the *Detector* wrote, "it is said that the dies were lately discovered in New Hampshire, for altering Belchertown Bank bills to those of the Globe and American Bank, Boston." Related accounts for other banks were common in the press at the time. Only selected notices are given in the present text.

In 1837 an act to continue banking corporations listed this bank as being rechartered with $500,000 capital.[34] Figures were given for January 1838: circulation $216,504; net profits on hand $9,090.71; balances due to other banks $38,180.02; cash deposited $63,296.91; cash deposited bearing interest $85,618.47; total amount due from banks $912,690.11; gold, silver, and other coined metals in the banking house $31,210.91; bills of other banks in this state $12,265.00; balance due from other banks $3,129.30; amount of all debts due $866,084.90; total amount of resources of the bank $912,690.11.

Matters were in disarray. A different set of figures for January 1838 was given in the *Financial Register*: bills in circulation $158,084; net profits on hand $31,545.28; balances due to other banks $60,218.20; cash deposited $148,637.92; cash deposited bearing interest $149,700; total amount due from banks $1,048,185.40; gold, silver, and other coined metals in the banking house $24,308.07; real estate $44,004.40; bills of other banks in this state $35,418; balance due from other banks $39,882.48; amount of all debts due $904,572.45; total amount of resources of the bank $1,048,185.40.

On January 30, 1838, the Suffolk Bank of Boston reported that bills of the American Bank would not be received.[35] This effectively ended its business, making it a victim of the Panic of 1837. It seems, however, that most notes were redeemed. By 1841 the Bank Commissioners reported a circulation of only $1,818.

Numismatic Commentary: Some well preserved, altered PSSP notes have surfaced in the last several decades and may be the only examples available from this bank.

Valid Issues

$1 • W-MA-240-001-G010
Left: Lathework panel. ***Center:*** 1 / 1 / Oval of flower garlands and gridwork segments / 1 / 1. ***Right:*** Lathework panel. ***Engraver:*** PSSP. ***Comments:*** H-MA-95-G2. 18__. 1820s.

Rarity: —

$1 • W-MA-240-001-G010a
Left: Narrow panel of lathework circle segments. ***Right:*** Narrow panel of lathework circle segments. ***Engraver:*** PSSP. ***Comments:*** H-MA-95-G4. Similar to W-MA-240-001-G010. 18__. 1820s–1830s.

Rarity: —

$1 • W-MA-240-001-G010b
Left: ONE / D / ONE vertically. ***Right:*** ONE / D / ONE vertically. ***Engraver:*** PSSP. ***Comments:*** H-MA-95-G6. Similar to W-MA-240-001-G010. 18__. 1830s.

Rarity: —

$2 • W-MA-240-002-G020
Left: Lathework panel. ***Center:*** 2 / 2 / Oval of flower garlands and gridwork segments / 2 / 2. ***Right:*** Lathework panel. ***Engraver:*** PSSP. ***Comments:*** H-MA-95-G10. 18__. 1820s.

Rarity: —

$2 • W-MA-240-002-G020a
Left: Narrow panel of lathework circle segments. ***Right:*** Narrow panel of lathework circle segments. ***Engraver:*** PSSP. ***Comments:*** H-MA-95-G12. Similar to W-MA-240-002-G020. 18__. 1820s–1830s.

Rarity: —

$2 • W-MA-240-002-G020b

Left: Five TWOs vertically. ***Right:*** Five TWOs vertically. ***Engraver:*** PSSP. ***Comments:*** H-MA-95-G14. Similar to W-MA-240-002-G020. 18__. 1830s.

Rarity: —

$3 • W-MA-240-003-G030

Left: Lathework panel. ***Center:*** 3 / 3 / Oval of flower garlands and gridwork segments / 3 / 3. ***Right:*** Lathework panel. ***Engraver:*** PSSP. ***Comments:*** H-MA-95-G18. 18__. 1820s.

Rarity: —

$3 • W-MA-240-003-G030a

Left: Narrow panel of lathework circle segments. ***Right:*** Narrow panel of lathework circle segments. ***Engraver:*** PSSP. ***Comments:*** H-MA-95-G20. Similar to W-MA-240-003-G030. 18__. 1820s–1830s.

Rarity: —

$3 • W-MA-240-003-G030b

Left: THREE vertically. ***Right:*** THREE vertically. ***Engraver:*** PSSP. ***Comments:*** H-MA-95-G22. Similar to W-MA-240-003-G030. 18__. 1830s.

Rarity: —

$5 • W-MA-240-005-G040

Left: Lathework chain bearing MASSACHUSETTS / 5 / 5. ***Center:*** Alternating flower garlands and gridwork segments. ***Right:*** 5 / 5. ***Engraver:*** PSSP. ***Comments:*** H-MA-95-G26. 18__. 1820s.

Rarity: URS-3
F $500

$5 • W-MA-240-005-G040a

Engraver: PSSP. ***Comments:*** H-MA-95-G28. Similar to W-MA-240-005-G040 but with zigzag ruled lines. 18__. 1820s–1830s.

Rarity: —

$5 • W-MA-240-005-G040b

Engraver: PSSP. ***Comments:*** H-MA-95-G30. Similar to W-MA-240-005-G040 but with spiral lathework lines. 18__. 1830s.

Rarity: —

$5 • W-MA-240-005-G040c

Comments: H-MA-95-G30a. Similar to W-MA-240-005-G040b but printed in blue. 18__. 1830s.

Rarity: —

$10 • W-MA-240-010-G050

Left: Lathework chain bearing MASSACHUSETTS / 10 / 10 vertically. ***Center:*** Alternating flower garlands and gridwork segments. ***Right:*** 10 / 10 vertically. ***Engraver:*** PSSP. ***Comments:*** H-MA-95-G34. 18__. 1820s.

Rarity: —

$10 • W-MA-240-010-G050a

Engraver: PSSP. ***Comments:*** H-MA-95-G36. Similar to W-MA-240-010-G050 but with zigzag ruled lines. 18__. 1820s–1830s.

Rarity: —

$10 • W-MA-240-010-G050b

Engraver: PSSP. ***Comments:*** H-MA-95-G38. Similar to W-MA-240-010-G050 but with spiral lathework lines. 18__. 1830s.

Rarity: —

$10 • W-MA-240-010-G050c

Engraver: PSSP. ***Comments:*** H-MA-95-G38a. Similar to W-MA-240-010-G050b but printed in blue. 18__. 1830s.

Rarity: —

$20 • W-MA-240-020-G060

Left: Lathework chain bearing MASSACHUSETTS / 20 / 20 vertically. ***Center:*** Alternating flower garlands and gridwork segments. ***Right:*** 20 / 20 vertically. ***Engraver:*** PSSP. ***Comments:*** H-MA-95-G42. 18__. 1820s–1830s.

Rarity: —

$50 • W-MA-240-050-G070

Left: Lathework chain bearing MASSACHUSETTS / 100 / 100 vertically. ***Center:*** Alternating flower garlands and gridwork segments. ***Right:*** 50 / 50 vertically. ***Engraver:*** PSSP. ***Comments:*** H-MA-95-G46. 18__. 1820s–1830s.

Rarity: —

$100 • W-MA-240-100-G080

Left: Lathework chain bearing MASSACHUSETTS / 100 / 100 vertically. ***Center:*** Alternating flower garlands and gridwork segments. ***Right:*** 100 / 100 vertically. ***Engraver:*** PSSP. ***Comments:*** H-MA-95-G50. 18__. 1820s–1830s.

Rarity: —

Non-Valid Issues

$5 • W-MA-240-005-A010

Engraver: PSSP. ***Comments:*** H-MA-95-A5. Altered from W-MA-175-005-G040 or G040a. 18__. 1824.

Rarity: —

$20 • W-MA-240-020-A020

Left: Statue of George Washington with scroll. ***Center:*** Portrait of Benjamin Franklin / Man in chariot drawn by four horses / 20. ***Bottom center:*** Dog, key, and strongbox. ***Right:*** Statesman standing with scroll lying on table. ***Engraver:*** PSSP / New England Bank Note Co. ***Comments:*** H-MA-95-A10. Altered from W-MA-520-020-G120. 18__. 1830s.

Rarity: —

Atlantic Bank

1824–1864

W-MA-250

History: The Atlantic Bank was incorporated in February 1828. It was located at 8 Kilby Street. The capital of the bank was $500,000 throughout its existence. Circulation ranged from $81,910 in November 1839 to $264,550 in 1849. It later decreased to $112,593 between 1857 and 1860.

In 1857 the bank reported these figures: bills of this bank and other New England states in the vault $29,873; real estate $45,000. According to the *Banker's Magazine*, the Atlantic Bank paid dividends of $17,500 in October 1848.

It was reported in the *Banker's Magazine* of June 1875 that Benjamin Dodd had died in Boston on April 29, aged 79. Mr. Dodd was a cashier from 1838 until his death, a period of 47 years.

The Atlantic Bank closed in 1864 when its business was succeeded by the Atlantic National Bank.

Numismatic Commentary: Notes from the Atlantic Bank are available to any collector who won't take "no" as an answer. With some effort and patience, several different denominations can be obtained.

As of 2003 the American Bank Note Co. archives had remaining a $1-$1-$2-$3 face plate.

Valid Issues

$1 • W-MA-250-001-G010

Left: Lathework panel. ***Center:*** 1 / 1 / Oval of flower garlands and gridwork segments / 1 / 1. ***Right:*** Lathework panel. ***Engraver:*** PSSP. ***Comments:*** H-MA-100-G2. 18__. 1820s.

Rarity: —

$1 • W-MA-250-001-G010a

Left: Narrow panel of lathework circle segments. ***Right:*** Narrow panel of lathework circle segments. ***Engraver:*** PSSP. ***Comments:*** H-MA-100-G4. Similar to W-MA-250-001-G010. 18__. 1820s–1830s.

Rarity: —

$1 • W-MA-250-001-G010b

Left: ONE / D / ONE vertically. ***Center:*** 1 / ONE / 1 / Flower garlands and gridwork segments / 1 / ONE / 1. ***Right:*** ONE / D / ONE vertically. ***Engraver:*** PSSP. ***Comments:*** H-MA-100-G6. Similar to W-MA-250-001-G010. 18__. 1830s.

Rarity: —

$1 • W-MA-250-001-G010c

Center: 1 / 1 / Oval of flower garlands and gridwork segments / 1 / 1. ***Engraver:*** PSSP. ***Comments:*** H-MA-100-G8. Similar to W-MA-250-001-G010. 18__. 1830s–1840s.

Rarity: —

$1 • W-MA-250-001-G020

HA

Engraver: Toppan, Carpenter & Co. ***Comments:*** H-MA-100-G12. Proof. 18__. 1840s–1850s.

Rarity: URS-2
Proof $2,000

$1 • W-MA-250-001-G020a

Left: Portrait of Zachary Taylor on 1. ***Center:*** Ships, Spread eagle, Ships / ONE. ***Right:*** 1 / Woman with spyglass seated on barrel. ***Overprint:*** Red ONE. ***Engraver:*** Toppan, Carpenter & Co. ***Comments:*** H-MA-100-G12a. Similar to W-MA-250-001-G020. 18__. 1850s.

Rarity: —

$1 • W-MA-250-001-G030

Left: 1 / Shield bearing arm and sword. ***Center:*** Sailors sitting with packages, INCORPORATED over 1 / ONE. ***Right:*** 1 / Woman with spyglass seated on barrel. ***Tint:*** Red-orange 1 and ONE. ***Engraver:*** American Bank Note Co. ***Comments:*** H-MA-100-G16a. May 1, 186_. 1860s.

Rarity: URS-2
VF $2,000

$2 • W-MA-250-002-G040

Left: Lathework panel. ***Center:*** 2 / 2 / Oval of flower garlands and gridwork segments / 2 / 2. ***Right:*** Lathework panel. ***Engraver:*** Toppan, Carpenter & Co. ***Comments:*** H-MA-100-G18. 18__. 1820s.

Rarity: —

$2 • W-MA-250-002-G040a

Left: Narrow panel of lathework circle segments. ***Right:*** Narrow panel of lathework circle segments. ***Engraver:*** PSSP. ***Comments:*** H-MA-100-G20. Similar to W-MA-250-002-G040. 18__. 1820s–1830s.

Rarity: —

$2 • W-MA-250-002-G040b

Left: Five TWOs vertically. ***Right:*** Five TWOs vertically. ***Engraver:*** PSSP. ***Comments:*** H-MA-100-G22. Similar to W-MA-250-002-G040. 18__. 1830s.

Rarity: —

$2 • W-MA-250-002-G040c

Left: Five TWOs vertically. ***Right:*** Five TWOs vertically. ***Engraver:*** PSSP. ***Comments:*** H-MA-100-G24. Similar to W-MA-250-002-G040. 18__. 1830s–1840s.

Rarity: —

$2 • W-MA-250-002-G050

HA

Engraver: Toppan, Carpenter & Co. ***Comments:*** H-MA-100-G28. Proof. 18__. 1840s–1850s.

Rarity: URS-3
Proof $2,000

$2 • W-MA-250-002-G050a

Left: 2 / Portrait of Zachary Taylor / TWO. ***Center:*** Three-masted steamship, Ships. ***Right:*** TWO / Woman with spyglass seated on barrel / TWO. ***Overprint:*** Red TWO. ***Engraver:*** Toppan, Carpenter & Co. ***Comments:*** H-MA-100-G28a. Similar to W-MA-250-002-G050. 18__. 1850s.

Rarity: —

$2 • W-MA-250-002-G060

Left: 2 / Eagle on shield. ***Center:*** Indian woman seated with shield and eagle, Ships. ***Right:*** TWO / Woman with spyglass seated on barrel. ***Tint:*** Red-orange 2. ***Engraver:*** American Bank Note Co. ***Comments:*** H-MA-100-G32a. May 1, 186_. 1860s.

Rarity: —

$3 • W-MA-250-003-G070

Left: Lathework panel. ***Center:*** 3 / 3 / Oval of flower garlands and gridwork segments / 3 / 3. ***Right:*** Lathework panel. ***Engraver:*** PSSP. ***Comments:*** H-MA-100-G34. 18__. 1820s.

Rarity: —

$3 • W-MA-250-003-G070a

Left: Narrow panel of lathework circle segments. ***Right:*** Narrow panel of lathework circle segments. ***Engraver:*** PSSP. ***Comments:*** H-MA-100-G36. Similar to W-MA-250-003-G070. 18__. 1820s–1830s.

Rarity: —

$3 • W-MA-250-003-G070b

Left: THREE vertically. ***Right:*** THREE vertically. ***Engraver:*** PSSP. ***Comments:*** H-MA-100-G38. Similar to W-MA-250-003-G070. 18__. 1830s.

Rarity: —

$3 • W-MA-250-003-G070c

Center: 3 / 3 / Oval of flower garlands and gridwork segments / 3 / 3. ***Engraver:*** PSSP. ***Comments:*** H-MA-100-G40. Similar to W-MA-250-003-G070. 18__. 1830s–1840s.

Rarity: —

$3 • W-MA-250-003-G080

HA

Engraver: Toppan, Carpenter & Co. ***Comments:*** H-MA-100-G44. Proof. 18__. 1840s–1850s.

Rarity: URS-3

Proof $2,500

$3 • W-MA-250-003-G080a

Left: Woman with spyglass seated on barrel. ***Center:*** 3 / Indian man and woman flanking eagle on globe / THREE. ***Right:*** 3 / Sailor seated with bales. ***Overprint:*** Red THREE. ***Engraver:*** Toppan, Carpenter & Co. ***Comments:*** H-MA-100-G44a. Similar to W-MA-250-003-G080. 18__. 1850s.

Rarity: —

Collectors and Researchers:

If you have new information about any banks or notes listed in this volume, contact Whitman Publishing, Attn: Obsolete Paper Money, 3101 Clairmont Road, Suite G, Atlanta, GA 30329.

$3 • W-MA-250-003-G090

CC

Tint: Red-orange. ***Engraver:*** American Bank Note Co. ***Comments:*** H-MA-100-G48a. May 1, 186_. 1860s.

Rarity: URS-4

F $1,000; **VF** $1,800

$3 • W-MA-250-003-G090a

Overprint: Red THREE. ***Tint:*** Red-orange. ***Engraver:*** American Bank Note Co. ***Comments:*** H-Unlisted. Similar to W-MA-250-003-G090. May 1, 186_. 1860s.

Rarity: URS-2

F $2,250

$5 • W-MA-250-005-G100

Left: Lathework chain bearing MASSACHUSETTS / 5 / 5 vertically. ***Center:*** Alternating flower garlands and gridwork segments. ***Right:*** 5 / 5 vertically. ***Engraver:*** PSSP. ***Comments:*** H-MA-100-G50. 18__. 1820s.

Rarity: —

$5 • W-MA-250-005-G100a

Engraver: PSSP. ***Comments:*** H-MA-100-G52. Similar to W-MA-250-005-G100 but with zigzag ruled lines. 18__. 1820s–1830s.

Rarity: —

$5 • W-MA-250-005-G100b

Engraver: PSSP. ***Comments:*** H-MA-100-G54. Similar to W-MA-250-005-G100 but with spiral lathework lines. 18__. 1830s.

Rarity: —

$5 • W-MA-250-005-G110

CC

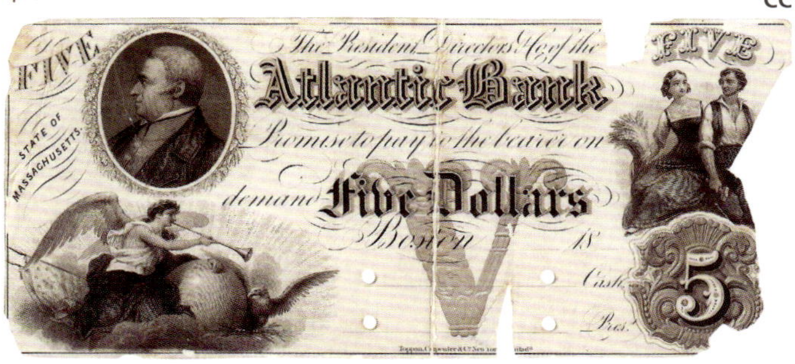

Engraver: PSSP. ***Comments:*** H-MA-100-G60. 18__. 1840s–1850s.

Rarity: URS-3

G $200

$5 • W-MA-250-005-G110a

Overprint: Red FIVE. ***Engraver:*** Toppan, Carpenter & Co. ***Comments:*** H-MA-100-G60a. Similar to W-MA-250-005-G110 but with different engraver imprint. 18__. 1850s.

Rarity: —

$5 • W-MA-250-005-G110b

JF

Overprint: Red FIVE. ***Tint:*** Red-orange. ***Engraver:*** American Bank Note Co. ***Comments:*** H-MA-100-G60c. Similar to W-MA-250-005-G110 but with different engraver imprint. 18__. 1860s.

Rarity: URS-2
Proof $3,500

$10 • W-MA-250-010-G120

Left: Lathework chain bearing MASSACHUSETTS / 10 / 10 vertically. ***Center:*** Alternating flower garlands and gridwork segments. ***Right:*** 10 / 10 vertically. ***Engraver:*** PSSP. ***Comments:*** H-MA-100-G62. 18__. 1820s.

Rarity: —

$10 • W-MA-250-010-G120a

Engraver: PSSP. ***Comments:*** H-MA-100-G64. Similar to W-MA-250-010-G120 but with zigzag ruled lines. 18__. 1820s–1830s.

Rarity: —

$10 • W-MA-250-010-G120b

Engraver: PSSP. ***Comments:*** H-MA-100-G66. Similar to W-MA-250-010-G120 but with spiral lathework lines. 18__. 1830s.

Rarity: —

$10 • W-MA-250-010-G130

Left: Woman seated with shield / X. ***Center:*** Portrait of Zachary Taylor. ***Right:*** TEN / Woman seated looking through spyglass. ***Engraver:*** Toppan, Carpenter & Co. ***Comments:*** H-MA-100-G72. 18__. 1840s–1850s.

Rarity: —

$10 • W-MA-250-010-G130a

CC

Overprint: Red TEN. ***Engraver:*** Toppan, Carpenter & Co. ***Comments:*** H-MA-100-G72a. Similar to W-MA-250-010-G130. 18__. 1850s.

Rarity: URS-6
VF $200; **Unc-Rem** $350

$10 • W-MA-250-010-G140

Left: 10 / Woman seated with wheel, Lamp and flowers. ***Center:*** Steamship and sailing ships at sea. ***Right:*** 10 / Justice. ***Tint:*** Red-orange. ***Engraver:*** American Bank Note Co. ***Comments:*** H-MA-100-G74a. May 1, 186_. 1860s.

Rarity: —

$20 • W-MA-250-020-G150

Left: Lathework chain bearing MASSACHUSETTS / 20 / 20 vertically. ***Center:*** Alternating flower garlands and gridwork segments. ***Right:*** 20 / 20 vertically. ***Engraver:*** PSSP. ***Comments:*** H-MA-100-G76. 18__. 1820s–1830s.

Rarity: —

$20 • W-MA-250-020-G160

CC

Tint: Red-orange dies bearing 20s, Panel of microlettering bearing XX / 20 / XX. ***Engraver:*** American Bank Note Co. ***Comments:*** H-MA-100-G80a. Proof. May 1, 186_. 1860s.

Rarity: URS-2
Proof $6,000

$50 • W-MA-250-050-G170

Left: Lathework chain bearing MASSACHUSETTS / 50 / 50 vertically. ***Center:*** Alternating flower garlands and gridwork segments. ***Right:*** 50 / 50 vertically. ***Engraver:*** PSSP. ***Comments:*** H-MA-100-G82. 18__. 1820s–1830s.

Rarity: —

$50 • W-MA-250-050-G180

CC

Engraver: American Bank Note Co. ***Comments:*** H-MA-100-G86. Image is Proof lacking tint used on circulated notes. May 1, 18__.

Rarity: URS-2
Proof $2,000

$50 • W-MA-250-050-G180a

Left: L. ***Center:*** Woman writing on tablet, Child at feet / Portrait of girl. ***Right:*** Men, wharf scene, barrels. ***Tint:*** Red-orange. ***Engraver:*** American Bank Note Co. ***Comments:*** H-MA-100-G86a. Similar to W-MA-250-050-G180. May 1, 18__. 1860s.

Rarity: —

$100 • W-MA-250-100-G190

Left: Lathework chain bearing MASSACHUSETTS / 100 / 100 vertically. ***Center:*** Alternating flower garlands and gridwork segments. ***Right:*** 100 / 100 vertically. ***Engraver:*** PSSP. ***Comments:*** H-MA-100-G88. 18__. 1820s–1830s.

Rarity: —

$100 • W-MA-250-100-G200

CC

Tint: Red-orange C C / HUNDRED. ***Engraver:*** American Bank Note Co. ***Comments:*** H-MA-100-G92a. Proof. May 1, 186_. 1860s.

Rarity: URS-2
Proof $5,500

$500 • W-MA-250-500-G210

Left: Lathework chain bearing MASSACHUSETTS / 500 / 500 vertically. ***Center:*** Alternating flower garlands and gridwork segments. ***Right:*** 500 / 500 vertically. ***Engraver:*** PSSP. ***Comments:*** H-MA-100-G94. 18__. 1820s–1830s.

Rarity: —

$500 • W-MA-250-500-G220

HA

Engraver: American Bank Note Co. ***Comments:*** H-MA-100-G98. Image is of Progressive Proof lacking tint used on circulated notes. May 1, 18__.

Rarity: URS-3
Proof $1,000

$500 • W-MA-250-500-G220a

Left: D / FIVE HUNDRED. ***Center:*** Man seated with boy, Man standing / 500. ***Right:*** 50 / FIVE HUNDRED. ***Tint:*** Red-orange. ***Engraver:*** American Bank Note Co. ***Comments:*** H-MA-100-G98a. Similar to W-MA-250-500-G220. May 1, 18__.

Rarity: —

$1,000 • W-MA-250-1000-G230

Left: Lathework chain bearing MASSACHUSETTS / 1000 / 1000 vertically. ***Center:*** Alternating flower garlands and gridwork segments. ***Right:*** 1000 / 1000 vertically. ***Engraver:*** American Bank Note Co. ***Comments:*** H-MA-100-G100. 18__. 1820s–1830s.

Rarity: —

Uncut Sheets

$1-$1-$2-$3 • W-MA-250-001.001.002.003-US010

HA

Engraver: Toppan, Carpenter & Co. ***Comments:*** H-MA-100-G12, G12, G28, G44. 18__. 1840s–1850s.

Rarity: URS-1
Proof $5,000

Non-Valid Issues

$1 • W-MA-250-001-C010c

ANS

Engraver: PSSP. ***Comments:*** H-MA-100-C8. Counterfeit of W-MA-250-001-G010c. 18__. 1840s.

Rarity: URS-6
F $65

$1 • W-MA-250-001-S010

CC

Tint: Brown. ***Comments:*** H-MA-100-S5.

Rarity: URS-7

VG $50; **VF** $100

$2 • W-MA-250-002-C040c

Engraver: PSSP. ***Comments:*** H-MA-100-C24. Counterfeit of W-MA-250-002-G040c. 18__. 1830s–1840s.

Rarity: —

F $100

$2 • W-MA-250-002-A010

Left: 2 / Justice standing / 2. ***Center:*** Steamship, Anchor, Four allegorical women seated and standing, Sheaf / Train. ***Right:*** 2 / Portrait of Benjamin Franklin / 2. ***Engraver:*** PSSP / New England Bank Note Co. ***Comments:*** H-MA-100-A5. Altered from W-MA-520-002-G040. 18__. 1830s.

Rarity: —

F $100

$2 • W-MA-250-002-A020

Left: Portrait of Thomas Jefferson. ***Center:*** Ship / Ship, Factory scene, Horse-drawn wagons. ***Right:*** Portrait of Marquis de Lafayette. ***Engraver:*** New England Bank Note Co. ***Comments:*** H-MA-100-A10. Altered from W-MA-680-002-G070. 18__. 1830s.

Rarity: —

F $100

$3 • W-MA-250-003-A030

Left: 3 / Woman seated / THREE. ***Center:*** Portrait of Benjamin Franklin / Spinning wheel, Allegorical woman receiving bag from cherub / Portrait of George Washington. ***Right:*** 3 / Woman seated / THREE. ***Engraver:*** PSSP / New England Bank Note Co. ***Comments:*** H-MA-100-A15. Altered from W-MA-520-003-G060. 18__. 1830s.

Rarity: —

F $100

$5 • W-MA-250-005-R010

Engraver: Toppan, Carpenter & Co. ***Comments:*** H-MA-100-R5. Raised from W-MA-250-001-G020. 18__. 1840s–1850s.

Rarity: —

F $75

$5 • W-MA-250-005-S020

Center: Three water nymphs and cherub. ***Right:*** Portrait of Henry Clay. ***Comments:*** H-MA-100-S10. From a modified plate, originally for a counterfeit $5 Atlantic Bank, New York City, New York.

Rarity: —

F $75

$5 • W-MA-250-005-A040

Left: 5 / Portrait of Zachary Taylor / 5. ***Center:*** 5 / Two allegorical women and three cherubs surrounding 5 / 5. ***Bottom center:*** Train. ***Right:*** FIVE / Woman standing / FIVE. ***Engraver:*** Rawdon, Wright, Hatch & Edson. ***Comments:*** H-MA-100-A20. Altered from $5 Merchants Bank, Washington, D.C. Dec. 1, 1852.

Rarity: —

F $75

$5 • W-MA-250-005-A050

Left: 5 / Portrait of George Washington / FIVE. ***Center:*** Ship, Factory scene, Horse-drawn wagons. ***Right:*** 5 / Portrait of Marquis de Lafayette / FIVE. ***Engraver:*** New England Bank Note Co. ***Comments:*** H-MA-100-A25. Altered from W-MA-680-005-G110. 18__. 1830s.

Rarity: —

F $75

$10 • W-MA-250-010-C130a

NJW

Overprint: Red TEN. ***Engraver:*** Toppan, Carpenter & Co. ***Comments:*** H-MA-100-C72a. Counterfeit of W-MA-250-010-G130a. 18__. 1861.

Rarity: URS-5

VG $59; **F** $75; **VF** $150

$10 • W-MA-250-010-R020

Engraver: Toppan, Carpenter & Co. ***Comments:*** H-MA-100-R10. Raised from W-MA-250-002-G050. 18__. 1840s–1850s.

Rarity: —

$10 • W-MA-250-010-N010

Left: Woman. ***Center:*** Street scene. ***Comments:*** H-MA-100-N5.

Rarity: —

Atlas Bank

1833–1864

W-MA-260

History: The Atlas Bank was incorporated in 1828 and chartered in March 1833. It was located at 65 State Street but moved in March 1850 to No. 10 Kilby Street, on the corner of Doane Street.

These figures were reported in the *Financial Register* in January 1838: capital paid in $500,000; bills in circulation $22,154; net profits on hand $49,728; balances due to other banks $21,837.89; cash deposited $95,170.30; cash deposited bearing interest $68,580.03; total amount due from banks $757,470.22; gold, silver, and other coined metals in the banking house $15,173.43; bills of other banks in this state $17,324; balance due from other banks $17,701.83; amount of all debts due $707,270.96; total amount of resources of the bank $757,470.22.

The capital of the bank remained at $500,000 until 1860, when it doubled to $1,000,000. Circulation ranged from $67,816 in 1839 to $166,819 in 1845. From 1857 to 1860 it averaged at $116,000. In 1857 the amount of bills of this bank and other New England states in the vault was $40,483.

In 1864 the Atlas Bank closed when its affairs were succeeded by the Atlas National Bank of Boston.

Numismatic Commentary: This bank will present a challenge to collectors, but chances are a nice, early note with the vignette of "Atlas Bearing the Globe Upon His Back" can be had. This interesting vignette would be a welcome addition to any collection.

Valid Issues

$1 • W-MA-260-001-G010

Left: 1 / ONE / 1. ***Center:*** ONE / Atlas kneeling, supporting globe on his shoulders / 1. ***Right:*** ONE DOLLAR vertically. ***Back:*** Check Plate. ***Engraver:*** New England Bank Note Co. ***Comments:*** H-MA-105-G6. 18__. 1830s.

Rarity: URS-1

F $1,000; **VF** $2,500

$1 • W-MA-260-001-G010a

Back: Plain. ***Engraver:*** New England Bank Note Co. ***Comments:*** H-MA-105-G6a. Similar to W-MA-260-001-G010. 18__. 1850s.

Rarity: —

$2 • W-MA-260-002-G020

Left: 2 / TWO / 2. ***Center:*** TWO / Atlas kneeling, supporting globe on his shoulders / 2. ***Right:*** TWO DOLLARS vertically. ***Back:*** Check Plate. ***Engraver:*** New England Bank Note Co. ***Comments:*** H-MA-105-G12. 18__. 1830s–1840s.

Rarity: URS-2

F $1,500; **EF** $2,500

$2 • W-MA-260-002-G020a

Back: Plain. ***Engraver:*** New England Bank Note Co. ***Comments:*** H-MA-105-G12a. Similar to W-MA-260-002-G020. 18__. 1850s.

Rarity: —

$2 • W-MA-260-002-G020b

CJF, CJF

Back: Check Plate. ***Engraver:*** New England Bank Note Co. / PSSP. ***Comments:*** H-Unlisted. Similar to W-MA-260-002-G020 but with additional engraver imprint. 18__. 1850s.

Rarity: URS-3

F $1,500

$3 • W-MA-260-003-G030

Left: 3 / THREE / 3. ***Center:*** THREE / Atlas kneeling, supporting globe on his shoulders / 3. ***Right:*** THREE DOLLARS vertically. ***Back:*** Check Plate. ***Engraver:*** New England Bank Note Co. ***Comments:*** H-MA-105-G18. 18__. 1830s–1840s.

Rarity: URS-2

F $1,500

$3 • W-MA-260-003-G030a

Back: Plain. ***Engraver:*** New England Bank Note Co. ***Comments:*** H-MA-105-G18a. Similar to W-MA-260-003-G030. 18__. 1850s.

Rarity: URS-2

F $1,500

$3 • W-MA-260-003-G030b

JF

Engraver: New England Bank Note Co. / ABNCo. monogram. ***Comments:*** H-Unlisted. Similar to W-MA-260-003-G030 but with additional engraver imprint. 18__. 1850s.

Rarity: URS-3

F $2,000

$5 • W-MA-260-005-G040

Left: 5 / FIVE / FIVE. ***Center:*** V / Atlas kneeling, supporting globe on his shoulders / 5. ***Right:*** FIVE DOLLARS vertically. ***Back:*** Check Plate. ***Engraver:*** New England Bank Note Co. ***Comments:*** H-MA-105-G26. 18__. 1830s–1840s.

Rarity: —

$5 • W-MA-260-005-G040a

Back: Plain. ***Engraver:*** New England Bank Note Co. ***Comments:*** H-MA-105-G26a. Similar to W-MA-260-005-G040. 18__. 1850s.

Rarity: —

$10 • W-MA-260-010-G050

Left: 10 / TEN / 10. ***Center:*** X / Atlas kneeling, supporting globe on his shoulders. ***Right:*** TEN DOLLARS vertically. ***Back:*** Check Plate. ***Engraver:*** New England Bank Note Co. ***Comments:*** H-MA-105-G34. 18__. 1830s–1840s.

Rarity: —

$10 • W-MA-260-010-G050a

Back: Plain. ***Engraver:*** New England Bank Note Co. ***Comments:*** H-MA-105-G34a. Similar to W-MA-260-010-G050. 18__. 1850s.

Rarity: —

$20 • W-MA-260-020-G060

Left: 20 / TWENTY vertically. ***Center:*** XX / Atlas kneeling, supporting globe on his shoulders / 20. ***Right:*** TWENTY vertically. ***Back:*** Check Plate. ***Engraver:*** New England Bank Note Co. ***Comments:*** H-MA-105-G42. 18__. 1830s–1840s.

Rarity: —

$20 • W-MA-260-020-G060a
Back: Plain. ***Engraver:*** New England Bank Note Co. ***Comments:*** H-MA-105-G42a. Similar to W-MA-260-020-G060. 18__. 1850s.

Rarity: —

$50 • W-MA-260-050-G070
Left: 50 / FIFTY vertically. ***Center:*** FIFTY / Atlas kneeling, supporting globe on his shoulders. ***Right:*** 50 / FIFTY DOLLARS vertically. ***Back:*** Check Plate. ***Engraver:*** New England Bank Note Co. ***Comments:*** H-MA-105-G50. 18__. 1830s–1840s.

Rarity: —

$50 • W-MA-260-050-G070a
Back: Plain. ***Engraver:*** New England Bank Note Co. ***Comments:*** H-MA-105-G50a. Similar to W-MA-260-050-G070. 18__. 1850s.

Rarity: —

$100 • W-MA-260-100-G080
Left: 100 / 100 / 100. ***Center:*** C / Atlas kneeling, supporting globe on his shoulders / 100. ***Right:*** ONE HUNDRED vertically. ***Back:*** Check Plate. ***Engraver:*** New England Bank Note Co. ***Comments:*** H-MA-105-G58. 18__. 1830s–1840s.

Rarity: —

$100 • W-MA-260-100-G080a
Back: Plain. ***Engraver:*** New England Bank Note Co. ***Comments:*** H-MA-105-G58a. Similar to W-MA-260-100-G080. 18__. 1850s.

Rarity: —

$500 • W-MA-260-500-G090
Left: 500 / 500 / 500. ***Center:*** FIVE HUNDRED / Atlas kneeling, supporting globe on his shoulders. ***Right:*** FIVE HUNDRED vertically. ***Back:*** Check Plate. ***Engraver:*** New England Bank Note Co. ***Comments:*** H-MA-105-G62. 18__. 1830s–1840s.

Rarity: —

$500 • W-MA-260-500-G090a
Back: Plain. ***Engraver:*** New England Bank Note Co. ***Comments:*** H-MA-105-G62a. Similar to W-MA-260-500-G090. 18__. 1850s.

Rarity: —

$1,000 • W-MA-260-1000-G100
Left: 1000 / 1000 / 1000. ***Center:*** M / Atlas kneeling, supporting globe on his shoulders. ***Right:*** ONE THOUSAND vertically. ***Engraver:*** New England Bank Note Co. ***Comments:*** H-MA-105-G66. 18__. 1830s–1840s.

Rarity: —

$1,000 • W-MA-260-1000-G100a
Back: Plain. ***Engraver:*** New England Bank Note Co. ***Comments:*** H-MA-105-G66a. Similar to W-MA-260-1000-G100. 18__. 1850s.

Rarity: —

Non-Valid Issues

$1 • W-MA-260-001-S010
Left: ONE / D / ONE vertically / 1 on gridwork triangle / 1 on gridwork triangle. ***Center:*** Alternating flower garlands and grid segments bearing ONE / ONE. ***Right:*** 1 on gridwork triangle / 1 on gridwork triangle / 1 on gridwork triangle / ONE / D / ONE vertically. ***Engraver:*** PSSP. ***Comments:*** H-MA-105-S5. 18__. 1840s.

Rarity: —

$2 • W-MA-260-002-S020

HA

Engraver: PSSP. ***Comments:*** H-MA-105-S10. 18__. 1840s.

Rarity: URS-5
F $150

$3 • W-MA-260-003-S030
Left: THREE vertically / 3 on gridwork triangle / 3 on gridwork triangle. ***Center:*** Alternating flower garlands and grid segments bearing THREE / THREE. ***Right:*** 3 on gridwork triangle / 3 on gridwork triangle / THREE vertically. ***Engraver:*** PSSP. ***Comments:*** H-MA-105-S15. 18__. 1840s.

Rarity: —

$5 • W-MA-260-005-R010
Center: Atlas kneeling, supporting globe on his shoulders. ***Comments:*** H-Unlisted. Raised from W-MA-260-001-G010.

Rarity: URS-3
F $750

$5 • W-MA-260-005-A010
Left: Ships / 5. ***Center:*** Four women seated. ***Right:*** 5 / Woman standing next to shield. ***Engraver:*** New England Bank Note Co. ***Comments:*** H-MA-105-A5. Altered from $5 Globe Bank, Bangor, Maine. 18__. 1836.

Rarity: —

Bank of Commerce
1850–1864
W-MA-270

History: In December 1849, it was reported by *Banker's Magazine* that a new bank was organizing in Boston to be called the Bank of Commerce, with a starting capital of $500,000. It was incorporated in 1850.

The bank was located at 85 State Street. The front was constructed of Connecticut sandstone, and the architecture was Italian in style. Capital was increased to $750,000 by 1851. In 1852 it was $1,500,000. By 1855 it had increased yet again to $2,000,000. An act to further increase the capital by $750,000 was published in 1860.

These values were reported in 1857: circulation $242,520; bills of this bank and other New England states in the vault $364,394; real estate $9,025.54. By March 1860, circulation had increased slightly to $277,531.

The Bank of Commerce wound down its affairs after the stockholders obtained a charter for what became the National Bank of Commerce of Boston.

Numismatic Commentary: Many interesting and unusual vignettes, some with multiple colors, are available on notes from this bank.

As of 2003 the American Bank Note Co. archives held a $1-$1-$2-$3 tint plate.

Valid Issues

$1 • W-MA-270-001-G010

CC

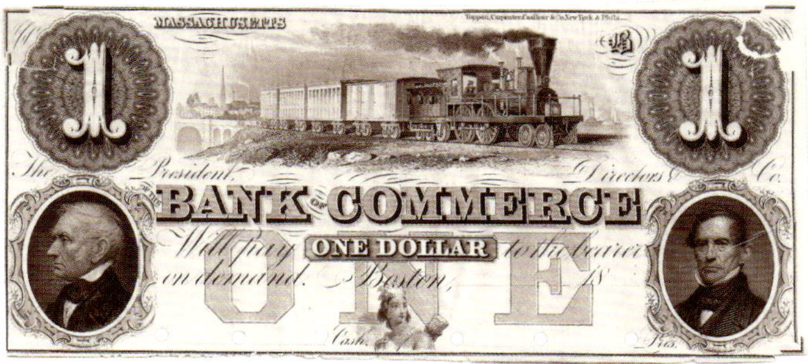

Engraver: Toppan, Carpenter, Casilear & Co. ***Comments:*** H-MA-145-G2. Proof. 18__. 1850s.

Rarity: URS-3
Proof $400

$1 • W-MA-270-001-G020

CC

Overprint: Red. ***Engraver:*** Danforth, Wright & Co. ***Comments:*** H-Unlisted. Proof. 18__.

Rarity: URS-3
Proof $3,500

$1 • W-MA-270-001-G020a

SBG

Tint: Brown-orange outlining white ONE. ***Engraver:*** Danforth, Wright & Co. ***Comments:*** H-MA-145-G4a. Similar to W-MA-270-001-G020. Proof. 18__. 1850s.

Rarity: URS-3
Proof $2,500
Selected auction price: Heritage, October 2013, Lot 15859, Choice New $2,232

$1 • W-MA-270-001-G020b

JF

Overprint: Red. ***Tint:*** Brown-orange outlining white ONE. ***Engraver:*** Danforth, Wright & Co. ***Comments:*** H-MA-145-G4b. Similar to W-MA-270-001-G020. Proof. 18__. 1850s.

Rarity: URS-3
Proof $2,500

$1 • W-MA-270-001-G020c

SI

Tint: Red-brown panel bearing ONE. ***Engraver:*** Danforth, Wright & Co. / American Bank Note Co. ***Comments:*** H-MA-145-G4c. Similar to W-MA-270-001-G020 but with additional engraver imprint. 18__. 1860s.

Rarity: URS-3
F $1,000

$2 • W-MA-270-002-G030

Left: 2 / Male portrait. ***Center:*** Eagle on limb, Ships. ***Bottom center:*** Ship. ***Right:*** 2 / Female portrait. ***Engraver:*** Toppan, Carpenter, Casilear & Co. ***Comments:*** H-MA-145-G6. 18__. 1850s.

Rarity: —

$2 • W-MA-270-002-G040

CC

Overprint: Red. ***Engraver:*** Danforth, Wright & Co. ***Comments:*** H-Unlisted. Proof. 18__.

Rarity: URS-3
Proof $1,200

$2 • W-MA-270-002-G040a

Left: 2 / Ship. ***Center:*** 2. ***Right:*** 2 / Portrait of Judge Joseph Story. ***Tint:*** Brown-orange outlining white TWO. ***Engraver:*** Danforth, Wright & Co. ***Comments:*** H-MA-145-G8a. Similar to W-MA-270-002-G040. 18__. 1850s.

Rarity: —

$2 • W-MA-270-002-G040b

JF

Overprint: Red. ***Tint:*** Brown-orange outlining white TWO. ***Engraver:*** Danforth, Wright & Co. ***Comments:*** H-MA-145-G8b. Similar to W-MA-270-002-G040. Proof. 18__. 1850s.

Rarity: URS-3
AG $350; **Proof** $3,500

$2 • W-MA-270-002-G040c

Tint: Red-brown panel bearing TWO. ***Engraver:*** Danforth, Wright & Co. / American Bank Note Co. ***Comments:*** H-MA-145-G8c. Similar to W-MA-270-002-G040 but with additional engraver imprint. 18__. 1860s.

Rarity: —

$3 • W-MA-270-003-G050

Left: 3 / Male portrait. ***Center:*** Eagle and shield, View of State Street and Faneuil Hall in Boston. ***Bottom center:*** State arms. ***Right:*** 3 / Mercury in clouds. ***Engraver:*** Toppan, Carpenter, Casilear & Co. ***Comments:*** H-MA-145-G10. 18__. 1850s.

Rarity: —

$3 • W-MA-270-003-G060

CC

Overprint: Red. ***Engraver:*** Danforth, Wright & Co. ***Comments:*** H-Unlisted. Proof. 18__.

Rarity: URS-2
Proof $5,000

$3 • W-MA-270-003-G060a

Left: THREE / Sailor leaning on capstan. ***Right:*** 3 / Male portrait. ***Tint:*** Brown-orange outlining white THREE. ***Engraver:*** Danforth, Wright & Co. ***Comments:*** H-MA-145-G12a. Similar to W-MA-270-003-G060. 18__. 1850s.

Rarity: —

$3 • W-MA-270-003-G060b

JF

Overprint: Red. ***Tint:*** Brown-orange outlining white TWO. ***Engraver:*** Danforth, Wright & Co. ***Comments:*** H-MA-145-G12b. Similar to W-MA-270-003-G060. Error overprint. Proof. 18__. 1850s.

Rarity: URS-3
Proof $3,000

$3 • W-MA-270-003-G060c

Tint: Red-brown panel bearing THREE. ***Engraver:*** Danforth, Wright & Co. / American Bank Note Co. ***Comments:*** H-MA-145-G12c. Similar to W-MA-270-003-G060 but with additional engraver imprint. 18__. 1860s.

Rarity: —

$5 • W-MA-270-005-G070

HA

Engraver: Toppan, Carpenter, Casilear & Co. ***Comments:*** H-MA-145-G14. 18__. 1850s.

Rarity: URS-3
Proof $2,000

$10 • W-MA-270-010-G080

Engraver: Toppan, Carpenter, Casilear & Co. ***Comments:*** H-MA-145-G16. Similar to W-MA-270-010-C080. 18__. 1850s.

Rarity: —

$20 • W-MA-270-020-G090

Left: 20 / Male portrait. ***Center:*** View of Customs House in Boston / Sailing ship. ***Right:*** 20 / Man standing. ***Engraver:*** Toppan, Carpenter, Casilear & Co. ***Comments:*** H-MA-145-G18. 18__. 1850s.

Rarity: URS-3
Proof $1,500

$50 • W-MA-270-050-G100

Left: 50 / Sailor standing. ***Center:*** Woman with wings blowing trumpet, Globe. ***Right:*** 50 / Portrait of George Washington. ***Engraver:*** Toppan, Carpenter, Casilear & Co. ***Comments:*** H-MA-145-G20. 18__. 1850s–1860s.

Rarity: URS-3
Proof $2,000

$100 • W-MA-270-100-G110

Left: Male portrait / C. ***Center:*** Three allegorical women reclining in clouds. ***Bottom center:*** Ship. ***Right:*** 100 / Female portrait. ***Engraver:*** Toppan, Carpenter, Casilear & Co. ***Comments:*** H-MA-145-G22. 18__. 1850s–1860s.

Rarity: —

$500 • W-MA-270-500-G120

Left: Male portrait / D. ***Center:*** Indian woman as Liberty seated with shield, eagle, and flags. ***Bottom center:*** Beehive. ***Right:*** 500 / Woman seated in clouds. ***Engraver:*** Toppan, Carpenter, Casilear & Co. ***Comments:*** H-MA-145-G24. 18__. 1850s–1860s.

Rarity: —

$1,000 • W-MA-270-1000-G130

Left: Woman reclining on parcels / 1000. ***Center:*** Male portrait. ***Right:*** 1000. ***Engraver:*** Toppan, Carpenter, Casilear & Co. ***Comments:*** H-MA-145-G26. 18__. 1850s–1860s.

Rarity: URS-3
Proof $3,500

Uncut Sheets

$1-$1-$2-$3 • W-MA-270-001.001.002.003-US010 HA

Overprint(s): Red. ***Engraver:*** Danforth, Wright & Co. ***Comments:*** All unlisted in Haxby. 18__.

Rarity: URS-1
Proof $12,000

How to Read the Whitman Numbering System

$1 • W-MA-010-001-G010a

Denomination: Value of the note shown.

W: Whitman number. This number is a sortable code unique to each bank and note.

MA: Abbreviation for the state under study.

010: Numerical designation specific to each bank.

001: The denomination in dollars.

G010a: G indicates a good or valid note. Other categories are indicated thus: C (counterfeit); R (raised); S (spurious); N (not-attributed); A (altered). Numbers are assigned starting with 010, 020, et seq. Terminal letters following the number indicate variations of a note: a series of different colored overprints, tints, payees, etc., all on the same design of note. For more information, see the "How to Use This Book" section at the front of the volume, page xiv.

Non-Valid Issues

$1 • W-MA-270-001-S010

Left: ONE / Portrait of William Henry Harrison. ***Center:*** Mercury seated with sailor, pointing out to sea / 1. ***Bottom center:*** Steamboat. ***Right:*** George Washington standing / ONE. ***Engraver:*** Toppan, Carpenter & Co. ***Comments:*** H-MA-145-S5. May 1, 1856.

Rarity: —

$1 • W-MA-270-001-N010

Left: Portrait of Henry Clay. ***Center:*** Woman and sailor, Ship. ***Right:*** Portrait of George Washington. ***Comments:*** H-MA-145-N5. 1850s.

Rarity: —

$1 • W-MA-270-001-A010

Left: 1 / Cattle, Telegraph poles, Train on bridge. ***Center:*** Trees and river, Young woman seated with two calves. ***Right:*** 1 / Woman with elbow on fence. ***Tint:*** Red-brown 1s and panel outlining white ONE DOLLAR. ***Engraver:*** Danforth, Wright & Co. ***Comments:*** H-MA-145-A5. Altered from $1 Southern Bank of Georgia, Bainbridge, Georgia. March 1, 1858.

Rarity: —

$1 • W-MA-270-001-A020

Left: ONE over 1 / Medallion head bearing 1 / ONE. ***Center:*** Portrait of baby / Woman seated / Shield bearing 1 / ONE. ***Right:*** 1 / Woman with elbow on fence. ***Tint:*** Red-brown 1s and panel outlining white ONE DOLLAR. ***Comments:*** H-MA-145-A10. Altered from $1 Southern Bank of Georgia, Bainbridge, Georgia. June 6, 1856.

Rarity: URS-6
F $125

$2 • W-MA-270-002-A030

Left: 2 / Two Indians on cliff viewing town. ***Center:*** Portrait of Andrew Jackson / Woman seated, right arm on shield bearing cotton plant. ***Right:*** 2 / CONSTITUTION on top of monument. ***Overprint:*** Red TWO. ***Engraver:*** Bald, Cousland & Co. / Baldwin, Bald & Cousland. ***Comments:*** H-MA-145-A15. Altered from $2 Southern Bank of Georgia, Bainbridge, Georgia. 18__. 1860s.

Rarity: —

$2 • W-MA-270-002-A040

Center: Seated woman / Portrait of George Washington / Seated woman. ***Right:*** Man. ***Comments:*** H-MA-145-A20. Altered from $2 Indiana State Mining and Manufacturing Co., Evansville, Indiana. June 6, 1856.

Rarity: —

$3 • W-MA-270-003-S020

CC

Overprint: Red THREE. ***Engraver:*** Toppan, Carpenter, Casilear & Co. ***Comments:*** H-MA-145-S10. July 1, 18__. 1850s.

Rarity: URS-4
F $125; **VF** $250

$3 • W-MA-270-003-N020

Center: Woman. ***Comments:*** H-MA-145-N10. 1850s.

Rarity: —

$3 • W-MA-270-003-A050

Left: 3 / Portrait of Benjamin Franklin. ***Center:*** Woman seated / 3 on shield. ***Right:*** 3 / Woman seated. ***Engraver:*** Danforth, Bald & Co. ***Comments:*** H-MA-145-A25. Altered from $3 Columbia Bank, Washington, D.C. 18__. 1850s.

Rarity: —
F $145

$5 • W-MA-270-005-C070

Engraver: Toppan, Carpenter & Co. ***Comments:*** H-MA-145-C14. Counterfeit of W-MA-270-005-G070. 18__. 1850s.

Rarity: —

$5 • W-MA-270-005-R010

Engraver: Toppan, Carpenter & Co. ***Comments:*** H-MA-145-R5. Raised from W-MA-270-001-G010. 18__. 1850s.

Rarity: —

$5 • W-MA-270-005-S030

HA

Engraver: Wellstood, Hanks & Co. ***Comments:*** H-Unlisted. 18__. 1850s.

Rarity: URS-5
VG $125

$5 • W-MA-270-005-N030

Left: Three women. ***Center:*** Ocean view with ships. ***Right:*** Woman / 5. ***Comments:*** H-MA-145-N15. 1850s.

Rarity: —

$5 • W-MA-270-005-A060

Left: 5 / State arms / FIVE. ***Center:*** View of U.S. Capitol / Portrait of Zachary Taylor / FIVE. ***Bottom center:*** Two quail. ***Right:*** 5 / Train and building, Liberty seated. ***Engraver:*** Danforth, Bald & Co. ***Comments:*** H-MA-145-A30. Altered from $5 Government Stock Bank, Ann Arbor, Michigan. June 1, 1852.

Rarity: —

$5 • W-MA-270-005-A070

Left: 5 / V / 5. ***Center:*** Boy lying down, Farmers seated, Girl standing, Horses. ***Right:*** 5 / V / 5. ***Overprint:*** Red FIVE. ***Engraver:*** Baldwin, Bald & Cousland / Bald, Cousland & Co. ***Comments:*** H-MA-145-A35. Altered from $5 Southern Bank of Georgia, Bainbridge, Georgia. 18__. 1850s.

Rarity: —

$5 • W-MA-270-005-A080

Left: 5 / Horse / FIVE. ***Center:*** Three figures, two seated on bales. ***Right:*** V / Portrait of Andrew Jackson / FIVE. ***Engraver:*** Danforth, Wright & Co. ***Comments:*** H-MA-145-A40. Altered from $5 Bank of the Ohio Savings Institute, Tiffin, Ohio. 185_. 1850s.

Rarity: —
F $100

$5 • W-MA-270-005-A090

Left: L / Portrait of Henry Clay. ***Center:*** Western river steamboat, Wharf. ***Right:*** 5 / Portrait of George Washington. ***Overprint:*** Red FIVE. ***Engraver:*** New England Bank Note Co. / Rawdon, Wright, Hatch & Edson. ***Comments:*** H-MA-145-A45. Altered from $5 Waubeek Bank, De Soto, Nebraska. 1857.

Rarity: —

$10 • W-MA-270-010-C080

Left: Man holding up woman / TEN. ***Center:*** Sailing ships. ***Right:*** 10 / Male portrait. ***Engraver:*** Toppan, Carpenter & Co. ***Comments:*** H-MA-145-C16. Counterfeit of W-MA-270-010-G080. 18__. Circa 1860.

Rarity: URS-6
F $175

$10 • W-MA-270-010-R020

Engraver: Toppan, Carpenter & Co. ***Comments:*** H-MA-145-R10. Raised from W-MA-270-002-G030. 18__. 1850s.

Rarity: —

$20 • W-MA-270-020-R030

Engraver: Toppan, Carpenter & Co. ***Comments:*** H-MA-145-R15. Raised from W-MA-270-001-G010. 18__. 1850s.

Rarity: —

$50 • W-MA-270-050-R040

Engraver: Toppan, Carpenter & Co. ***Comments:*** H-MA-145-R20. Raised from W-MA-270-001-G010. 18__. 1850s.

Rarity: —

Bank of the Metropolis

1858–1864

W-MA-280

History: The Bank of the Metropolis was established under the General Banking Law and was located at 39 State Street. Its president was Samuel A. Way and its cashier William H. Foster, who served together through 1862. Samuel Way died on Tuesday, June 4, 1872, at age 56.[36]

In 1857 the *Congressional Serial Set* reported these figures: capital $200,000; bills of this bank and other New England states in the vault $38,479.22; specie $40,176.05. The next year circulation was down to $87,590, and specie had doubled to $80,004.46. Circulation ranged from $102,733 in 1857 to $63,619 in 1862. The amount of specie was only $6,438.29 in 1861, but it was back up to $35,241.59 in 1862.

Numismatic Commentary: This short-lived bank had its notes printed by the American Bank Note Co. Its issues were some of the most pleasant in appearance. Benjamin Franklin, Christopher Columbus, and the Declaration of Independence are but a few of the beautiful vignettes used on notes from this bank.

Valid Issues

$1 • W-MA-280-001-G010

HA

Tint: Green. ***Engraver:*** American Bank Note Co. ***Comments:*** H-MA-290-G2a. 18__. 1858–1860s.

Rarity: URS-3
VG $1,250

$2 • W-MA-280-002-G020

CJF

Tint: Green. ***Engraver:*** American Bank Note Co. ***Comments:*** H-MA-290-G4a. 18__. 1858–1860s.

Rarity: URS-3
F $2,000

$3 • W-MA-280-003-G030

Left: Panel bearing THREE vertically. ***Center:*** State arms / View of State House in Boston / 3. ***Right:*** Panel bearing THREE vertically. ***Engraver:*** American Bank Note Co. ***Comments:*** H-MA-290-G6a. 18__. 1858–1860s.

Rarity: —

$5 • W-MA-280-005-G040

Left: Panel bearing FIVE vertically. ***Center:*** "Presentation of the Declaration of Independence". ***Right:*** 5 / State arms. ***Tint:*** Green. ***Engraver:*** American Bank Note Co. ***Comments:*** H-MA-290-G8a. 18__. 1858–1860s.

Rarity: —

$10 • W-MA-280-010-G050

Left: Panel bearing TEN vertically. ***Center:*** View of U.S. Capitol. ***Right:*** 10 / State arms. ***Tint:*** Green or red. ***Engraver:*** American Bank Note Co. ***Comments:*** H-MA-290-G10a. 18__. 1859–1860s.

Rarity: —

$20 • W-MA-280-020-G060

Left: TWENTY / XX. ***Center:*** State arms. ***Right:*** TWENTY / XX. ***Tint:*** Red bank title and red dies bearing white 20s. ***Engraver:*** American Bank Note Co. ***Comments:*** H-MA-290-G12a. 18__. 1859–1860s.

Rarity: —

$50 • W-MA-280-050-G070

Left: State arms. *Center:* Three sailors, one reclining, one seated on broken mast, one standing looking through spyglass. *Right:* Eagle. *Tint:* Red bank title and red dies bearing white 50s. *Engraver:* American Bank Note Co. *Comments:* H-MA-290-G14a. 18__. 1859–1860s.

Rarity: —

$100 • W-MA-280-100-G080

Left: State arms. *Center:* Anchor, bales, barrels, and masts. *Right:* Portrait of girl. *Tint:* Red bank title and red dies bearing white C and white 100. *Engraver:* American Bank Note Co. *Comments:* H-MA-290-G16a. 18__. 1858–1860s.

Rarity: —

$500 • W-MA-280-500-G090

Center: Horse, Eagle / Ocean scene, Sailing ship and other ships. *Right:* State arms. *Tint:* Red dies bearing white 500s. *Engraver:* American Bank Note Co. *Comments:* H-MA-290-G18a. 18__. 1858–1860s.

Rarity: —

Non-Valid Issues

$5 • W-MA-280-005-A010

CC

Overprint: Red FIVE. *Engraver:* New England Bank Note Co. / Rawdon, Wright, Hatch & Edson. *Comments:* H-MA-290-A5. Altered from $5 Waubeek Bank, De Soto, Nebraska. 1857.

Rarity: URS-7
VG $50; **F** $150

$10 • W-MA-280-010-A020

Left: 10 / Justice seated. *Center:* Indian family, woman kneeling and pointing at plow. *Right:* 10 / Woman reclining on cornucopia. *Back:* Ten orange dies bearing Xs. *Engraver:* W.L. Ormsby. *Comments:* H-MA-290-A10. Altered from $10 Farmers and Drovers Bank, Petersburg, Indiana. Oct. 1, 1858.

Rarity: —

Bank of Mutual Redemption

CIRCA 1855–1864

W-MA-290

History: By 1855 the Suffolk Bank System, W-MA-960, had garnered such opposition that an organized resistance had come about. Smaller country banks were profitable for the Suffolk Bank but little regarded in return, and so the Bank of Mutual Redemption was established as a cooperative bank, owned by country institutions, by them and for them. It was located at 91 State Street.

To many, the Bank of Mutual Redemption was a triumph. But by 1863 trouble was brewing, and it was reported that the bank was borrowing specie to satisfy the requirements by law instead of keeping it on hand for the redemption of funds. The bank had little circulation to claim, as most of its large transactions were with other banks only, and it was considered in violation of the Massachusetts Specie Reserve Law.[37] A petition by the Bank Commissioners of the Commonwealth was signed against the Bank of Mutual Redemption, accusing it of going over its limit of power and failing to comply with the rules that were set down by law. The petition further requested that an injunction be placed against the bank.

In 1863 it was reported by the *Annual Report of the Secretary of the Treasury on the Condition of the Banks* that the Bank of Mutual Redemption "had been almost constantly a debtor at the clearing-house for more than a year previous." All turned out well, however. The shareholders secured a charter on September 12, 1864, for the National Bank of Redemption of Boston, after which the notes of the state bank were retired at full value.

Numismatic Commentary: The Bank of Mutual Redemption was a relatively short-lived bank. Collectors should note the lack of low-denomination bills that this bank issued. This shortage was probably due to the fact that the bank was formed primarily to act as a clearing house for country banks, the successor to most of the business earlier enjoyed by the Suffolk Bank. As such, it will be much easier to locate altered or spurious issues for a collection than the real thing. Genuine notes are extremely hard to find.

Valid Issues

$5 • W-MA-290-005-G010

QDB

Engraver: Edmonds, Jones, & Smillie. *Comments:* H-Unlisted. Proof. 18__. 1860s.

Rarity: URS-2
Proof $2,500

$5 • W-MA-290-005-G010a

Left: Indian on shield / 5. *Center:* FIVE / 5. *Right:* 5 / Indian on shield. *Overprint:* Green FIVE. *Engraver:* American Bank Note Co. *Comments:* H-MA-305-G6b. Similar to W-MA-290-005-G010 but with different engraver imprint. 18__. 1860s.

Rarity: —

$20 • W-MA-290-020-G020

Left: MASSACHUSETTS and 20 / 20. *Center:* Text. *Right:* 20 / 20. *Engraver:* American Bank Note Co. *Comments:* H-MA-305-G12. 18__. 1860s.

Rarity: —

$50 • W-MA-290-050-G030

Left: MASSACHUSETTS vertically. ***Center:*** Text. ***Right:*** 50 / 50. ***Engraver:*** American Bank Note Co. ***Comments:*** H-MA-305-G18. 18__. 1860s.

Rarity: —

Non-Valid Issues

$5 • W-MA-290-005-N010

Center: Three women reclining with instruments / FIVE. ***Right:*** Woman holding pole and globe surmounted by eagle. ***Comments:*** H-MA-305-N5. 1850s.

Rarity: —

$5 • W-MA-290-005-A010

Left: Several men with sticks driving herd of cattle into stream / 5. ***Center:*** Five men raking and loading hay, Ox wagon. ***Right:*** 5. ***Tint:*** Red-brown lathework outlining white 5. ***Engraver:*** Bald, Cousland & Co. ***Comments:*** H-MA-305-A15. Altered from $5 Pioneer Association, Lafayette, Indiana. 18__. 1850s.

Rarity: —

$5 • W-MA-290-005-A020

Left: V / Portrait of Henry Clay. ***Center:*** Steamship. ***Right:*** 5 / Portrait of George Washington. ***Overprint:*** Red FIVE. ***Engraver:*** New England Bank Note Co. / Rawdon, Wright, Hatch & Edson. ***Comments:*** H-MA-305-A20. Altered from $5 Waubeek Bank, De Soto, Nebraska. 1857.

Rarity: —

$10 • W-MA-290-010-A030

Left: 10 / Justice seated. ***Center:*** Indian family, woman kneeling and pointing at plow. ***Right:*** 10 / Woman reclining on cornucopia. ***Back:*** Ten orange dies bearing white Xs. ***Engraver:*** W.L. Ormsby. ***Comments:*** H-MA-305-A30. Altered from $10 Farmers and Drovers Bank, Petersburg, Indiana. Oct. 1, 1858.

Rarity: —

$20 • W-MA-290-020-A040

Left: Woman floating in clouds holding U.S. shield and flowers above head / XX. ***Center:*** XX / Slain deer, Indian man with headdress reclining, arm raised. ***Right:*** 20 / Portrait of George Washington. ***Engraver:*** Rawdon, Wright, Hatch & Edson. ***Comments:*** H-MA-305-A40. Altered from $20 New England Bank, Fairmount, Maine. Oct. 1, 1857.

Rarity: —

Bank of Mutual Redemption of Boston

1850s

W-MA-300

History: A non-existent bank represented only by fraudulent notes intended to pass for those of the Bank of Mutual Redemption, W-MA-290.

Issues

$2 • W-MA-300-002-A010

CC

Overprint: Blue TWO. ***Comments:*** H-MA-306-A5. Altered from $2 Farmers and Merchants Bank of Memphis, Memphis, Tennessee series. 18__. 1850s.

Rarity: URS-7

F $100

$3 • W-MA-300-003-S010

Left: 3 / Portrait of George Washington. ***Center:*** Woman seated / 3 / Woman seated. ***Right:*** 3 / Man seated. ***Comments:*** H-MA-306-S5. Jan. __, 185_. 1850s.

Rarity: —

$3 • W-MA-300-003-A020

HA

Overprint: Red THREE. ***Engraver:*** Rawdon, Wright, Hatch & Edson. ***Comments:*** H-MA-306-A10. Altered from $3 Farmers and Merchants Bank of Memphis, Memphis, Tennessee. 18__. 1850s.

Rarity: URS-5

F $150

$5 • W-MA-300-005-A030

CC

Overprint: Blue FIVE. ***Engraver:*** Rawdon, Wright, Hatch & Edson. ***Comments:*** H-MA-306-A25. Altered from $5 Farmers and Merchants Bank of Memphis, Memphis, Tennessee series. 18__. 1850s.

Rarity: URS-7

F $100

$10 • **W-MA-300-010-A040** CC

Overprint: Red TEN. ***Engraver:*** Rawdon, Wright, Hatch & Edson. ***Comments:*** H-MA-306-A35. Altered from $10 Farmers and Merchants Bank of Memphis, Tennessee series. Handwritten 9 over 4 in date. 1 Aug. 1854. 1850s.

Rarity: URS-7
F $100

Bank of North America
1850–1864
W-MA-310

History: The Bank of North America was chartered in Massachusetts in 1850, by which time banks of the same name had been established elsewhere. The capital was set at $50,000.

The bank was located at 99 State Street. By 1855 its capital was $750,000, where it remained throughout 1864. In 1857 these figures were reported: bills in circulation $147,183; bills of this bank and other New England states in the vault $33,698; specie $64,530.27.

The bank's first president was George W. Crockett, accompanied by cashier John R. Hall. In 1863 W.W. Kendrick became the president of the bank, and 1864 saw yet another change when R.W. Shapleigh took the presidency.

The stockholders voted to liquidate and establish a National Banking Association. The National Bank of North America was chartered on December 30, 1864, and succeeded the state bank's business.

Numismatic Commentary: The Bank of North America is an example of another large city bank with only hard-to-find issues available in the genuine category.

Valid Issues

$1 • **W-MA-310-001-G010** CC

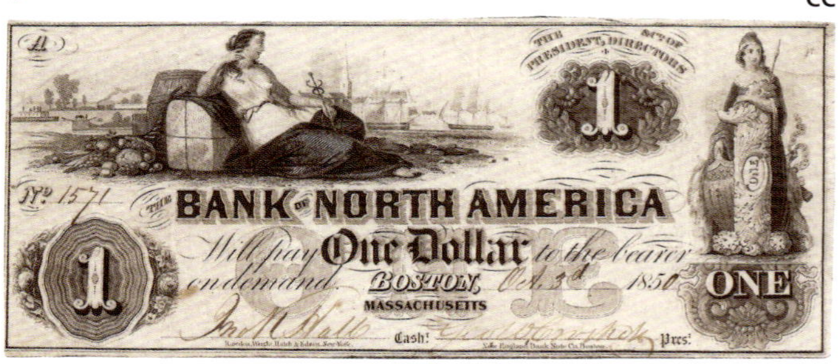

Engraver: New England Bank Note Co. / Rawdon, Wright, Hatch & Edson. ***Comments:*** H-MA-325-G2. 185_. 1850s.

Rarity: URS-5
F $500; **VF** $1,000

$1 • **W-MA-310-001-G020**
Left: Woman reclining with arm on bale, Barrel and cornucopia, Train, Canal and ships / 1. ***Center:*** 1. ***Right:*** 1 / Indian woman, Trees and rocks. ***Engraver:*** American Bank Note Co. ***Comments:*** H-MA-325-G4. 18__. 1860s.

Rarity: —

$2 • **W-MA-310-002-G030**
Left: Sailor seated on wharf holding spyglass, Two barrels and bale / 2. ***Center:*** 2. ***Right:*** 2 / State arms. ***Engraver:*** New England Bank Note Co. / Rawdon, Wright, Hatch & Edson. ***Comments:*** H-MA-325-G6. 185_. 1850s.

Rarity: —

$2 • **W-MA-310-002-G040**
Left: Sailor seated on wharf holding spyglass, Two barrels and bale / 2. ***Center:*** 2. ***Right:*** 2 / Woman with shield and scales. ***Engraver:*** American Bank Note Co. ***Comments:*** H-MA-325-G8. 18__. 1860s.

Rarity: —

$3 • **W-MA-310-003-G050**
Left: 3 / Indian woman and white woman flanking shield surmounted by bust of George Washington. ***Center:*** 3. ***Right:*** 3 / Woman in clouds holding flag with three cherubs. ***Engraver:*** New England Bank Note Co. / Rawdon, Wright, Hatch & Edson. ***Comments:*** H-MA-325-G10. 185_. 1850s.

Rarity: —

$3 • **W-MA-310-003-G060**
Left: Indian woman and white woman flanking shield surmounted by bust of George Washington / 3. ***Center:*** 3 on die bearing 3s. ***Right:*** THREE / Sailor aloft with spyglass holding rigging. ***Engraver:*** American Bank Note Co. ***Comments:*** H-MA-325-G12. 18__. 1860s.

Rarity: —

$5 • **W-MA-310-005-G070**
Left: FIVE / Cherub, Woman seated holding 5 overhead. ***Center:*** Eagle on shield, Ships. ***Right:*** FIVE / Cherub, Woman seated holding 5 overhead. ***Engraver:*** New England Bank Note Co. / Rawdon, Wright, Hatch & Edson. ***Comments:*** H-MA-325-G14. 185_. 1850s.

Rarity: —

$5 • **W-MA-310-005-G080**
Left: FIVE / Woman. ***Center:*** Two women seated on bale, Factories and cotton field. ***Right:*** 5 / Seal of the city of Boston. ***Engraver:*** American Bank Note Co. ***Comments:*** H-MA-325-G16. 18__. 1860s.

Rarity: —

$10 • **W-MA-310-010-G090**
Left: Train / TEN. ***Center:*** 10 / TEN. ***Right:*** TEN / Woman shading eyes with hand and holding staff. ***Engraver:*** New England Bank Note Co. / Rawdon, Wright, Hatch & Edson. ***Comments:*** H-MA-325-G18. 185_. 1850s.

Rarity: —

$10 • **W-MA-310-010-G100**
Left: Woman seated with scroll, Child with wreath / TEN. ***Center:*** Indian woman reclining with shield and eagle, Steamship. ***Right:*** 10 / Eagle on rock. ***Engraver:*** American Bank Note Co. ***Comments:*** H-MA-325-G20. 18__. 1860s.

Rarity: —

$20 • W-MA-310-020-G110

Left: 20 / Woman seated. ***Center:*** Two women flanking shield bearing scene, Boxes and bales, Steamboat and train. ***Right:*** 20 / Sailor standing by capstan and barrels. ***Engraver:*** New England Bank Note Co. / Rawdon, Wright, Hatch & Edson. ***Comments:*** H-MA-325-G22. 185_. 1850s.

Rarity: —

$20 • W-MA-310-020-G120

Left: 20 / Woman seated on rock. ***Center:*** Two women flanking shield bearing scene, Boxes and barrels, Steamboat and train. ***Right:*** 20 / Liberty reclining on shield. ***Engraver:*** American Bank Note Co. ***Comments:*** H-MA-325-G24. 18__. 1860s.

Rarity: —

$50 • W-MA-310-050-G130

Left: Milkmaid seated with pail, Farmer standing with grain. ***Center:*** 50 / Woman placing wreath on eagle and holding Portrait of George Washington, Boxes and bales, Ship and train. ***Right:*** Woman seated and sailor standing, Boxes and bales. ***Engraver:*** New England Bank Note Co. / Rawdon, Wright, Hatch & Edson. ***Comments:*** H-MA-325-G26. 185_. 1850s.

Rarity: —

$100 • W-MA-310-100-G140

Left: 100 / Woman leaning on shield. ***Center:*** Steamship and other ships. ***Right:*** 100 / Woman standing with anchor. ***Engraver:*** New England Bank Note Co. / Rawdon, Wright, Hatch & Edson. ***Comments:*** H-MA-325-G28. 185_. 1850s.

Rarity: —

$500 • W-MA-310-500-G150

Left: 500 / Woman seated with wreath and balance, Eagle and shield. ***Center:*** Woman floating in clouds with eagle and shield. ***Right:*** 500 / Indian woman seated on rock, holding papoose. ***Engraver:*** New England Bank Note Co. / Rawdon, Wright, Hatch & Edson. ***Comments:*** H-MA-325-G30. 185_. 1850s.

Rarity: —

Non-Valid Issues

$1 • W-MA-310-001-A010

Left: ONE / Woman holding cornucopia of flowers and standing by 1. ***Center:*** Capitol / Eagle on U.S. shield and branches / Steamship. ***Bottom center:*** Eagle with shield and motto. ***Right:*** 1 on medallion U.S. shield / ONE / Portrait of George Washington. ***Engraver:*** Wellstood, Hanks, Hay & Whiting. ***Comments:*** H-MA-325-A5. Altered from $1 People's Bank of North America, Washington, D.C. 18__. 1850s.

Rarity: —

$2 • W-MA-310-002-N010

Left: Woman. ***Center:*** Woman seated with bale and shield. ***Right:*** Woman. ***Comments:*** H-MA-325-N10.

Rarity: —

$2 • W-MA-310-002-A020

Left: TWO / Justice seated on die bearing 2. ***Center:*** Capitol, Eagle on U.S. shield and branches, Steamship. ***Bottom center:*** Sailboat. ***Right:*** 2 on medallion U.S. shield / TWO / Portrait of Henry Clay. ***Engraver:*** Wellstood, Hanks, Hay & Whiting. ***Comments:*** H-MA-325-A10. Altered from $2 People's Bank of North America, Washington, D.C. 18__. 1850s.

Rarity: —

$3 • W-MA-310-003-A030

CC

Overprint: Red THREE. ***Engraver:*** New England Bank Note Co. / Rawdon, Wright, Hatch & Edson. ***Comments:*** H-MA-325-A15. Altered from $3 Waubeek Bank, De Soto, Nebraska. 1857.

Rarity: URS-6

VG $200; **F** $300

$5 • W-MA-310-005-C070

Engraver: New England Bank Note Co. / Rawdon, Wright, Hatch & Edson. ***Comments:*** H-MA-325-C14. Counterfeit of W-MA-310-005-G070. 185_. 1850s.

Rarity: —

$5 • W-MA-310-005-R010

Comments: H-MA-325-R5. Raised from W-MA-310-001-G010. 18__. 1850s.

Rarity: —

$10 • W-MA-310-010-C090

CC

Engraver: New England Bank Note Co. / Rawdon, Wright, Hatch & Edson. ***Comments:*** H-MA-325-C18. Counterfeit of W-MA-310-010-G090. Handwritten 6 over 5 in date. 185_. 1850s–1860s.

Rarity: URS-5

VG $400; **F** $500; **VF** $700

$10 • W-MA-310-010-AR010

Left: Woman with dividers and book / 10. ***Center:*** Angel in clouds blowing trumpet, Globe and eagle. ***Right:*** 1 / Portrait of General David Humphreys. ***Engraver:*** Toppan, Carpenter, Casilear & Co. ***Comments:*** H-MA-325-AR20. Altered and raised from $1 Bank of North America, Seymour, Connecticut. 18__. 1850s.

Rarity: —

$50 • W-MA-310-050-R020

Engraver: New England Bank Note Co. / Rawdon, Wright, Hatch & Edson. ***Comments:*** H-MA-325-R10. Raised from W-MA-310-002-G030. 18__. 1850s.

Rarity: —

$500 • W-MA-310-500-N020

Center: White woman and Indian man seated. ***Comments:*** H-MA-325-N20.

Rarity: —

Bank of the Republic

1860–1864

W-MA-320

History: The Bank of the Republic was organized in 1859 and opened for business at 77 State Street in Boston. The initial capital was recorded at $1,000,000. David Snow was the first president, and Theo C. Severance was the first cashier. William Bassett Jr. became president in 1863. In 1864 Charles A. Vialle became cashier.

These figures were given for 1862: circulation $102,933; specie $56,941.69; real estate $4,000. In 1864 the *Boston Directory* reported the directors to be David Snow, Asa Jacobs, Thomas Nickerson, Horatio Chickering, F.L. Fay, Harrison O. Briggs, Moses B. Sewell, J.M. Murdock, Sandford Gilmore, Avery Plumer, and Frederick D. Allen.

On April 13, 1864, the National Bank of the Republic was chartered and assumed the business of the state bank, whose notes were redeemed at face value and burned.

Numismatic Commentary: All genuine issues from this bank are hard to find. The few that have been reported have handsome vignettes executed by the American Bank Note Co. The $1 note bears a vignette titled in Roger Durand's reference as "Major Waldron's Terrible Fight."

Valid Issues

$1 • W-MA-320-001-G010

Left: 1 / State arms. ***Center:*** Three women, child, and man at table, Dog. ***Right:*** 1 / Spread eagle. ***Comments:*** H-Unlisted.

Rarity: —

EF $895

$1 • W-MA-320-001-G010a

CC

Tint: Orange counter, text, and panel of microlettering. ***Engraver:*** American Bank Note Co. ***Comments:*** H-MA-335-G2a. Similar to W-MA-320-001-G010. Proof. 186_. 1860s.

Rarity: URS-5

VG $1,500; **VF** $2,500; **Unc-S&D** $6,000

Collectors and Researchers:

If you have new information about any banks or notes listed in this volume, contact Whitman Publishing, Attn: Obsolete Paper Money, 3101 Clairmont Road, Suite G, Atlanta, GA 30329.

$1 • W-MA-320-001-G010b

CJF

Tint: Green counters and panel of dies. ***Engraver:*** American Bank Note Co. ***Comments:*** H-Unlisted. Similar to W-MA-320-001-G010. Feb. 3, 1860. 1860s.

Rarity: URS-3

VG $1,000; **VF** $2,000

$2 • W-MA-320-002-G020

Left: 2 / State arms. ***Center:*** Fleet of small sailing ships. ***Right:*** 2 / Sailor standing by capstan and anchor. ***Tint:*** Orange counter and panel of microlettering. ***Engraver:*** American Bank Note Co. ***Comments:*** H-MA-335-G4a. 186_. 1860s.

Rarity: —

$3 • W-MA-320-003-G030

JF

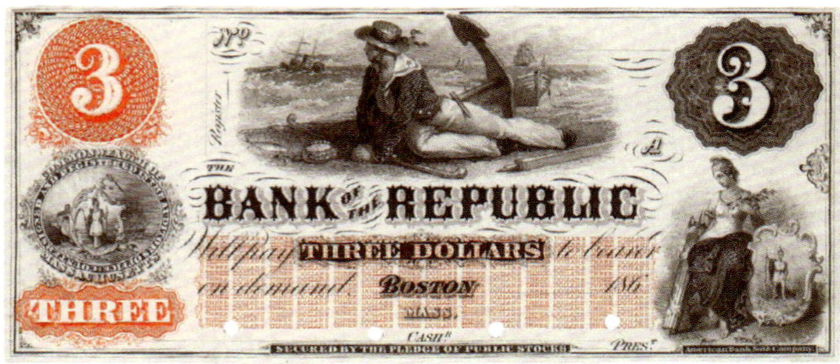

Tint: Orange counters and panel of microlettering. ***Engraver:*** American Bank Note Co. ***Comments:*** H-MA-335-G6a. Proof. 186_. 1860s.

Rarity: URS-3

Proof $1,500

$5 • W-MA-320-005-G040

HA

Tint: Orange counter and panel of microlettering. ***Engraver:*** American Bank Note Co. ***Comments:*** H-MA-335-G8a. Proof. 186_. 1860s.

Rarity: URS-1

Proof $3,800

$10 • W-MA-320-010-G050

Left: X / State arms. ***Center:*** Ships in harbor. ***Right:*** 10 / Man with child and bust of George Washington. ***Tint:*** Orange counter and panel of microlettering. ***Engraver:*** American Bank Note Co. ***Comments:*** H-MA-335-G10a. 186_. 1860s.

Rarity: URS-3

Proof $800

$20 • W-MA-320-020-G060

HA

Tint: Orange counters, text, and frames. ***Engraver:*** American Bank Note Co. ***Comments:*** H-MA-335-G12a. Proof. February 3, 186_. 1860s.

Rarity: URS-2
Proof $7,500

$50 • W-MA-320-050-G070

CC

Tint: Orange frames, ornate panel, lathework panel, and panel outlining white 50 Dolls. ***Engraver:*** American Bank Note Co. ***Comments:*** H-MA-335-G14a. Proof. February 3, 186_. 1860s.

Rarity: URS-2
Proof $8,000

$100 • W-MA-320-100-G080

CC

Tint: Orange ornate panel, lathework panel, and panel outlining white 100 Dolls. ***Engraver:*** American Bank Note Co. ***Comments:*** H-MA-335-G16a. Proof. February 3, 186_. 1860s.

Rarity: URS-2
Proof $10,000

$500 • W-MA-320-500-G090

Left: 500 / State arms. ***Right:*** 500 / Male portrait. ***Tint:*** Red-orange counters and panel of microlettering, 500 DOLLS. ***Engraver:*** American Bank Note Co. ***Comments:*** H-MA-335-G18a. Feb. 3, 186_. 1860s.

Rarity: —

Uncut Sheets

$1-$1-$2-$3 • W-MA-470-001.001.002.003-US010

Vignette(s): ***($1)*** State arms / Two men at table / Spread eagle. ***($1)*** State arms / Two men at table / Spread eagle. ***($2)*** State arms / Sailing ships / Sailor. ***($3)*** State arms / Sailor /Woman. ***Tint(s):*** Orange. ***Comments:*** H-MA-335-G2a, G2a, G4a, G6a.

Rarity: —

Selected auction price: Heritage, January 2011, Lot 15542, CU $5,462

Non-Valid Issues

$1 • W-MA-320-001-A010

Left: ONE vertically. ***Center:*** Scene of men on horseback / Hunting scene / ONE DOLLAR over ONE. ***Right:*** 1 / Portrait of girl. ***Engraver:*** Bald, Cousland & Co. / Baldwin, Bald & Cousland. ***Comments:*** H-MA-335-A5. 18__. 1860s.

Rarity: URS-5
F $30

$1 • W-MA-320-001-A020

Left: 1 / State arms / ONE. ***Center:*** Three allegorical women reclining around shield surmounted by eagle, Ship. ***Right:*** 1 / Dog, Two farmers walking. ***Engraver:*** Danforth, Wright & Co. ***Comments:*** H-MA-335-A10. Altered from $1 Bank of Washtenaw, Washtenaw, Michigan series. 1850s.

Rarity: —

$2 • W-MA-320-002-N010

Left: 2 / Male portrait. ***Center:*** Liberty seated, Ships. ***Right:*** 2 / Male portrait. ***Comments:*** H-MA-335-N5.

Rarity: —

$2 • W-MA-320-002-A030

Left: 2 / Farmer plowing with black and white horses. ***Center:*** Two men loading wagon with sheaves, Three men cradling and binding. ***Right:*** 2 / Two floating cherubs with caduceus and sheaf. ***Tint:*** Red-brown 2s and TWO DOLLARS. ***Engraver:*** Danforth, Wright & Co. ***Comments:*** H-MA-335-A20. Altered from $2 Southern Bank of Georgia, Bainbridge, Georgia. March 1, 1858.

Rarity: —

$3 • W-MA-320-003-C030

Engraver: American Bank Note Co. ***Comments:*** H-MA-335-C6a. Counterfeit of W-MA-320-003-G030. 186_. 1860s.

Rarity: —

$3 • W-MA-320-003-A040

CC

Overprint: Red THREE. ***Engraver:*** Danforth, Bald & Co. ***Comments:*** H-MA-335-A25. Altered from $3 Columbia Bank, Washington, D.C. 18__. 1850s.

Rarity: URS-7
F $125

$5 • W-MA-320-005-A050

Left: Horses running / V. ***Center:*** Liberty and Ceres flanking shield surmounted by horse's head. ***Bottom center:*** Sleeping dog. ***Right:*** 5 / Portrait of girl shading eyes. ***Overprint:*** Red FIVE. ***Engraver:*** Bald, Cousland & Co. / Baldwin, Bald & Cousland. ***Comments:*** H-MA-335-A30. Altered from $5 Bank of Morgan, Morgan, Georgia. 18__. 1850s.

Rarity: —

$20 • W-MA-320-020-R010

Engraver: American Bank Note Co. ***Comments:*** H-MA-335-R5. Raised from W-MA-320-001-G010a. 186_. 1860s.

Rarity: —

Bank of the United States {1st} (branch)

1792–1811

W-MA-330

History: The first Bank of the United States, chartered in 1791, operated until its charter expired in 1811. The Boston branch opened for business in 1792 with a capital of $700,000. It was among the first of the branches to start business, the others being located in New York City, Baltimore, and Charleston.

An early account noted: "The Boston Branch consists of the following officers, thirteen directors, one of whom is president, one cashier, two tellers, two book keepers, one discount clerk, one messenger." Into the early 1800s, the Boston branch also exchanged bills of other banks in the city.

In 1806 the Bank of the United States competed in Boston with the Massachusetts Bank, the Boston Bank, and the Union Bank. While those state-chartered banks were well-operated, they did not give the public the assurance that the Bank of the United States did. Nevertheless, in 1809 the Bank of the United States began to wind down its affairs, as it seemed the charter would not be renewed. Various state-chartered banks, often with politically connected shareholders and officers, viewed the bank as a threat to their businesses and an unfair competitor due to the fact that it had government backing, even though most of the bank's shares were held by others.

A Treasury statement of March 2, 1809, noted the following concerning branches: "There are at present eight of those offices, viz. at Boston, New York, Baltimore, Norfolk, Charleston, Savannah, the city of Washington, and New Orleans. The two last were established at the request of the secretary of the Treasury."

The Boston branch closed out its affairs in 1811 when Congress failed to renew the charter for the Bank of the United States.

Numismatic Commentary: Paper money for the bank was printed in Philadelphia and carried the same designs as all of the other branches but with the imprint of Boston. As bills of the bank could be spent anywhere, they were widely counterfeited. Nearly all genuine notes were redeemed, with the result that many years may pass between market appearances of even a single bill. Nearly all offered are counterfeits.

Valid Issues

$5 • W-MA-330-005-G010

Left: Portraits. ***Center:*** Eagle perched on shield, Ship, Nymphs holding frame bearing 5. ***Bottom center:*** 5. ***Right:*** Portraits. ***Engraver:*** Murray, Draper, Fairman & Co. ***Comments:*** H-US1-G140. Design 5A.

Rarity: *None known*

$5 • W-MA-330-005-G020

Left: FIVE vertically. ***Center:*** 5 / Eagle perched on shield, Ships / V. ***Right:*** FIVE vertically. ***Engraver:*** Fairman, Draper, Underwood & Co. ***Comments:*** H-US1-G142. Design 5B.

Rarity: *None known*

$5 • W-MA-330-005-G025

Engraver: Fairman, Draper, Underwood & Co. ***Comments:*** H-US1-G144. Design 5C. No description available.

Rarity: *None known*

$10 • W-MA-330-010-G030

Left: Portraits. ***Center:*** 10 / Eagle perched on shield, Ship / 10. ***Right:*** Portraits. ***Engraver:*** Murray, Draper, Fairman & Co. ***Comments:*** H-US1-G148. Design 10A.

Rarity: *None known*

$10 • W-MA-330-010-G040

Engraver: Fairman, Draper, Underwood & Co. ***Comments:*** H-US1-G150. Design 10B.

Rarity: *None known*

$10 • W-MA-330-010-G045

Engraver: Fairman, Draper, Underwood & Co. ***Comments:*** H-US1-G152. Design 10C. No description available.

Rarity: *None known*

$20 • W-MA-330-020-G050

Left: Portraits. ***Center:*** 20 / Eagle perched on shield, Ship / 20. ***Right:*** Portraits. ***Engraver:*** Murray, Draper, Fairman & Co. ***Comments:*** H-US1-G156. Design 20A.

Rarity: *None known*

$20 • W-MA-330-020-G060

MR

Engraver: Fairman, Draper, Underwood & Co. ***Comments:*** H-US1-G158. Design 20B. 1___. 1800s.

Rarity: URS-1

F $2,000

$20 • W-MA-330-020-G070

Engraver: Draper, Underwood, Bald & Spencer. ***Comments:*** H-US1-G160. Design 20C.

Rarity: *None known*

$50 • W-MA-330-050-G080

Left: Portraits. ***Center:*** 50 / Eagle perched on shield, Ship / 50. ***Right:*** Portraits. ***Engraver:*** Murray, Draper, Fairman & Co. ***Comments:*** H-US1-G164. Design 50A.

Rarity: *None known*

$50 • W-MA-330-050-G090

Left: Eagle / Portrait of Martha Washington / Minerva. ***Center:*** 50 / Eagle perched on shield, Ship / 50. ***Right:*** Eagle / Portrait of Benjamin Franklin / Female portrait. ***Engraver:*** Fairman, Draper, Underwood & Co. ***Comments:*** H-US1-G166. Design 50B.

Rarity: *None known*

$50 • W-MA-330-050-G100

Left: L / Male portrait / 50. ***Center:*** 50 / Eagle perched on shield / L. ***Right:*** 50 / Male portrait / L. ***Engraver:*** Draper, Underwood, Bald & Spencer. ***Comments:*** H-US1-G168. Design 50C.

Rarity: *None known*

$100 • W-MA-330-100-G110

Left: Portraits. ***Center:*** 100 / Eagle perched on shield, Ship / 100. ***Right:*** Portraits. ***Engraver:*** Murray, Draper, Fairman & Co. ***Comments:*** H-US1-G172. Design 100A.

Rarity: *None known*

$100 • W-MA-330-100-G120

Left: Eagle / Portrait of George Washington / Minerva. ***Center:*** 100 / Eagle perched on shield, Ship / 100. ***Right:*** Eagle / Portrait of Benjamin Franklin / Female portrait. ***Engraver:*** Fairman, Draper, Underwood & Co. ***Comments:*** H-US1-G174. Design 100B.

Rarity: *None known*

$100 • W-MA-330-100-G130

Left: 100 / Male portrait / C. ***Center:*** 100 / Eagle perched on shield / 100. ***Right:*** C / Male portrait / 100. ***Engraver:*** Draper, Underwood, Bald & Spencer. ***Comments:*** H-US1-G176. Design 100C.

Rarity: *None known*

NON-VALID ISSUES

$10 • W-MA-330-010-C035

MR

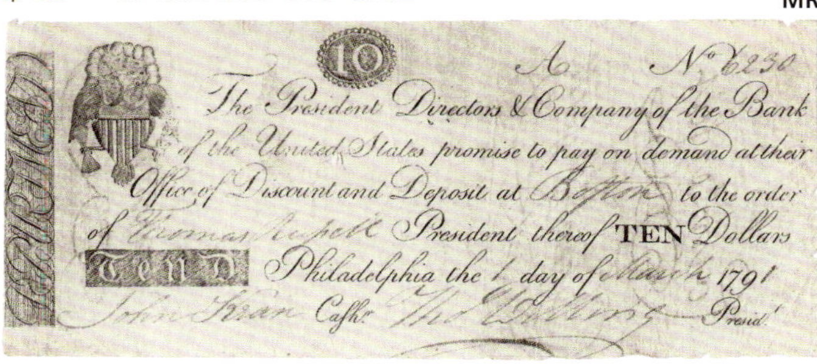

Engraver: Murray, Draper, Fairman & Co. ***Comments:*** H-Unlisted. Counterfeit of Philadelphia, Pennsylvania issue, payable in Boston. 179_. 1790s.

Rarity: URS-1

F $2,000

$50 • W-MA-330-050-C075

CJF, CJF

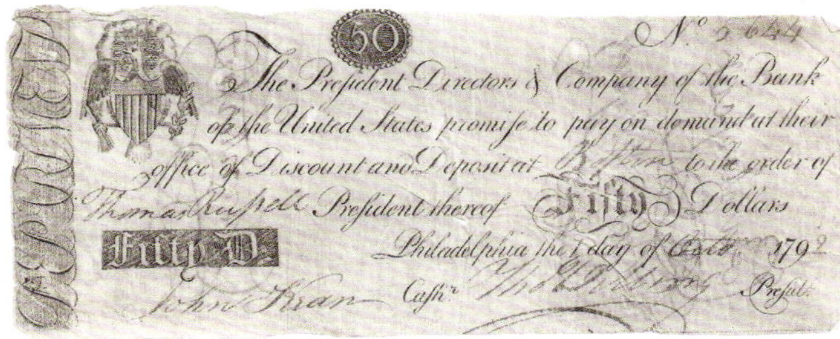

Engraver: Murray, Draper, Fairman & Co. ***Comments:*** H-Unlisted. Counterfeit of Philadelphia, Pennsylvania issue, payable in Boston. 179_. 1790s.

Rarity: URS-1

F $2,000

$50 • W-MA-330-050-C080

Left: Portraits. ***Center:*** 50 / Eagle perched on shield, Ship / 50. ***Right:*** Portraits. ***Engraver:*** Murray, Draper, Fairman & Co. ***Comments:*** H-US1-C164. Counterfeit of W-MA-330-050-G080.

Rarity: *None known*

$50 • W-MA-330-050-C085

SI

Engraver: Murray, Draper, Fairman & Co. ***Comments:*** H-Unlisted. 1___. 1800s.

Rarity: URS-1

F $2,000

$50 • W-MA-330-050-C090

Left: Eagle / Portrait of Martha Washington / Minerva. ***Center:*** 50 / Eagle perched on shield, Ship / 50. ***Right:*** Eagle / Portrait of Benjamin Franklin / Female portrait. ***Engraver:*** Fairman, Draper, Underwood & Co. ***Comments:*** H-US1-C166. Counterfeit of W-MA-330-050-G090.

Rarity: *None known*

Collectors and Researchers:

If you have new information about any banks or notes listed in this volume, contact Whitman Publishing, Attn: Obsolete Paper Money, 3101 Clairmont Road, Suite G, Atlanta, GA 30329.

Bank of the United States {2nd} (branch)

1817–1835

W-MA-340

History: The Boston branch of the second Bank of the United States opened on January 1, 1817, and began business on February 20. The first president was William Gray, and the founding cashier was Samuel Frothingham.

The bank began taking in and paying out bills of other banks but was soon ordered to curtail this practice. At the time, specie had been withdrawn from circulation by the public and speculators, and it was trading at an average premium of 14 percent in good bank notes. The premium soon fell as monetary conditions improved. By the end of December 1818, $1,622,800 in gold and silver coins had been taken in. In December 1822, the capital of the Boston branch was $1,500,000. The capital of the main office in Philadelphia was over $24,000,000.

On July 4, 1824, the cornerstone was laid for the bank's building. In January 1827, the branch conducted $4,150,000 in business. By January 1829, the monthly business fell to just $629,000 due to competitive banks with large amounts of capital on hand offering better terms for loans. The Boston branch constantly received bills of other branches and posted figures. In 1830 the amount was $1,794.

In 1832 President Andrew Jackson vetoed the 1836 renewal of the Bank of the United States which had been brought up before Congress. This instituted a period of great debate and political turmoil. In late 1833 and early 1834 there was a depression in some areas of business which only served to strengthen the bank, as it was backed by the government. The branches began closing and selling their buildings. By March 1836, only the Boston, New York City, Savannah, Nashville, and main Philadelphia facilities remained unsold.

Numismatic Commentary: Although no specific, unique designs were created for the Boston branch, certain generic notes of the Bank of the United States had a space where the branch office of discount and deposit could be inked in. In addition to notes, "drafts" resembling bank notes were issued. Some financial capers may have been practiced with these drafts.

Valid Issues

$5 • W-MA-340-005-G010

Left: Portraits. ***Center:*** Eagle perched on shield, Ship, Nymphs holding frame bearing 5. ***Bottom center:*** 5. ***Right:*** Portraits. ***Engraver:*** Murray, Draper, Fairman & Co. ***Comments:*** H-US2-G80. Design 5A.

Rarity: *None known*

$5 • W-MA-340-005-G020

Left: FIVE vertically. ***Center:*** 5 / Eagle perched on shield, Ships / V. ***Right:*** FIVE vertically. ***Engraver:*** Fairman, Draper, Underwood & Co. ***Comments:*** H-US2-G82. Design 5B.

Rarity: *None known*

$10 • W-MA-340-010-G030

Left: Portraits. ***Center:*** 10 / Eagle perched on shield, Ship / 10. ***Right:*** Portraits. ***Engraver:*** Murray, Draper, Fairman & Co. ***Comments:*** H-US2-G86. Design 10A.

Rarity: *None known*

$10 • W-MA-340-010-G040

Engraver: Fairman, Draper, Underwood & Co. ***Comments:*** H-US2-G88. Design 10B.

Rarity: *None known*

$20 • W-MA-340-020-G050

Left: Portraits. ***Center:*** 20 / Eagle perched on shield, Ship / 20. ***Right:*** Portraits. ***Engraver:*** Murray, Draper, Fairman & Co. ***Comments:*** H-US2-G92 Design 20A.

Rarity: *None known*

$20 • W-MA-340-020-G060

Engraver: Fairman, Draper, Underwood & Co. ***Comments:*** H-US2-G94. Design 20B.

Rarity: *None known*

$20 • W-MA-340-020-G070

Engraver: Draper, Underwood, Bald & Spencer. ***Comments:*** H-US2-G96. Design 20C.

Rarity: *None known*

$50 • W-MA-340-050-G080

Left: Portraits. ***Center:*** 50 / Eagle perched on shield, Ship / 50. ***Right:*** Portraits. ***Engraver:*** Murray, Draper, Fairman & Co. ***Comments:*** H-US2-G100. Design 50A.

Rarity: *None known*

$50 • W-MA-340-050-G090

Left: Eagle / Portrait of Martha Washington / Minerva. ***Center:*** 50 / Eagle perched on shield, Ship / 50. ***Right:*** Eagle / Portrait of Benjamin Franklin / Female portrait. ***Engraver:*** Fairman, Draper, Underwood & Co. ***Comments:*** H-US2-G102. Design 50B.

Rarity: *None known*

$50 • W-MA-340-050-G100

Left: L / Male portrait / 50. ***Center:*** 50 / Eagle perched on shield / L. ***Right:*** 50 / Male portrait / L. ***Engraver:*** Draper, Underwood, Bald & Spencer. ***Comments:*** H-US2-G104. Design 50C.

Rarity: *None known*

$100 • W-MA-340-100-G110

Left: Portraits. ***Center:*** 100 / Eagle perched on shield, Ship / 100. ***Right:*** Portraits. ***Engraver:*** Murray, Draper, Fairman & Co. ***Comments:*** H-US2-G108. Design 100A.

Rarity: *None known*

$100 • W-MA-340-100-G120

Left: Eagle / Portrait of George Washington / Minerva. ***Center:*** 100 / Eagle perched on shield, Ship / 100. ***Right:*** Eagle / Portrait of Benjamin Franklin / Female portrait. ***Engraver:*** Fairman, Draper, Underwood & Co. ***Comments:*** H-US2-G110. Design 100B.

Rarity: *None known*

$100 • W-MA-340-100-G130
Left: 100 / Male portrait / C. ***Center:*** 100 / Eagle perched on shield / 100. ***Right:*** C / Male portrait / 100. ***Engraver:*** Draper, Underwood, Bald & Spencer. ***Comments:*** H-US2-G112. Design 100C.
Rarity: *None known*

NON-VALID ISSUES

$5 • W-MA-340-005-C010
Left: Portraits. ***Center:*** Eagle perched on shield, Ship, Nymphs holding frame bearing 5. ***Bottom center:*** 5. ***Right:*** Portraits. ***Engraver:*** Murray, Draper, Fairman & Co. ***Comments:*** H-US2-C80. Design 5A. Counterfeit of W-MA-340-005-G010.
Rarity: *None known*

$10 • W-MA-340-010-C030
Left: Portraits. ***Center:*** 10 / Eagle perched on shield, Ship / 10. ***Right:*** Portraits. ***Engraver:*** Murray, Draper, Fairman & Co. ***Comments:*** H-US2-C86. Design 10A. Counterfeit of W-MA-340-010-G030.
Rarity: *None known*

$20 • W-MA-340-020-C050
Left: Portraits. ***Center:*** 20 / Eagle perched on shield, Ship / 20. ***Right:*** Portraits. ***Engraver:*** Murray, Draper, Fairman & Co. ***Comments:*** H-US2-C92 Design 20A. Counterfeit of W-MA-340-020-G050.
Rarity: *None known*

$50 • W-MA-340-050-C090
Left: Eagle / Portrait of Martha Washington / Minerva. ***Center:*** 50 / Eagle perched on shield, Ship / 50. ***Right:*** Eagle / Portrait of Benjamin Franklin / Female portrait. ***Engraver:*** Fairman, Draper, Underwood & Co. ***Comments:*** H-US2-C102. Design 50B. Counterfeit of W-MA-340-050-G090.
Rarity: *None known*

$100 • W-MA-340-100-C110
Left: Portraits. ***Center:*** 100 / Eagle perched on shield, Ship / 100. ***Right:*** Portraits. ***Engraver:*** Murray, Draper, Fairman & Co. ***Comments:*** H-US2-C108. Design 100A. Counterfeit of W-MA-340-100-G110.
Rarity: *None known*

$100 • W-MA-340-100-C120
Left: Eagle / Portrait of George Washington / Minerva. ***Center:*** 100 / Eagle perched on shield, Ship / 100. ***Right:*** Eagle / Portrait of Benjamin Franklin / Female portrait. ***Engraver:*** Fairman, Draper, Underwood & Co. ***Comments:*** H-US2-C110. Design 100B. Counterfeit of W-MA-340-100-G120.
Rarity: *None known*

Blackstone Bank
1851–1864
W-MA-350

History: The Blackstone Bank commenced business on September 16, 1851, at the corner of Blackstone and Hanover streets.[38] In 1864 the bank was located on Union Street.

The bank's capital was authorized at $250,000, of which only $150,000 was paid in. It was increased to $350,000 in 1853. By 1855 it was $750,000, where it remained until 1864. Profits in 1853 amounted to $16,475, and stocks were valued at $105.

The *Annual Report of Bank Commissioners* reported these figures for 1854: circulation $233,995; specie $34,019.34; real estate $4,120.73. Circulation increased to $265,726 in 1857, where it remained through 1860. Bills of this bank and other New England states amounted to $92,362.15.

The Blackstone National Bank was chartered on September 10, 1864, and assumed the interests of the Blackstone Bank.

Numismatic Commentary: Genuine notes of the Blackstone Bank are very hard to locate. Collectors lucky enough may come across one with a vignette of the Quincy Market Place or Haymarket Square.

VALID ISSUES

$1 • W-MA-350-001-G010
Left: View of Haymarket Square / 1. ***Center:*** 1 on 1. ***Right:*** ONE / Woman shading eyes with hand. ***Engraver:*** New England Bank Note Co. / Rawdon, Wright, Hatch & Edson. ***Comments:*** H-MA-110-G2. Aug. 1, 185_. 1850s.
Rarity: —

$1 • W-MA-350-001-G010a CC

Overprint: Red ONE. ***Engraver:*** New England Bank Note Co. / Rawdon, Wright, Hatch & Edson. ***Comments:*** H-MA-110-G2a. Similar to W-MA-350-001-G010. Proof. August 1, 185_. 1850s.
Rarity: URS-2
Proof $1,500
Selected auction price: Stack's Bowers Galleries, August 2014, Lot 2054, Proof $1,410

$1 • W-MA-350-001-G020
Left: 1 / Sailing ship. ***Center:*** Shipyard scene, Man seated on timber working, Child picking up chips. ***Right:*** 1 / Blacksmith with sledge on shoulder. ***Engraver:*** New England Bank Note Co. ***Comments:*** H-MA-110-G4. Aug. __, 18__. 1850s.
Rarity: —

$1 • W-MA-350-001-G020a
Tint: Green. ***Engraver:*** New England Bank Note Co. / American Bank Note Co. ***Comments:*** H-MA-110-G4a. Similar to W-MA-350-001-G020 but with additional engraver imprint. Aug. __, 18__. 1860s.
Rarity: URS-2
VG $1,000

$2 • W-MA-350-002-G030

Left: View of Haymarket Square / TWO. ***Center:*** 2. ***Right:*** 2 / Sailor standing. ***Engraver:*** New England Bank Note Co. / Rawdon, Wright, Hatch & Edson. ***Comments:*** H-MA-110-G6. Aug. 1, 185_. 1850s.

Rarity: URS-3
Proof $2,000

$2 • W-MA-350-002-G030a

CC

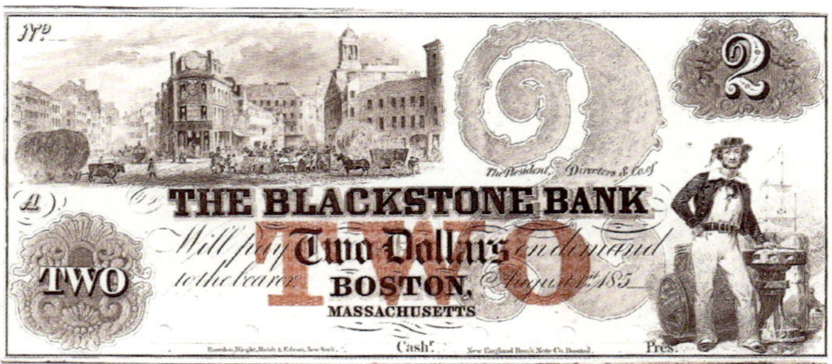

Overprint: Red TWO. ***Engraver:*** New England Bank Note Co. / Rawdon, Wright, Hatch & Edson. ***Comments:*** H-MA-110-G6a. Similar to W-MA-350-002-G030. Proof. August 1, 185_. 1850s.

Rarity: URS-2
Proof $3,000

$2 • W-MA-350-002-G040

Left: TWO / Sailor seated on bale holding spyglass, Woman in clouds / TWO. ***Right:*** 2 / Child with rabbits. ***Engraver:*** New England Bank Note Co. ***Comments:*** H-MA-110-G8. Aug. __, 18__.

Rarity: —

$2 • W-MA-350-002-G040a

Tint: Green. ***Engraver:*** New England Bank Note Co. / American Bank Note Co. ***Comments:*** H-MA-110-G8a. Similar to W-MA-350-002-G040 but with additional engraver imprint. Aug. __, 18__. 1860s.

Rarity: —

$3 • W-MA-350-003-G050

Left: View of Haymarket Square / 3. ***Center:*** 3. ***Right:*** 3 / Sailing ship. ***Engraver:*** New England Bank Note Co. / Rawdon, Wright, Hatch & Edson. ***Comments:*** H-MA-110-G10. Aug. 1, 185_. 1850s.

Rarity: —

$3 • W-MA-350-003-G050a

CC

Overprint: Red THREE. ***Engraver:*** New England Bank Note Co. / Rawdon, Wright, Hatch & Edson. ***Comments:*** H-MA-110-G10a. Similar to W-MA-350-003-G050. Proof. August 1, 185_. 1850s.

Rarity: URS-2
Proof $3,000

$3 • W-MA-350-003-G060

CC

Engraver: New England Bank Note Co. ***Comments:*** H-MA-110-G12. August __, 18__. 1850s.

Rarity: URS-4
Proof $3,000

$3 • W-MA-350-003-G060a

Tint: Green. ***Engraver:*** New England Bank Note Co. / American Bank Note Co. ***Comments:*** H-MA-110-G12a. Similar to W-MA-350-003-G060 but with additional engraver imprint. Aug. __, 18__. 1860s.

Rarity: —

$5 • W-MA-350-005-G070

Left: View of Haymarket Square / FIVE. ***Center:*** FIVE on 5. ***Right:*** 5 / MASSACHUSETTS / Indian woman on shield. ***Engraver:*** New England Bank Note Co. / Rawdon, Wright, Hatch & Edson. ***Comments:*** H-MA-110-G14. Aug. 1, 185_. 1850s.

Rarity: —

$5 • W-MA-350-005-G070a

HA

Overprint: Red FIVE. ***Engraver:*** New England Bank Note Co. / Rawdon, Wright, Hatch & Edson. ***Comments:*** H-MA-110-G14a. Similar to W-MA-350-005-G070. Proof. August 1, 185_. 1850s.

Rarity: URS-3
Proof $1,500

$5 • W-MA-350-005-G080

JF

Tint: Green FIVE on panel of microlettering. ***Engraver:*** New England Bank Note Co. / American Bank Note Co. ***Comments:*** H-MA-110-G16a. Proof. August __, 18__. 1860s.

Rarity: URS-3
Proof $2,500

$10 • W-MA-350-010-G090

Left: View of Haymarket Square / 10. ***Center:*** Medallion X bearing female portrait. ***Right:*** 10 / Woman standing. ***Engraver:*** New England Bank Note Co. / Rawdon, Wright, Hatch & Edson. ***Comments:*** H-MA-110-G18. Aug. 1, 185_. 1850s.

Rarity: —

$10 • W-MA-350-010-G090a CC

Overprint: Red TEN. ***Engraver:*** New England Bank Note Co. / Rawdon, Wright, Hatch & Edson. ***Comments:*** H-MA-110-G18a. Similar to W-MA-350-010-G090. Proof. August 1, 185_. 1850s.

Rarity: URS-3

Proof $3,000

$10 • W-MA-350-010-G100 HA

Tint: Green counters and panel of microlettering. ***Engraver:*** New England Bank Note Co. / American Bank Note Co. ***Comments:*** H-MA-110-G20a. Proof. Aug. __, 18__. 1860s.

Rarity: URS-2

Proof $3,800

Selected auction price: Stack's Bowers Galleries, August 2014, Lot 2055, Proof $3,818

$20 • W-MA-350-020-G110

Left: 20 / Woman, eagle, and shield. ***Center:*** View of Haymarket Square. ***Right:*** 20. ***Engraver:*** New England Bank Note Co. / Rawdon, Wright, Hatch & Edson. ***Comments:*** H-MA-110-G22. Aug. 1, 185_. 1850s.

Rarity: —

$20 • W-MA-350-020-G120 CC

Tint: Green TWENTY on panel of microlettering. ***Engraver:*** New England Bank Note Co. / American Bank Note Co. ***Comments:*** H-MA-110-G24a. 18__. 1860s.

Rarity: URS-2

Proof $4,500

Selected auction price: Stack's Bowers Galleries, August 2014, Lot 2056, Proof $4,700

$50 • W-MA-350-050-G130

Left: View of Haymarket Square. ***Center:*** 50 / Cherub. ***Right:*** FIFTY / Woman seated holding shield bearing 50. ***Engraver:*** New England Bank Note Co. / Rawdon, Wright, Hatch & Edson. ***Comments:*** H-MA-110-G26. Aug. 1, 185_. 1850s.

Rarity: —

$50 • W-MA-350-050-G140 HA

Tint: Green FIFTY on panel of microlettering. ***Engraver:*** New England Bank Note Co. / American Bank Note Co. ***Comments:*** H-MA-110-G28a. Proof. 18__. 1860s.

Rarity: URS-2

Proof $7,000

Selected auction price: Stack's Bowers Galleries, August 2014, Lot 2057, Proof $7,050

$100 • W-MA-350-100-G150

Left: Woman seated / 100. ***Center:*** View of Haymarket Square. ***Right:*** 100 / Woman with anchor. ***Engraver:*** New England Bank Note Co. / Rawdon, Wright, Hatch & Edson. ***Comments:*** H-MA-110-G30. Aug. 1, 185_. 1850s.

Rarity: —

$100 • W-MA-350-100-G160

Left: C / Female portrait. ***Center:*** Train and steamboat / Justice seated by shield and strongbox. ***Right:*** 100. ***Tint:*** Green. ***Engraver:*** New England Bank Note Co. / American Bank Note Co. ***Comments:*** H-MA-110-G32a. 18__. 1860s.

Rarity: —

$500 • W-MA-350-500-G170

Left: 500 / Eagle and shield. ***Center:*** Haymarket Square. ***Right:*** 500 / Male portrait. ***Engraver:*** New England Bank Note Co. / Rawdon, Wright, Hatch & Edson. ***Comments:*** H-MA-110-G34. 18__. 1850s.

Rarity: —

$500 • W-MA-350-500-G180

Left: Marine view with ships / 500. ***Center:*** D. ***Right:*** 500 / Portrait of Benjamin Franklin. ***Tint:*** Green. ***Engraver:*** New England Bank Note Co. / American Bank Note Co. ***Comments:*** H-MA-110-G36a. 18__. 1860s.

Rarity: —

Non-Valid Issues

$3 • W-MA-350-003-C060

Left: Portrait of George Washington / 3. ***Center:*** Two men, one woman. ***Right:*** 3 / Woman with 3. ***Engraver:*** New England Bank Note Co. ***Comments:*** H-Unlisted. Counterfeit of W-MA-350-003-G060. Photographic counterfeit. Aug. __, 18__. 1850s.

Rarity: —

$3 • W-MA-350-003-R010

Engraver: New England Bank Note Co. / Rawdon, Wright, Hatch & Edson. ***Comments:*** H-MA-110-R5. Raised from W-MA-350-001-G010 or G010a. Aug. 1, 185_. 1850s.

Rarity: —

$3 • W-MA-350-003-S010

Left: Spread eagle on shield / 3. ***Center:*** 3. ***Right:*** THREE / Female portrait. ***Comments:*** H-MA-110-S5. 18__. 1850s.

Rarity: —

$5 • W-MA-350-005-S020

Left: Eagle with ribbon in its beak on shield / FIVE. ***Center:*** V. ***Right:*** 5 / Woman leaning on column. ***Engraver:*** Baldwin, Adams & Co. ***Comments:*** H-MA-110-S10. 185_. 1850s.

Rarity: —

$10 • W-MA-350-010-R020

Engraver: New England Bank Note Co. / Rawdon, Wright, Hatch & Edson. ***Comments:*** H-MA-110-R10. Raised from W-MA-350-001-G010 or G010a. Aug. 1, 185_. 1850s.

Rarity: —

$50 • W-MA-350-050-R030

Engraver: New England Bank Note Co. / Rawdon, Wright, Hatch & Edson. ***Comments:*** H-MA-110-R15. Raised from W-MA-350-001-G010 or G010a. Aug. 1, 185_. 1850s.

Rarity: —

$50 • W-MA-350-050-S030

Left: Portrait of George Washington. ***Center:*** Battle of Bunker Hill. ***Right:*** Portrait of George Washington. ***Engraver:*** New England Bank Note Co. ***Comments:*** H-MA-110-S15. 18__. 1850s.

Rarity: —

Boston Bank

1803–1865

W-MA-360

History: The Boston Bank was incorporated on June 23, 1803. It was located at 48 State Street in a building held by the U.S. branch bank. In July that year, the Boston Bank moved to the estate of Christopher Marshall, 50 State Street, and there erected its first building. Operations opened there in September 1804. Initially, the Commonwealth of Massachusetts was listed as a stockholder, resulting in complaints that the state should not be a partner in a bank.

On April 13, 1803, Jonathan Jackson was elected president, accompanied by Peleg Coffin as cashier. Other officers elected included Thomas C. Amory, Samuel P. Gardner, Joseph Hall, Peter C. Brooks, John Codman, Thomas K. Jones, James Lloyd Jr., James Perkins, Daniel Sargent Jr., Jonathan Mason, Adam Babcock, and Jonathan Jackson. In 1807 capital was $1,800,000. The charter was renewed in 1812. Capital was decreased to $900,000 by 1823. The bank's charter was renewed again in 1827 with a capital of $600,000. The figure after that was $900,000 until 1857.

By 1857 the bank's bills in circulation amounted to $250,826, bills of this bank and other New England states was $131,878.67, and real estate was valued at $65,000.

In April 1865, the stockholders were given a charter for a National Banking Association. As the name Boston National Bank was already taken, the founders had to settle for the title of the Old National Bank. This firm succeeded the business of the state bank.

Numismatic Commentary: At present, there are plenty of issues in the marketplace from the Boston Bank, non-valid included, to satisfy a certain amount of collector demand. The longevity of the bank assured this.

Valid Issues

$1 • W-MA-360-001-G010

CC

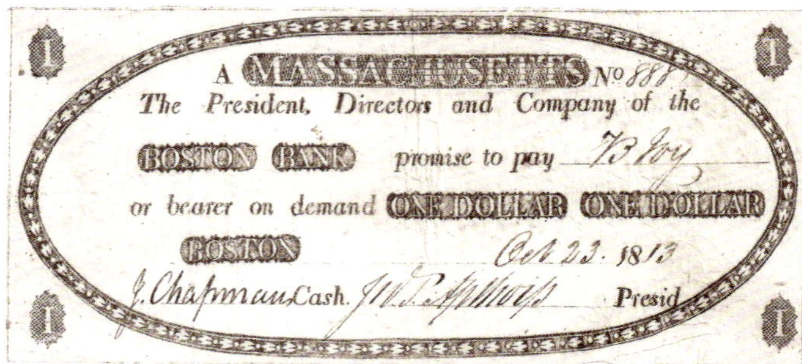

Engraver: Perkins. ***Comments:*** H-MA-115-G20. 18__. 1810s.

Rarity: URS-6

F $250; **EF** $350

$1 • W-MA-360-001-G020

Center: 1 / 1 / Oval bearing white flower buds / ONE / 1 / 1. ***Engraver:*** PSSP. ***Comments:*** H-MA-115-G22. 18__. 1810s.

Rarity: —

$1 • W-MA-360-001-G030

Comments: H-MA-115-G24. No description available. 18__. 1820s–1830s.

Rarity: *None known*

$1 • W-MA-360-001-G040

Left: ONE on 1 / Indian standing / ONE. ***Center:*** 1 / Ships / 1. ***Right:*** ONE on 1 / Ship / ONE. ***Engraver:*** PSSP / New England Bank Note Co. ***Comments:*** H-MA-115-G28. 18__. 1830s–1850s.

Rarity: —

$1 • W-MA-360-001-G040a

Overprint: Red ONE. ***Engraver:*** PSSP / New England Bank Note Co. ***Comments:*** H-MA-115-G28a. Similar to W-MA-350-001-G040. 18__. 1850s.

Rarity: —

$1 • W-MA-360-001-G040b

HA

Overprint: Red ONE. ***Engraver:*** PSSP / New England Bank Note Co. / ABNCo. monogram. ***Comments:*** H-MA-115-G28b. Similar to W-MA-350-001-G040 but with additional engraver imprint. 18__. 1850s–1860s.

Rarity: URS-3
F $500; **VF** $800

$2 • W-MA-360-002-G050

Center: 2 / 2 / Oval bearing white flower buds / 2 / 2. ***Engraver:*** PSSP. ***Comments:*** H-MA-115-G36. 18__. 1800s.

Rarity: —

$2 • W-MA-360-002-G060

Center: 2 / 2 / Oval bearing white flower buds / TWO / 2 / 2. ***Engraver:*** PSSP. ***Comments:*** H-MA-115-G38. 18__. 1810s.

Rarity: —

$2 • W-MA-360-002-G070

Comments: H-MA-115-G40. No description available. 18__. 1820s–1830s.

Rarity: *None known*

$2 • W-MA-360-002-G080

Left: 2 / Mercury standing / TWO. ***Center:*** 2 / View of Boston Harbor / 2. ***Right:*** 2 / Indian in shield / TWO. ***Engraver:*** PSSP / New England Bank Note Co. ***Comments:*** H-MA-115-G44. 18__. 1830s–1850s.

Rarity: URS-3
F $500; **VF** $800

$2 • W-MA-360-002-G080a

Overprint: Red TWO. ***Engraver:*** PSSP / New England Bank Note Co. ***Comments:*** H-MA-115-G44a. Similar to W-MA-360-002-G080. 18__. 1850s.

Rarity: —

$2 • W-MA-360-002-G080b

CC

Overprint: Red TWO. ***Engraver:*** PSSP / New England Bank Note Co. / ABNCo. monogram. ***Comments:*** H-MA-115-G44b. Similar to W-MA-360-002-G080 but with additional engraver imprint. 18__. 1850s–1860s.

Rarity: URS-3
VF $500

$3 • W-MA-360-003-G090

Center: 3 / 3 / Oval bearing white flower buds / 3 / 3. ***Engraver:*** PSSP. ***Comments:*** H-MA-115-G50. 18__. 1800s.

Rarity: —

$3 • W-MA-360-003-G100

Center: 3 / 3 / Oval bearing white flower buds / THREE / 3 / 3. ***Engraver:*** PSSP. ***Comments:*** H-MA-115-G52. 18__. 1810s.

Rarity: —

$3 • W-MA-360-003-G110

Comments: H-MA-115-G54. No description available. 18__. 1820s–1830s.

Rarity: *None known*

$3 • W-MA-360-003-G120

Left: 3 / Justice. ***Center:*** 3 / View of Boston Harbor / 3. ***Right:*** 3 / Woman with shield bearing 3. ***Engraver:*** PSSP / New England Bank Note Co. ***Comments:*** H-MA-115-G58. 18__. 1830s–1850s.

Rarity: —

$3 • W-MA-360-003-G120a

Overprint: Red THREE. ***Engraver:*** PSSP / New England Bank Note Co. ***Comments:*** H-MA-115-G58a. Similar to W-MA-360-003-G120. 18__. 1850s.

Rarity: —

$3 • W-MA-360-003-G120b

NJW

Overprint: Red THREE. ***Engraver:*** PSSP / New England Bank Note Co. / ABNCo. monogram. ***Comments:*** H-MA-115-G58b. Similar to W-MA-360-003-G120 but with additional engraver imprint. 18__. 1850s–1860s.

Rarity: URS-3
F $750

$5 • W-MA-360-005-G130

Left: 5 / FIVE / 5 vertically. ***Center:*** Eagle atop wreath / Indian. ***Right:*** 5 / 5. ***Comments:*** H-MA-115-G64. 1800s–1810s.

Rarity: URS-7
F $250; **EF** $400

$5 • W-MA-360-005-G130a

Comments: H-MA-115-G68. Similar to W-MA-360-005-G130 but with different date. 1810s–1820s.

Rarity: URS-7
F $250; **EF** $400

$5 • W-MA-360-005-G140

Left: 5 / Man standing, woman seated / FIVE. ***Center:*** 5 / View of Boston Harbor / 5. ***Right:*** 5 / Ships / FIVE. ***Engraver:*** PSSP / New England Bank Note Co. ***Comments:*** H-MA-115-G74. 18__. 1830s–1850s.

Rarity: —

$5 • W-MA-360-005-G140a

JF

Overprint: Red FIVE. ***Engraver:*** PSSP / New England Bank Note Co. ***Comments:*** H-MA-115-G74a. Similar to W-MA-360-005-G140. 18__. 1850s.

Rarity: URS-4
F $350; **EF** $600

$5 • W-MA-360-005-G140b

Overprint: Red FIVE. ***Engraver:*** PSSP / New England Bank Note Co. / ABNCo. monogram. ***Comments:*** H-MA-115-G74b. Similar to W-MA-360-005-G140 but with additional engraver imprint. 18__. 1850s–1860s.

Rarity: —

$10 • W-MA-360-010-G150

Comments: H-MA-115-G80. Similar to W-MA-360-005-G130 but with different denomination. 1800s–1810s.

Rarity: —

$10 • W-MA-360-010-G150a

Comments: H-MA-115-G84. Similar to W-MA-360-005-G130a but with different denomination. 1810s–1820s.

Rarity: —

$10 • W-MA-360-010-G160

Left: Woman kneeling, unveiling shield bearing X / 10. ***Center:*** X. ***Right:*** Panel bearing 10. ***Comments:*** H-MA-115-G90. 18__. 1850s.

Rarity: —

$20 • W-MA-360-020-G170

Left: Panel bearing state arms / 20 vertically. ***Center:*** Alternating flower garlands and gridwork segments. ***Right:*** 20 / 20 vertically. ***Comments:*** H-MA-115-G96. 18__. 1810s

Rarity: —

$20 • W-MA-360-020-G180

Left: Sailor at wheel of ship / 20. ***Right:*** Panel bearing TWENTY vertically. ***Comments:*** H-MA-115-G100. 18__. 1850s.

Rarity: —

$50 • W-MA-360-050-G190

Left: Panel bearing state arms / 50 / 50 vertically. ***Center:*** Alternating flower garlands and gridwork segments. ***Right:*** 50 / 50 vertically. ***Comments:*** H-MA-115-G106. 18__. 1810s.

Rarity: —

$50 • W-MA-360-050-G200

Left: 50 / Girl in shield with sword. ***Center:*** Sailing ship / FIFTY. ***Right:*** 50 / Woman holding shield. ***Tint:*** Green die bearing 50 and FIFTY. ***Engraver:*** American Bank Note Co. ***Comments:*** H-MA-115-G110a. 186_. 1860s.

Rarity: URS-2
Proof $5,000

$100 • W-MA-360-100-G210

Left: Panel bearing state arms / 100 / 100 vertically. ***Center:*** Alternating flower garlands and gridwork segments. ***Right:*** 100 / 100 vertically. ***Comments:*** H-MA-115-G112. 18__. 1810s.

Rarity: —

$100 • W-MA-360-100-G220

Left: 100 / Sailor with horn leaning on side of ship. ***Center:*** View of Boston Bay. ***Right:*** 100 / Beehive. ***Tint:*** Green C C. ***Engraver:*** American Bank Note Co. ***Comments:*** H-MA-115-G116a. 186_. 1860s.

Rarity: —

$500 • W-MA-360-500-G230

Left: 500 / Sailor standing beside capstan. ***Center:*** 500. ***Right:*** Ships / 500. ***Engraver:*** American Bank Note Co. ***Comments:*** H-MA-115-G120. 1850s–1860s.

Rarity: —

$1,000 • W-MA-360-1000-G240

Left: M / Woman with balance, eagle, and wreath. ***Center:*** 1000. ***Right:*** Ships / 1000. ***Engraver:*** American Bank Note Co. ***Comments:*** H-MA-115-G124. 1850s–1860s.

Rarity: —

Non-Valid Issues

$1 • W-MA-360-001-S010

Left: ONE vertically. ***Center:*** 1 / Spread eagle / 1. ***Bottom center:*** ONE. ***Right:*** 1 / ONE / 1. ***Engraver:*** Hatch & Co. ***Comments:*** H-MA-115-S5. July 1, 18__. 1847.

Rarity: URS-5
VG $30; **F** $295

$1 • W-MA-360-001-A010

SI

Engraver: Wellstood, Hanks, Hay & Whiting. ***Comments:*** H-MA-115-A5. Altered from $1 Merchants Bank, Stillwater, Minnesota. July 20, 1855.

Rarity: URS-6
F $150

$2 • W-MA-360-002-S020

NJW

Engraver: PSSP. ***Comments:*** H-MA-115-S10. 18__. 1820s.

Rarity: URS-8
VF $75

$2 • W-MA-360-002-N010

Center: Train on bridge. ***Comments:*** H-MA-115-N5.

Rarity: —

$2 • W-MA-360-002-A020

CC

Comments: H-MA-115-A10. Altered from $2 Merchants Bank, Stillwater, Minnesota. July 20, 1855.

Rarity: URS-8
VF $75

$5 • W-MA-360-005-C130

CC

Comments: H-MA-115-C64. Counterfeit of W-MA-360-005-G130. 1810s.

Rarity: URS-4
F $200

$5 • W-MA-360-005-C130a

CC

Comments: H-MA-115-C68. Counterfeit of W-MA-360-005-G130a. Similar to W-MA-360-005-C130 but with different date. 1820s.

Rarity: URS-4
F $200

$5 • W-MA-360-005-S030

ANS

Engraver: Draper, Toppan & Co. ***Comments:*** H-MA-115-S15. From a modified plate originally for $5 Lebanon Miami Banking Co., Lebanon, Ohio. 18__. 1850s.

Rarity: URS-6
VG $45; **F** $75

$5 • W-MA-360-005-A030

Left: Panel bearing FIVE vertically. ***Center:*** 5 / Ships, Eagle on shield and laurel, Ships / FIVE. ***Right:*** 5 on die supported by boy riding on dolphin. ***Engraver:*** Wellstood, Hanks, Hay & Whiting. ***Comments:*** H-MA-115-A15. Altered from $5 Citizens Bank, Washington, D.C. 18__. 1850s.

Rarity: —

$10 • W-MA-360-010-C160

Comments: H-MA-115-C90. Counterfeit of W-MA-360-010-G160. 18__. 1850s.

Rarity: —

$10 • W-MA-360-010-R010

Engraver: PSSP / New England Bank Note Co. ***Comments:*** H-MA-115-R5. Raised likely from W-MA-360-001-G040. 18__. 1850s.

Rarity: —

$10 • W-MA-360-010-A040

Left: Diagonal X / TEN. ***Center:*** Woman seated on rock, Train / Ceres with sheaf on back. ***Right:*** 10 / Portrait of George Washington. ***Overprint:*** Red TEN. ***Engraver:*** Bald, Cousland & Co. / Baldwin, Bald & Cousland. ***Comments:*** H-MA-115-A20. Altered from $10 Southern Bank of Georgia, Bainbridge, Georgia. 18__. 1860s.

Rarity: —

$20 • W-MA-360-020-R020

Engraver: PSSP / New England Bank Note Co. ***Comments:*** H-MA-115-R10. Raised likely from W-MA-360-001-G040. 18__. 1850s.

Rarity: —

$50 • W-MA-360-050-R030

Engraver: New England Bank Note Co. ***Comments:*** H-MA-115-R15. Raised likely from W-MA-360-001-G040. 18__. 1850s.

Rarity: —

$100 • W-MA-360-100-R040

Engraver: PSSP / New England Bank Note Co. ***Comments:*** H-MA-115-R20. Raised likely from W-MA-360-001-G040. 18__. 1840s–1850s.

Rarity: —

Boylston Bank
1845–1864
W-MA-370

History: The Boylston Bank was chartered in March 1845. It opened for business located on the corner of Washington and Boylston streets. The beginning capital for the bank was $150,000. By 1849 it had increased to $200,000 and to $250,000 in 1852. In 1855 the capital was $400,000, where it remained through 1864. In October 1849, bills in circulation were $135,790. From 1857 to 1860 the same was $191,077.

The bank continued under its state charter until its affairs were assumed after January 1, 1875, by the Boylston National Bank of Boston.[39]

Numismatic Commentary: Genuine notes are fairly hard to obtain. A collector might have to settle for a non-valid note, at least temporarily.

Valid Issues

$1 • W-MA-370-001-G010

CC

Engraver: New England Bank Note Co. ***Comments:*** H-MA-120-G2. 18__. 1845–1850s.

Rarity: URS-6
VG $100; **VF** $250; **EF** $1,200

$1 • W-MA-370-001-G010a

Left: Woman in 1 with basket on head / ONE. ***Center:*** Portrait of George Washington, Ships. ***Right:*** Woman in 1 with basket on head / ONE ONE. ***Engraver:*** New England Bank Note Co. / ABNCo. monogram. ***Comments:*** H-MA-120-G2a. Similar to W-MA-370-001-G010 but with additional engraver imprint. 18__. 1850s–1860s.

Rarity: —

$1 • W-MA-370-001-G010b

CJF

Overprint: Green ONE. ***Engraver:*** New England Bank Note Co. / ABNCo. monogram. ***Comments:*** H-Unlisted. Similar to W-MA-370-001-G010 but with different date and additional engraver imprint. Remainder. January 1, 1859. 1850s–1860s.

Rarity: URS-3
Unc-Rem $500

$2 • W-MA-370-002-G020

Left: TWO / Eagle on 2 / TWO. ***Center:*** Blacksmith with anvil. ***Right:*** TWO / Eagle on 2 / TWO. ***Engraver:*** New England Bank Note Co. ***Comments:*** H-MA-120-G4. 18__. 1845–1850s.

Rarity: —

$2 • W-MA-370-002-G020a

Engraver: New England Bank Note Co. / ABNCo. monogram. ***Comments:*** H-MA-120-G4a. Similar to W-MA-370-002-G020 but with additional engraver imprint. 18__. 1850s–1860s.

Rarity: —

$3 • W-MA-370-003-G030

Left: Eagle beside 3 / THREE. ***Center:*** Steamship and sailing ships. ***Right:*** THREE / Indian man standing beside 3. ***Comments:*** H-MA-120-G6. Beware of spurious imitation W-MA-370-003-S030. 18__. 1840s–1850s.

Rarity: —

$3 • W-MA-370-003-G030a

Engraver: ABNCo. monogram. ***Comments:*** H-MA-120-G6a. Similar to W-MA-370-003-G030 but with additional engraver imprint. 18__. 1850s–1860s.

Rarity: —

$5 • W-MA-370-005-G040

Left: FIVE across V / Man, boy, and sheep on V. ***Center:*** Eagle. ***Right:*** 5 / Man, boy, and sheep on V. ***Comments:*** H-MA-120-G8. 18__. 1840s–1850s.

Rarity: —

$5 • W-MA-370-005-G040a

Engraver: ABNCo. monogram. ***Comments:*** H-MA-120-G8a. Similar to W-MA-370-005-G040 but with additional engraver imprint. 18__. 1850s–1860s.

Rarity: —

$10 • W-MA-370-010-G050

Left: X / Two men with horses. ***Center:*** Portrait of Christopher Columbus / X / Portrait of George Washington. ***Right:*** 10 / Men and horses on wharf. ***Engraver:*** New England Bank Note Co. ***Comments:*** H-MA-120-G10. 18__. 1840s–1850s.

Rarity: —

$10 • W-MA-370-010-G050a

JF

Overprint: Red TEN. ***Engraver:*** New England Bank Note Co. / ABNCo. monogram. ***Comments:*** H-MA-120-G10a. Similar to W-MA-370-010-G050 but with additional engraver imprint. 18__. 1850s–1860s.

Rarity: URS-2
VF $4,000

$20 • W-MA-370-020-G060

Left: 20 / Woman seated with book on lap, opening chest. *Center:* XX / Eagle on rock / XX. *Right:* 20 / Ship in harbor. *Engraver:* New England Bank Note Co. *Comments:* H-MA-120-G12. 18__. 1840s–1850s.

Rarity: —

$20 • W-MA-370-020-G070

Left: 20 / Woman seated. *Center:* Woman stepping into stream. *Right:* 20 / Female portrait. *Tint:* Green 20 / 20. *Engraver:* American Bank Note Co. *Comments:* H-MA-120-G14a. 1860s.

Rarity: —

$50 • W-MA-370-050-G080

Left: FIFTY / Woman standing with wreath and flowers / FIFTY. *Center:* 50 / Man restraining prancing horse / 50. *Right:* FIFTY / Woman standing with cornucopia against shoulder / FIFTY. *Engraver:* New England Bank Note Co. *Comments:* H-MA-120-G16. 18__. 1840s–1850s.

Rarity: —

$50 • W-MA-370-050-G090

Left: Street scene, Men loading wagon. *Center:* State arms. *Right:* 50 / Woman leaning on column, holding torch. *Tint:* 50 and FIFTY. *Engraver:* American Bank Note Co. *Comments:* H-MA-120-G18a. 1860s.

Rarity: —

$100 • W-MA-370-100-G100

Left: ONE HUNDRED on 100 / Portrait of William Henry Harrison. *Center:* Wharf scene, Men loading wagon with barrels. *Right:* ONE HUNDRED on 100 / Portrait of Christopher Columbus. *Engraver:* New England Bank Note Co. *Comments:* H-MA-120-G20. 18__. 1840s–1850s.

Rarity: —

$100 • W-MA-370-100-G110

Left: 100 / Woman standing by column. *Center:* Soldier talking, one seated on cannon, Fort. *Right:* C / Woman seated with shield bearing view of Boston. *Tint:* Green. *Engraver:* American Bank Note Co. *Comments:* H-MA-120-G22a. 1860s.

Rarity: —

$500 • W-MA-370-500-G120

Left: Woman seated on sheaves, Men reaping, Man on horse / 500. *Center:* 500 / D. *Right:* 500 vertically. *Engraver:* Rawdon, Wright, Hatch & Edson. *Comments:* H-MA-120-G24. 18__. 1850s.

Rarity: —

$500 • W-MA-370-500-G130

Left: D / D. *Center:* "Landing of the Pilgrims" / Female portrait. *Right:* Woman seated with globe and book. *Tint:* Green. *Engraver:* American Bank Note Co. *Comments:* H-MA-120-G26a. 1860s.

Rarity: —

Non-Valid Issues

$1 • W-MA-370-001-C010

Comments: H-MA-120-C2. Counterfeit of W-MA-370-001-G010.

Rarity: —

F $165

$1 • W-MA-370-001-A010

HA

Overprint: Red ONE. *Engraver:* Danforth, Wright & Co. *Comments:* H-MA-120-A5. Altered from $1 Bank of Washtenaw, Washtenaw, Michigan series. May 1, 1854. 1850s.

Rarity: URS-8

VG $75; **F** $100; **EF** $150

$2 • W-MA-370-002-S010

Left: Portrait / 2. *Center:* Train. *Right:* Portrait of Benjamin Franklin / 2. *Comments:* H-MA-120-S5.

Rarity: —

$2 • W-MA-370-002-S020

Left: TWO / Portrait. *Center:* Man and child under the tree, Boy and horses, Town and canal locks. *Right:* Soldier. *Engraver:* New England Bank Note Co. *Comments:* H-MA-120-S10. 18__. 1850s.

Rarity: —

$2 • W-MA-370-002-N010

Left: Woman. *Center:* Portrait of George Washington. *Right:* Woman. *Comments:* H-MA-120-N5.

Rarity: —

$3 • W-MA-370-003-S030

ANS

Engraver: Rawdon, Wright, Hatch & Edson. *Comments:* H-MA-120-S15. Spurious design imitating a rough verbal description of W-MA-370-003-G030. 18__. 1861.

Rarity: URS-8

VG $75; **F** $100

$10 • W-MA-370-010-N020

Center: Two women flanking sheaf and sickle. ***Overprint:*** Red X X. ***Comments:*** H-MA-120-N10.

Rarity: URS-6
G $14; **F** $100

$10 • W-MA-370-010-N030

Center: Eagle. ***Comments:*** H-MA-120-N20.

Rarity: —

$10 • W-MA-370-010-N040

Center: X / Woman with shield, Ship / Male portrait. ***Comments:*** H-MA-120-N25.

Rarity: —

Broadway Bank
1853–1864
W-MA-380

History: The Broadway Bank was incorporated on April 28, 1853, with an authorized capital of $100,000. It was located at 10 Broadway in South Boston and commenced business in December of the same year. Selected values in 1851 included: capital $150,000; circulation $50,857; specie $5,912.84; real estate $8,644.10.

By 1853 capital had decreased to $100,000. In 1854 the capital was increased to $150,000, where it remained through 1864.[40] The circulation of the bank amounted to $92,818 in 1857 and was $112,371 in 1863. Specie was $5,401.53 in 1857.

After the charter of the Broadway National Bank on October 25, 1864, the national bank assumed the business of the state bank.

See also listing under South Boston, W-MA-3030.

Numismatic Commentary: This is one of the hardest Boston banks to acquire a note from. Obtaining two or three in a collecting lifetime would be a challenge.

VALID ISSUES

$1 • W-MA-380-001-G010 CJF

Overprint: Red ONE. ***Engraver:*** Rawdon, Wright, Hatch & Edson / ABNCo. monogram. ***Comments:*** H-MA-1150-G2b. Similar to W-MA-3030-001-G010 but with additional engraver imprint. 18__. 1850s–1860s.

Rarity: URS-3
F $700; **VF** $1,000

$2 • W-MA-380-002-G020 CC

Overprint: Red TWO. ***Engraver:*** Rawdon, Wright, Hatch & Edson / New England Bank Note Co. / ABNCo. monogram. ***Comments:*** H-Unlisted. Similar to W-MA-3030-002-G020 but with additional engraver imprint. 18__. 1850s–1860s.

Rarity: —

NON-VALID ISSUES

$10 • W-MA-380-010-R010 CC

Engraver: Rawdon, Wright, Hatch & Edson / New England Bank Note Co. ***Comments:*** H-MA-1150-R10. Raised from W-MA-3030-001-G010. 18__. 1850s.

Rarity: URS-3
VG $500; **F** $750

City Bank
1822–1864
W-MA-390

History: The City Bank was chartered in February 1822. Its office was located at 61 State Street. The authorized capital was $1,000,000.

By 1838 the full amount of capital was paid in, where it remained through 1864. Bank figures for 1838 included these: bills in circulation $128,375; net profits on hand $107,055.48; balances due to other banks $34,025.57; cash deposited $442,360.12; cash deposited bearing interest $567,475.22; total amount due from banks $2,379,324.30; gold, silver, and other coined metals in the banking house $58,757.20; real estate $31,624.68; bills of other banks incorporated in this state $105,836; bills of other banks incorporated elsewhere $2,002; balance due from other banks $112,427.48; amount of all debts due $2,068,677.03; total amount of bank resources $2,379,324.39.

Circulation ranged from $106,520 in 1839 to $208,121 in 1845. From 1857 to 1860 it remained at $116,352. Other figures for 1857 included bills of this bank and other New England states totaling at $29,415. Real estate was valued at $30,000.

In addition to the notes listed below, this bank issued interest-bearing *time checks* during the 1820s. These were essentially drafts payable at a future date. They closely resembled bank notes, with known denominations of $30, $50, and $500.[41]

The business of the City Bank was succeeded by the National City Bank of Boston in November 1864, which was approved with a capital of $1,000,000 authorized up to $2,000,000.

Numismatic Commentary: Notes from the City Bank in general are fairly rare. On occasion one will become available and will probably show a scene of the Boston harbor with ships.

Valid Issues

$1 • W-MA-390-001-G010

Center: 1 / 1 / Flower garlands and gridwork segments / ONE / 1 / 1. ***Engraver:*** PSSP. ***Comments:*** H-MA-125-G2. 18__. 1820s.

Rarity: —

$1 • W-MA-390-001-G010a

Left: Narrow panel of lathework circle segments. ***Right:*** Narrow panel of lathework circle segments. ***Engraver:*** PSSP. ***Comments:*** H-MA-125-G4. Similar to W-MA-390-001-G010. 18__. 1820s.

Rarity: —

$1 • W-MA-390-001-G010b

Left: Narrow panel of lathework circle segments. ***Right:*** Narrow panel of lathework circle segments. ***Engraver:*** PSSP. ***Comments:*** H-MA-125-G6. Similar to W-MA-390-001-G010. 18__. 1820s–1830s.

Rarity: —

$1 • W-MA-390-001-G010c

Left: ONE / D / ONE vertically. ***Right:*** ONE / D / ONE vertically. ***Engraver:*** PSSP. ***Comments:*** H-MA-125-G8. Similar to W-MA-390-001-G010. 18__. 1830s.

Rarity: —

$1 • W-MA-390-001-G010d

Left: MASSACHUSETTS / ONE. ***Engraver:*** PSSP. ***Comments:*** H-MA-125-G10. Similar to W-MA-390-001-G010c. 18__. 1830s.

Rarity: —

$1 • W-MA-390-001-G020

Left: 1 / Steamship. ***Center:*** View of Boston Harbor, Sailing ship. ***Right:*** 1 / Sailing ship. ***Engraver:*** New England Bank Note Co. / Rawdon, Wright, Hatch & Edson. ***Comments:*** H-MA-125-G12. 18__. 1840s–1850s.

Rarity: —

$1 • W-MA-390-001-G020a

CC

Overprint: Red ONE. ***Engraver:*** New England Bank Note Co. / American Bank Note Co. ***Comments:*** H-Unlisted. Similar to W-MA-390-001-G020 but with different engraver imprint. 18__. 1850s.

Rarity: URS-3
VG $750; **F** $1,000; **VF** $1,200

$1 • W-MA-390-001-G020b

CJF

Overprint: Green ONE. ***Engraver:*** New England Bank Note Co. / American Bank Note Co. ***Comments:*** H-MA-125-G12c. Similar to W-MA-390-001-G020 but with different engraver imprint. 18__. 1860s.

Rarity: URS-3
VF $1,500

$2 • W-MA-390-002-G030

Center: 2 / 2 / Flower garlands and gridwork segments / TWO / 2 / 2. ***Engraver:*** PSSP. ***Comments:*** H-MA-125-G14. 18__. 1820s.

Rarity: —

$2 • W-MA-390-002-G030a

Left: Narrow panel of lathework circle segments. ***Right:*** Narrow panel of lathework circle segments. ***Engraver:*** PSSP. ***Comments:*** H-MA-125-G16. Similar to W-MA-390-002-G030. 18__. 1820s.

Rarity: —

How to Read the Whitman Numbering System

$1 • W-MA-010-001-G010a

Denomination: Value of the note shown.

W: Whitman number. This number is a sortable code unique to each bank and note.

MA: Abbreviation for the state under study.

010: Numerical designation specific to each bank.

001: The denomination in dollars.

G010a: G indicates a good or valid note. Other categories are indicated thus: C (counterfeit); R (raised); S (spurious); N (not-attributed); A (altered). Numbers are assigned starting with 010, 020, et seq. Terminal letters following the number indicate variations of a note: a series of different colored overprints, tints, payees, etc., all on the same design of note. For more information, see the "How to Use This Book" section at the front of the volume, page xiv.

$2 • W-MA-390-002-G030b

Left: Narrow panel of lathework circle segments. ***Right:*** Narrow panel of lathework circle segments. ***Engraver:*** PSSP. ***Comments:*** H-MA-125-G18. Similar to W-MA-390-002-G030. 18__. 1820s–1830s.

Rarity: —

$2 • W-MA-390-002-G030c

Left: Five TWOs vertically. ***Right:*** Five TWOs vertically. ***Engraver:*** PSSP. ***Comments:*** H-MA-125-G20. Similar to W-MA-390-002-G030. 18__. 1830s.

Rarity: —

$2 • W-MA-390-002-G030d

Left: MASSACHUSETTS / TWO. ***Engraver:*** PSSP. ***Comments:*** H-MA-125-G22. Similar to W-MA-390-002-G030c. 18__. 1830s.

Rarity: URS-3
VF $1,750

$2 • W-MA-390-002-G040

Left: 2 / Medallion head. ***Center:*** View of Boston and harbor. ***Right:*** 2 / Medallion head. ***Engraver:*** New England Bank Note Co. ***Comments:*** H-MA-125-G24. 18__. 1840s–1850s.

Rarity: —

$2 • W-MA-390-002-G040a

Overprint: Green TWO. ***Engraver:*** New England Bank Note Co. / American Bank Note Co. ***Comments:*** H-MA-125-G24c. Similar to W-MA-390-002-G040. 18__. 1860s.

Rarity: —

$3 • W-MA-390-003-G050

Center: 3 / 3 / Flower garlands and gridwork segments / 3 / 3. ***Engraver:*** PSSP. ***Comments:*** H-MA-125-G26. 18__. 1820s.

Rarity: —

$3 • W-MA-390-003-G050a

Left: Narrow panel of lathework circle segments. ***Right:*** Narrow panel of lathework circle segments. ***Engraver:*** PSSP. ***Comments:*** H-MA-125-G28. Similar to W-MA-390-003-G050. 18__. 1820s.

Rarity: —

$3 • W-MA-390-003-G050b

Left: Narrow panel of lathework circle segments. ***Right:*** Narrow panel of lathework circle segments. ***Engraver:*** PSSP. ***Comments:*** H-MA-125-G30. Similar to W-MA-390-003-G050. 18__. 1820s–1830s.

Rarity: —

$3 • W-MA-390-003-G050c

Left: THREE vertically. ***Right:*** THREE vertically. ***Engraver:*** PSSP. ***Comments:*** H-MA-125-G32. Similar to W-MA-390-003-G050. 18__. 1830s.

Rarity: —

$3 • W-MA-390-003-G050d

Left: MASSACHUSETTS / THREE. ***Engraver:*** PSSP. ***Comments:*** H-MA-125-G34. Similar to W-MA-390-003-G050c. 18__. 1830s.

Rarity: —

$3 • W-MA-390-003-G060

Left: 3 / Medallion head / 3. ***Center:*** View of Boston and harbor. ***Right:*** 3 / Medallion head. ***Engraver:*** New England Bank Note Co. / Rawdon, Wright, Hatch & Edson. ***Comments:*** H-MA-125-G36. 18__. 1840s–1850s.

Rarity: —

$3 • W-MA-390-003-G060a

Overprint: Green THREE. ***Engraver:*** New England Bank Note Co. / American Bank Note Co. ***Comments:*** H-MA-125-G36c. Similar to W-MA-390-003-G060 but with different engraver imprint. 18__. 1860s.

Rarity: —

$5 • W-MA-390-005-G070

Left: Lathework chain bearing MASSACHUSETTS / 5 / 5. ***Center:*** Alternating flower garlands and gridwork segments. ***Right:*** 5 / 5. ***Engraver:*** PSSP. ***Comments:*** H-MA-125-G38. 18__. 1820s.

Rarity: —

$5 • W-MA-390-005-G070a

Center: White boxes flanking FIVE DOLLARS. ***Engraver:*** PSSP. ***Comments:*** H-MA-125-G40. Similar to W-MA-390-005-G070. 18__. 1820s.

Rarity: —

$5 • W-MA-390-005-G070b

Engraver: PSSP. ***Comments:*** H-MA-125-G42. Similar to W-MA-390-005-G070 but with zigzag ruled lines. 18__. 1820s–1830s.

Rarity: —

$5 • W-MA-390-005-G070c

Engraver: PSSP. ***Comments:*** H-MA-125-G44. Similar to W-MA-390-005-G070 but with spiral lathework lines. 18__. 1830s.

Rarity: —

$5 • W-MA-390-005-G080

Left: 5 / Medallion head / FIVE. ***Center:*** View of Boston and harbor. ***Bottom center:*** State arms. ***Right:*** 5 / Medallion head. ***Engraver:*** New England Bank Note Co. / Rawdon, Wright, Hatch & Edson. ***Comments:*** H-MA-125-G46. 18__. 1840s–1850s.

Rarity: URS-2
Proof $1,500

$5 • W-MA-390-005-G080a

Overprint: Green FIVE. ***Engraver:*** New England Bank Note Co. / American Bank Note Co. ***Comments:*** H-MA-125-G46c. Similar to W-MA-390-005-G080 but with different engraver imprint. 18__. 1860s.

Rarity: —

$10 • W-MA-390-010-G090

Left: Lathework chain bearing MASSACHUSETTS / 10 / 10 vertically. ***Center:*** Alternating flower garlands and gridwork segments. ***Right:*** 10 / 10 vertically. ***Comments:*** H-MA-125-G48. 18__. 1820s.

Rarity: —

$10 • W-MA-390-010-G090a

Center: White boxes flanking TEN DOLLARS. ***Comments:*** H-MA-125-G50. Similar to W-MA-390-010-G090. 18__. 1820s.

Rarity: —

$10 • W-MA-390-010-G090b

Engraver: PSSP. ***Comments:*** H-MA-125-G52. Similar to W-MA-390-010-G090a but with zigzag ruled lines. 18__. 1820s–1830s.

Rarity: —

$10 • W-MA-390-010-G090c

Engraver: PSSP. ***Comments:*** H-MA-125-G54. Similar to W-MA-390-010-G090a but with spiral lathework lines. 18__. 1830s.

Rarity: —

$10 • W-MA-390-010-G100

Left: TEN / Medallion head bearing TEN. ***Center:*** View of Boston and harbor. ***Right:*** 10 / Medallion head. ***Engraver:*** New England Bank Note Co. / Rawdon, Wright, Hatch & Edson. ***Comments:*** H-MA-125-G56. 18__. 1840s–1850s.

Rarity: —

$10 • W-MA-390-010-G100a

Overprint: Green TEN. ***Engraver:*** New England Bank Note Co. / American Bank Note Co. ***Comments:*** H-MA-125-G56c. Similar to W-MA-390-010-G100 but with different engraver imprint. 18__. 1860s.

Rarity: —

$20 • W-MA-390-020-G110

Left: Panel bearing state arms / 20 / 20 vertically. ***Center:*** Alternating flower garlands and gridwork segments. ***Right:*** 20 / 20 vertically. ***Comments:*** H-MA-125-G58. 18__. 1820s.

Rarity: —

$20 • W-MA-390-020-G110a

Left: Lathework chain bearing MASSACHUSETTS vertically. ***Engraver:*** PSSP. ***Comments:*** H-MA-125-G60. Similar to W-MA-390-020-G110. 18__. 1820s–1830s.

Rarity: —

$50 • W-MA-390-050-G120

Left: Panel bearing state arms / 50 / 50 vertically. ***Center:*** Alternating flower garlands and gridwork segments. ***Right:*** 50 / 50 vertically. ***Comments:*** H-MA-125-G62. 18__. 1820s.

Rarity: —

$50 • W-MA-390-050-G120a

Left: Lathework chain bearing MASSACHUSETTS vertically. ***Comments:*** H-MA-125-G64. Similar to W-MA-390-050-G120. 18__. 1820s.

Rarity: —

$100 • W-MA-390-100-G130

Left: Panel bearing state arms / 100 / 100 vertically. ***Center:*** Alternating flower garlands and gridwork segments. ***Right:*** 100 / 100 vertically. ***Comments:*** H-MA-125-G66. 18__. 1820s.

Rarity: —

$100 • W-MA-390-100-G130a

Left: Lathework chain bearing MASSACHUSETTS vertically. ***Comments:*** H-MA-125-G68. Similar to W-MA-390-100-G130. 18__. 1820s–1830s.

Rarity: —

$500 • W-MA-390-500-G140

Left: Lathework chain bearing MASSACHUSETTS / 500 / 500 vertically. ***Center:*** Alternating flower garlands and gridwork segments. ***Right:*** 500 / 500 vertically. ***Engraver:*** PSSP. ***Comments:*** H-MA-125-G70. 18__. 1820s–1830s.

Rarity: URS-4

Proof $1,500

$500 • W-MA-390-500-G150

CC

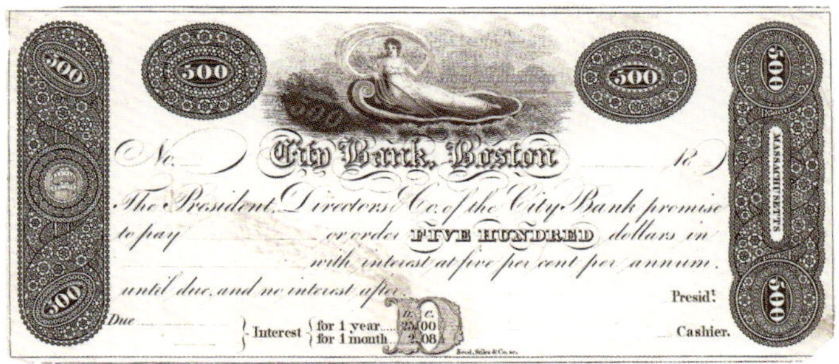

Engraver: Reed, Stiles & Co. ***Comments:*** H-Unlisted. Promissory note. 18__.

Rarity: URS-2

Proof $1,200

$1,000 • W-MA-390-1000-G160

QDB

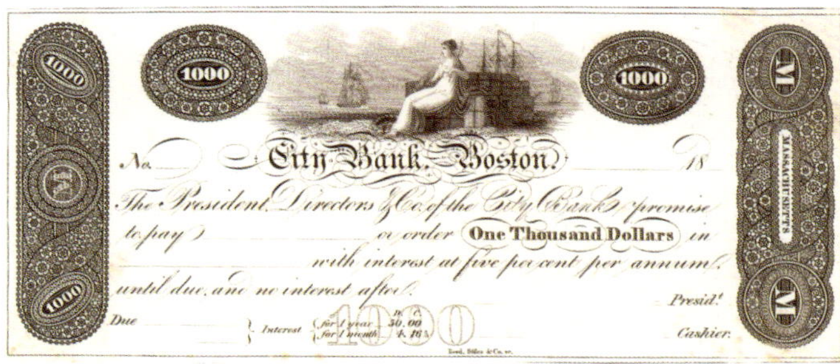

Engraver: Reed, Stiles & Co. ***Comments:*** H-Unlisted. Promissory note. 18__.

Rarity: URS-1

EF $1,650; **Proof** $3,000

Non-Valid Issues

$1 • W-MA-390-001-C020

Engraver: New England Bank Note Co. / Rawdon, Wright, Hatch & Edson. ***Comments:*** H-MA-125-C12. Counterfeit of W-MA-390-001-G020. 18__. 1850s.

Rarity: —

$2 • W-MA-390-002-A010

Left: 2 / Cornucopia, Woman standing with staff / TWO. ***Center:*** TWO / Machinery and merchandise flanking Ceres seated holding sickle and rake, Factories and harbor. ***Engraver:*** New England Bank Note Co. ***Comments:*** H-MA-125-A5. Altered from $2 Washington County Bank, Calais, Maine, or from notes of other failed banks using the same plate. 18__. 1840s.

Rarity: —

$3 • **W-MA-390-003-A020**

Left: THREE / Beehive and foliage / THREE. ***Center:*** Machinery and merchandise flanking Ceres seated holding sickle and rake, Factories and harbor / THREE. ***Right:*** 3 on THREE / Two reapers / 3 on THREE. ***Engraver:*** New England Bank Note Co. ***Comments:*** H-MA-125-A10. Altered from $3 Washington County Bank, Calais, Maine, or from notes of other failed banks using the same plate. 18__. 1840s.

Rarity: —

$3 • **W-MA-390-003-A030**

Center: REAL ESTATE SECURITY. ***Comments:*** H-MA-125-A15. Altered from a Michigan bank. 18__. 1830s.

Rarity: —

$5 • **W-MA-390-005-R010**

Engraver: New England Bank Note Co. / Rawdon, Wright, Hatch & Edson. ***Comments:*** H-MA-125-R5. Raised from W-MA-390-001-G020. 18__. 1840s.

Rarity: —

$5 • **W-MA-390-005-A040**

Left: 5 / Blacksmith at anvil / FIVE. ***Center:*** Mercury standing with 5, Cornucopia and merchandise, Factories and ship / V. ***Right:*** 5 / Ceres kneeling / FIVE. ***Engraver:*** New England Bank Note Co. ***Comments:*** H-MA-125-A20. Altered from $5 Washington County Bank, Calais, Maine, or from notes of other failed banks using the same plate. 18__. 1840s.

Rarity: —

$5 • **W-MA-390-005-A050**

Center: REAL ESTATE SECURITY. ***Comments:*** H-MA-125-A25. Altered from a Michigan bank. 18__. 1830s.

Rarity: —

$10 • **W-MA-390-010-R020**

Engraver: New England Bank Note Co. ***Comments:*** H-MA-125-R10. Raised from W-MA-390-002-G040. 18__. 1840s.

Rarity: —

$10 • **W-MA-390-010-A060**

Left: 10 / Portrait of George Washington held by cherub / 10. ***Center:*** X / Spread eagle with shield and arrows, E PLURIBUS UNUM / X. ***Bottom center:*** Ship. ***Right:*** 10 / Indian man / 10. ***Engraver:*** Terry, Pelton & Co. ***Comments:*** H-MA-125-A30. Altered from W-MA-2860-010-A010. 18__. 1830s.

Rarity: —

$10 • **W-MA-390-010-A070**

Center: REAL ESTATE SECURITY. ***Comments:*** H-MA-125-A35. Altered from a Michigan bank. 18__. 1830s.

Rarity: —

Cochituate Bank

1849–1854

W-MA-400

History: The Cochituate Bank was chartered in 1849. By year's end it was open for business in the U.S. Hotel building. Calvin S. Lane was the founding cashier. In July 1851, the bank moved to the corner of Washington and Summer streets.[42]

In 1850 the bank's capital was $150,000, but this had increased by $100,000 a mere year later. The amount was to be paid in on or before October 1. It remained at $250,000 through 1854. Circulation of that year was $275,027, and specie was valued at $28,251.07. However, all was not well. The president of the bank had engaged in fraudulent activities and others were involved as accomplices.

The *Banker's Magazine* reported that on Saturday, April 15, 1854, the Cochituate Bank had officially suspended business. It was thought that the funds were in good order, but that the bank had merely been unwisely managed, and no loss would result for the public. The court ordered an injunction that was made permanent, and the affairs of the bank were wound up. The report was overly optimistic. The bills became worthless, and thousands of bills remained to later end up in numismatic hands, making them available to a later generation of collectors.

Numismatic Commentary: Fortunately, collectors should have little trouble assembling an almost complete collection of issues from this bank. The $500 and $1,000 varieties may pose some problem, but they are certainly attainable. All of the notes are attractive, and many have been put into frames for wall decorating. As is usually the case, news that was bad for stockholders and original holders of bills was good for numismatists.

Valid Issues

$1 • **W-MA-400-001-G010**

Left: Woman seated with trident / ONE. ***Center:*** Spread eagle / 1. ***Bottom center:*** State arms. ***Right:*** 1 / Ceres standing with anchor and cornucopia, Bales and ship. ***Engraver:*** New England Bank Note Co. / Rawdon, Wright, Hatch & Edson. ***Comments:*** H-MA-130-G2. 18__. 1849–1850s.

Rarity: URS-10

VG $60; **F** $65; **VF** $85

$1 • **W-MA-400-001-G010a**

QDB

Overprint: Red ONE. ***Engraver:*** New England Bank Note Co. / Rawdon, Wright, Hatch & Edson. ***Comments:*** H-MA-130-G2a. Similar to W-MA-400-001-G010 but with different date and engraved payee's name. Jan. 1, 18__. 1850s.

Rarity: (Rem) URS-2; URS-12

Unc-Rem $400

VG $45; **VF** $60; **EF** $85

$2 • **W-MA-400-002-G020**

Left: Man reclining with sledge / 2. ***Center:*** 2. ***Bottom center:*** Bales and cogs. ***Right:*** TWO / Woman with flag, Cherubs with cornucopias. ***Engraver:*** New England Bank Note Co. / Rawdon, Wright, Hatch & Edson. ***Comments:*** H-MA-130-G4. 18__. 1849–1850s.

Rarity: URS-10

VG $60; **F** $75; **VF** $100

$2 • W-MA-400-002-G020a

QDB

Overprint: Red TWO. ***Engraver:*** New England Bank Note Co. / Rawdon, Wright, Hatch & Edson. ***Comments:*** H-MA-130-G4a. Similar to W-MA-400-002-G020 but with different date and engraved payee's name. Jan. 1, 18__. 1850s.

Rarity: URS-12
VG $25; **F** $50; **VF** $75; **Unc-S&D** $100

$3 • W-MA-400-003-G030

Left: Train on bridge, Shield bearing Portrait of George Washington, Liberty seated with shield, Eagle, Barrels, Ship / 3. ***Center:*** 3. ***Bottom center:*** Train. ***Right:*** THREE / Blacksmith standing. ***Engraver:*** New England Bank Note Co. / Rawdon, Wright, Hatch & Edson. ***Comments:*** H-MA-130-G6. 18__. 1849–1850s.

Rarity: URS-10
F $50; **VF** $75

$3 • W-MA-400-003-G030a

QDB

Overprint: Red THREE. ***Engraver:*** New England Bank Note Co. / Rawdon, Wright, Hatch & Edson. ***Comments:*** H-MA-130-G6a. Similar to W-MA-400-003-G030 but with different date and engraved payee's name. Jan. 1, 18__. 1850s.

Rarity: URS-12
F $50; **VF** $75

$5 • W-MA-400-005-G040

HA

Engraver: New England Bank Note Co. / Rawdon, Wright, Hatch & Edson. ***Comments:*** H-MA-130-G8. 18__. 1849–1850s.

Rarity: URS-10
VG $25; **F** $50; **VF** $75

$5 • W-MA-400-005-G040a

Left: Ships / 5. ***Center:*** Sailing ship / FIVE on 5. ***Bottom center:*** Ship. ***Right:*** FIVE / Sailor standing. ***Overprint:*** Red FIVE and panel over white FIVE. ***Engraver:*** New England Bank Note Co. / Rawdon, Wright, Hatch & Edson. ***Comments:*** H-MA-130-G8a. Similar to W-MA-400-005-G040 but with different date and engraved payee's name. Jan. 1, 18__. 1850s.

Rarity: URS-9
F $50; **VF** $75

$5 • W-MA-400-005-G040b

QDB

Overprint: Red FIVE. ***Engraver:*** New England Bank Note Co. / Rawdon, Wright, Hatch & Edson. ***Comments:*** H-MA-130-G8b. Similar to W-MA-400-005-G040 but with different date. Jan. 1, 18__. 1850s.

Rarity: URS-9
VG $30; **F** $50; **VF** $75; **EF** $150

$5 • W-MA-400-005-G040c

HA

Overprint: Blue scalloped FIVE. ***Engraver:*** New England Bank Note Co. / Rawdon, Wright, Hatch & Edson. ***Comments:*** H-MA-130-G8c. Similar to W-MA-400-005-G040 but with different date. Jan. 1, 18__. 1850s.

Rarity: URS-9
F $50; **VF** $75

$5 • W-MA-400-005-G040d

QDB

Overprint: Blue FIVE. ***Engraver:*** New England Bank Note Co. / Rawdon, Wright, Hatch & Edson. ***Comments:*** H-MA-130-G8d. Similar to W-MA-400-005-G040 but with different date. Jan. 1, 18__. 1850s.

Rarity: URS-12
F $40; **VF** $60

$5 • W-MA-400-005-G040e

QDB

Overprint: Blue block FIVE. ***Engraver:*** New England Bank Note Co. / Rawdon, Wright, Hatch & Edson. ***Comments:*** H-MA-130-G8e. Similar to W-MA-400-005-G040 but with different date. Jan. 1, 18__. 1850s.

Rarity: URS-9
F $50; **VF** $75

$10 • W-MA-400-010-G050

SI

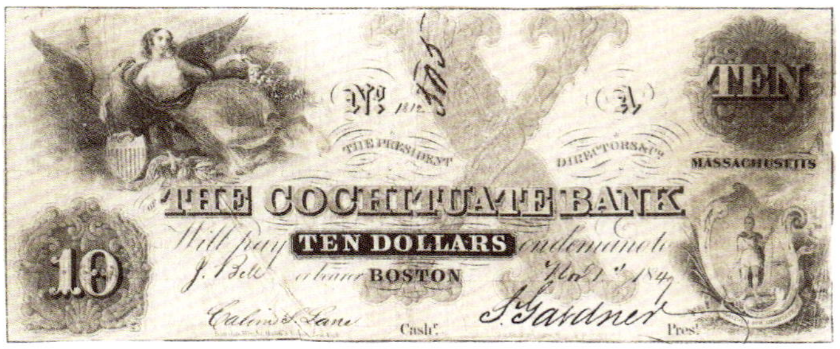

Engraver: New England Bank Note Co. / Rawdon, Wright, Hatch & Edson. ***Comments:*** H-MA-130-G10. 18__. 1849–1850s.

Rarity: URS-10
VG $26; **F** $50; **VF** $75

$10 • W-MA-400-010-G050a

QDB

Overprint: Red TEN. ***Engraver:*** New England Bank Note Co. / Rawdon, Wright, Hatch & Edson. ***Comments:*** H-MA-130-G10a. Similar to W-MA-400-010-G050 but with different date and engraved payee's name. Jan. 1, 18__. 1850s.

Rarity: URS-8
VG $24; **F** $50; **VF** $110; **Unc-Rem** $175

$20 • W-MA-400-020-G060

CC

Engraver: New England Bank Note Co. / Rawdon, Wright, Hatch & Edson. ***Comments:*** H-MA-130-G12. 185_. 1850s.

Rarity: URS-6
F $50; **VF** $175; **EF** $200

$50 • W-MA-400-050-G070

QDB

Engraver: Rawdon, Wright, Hatch & Edson. ***Comments:*** H-MA-130-G14. 18__. 1849–1850s.

Rarity: URS-9
F $60; **VF** $80; **Unc-Rem** $150

$100 • W-MA-400-100-G080

QDB

Engraver: New England Bank Note Co. ***Comments:*** H-MA-130-G16. 18__. 1849–1850s.

Rarity: URS-6
VG $100; **F** $150; **VF** $200

$500 • W-MA-400-500-G090

HA

Engraver: New England Bank Note Co. ***Comments:*** H-MA-130-G18. 18__. 1849–1850s.

Rarity: URS-5
F $500; **VF** $750; **Proof** $1,500

$500 • W-MA-400-500-G100

CC

Engraver: New England Bank Note Co. ***Comments:*** H-Unlisted. 18__. 1849–1850s.

Rarity: URS-4
VF $1,000

$1,000 • W-MA-400-1000-G110

CC

Engraver: New England Bank Note Co. ***Comments:*** H-MA-130-G20. 18__. 1849–1850s.

Rarity: URS-4
VG $600; **F** $800; **VF** $1,200; **Proof** $2,000
Selected auction price(s): Heritage, January 2008, Lot 13035, CF $2,530; Heritage, January 2014, Lot 15347, F $1,057

$1,000 • W-MA-400-1000-G120

CC

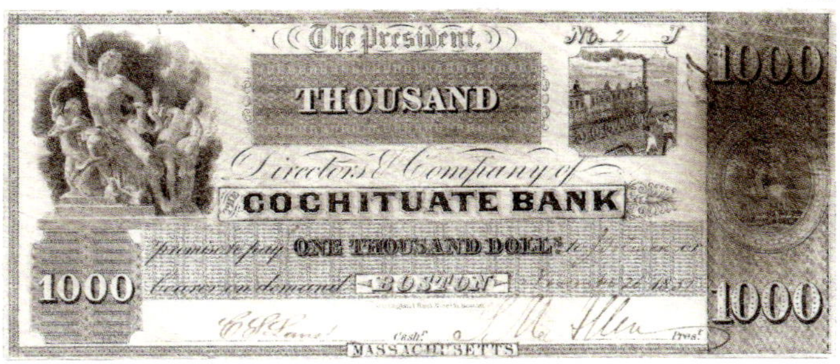

Engraver: New England Bank Note Co. ***Comments:*** H-Unlisted. 18__. 1849–1850s.

Rarity: URS-3
VF $2,000

Non-Valid Issues

$5 • W-MA-400-005-N010

Left: V / Woman / FIVE. ***Center:*** Woman floating with V and emblems of commerce and agriculture. ***Right:*** 5 / Woman / 5. ***Comments:*** H-MA-130-N5. 18__. 1850s.

Rarity: URS-8
F $75; **EF** $125

$10 • W-MA-400-010-R010

Engraver: New England Bank Note Co. / Rawdon, Wright, Hatch & Edson. ***Comments:*** H-Unlisted. Raised from W-MA-400-002-G020. 18__. 1850s.

Rarity: —

Columbia Bank

Late 1850s

W-MA-410

History: A non-existent bank represented only by notes altered from those of other banks.

Issues

$1 • W-MA-410-001-A010

Left: ONE / Woman holding up spread eagle / ONE. ***Center:*** Perched eagle / ONE. ***Right:*** 1 / Woman. ***Engraver:*** Danforth, Bald & Co. ***Comments:*** H-MA-135-A5. Altered from $1 Columbia Bank, Washington, D.C. 185_. 1850s.

Rarity: URS-8
VG $75; **VF** $150

Columbian Bank

1822–1865

W-MA-420

History: The Columbian Bank was chartered in February 1822. It was located at 34 State Street until 1864, when it moved to 40 State Street. The bank's charter was renewed in 1827 with $500,000 in starting capital.[43] The capital was increased to $750,000 in 1857 and to $1,000,000 in 1863.

Circulation in 1838 was $72,093; net profits on hand $58,916.22; balances due to other banks $4,000; cash deposited $147,108.57; cash deposited bearing interest $60,200; total amount due from banks $842,317.79; gold, silver, and other coined metals in the banking house $24,931.43; bills of other banks incorporated in this state $58,104; balance due from other banks $20,620.02; amount of all debts due $738,662.34; total amount of resources of the bank $842,317.79.

Circulation had decreased to $31,412 by 1839, and in 1845 it amounted to $134,416. In 1857 it was $124,907. Bills of this bank and other New England states totaled $67,675.

The Columbian National Bank of Boston was chartered on April 17, 1865, and assumed the state bank's business interests.

Numismatic Commentary: The Columbian Bank will be another difficult entity from which to find a genuine note, even though this institution was in business for many years. PSSP style notes may be the easiest to obtain.

Valid Issues

$1 • W-MA-420-001-G010

Center: 1 / 1 / Flower garlands and gridwork segments / ONE / 1 / 1. ***Engraver:*** PSSP. ***Comments:*** H-MA-140-G2. 18__. 1820s.

Rarity: —

$1 • **W-MA-420-001-G010a**

Left: Narrow panel of lathework circle segments. ***Right:*** Narrow panel of lathework circle segments. ***Engraver:*** PSSP. ***Comments:*** H-MA-140-G4. Similar to W-MA-420-001-G010. 18__. 1820s.

Rarity: —

$1 • **W-MA-420-001-G010b**

Left: Narrow panel of lathework circle segments. ***Right:*** Narrow panel of lathework circle segments. ***Engraver:*** PSSP. ***Comments:*** H-MA-140-G6. Similar to W-MA-420-001-G010. 18__. 1820s–1830s.

Rarity: —

$1 • **W-MA-420-001-G010c**

Left: ONE / D / ONE vertically. ***Right:*** ONE / D / ONE vertically. ***Engraver:*** PSSP. ***Comments:*** H-MA-140-G8. Similar to W-MA-420-001-G010. 18__. 1830s.

Rarity: —

$1 • **W-MA-420-001-G020**

Left: ONE / Bust of George Washington / ONE. ***Center:*** 1 / Two blacksmiths at anvil in front of forge, 1 / Panel outlining white ONE. ***Right:*** ONE / Woman / ONE. ***Engraver:*** New England Bank Note Co. ***Comments:*** H-MA-140-G12. 18__. 1840s–1850s.

Rarity: —

$1 • **W-MA-420-001-G030**

Left: Female portrait / 1. ***Center:*** 1 / Woman seated with fasces and shield, 1. ***Right:*** 1 / Male portrait. ***Engraver:*** Toppan, Carpenter & Co. ***Comments:*** H-MA-140-G16. 18__. 1850s.

Rarity: —

$1 • **W-MA-420-001-G030a**

Overprint: Red 1 / 1. ***Engraver:*** Toppan, Carpenter & Co. ***Comments:*** H-MA-140-G16a. Similar to W-MA-420-001-G030. 18__. 1850s–1860s.

Rarity: —

$2 • **W-MA-420-002-G040**

Center: 2 / 2 / Flower garlands and gridwork segments / TWO / 2 / 2. ***Engraver:*** PSSP. ***Comments:*** H-MA-140-G20. 18__. 1820s.

Rarity: —

$2 • **W-MA-420-002-G040a**

Left: Narrow panel of lathework circle segments. ***Right:*** Narrow panel of lathework circle segments. ***Engraver:*** PSSP. ***Comments:*** H-MA-140-G22. Similar to W-MA-420-002-G040. 18__. 1820s.

Rarity: —

$2 • **W-MA-420-002-G040b**

Left: Narrow panel of lathework circle segments. ***Right:*** Narrow panel of lathework circle segments. ***Engraver:*** PSSP. ***Comments:*** H-MA-140-G24. Similar to W-MA-420-002-G040. 18__. 1820s–1830s.

Rarity: —

$2 • **W-MA-420-002-G040c**

Left: Five TWOs vertically. ***Right:*** Five TWOs vertically. ***Engraver:*** PSSP. ***Comments:*** H-MA-140-G26. Similar to W-MA-420-002-G040. 18__. 1830s.

Rarity: —

$2 • **W-MA-420-002-G050**

Left: TWO / Woman / 2. ***Center:*** 2 / Woman giving drink to one of two men / 2 / Panel outlining white TWO. ***Right:*** TWO / Bust of female reaper. ***Engraver:*** New England Bank Note Co. ***Comments:*** H-MA-140-G30. 18__. 1840s–1850s.

Rarity: —

$2 • **W-MA-420-002-G060**

Left: Indian / 2. ***Center:*** TWO / Sailing ship / Dollars. ***Right:*** 2 / Male portrait. ***Engraver:*** Toppan, Carpenter & Co. ***Comments:*** H-MA-140-G34. 18__. 1850s.

Rarity: URS-2
Proof $2,500

$2 • **W-MA-420-002-G060a** CC

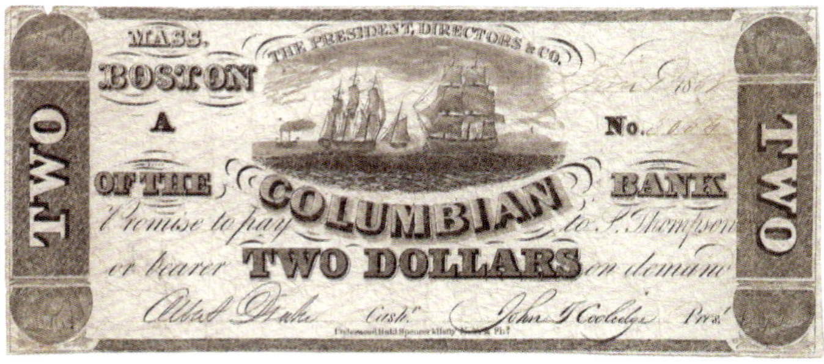

Overprint: Red 2 / 2. ***Engraver:*** Toppan, Carpenter & Co. ***Comments:*** H-MA-140-G34a. Similar to W-MA-420-002-G060. 18__. 1850s.

Rarity: URS-3
F $300; **VF** $1,250

$3 • **W-MA-420-003-G070**

Center: 3 / 3 / Flower garlands and gridwork segments / 3 / 3. ***Engraver:*** PSSP. ***Comments:*** H-MA-140-G38. 18__. 1820s.

Rarity: —

$3 • **W-MA-420-003-G070a**

Left: Narrow panel of lathework circle segments. ***Right:*** Narrow panel of lathework circle segments. ***Engraver:*** PSSP. ***Comments:*** H-MA-140-G40. Similar to W-MA-420-003-G070. 18__. 1820s.

Rarity: —

$3 • **W-MA-420-003-G070b**

Left: Narrow panel of lathework circle segments. ***Right:*** Narrow panel of lathework circle segments. ***Engraver:*** PSSP. ***Comments:*** H-MA-140-G42. Similar to W-MA-420-003-G070. 18__. 1820s–1830s.

Rarity: —

$3 • **W-MA-420-003-G070c**

Left: THREE vertically. ***Right:*** THREE vertically. ***Engraver:*** PSSP. ***Comments:*** H-MA-140-G44. Similar to W-MA-420-003-G070. 18__. 1830s.

Rarity: —

$3 • **W-MA-420-003-G080**

Left: THREE / Farmer standing sharpening scythe / 3 across THREE. ***Center:*** 3 / Beehive and cornucopia, Woman seated placing garland on eagle / 3 / Panel outlining white THREE. ***Right:*** THREE / Sailor standing on wharf with hat / 3 across THREE. ***Engraver:*** New England Bank Note Co. ***Comments:*** H-MA-140-G48. 18__. 1840s–1850s.

Rarity: —

$3 • W-MA-420-003-G090 JF

Engraver: Toppan, Carpenter, Casilear & Co. ***Comments:*** H-MA-140-G52. 18__. 1850s.

Rarity: URS-2
Proof $2,500

$3 • W-MA-420-003-G090a

Left: Ceres seated with sheaf and sickle, 3 / THREE. ***Center:*** 3 / Male portrait / 3. ***Right:*** Woman seated with bales and barrel, Ship, 3 / THREE. ***Overprint:*** Red 3 3. ***Engraver:*** Toppan, Carpenter & Co. ***Comments:*** H-MA-140-G52a. Similar to W-MA-420-003-G090. 18__. 1850s.

Rarity: —

$5 • W-MA-420-005-G100

Left: Lathework chain bearing MASSACHUSETTS / 5 / 5. ***Center:*** Alternating flower garlands and gridwork segments. ***Right:*** 5 / 5. ***Engraver:*** PSSP. ***Comments:*** H-MA-140-G56. 18__. 1820s.

Rarity: —

$5 • W-MA-420-005-G100a

Engraver: PSSP. ***Comments:*** H-MA-140-G58. Similar to W-MA-420-005-G100. 18__. 1820s.

Rarity: —

$5 • W-MA-420-005-G100b

Engraver: PSSP. ***Comments:*** H-MA-140-G60. Similar to W-MA-420-005-G100 but with zigzag ruled lines. 18__. 1820s–1830s.

Rarity: —

$5 • W-MA-420-005-G100c

Engraver: PSSP. ***Comments:*** H-MA-140-G62. Similar to W-MA-420-005-G100 but with spiral lathework lines. 18__. 1830s.

Rarity: —

$5 • W-MA-420-005-G110

Left: 5 / Portrait of George Washington / 5. ***Center:*** 5 / Woman / Landing of Christopher Columbus / 5. ***Right:*** 5 / Portrait of Christopher Columbus / 5. ***Engraver:*** New England Bank Note Co. ***Comments:*** H-MA-140-G66. 18__. 1840s–1850s.

Rarity: —

$5 • W-MA-420-005-G120

Left: Male portrait / 5. ***Center:*** Shipyard scene, Two ships on stocks. ***Right:*** 5 / Woman seated in 5. ***Engraver:*** Toppan, Carpenter & Co. ***Comments:*** H-MA-140-G70. 18__. 1850s.

Rarity: —

$5 • W-MA-420-005-G120a

Overprint: Red. ***Engraver:*** Toppan, Carpenter & Co. ***Comments:*** H-MA-140-G70a. Similar to W-MA-420-005-G120. 18__. 1850s.

Rarity: —

$10 • W-MA-420-010-G130

Left: MASSACHUSETTS / 10 / 10 vertically. ***Center:*** Alternating flower garlands and gridwork segments. ***Right:*** 10 / 10 vertically. ***Comments:*** H-MA-140-G74. 18__. 1820s.

Rarity: —

$10 • W-MA-420-010-G130a

Comments: H-MA-140-G76. Similar to W-MA-420-010-G130. 18__. 1820s.

Rarity: —

$10 • W-MA-420-010-G130b

Engraver: PSSP. ***Comments:*** H-MA-140-G78. Similar to W-MA-420-010-G130 but with zigzag ruled lines. 18__. 1820s–1830s.

Rarity: —

$10 • W-MA-420-010-G130c

Engraver: PSSP. ***Comments:*** H-MA-140-G80. Similar to W-MA-420-010-G130 but with spiral lathework lines. 18__. 1830s.

Rarity: —

$10 • W-MA-420-010-G140

Left: 10 / Portrait of George Washington / 10. ***Center:*** TEN / X / TEN. ***Right:*** 10 / Portrait of Christopher Columbus / 10. ***Comments:*** H-MA-140-G84. 18__. 1840s–1850s.

Rarity: —

$10 • W-MA-420-010-G150

Left: Three women on cliff with anchor. ***Center:*** Two women tending looms. ***Right:*** 10 / Male portrait. ***Engraver:*** Toppan, Carpenter & Co. ***Comments:*** H-MA-140-G88. 18__. 1850s.

Rarity: —

$10 • W-MA-420-010-G150a

Overprint: Red. ***Engraver:*** Toppan, Carpenter & Co. ***Comments:*** H-MA-140-G88a. Similar to W-MA-420-010-G150. 18__. 1850s.

Rarity: —

$20 • W-MA-420-020-G160

Left: Panel bearing state arms / 20 / 20 vertically. ***Center:*** Alternating flower garlands and gridwork segments. ***Right:*** 20 / 20 vertically. ***Comments:*** H-MA-140-G92. 18__. 1820s.

Rarity: —

$20 • W-MA-420-020-G160a

Left: Panel with lathework chain bearing MASSACHUSETTS vertically. ***Engraver:*** PSSP. ***Comments:*** H-MA-140-G94. Similar to W-MA-420-020-G160. 18__. 1820s–1830s.

Rarity: —

$20 • W-MA-420-020-G170

Left: Woman seated on barrel holding 20 on die overhead. ***Center:*** Eagle with sheaf and cog wheel. ***Right:*** 20 / Woman. ***Comments:*** H-MA-140-G98. 18__. 1860s.

Rarity: —

$50 • W-MA-420-050-G180

Left: Panel bearing state arms / 50 / 50 vertically. ***Center:*** Alternating flower garlands and gridwork segments. ***Right:*** 50 / 50 vertically. ***Comments:*** H-MA-140-G102. 18__. 1820s.

Rarity: —

$50 • W-MA-420-050-G180a

Left: Panel with lathework chain bearing MASSACHUSETTS vertically. ***Engraver:*** PSSP. ***Comments:*** H-MA-140-G104. Similar to W-MA-420-050-G180. 18__. 1820s–1830s.

Rarity: —

$50 • W-MA-420-050-G190

Left: 50 / Woman / 50. ***Center:*** Steamship. ***Bottom center:*** Farm tools and products. ***Right:*** 50. ***Comments:*** H-MA-140-G108. 18__. 1860s.

Rarity: —

$100 • W-MA-420-100-G200

Left: Panel bearing state arms / 100 / 100 vertically. ***Center:*** Alternating flower garlands and gridwork segments. ***Right:*** 100 / 100 vertically. ***Comments:*** H-MA-140-G112. 18__. 1820s.

Rarity: —

$100 • W-MA-420-100-G200a

Left: Panel with lathework chain bearing MASSACHUSETTS vertically. ***Comments:*** H-MA-140-G114. Similar to W-MA-420-100-G200. 18__. 1820s–1830s.

Rarity: —

$100 • W-MA-420-100-G210

CJF

Comments: H-MA-140-G118. Proof. 18__. 1860s.

Rarity: URS-2

Proof $3,250

$500 • W-MA-420-500-G220

Left: 500 / Mercury in clouds with cornucopia / 500. ***Center:*** Landing of Christopher Columbus. ***Right:*** 500. ***Comments:*** H-MA-140-G122. 1850s–1860s.

Rarity: —

Non-Valid Issues

$2 • W-MA-420-002-S010

CC

Engraver: Underwood, Bald, Spencer & Hufty. ***Comments:*** H-MA-140-S5. From a modified plate, originally for a counterfeit $2 Massachusetts Bank, Boston. 18__. 1830s.

Rarity: URS-7

F $50; **VF** $75

$2 • W-MA-420-002-A010

Left: 2 / Woman standing. ***Center:*** Eagle with motto and shield / Bales, Sailor standing on wharf, hat in hand. ***Right:*** 2 / Portrait of Marquis de Lafayette / TWO. ***Engraver:*** New England Bank Note Co. ***Comments:*** H-MA-140-A10. Altered from W-MA-680-002-G070. 18__. 1840s.

Rarity: —

$3 • W-MA-420-003-A020

Left: 3 / Woman standing with both hands on harp. ***Center:*** Eagle with motto and shield / Bales, Sailor standing on wharf, hat in hand. ***Right:*** 3 / Portrait of Marquis de Lafayette / THREE. ***Engraver:*** New England Bank Note Co. ***Comments:*** H-MA-140-A15. Altered from W-MA-680-003-G090. 18__. 1840s.

Rarity: —

$5 • W-MA-420-005-C100b

CJF

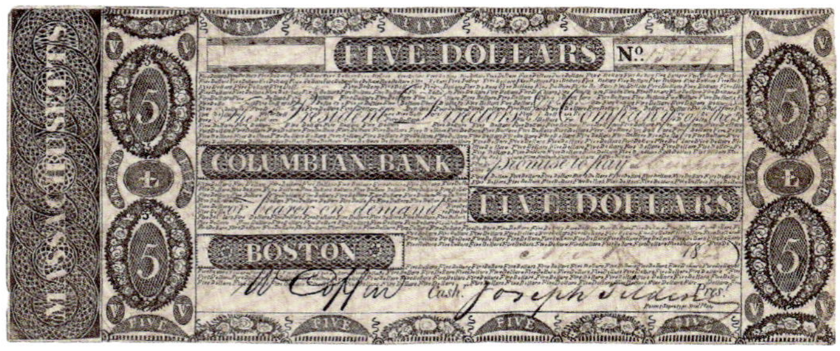

Engraver: PSSP. ***Comments:*** H-MA-140-C60. Counterfeit of W-MA-420-005-G100b. 18__. 1828.

Rarity: URS-5

F $125

$5 • W-MA-420-005-C110

Engraver: New England Bank Note Co. ***Comments:*** H-MA-140-C66. Counterfeit of W-MA-420-005-G110. 18__. 1850s.

Rarity: —

$5 • W-MA-420-005-A030

Left: Panel bearing FIVE vertically. ***Center:*** 5 / Ships, Eagle on shield and laurel, Ships / FIVE. ***Right:*** 5 on die supported by boy riding on dolphin. ***Engraver:*** Wellstood, Hanks, Hay & Whiting. ***Comments:*** H-MA-140-A20. Altered from $5 Citizens Bank, Washington, D.C. 18__. 1850s.

Rarity: —

$5 • W-MA-420-005-A040

Left: 5 / Portrait of George Washington / FIVE. ***Center:*** Ship, Factory scene, Horse-drawn wagons. ***Right:*** 5 / Portrait of Marquis de Lafayette / FIVE. ***Engraver:*** New England Bank Note Co. ***Comments:*** H-MA-140-A25. Altered from W-MA-680-005-G110. 18__. 1840s.

Rarity: —

Collectors and Researchers:

If you have new information about any banks or notes listed in this volume, contact Whitman Publishing, Attn: Obsolete Paper Money, 3101 Clairmont Road, Suite G, Atlanta, GA 30329.

$10 • W-MA-420-010-A050

Left: X / Portrait of Marquis de Lafayette / TEN. ***Center:*** Ship, Factory scene, Horse-drawn wagons. ***Right:*** 10 / Male portrait / TEN. ***Engraver:*** New England Bank Note Co. ***Comments:*** H-MA-140-A30. Altered from W-MA-680-010-G130. 18__. 1840s.

Rarity: —

$20 • W-MA-420-020-R010

Engraver: Toppan, Carpenter & Co. ***Comments:*** H-MA-140-R5. Raised from W-MA-420-001-G030 series. 18__. 1850s.

Rarity: —

Commercial Bank

1831–1838

W-MA-430

History: The Commercial Bank was chartered on August 15, 1831. The first president was Parker H. Pierce, and its first cashier was Joseph Andrews. The directors were Parker H. Pierce, John Albree, William Graves, J. Scholfield Jr., A.B. Weston, Joseph Andrews, Charles Valentine, and A.C. Lombard.

It was learned in early 1838 that the president and the cashier had absconded with bank funds. In 1838 the *Financial Register* reported that "at a stated meeting of the stockholder of the Commercial Bank of Boston, held on Wednesday, March 8, it was unanimously resolved to wind up the affairs of the bank."

An examination into the affairs and property of the bank took place, and it was found that the president and cashier had, without the knowledge of the directors, put $120,000 dollars in post-notes into circulation, as well as $40,000 dollars of their old bank notes, which the directors had ordered to be burnt but which were not.

Numismatic Commentary: Notes of this short-lived bank are very hard to find. All are of the PSSP design.

Valid Issues

$1 • W-MA-430-001-G010

Left: Lathework panel bearing MASSACHUSETTS vertically. ***Center:*** 1 / 1 / Alternating flower garlands and gridwork segments / ONE / 1 / 1. ***Right:*** Lathework panel bearing ONE / D / ONE vertically. ***Engraver:*** PSSP. ***Comments:*** H-MA-150-G2. 18__. 1830s.

Rarity: —

$2 • W-MA-430-002-G020

Left: Lathework panel bearing MASSACHUSETTS vertically. ***Center:*** Alternating flower garlands and gridwork segments. ***Right:*** Lathework panel bearing five TWOs vertically. ***Engraver:*** PSSP. ***Comments:*** H-MA-150-G4. 18__. 1830s.

Rarity: —

$3 • W-MA-430-003-G030

Left: Lathework panel bearing MASSACHUSETTS vertically. ***Center:*** 3 / 3 / Alternating flower garlands and gridwork segments / THREE / 3 / 3. ***Right:*** Lathework panel bearing THREE vertically. ***Engraver:*** PSSP. ***Comments:*** H-MA-150-G6. 18__. 1830s.

Rarity: —

$5 • W-MA-430-005-G040

Left: Lathework chain bearing MASSACHUSETTS / 5 / 5. ***Center:*** Alternating flower garlands and gridwork segments / FIVE DOLLARS with spiral lathework lines. ***Right:*** 5 / 5. ***Engraver:*** PSSP. ***Comments:*** H-MA-150-G8. 18__. 1830s.

Rarity: —

$10 • W-MA-430-010-G050

Left: Lathework chain bearing MASSACHUSETTS / 10 / 10 vertically. ***Center:*** Alternating flower garlands and gridwork segments / TEN DOLLARS with spiral lathework lines. ***Right:*** 10 / 10 vertically. ***Engraver:*** PSSP. ***Comments:*** H-MA-150-G10. 18__. 1830s.

Rarity: —

$20 • W-MA-430-020-G060

Left: Lathework chain bearing MASSACHUSETTS / 20 / 20 vertically. ***Center:*** Alternating flower garlands and gridwork segments. ***Right:*** 20 / 20 vertically. ***Engraver:*** PSSP. ***Comments:*** H-MA-150-G12. 18__. 1830s.

Rarity: —

$50 • W-MA-430-050-G070

Left: Lathework chain bearing MASSACHUSETTS / 50 / 50 vertically. ***Center:*** Alternating flower garlands and gridwork segments. ***Right:*** 50 / 50 vertically. ***Engraver:*** PSSP. ***Comments:*** H-MA-150-G14. 18__. 1830s.

Rarity: —

$100 • W-MA-430-100-G080

Left: Lathework chain bearing MASSACHUSETTS / 100 / 100 vertically. ***Center:*** Alternating flower garlands and gridwork segments. ***Right:*** 100 / 100 vertically. ***Comments:*** H-MA-150-G16. 18__. 1830s.

Rarity: —

Non-Valid Issues

$5 • W-MA-430-005-A010

Left: FIVE. ***Center:*** 5 / Two figures / 5. ***Bottom center:*** Steamboat. ***Right:*** V / Scene / V. ***Engraver:*** Rawdon, Wright & Hatch. ***Comments:*** H-MA-150-A5. Altered from $5 Commercial Bank of Millington, Maryland. 18__. 1830s.

Rarity: —

Commonwealth Bank

1824–1838

W-MA-440

History: The Commonwealth Bank was incorporated on February 20, 1824. It was located at 47 State Street in Boston and was a depository for the public moneys.

In 1833 capital was listed at $500,000, and the bank's charter was renewed in 1834. Circulation at the time was $101,984. In 1835 it was $120,140, and in 1836 it had risen to $132,712.

By 1837 the Commonwealth Bank had become a bank of deposit for the Treasury Department, with $24,920.98 on deposit as of August that year. It then was found on the "list of deposite banks discontinued under the Deposite Act of June 1836."[44] On January 12, 1838, a report was heard that the Commonwealth

Bank had stopped its specie payments, which was considered a serious problem in light of its status as a deposit bank, with a capital of $1,750,000.[45] The Commonwealth Bank closed its doors on January 12, 1838.[46]

Numismatic Commentary: All notes from this bank are of the PSSP design. However, the vignettes used made them more attractive than what appeared on most other bank notes made by Perkins and, later, the New England Bank Note Co. Issues from this bank are quite handsome.

Valid Issues

$1 • W-MA-440-001-G010

Left: Lathework panel. *Center:* 1 / 1 / Flower garlands and gridwork segments / 1 / 1. *Right:* Lathework panel. *Engraver:* PSSP. *Comments:* H-MA-155-G2. 18__. 1820s.

Rarity: —

$1 • W-MA-440-001-G010a

Left: Narrow panel of lathework circle segments. *Right:* Narrow panel of lathework circle segments. *Engraver:* PSSP. *Comments:* H-MA-155-G4. Similar to W-MA-440-001-G010. 18__. 1820s–1830s.

Rarity: —

$1 • W-MA-440-001-G010b

CC

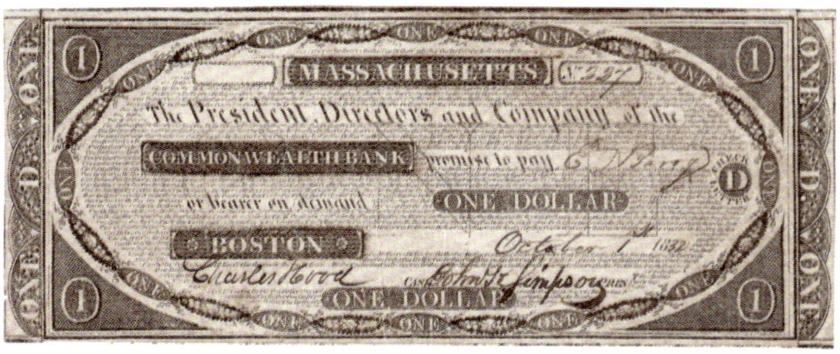

Engraver: PSSP. *Comments:* H-MA-155-G6. Similar to W-MA-440-001-G010. 18__. 1830s.

Rarity: URS-5
Proof $500

$1 • W-MA-440-001-G020

SBG

Engraver: PSSP. *Comments:* H-Unlisted. 18__. 1820s–1830s.

Rarity: URS-4
VG $400

$2 • W-MA-440-002-G030

Left: Lathework panel. *Center:* 2 / 2 / Flower garlands and gridwork segments / 2 / 2. *Right:* Lathework panel. *Engraver:* PSSP. *Comments:* H-MA-155-G10. 18__. 1820s.

Rarity: —

$2 • W-MA-440-002-G030a

Left: Narrow panel of lathework circle segments. *Right:* Narrow panel of lathework circle segments. *Engraver:* PSSP. *Comments:* H-MA-155-G12. Similar to W-MA-440-002-G030. 18__. 1820s–1830s.

Rarity: —

$2 • W-MA-440-002-G030b

Left: Five TWOs vertically. *Right:* Five TWOs vertically. *Engraver:* PSSP. *Comments:* H-MA-155-G14. Similar to W-MA-440-002-G030. 18__. 1830s.

Rarity: —

$3 • W-MA-440-003-G040

Left: Lathework panel. *Center:* 3 / 3 / Flower garlands and gridwork segments / 3 / 3. *Right:* Lathework panel. *Engraver:* PSSP. *Comments:* H-MA-155-G18. 18__. 1820s.

Rarity: —

$3 • W-MA-440-003-G040a

Left: Narrow panel of lathework circle segments. *Right:* Narrow panel of lathework circle segments. *Engraver:* PSSP. *Comments:* H-MA-155-G20. Similar to W-MA-440-003-G040. 18__. 1820s–1830s.

Rarity: —

$3 • W-MA-440-003-G040b

Left: THREE vertically. *Right:* THREE vertically. *Engraver:* PSSP. *Comments:* H-MA-155-G22. Similar to W-MA-440-003-G040. 18__. 1830s.

Rarity: —

$5 • W-MA-440-005-G050

Left: Lathework chain bearing MASSACHUSETTS / 5 / 5. *Center:* Alternating flower garlands and gridwork segments. *Right:* 5 / 5. *Engraver:* PSSP. *Comments:* H-MA-155-G26. 18__. 1820s.

Rarity: —

$5 • W-MA-440-005-G050a

Engraver: PSSP. *Comments:* H-MA-155-G28. Similar to W-MA-440-005-G050 but with zigzag ruled lines. 18__. 1820s–1830s.

Rarity: —

$5 • W-MA-440-005-G050b

Engraver: PSSP. *Comments:* H-MA-155-G30. Similar to W-MA-440-005-G050 but with spiral lathework lines. 18__. 1830s.

Rarity: —

$5 • W-MA-440-005-G060

CC

Engraver: PSSP. *Comments:* H-MA-155-G32. 18__. 1830s.

Rarity: URS-6
F $400; **VF** $750

$10 • **W-MA-440-010-G070**

Left: Lathework chain bearing MASSACHUSETTS / 10 / 10 vertically. ***Center:*** Alternating flower garlands and gridwork segments. ***Right:*** 10 / 10 vertically. ***Comments:*** H-MA-155-G36. 18__. 1820s.

Rarity: URS-6
F $400; **VF** $750

$10 • **W-MA-440-010-G070a**

Engraver: PSSP. ***Comments:*** H-MA-155-G38. Similar to W-MA-440-010-G070. 18__. 1820s–1830s.

Rarity: —

$10 • **W-MA-440-010-G070b**

Engraver: PSSP. ***Comments:*** H-MA-155-G40. Similar to W-MA-440-010-G070 but with spiral lathework lines. 18__. 1830s.

Rarity: —

$10 • **W-MA-440-010-G080**

Left: MASSACHUSETTS. ***Center:*** 10 / Woman reclining / 10. ***Right:*** 10 / Shield / 10. ***Engraver:*** PSSP. ***Comments:*** H-MA-155-G42. 18__. 1830s.

Rarity: —

$20 • **W-MA-440-020-G090**

Left: Lathework chain bearing MASSACHUSETTS / 20 / 20 vertically. ***Center:*** Alternating flower garlands and gridwork segments. ***Right:*** 20 / 20 vertically. ***Comments:*** H-MA-155-G46. 18__. 1820s–1830s.

Rarity: —

$20 • **W-MA-440-020-G100**

Left: MASSACHUSETTS. ***Center:*** 20 / Woman reclining / 20. ***Right:*** 20 / Shield / 20. ***Engraver:*** PSSP. ***Comments:*** H-MA-155-G48. Similar to W-MA-440-010-G080. 18__. 1830s.

Rarity: —

$50 • **W-MA-440-050-G110**

Left: Lathework chain bearing MASSACHUSETTS / 50 / 50 vertically. ***Center:*** Alternating flower garlands and gridwork segments. ***Right:*** 50 / 50 vertically. ***Engraver:*** PSSP. ***Comments:*** H-MA-155-G52. 18__. 1820s–1830s.

Rarity: —

$50 • **W-MA-440-050-G120**

Left: MASSACHUSETTS. ***Center:*** 50 / Woman reclining / 50. ***Right:*** 50 / Shield / 50. ***Engraver:*** PSSP. ***Comments:*** H-MA-155-G54. Similar to W-MA-440-010-G080. 18__. 1830s.

Rarity: URS-4
F $750

$100 • **W-MA-440-100-G130**

Left: Lathework chain bearing MASSACHUSETTS / 100 / 100 vertically. ***Center:*** Alternating flower garlands and gridwork segments. ***Right:*** 100 / 100 vertically. ***Comments:*** H-MA-155-G58. 18__. 1820s–1830s.

Rarity: —

$100 • **W-MA-440-100-G140**

Left: MASSACHUSETTS. ***Center:*** 100 / Woman seated / 100. ***Right:*** 100 / Shield / 100. ***Engraver:*** PSSP. ***Comments:*** H-MA-155-G60. Similar to W-MA-440-010-G080. 18__. 1830s.

Rarity: URS-4
F $1,000

$500 • **W-MA-440-500-G150**

Left: MASSACHUSETTS. ***Center:*** 500 / Woman seated / 500. ***Right:*** 500 / Shield / 500. ***Engraver:*** PSSP. ***Comments:*** H-MA-155-G64. Similar to W-MA-440-010-G080. 18__. 1830s.

Rarity: —

Continental Bank
1860–1864
W-MA-450

History: The Continental Bank was founded in 1860 by E.R. Secomb and James Swan, who became the president and cashier, respectively. It was located at 238 Washington Street and had an $800,000 authorized capital. By 1861 the capital had risen to $900,000.

In 1862 circulation was listed at $37,027 and specie was $39,887.19.[47] The president of the bank in 1863 was Oliver Ditson.

On October 1, 1864, the interests of the Continental Bank were succeeded by the Continental National Bank of Boston, which opened with a capital of $300,000.

Numismatic Commentary: All issues from this short-lived bank were engraved by the American Bank Note Co. and are pleasantly attractive, with plenty of green color added. The Continental Bank is one of the few banks that issued notes with the Polar Bear vignette, a numismatic favorite. Uncut Sheets are available on occasion.

Valid Issues

$1 • **W-MA-450-001-G010**

CJF

Tint: Green frame and panel of microlettering. ***Engraver:*** American Bank Note Co. ***Comments:*** H-MA-160-G2a. Remainder. Oct. __, 18__. 1860s.

Rarity: URS-6
VF $300; **EF** $350; **Unc-Rem** $500

$2 • W-MA-450-002-G020 HA

Tint: Green frame and panel of microlettering. ***Engraver:*** American Bank Note Co. ***Comments:*** H-MA-160-G4a. Remainder. Oct. __, 18__. 1860s.

Rarity: URS-8

VF $300; **EF** $350; **Unc-Rem** $600

Selected auction price: Heritage, April–May 2011, Lot 15225, Gem Unc $632

$3 • W-MA-450-003-G030 HA

Tint: Green frame and panel of microlettering. ***Engraver:*** American Bank Note Co. ***Comments:*** H-MA-160-G6a. Remainder. Oct. __, 18__. 1860s.

Rarity: URS-8

F $1,500; **Unc-Rem** $5,000; **Proof** $6,000

Selected auction price(s): Heritage, January 2008, Lot 13036, AU $4,600; Heritage, September 2009, Lot 14608, CU $6,325; Stack's Bowers Galleries, August 2012, Lot 7129, AU $5,175; Stack's Bowers Galleries, November 2013, Lot 1050, EF $1,997; Stack's Bowers Galleries, November 2013, Lot 1049, Gem Unc $6,462

$5 • W-MA-450-005-G040

Left: 5 / State arms. ***Center:*** White 5 / Three men near wharf / White 5. ***Bottom center:*** FI5VE. ***Right:*** 5 / Portrait of Benjamin Franklin. ***Tint:*** Green frame, 5 5, and die bearing FI5VE. ***Engraver:*** American Bank Note Co. ***Comments:*** H-MA-160-G8a. Oct. __, 18__. 1860s.

Rarity: URS-8

VF $300; **Unc-Rem** $400

$10 • W-MA-450-010-G050 HA

Tint: Green dies bearing Xs, and TEN / 10 / TEN. ***Engraver:*** American Bank Note Co. ***Comments:*** H-MA-160-G10a. Proof. Oct. __, 18__. 1860s.

Rarity: URS-3

VF $1,500; **Proof** $3,000

$20 • W-MA-450-020-G060

Left: MASSACHUSETTS across XX / State arms. ***Center:*** Surrender of Cornwallis. ***Right:*** 20 / Soldier with gun. ***Tint:*** Green. ***Engraver:*** American Bank Note Co. ***Comments:*** H-MA-160-G12a. Oct. __, 18__. 1860s.

Rarity: —

$50 • W-MA-450-050-G070

Left: 50 / State arms. ***Center:*** George Washington on horseback, Soldiers, Tents, Cannons and horses. ***Right:*** 50 / Male portrait. ***Tint:*** Green. ***Engraver:*** American Bank Note Co. ***Comments:*** H-MA-160-G14a. Oct. __, 18__. 1860s.

Rarity: —

$100 • W-MA-450-100-G080

Left: 100 / State arms. ***Tint:*** Green panel and die bearing 100. ***Engraver:*** American Bank Note Co. ***Comments:*** H-MA-160-G16a. Oct. __, 18__. 1860s.

Rarity: URS-3

VF $1,600; **Proof** $2,500

$500 • W-MA-450-500-G090

Left: 500 / State arms. ***Center:*** Statue of woman with sword and shield. ***Right:*** 500 / Eagle. ***Tint:*** Green die bearing 500. ***Engraver:*** American Bank Note Co. ***Comments:*** H-MA-160-G18a. Oct. __, 18__. 1860s.

Rarity: —

How to Read the Whitman Numbering System

$1 • W-MA-010-001-G010a

Denomination: Value of the note shown.

W: Whitman number. This number is a sortable code unique to each bank and note.

MA: Abbreviation for the state under study.

010: Numerical designation specific to each bank.

001: The denomination in dollars.

G010a: G indicates a good or valid note. Other categories are indicated thus: C (counterfeit); R (raised); S (spurious); N (not-attributed); A (altered). Numbers are assigned starting with 010, 020, et seq. Terminal letters following the number indicate variations of a note: a series of different colored overprints, tints, payees, etc., all on the same design of note. For more information, see the "How to Use This Book" section at the front of the volume, page xiv.

Uncut Sheets

$1-$1-$2-$3 • W-MA-450-001.001.002.003-US010 JF

Tint(s): Green. ***Engraver:*** American Bank Note Co. ***Comments:*** H-MA-160-G2a, G2a, G4a, G6a. Oct. __, 18__. 1860s.

Rarity: URS-4
Unc-Rem $6,000

Non-Valid Issues

$3 • W-MA-450-003-C030

Engraver: American Bank Note Co. ***Comments:*** H-MA-160-C6a Counterfeit of W-MA-450-003-G030. Oct. __, 18__. 1860s.

Rarity: —

$3 • W-MA-450-003-S010

Left: 3 / Portrait of girl / THREE. ***Center:*** White 3 / Boy with dog / White 3. ***Right:*** THREE / Man. ***Tint:*** Brown lathework. ***Comments:*** H-MA-160-S5a. Sept. 10, 18__. 1860.

Rarity: —

$5 • W-MA-450-005-A010 SI

Tint: Red-brown lathework outlining white 5. ***Engraver:*** Bald, Cousland & Co. ***Comments:*** H-MA-160-A5. Altered from $5 Pioneer Association, Lafayette, Indiana. 18__. 1850s–1860s.

Rarity: URS-7
F $75

Continental Bank of Boston
1860s
W-MA-460

History: A non-existent bank represented only by notes altered from those of other banks and intended to pass for those of the Continental Bank, W-MA-450.

Issues

$5 • W-MA-460-005-A010

Left: 5 / FIVE / FIVE. ***Center:*** Man and woman with three cherubs, Five silver dollars / FIVE. ***Right:*** 5 / Female portrait / FIVE. ***Overprint:*** FIVE. ***Engraver:*** Rawdon, Wright, Hatch & Edson. ***Comments:*** H-MA-161-A10. Altered from $5 Farmers and Merchants Bank of Memphis, Memphis, Tennessee series. Oct. __, 18__. 1850s–1860s.

Rarity: —

Eagle Bank
1822–1865
W-MA-470

History: The Eagle Bank was chartered in February 1822. It was located at 70 State Street in Boston until 1864, when it was located at 16 Kilby Street.

In 1837 the Eagle Bank's charter was renewed until January 1, 1870, with $500,000 in authorized capital. Circulation in 1838 was $160,368. Net profits on hand were $95,944.64; balances due to other banks $95,944.64; cash deposited $276,714.20; cash deposited bearing interest $252,741.71; total amount due from banks $1,410,576.74; gold, silver, and other coined metals in the banking house $22,148.51; bills of other banks incorporated in this state $163,034; balance due from other banks $125,000; amount of all debts due $1,100,394.23; total amount of resources of the bank $1,410,576.74.

Between 1839 and 1860 circulation ranged from $131,596 to $152,861. In 1841 the bank suffered a loss of several tens of thousands of dollars when a teller made secret loans.

In 1849 the bank petitioned the legislature and was approved for a renewal of its charter. In 1852 the bank's capital was $500,000. A bill proposed in the Senate on May 14 to increase the capital stock of the Eagle Bank was rejected.[48] Nevertheless, by 1857 it was $700,000. In December 1860, it had reached $1,000,000.

After the National Eagle Bank of Boston was chartered on April 1, 1865, the state bank wound up its affairs.

Numismatic Commentary: Genuine notes from this bank are hard to locate. Some of the later issues have a vignette of a spread eagle resting on various boxes of merchandise.

VALID ISSUES

$1 • W-MA-470-001-G010
Center: 1 / 1 / Flower garlands and gridwork segments / ONE / 1 / 1. ***Engraver:*** PSSP. ***Comments:*** H-MA-165-G2. 18__. 1820s.

Rarity: —

$1 • W-MA-470-001-G010a
Left: Narrow panel of lathework circle segments. ***Right:*** Narrow panel of lathework circle segments. ***Engraver:*** PSSP. ***Comments:*** H-MA-165-G4. Similar to W-MA-470-001-G010. 18__. 1820s.

Rarity: —

$1 • W-MA-470-001-G010b
Left: Narrow panel of lathework circle segments. ***Right:*** Narrow panel of lathework circle segments. ***Engraver:*** PSSP. ***Comments:*** H-MA-165-G6. Similar to W-MA-470-001-G010. 18__. 1820s–1830s.

Rarity: —

$1 • W-MA-470-001-G010c
Left: ONE / D / ONE vertically. ***Right:*** ONE / D / ONE vertically. ***Engraver:*** PSSP. ***Comments:*** H-MA-165-G8. Similar to W-MA-470-001-G010. 18__. 1830s.

Rarity: —

$1 • W-MA-470-001-G010d
Left: Panel bearing MASSACHUSETTS. ***Center:*** ONE. ***Right:*** ONE / D / ONE vertically. ***Engraver:*** PSSP. ***Comments:*** H-MA-165-G10. Similar to W-MA-470-001-G010. 18__. 1830s.

Rarity: —

$1 • W-MA-470-001-G020

CJF

Engraver: New England Bank Note Co. ***Comments:*** H-MA-165-G14. 18__. 1830s–1850s.

Rarity: URS-3
F $750

$1 • W-MA-470-001-G020a

CJF

Overprint: Red ONE. ***Engraver:*** New England Bank Note Co. / ABNCo. monogram. ***Comments:*** H-MA-165-G14a. Similar to W-MA-470-001-G020 but with additional engraver imprint. 18__. 1850s–1860s.

Rarity: URS-3
F $750

$2 • W-MA-470-002-G030
Center: 2 / 2 / Flower garlands and gridwork segments / TWO / 2 / 2. ***Engraver:*** PSSP. ***Comments:*** H-MA-165-G18. 18__. 1820s.

Rarity: —

$2 • W-MA-470-002-G030a
Left: Narrow panel of lathework circle segments. ***Right:*** Narrow panel of lathework circle segments. ***Engraver:*** PSSP. ***Comments:*** H-MA-165-G20. Similar to W-MA-470-002-G030. 18__. 1820s.

Rarity: —

$2 • W-MA-470-002-G030b
Left: Narrow panel of lathework circle segments. ***Right:*** Narrow panel of lathework circle segments. ***Engraver:*** PSSP. ***Comments:*** H-MA-165-G22. Similar to W-MA-470-002-G030. 18__. 1820s–1830s.

Rarity: —

$2 • W-MA-470-002-G030c
Left: Five TWOs vertically. ***Right:*** Five TWOs vertically. ***Engraver:*** PSSP. ***Comments:*** H-MA-165-G24. Similar to W-MA-470-002-G030. 18__. 1830s.

Rarity: —

$2 • W-MA-470-002-G030d
Left: Panel bearing MASSACHUSETTS. ***Center:*** TWO. ***Right:*** Five TWOs vertically. ***Engraver:*** PSSP. ***Comments:*** H-MA-165-G26. Similar to W-MA-470-002-G030. 18__. 1830s.

Rarity: URS-2
F $750

$2 • W-MA-470-002-G040
Left: 2 / Woman with basket of flowers on shoulder / TWO. ***Center:*** Spread eagle on pile of merchandise / TWO. ***Right:*** 2 / TWO / Female portrait. ***Engraver:*** PSSP. ***Comments:*** H-MA-165-G30. 18__. 1830s–1850s.

Rarity: —

$2 • W-MA-470-002-G040a
Engraver: New England Bank Note Co. / ABNCo. monogram. ***Comments:*** H-MA-165-G30a. Similar to W-MA-470-002-G040 but with additional engraver imprint. 18__. 1850s–1860s.

Rarity: —

$3 • W-MA-470-003-G050

Center: 3 / 3 / Flower garlands and gridwork segments / 3 / 3. ***Engraver:*** PSSP. ***Comments:*** H-MA-165-G34. 18__. 1820s.

Rarity: URS-2
F $750

$3 • W-MA-470-003-G050a

Left: Narrow panel of lathework circle segments. ***Right:*** Narrow panel of lathework circle segments. ***Engraver:*** PSSP. ***Comments:*** H-MA-165-G36. Similar to W-MA-470-003-G050. 18__. 1820s.

Rarity: —

$3 • W-MA-470-003-G050b

Left: Narrow panel of lathework circle segments. ***Right:*** Narrow panel of lathework circle segments. ***Engraver:*** PSSP. ***Comments:*** H-MA-165-G38. Similar to W-MA-470-003-G050. 18__. 1820s–1830s.

Rarity: —

$3 • W-MA-470-003-G050c

Left: THREE vertically. ***Right:*** THREE vertically. ***Engraver:*** PSSP. ***Comments:*** H-MA-165-G40. Similar to W-MA-470-003-G050. 18__. 1830s.

Rarity: —

$3 • W-MA-470-003-G050d

Left: Panel bearing MASSACHUSETTS. ***Center:*** THREE. ***Right:*** THREE vertically. ***Engraver:*** PSSP. ***Comments:*** H-MA-165-G42. Similar to W-MA-470-003-G050. 18__. 1830s.

Rarity: —

$5 • W-MA-470-005-G060

Left: Lathework chain bearing MASSACHUSETTS / 5 / 5. ***Center:*** Alternating flower garlands and gridwork segments. ***Right:*** 5 / 5. ***Engraver:*** PSSP. ***Comments:*** H-MA-165-G46. 18__. 1820s.

Rarity: URS-2
F $750

$5 • W-MA-470-005-G060a

Engraver: PSSP. ***Comments:*** H-MA-165-G48. Similar to W-MA-470-005-G060 but with white boxes at top. 18__. 1820s.

Rarity: —

$5 • W-MA-470-005-G060b

Engraver: PSSP. ***Comments:*** H-MA-165-G50. Similar to W-MA-470-005-G060 but with zigzag ruled lines. 18__. 1820s–1830s.

Rarity: —

$5 • W-MA-470-005-G060c

Engraver: PSSP. ***Comments:*** H-MA-165-G52. Similar to W-MA-470-005-G060 but with spiral, lathework lines. 18__. 1830s.

Rarity: URS-5
F $300

$5 • W-MA-470-005-G070

Left: Spread eagle on pile of merchandise / 5. ***Center:*** Two cherubs flanking V. ***Right:*** FIVE / Woman standing with arm on pedestal. ***Engraver:*** New England Bank Note Co. ***Comments:*** H-MA-165-G56. 18__. 1830s–1850s.

Rarity: —

$5 • W-MA-470-005-G070a

Engraver: PSSP. ***Comments:*** H-MA-165-G56a. Similar to W-MA-470-005-G070 but with different engraver imprint. 18__. 1850s–1860s.

Rarity: —

$10 • W-MA-470-010-G080

Left: Lathework chain bearing MASSACHUSETTS / 10 / 10 vertically. ***Center:*** Alternating flower garlands and gridwork segments. ***Right:*** 10 / 10 vertically. ***Comments:*** H-MA-165-G60. 18__. 1820s.

Rarity: —

$10 • W-MA-470-010-G080a

Comments: H-MA-165-G62. Similar to W-MA-470-010-G080 but with white boxes at top. 18__. 1820s.

Rarity: —

$10 • W-MA-470-010-G080b

Engraver: PSSP. ***Comments:*** H-MA-165-G64. Similar to W-MA-470-010-G080a but with zigzag ruled lines. 18__. 1820s–1830s.

Rarity: —

$10 • W-MA-470-010-G080c

Engraver: PSSP. ***Comments:*** H-MA-165-G66. Similar to W-MA-470-010-G080a but with spiral lathework lines. 18__. 1830s.

Rarity: —

$10 • W-MA-470-010-G090

Left: Spread eagle on pile of merchandise / X. ***Center:*** Dog with key lying by strongbox, Houses. ***Right:*** 10 / Woman drawing water from well. ***Engraver:*** PSSP / New England Bank Note Co. ***Comments:*** H-MA-165-G70. 18__. 1830s–1850s.

Rarity: —

$10 • W-MA-470-010-G090a

Engraver: New England Bank Note Co. / ABNCo. monogram. ***Comments:*** H-MA-165-G70a. Similar to W-MA-470-010-G090 but with additional engraver imprint. 18__. 1850s–1860s.

Rarity: —

$20 • W-MA-470-020-G100

Left: Panel bearing state arms / 20 / 20 vertically. ***Center:*** Alternating flower garlands and gridwork segments. ***Right:*** 20 / 20 vertically. ***Comments:*** H-MA-165-G74. 18__. 1820s.

Rarity: —

$20 • W-MA-470-020-G100a

Left: Lathework chain bearing MASSACHUSETTS vertically. ***Engraver:*** PSSP. ***Comments:*** H-MA-165-G76. Similar to W-MA-470-020-G100. 18__. 1820s–1830s.

Rarity: —

$20 • W-MA-470-020-G110

Left: Spread eagle on pile of merchandise / 20. ***Center:*** Two cherubs flanking XX. ***Right:*** 20 / Woman. ***Engraver:*** New England Bank Note Co. ***Comments:*** H-MA-165-G80. 18__. 1830s–1850s.

Rarity: —

$50 • W-MA-470-050-G120

Left: Panel bearing state arms vertically. ***Center:*** Alternating flower garlands and gridwork segments. ***Right:*** 50 / 50 vertically. ***Comments:*** H-MA-165-G84. 18__. 1820s.

Rarity: —

$50 • W-MA-470-050-G120a

Left: Lathework chain bearing MASSACHUSETTS vertically. ***Engraver:*** PSSP. ***Comments:*** H-MA-165-G86. Similar to W-MA-470-050-G120. 18__. 1820s–1830s.

Rarity: —

$50 • W-MA-470-050-G130

Left: L / Steamboat / 50. ***Center:*** Spread eagle and pile of merchandise / Female portrait. ***Right:*** 50 / Reapers / L. ***Engraver:*** New England Bank Note Co. ***Comments:*** H-MA-165-G90. 18__. 1830s–1850s.

Rarity: —

$100 • W-MA-470-100-G140

Left: Panel bearing state arms / 100 / 100 vertically. ***Center:*** Alternating flower garlands and gridwork segments. ***Right:*** 100 / 100 vertically. ***Comments:*** H-MA-165-G94. 18__. 1820s.

Rarity: —

$100 • W-MA-470-100-G140a

Left: Lathework chain bearing MASSACHUSETTS vertically. ***Comments:*** H-MA-165-G96. Similar to W-MA-470-100-G140. 18__. 1820s–1830s.

Rarity: —

$100 • W-MA-470-100-G150

Left: 100 / Woman / 100. ***Center:*** Spread eagle on pile of merchandise. ***Right:*** 100 / Woman / 100. ***Engraver:*** New England Bank Note Co. ***Comments:*** H-MA-165-G100. 18__. 1830s–1850s.

Rarity: —

Non-Valid Issues

$2 • W-MA-470-002-C030d

CC

Engraver: PSSP. ***Comments:*** H-MA-165-C26. Counterfeit of W-MA-470-002-G030d. 18__. 1830s.

Rarity: URS-8

VG $45; **F** $50; **VF** $75; **EF** $100

$2 • W-MA-470-002-S010

Left: MASSACHUSETTS on banner. ***Center:*** 2 / Spread eagle / 2. ***Right:*** 2 / 2. ***Engraver:*** Graphic Co. ***Comments:*** H-MA-165-S5. 18__. 1820s.

Rarity: —

$3 • W-MA-470-003-C050d

Engraver: PSSP. ***Comments:*** H-MA-165-C42. Counterfeit of W-MA-470-003-G050d. 18__. 1830s.

Rarity: —

$5 • W-MA-470-005-R010

Overprint: Red FIVE. ***Engraver:*** New England Bank Note Co. / ABNCo. monogram. ***Comments:*** H-MA-165-R5. Raised from W-MA-470-001-G020a. 18__. 1860s.

Rarity: URS-4

F $150

$5 • W-MA-470-005-S020

Left: MASSACHUSETTS on banner. ***Center:*** 5 / Spread eagle with white 5 at feet / 5. ***Bottom center:*** White 5. ***Right:*** 5 / 5. ***Engraver:*** Graphic Co. ***Comments:*** H-MA-165-S10. Similar to W-MA-470-005-S010. 18__. 1820s.

Rarity: URS-4

F $150; **VF** $175

$5 • W-MA-470-005-A010

CC

Engraver: Graphic Co. ***Comments:*** H-MA-165-A5. Altered from $5 Eagle Bank, New Haven, Connecticut. 18__. 1820s.

Rarity: URS-3

F $150

$10 • W-MA-470-010-C080b

CC

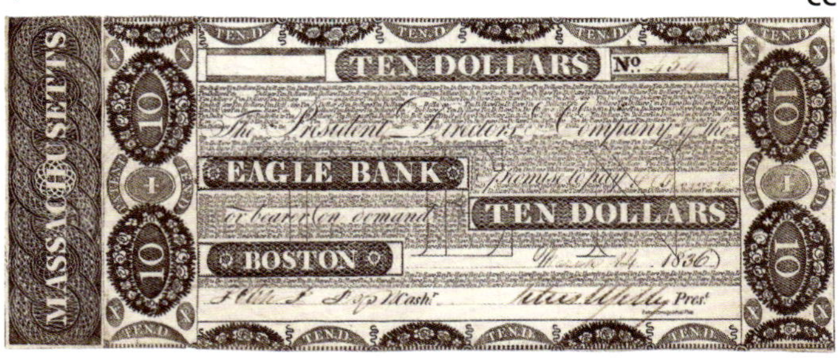

Engraver: PSSP. ***Comments:*** H-MA-165-C64. Counterfeit of W-MA-470-010-G080b. 18__. 1830s.

Rarity: URS-6

F $100; **VF** $175

$10 • W-MA-470-010-R020

Engraver: New England Bank Note Co. ***Comments:*** H-MA-165-R10. Raised from W-MA-470-001-G020 or W-MA-470-002-G040. 18__. 1840s.

Rarity: —

$20 • W-MA-470-020-R030

Engraver: PSSP. ***Comments:*** H-MA-165-R15. Raised from W-MA-470-001-G020 or W-MA-470-002-G040. 18__. 1840s.

Rarity: —

$50 • W-MA-470-050-R040

Engraver: New England Bank Note Co. ***Comments:*** H-MA-165-R20. Raised from W-MA-470-001-G020. 18__. 1840s.

Rarity: —

Eliot Bank

1853–1864

W-MA-480

History: The Eliot Bank commenced business on October 6, 1853, with an authorized capital of $300,000. It was located at 23 Kilby Street in Boston. By 1863 the address was 13 Kilby Street. Later in 1864 the address was changed to 18 Kilby Street.

By 1855 the Eliot Bank's capital had increased to $600,000. Later it rose as high as $750,000. Circulation ranged from $149,939.50 in 1854 to $87,627 in 1858. Other values in 1854 included specie $36,454.87; bills of this bank and other New England states $73,095.09. By 1858 specie was $65,353.65.

After the Eliot National Bank of Boston was chartered in 1864, it assumed the state bank's business.

Numismatic Commentary: These notes are among the most coveted of the entire state of Massachusetts. The historical vignette of "John Eliot Preaching to the Indians" is especially popular and in demand, making these and other notes from this bank very hard to locate.

Valid Issues

$1 • W-MA-480-001-G010

CC

Engraver: Baldwin, Adams & Co. ***Comments:*** H-Unlisted. Proof. 18__. 1850s.

Rarity: URS-2
Proof $2,000

$1 • W-MA-480-001-G010a

CC

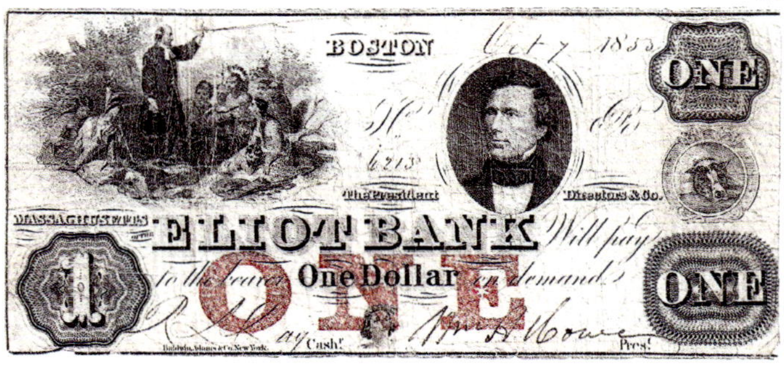

Overprint: Red ONE. ***Engraver:*** Baldwin, Adams & Co. ***Comments:*** H-MA-170-G2a. Similar to W-MA-480-001-G010. 18__. 1850s.

Rarity: URS-3
F $600; **Proof** $2,200

$1 • W-MA-480-001-G010b

Left: Eliot preaching to the Indians / 1. ***Center:*** Portrait of Franklin Pierce. ***Right:*** ONE / Dog with key / ONE. ***Engraver:*** Baldwin, Adams & Co. / ABNCo. monogram. ***Comments:*** H-MA-170-G2b. Similar to W-MA-480-001-G010 but with additional engraver imprint. 18__. 1850s–1860s.

Rarity: URS-5
F $750; **EF** $1,500

$2 • W-MA-480-002-G020

Left: 2 / Eliot preaching to Indians. ***Center:*** 2. ***Right:*** TWO / Sailor and carpenter on ship. ***Overprint:*** Red 2. ***Engraver:*** Baldwin, Adams & Co. ***Comments:*** H-MA-170-G4a. 18__. 1850s.

Rarity: —

$2 • W-MA-480-002-G020a

QDB

Overprint: Red 2. ***Engraver:*** Baldwin, Adams & Co. / ABNCo. monogram. ***Comments:*** H-MA-170-G4b. Similar to W-MA-480-002-G020 but with additional engraver imprint. 18__. 1850s–1860s.

Rarity: URS-3
VG $350; **F** $600; **VF** $800

$3 • W-MA-480-003-G030

HA

Overprint: Red lazy 3. ***Engraver:*** Baldwin, Adams & Co. ***Comments:*** H-MA-170-G6a. Proof. 18__. 1850s.

Rarity: URS-2
Proof $2,000

$3 • W-MA-480-003-G030a

Left: 3 / Woman with sheaf and sickle. ***Center:*** Eliot preaching to the Indians. ***Right:*** 3 / Portrait of Daniel Webster. ***Engraver:*** Baldwin, Adams & Co. / ABNCo. monogram. ***Comments:*** H-MA-170-G6b. Similar to W-MA-480-003-G030 but with additional engraver imprint. 18__. 1850s–1860s.

Rarity: —

$5 • W-MA-480-005-G040

QDB

Engraver: Baldwin, Adams & Co. ***Comments:*** H-Unlisted. Proof. 18__. 1850s.

Rarity: URS-5
Proof $400

$5 • W-MA-480-005-G040a

Left: FIVE / Indian man kneeling. ***Center:*** Female portrait / Eliot preaching to the Indians. ***Right:*** 5 / 5. ***Overprint:*** Red. ***Engraver:*** Baldwin, Adams & Co. ***Comments:*** H-MA-170-G8a. Similar to W-MA-480-005-G040. 18__. 1850s.

Rarity: URS-4
F $500

$5 • W-MA-480-005-G040b

Engraver: Baldwin, Adams & Co. / ABNCo. monogram. ***Comments:*** H-MA-170-G8b. Similar to W-MA-480-005-G040 but with additional engraver imprint. 18__. 1850s–1860s.

Rarity: —

$10 • W-MA-480-010-G050

HA

Overprint: Red TEN. ***Engraver:*** Baldwin, Adams & Co. ***Comments:*** H-MA-170-G10a. Proof. 18__. 1850s.

Rarity: URS-2
Proof $2,000

$10 • W-MA-480-010-G050a

Left: TEN / Hunter warming hands by fire, Dog. ***Center:*** TEN / X / X. ***Right:*** TEN / Hunter drinking from stream. ***Engraver:*** Baldwin, Adams & Co. / ABNCo. monogram. ***Comments:*** H-MA-170-G10b. Similar to W-MA-480-010-G050 but with additional engraver imprint. 18__. 1850s–1860s.

Rarity: URS-6
F $150

$20 • W-MA-480-020-G060

CC

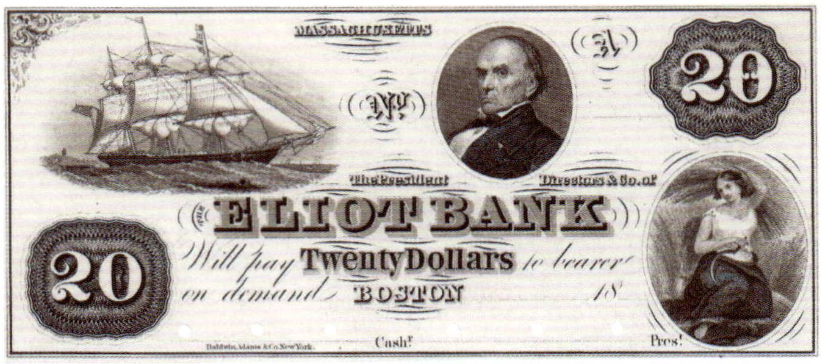

Engraver: Baldwin, Adams & Co. ***Comments:*** H-Unlisted. Proof. 18__. 1850s.

Rarity: URS-2
Proof $1,500

$20 • W-MA-480-020-G060a

Left: Clipper ship under sail / 20. ***Center:*** Portrait of Daniel Webster. ***Right:*** 20 / Ceres seated. ***Overprint:*** Red. ***Engraver:*** Baldwin, Adams & Co. ***Comments:*** H-MA-170-G12a. Similar to W-MA-480-020-G060. 18__. 1850s.

Rarity: URS-3
Proof $1,750

$20 • W-MA-480-020-G060b

Engraver: Baldwin, Adams & Co. / ABNCo. monogram. ***Comments:*** H-MA-170-G12b. Similar to W-MA-480-020-G060 but with additional engraver imprint. 18__. 1850s–1860s.

Rarity: —

$50 • W-MA-480-050-G070

QDB

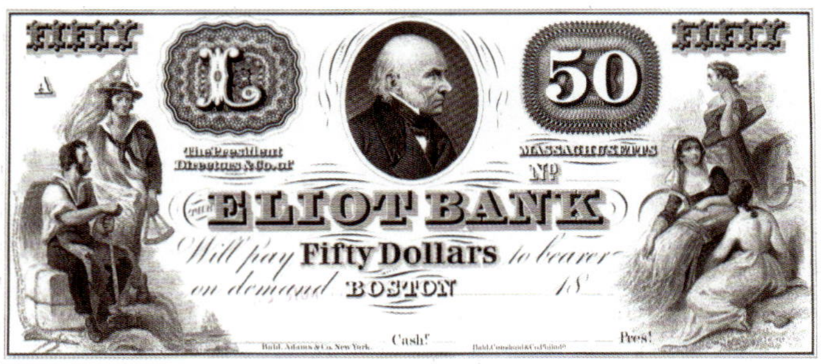

Engraver: Bald, Adams & Co. / Bald, Cousland & Co. ***Comments:*** H-Unlisted. Proof. 18__. 1850s.

Rarity: URS-2
Proof $1,750

$50 • W-MA-480-050-G070a

Left: FIFTY / Mechanic seated and sailor standing with flag. ***Center:*** L / Portrait of John Quincy Adams / 50. ***Right:*** FIFTY / Two women seated and one standing by anchor. ***Engraver:*** Bald, Adams & Co. / Bald, Cousland & Co. ***Comments:*** H-MA-170-G14a. Similar to W-MA-480-050-G070. 18__. 1850s.

Rarity: URS-2
Proof $1,750

$50 • W-MA-480-050-G070b

Engraver: Baldwin, Adams & Co. / ABNCo. monogram. ***Comments:*** H-MA-170-G14b. Similar to W-MA-480-050-G070 but with different engraver imprint. 18__. 1850s–1860s.

Rarity: —

$100 • W-MA-480-100-G080

HA

Engraver: Baldwin, Adams & Co. ***Comments:*** H-MA-170-G16. Proof. 18__. 1850s.

Rarity: URS-4
Proof $2,500

$100 • W-MA-480-100-G090

CC

Engraver: Bald, Adams & Co. / Bald, Cousland & Co. ***Comments:*** H-Unlisted. Proof. 18__. 1850s–1860s.

Rarity: URS-4
Proof $2,000

$100 • W-MA-480-100-G090a

Left: 100 / Indian man standing with bow and arrow. ***Center:*** Indians on cliff viewing city in distance. ***Right:*** 100 / C. ***Engraver:*** American Bank Note Co. ***Comments:*** H-MA-170-G18. Similar to W-MA-480-100-G090 but with different engraver imprint. 18__. 1850s–1860s.

Rarity: URS-3
Proof $2,000

$500 • W-MA-480-500-G100

CC

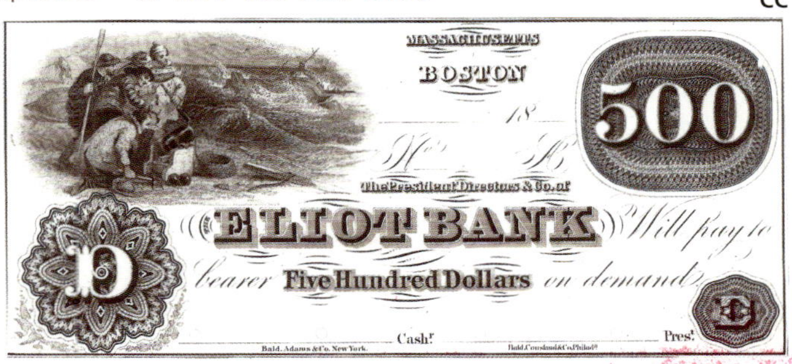

Engraver: Bald, Adams & Co. / Bald, Cousland & Co. ***Comments:*** H-Unlisted. Proof. 18__. 1850s–1860s.

Rarity: URS-5
Proof $2,500

$500 • W-MA-480-500-G100a

Left: Shipwreck scene, Five men on beach / D. ***Right:*** 500 / D. ***Engraver:*** American Bank Note Co. ***Comments:*** H-MA-170-G20. Similar to W-MA-480-500-G100 but with different engraver imprint. 18__. 1850s–1860s.

Rarity: URS-3
Proof $3,500
Selected auction price: Lyn Knight, June 2012, Lot 660, Choice AN $600

Uncut Sheets

$1-$1-$2-$5 • W-MA-480-001.001.002.005-US010

Vignette(s): ($1) Eliot preaching to the Indians / Portrait of Franklin Pierce. ***($1)*** Eliot preaching to the Indians / Portrait of Franklin Pierce. ***($2)*** Eliot preaching to Indians / Sailor and carpenter on ship. ***($5)*** Indian man kneeling / Female portrait / Eliot preaching to the Indians. ***Overprint(s):*** None. ***Engraver:*** Baldwin, Adams & Co. ***Comments:*** Similar to H-MA-170-G2a, G2a, G4a, G8a. 18__. 1850s.

Rarity: URS-3
Proof $1,500

$1-$2-$3-$5 • W-MA-480-001.002.003.005-US020

Vignette(s): ($1) Eliot preaching to the Indians / Portrait of Franklin Pierce. ***($2)*** Eliot preaching to Indians / Sailor and carpenter on ship. ***($3)*** Woman / Eliot preaching to the Indians / Male portrait. ***($5)*** Indian man kneeling / Female portrait / Eliot preaching to the Indians. ***Overprint(s):*** None. ***Engraver:*** Baldwin, Adams & Co. ***Comments:*** Similar to H-MA-170-G2a, G4a, G6a, G8a. 18__. 1850s.

Rarity: URS-3
Proof $1,500

$3-$10 • W-MA-480-003.010-US030

Vignette(s): ($3) Woman / Eliot preaching to the Indians / Male portrait. ***($10)*** Hunter at fire / Hunter drinking. ***Overprint(s):*** None. ***Engraver:*** Baldwin, Adams & Co. ***Comments:*** Similar to H-MA-170-G6a, G10a. Partial sheet. 18__. 1850s.

Rarity: URS-4
Proof $800

$3-$10 • W-MA-480-003.010-US030a

Overprint(s): Red. ***Engraver:*** Baldwin, Adams & Co. ***Comments:*** All unlisted in Haxby. Similar to W-MA-480-003.010-US030. Partial sheet. 18__. 1850s.

Rarity: URS-4
Proof $1,000

$20-$50-$100-$500 • W-MA-480-020.050.100.500-US040

SBG

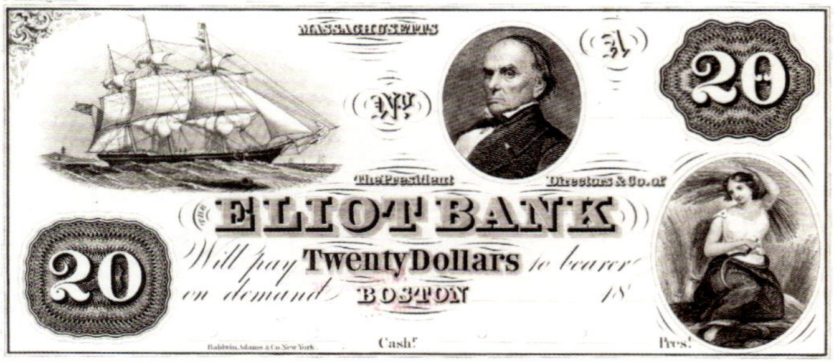

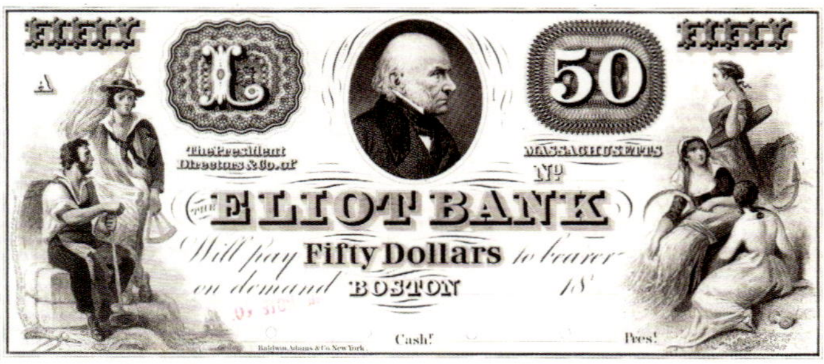

Overprint(s): None. ***Engraver:*** Baldwin, Adams & Co. ***Comments:*** All unlisted in Haxby. Proof. 18__. 1850s.

Rarity: URS-2
Proof $7,000

$20-$50-$100-$500 • W-MA-480-020.050.100.500-US040a

Vignette(s): ($20) Clipper ship / Portrait of Daniel Webster / Ceres seated. ***($50)*** Mechanic and sailor / Portrait of John Quincy Adams / Three women. ***($100)*** Indian man / Ship. ***($500)*** Shipwreck scene, Five men. ***Overprint(s):*** Red. ***Comments:*** H-MA-170-G12b, G14b, G16, G20. Similar to W-MA-480-020.050.100.500-US040.

Rarity: —

Selected auction price: Heritage, January 2014, Lot 15348, Choice AN $1,410

Non-Valid Issues

$2 • W-MA-480-002-C020

Engraver: Bald, Adams & Co. ***Comments:*** H-MA-170-C4a. Counterfeit of W-MA-480-002-G020 or G020a. 18__. 1850s.

Rarity: —

$5 • W-MA-480-005-N010

Left: Woman. ***Center:*** Woman and man with eagle and agricultural implements. ***Right:*** Five women. ***Comments:*** H-MA-170-N5. 1850s.

Rarity: —

Exchange Bank

1847–1864

W-MA-490

History: The Exchange Bank was chartered in April 1847 and opened for business in January 1848 at 28 State Street in the Merchants Bank Building.

Capital in February 1848 amounted to $383,650. By 1852 it was $1,000,000, where it remained through 1864. Circulation of the bank from 1857 to 1860 was $268,103. Bills of this bank and other New England states in the vault amounted to $134,958.22. In 1860 the bank's charter was renewed. The National Exchange Bank of Boston was chartered on October 10, 1864, and assumed the state bank's business.

Numismatic Commentary: Genuine notes of this bank are very hard to locate as nearly all were redeemed and destroyed, a familiar litany for Massachusetts obsolete currency.

Valid Issues

$1 • W-MA-490-001-G010

CC

Engraver: New England Bank Note Co. ***Comments:*** H-MA-175-G2. 18__. 1847–1850s.

Rarity: —

$1 • W-MA-490-001-G010a

Overprint: Red ONE. ***Engraver:*** New England Bank Note Co. ***Comments:*** H-MA-175-G2a. Similar to W-MA-490-001-G010. 18__. 1850s.

Rarity: —

$1 • W-MA-490-001-G010b

CJF

Overprint: Red ONE. ***Engraver:*** New England Bank Note Co. / ABNCo. monogram. ***Comments:*** H-MA-175-G2b. Similar to W-MA-490-001-G010 but with additional engraver imprint. 18__. 1850s–1860s.

Rarity: URS-3
VF $750

$2 • W-MA-490-002-G020

Left: Steamship sailing / 2. ***Center:*** 2 bearing female portrait. ***Right:*** 2 / Woman seated. ***Engraver:*** New England Bank Note Co. ***Comments:*** H-MA-175-G4. 18__. 1847–1850s.

Rarity: URS-2
F $1,000

$2 • W-MA-490-002-G020a

Overprint: Red. ***Engraver:*** New England Bank Note Co. ***Comments:*** H-MA-175-G4a. Similar to W-MA-490-002-G020. 18__. 1850s.

Rarity: —

$2 • W-MA-490-002-G020b

Overprint: Red. ***Engraver:*** New England Bank Note Co. / ABNCo. monogram. ***Comments:*** H-MA-175-G4b. Similar to W-MA-490-002-G020 but with additional engraver imprint. 18__. 1850s–1860s.

Rarity: —

$3 • W-MA-490-003-G030

Left: Eagle on 3 / THREE. ***Center:*** Ships / THREE. ***Right:*** 3 / Man / THREE. ***Engraver:*** New England Bank Note Co. ***Comments:*** H-MA-175-G6. 18__. 1847–1850s.

Rarity: —

$3 • W-MA-490-003-G030a

Overprint: Red. ***Engraver:*** New England Bank Note Co. ***Comments:*** H-MA-175-G6a. Similar to W-MA-490-003-G030. 18__. 1850s.

Rarity: —

$3 • W-MA-490-003-G030b

HA

Overprint: Red THREE. ***Engraver:*** New England Bank Note Co. / ABNCo. monogram. ***Comments:*** H-MA-175-G6b. Similar to W-MA-490-003-G030 but with additional engraver imprint. 18__. 1850s–1860s.

Rarity: URS-3
F $750

$5 • W-MA-490-005-G040

Left: 5 / Female portrait. ***Center:*** Eagle on shield, Factory and ship. ***Right:*** Woman and cherub in V / 5. ***Engraver:*** New England Bank Note Co. ***Comments:*** H-MA-175-G8. 18__. 1847–1850s.

Rarity: —

$5 • W-MA-490-005-G040a

Overprint: Red. ***Engraver:*** New England Bank Note Co. ***Comments:*** H-MA-175-G8a. Similar to W-MA-490-005-G040. 18__. 1850s.

Rarity: —

$5 • W-MA-490-005-G040b

Overprint: Red. ***Engraver:*** New England Bank Note Co. / ABNCo. monogram. ***Comments:*** H-MA-175-G8b. Similar to W-MA-490-005-G040 but with additional engraver imprint. 18__. 1850s–1860s.

Rarity: —

$10 • W-MA-490-010-G050

Left: Group of women with chariot / 10. ***Center:*** X. ***Right:*** 10 / Steamship / TEN. ***Engraver:*** New England Bank Note Co. ***Comments:*** H-MA-175-G10. 18__. 1847–1850s.

Rarity: —

$10 • W-MA-490-010-G050a

Overprint: Red. ***Engraver:*** New England Bank Note Co. ***Comments:*** H-MA-175-G10a. Similar to W-MA-490-010-G050. 18__. 1850s.

Rarity: —

$10 • W-MA-490-010-G050b

Overprint: Red. ***Engraver:*** New England Bank Note Co. / ABNCo. monogram. ***Comments:*** H-MA-175-G10b. Similar to W-MA-490-010-G050 but with additional engraver imprint. 18__. 1850s–1860s.

Rarity: —

$20 • W-MA-490-020-G060

Left: TWENTY across 20 / Portrait of Christopher Columbus. ***Center:*** Cherub standing on bale, dropping gold onto scales held by woman, Shield bearing state arms. ***Right:*** TWENTY across 20 / Portrait of George Washington. ***Engraver:*** New England Bank Note Co. ***Comments:*** H-MA-175-G12. 18__. 1847–1850s.

Rarity: —

$20 • W-MA-490-020-G060a

Overprint: Red. ***Engraver:*** New England Bank Note Co. ***Comments:*** H-MA-175-G12a. Similar to W-MA-490-020-G060. 18__. 1850s.

Rarity: —

$20 • W-MA-490-020-G060b

Overprint: Red. ***Engraver:*** New England Bank Note Co. / ABNCo. monogram. ***Comments:*** H-MA-175-G12b. Similar to W-MA-490-020-G060 but with additional engraver imprint. 18__. 1850s–1860s.

Rarity: —

$50 • W-MA-490-050-G070 HA

Engraver: New England Bank Note Co. ***Comments:*** H-MA-175-G14. Proof. 18__. 1847–1850s.

Rarity: URS-2
Proof $3,500
Selected auction price: Stack's Bowers Galleries, August 2014, Lot 2058, Proof $3,818

$50 • W-MA-490-050-G070a

Left: View of Customs House in Boston / FIFTY across 50. ***Center:*** 50. ***Right:*** 50 / Portrait of Benjamin Franklin. ***Overprint:*** Red. ***Engraver:*** New England Bank Note Co. ***Comments:*** H-MA-175-G14a. Similar to W-MA-490-050-G070. 18__. 1850s.

Rarity: URS-1
Proof $3,000

$50 • W-MA-490-050-G070b

Overprint: Red. ***Engraver:*** New England Bank Note Co. / ABNCo. monogram. ***Comments:*** H-MA-175-G14b. Similar to W-MA-490-050-G070 but with additional engraver imprint. 18__. 1850s–1860s.

Rarity: —

$100 • W-MA-490-100-G080

Left: 100. ***Center:*** Woman seated with arm on barrel, Ship and train. ***Right:*** HUNDRED across 100. ***Engraver:*** New England Bank Note Co. ***Comments:*** H-MA-175-G16. 18__. 1847–1850s.

Rarity: —

$100 • W-MA-490-100-G080a

Overprint: Red. ***Engraver:*** New England Bank Note Co. ***Comments:*** H-MA-175-G16a. Similar to W-MA-490-100-G080. 18__. 1850s.

Rarity: —

$100 • W-MA-490-100-G080b

Overprint: Red. ***Engraver:*** New England Bank Note Co. / ABNCo. monogram. ***Comments:*** H-MA-175-G16b. Similar to W-MA-490-100-G080 but with additional engraver imprint. 18__. 1850s–1860s.

Rarity: —

$500 • W-MA-490-500-G090

Left: Steamship / Ship / 500. ***Right:*** 500 / Woman standing with cornucopia and anchor. ***Comments:*** H-MA-175-G18. 1850s–1860s.

Rarity: —

$1,000 • W-MA-490-1000-G100

Left: Woman holding balance and fasces, Cornucopia, Shield and strongbox, Steamship and train on bridge. ***Right:*** 1000 / 1000. ***Comments:*** H-MA-175-G20. 1850s–1860s.

Rarity: URS-1
VF $3,500

Non-Valid Issues

$1 • W-MA-490-001-A010

Left: ONE across 1 / Female portrait. ***Center:*** Man binding sheaf, woman holding sheaf. ***Right:*** ONE across 1 / Female portrait. ***Engraver:*** W.L. Ormsby. ***Comments:*** H-MA-175-A5. Altered from a spurious issue of the Exchange Bank, Hartford, Connecticut. Dec. 1, 1856.

Rarity: —

$2 • W-MA-490-002-A020

Left: TWO across 2 / Ceres. ***Center:*** Hill and tree, Train, Two men. ***Right:*** TWO across 2 / Woman seated, Shield. ***Engraver:*** W.L. Ormsby. ***Comments:*** H-MA-175-A10. Altered from a spurious issue of the Exchange Bank, Hartford, Connecticut. Dec. 1, 1856.

Rarity: —

$3 • W-MA-490-003-C030a

Engraver: ABNCo. monogram. ***Comments:*** H-MA-175-C6b. Counterfeit of W-MA-490-003-G030a or G030b. 18__. 1850s–1860s.

Rarity: —

$3 • W-MA-490-003-R010

Engraver: New England Bank Note Co. ***Comments:*** H-MA-175-R5. Raised from W-MA-490-001-G010 or G010a. 18__. 1850s.

Rarity: —

$3 • W-MA-490-003-A030

Left: 3 / Cliff and trees, Hotel. ***Center:*** Town, Suspension bridge with two trains and carriage on it. ***Right:*** 3 / Portrait of young Queen Victoria. ***Overprint:*** Red THREE. ***Engraver:*** American Bank Note Co. ***Comments:*** H-MA-175-A15. Altered from $3 Bank of Clifton, Clifton, Canada. 18__. 1859.

Rarity: —

$3 • W-MA-490-003-A040

Left: 3 / Portrait of Benjamin Franklin. ***Center:*** Woman seated next to shield bearing 3 / THREE. ***Right:*** 3 / Woman seated. ***Engraver:*** Danforth, Bald & Co. ***Comments:*** H-MA-175-A20. Altered from $3 Columbia Bank, Washington, D.C. 185_. 1850s.

Rarity: —

$5 • W-MA-490-005-R020

Engraver: New England Bank Note Co. ***Comments:*** H-MA-175-R10. Raised from W-MA-490-001-G010 or G010a. 18__. 1850s.

Rarity: —

$5 • W-MA-490-005-N010

Left: Woman. ***Center:*** Three women. ***Right:*** Woman. ***Comments:*** H-MA-175-N5. 1850s.

Rarity: —

$5 • W-MA-490-005-A050

Left: 5 / 5. ***Center:*** Two allegorical women in clouds, U.S. shield and eagle. ***Right:*** 5 / 5. ***Engraver:*** W.L. Ormsby. ***Comments:*** H-MA-175-A25. Altered from a spurious issue of the Exchange Bank, Hartford, Connecticut. Dec. 1, 1856.

Rarity: —

$10 • W-MA-490-010-R030

Engraver: New England Bank Note Co. ***Comments:*** H-MA-175-R15. Raised from W-MA-490-002-G020 or G020a. 18__. 1850s.

Rarity: —

$10 • W-MA-490-010-A060

CC

Engraver: W.L. Ormsby. ***Comments:*** H-MA-175-A30. Altered from $10 Exchange Bank, Hartford, Connecticut. Dec. 1, 1856.

Rarity: URS-4
F $250

$10 • W-MA-490-010-A070

Left: X / Sailor standing by barrel, Bale and anchor, Flag. ***Center:*** Three allegorical women seated with cornucopia, caduceus, sword and balance. ***Bottom center:*** Train. ***Right:*** 10 / Woman with sheaf on back. ***Engraver:*** Toppan, Carpenter, Casilear & Co. ***Comments:*** H-MA-175-A35. Altered from $10 Exchange Bank, Bangor, Maine. 18__. 1850s.

Rarity: —

$20 • W-MA-490-020-C060a

Engraver: New England Bank Note Co. ***Comments:*** H-MA-175-C12a. Counterfeit of W-MA-490-020-G060a. 18__. 1850s.

Rarity: —

Faneuil Hall Bank

1851–1865

W-MA-500

History: The Faneuil Hall Bank commenced business on September 1, 1851, and was open to the public in October. It was located at 4 Market Square on the south side of Faneuil Hall, the most famous public building in the city. The capital of the bank was $500,000, of which $400,000 had been paid in. It remained at this figure through 1864.

The bank's circulation in 1857 was $231,015. By 1858 the value had dropped to $179,756. In 1860 it was back up to $231,015. Other figures for 1857 included: bills of this bank and other New England states $64,283; real estate $60,000. In 1858 specie was valued at $41,286.82, and real estate was worth $60,000.

The Faneuil Hall National Bank was chartered on February 27, 1865, and succeeded the state bank's interests.

Numismatic Commentary: All of the genuine issues of the Faneuil Hall Bank are high in rarity and in demand due to their historical content. Many of the issues will show Faneuil Hall and at least part of Quincy Market.

All valid notes were engraved by Rawdon, Wright, Hatch & Edson and the New England Bank Note Co.

Valid Issues

$1 • W-MA-500-001-G010

Left: 1 / Liberty holding 1. ***Center:*** View of Faneuil Hall and Quincy Market. ***Right:*** 1 / Woman with flag, Cherubs with cornucopias. ***Comments:*** H-MA-180-G2. 18__. 1850s.

Rarity: —

$1 • W-MA-500-001-G010a

Overprint: Red ONE. ***Comments:*** H-MA-180-G2a. Similar to W-MA-500-001-G010. 18__. 1850s.

Rarity: URS-3
F $600; **VF** $800

$1 • W-MA-500-001-G010b

CJF

Overprint: Red ONE. ***Engraver:*** ABNCo. monogram. ***Comments:*** H-MA-180-G2b. Similar to W-MA-500-001-G010 but with additional engraver imprint. 18__. 1860s.

Rarity: URS-3
F $600; **VF** $800

$2 • W-MA-500-002-G020

Left: 2 / Portrait of George Washington standing with horse. ***Center:*** View of Faneuil Hall, Houses, men, horses, and wagons. ***Right:*** 2 / Woman seated by cornucopia. ***Comments:*** H-MA-180-G4. 18__. 1850s.

Rarity: —

$2 • W-MA-500-002-G020a

Overprint: Red TWO. ***Comments:*** H-MA-180-G4a. Similar to W-MA-500-002-G020. 18__. 1850s.

Rarity: URS-4
F $800; **VF** $1,000

$2 • W-MA-500-002-G020b

Overprint: Red TWO. ***Engraver:*** ABNCo. monogram. ***Comments:*** H-MA-180-G4b. Similar to W-MA-500-002-G020 but with additional engraver imprint. 18__.

Rarity: URS-4
F $800; **VF** $1,000

$3 • W-MA-500-003-G030

Left: 3 / Woman seated on barrel. ***Center:*** View of Faneuil Hall, Houses, men, horses, and wagons. ***Right:*** 3 / Farmer, sailor, and mechanic standing with 3. ***Comments:*** H-MA-180-G6. 18__. 1850s.

Rarity: —

$3 • W-MA-500-003-G030a

Overprint: Red THREE. ***Comments:*** H-MA-180-G6a. Similar to W-MA-500-003-G030. 18__. 1850s.

Rarity: —

$5 • W-MA-500-005-G040

Left: View of Faneuil Hall / 5. ***Center:*** V. ***Right:*** FIVE / 5 with woman seated and two women standing. ***Comments:*** H-MA-180-G8. 18__. 1850s.

Rarity: URS-2
VG $1,250

$5 • W-MA-500-005-G040a
Overprint: Red FIVE. ***Comments:*** H-MA-180-G8a. Similar to W-MA-500-005-G040. 18__. 1850s.
Rarity: —

$10 • W-MA-500-010-G050
Left: View of Quincy Market, Men, horses, and wagons / TEN. ***Center:*** X. ***Right:*** X / Men and livestock. ***Comments:*** H-MA-180-G10. 18__. 1850s.
Rarity: —

$10 • W-MA-500-010-G050a
Overprint: Red. ***Comments:*** H-MA-180-G10a. Similar to W-MA-500-010-G050. 18__. 1850s.
Rarity: —

$20 • W-MA-500-020-G060
Left: Ship / 20. ***Center:*** Milkmaid and cows. ***Right:*** 20 / Woman. ***Comments:*** H-MA-180-G12. 18__. 1850s.
Rarity: —

$50 • W-MA-500-050-G070
Left: 50 / Woman. ***Center:*** Cows and sheep. ***Right:*** 50 / State arms. ***Comments:*** H-MA-180-G14. 18__. 1850s.
Rarity: —

$100 • W-MA-500-100-G080
Left: 100 / Train. ***Center:*** Farm scene, Woman and man seated, Two men with sickle and scythe, Man lying down, Hay wagon. ***Right:*** 100 / Livestock. ***Comments:*** H-MA-180-G16. 18__. 1850s.
Rarity: —

$500 • W-MA-500-500-G090
Left: 500 / Portrait of George Washington on horseback. ***Center:*** Woman reclining on bale holding distaff, Ships, city, canal scene, and train. ***Right:*** 500 / 500. ***Comments:*** H-MA-180-G18. 18__. 1850s.
Rarity: —

Non-Valid Issues

$1 • W-MA-500-001-S010

SI

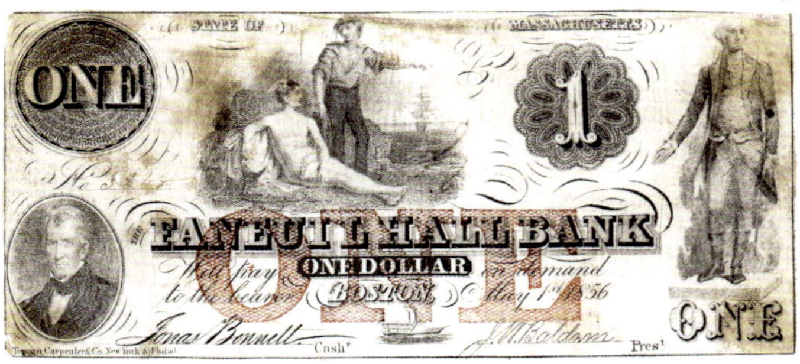

Overprint: Red ONE. ***Engraver:*** Toppan, Carpenter & Co. ***Comments:*** H-MA-180-S5. May 1, 1856.
Rarity: URS-7
VG $125

$5 • W-MA-500-005-N010
Left: 5. ***Center:*** Woman reclining. ***Right:*** 5. ***Comments:*** H-MA-180-N5. 18__. 1850s.
Rarity: —

$20 • W-MA-500-020-R010
Engraver: Rawdon, Wright, Hatch & Edson / New England Bank Note Co. ***Comments:*** H-MA-180-R5. Raised from W-MA-500-002-G020. 18__. 1850s.
Rarity: —

Farmers Bank
1820s
W-MA-510

History: A non-existent bank represented only by notes altered from those of other banks.

Issues

$1 • W-MA-510-001-A010
Left: Panel of lathework bearing MASSACHUSETTS vertically / 5 / 5. ***Center:*** Alternating garlands of flowers and grid segments / FIVE. ***Right:*** 5 / 5. ***Engraver:*** PSSP. ***Comments:*** H-MA-185-A5. Altered from W-MA-175-005-G040 or G040a. 18__. 1820s.
Rarity: URS-7
F $100

Franklin Bank
1828–1837
W-MA-520

History: The Franklin Bank was incorporated on March 18, 1828, with an authorized capital of $100,000. As of the January session of the legislature in 1832, the capital was increased to $150,000. The whole amount was paid in and the bank experienced a prosperous existence until 1834, when there was a change in direction of the bank.

Thomas Richardson, Josiah Dunham, and Benjamin F. Hathorne, accompanied by Ebenezer Stevens and Ebenezer Hayward, decided to place the management into other hands—namely, theirs. They bought out the majority of the stock in order to do this, putting Hathorne in place as cashier and also in a severe state of debt. This proved no deterrent, however, as Hathorne sustained himself by taking out loans from the bank. When he could not repay the loans at their conclusion, the deficiency was provided for out of the cash box of the bank itself, until the resources of the Franklin Bank were so weakened that the customers could not apply for discounts. This continued until 1837, when Hathorne left his position as cashier of the bank, leaving behind a loss of $820,000. It thus failed in July of 1837 and was placed on the "list of deposite banks discontinued under the Deposite Act of June 1836."[49]

In 1838 the Suffolk Bank reported that bills of the Franklin bank would not be received.[50] Further, on February 14 of that year, it was reported that "the grand jury found an indictment, for official misconduct, against Josiah Dunham, president of the Franklin Bank, and Ebenezer Stevens, Samuel S. Ridgway, Thomas H. Dunham, and Ebenezer Hayward, directors. . . ."[51]

Numismatic Commentary: When banks failed due to mismanagement or criminal activities, they tended to leave behind a great amount of unredeemed bank notes. Such was the case for the Franklin Bank. Collectors should have no trouble locating examples of its notes. Many remain in the marketplace ready to satisfy collector demand.

Valid Issues

$1 • W-MA-520-001-G010

Left: Panel of lathework circle segments. ***Center:*** 1 / 1 / Flower garlands and gridwork segments / 1 / 1. ***Right:*** Panel of lathework circle segments. ***Engraver:*** PSSP. ***Comments:*** H-MA-190-G2. 18__. 1828–1830s.

Rarity: —

$1 • W-MA-520-001-G010a

Left: ONE / D / ONE vertically. ***Right:*** ONE / D / ONE vertically. ***Engraver:*** PSSP. ***Comments:*** H-MA-190-G4. Similar to W-MA-520-001-G010. 18__. 1830s.

Rarity: —

$1 • W-MA-520-001-G010b

Left: Lathework panel bearing MASSACHUSETTS / ONE. ***Right:*** Panel of lathework circle segments. ***Engraver:*** PSSP. ***Comments:*** H-MA-190-G6. Similar to W-MA-520-001-G010. 18__. 1830s.

Rarity: —

$1 • W-MA-520-001-G020

SI

Engraver: PSSP / New England Bank Note Co. ***Comments:*** H-MA-190-G16. 18__. 1833–1837.

Rarity: URS-9
VF $100

$2 • W-MA-520-002-G030

Left: Panel of lathework circle segments. ***Center:*** 2 / 2 / Flower garlands and gridwork segments / 2 / 2. ***Right:*** Panel of lathework circle segments. ***Engraver:*** PSSP. ***Comments:*** H-MA-190-G18. 18__. 1828–1830s.

Rarity: —

$2 • W-MA-520-002-G030a

SI

Engraver: PSSP. ***Comments:*** H-MA-190-G20. Similar to W-MA-520-002-G030. 18__. 1830s.

Rarity: URS-7
F $25; **VF** $125

$2 • W-MA-520-002-G030b

Left: Lathework panel bearing MASSACHUSETTS / TWO. ***Right:*** Panel of lathework circle segments. ***Engraver:*** PSSP. ***Comments:*** H-MA-190-G22. Similar to W-MA-520-002-G030. 18__. 1830s.

Rarity: URS-5
F $125

$2 • W-MA-520-002-G040

CC

Engraver: PSSP / New England Bank Note Co. ***Comments:*** H-MA-190-G32. 18__. 1833–1837.

Rarity: URS-9
VG $50; **VF** $75; **Unc-Rem** $150

$3 • W-MA-520-003-G050

Left: Panel of lathework circle segments. ***Center:*** 3 / 3 / Flower garlands and gridwork segments / 3 / 3. ***Right:*** Panel of lathework circle segments. ***Engraver:*** PSSP. ***Comments:*** H-MA-190-G34. 18__. 1828–1830s.

Rarity: —

$3 • W-MA-520-003-G050a

Left: THREE vertically. ***Right:*** THREE vertically. ***Engraver:*** PSSP. ***Comments:*** H-MA-190-G36. Similar to W-MA-520-003-G050. 18__. 1830s.

Rarity: —

$3 • W-MA-520-003-G050b

Left: Lathework panel bearing MASSACHUSETTS / THREE. ***Right:*** Panel of lathework circle segments. ***Engraver:*** PSSP. ***Comments:*** H-MA-190-G38. Similar to W-MA-520-003-G050. 18__. 1830s.

Rarity: —

$3 • W-MA-520-003-G060

CC

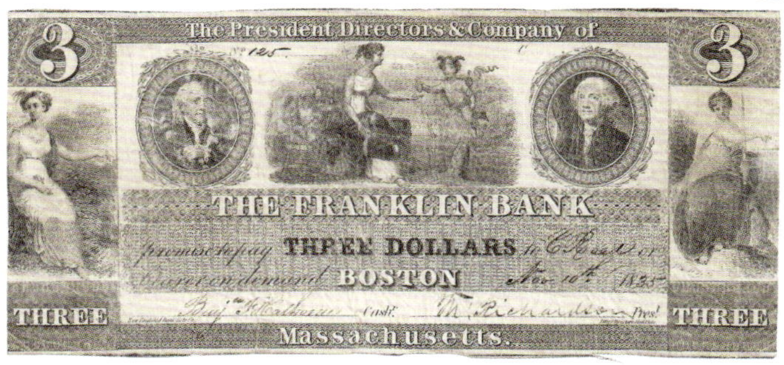

Engraver: PSSP / New England Bank Note Co. ***Comments:*** H-MA-190-G48. 18__. 1833–1837.

Rarity: URS-8
VG $75; **F** $100; **VF** $125; **Unc-Rem** $200

$5 • W-MA-520-005-G070

Left: MASSACHUSETTS vertically / 5 / 5. ***Center:*** White boxes flanking FIVE DOLLARS lined by zigzag ruled lines. ***Right:*** 5 / 5. ***Engraver:*** PSSP. ***Comments:*** H-MA-190-G50. 18__. 1828–1830s.

Rarity: URS-9
F $75

$5 • W-MA-520-005-G070a

SI

Engraver: PSSP. ***Comments:*** H-MA-190-G56. Similar to W-MA-520-005-G070 but with spiral lathework lines. 18__. 1830s.

Rarity: URS-8
F $100

$5 • W-MA-520-005-G080

HA

Engraver: PSSP / New England Bank Note Co. ***Comments:*** H-MA-190-G60. 18__. 1833–1837.

Rarity: URS-9
F $50; **VF** $75

$10 • W-MA-520-010-G090

Left: Lathework chain bearing MASSACHUSETTS / 10 / 10 vertically. ***Center:*** Alternating flower garlands and gridwork segments / TEN DOLLARS. ***Right:*** 10 / 10 vertically. ***Engraver:*** PSSP. ***Comments:*** H-MA-190-G62. 18__. 1828–1830s.

Rarity: —

$10 • W-MA-520-010-G090a

SI

Engraver: PSSP. ***Comments:*** H-MA-190-G68. Similar to W-MA-520-010-G090 but with spiral lathework lines. 18__. 1830s.

Rarity: URS-9
VF $100

$10 • W-MA-520-010-G100

QDB

Engraver: PSSP / New England Bank Note Co. ***Comments:*** H-MA-190-G72. 18__. 1833–1837.

Rarity: URS-9
F $75; **VF** $100; **Unc-S&D** $175; **Proof** $750

$20 • W-MA-520-020-G110

SI

Engraver: PSSP. ***Comments:*** H-MA-190-G76. 18__. 1828–1830s.

Rarity: URS-9
F $75; **VF** $100

$20 • W-MA-520-020-G120

CC

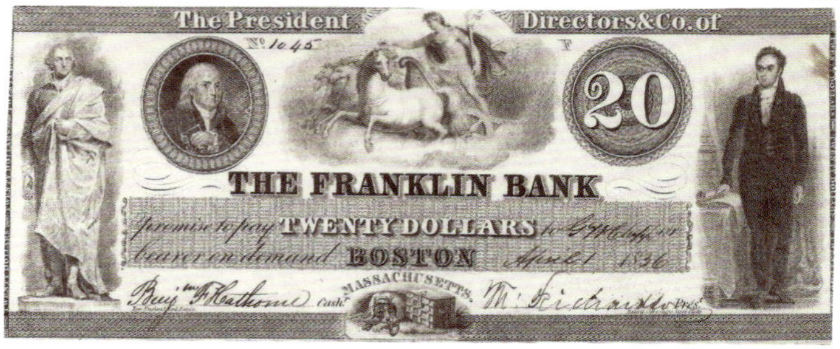

Engraver: PSSP / New England Bank Note Co. ***Comments:*** H-MA-190-G80. 18__. 1833–1837.

Rarity: URS-9
F $50; **VF** $100; **Unc-S&D** $175

$50 • W-MA-520-050-G130

CC

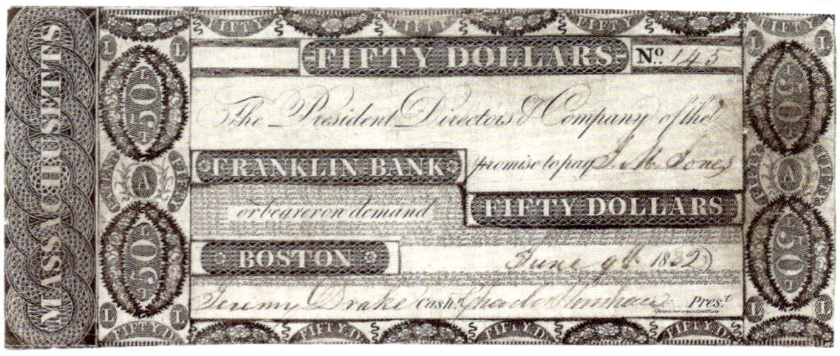

Engraver: PSSP. ***Comments:*** H-MA-190-G84. Similar to W-MA-520-010-G090 but with different denomination. 18__. 1828–1830s.

Rarity: URS-8
F $75; **VF** $125; **EF** $175

$50 • W-MA-520-050-G140 CC

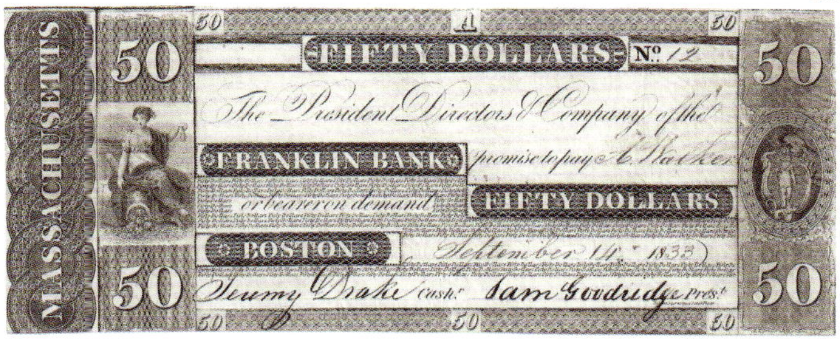

Engraver: PSSP. ***Comments:*** H-MA-190-G88. 18__. 1830s.

Rarity: URS-8
F $100; **VF** $150; **EF** $175

$100 • W-MA-520-100-G150

Comments: H-MA-190-G92. Similar to W-MA-520-010-G090 but with different denomination. 18__. 1828–1830s.

Rarity: URS-7
F $125; **VF** $150; **EF** $185

$100 • W-MA-520-100-G160 CC

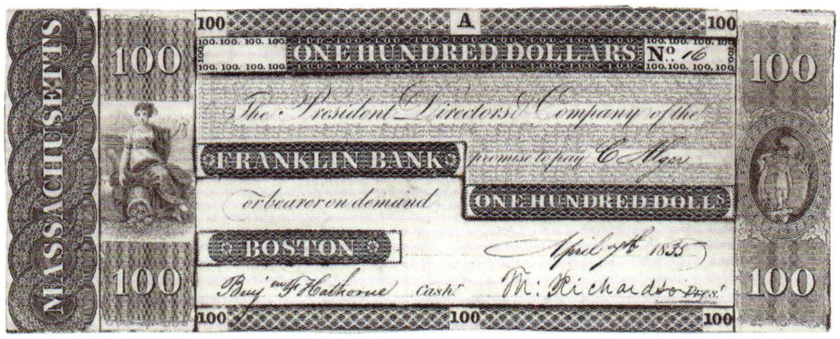

Engraver: PSSP. ***Comments:*** H-MA-190-G96. Similar to W-MA-520-050-G140 but with different denomination. 18__. 1830s.

Rarity: URS-7
F $125; **VF** $150; **EF** $185

$500 • W-MA-520-500-G170 CC

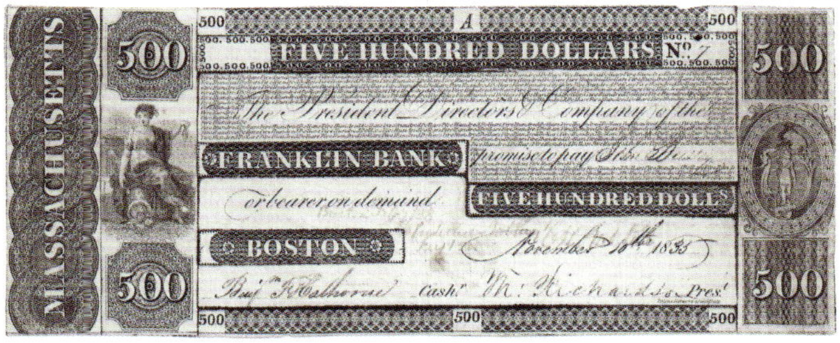

Engraver: PSSP. ***Comments:*** H-MA-190-G100. Similar to W-MA-520-050-G140 but with different denomination. 18__. 1830s

Rarity: URS-4
F $750; **VF** $1,000

$1,000 • W-MA-520-1000-G180 CC

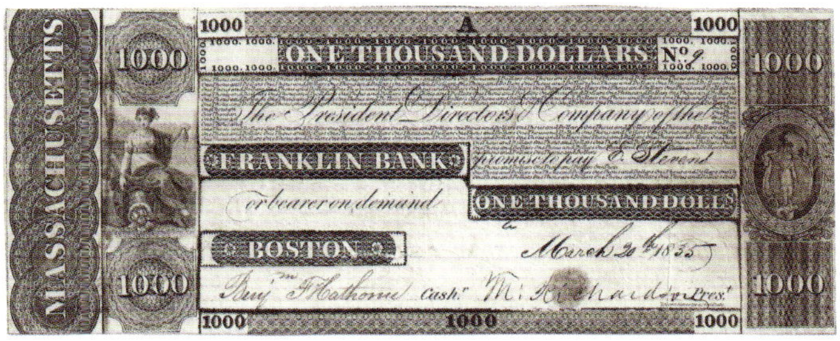

Engraver: PSSP. ***Comments:*** H-MA-190-G104. Similar to W-MA-520-050-G140 but with different denomination. 18__. 1830s.

Rarity: URS-4
F $1,000; **VF** $1,250

Freemans Bank

1836–1860s

W-MA-530

History: Chartered in April 1836, the Freeman's Bank was located at 5 Sea Street in Boston. In 1863 its location changed to 217 Federal Street. Starting capital was set at $150,000 until 1845, when it was increased to $200,000. From 1854 to 1864 the capital rose to and remained at $400,000.

The bank's charter was renewed in 1837, to remain in business until January 1, 1870. Figures from the *Financial Register* of February 14, 1838, included these: bills in circulation $69,518; net profits on hand $5,313.33; cash deposited $33,290.87; total amount due from banks $258,122.20; gold, silver, and other coined metals in the banking house $10,658.28; bills of other banks incorporated in this state $11,494; bills of other banks incorporated elsewhere $158; balance due from other banks $17,584.09; amount of all debts due $218,227.83; total amount of resources of the bank $258,122.20.

Circulation in 1839 amounted to $58,885. In 1854 specie was valued at $18,903.88. Between 1845 and 1860 it averaged at $215,000.

The Freeman's National Bank of Boston, chartered on December 30, 1864, succeeded the interests of the state bank.

Numismatic Commentary: Notes from this bank are extremely hard to locate, but the persistent collector may find a note bearing a vignette of Quincy Market or the Battle of Bunker Hill. Most notes found are low in quality. A Very Fine note or higher would be the exception.

Valid Issues

$1 • W-MA-530-001-G010 CC

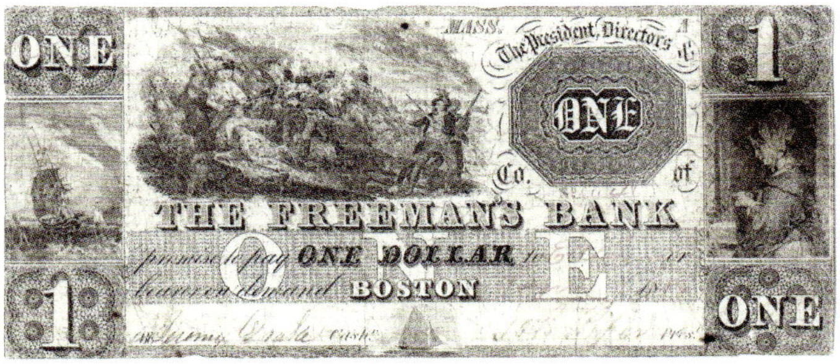

Engraver: New England Bank Note Co. ***Comments:*** H-MA-195-G4. 18__. 1830s–1850s.

Rarity: URS-3
F $1,750; **VF** $1,800

$1 • W-MA-530-001-G010a

Left: ONE / Sailing ship / 1. ***Center:*** Battle of Bunker Hill / ONE. ***Bottom center:*** Sloop. ***Right:*** 1 / Female portrait / ONE. ***Engraver:*** New England Bank Note Co. / ABNCo. monogram. ***Comments:*** H-MA-195-G4a. Similar to W-MA-530-001-G010 but with additional engraver imprint. 18__. 1860s.

Rarity: —

$2 • W-MA-530-002-G020
Left: TWO / Woman / 2. ***Center:*** George Washington on horseback, Man chopping wood / TWO. ***Right:*** 2 / Portrait of Benjamin Franklin / TWO. ***Engraver:*** New England Bank Note Co. ***Comments:*** H-MA-195-G8. 18__. 1830s–1850s.

Rarity: —

$2 • W-MA-530-002-G020a
Engraver: New England Bank Note Co. / ABNCo. monogram. ***Comments:*** H-MA-195-G8a. Similar to W-MA-530-002-G020 but with additional engraver imprint. 18__. 1860s.

Rarity: URS-4
F $300

$3 • W-MA-530-003-G030
Left: THREE / Woman standing with basket and pail / 3. ***Center:*** Steamboat landing, Sailing ships / THREE. ***Bottom center:*** Sloop. ***Right:*** 3 / Portrait of George Washington standing by horse / THREE. ***Engraver:*** New England Bank Note Co. ***Comments:*** H-MA-195-G12. 18__. 1830s–1850s.

Rarity: —

$3 • W-MA-530-003-G030a
Engraver: New England Bank Note Co. / ABNCo. monogram. ***Comments:*** H-MA-195-G12a. Similar to W-MA-530-003-G030 but with additional engraver imprint. 18__. 1860s.

Rarity: —

$5 • W-MA-530-005-G040

CC

Engraver: New England Bank Note Co. ***Comments:*** H-MA-195-G16. 18__. 1830s–1850s.

Rarity: URS-2
VF $7,500

$5 • W-MA-530-005-G040a
Left: 5 / Ship / FIVE. ***Center:*** View of Quincy Market / FIVE. ***Bottom center:*** Steer. ***Right:*** 5 / Woman with stool. ***Comments:*** H-MA-195-G16a. Similar to W-MA-530-005-G040 but with additional engraver imprint. 18__. 1860s.

Rarity: —

$10 • W-MA-530-010-G050
Left: TEN / Blacksmith in ship, Anvil / 10. ***Center:*** X / Ships at sea / TEN. ***Right:*** 10 / Woman standing and man seated / TEN. ***Engraver:*** New England Bank Note Co. ***Comments:*** H-MA-195-G20. 18__. 1830s–1850s.

Rarity: —

$10 • W-MA-530-010-G050a
Engraver: New England Bank Note Co. / ABNCo. monogram. ***Comments:*** H-MA-195-G20a. Similar to W-MA-530-010-G050 but with additional engraver imprint. 18__. 1860s.

Rarity: —

$50 • W-MA-530-050-G060
Engraver: Unverified, but likely New England Bank Note Co. ***Comments:*** H-MA-195-G24. No description available. 18__. 1830s–1840s.

Rarity: *None known*

$50 • W-MA-530-050-G070
Left: FIFTY / Woman standing with wreath and flowers / FIFTY. ***Center:*** 50 / Man restraining prancing horse / 50. ***Right:*** FIFTY / Woman standing with cornucopia against left shoulder / FIFTY. ***Engraver:*** New England Bank Note Co. ***Comments:*** H-MA-195-G28. 18__. 1840s–1850s.

Rarity: —

$50 • W-MA-530-050-G080
Left: 50 / Woman seated by bale holding Liberty cap. ***Right:*** 50 / Male portrait. ***Tint:*** Color unknown. ***Engraver:*** American Bank Note Co. ***Comments:*** H-MA-195-G32. 1860s.

Rarity: —

$100 • W-MA-530-100-G090
Engraver: Unverified, but likely New England Bank Note Co. ***Comments:*** H-MA-195-G36. No description available. 18__. 1830s–1840s.

Rarity: *None known*

$100 • W-MA-530-100-G100
Left: ONE HUNDRED on 100 / Portrait of William Henry Harrison. ***Center:*** Wharf scene, Men loading wagon with barrels. ***Right:*** ONE HUNDRED on 100 / Portrait of Christopher Columbus. ***Engraver:*** New England Bank Note Co. ***Comments:*** H-MA-195-G40. 18__. 1840s–1850s.

Rarity: —

$100 • W-MA-530-100-G110
Left: C / Male portrait. ***Center:*** 100 / State arms. ***Tint:*** Color unknown. ***Engraver:*** American Bank Note Co. ***Comments:*** H-MA-195-G44. 1860s.

Rarity: —

$500 • W-MA-530-500-G120
Left: Woman seated on sheaves, Men reaping, Man on horse. ***Center:*** 500 / D. ***Right:*** 500 vertically. ***Engraver:*** Rawdon, Wright, Hatch & Edson. ***Comments:*** H-MA-195-G48. 18__. 1850s.

Rarity: —

$500 • W-MA-530-500-G130
Left: 500 / 500 / 500. ***Center:*** 500 / Woman seated with shield bearing D, Fasces, cornucopia, lyre, and sheaf on ground / 500. ***Right:*** 500 / D / 500. ***Engraver:*** New England Bank Note Co. / PSSP. ***Comments:*** H-MA-195-G52. 18__. 1830s–1840s.

Rarity: —

$500 • W-MA-530-500-G140
Left: State arms. ***Center:*** D / Male portrait / D. ***Right:*** 500 / Sloop under sail. ***Engraver:*** American Bank Note Co. ***Comments:*** H-MA-195-G56. 1860s.

Rarity: —

$1,000 • W-MA-530-1000-G150
Left: THOUSAND vertically. ***Center:*** 1000 / Woman standing with legs crossed, lyre, and cornucopia. ***Right:*** 1000 / M / 1000. ***Engraver:*** New England Bank Note Co. / PSSP. ***Comments:*** H-MA-195-G60. 18__. 1830s–1840s.

Rarity: —

Non-Valid Issues

$1 • W-MA-530-001-A010

Left: 1 / Steamboat / 1. ***Center:*** Medallion head with 1 / Train backed up to wharf / Medallion head with 1. ***Bottom center:*** Dog and strongbox. ***Right:*** 1 / Cherub with arms upraised seated on lion / 1. ***Engraver:*** Unverified, but likely Chas. E. Ely. ***Comments:*** H-MA-195-A5. Altered from $1 Geauga Insurance Co., Painesville, Ohio. 18__. 1840s.

Rarity: —

$2 • W-MA-530-002-A020

SI

Engraver: Toppan, Carpenter, Casilear & Co. ***Comments:*** H-MA-195-A10. Altered from $2 Freeman's Bank, Washington, D.C. 18__. 1850s.

Rarity: URS-6
VG $75

$3 • W-MA-530-003-R010

Engraver: New England Bank Note Co. ***Comments:*** H-MA-195-R5. Raised from W-MA-530-001-G010. 18__. 1850s.

Rarity: —

$3 • W-MA-530-003-A030

Left: 3 / Woman seated with arm around eagle / 3. ***Center:*** Medallion head / Steamboat / Medallion head. ***Bottom center:*** Dog and strongbox. ***Right:*** 3 / Train backed up to wharf. ***Engraver:*** Unverified, but likely Chas. E. Ely. ***Comments:*** H-MA-195-A15. Altered from $3 Geauga Insurance Co., Painesville, Ohio. 18__. 1840s.

Rarity: —

$5 • W-MA-530-005-R020

HA

Engraver: New England Bank Note Co. / ABNCo. monogram. ***Comments:*** H-Unlisted. Raised from W-MA-530-001-G010. 18__. 1860s.

Rarity: URS-1
F $500

$5 • W-MA-530-005-A040

Left: Dog, Indian man seated on rock with box. ***Center:*** Large warehouse, Ships in harbor / 5. ***Right:*** FIVE on die, Panel of wheat ears and fruit. ***Engraver:*** Durand & Co. ***Comments:*** H-MA-195-A20. Altered from $5 Globe Bank, New York City, New York. 18__. 1840s.

Rarity: —

$5 • W-MA-530-005-A050

HA

Engraver: Chas. E. Ely. ***Comments:*** H-MA-195-A25. Altered from $5 Geauga Insurance Co., Painesville, Ohio. 18__. 1840s.

Rarity: URS-6
VG $100

$10 • W-MA-530-010-AR010

SI

Engraver: Toppan, Carpenter, Casilear & Co. ***Comments:*** H-Unlisted. Altered and raised from $2 Freeman's Bank, Washington, D.C. 18__. 1850s.

Rarity: —

Freemens Bank

LATE 1850s

W-MA-540

History: A non-existent bank represented only by notes altered from those of other banks.

Numismatic Commentary: This non-existent bank is easy to ignore, as no genuine notes were ever made.

Issues

$2 • W-MA-540-002-A010

Left: Woman resting stone tablet on column, Cogwheel. ***Center:*** Eagle with U.S. shield and olive branches. ***Bottom center:*** Horse. ***Right:*** 2 / Farmer picking corn. ***Comments:*** H-MA-200-A10. Altered from $2 Freemen's Bank, Washington, D.C.

Rarity: —

Collectors and Researchers:

If you have new information about any banks or notes listed in this volume, contact Whitman Publishing, Attn: Obsolete Paper Money, 3101 Clairmont Road, Suite G, Atlanta, GA 30329.

Fulton Bank

1835–1838

W-MA-550

History: By an act of the legislature the name of the Winnisimmet Bank, W-MA-1070, was changed to the Fulton Bank on March 6, 1835. Capital at this time was $500,000, and the bank's circulation was $259,431. Charles Henshaw was president of the bank in 1837, accompanied by J.C. Brodhead as cashier. The Treasury Department declared the Fulton Bank an official bank of deposit in 1837, with $17,736.67 reported on deposit by *Niles' National Register*. But another report of the same year declared that the bank had been discontinued as a deposit bank.[52]

This was reported in the *Financial Register of the United States* in 1838:

> Joseph D. Adams, late cashier of the Fulton Bank, in this city, appeared yesterday before the Municipal Court to answer seven indictments for defrauding that institution, on which he was arraigned. He gave bail in $23,000 for his appearance at trial next term.— *Bolton Journal, Aug. 11.*

In 1838 it was also noted that the American Bible Society owed the Fulton Bank $11,000, which it had borrowed.[53]

Circulation was reported to be $171,073 in 1838. By 1841 it had dropped drastically down to $5,084. The next year it was even lower at $4,617.

Other figures for 1838 included: net profits on hand $9,959.30; balances due to other banks $80,000; cash deposited $60,292.88; cash deposited bearing interest $102,329; total amount due from banks $923,654.18; gold, silver, and other coined metals in the banking house $25,107.50; bills of other banks incorporated in this state $18,023; balance due from other banks $5,000; amount of all debts due $875,523.68; total amount of resources of the bank $923,654.18.

On January 18, 1838, the stockholders voted to surrender the charter of the bank. The capital was $500,000, of which it was believed that at least $450,000 would be lost to the stockholders.[54]

Numismatic Commentary: Notes from this short-lived bank are quite hard to locate and not especially attractive, artistically. The lower denominations, such as the $1, $2, and $3, are most likely to be encountered.

Valid Issues

$1 • W-MA-550-001-G010

CC

Engraver: New England Bank Note Co. / PSSP. ***Comments:*** H-MA-205-G4. 18__. 1830s.

Rarity: URS-6

F $125; **VF** $250; **EF** $375

$2 • W-MA-550-002-G020

SI

Engraver: New England Bank Note Co. / PSSP. ***Comments:*** H-MA-205-G8. 18__. 1830s.

Rarity: URS-3

VG $500

$3 • W-MA-550-003-G030

Left: Woman leaning on flowerpot / Beehive. ***Center:*** 3 / Woman standing, Man plowing / 3. ***Right:*** Ship / Eagle. ***Engraver:*** New England Bank Note Co. / PSSP. ***Comments:*** H-MA-205-G12. Similar to W-MA-550-003-C030. 18__. 1830s.

Rarity: URS-7

F $175; **VF** $250

$3 • W-MA-550-003-G040

CC

Engraver: New England Bank Note Co. / PSSP. ***Comments:*** H-Unlisted. 18__. 1830s.

Rarity: URS-4

Proof $400

$5 • W-MA-550-005-G050

Engraver: Unverified, but likely New England Bank Note Co. / PSSP. ***Comments:*** H-MA-205-G16. No description available. 18__. 1830s.

Rarity: *None known*

$10 • W-MA-550-010-G060

Engraver: Unverified, but likely New England Bank Note Co. / PSSP. ***Comments:*** H-MA-205-G20. No description available. 18__. 1830s.

Rarity: *None known*

$20 • W-MA-550-020-G070

Engraver: Unverified, but likely New England Bank Note Co. / PSSP. ***Comments:*** H-MA-205-G24. No description available. 18__. 1830s.

Rarity: *None known*

$50 • W-MA-550-050-G080

Engraver: Unverified, but likely New England Bank Note Co. / PSSP. ***Comments:*** H-MA-205-G28. No description available. 18__. 1830s.

Rarity: *None known*

$50 • W-MA-550-050-G090

Engraver: Unverified, but likely New England Bank Note Co. / PSSP. *Comments:* H-MA-205-G32. No description available. 18__. 1830s.

Rarity: *None known*

$100 • W-MA-550-100-G100

Engraver: Unverified, but likely New England Bank Note Co. / PSSP. *Comments:* H-MA-205-G36. No description available. 18__. 1830s.

Rarity: *None known*

$500 • W-MA-550-500-G110

Left: 500, 500 / 500. *Center:* 500 / Woman seated with shield bearing D, Fasces, cornucopia, lyre, and shear on ground / 500. *Right:* 500 / D / 500. *Engraver:* New England Bank Note Co. / PSSP. *Comments:* H-MA-205-G40. 18__. 1830s.

Rarity: —

$1,000 • W-MA-550-1000-G120

Left: THOUSAND vertically. *Center:* 1000 / Woman standing with legs crossed, Lyre and cornucopia / 1000. *Right:* 1000 / M / 1000. *Engraver:* New England Bank Note Co. / PSSP. *Comments:* H-MA-205-G44. 18__. 1830s.

Rarity: —

Non-Valid Issues

$3 • W-MA-550-003-C030

CC

Engraver: New England Bank Note Co. *Comments:* H-MA-205-C12. Counterfeit of W-MA-550-003-G030. 18__. 1830s.

Rarity: URS-5
VF $250

$5 • W-MA-550-005-C050

Engraver: New England Bank Note Co. / PSSP. *Comments:* H-MA-205-C16. Counterfeit of W-MA-550-005-G050. 18__. 1830s

Rarity: —

Globe Bank
1824–1864
W-MA-560

History: The Globe Bank was incorporated in June 1824. Its charter was renewed in 1831 to operate until January 1, 1875.[55] It was located at 40 State Street, although from 1837 to 1846 the bank's location was given as 22 State Street. In 1864 it was listed as 40 State Street again.

Capital was approved at $1,000,000, where it remained throughout the bank's existence.

In 1830 *Bicknell's Counterfeit Detector* reported this:

> It is ascertained that the bills, Perkins's stereotype plate, on the Globe Bank, Boston, recently discovered to have been counterfeited, are bills of a broken bank ingeniously altered. It is said that the dies were lately discovered in New Hampshire, for altering Belchertown Bank bills to those of the Globe and American Bank, Boston.

Circulation of the bank amounted to $87,949 in 1838. By 1839 it had risen to $114,736. In 1845 it was still higher at $247,881, but it decreased to $171,241 by 1857. Other figures for 1838 included: net profits on hand $93,001.40; balances due to other banks $800,446.29; cash deposited $172,709.34; cash deposited bearing interest $187,424.31; total amount due from banks $2,395,530.40; gold, silver, and other coined metals in the banking house $122,000.92; real estate $40,000; bills of other banks incorporated in this state $210,481; balance due from other banks $209,186.03; amount of all debts due $1,813,862.45; total amount of resources of the bank $2,395,530.40.

In July 1854, it was reported that the Globe Bank would be making extensive alterations and improvements in their building at the corner of State Street and Wilson's Lane. "The block is to be raised in height, and entirely remodeled in its interior arrangements. On the second story the bank will provide for itself much more convenient quarters than it now occupies . . . The work of remodeling the building will be commenced about the first of July."[56]

The Globe National Bank of Boston, chartered on March 25, 1865, assumed the business of the state bank.

Numismatic Commentary: Many of this bank's notes were produced by the New England Bank Note Co. and retain the flavor of the older PSSP designs. Some of these later dated plates will show the addition of the ABNCo. monogram. These notes should be attainable for the average collector. The higher denominations, as with notes from most banks, will be much harder to locate.

Valid Issues

$1 • W-MA-560-001-G010

Left: Lathework panel. *Center:* 1 / 1 / Oval of flower garlands and gridwork segments / 1 / 1. *Right:* Lathework panel. *Engraver:* PSSP. *Comments:* H-MA-210-G2. 18__. 1820s.

Rarity: —

$1 • W-MA-560-001-G010a

Left: Narrow panel of lathework circle segments. *Right:* Narrow panel of lathework circle segments. *Engraver:* PSSP. *Comments:* H-MA-210-G4. Similar to W-MA-560-001-G010. 18__. 1820s–1830s.

Rarity: URS-3
VF $600

$1 • W-MA-560-001-G010b

Left: ONE / D / ONE vertically. *Right:* ONE / D / ONE vertically. *Engraver:* PSSP. *Comments:* H-MA-210-G6. Similar to W-MA-560-001-G010. 18__. 1830s.

Rarity: —

$1 • **W-MA-560-001-G020**

CC

Engraver: New England Bank Note Co. ***Comments:*** H-MA-210-G10. 18__. 1840s–1850s.

Rarity: URS-3
VF $600

$1 • **W-MA-560-001-G020a**

Left: ONE / 1 / ONE. ***Center:*** Text. ***Right:*** 1 / ONE / 1. ***Engraver:*** New England Bank Note Co. / ABNCo. monogram. ***Comments:*** H-MA-210-G10a. Similar to W-MA-560-001-G020 but with additional engraver imprint. 18__. 1850s–1860s.

Rarity: URS-4
VG $250; **F** $500

$2 • **W-MA-560-002-G030**

Left: Lathework panel. ***Center:*** 2 / 2 / Oval of flower garlands and gridwork segments / 2 / 2. ***Right:*** Lathework panel. ***Engraver:*** PSSP. ***Comments:*** H-MA-210-G12. 18__. 1820s.

Rarity: —

$2 • **W-MA-560-002-G030a**

Left: Narrow panel of lathework circle segments. ***Right:*** Narrow panel of lathework circle segments. ***Engraver:*** PSSP. ***Comments:*** H-MA-210-G14. Similar to W-MA-560-002-G030. 18__. 1820s–1830s.

Rarity: —

$2 • **W-MA-560-002-G030b**

Left: Five TWOs vertically. ***Right:*** Five TWOs vertically. ***Engraver:*** PSSP. ***Comments:*** H-MA-210-G16. Similar to W-MA-560-002-G030. 18__. 1830s.

Rarity: —

$2 • **W-MA-560-002-G040**

Left: TWO / 2 / TWO. ***Center:*** Text. ***Right:*** 2 / TWO / 2. ***Engraver:*** New England Bank Note Co. ***Comments:*** H-MA-210-G20. 18__. 1838–1850s.

Rarity: —

$2 • **W-MA-560-002-G040a**

Engraver: New England Bank Note Co. / ABNCo. monogram. ***Comments:*** H-MA-210-G20a. Similar to W-MA-560-002-G040 but with additional engraver imprint. 18__. 1850s–1860s.

Rarity: URS-4
VF $600

$3 • **W-MA-560-003-G050**

Left: Lathework panel. ***Center:*** 3 / 3 / Oval of flower garlands and gridwork segments / 3 / 3. ***Right:*** Lathework panel. ***Engraver:*** PSSP. ***Comments:*** H-MA-210-G22. 18__. 1820s.

Rarity: URS-3
Proof $750

$3 • **W-MA-560-003-G050a**

Left: Narrow panel of lathework circle segments. ***Right:*** Narrow panel of lathework circle segments. ***Engraver:*** PSSP. ***Comments:*** H-MA-210-G24. Similar to W-MA-560-003-G050. 18__. 1820s–1830s.

Rarity: —

$3 • **W-MA-560-003-G050b**

Left: THREE vertically. ***Right:*** THREE vertically. ***Engraver:*** PSSP. ***Comments:*** H-MA-210-G26. Similar to W-MA-560-003-G050. 18__. 1830s.

Rarity: —

$3 • **W-MA-560-003-G060**

Left: THREE / 3 / THREE. ***Center:*** Text. ***Right:*** 3 / THREE / 3. ***Engraver:*** New England Bank Note Co. ***Comments:*** H-MA-210-G30. 18__. 1838–1850s.

Rarity: URS-4
VF $500

$3 • **W-MA-560-003-G060a**

JF

Engraver: New England Bank Note Co. / ABNCo. monogram. ***Comments:*** H-MA-210-G30a. Similar to W-MA-560-003-G060 but with additional imprint. 18__. 1850s–1860s.

Rarity: URS-2
VF $1,250

$5 • **W-MA-560-005-G070**

Left: Lathework chain bearing MASSACHUSETTS / 5 / 5. ***Center:*** Alternating flower garlands and gridwork segments. ***Right:*** 5 / 5. ***Engraver:*** PSSP. ***Comments:*** H-MA-210-G32. 18__. 1820s.

Rarity: URS-5
VF $300

$5 • **W-MA-560-005-G070a**

Engraver: PSSP. ***Comments:*** H-MA-210-G34. Similar to W-MA-560-005-G070 but with zigzag ruled lines. 18__. 1820s–1830s.

Rarity: —

$5 • **W-MA-560-005-G070b**

Engraver: PSSP. ***Comments:*** H-MA-210-G36. Similar to W-MA-560-005-G070 but with spiral lathework lines. 18__. 1830s.

Rarity: —

$5 • **W-MA-560-005-G080**

Left: FIVE / 5 / FIVE. ***Center:*** Text. ***Right:*** 5 / FIVE / 5. ***Engraver:*** New England Bank Note Co. ***Comments:*** H-MA-210-G40. 18__. 1838–1850s.

Rarity: URS-3
F $400; **Proof** $750

$5 • **W-MA-560-005-G080a**

CC

Engraver: New England Bank Note Co. / ABNCo. monogram. ***Comments:*** H-MA-210-G40a. Similar to W-MA-560-005-G080 but with additional engraver imprint. 18__. 1850s–1860s.

Rarity: URS-4
VF $400

$10 • **W-MA-560-010-G090**

Left: Lathework chain bearing MASSACHUSETTS / 10 / 10 vertically. ***Center:*** Alternating flower garlands and gridwork segments. ***Right:*** 10 / 10 vertically. ***Comments:*** H-MA-210-G42. 18__. 1820s.

Rarity: —

$10 • **W-MA-560-010-G090a**

Engraver: PSSP. ***Comments:*** H-MA-210-G44. Similar to W-MA-560-010-G090 but with zigzag ruled lines. 18__. 1820s–1830s.

Rarity: —

$10 • **W-MA-560-010-G090b**

Engraver: PSSP. ***Comments:*** H-MA-210-G46. Similar to W-MA-560-010-G090 but with spiral lathework lines. 18__. 1830s.

Rarity: —

$10 • **W-MA-560-010-G100**

Left: TEN / X / TEN. ***Center:*** Text. ***Right:*** 10 / TEN / 10. ***Engraver:*** New England Bank Note Co. ***Comments:*** H-MA-210-G50. 18__. 1838–1850s.

Rarity: —

$10 • **W-MA-560-010-G100a**

Engraver: New England Bank Note Co. / ABNCo. monogram. ***Comments:*** H-MA-210-G50a. Similar to W-MA-560-010-G100 but with additional engraver imprint. 18__. 1850s–1860s.

Rarity: URS-2
F $1,000

$20 • **W-MA-560-020-G110**

Left: Lathework chain bearing MASSACHUSETTS / 20 / 20 vertically. ***Center:*** Alternating flower garlands and gridwork segments. ***Right:*** 20 / 20 vertically. ***Engraver:*** PSSP. ***Comments:*** H-MA-210-G52. 18__. 1820s–1830s.

Rarity: —

$50 • **W-MA-560-050-G120**

Left: Lathework chain bearing MASSACHUSETTS / 50 / 50. ***Center:*** Alternating flower garlands and gridwork segments / FIFTY. ***Right:*** 50 / 50 vertically. ***Engraver:*** PSSP. ***Comments:*** H-MA-210-G54. 18__. 1820s–1830s.

Rarity: —

$50 • **W-MA-560-050-G130**

Left: FIFTY / 50 / FIFTY. ***Center:*** Text. ***Right:*** 50 / FIFTY / 50. ***Engraver:*** New England Bank Note Co. ***Comments:*** H-MA-210-G56. 18__. 1838–1850s.

Rarity: —

$50 • **W-MA-560-050-G130a**

Engraver: New England Bank Note Co. / ABNCo. monogram. ***Comments:*** H-MA-210-G56a. Similar to W-MA-560-050-G130 but with additional engraver imprint. 18__. 1850s–1860s.

Rarity: —

$100 • **W-MA-560-100-G140**

Left: Lathework chain bearing MASSACHUSETTS / 100 / 100 vertically. ***Center:*** Alternating flower garlands and gridwork segments / 100. ***Right:*** 100 / 100 vertically. ***Comments:*** H-MA-210-G58. 18__. 1820s–1830s.

Rarity: —

$100 • **W-MA-560-100-G150**

CC

Engraver: New England Bank Note Co. ***Comments:*** H-MA-210-G60. 18__. 1838–1850s.

Rarity: URS-4
F $950; **VF** $1,250

$100 • **W-MA-560-100-G150a**

Left: C / 100 / C. ***Center:*** Text. ***Right:*** 100 / C / 100. ***Engraver:*** New England Bank Note Co. / ABNCo. monogram. ***Comments:*** H-MA-210-G60a. Similar to W-MA-560-100-G150 but with additional engraver imprint. 18__. 1850s–1860s.

Rarity: —

$500 • **W-MA-560-500-G160**

Left: D / 500 / D. ***Center:*** Text. ***Right:*** 500 / D / 500. ***Engraver:*** New England Bank Note Co. ***Comments:*** H-MA-210-G62. 18__. 1838–1850s.

Rarity: —

$500 • **W-MA-560-500-G160a**

Engraver: New England Bank Note Co. / ABNCo. monogram. ***Comments:*** H-MA-210-G62a. Similar to W-MA-560-500-G160 but with additional engraver imprint. 18__. 1850s–1860s.

Rarity: URS-2
Proof $1,500

$1,000 • **W-MA-560-1000-G170**

Left: M / 1000 / M. ***Center:*** Text. ***Right:*** 1000 / M / 1000. ***Engraver:*** New England Bank Note Co. ***Comments:*** H-MA-210-G64. 18__. 1838–1850s.

Rarity: —

$1,000 • W-MA-560-1000-G170a

Engraver: New England Bank Note Co. / ABNCo. monogram. ***Comments:*** H-MA-210-G64a. Similar to W-MA-560-1000-G170 but with additional engraver imprint. 18__. 1850s–1860s.

Rarity: —

Non-Valid Issues

$1 • W-MA-560-001-A010

Left: 1 / Woman wearing bonnet standing by pail / ONE. ***Center:*** Machinery and merchandise flanking Ceres seated holding sickle and rake, Factories and harbor / ONE. ***Right:*** 1 / Ship / ONE. ***Engraver:*** PSSP. ***Comments:*** H-MA-210-A5. Altered from $1 Globe Bank, Bangor, Maine. 18__. 1820s.

Rarity: URS-7
VG $125

$2 • W-MA-560-002-A020

CC

Engraver: New England Bank Note Co. ***Comments:*** H-MA-210-A10. Altered from $2 Globe Bank, Bangor, Maine. 18__. 1830s.

Rarity: URS-7
F $75

$3 • W-MA-560-003-A030

Engraver: New England Bank Note Co. ***Comments:*** H-MA-210-A15. Altered from $3 Globe Bank, Bangor, Maine. 18__. 1840s.

Rarity: —

$5 • W-MA-560-005-A040

Engraver: PSSP. ***Comments:*** H-MA-210-A18. Altered from W-MA-175-005-G040 or G040a. 18__. 1820s.

Rarity: —

$5 • W-MA-560-005-A050

Left: Sailing ships at sea / 5. ***Center:*** Four women of different races seated on globe. ***Right:*** 5 / Woman standing with oval bearing 5. ***Engraver:*** PSSP. ***Comments:*** H-MA-210-A20. Altered from $5 Globe Bank, Bangor, Maine. 18__. 1820s.

Rarity: —

$10 • W-MA-560-010-N010

Center: Amphitrite and Neptune in car drawn by sea horses. ***Comments:*** H-MA-210-N5.

Rarity: —

$10 • W-MA-560-010-A060

Left: Primitive train passing cliffs, Men with wheelbarrows and picks / Portrait of Benjamin Franklin. ***Center:*** Four women of different races seated on globe. ***Right:*** 10 / 10. ***Engraver:*** New England Bank Note Co. ***Comments:*** H-MA-210-A25. Altered from $10 Globe Bank, Bangor, Maine. 18__.

Rarity: —

$20 • W-MA-560-020-A070

Left: Steamboat / XX / Train. ***Center:*** Three women seated with eagle, pole and cap, Shield, scales, and book / 20 / Panel outlining white TWENTY. ***Right:*** XX / Milkmaid standing with pail. ***Engraver:*** New England Bank Note Co. ***Comments:*** H-MA-210-A30. Altered from $20 Hamilton Bank, Scituate, Rhode Island, or from notes of other failed banks using the same plate. 18__. 1840s.

Rarity: —

Granite Bank

1833–1864

W-MA-570

History: The Granite Bank was chartered in March 1832 and set up business at 1 Commercial Wharf. Authorized capital was listed at $500,000, from which it rose to $700,000 in 1853. Between 1853 and 1864 it was as high as $900,000.

Circulation in 1838 was $105,403. By 1839 it had peaked at $485,693. Between 1845 and 1861 it fluctuated between $267,638 and $124,174.

Other figures for 1838 included these: net profits on hand $11,706.38; balances due to other banks $9,519.40; cash deposited $64,824.43; cash deposited bearing interest $41,397.51; total amount due from banks $732,851.26; gold, silver, and other coined metals in the banking house $22,939.77; bills of other banks incorporated in this state $12,961; bills of other banks incorporated elsewhere $270; balance due from other banks $19,953.28; amount of all debts due $676,727.21; total amount of resources of the bank $732,851.26.

On March 16, 1864, the Second National Bank of Boston was chartered. It was the successor to the state bank's business.

Numismatic Commentary: Genuine notes from this bank are very hard to find.

Valid Issues

$1 • W-MA-570-001-G010

SBG

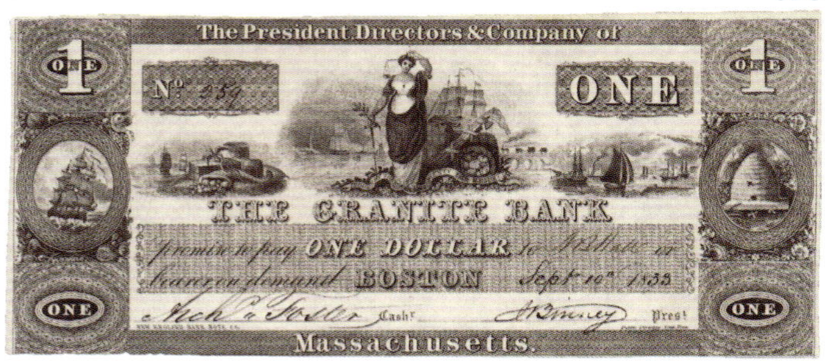

Engraver: New England Bank Note Co. / PSSP. ***Comments:*** H-MA-215-G4. 18__. 1830s–1850s.

Rarity: URS-2
VF $2,000

$1 • W-MA-570-001-G010a

Left: 1 / Ship / ONE. ***Center:*** Ship, dock, merchandise / Justice holding scale, Ship / ONE, Ships. ***Bottom center:*** ONE. ***Right:*** 1 / Beehive / ONE. ***Overprint:*** Red. ***Engraver:*** New England Bank Note Co. / PSSP. ***Comments:*** H-MA-215-G4a. Similar to W-MA-570-001-G010. 18__. 1850s.

Rarity: —

$1 • W-MA-570-001-G010b

Overprint: Red. ***Engraver:*** New England Bank Note Co. / PSSP / ABNCo. monogram. ***Comments:*** H-MA-215-G4b. Similar to W-MA-570-001-G010 but with additional engraver imprint. 18__. 1850s–1860s.

Rarity: URS-3
VF $750

$2 • W-MA-570-002-G020

Left: 2 / Ship / TWO. ***Center:*** 2 / Justice standing / TWO / 2. ***Bottom center:*** TWO. ***Right:*** 2 / Beehive / TWO. ***Engraver:*** New England Bank Note Co. / PSSP. ***Comments:*** H-MA-215-G8. 18__. 1830s–1850s.

Rarity: —

$2 • W-MA-570-002-G020a

Overprint: Red TWO. ***Engraver:*** New England Bank Note Co. / PSSP. ***Comments:*** H-MA-215-G8a. Similar to W-MA-570-002-G020. 18__. 1850s.

Rarity: —

$2 • W-MA-570-002-G020b

CC

Overprint: Red TWO. ***Engraver:*** New England Bank Note Co. / PSSP / ABNCo. monogram. ***Comments:*** H-MA-215-G8b. Similar to W-MA-570-002-G020 but with additional engraver imprint. 18__. 1850s–1860s.

Rarity: URS-3
VF $500; **Proof** $600

$3 • W-MA-570-003-G030

Left: 3 / Ship / THREE. ***Center:*** Justice standing. ***Right:*** 3 / Beehive / THREE. ***Engraver:*** New England Bank Note Co. / PSSP. ***Comments:*** H-MA-215-G12. 18__. 1830s–1850s.

Rarity: —

$3 • W-MA-570-003-G030a

Overprint: Red. ***Engraver:*** New England Bank Note Co. / PSSP. ***Comments:*** H-MA-215-G12a. Similar to W-MA-570-003-G030. 18__. 1850s.

Rarity: —

$3 • W-MA-570-003-G030b

Overprint: Red. ***Engraver:*** New England Bank Note Co. / PSSP / ABNCo. monogram. ***Comments:*** H-MA-215-G12b. Similar to W-MA-570-003-G030 but with additional engraver imprint. 18__. 1850s–1860s.

Rarity: —

$5 • W-MA-570-005-G040

Left: 5 / Ship / FIVE. ***Center:*** Justice standing / FIVE. ***Right:*** 5 / Beehive / FIVE. ***Engraver:*** New England Bank Note Co. / PSSP. ***Comments:*** H-MA-215-G16. 18__. 1830s–1850s.

Rarity: —

$5 • W-MA-570-005-G040a

Overprint: Red. ***Engraver:*** New England Bank Note Co. / PSSP. ***Comments:*** H-MA-215-G16a. Similar to W-MA-570-005-G040. 18__. 1850s.

Rarity: —

$5 • W-MA-570-005-G040b

Overprint: Red. ***Engraver:*** New England Bank Note Co. / PSSP / ABNCo. monogram. ***Comments:*** H-MA-215-G16b. Similar to W-MA-570-005-G040 but with additional engraver imprint. 18__. 1850s–1860s.

Rarity: —

$10 • W-MA-570-010-G050

Left: 10 / Ship / TEN. ***Center:*** Justice standing / TEN. ***Right:*** 10 / Beehive / TEN. ***Engraver:*** New England Bank Note Co. / PSSP. ***Comments:*** H-MA-215-G20. 18__. 1830s–1850s.

Rarity: —

$10 • W-MA-570-010-G050a

Overprint: Red. ***Engraver:*** New England Bank Note Co. / PSSP. ***Comments:*** H-MA-215-G20a. Similar to W-MA-570-010-G050. 18__. 1850s.

Rarity: —

$10 • W-MA-570-010-G050b

Overprint: Red. ***Engraver:*** New England Bank Note Co. / PSSP / ABNCo. monogram. ***Comments:*** H-MA-215-G20b. Similar to W-MA-570-010-G050 but with additional engraver imprint. 18__. 1850s–1860s.

Rarity: —

$20 • W-MA-570-020-G060

Left: 20 / Ship / TWENTY. ***Center:*** Justice standing. ***Right:*** 20 / Beehive / TWENTY. ***Engraver:*** New England Bank Note Co. / PSSP. ***Comments:*** H-MA-215-G24. 18__. 1830s–1850s.

Rarity: —

$20 • W-MA-570-020-G060a

Overprint: Red. ***Engraver:*** New England Bank Note Co. / PSSP. ***Comments:*** H-MA-215-G24a. Similar to W-MA-570-020-G060. 18__. 1850s.

Rarity: —

$20 • W-MA-570-020-G060b

Overprint: Red. ***Engraver:*** New England Bank Note Co. / PSSP / ABNCo. monogram. ***Comments:*** H-MA-215-G24b. Similar to W-MA-570-020-G060 but with additional engraver imprint. 18__. 1850s–1860s.

Rarity: —

$50 • W-MA-570-050-G070

Left: 50 / Woman standing with ankles crossed, staff, cornucopia, and anchor / 50. ***Center:*** FIFTY DOLLARS / 50. ***Right:*** FIFTY vertically. ***Engraver:*** New England Bank Note Co. / PSSP. ***Comments:*** H-MA-215-G28. 18__. 1830s–1840s.

Rarity: —

$50 • W-MA-570-050-G080

Left: FIFTY / Woman standing with wreath and flower / FIFTY. ***Center:*** 50 / Man restraining prancing horse / 50. ***Right:*** FIFTY / Woman standing with cornucopia against shoulder / FIFTY. ***Engraver:*** New England Bank Note Co. ***Comments:*** H-MA-215-G32. 18__. 1840s–1850s.

Rarity: —

$100 • W-MA-570-100-G090

Left: Lathework panel bearing C / Portrait of George Washington / C. ***Center:*** 100 / Manhattan reclining pouring water, Ship / 100. ***Right:*** Lathework panel bearing ONE HUNDRED vertically. ***Engraver:*** New England Bank Note Co. / PSSP. ***Comments:*** H-MA-215-G36. 18__. 1830s–1840s.

Rarity: —

$100 • W-MA-570-100-G100

Left: ONE HUNDRED on 100 / Portrait of William Henry Harrison. ***Center:*** Wharf scene, Men loading wagon with barrels. ***Right:*** ONE HUNDRED on 100 / Portrait of Christopher Columbus. ***Engraver:*** New England Bank Note Co. ***Comments:*** H-MA-215-G40. 18__. 1840s–1850s.

Rarity: —

$100 • W-MA-570-100-G110

Left: 100 / Vulcan seated with sledge and anchor. ***Center:*** Train on bridge / Eagle on limb / Canal locks. ***Bottom center:*** 100. ***Right:*** 100 / Ceres seated, Cornucopia. ***Engraver:*** Rawdon, Wright, Hatch & Edson. ***Comments:*** H-MA-215-G44. 18__. 1850s.

Rarity: —

$500 • W-MA-570-500-G120

Left: 500 / 500 vertically. ***Center:*** 500 / Woman seated with shield bearing D, Fasces, cornucopia, lyre, and sheaf on ground / 500. ***Right:*** 500 / D / 500. ***Engraver:*** New England Bank Note Co. / PSSP. ***Comments:*** H-MA-215-G48. 18__. 1830s–1840s.

Rarity: —

$500 • W-MA-570-500-G130

Left: Woman reclining / 500. ***Center:*** 500 / D. ***Right:*** 500 vertically. ***Engraver:*** Rawdon, Wright, Hatch & Edson. ***Comments:*** H-MA-215-G52. 18__. 1850s.

Rarity: URS-2
VF $1,600

$1,000 • W-MA-570-1000-G140

Left: THOUSAND vertically. ***Center:*** 1000 / Woman standing with legs crossed, lyre, and cornucopia / 1000. ***Right:*** 1000 / M / 1000. ***Engraver:*** New England Bank Note Co. / PSSP. ***Comments:*** H-MA-215-G56. 18__. 1830s–1840s.

Rarity: —

$1,000 • W-MA-570-1000-G150

Left: Laocoon and sons strangled by serpents / 1000. ***Center:*** THOUSAND / Train and laborers. ***Right:*** 1000 / Ship / 1000. ***Engraver:*** Rawdon, Wright, Hatch & Edson. ***Comments:*** H-MA-215-G60. 18__. 1850s.

Rarity: —

Non-Valid Issues

$2 • W-MA-570-002-A010

Left: Two girls carrying sheaves / 2. ***Center:*** Sailor and mechanic flanking U.S. shield surmounted by badger. ***Right:*** 2 / Indian woman kneeling, Liberty standing. ***Overprint:*** Red TWO. ***Engraver:*** New England Bank Note Co. / Rawdon, Wright, Hatch & Edson. ***Comments:*** H-MA-215-A5. Altered from $2 Waubeek Bank, De Soto, Nebraska. 1857.

Rarity: —

$3 • W-MA-570-003-A020

Left: 3 / Woman standing with branch, Trident and oval bearing THREE / THREE. ***Center:*** Three women seated with pole and cap by globe. ***Right:*** 5 / Portrait of Jenny Lind. ***Tint:*** Orange dies outlining white 5s. ***Engraver:*** Terry, Pelton & Co. ***Comments:*** H-MA-215-A10. Altered from $5 Arlington Bank, Washington, D.C. 18__. 1840s.

Rarity: —

$5 • W-MA-570-005-A030

Left: U.S. flag, Woman seated, eagle / DOLLARS across V. ***Center:*** Three women seated with pole and cap by globe. ***Right:*** 5 / Portrait of Jenny Lind. ***Tint:*** Orange dies outlining white 5s. ***Engraver:*** Danforth, Wright & Co. ***Comments:*** H-MA-215-A15. Altered from $5 Arlington Bank, Washington, D.C. 18__. 1850s.

Rarity: —

$5 • W-MA-570-005-A040

SI

Overprint: Red FIVE. ***Engraver:*** Bald, Cousland & Co. / Baldwin, Bald & Cousland. ***Comments:*** H-MA-215-A20. 18__. 1850s.

Rarity: URS-6
F $150

$5 • W-MA-570-005-A050

Left: Portrait of Henry Clay. ***Right:*** Portrait of George Washington. ***Engraver:*** New England Bank Note Co. / Rawdon, Wright, Hatch & Edson. ***Comments:*** H-MA-215-A25. Altered from $5 Waubeek Bank, De Soto, Nebraska. 18__. 1857.

Rarity: URS-6
EF $250

How to Read the Whitman Numbering System

$1 • W-MA-010-001-G010a

Denomination: Value of the note shown.

W: Whitman number. This number is a sortable code unique to each bank and note.

MA: Abbreviation for the state under study.

010: Numerical designation specific to each bank.

001: The denomination in dollars.

G010a: G indicates a good or valid note. Other categories are indicated thus: C (counterfeit); R (raised); S (spurious); N (not-attributed); A (altered). Numbers are assigned starting with 010, 020, et seq. Terminal letters following the number indicate variations of a note: a series of different colored overprints, tints, payees, etc., all on the same design of note. For more information, see the "How to Use This Book" section at the front of the volume, page xiv.

$10 • W-MA-570-010-N010

Left: 10 / Sailor. ***Center:*** Three men, Ship. ***Comments:*** H-MA-215-N10.

Rarity: —

$10 • W-MA-570-010-A060

Left: X / TEN vertically. ***Center:*** Men and animals, Farming scene. ***Right:*** 10 / Woman seated. ***Engraver:*** Danforth, Wright & Co. ***Comments:*** H-MA-215-A30. Altered from $10 Brownville Bank and Land Co., Omaha City, Nebraska. Sept. 1, 1857.

Rarity: URS-6
VG $125

Grocers Bank
1848–1855
W-MA-580

History: The Grocers Bank commenced business on September 12, 1848, with a starting capital of $250,000. It was located at 70 State Street. Its capital was increased to $300,000 in 1851, to $650,000 in 1854, and to $750,000 in 1855.

According to the *Annual Report of the Secretary of the Treasury on the Condition of Banks*, circulation in 1849 was $178,910. By 1854 it had risen to $282,316. In the same year real estate was valued at $30,246.88 and specie at $50,249.92.

On December 3, 1855, the Grocers Bank ceased operations. It went into receivership and was later liquidated.

Numismatic Commentary: Notes from this bank are occasionally attainable, with the $5 note showing a distant view of Quincy Market. It is probably the note that will most likely fall into a collector's hands.

Valid Issues

$1 • W-MA-580-001-G010

JF

Engraver: Toppan, Carpenter & Co. ***Comments:*** H-MA-220-G2. Proof. 18__. 1848–1850s.

Rarity: URS-3
VF $500; **Proof** $1,250

$1 • W-MA-580-001-G010a

Left: 1 / Indian in shield. ***Center:*** Woman on dock with merchandise, Ships / ONE. ***Bottom center:*** Train. ***Right:*** 1 / Indian woman as liberty holding staff. ***Overprint:*** Red. ***Engraver:*** Toppan, Carpenter & Co. ***Comments:*** H-MA-220-G2a. Similar to W-MA-580-001-G010. 18__. 1850s.

Rarity: —

$2 • W-MA-580-002-G020

Left: 2 / Portrait of John Hancock. ***Center:*** Indian man with gun and woman with sickle. ***Right:*** 2 / Portrait of John Quincy Adams. ***Engraver:*** Toppan, Carpenter & Co. ***Comments:*** H-MA-220-G4. 18__. 1848–1850s.

Rarity: —

$2 • W-MA-580-002-G020a

Overprint: Red. ***Engraver:*** Toppan, Carpenter & Co. ***Comments:*** H-MA-220-G4a. Similar to W-MA-580-002-G020. 18__. 1850s.

Rarity: —

$3 • W-MA-580-003-G030

HA

Engraver: Toppan, Carpenter & Co. ***Comments:*** H-MA-220-G6. 18__. 1848–1850s.

Rarity: URS-3
F $540; **VF** $750

$3 • W-MA-580-003-G030a

Left: Woman holding up 3. ***Center:*** Eagle / THREE. ***Right:*** 3 / Woman. ***Overprint:*** Red. ***Engraver:*** Toppan, Carpenter & Co. ***Comments:*** H-MA-220-G6a. Similar to W-MA-580-003-G030. 18__. 1850s.

Rarity: —

$5 • W-MA-580-005-G040

CC

Engraver: Toppan, Carpenter & Co. ***Comments:*** H-MA-220-G8. Proof. 18__. 1848–1850s.

Rarity: URS-3
F $645; **Proof** $1,500

$5 • W-MA-580-005-G040a

Left: Train / Hall, Horses pulling wagon / 5. ***Center:*** FIVE on 5. ***Bottom center:*** Female portrait. ***Right:*** 5 / Male portrait. ***Overprint:*** Red FIVE. ***Engraver:*** Toppan, Carpenter & Co. ***Comments:*** H-MA-220-G8a. Similar to W-MA-580-005-G040. 18__. 1850s.

Rarity: URS-3
F $600

$10 • W-MA-580-010-G050

Left: George Washington on horseback / TEN. ***Center:*** Woman leaning on bale, Ships. ***Right:*** 10 / Portrait of Daniel Webster / TEN. ***Engraver:*** Toppan, Carpenter & Co. ***Comments:*** H-MA-220-G10. 18__. 1848–1850s.

Rarity: —

$10 • W-MA-580-010-G050a

Overprint: Red. ***Engraver:*** Toppan, Carpenter & Co. ***Comments:*** H-MA-220-G10a. Similar to W-MA-580-010-G050. 18__. 1850s.

Rarity: —

$20 • W-MA-580-020-G060

Left: Woman with sheaf / TWENTY. ***Center:*** 20 / Woman, eagle, and globe. ***Right:*** 20 / Ship. ***Engraver:*** Toppan, Carpenter & Co. ***Comments:*** H-MA-220-G12. 18__. 1848–1850s.

Rarity: —

$20 • W-MA-580-020-G060a

Overprint: Red. ***Engraver:*** Toppan, Carpenter & Co. ***Comments:*** H-MA-220-G12a. Similar to W-MA-580-020-G060. 18__. 1850s.

Rarity: —

$50 • W-MA-580-050-G070

Left: 50 / Woman, Shipping scene. ***Center:*** Three women. ***Right:*** 50 / Train. ***Engraver:*** Toppan, Carpenter & Co. ***Comments:*** H-MA-220-G14. 18__. 1848–1850s.

Rarity: —

$50 • W-MA-580-050-G070a

Overprint: Red. ***Engraver:*** Toppan, Carpenter & Co. ***Comments:*** H-MA-220-G14a. Similar to W-MA-580-050-G070. 18__. 1850s.

Rarity: —

$100 • W-MA-580-100-G080

Left: Woman reclining / 100. ***Center:*** C / Woman seated / 100. ***Bottom center:*** Portrait of girl. ***Right:*** 100 / Portrait of Benjamin Franklin. ***Engraver:*** Toppan, Carpenter & Co. ***Comments:*** H-MA-220-G16. 18__. 1848–1850s.

Rarity: URS-2

Proof $2,500

Selected auction price: Stack's Bowers Galleries, August 2014, Lot 2059, Proof $2,350

$100 • W-MA-580-100-G080a

Overprint: Red. ***Engraver:*** Toppan, Carpenter & Co. ***Comments:*** H-MA-220-G16a. Similar to W-MA-580-100-G080. 18__. 1850s.

Rarity: —

$500 • W-MA-580-500-G090

Engraver: Unverified, but likely Toppan, Carpenter & Co. ***Comments:*** H-MA-220-G18. No description available. 18__. 1850s.

Rarity: *None known*

$1,000 • W-MA-580-1000-G100

Left: Female portrait / 1000. ***Center:*** ONE / Sailing ship / THOUSAND. ***Right:*** 1000. ***Engraver:*** Toppan, Carpenter & Co. ***Comments:*** H-MA-220-G20. 18__. 1850s.

Rarity: URS-2

Proof $3,500

Non-Valid Issues

$3 • W-MA-580-003-S010

NJW

Engraver: Terry, Pelton & Co. ***Comments:*** H-MA-220-S5. 18__. 1849.

Rarity: URS-7

VG $75; **F** $100

$10 • W-MA-580-010-R010

Engraver: Toppan, Carpenter & Co. ***Comments:*** H-MA-220-R5. Raised from W-MA-580-001-G010. 18__. 1840s.

Rarity: —

Hamilton Bank

1831–1865

W-MA-590

History: The Hamilton Bank was chartered in March 1828. It opened for business at 53 State Street, but beginning in 1846 the bank was at 66 State Street. In 1837 the bank's charter was extended until January 1, 1875.

Figures for 1838 included: net profits on hand $38,474.89; balances due to other banks $33,055.72; cash deposited $90,776.99; cash deposited bearing interest $125,000; total amount due from banks $895,303.60; gold, silver, and other coined metals in the banking house $30,410.46; bills of other banks incorporated in this state $84,544; balance due from other banks $10,960.13; amount of all debts due $769,389.01; total amount of resources of the bank $895,303.60. Circulation ranged from $86,773 in 1839 to $222,540 in 1845. Profits were $78,000 in 1851.

The Hamilton Bank closed its affairs after it was succeeded by the Hamilton National Bank of Boston on February 2, 1865.

Numismatic Commentary: The only genuine note from this bank that shows up with any frequency is the $1 note with the Alexander Hamilton portrait.

Valid Issues

$1 • W-MA-590-001-G010

Engraver: PSSP. ***Comments:*** H-MA-225-G4. 18__. 1830s–1840s.

Rarity: —

$1 • W-MA-590-001-G020

CC

Engraver: New England Bank Note Co. ***Comments:*** H-MA-225-G8. 18__. 1840s–1850s.

Rarity: URS-5
F $200; **VF** $350; **AU** $750; **CU** $900
Selected auction price: Heritage, January 2009, Lot 12416, CU $862

$2 • W-MA-590-002-G030

Left: Lathework panel bearing MASSACHUSETTS vertically. ***Center:*** 2 / 2 / Alternating flower garlands and gridwork segments / TWO / 2 / 2. ***Right:*** Lathework panel bearing five TWOs vertically. ***Engraver:*** PSSP. ***Comments:*** H-MA-225-G12. 18__. 1830s.

Rarity: —

$2 • W-MA-590-002-G040

SBG

Engraver: New England Bank Note Co. ***Comments:*** H-MA-225-G16. 18__. 1840s–1850s.

Rarity: URS-3
VG $850; **F** $1,500

$3 • W-MA-590-003-G050

Left: Lathework panel bearing MASSACHUSETTS vertically. ***Center:*** 3 / 3 / Alternating flower garlands and gridwork segments / 3 / 3. ***Right:*** Lathework panel bearing THREE vertically. ***Engraver:*** PSSP. ***Comments:*** H-MA-225-G20. 18__. 1830s.

Rarity: —

$3 • W-MA-590-003-G060

CC

Engraver: New England Bank Note Co. ***Comments:*** H-MA-225-G24. 18__. 1840s–1850s.

Rarity: URS-4
VF $850

$5 • W-MA-590-005-G070

QDB

Engraver: PSSP. ***Comments:*** H-MA-225-G28. Proof. 18__. 1830s.

Rarity: URS-3
Proof $2,250

$10 • W-MA-590-010-G080

CC

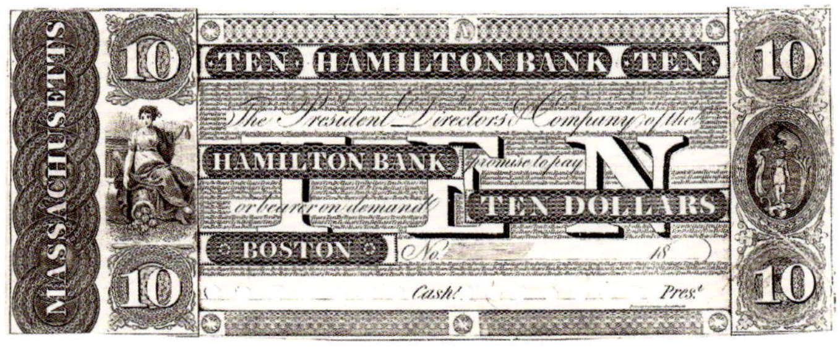

Engraver: PSSP. ***Comments:*** H-MA-225-G30. Proof. 18__. 1830s.

Rarity: URS-2
Proof $1,000

$20 • W-MA-590-020-G090

Left: Lathework chain bearing MASSACHUSETTS / 20 / 20 vertically. ***Center:*** Alternating flower garlands and gridwork segments. ***Right:*** 20 / 20 vertically. ***Engraver:*** PSSP. ***Comments:*** H-MA-225-G34. 18__. 1830s.

Rarity: —

$20 • W-MA-590-020-G100

Left: 20 / Male portrait / XX. ***Center:*** XX / Male portrait / XX. ***Right:*** 20 / Male portrait / XX. ***Engraver:*** PSSP. ***Comments:*** H-MA-225-G36. 18__. 1840s–1850s.

Rarity: —

$50 • W-MA-590-050-G110

Left: Lathework chain bearing MASSACHUSETTS / 50 / 50 vertically. ***Center:*** Alternating flower garlands and gridwork segments. ***Right:*** 50 / 50 vertically. ***Engraver:*** PSSP. ***Comments:*** H-MA-225-G40. 18__. 1830s.

Rarity: —

$50 • W-MA-590-050-G120

CC

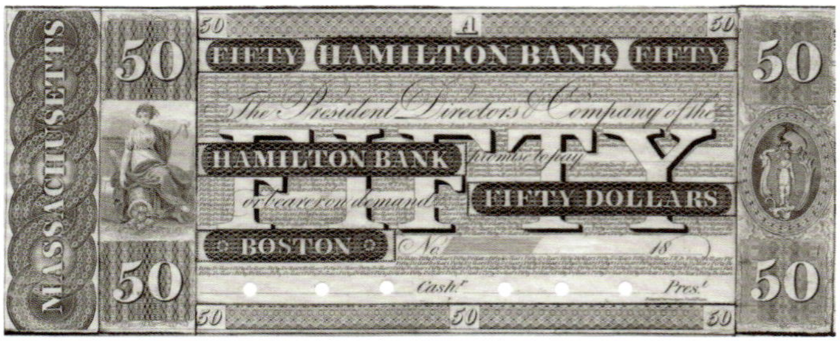

Engraver: PSSP. ***Comments:*** H-MA-225-G44. Similar to W-MA-590-050-G080 but with different denomination. 18__. 1830s.

Rarity: URS-2
Proof $1,250
Selected auction price: Stack's Bowers Galleries, August 2014, Lot 2060, Proof $1,116

$100 • W-MA-590-100-G130

Left: Lathework chain bearing MASSACHUSETTS / 100 / 100 vertically. ***Center:*** Alternating flower garlands and gridwork segments. ***Right:*** 100 / 100 vertically. ***Engraver:*** Perkins. ***Comments:*** H-MA-225-G48. 18__. 1830s.

Rarity: —

$100 • W-MA-590-100-G140

JF

Engraver: PSSP. ***Comments:*** H-MA-225-G52. Similar to W-MA-590-050-G080 but with different denomination. Proof. 18__. 1830s.

Rarity: URS-2
Proof $2,000
Selected auction price: Stack's Bowers Galleries, August 2014, Lot 2061, Proof $1,897

$500 • W-MA-590-500-G150

Left: Lathework chain bearing MASSACHUSETTS / 500 / Ceres / 500 vertically. ***Center:*** Alternating flower garlands and gridwork segments / FIVE HUNDRED DOLLARS lined by spiral lathework lines. ***Right:*** 500 / State arms / 500. ***Engraver:*** PSSP. ***Comments:*** H-MA-225-G56. Similar to W-MA-590-050-G080 but with different denomination. 18__. 1830s.

Rarity: —

$500 • W-MA-590-500-G160

Left: 500 / Male portrait / 500. ***Center:*** Two women flanking state arms. ***Right:*** 500 / Ship. ***Engraver:*** American Bank Note Co. ***Comments:*** H-MA-225-G60. 1860s.

Rarity: —

Non-Valid Issues

$1 • W-MA-590-001-A010

Left: ONE / Sailboat / 1. ***Center:*** Houses with smoke coming out of chimneys. ***Right:*** 1 / Portrait of Marquis de Lafayette / ONE. ***Engraver:*** New England Bank Note Co. ***Comments:*** H-MA-225-A5. Altered from W-MA-680-001-G020. 18__. 1830s.

Rarity: URS-3
VG $175

$2 • W-MA-590-002-A020

Left: TWO DOLLARS / Portrait of Thomas Jefferson / TWO DOLLARS. ***Center:*** Ship, Factory scene, Horse-drawn wagons. ***Right:*** TWO DOLLARS / Portrait of Marquis de Lafayette. ***Engraver:*** New England Bank Note Co. ***Comments:*** H-MA-225-A10. Altered from W-MA-680-002-G070. 18__. 1830s.

Rarity: —

$2 • W-MA-590-002-A030

ANS

Overprint: Red TWO. ***Engraver:*** Baldwin, Bald & Cousland / Bald, Cousland & Co. ***Comments:*** H-MA-225-A15. Altered from $2 Tiverton Bank, Tiverton, Rhode Island. 18__. 1850s.

Rarity: URS-6
F $150

$3 • W-MA-590-003-A040

Left: 3 / Woman standing. ***Center:*** Eagle and U.S. shield / Sailor standing on wharf with bales, Ships. ***Right:*** 3 / Portrait of Marquis de Lafayette / THREE. ***Engraver:*** New England Bank Note Co. ***Comments:*** H-MA-225-A20. Altered from W-MA-680-003-G090. 18__. 1830s.

Rarity: —

$5 • W-MA-590-005-A050

Left: 5 / Portrait of George Washington / FIVE. ***Center:*** Ship, Factory scene, Horse-drawn wagons. ***Right:*** 5 / Portrait of Marquis de Lafayette / FIVE. ***Engraver:*** New England Bank Note Co. ***Comments:*** H-MA-225-A25. Altered from W-MA-680-005-G110. 18__. Circa 1840.

Rarity: —

$10 • W-MA-590-010-A060

Left: X / Portrait of Marquis de Lafayette / TEN. ***Center:*** Ship, Factory scene, Horse-drawn wagons. ***Right:*** 10 / Male portrait / TEN. ***Engraver:*** New England Bank Note Co. ***Comments:*** H-MA-225-A30. Altered from W-MA-680-010-G130. 18__. Circa 1840.

Rarity: —

$10 • W-MA-590-010-A070

Engraver: New England Bank Note Co. ***Comments:*** H-MA-225-A35. Altered from $10 Hamilton Bank, Scituate, Rhode Island, or from notes of other failed banks using the same plate. 18__. 1830s–1840s.

Rarity: URS-5
F $150; **VF** $245

$20 • W-MA-590-020-A080

Left: TWENTY / Justice holding sword and balance. ***Center:*** Ship, Factory scene, Horse-drawn wagons. ***Right:*** 20 / Portrait of Marquis de Lafayette / 20. ***Engraver:*** New England Bank Note Co. ***Comments:*** H-MA-225-A40. Altered from W-MA-680-020-G150. 18__. Circa 1840.

Rarity: —

$20 • W-MA-590-020-A090

Engraver: New England Bank Note Co. ***Comments:*** H-MA-225-A45. Altered from $20 Hamilton Bank, Scituate, Rhode Island, or from notes of other failed banks using the same plate. 18__. 1840s.

Rarity: URS-5
F $150; **VF** $350

$50 • W-MA-590-050-A100

Left: 50 / Woman standing, Cornucopia, Anchor and steamboat / 50. ***Center:*** FIFTY DOLLARS / 50. ***Right:*** FIFTY vertically. ***Engraver:*** New England Bank Note Co. ***Comments:*** H-MA-225-A50. Altered from W-MA-680-050-G160. 18__. Circa 1840.

Rarity: —

Hancock Bank
1833–1837
W-MA-600

History: The Hancock Bank was incorporated on March 25, 1833, with an authorized capital of $500,000. Soon it became a "pet bank" for the Jackson administration's movement of federal funds from the Bank of the United States. It maintained that status until 1836, when rumors about the bank arose. There were management difficulties, and a new board of directors was elected. Matters grew worse, and in 1838 it was learned that the bank's entire capital of $500,000 had been loaned to the president and to two directors in the sums of $210,000, $160,000, and $140,000, respectively. Shortly afterward, the stockholders voted to close the bank.

Numismatic Commentary: Notes from this bank are virtually non-existent.

Valid Issues

$1 • W-MA-600-001-G010

Engraver: Unverified, but likely New England Bank Note Co. ***Comments:*** H-MA-230-G2. No description available. 18__. 1830s.

Rarity: *None known*

$2 • W-MA-600-002-G020

Engraver: Unverified, but likely New England Bank Note Co. ***Comments:*** H-MA-230-G4. No description available. 18__. 1830s.

Rarity: *None known*

$3 • W-MA-600-003-G030

Engraver: Unverified, but likely New England Bank Note Co. ***Comments:*** H-MA-230-G6. No description available. 18__. 1830s.

Rarity: *None known*

$5 • W-MA-600-005-G040

Engraver: Unverified, but likely New England Bank Note Co. ***Comments:*** H-MA-230-G8. No description available. 18__. 1830s.

Rarity: *None known*

$10 • W-MA-600-010-G050

Engraver: Unverified, but likely New England Bank Note Co. ***Comments:*** H-MA-230-G10. No description available. 18__. 1830s.

Rarity: *None known*

$20 • W-MA-600-020-G060

Engraver: Unverified, but likely New England Bank Note Co. ***Comments:*** H-MA-230-G12. No description available. 18__. 1830s.

Rarity: *None known*

$50 • W-MA-600-050-G070

Engraver: Unverified, but likely New England Bank Note Co. ***Comments:*** H-MA-230-G14. No description available. 18__. 1830s.

Rarity: *None known*

$50 • W-MA-600-050-G080

Left: 50 / Steamboat and schooner. ***Center:*** Farmyard scene, Load of hay with two men on it, Man with rake and pail. ***Right:*** L / Justice kneeling. ***Engraver:*** New England Bank Note Co. ***Comments:*** H-MA-230-G16. 18__. 1830s.

Rarity: —

$100 • W-MA-600-100-G090

Engraver: Unverified, but likely New England Bank Note Co. ***Comments:*** H-MA-230-G18. No description available. 18__. 1830s.

Rarity: *None known*

$100 • W-MA-600-100-G100

Engraver: Unverified, but likely New England Bank Note Co. ***Comments:*** H-MA-230-G20. No description available. 18__. 1830s.

Rarity: *None known*

$500 • W-MA-600-500-G110

Left: 500 / 500 vertically. ***Center:*** 500 / Woman seated with right arm on shield bearing D, Fasces, cornucopia, lyre, and sheaf on ground. ***Right:*** 500 / D / 500. ***Engraver:*** PSSP / New England Bank Note Co. ***Comments:*** H-MA-230-G22. 18__. 1830s.

Rarity: —

$1,000 • W-MA-600-1000-G120

Left: THOUSAND vertically. ***Center:*** 1000 / Woman standing with legs crossed and lyre, Cornucopia / 1000. ***Right:*** 1000 / M / 1000. ***Engraver:*** PSSP / New England Bank Note Co. ***Comments:*** H-MA-230-G26. 18__. 1830s.

Rarity: —

Non-Valid Issues

$20 • W-MA-600-020-A010

Engraver: New England Bank Note Co. ***Comments:*** H-MA-230-A5. Altered from W-MA-520-020-G110 or G120. 18__. 1830s.

Rarity: —

Haymarket Square Bank
1850s
W-MA-610

History: The Haymarket Square Bank was chartered on April 9, 1850, with an authorized capital of $150,000, to operate in or near Haymarket Square. Samuel A. Way was the chief organizer. It was soon realized that he was a man "of notoriously bad character." Pressured to resign his directorship, he did so, but he was alleged to have continued to maintain control over a majority of the stock subscriptions. Certain other stockholders, namely Chamberlain, Holden, and Chilson, petitioned the Supreme Judicial Court of Massachusetts to issue an injunction, which was done in August. By that time $40,000 had been paid in. The bank was thereby prevented from opening and ordered to liquidate. After expenses were paid, proportional refunds were given to those who had paid for stock.

Numismatic Commentary: All known genuine notes are Proofs. Only two or three of these notes are still known to exist. The central vignette on these notes shows Haymarket Square in Boston. Certain notes are imprinted "Hay Market Bank."

Issues

$5 • W-MA-610-005-G010

Left: View of Haymarket Square / FIVE. ***Center:*** 5. ***Right:*** 5 / MASSACHUSETTS / Woman standing. ***Engraver:*** Rawdon, Wright, Hatch & Edson / New England Bank Note Co. ***Comments:*** H-MA-235-G8. Aug. 1, 185_. 1850s.

Rarity: URS-3
Proof $2,500

$500 • W-MA-610-500-G020 CC

Engraver: New England Bank Note Co. ***Comments:*** H-Unlisted. Remainder. 18__.

Rarity: URS-2
Proof $2,200

Hide and Leather Bank
1857–1864
W-MA-620

History: The Hide and Leather Bank was chartered in 1857 with a capital of $1,000,000. The bank opened in October at 60 State Street. Later, by 1864, it was located at 51 Congress Street.

Circulation amounted to $235,595 in 1857. By 1858 it was $128,681, and in 1860 it was $236,595. Specie totaled $99,861.42 at the same time.

In October 1864, the Hide and Leather Bank was on the list of state banks that had become National Banks. It closed its affairs after the National Hide and Leather Bank of Boston, chartered on June 8, 1864, commenced business.

Numismatic Commentary: Notes of this bank are great rarities, as most were redeemed and destroyed.

As of 2003, there was a $1-$1-$2-$3 tint, a $1-$1-$2-$3 tint, a $1-$1-$2-$3 tint, and a $5-$5-$5-$5 tint plate remaining in the archives of the American Bank Note Co.

Valid Issues

$1 • W-MA-620-001-G010 CC

Tint: Red ONE and panel of microlettering. ***Engraver:*** Danforth, Wright & Co. ***Comments:*** H-MA-240-G2a. August 1, 1862.

Rarity: URS-3
VF $2,000; **Proof** $2,500
Selected auction price: Heritage, January 2011, Lot 15543, VF $1,955

$2 • W-MA-620-002-G020

Center: TWO / Indian man on horse shooting buffalo with bow and arrow. ***Right:*** 2 / Bull's head. ***Tint:*** Red TWO. ***Engraver:*** Danforth, Wright & Co. ***Comments:*** H-MA-240-G4a. 18__. 1850s.

Rarity: URS-2
Proof $3,500

$3 • W-MA-620-003-G030 CC

Tint: Red THREE and panel of microlettering. ***Engraver:*** Danforth, Wright & Co. ***Comments:*** H-MA-240-G6a. August 1, 1858. 1850s.

Rarity: URS-3
F $2,500; **Proof** $4,500

$5 • W-MA-620-005-G040

CC

Tint: Red panel of microlettering outlining white FIVE. ***Engraver:*** Danforth, Wright & Co. ***Comments:*** H-MA-240-G8a. Proof. October 1, 1857.

Rarity: URS-2
Proof $6,500

$10 • W-MA-620-010-G050

Left: 10 / Steamship. ***Center:*** Man dressing leather / 10. ***Tint:*** Red die bearing X. ***Engraver:*** Danforth, Wright & Co. ***Comments:*** H-MA-240-G10a. 18__. 1850s

Rarity: —

$20 • W-MA-620-020-G060

Left: XX / Cattle in stream. ***Right:*** 20 / Boy, Old man seated under tree, Dog. ***Tint:*** Red die bearing 20. ***Engraver:*** Danforth, Wright & Co. ***Comments:*** H-MA-240-G12a. 18__. 1850s.

Rarity: —

$50 • W-MA-620-050-G070

Left: 50 / Farmer, sailor, and mechanic standing, Ships. ***Right:*** 50. ***Tint:*** Red FIFTY and die bearing L. ***Engraver:*** Danforth, Wright & Co. ***Comments:*** H-MA-240-G14a. 18__. 1850s.

Rarity: —

$100 • W-MA-620-100-G080

Left: Panel bearing ONE HUNDRED vertically. ***Center:*** Four women, three seated and one reading book. ***Right:*** 100. ***Tint:*** Red panel bearing C. ***Engraver:*** Danforth, Wright & Co. ***Comments:*** H-MA-240-G16a. 18__. 1850s.

Rarity: URS-2
Proof $10,000

$500 • W-MA-620-500-G090

Left: Woman seated with book on lap pointing upward / 500. ***Right:*** 500 / Sailing ship. ***Tint:*** Red die surrounding ship. ***Engraver:*** Danforth, Wright & Co. ***Comments:*** H-MA-240-G18a. 18__. 1850s.

Rarity: URS-1
Proof $15,000

$1,000 • W-MA-620-1000-G100

Left: Liberty standing with pole and cap. ***Right:*** 100 / Two cherubs flying with sheaf, purse, and wand. ***Tint:*** Red ring composed of ONE THOUSANDs. ***Engraver:*** Danforth, Wright & Co. ***Comments:*** H-MA-240-G20a. 18__. 1850s.

Rarity: URS-1
Proof $15,000

Uncut Sheets

$1-$1-$2-$3 • W-MA-620-001.001.002.003-US010

Vignette(s): ***($1)*** Indian man standing / Cowboy on horse lassoing wild cow / Sailor. ***($1)*** Indian man standing / Cowboy on horse lassoing wild cow / Sailor. ***($2)*** Indian man on horse shooting buffalo with bow and arrow / Bull's head. ***($3)*** Woman seated in clouds with cornucopia and shield / Woman sewing shoes, Two men dressing leather. ***Tint(s):*** Red. ***Engraver:*** Danforth, Wright & Co. ***Comments:*** H-MA-240-G2a, G2a, G4a, G6a. October 3, 1857.

Rarity: —
Proof $1,000

$5-$5-$5-$5 • W-MA-620-005.005.005.005-US020

Vignette(s): ***($5)*** Scene in tannery, Men dressing leather. ***($5)*** Scene in tannery, Men dressing leather. ***($5)*** Scene in tannery, Men dressing leather. ***($5)*** Scene in tannery, Men dressing leather. ***Tint(s):*** Red. ***Engraver:*** Danforth, Wright & Co. ***Comments:*** H-MA-240-G8a, G8a, G8a, G8a. October 1, 1857.

Rarity: —
Proof $1,000

$100-$100-$500-$1,000 • W-MA-620-100.100.500.1000-US030

Vignette(s): ***($100)*** Four women, three seated and one standing reading book. ***($100)*** Four women, three seated and one standing reading book. ***($500)*** Woman seated with book on lap pointing upward / Sailing ship. ***($1,000)*** Liberty standing with pole and cap / Two cherubs flying with sheaf, purse, and wand. ***Tint(s):*** Red. ***Engraver:*** Danforth, Wright & Co. ***Comments:*** H-MA-240-G16a, G16a, G18a, G20a. October 1, 1857.

Rarity: —
Proof $1,000

Non-Valid Issues

$2 • W-MA-620-002-A010

Left: TWO / Eagle on shield / 2. ***Center:*** 2 / Building, Woman seated with caduceus and Ceres standing with tall sheaf, Wagon and team / 2. ***Right:*** Woman walking with staff and pitcher / TWO. ***Engraver:*** Doolittle & Munson, Cincinnati. ***Comments:*** H-MA-240-A5. Altered from $2 Bank of West Union, West Union, Ohio. 18__. 1830s.

Rarity: —

$3 • W-MA-620-003-A020

Left: 3 / Portrait of Daniel Webster. ***Center:*** Ceres and Liberty flanking U.S. shield surmounted by eagle. ***Right:*** THREE across 3 / Female portrait. ***Overprint:*** Red THREE. ***Engraver:*** New England Bank Note Co. / Rawdon, Wright, Hatch & Edson. ***Comments:*** H-MA-240-A10. Altered from $3 Waubeek Bank, De Soto, Nebraska. 1857.

Rarity: —

$5 • W-MA-620-005-A030

Left: Panel bearing FIVE vertically. ***Center:*** 5 / Griffin on chest, Moneta receiving bag of coin from Mercury in clouds / 5. ***Bottom center:*** Arm and hammer. ***Right:*** FIVE / Six milkmaids standing and seated / V. ***Engraver:*** Rawdon, Wright, Hatch & Edson. ***Comments:*** H-MA-240-A15. Altered from $5 Bank of West Union, West Union, Ohio. 18__. 1859.

Rarity: —

Howard Bank

1859–1865

W-MA-630

History: By legislative action in 1859, the name of the Howard Banking Company, W-MA-640, was changed to the Howard Bank. Reuben E. Demmon was the president, and the cashier was George E. Hersey. The *Boston Directory* listed the directors of the Howard Bank in 1861 as: Reuben E. Demmon, Abijah W. Farrar, Abram French, Elisha Atkins, Darius B. Rising, Leister M. Clark, Francis K. Fisher, A.B. Butterfield, and William Hilton.

Circulation ranged from a low of $114,013 in 1858 to a high of $254,279 in 1851. Specie ranged between $49,681.24 in 1851 to $75,014.45 in 1858.

On November 19, 1864, the business of the Howard Bank was succeeded by the Howard National Bank of Boston. As was usually the case, the same officers remained in place.

Numismatic Commentary: Genuine notes from this bank are very hard to locate. Some of these issues bear the portrait of John Howard.

Valid Issues

$1 • W-MA-630-001-G010

QDB

Overprint: Red ONE. ***Engraver:*** American Bank Note Co. ***Comments:*** H-MA-245-G2a. 18__. 1850s–1860s.

Rarity: URS-4

F $400; **VF** $650; **EF** $775

$1 • W-MA-630-001-G010a

JF

Overprint: Green ONE. ***Engraver:*** American Bank Note Co. ***Comments:*** H-MA-245-G2b. Similar to W-MA-630-001-G010 but with printed serial number. June 16, 1862.

Rarity: URS-4

F $500; **VF** $750

$2 • W-MA-630-002-G020

Left: 2 / Portrait of girl. ***Center:*** Portrait of George Washington / TWO. ***Right:*** 2 / Man standing. ***Overprint:*** Red TWO. ***Engraver:*** American Bank Note Co. ***Comments:*** H-MA-245-G4a. 18__. 1850s–1860s.

Rarity: URS-4

F $750; **VF** $1,000

$2 • W-MA-630-002-G020a

Overprint: Green. ***Engraver:*** American Bank Note Co. ***Comments:*** H-MA-245-G4b. Similar to W-MA-630-002-G020 but with different date. June 6, 1862.

Rarity: —

$3 • W-MA-630-003-G030

CC

Overprint: Red 3. ***Engraver:*** American Bank Note Co. ***Comments:*** H-MA-245-G6a. 18__. 1850s–1860s.

Rarity: URS-3

VG $400; **F** $1,200; **EF** $1,600

$3 • W-MA-630-003-G030a

Left: 3 / Three women / THREE. ***Center:*** 3. ***Right:*** 3 / Portrait of John Howard. ***Overprint:*** Green. ***Engraver:*** American Bank Note Co. ***Comments:*** H-MA-245-G6b. Similar to W-MA-630-003-G030 but with different date. June 6, 1862.

Rarity: —

$5 • W-MA-630-005-G040

HA

Overprint: Red FIVE. ***Engraver:*** American Bank Note Co. ***Comments:*** H-MA-245-G8a. 18__. 1850s–1860s.

Rarity: URS-3

F $800

$5 • W-MA-630-005-G040a

Left: V / Man tanning leather. ***Center:*** Sailor reclining next to anchor. ***Right:*** 5 / Helmeted woman seated with V. ***Overprint:*** Green. ***Engraver:*** American Bank Note Co. ***Comments:*** H-MA-245-G8b. Similar to W-MA-630-005-G040 but with different date. June 6, 1862.

Rarity: URS-2

F $1,500

$10 • W-MA-630-010-G050

Left: 10 / Woman standing by column, Steamboat. ***Center:*** Two women flanking shield bearing rising sun surmounted by eagle. ***Right:*** 10 / Portrait of John Howard. ***Overprint:*** Red. ***Engraver:*** American Bank Note Co. ***Comments:*** H-MA-245-G10a. 18__. 1850s–1860s.

Rarity: —

$10 • W-MA-630-010-G050a

Overprint: Green. ***Engraver:*** American Bank Note Co. ***Comments:*** H-MA-245-G10b. Similar to W-MA-630-010-G050 but with different date. June 6, 1862.

Rarity: —

$20 • W-MA-630-020-G060

Left: Sailing ship / 20. ***Right:*** 20 / Male portrait. ***Overprint:*** Red. ***Engraver:*** American Bank Note Co. ***Comments:*** H-MA-245-G12a. 18__. 1850s–1860s.

Rarity: —

$20 • W-MA-630-020-G060a

Overprint: Green. ***Engraver:*** American Bank Note Co. ***Comments:*** H-MA-245-G12b. Similar to W-MA-630-020-G060 but with different date. June 6, 1862.

Rarity: —

$50 • W-MA-630-050-G070

Left: 50 / Sailing ships, City / L. ***Right:*** 50 / Indian woman reclining. ***Engraver:*** American Bank Note Co. ***Comments:*** H-MA-245-G14. 18__. 1850s–1860s.

Rarity: —

$100 • W-MA-630-100-G080

Left: 100 / Steamship and sailing ship. ***Right:*** C / HUNDRED. ***Engraver:*** American Bank Note Co. ***Comments:*** H-MA-245-G16. 18__. 1850s–1860s.

Rarity: —

$500 • W-MA-630-500-G090

Left: 500 / Woman, Globe and chart, Ship. ***Right:*** 500 / Portrait. ***Engraver:*** American Bank Note Co. ***Comments:*** H-MA-245-G18. 18__. 1850s–1860s.

Rarity: —

Non-Valid Issues

$5 • W-MA-630-005-R010

Engraver: American Bank Note Co. ***Comments:*** H-MA-245-R5. Raised from W-MA-630-001-G010. 18__. 1850s.

Rarity: —

$5 • W-MA-630-005-N010

Center: Liberty reclining. ***Comments:*** H-MA-245-N5. 1850s.

Rarity: —

Howard Banking Company

1853–1859

W-MA-640

History: The Howard Banking Company commenced business on August 23, 1853, with a capital of $500,000, which was then increased to $750,000 with an authorized limit of $1,000,000. The amount was to be paid in $50 per share, the balance payable on September 7.[57] It was located at 97 State Street.

By legislative action in 1859, the name was changed to the Howard Bank, W-MA-630.

Numismatic Commentary: The Howard Banking Company issued $5 notes with a vignette of Santa Claus. Fortunately for collectors, this issue has been counterfeited, making these notes the least expensive of all Santa Claus notes from any bank due to their availability. Of course, a genuine note is rarer and more expensive. Some of these issues also bear the portrait of John Howard. Genuine notes from this bank are very hard to locate.

Valid Issues

$1 • W-MA-640-001-G010

Left: Liberty / 1. ***Center:*** Indian man reclining with arm on shield, Quiver and bow, Deer. ***Right:*** 1 / Portrait of John Howard. ***Overprint:*** Red ONE. ***Engraver:*** New England Bank Note Co. / Rawdon, Wright, Hatch & Edson. ***Comments:*** H-MA-246-G2a. 18__. 1850s.

Rarity: —

$2 • W-MA-640-002-G020

HA

Overprint: Red TWO. ***Engraver:*** New England Bank Note Co. / Rawdon, Wright, Hatch & Edson. ***Comments:*** H-MA-246-G4a. 18__. 1850s.

Rarity: URS-3
VF $1,000

$3 • W-MA-640-003-G030

Center: 3 / Train, Woman reclining by shield, Milkmaid and cows. ***Right:*** 3 / 3. ***Overprint:*** Red THREE. ***Engraver:*** New England Bank Note Co. / Rawdon, Wright, Hatch & Edson. ***Comments:*** H-MA-246-G6a. 18__. 1850s.

Rarity: —

$5 • W-MA-640-005-G040

HA

Overprint: Red FIVE. ***Engraver:*** New England Bank Note Co. / Rawdon, Wright, Hatch & Edson. ***Comments:*** H-MA-246-G8a. A coveted Santa Claus note. 18__. 1850s.

Rarity: URS-2
VF $10,000

$10 • W-MA-640-010-G050

Left: X / Steamship, Steamship and sailing ship. ***Right:*** X / Portrait of John Howard. ***Engraver:*** New England Bank Note Co. / Rawdon, Wright, Hatch & Edson. ***Comments:*** H-MA-246-G10. 18__. 1850s.

Rarity: —

$20 • W-MA-640-020-G060

Left: 2 / Steamship and six sailing ships at sea. ***Right:*** 20 / Portrait of John Howard. ***Engraver:*** New England Bank Note Co. / Rawdon, Wright, Hatch & Edson. ***Comments:*** H-MA-246-G12. 18__. 1850s.

Rarity: —

$50 • W-MA-640-050-G070

Left: 50 / L. ***Center:*** Shipping, City. ***Right:*** 50 / Indian woman. ***Engraver:*** New England Bank Note Co. / Rawdon, Wright, Hatch & Edson. ***Comments:*** H-MA-246-G14. 18__. 1850s.

Rarity: —

$100 • W-MA-640-100-G080

Left: 100 / Steamship and sailing ships. ***Right:*** C. ***Engraver:*** New England Bank Note Co. / Rawdon, Wright, Hatch & Edson. ***Comments:*** H-MA-246-G16. 18__. 1850s.

Rarity: —

$500 • W-MA-640-500-G090

Left: 500 / Neptune with globe, Ship / 500. ***Right:*** 500 / Woman reading book. ***Engraver:*** New England Bank Note Co. / Rawdon, Wright, Hatch & Edson. ***Comments:*** H-MA-246-G18. 18__. 1850s.

Rarity: —

Non-Valid Issues

$1 • W-MA-640-001-A010

Left: 1 / Eagle with shield standing on rock in ocean / ONE. ***Center:*** Eagle and shield, Justice seated and Liberty reclining, Cornucopia. ***Bottom center:*** Steamship. ***Right:*** 1 / Sailing ship. ***Overprint:*** Red 1 / ONE / 1. ***Engraver:*** Wellstood, Hanks, Hay & Whiting. ***Comments:*** H-MA-246-A5. Altered from $1 Merchants Exchange Bank, Anacostia, D.C. series. Jan. 2, 1854.

Rarity: —

$2 • W-MA-640-002-A020

Left: Sailor standing / 2. ***Center:*** Two women seated / TWO. ***Right:*** ONE / Woman standing / 2. ***Overprint:*** Red TWO. ***Engraver:*** Wellstood, Hanks, Hay & Whiting. ***Comments:*** H-MA-246-A10. Altered from $2 Merchants Exchange Bank, Anacostia, D.C. series. Jan. 2, 185_. 1850s.

Rarity: URS-3
F $300

$2 • W-MA-640-002-A030

Left: Two girls carrying sheaves / 2. ***Center:*** Sailor and mechanic flanking U.S. shield surmounted by badger. ***Right:*** 2 / Liberty standing, Indian woman kneeling. ***Overprint:*** Red TWO. ***Engraver:*** New England Bank Note Co. / Rawdon, Wright, Hatch & Edson. ***Comments:*** H-MA-246-A15. Altered from $2 Waubeek Bank, De Soto, Nebraska. 1857.

Rarity: —

Collectors and Researchers:

If you have new information about any banks or notes listed in this volume, contact Whitman Publishing, Attn: Obsolete Paper Money, 3101 Clairmont Road, Suite G, Atlanta, GA 30329.

$3 • W-MA-640-003-A040 CC

Overprint: Red THREE. ***Engraver:*** Wellstood, Hanks, Hay & Whiting. ***Comments:*** H-MA-246-A20. Altered from $3 Merchants Exchange Bank, Anacostia, D.C. series. Jan. 2, 185_. 1850s.

Rarity: URS-5
F $75

$5 • W-MA-640-005-C040 SI

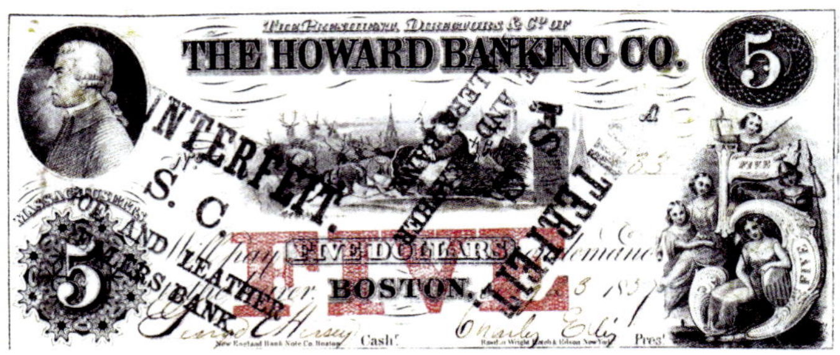

Overprint: Red FIVE. ***Engraver:*** New England Bank Note Co. / Rawdon, Wright, Hatch & Edson. ***Comments:*** H-MA-246-C8a. Counterfeit of W-MA-640-005-G040. A coveted Santa Claus note. 18__. 1857.

Rarity: URS-4
F $1,000
Selected auction price(s): Heritage, April–May 2011, Lot 15226, F $632; Stack's Bowers Galleries, November 2013, Lot 1051, VG $940

India Bank {1st}
1828
W-MA-650

History: The India Bank was chartered in 1828 with an authorized capital of $500,000. It never went into operation.

India Bank {2nd}
1836
W-MA-660

History: The second India Bank was chartered in 1836 with an authorized capital of $1,000,000. It too never went into operation.

Kilby Bank
1836 and 1837
W-MA-670

History: The Kilby Bank was incorporated on April 15, 1836. Its capital was authorized at $500,000.

Bills in circulation in 1838 amounted to $112,082. Other figures for 1838 included: net profits on hand $10,626.29; balances due to other banks $56,845.42; cash deposited $85,667.48; cash deposited bearing interest $39,000; total amount due from banks $804,221.19; gold, silver, and other coined metals in the banking house $25,351.37; bills of other banks incorporated in this state $25,494; bills of other banks incorporated elsewhere $19,422; balance due from other banks $32,305.72; amount of all debts due $701,648.10; total amount of resources of the bank $804,221.19.

On January 30, 1838, the Suffolk Bank, Boston, reported that bills of this bank would not be received.[58] The Kilby Bank was on the list of broken and closed banks in the *Farmer's Monthly Visitor* of 1838.

Numismatic Commentary: Notes from this bank are extremely hard to find. There are only a few remaining today.

Valid Issues

$1 • W-MA-670-001-G010

ANS

Back: Plain. ***Engraver:*** New England Bank Note Co. ***Comments:*** H-MA-250-G2. 18__. 1836 and 1837.

Rarity: URS-3
VF $600

$1 • W-MA-670-001-G010a

Left: 1 / ONE / 1. ***Center:*** Eagle / ONE. ***Right:*** 1 / Sailboat. ***Back:*** Check Plate. ***Engraver:*** New England Bank Note Co. ***Comments:*** H-MA-250-G2a. Similar to W-MA-670-001-G010. 18__. 1837.

Rarity: URS-3
VF $600

$2 • W-MA-670-002-G020

HA

Back: Plain. ***Engraver:*** New England Bank Note Co. ***Comments:*** H-MA-250-G4. 18__. 1836 and 1837.

Rarity: URS-3
VF $600

$2 • W-MA-670-002-G020a

Left: 2 / TWO / 2. ***Center:*** Eagle / TWO. ***Right:*** 2 / Woman. ***Back:*** Check Plate. ***Engraver:*** New England Bank Note Co. ***Comments:*** H-MA-250-G4a. Similar to W-MA-670-002-G020. 18__. 1837.

Rarity: —

$3 • W-MA-670-003-G030

Left: Panel bearing 3 / THREE / 3. ***Center:*** Eagle perched on cannon, Anchor and merchandise / THREE. ***Right:*** 3. ***Engraver:*** New England Bank Note Co. ***Comments:*** H-MA-250-G6. 18__. 1836 and 1837.

Rarity: —

$5 • W-MA-670-005-G040

Engraver: Unverified, but likely New England Bank Note Co. ***Comments:*** H-MA-250-G8. No description available. 18__. 1836 and 1837.

Rarity: *None known*

$10 • W-MA-670-010-G050

Engraver: Unverified, but likely New England Bank Note Co. ***Comments:*** H-MA-250-G10. No description available. 18__. 1836 and 1837.

Rarity: *None known*

$50 • W-MA-670-050-G060

Engraver: Unverified, but likely New England Bank Note Co. ***Comments:*** H-MA-250-G12. No description available. 18__. 1836 and 1837.

Rarity: *None known*

$100 • W-MA-670-100-G070

Engraver: Unverified, but likely New England Bank Note Co. ***Comments:*** H-MA-250-G14. No description available. 18__. 1836 and 1837.

Rarity: *None known*

$1,000 • W-MA-670-1000-G080

Engraver: Unverified, but likely New England Bank Note Co. ***Comments:*** H-MA-250-G16. 18__. 1836 and 1837.

Rarity: URS-7
VG $75; **F** $150; **Unc-Rem** $250

Lafayette Bank

1836 and 1837

W-MA-680

History: The Lafayette Bank, located in South Boston, began business on July 13, 1835, but was not incorporated until April 16, 1836. The bank's capital was $150,000. In 1837 this amount had increased to $500,000, but by 1838 it had dropped again to $100,000.

In June 1837, the bank was unable to meet its obligations and discontinued its business. The *Annual Bank Commissioners Report* stated that the circulation had amounted to $63,728. In 1838 it had dropped to $13,955. Specie totaled $3,131.44 at the time.

The Legislature appointed a special committee to investigate the affairs of the bank.[59] It was found that the bank's ledgers had been in disarray since the beginning of business; that false reports had been filed by the cashier, Dunham; that pages were missing from the ledgers; and that bills that were reported as unissued had in fact been placed into circulation to an amount far greater than legally permitted. It was presumed that the entire capital had been lost, although in fact much had never been paid in the first place.

Numismatic Commentary: This short-lived bank issued paper with impunity and failed. Many notes, once worthless, are available for today's collector. Some show an interesting vignette of Alger's Iron Foundry in South Boston.

Valid Issues

$1 • W-MA-680-001-G010

Left: 2 / Woman with pail / ONE. ***Center:*** Woman with rake, Shield, Train / ONE. ***Right:*** 1 / Sailing ship / ONE. ***Engraver:*** PSSP / New England Bank Note Co. ***Comments:*** H-MA-255-G2. 18__. 1836.

Rarity: URS-7
VF $75

$1 • W-MA-680-001-G020

PEM

Engraver: New England Bank Note Co. ***Comments:*** H-MA-255-G4. 18__. 1837.

Rarity: URS-7
VF $125

$1.25 • W-MA-680-001.25-G030

Left: 1 25/100 / Train / 1 25/100. ***Center:*** Sailing ships / $1.25. ***Right:*** 1 25/100 / Perched eagle. ***Engraver:*** New England Bank Note Co. ***Comments:*** H-MA-255-G6. 18__. 1837.

Rarity: URS-4
VF $500; **EF** $800

$1.50 • W-MA-680-001.50-G040

CC

Engraver: New England Bank Note Co. ***Comments:*** H-MA-255-G7. 18__. 1837.

Rarity: URS-5
VG $250; **VF** $350

$1.75 • W-MA-680-001.75-G050

Left: $1.75 Ct / Two women / 1 75/100. ***Center:*** Sailing ships. ***Right:*** $1.75 Ct / Woman standing / 1 / 75/100. ***Engraver:*** New England Bank Note Co. ***Comments:*** H-MA-255-G8. 18__. 1837.

Rarity: URS-4
G $25; **VF** $350

$2 • W-MA-680-002-G060

HA

Engraver: New England Bank Note Co. / PSSP. ***Comments:*** H-MA-255-G10. 18__. 1836.

Rarity: —

$2 • W-MA-680-002-G070

Left: 2 / Portrait of Thomas Jefferson / TWO. ***Center:*** Factory scene. ***Right:*** 2 / Portrait of Marquis de Lafayette / TWO. ***Engraver:*** New England Bank Note Co. ***Comments:*** H-MA-255-G12. 18__. 1837.

Rarity: —
VG $39

$3 • W-MA-680-003-G080

JF

Engraver: PSSP / New England Bank Note Co. ***Comments:*** H-MA-255-G14. 18__. 1836.

Rarity: URS-4
VF $500

$3 • W-MA-680-003-G090

CC

Engraver: New England Bank Note Co. ***Comments:*** H-MA-255-G16. 18__. 1837.

Rarity: URS-6
F $100; **VF** $300

$5 • W-MA-680-005-G100

Left: 5 / Blacksmith at anvil / FIVE. ***Center:*** Mercury standing with 5 / Cornucopia and merchandise, Factories and ship / V / Panel outlining white FIVE. ***Right:*** 5 / Ceres kneeling / FIVE. ***Engraver:*** PSSP / New England Bank Note Co. ***Comments:*** H-MA-255-G18. 18__. 1836.

Rarity: —

$5 • W-MA-680-005-G110

QDB

Engraver: New England Bank Note Co. ***Comments:*** H-MA-255-G20. 18__. 1837.

Rarity: URS-10
VG $40; **VF** $75

$10 • W-MA-680-010-G120

Left: 10 / Man standing / TEN. ***Center:*** Figure holding shield / Boat scene. ***Right:*** 10 / TEN. ***Engraver:*** PSSP / New England Bank Note Co. ***Comments:*** H-MA-255-G22. 18__. 1836.

Rarity: URS-5
VF $125

$10 • W-MA-680-010-G130

QDB

Engraver: New England Bank Note Co. ***Comments:*** H-MA-255-G24. 18__. 1837.

Rarity: URS-10
VF $75

$20 • W-MA-680-020-G140

Engraver: Unverified, but likely PSSP / New England Bank Note Co. ***Comments:*** H-MA-255-G26. 18__. 1836.

Rarity: URS-7
VF $75

$20 • W-MA-680-020-G150

CC

Engraver: New England Bank Note Co. ***Comments:*** H-MA-255-G28. 18__. 1837.

Rarity: URS-7
F $29; **VF** $75; **Unc-S&D** $150

$50 • W-MA-680-050-G160

QDB

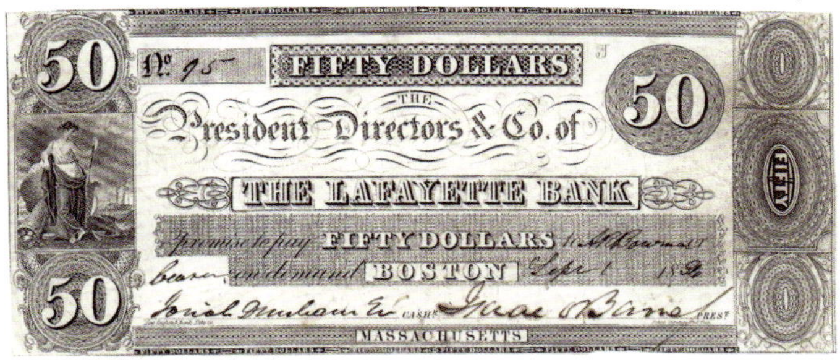

Engraver: PSSP / New England Bank Note Co. ***Comments:*** H-MA-255-G30. Printed on white paper. 18__. 1836.

Rarity: URS-4
F $400; **VF** $750; **EF** $1,100
Selected auction price: Heritage, January 2009, Lot 12417, F $632

$50 • W-MA-680-050-G160a

Left: 50 / Woman standing / 50. ***Center:*** Text / 50. ***Right:*** Die / FIFTY vertically / Die. ***Engraver:*** New England Bank Note Co. ***Comments:*** H-MA-255-G30a. Similar to W-MA-680-050-G160 but printed on pink paper. 18__. 1837.

Rarity: —

$100 • W-MA-680-100-G170

Left: C / Portrait of George Washington / C. ***Center:*** 100 / Woman standing / 100. ***Right:*** ONE HUNDRED vertically. ***Engraver:*** PSSP / New England Bank Note Co. ***Comments:*** H-MA-255-G32. 18__. 1836.

Rarity: —

$100 • W-MA-680-100-G170a

Engraver: New England Bank Note Co. ***Comments:*** H-MA-255-G32a. Similar to W-MA-680-100-G170 but printed on pink paper. 18__. 1836 and 1837.

Rarity: URS-4
VG $400; **F** $1,000; **VF** $1,500

$500 • W-MA-680-500-G180

HA

Engraver: PSSP / New England Bank Note Co. ***Comments:*** H-MA-255-G34. 18__. 1836 and 1837.

Rarity: URS-1
VG $4,000

$1,000 • W-MA-680-1000-G190

Left: THOUSAND vertically. ***Center:*** 1000 / Woman standing with legs crossed and lyre, Cornucopia / 1000. ***Right:*** 1000 / M / 1000. ***Engraver:*** PSSP / New England Bank Note Co. ***Comments:*** H-MA-255-G36. 18__. 1836 and 1837.

Rarity: URS-1
F $6,000

Non-Valid Issues

$2 • W-MA-680-002-C070

Comments: H-Unlisted. Counterfeit of W-MA-680-002-G070.

Rarity: —
VF $65

Manufacturers and Mechanics Bank

1814–1830

W-MA-690

History: The Manufacturers and Mechanics Bank was incorporated on February 8, 1814, with a capital of $1,500,000. In 1823 capital was $750,000. The bank was located at 41 State Street. In 1818 a gang of counterfeiters in Batavia, New York, produced counterfeits of this bank. The perpetrators were convicted and jailed.

On March 8, 1830, the Legislature reduced the authorized capital of the Manufacturers and Mechanics Bank and allowed the name to be changed to the Tremont Bank, W-MA-1000.

Numismatic Commentary: Most notes encountered from this bank are either Proofs by Reed or counterfeit PSSP style notes. Genuine notes are very hard to locate.

In addition to the notes listed below, this bank issued *time checks,* drafts payable at a future date. $200 and $500 denominations have been seen.[60]

Valid Issues

$1 • W-MA-690-001-G010

Center: 1 / 1 / Oval of flower garlands and gridwork segments / ONE / 1 / 1. ***Engraver:*** PSSP. ***Comments:*** H-MA-260-G20. 18__. 1810s.

Rarity: —

$1 • W-MA-690-001-G020

CC

Engraver: A. Reed / Reed. ***Comments:*** H-MA-260-G24. Proof. 18__. 1810s–1820s.

Rarity: URS-3
Proof $750

$1 • W-MA-690-001-G030

Comments: H-MA-260-G28. No description available. 18__. 1820s.

Rarity: *None known*

$2 • W-MA-690-002-G040

Center: 2 / TWO / 2 / Oval of flower garlands and gridwork segments / TWO / 2 / 2. ***Engraver:*** PSSP. ***Comments:*** H-MA-260-G32. 18__. 1810s.

Rarity: —

$2 • W-MA-690-002-G050

Left: TWO / 2 / TWO. ***Center:*** 2 / Figure on shield next to building / 2. ***Right:*** 2 / MASSACHUSETTS / 2. ***Engraver:*** A. Reed / Reed. ***Comments:*** H-MA-260-G36. 18__. 1810s–1820s.

Rarity: URS-2
Proof $1,500

$2 • W-MA-690-002-G060

Comments: H-MA-260-G40. No description available. 18__. 1820s.

Rarity: *None known*

$3 • W-MA-690-003-G070

Center: 3 / 3 / Oval of flower garlands and gridwork segments / 3 / 3. ***Engraver:*** PSSP. ***Comments:*** H-MA-260-G44. 18__. 1810s.

Rarity: —

$3 • W-MA-690-003-G080

Left: 3 / THREE / 3. ***Center:*** 3 / THREE / Figure on shield next to building / 3. ***Right:*** 3 / MASSACHUSETTS / 3. ***Engraver:*** A. Reed / Reed. ***Comments:*** H-MA-260-G48. 18__. 1810s–1820s.

Rarity: URS-3
Proof $1,000

$3 • W-MA-690-003-G090

Comments: H-MA-260-G52. No description available. 18__. 1820s.

Rarity: *None known*

$5 • W-MA-690-005-G100

Left: Lathework panel bearing MASSACHUSETTS / 5 / 5 vertically. ***Center:*** Alternating flower garlands and gridwork segments. ***Right:*** 5 / 5. ***Engraver:*** PSSP. ***Comments:*** H-MA-260-G56. 18__. 1810s.

Rarity: —

$5 • W-MA-690-005-G110

Left: FIVE vertically. ***Center:*** 5 / Ship, Justice seated with shield / 5. ***Bottom center:*** V. ***Right:*** 5 / MASSACHUSETTS / 5 vertically. ***Payee:*** J. Jackson. ***Engraver:*** A. Reed / Reed. ***Comments:*** H-MA-260-G60. 18__. 1810s–1820s.

Rarity: URS-5
Proof $1,100

$5 • W-MA-690-005-G110a

CC

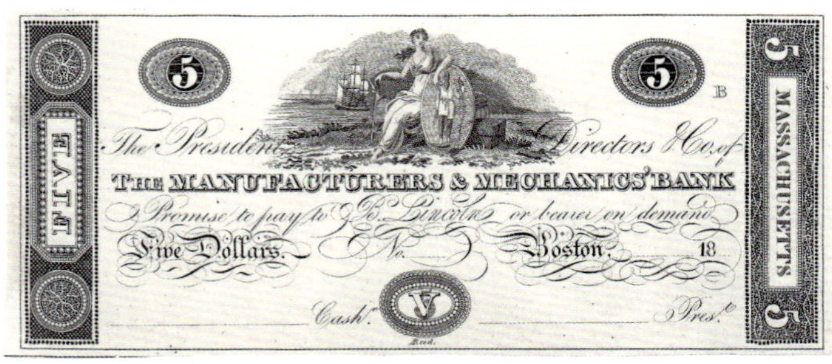

Engraver: A. Reed / Reed. ***Comments:*** H-MA-260-G60a. Similar to W-MA-690-005-G110 but with engraved payee of B. Lincoln (Letter B). Proof. 18__. 1810s–1820s.

Rarity: URS-4
Proof $1,250

$5 • W-MA-690-005-G120

Comments: H-MA-260-G64. No description available. 18__. 1820s.

Rarity: *None known*

$10 • W-MA-690-010-G130

Left: Lathework panel bearing MASSACHUSETTS / 10 / 10 vertically. ***Center:*** Alternating flower garlands and gridwork segments / TEN. ***Right:*** 10 / 10 vertically. ***Engraver:*** Perkins. ***Comments:*** H-MA-260-G66. 18__. 1810s.

Rarity: —

$10 • W-MA-690-010-G140

JF

Payee: T. Parsons. ***Engraver:*** A. Reed / Reed. ***Comments:*** H-MA-260-G68. Proof. 18__. 1810s–1820s.

Rarity: URS-5

$10 • W-MA-690-010-G140a

Left: TEN vertically. ***Center:*** 10 / Ship, Justice leaning against shield bearing Indian / 10. ***Bottom center:*** X. ***Right:*** X / MASSACHUSETTS / X vertically. ***Engraver:*** A. Reed / Reed. ***Comments:*** H-MA-260-G68a. Similar to W-MA-690-010-G140 but with engraved payee of O. Ellsworth (Letter B). 18__. 1810s–1820s.

Rarity: —

$10 • W-MA-690-010-G150

Comments: H-MA-260-G76. No description available. 18__. 1820s.

Rarity: *None known*

$20 • W-MA-690-020-G160

Left: Panel bearing state arms / 20 / 20 vertically. ***Center:*** Alternating flower garlands and gridwork segments. ***Right:*** 20 / 20 vertically. ***Engraver:*** Perkins. ***Comments:*** H-MA-260-G80. 18__. 1810s.

Rarity: —

$20 • W-MA-690-020-G170

Left: TWENTY vertically. ***Center:*** 20 / Justice with shield bearing Indian, Ship / 20. ***Bottom center:*** XX. ***Right:*** XX / MASSACHUSETTS / XX vertically. ***Payee:*** A. Hamilton. ***Engraver:*** A. Reed / Reed. ***Comments:*** H-MA-260-G84. 18__. 1810s–1820s.

Rarity: URS-3
Proof $1,500

$20 • W-MA-690-020-G170a

CC

Engraver: A. Reed / Reed. ***Comments:*** H-MA-260-G84a. Similar to W-MA-690-020-G170 but with engraved payee of H. Knox (Letter B). Proof. 18__. 1810s–1820s.

Rarity: URS-4
Proof $1,000

$50 • W-MA-690-050-G180

Left: Panel bearing state arms / 50 / 50 vertically. ***Center:*** Alternating flower garlands and gridwork segments. ***Right:*** 50 / 50 vertically. ***Engraver:*** Perkins. ***Comments:*** H-MA-260-G86. 18__. 1810s.

Rarity: —

$50 • W-MA-690-050-G190

HA

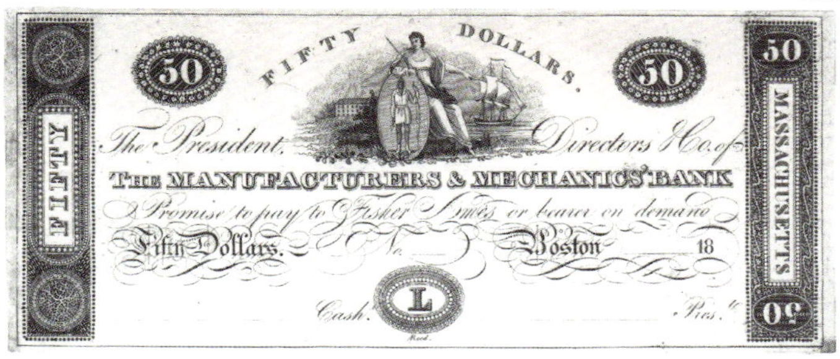

Engraver: A. Reed / Reed. ***Comments:*** H-MA-260-G88. Proof. 18__. 1810s–1820s.

Rarity: URS-3
Proof $2,000

$100 • W-MA-690-100-G200

Left: Panel bearing state arms / 100 / 100 vertically. ***Center:*** Alternating flower garlands and gridwork segments. ***Right:*** 100 / 100 vertically. ***Engraver:*** Perkins. ***Comments:*** H-MA-260-G90. 18__. 1810s.

Rarity: —

$100 • W-MA-690-100-G210

CC

Engraver: A. Reed / Reed. ***Comments:*** H-MA-260-G92. Proof. 18__. 1810s–1820s.

Rarity: URS-5
Proof $1,000

Post Notes

$200 • W-MA-690-200-G220

CC

Engraver: Murray, Draper, Fairman & Co. ***Comments:*** H-Unlisted. Proof. 181_. 1810s.

Rarity: URS-1
Proof $5,000
Selected auction price: Stack's Bowers Galleries, August 2014, Lot 2062, Proof $4,700

$500 • W-MA-690-500-G230

Left: 500 vertically. ***Center:*** 500 / Three allegorical women. ***Right:*** Five Hundred Dollars. ***Engraver:*** Murray, Draper, Fairman & Co. ***Comments:*** H-Unlisted. Proof. 18__. 1810s–1820s.

Rarity: URS-1
Proof $5,000

Non-Valid Issues

$2 • W-MA-690-002-C040

CC

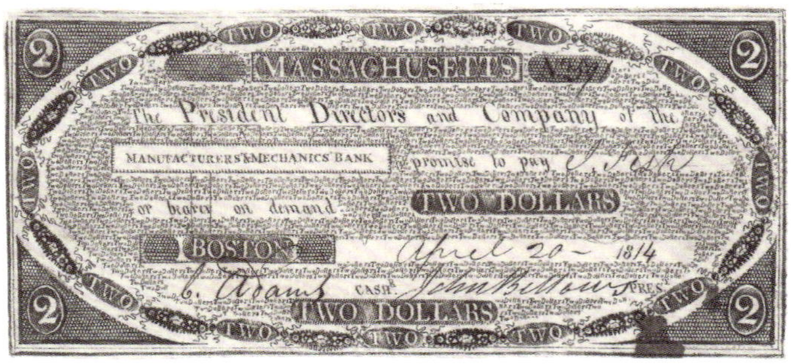

Engraver: PSSP. ***Comments:*** H-MA-260-C32. Counterfeit of W-MA-690-002-G040. 18__. 1810s.

Rarity: URS-7
G $50; **EF** $100

$3 • W-MA-690-003-C070

Engraver: PSSP. ***Comments:*** H-MA-260-C44. Counterfeit of W-MA-690-003-G070. 18__. 1810s.

Rarity: —

Market Bank

1832–1865

W-MA-700

History: The Market Bank was chartered on March 1, 1832, with an authorized capital of $500,000. Business was conducted at 1 Exchange Street. The capital remained at $500,000 until 1857, when it was increased to $560,000. An odd figure of $563,000 was given for 1863.

Circulation in 1838 totaled $150,537. In 1839 it was $68,412. By 1845 it was $227,696, only to decrease again to $149,375 in 1849. It averaged about $116,000 from 1857 to 1860. Specie in 1858 totaled $52,545.63.

Other figures for 1838 included: net profits on hand $44,370.58; balances due to other banks $9,000; cash deposited $283,630.34; cash deposited bearing interest $304,000; total amount due from banks $1,791,537.92; gold, silver, and other coined metals in the banking house $23,577.38; bills of other banks incorporated in this state $80,180; balance due from other banks $83,000; amount of all debts due $1,604,780.54; total amount of resources of the bank $1,791,537.92.

After the National Market Bank of Boston was chartered on August 26, 1864, the state bank wound down its operations.

Numismatic Commentary: Most genuine notes are hard to find or non-existent. One exception is a colorful $3 National Bank Note Co. note with a red-orange tint.

Valid Issues

$1 • W-MA-700-001-G010

Left: Lathework panel bearing MASSACHUSETTS vertically. ***Center:*** 1 / 1 / Alternating flower garlands and gridwork segments / ONE / 1 / 1. ***Right:*** Lathework panel bearing ONE / D / ONE vertically. ***Engraver:*** PSSP. ***Comments:*** H-MA-265-G2. 18__. 1830s.

Rarity: —

$1 • W-MA-700-001-G020

Engraver: Unverified, but likely New England Bank Note Co. ***Comments:*** H-MA-265-G4. No description available. 18__. 1830s–1840s.

Rarity: *None known*

$1 • W-MA-700-001-G030

Left: Two horses, cart, and men / ONE / Man on horse, farmer, dog, and cattle. ***Center:*** 1 / 1 bearing Indian / 1. ***Right:*** Cattle and drover on horse / ONE / View of Quincy Market, Horses and wagons, Shipping. ***Comments:*** H-MA-265-G6. 18__. 1850s.

Rarity: —

$1 • W-MA-700-001-G040

CJF

Tint: Red-orange. ***Engraver:*** National Bank Note Co. ***Comments:*** H-MA-265-G8a. Proof. 18__. 1860s.

Rarity: URS-3
Proof $11,000
Selected auction price: Stack's Bowers Galleries, March 2013, CU $3,525

$1 • W-MA-700-001-G050

QDB

Engraver: New England Bank Note Co. / PSSP. ***Comments:*** H-Unlisted. 18__. 1830s.

Rarity: URS-2
F $1,000

$2 • W-MA-700-002-G060

Left: Lathework panel bearing MASSACHUSETTS vertically. ***Center:*** 2 / 2 / Alternating flower garlands and gridwork segments / TWO / 2 / 2. ***Right:*** Lathework panel bearing five TWOs vertically. ***Engraver:*** PSSP. ***Comments:*** H-MA-265-G10. 18__. 1830s.

Rarity: —

$2 • W-MA-700-002-G070

Engraver: Unverified, but likely New England Bank Note Co. ***Comments:*** H-MA-265-G12. No description available. 18__. 1830s–1840s.

Rarity: *None known*

$2 • W-MA-700-002-G080

Left: Vase of flowers / 2. ***Center:*** TWO / 2 / TWO. ***Right:*** Ship under sail / 2. ***Comments:*** H-MA-265-G14. 18__. 1850s.

Rarity: —

$2 • W-MA-700-002-G090

CJF

Tint: Red-orange. ***Engraver:*** National Bank Note Co. ***Comments:*** H-MA-265-G16a. Proof. 18__. 1860s.

Rarity: URS-2
Proof $7,500
Selected auction price: Stack's Bowers Galleries, March 2013, Gem Unc $4,993

$3 • W-MA-700-003-G100

Center: 3 / 3 / Alternating flower garlands and gridwork segments / THREE / 3 / 3. ***Engraver:*** PSSP. ***Comments:*** H-MA-265-G18. 18__. 1830s.

Rarity: URS-4
F $200

$3 • W-MA-700-003-G110

Engraver: Unverified, but likely New England Bank Note Co. ***Comments:*** H-MA-265-G20. No description available. 18__. 1830s–1840s.

Rarity: *None known*

$3 • W-MA-700-003-G120

Left: 3 / Vase of flowers. ***Center:*** Bust of George Washington / 3 / Female portrait. ***Right:*** 3 / Vase of flowers. ***Comments:*** H-MA-265-G22. 18__. 1850s.

Rarity: —

$3 • W-MA-700-003-G130

Left: 3 / Justice seated. ***Center:*** Two women flanking anvil, Hammer and cornucopia. ***Right:*** 3 / 3. ***Tint:*** Likely red-orange. ***Engraver:*** National Bank Note Co. ***Comments:*** H-MA-265-G24a. 18__. 1860s.

Rarity: —

$3 • W-MA-700-003-G140

CC

Tint: Red-orange. ***Engraver:*** National Bank Note Co. ***Comments:*** H-MA-265-G26a. Proof. 18__. 1860s.

Rarity: URS-2
Proof $7,500

$5 • W-MA-700-005-G150

Left: Lathework chain bearing MASSACHUSETTS / 5 / 5 vertically. ***Center:*** Alternating flower garlands and gridwork segments / FIVE. ***Right:*** 5 / 5. ***Engraver:*** PSSP. ***Comments:*** H-MA-265-G28. 18__. 1830s.

Rarity: —

$5 • W-MA-700-005-G160

Engraver: Unverified, but likely New England Bank Note Co. ***Comments:*** H-MA-265-G30. No description available. 18__. 1830s–1840s.

Rarity: *None known*

$5 • W-MA-700-005-G170

Left: 5 / FIVE. ***Center:*** View of Quincy Market, Horses and wagons, Shipping / V. ***Right:*** 5 / Cows / FIVE. ***Comments:*** H-MA-265-G32. 18__. 1850s.

Rarity: —

$5 • W-MA-700-005-G180

Left: Train / FIVE. ***Center:*** Portrait of Martha Washington / 5 / Portrait of George Washington. ***Bottom center:*** Bull. ***Right:*** 5 / Eagle on shield bearing FIVE. ***Comments:*** H-MA-265-G34. 18__. 1850s.

Rarity: —

$10 • W-MA-700-010-G190

Left: Lathework chain bearing MASSACHUSETTS / 10 / 10 vertically. ***Center:*** Alternating flower garlands and gridwork segments / TEN. ***Right:*** 10 / 10 vertically. ***Engraver:*** PSSP. ***Comments:*** H-MA-265-G36. 18__. 1830s.

Rarity: —

$10 • W-MA-700-010-G200

Engraver: Unverified, but likely New England Bank Note Co. ***Comments:*** H-MA-265-G38. No description available. 18__. 1830s–1840s.

Rarity: *None known*

$10 • W-MA-700-010-G210

Left: 10 / Women / TEN. ***Center:*** View of Quincy Market, Horses and wagons, Shipping / X. ***Right:*** 10 / Ship / TEN. ***Comments:*** H-MA-265-G40. 18__. 1850s.

Rarity: —

$10 • W-MA-700-010-G220

Left: Ship under sail / X. ***Center:*** X. ***Bottom center:*** Bull. ***Right:*** 10 / Female portrait / TEN. ***Comments:*** H-MA-265-G42. 18__. 1850s.

Rarity: —

$20 • W-MA-700-020-G230

Left: Lathework chain bearing MASSACHUSETTS / 20 / 20 vertically. ***Center:*** Alternating flower garlands and gridwork segments / TWENTY. ***Right:*** 20 / 20 vertically. ***Engraver:*** PSSP. ***Comments:*** H-MA-265-G44. 18__. 1830s.

Rarity: —

$20 • W-MA-700-020-G240

Engraver: Unverified, but likely New England Bank Note Co. ***Comments:*** H-MA-265-G46. No description available. 18__. 1830s–1840s.

Rarity: *None known*

$20 • W-MA-700-020-G250

Left: 20 / Portrait of George Washington / TWENTY. ***Center:*** Eagle on limb, Canal and train. ***Bottom center:*** Steamship. ***Right:*** 20 / Male portrait / TWENTY. ***Comments:*** H-MA-265-G48. 18__. 1850s.

Rarity: —

$50 • W-MA-700-050-G260

Left: Lathework chain bearing MASSACHUSETTS / 50 / 50 vertically. ***Center:*** Alternating flower garlands and gridwork segments / FIFTY. ***Right:*** 50 / 50 vertically. ***Engraver:*** PSSP. ***Comments:*** H-MA-265-G50. 18__. 1830s.

Rarity: —

$50 • W-MA-700-050-G270

Engraver: Unverified, but likely New England Bank Note Co. ***Comments:*** H-MA-265-G52. No description available. 18__. 1830s–1850s.

Rarity: *None known*

$50 • W-MA-700-050-G280

Left: Steamship / 50. ***Center:*** 50. ***Right:*** FIFTY / Portrait of Christopher Columbus / FIFTY. ***Comments:*** H-MA-265-G54. 18__. 1850s.

Rarity: —

$100 • W-MA-700-100-G290

Left: Lathework chain bearing MASSACHUSETTS / 100 / 100 vertically. ***Center:*** Alternating flower garlands and gridwork segments / HUNDRED. ***Right:*** 100 / 100 vertically. ***Engraver:*** PSSP. ***Comments:*** H-MA-265-G56. 18__. 1830s.

Rarity: —

$100 • W-MA-700-100-G300

Engraver: Unverified, but likely New England Bank Note Co. ***Comments:*** H-MA-265-G58. No description available. 18__. 1830s–1840s

Rarity: *None known*

$100 • W-MA-700-100-G310

Left: 100 / Neptune / 100. ***Center:*** Steamship. ***Right:*** 100 / Portrait of Benjamin Franklin / 100. ***Comments:*** H-MA-265-G60. 18__. 1850s.

Rarity: —

$500 • W-MA-700-500-G320

Engraver: Unverified, but likely New England Bank Note Co. ***Comments:*** H-MA-265-G62. No description available. 18__. 1830s–1840s.

Rarity: *None known*

$500 • W-MA-700-500-G330

Left: 500 / Medallion head / 500. ***Center:*** Ceres seated, Train and ship. ***Right:*** 500 / Portrait of George Washington. ***Comments:*** H-MA-265-G64. 18__. 1850s.

Rarity: —

Non-Valid Issues

$1 • W-MA-700-001-A010

Left: Woman standing with apron full of flowers / ONE across 1. ***Center:*** Two reapers, Reaper seated by cradle, Hay wagon / 1. ***Right:*** ONE / Indian standing on cliff. ***Overprint:*** Red ONE. ***Engraver:*** New England Bank Note Co. / Rawdon, Wright, Hatch & Edson. ***Comments:*** H-MA-265-A5. Altered from $1 Waubeek Bank, De Soto, Nebraska. 1857.

Rarity: —

$2 • W-MA-700-002-A020

CC

Engraver: Rawdon, Wright, Hatch & Edson. ***Comments:*** H-MA-265-A10. Altered from $2 Bank of America, Georgetown, D.C. series. Oct. 19, 1852.

Rarity: URS-6
F $100

$2 • W-MA-700-002-A030

Left: Two girls carrying sheaves / 2. ***Center:*** Sailor and mechanic flanking U.S. shield surmounted by badger. ***Right:*** 2 / Liberty standing, Indian woman kneeling. ***Overprint:*** Red TWO. ***Engraver:*** New England Bank Note Co. / Rawdon, Wright, Hatch & Edson. ***Comments:*** H-MA-265-A15. Altered from $2 Waubeek Bank, De Soto, Nebraska. 1857.

Rarity: —

$3 • W-MA-700-003-C120

Comments: H-MA-265-C22. Counterfeit of W-MA-700-003-G120. 18__. 1850s.

Rarity: —

$3 • W-MA-700-003-A040

Left: 3 / Portrait of George Washington / THREE. ***Center:*** Spread eagle, Woman with shield. ***Right:*** 3 / Woman standing. ***Engraver:*** Rawdon, Wright, Hatch & Edson. ***Comments:*** H-MA-265-A20a. Altered from $3 Bank of America, Georgetown, D.C. series. Oct. 19, 1852.

Rarity: URS-4
F $150

$5 • W-MA-700-005-S010

Left: FIVE / Woman seated on V / 5. ***Center:*** 5 / Herd of livestock, Drover on horse and covered bridge / 5. ***Bottom center:*** Horse. ***Right:*** Panel bearing FIVE vertically. ***Engraver:*** Draper, Toppan & Co. ***Comments:*** H-MA-265-S5. 1840s.

Rarity: —

$5 • W-MA-700-005-A050

Left: V / Portrait of Henry Clay. ***Center:*** Steamship / FIVE. ***Right:*** 5 / Portrait of George Washington. ***Overprint:*** Red FIVE. ***Engraver:*** New England Bank Note Co. / Rawdon, Wright, Hatch & Edson. ***Comments:*** H-MA-265-A25. Altered from $5 Waubeek Bank, De Soto, Nebraska. 1857.

Rarity: URS-5
F $125

$10 • W-MA-700-010-N010

Left: Two children / 10. ***Center:*** Indian man on cliff viewing town. ***Right:*** Woman / TEN. ***Comments:*** H-MA-265-N5.

Rarity: —

$10 • W-MA-700-010-N020

Left: Ship / X. ***Center:*** 10 on die. ***Right:*** Woman / TEN. ***Overprint:*** Green X / X. ***Comments:*** H-MA-265-N10.

Rarity: —

Massachusetts Bank

1784–1865

W-MA-710

History: Organized in Boston, the Massachusetts Bank obtained a charter from the Legislature on February 7, 1784. It was the first bank to open in Boston and was organized primarily to facilitate those engaged in trade. The Massachusetts Bank was also the second bank established in the United States. It had a capital of $200,000, limited at $300,000. An amount of $253,500 had been paid in at the commencement of business on July 5. The charter was renewed and extended from time to time. Later the capital increased to $400,000.[61]

The bank had a capital of $1,600,000 by 1814. In 1837 its charter was renewed with $800,000 capital, where it stayed until 1839.[62] Circulation ranged from a low in 1839 of $45,909 to a high of $124,404 a decade later. From 1857 to 1860 it averaged $108,000. Other figures for 1857 included: bills of this bank and other New England states $19,768; real estate $75,812.24.

On April 4, 1865, the assets of the corporation passed to the newly chartered Massachusetts National Bank of Boston. The new entity did not last long, and the company was absorbed by the First National Bank of Boston.

Numismatic Commentary: The earliest bills of this bank bear no imprint or engraver's signature, while certain others are the work of Abner Reed and signed as such. Still others were by William Hoagland, sometimes cited as Hoogland or Hoegland, a Boston engraver. He engraved primarily on wood and worked for a time with Abel Bowen. Many notes were printed from the PSSP style devised by Jacob Perkins when the use of such engraving was made mandatory by all Massachusetts banks. This turned out to be a misguided piece of legislation, as counterfeiters found it particularly easy to alter these slug-plate type notes by removing the ink from Perkins's bills of failed banks and imprinting the names of good banks in the same spaces. One band of counterfeiters created its own stereotype plates from scratch (albeit with somewhat crude lettering) and merrily set about creating bills for many different banks. Today those of the $2 denomination are particularly common. Among the authentic notes made for this bank were such unusual denominations as $1.50, $2.50, $3.50, $4.50, $6, $7, $8, $9, $15, $25, $30, $35, and $40.

VALID ISSUES

$1 • W-MA-710-001-G010 SBG

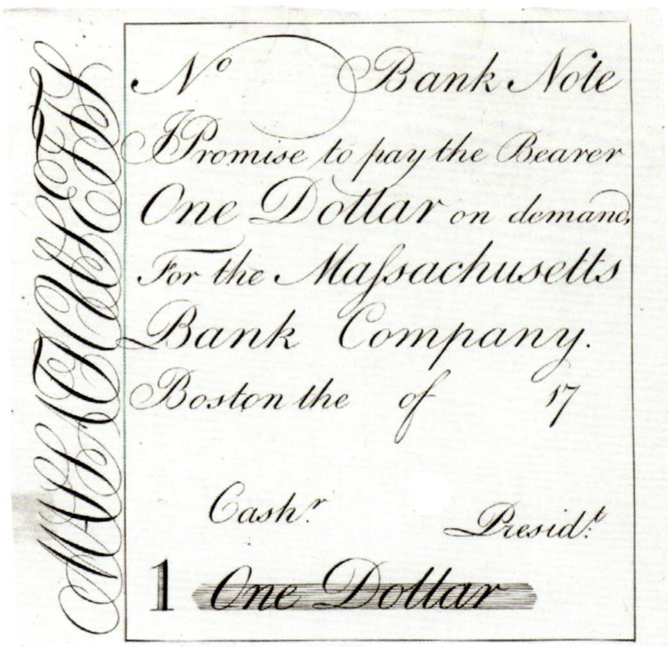

Comments: H-MA-270-G30. Square note with script text. Reprint. 17__. 1780s–1790s.

Rarity: URS-7
Proof $500
Selected auction price: Stack's Bowers Galleries, March 2012, Lot 5177, EF $977

$1 • W-MA-710-001-G020

HS

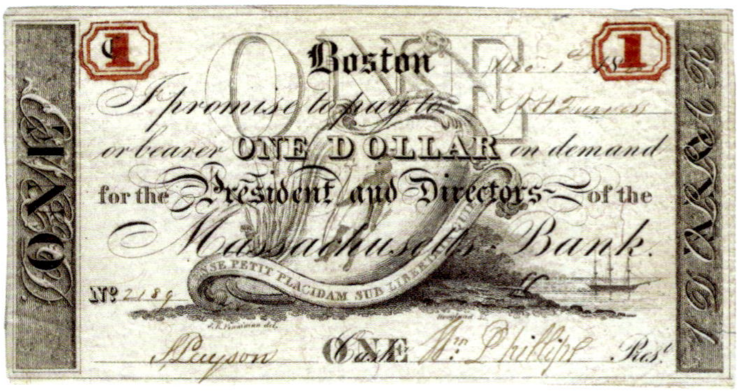

Overprint: Red. ***Engraver:*** Hoogland. ***Comments:*** H-MA-270-G36. 18__. 1810s–1820s.

Rarity: URS-3
EF $1,000

$1 • W-MA-710-001-G030

QDB

Engraver: A. Reed / Reed. ***Comments:*** H-MA-270-G42. Proof. 18__. 1810s–1820s.

Rarity: URS-3
Proof $1,100

$1 • W-MA-710-001-G030a

Left: 1 / ONE / 1. ***Center:*** 1 / Woman holding shield bearing ONE / 1. ***Bottom center:*** State arms. ***Right:*** 1 / MASSACHUSETTS / 1. ***Engraver:*** A. Reed / Reed. ***Comments:*** H-MA-270-G42a. Similar to W-MA-710-001-G030 but with engraved payee of J. Walley (Letter B). 18__. 1810s–1820s.

Rarity: URS-5
VG $200

$1 • W-MA-710-001-G040

Comments: H-MA-270-G48. No description available. 18__. 1830s.

Rarity: *None known*

$1 • W-MA-710-001-G050

JF

Engraver: Underwood, Bald, Spencer & Hufty. ***Comments:*** H-MA-270-G56. 18__. 1830s–1850s.

Rarity: URS-5
VF $500

$1 • W-MA-710-001-G050a

Left: 1 on medallion head / ONE / 1 on medallion head. ***Center:*** Indian seated. ***Right:*** 1 on medallion head / ONE / 1 on medallion head. ***Overprint:*** Red 1 / 1. ***Engraver:*** Underwood, Bald, Spencer & Hufty. ***Comments:*** H-MA-270-G56a. Similar to W-MA-710-001-G050. 18__. 1850s.

Rarity: URS-3
VF $650; **Proof** $1,000

$1 • W-MA-710-001-G060

Left: 1 / ONE. ***Center:*** 1 / Figure in shield / 1. ***Right:*** 1 / ONE. ***Overprint:*** Red. ***Engraver:*** Rawdon, Wright, Hatch & Edson / New England Bank Note Co. ***Comments:*** H-MA-270-G62a. June __, 18__. 1850s.

Rarity: URS-3
VF $750

$1 • W-MA-710-001-G060a

Overprint: Green 1 / 1. ***Engraver:*** Rawdon, Wright, Hatch & Edson / New England Bank Note Co. / ABNCo. monogram. ***Comments:*** H-MA-270-G62b. Similar to W-MA-710-001-G060 but with additional engraver imprint. June __, 18__. 1860s.

Rarity: URS-3
F $600

$1.50 • W-MA-710-001.50-G070

Comments: H-MA-270-G68. Square note with script text. 17__. 1780s–1790s.

Rarity: —

$2 • W-MA-710-002-G080

Comments: H-MA-270-G74. Square note with script text. 17__. 1780s–1790s.

Rarity: —

How to Read the Whitman Numbering System

$1 • W-MA-010-001-G010a

Denomination: Value of the note shown.

W: Whitman number. This number is a sortable code unique to each bank and note.

MA: Abbreviation for the state under study.

010: Numerical designation specific to each bank.

001: The denomination in dollars.

G010a: G indicates a good or valid note. Other categories are indicated thus: C (counterfeit); R (raised); S (spurious); N (not-attributed); A (altered). Numbers are assigned starting with 010, 020, et seq. Terminal letters following the number indicate variations of a note: a series of different colored overprints, tints, payees, etc., all on the same design of note. For more information, see the "How to Use This Book" section at the front of the volume, page xiv.

$2 • W-MA-710-002-G090

Engraver: Hoogland. ***Comments:*** H-MA-270-G80. Square note with script text. 18__. 1810s.

Rarity: —

$2 • W-MA-710-002-G100

QDB

Engraver: A. Reed / Reed. ***Comments:*** H-MA-270-G86. Proof. Reprint. 18__. 1810s–1820s.

Rarity: URS-4
Proof $750

$2 • W-MA-710-002-G110

Comments: H-MA-270-G92. No description available. 18__. 1830s.

Rarity: *None known*

$2 • W-MA-710-002-G120

SI

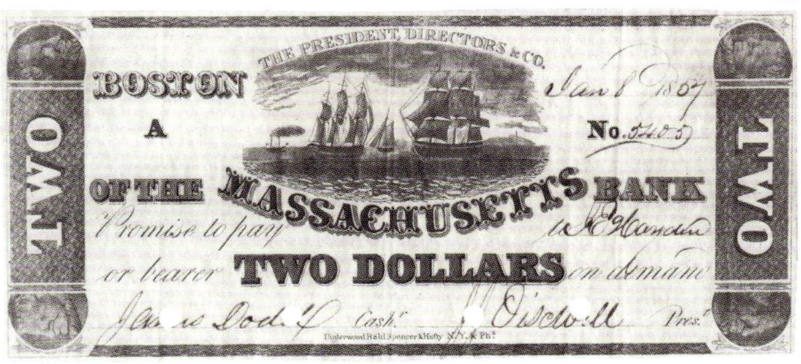

Engraver: Underwood, Bald, Spencer & Hufty. ***Comments:*** H-MA-270-G98. 18__. 1830s–1850s.

Rarity: URS-4
VF $400

$2 • W-MA-710-002-G120a

Left: TWO vertically. ***Center:*** Ships in harbor. ***Right:*** TWO vertically. ***Overprint:*** Red 2 / 2. ***Engraver:*** Underwood, Bald, Spencer & Hufty. ***Comments:*** H-MA-270-G98a. Similar to W-MA-710-002-G120. 18__. 1850s.

Rarity: URS-3
VF $500

$2 • W-MA-710-002-G120b

CC

Overprint: Red TWO. ***Engraver:*** Underwood, Bald, Spencer & Hufty. ***Comments:*** H-Unlisted. Similar to W-MA-710-002-G120. 18__. 1850s.

Rarity: URS-4
VF $400

$2 • W-MA-710-002-G130

Left: TWO / 2 / TWO. ***Center:*** 2 / Indian in shield / 2. ***Right:*** TWO / 2 / TWO. ***Overprint:*** Likely red. ***Engraver:*** Rawdon, Wright, Hatch & Edson / New England Bank Note Co. ***Comments:*** H-MA-270-G104a. June __, 18__. 1850s.

Rarity: —

$2 • W-MA-710-002-G130a

Overprint: Likely red. ***Engraver:*** Rawdon, Wright, Hatch & Edson / New England Bank Note Co. / ABNCo. monogram. ***Comments:*** H-MA-270-G104b. Similar to W-MA-710-002-G130 but with additional engraver imprint. June __, 18__. 1860s.

Rarity: URS-3
VF $600

$2.50 • W-MA-710-002.50-G140

SBG

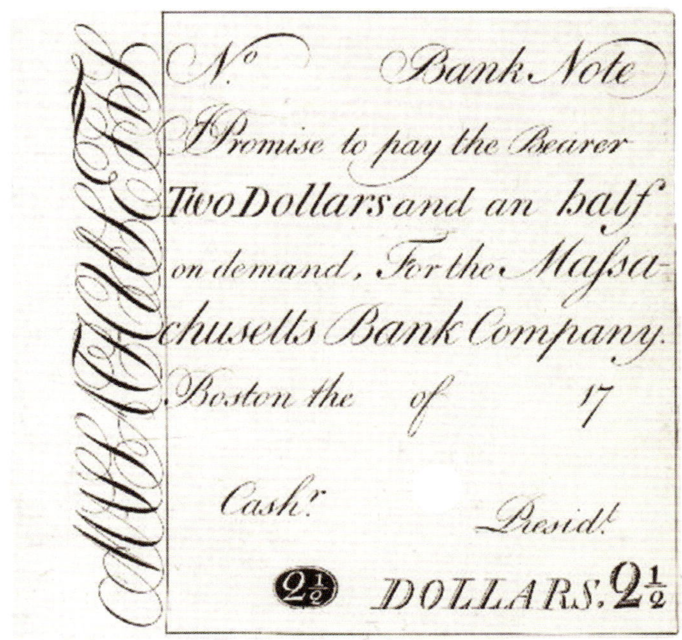

Comments: H-MA-270-G110. Square note with script text. Reprint. 17__. 1780s–1790s.

Rarity: URS-7
Proof $500

$3 • W-MA-710-003-G150 SBG

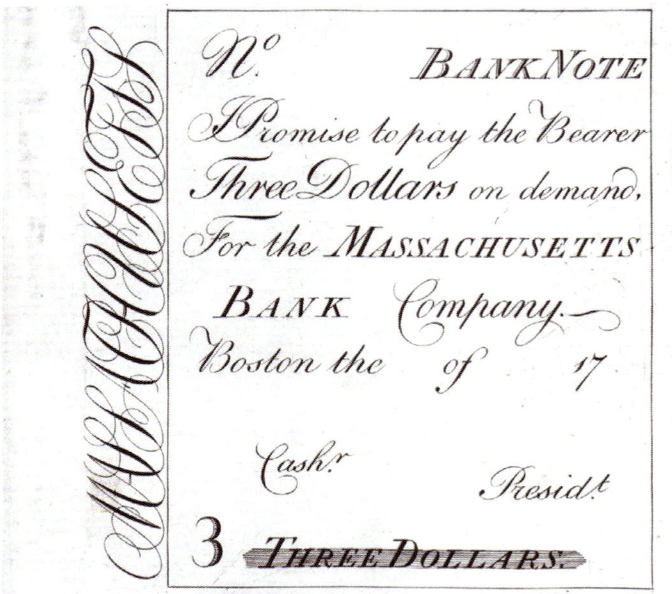

Comments: H-MA-270-G116. Square note with script text. Reprint. 17__. 1780s–1790s.

Rarity: URS-7
Proof $400

$3 • W-MA-710-003-G160 CC

Engraver: A. Reed / Reed. ***Comments:*** H-MA-270-G122. Proof. 18__. 1810s–1820s.

Rarity: URS-4
Proof $750

$3.50 • W-MA-710-003.50-G170 SBG

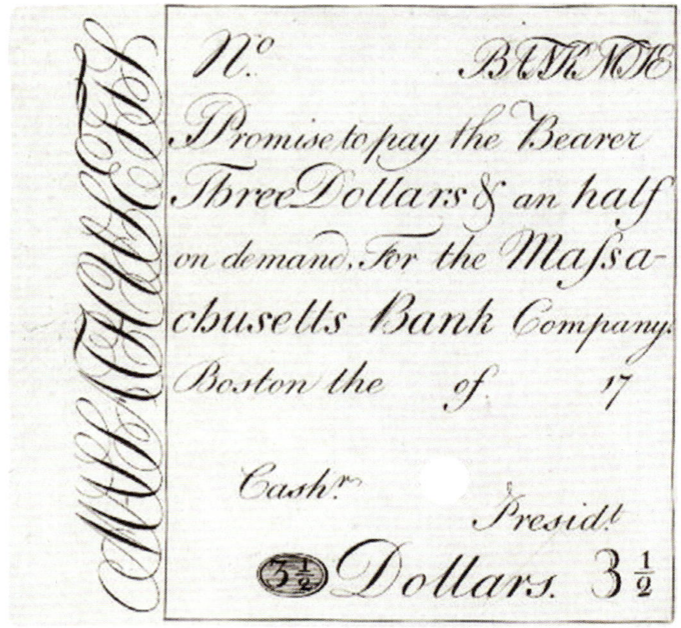

Comments: H-MA-270-G134. Square note with script text. Reprint. 17__. 1780s–1790s.

Rarity: URS-7
Proof $500

$4 • W-MA-710-004-G180 SBG

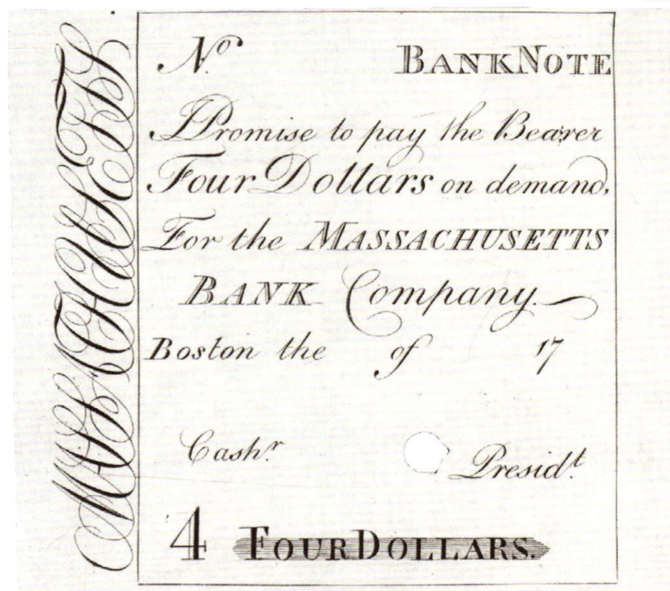

Comments: H-MA-270-G140. Square note with script text. Reprint. 17__. 1780s–1790s.

Rarity: URS-7
Proof $500
Selected auction price: Stack's Bowers Galleries, March 2012, Lot 5179, Choice AU $1,380

$4.50 • W-MA-710-004.50-G190

SBG

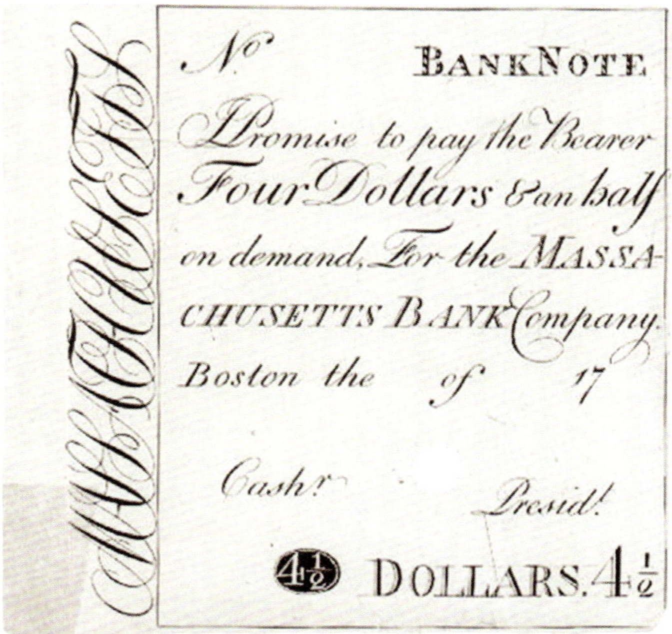

Comments: H-MA-270-G146. Square note with script text. Reprint. 17__. 1780s–1790s.

Rarity: URS-7
Proof $1,000

$5 • W-MA-710-005-G200

Comments: H-MA-270-G152. Square note with script text. 178_. 1780s.

Rarity: —

$5 • W-MA-710-005-G210

Right: Wreath. ***Comments:*** H-MA-270-G158. Square note with script text. 17__. 1780s–1790s.

Rarity: —

$5 • W-MA-710-005-G220

CJF

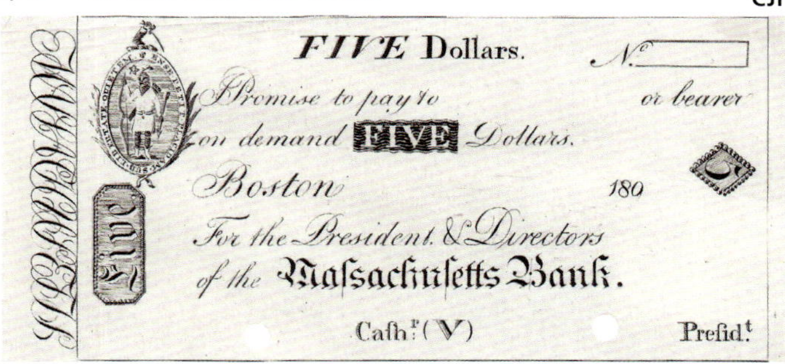

Comments: H-MA-270-G164. Reprint. 180_. 1800s.

Rarity: URS-7

$5 • W-MA-710-005-G220a

SI

Comments: H-Unlisted. Similar to W-MA-710-005-G220. 179_. 1790s.

Rarity: —

$5 • W-MA-710-005-G230

Left: MASSACHUSETTS BANK vertically. ***Center:*** 5 / State arms / 5. ***Right:*** FIVE vertically. ***Engraver:*** Reed. ***Comments:*** H-MA-270-G170. 181_. 1810s.

Rarity: —

$5 • W-MA-710-005-G240

TD

Engraver: A. Reed / Reed. ***Comments:*** H-MA-270-G176. Proof. Reprint. 18__. 1810s–1820s.

Rarity: URS-5
Proof $1,000

$5 • W-MA-710-005-G240a

Left: 5 / FIVE / 5 vertically. ***Center:*** 5 / Woman reclining, Ships / 5. ***Bottom center:*** State arms. ***Right:*** 5 / MASSACHUSETTS / 5 vertically. ***Engraver:*** A. Reed / Reed. ***Comments:*** H-MA-270-G176a. Similar to W-MA-710-005-G240 but with engraved payee of J. Dodd (Letter B). 18__. 1810s–1820s.

Rarity: —

$5 • W-MA-710-005-G240b

CC

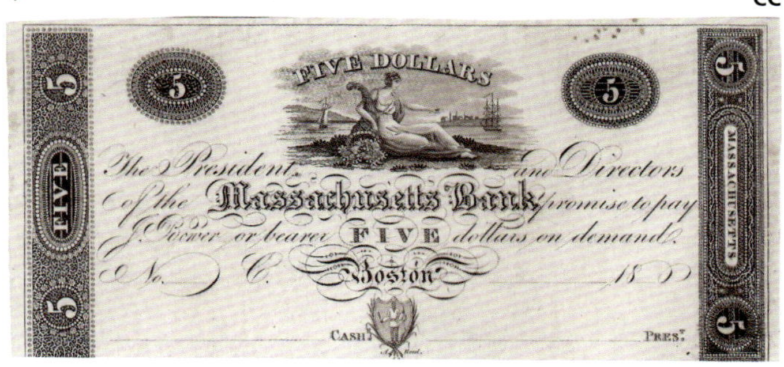

Engraver: A. Reed / Reed. ***Comments:*** H-MA-270-G176b. Similar to W-MA-710-005-G240 but with engraved payee of J. Bower (Letter C). Proof. 18__. 1810s–1820s.

Rarity: URS-3
Proof $700

$5 • W-MA-710-005-G240c

Engraver: A. Reed / Reed. ***Comments:*** H-MA-270-G176c. Similar to W-MA-710-005-G240 but with engraved payee of T. Chase (Letter D). 18__. 1810s–1820s.

Rarity: URS-5
Proof $500

$5 • W-MA-710-005-G250

HA

Engraver: New England Bank Note Co. ***Comments:*** H-MA-270-G182. 18__. 1830s.

Rarity: URS-4
VF $350

Selected auction price: Heritage, January 2010, Lot 12821, AU $546

$5 • W-MA-710-005-G250a

Left: V / Medallion head of George Washington / 5. ***Center:*** State arms surmounted by arm and sword. ***Bottom center:*** FIVEs. ***Right:*** 5 / Portrait of John Adams / V. ***Overprint:*** Red V V. ***Engraver:*** New England Bank Note Co. ***Comments:*** H-MA-270-G182b. Similar to W-MA-710-005-G250. 18__. 1850s.

Rarity: URS-4
VF $350

$5 • W-MA-710-005-G250b

Tint: Ochre. ***Engraver:*** New England Bank Note Co. / ABNCo. monogram. ***Comments:*** H-MA-270-G182c. Similar to W-MA-710-005-G250 but with additional engraver imprint. 18__. 1850s.

Rarity: URS-4
VF $450

$5 • W-MA-710-005-G250c

CC

Overprint: Green 5 / 5. ***Engraver:*** New England Bank Note Co. / ABNCo. monogram. ***Comments:*** H-MA-270-G182d. Similar to W-MA-710-005-G250 but with additional engraver imprint. 18__. 1860s.

Rarity: URS-5
F $350; **VF** $550

$6 • W-MA-710-006-G260

Left: Script vertically. ***Center:*** State arms / SIX. ***Right:*** Six / VI. ***Comments:*** H-MA-270-G188. 181_. 1810s.

Rarity: —

$7 • W-MA-710-007-G270

Left: Script vertically. ***Center:*** Wreath / SEVEN. ***Right:*** Seven / 7. ***Comments:*** H-MA-270-G194. 181_. 1810s.

Rarity: —

$8 • W-MA-710-008-G280

Left: Script vertically. ***Center:*** Wreath / EIGHT. ***Right:*** Eight / 8. ***Comments:*** H-MA-270-G200. 181_. 1810s.

Rarity: —

$9 • W-MA-710-009-G290

Left: Script vertically. ***Center:*** Wreath / NINE. ***Right:*** Nine / IX. ***Comments:*** H-MA-270-G206. 181_. 1810s.

Rarity: —

$10 • W-MA-710-010-G300

Left: Script vertically. ***Center:*** Text. ***Right:*** Wreath. ***Comments:*** H-MA-270-G212. 178_. 1780s.

Rarity: —

$10 • W-MA-710-010-G310

SBG

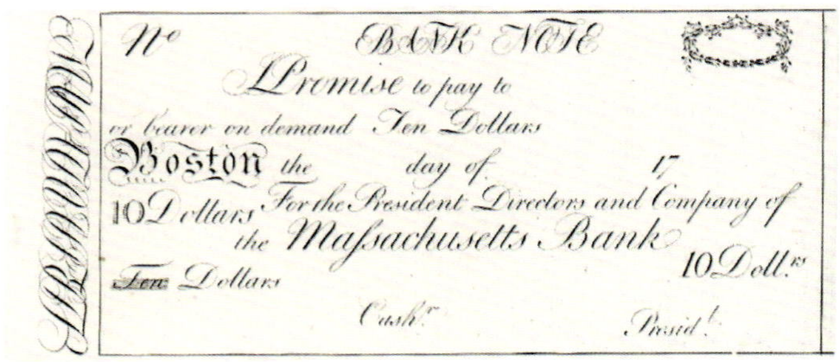

Comments: H-MA-270-G218. Proof. Reprint. 17__. 1780s–1790s.

Rarity: URS-7
Proof $250

$10 • W-MA-710-010-G320

CJF

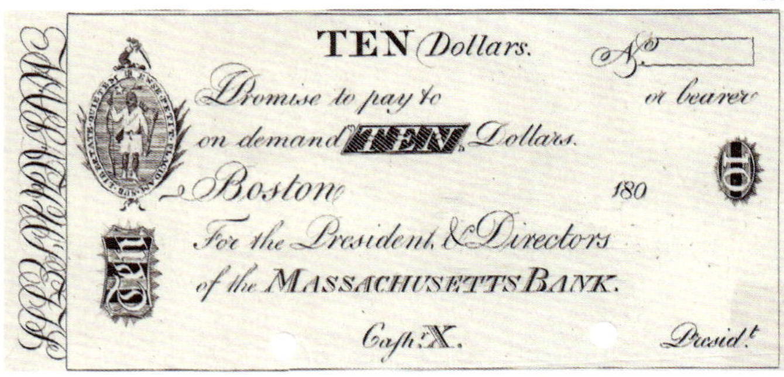

Comments: H-MA-270-G224. Proof. Reprint. 180_. 1800s.

Rarity: URS-7
Proof $250

$10 • W-MA-710-010-G330

CC

Engraver: A. Reed / Reed. ***Comments:*** H-MA-270-G230. Reprint. 181_. 1810s.

Rarity: URS-5
Proof $600

$10 • W-MA-710-010-G340

Left: X / Portrait of John Adams / 10. ***Center:*** Figure on shield. ***Right:*** 10 / Medallion head of George Washington / X. ***Engraver:*** New England Bank Note Co. ***Comments:*** H-MA-270-G236. 18__. 1830s.

Rarity: URS-5
VF $400

$10 • W-MA-710-010-G340a

Bottom center: TENs. ***Overprint:*** Red X X. ***Engraver:*** New England Bank Note Co. ***Comments:*** H-MA-270-G236b. Similar to W-MA-710-010-G340. 18__. 1850s.

Rarity: URS-5
VF $400

$10 • W-MA-710-010-G340b

Bottom center: TENs. ***Tint:*** Ochre. ***Engraver:*** New England Bank Note Co. / ABNCo. monogram. ***Comments:*** H-MA-270-G236c. Similar to W-MA-710-010-G340 but with additional engraver imprint. 18__. 1850s.

Rarity: URS-4
VF $500

$10 • W-MA-710-010-G340c

CC

Overprint: Green X / X. ***Engraver:*** New England Bank Note Co. / ABNCo. monogram. ***Comments:*** H-MA-270-G236d. Similar to W-MA-710-010-G340 but with additional engraver imprint. 18__. 1860s.

Rarity: URS-4
F $500; **VF** $850

$15 • W-MA-710-015-G350

Left: Script vertically. ***Center:*** Text. ***Right:*** Wreath. ***Comments:*** H-MA-270-G242. 178_. 1780s.

Rarity: —

$15 • W-MA-710-015-G360

Left: Script vertically. ***Center:*** Text. ***Right:*** Wreath. ***Comments:*** H-MA-270-G248. 17__. 1780s–1790s.

Rarity: —

$20 • W-MA-710-020-G370

Left: Script vertically. ***Center:*** Text. ***Right:*** Wreath. ***Comments:*** H-MA-270-G254. 178_. 1780s.

Rarity: —

$20 • W-MA-710-020-G380

SBG

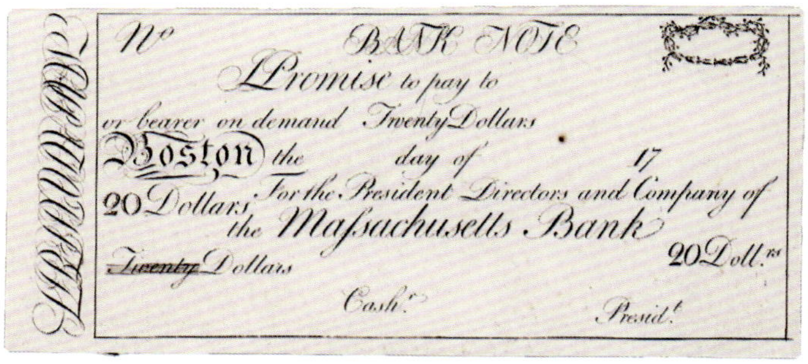

Comments: H-MA-270-G260. Proof. Reprint. 17__. 1780s–1790s.

Rarity: URS-7
Proof $300

$20 • W-MA-710-020-G390

Left: Script vertically. ***Center:*** TWENTY / State arms. ***Right:*** Wreath. ***Comments:*** H-MA-270-G266. 1799.

Rarity: —

$20 • W-MA-710-020-G400

Comments: H-MA-270-G272. No description available. 18__. 1800s.

Rarity: *None known*

$20 • W-MA-710-020-G410

CC

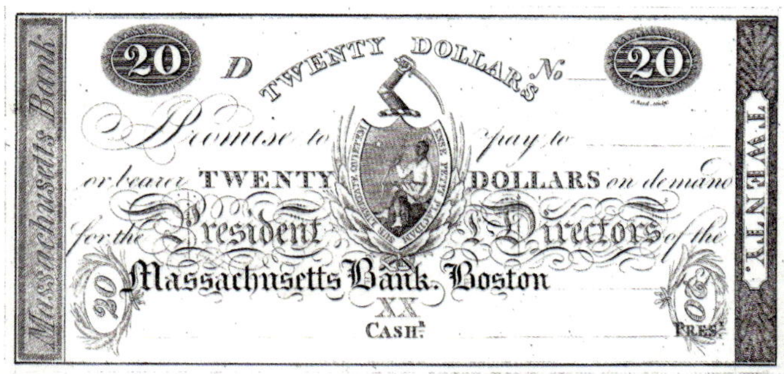

Engraver: A. Reed / Reed. ***Comments:*** H-MA-270-G278. Proof. Reprint. 181_. 1810s.

Rarity: URS-4
Proof $1,250

$20 • W-MA-710-020-G410a

CC

Tint: Red. ***Engraver:*** A. Reed / Reed. ***Comments:*** H-Unlisted. Similar to W-MA-710-020-G410. Proof. 181_. 1850s.

Rarity: URS-2
Proof $3,500

$20 • W-MA-710-020-G410b

Left: Massachusetts Bank vertically. ***Center:*** 20 / Shield with arm and sword / 20. ***Right:*** TWENTY vertically. ***Tint:*** Ochre. ***Engraver:*** A. Reed / Reed. ***Comments:*** H-MA-270-G278c. Similar to W-MA-710-020-G410. 181_. 1850s.

Rarity: —

$20 • W-MA-710-020-G410c

CC

Overprint: Green TWENTY. ***Engraver:*** A. Reed / Reed. ***Comments:*** H-MA-270-G278d. Similar to W-MA-710-020-G410. 181_. Handwritten 6 over 1 in date. 1860s.

Rarity: URS-3
VF $850

$20 • W-MA-710-020-G410d

QDB

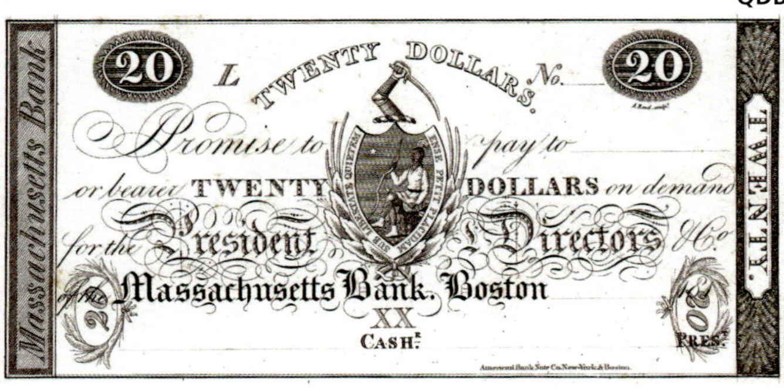

Engraver: American Bank Note Co. ***Comments:*** H-MA-270-G278e. Similar to W-MA-710-020-G410 but with different engraver imprint. Reprint. 181_. 1860s.

Rarity: URS-4
VF $500; **Proof** $1,000

$20 • W-MA-710-020-G420

Comments: H-MA-270-G284. No description available. 18__. 1820s.

Rarity: *None known*

$20 • W-MA-710-020-G430

Comments: H-MA-270-G290. No description available. 18__. 1830s.

Rarity: *None known*

$25 • W-MA-710-025-G440

Left: Script vertically. ***Center:*** Text. ***Right:*** Wreath. ***Comments:*** H-MA-270-G296. 178_. 1780s.

Rarity: —

$25 • W-MA-710-025-G450

Left: Script vertically. ***Center:*** Text. ***Right:*** Wreath. ***Comments:*** H-MA-270-G302. 17__. 1780s–1790s.

Rarity: —

$30 • W-MA-710-030-G460

Left: Script vertically. ***Center:*** Text. ***Right:*** Wreath. ***Comments:*** H-MA-270-G308. 178_. 1780s.

Rarity: —

$30 • W-MA-710-030-G470

Left: Script vertically. ***Center:*** Text. ***Right:*** Wreath. ***Comments:*** H-MA-270-G314. 17__. 1780s–1790s.

Rarity: —

$30 • W-MA-710-030-G480

Left: Script vertically. ***Center:*** THIRTY / State arms. ***Right:*** Wreath. ***Comments:*** H-MA-270-G320. 1799.

Rarity: —

$35 • W-MA-710-035-G490

Left: Script vertically. ***Center:*** Text. ***Right:*** Wreath. ***Comments:*** H-MA-270-G326. 17__. 1780s–1790s.

Rarity: —

$40 • W-MA-710-040-G500

Left: Script vertically. ***Center:*** Text vertically. ***Right:*** Wreath. ***Comments:*** H-MA-270-G332. 17__. 1780s–1790s.

Rarity: —

$50 • W-MA-710-050-G510

Comments: H-MA-270-G334. Square note with script text. 17__. 1790s.

Rarity: —

$50 • W-MA-710-050-G520

Left: Script vertically. ***Center:*** Text vertically. ***Right:*** Wreath. ***Comments:*** H-MA-270-G338. 178_. 1780s.

Rarity: —

$50 • W-MA-710-050-G530

SBG

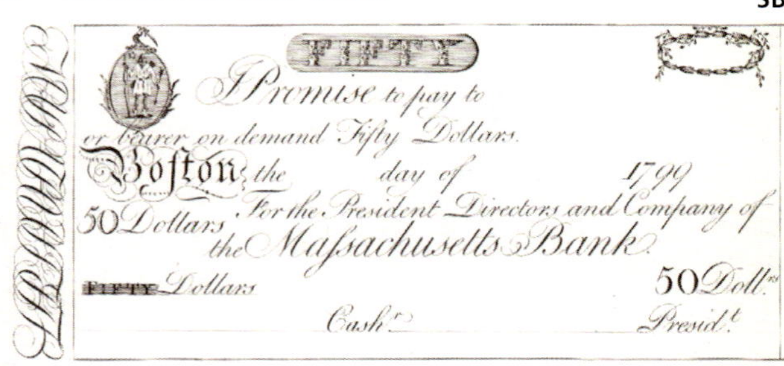

Comments: H-MA-270-G350. Proof. Reprint. 1799.

Rarity: URS-7
Proof $400

$50 • W-MA-710-050-G540

Comments: H-MA-270-G356. No description available. 18__. 1800s.

Rarity: *None known*

$50 • W-MA-710-050-G550

Left: Massachusetts Bank vertically. ***Center:*** State arms. ***Right:*** FIFTY DOLLARS vertically. ***Engraver:*** A. Reed / Reed. ***Comments:*** H-MA-270-G362. 181_. 1810s.

Rarity: —

$50 • W-MA-710-050-G550a

HA

Tint: Red. ***Engraver:*** A. Reed / Reed. ***Comments:*** H-Unlisted. Similar to W-MA-710-050-G550. Proof. 18__. 1850s.

Rarity: URS-2

Proof $3,200

$50 • W-MA-710-050-G550b

Tint: Ochre. ***Engraver:*** A. Reed / Reed. ***Comments:*** H-MA-270-G362c. Similar to W-MA-710-050-G550. 181_. 1850s.

Rarity: URS-2

Proof $3,000

$50 • W-MA-710-050-G550c

Overprint: Green. ***Engraver:*** A. Reed / Reed. ***Comments:*** H-MA-270-G362d. Similar to W-MA-710-050-G550. 181_. 1860s.

Rarity: —

$50 • W-MA-710-050-G550d

Engraver: American Bank Note Co. ***Comments:*** H-MA-270-G362e. Similar to W-MA-710-050-G550 but with different engraver imprint. 181_. 1860s.

Rarity: —

$50 • W-MA-710-050-G560

Comments: H-MA-270-G368. No description available. 18__. 1820s.

Rarity: *None known*

$50 • W-MA-710-050-G570

Comments: H-MA-270-G374. No description available. 18__. 1830s.

Rarity: *None known*

$100 • W-MA-710-100-G580

Left: Script vertically. ***Right:*** Text / Bank Note. ***Comments:*** H-MA-270-G380. 178_. 1780s.

Rarity: —

$100 • W-MA-710-100-G590

Comments: H-MA-270-G386. Square note with script text. 17__. 1780s–1790s.

Rarity: —

$100 • W-MA-710-100-G600

Left: Script vertically. ***Center:*** State arms / ONE HUNDRED. ***Right:*** Wreath. ***Comments:*** H-MA-270-G392. 1799.

Rarity: —

$100 • W-MA-710-100-G610

Comments: H-MA-270-G398. No description available. 18__. 1800s.

Rarity: *None known*

$100 • W-MA-710-100-G620

Left: Massachusetts Bank vertically. ***Center:*** 100 / State arms / 100. ***Right:*** ONE HUNDRED vertically. ***Engraver:*** A. Reed / Reed. ***Comments:*** H-MA-270-G404. 181_. 1810s.

Rarity: —

$100 • W-MA-710-100-G620a

CC

Tint: Ochre. ***Engraver:*** A. Reed / Reed. ***Comments:*** H-MA-270-G404c. Similar to W-MA-710-100-G620. 18__. 1850s.

Rarity: URS-3

Proof $1,750

Selected auction price: Heritage, January 2010, Lot 12822, VF-EF $1,150

$100 • W-MA-710-100-G620b

CC

Tint: Red-brown. ***Engraver:*** A. Reed / Reed. ***Comments:*** H-Unlisted. Similar to W-MA-710-100-G620. 18__.

Rarity: URS-2

Proof $3,700

$100 • W-MA-710-100-G620c

Overprint: Green. ***Engraver:*** A. Reed / Reed. ***Comments:*** H-MA-270-G404d. Similar to W-MA-710-100-G620. 181_. 1860s.

Rarity: —

$100 • W-MA-710-100-G620d

Engraver: American Bank Note Co. ***Comments:*** H-MA-270-G404e. Similar to W-MA-710-100-G620 but with different engraver imprint. 181_. 1860s.

Rarity: —

$100 • W-MA-710-100-G630

Comments: H-MA-270-G410. No description available. 18__. 1820s.

Rarity: *None known*

$100 • W-MA-710-100-G640

Comments: H-MA-270-G416. No description available. 18__. 1830s.

Rarity: *None known*

$500 • W-MA-710-500-G650

CC

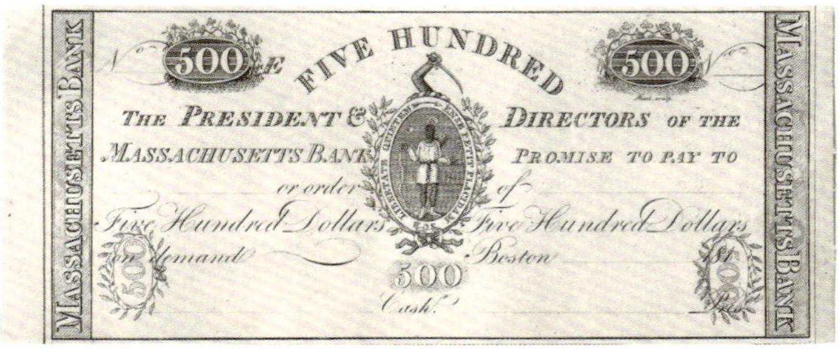

Engraver: A. Reed / Reed. ***Comments:*** H-MA-270-G428. Proof. 181_. 1810s.

Rarity: URS-3
Proof $3,000

$500 • W-MA-710-500-G650a

Left: Massachusetts Bank vertically. ***Center:*** 500 vertically / 500 / State arms / 500 / 500 vertically. ***Right:*** Massachusetts Bank vertically. ***Tint:*** Ochre. ***Engraver:*** A. Reed / Reed. ***Comments:*** H-MA-270-G428c. Similar to W-MA-710-500-G650. 18__. 1850s.

Rarity: —

$500 • W-MA-710-500-G650b

Overprint: Green. ***Engraver:*** A. Reed / Reed. ***Comments:*** H-MA-270-G428d. Similar to W-MA-710-500-G650. 18__. 1860s.

Rarity: —

$500 • W-MA-710-500-G650c

Engraver: American Bank Note Co. ***Comments:*** H-MA-270-G428e. Similar to W-MA-710-500-G650 but with different engraver imprint. 18__. 1860s.

Rarity: —

$500 • W-MA-710-500-G660

CC

Engraver: American Bank Note Co. ***Comments:*** H-MA-270-G434. 18__. 1860s.

Rarity: URS-3
Proof $3,500

$1,000 • W-MA-710-1000-G670

CC

Engraver: A. Reed / Reed. ***Comments:*** H-MA-270-G446. Proof. 181_. 1810s.

Rarity: URS-3
Proof $2,750

$1,000 • W-MA-710-1000-G670a

Left: MASSACHUSETTS BANK vertically. ***Center:*** 1000 vertically / 1000 / State arms with arm and sword / 1000 / 1000 vertically. ***Right:*** MASSACHUSETTS BANK vertically. ***Tint:*** Ochre. ***Engraver:*** A. Reed / Reed. ***Comments:*** H-MA-270-G446c. Similar to W-MA-710-1000-G670. 18__. 1850s.

Rarity: —

$1,000 • W-MA-710-1000-G670b

Overprint: Green. ***Engraver:*** A. Reed / Reed. ***Comments:*** H-MA-270-G446d. Similar to W-MA-710-1000-G670. 18__. 1860s.

Rarity: —

$1,000 • W-MA-710-1000-G670c

Engraver: American Bank Note Co. ***Comments:*** H-MA-270-G446e. Similar to W-MA-710-1000-G670. 18__. 1860s.

Rarity: —

Uncut Sheets

$1-$1-$2-$2 • W-MA-710-001.001.002.002-US010

Vignette(s): ($1) Indian seated. ***($1)*** Indian seated. ***($2)*** Ships in harbor. ***($2)*** Ships in harbor. ***Comments:*** H-MA-270-G56, G56, G98, G98. 18__. 1830s–1850s.

Rarity: URS-2
Proof $3,500

$1-$1-$2-$3 • W-MA-710-001.001.002.003-US020

Vignette(s): ($1) ONE / Woman holding shield bearing ONE / State arms / MASSACHUSETTS. ***($1)*** ONE / Woman holding shield bearing ONE / State arms / MASSACHUSETTS. ***($2)*** TWO / TWO / Woman seated next to shield bearing TWO / State arms / MASSACHUSETTS. ***($3)*** THREE vertically. ***Center:*** Woman seated / State arms / MASSACHUSETTS. ***Engraver:*** Hoogland. ***Comments:*** H-MA-270-G42, G42, G86, G122. Reprint.

Rarity: —

$1-$1.50-$2-$2.50-$3-$3.50-$4-$4.50 • W-MA-710-001.001.50.002.002.50.003.003.50.004.004.50-US030

Vignette(s): ($1) Square note with script text. ***($1.50)*** Square note with script text. ***($2)*** Square note with script text. ***($2.50)*** Square note with script text. ***($3)*** Square note with script text. ***($3.50)*** Square note with script text. ***($4)*** Square note with script text. ***($4.50)*** Square note with script text. ***Engraver:*** A. Reed / Reed. ***Comments:*** H-MA-270-G30, G68, G74, G110, G116, G134, G140, G146. Reprint.

Rarity: —

Selected auction price: Heritage, January 2010, Lot 12823, AU $1,006

$2-$2-$1-$1 • W-MA-710-002.002.001.001-US040

Vignette(s): ($2) Square note with script text. ***($2)*** Square note with script text. ***($1)*** ONE in script vertically / Script letters. ***($1)*** ONE in script vertically / Script letters. ***Comments:*** H-MA-270-G80, G80, G36, G36. Reprint.

Rarity: —

$5-$5-$5-$5 • W-MA-710-005.005.005.005-US050

Vignette(s): ($5) / FIVE across / Woman reclining, Boats / Shield / MASSACHUSETTS. ***($5)*** FIVE across / Woman reclining, Boats / Shield / MASSACHUSETTS. ***($5)*** FIVE across / Woman reclining, Boats / Shield / MASSACHUSETTS. ***($5)*** FIVE across / Woman reclining, Boats / Shield / MASSACHUSETTS. ***Engraver:*** A. Reed / Reed. ***Comments:*** H-MA-270-G176, G176, G176, G176. Reprint.

Rarity: —

$5-$10-$5-$5 • W-MA-710-005.010.005.005-US060

CJF

Comments: H-MA-270-G164, G224, G164, G164. Reprint. 180_. 1800s.

Rarity: URS-5
Proof $1,200

$5-$10-$15-$20 • W-MA-710-005.010.015.020-US070

Vignette(s): ($5) Square note with script text. ***($10)*** Script vertically / Text / Wreath. ***($15)*** Script vertically / Text / Wreath. ***($20)*** Script vertically / Text / Wreath. ***Comments:*** H-MA-270-G152, G212, G242, G254. Reprint.

Rarity: URS-5
Proof $1,500

$5-$10-$15-$20 • W-MA-710-005.010.015.020-US080

Vignette(s): ($5) Square note with script text. ***($10)*** Script vertically / Text / Wreath. ***($15)*** Script vertically / Text / Wreath. ***($20)*** Script vertically / Text / Wreath. ***Comments:*** H-MA-270-G158, G218, G248, G260. Reprint.

Rarity: —

$6-$7-$8-$9 • W-MA-710-006.007.008.009-US090

Vignette(s): ($6) Script vertically / State arms / SIX / Six / VI. ***($7)*** Script vertically / Wreath / SEVEN / Seven / 7. ***($8)*** Script vertically / Wreath / EIGHT / Eight / 8. ***($9)*** Script vertically / Wreath / NINE / Nine / IX. ***Comments:*** H-MA-270-G188, G194, G200, G206. Reprint.

Rarity: —

$10-$10-$10-$10 • W-MA-710-010.010.010.010-US100

Vignette(s): ($10) MASSACHUSETTS BANK vertically / Shield / 10 / TEN vertically. ***($10)*** MASSACHUSETTS BANK vertically / Shield / 10 / TEN vertically. ***($10)*** MASSACHUSETTS BANK vertically / Shield / 10 / TEN vertically. ***($10)*** MASSACHUSETTS BANK vertically / Shield / 10 / TEN vertically. ***Engraver:*** A. Reed / Reed. ***Comments:*** H-MA-270-G230, G230, G230, G230. Reprint.

Rarity: —

$20-$20-$20-$20 • W-MA-710-020.020.020.020-US110

Vignette(s): ($20) Massachusetts Bank vertically / Shield with arm and sword / TWENTY vertically. ***($20)*** Massachusetts Bank vertically / Shield with arm and sword / TWENTY vertically. ***($20)*** Massachusetts Bank vertically / Shield with arm and sword / TWENTY vertically. ***($20)*** Massachusetts Bank vertically / Shield with arm and sword / TWENTY vertically. ***Engraver:*** American Bank Note Co. ***Comments:*** H-MA-270-G278e, G278e, G278e, G278e. Reprint.

Rarity: —

$20-$30-$50-$100 • W-MA-710-020.030.050.100-US120

Vignette(s): ($20) Script vertically / TWENTY / State arms / Wreath. ***($30)*** Script vertically / THIRTY / State arms / Wreath. ***($50)*** Script vertically / FIFTY / State arms / Wreath. ***($100)*** Script vertically / State arms / ONE HUNDRED / Wreath. ***Comments:*** H-MA-270-G266, G320, G350, G392. Reprint.

Rarity: —

$25-$30-$35-$40 • W-MA-710-025.030.035.040-US130

Vignette(s): ($25) Script vertically / Text / Wreath. ***($30)*** Script vertically / Text / Wreath. ***($35)*** Script vertically / Text / Wreath. ***($40)*** Script vertically / Text / Wreath. ***Comments:*** H-MA-270-G302, G314, G326, G332. Reprint.

Rarity: —

Selected auction price: Heritage, January 2010, Lot 12824, Unc $1,265

$25-$30-$50-$100 • W-MA-710-025.030.050.100-US140

Vignette(s): ($25) Script vertically / Text / Wreath. ***($30)*** Script vertically / Text / Wreath. ***($50)*** Script vertically / Text vertically / Wreath. ***($100)*** Script vertically / Text / Bank Note. ***Comments:*** H-MA-270-G296, G308, G338, G380. Reprint.

Rarity: —

Non-Valid Issues

$1 • W-MA-710-001-C030a

Engraver: A. Reed / Reed. ***Comments:*** H-MA-270-C42a. Counterfeit of W-MA-710-001-G030a. 18__. 1820s.

Rarity: —

$2 • W-MA-710-002-C120

Engraver: Underwood, Bald, Spencer & Hufty. ***Comments:*** H-MA-270-C98. Counterfeit of W-MA-710-002-G120. 18__. 1850s.

Rarity: —
VF $75

$2 • W-MA-710-002-C120a

Overprint: Red. ***Comments:*** H-Unlisted. Counterfeit of W-MA-710-002-G120a.

Rarity: —
F $95

$2 • W-MA-710-002-C130a

Engraver: Rawdon, Wright, Hatch & Edson / New England Bank Note Co. ***Comments:*** H-MA-270-C104b. Counterfeit of W-MA-710-002-G130a or variety. June __, 18__. 1860s.

Rarity: —

$5 • W-MA-710-005-R010

Engraver: Rawdon, Wright, Hatch & Edson / New England Bank Note Co. ***Comments:*** H-MA-270-R5. Raised from W-MA-710-001-G060 or G060a. June __, 18__. 1860s.

Rarity: —

$10 • W-MA-710-010-C320

CC

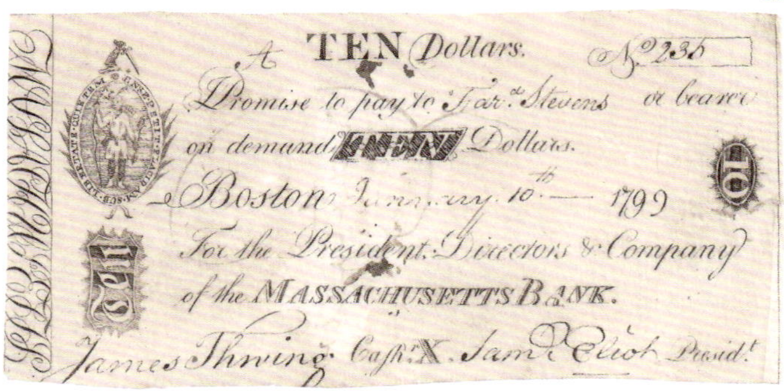

Comments: H-MA-270-C224. Counterfeit of W-MA-710-010-G320. 179_.

Rarity: URS-7
VF $750

$10 • W-MA-710-010-R020

Engraver: Underwood, Bald, Spencer & Hufty. ***Comments:*** H-MA-270-R10. Raised from W-MA-710-001-G050. 18__. 1830s–1840s.

Rarity: —

$20 • W-MA-710-020-R030

Engraver: Underwood, Bald, Spencer & Hufty. ***Comments:*** H-MA-270-R15. Raised from W-MA-710-001-G050. 18__. 1830s–1840s.

Rarity: —

$50 • W-MA-710-050-R040

Engraver: Underwood, Bald, Spencer & Hufty. ***Comments:*** H-MA-270-R20. Raised from W-MA-710-001-G050. 18__. 1830s–1840s.

Rarity: —

$100 • W-MA-710-100-R050

Engraver: Underwood, Bald, Spencer & Hufty. ***Comments:*** H-MA-270-R25. Raised from W-MA-710-002-G120 or G120a. 18__. 1830s–1840s

Rarity: —

Maverick Bank
1854–1864
W-MA-720

History: The Maverick Bank was conceived in 1849, but it was not chartered until March 28, 1854. The institution had an authorized capital of $400,000, a figure that the bank maintained throughout its existence. Business commenced on August 1.

In June 1856, the bank moved from East Boston to 75 State Street in the heart of Boston's financial district. Circulation in 1857 was $100,766. In 1860 it was $100,676. Specie amounted to $47,104.81.

On December 31, 1864, the Maverick National Bank of Boston was chartered to succeed the interests of the Maverick Bank. There had been some delays in the application due to the fact that certain British stockholders had objected to the idea.

See also listing under East Boston, W-MA-1490.

Numismatic Commentary: Collectors will find it hard to locate examples from this bank, but when notes do arise on the market, they are resplendent with vignettes of local scenery in East Boston, including a ship yard, a commercial block, and a ferry slip.

Valid Issues

$1 • W-MA-720-001-G010

JF

Overprint: Red ONE. ***Engraver:*** Rawdon, Wright, Hatch & Edson / New England Bank Note Co. ***Comments:*** H-MA-275-G2a. 185_. 1850s.

Rarity: URS-2
F $3,000

$2 • W-MA-720-002-G020

Left: 2 / TWO / 2. ***Center:*** Ships in harbor. ***Right:*** 2 / Sailor standing. ***Overprint:*** Red TWO. ***Engraver:*** Rawdon, Wright, Hatch & Edson / New England Bank Note Co. ***Comments:*** H-MA-275-G4a. 185_. 1850s.

Rarity: URS-2
VG $1,500

$3 • W-MA-720-003-G030

Left: 3 / Barrel, bale, and anchor / 3. ***Center:*** 3 / River scene, Ship on stocks, City, Ships. ***Right:*** 3. ***Overprint:*** Red THREE. ***Engraver:*** Rawdon, Wright, Hatch & Edson / New England Bank Note Co. ***Comments:*** H-MA-275-G6a. 185_. 1850s.

Rarity: —

$5 • W-MA-720-005-G040

Left: 5 / V. ***Center:*** East Boston Ferry landing, Two ferry boats, Ships. ***Right:*** 5 / Portrait of Daniel Webster. ***Overprint:*** Red. ***Engraver:*** Rawdon, Wright, Hatch & Edson / New England Bank Note Co. ***Comments:*** H-MA-275-G8a. 185_. 1850s.

Rarity: —

$10 • W-MA-720-010-G050

Left: 10 / X. ***Center:*** East Boston ferry landing, Two ferry boats, Ships. ***Right:*** 10 / Sailor and Indian man flanking shield bearing TEN. ***Engraver:*** Rawdon, Wright, Hatch & Edson / New England Bank Note Co. ***Comments:*** H-MA-275-G10a. 185_. 1850s.

Rarity: —

$20 • W-MA-720-020-G060

HA

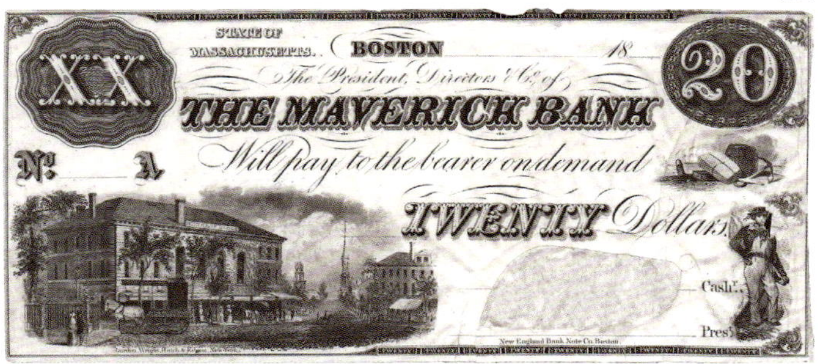

Engraver: Rawdon, Wright, Hatch & Edson / New England Bank Note Co. ***Comments:*** H-MA-275-G12. Proof. 18__. 1850s.

Rarity: URS-2
Proof $2,000

$50 • W-MA-720-050-G070

Left: 50 / FIFTY. ***Center:*** Winthrop Block and street in East Boston. ***Right:*** 50 / Navy Yard, Ship and warehouses. ***Overprint:*** Red. ***Engraver:*** Rawdon, Wright, Hatch & Edson / New England Bank Note Co. ***Comments:*** H-MA-275-G14a. 185_. 1850s.

Rarity: —

$100 • W-MA-720-100-G080

Left: 100 / Woman standing with hand on capstan / HUNDRED. ***Center:*** Winthrop Block and street in East Boston. ***Right:*** 100 / Woman reclining on bale pointing to ship. ***Overprint:*** Red. ***Engraver:*** Rawdon, Wright, Hatch & Edson / New England Bank Note Co. ***Comments:*** H-MA-275-G16a. 185_. 1850s.

Rarity: —

$500 • W-MA-720-500-G090

Left: FIVE HUNDRED / Portrait of George Washington / 500. ***Center:*** D / Winthrop Block and street in East Boston. ***Right:*** 500. ***Engraver:*** Rawdon, Wright, Hatch & Edson / New England Bank Note Co. ***Comments:*** H-MA-275-G18. 185_. 1850s.

Rarity: —

Non-Valid Issues

$5 • W-MA-720-005-R010

Engraver: Rawdon, Wright, Hatch & Edson / New England Bank Note Co. ***Comments:*** H-MA-275-R5. Raised from W-MA-720-001-G010. 185_. 1850s.

Rarity: —

Mechanics Bank

1836–1865

W-MA-730

History: The Mechanics Bank was chartered on March 31, 1836, with an authorized capital of $150,000. By 1854 the capital was $200,000. The bank was located at No. 27 Turnpike at the corner of Division Street in 1854. By 1855 it had moved to 95 Dorchester Avenue.

Between the years of 1838 and 1860, circulation fluctuated between a low of $63,875 and a high of $106,970. Selected figures for 1838 included: net profits on hand $3,569.48; cash deposited $4,198.18; total amount due from banks $237,655.66; gold, silver, and other coined metals in the banking house $10,007.78; real estate $13,376.55; bills of other banks incorporated in this state $2,300; balance due from other banks $11,262.85; amount of all debts due $200,708.48; total amount of resources of the bank $237,655.66.

The business of the Mechanics Bank was succeeded by the Mechanics National Bank of Boston, chartered on March 24, 1865.

See also listing under South Boston, W-MA-3040.

Numismatic Commentary: All notes of the Mechanics Bank are extremely hard to locate.

Valid Issues

$1 • W-MA-730-001-G010

Engraver: Unverified, but likely New England Bank Note Co. ***Comments:*** H-MA-280-G4. No description available. 18__. 1830s.

Rarity: *None known*

$1 • W-MA-730-001-G020

Left: Fishing ships / Statue of George Washington. ***Center:*** Woman. ***Right:*** 1 / ONE / 1. ***Engraver:*** New England Bank Note Co. ***Comments:*** H-MA-280-G8. 18__. 1840s–1850s.

Rarity: —

$1 • W-MA-730-001-G030

Left: 1 / Mechanic seated on safe with hammer. ***Center:*** Gold dollar, Woodcutter leaning on axe, Log at right. ***Right:*** 1 / Ship. ***Engraver:*** Rawdon, Wright, Hatch & Edson / New England Bank Note Co. ***Comments:*** H-MA-280-G12. 18__. 1850s.

Rarity: —

$2 • W-MA-730-002-G040

Engraver: Unverified, but likely New England Bank Note Co. ***Comments:*** H-MA-280-G16. No description available. 18__. 1830s.

Rarity: *None known*

$2 • W-MA-730-002-G050

Left: 2. ***Center:*** TWO / Interior of blacksmith's shop, Men at work / TWO. ***Right:*** 2 / Female portrait / 2. ***Engraver:*** New England Bank Note Co. ***Comments:*** H-MA-280-G20. 18__. 1840s–1850s.

Rarity: —

$2 • W-MA-730-002-G060

Left: 2 / Blacksmith standing at anvil and forge. ***Center:*** Milkmaid seated with pail on arm, Farmer reclining, Cows, Two gold dollars. ***Right:*** 2 / Train. ***Engraver:*** Rawdon, Wright, Hatch & Edson / New England Bank Note Co. ***Comments:*** H-MA-280-G24. 18__. 1850s.

Rarity: —

$3 • W-MA-730-003-G070

Engraver: Unverified, but likely New England Bank Note Co. ***Comments:*** H-MA-280-G28. No description available. 18__. 1830s–1840s.

Rarity: *None known*

$3 • W-MA-730-003-G080

Left: THREE / George Washington and staff on Dorchester Heights / THREE. ***Center:*** Shipyard scene / Steamboat. ***Right:*** 3 / Man on horseback, Cattle. ***Engraver:*** New England Bank Note Co. ***Comments:*** H-MA-280-G32. 18__. 1840s–1850s.

Rarity: —

$3 • W-MA-730-003-G090

Left: 3 / Woman seated. ***Center:*** Farmer with scythe, Sailor by bale, Blacksmith, Three gold dollars. ***Right:*** 3 / Stonecutter at work. ***Engraver:*** Rawdon, Wright, Hatch & Edson / New England Bank Note Co. ***Comments:*** H-MA-280-G36. 18__. 1850s.

Rarity: —

$5 • W-MA-730-005-G100

Engraver: Unverified, but likely New England Bank Note Co. ***Comments:*** H-MA-280-G40. No description available. 18__. 1830s–1840s.

Rarity: *None known*

$5 • W-MA-730-005-G110

Left: FIVE vertically. ***Center:*** George Washington and staff on Dorchester Heights. ***Right:*** 5 / Portrait of George Washington. ***Engraver:*** New England Bank Note Co. ***Comments:*** H-MA-280-G44. 18__. 1840s–1850s.

Rarity: URS-3
F $750

$5 • W-MA-730-005-G120

Left: FIVE / Liberty standing. ***Center:*** Indian woman and hunter flanking five gold dollars and three cherubs. ***Right:*** 5 / Portrait of Daniel Webster. ***Engraver:*** Rawdon, Wright, Hatch & Edson / New England Bank Note Co. ***Comments:*** H-MA-280-G48. 18__. 1850s.

Rarity: —

$10 • W-MA-730-010-G130

Engraver: Unverified, but likely New England Bank Note Co. ***Comments:*** H-MA-280-G52. No description available. 18__. 1830s–1840s.

Rarity: *None known*

$10 • W-MA-730-010-G140

Left: Ships / 10. ***Center:*** Steamboat landing and sailing ships / George Washington on horseback. ***Bottom center:*** Shipping. ***Right:*** 10 / Train / TEN. ***Engraver:*** New England Bank Note Co. ***Comments:*** H-MA-280-G56. 18__. 1840s–1850s.

Rarity: —

$20 • W-MA-730-020-G150

Engraver: Unverified, but likely New England Bank Note Co. ***Comments:*** H-MA-280-G60. No description available. 18__. 1840s.

Rarity: *None known*

$20 • W-MA-730-020-G160

Left: XX / Milkmaid standing with pail and stool. ***Center:*** Man on horseback, Cattle and sheep, Man standing with dog, Train. ***Right:*** 20 / Girl and boy seated, Sailing boats in tub. ***Engraver:*** New England Bank Note Co. ***Comments:*** H-MA-280-G64. 18__. 1840s–1850s.

Rarity: —

$50 • W-MA-730-050-G170

Engraver: Unverified, but likely New England Bank Note Co. ***Comments:*** H-MA-280-G68. No description available. 18__. 1830s–1840s.

Rarity: *None known*

$50 • W-MA-730-050-G180

Left: FIFTY / Woman standing with wreath and flowers / FIFTY. ***Center:*** 50 / Man restraining prancing horse / 50. ***Right:*** FIFTY / Woman standing with cornucopia against shoulder / FIFTY. ***Engraver:*** New England Bank Note Co. ***Comments:*** H-MA-280-G72. 18__. 1840s–1850s.

Rarity: —

$50 • W-MA-730-050-G190

Left: Train / 50. ***Center:*** Sailor seated on yard-arm with spyglass. ***Bottom center:*** 50. ***Right:*** 50. ***Engraver:*** American Bank Note Co. ***Comments:*** H-MA-280-G76. 1860s.

Rarity: —

$100 • W-MA-730-100-G200

Engraver: Unverified, but likely New England Bank Note Co. ***Comments:*** H-MA-280-G80. No description available. 18__. 1830s–1840s.

Rarity: *None known*

$100 • W-MA-730-100-G210

Left: ONE HUNDRED on 100 / Portrait of William Henry Harrison. ***Center:*** Wharf scene, Men loading wagon with barrels. ***Right:*** ONE HUNDRED on 100 / Portrait of Christopher Columbus. ***Engraver:*** New England Bank Note Co. ***Comments:*** H-MA-280-G84. 18__. 1840s–1850s.

Rarity: —

$100 • W-MA-730-100-G220

Left: 100 / Woman seated on bale with shield bearing view of Boston. ***Center:*** Shipyard scene. ***Right:*** 100 / Mechanic at work. ***Engraver:*** American Bank Note Co. ***Comments:*** H-MA-280-G88. 1860s.

Rarity: —

$500 • W-MA-730-500-G230

Engraver: Unverified, but likely New England Bank Note Co. ***Comments:*** H-MA-280-G92. No description available. 18__. 1830s–1840s.

Rarity: *None known*

$500 • **W-MA-730-500-G240**

Left: 500. ***Center:*** Indian man paddling canoe, Forest and mountains / 500 / D D. ***Right:*** 500 / Justice. ***Engraver:*** New England Bank Note Co. ***Comments:*** H-MA-280-G96. 18__. 1840s–1850s.

Rarity: —

$500 • **W-MA-730-500-G250**

Left: 500 / Sculptor at work on bust. ***Center:*** Steamship and sailing ships. ***Right:*** 500 / State arms. ***Engraver:*** American Bank Note Co. ***Comments:*** H-MA-280-G100. 1860s.

Rarity: —

$1,000 • **W-MA-730-1000-G260**

Engraver: Unverified, but likely New England Bank Note Co. ***Comments:*** H-MA-280-G104. No description available. 18__. 1830s–1840s.

Rarity: *None known*

Non-Valid Issues

$1 • **W-MA-730-001-A010**

Left: ONE / Woman standing / ONE. ***Center:*** 1 / Woman standing / 1, MASSACHUSETTS. ***Right:*** ONE / Ships / ONE. ***Engraver:*** Durand & Co. ***Comments:*** H-MA-280-A5. Altered from $1 Pennsylvania Savings Bank, Philadelphia, Pennsylvania. 185_. 1850s.

Rarity: URS-6
F $75

$2 • **W-MA-730-002-A020**

Left: 2 / Portrait of George Washington / TWO. ***Center:*** Globe, Woman seated with scroll and U.S. shield, Sheaves. ***Right:*** TWO / Mercury in clouds with caduceus and cornucopia of coins. ***Overprint:*** Brown or red TWO. ***Engraver:*** Wellstood, Hanks, Hay & Whiting. ***Comments:*** H-MA-280-A10. Altered from $2 Mechanics Bank, Georgetown, D.C. 18__. 1850s.

Rarity: URS-6
F $100

$3 • **W-MA-730-003-A030**

Left: Eagle on U.S. shield and laurel / 3. ***Center:*** 3 / Portrait of George Washington. ***Right:*** 3 / Mercury holding cornucopia of flowers and caduceus. ***Overprint:*** Brown or red THREE. ***Engraver:*** Wellstood, Hanks, Hay & Whiting. ***Comments:*** H-MA-280-A15. Altered from $3 Mechanics Bank, Georgetown, D.C. 18__. 1850s.

Rarity: —

$5 • **W-MA-730-005-R010**

TD

Overprint: Red FIVE. ***Engraver:*** Rawdon, Wright, Hatch & Edson / New England Bank Note Co. ***Comments:*** H-MA-280-R5. Raised from W-MA-730-001-G030. 18__. 1860s.

Rarity: URS-2
F $100

$5 • **W-MA-730-005-R020**

Engraver: Rawdon, Wright, Hatch & Edson / New England Bank Note Co. ***Comments:*** H-MA-280-R10. Raised from W-MA-730-002-G060. 18__. 1850s.

Rarity: —

$5 • **W-MA-730-005-A040**

Left: 5 / Script FIVE / FIVE. ***Center:*** Three women and two cherubs, Five silver dollars / FIVE. ***Right:*** 5 / Female portrait / FIVE. ***Engraver:*** Rawdon, Wright, Hatch & Edson. ***Comments:*** H-MA-280-A20. Altered from $5 Farmers and Merchants Bank of Memphis, Memphis, Tennessee series. May 14, 1858.

Rarity: URS-6
F $75

$10 • **W-MA-730-010-R030**

Engraver: Rawdon, Wright, Hatch & Edson / New England Bank Note Co. ***Comments:*** H-MA-280-R15. Raised from W-MA-730-001-G030. 18__. 1850s.

Rarity: —

$10 • **W-MA-730-010-S010**

Left: TEN on three dies. ***Center:*** 10 / Steamboat, Sailing ships / 10. ***Right:*** TEN / Portrait of George Washington / TEN. ***Engraver:*** Rawdon, Wright & Hatch. ***Comments:*** H-MA-280-S5. Aug. 1, 1849.

Rarity: —

$20 • **W-MA-730-020-A050**

Left: Blacksmith at anvil. ***Center:*** Paddlewheel steamship with U.S. flag. ***Right:*** Allegorical woman. ***Engraver:*** Rawdon, Wright & Hatch. ***Comments:*** H-MA-280-A25. Altered from $20 Mechanics Bank of St. John's, St. John's, Canada. 18__. 1830s.

Rarity: —

Mechanics Bank of Boston

1850s

W-MA-740

History: A non-existent bank represented only by notes altered from other banks. The notes were intended to pass for those of the Mechanics Bank, W-MA-730.

Issues

$5 • **W-MA-740-005-A010**

Left: FIVE / Portrait of Benjamin Franklin / FIVE. ***Center:*** Two women flanking portrait of George Washington. ***Right:*** 5 / Portrait of Andrew Jackson / 5. ***Engraver:*** Danforth, Wright & Co. ***Comments:*** H-MA-281-A5. Altered from $5 Mechanics Bank of Memphis, Memphis, Tennessee series. 1850s.

Rarity: URS-7
F $100

Collectors and Researchers:

If you have new information about any banks or notes listed in this volume, contact Whitman Publishing, Attn: Obsolete Paper Money, 3101 Clairmont Road, Suite G, Atlanta, GA 30329.

$10 • W-MA-740-010-A020 SI

Overprint: Red X. ***Engraver:*** Danforth, Wright & Co. ***Comments:*** H-MA-281-A10. Altered from $10 Mechanics Bank of Memphis, Memphis, Tennessee series. 185_. 1850s.

Rarity: URS-5
F $125

Mechanics and Traders Bank
1824
W-MA-750

History: According to the *Banker's Magazine*, the Mechanics and Traders Bank was chartered in 1824 but never went into operation. There was an unrelated bank of the same name in Salem, Massachusetts.

Merchants Bank
1831–1864
W-MA-760

History: The Merchants Bank was chartered in February 1828. Its office was at 28 State Street. In the mid-1830s it became one of many "pet banks" used by the Jackson administration to hold federal funds. In 1835 capital was $750,000, and by 1836 it had risen to $1,500,000. By 1839 it was $2,000,000, rising again to $3,000,000 from 1845 to 1848. It peaked at $5,000,000 but went back down to $4,000,000 by June 1855.

Circulation in 1835 amounted to $238,045. Between 1838 and 1860 it fluctuated between a low of $97,928 and a high of $818,440. The charter was extended until 1875.

Figures for 1838 included: net profits on hand $206,570.88; balances due to other banks $558,018; cash deposited $378,258.39; cash deposited bearing interest $30,000; total amount due from banks $2,770,775.27; gold, silver, and other coined metals in the banking house $165,191.54; real estate $100,000; bills of other banks incorporated in this state $183,426; balance due from other banks $246,596.88; amount of all debts due $2,075,560.85; total amount of resources of the bank $2,770,775.27. In 1853 it was reported that William W. Wilson, employed by the regional Banking Association to track down counterfeiters and plates, had used the acquired plates to make more counterfeits of this bank and the Tradesmans Bank of Chelsea.[63]

In March 1855, Thomas W. Hooper, the paying teller of the bank, was found to have large irregularities in his cash account. Shortly after this was learned, he committed suicide by hanging himself in the bank's cellar.[64]

The business of the Merchants Bank was succeeded by the Merchants National Bank of Boston, chartered on July 2, 1864.

Numismatic Commentary: Collectors might find nice examples of Merchants Bank notes showing scenes of the bank building, the Boston Customs House, and the U.S. Capitol building. The older, four-columned bank building shown was previously owned and occupied by the Boston branch of the second Bank of the United States, W-MA-340. The newer, multi-storied building was the second home of the Merchants Bank. In the vignette showing this bank location, one can see part of the "back porch" on the Old State House building. The nearby square is where the Boston Massacre took place.

Valid Issues

$1 • W-MA-760-001-G10

Left: Lathework panel bearing MASSACHUSETTS vertically. ***Center:*** 1 / 1 / Alternating flower garlands and gridwork segments / ONE / 1 / 1. ***Right:*** Lathework panel bearing ONE / D / ONE vertically. ***Engraver:*** PSSP. ***Comments:*** H-MA-285-G2. 18__. 1830s.

Rarity: —

$1 • W-MA-760-001-G020

Left: 1 / Shield / 1. ***Center:*** Man standing / Ship / 1 in die. ***Right:*** ONE / Two women standing / ONE. ***Engraver:*** New England Bank Note Co. / PSSP. ***Comments:*** H-MA-285-G4. 18__. 1830s–1850s.

Rarity: URS-2
Proof $2,500

$2 • W-MA-760-002-G030

Left: Lathework panel bearing MASSACHUSETTS vertically. ***Center:*** 2 / 2 / Alternating flower garlands and gridwork segments / TWO / 2 / 2. ***Right:*** Lathework panel bearing five TWOs vertically. ***Engraver:*** PSSP. ***Comments:*** H-MA-285-G6. 18__. 1830s.

Rarity: —

$2 • W-MA-760-002-G040

Engraver: Unverified, but likely New England Bank Note Co. / PSSP. ***Comments:*** H-MA-285-G8. No description available. 18__. 1830s–1850s.

Rarity: *None known*

$3 • W-MA-760-003-G050

Left: Lathework panel bearing MASSACHUSETTS vertically. ***Center:*** 3 / 3 / Alternating flower garlands and gridwork segments / THREE / 3 / 3. ***Right:*** Lathework panel bearing THREE vertically. ***Engraver:*** PSSP. ***Comments:*** H-MA-285-G10. 18__. 1830s.

Rarity: —

$3 • W-MA-760-003-G060

Engraver: Unverified, but likely New England Bank Note Co. / PSSP. ***Comments:*** H-MA-285-G12. No description available. 18__. 1830s–1850s.

Rarity: *None known*

$5 • W-MA-760-005-G070

Left: Lathework chain bearing MASSACHUSETTS / 5 / 5. ***Center:*** Alternating flower garlands and gridwork segments / FIVE DOLLARS lined by lathework lines. ***Right:*** 5 / 5. ***Engraver:*** PSSP. ***Comments:*** H-MA-285-G14. 18__. 1830s.

Rarity: —

$5 • **W-MA-760-005-G080**

Engraver: Unverified, but likely New England Bank Note Co. / PSSP. ***Comments:*** H-MA-285-G18. No description available. 18__. 1830s.

Rarity: *None known*

$5 • **W-MA-760-005-G090**

CC

Tint: Red. ***Engraver:*** New England Bank Note Co. / Rawdon, Wright, Hatch & Edson. ***Comments:*** H-MA-285-G20. July 1, 18__. 1850s.

Rarity: URS-2
VF $750

$5 • **W-MA-760-005-G100**

CC

Engraver: Rawdon, Wright & Hatch. ***Comments:*** H-MA-285-G22. 18__. 1840s–1850s.

Rarity: URS-4
VG $150; **F** $300; **Proof** $2,000

$5 • **W-MA-760-005-G110**

Left: V bearing cherub / Justice seated on chest. ***Center:*** Street scene in Boston. ***Right:*** FIVE / 5 bearing eagle, Woman seated, Portrait of George Washington. ***Engraver:*** New England Bank Note Co. / Rawdon, Wright, Hatch & Edson. ***Comments:*** H-MA-285-G24. July 1, 18__. 1850s.

Rarity: —

$5 • **W-MA-760-005-G110a**

HA

Tint: Red-brown lathework outlining white FIVE. ***Engraver:*** New England Bank Note Co. / Rawdon, Wright, Hatch & Edson / ABNCo. monogram. ***Comments:*** H-MA-285-G24b. Similar to W-MA-760-005-G110 but with additional engraver imprint. July 1, 18__. 1850s–1860s.

Rarity: URS-5
VF $1,000

$5 • **W-MA-760-005-G110b**

Tint: Red-brown lathework outlining white FIVE. ***Engraver:*** New England Bank Note Co. / American Bank Note Co. ***Comments:*** H-MA-285-G24c. Similar to W-MA-760-005-G110 but with different engraver imprint. July 1, 18__. 1860s.

Rarity: —

$10 • **W-MA-760-010-G120**

Left: Lathework chain bearing MASSACHUSETTS / 10 / 10 vertically. ***Center:*** Alternating flower garlands and gridwork segments / TEN DOLLARS lined by lathework lines. ***Right:*** 10 / 10 vertically. ***Engraver:*** PSSP. ***Comments:*** H-MA-285-G26. 18__. 1830s.

Rarity: —

$10 • **W-MA-760-010-G130**

Engraver: Unverified, but likely New England Bank Note Co. / PSSP. ***Comments:*** H-MA-285-G28. No description available. 18__. 1830s.

Rarity: *None known*

$10 • **W-MA-760-010-G140**

Engraver: Unverified, but likely New England Bank Note Co. ***Comments:*** H-MA-285-G30. No description available. 18__. 1830s.

Rarity: *None known*

$10 • **W-MA-760-010-G150**

JF

Engraver: Rawdon, Wright & Hatch. ***Comments:*** H-MA-285-G32. 18__. 1840s–1850s.

Rarity: URS-4
VF $750; **Proof** $2,000

$10 • **W-MA-760-010-G160**

Left: TEN / Sailor resting sextant on capstan / TEN. ***Center:*** Liberty flanked by two women reclining, U.S. shield, Cotton plant. ***Right:*** 10 / Steamship. ***Engraver:*** New England Bank Note Co. ***Comments:*** H-MA-285-G34. July 1, 18__. 1850s.

Rarity: —

$10 • **W-MA-760-010-G160a**

Tint: Red-brown lathework outlining white TEN. ***Engraver:*** New England Bank Note Co. / ABNCo. monogram. ***Comments:*** H-MA-285-G34b. Similar to W-MA-760-010-G160 but with additional engraver imprint. July 1, 18__. 1850s–1860s.

Rarity: —

$10 • W-MA-760-010-G160b

Tint: Red-brown lathework outlining white TEN. ***Engraver:*** New England Bank Note Co. / American Bank Note Co. ***Comments:*** H-MA-285-G34c. Similar to W-MA-760-010-G160 but with different engraver imprint. July 1, 18__. 1860s.

Rarity: URS-4
VF $1,000

$20 • W-MA-760-020-G170

Left: Lathework chain bearing MASSACHUSETTS / 20 / 20 vertically. ***Center:*** Alternating flower garlands and gridwork segments. ***Right:*** 20 / 20 vertically. ***Engraver:*** PSSP. ***Comments:*** H-MA-285-G36. 18__. 1830s.

Rarity: —

$20 • W-MA-760-020-G180

Engraver: Unverified, but likely New England Bank Note Co. / PSSP. ***Comments:*** H-MA-285-G38. No description available. 18__. 1830s.

Rarity: *None known*

$20 • W-MA-760-020-G190

Left: 20 / Woman seated / TWENTY. ***Center:*** 20 / War ship and sailboats / 20. ***Bottom center:*** Portrait of George Washington. ***Right:*** 20 / Eagle on shield, Cornucopia / TWENTY. ***Engraver:*** Rawdon, Wright & Hatch. ***Comments:*** H-MA-285-G40. 18__. 1840s–1850s.

Rarity: —

$20 • W-MA-760-020-G200

Left: 20 / TWENTY / 20. ***Center:*** View of U.S. Capitol. ***Bottom center:*** TWENTY. ***Right:*** 20 / Sailor boy raising hat. ***Tint:*** Color unknown. ***Engraver:*** American Bank Note Co. ***Comments:*** H-MA-285-G42a. 1860s.

Rarity: —

$50 • W-MA-760-050-G210

Left: Lathework chain bearing MASSACHUSETTS / 50 / 50 vertically. ***Center:*** Alternating flower garlands and gridwork segments. ***Right:*** 50 / 50 vertically. ***Engraver:*** PSSP. ***Comments:*** H-MA-285-G44. 18__. 1830s.

Rarity: —

$50 • W-MA-760-050-G220

Engraver: Unverified, but likely New England Bank Note Co. / PSSP. ***Comments:*** H-MA-285-G46. No description available. 18__. 1830s–1840s.

Rarity: *None known*

$50 • W-MA-760-050-G230

Left: Woman kneeling / 50. ***Center:*** Ceres with sickle and sheaf, Factory and train. ***Bottom center:*** Cornucopia. ***Right:*** L / Cherub in sailboat / 50. ***Comments:*** H-MA-285-G50. 18__. 1850s.

Rarity: —

$100 • W-MA-760-100-G240

Left: Lathework chain bearing MASSACHUSETTS / 100 / 100 vertically. ***Center:*** Alternating flower garlands and gridwork segments. ***Right:*** 100 / 100 vertically. ***Engraver:*** Perkins. ***Comments:*** H-MA-285-G52. 18__. 1830s.

Rarity: —

$100 • W-MA-760-100-G250

Engraver: Unverified, but likely New England Bank Note Co. / PSSP. ***Comments:*** H-MA-285-G54. No description available. 18__. 1830s.

Rarity: *None known*

$100 • W-MA-760-100-G260

Left: Woman seated / 100. ***Center:*** View of Merchants Bank building / Ship. ***Right:*** Indian on shield / C. ***Engraver:*** Rawdon, Wright & Hatch. ***Comments:*** H-MA-285-G56. 18__. 1840s–1850s.

Rarity: URS-3
Proof $2,000

$500 • W-MA-760-500-G270

Left: 500 / Eagle / 500. ***Center:*** Sailing ship, Sailor standing on wharf with U.S. flag, Man, horse, cart, and warehouse / 500. ***Right:*** 500 / Ship / 500. ***Engraver:*** New England Bank Note Co. / PSSP. ***Comments:*** H-MA-285-G60. 18__. 1830s–1850s.

Rarity: —

$500 • W-MA-760-500-G280 CC

Tint: Green. ***Engraver:*** American Bank Note Co. ***Comments:*** H-MA-285-G60a. July __, 186_. 1860s.

Rarity: URS-2
EF $17,500; **Proof** $20,000

$1,000 • W-MA-760-1000-G290

Left: 1000 / Eagle / 1000. ***Center:*** Sailing ship, Sailor standing on wharf with U.S. flag, Man, horse, cart, and warehouse. ***Right:*** 1000 / Woman with 1000 / 1000. ***Engraver:*** New England Bank Note Co. / PSSP. ***Comments:*** H-MA-285-G64. 18__. 1830s–1850s.

Rarity: —

$1,000 • W-MA-760-1000-G300

Left: 1000 / Eagle. ***Right:*** 1000 / Woman seated with sword, pole and cap, Child. ***Tint:*** Green die bearing M and white 1000. ***Engraver:*** American Bank Note Co. ***Comments:*** H-MA-285-G64a. July __, 186_. 1860s.

Rarity: —

Non-Valid Issues

$1 • W-MA-760-001-A010

PEM

Engraver: Rawdon, Wright, Hatch & Edson. ***Comments:*** H-MA-285-A5. Altered from $1 Merchants Bank, Washington, D.C. July 1, 1852.

Rarity: URS-7
F $75

$1 • W-MA-760-001-A020

Left: 1 / Portrait of William Henry Harrison. ***Center:*** Female portrait, Man on horse. ***Right:*** 1 / Indian standing. ***Engraver:*** Doty & Bergen. ***Comments:*** H-MA-285-A10. Altered from $1 Merchants Bank, Mankato City, Minnesota. Sept. 1, 185_. 1850s.

Rarity: URS-5
F $75

$1 • W-MA-760-001-A030

Left: Woman leaning on shield bearing 1. ***Center:*** 1 / Bull. ***Right:*** Indian dancing / 1. ***Engraver:*** Doty & Bergen. ***Comments:*** H-MA-285-A15. Altered from $1 Merchants Bank, Stillwater, Minnesota. Oct. 20, 185_. 1850s.

Rarity: URS-5
F $75

$2 • W-MA-760-002-S010

Left: 2 / Portrait of George Washington / 2. ***Center:*** Public buildings, people, and horses. ***Bottom center:*** Horse's head. ***Right:*** 2 / Laureate woman leaning on shield. ***Comments:*** H-MA-285-S5. 185_. 1850s.

Rarity: —

$2 • W-MA-760-002-A040

Left: 2 / Two Indians on cliff viewing town. ***Center:*** Portrait of Andrew Jackson / Woman seated with shield bearing cotton plant. ***Right:*** 2 / CONSTITUTION, Monument. ***Overprint:*** Red TWO. ***Engraver:*** Bald, Cousland & Co. / Baldwin, Bald & Co. ***Comments:*** H-MA-285-A20. Altered from $2 Southern Bank of Georgia, Bainbridge, Georgia. 18__. 1860s.

Rarity: —

$2 • W-MA-760-002-A050

SI

Overprint: Red-orange TWO. ***Engraver:*** Doty & Bergen. ***Comments:*** H-MA-285-A25. Altered from $2 Merchants Bank, Mankato City, Minnesota. Sept. 1, 185_. 1850s.

Rarity: URS-7
F $75

$3 • W-MA-760-003-N010

Left: Man seated with scroll. ***Right:*** Cherub. ***Comments:*** H-MA-285-N5. 1840s.

Rarity: —

$3 • W-MA-760-003-A060

Left: Two men, one seated, one standing, Woman seated / 3. ***Center:*** 3 / Woman seated / 3. ***Right:*** 3 / Farmer plowing / Man tending to horse. ***Engraver:*** Rawdon, Wright & Hatch. ***Comments:*** H-MA-285-A30. Altered from $3 Farmers and Merchants Bank of St. Joseph, St. Joseph, Michigan. 18__. 1840s.

Rarity: URS-6
F $100

$5 • W-MA-760-005-N020

Center: Farm, Woman and man, Cattle. ***Comments:*** H-MA-285-N10.

Rarity: —

$5 • W-MA-760-005-N030

Center: Ship under sail / MASSACHUSETTS SAFETY FUND. ***Right:*** Medallion head of George Washington. ***Engraver:*** New England Bank Note Co. ***Comments:*** H-MA-285-N15. 18__. 1839.

Rarity: —

$5 • W-MA-760-005-A070

SI

Engraver: Rawdon, Wright, Hatch & Edson. ***Comments:*** H-MA-285-A35. Altered from $5 Merchants Bank, Washington, D.C. March 2, 1859.

Rarity: URS-7
F $75

$5 • W-MA-760-005-A080

Left: Indian woman holding bow. ***Center:*** Eagle on branch / Indian man standing on cliff watching train. ***Bottom center:*** Indian in canoe. ***Right:*** 5 / Ship, Woman seated with anchor. ***Engraver:*** Doty & Bergen. ***Comments:*** H-MA-285-A40. Altered from $5 Merchants Bank, Mankato City, Minnesota. Sept. 1, 185_. 1850s.

Rarity: URS-6
F $75

$5 • W-MA-760-005-A090

Left: FIVE vertically. ***Center:*** 5 / Eagle. ***Right:*** Woman standing / FIVE. ***Engraver:*** Doty & Bergen. ***Comments:*** H-MA-285-A45. Altered from $5 Merchants Bank, Stillwater, Minnesota. Oct. 20, 185_. 1850s.

Rarity: URS-6
F $75

$5 • W-MA-760-005-A100
Left: V / Portrait of Henry Clay. ***Center:*** Western river steamboat, Wharf. ***Right:*** 5 / Portrait of George Washington. ***Overprint:*** Red FIVE. ***Engraver:*** New England Bank Note Co. / Rawdon, Wright, Hatch & Co. ***Comments:*** H-MA-285-A50. Altered from $5 Waubeek Bank, De Soto, Nebraska. 1857.

Rarity: —

$10 • W-MA-760-010-R010
Engraver: New England Bank Note Co. / PSSP. ***Comments:*** H-MA-285-R5. Raised likely from W-MA-760-001-G020. 18__. 1830s.

Rarity: —

$10 • W-MA-760-010-S020
Left: X / Portrait of child. ***Center:*** X / Man seated with flag, Ship / X. ***Bottom center:*** Ship. ***Right:*** X / Ship on stocks. ***Engraver:*** Rawdon, Wright & Hatch. ***Comments:*** H-MA-285-S10. 18__. 1850s.

Rarity: URS-10
F $50

$10 • W-MA-760-010-S030
Center: Griffin on chest, Two persons seated. ***Comments:*** H-MA-285-S15.

Rarity: —

$10 • W-MA-760-010-N040
Center: Farmer and woman, cattle. ***Comments:*** H-MA-285-N20.

Rarity: —

$20 • W-MA-760-020-C200
Engraver: American Bank Note Co. ***Comments:*** H-MA-285-C42a. Counterfeit of W-MA-760-020-G200. 1860s.

Rarity: —

$20 • W-MA-760-020-S040
Center: Griffin on chest, Two persons seated. ***Comments:*** H-MA-285-S20.

Rarity: —

$50 • W-MA-760-050-C230
Comments: H-MA-285-C50. Counterfeit of W-MA-760-050-G230. 18__. 1850s.

Rarity: —

$50 • W-MA-760-050-R020
Engraver: New England Bank Note Co. / PSSP. ***Comments:*** H-MA-285-R10. 18__. 1830s.

Rarity: —

$50 • W-MA-760-050-S050
Center: Griffin on chest, Two persons seated. ***Comments:*** H-MA-285-S25.

Rarity: —

$50 • W-MA-760-050-S060
Left: 50 / Portrait of Benjamin Franklin. ***Center:*** Sailor with flag seated on bales. ***Bottom center:*** Eagle. ***Right:*** 50 / Portrait of George Washington. ***Engraver:*** Boston Bank Note Co. ***Comments:*** H-MA-285-S30. 18__. 1850s.

Rarity: —

$50 • W-MA-760-050-N050
Left: Woman kneeling. ***Center:*** Woman seated with sheaf. ***Right:*** Cherub in boat. ***Comments:*** H-MA-285-N25.

Rarity: —

$500 • W-MA-760-500-S070
Left: Die bearing 500. ***Center:*** Eagle on rock in ocean, Ships. ***Right:*** Die bearing 500. ***Comments:*** H-MA-285-S35. 18__. 1850s.

Rarity: —

Metropolitan Bank
1854
W-MA-770

History: In 1854 Robert B. Williams and others applied for a charter for the Metropolitan Bank. However, the Legislature, which regulated the amount of bank capital, did not have a provision for the extra amount needed, and the charter was never approved.

Middling Interest Bank
1836–1840
W-MA-780

History: The Middling Interest Bank was incorporated on April 12, 1836. Its office was established on Commercial Street. In 1837 the capital totaled $150,000. The founding president was John M. Fiske, and the first cashier was James Steele. Figures for 1838 included: capital paid in $1,000,000; net profits on hand $1,535.68; cash deposited $9,262.59; total amount due from banks $220,953.27; gold, silver, and other coined metals in the banking house $12,648.18; real estate $1,452.01; bills of other banks incorporated in this state $5,616; balance due from other banks $9,995.29; amount of all debts due $191,241.79; total amount of resources of the bank $220,953.27.[65]

Bills in circulation totaled $60,155 in 1838. During that year there were many unfavorable rumors about the bank, and the Suffolk Bank stopped redeeming and exchanging its bills. On August 5, 1839, news that the bank had been closed by injunction surprised local bankers. Notes on the bank dropped to 50 percent of their value when accepted by exchange brokers. On August 7, the bank closed its doors, blaming the Suffolk Bank for its problems. In actuality, the bank had commenced business before its capital was paid in and had issued too many bills: there were $121,000 in circulation backed by just $11,000 in assets. In months previous, the bank did redeem some of its small-denomination notes in specie. An effort to remain in business failed, and the Legislature revoked the charter in January 1840.

Numismatic Commentary: Genuine notes of the Middling Interest Bank are quite rare, but collectors should have no trouble locating some of the odd denomination, altered notes that appear in the marketplace from time to time.

Valid Issues

$1 • W-MA-780-001-G010

QDB

Engraver: New England Bank Note Co. ***Comments:*** H-MA-295-G2. 18__. 1830s

Rarity: URS-3
F $500; **VF** $750

$2 • W-MA-780-002-G020

Left: TWO / Woman standing. ***Center:*** Farming scene / TWO. ***Right:*** 2 / Man standing / TWO. ***Engraver:*** New England Bank Note Co. ***Comments:*** H-MA-295-G4. 18__. 1830s.

Rarity: URS-3
F $500

$3 • W-MA-780-003-G030

Engraver: Unverified, but likely New England Bank Note Co. ***Comments:*** H-MA-295-G6. 18__. 1830s.

Rarity: URS-3
F $500

$5 • W-MA-780-005-G040

Left: 5 / FIVE. ***Center:*** V. ***Right:*** 5. ***Engraver:*** New England Bank Note Co. ***Comments:*** H-MA-295-G8. 18__. 1830s.

Rarity: URS-3
VG $400

$10 • W-MA-780-010-G050

Left: TEN / White horse, Covered wagon / TEN. ***Center:*** Ship, Buildings / 10. ***Right:*** TEN / TEN. ***Engraver:*** New England Bank Note Co. ***Comments:*** H-MA-295-G10. 18__. 1830s.

Rarity: URS-3
VF $500

$20 • W-MA-780-020-G060

Engraver: Unverified, but likely New England Bank Note Co. ***Comments:*** H-MA-295-G12. No description available. 18__. 1830s.

Rarity: *None known*

$50 • W-MA-780-050-G070

Engraver: Unverified, but likely New England Bank Note Co. ***Comments:*** H-MA-295-G14. No description available. 18__. 1830s.

Rarity: *None known*

Non-Valid Issues

$1.25 • W-MA-780-001.25-A010

CC

Engraver: Terry, Pelton & Co. ***Comments:*** H-MA-295-A5. Altered from a check of the New York Lumber Ass'n. 18__. 1830s.

Rarity: URS-7
F $100

$1.50 • W-MA-780-001.50-A020

QDB

Engraver: Terry, Pelton & Co. ***Comments:*** H-MA-295-A10. Altered from a check of the New York Lumber Ass'n. 18__. 1830s.

Rarity: URS-7
VG $100; **F** $150; **VF** $225

$1.75 • W-MA-780-001.75-A030

CC

Engraver: Terry, Pelton & Co. ***Comments:*** H-MA-295-A15. 18__. 1830s.

Rarity: URS-7
VG $100; **F** $150

Mount Vernon Bank of Boston

1850s

W-MA-790

History: A non-existent bank represented only by notes altered from other banks. The notes were intended to pass for those of the Mount Vernon Bank of the City of Boston, W-MA-800.

Issues

$1 • W-MA-790-001-A010

Left: 1 / Scene. ***Center:*** Woman with cow and basket. ***Right:*** 1 / Female portrait. ***Tint:*** Red-brown 1s and panel outlining white ONE DOLLAR. ***Engraver:*** Danforth, Wright & Co. ***Comments:*** H-MA-299-A5. Altered from $1 Southern Bank of Georgia, Bainbridge, Georgia. March 1, 18__. 1860s.

Rarity: URS-7
F $100; **VF** $125

$2 • W-MA-790-002-A020

Left: 2 / Two Indians on cliff viewing town. ***Center:*** Portrait of Andrew Jackson / Woman seated with shield bearing cotton plant. ***Right:*** 2 / CONSTITUTION, Monument. ***Overprint:*** Red TWO. ***Engraver:*** Bald, Cousland & Co. / Baldwin, Bald & Cousland. ***Comments:*** H-MA-299-A10. Altered from $2 Southern Bank of Georgia, Bainbridge, Georgia. 18__. 1860s.

Rarity: —

$2 • W-MA-790-002-A030

CC

Tint: Red dies outlining 2s and TWO DOLLARS. ***Engraver:*** Danforth, Wright & Co. ***Comments:*** H-MA-299-A15. Jan. 1, 1862. 1830s.

Rarity: URS-7
F $100

Mount Vernon Bank of the City of Boston

1860–1864

W-MA-800

History: The Mount Vernon Bank of the City of Boston was chartered on September 11, 1860. It was voted to increase the capital from $100,000 to $200,000 early on, due to the fact that so many people had an interest in buying stock. Henry W. Perkins Jr. was elected cashier. The bank had a location at 160 Washington Street.

This bank was a latecomer to the note-issuing scene, but in the 1860s it made good use of the privilege. Certain of its bills depicted Mount Vernon, George Washington's home on the Potomac River. The bank name reflected one of the popular causes of the late 1850s—the restoration of Mount Vernon, which had lapsed into desuetude. Edward Everett, a famous Boston politician and orator (he who gave a two hour speech at the dedication of the Gettysburg Battlefield in 1863—a speech sure to be remembered—followed by some brief remarks given by President Lincoln), toured the country and gave more than 200 presentations on Mount Vernon.

On January 12, 1865, the bank's interests were succeeded by the Mount Vernon National Bank of Boston.

Numismatic Commentary: All issues are hard to locate. The bank only issued nine different denominations, all attractive and very colorful.

Valid Issues

$1 • W-MA-800-001-G010

CC

Tint: Green. ***Engraver:*** American Bank Note Co. ***Comments:*** H-MA-300-G2a. 18__. 1860s.

Rarity: URS-4
VF $500; **Proof** $3,000
Selected auction price: Stack's Bowers Galleries, August 2014, Lot 2820, Proof $2,820

$2 • W-MA-800-002-G020

CC

Tint: Green. ***Engraver:*** American Bank Note Co. ***Comments:*** H-MA-300-G4a. Proof. 1860s.

Rarity: URS-3
VF $1,000; **Proof** $4,000

$3 • W-MA-800-003-G030

CC

Tint: Green. ***Engraver:*** American Bank Note Co. ***Comments:*** H-MA-300-G6a. Oct. 1, Proof. Oct. 1, 18__. 1860s.

Rarity: URS-2
VF $1,250; **Proof** $4,800

$5 • W-MA-800-005-G040

HA

Tint: Green. ***Engraver:*** American Bank Note Co. ***Comments:*** H-MA-300-G8a. Proof. Dec. 1, 1860. 1860s.

Rarity: URS-3

Proof $2,500

$10 • W-MA-800-010-G050

JF

Tint: Green. ***Engraver:*** American Bank Note Co. ***Comments:*** H-MA-300-G10a. Dec. 1, 1860.

Rarity: URS-3

Proof $3,200

$20 • W-MA-800-020-G060

Left: 20 / State arms. ***Center:*** TWENTY on seven dies. ***Right:*** 20 / Female portrait. ***Tint:*** Likely green. ***Engraver:*** American Bank Note Co. ***Comments:*** H-MA-300-G12a. 1860s.

Rarity: —

$50 • W-MA-800-050-G070

Left: 50 / State arms / FIFTY / 50. ***Center:*** Wharf scene, Men, horse and wagon, Ships. ***Right:*** 50 / Woman. ***Tint:*** Likely green. ***Engraver:*** American Bank Note Co. ***Comments:*** H-MA-300-G14a. 1860s.

Rarity: —

$100 • W-MA-800-100-G080

Left: 100 / State arms. ***Center:*** C / State arms / C. ***Right:*** 100 / Male portrait. ***Tint:*** Likely green. ***Engraver:*** American Bank Note Co. ***Comments:*** H-MA-300-G16a. 1860s.

Rarity: URS-2

Proof $5,000

$500 • W-MA-800-500-G090

Left: 500 / State arms. ***Center:*** D / Female portrait / D. ***Right:*** 500 / Male portrait. ***Tint:*** Likely green. ***Engraver:*** American Bank Note Co. ***Comments:*** H-MA-300-G18a. 1860s.

Rarity: —

Non-Valid Issues

$3 • W-MA-800-003-C030

Engraver: American Bank Note Co. ***Comments:*** H-MA-300-C6a. Counterfeit of W-MA-800-003-G030. Oct. 1, 18__. 1860s.

Rarity: —

National Bank

1850s

W-MA-810

History: A non-existent bank represented only by notes altered from those of other banks. The notes were intended to pass for those of the National Bank of Boston, W-MA-820.

Issues

$1 • W-MA-810-001-A010

CC

Overprint: Red ONE. ***Engraver:*** New England Bank Note Co. / Rawdon, Wright, Hatch & Edson. ***Comments:*** H-MA-309-A5. Altered from $1 Waubeek Bank, De Soto, Nebraska. 1857.

Rarity: URS-6

F $150

$2 • W-MA-810-002-A020

Left: 2 / Female portrait. ***Center:*** Lathework die / Lathework die. ***Bottom center:*** Sleeping dog. ***Right:*** 2 / Portrait of Franklin Pierce. ***Overprint:*** Red 2. ***Engraver:*** Baldwin, Adams & Co. ***Comments:*** H-MA-309-A10. Altered from $2 Bank of Anacostia, Anacostia, D.C. Aug. 1, 1854.

Rarity: —

$3 • W-MA-810-003-A030

Left: 3 / Portrait of George Washington / THREE. ***Center:*** Liberty standing with portrait of George Washington / Eagle and U.S. shield. ***Bottom center:*** Anchor on shield. ***Right:*** 3 / Liberty standing. ***Engraver:*** Rawdon, Wright, Hatch & Edson. ***Comments:*** H-MA-309-A15. Altered from $3 Bank of America, Georgetown, D.C. series. Oct. 19, 1852.

Rarity: URS-6

F $100

$3 • W-MA-810-003-A040

Left: Panel bearing THREE / Woman seated with scroll and pen / THREE. ***Center:*** Train / Woman in clouds with shield and eagle. ***Right:*** THREE / Laureate woman standing with legs crossed and shield bearing 3. ***Engraver:*** W.L. Ormsby. ***Comments:*** H-MA-309-A20. Altered from $3 Potomac River Bank, Georgetown, D.C. 18__. 1850s.

Rarity: —

$5 • W-MA-810-005-S010

HA

Overprint: Red FIVE. ***Engraver:*** Toppan, Carpenter & Co. ***Comments:*** H-MA-309-S5a. May 1, 185_. 1850s.

Rarity: URS-8
F $75

$5 • W-MA-810-005-A050

Left: FIVE / Woman leaning on shield bearing 5. ***Center:*** Steamship, Woman in clouds with eagle / 5. ***Right:*** FIVE / Woman standing. ***Engraver:*** W.L. Ormsby. ***Comments:*** H-MA-309-A25. Altered from $5 Potomac River Bank, Georgetown, D.C. 185_. 1850s.

Rarity: URS-5
F $100

$5 • W-MA-810-005-A060

CC

Overprint: Red FIVE. ***Engraver:*** Rawdon, Wright, Hatch & Edson. ***Comments:*** H-MA-309-A30. Altered from $5 Farmers and Merchants Bank of Memphis, Memphis, Tennessee series. 1850s.

Rarity: URS-7
F $100

$10 • W-MA-810-010-N010

Center: Mechanic and anvil. ***Comments:*** H-MA-309-N5.

Rarity: —

$10 • W-MA-810-010-A070

Left: 10 / Woman seated. ***Center:*** X / Three women standing, one pointing. ***Right:*** 10 / Street scene. ***Engraver:*** Danforth, Bald & Co. ***Comments:*** H-MA-309-A35. 185_. 1850s.

Rarity: URS-5
F $100

$10 • W-MA-810-010-A080

Left: Militiaman standing with musket. ***Center:*** Eagle on shield, Flags bearing state names. ***Bottom center:*** Woman bathing. ***Right:*** 10 / Indian drawing arrow from quiver. ***Overprint:*** Red TEN. ***Engraver:*** Bald, Cousland & Co. / Baldwin, Bald & Cousland. ***Comments:*** H-MA-309-A40. Altered from $10 Bank of Morgan, Morgan, Georgia. 18__. 1850s.

Rarity: —

$10 • W-MA-810-010-A090

Left: 10 / Allegorical woman and Justice flanking shield bearing anchor. ***Center:*** Man in white shirt standing over boy gathering corn, Horse-drawn wagon. ***Right:*** 10 / Portrait of girl with ringlets. ***Overprint:*** Red X X. ***Engraver:*** Toppan, Carpenter & Co. ***Comments:*** H-MA-309-A45. Altered from $10 Farmers Bank, Wickford, Rhode Island. 18__. 1855.

Rarity: —

National Bank of Boston

1853–1864

W-MA-820

History: The National Bank of Boston was chartered in 1853 and started business on August 1, 1854. It had an authorized starting capital of $300,000. John H. Wilkins was elected president, and Charles B. Hall was chosen as the cashier. Hall was the late treasurer of the Commonwealth of Massachusetts. In 1857 the National Bank had a capital of $750,000. Bills in circulation amounted to $146,667, bills of this bank and other New England states totaled $43,830.38, and specie was $66,860.80.

The National Bank of Boston was succeeded by the Boston National Bank, chartered on April 30, 1864.

Numismatic Commentary: All issued, genuine notes are extremely hard to find. Despite the name, this bank was not a "national" bank, but was state-chartered.

Valid Issues

$1 • W-MA-820-001-G010

JF

Engraver: Rawdon, Wright, Hatch & Edson / New England Bank Note Co. / ABNCo. monogram. ***Comments:*** H-MA-310-G2a. 18__. 1860s.

Rarity: URS-3
VG $1,500; **VF** $3,000

$2 • W-MA-820-002-G020

Left: Woman seated / 2. ***Center:*** Cows, Milkmaid seated with pail, Farmer reclining with rake, Two gold dollars. ***Right:*** 2 / Sailor standing with spyglass. ***Overprint:*** Red TWO. ***Engraver:*** Rawdon, Wright, Hatch & Edson / New England Bank Note Co. ***Comments:*** H-MA-310-G4a. 18__. 1850s.

Rarity: —

$3 • W-MA-820-003-G030

Left: 3 / Mermaid and Triton / Steamship. ***Center:*** Farmer, sailor, and blacksmith. ***Right:*** 3 / Portrait of George Washington. ***Overprint:*** Red THREE. ***Engraver:*** Rawdon, Wright, Hatch & Edson / New England Bank Note Co. ***Comments:*** H-MA-310-G6a. 18__. 1850s.

Rarity: —

$5 • W-MA-820-005-G040

Left: FIVE / Woman standing. ***Center:*** Two women, one man, Two cherubs, Five silver dollars / FIVE. ***Right:*** 5 / Building. ***Overprint:*** Red FIVE. ***Engraver:*** Rawdon, Wright, Hatch & Edson / New England Bank Note Co. ***Comments:*** H-MA-310-G8a. 18__. 1850s.

Rarity: URS-3
F $150; **VF** $2,000

$10 • W-MA-820-010-G050

Center: X / View of U.S. Capitol. ***Right:*** X / Portrait of Benjamin Franklin. ***Overprint:*** Red TEN. ***Engraver:*** Rawdon, Wright, Hatch & Edson / New England Bank Note Co. ***Comments:*** H-MA-310-G10a. 18__. 1850s.

Rarity: —

$20 • W-MA-820-020-G060

Left: Hebe watering eagle from cup / XX. ***Center:*** View of U.S. Capitol. ***Right:*** 20 / Woman feeding horse. ***Engraver:*** Rawdon, Wright, Hatch & Edson / New England Bank Note Co. ***Comments:*** H-MA-310-G12. 18__. 1850s.

Rarity: —

$50 • W-MA-820-050-G070

Left: Fountain / 50. ***Center:*** Ship and two steamships. ***Right:*** 50 / Female portrait. ***Engraver:*** Rawdon, Wright, Hatch & Edson / New England Bank Note Co. ***Comments:*** H-MA-310-G14. 18__. 1850s.

Rarity: —

$100 • W-MA-820-100-G080

Left: 100 / Minerva. ***Center:*** Eagle and shield, Steamship / U.S. Capitol. ***Right:*** C / Portrait. ***Engraver:*** Rawdon, Wright, Hatch & Edson / New England Bank Note Co. ***Comments:*** H-MA-310-G16. 18__. 1850s.

Rarity: —

$500 • W-MA-820-500-G090

Center: Justice seated, Shield, Steamship, train, and city. ***Right:*** 500 / Female portrait. ***Engraver:*** Rawdon, Wright, Hatch & Edson / New England Bank Note Co. ***Comments:*** H-MA-310-G18. 18__. 1850s.

Rarity: —

$1,000 • W-MA-820-1000-G100

Center: M / Two women flanking shield bearing 1000 and surmounted by eagle, Train and steamboat. ***Right:*** 1000 / Woman with sheaf. ***Engraver:*** American Bank Note Co. ***Comments:*** H-MA-310-G20. 18__. 1860s.

Rarity: —

Non-Valid Issues

$5 • W-MA-820-005-R010

Engraver: Rawdon, Wright, Hatch & Edson / New England Bank Note Co. ***Comments:*** H-MA-310-R5. Raised from W-MA-820-001-G010. 18__. 1850s.

Rarity: —

National Hide and Leather Bank

1857–1863

W-MA-830

History: On May 27, 1857, the Legislature approved the incorporation of the National Hide and Leather Bank with $1,000,000 authorized capital. The Panic of 1857 slowed down banking all across the United States, and this bank was no exception. On March 24, 1858, the Massachusetts Legislature extended the time for the bank to raise its capital until May 1, 1859, due to the economic conditions. The bank went into business later that year.

In 1860 the amount of bills in circulation of denominations $5 and up totaled $181,395. Bills of a smaller denomination totaled $55,200.

In October 1863, during the annual meeting of shareholders, it was authorized by the directors to shut down the National Hide and Leather Bank and pursue a national banking charter as the National Hide and Leather Bank of Boston. This was done, and on June 8, 1864, the charter was granted.

New England Bank

1813–1865

W-MA-840

History: The New England Bank was chartered in June 1813 and renewed in 1827. Business was conducted at 67 State Street.

In 1814 the New England Bank set up a program to redeem bills of various other banks in the New England states as a precursor of the Suffolk Bank system. It was not ultimately successful. In early 1836 the bank's officers were called upon by a special investigative committee of state officials, charging that this and certain other banks had "transcended the limits of their charters" in certain activities. However, the matter was soon forgotten.

By January 1838, the capital was $1,000,000 paid in full. Bills in circulation amounted to $36,259 in 1838, ranging from $66,158 in 1839 to $172,684 in 1849. Other figures for 1838 included: net profits on hand $106,457.32; balances due to other banks $388,119.63; cash deposited $132,707.94; cash deposited bearing interest $32,000; total amount due from banks $1,663,843.89; gold, silver, and other coined metals in the banking house $63,206.68; real estate $20,000; bills of other banks incorporated in this state $134,911; balance due from other banks $149,751.97; amount of all debts due $1,295,974.24; total amount of resources of the bank $1,663,843.89.

In the spring of 1847, the city was stunned to learn the details of a scandal involving Philip Maret, president of the bank, who had served the institution for 21 years. It was revealed that in the preceding October the directors had learned that he had used bank funds for his own investment scheme, defaulting in the amount of $60,000. He repaid the funds but fled the city.

The business of the bank was succeeded in 1864 by the New England National Bank of Boston.

Numismatic Commentary: The early PSSP style notes are easier to find than the later notes with scenic vignettes.

Valid Issues

$1 • W-MA-840-001-G010

Center: 1 / 1 / Flower garlands and gridwork segments / ONE / 1 / 1. ***Engraver:*** PSSP. ***Comments:*** H-MA-315-G20. 18__. 1810s–1820s.

Rarity: —

$1 • W-MA-840-001-G010a

Left: Narrow panel of lathework circle segments. ***Right:*** Narrow panel of lathework circle segments. ***Engraver:*** PSSP. ***Comments:*** H-MA-315-G22. Similar to W-MA-840-001-G010. 18__. 1820s.

Rarity: —

$1 • W-MA-840-001-G010b

Left: Narrow panel of lathework circle segments. ***Right:*** Narrow panel of lathework circle segments. ***Engraver:*** PSSP. ***Comments:*** H-MA-315-G24. Similar to W-MA-840-001-G010. 18__. 1820s–1830s.

Rarity: —

$1 • W-MA-840-001-G010c

Left: ONE / D / ONE vertically. ***Right:*** ONE / D / ONE vertically. ***Engraver:*** PSSP. ***Comments:*** H-MA-315-G26. Similar to W-MA-840-001-G010. 18__. 1830s.

Rarity: —

$1 • W-MA-840-001-G010d

Left: ONE / D / ONE vertically. ***Right:*** ONE / D / ONE vertically. ***Engraver:*** PSSP. ***Comments:*** H-MA-315-G28. Similar to W-MA-840-001-G010. 18__. 1830s–1840s.

Rarity: —

$1 • W-MA-840-001-G020

CC

Engraver: Draper, Toppan & Co. ***Comments:*** H-MA-315-G32. 18__. 1840s–1850s.

Rarity: URS-5
F $250

$1 • W-MA-840-001-G020a

Left: 1 on reverse 1. ***Center:*** Man seated, Eagle. ***Right:*** 1 on 1. ***Engraver:*** Draper, Toppan & Co. / ABNCo. monogram. ***Comments:*** H-MA-315-G32a. Similar to W-MA-840-001-G020 but with additional engraver imprint. 18__. 1850s–1860s.

Rarity: —

$1 • W-MA-840-001-G030

Left: ONE / Woman with arm raised. ***Center:*** 1 / Woman holding up shield bearing Indian / 1. ***Right:*** ONE on 1. ***Back:*** Green. ***Engraver:*** American Bank Note Co. ***Comments:*** H-MA-315-G36a. Jan. 1, 1864.

Rarity: URS-3
F $250; **VF** $1,250

$2 • W-MA-840-002-G040

Center: 2 / 2 / Flower garlands and gridwork segments / TWO / 2 / 2. ***Engraver:*** PSSP. ***Comments:*** H-MA-315-G38. 18__. 1810s–1820s.

Rarity: —

$2 • W-MA-840-002-G040a

Left: Narrow panel of lathework circle segments. ***Right:*** Narrow panel of lathework circle segments. ***Engraver:*** PSSP. ***Comments:*** H-MA-315-G40. Similar to W-MA-840-002-G040. 18__. 1820s.

Rarity: —

$2 • W-MA-840-002-G040b

Left: Narrow panel of lathework circle segments. ***Right:*** Narrow panel of lathework circle segments. ***Engraver:*** PSSP. ***Comments:*** H-MA-315-G42. Similar to W-MA-840-002-G040. 18__. 1820s–1830s.

Rarity: —

$2 • W-MA-840-002-G040c

Left: Five TWOs vertically. ***Right:*** Five TWOs vertically. ***Engraver:*** PSSP. ***Comments:*** H-MA-315-G44. Similar to W-MA-840-002-G040. 18__. 1830s.

Rarity: —

$2 • W-MA-840-002-G040d

HA

Engraver: PSSP. ***Comments:*** H-MA-315-G46. Similar to W-MA-840-002-G040. 18__. 1830s–1840s.

Rarity: URS-5
F $250

How to Read the Whitman Numbering System

$1 • W-MA-010-001-G010a

Denomination: Value of the note shown.

W: Whitman number. This number is a sortable code unique to each bank and note.

MA: Abbreviation for the state under study.

010: Numerical designation specific to each bank.

001: The denomination in dollars.

G010a: G indicates a good or valid note. Other categories are indicated thus: C (counterfeit); R (raised); S (spurious); N (not-attributed); A (altered). Numbers are assigned starting with 010, 020, et seq. Terminal letters following the number indicate variations of a note: a series of different colored overprints, tints, payees, etc., all on the same design of note. For more information, see the "How to Use This Book" section at the front of the volume, page xiv.

$2 • W-MA-840-002-G050 QDB

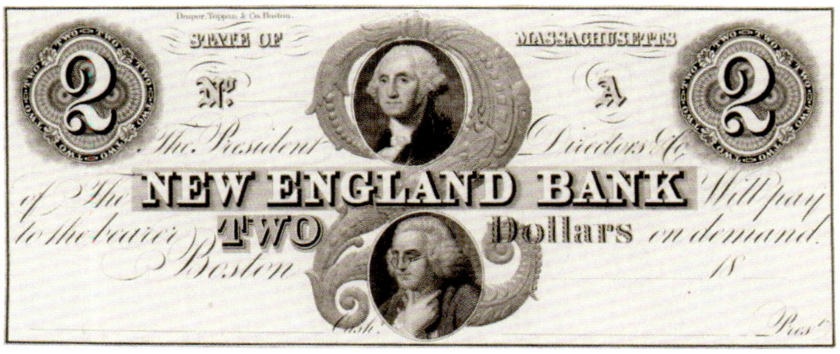

Engraver: Draper, Toppan & Co. ***Comments:*** H-MA-315-G50. Proof. 18__. 1840s–1850s.

Rarity: URS-3
Proof $1,250

$2 • W-MA-840-002-G050a

Left: 2. ***Center:*** 2 bearing portraits of George Washington and Benjamin Franklin. ***Right:*** 2. ***Engraver:*** Draper, Toppan & Co. / ABNCo. monogram. ***Comments:*** H-MA-315-G50a. Similar to W-MA-840-002-G050 but with additional engraver imprint. 18__. 1850s–1860s.

Rarity: —

$2 • W-MA-840-002-G060

Left: Woman seated with scroll, Child. ***Center:*** Woman reclining with books, chart, and globe. ***Right:*** 2 / Bust of George Washington. ***Tint:*** Green medallion 2s. ***Engraver:*** American Bank Note Co. ***Comments:*** H-MA-315-G54a. Jan. 1, 1864.

Rarity: —

$3 • W-MA-840-003-G070

Center: 3 / 3 / Oval of flower garlands and gridwork segments / 3 / 3. ***Engraver:*** PSSP. ***Comments:*** H-MA-315-G56. 18__. 1810s–1820s.

Rarity: —

$3 • W-MA-840-003-G070a

Left: Narrow panel of lathework circle segments. ***Right:*** Narrow panel of lathework circle segments. ***Engraver:*** PSSP. ***Comments:*** H-MA-315-G58. Similar to W-MA-840-003-G070. 18__. 1820s.

Rarity: —

$3 • W-MA-840-003-G070b

Left: Narrow panel of lathework circle segments. ***Right:*** Narrow panel of lathework circle segments. ***Engraver:*** PSSP. ***Comments:*** H-MA-315-G60. Similar to W-MA-840-003-G070. 18__. 1820s–1830s.

Rarity: —

$3 • W-MA-840-003-G070c

Left: THREE vertically. ***Right:*** THREE vertically. ***Engraver:*** PSSP. ***Comments:*** H-MA-315-G62. Similar to W-MA-840-003-G070. 18__. 1830s.

Rarity: —

$3 • W-MA-840-003-G070d

Left: THREE vertically. ***Right:*** THREE vertically. ***Engraver:*** PSSP. ***Comments:*** H-MA-315-G64. Similar to W-MA-840-003-G070. 18__. 1830s–1840s.

Rarity: —

$3 • W-MA-840-003-G080 JF

Engraver: Toppan, Carpenter & Co. ***Comments:*** H-MA-315-G68. Proof. 18__. 1840s–1850s.

Rarity: URS-3
Proof $1,500

$3 • W-MA-840-003-G080a

Left: 3 / Train. ***Center:*** Woman seated with parcels / Portrait of Indian. ***Right:*** 3 / Ship. ***Engraver:*** Toppan, Carpenter & Co. / ABNCo. monogram. ***Comments:*** H-MA-315-G68a. Similar to W-MA-840-003-G080 but with additional engraver imprint. 18__. 1850s–1860s.

Rarity: —

$3 • W-MA-840-003-G080b

Back: Green back dies bearing 3 / Bank title / 3. ***Engraver:*** American Bank Note Co. ***Comments:*** H-MA-315-G68c. Similar to W-MA-840-003-G080 but with different date and imprint. Jan. 1, 1864.

Rarity: URS-3
F $1,000

$5 • W-MA-840-005-G090

Left: Lathework panel bearing MASSACHUSETTS / 5 / 5 vertically. ***Center:*** Alternating flower garlands and gridwork segments. ***Right:*** 5 / 5. ***Engraver:*** PSSP. ***Comments:*** H-MA-315-G70. 18__. 1810s–1820s.

Rarity: —

$5 • W-MA-840-005-G100

Center: Alternating flower garlands and gridwork segments / White boxes flanking FIVE DOLLARS. ***Engraver:*** PSSP. ***Comments:*** H-MA-315-G72. 18__. 1820s.

Rarity: —

$5 • W-MA-840-005-G100a

Engraver: PSSP. ***Comments:*** H-MA-315-G74. Similar to W-MA-840-005-G100 but with zigzag ruled lines. 18__. 1820s–1830s.

Rarity: —

$5 • W-MA-840-005-G100b

Engraver: PSSP. ***Comments:*** H-MA-315-G76. Similar to W-MA-840-005-G100 but with spiral lathework lines. 18__. 1830s.

Rarity: —

$5 • W-MA-840-005-G100c

Back: Check Plate. ***Engraver:*** PSSP. ***Comments:*** H-MA-315-G76a. Similar to W-MA-840-005-G100 but with spiral lathework lines. 18__. 1830s–1840s.

Rarity: —

$5 • W-MA-840-005-G110 CC

Engraver: Draper, Toppan & Co. ***Comments:*** H-MA-315-G80. 18__. 1840s–1850s.

Rarity: URS-4
VF $500; **Proof** $900

$5 • W-MA-840-005-G110a
Engraver: Draper, Toppan & Co. / ABNCo. monogram. ***Comments:*** H-MA-315-G80a. Similar to W-MA-840-005-G110 but with additional engraver imprint. 18__. 1850s–1860s.

Rarity: —

$5 • W-MA-840-005-G120
Left: 5. ***Center:*** Bust of George Washington on pedestal flanked by woman and sailor standing with spyglass, Train and ship. ***Right:*** 5. ***Back:*** Green. ***Engraver:*** American Bank Note Co. ***Comments:*** H-MA-315-G84a. Jan. 1, 1864.

Rarity: —

$10 • W-MA-840-010-G130
Left: Lathework panel bearing MASSACHUSETTS / 10 / 10 vertically. ***Center:*** Alternating flower garlands and gridwork segments / TEN. ***Right:*** 10 / 10 vertically. ***Engraver:*** Perkins. ***Comments:*** H-MA-315-G86. 18__. 1810s–1820s.

Rarity: —

$10 • W-MA-840-010-G130a
Center: Alternating flower garlands and gridwork segments / TEN / White boxes flanking TEN DOLLARS. ***Engraver:*** Perkins. ***Comments:*** H-MA-315-G88. Similar to W-MA-840-010-G130. 18__. 1820s.

Rarity: —

$10 • W-MA-840-010-G130b
Engraver: PSSP. ***Comments:*** H-MA-315-G90. Similar to W-MA-840-010-G130 but with zigzag ruled lines. 18__. 1820s–1830s.

Rarity: —

$10 • W-MA-840-010-G130c
Engraver: PSSP. ***Comments:*** H-MA-315-G92. Similar to W-MA-840-010-G130 but with spiral lathework lines. 18__. 1830s.

Rarity: —

$10 • W-MA-840-010-G140
Left: X. ***Center:*** Spread eagle / X. ***Right:*** Panel bearing TEN DOLLARS vertically. ***Engraver:*** New England Bank Note Co. ***Comments:*** H-MA-315-G96. 18__. 1830s–1850s.

Rarity: —

$10 • W-MA-840-010-G150 HSPA

Comments: H-Unlisted. 181_. 1810s.

Rarity: URS-2
Proof $750

$10 • W-MA-840-010-G160
Left: Panel bearing TEN DOLLARS vertically. ***Center:*** Eagle on rock / Ship. ***Right:*** 10 / Woman standing with spear and shield. ***Engraver:*** American Bank Note Co. ***Comments:*** H-MA-315-G100. 18__. 1850s–1860s.

Rarity: —

$20 • W-MA-840-020-G170
Left: Panel bearing state arms / 20 / 20 vertically. ***Center:*** Alternating flower garlands and gridwork segments. ***Right:*** 20 / 20 vertically. ***Engraver:*** Perkins. ***Comments:*** H-MA-315-G102. 18__. 1810s–1820s.

Rarity: URS-4
Proof $1,500

$20 • W-MA-840-020-G170a
Left: Lathework chain bearing MASSACHUSETTS vertically. ***Engraver:*** PSSP. ***Comments:*** H-MA-315-G104. Similar to W-MA-840-020-G170. 18__. 1820s–1830s.

Rarity: —

$20 • W-MA-840-020-G180
Left: 20 / TWENTY DOLLARS / 20. ***Center:*** Eagle on rock, Ship. ***Right:*** 20 / Woman with spear and shield bearing 20. ***Engraver:*** New England Bank Note Co. ***Comments:*** H-MA-315-G106. 18__. 1830s–1850s.

Rarity: —

$20 • W-MA-840-020-G190 CC

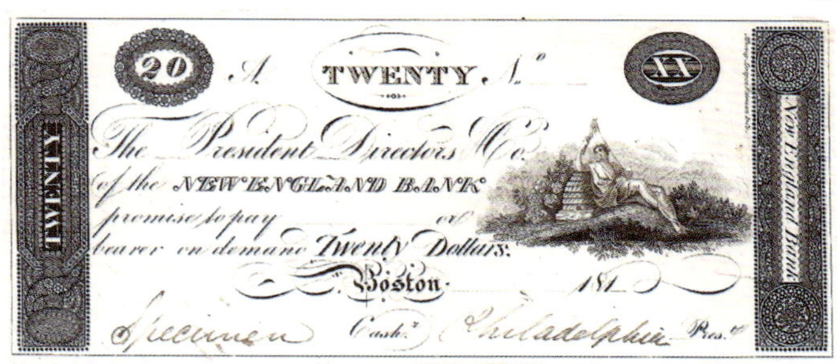

Engraver: Murray, Draper, Fairman & Co. ***Comments:*** H-Unlisted. 181_. 1810s.

Rarity: URS-2
Proof $1,200

$50 • W-MA-840-050-G200
Left: Panel bearing state arms / 50 vertically. ***Center:*** Alternating flower garlands and gridwork segments. ***Right:*** 50 / 50 vertically. ***Engraver:*** Perkins. ***Comments:*** H-MA-315-G108. 18__. 1810s–1820s.
Rarity: —

$50 • W-MA-840-050-G200a
Left: Lathework chain bearing MASSACHUSETTS vertically. ***Engraver:*** PSSP. ***Comments:*** H-MA-315-G110. Similar to W-MA-840-050-G200. 18__. 1820s–1830s.
Rarity: —

$50 • W-MA-840-050-G210
Left: Indian man in canoe. ***Center:*** FIFTY DOLLARS / 50. ***Right:*** FIFTY vertically. ***Engraver:*** New England Bank Note Co. ***Comments:*** H-MA-315-G114. 18__. 1830s–1850s.
Rarity: —

$100 • W-MA-840-100-G220
Left: Panel bearing state arms / 100 / 100 vertically. ***Center:*** Alternating flower garlands and gridwork segments. ***Right:*** 100 / 100 vertically. ***Engraver:*** Perkins. ***Comments:*** H-MA-315-G116. 18__. 1810s–1820s.
Rarity: —

$100 • W-MA-840-100-G220a
Left: Lathework chain bearing MASSACHUSETTS vertically. ***Engraver:*** Perkins. ***Comments:*** H-MA-315-G118. Similar to W-MA-840-100-G220. 18__. 1820s–1830s.
Rarity: —

$100 • W-MA-840-100-G230
Left: Indian man in canoe, Mountains / 100. ***Center:*** 100. ***Right:*** 100 vertically. ***Engraver:*** New England Bank Note Co. ***Comments:*** H-MA-315-G122. 18__. 1830s–1850s.
Rarity: —

$500 • W-MA-840-500-G240
Left: FIVE HUN. vertically. ***Center:*** D, Woman seated with boxes and bales, Ship. ***Right:*** NEW ENGLAND BANK vertically. ***Engraver:*** American Bank Note Co. ***Comments:*** H-MA-315-G126. 1860s.
Rarity: URS-1
Proof $5,500
Selected auction price: Stack's Bowers Galleries, August 2014, Lot 2064, Proof $5,287

$1,000 • W-MA-840-1000-G250
Left: Justice seated next to pedestal / 1000. ***Center:*** Harbor scene, Sail ships, City. ***Right:*** 1000 / Portrait of George Washington. ***Engraver:*** American Bank Note Co. ***Comments:*** H-MA-315-G130. 1860s.
Rarity: —

NON-VALID ISSUES

$1 • W-MA-840-001-C010d
SI

Engraver: PSSP. ***Comments:*** H-MA-315-C28. Counterfeit of W-MA-840-001-G010d. 18__. 1830s–1840s.
Rarity: URS-7
VG $50

$2 • W-MA-840-002-C040d
HA

Engraver: PSSP. ***Comments:*** H-MA-315-C46. Counterfeit of W-MA-840-002-G040d. Remainder. 18__. 1840s.
Rarity: URS-6
VG $75; **Unc-Rem** $50

$2 • W-MA-840-002-C050
Engraver: Draper, Toppan & Co. ***Comments:*** H-MA-315-C50. Counterfeit of W-MA-840-002-G050 or G050a. 18__. 1850s.
Rarity: —

$3 • W-MA-840-003-C070d
Engraver: PSSP. ***Comments:*** H-MA-315-C64. Counterfeit of W-MA-840-003-G070d. 18__. 1840s.
Rarity: —
F $100

$5 • W-MA-840-005-C110a
SI

Engraver: Draper, Toppan & Co. / ABNCo. monogram. ***Comments:*** H-MA-315-C80a. Counterfeit of W-MA-840-005-G110a. 18__. 1860s.
Rarity: URS-8
VF $90

$5 • W-MA-840-005-A010

Left: 5 / Train / 5. ***Center:*** 5 / Indian seated / 5. ***Bottom center:*** Dog and strongbox. ***Right:*** 5 / Train / 5. ***Engraver:*** Chas. E. Ely, Philadelphia. ***Comments:*** H-MA-315-A5. Altered from $5 Geauga Insurance Co., Painesville, Ohio. 18__. 1840s.

Rarity: URS-4
VG $75

$10 • W-MA-840-010-A020 CC

Engraver: Rawdon, Wright, Hatch & Edson. ***Comments:*** H-MA-315-A10. Altered from $10, New England Bank, Fairmount, Maine. October 1, 185_.

Rarity: URS-7
EF $100

$20 • W-MA-840-020-A030 CC

Engraver: Rawdon, Wright, Hatch & Edson. ***Comments:*** H-MA-315-A15. Altered, including replacement of center vignette, from $20 New England Bank, Fairmount, Maine. October 1, 1857.

Rarity: URS-7
F $125

North Bank
1825–1864
W-MA-850

History: The North Bank was incorporated in June 1825 and was located at 26 North Market Street. Its charter was renewed in 1827 with a $750,000 capital. In 1838 a teller at the bank confessed to embezzling $28,000, but the bank was not seriously affected. In the same year it was reported that the bank was manipulating the price of its stock. This too passed, and the bank continued onward.[66]

Figures for 1838 included: net profits on hand $38,828.96; balances due to other banks $13,849.33; cash deposited $157,348.54; cash deposited bearing interest $17,000; total amount due from banks $1,185,120.83; gold, silver, and other coined metals in the banking house $300,100.54; real estate $22,425.06; bills of other banks incorporated in this state $60,608; balance due from other banks $75,446.17; amount of all debts due $996,541.06; total amount of resources of the bank $1,185,120.83.

The North Bank was succeeded by the North National Bank of Boston, chartered on October 5, 1864.

Numismatic Commentary: Genuine signed and dated notes are hard to locate, but quite a few unissued remainder notes have been circulating among collectors for quite a few years.

Valid Issues

$1 • W-MA-850-001-G010

Left: Lathework panel. ***Center:*** 1 / 1 / Oval of flower garlands and gridwork segments / 1 / 1. ***Right:*** Lathework panel. ***Engraver:*** PSSP. ***Comments:*** H-MA-320-G2. 18__. 1820s.

Rarity: —

$1 • W-MA-850-001-G010a

Left: Narrow panel of lathework circle segments. ***Right:*** Narrow panel of lathework circle segments. ***Engraver:*** PSSP. ***Comments:*** H-MA-320-G4. Similar to W-MA-850-001-G010. 18__. 1820s–1830s.

Rarity: —

$1 • W-MA-850-001-G010b

Left: ONE / D / ONE vertically. ***Right:*** ONE / D / ONE vertically. ***Engraver:*** PSSP. ***Comments:*** H-MA-320-G6. Similar to W-MA-850-001-G010. 18__. 1830s.

Rarity: —

$1 • W-MA-850-001-G020 CC

Engraver: New England Bank Note Co. / PSSP. ***Comments:*** H-MA-320-G10. 18__. 1830s–1850s.

Rarity: URS-4
VG $250; **F** $400

$1 • W-MA-850-001-G030 CC

Engraver: Rawdon, Wright, Hatch & Edson / New England Bank Note Co. ***Comments:*** H-MA-320-G14. Proof. 18__. 1850s.

Rarity: URS-4
F $200; **EF** $375; **Unc-Rem** $750; **Proof** $1,600

$1 • W-MA-850-001-G030a

Left: 1 / Woman standing with hat, 1, and bucket. ***Center:*** Woman seated with portrait of Benjamin Franklin / ONE. ***Right:*** 1 / Woman leaning on 1. ***Overprint:*** Red ONE. ***Engraver:*** Rawdon, Wright, Hatch & Edson / New England Bank Note Co. ***Comments:*** H-MA-320-G14a. Similar to W-MA-850-001-G030. 18__. 1850s.

Rarity: —

$1 • W-MA-850-001-G030b

JF

Overprint: Red ONE. ***Engraver:*** Rawdon, Wright, Hatch & Edson / New England Bank Note Co. / ABNCo. monogram. ***Comments:*** H-MA-320-G14b. Similar to W-MA-850-001-G030 but with additional engraver imprint. 18__. 1850s–1860s.

Rarity: URS-3
F $2,000

$2 • W-MA-850-002-G040

Left: Lathework panel. ***Center:*** 2 / 2 / Oval of flower garlands and gridwork segments / 2 / 2. ***Right:*** Lathework panel. ***Engraver:*** PSSP. ***Comments:*** H-MA-320-G16. 18__. 1820s.

Rarity: URS-5
Unc-Rem $1,000

$2 • W-MA-850-002-G040a

Left: Narrow panel of lathework circle segments. ***Right:*** Narrow panel of lathework circle segments. ***Engraver:*** PSSP. ***Comments:*** H-MA-320-G18. Similar to W-MA-850-002-G040. 18__. 1820s–1830s.

Rarity: —

$2 • W-MA-850-002-G040b

Left: Five TWOs vertically. ***Right:*** Five TWOs vertically. ***Engraver:*** PSSP. ***Comments:*** H-MA-320-G20. Similar to W-MA-850-002-G040. 18__. 1830s.

Rarity: —

$2 • W-MA-850-002-G050

Left: 2 / Ship / 2. ***Center:*** Woman / View of State House and Boston Common. ***Right:*** 2 / Ship / 2. ***Engraver:*** New England Bank Note Co. / PSSP. ***Comments:*** H-MA-320-G24. 18__. 1830s–1850s.

Rarity: —

$2 • W-MA-850-002-G060

CC

Engraver: Rawdon, Wright, Hatch & Edson / New England Bank Note Co. ***Comments:*** H-MA-320-G28. Proof. 18__. 1850s.

Rarity: URS-3
F $200; **EF** $375; **Proof** $2,000

$2 • W-MA-850-002-G060a

Left: TWO / Hebe seated on cornucopia watering eagle from cup. ***Center:*** Train / Woman seated with telegraph transmitter, Portrait of Benjamin Franklin / Men. ***Right:*** 2 / Portrait of George Washington. ***Overprint:*** Red TWO. ***Engraver:*** Rawdon, Wright, Hatch & Edson / New England Bank Note Co. ***Comments:*** H-MA-320-G28a. Similar to W-MA-850-002-G060. 18__. 1850s.

Rarity: —

$2 • W-MA-850-002-G060b

Overprint: Red TWO. ***Engraver:*** Rawdon, Wright, Hatch & Edson / New England Bank Note Co. / ABNCo. monogram. ***Comments:*** H-MA-320-G28b. Similar to W-MA-850-002-G060 but with additional engraver imprint. 18__. 1850s–1860s.

Rarity: —

$3 • W-MA-850-003-G070

Left: Lathework panel. ***Center:*** 3 / 3 / Oval of flower garlands and gridwork segments / 3 / 3. ***Right:*** Lathework panel. ***Engraver:*** PSSP. ***Comments:*** H-MA-320-G30. 18__. 1820s.

Rarity: —

$3 • W-MA-850-003-G070a

Left: Narrow panel of lathework circle segments. ***Right:*** Narrow panel of lathework circle segments. ***Engraver:*** PSSP. ***Comments:*** H-MA-320-G32. Similar to W-MA-850-003-G070. 18__. 1820s–1830s.

Rarity: —

$3 • W-MA-850-003-G070b

Left: THREE vertically. ***Right:*** THREE vertically. ***Engraver:*** PSSP. ***Comments:*** H-MA-320-G34. Similar to W-MA-850-003-G070. 18__. 1830s.

Rarity: —

$3 • W-MA-850-003-G080

Left: 3 / Reapers / 3. ***Center:*** View of State House and Boston Common. ***Right:*** 3 / 3. ***Engraver:*** New England Bank Note Co. / PSSP. ***Comments:*** H-MA-320-G38. 18__. 1830s–1850s.

Rarity: —

$3 • W-MA-850-003-G090

CC

Engraver: Rawdon, Wright, Hatch & Edson / New England Bank Note Co. ***Comments:*** H-MA-320-G42. 18__. 1850s.

Rarity: URS-5

F $175; **EF** $350; **Unc-Rem** $400; **Proof** $1,500

$3 • W-MA-850-003-G090a

Overprint: Red THREE. ***Engraver:*** Rawdon, Wright, Hatch & Edson / New England Bank Note Co. ***Comments:*** H-MA-320-G42a. Similar to W-MA-850-003-G090. 18__. 1850s.

Rarity: —

$3 • W-MA-850-003-G090b

Overprint: Red THREE. ***Engraver:*** Rawdon, Wright, Hatch & Edson / New England Bank Note Co. / ABNCo. monogram. ***Comments:*** H-MA-320-G42b. Similar to W-MA-850-003-G090 but with additional engraver imprint. 18__. 1850s–1860s.

Rarity: —

$5 • W-MA-850-005-G100

Left: Lathework chain bearing MASSACHUSETTS / 5 / 5. ***Center:*** Alternating flower garlands and gridwork segments. ***Right:*** 5 / 5. ***Engraver:*** Rawdon, Wright, Hatch & Edson / New England Bank Note Co. ***Comments:*** H-MA-320-G44. 18__. 1820s.

Rarity: —

$5 • W-MA-850-005-G100a

CC

Engraver: PSSP. ***Comments:*** H-MA-320-G46. Similar to W-MA-850-005-G100 but with zigzag, ruled lines. 18__. 1820s–1830s.

Rarity: URS-5

EF $200

$5 • W-MA-850-005-G100b

Engraver: PSSP. ***Comments:*** H-MA-320-G48. Similar to W-MA-850-005-G100 but with spiral lathework lines. 18__. 1830s.

Rarity: —

$5 • W-MA-850-005-G110

Left: 5 / Ship / 5. ***Center:*** FIVE / View of State House and Boston Common / FIVE. ***Right:*** 5 / Woman / 5. ***Engraver:*** New England Bank Note Co. / PSSP. ***Comments:*** H-MA-320-G52. 18__. 1830s–1850s.

Rarity: —

$5 • W-MA-850-005-G120

CC

Engraver: New England Bank Note Co. / PSSP. ***Comments:*** H-MA-320-G56. 18__. 1850s.

Rarity: URS-1

Proof $4,000

$5 • W-MA-850-005-G120a

Overprint: Red FIVE. ***Engraver:*** New England Bank Note Co. / PSSP. ***Comments:*** H-MA-320-G56a. Similar to W-MA-850-005-G120. 18__. 1850s.

Rarity: —

$5 • W-MA-850-005-G120b

Overprint: Red FIVE. ***Engraver:*** Rawdon, Wright, Hatch & Edson / New England Bank Note Co. / ABNCo. monogram. ***Comments:*** H-MA-320-G56b. Similar to W-MA-850-005-G120 but with additional engraver imprint. 18__. 1850s–1860s.

Rarity: —

$10 • W-MA-850-010-G130

Left: Lathework chain bearing MASSACHUSETTS / 10 / 10 vertically. ***Center:*** Alternating flower garlands and gridwork segments. ***Right:*** 10 / 10 vertically. ***Engraver:*** Perkins. ***Comments:*** H-MA-320-G58. 18__. 1820s.

Rarity: —

$10 • W-MA-850-010-G130a

Engraver: PSSP. ***Comments:*** H-MA-320-G60. Similar to W-MA-850-010-G130 but with zigzag ruled lines. 18__. 1820s–1830s.

Rarity: —

$10 • W-MA-850-010-G130b

Engraver: PSSP. ***Comments:*** H-MA-320-G62. Similar to W-MA-850-010-G130 but with spiral lathework lines. 18__. 1830s.

Rarity: —

$10 • W-MA-850-010-G140

Left: 10 / 10. ***Center:*** Ship / View of State House and Boston Common. ***Right:*** 10 / Farm tools. ***Engraver:*** New England Bank Note Co. / PSSP. ***Comments:*** H-MA-320-G66. 18__. 1830s–1850s.

Rarity: —

$10 • W-MA-850-010-G150

CC

Engraver: Rawdon, Wright, Hatch & Edson / New England Bank Note Co. ***Comments:*** H-MA-320-G70. 18__. 1850s.

Rarity: URS-1
Proof $4,000

$10 • W-MA-850-010-G150a

Overprint: Red TEN. ***Engraver:*** Rawdon, Wright, Hatch & Edson / New England Bank Note Co. ***Comments:*** H-MA-320-G70a. Similar to W-MA-850-010-G150. 18__. 1850s.

Rarity: —

$10 • W-MA-850-010-G150b

Overprint: Red TEN. ***Engraver:*** Rawdon, Wright, Hatch & Edson / New England Bank Note Co. / ABNCo. monogram. ***Comments:*** H-MA-320-G70b. Similar to W-MA-850-010-G150 but with additional engraver imprint. 18__. 1850s–1860s.

Rarity: —

$20 • W-MA-850-020-G160

Left: Lathework chain bearing MASSACHUSETTS / 20 / 20 vertically. ***Center:*** Alternating flower garlands and gridwork segments. ***Right:*** 20 / 20. ***Engraver:*** PSSP. ***Comments:*** H-MA-320-G72. 18__. 1820s–1830s.

Rarity: —

$20 • W-MA-850-020-G170

Left: 20 / XX vertically / 20. ***Center:*** 20 / Men plowing, Woman seated with scales, Sheaf and bales, Ship / 20. ***Right:*** TWENTY vertically. ***Engraver:*** PSSP / New England Bank Note Co. ***Comments:*** H-MA-320-G76. 18__. 1830s.

Rarity: —

$20 • W-MA-850-020-G180

Left: Steamboat / XX / Train. ***Center:*** Three women seated with eagle, pole and cap, shield, scales and book / 20 / Panel outlining white TWENTY. ***Right:*** XX / Milkmaid standing with pail. ***Engraver:*** New England Bank Note Co. ***Comments:*** H-MA-320-G80. Beware of altered notes from the same plate as the genuine. 18__. 1840s.

Rarity: URS-6
VG $200; **F** $400

$20 • W-MA-850-020-G190

Left: 20 / Woman seated with book on lap opening chest. ***Center:*** XX / Eagle on rock / XX. ***Right:*** 20 / Ship in harbor. ***Engraver:*** New England Bank Note Co. ***Comments:*** H-MA-320-G82. 18__. 1840s–1850s.

Rarity: —

$20 • W-MA-850-020-G200

CC

Engraver: Rawdon, Wright, Hatch & Edson / New England Bank Note Co. ***Comments:*** H-MA-320-G84. 18__. 1850s.

Rarity: URS-1
Proof $4,000

$20 • W-MA-850-020-G200a

Overprint: Red TWENTY. ***Engraver:*** Rawdon, Wright, Hatch & Edson / New England Bank Note Co. ***Comments:*** H-MA-320-G84a. Similar to W-MA-850-020-G200. 18__. 1850s.

Rarity: —

$20 • W-MA-850-020-G200b

Overprint: Red TWENTY. ***Engraver:*** American Bank Note Co. ***Comments:*** H-MA-320-G84b. Similar to W-MA-850-020-G200 but with different date and engraver imprint. Jan. 1, 1863.

Rarity: —

$20 • W-MA-850-020-G200c

Tint: Green. ***Engraver:*** American Bank Note Co. ***Comments:*** H-MA-320-G84c. Similar to W-MA-850-020-G200 but with different date and engraver imprint. Jan. 1, 1863.

Rarity: —

$50 • W-MA-850-050-G210

Left: Lathework chain bearing MASSACHUSETTS / 50 / 50 vertically. ***Center:*** Alternating flower garlands and gridwork segments. ***Right:*** 50 / 50 vertically. ***Engraver:*** PSSP. ***Comments:*** H-MA-320-G86. 18__. 1820s–1830s.

Rarity: —

$50 • W-MA-850-050-G220

Left: 50 / Cornucopia, Woman standing with ankles crossed, staff, and anchor / 50. ***Center:*** FIFTY DOLLARS, 50. ***Right:*** FIFTY vertically. ***Engraver:*** New England Bank Note Co. / PSSP. ***Comments:*** H-MA-320-G90. 18__. 1830s–1840s.

Rarity: —

$50 • W-MA-850-050-G230

CC

Engraver: Rawdon, Wright, Hatch & Edson / New England Bank Note Co. ***Comments:*** H-MA-320-G92. 18__. 1850s.

Rarity: URS-1
Proof $4,000

$50 • **W-MA-850-050-G230a**

Overprint: Red FIFTY. ***Engraver:*** Rawdon, Wright, Hatch & Edson / New England Bank Note Co. ***Comments:*** H-MA-320-G92a. Similar to W-MA-850-050-G230. 18__. 1850s.

Rarity: —

$50 • **W-MA-850-050-G230b**

Overprint: Red FIFTY. ***Engraver:*** New England Bank Note Co. ***Comments:*** H-MA-320-G92b. Similar to W-MA-850-050-G230 but with different date and engraver imprint. January 1, 1863.

Rarity: —

$50 • **W-MA-850-050-G230c**

CC

Tint: Green. ***Engraver:*** American Bank Note Co. ***Comments:*** H-MA-320-G92c. Similar to W-MA-850-050-G230 but with different date and engraver imprint. Proof. January 1, 1863.

Rarity: URS-2
Proof $3,000

$100 • **W-MA-850-100-G240**

Left: Lathework chain bearing MASSACHUSETTS / 100 / 100 vertically. ***Center:*** Alternating flower garlands and gridwork segments. ***Right:*** 100 / 100 vertically. ***Engraver:*** Perkins. ***Comments:*** H-MA-320-G94. 18__. 1820s–1830s.

Rarity: —

$100 • **W-MA-850-100-G250**

Left: Lathework panel bearing C / Portrait of George Washington / C. ***Center:*** 100 / Manhattan reclining, pouring water, Ship / 100. ***Right:*** Lathework panel bearing ONE HUNDRED vertically. ***Engraver:*** New England Bank Note Co. / PSSP. ***Comments:*** H-MA-320-G98. 18__. 1830s–1840s.

Rarity: —

$100 • **W-MA-850-100-G260**

CC

Engraver: Rawdon, Wright, Hatch & Edson / New England Bank Note Co. ***Comments:*** H-MA-320-G102. 18__. 1850s.

Rarity: URS-1
Proof $4,000

$100 • **W-MA-850-100-G260a**

Overprint: Red HUNDRED. ***Engraver:*** Rawdon, Wright, Hatch & Edson / New England Bank Note Co. ***Comments:*** H-MA-320-G102a. Similar to W-MA-850-100-G260. 18__. 1850s.

Rarity: —

$100 • **W-MA-850-100-G260b**

CC

Overprint: Red HUNDRED. ***Engraver:*** American Bank Note Co. ***Comments:*** H-MA-320-G102b. Similar to W-MA-850-100-G260 but with different date and engraver imprint. January 1, 1863.

Rarity: URS-4
F $750; **VF** $1,000

$100 • **W-MA-850-100-G260c**

CC

Tint: Green. ***Engraver:*** American Bank Note Co. ***Comments:*** H-MA-320-G102c. Similar to W-MA-850-100-G260 but with different date and engraver imprint. Proof. January 1, 1863.

Rarity: URS-4
Proof $4,000

$500 • **W-MA-850-500-G270**

Left: 500 / 500 / 500. ***Center:*** 500 / Woman seated with shield bearing D, Fasces, cornucopia, lyre, and sheaf on ground / 500. ***Right:*** 500 / D / 500. ***Engraver:*** PSSP / New England Bank Note Co. ***Comments:*** H-MA-320-G106. 18__. 1830s–1840s.

Rarity: —

$500 • **W-MA-850-500-G280**

CC

Engraver: American Bank Note Co. ***Comments:*** H-Unlisted. 18__. 1850s–1860s.

Rarity: URS-1
Proof $6,000

$500 • **W-MA-850-500-G280a**
Tint: Green. ***Engraver:*** American Bank Note Co. ***Comments:*** H-MA-320-G110. Similar to W-MA-850-500-G280. 18__. 1850s–1860s.

Rarity: —

$1,000 • **W-MA-850-1000-G290**
Left: THOUSAND vertically. ***Center:*** 1000 / Woman standing with legs crossed and lyre, Cornucopia / 1000. ***Right:*** 1000 / M / 1000. ***Engraver:*** PSSP / New England Bank Note Co. ***Comments:*** H-MA-320-G114. 18__. 1830s–1840s.

Rarity: —

$1,000 • **W-MA-850-1000-G300** CC

Engraver: American Bank Note Co. ***Comments:*** H-Unlisted. 18__. 1850s–1860s.

Rarity: URS-1
Proof $7,500

$1,000 • **W-MA-850-1000-G300a**
Tint: Green. ***Engraver:*** American Bank Note Co. ***Comments:*** H-MA-320-G118. Similar to W-MA-850-1000-G300. 18__. 1850s–1860s.

Rarity: —

Uncut Sheets

$50-$100 • **W-MA-850-050.100-US010** HA

Tint(s): Green. ***Engraver:*** American Bank Note Co. ***Comments:*** H-MA-320-G92c, G102c. January 1, 1863.

Rarity: URS-1
Proof $6,500

Non-Valid Issues

$5 • **W-MA-850-005-C100b**
Engraver: PSSP. ***Comments:*** H-MA-320-C48. Counterfeit of W-MA-850-005-G100b. 18__. 1830s.

Rarity: —

$5 • **W-MA-850-005-R010**
Engraver: New England Bank Note Co. / PSSP. ***Comments:*** H-MA-320-R5. Raised from W-MA-850-001-G020. 18__. 1840s.

Rarity: —

$5 • **W-MA-850-005-R020**
Overprint: Red FIVE. ***Engraver:*** Rawdon, Wright, Hatch & Edson / New England Bank Note Co. / ABNCo. monogram. ***Comments:*** H-MA-320-R10. Raised from W-MA-850-001-G030b. 18__. 1860s.

Rarity: URS-3
VG $200

$10 • **W-MA-850-010-R030**
Engraver: New England Bank Note Co. / PSSP. ***Comments:*** H-MA-320-R15. Raised from W-MA-850-002-G050. 18__. 1850s.

Rarity: —

$20 • **W-MA-850-020-R040**
Engraver: New England Bank Note Co. / PSSP. ***Comments:*** H-MA-320-R25. Raised from W-MA-850-002-G050. 18__. 1850s.

Rarity: —

$20 • **W-MA-850-020-A010** CC

Engraver: New England Bank Note Co. ***Comments:*** H-MA-320-A10. Altered from $20 Hamilton Bank, Scituate, Rhode Island, or from notes of other failed banks using the same plate. Genuine notes of this design were used. 18__. 1840s.

Rarity: URS-6
F $350

$50 • **W-MA-850-050-R050**
Engraver: New England Bank Note Co. / PSSP. ***Comments:*** H-MA-320-R30. Raised from W-MA-850-001-G020. 18__. 1840s.

Rarity: —

Collectors and Researchers:

If you have new information about any banks or notes listed in this volume, contact Whitman Publishing, Attn: Obsolete Paper Money, 3101 Clairmont Road, Suite G, Atlanta, GA 30329.

$50 • W-MA-850-050-R060

Engraver: New England Bank Note Co. / PSSP. ***Comments:*** H-MA-320-R35. Raised from W-MA-850-002-G050. 18__. 1850s.

Rarity: —

$100 • W-MA-850-100-C260b

Left: 100 / Woman. ***Center:*** Woman seated with portrait of Benjamin Franklin / HUNDRED. ***Right:*** Woman standing with staff / 100. ***Engraver:*** American Bank Note Co. ***Comments:*** H-MA-320-C102b. Counterfeit of W-MA-850-100-G260b. Jan. 1, 1863.

Rarity: URS-3
VF $300

$100 • W-MA-850-100-R070

Engraver: New England Bank Note Co. / PSSP. ***Comments:*** H-MA-320-R40. Raised from W-MA-850-001-G020. 18__. 1840s.

Rarity: —

$500 • W-MA-850-500-C280a

Engraver: American Bank Note Co. ***Comments:*** H-MA-320-C110. Counterfeit of W-MA-850-500-G280a. 18__. Circa 1860.

Rarity: —

$500 • W-MA-850-500-R080

Engraver: New England Bank Note Co. / PSSP. ***Comments:*** H-MA-320-R45. Raised from W-MA-850-001-G020. 18__. 1840s.

Rarity: —

Oriental Bank

1831–1838

W-MA-860

History: The Oriental Bank was incorporated on June 23, 1831. Its office was at 61 Kilby Street. By 1837 the bank was at 88 State Street. Capital began at the amount of $750,000, but later dropped to $500,000. In early 1838 the shareholders voted to surrender the charter and close the business.[67]

Numismatic Commentary: Notes from this bank have always been hard to locate. Most seen are unsigned remainders.

Valid Issues

$1 • W-MA-860-001-G010

Left: Lathework panel bearing MASSACHUSETTS vertically. ***Center:*** 1 / 1 / Alternating flower garlands and gridwork segments / ONE / 1 / 1. ***Right:*** Lathework panel bearing ONE / D / ONE vertically. ***Engraver:*** PSSP. ***Comments:*** H-MA-330-G2. 18__. 1830s.

Rarity: —

$1 • W-MA-860-001-G020

Left: 1 / Ship / ONE. ***Center:*** Woman leaning against shield holding sheaf / Farm scene with ONE / Plow with ONE. ***Right:*** 1 / Plow and tree / ONE. ***Engraver:*** New England Bank Note Co. / PSSP. ***Comments:*** H-MA-330-G4. 18__. 1830s.

Rarity: URS-3
Proof $1,250

$1 • W-MA-860-001-G020a

Back: Check Plate. ***Engraver:*** New England Bank Note Co. / PSSP. ***Comments:*** H-MA-330-G4a. Similar to W-MA-860-001-G020. 18__. 1830s.

Rarity: —

$1.25 • W-MA-860-001.25-G030

Left: 1 25/100 / Train / 1 25/100. ***Center:*** Sloop and other ships at sea / $1 25 cts. ***Right:*** 1 25/100 / Eagle. ***Engraver:*** New England Bank Note Co. ***Comments:*** H-MA-330-G6. 18__. 1830s.

Rarity: —

$1.50 • W-MA-860-001.50-G040

CJF

Engraver: New England Bank Note Co. ***Comments:*** H-MA-330-G8. 18__. 1830s.

Rarity: URS-1
F $2,000

$1.75 • W-MA-860-001.75-G050

Left: $1.75 Cts / Hebe watering eagle / 1 75/100. ***Center:*** Three sloops at sea. ***Right:*** $1.75 Cts. / Dog, Woman seated with grain / 1 75/100. ***Engraver:*** New England Bank Note Co. ***Comments:*** H-MA-330-G10. 18__. 1830s.

Rarity: —

$2 • W-MA-860-002-G060

Left: Lathework panel bearing MASSACHUSETTS vertically. ***Center:*** 2 / 2 / Alternating flower garlands and gridwork segments / TWO / 2 / 2. ***Right:*** Lathework panel bearing five TWOs vertically. ***Engraver:*** PSSP. ***Comments:*** H-MA-330-G12. 18__. 1830s.

Rarity: —

$2 • W-MA-860-002-G070

Left: Woman holding bag and staff, Wreath, ONE with swan. ***Center:*** 2 / Indian standing / 2. ***Right:*** Wreath / Woman seated / ONE with swan. ***Engraver:*** New England Bank Note Co. / PSSP. ***Comments:*** H-MA-330-G14. 18__. 1830s.

Rarity: URS-3
F $1,000; **Proof** $1,250

$2 • W-MA-860-002-G070a

Back: Check Plate. ***Engraver:*** New England Bank Note Co. / PSSP. ***Comments:*** H-MA-330-G14a. Similar to W-MA-860-002-G070. 18__. 1830s.

Rarity: —

$3 • W-MA-860-003-G080

Left: Lathework panel bearing MASSACHUSETTS vertically. ***Center:*** 3 / 3 / Alternating flower garlands and gridwork segments / THREE / 3 / 3. ***Right:*** Lathework panel bearing THREE vertically. ***Engraver:*** PSSP. ***Comments:*** H-MA-330-G16. 18__. 1830s.

Rarity: —

$3 • W-MA-860-003-G090

HA

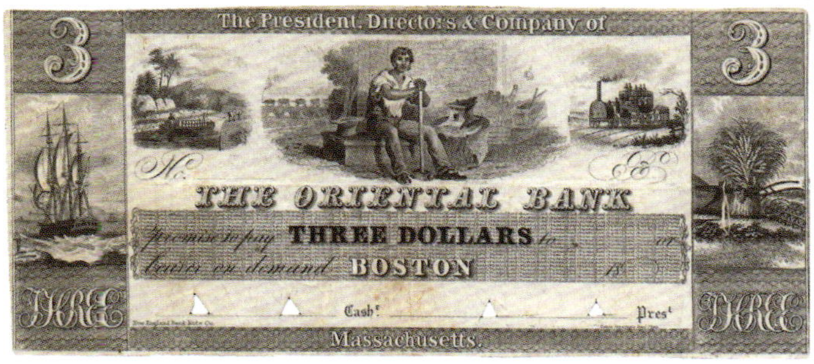

Back: Plain. ***Engraver:*** New England Bank Note Co. / PSSP. ***Comments:*** H-MA-330-G18. Remainder. 18__. 1830s.

Rarity: URS-2
Proof $1,000

$3 • W-MA-860-003-G090a

Left: 3 / Ship / THREE. ***Center:*** Canal / Mechanic seated / Train. ***Right:*** 3 / Sheaf / THREE. ***Back:*** Check Plate. ***Engraver:*** New England Bank Note Co. / PSSP. ***Comments:*** H-MA-330-G18a. Similar to W-MA-860-003-G090. 18__. 1830s.

Rarity: —

$5 • W-MA-860-005-G100

Left: Lathework chain bearing MASSACHUSETTS / 5 / 5. ***Center:*** Alternating flower garlands and gridwork segments / FIVE DOLLARS with spiral lathework lines. ***Right:*** 5 / 5. ***Engraver:*** PSSP. ***Comments:*** H-MA-330-G20. 18__. 1830s.

Rarity: —

$5 • W-MA-860-005-G110

Left: Eagle / FIVE. ***Center:*** 5 / Steamboat / 5. ***Right:*** Statue of George Washington. ***Back:*** Plain. ***Engraver:*** New England Bank Note Co. / PSSP. ***Comments:*** H-MA-330-G22. 18__. 1830s.

Rarity: URS-3
Proof $1,000

$5 • W-MA-860-005-G110a

Back: Check Plate. ***Engraver:*** New England Bank Note Co. / PSSP. ***Comments:*** H-MA-330-G22a. Similar to W-MA-860-005-G110. 18__. 1830s.

Rarity: —

$10 • W-MA-860-010-G120

Left: Lathework chain bearing MASSACHUSETTS / 10 / 10 vertically. ***Center:*** Alternating flower garlands and gridwork segments / TEN DOLLARS with spiral lathework lines. ***Right:*** 10 / 10 vertically. ***Engraver:*** PSSP. ***Comments:*** H-MA-330-G24. 18__. 1830s.

Rarity: —

$10 • W-MA-860-010-G130

Back: Plain. ***Engraver:*** New England Bank Note Co. / PSSP. ***Comments:*** H-MA-330-G26. 18__. 1830s.

Rarity: —

$10 • W-MA-860-010-G130a

Back: Check Plate. ***Engraver:*** New England Bank Note Co. / PSSP. ***Comments:*** H-MA-330-G26a. Similar to W-MA-860-010-G130. 18__. 1830s.

Rarity: —

$20 • W-MA-860-020-G140

Left: Lathework chain bearing MASSACHUSETTS / 20 / 20 vertically. ***Center:*** Alternating flower garlands and gridwork segments. ***Right:*** 20 / 20 vertically. ***Engraver:*** PSSP. ***Comments:*** H-MA-330-G28. 18__. 1830s.

Rarity: —

$20 • W-MA-860-020-G150

Back: Plain. ***Engraver:*** New England Bank Note Co. / PSSP. ***Comments:*** H-MA-330-G30. 18__. 1830s.

Rarity: —

$20 • W-MA-860-020-G150a

Back: Check Plate. ***Engraver:*** New England Bank Note Co. / PSSP. ***Comments:*** H-MA-330-G30a. Similar to W-MA-860-020-G150. 18__. 1830s.

Rarity: —

$50 • W-MA-860-050-G160

Left: Lathework chain bearing MASSACHUSETTS / 50 / 50 vertically. ***Center:*** Alternating flower garlands and gridwork segments. ***Right:*** 50 / 50 vertically. ***Engraver:*** PSSP. ***Comments:*** H-MA-330-G32. 18__. 1830s.

Rarity: —

$50 • W-MA-860-050-G170

Left: 50 / Cornucopia, Woman standing with ankles crossed and staff, Anchor / 50. ***Center:*** FIFTY DOLLARS / 50. ***Right:*** FIFTY vertically. ***Engraver:*** New England Bank Note Co. / PSSP. ***Comments:*** H-MA-330-G34. 18__. 1830s.

Rarity: —

$100 • W-MA-860-100-G180

Left: Lathework chain bearing MASSACHUSETTS / 100 / 100 vertically. ***Center:*** Alternating flower garlands and gridwork segments. ***Right:*** 100 / 100 vertically. ***Engraver:*** Perkins. ***Comments:*** H-MA-330-G36. 18__. 1830s.

Rarity: —

$100 • W-MA-860-100-G190

Left: Lathework panel bearing C / Portrait of George Washington / C. ***Center:*** 100 / Manhattan reclining, pouring water, Ship / 100. ***Right:*** Lathework panel bearing ONE HUNDRED vertically. ***Engraver:*** New England Bank Note Co. / PSSP. ***Comments:*** H-MA-330-G38. 18__. 1830s.

Rarity: —

$500 • W-MA-860-500-G200

Left: 500 / 500 / 500. ***Center:*** 500 / Woman seated with right arm on shield bearing D, Fasces, cornucopia, lyre, and sheaf on ground / 500. ***Right:*** 500 / D / 500. ***Engraver:*** PSSP / New England Bank Note Co. ***Comments:*** H-MA-330-G42. 18__. 1830s.

Rarity: —

$1,000 • W-MA-860-1000-G210

Left: THOUSAND vertically. ***Center:*** 1000 / Woman standing with legs crossed and lyre, Cornucopia / 1000. ***Right:*** 1000 / M / 1000. ***Engraver:*** PSSP / New England Bank Note Co. ***Comments:*** H-MA-330-G46. 18__. 1830s.

Rarity: —

Uncut Sheets

$5-$5-$10-$20 • W-MA-860-005.005.010.020-US010

Engraver: Danforth, Underwood, Bald & Spencer. ***Comments:*** All unlisted in Haxby. Vignettes for notes which were never issued.

Rarity: —

Non-Valid Issues

$2 • W-MA-860-002-C060

CC

Engraver: PSSP. ***Comments:*** H-MA-330-C12. Counterfeit of W-MA-860-002-G060. 18__. 1832.

Rarity: URS-6
VG $100; **VF** $175

$3 • W-MA-860-003-C080

Engraver: PSSP. ***Comments:*** H-MA-330-C16. Counterfeit of W-MA-860-003-G080. 18__. 1830s.

Rarity: —

Pawners Bank
1860–1869
W-MA-875

History: The Pawners Bank was organized on November 30, 1859, and opened for business on January 2, 1860. As reported by the *Banker's Magazine*, the inception of the Pawners Bank was established as an institution for the poor, based on the "Mont de Piete" Banks of Charity in Paris, France. The *Boston Traveller* gave the following description of the means of business for the company:

> This bank will loan money on all goods and chattels at the rate of one and a half percent per month, which includes the cost of storage, insurance, etc.[68]

In 1860 the capital stock was $74,700. The bank was considered beneficial as it engaged in pawnbrokering, essentially, but at cheaper rates. Cash on hand was $1,204.27, and total resources were $76,266.81.[69] In 1866 the capital was listed at $113,500, unclaimed dividends were $940, and the total amount due from the bank was $123,166.21.[70]

The bank closed up its affairs and became known as the Collateral Loan Company in 1869.

Revere Bank
1859–1865
W-MA-890

History: The Revere Bank was established under the provisions of the Act of 1851, otherwise known as the Free Banking Law. The capital in 1859 was $1,000,000. Its office was at 74 Franklin Street.

Circulation in 1859 amounted to $97,182, rising to $200,538. By 1861 it was back down to $115,293.

Other figures for 1859 were: bills of this bank and other New England states $85,615; specie $95,222.36. In 1861 specie had dropped to $81,005.17.

The business of the Revere Bank was succeeded by the National Bank of Boston, chartered on June 16, 1865.

Numismatic Commentary: All issues have an engraving of Paul Revere.

Valid Issues

$1 • W-MA-890-001-G010

HA

Tint: Green. ***Engraver:*** American Bank Note Co. ***Comments:*** H-MA-340-G2a. June 1, 18__. 1859–1860s.

Rarity: URS-4
F $1,000; **VF** $1,500

$2 • W-MA-890-002-G020

JF

Tint: Red. ***Engraver:*** American Bank Note Co. ***Comments:*** H-MA-340-G4a. June 1, 18__. 1859–1860s.

Rarity: URS-4
F $2,500

$3 • W-MA-890-003-G030

Left: 3 / Portrait of sailor boy. ***Center:*** Steamship, sailboats, and steamboat, City. ***Right:*** 3 / State arms. ***Tint:*** Likely green. ***Engraver:*** American Bank Note Co. ***Comments:*** H-MA-340-G6a. June 1, 18__. 1859–1860s.

Rarity: —

$3 • W-MA-890-003-G030a

CC

Tint: Red. *Engraver:* American Bank Note Co. *Comments:* H-Unlisted. Similar to W-MA-890-003-G030. June 1, 18__. 1859–1860s.

Rarity: URS-3
F $1,500

$5 • W-MA-890-005-G040

SBG

Tint: Red. *Engraver:* American Bank Note Co. *Comments:* H-MA-340-G8a. June 1, 18__. 1859–1860s.

Rarity: URS-3
F $3,000

Selected auction price(s): Heritage, January 2011, Lot 15545, VF $2,990; Stack's Bowers Galleries, August 2012, Lot 7130, Choice F-VF $2,760

$10 • W-MA-890-010-G050

Left: 10 / State arms. *Center:* Men at work in iron foundry. *Right:* 10 / Portrait of Paul Revere. *Tint:* Likely green. *Engraver:* American Bank Note Co. *Comments:* H-MA-340-G10. June 1, 18__. 1859–1860s.

Rarity: —

$20 • W-MA-890-020-G060

Left: 20 / State arms. *Center:* Text / 20 Dolls. *Right:* 20 / Portrait of Paul Revere. *Engraver:* American Bank Note Co. *Comments:* H-MA-340-G12a. June 1, 18__. 1859–1860s.

Rarity: URS-2
Proof $10,000

Selected auction price: Stack's Bowers Galleries, August 2014, Lot 2067, Proof $10,575

$50 • W-MA-890-050-G070

Left: 50 / State arms. *Center:* Portrait of Paul Revere. *Right:* 50 / Sailor seated and mechanic standing, Shipping. *Tint:* Red L / L. *Engraver:* American Bank Note Co. *Comments:* H-MA-340-G14a. June 1, 18__. 1859–1860s.

Rarity: —

$100 • W-MA-890-100-G080

HA

Tint: Red. *Engraver:* American Bank Note Co. *Comments:* H-MA-340-G16a. Proof. June 1, 18__. 1859–1860s.

Rarity: URS-2
Proof $12,500

$500 • W-MA-890-500-G090

Left: State arms. *Center:* Hogshead, bales, rope, masts, Shipping. *Right:* 500 / Portrait of Paul Revere. *Tint:* Red 500. *Engraver:* American Bank Note Co. *Comments:* H-MA-340-G18a. June 1, 18__. 1859–1860s.

Rarity: URS-1
Proof $17,500

Non-Valid Issues

$2 • W-MA-890-002-A010

Left: 2 / Farmer plowing with black and white horses. *Center:* Two men loading wagon with sheaves, Three men cradling and binding. *Right:* 2 / Two floating cherubs with caduceus and sheaf. *Tint:* Red-brown 2s and TWO DOLLARS. *Engraver:* Danforth, Wright & Co. *Comments:* H-MA-340-A5. Altered from $2 Southern Bank of Georgia, Bainbridge, Georgia. March 1, 1858.

Rarity: —

Safety Fund Bank
1857–1864
W-MA-900

History: The Safety Fund Bank was established in February 1857 under the provisions of the Act of 1851, also known as the Free Banking Law. It was located at 41 State Street and had a capital of $1,000,000. By 1858 the same had been decreased to $600,000. Bills in circulation ranged from $89,980 in 1858 to $115,914 in 1860. By 1861 it had increased to $180,411.

Other figures for 1857 included: bills of this bank and other New England states $88,960.42; specie $68,769.58; real estate $64,348.51. The figures recorded in 1858 were much lower: real estate $8,222.49; specie $7,412.94. By 1861 the amount of specie had skyrocketed to $117,276.31. In 1863 the directors of the bank were the first in the state to gain a charter under the National Banking Act. The First National Bank of Boston was chartered on February 1, 1864, and succeeded the interests of the state bank.

Numismatic Commentary: Genuine notes are particularly hard to locate. In the second decade of the 21st century, punch-canceled notes made their way into the marketplace, increasing the supply.

VALID ISSUES

$1 • W-MA-900-001-G010

Left: Three women bathing and cherub / ONE. ***Center:*** 1 / ONE. ***Right:*** 1 / State arms. ***Overprint:*** Red. ***Engraver:*** American Bank Note Co. ***Comments:*** H-MA-345-G2a. 18__. 1859–1860s.

Rarity: URS-3
F $800

$1 • W-MA-900-001-G010a

Overprint: Green 1 and panel outlining white ONE. ***Engraver:*** American Bank Note Co. ***Comments:*** H-MA-345-G2b. Similar to W-MA-900-001-G010. 18__. 1860s.

Rarity: URS-3
F $800

$2 • W-MA-900-002-G020

Left: 1 / Woman. ***Center:*** Dr. Kane's Arctic Expedition / TWO. ***Right:*** 2 / State arms. ***Overprint:*** Red. ***Engraver:*** American Bank Note Co. ***Comments:*** H-MA-345-G4a. 18__. 1859–1860s.

Rarity: —

$2 • W-MA-900-002-G020a

HA

Overprint: Green panel outlining white TWO. ***Engraver:*** American Bank Note Co. ***Comments:*** H-MA-345-G4b. Similar to W-MA-900-002-G020. 18__. 1860s.

Rarity: URS-3
F $1,250; **VF** $1,750
Selected auction price: Heritage, January 2013, Lot 15817, VF $1,116

$3 • W-MA-900-003-G030

Left: THREE on 3 / Bird. ***Center:*** Three men and wagon wheels / Eagle / THREE. ***Right:*** 3 / State arms / 3. ***Overprint:*** Red. ***Engraver:*** American Bank Note Co. ***Comments:*** H-MA-345-G6a. 18__. 1859–1860s.

Rarity: —

$3 • W-MA-900-003-G030a

Overprint: Green panel outlining THREE. ***Engraver:*** American Bank Note Co. ***Comments:*** H-MA-345-G6b. Similar to W-MA-900-003-G030. 18__. 1860s.

Rarity: URS-3
F $1,000

$5 • W-MA-900-005-G040

Left: State arms / 5. ***Center:*** Soldier and Liberty showing portrait of George Washington to two Indians. ***Right:*** 5 / Dog and strongbox. ***Engraver:*** American Bank Note Co. ***Comments:*** H-MA-345-G8. 18__. 1859.

Rarity: URS-4
Unc-Rem $500

$5 • W-MA-900-005-G040a

TD

Overprint: Red V / V. ***Engraver:*** American Bank Note Co. ***Comments:*** H-MA-345-G8a. Similar to W-MA-900-005-G040. 18__. 1859–1860s.

Rarity: URS-4
VF $1,250

$5 • W-MA-900-005-G040b

CC

Overprint: Green 5 / 5. ***Engraver:*** American Bank Note Co. ***Comments:*** H-MA-345-G8b. Similar to W-MA-900-005-G040. 18__. 1860s.

Rarity: URS-3
VF $1,100
Selected auction price: Heritage, January 2013, Lot 15818, VF $1,057

How to Read the Whitman Numbering System

$1 • W-MA-010-001-G010a

Denomination: Value of the note shown.

W: Whitman number. This number is a sortable code unique to each bank and note.

MA: Abbreviation for the state under study.

010: Numerical designation specific to each bank.

001: The denomination in dollars.

G010a: G indicates a good or valid note. Other categories are indicated thus: C (counterfeit); R (raised); S (spurious); N (not-attributed); A (altered). Numbers are assigned starting with 010, 020, et seq. Terminal letters following the number indicate variations of a note: a series of different colored overprints, tints, payees, etc., all on the same design of note. For more information, see the "How to Use This Book" section at the front of the volume, page xiv.

$10 • W-MA-900-010-G050

CC

Engraver: American Bank Note Co. ***Comments:*** H-MA-345-G10. Proof. 18__. 1860s.

Rarity: URS-4
Unc-Rem $700

$10 • W-MA-900-010-G050a

CC

Overprint: Green TEN. ***Engraver:*** American Bank Note Co. ***Comments:*** H-MA-345-G10b. Similar to W-MA-900-010-G050. 18__. 1860s.

Rarity: URS-4
Unc-Rem $900

$20 • W-MA-900-020-G060

CC

Engraver: American Bank Note Co. ***Comments:*** H-Unlisted. Proof. 18__. 1860s.

Rarity: URS-5
F $200; **EF** $350; **AU** $500

$20 • W-MA-900-020-G060a

Left: 20 / State arms vertically. ***Center:*** Woman with cap and pole / Two women / TWENTY. ***Right:*** 20 / Portrait of Henry Clay. ***Overprint:*** Green TWENTY. ***Engraver:*** American Bank Note Co. ***Comments:*** H-MA-345-G12b. Similar to W-MA-900-020-G060. 18__. 1860s.

Rarity: URS-3
VF $700

$50 • W-MA-900-050-G070

CC

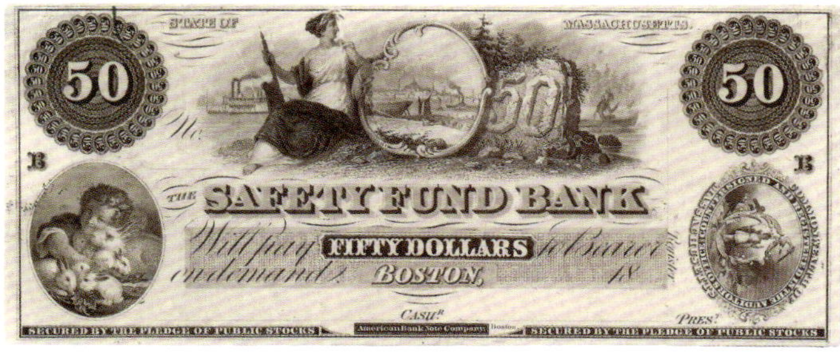

Engraver: American Bank Note Co. ***Comments:*** H-Unlisted. Proof. 18__. 1860s.

Rarity: URS-3
Unc-Rem $1,400

$50 • W-MA-900-050-G070a

Left: 50 / Portrait of child with rabbits. ***Center:*** Woman next to frame and rock. ***Right:*** 50 / State arms vertically. ***Overprint:*** Green FIFTY. ***Engraver:*** American Bank Note Co. ***Comments:*** H-MA-345-G14b. Similar to W-MA-900-050-G070. 18__. 1860s.

Rarity: URS-4
EF $1,000; **Unc-S&D** $1,500

$100 • W-MA-900-100-G080

CC

Engraver: American Bank Note Co. ***Comments:*** H-Unlisted. Proof. 18__. 1860s.

Rarity: URS-2
Unc-Rem $1,700

$100 • W-MA-900-100-G080a

Left: C / State arms vertically. ***Center:*** Four women. ***Right:*** 100 / Portrait of Daniel Webster. ***Overprint:*** Green C C. ***Engraver:*** American Bank Note Co. ***Comments:*** H-MA-345-G16b. Similar to W-MA-900-100-G080. 18__. 1860s.

Rarity: URS-3
Unc-S&D $1,750

$500 • W-MA-900-500-G090

Left: 500 / Woman seated with globe. ***Center:*** State arms / 500. ***Right:*** 500 / Man seated with boy and bust of George Washington. ***Engraver:*** American Bank Note Co. ***Comments:*** H-MA-345-G18a. 18__. 1860s.

Rarity: URS-3
VF $1,750

Uncut Sheets

$10-$20-$50-$100 • W-MA-900-010.020.050.100-US010

CJF

Comments: H-MA-345-G10, H-Unlisted, H-Unlisted, H-Unlisted. 18__. 1860s.

Rarity: URS-3
Unc-Rem $2,500

Non-Valid Issues

$1 • W-MA-900-001-A010

Left: 1 / Milkmaid seated with pail. ***Center:*** Two cows, one lying down and one standing, Horse and cows. ***Bottom center:*** Obverse of U.S. gold dollar. ***Right:*** ONE / Girl / 1. ***Overprint:*** Red ONE. ***Engraver:*** Wellstood, Hay & Whiting. ***Comments:*** H-MA-345-A5. Altered from $1 Thames Bank, Laurel, Indiana. 1850s.

Rarity: —

$2 • W-MA-900-002-A020

Left: 2 / Man carrying basket of cotton. ***Center:*** TWO on die. ***Right:*** 2 / Cornucopia, Woman reclining. ***Comments:*** H-MA-345-A10. Altered from $2 Bank of Greensborough, Georgia, series. 1850s.

Rarity: —

$2 • W-MA-900-002-A030

SI

Overprint: Red TWO. ***Engraver:*** Wellstood, Hay & Whiting. ***Comments:*** H-MA-345-A15. Altered from $2 Thames Bank, Laurel, Indiana. August 12, 1856.

Rarity: URS-7
F $100

$2 • W-MA-900-002-A040

CC

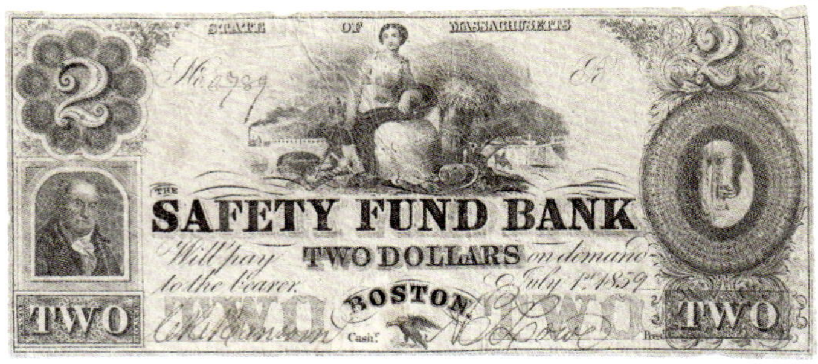

Engraver: Doty & Bergen. ***Comments:*** H-MA-345-A20. Altered from $2 Delaware City Bank, Delaware, Kansas. July 1, 185_. 1850s.

Rarity: URS-7
F $100

$5 • W-MA-900-005-A050

Left: Portrait of Henry Clay / V. ***Center:*** Train. ***Bottom center:*** Dog lying down. ***Right:*** 5 / Farmer carrying basket of corn. ***Overprint:*** Red FIVE. ***Engraver:*** Wellstood, Hay & Whiting. ***Comments:*** H-MA-345-A25. Altered from $5 Thames Bank, Laurel, Indiana, with center vignette changed. 1850s.

Rarity: URS-7
F $75

$20 • W-MA-900-020-A060

Left: 20 / Woman seated, resting right arm and scroll on chest. ***Center:*** Indian woman reclining on cliff, gazing at canal locks and distant city. ***Right:*** 20 / Train. ***Overprint:*** Red TWENTY. ***Engraver:*** Danforth, Bald & Co. ***Comments:*** H-MA-345-A30. Altered from $20 Columbia Bank, Washington, D.C. 1850s.

Rarity: —

Shawmut Bank

1836–1864

W-MA-910

History: The Shawmut Bank was formerly the Warren Bank, W-MA-1020. It was chartered and incorporated in April 1836 and was located at 39 State Street. In June 1838, the bank had $500,000 capital paid in with a circulation of $89,399. Capital was raised to $750,000 in 1854. Bills in circulation amounted to $83,660 as of November 1839. In 1845 the total was $175,812.

Other figures for 1838 included: net profits on hand $16,392.08; balances due to other banks $26,768.39; cash deposited $67,566.71; cash deposited bearing interest $36,000; total amount due from banks $736,356.18; gold, silver, and other coined metals in the banking house $17,470.79; bills of other banks incorporated in this state $21,357; balance due from other banks $8,166.33; amount of all debts due $689,362.06; total amount of resources of the bank $736,356.18. The bank was succeeded by the Shawmut National Bank of Boston on November 22, 1864. Later this entity changed its name to the National Shawmut Bank of Boston on November 25, 1898.

Numismatic Commentary: All genuine issues show a vignette of an Indian, presumably Chief Obbatinewat. Some notes will show a smaller engraving of Merchant's Row and the Warren Bank building. All issues are extremely hard to locate.

Valid Issues

$1 • W-MA-910-001-G010

Left: ONE / View of Merchants Row / 1. ***Center:*** Indian man seated on shore, viewing ship. ***Bottom center:*** Boat and men. ***Right:*** 1 / View of Boston Harbor / ONE. ***Engraver:*** Terry, Pelton & Co. ***Comments:*** H-MA-350-G2. 18__. 1830s–1850s.

Rarity: —

$1 • W-MA-910-001-G010a

Overprint: Red ONE. ***Engraver:*** Terry, Pelton & Co. ***Comments:*** H-MA-350-G2a. Similar to W-MA-910-001-G010. 18__. 1850s.

Rarity: —

$1 • W-MA-910-001-G010b

CC

Overprint: Red ONE. ***Engraver:*** Terry, Pelton & Co. / ABNCo. monogram. ***Comments:*** H-MA-350-G2b. Similar to W-MA-910-001-G010 but with additional engraver imprint. 18__. 1850s–1860s.

Rarity: URS-4
F $1,250

$2 • W-MA-910-002-G020

Left: 2 / View of Merchants Row / TWO. ***Center:*** Indian man seated on shore, viewing ship. ***Bottom center:*** Men in boat. ***Right:*** 2 / View of Boston from the harbor / TWO. ***Engraver:*** Terry, Pelton & Co. ***Comments:*** H-MA-350-G4. 18__. 1830s–1850s.

Rarity: —

$2 • W-MA-910-002-G020a

Overprint: Red TWO. ***Engraver:*** Terry, Pelton & Co. ***Comments:*** H-MA-350-G4a. Similar to W-MA-910-002-G020. 18__. 1850s.

Rarity: —

$2 • W-MA-910-002-G020b

Overprint: Red TWO. ***Engraver:*** Terry, Pelton & Co. / ABNCo. monogram. ***Comments:*** H-MA-350-G4b. Similar to W-MA-910-002-G020 but with additional engraver imprint. 18__. 1850s–1860s.

Rarity: —

$3 • W-MA-910-003-G030

Left: THREE / View of Boston from the Harbor / THREE. ***Center:*** Indian man seated on shore, viewing ship. ***Bottom center:*** Eagle. ***Right:*** 3 / View of Merchants Row. ***Engraver:*** Terry, Pelton & Co. ***Comments:*** H-MA-350-G6. 18__. 1830s–1850s.

Rarity: —

$3 • W-MA-910-003-G030a

CC

Overprint: Red THREE. ***Engraver:*** Terry, Pelton & Co. ***Comments:*** H-MA-350-G6a. Similar to W-MA-910-003-G030. 18__. 1850s.

Rarity: —

$3 • W-MA-910-003-G030b

Overprint: Red THREE. ***Engraver:*** Terry, Pelton & Co. / ABNCo. monogram. ***Comments:*** H-MA-350-G6b. Similar to W-MA-910-003-G030 but with additional engraver imprint. 18__. 1850s–1860s.

Rarity: URS-3
F $1,200

$5 • W-MA-910-005-G040

Left: 5 / View of Boston from the harbor / FIVE. ***Center:*** Indian man seated on shore, viewing ship. ***Bottom center:*** Anchor. ***Right:*** 5 / View of Merchants Row. ***Engraver:*** Terry, Pelton & Co. ***Comments:*** H-MA-350-G8. 18__. 1830s–1850s.

Rarity: —

$5 • W-MA-910-005-G040a

Overprint: Red FIVE. ***Engraver:*** Terry, Pelton & Co. ***Comments:*** H-MA-350-G8a. Similar to W-MA-910-005-G040. 18__. 1850s.

Rarity: —

$5 • W-MA-910-005-G040b

Overprint: Red FIVE. ***Engraver:*** Terry, Pelton & Co. / ABNCo. monogram. ***Comments:*** H-MA-350-G8b. Similar to W-MA-910-005-G040 but with additional engraver imprint. 18__. 1850s–1860s.

Rarity: —

$10 • W-MA-910-010-G050

Left: 10 / View of Boston Harbor / 10. ***Center:*** Indian seated looking at cliff / 10. ***Right:*** 10 / View of Merchants Row / 10. ***Engraver:*** Terry, Pelton & Co. ***Comments:*** H-MA-350-G10. 18__. 1830s–1850s.

Rarity: URS-3
Proof $800

$10 • W-MA-910-010-G050a

CC

Overprint: Red TEN. ***Engraver:*** Terry, Pelton & Co. ***Comments:*** H-MA-350-G10a. Similar to W-MA-910-010-G050. 18__. 1850s.

Rarity: URS-3
F $1,500; **VF** $2,000

$10 • W-MA-910-010-G050b

Overprint: Red TEN. ***Engraver:*** Terry, Pelton & Co. / ABNCo. monogram. ***Comments:*** H-MA-350-G10b. Similar to W-MA-910-010-G050 but with additional engraver imprint. 18__. 1850s–1860s.

Rarity: —

$20 • W-MA-910-020-G060

Left: View of Merchants Row / XX. ***Center:*** Indian seated looking at cliff. ***Right:*** 20 / View of Boston from the harbor / 20. ***Engraver:*** Terry, Pelton & Co. ***Comments:*** H-MA-350-G12. 18__. 1830s–1850s.

Rarity: URS-3
Proof $1,750

$20 • W-MA-910-020-G060a

Overprint: Red TWENTY. ***Engraver:*** Terry, Pelton & Co. ***Comments:*** H-MA-350-G12a. Similar to W-MA-910-020-G060. 18__. 1850s.

Rarity: —

$20 • W-MA-910-020-G060b

Overprint: Red TWENTY. ***Engraver:*** Terry, Pelton & Co. / ABNCo. monogram. ***Comments:*** H-MA-350-G12b. Similar to W-MA-910-020-G060 but with additional engraver imprint. 18__. 1850s–1860s.

Rarity: —

$50 • W-MA-910-050-G070

Left: 50 / View of Merchants Row / 50. ***Center:*** Indian seated looking at cliff. ***Right:*** 50 / View of Boston from harbor / 50. ***Engraver:*** Terry, Pelton & Co. ***Comments:*** H-MA-350-G14. 18__. 1830s–1850s.

Rarity: URS-3
Proof $2,000

$50 • W-MA-910-050-G070a

Overprint: Red FIFTY. ***Engraver:*** Terry, Pelton & Co. ***Comments:*** H-MA-350-G14a. Similar to W-MA-910-050-G070. 18__. 1850s.

Rarity: —

$50 • W-MA-910-050-G070b

Overprint: Red FIFTY. ***Engraver:*** Terry, Pelton & Co. / ABNCo. monogram. ***Comments:*** H-MA-350-G14b. Similar to W-MA-910-050-G070 but with additional engraver imprint. 18__. 1850s–1860s.

Rarity: —

$100 • W-MA-910-100-G080

Left: C / View of Boston from the harbor / C. ***Center:*** Indian man seated on shore, viewing ship. ***Right:*** 100 / View of Merchants Row / 100. ***Engraver:*** Terry, Pelton & Co. ***Comments:*** H-MA-350-G16. 18__. 1830s–1850s.

Rarity: —

$100 • W-MA-910-100-G080a

Overprint: Red HUNDRED. ***Engraver:*** Terry, Pelton & Co. ***Comments:*** H-MA-350-G16a. Similar to W-MA-910-100-G080. 18__. 1850s.

Rarity: —

$100 • W-MA-910-100-G080b

Overprint: Red HUNDRED. ***Engraver:*** Terry, Pelton & Co. / ABNCo. monogram. ***Comments:*** H-MA-350-G16b. Similar to W-MA-910-100-G080 but with additional engraver imprint. 18__. 1850s–1860s.

Rarity: —

$500 • W-MA-910-500-G090

Left: FIVE HUNDRED vertically. ***Center:*** Eagle and shield. ***Right:*** 500 / Male portrait / 500. ***Engraver:*** American Bank Note Co. ***Comments:*** H-MA-350-G18. 18__. 1860s.

Rarity: —

$1,000 • W-MA-910-1000-G100

Left: 1000 vertically. ***Center:*** Eagle, shield, and motto E PLURIBUS UNUM. ***Right:*** 1000 / Portrait of George Washington / 1000. ***Engraver:*** American Bank Note Co. ***Comments:*** H-MA-350-G20. 18__. 1860s.

Rarity: —

Non-Valid Issues

$2 • W-MA-910-002-R010

Engraver: Terry, Pelton & Co. ***Comments:*** H-MA-350-R5. Raised from W-MA-910-001-G010 or G010a. 18__. 1840s–1850s.

Rarity: —

$5 • W-MA-910-005-R020

Engraver: Terry, Pelton & Co. ***Comments:*** H-MA-350-R10. Raised from W-MA-910-001-G010 or G010a. 18__. 1840s–1850s.

Rarity: —

$10 • W-MA-910-010-R030

Engraver: Terry, Pelton & Co. ***Comments:*** H-MA-350-R15. Raised from W-MA-910-001-G010 or G010a. 18__. 1840s–1850s.

Rarity: —

$10 • W-MA-910-010-R040

Engraver: Terry, Pelton & Co. ***Comments:*** H-MA-350-R20. Raised from W-MA-910-001-G010 or G010a. 18__. 1850s.

Rarity: —

Shoe and Leather Dealers Bank

1836–1864

W-MA-920

History: The Shoe and Leather Dealers Bank was chartered in April 1836. Its office was at 53 State Street in the financial district. The bank was one of many institutions named after a commercial trade, the business plan being that those involved in such commerce would find bank officers understanding in matters of loans and finance. It specialized in facilitating trade between business people from Boston and commercial interests in the South and West.

The bank had a starting capital of $500,000. In 1849 the capital was authorized to increase to $750,000. In 1852 the same was increased again to $1,000,000.

Circulation in 1838 amounted to $148,166. In 1839 it had decreased to $45,420, but by 1845 it had again increased to $246,916. By 1860 it was $197,232. Other figures for 1838 included: net profits on hand $23,538.50; balances due to other banks $64,045.78; cash deposited $47,659.34; total amount due from banks $783,409.62; gold, silver, and other coined metals in the banking house $9,787.30; bills of other banks incorporated in this state $43,586.15; balance due from other banks $37,477.32; amount of all debts due $692,558.85; total amount of resources of the bank $783,409.62.

On December 31, 1864, the Shoe and Leather National Bank of Boston was chartered, after which it assumed the business of the state bank.

Numismatic Commentary: Most of the genuine notes collectors will encounter show a vignette of the Shoe and Leather Dealers building near the Boston waterfront. All denominations are hard to locate, but this pleasant vignette will make the search worthwhile.

Valid Issues

$1 • W-MA-920-001-G010

Left: 1 / Man dressing leather / ONE. ***Center:*** Horses and wagon / Shoe and Leather Dealers Store in Boston / Men and boxes, Ship / Black lathework ONE. ***Right:*** 1 / Interior of shoemaker's shop, Two men at work / ONE. ***Engraver:*** New England Bank Note Co. ***Comments:*** H-MA-355-G2. 18__. 1830s–1850s.

Rarity: URS-3
F $450

$1 • W-MA-920-001-G010a

Overprint: Red ONE. ***Engraver:*** New England Bank Note Co. ***Comments:*** H-MA-355-G2a. Similar to W-MA-920-001-G010. 18__. 1850s.

Rarity: URS-4
F $500; **VF** $750

$1 • W-MA-920-001-G010b

CC

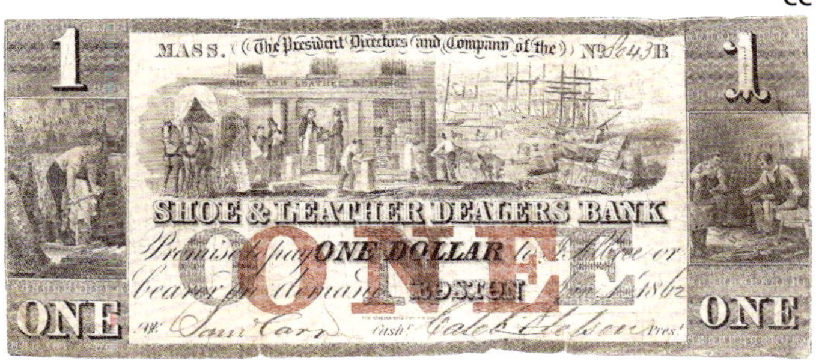

Overprint: Red ONE. ***Engraver:*** New England Bank Note Co. / ABNCo. monogram. ***Comments:*** H-MA-355-G2b. Similar to W-MA-920-001-G010 but with additional engraver imprint. 18__. 1850s–1860s.

Rarity: URS-3
VF $950

$2 • W-MA-920-002-G020

Left: 2 / Interior of shoemaker's shop, Two men at work / TWO. ***Center:*** Shoe and Leather Dealers Store / Black lathework TWO. ***Right:*** 2 / Man dressing leather / TWO. ***Engraver:*** New England Bank Note Co. ***Comments:*** H-MA-355-G4. 18__. 1830s–1850s.

Rarity: —

$2 • W-MA-920-002-G020a

Overprint: Red TWO. ***Engraver:*** New England Bank Note Co. ***Comments:*** H-MA-355-G4a. Similar to W-MA-920-002-G020. 18__. 1850s.

Rarity: —

$2 • W-MA-920-002-G020b

Overprint: Red TWO. ***Engraver:*** New England Bank Note Co. / ABNCo. monogram. ***Comments:*** H-MA-355-G4b. Similar to W-MA-920-002-G020 but with additional engraver imprint. 18__. 1850s–1860s.

Rarity: —

$3 • W-MA-920-003-G030

JF

Engraver: New England Bank Note Co. ***Comments:*** H-MA-355-G6. 18__. 1830s–1850s.

Rarity: URS-3
F $1,250
Selected auction price: Heritage, January 2010, Lot 12820, F+ $1,150

$3 • W-MA-920-003-G030a

Left: 3 / Cattle / THREE. ***Center:*** Shoe and Leather Dealers Store / Black lathework THREE. ***Right:*** 3 / Interior of shoemaker's shop, Two men at work / THREE. ***Overprint:*** Red THREE. ***Engraver:*** New England Bank Note Co. ***Comments:*** H-MA-355-G6a. Similar to W-MA-920-003-G030. 18__. 1850s.

Rarity: —

$3 • W-MA-920-003-G030b

Overprint: Red THREE. ***Engraver:*** New England Bank Note Co. / ABNCo. monogram. ***Comments:*** H-MA-355-G6b. Similar to W-MA-920-003-G030 but with additional engraver imprint. 18__. 1850s–1860s.

Rarity: —

$5 • W-MA-920-005-G040

Left: 5 / Man tanning leather. ***Center:*** Shoe and Leather Dealers Store / FIVE. ***Right:*** 5 / Justice standing with scales. ***Engraver:*** New England Bank Note Co. ***Comments:*** H-MA-355-G8. 18__. 1830s–1850s.

Rarity: —

$5 • W-MA-920-005-G040a

Overprint: Red FIVE. ***Engraver:*** New England Bank Note Co. ***Comments:*** H-MA-355-G8a. Similar to W-MA-920-005-G040. 18__. 1850s.

Rarity: —

$5 • W-MA-920-005-G040b

TD

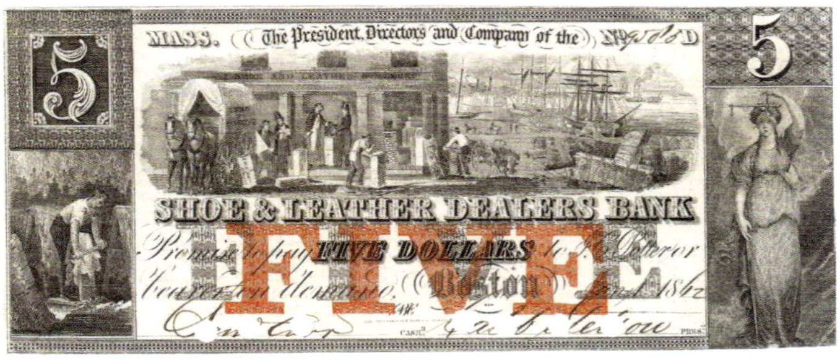

Overprint: Red FIVE. ***Engraver:*** New England Bank Note Co. / ABNCo. monogram. ***Comments:*** H-MA-355-G8b. Similar to W-MA-920-005-G040 but with additional engraver imprint. 18__. 1850s–1860s.

Rarity: URS-3
VF $1,250

$10 • W-MA-920-010-G050

Left: 10 / George Washington at Dorchester Heights, 1775 / TEN. ***Center:*** Shoe and Leather Dealers Store / TEN. ***Right:*** 10 / Ships / TEN. ***Engraver:*** New England Bank Note Co. ***Comments:*** H-MA-355-G10. 18__. 1830s–1850s.

Rarity: —

$10 • W-MA-920-010-G050a

CC

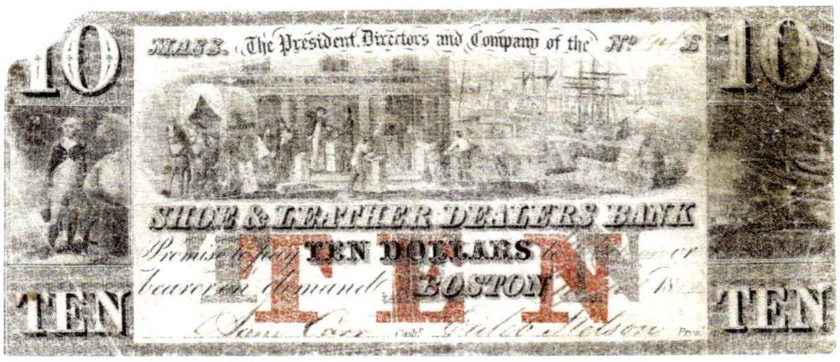

Overprint: Red TEN. ***Engraver:*** New England Bank Note Co. ***Comments:*** H-MA-355-G10a. Similar to W-MA-920-010-G050. 18__. 1850s.

Rarity: URS-4
VG $375; **F** $450; **VF** $500

$10 • W-MA-920-010-G050b

Overprint: Red TEN. ***Engraver:*** New England Bank Note Co. / ABNCo. monogram. ***Comments:*** H-MA-355-G10b. Similar to W-MA-920-010-G050 but with additional engraver imprint. 18__. 1850s–1860s.

Rarity: —

$20 • W-MA-920-020-G060

Left: XX / Indian man with bow / 20. ***Center:*** Shoe and Leather Dealers Store / Black lathework TWENTY. ***Right:*** 20 / Eagle / XX. ***Engraver:*** New England Bank Note Co. ***Comments:*** H-MA-355-G12. 18__. 1830s–1850s.

Rarity: —

$20 • W-MA-920-020-G060a

Overprint: Red TWENTY. ***Engraver:*** New England Bank Note Co. ***Comments:*** H-MA-355-G12a. Similar to W-MA-920-020-G060. 18__. 1850s.

Rarity: —

$20 • W-MA-920-020-G060b

Overprint: Red TWENTY. ***Engraver:*** New England Bank Note Co. / ABNCo. monogram. ***Comments:*** H-MA-355-G12b. Similar to W-MA-920-020-G060 but with additional engraver imprint. 18__. 1850s–1860s.

Rarity: —

$50 • W-MA-920-050-G070

Left: FIFTY / Portrait of George Washington / 50. ***Center:*** Shoe and Leather Dealers Store / FIFTY. ***Right:*** 50 / Portrait of Benjamin Franklin / FIFTY. ***Engraver:*** New England Bank Note Co. ***Comments:*** H-MA-355-G14. 18__. 1830s–1840s.

Rarity: —

$50 • W-MA-920-050-G070a

Overprint: White FIFTY. ***Engraver:*** New England Bank Note Co. ***Comments:*** H-MA-355-G14a. Similar to W-MA-920-050-G070. 18__. 1850s.

Rarity: —

$50 • W-MA-920-050-G070b

Overprint: Red FIFTY. ***Engraver:*** New England Bank Note Co. ***Comments:*** H-MA-355-G14b. Similar to W-MA-920-050-G070. 18__. 1850s.

Rarity: —

$50 • W-MA-920-050-G070c

Overprint: Red FIFTY. ***Engraver:*** New England Bank Note Co. / ABNCo. monogram. ***Comments:*** H-MA-355-G14c. Similar to W-MA-920-050-G070 but with additional engraver imprint. 18__. 1850s–1860s.

Rarity: URS-3
EF $900

$100 • W-MA-920-100-G080

Engraver: Unverified, but likely New England Bank Note Co. ***Comments:*** H-MA-355-G18. No description available. 18__. 1830s–1840s.

Rarity: *None known*

$100 • W-MA-920-100-G090

Left: ONE HUNDRED on 100 / Portrait of William Henry Harrison. ***Center:*** Wharf scene, Men loading wagon with barrels. ***Right:*** ONE HUNDRED on 100 / Portrait of Christopher Columbus. ***Engraver:*** New England Bank Note Co. ***Comments:*** H-MA-355-G22. 18__. 1840s–1850s.

Rarity: —

$100 • W-MA-920-100-G100

Left: 100 / Justice seated. ***Center:*** Shoe and Leather Dealers Store. ***Right:*** 100 / Female portrait. ***Engraver:*** New England Bank Note Co. ***Comments:*** H-MA-355-G26. 18__. 1850s.

Rarity: —

$500 • W-MA-920-500-G110

Engraver: Unverified, but likely New England Bank Note Co. ***Comments:*** H-MA-355-G30. No description available. 18__. 1830s–1840s.

Rarity: *None known*

$500 • W-MA-920-500-G120

Center: Shoe and Leather Dealers Store / 500. ***Right:*** 500 / Cattle. ***Engraver:*** New England Bank Note Co. ***Comments:*** H-MA-355-G34. 18__. 1850s.

Rarity: —

$1,000 • W-MA-920-1000-G130
Engraver: Unverified, but likely New England Bank Note Co. ***Comments:*** H-MA-355-G38. No description available. 18__. 1830s–1840s.
Rarity: *None known*

NON-VALID ISSUES

$5 • W-MA-920-005-R010
Engraver: New England Bank Note Co. ***Comments:*** H-MA-355-R5. Raised from W-MA-920-001-G010 or G010a. 18__. 1840s–1850s.
Rarity: —

$10 • W-MA-920-010-R020
Engraver: New England Bank Note Co. ***Comments:*** H-MA-355-R10. Raised from W-MA-920-001-G010 or G010a. 18__. 1840s–1850s.
Rarity: —

$10 • W-MA-920-010-R030
Engraver: New England Bank Note Co. ***Comments:*** H-MA-355-R15. Raised from W-MA-920-002-G020 or G020a. 18__. 1850s.
Rarity: —

$10 • W-MA-920-010-S010
Left: X / Portrait of Thomas Jefferson / X. ***Center:*** X / Four women / X. ***Bottom center:*** Dog and strongbox. ***Right:*** X / Portrait of William Henry Harrison. ***Engraver:*** Draper, Toppan & Co. ***Comments:*** H-MA-355-S5. June 1, 1848.
Rarity: URS-5
VG $125

$50 • W-MA-920-050-R040
Engraver: New England Bank Note Co. ***Comments:*** H-MA-355-R20. Raised from W-MA-920-001-G010 or G010a. 18__. 1840s–1850s.
Rarity: —

$100 • W-MA-920-100-R050
Engraver: New England Bank Note Co. ***Comments:*** H-MA-355-R25. Raised from W-MA-920-001-G010 or G010a. 18__. 1840s–1850s.
Rarity: —

$500 • W-MA-920-500-R060
Engraver: New England Bank Note Co. ***Comments:*** H-MA-355-R30. Raised from W-MA-920-001-G010 or G010a. 18__. 1840s–1850s
Rarity: —

South Bank
1833–1843
W-MA-930

History: The South Bank was chartered on March 25, 1833, with an authorized capital of $500,000. Its office was in the financial district at 40 State Street. Circulation in 1838 amounted to $147,276. In 1839 it was $46,320.

Other figures for 1838 included: net profits on hand $8,527.50; balances due to other banks $54,560.55; cash deposited $17,691.36; cash deposited bearing interest $54,500; total amount due from banks $782,555.41; gold, silver, and other coined metals in the banking house $10,622.16; bills of other banks incorporated in this state $32,171.60; amount of all debts due $739,761.65; total amount of resources of the bank $782,555.41.

In October 1842, the stockholders voted unanimously to close the bank and surrender the charter. The bank wound down its operations in 1843.

Numismatic Commentary: The South Bank notes are very hard to locate. This bank also issued notes with a vignette of the "Landing of the Pilgrims," a prized addition to any collection. The vignette, seen on the notes illustrated below, seems to be a copy of the motif created by Michel Felice Corne.

VALID ISSUES

$1 • W-MA-930-001-G010
Back: Check Plate. ***Engraver:*** New England Bank Note Co. / PSSP. ***Comments:*** H-MA-360-G2. 18__. 1830s.
Rarity: —

$1 • W-MA-930-001-G010a HA

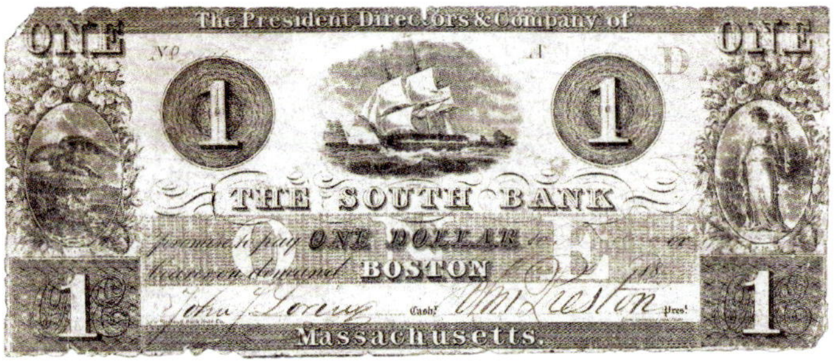

Back: Plain. ***Engraver:*** New England Bank Note Co. / PSSP. ***Comments:*** H-MA-360-G2a. Similar to W-MA-930-001-G010. 18__. 1830s.
Rarity: URS-2
F $2,500

$2 • W-MA-930-002-G020
Back: Check Plate. ***Engraver:*** New England Bank Note Co. / PSSP. ***Comments:*** H-MA-360-G6. 18__. 1830s.
Rarity: —

$2 • W-MA-930-002-G020a
Back: Plain. ***Engraver:*** New England Bank Note Co. / PSSP. ***Comments:*** H-MA-360-G6a. Similar to W-MA-930-002-G020. 18__. 1830s.
Rarity: —

$3 • W-MA-930-003-G030
Left: Eagle / THREE. ***Center:*** Train / Ship / 3. ***Right:*** Woman with cornucopia / THREE. ***Back:*** Check Plate. ***Engraver:*** New England Bank Note Co. / PSSP. ***Comments:*** H-MA-360-G10. 18__. 1830s.
Rarity: —

$3 • W-MA-930-003-G030a

HA

Back: Plain. ***Engraver:*** New England Bank Note Co. / PSSP. ***Comments:*** H-MA-360-G10a. Similar to W-MA-930-003-G030. Proof. 18__. 1830s.

Rarity: URS-1
Proof $3,500

$5 • W-MA-930-005-G040

Back: Check Plate. ***Engraver:*** New England Bank Note Co. / PSSP. ***Comments:*** H-MA-360-G14. 18__. 1830s.

Rarity: —

$5 • W-MA-930-005-G040a

Back: Plain. ***Engraver:*** New England Bank Note Co. / PSSP. ***Comments:*** H-MA-360-G14a. Similar to W-MA-930-005-G040. 18__. 1830s.

Rarity: —

$10 • W-MA-930-010-G055

Back: Check Plate. ***Engraver:*** New England Bank Note Co. / PSSP. ***Comments:*** H-MA-360-G18. 18__. 1830s.

Rarity: —

$10 • W-MA-930-010-G055a

Back: Plain. ***Engraver:*** New England Bank Note Co. / PSSP. ***Comments:*** H-MA-360-G18a. Similar to W-MA-930-010-G055. 18__. 1830s.

Rarity: —

$20 • W-MA-930-020-G070

Back: Check Plate. ***Engraver:*** New England Bank Note Co. / PSSP. ***Comments:*** H-MA-360-G22. 18__. 1830s.

Rarity: —

$20 • W-MA-930-020-G070a

Back: Plain. ***Engraver:*** New England Bank Note Co. / PSSP. ***Comments:*** H-MA-360-G22a. Similar to W-MA-930-020-G070. 18__. 1830s.

Rarity: —

$50 • W-MA-930-050-G080

Left: 50 / Cornucopia, Woman standing with ankles crossed and staff, Anchor / 50. ***Center:*** FIFTY DOLLARS / 50. ***Right:*** FIFTY vertically. ***Back:*** Check Plate. ***Engraver:*** New England Bank Note Co. / PSSP. ***Comments:*** H-MA-360-G26. 18__. 1830s.

Rarity: —

$50 • W-MA-930-050-G080a

Back: Plain. ***Engraver:*** New England Bank Note Co. / PSSP. ***Comments:*** H-MA-360-G26a. Similar to W-MA-930-050-G080. 18__. 1830s.

Rarity: —

$100 • W-MA-930-100-G090

Left: Panel bearing C / Portrait of George Washington / C. ***Center:*** 100 / Manhattan reclining pouring water from jug, Ship / 100. ***Right:*** Panel bearing ONE HUNDRED vertically. ***Back:*** Check Plate. ***Engraver:*** New England Bank Note Co. / PSSP. ***Comments:*** H-MA-360-G30. 18__. 1830s.

Rarity: —

$100 • W-MA-930-100-G090a

Back: Plain. ***Engraver:*** New England Bank Note Co. / PSSP. ***Comments:*** H-MA-360-G30a. Similar to W-MA-930-100-G090. 18__. 1830s.

Rarity: —

$500 • W-MA-930-500-G100

Left: 500 / 500 / 500. ***Center:*** 500 / Woman seated with shield bearing D, Fasces, cornucopia, lyre, and sheaf on ground. ***Right:*** 500 / D / 500. ***Engraver:*** New England Bank Note Co. / PSSP. ***Comments:*** H-MA-360-G34. 18__. 1830s.

Rarity: —

$500 • W-MA-930-500-G100a

Back: Plain. ***Engraver:*** New England Bank Note Co. / PSSP. ***Comments:*** H-MA-360-G34a. Similar to W-MA-930-500-G100. 18__. 1830s.

Rarity: —

$1,000 • W-MA-930-1000-G110

Left: THOUSAND vertically. ***Center:*** 1000 / Woman standing with legs crossed and lyre, Cornucopia / 1000. ***Right:*** 1000 / M / 1000. ***Back:*** Check Plate. ***Engraver:*** New England Bank Note Co. / PSSP. ***Comments:*** H-MA-360-G38. 18__. 1830s.

Rarity: —

$1,000 • W-MA-930-1000-G110a

Back: Plain. ***Engraver:*** New England Bank Note Co. ***Comments:*** H-MA-360-G38a. Similar to W-MA-930-1000-G110. 18__. 1830s.

Rarity: —

Non-Valid Issues

$10 • W-MA-930-010-R010

Engraver: New England Bank Note Co. / PSSP. ***Comments:*** H-MA-360-R5. Raised from W-MA-930-001-G010 or G010a. 18__. 1830s.

Rarity: —

$50 • W-MA-930-050-R020

Engraver: New England Bank Note Co. / PSSP. ***Comments:*** H-MA-360-R10. Raised from W-MA-930-001-G010 or G010a. 18__. 1830s.

Rarity: —

South Boston Bank
1827
W-MA-940

History: The South Boston Bank was chartered in 1827 according to *Banker's Magazine*. It had an authorized capital of $500,000 but never went into operation.

State Bank
1811–1865
W-MA-950

History: The State Bank was incorporated on June 27, 1811, with capital authorized at $1,800,000, where it remained throughout the bank's existence.

On June 10, 1812, there was a loan made to the federal government in the amount of $500,000 to be repaid in the amount of $250,000 on December 15, 1813, and $250,000 on December 15, 1814. The first payment was made early, on November 15, 1813, but the second payment was missed.[71]

Circulation totaled $376,932 in 1838. In 1839 it had dropped down to $161,418, but by 1845 it had again increased to $405,076. Other figures for 1838 included: net profits on hand $137,217.07; balances due to other banks $32,000; cash deposited $351,288.87; cash deposited bearing interest $139,000; total amount due from banks $2,736,437.94; gold, silver, and other coined metals in the banking house $24,813.98; bills of other banks incorporated in this state $97,315; balance due from other banks $36,000; amount of all debts due $2,578,308.96; total amount of resources of the bank $2,736,437.94. In 1846 the bank was at 47 State Street.

On April 17, 1865, the State National Bank (seemingly an oxymoronic title, but widely used elsewhere) was incorporated and in time succeeded the interests of the State Bank.

Numismatic Commentary: There should be ample opportunity to add notes of this long-lived institution to a collection. On many of the earlier issues engraved by Reed is the bank building designed by the noted Boston architect Charles Bulfinch, which is a design copy of the Strand front of Somerset House in London. This bank building was acquired from the first Bank of the United States, W-MA-330, after its charter expired.

Valid Issues

$1 • W-MA-950-001-G010
Left: 1 vertically. ***Center:*** 1 / Indian standing / ONE. ***Right:*** Lathework panel. ***Engraver:*** Leney & Rollinson. ***Comments:*** H-MA-365-G20. 18__. 1810s.

Rarity: —

$1 • W-MA-950-001-G020
Left: ONE / 1 / ONE. ***Center:*** 1 / Bank building / 1 / Figure in branches. ***Right:*** 1 / MASSACHUSETTS / 1. ***Engraver:*** A. Reed / Reed. ***Comments:*** H-MA-365-G24. 18__. 1820s.

Rarity: URS-3
Proof $1,500

$1 • W-MA-950-001-G030
Left: Narrow panel of lathework circle segments. ***Center:*** 1 / 1 / Flower garlands and gridwork segments / 1 / 1. ***Right:*** Narrow panel of lathework circle segments. ***Engraver:*** PSSP. ***Comments:*** H-MA-365-G26. 18__. 1820s–1830s.

Rarity: —

$1 • W-MA-950-001-G030a
Left: ONE / D / ONE vertically. ***Right:*** ONE / D / ONE vertically. ***Engraver:*** PSSP. ***Comments:*** H-MA-365-G28. Similar to W-MA-950-001-G030. 18__. 1830s.

Rarity: —

$1 • W-MA-950-001-G030b
Left: Lathework bearing MASSACHUSETTS vertically / ONE. ***Right:*** ONE / D / ONE vertically. ***Engraver:*** PSSP. ***Comments:*** H-MA-365-G30. Similar to W-MA-950-001-G030. 18__. 1830s.

Rarity: —

$1 • W-MA-950-001-G040
Comments: H-MA-365-G36. No description available. 18__. 1840s.

Rarity: *None known*

$1 • W-MA-950-001-G050
Left: 1 / Ship under sail. ***Center:*** Angel flying in clouds holding sword, balance, and figure / ONE. ***Bottom center:*** Steamship. ***Right:*** 1 / State arms. ***Engraver:*** Draper, Toppan & Co. ***Comments:*** H-MA-365-G40. 18__. 1840s–1850s.

Rarity: —

$1.25 • W-MA-950-001.25-G060
Left: 1 25/100 / Train / 1 25/100. ***Center:*** Sloop and other ships at sea / $1.25 cts. ***Right:*** 1 25/100 / Eagle. ***Engraver:*** New England Bank Note Co. ***Comments:*** H-MA-365-G42. 18__. 1830s.

Rarity: —

$1.50 • W-MA-950-001.50-G070
Left: 1 Doll. 50 Cts. vertically. ***Center:*** Eagle on rock in ocean / $1 50/100. ***Right:*** 1 50/100 / Justice. ***Engraver:*** New England Bank Note Co. ***Comments:*** H-MA-365-G44. 18__. 1830s.

Rarity: —

$1.75 • W-MA-950-001.75-G080
Left: $1.75 Cts. / Hebe watering eagle / 1 75/100. ***Center:*** Three sloops at sea. ***Right:*** $1.75 Cts. / Dog, Woman seated with grain / 1 75/100. ***Engraver:*** New England Bank Note Co. ***Comments:*** H-MA-365-G46. 18__. 1830s.

Rarity: —

$2 • W-MA-950-002-G090
Left: 2 vertically. ***Center:*** 2 / Indian standing / TWO. ***Right:*** Lathework panel. ***Engraver:*** Leney & Rollinson. ***Comments:*** H-MA-365-G50. 18__. 1810s.

Rarity: URS-2
Proof $1,500

$2 • W-MA-950-002-G100

QDB

Engraver: A. Reed / Reed. ***Comments:*** H-MA-365-G54. Proof. 18__. 1820s.

Rarity: URS-4
Proof $750

$2 • W-MA-950-002-G110
Left: Narrow panel of lathework circle segments. ***Center:*** 2 / 2 / Flower garlands and gridwork segments / 2 / 2. ***Right:*** Narrow panel of lathework circle segments. ***Engraver:*** PSSP. ***Comments:*** H-MA-365-G56. 18__. 1820s–1830s.

Rarity: —

$2 • W-MA-950-002-G110a

Left: Five TWOs vertically. ***Right:*** Five TWOs vertically. ***Engraver:*** PSSP. ***Comments:*** H-MA-365-G58. Similar to W-MA-950-002-G110. 18__. 1830s.

Rarity: —

$2 • W-MA-950-002-G110b

Left: Lathework bearing MASSACHUSETTS vertically / TWO. ***Right:*** Five TWOs vertically. ***Engraver:*** PSSP. ***Comments:*** H-MA-365-G60. Similar to W-MA-950-002-G110. 18__. 1830s.

Rarity: —

$2 • W-MA-950-002-G120

Comments: H-MA-365-G66.

Rarity: URS-4
VF $450

$2 • W-MA-950-002-G130 HA

Engraver: Draper, Toppan & Co. ***Comments:*** H-MA-365-G70. Proof. 18__. 1840s–1850s.

Rarity: URS-3
Proof $750

$3 • W-MA-950-003-G140

Left: 3 vertically. ***Center:*** 3 / Indian standing / THREE. ***Right:*** Lathework panel. ***Engraver:*** Leney & Rollinson. ***Comments:*** H-MA-365-G74. 18__. 1810s.

Rarity: —

$3 • W-MA-950-003-G150

Left: III / THREE DOLLARS / 3. ***Center:*** 3 / Bank building / 3 / State arms. ***Right:*** 3 / MASSACHUSETTS / 3. ***Engraver:*** A. Reed / Reed. ***Comments:*** H-MA-365-G78. 18__. 1820s.

Rarity: URS-2
Proof $900

$3 • W-MA-950-003-G160

Left: Narrow panel of lathework circle segments. ***Center:*** 3 / 3 / Flower garlands and gridwork segments / 3 / 3. ***Right:*** Narrow panel of lathework circle segments. ***Engraver:*** PSSP. ***Comments:*** H-MA-365-G80. 18__. 1820s–1830s.

Rarity: —

$3 • W-MA-950-003-G160a

Left: THREE vertically. ***Right:*** THREE vertically. ***Engraver:*** PSSP. ***Comments:*** H-MA-365-G82. Similar to W-MA-950-003-G160. 18__. 1830s.

Rarity: —

$3 • W-MA-950-003-G160b

Left: Lathework bearing MASSACHUSETTS vertically / THREE. ***Right:*** THREE vertically. ***Engraver:*** PSSP. ***Comments:*** H-MA-365-G84. Similar to W-MA-950-003-G160. 18__. 1830s.

Rarity: —

$3 • W-MA-950-003-G170

Comments: H-MA-365-G90. No description available. 18__. 1840s.

Rarity: *None known*

$3 • W-MA-950-003-G180 CC

Engraver: Draper, Toppan & Co. ***Comments:*** H-MA-365-G94. Proof. 18__. 1840s–1850s.

Rarity: URS-3
Proof $1,500

$5 • W-MA-950-005-G190

Left: 5 vertically. ***Center:*** 5 / Indian standing / FIVE. ***Right:*** Lathework panel. ***Engraver:*** Leney & Rollinson. ***Comments:*** H-MA-365-G98. 18__. 1810s.

Rarity: —

$5 • W-MA-950-005-G200

Left: 5 / FIVE / 5. ***Center:*** Indian standing with staff. ***Right:*** 5. ***Engraver:*** Perkins. ***Comments:*** H-MA-365-G102. 18__. 1810s–1820s.

Rarity: —

$5 • W-MA-950-005-G210

Left: FIVE / FIVE DOLLARS / 5. ***Center:*** 5 / Bank building / 5 / State arms. ***Right:*** 5 / MASSACHUSETTS / 5. ***Engraver:*** A. Reed / Reed. ***Comments:*** H-MA-365-G106. 18__. 1820s.

Rarity: —

$5 • W-MA-950-005-G220

Left: Lathework chain bearing MASSACHUSETTS / 5 / 5. ***Center:*** Alternating flower garlands and gridwork segments / FIVE DOLLARS with zigzag ruled lines. ***Right:*** 5 / 5. ***Engraver:*** PSSP. ***Comments:*** H-MA-365-G108. 18__. 1820s.

Rarity: —

$5 • W-MA-950-005-G220a

Engraver: PSSP. ***Comments:*** H-MA-365-G110. Similar to W-MA-950-005-G220 but with spiral lathework lines. 18__. 1830s.

Rarity: —

$5 • W-MA-950-005-G230

Comments: H-MA-365-G114. No description available. 18__. 1840s.

Rarity: *None known*

$5 • W-MA-950-005-G240

HA

Engraver: Draper, Toppan & Co. ***Comments:*** H-MA-365-G118. Proof. 18__. 1840s.

Rarity: URS-3
Proof $1,250

$5 • W-MA-950-005-G250

Left: Indian / 5. ***Center:*** 5 / Portrait of Rachel Jackson / Female portrait. ***Right:*** 5 / Portrait of Indian. ***Engraver:*** Toppan, Carpenter & Co. ***Comments:*** H-MA-365-G122. 18__. 1840s–1850s.

Rarity: URS-3
VF $400

$6 • W-MA-950-006-G260

Left: 6 vertically. ***Center:*** 6 / Indian standing / SIX. ***Right:*** Lathework panel. ***Engraver:*** Leney & Rollinson. ***Comments:*** H-MA-365-G126. 18__. 1810s.

Rarity: —

$7 • W-MA-950-007-G270

Left: 7 vertically. ***Center:*** 7 / Indian standing / SEVEN. ***Right:*** Lathework panel. ***Engraver:*** Leney & Rollinson. ***Comments:*** H-MA-365-G130. 18__. 1810s.

Rarity: —

$8 • W-MA-950-008-G280

Left: 8 vertically. ***Center:*** 8 / Indian standing / EIGHT. ***Right:*** Lathework panel. ***Engraver:*** Leney & Rollinson. ***Comments:*** H-MA-365-G134. 18__. 1810s.

Rarity: —

$9 • W-MA-950-009-G290

Left: 9 vertically. ***Center:*** 9 / Indian standing / NINE. ***Right:*** Lathework panel. ***Engraver:*** Leney & Rollinson. ***Comments:*** H-MA-365-G136. 18__. 1810s.

Rarity: —

$10 • W-MA-950-010-G300

Left: X / 10 vertically. ***Center:*** 10 / Indian with TEN / TEN. ***Right:*** Lathework panel. ***Engraver:*** Leney & Rollinson. ***Comments:*** H-MA-365-G138. 18__. 1810s.

Rarity: —

$10 • W-MA-950-010-G310

Left: TEN / 10 / TEN. ***Center:*** 10 / Scene with Indian and sailing ship. ***Right:*** 10. ***Engraver:*** Perkins. ***Comments:*** H-MA-365-G142. 18__. 1810s–1820s.

Rarity: —

$10 • W-MA-950-010-G320

SI

Engraver: PSSP. ***Comments:*** H-MA-365-G148. 18__. 1830s.

Rarity: URS-4
VG $250

$10 • W-MA-950-010-G320a

Left: MASSACHUSETTS on lathework panel / 10 / 10 vertically. ***Center:*** White boxes flanking TEN DOLLARS with straight lines. ***Right:*** 10 / 10 vertically. ***Engraver:*** PSSP. ***Comments:*** H-MA-365-G150. Similar to W-MA-950-010-G320 but with spiral lathework lines. 18__. 1830s.

Rarity: —

$10 • W-MA-950-010-G330

Comments: H-MA-365-G154. No description available. 18__. 1840s.

Rarity: *None known*

$10 • W-MA-950-010-G340

HA

Engraver: Draper, Toppan & Co. ***Comments:*** H-MA-365-G158. Proof. 18__. 1840s–1850s.

Rarity: URS-3
Proof $1,250

$10 • W-MA-950-010-G350

Left: 10 / Portrait of George Washington. ***Center:*** Two women flanking state arms, Shipping and factories. ***Right:*** 10 / State arms. ***Comments:*** H-MA-365-G162. 18__. 1850s.

Rarity: —

$20 • W-MA-950-020-G360

Left: 20 vertically. ***Center:*** 20 / Indian standing / TWENTY. ***Right:*** Lathework panel. ***Engraver:*** Leney & Rollinson. ***Comments:*** H-MA-365-G166. 18__. 1810s.

Rarity: —

$20 • W-MA-950-020-G370

CC

Engraver: Perkins. ***Comments:*** H-MA-365-G170. 18__. 1810s–1820s.

Rarity: URS-3
Proof $3,750

$20 • W-MA-950-020-G380

Left: Lathework chain bearing MASSACHUSETTS / 20 / 20 vertically. ***Center:*** Alternating flower garlands and gridwork segments. ***Right:*** 20 / 20 vertically. ***Engraver:*** PSSP. ***Comments:*** H-MA-365-G172. 18__. 1820s–1830s.

Rarity: —

$20 • W-MA-950-020-G390

Comments: H-MA-365-G174. No description available. 18__. 1830s–1840s.

Rarity: *None known*

$20 • W-MA-950-020-G400

Comments: H-MA-365-G178. No description available. 18__. 1840s.

Rarity: *None known*

$20 • W-MA-950-020-G410

HA

Engraver: Draper, Toppan & Co. ***Comments:*** H-MA-365-G182. Proof. 18__. 1840s–1850s.

Rarity: URS-3
Proof $2,500

$50 • W-MA-950-050-G420

HA

Tint: Brown. ***Engraver:*** Perkins. ***Comments:*** H-MA-365-G186. 18__. 1810s–1820s.

Rarity: URS-2
Proof $3,000

$50 • W-MA-950-050-G430

Left: Lathework chain bearing MASSACHUSETTS / 50 / 50 vertically. ***Center:*** Alternating flower garlands and gridwork segments. ***Right:*** 50 / 50 vertically. ***Engraver:*** PSSP. ***Comments:*** H-MA-365-G188. 18__. 1820s–1830s.

Rarity: —

$50 • W-MA-950-050-G440

Comments: H-MA-365-G190. No description available. 18__. 1830s–1840s.

Rarity: *None known*

$50 • W-MA-950-050-G450

Comments: H-MA-365-G194. No description available. 18__. 1840s.

Rarity: *None known*

$50 • W-MA-950-050-G460

Left: State arms / 50. ***Center:*** Three women, one seated pointing to train, one kneeling with sheaf, one reclining with rudder. ***Bottom center:*** Horse. ***Right:*** 50 / Sailor with spyglass. ***Engraver:*** Draper, Toppan & Co. ***Comments:*** H-MA-365-G198. 18__. 1840s–1850s.

Rarity: —

$100 • W-MA-950-100-G470

Left: Lathework chain bearing MASSACHUSETTS / 100 / 100 vertically. ***Center:*** Alternating flower garlands and gridwork segments. ***Right:*** 100 / 100 vertically. ***Engraver:*** Perkins. ***Comments:*** H-MA-365-G200. 18__. 1820s–1830s.

Rarity: —

$100 • W-MA-950-100-G480

Comments: H-MA-365-G206. No description available. 18__. 1830s–1840s.

Rarity: *None known*

$100 • W-MA-950-100-G490

Comments: H-MA-365-G210. No description available. 18__. 1840s.

Rarity: *None known*

$100 • W-MA-950-100-G500

Left: State arms / 50. ***Center:*** Woman seated on bale, arms resting on another bale, pointing to ships and lighthouse. ***Right:*** 100 / Justice and Liberty seated with eagle on globe. ***Engraver:*** Draper, Toppan & Co. ***Comments:*** H-MA-365-G214. 18__. 1840s–1850s.

Rarity: —

$500 • W-MA-950-500-G510

Comments: H-MA-365-G226. No description available. 18__. 1830s–1840s.

Rarity: *None known*

$500 • W-MA-950-500-G520

Left: 500 / Medallion head / 500. ***Center:*** Commerce reclining with anchor, Lighthouse, Ship and rainbow. ***Right:*** 500 / State arms / 500. ***Engraver:*** Draper, Toppan & Co. ***Comments:*** H-MA-365-G238. 18__. 1840s–1850s.

Rarity: —

$1,000 • W-MA-950-1000-G530

Left: Justice leaning on pedestal / 1000. ***Center:*** Eagle on limb, Ships. ***Bottom center:*** Ships. ***Right:*** 1000 / State arms. ***Comments:*** H-MA-365-G250. 18__. 1840s.

Rarity: —

Non-Valid Issues

$1 • W-MA-950-001-S010

Left: ONE / Woman standing next to pedestal / ONE. ***Center:*** ONE / Group of three people / Dollar. ***Right:*** Portrait of Christopher Columbus. ***Engraver:*** Draper, Toppan & Co. ***Comments:*** H-MA-365-S5. From a modified, fraudulent plate, originally for a counterfeit $1 of the State Bank of Indiana. Jan. 1, 1849.

Rarity: URS-7
F $75

$1 • W-MA-950-001-A010

Left: ONE / Woman / ONE. ***Center:*** Train / 1 / ONE / ONE. ***Right:*** ONE / Woman standing. ***Engraver:*** W.L. Ormsby. ***Comments:*** H-MA-365-A5. Altered from $1 Potomac River Bank, Georgetown, D.C. 18__. 1850s.

Rarity: URS-6
F $75

$2 • W-MA-950-002-C110b

SI

Engraver: PSSP. ***Comments:*** H-MA-365-C60. Counterfeit of W-MA-950-002-G110b. 18__. 1830s.

Rarity: URS-6
F $100

$2 • W-MA-950-002-C130

Engraver: Draper, Toppan & Co. ***Comments:*** H-MA-365-C70. Counterfeit of W-MA-950-002-G130. 18__. 1840s–1850s.

Rarity: —

$2 • W-MA-950-002-A020

Left: 2 / Eagle in die. ***Center:*** Man and woman, Fence, Trough / TWO. ***Right:*** 2 / Woman. ***Overprint:*** Red TWO. ***Engraver:*** Wellstood, Hays & Whiting. ***Comments:*** H-MA-365-A10. Altered from $2 Thames Bank, Laurel, Indiana. Aug. 12, 185_. 1859.

Rarity: URS-8
F $75

$3 • W-MA-950-003-C150

CC

Engraver: A. Reed / Reed. ***Comments:*** H-MA-365-C78. Counterfeit of W-MA-950-003-G150. 18__. 1820s.

Rarity: URS-7
F $150

$3 • W-MA-950-003-N010

Center: Portrait of George Washington. ***Comments:*** H-MA-365-N5.

Rarity: —

$5 • W-MA-950-005-C210

Engraver: A. Reed / Reed. ***Comments:*** H-MA-365-C106. Counterfeit of W-MA-950-005-G210. 18__. 1826.

Rarity: —

$5 • W-MA-950-005-C240

Engraver: Draper, Toppan & Co. ***Comments:*** H-MA-365-C118. Counterfeit of W-MA-950-005-G240. 18__. 1840s.

Rarity: URS-5
F $75

$5 • W-MA-950-005-R010

Engraver: Draper, Toppan & Co. ***Comments:*** H-MA-365-R5. Raised from W-MA-950-001-G050. 18__. 1840s.

Rarity: —

$5 • W-MA-950-005-A030

Left: V / Portrait of Henry Clay. ***Center:*** Steamboat / FIVE. ***Right:*** 5 / Portrait of George Washington. ***Overprint:*** Red FIVE. ***Engraver:*** New England Bank Note Co. / Rawdon, Wright, Hatch & Edson. ***Comments:*** H-MA-365-A15. Altered from $5 Waubeek Bank, De Soto, Nebraska. 18__. 1857.

Rarity: URS-5
F $75

$7 • W-MA-950-007-C260

QDB

Engraver: Leney & Rollinson. ***Comments:*** H-MA-365-C126. Counterfeit of W-MA-950-007-G260. 18__. 1810s.

Rarity: URS-5
F $750

$8 • W-MA-950-008-C280

CC

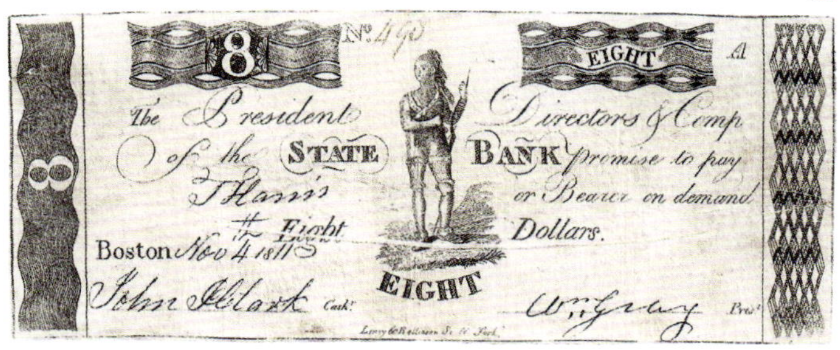

Engraver: Leney & Rollinson. ***Comments:*** H-MA-365-C134. Counterfeit of W-MA-950-008-G280. 18__. 1810s.

Rarity: URS-5
F $750

$10 • W-MA-950-010-C300

MR

Engraver: Leney & Rollinson. *Comments:* H-MA-365-C138. Counterfeit of W-MA-950-010-G300. 18__. 1810s.

Rarity: URS-5
F $400

$10 • W-MA-950-010-C310

Left: TEN / 10 / TEN. *Center:* 10 / Scene with Indian and sailing ship. *Right:* 10. *Engraver:* Perkins. *Comments:* H-MA-365-C142. Counterfeit of W-MA-950-010-G310. 18__. 1810s–1820s.

Rarity: URS-5
F $100

$10 • W-MA-950-010-C320

Left: MASSACHUSETTS. *Center:* Text. *Right:* 10 / 10. *Engraver:* PSSP. *Comments:* H-MA-365-C148. Counterfeit of W-MA-950-010-G320. 18__. 1830s.

Rarity: URS-5
F $100

$10 • W-MA-950-010-R020

Engraver: Draper, Toppan & Co. *Comments:* H-MA-365-R10. Raised from W-MA-950-001-G050. 18__. 1840s.

Rarity: —

$10 • W-MA-950-010-S020

Left: TEN on three dies. *Center:* 10 / Steamboat, Sailing ships / 10. *Right:* TEN / Portrait of George Washington / TEN. *Engraver:* Draper, Toppan & Co. *Comments:* H-MA-365-S10. Aug. 1, 1849.

Rarity: —

Suffolk Bank
1819–1865
W-MA-960

History: The Suffolk Bank was chartered on February 10, 1818, with an authorized capital of $500,000. The founding president was Ebenezer Francis, and Matthew S. Parker was the first cashier. The bank's office was located at 6 State Street.

In 1819 the Suffolk Bank set up an operation to act as a clearing house for bills of other regional banks which posted a deposit for their redemption. In 1824 this was expanded and became known as the Suffolk Bank System, a clearing house for almost all New England banks. Each bank posted a deposit of $2,000 or more, depending on the size of the bank and the amount of its circulating bills. This permitted the bills of member banks to circulate throughout New England at only a small discount from face value. However, the bank was not without its problems: during the Panic of 1837, the smooth flow of redemptions was interrupted on occasion. In 1852 two employees of the bank stole $205,718. In the mid-1850s the Bank of Mutual Redemption, W-MA-290, became dominant in the field, and the Suffolk Bank System faded.

The interests of this bank were succeeded by the Suffolk National Bank of Boston, chartered on December 17, 1864.

Numismatic Commentary: There should be many opportunities to add bills of this bank to any collection. Over a long period of years, this bank used many engraving firms, and examples of their notes are still available.

VALID ISSUES

$1 • W-MA-960-001-G010

HA

Engraver: Reed. *Comments:* H-MA-370-G20. 18__. 1819–1820s.

Rarity: URS-5
F $350; **Proof** $850

$1 • W-MA-960-001-G020

Center: Flower garlands and gridwork segments. *Engraver:* PSSP. *Comments:* H-MA-370-G22. 18__. 1820s.

Rarity: URS-5
VG $200

$1 • W-MA-960-001-G020a

Left: Narrow panel of lathework circle segments. *Right:* Narrow panel of lathework circle segments. *Engraver:* PSSP. *Comments:* H-MA-370-G24. Similar to W-MA-960-001-G020. 18__. 1820s.

Rarity: —

$1 • W-MA-960-001-G020b

Left: Narrow panel of lathework circle segments. *Right:* Narrow panel of lathework circle segments. *Engraver:* PSSP. *Comments:* H-MA-370-G26. Similar to W-MA-960-001-G020. 18__. 1820s–1830s.

Rarity: —

$1 • W-MA-960-001-G020c

Left: ONE / D / ONE vertically. *Right:* ONE / D / ONE vertically. *Comments:* H-MA-370-G28. Similar to W-MA-960-001-G020. 18__. 1830s.

Rarity: —

$1 • W-MA-960-001-G020d

Left: MASSACHUSETTS vertically. *Right:* ONE / D / ONE vertically. *Engraver:* PSSP. *Comments:* H-MA-370-G30. Similar to W-MA-960-001-G020. 18__. 1830s.

Rarity: URS-2
F $800

$1 • **W-MA-960-001-G020e**

Left: ONE / D / ONE vertically. ***Center:*** ONE. ***Right:*** ONE / D / ONE vertically. ***Engraver:*** PSSP. ***Comments:*** H-MA-370-G32. Similar to W-MA-960-001-G020. 18__. 1830s–1840s.

Rarity: —

$1 • **W-MA-960-001-G030**

CC

Engraver: New England Bank Note Co. ***Comments:*** H-MA-370-G36. 18__. 1840s–1850s.

Rarity: URS-3
VF $500

$1 • **W-MA-960-001-G030a**

Left: 1 / George Washington with horse. ***Center:*** Female portrait / 1 / Female portrait. ***Right:*** ONE / Eagle / ONE. ***Overprint:*** Red ONE. ***Engraver:*** New England Bank Note Co. ***Comments:*** H-MA-370-G36a. Similar to W-MA-960-001-G030. 18__. 1850s.

Rarity: —

$1 • **W-MA-960-001-G030b**

Overprint: Green ONE. ***Engraver:*** New England Bank Note Co. / ABNCo. monogram. ***Comments:*** H-MA-370-G36b. Similar to W-MA-960-001-G030 but with additional engraver imprint. 18__. 1850s–1860s.

Rarity: URS-4
F $500

$2 • **W-MA-960-002-G040**

QDB

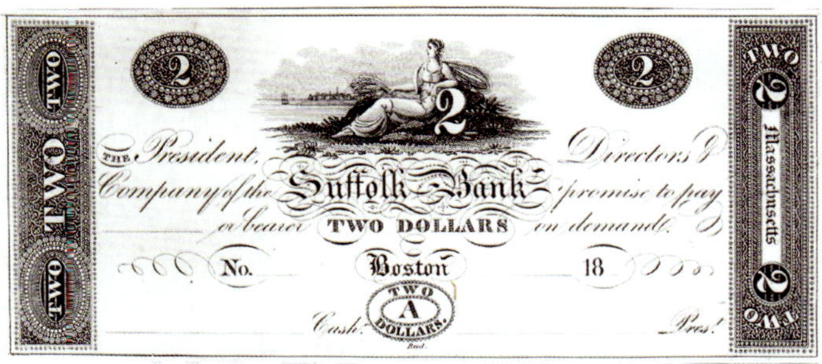

Engraver: Reed. ***Comments:*** H-MA-370-G40. Proof. 18__. 1819–1820s.

Rarity: URS-3
Proof $2,000

$2 • **W-MA-960-002-G050**

Center: 2 / 2 / Flower garlands and gridwork segments / TWO / 2 / 2. ***Engraver:*** PSSP. ***Comments:*** H-MA-370-G42. 18__. 1820s.

Rarity: —

$2 • **W-MA-960-002-G050a**

Left: Narrow panel of lathework circle segments. ***Right:*** Narrow panel of lathework circle segments. ***Engraver:*** PSSP. ***Comments:*** H-MA-370-G44. Similar to W-MA-960-002-G050. 18__. 1820s.

Rarity: —

$2 • **W-MA-960-002-G050b**

Left: Narrow panel of lathework circle segments. ***Right:*** Narrow panel of lathework circle segments. ***Engraver:*** PSSP. ***Comments:*** H-MA-370-G46. Similar to W-MA-960-002-G050. 18__. 1820s–1830s.

Rarity: —

$2 • **W-MA-960-002-G050c**

Left: Five TWOs vertically. ***Right:*** Five TWOs vertically. ***Engraver:*** PSSP. ***Comments:*** H-MA-370-G48. Similar to W-MA-960-002-G050. 18__. 1830s.

Rarity: —

$2 • **W-MA-960-002-G050d**

Left: MASSACHUSETTS vertically. ***Right:*** Five TWOs vertically. ***Engraver:*** PSSP. ***Comments:*** H-MA-370-G50. Similar to W-MA-960-002-G050. 18__. 1830s.

Rarity: —

$2 • **W-MA-960-002-G050e**

Left: Five TWOs vertically. ***Right:*** Five TWOs vertically. ***Engraver:*** PSSP. ***Comments:*** H-MA-370-G52. Similar to W-MA-960-002-G050. 18__. 1830s–1840s.

Rarity: —

$2 • **W-MA-960-002-G060**

Left: TWO / George Washington at Dorchester Heights, 1775 / TWO. ***Center:*** 2 / 2 / 2. ***Right:*** TWO / Female portrait / TWO. ***Engraver:*** New England Bank Note Co. ***Comments:*** H-MA-370-G56. 18__. 1840s–1850s.

Rarity: URS-4
F $500

$2 • **W-MA-960-002-G060a**

Overprint: Red TWO. ***Engraver:*** New England Bank Note Co. ***Comments:*** H-MA-370-G56a. Similar to W-MA-960-002-G060. 18__. 1850s.

Rarity: —

$2 • **W-MA-960-002-G060b**

Overprint: Green TWO. ***Engraver:*** New England Bank Note Co. / ABNCo. monogram. ***Comments:*** H-MA-370-G56b. Similar to W-MA-960-002-G060 but with additional engraver imprint. 18__. 1850s–1860s.

Rarity: —

$3 • **W-MA-960-003-G070**

TD

Engraver: Reed. ***Comments:*** H-MA-370-G60. 18__. 1819–1820s.

Rarity: URS-3
Proof $1,000

$3 • W-MA-960-003-G080

Center: 3 / 3 / Oval of flower garlands and gridwork segments / 3 / 3. ***Engraver:*** PSSP. ***Comments:*** H-MA-370-G62. 18__. 1820s.

Rarity: —

$3 • W-MA-960-003-G080a

Left: Narrow panel of lathework circle segments. ***Right:*** Narrow panel of lathework circle segments. ***Engraver:*** PSSP. ***Comments:*** H-MA-370-G64. Similar to W-MA-960-003-G080. 18__. 1820s.

Rarity: —

$3 • W-MA-960-003-G080b

Left: Narrow panel of lathework circle segments. ***Right:*** Narrow panel of lathework circle segments. ***Engraver:*** PSSP. ***Comments:*** H-MA-370-G66. Similar to W-MA-960-003-G080. 18__. 1820s–1830s.

Rarity: —

$3 • W-MA-960-003-G080c

Left: THREE vertically. ***Right:*** THREE vertically. ***Engraver:*** PSSP. ***Comments:*** H-MA-370-G68. Similar to W-MA-960-003-G080. 18__. 1830s.

Rarity: —

$3 • W-MA-960-003-G080d

ANS

Engraver: PSSP. ***Comments:*** H-MA-370-G70. Similar to W-MA-960-003-G080. 18__. 1830s.

Rarity: URS-5

F $500

$3 • W-MA-960-003-G080e

Left: THREE vertically. ***Right:*** THREE vertically. ***Engraver:*** PSSP. ***Comments:*** H-MA-370-G72. Similar to W-MA-960-003-G080. 18__. 1830s–1840s.

Rarity: URS-6

VG $100; **VF** $200

$3 • W-MA-960-003-G090

HA

Engraver: New England Bank Note Co. ***Comments:*** H-MA-370-G76. 18__. 1840s–1850s.

Rarity: URS-4

F $750

$3 • W-MA-960-003-G090a

Left: Woman. ***Center:*** THREE / 3 / THREE. ***Right:*** 3 / Dog with strongbox / 3. ***Overprint:*** Red THREE. ***Engraver:*** New England Bank Note Co. ***Comments:*** H-MA-370-G76a. Similar to W-MA-960-003-G090. 18__. 1850s.

Rarity: URS-4

VF $1,000

$3 • W-MA-960-003-G090b

Overprint: Green THREE. ***Engraver:*** New England Bank Note Co. / ABNCo. monogram. ***Comments:*** H-MA-370-G76b. Similar to W-MA-960-003-G090 but with additional engraver imprint. 18__. 1850s–1860s.

Rarity: —

$5 • W-MA-960-005-G100

Left: FIVE / 5 / FIVE vertically. ***Center:*** 5 / Woman holding 5 / 5. ***Bottom center:*** V. ***Right:*** 5 / Massachusetts / V vertically. ***Engraver:*** Reed. ***Comments:*** H-MA-370-G80. 18__. 1819–1820s.

Rarity: URS-3

Proof $700

$5 • W-MA-960-005-G110

Left: FIVE / 5 / FIVE. ***Center:*** 5 / Ship / FIVE / Ship / 5. ***Bottom center:*** V. ***Right:*** 5 / Massachusetts / V. ***Engraver:*** A. Reed / Reed. ***Comments:*** H-MA-370-G81. 18__. 1819–1820s.

Rarity: URS-3

Proof $750

$5 • W-MA-960-005-G120

CC

Engraver: A. Reed / Reed. ***Comments:*** H-MA-370-G82. 18__. 1819–1820s.

Rarity: URS-3

Proof $750

$5 • W-MA-960-005-G130

Left: Lathework panel bearing MASSACHUSETTS / 5 / 5. ***Center:*** Alternating flower garlands and gridwork segments. ***Right:*** 5 / 5. ***Engraver:*** PSSP. ***Comments:*** H-MA-370-G84. 18__. 1820s.

Rarity: —

$5 • W-MA-960-005-G130a

Center: White boxes flanking FIVE DOLLARS. ***Engraver:*** PSSP. ***Comments:*** H-MA-370-G86. Similar to W-MA-960-005-G130. 18__. 1820s.

Rarity: —

$5 • W-MA-960-005-G130b

Center: White boxes flanking FIVE DOLLARS. ***Engraver:*** PSSP. ***Comments:*** H-MA-370-G88. Similar to W-MA-960-005-G130 but with zigzag ruled lines. 18__. 1820s–1830s.

Rarity: —

$5 • W-MA-960-005-G130c

Center: White boxes flanking FIVE DOLLARS. ***Engraver:*** PSSP. ***Comments:*** H-MA-370-G90. Similar to W-MA-960-005-G130 but with spiral lathework lines. 18__. 1830s.

Rarity: —

$5 • W-MA-960-005-G130d

Center: White boxes flanking FIVE DOLLARS. ***Engraver:*** PSSP. ***Comments:*** H-MA-370-G92. Similar to W-MA-960-005-G130. 18__. 1830s.

Rarity: URS-7
VF $150

$5 • W-MA-960-005-G140

Left: 5 / Two women seated / V. ***Center:*** Portrait of George Washington / Angel with trumpet and globe / Portrait of Christopher Columbus. ***Bottom center:*** Eagle. ***Right:*** 5 / Portrait of Indian / V. ***Engraver:*** Draper, Toppan & Co. ***Comments:*** H-MA-370-G100. 18__. 1840s–1850s.

Rarity: —

$5 • W-MA-960-005-G140a

SI

Tint: Green outlined FIVE. ***Engraver:*** Draper, Toppan & Co. / ABNCo. monogram. ***Comments:*** H-MA-370-G100b. Similar to W-MA-960-005-G140 but with additional engraver imprint. 18__. 1850s–1860s.

Rarity: URS-3
VF $600

$10 • W-MA-960-010-G150

HA

Engraver: Reed. ***Comments:*** H-MA-370-G104. Proof. 18__. 1819–1820s.

Rarity: URS-3
Proof $400

$10 • W-MA-960-010-G160

Left: Lathework panel bearing MASSACHUSETTS / 10 / 10 vertically. ***Center:*** Alternating flower garlands and gridwork segments. ***Right:*** 10 / 10 vertically. ***Engraver:*** Perkins. ***Comments:*** H-MA-370-G106. 18__. 1820s.

Rarity: —

$10 • W-MA-960-010-G160a

ANS

Engraver: Perkins. ***Comments:*** H-MA-370-G108. Similar to W-MA-960-010-G160. 18__. 1820s.

Rarity: URS-4
VF $600

$10 • W-MA-960-010-G160b

Center: White boxes flanking TEN DOLLARS. ***Engraver:*** PSSP. ***Comments:*** H-MA-370-G110. Similar to W-MA-960-010-G160 but with zigzag ruled lines. 18__. 1820s–1830s.

Rarity: —

$10 • W-MA-960-010-G160c

Center: White boxes flanking TEN DOLLARS. ***Engraver:*** PSSP. ***Comments:*** H-MA-370-G112. Similar to W-MA-960-010-G160 but with spiral lathework lines. 18__. 1830s.

Rarity: —

$10 • W-MA-960-010-G160d

Center: White boxes flanking TEN DOLLARS. ***Engraver:*** PSSP. ***Comments:*** H-MA-370-G114. Similar to W-MA-960-010-G160. 18__. 1830s.

Rarity: —

$10 • W-MA-960-010-G160e

Center: White boxes flanking TEN DOLLARS. ***Engraver:*** PSSP. ***Comments:*** H-MA-370-G116. Similar to W-MA-960-010-G160. 18__. 1830s–1840s.

Rarity: —

$10 • W-MA-960-010-G170

QDB

Engraver: Draper, Toppan & Co. ***Comments:*** H-MA-370-G120. Proof. 18__. 1840s–1850s.

Rarity: URS-3
Proof $1,250

Collectors and Researchers:

If you have new information about any banks or notes listed in this volume, contact Whitman Publishing, Attn: Obsolete Paper Money, 3101 Clairmont Road, Suite G, Atlanta, GA 30329.

$10 • W-MA-960-010-G170a
Left: Portrait of George Washington on medallion scrolls. *Center:* 10 / Woman seated with arm on shield, Eagle, pole, and cap. *Bottom center:* Building. *Right:* 10 / Male portrait. *Tint:* Green. *Engraver:* Draper, Toppan & Co. / ABNCo. monogram. *Comments:* H-MA-370-G120b. Similar to W-MA-960-010-G170 but with additional engraver imprint. 18__. 1850s–1860s.
Rarity: —

$20 • W-MA-960-020-G180

HA

Engraver: Reed. *Comments:* H-MA-370-G124. Proof. 18__. 1819–1820s.
Rarity: URS-3
Proof $750

$20 • W-MA-960-020-G190
Left: Panel bearing state arms / 20 / 20 vertically. *Center:* Alternating flower garlands and gridwork segments. *Right:* 20 / 20 vertically. *Engraver:* Perkins. *Comments:* H-MA-370-G126. 18__. 1810s–1820s.
Rarity: —

$20 • W-MA-960-020-G190a
Left: Lathework chain bearing MASSACHUSETTS vertically. *Engraver:* PSSP. *Comments:* H-MA-370-G128. Similar to W-MA-960-020-G190. 18__. 1820s–1830s.
Rarity: —

$20 • W-MA-960-020-G200
Left: XX / Female portrait / XX. *Center:* Woman on rock, Cherubs and dolphins playing in water. *Right:* 20 / Dog's head / XX. *Engraver:* American Bank Note Co. *Comments:* H-MA-370-G132. 18__. 1860s.
Rarity: —

$30 • W-MA-960-030-G210

JF

Engraver: Reed. *Comments:* H-Unlisted. Promissory note. 18__.
Rarity: URS-2
Proof $2,500
Selected auction price: Heritage, January 2008, Lot 13037, EF-AU $1,092

$50 • W-MA-960-050-G220
Left: L / Massachusetts / L. *Center:* 50 / Woman leaning on shield bearing 50 / 50. *Bottom center:* 50. *Right:* 50 / FIFTY / 50. *Engraver:* A. Reed / Reed. *Comments:* H-MA-370-G136. 18__. 1819–1820s.
Rarity: URS-3
Proof $400

$50 • W-MA-960-050-G230
Left: Panel bearing state arms / 50 / 50 vertically. *Center:* Alternating flower garlands and gridwork segments. *Right:* 50 / 50 vertically. *Engraver:* Perkins. *Comments:* H-MA-370-G138. 18__. 1810s–1820s.
Rarity: —

$50 • W-MA-960-050-G230a
Left: Lathework chain bearing MASSACHUSETTS vertically. *Engraver:* PSSP. *Comments:* H-MA-370-G140. Similar to W-MA-960-050-G230. 18__. 1820s–1830s.
Rarity: —

$50 • W-MA-960-050-G240
Left: 50 / Minerva standing. *Center:* FIFTY on panel of microlettering. *Bottom center:* L. *Right:* 50 / Eagle / FIFTY. *Engraver:* American Bank Note Co. *Comments:* H-MA-370-G144. 18__. 1860s.
Rarity: —

$100 • W-MA-960-100-G250
Left: C / Massachusetts / C. *Center:* 100 / Woman reclining holding C / 100. *Bottom center:* 100. *Right:* 100 / ONE HUNDRED / 100. *Engraver:* A. Reed / Reed. *Comments:* H-MA-370-G148. 18__. 1819–1820s.
Rarity: URS-3
Proof $400

$100 • W-MA-960-100-G260
Left: Panel bearing state arms / 100 / 100 vertically. *Center:* Alternating flower garlands and gridwork segments. *Right:* 100 / 100 vertically. *Engraver:* Perkins. *Comments:* H-MA-370-G150. 18__. 1810s–1820s.
Rarity: —

$100 • W-MA-960-100-G260a
Left: Lathework chain bearing MASSACHUSETTS vertically. *Engraver:* Perkins. *Comments:* H-MA-370-G152. Similar to W-MA-960-100-G260. 18__. 1820s–1830s.
Rarity: —

$100 • W-MA-960-100-G270
Left: 100 / 100 / 100. *Center:* ONE HUNDRED on panel of microlettering. *Right:* 100 / 100 / 100. *Engraver:* American Bank Note Co. *Comments:* H-MA-370-G156. 18__. 1860s.
Rarity: —

$500 • W-MA-960-500-G280
Left: Lathework chain bearing MASSACHUSETTS / 500 / 500 vertically. *Center:* Alternating flower garlands and gridwork segments. *Right:* 500 / 500 vertically. *Engraver:* PSSP. *Comments:* H-MA-370-G158. 18__. 1820s–1830s.
Rarity: —

$500 • W-MA-960-500-G290

Left: 500 / Liberty with view of Boston. ***Center:*** Five Ds on panel of microlettering. ***Bottom center:*** D. ***Right:*** 500 / Woman seated with state arms. ***Engraver:*** American Bank Note Co. ***Comments:*** H-MA-370-G164. 18__. 1860s.

Rarity: —

$1,000 • W-MA-960-1000-G300

Left: Lathework chain bearing MASSACHUSETTS / 1000 / 1000 vertically. ***Center:*** Alternating flower garlands and gridwork segments. ***Right:*** 1000 / 1000 vertically. ***Engraver:*** PSSP. ***Comments:*** H-MA-370-G166. 18__. 1820s–1830s.

Rarity: —

$1,000 • W-MA-960-1000-G310

Left: 1000 / Woman seated. ***Center:*** Text / 1000. ***Right:*** 1000 / M on die / 1000. ***Engraver:*** American Bank Note Co. ***Comments:*** H-MA-370-G172. 18__. 1860s.

Rarity: URS-1

Proof $4,000

NON-VALID ISSUES

$2 • W-MA-960-002-C050e

CC

Engraver: PSSP. ***Comments:*** H-MA-370-C52. Counterfeit of W-MA-960-002-G050e. 18__. 1830s–1840s.

Rarity: URS-6

F $100; **VF** $150

$3 • W-MA-960-003-C070

SI

Engraver: Reed. ***Comments:*** H-MA-370-C60. Counterfeit of W-MA-960-003-G070. 18__. 1819–1820s.

Rarity: URS-6

F $100; **VF** $375

$3 • W-MA-960-003-C080e

CC

Engraver: PSSP. ***Comments:*** H-MA-370-C72. Counterfeit of W-MA-960-003-G080e. 18__. 1830s–1840s.

Rarity: URS-6

F $100

$5 • W-MA-960-005-C100

ANS

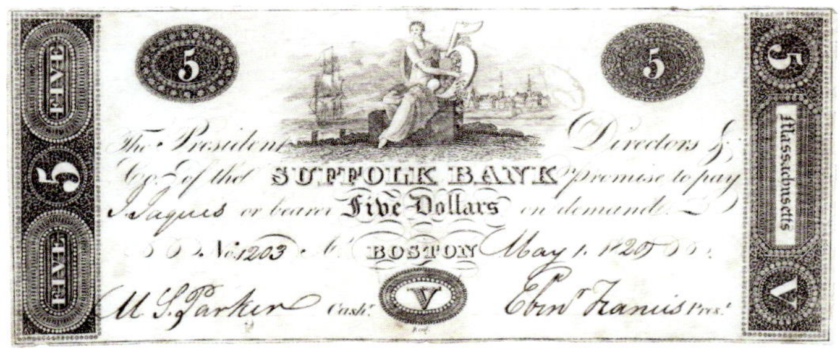

Engraver: A. Reed / Reed. ***Comments:*** H-MA-370-C80. Counterfeit of W-MA-960-005-G100. 18__. 1819–1820s.

Rarity: URS-6

F $100; **AU** $125

$5 • W-MA-960-005-C130d

SI

Engraver: PSSP. ***Comments:*** H-MA-370-C92. Counterfeit of W-MA-960-005-G130d. 18__. 1830s–1840s.

Rarity: URS-6

F $75

$5 • W-MA-960-005-C140

Engraver: Draper, Toppan & Co. ***Comments:*** H-MA-370-C100. Counterfeit of W-MA-960-005-G140. 18__. 1840s–1850s.

Rarity: URS-6

F $100

$5 • W-MA-960-005-A010

Engraver: PSSP. ***Comments:*** H-MA-370-A5. Altered from W-MA-175-005-G040 or G040a. 18__. 1820s.

Rarity: —

$10 • W-MA-960-010-C150

Engraver: A. Reed / Reed. ***Comments:*** H-MA-370-C104. Counterfeit of W-MA-960-010-G150. 18__. 1819–1820s.

Rarity: —

$10 • W-MA-960-010-C160e

Engraver: PSSP. ***Comments:*** H-MA-370-C116. Counterfeit of W-MA-960-010-G160e. 18__. 1830s–1840s.

Rarity: —

$10 • W-MA-960-010-C170

Engraver: Draper, Toppan & Co. ***Comments:*** H-MA-370-C120. Counterfeit of W-MA-960-010-G170 or variety. 18__. 1850s.

Rarity: —

$10 • W-MA-960-010-A020

Left: 10 / Hebe watering eagle in clouds / TEN. ***Center:*** Harbor scene / Portrait of Benjamin Franklin flanked by scientific instruments / Harvesting scene. ***Right:*** 10 / Dog, Woman standing with grain / TEN. ***Engraver:*** New England Bank Note Co. / PSSP. ***Comments:*** H-MA-370-A10. Altered from W-MA-520-010-G100. 18__. 1830s.

Rarity: —

Suffolk Bank of Boston

1840s

W-MA-970

History: A non-existent bank represented only by fraudulent notes intended to pass for those of the Suffolk Bank, W-MA-960.

Issues

$100 • W-MA-970-100-S010

Left: Medallion head. ***Center:*** 100 / Men working, Train cars / 100. ***Right:*** Woman / Portrait of Benjamin Franklin / Woman. ***Engraver:*** Spencer, Hufty & Danforth / Danforth, Spencer & Hufty. ***Comments:*** H-MA-371-G10. 18__. 1840s.

Rarity: —

Sutton Bank

1828–1829

W-MA-980

History: The Sutton Bank was incorporated on March 11, 1828, with an authorized capital of $100,000.

On September 26, 1828, the governor of Massachusetts agreed to have the paid-in capital stock examined, to assure that the oaths of the directors were sound regarding the payments of their shares.[72] This was done out of fear—justly founded—that the subscriptions had been made in the forms of loans, rather than in specie. It was discovered that the Sutton Bank had borrowed an amount of $51,000 to be used as the specie under examination, allowing the commissioners to write a report confirming that there was, indeed, $50,000 in specie in the vaults of the Sutton Bank. The borrowed funds were returned after the inspection was made.[73] Shortly after, the Sutton Bank failed in 1829.

See also listing under Wilkinsonville, W-MA-3330.

Traders Bank

1831–1865

W-MA-990

History: The Traders Bank was chartered in March 1831. Its office was located at 9 India Street. The capital was $500,000 until 1845, when it was decreased to $400,000.

Figures for 1838 were: net profits on hand $47,723.55; balances due to other banks $54,039.49; cash deposited $154,618.54; cash deposited bearing interest $17,754.88; total amount due from banks $935,553.46; gold, silver, and other coined metals in the banking house $21,181.02; bills of other banks incorporated in this state $27,349; balance due from other banks $37,573.21; amount of all debts due $849,450.23; total amount of resources of the bank $935,553.46.

The business of the Traders Bank was succeeded by the Traders National Bank of Boston, chartered on July 15, 1865.

Numismatic Commentary: Many of this bank's genuine notes carry identical vignettes of a wharf scene on the East Boston side of the harbor looking toward the State House. The area depicted on these notes looks very much the same today.

Valid Issues

$1 • W-MA-990-001-G010

Left: Lathework panel bearing MASSACHUSETTS vertically. ***Center:*** 1 / 1 / Alternating flower garlands and gridwork segments / ONE / 1 / 1. ***Right:*** Lathework panel bearing ONE / D / ONE vertically. ***Engraver:*** PSSP. ***Comments:*** H-MA-375-G4. 18__. 1830s.

Rarity: —

$1 • W-MA-990-001-G020

Left: 1 / Carpenter / ONE. ***Center:*** Wharf scene and harbor view / ONE. ***Right:*** 1 / Woman standing, Man seated / ONE. ***Engraver:*** New England Bank Note Co. / PSSP. ***Comments:*** H-MA-375-G6. 18__. 1830s–1850s.

Rarity: —

$1 • W-MA-990-001-G020a

Engraver: New England Bank Note Co. / PSSP. ***Comments:*** H-MA-375-G6a. Similar to W-MA-990-001-G020 but printed on pink paper. 18__. 1830s.

Rarity: —

$1 • W-MA-990-001-G020b

Engraver: New England Bank Note Co. ***Comments:*** H-MA-375-G6b. Similar to W-MA-990-001-G020 but with different engraver imprint. 18__. 1830s–1850s.

Rarity: URS-6
VF $450

$1 • W-MA-990-001-G020c

Engraver: New England Bank Note Co. / ABNCo. monogram. ***Comments:*** H-MA-375-G6c. Similar to W-MA-990-001-G020b but with additional engraver imprint. 18__. 1850s–1860s.

Rarity: —

$1 • W-MA-990-001-G020d

Engraver: American Bank Note Co. ***Comments:*** H-MA-375-G6d. Similar to W-MA-990-001-G020 but with different engraver imprint. 18__. 1860s.

Rarity: URS-6
VF $450

$2 • W-MA-990-002-G030

Left: Lathework panel bearing MASSACHUSETTS vertically. ***Center:*** 2 / 2 / Alternating flower garlands and gridwork segments / TWO / 2 / 2. ***Right:*** Lathework panel bearing five TWOs vertically. ***Engraver:*** PSSP. ***Comments:*** H-MA-375-G10. 18__. 1830s.

Rarity: —

$2 • W-MA-990-002-G040

Left: 2 / Two men at work / TWO. ***Center:*** Wharf scene and harbor view / 2. ***Right:*** 2 / Woman seated / TWO. ***Engraver:*** New England Bank Note Co. / PSSP. ***Comments:*** H-MA-375-G12. 18__. 1830s–1850s.

Rarity: —

$2 • W-MA-990-002-G040a

Engraver: New England Bank Note Co. / PSSP. ***Comments:*** H-MA-375-G12a. Similar to W-MA-990-002-G040 but printed on pink paper. 18__. 1830s.

Rarity: —

$2 • W-MA-990-002-G040b

CC

Engraver: New England Bank Note Co. / PSSP / ABNCo. monogram. ***Comments:*** H-MA-375-G12c. Similar to W-MA-990-002-G040 but with additional engraver imprint. 18__. 1850s–1860s.

Rarity: URS-6
VF $450

$3 • W-MA-990-003-G050

Left: Lathework panel bearing MASSACHUSETTS vertically. ***Center:*** 3 / 3 / Alternating flower garlands and gridwork segments / THREE / 3 / 3. ***Right:*** Lathework panel bearing THREE vertically. ***Engraver:*** PSSP. ***Comments:*** H-MA-375-G16. 18__. 1830s.

Rarity: —

$3 • W-MA-990-003-G060

Left: 3 / Man with anvil / THREE. ***Center:*** Wharf scene and harbor view / 3. ***Right:*** 3 / Woman standing with basket / THREE. ***Engraver:*** New England Bank Note Co. / PSSP. ***Comments:*** H-MA-375-G18. 18__. 1840s–1850s.

Rarity: —

$3 • W-MA-990-003-G060a

Engraver: New England Bank Note Co. / PSSP. ***Comments:*** H-MA-375-G18a. Similar to W-MA-990-003-G060 but printed on pink paper. 18__. 1830s.

Rarity: —

$3 • W-MA-990-003-G060b

HA

Engraver: New England Bank Note Co. / PSSP / ABNCo. monogram. ***Comments:*** H-MA-375-G18c. Similar to W-MA-990-003-G060 but with additional engraver imprint. 18__. 1850s–1860s.

Rarity: URS-4
VF $700

$5 • W-MA-990-005-G070

Left: Lathework chain bearing MASSACHUSETTS / 5 / 5. ***Center:*** Alternating flower garlands and gridwork segments / FIVE DOLLARS with spiral lathework lines. ***Right:*** 5 / 5. ***Engraver:*** PSSP. ***Comments:*** H-MA-375-G22. 18__. 1830s.

Rarity: —

$5 • W-MA-990-005-G080

Left: FIVE / Justice with scales. ***Center:*** Wharf scene and harbor view / 5. ***Right:*** 5 / Portrait of Daniel Webster / FIVE. ***Engraver:*** New England Bank Note Co. / PSSP. ***Comments:*** H-MA-375-G24. 18__. 1830s–1850s.

Rarity: —

$5 • W-MA-990-005-G080a

Engraver: New England Bank Note Co. / PSSP. ***Comments:*** H-MA-375-G24a. Similar to W-MA-990-005-G080 but printed on pink paper. 18__. 1830s.

Rarity: —

$5 • W-MA-990-005-G080b

QDB

Engraver: New England Bank Note Co. / PSSP / ABNCo. monogram. ***Comments:*** H-MA-375-G24c. Similar to W-MA-990-005-G080 but with additional engraver imprint. 18__. 1850s–1860s.

Rarity: URS-5
F $350; **VF** $500

$10 • W-MA-990-010-G090

Left: Lathework chain bearing MASSACHUSETTS / 10 / 10 vertically. ***Center:*** Alternating flower garlands and gridwork segments / TEN DOLLARS with spiral lathework lines. ***Right:*** 10 / 10 vertically. ***Engraver:*** New England Bank Note Co. / PSSP. ***Comments:*** H-MA-375-G26. 18__. 1830s.

Rarity: —

$10 • W-MA-990-010-G100

Left: TEN / Woman with harp. ***Center:*** Wharf scene and harbor view / X. ***Right:*** 10 / Female portrait / TEN. ***Engraver:*** New England Bank Note Co. / PSSP. ***Comments:*** H-MA-375-G30. 18__. 1830s–1850s.

Rarity: —

$10 • **W-MA-990-010-G100a**

TD

Engraver: New England Bank Note Co. / PSSP / ABNCo. monogram. ***Comments:*** H-MA-375-G30c. Similar to W-MA-990-010-G100 but with additional engraver imprint. 18__. 1850s–1860s.

Rarity: URS-4
F $300; **VF** $650

$20 • **W-MA-990-020-G110**

Left: Lathework chain bearing MASSACHUSETTS / 20 / 20 vertically. ***Center:*** Alternating flower garlands and gridwork segments. ***Right:*** 20 / 20 vertically. ***Engraver:*** PSSP. ***Comments:*** H-MA-375-G32. 18__. 1830s.

Rarity: —

$20 • **W-MA-990-020-G120**

Left: 20 / Woman / XX. ***Center:*** Wharf scene and harbor view / TWENTY on panel of microlettering. ***Right:*** 20 / Indian woman as Justice / XX. ***Engraver:*** New England Bank Note Co. / PSSP. ***Comments:*** H-MA-375-G36. Center vignette same as W-MA-990-001-G020. 18__. 1830s–1850s.

Rarity: —

$20 • **W-MA-990-020-G120a**

Engraver: New England Bank Note Co. / PSSP / ABNCo. monogram. ***Comments:*** H-MA-375-G36a. Similar to W-MA-990-020-G120 but with additional engraver imprint. 18__. 1850s–1860s.

Rarity: —

$20 • **W-MA-990-020-G120b**

TD

Overprint: Red TWENTY. ***Engraver:*** American Bank Note Co. ***Comments:*** H-Unlisted. Similar to W-MA-990-020-G120. Center vignette same as W-MA-990-001-G020. 18__. 1860s.

Rarity: URS-3
VF $1,750

$50 • **W-MA-990-050-G130**

Left: Lathework chain bearing MASSACHUSETTS / 50 / 50 vertically. ***Center:*** Alternating flower garlands and gridwork segments. ***Right:*** 50 / 50 vertically. ***Engraver:*** PSSP. ***Comments:*** H-MA-375-G38. 18__. 1830s.

Rarity: —

$50 • **W-MA-990-050-G140**

Left: 50. ***Center:*** Wharf scene and harbor view / 50. ***Right:*** 50 / Covered wagon and merchandise. ***Engraver:*** New England Bank Note Co. ***Comments:*** H-MA-375-G42. Center vignette same as W-MA-990-001-G020. 18__. 1840s–1850s.

Rarity: —

$50 • **W-MA-990-050-G140a**

Overprint: Red. ***Engraver:*** New England Bank Note Co. ***Comments:*** H-MA-375-G42a. Similar to W-MA-990-050-G140. 18__. 1850s.

Rarity: —

$50 • **W-MA-990-050-G140b**

Overprint: Red. ***Engraver:*** New England Bank Note Co. / ABNCo. monogram. ***Comments:*** H-MA-375-G42b. Similar to W-MA-990-050-G140 but with additional engraver imprint. 18__. 1850s–1860s.

Rarity: —

$100 • **W-MA-990-100-G150**

Left: Lathework chain bearing MASSACHUSETTS / 100 / 100 vertically. ***Center:*** Alternating flower garlands and gridwork segments. ***Right:*** 100 / 100 vertically. ***Engraver:*** Perkins ***Comments:*** H-MA-375-G44. 18__. 1830s.

Rarity: —

$100 • **W-MA-990-100-G160**

Left: Wharf scene and harbor view / 100. ***Center:*** ONE HUND. ***Right:*** HUNDRED over 100 / Portrait of George Washington. ***Engraver:*** New England Bank Note Co. ***Comments:*** H-MA-375-G48. 18__. 1840s–1850s.

Rarity: —

$100 • **W-MA-990-100-G160a**

JF

Overprint: Red HUNDRED. ***Engraver:*** New England Bank Note Co. ***Comments:*** H-MA-375-G48a. Similar to W-MA-990-100-G160. 18__. 1850s–1860s.

Rarity: URS-3
VF $2,000

$100 • **W-MA-990-100-G160b**

Overprint: Red HUNDRED. ***Engraver:*** New England Bank Note Co. / ABNCo. monogram. ***Comments:*** H-MA-375-G48b. Similar to W-MA-990-100-G160 but with additional engraver imprint. 18__. 1850s–1860s.

Rarity: URS-3
VF $1,500

$500 • **W-MA-990-500-G170**

Left: Lathework chain bearing MASSACHUSETTS / 500 / 500 vertically. ***Center:*** Alternating flower garlands and gridwork segments. ***Right:*** 500 / 500 vertically. ***Engraver:*** PSSP. ***Comments:*** H-MA-375-G50. 18__. 1820s–1830s.

Rarity: —

$500 • W-MA-990-500-G180

Left: 500. ***Center:*** Wharf scene and harbor view / 500. ***Right:*** 500 / Eagle and shield. ***Engraver:*** ABNCo. monogram. ***Comments:*** H-MA-375-G54. Center vignette same as W-MA-990-001-G020. 18__. 1850s–1860s.

Rarity: —

Non-Valid Issues

$1 • W-MA-990-001-N010

Center: Farmer seated with scythe. ***Right:*** Portrait. ***Overprint:*** Red ONE. ***Comments:*** H-MA-375-N5. 1850s.

Rarity: —

$1 • W-MA-990-001-A010

Left: 1 / Milkmaid seated with pail. ***Center:*** Two cows, one lying down and one standing, Horse and cows. ***Bottom center:*** Obverse of U.S. gold dollar. ***Right:*** ONE / Girl / 1. ***Engraver:*** Wellstood, Hay & Whiting. ***Comments:*** H-MA-375-A5. Altered from $1 Thames Bank, Laurel, Indiana. 1850s.

Rarity: —

$1 • W-MA-990-001-A020

Left: Woman / ONE on 1. ***Center:*** Man seated with rake, Farmers / ONE. ***Right:*** ONE / Indian / ONE. ***Overprint:*** Red ONE. ***Engraver:*** New England Bank Note Co. / Rawdon, Wright, Hatch & Edson. ***Comments:*** H-MA-375-A10. Altered from $1 Waubeek Bank, De Soto, Nebraska. May 1, 1857.

Rarity: URS-5

F $125

$2 • W-MA-990-002-N020

Center: Wagon and four horses. ***Comments:*** H-MA-375-N10. 1850s.

Rarity: —

$2 • W-MA-990-002-N030

Center: Shield, Steamboat. ***Right:*** Woman standing with flag. ***Comments:*** H-MA-375-N15.

Rarity: —

$2 • W-MA-990-002-A030

Left: 2 / Two Indians on cliff viewing town. ***Center:*** Portrait of Andrew Jackson / Woman seated with shield bearing cotton plant. ***Right:*** 2 / CONSTITUTION, Monument. ***Overprint:*** Red TWO. ***Engraver:*** Bald, Cousland & Co. / Baldwin, Bald & Cousland. ***Comments:*** H-MA-375-A15. Altered from $2 Southern Bank of Georgia, Bainbridge, Georgia. 18__. 1860s.

Rarity: —

$2 • W-MA-990-002-A040

SI

Overprint: Red TWO. ***Engraver:*** Wellstood, Hays & Whiting. ***Comments:*** H-MA-375-A20. Altered from $2 Thames Bank, Laurel, Indiana. August 12, 185_. 1850s.

Rarity: URS-7

F $100; **VF** $1,750

$2 • W-MA-990-002-A050

Left: Two girls carrying sheaves / 2. ***Center:*** Sailor and mechanic flanking U.S. shield surmounted by badger. ***Right:*** 2 / Liberty standing, Indian woman kneeling. ***Overprint:*** Red TWO. ***Engraver:*** New England Bank Note Co. / Rawdon, Wright, Hatch & Edson. ***Comments:*** H-MA-375-A25. Altered from $2 Waubeek Bank, De Soto, Nebraska. 1857.

Rarity: —

$3 • W-MA-990-003-A060

Left: THREE / Woman seated with scroll and pen / THREE. ***Center:*** Train / Woman in clouds with shield and eagle. ***Right:*** THREE / Laureate woman standing with legs crossed and shield bearing 3. ***Engraver:*** New England Bank Note Co. / PSSP. ***Comments:*** H-MA-375-A30. Altered from $3 Potomac River Bank, Georgetown, D.C. 18__. 1830s–1850s

Rarity: —

$5 • W-MA-990-005-S010

Left: Portrait of Benjamin Franklin. ***Center:*** Farmer reclining under tree, Canal scene and horses. ***Right:*** Woman leaning on 5. ***Engraver:*** Toppan, Carpenter & Co. ***Comments:*** H-MA-375-S5. 18__. 1850s.

Rarity: —

$5 • W-MA-990-005-A070

Left: Portrait of Henry Clay / V. ***Center:*** Farmer feeding hogs. ***Bottom center:*** Dog lying down. ***Right:*** 5 / Farmer carrying basket of corn. ***Overprint:*** Red FIVE. ***Engraver:*** Wellstood, Hays & Whiting. ***Comments:*** H-MA-375-A35. Altered from $5 Thames Bank, Laurel, Indiana. 1850s.

Rarity: —

How to Read the Whitman Numbering System

$1 • W-MA-010-001-G010a

Denomination: Value of the note shown.

W: Whitman number. This number is a sortable code unique to each bank and note.

MA: Abbreviation for the state under study.

010: Numerical designation specific to each bank.

001: The denomination in dollars.

G010a: G indicates a good or valid note. Other categories are indicated thus: C (counterfeit); R (raised); S (spurious); N (not-attributed); A (altered). Numbers are assigned starting with 010, 020, et seq. Terminal letters following the number indicate variations of a note: a series of different colored overprints, tints, payees, etc., all on the same design of note. For more information, see the "How to Use This Book" section at the front of the volume, page xiv.

$5 • W-MA-990-005-A080 HA

Engraver: Rawdon, Wright & Hatch. ***Comments:*** H-MA-375-A40. Altered from $5 Commercial Bank of Millington, Millington, Maryland. 18__. Circa 1840.

Rarity: URS-5
F $125

$10 • W-MA-990-010-N040

Left: Portrait of George Washington. ***Right:*** Coins. ***Comments:*** H-MA-375-N20.

Rarity: —

$10 • W-MA-990-010-N050

Center: Female portrait, State arms. ***Comments:*** H-MA-375-N25.

Rarity: —

$10 • W-MA-990-010-N060

Left: X / X. ***Center:*** Liberty reclining on shield. ***Right:*** TEN. ***Comments:*** H-MA-375-N30.

Rarity: —

$20 • W-MA-990-020-R010

Engraver: New England Bank Note Co. / PSSP. ***Comments:*** H-MA-375-R10. Raised from W-MA-990-001-G020 or variety. 18__. 1840s–1850s.

Rarity: —

$20 • W-MA-990-020-A090

Left: Steamboat / XX / Train. ***Center:*** Three women seated with eagle, pole and cap, shield, scales, and book / 20 / Panel outlining white TWENTY. ***Right:*** XX / Milkmaid with pail. ***Engraver:*** New England Bank Note Co. ***Comments:*** H-MA-375-A45. Altered from $20 Hamilton Bank, Scituate, Rhode Island, or from notes of other failed banks using the same plate. 18__. 1840s.

Rarity: —

Tremont Bank

1830–1864

W-MA-1000

History: The Tremont Bank was formerly known as the Manufacturers and Mechanics Bank, W-MA-690. On March 8, 1830, the Legislature reduced the authorized capital of the bank and allowed the name to be changed to the Tremont Bank. Later, the bank's charter was renewed in 1837 with an authorized capital of $500,000. It was increased to $1,000,000 in 1851. In 1855 it was even higher at $1,250,000. Circulation averaged at $45,000 between 1838 and 1840, and from 1845 to 1860 it ranged from $219,809 to $260,452.

Other figures for 1838 included: net profits on hand $28,702.67; balances due to other banks $25,507.18; cash deposited $100,131.25; cash deposited bearing interest $2,000; total amount due from banks $775,492.10; gold, silver, and other coined metals in the banking house $20,833.25; real estate $34,363.03; bills of other banks incorporated in this state $12,601; balance due from other banks $9,056.27; amount of all debts due $698,638.55; total amount of resources of the bank $775,492.10.

In the summer of 1852, a caper was discovered involving the stealing of duplicate keys of the Tremont Bank that had been deposited for safekeeping with the cashier of the Shoe and Leather Dealers Bank. It seemed that a trusted expressman was involved who was tied in with some fellow miscreants located in New York City. Apparently, the group planned to burgle both of the banks. However, after cashing a false check for $2,300 at the Tremont Bank, the expressman fled to California without sharing his spoils with his fellow conspirators. The banks never were burgled. Whether the expressman found riches is not recorded. His New York City friends were hauled off to jail.

The interests of the Tremont Bank were succeeded by the Tremont National Bank on December 14, 1864.

Numismatic Commentary: Some of the genuine notes of this bank will show a street scene of the financial district on State Street looking toward Long Wharf. Notes showing local scenes like this are highly prized by collectors.

Valid Issues

$1 • W-MA-1000-001-G010

Left: Lathework panel bearing ONE / D / ONE vertically. ***Center:*** 1 / 1 / 1 on a gridwork triangle / Alternating flower garlands and gridwork segments bearing ONE / 1 / 1. ***Right:*** Lathework panel bearing ONE / D / ONE vertically. ***Engraver:*** PSSP. ***Comments:*** H-MA-380-G4. 18__. 1830s.

Rarity: —

$1 • W-MA-1000-001-G020

Left: 1 / Woman wearing bonnet with pail / ONE. ***Center:*** Machinery and merchandise flanking Ceres seated holding sickle and rake, Factories and harbor / Panel outlining white ONE. ***Right:*** 1 / Ship / ONE. ***Engraver:*** PSSP / New England Bank Note Co. ***Comments:*** H-MA-380-G8. 18__. 1830s–1840s.

Rarity: —

$1 • W-MA-1000-001-G030

Left: ONE / Liberty / ONE. ***Center:*** View of Boston in 1630 / Neptune / View of Boston in 1852. ***Right:*** 1 / Woman. ***Comments:*** H-MA-380-G12. 18__. 1850s.

Rarity: —

$1 • W-MA-1000-001-G040 CC

Back: Plain. ***Engraver:*** Danforth, Wright & Co. ***Comments:*** H-MA-380-G16. Remainder. 18__. 1850s.

Rarity: URS-3
EF $1,500

$1 • W-MA-1000-001-G040a

Left: 1 / ONE / 1. ***Center:*** View of street in Boston. ***Right:*** ONE on 1 / Male portrait / ONE. ***Back:*** Brown lathework bearing "NEPONSET BANK, INCORPORATED 1836, MASSACHUSETTS." ***Engraver:*** Danforth, Wright & Co. ***Comments:*** H-MA-380-G16a. Similar to W-MA-1000-001-G040. Back presumably printed in error. 18__.

Rarity: URS-3
F $1,500; **Unc-Rem** $600

$1 • W-MA-1000-001-G040b

Tint: Red-brown. ***Engraver:*** Danforth, Wright & Co. ***Comments:*** H-MA-380-G16b. Similar to W-MA-1000-001-G040. 18__. 1850s.

Rarity: URS-4
F $1,500; **Proof** $2,500

$2 • W-MA-1000-002-G050

Left: Lathework panel bearing five TWOs vertically. ***Center:*** 2 / 2 / 2 on a gridwork triangle / Alternating flower garlands and gridwork segments bearing TWO / 2 / 2. ***Right:*** Lathework panel bearing five TWOs vertically. ***Engraver:*** PSSP. ***Comments:*** H-MA-380-G18. 18__. 1830s.

Rarity: —

$2 • W-MA-1000-002-G060

Left: 2 / Cornucopia, Woman standing with staff / TWO. ***Center:*** TWO / Machinery and merchandise flanking Ceres seated holding sickle and rake, Factories and harbor / Panel outlining white TWO. ***Right:*** 2 / Woman wearing hat, Trees / TWO. ***Engraver:*** New England Bank Note Co. / PSSP. ***Comments:*** H-MA-380-G24. 18__. 1830s–1840s.

Rarity: —

$2 • W-MA-1000-002-G070

Left: Woman composed of names of states / TWO. ***Center:*** View of Boston in 1630 / Neptune / View of Boston in 1852. ***Right:*** 2 / Two women. ***Comments:*** H-MA-380-G28. 18__. 1850s.

Rarity: —

$2 • W-MA-1000-002-G080

HA

Back: Plain. ***Engraver:*** Danforth, Wright & Co. ***Comments:*** H-MA-380-G32. Proof. 18__. 1830s.

Rarity: URS-3
Proof $2,000
Selected auction price: Stack's Bowers Galleries, August 2014, Lot 2068, Proof $1,880

$2 • W-MA-1000-002-G080a

Left: 2. ***Center:*** View of street in Boston / 2. ***Right:*** 2 / Two women. ***Back:*** Brown lathework bearing "NEPONSET BANK, INCORPORATED 1836, MASSACHUSETTS." ***Engraver:*** Danforth, Wright & Co. ***Comments:*** H-MA-380-G32a. Similar to W-MA-1000-002-G080. Back presumably printed in error. 18__.

Rarity: URS-4
VG $750; **EF** $1,500

$2 • W-MA-1000-002-G080b

JF

Tint: Red-brown. ***Engraver:*** Danforth, Wright & Co. ***Comments:*** H-MA-380-G32b. Similar to W-MA-1000-002-G080. Proof. 18__. 1850s.

Rarity: URS-3
Proof $5,000

$3 • W-MA-1000-003-G090

Left: Lathework panel bearing THREE vertically. ***Center:*** 3 / 3 / 3 on a gridwork triangle / Alternating flower garlands and gridwork segments bearing THREE / 3 / 3. ***Right:*** Lathework panel bearing THREE vertically. ***Engraver:*** PSSP. ***Comments:*** H-MA-380-G34. 18__. 1830s.

Rarity: —

$3 • W-MA-1000-003-G100

Left: 3 / Woman seated on barrel with bale. ***Center:*** View of Boston in 1632 / Neptune / View of Boston in 1852. ***Right:*** 3 / Mechanic, sailor, and farmer standing with 3. ***Comments:*** H-MA-380-G40. 18__. 1850s.

Rarity: —

$3 • W-MA-1000-003-G110

CC

Back: Plain. ***Engraver:*** Danforth, Wright & Co. ***Comments:*** H-MA-380-G44. 18__. 1850s.

Rarity: URS-3
Proof $2,500

$3 • W-MA-1000-003-G110a

Left: 3 / THREE / 3. ***Center:*** 3 / Street scene in Boston. ***Right:*** 3 over III / Three women. ***Back:*** Brown lathework bearing "NEPONSET BANK, INCORPORATED 1836, MASSACHUSETTS." ***Engraver:*** Danforth, Wright & Co. ***Comments:*** H-MA-380-G44a. Similar to W-MA-1000-003-G110. Back presumably printed in error. 18__.

Rarity: URS-4
F $1,250; **EF** $2,250

$3 • W-MA-1000-003-G110b

Tint: Red-brown. ***Engraver:*** Danforth, Wright & Co. ***Comments:*** H-MA-380-G44b. Similar to W-MA-1000-003-G110. 18__. 1850s.

Rarity: URS-2
Proof $4,000

$5 • W-MA-1000-005-G120

Left: Lathework chain bearing MASSACHUSETTS / 5 / 5. ***Center:*** Alternating flower garlands and gridwork segments / White boxes flanking FIVE DOLLARS with zigzag ruled lines. ***Right:*** 5 / 5. ***Engraver:*** PSSP. ***Comments:*** H-MA-380-G46. 18__. 1830s.

Rarity: —

$5 • W-MA-1000-005-G120a

Engraver: PSSP. ***Comments:*** H-MA-380-G48. Similar to W-MA-1000-005-G120 but with spiral lathework lines. 18__. 1830s.

Rarity: —

$5 • W-MA-1000-005-G130

Left: MASSACHUSETTS on lathework strip. ***Center:*** 5 / Woman / FIVE. ***Right:*** 5 / Indian / 5. ***Engraver:*** PSSP. ***Comments:*** H-MA-380-G52. 18__. 1840s–1850s.

Rarity: URS-4
F $400

$10 • W-MA-1000-010-G140

Left: Lathework chain bearing MASSACHUSETTS / 10 / 10 vertically. ***Center:*** Alternating flower garlands and gridwork segments / White boxes flanking TEN DOLLARS with zigzag ruled lines. ***Right:*** 10 / 10 vertically. ***Engraver:*** PSSP. ***Comments:*** H-MA-380-G54. 18__. 1830s.

Rarity: —

$10 • W-MA-1000-010-G140a

Engraver: PSSP. ***Comments:*** H-MA-380-G56. Similar to W-MA-1000-010-G140 but with spiral lathework lines. 18__. 1830s.

Rarity: —

$10 • W-MA-1000-010-G150

Left: MASSACHUSETTS on circular dies. ***Center:*** 10 / Woman standing / 10 / Text on microletter background. ***Right:*** 10 / Indian / 10. ***Engraver:*** PSSP. ***Comments:*** H-MA-380-G60. 18__. 1840s–1850s.

Rarity: URS-2
Proof $1,200

$20 • W-MA-1000-020-G160

Left: Lathework chain bearing MASSACHUSETTS / 20 / 20 vertically. ***Center:*** Alternating flower garlands and gridwork segments. ***Right:*** 20 / 20 vertically. ***Engraver:*** PSSP. ***Comments:*** H-MA-380-G64. 18__. 1830s.

Rarity: —

$50 • W-MA-1000-050-G170

CC

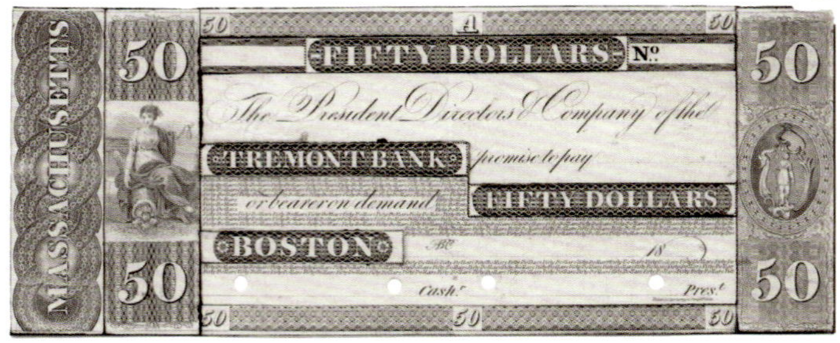

Engraver: PSSP. ***Comments:*** H-MA-380-G66. 18__. 1830s.

Rarity: URS-1
Proof $1,500
Selected auction price: Stack's Bowers Galleries, August 2014, Lot 2069, Proof $1,116

$100 • W-MA-1000-100-G180

CC

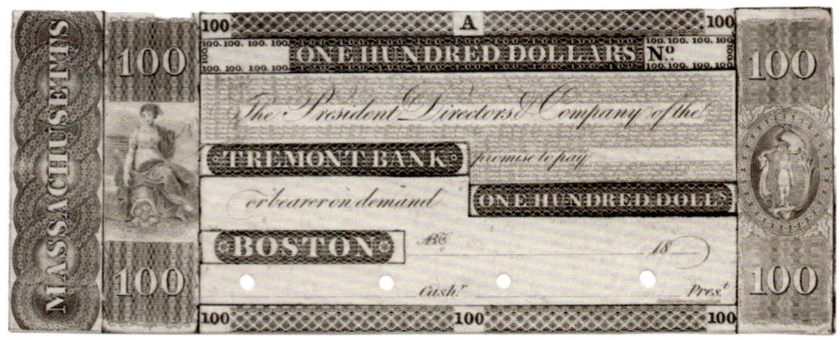

Engraver: Perkins. ***Comments:*** H-MA-380-G68. 18__. 1830s.

Rarity: URS-1
Proof $2,000
Selected auction price: Stack's Bowers Galleries, August 2014, Lot 2070, Proof $1,527

$500 • W-MA-1000-500-G190

CC

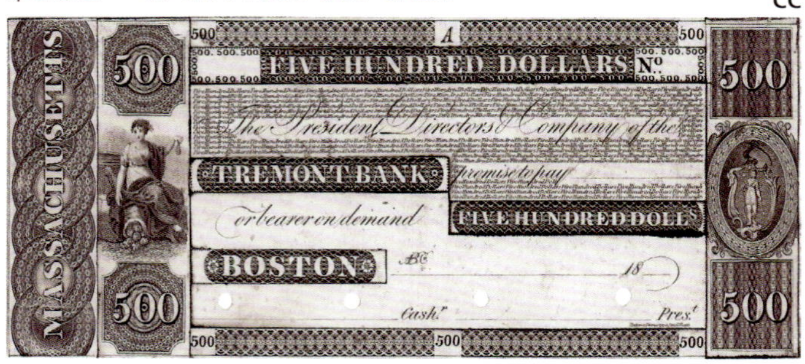

Engraver: PSSP. ***Comments:*** H-MA-380-G70. 18__. 1830s.

Rarity: URS-1
Proof $4,000
Selected auction price: Stack's Bowers Galleries, August 2014, Lot 2071, Proof $3,525

$1,000 • W-MA-1000-1000-G200

Left: Lathework chain bearing MASSACHUSETTS / 1000 / Ceres / 1000. ***Center:*** ONE THOUSAND DOLLARS. ***Right:*** 1000 / State arms / 1000. ***Engraver:*** PSSP. ***Comments:*** H-MA-380-G72. 18__. 1820s–1830s.

Rarity: —
CU $475

$1,000 • W-MA-1000-1000-G200a

TD

Engraver: PSSP / ABNCo. monogram. ***Comments:*** H-Unlisted. Similar to W-MA-1000-1000-G200 but with additional engraver imprint. 18__.

Rarity: URS-1
Proof $4,500

Uncut Sheets

$1-$1-$2-$3 • W-MA-1000-001.001.002.003-US010

Vignette(s): ***($1)*** ONE / View of street in Boston / ONE / Male portrait / ONE. ***($1)*** ONE / View of street in Boston / ONE / Male portrait / ONE. ***($2)*** View of street in Boston / Two women. ***($3)*** THREE / Street scene in Boston / Three women. ***Back:*** Brown lathework bearing "NEPONSET BANK, INCORPORATED 1836, MASSACHUSETTS." ***Engraver:*** Danforth, Wright & Co. ***Comments:*** H-MA-380-G16a, G16a, G32a, G44a. Back presumably printed in error.

Rarity: —

$1-$1-$2-$3 • W-MA-1000-001.001.002.003-US010a

Tint(s): Red-brown. ***Engraver:*** Danforth, Wright & Co. ***Comments:*** H-MA-380-G16b, G16b, G32b, G44b. Similar to W-MA-1000-001.001.002.003-US010. 18__. 1850s.

Rarity: —

Non-Valid Issues

$1 • W-MA-1000-001-S010

SI

Engraver: Draper, Toppan & Co. ***Comments:*** H-MA-380-S5. From a modified, fraudulent plate originally for a $1 counterfeit of the State Bank of Indiana. July 1, 1850.

Rarity: URS-7
VG $75

$1 • W-MA-1000-001-A010

Left: 1 / Milkmaid seated with pail. ***Center:*** Two cows, one lying down and one standing, Horse and cows. ***Bottom center:*** Obverse of U.S. gold dollar. ***Right:*** ONE / Girl / 1. ***Overprint:*** Red ONE. ***Engraver:*** Wellstood, Hay & Whiting. ***Comments:*** H-MA-380-A5. Altered from $1 Thames Bank, Laurel, Indiana. 1850s.

Rarity: —

$3 • W-MA-1000-003-S020

Left: THREE / Woman reading book resting on column / THREE. ***Center:*** Three men at work in foundry. ***Right:*** THREE / Portrait of Christopher Columbus / THREE. ***Engraver:*** Draper, Toppan & Co. ***Comments:*** H-MA-380-S10. From a modified, fraudulent plate originally for a $1 counterfeit of the State Bank of Indiana. July 1, 1850.

Rarity: —

$3 • W-MA-1000-003-S030

CC

Engraver: New England Bank Note Co. ***Comments:*** H-MA-380-S15. Remainder. 18__. Circa 1850.

Rarity: URS-7
VG $100

$5 • W-MA-1000-005-S040

Left: 5 / FIVE / 5. ***Center:*** V / Eagle on wharf with plow, Cannon and anchor, Ships / V / Panel outlining white FIVE. ***Right:*** 5 / FIVE / 5. ***Engraver:*** New England Bank Note Co. ***Comments:*** H-MA-380-S20. 18__. Circa 1850.

Rarity: —

$10 • W-MA-1000-010-S050

Left: TEN / Woman reading book resting on column / TEN. ***Center:*** Three men at work in foundry. ***Right:*** TEN / Portrait of Christopher Columbus / TEN. ***Engraver:*** Draper, Toppan & Co. ***Comments:*** H-MA-380-S25. From a modified, fraudulent plate originally for a $1 counterfeit of the State Bank of Indiana. July 1, 1850.

Rarity: —

$10 • W-MA-1000-010-A020

Left: 10 / Hebe watering eagle in clouds / TEN. ***Center:*** Harbor scene / Portrait of Benjamin Franklin flanked by scientific instruments / Harvesting scene. ***Right:*** 10 / Dog, Woman standing with grain / TEN. ***Engraver:*** New England Bank Note Co. / PSSP. ***Comments:*** H-MA-380-A10. Altered from W-MA-520-010-G100. 18__. 1830s.

Rarity: —

$20 • W-MA-1000-020-R010

Comments: H-MA-380-R5. Raised likely from W-MA-1000-002-G070. 18__. 1850s.

Rarity: —

Union Bank

1792–1865

W-MA-1010

History: The Union Bank was incorporated by the General Court in 1792 for the purpose of accommodating agricultural interests. Its long span of continued business is remarkable in the annals of state-chartered banking. The bank was located at

40 State Street, Boston, with branches located in Salem and Worcester. It was chartered on June 23, 1812, with a capital of $1,200,000, of which the State subscribed to $500,000. It was the second bank chartered by the state of Massachusetts. The issue of notes in smaller denominations than $5 was prohibited. The bank was also made the depositary of state funds. It was required to loan a sum not to exceed $100,000 to the state at any time.[74] On June 26, 1811, the *Columbian Centinel* reported that the state held $1,000,000 worth of stock in the Union Bank and the Boston Bank, and that this investment was worth nearly a 20 percent premium. Such matters worked against others who desired to form banks, for it was feared that this would dilute the profits of the Boston and Union institutions. At the time, politics was probably the largest single creative factor in the acquiring of a bank charter.

The paid-in capital was $800,000 in 1838. Other figures for 1838 included: net profits on hand $34,485.69; balances due to other banks $75,033.14; cash deposited $153,081.60; cash deposited bearing interest $47,714.00; total amount due from banks $1,179,635.46; gold, silver, and other coined metals in the banking house $32,222.48; real estate $128,178.40; bills of other banks incorporated in this state $45,795; balance due from other banks $27,106.12; amount of all debts due $946,333.46; total amount of resources of the bank $1,179,635.46. The capital was increased to $1,000,000 in 1852.

The business of this institution was succeeded by the National Union Bank of Boston, chartered on April 6, 1865.

See also branches under Salem, W-MA-2985, and Worcester, W-MA-3440.

Numismatic Commentary: There is an ample supply of this bank's notes in the marketplace to satisfy the needs of collectors. The Union Bank is one of the nation's oldest banking institutions, and it used a variety of engravers and bank-note companies to engrave its issues.

Valid Issues

$1 • W-MA-1010-001-G010

HA

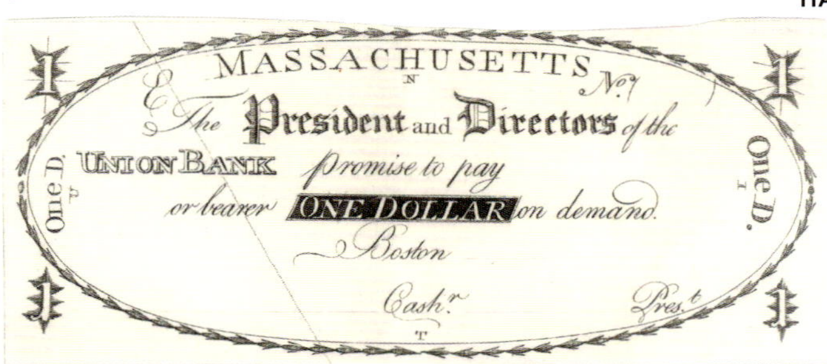

Comments: H-MA-385-G20. Reprint. 1800s.

Rarity: URS-4

CU $350; **Proof** $500

$1 • W-MA-1010-001-G020

Left: Narrow panel of lathework circle segments. ***Center:*** 1 / 1 / Flower garlands and gridwork segments / 1 / 1. ***Right:*** Narrow panel of lathework circle segments. ***Engraver:*** PSSP. ***Comments:*** H-MA-385-G30. 18__. 1820s–1830s.

Rarity: —

$1 • W-MA-1010-001-G020a

CC

Engraver: PSSP. ***Comments:*** H-Unlisted. Similar to W-MA-1010-001-G020. Remainder. 18__.

Rarity: —

$1 • W-MA-1010-001-G020b

Left: ONE / D / ONE vertically. ***Right:*** ONE / D / ONE vertically. ***Engraver:*** PSSP. ***Comments:*** H-MA-385-G32. Similar to W-MA-1010-001-G020. 18__. 1830s.

Rarity: URS-5

VG $350; **VF** $600

$1 • W-MA-1010-001-G030

Left: 1 / Portrait of Millard Fillmore. ***Center:*** Steamboat, Two women flanking state arms surmounted by eagle, Train. ***Right:*** Woman standing with 1 / ONE. ***Comments:*** H-MA-385-G36. 18__. 1850s.

Rarity: —

$1 • W-MA-1010-001-G030a

Engraver: ABNCo. monogram. ***Comments:*** H-MA-385-G36a. Similar to W-MA-1010-001-G030 but with additional engraver imprint. 18__. 1850s–1860s.

Rarity: —

$2 • W-MA-1010-002-G040

CJF

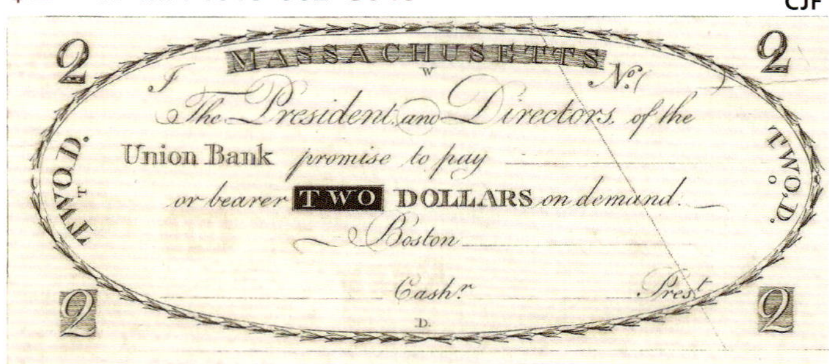

Comments: H-MA-385-G48. Proof. Reprint. 1800s.

Rarity: URS-4

VF $175; **Proof** $750

$2 • W-MA-1010-002-G050

Left: Narrow panel of lathework circle segments. ***Center:*** 2 / 2 / Flower garlands and gridwork segments / 2 / 2. ***Right:*** Narrow panel of lathework circle segments. ***Engraver:*** PSSP. ***Comments:*** H-MA-385-G50. 18__. 1820s–1830s.

Rarity: —

$2 • W-MA-1010-002-G050a

Left: Five TWOs vertically. ***Right:*** Five TWOs vertically. ***Engraver:*** PSSP. ***Comments:*** H-MA-385-G52. Similar to W-MA-1010-002-G050. 18__. 1830s.

Rarity: —

$2 • W-MA-1010-002-G060

Left: TWO / Indian woman standing with bow and spear. ***Center:*** Woman reclining on bale holding caduceus, Railroad, Ships and city. ***Right:*** 2 / Portrait of Zachary Taylor. ***Comments:*** H-MA-385-G64. 18__. 1850s.

Rarity: —

$2 • W-MA-1010-002-G060a

Engraver: ABNCo. monogram. ***Comments:*** H-MA-385-G64a. Similar to W-MA-1010-002-G060 but with additional engraver imprint. 18__. 1850s–1860s.

Rarity: —

$3 • W-MA-1010-003-G070

CC

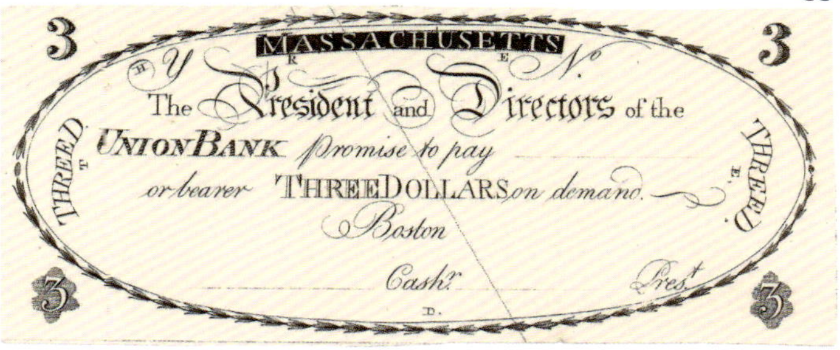

Comments: H-MA-385-G72. Proof. Reprint. 1800s.

Rarity: URS-4

F $150; **Unc-S&D** $400; **Proof** $750

$3 • W-MA-1010-003-G080

Left: Narrow panel of lathework circle segments. ***Center:*** 3 / 3 / Flower garlands and gridwork segments / 3 / 3. ***Right:*** Narrow panel of lathework circle segments. ***Engraver:*** PSSP. ***Comments:*** H-MA-385-G76. 18__. 1820s–1830s.

Rarity: —

$3 • W-MA-1010-003-G080a

Left: THREE vertically. ***Right:*** THREE vertically. ***Engraver:*** PSSP. ***Comments:*** H-MA-385-G78. Similar to W-MA-1010-003-G080. 18__. 1830s.

Rarity: —

$3 • W-MA-1010-003-G090

Engraver: PSSP. ***Comments:*** H-MA-385-G80. 18__. 1840s.

Rarity: —

$3 • W-MA-1010-003-G100

Left: 3 / Woman seated with spear, olive branch, and shield. ***Center:*** Eagle on shield, Ship and steamship. ***Right:*** 3 / Portrait of Daniel Webster. ***Comments:*** H-MA-385-G88. 18__. 1850s.

Rarity: —

$3 • W-MA-1010-003-G100a

Engraver: ABNCo. monogram. ***Comments:*** H-MA-385-G88a. Similar to W-MA-1010-003-G100 but with additional engraver imprint. 18__. 1850s–1860s.

Rarity: —

$5 • W-MA-1010-005-G110

Left: FIVE vertically. ***Center:*** State arms / Plow / 5 / Ship. ***Right:*** Text / 5. ***Comments:*** H-MA-385-G96. 17__. 1700s.

Rarity: —

$5 • W-MA-1010-005-G110a

Comments: H-MA-385-G96a. Similar to W-MA-1010-005-G110 but with different style of legend. 18__. 1800s.

Rarity: URS-5

Proof $300

$5 • W-MA-1010-005-G120

SI

Payee: Benj.n Franklin. ***Engraver:*** A. Reed / Reed. ***Comments:*** H-MA-385-G104. Proof. 181_. 1810s.

Rarity: URS-4

Proof $500

$5 • W-MA-1010-005-G120a

Left: FIVE vertically. ***Center:*** 5 / Shield bearing Indian / 5. ***Bottom center:*** V. ***Right:*** 5 / MASSACHUSETTS / 5 vertically. ***Engraver:*** A. Reed / Reed. ***Comments:*** H-MA-385-G104a. Similar to W-MA-1010-005-G120 but with different engraved payee. 181_. 1810s.

Rarity: —

$5 • W-MA-1010-005-G120b

Engraver: A. Reed / Reed. ***Comments:*** H-MA-385-G104b. Similar to W-MA-1010-005-G120 but with engraved payee of Joseph Warren (Letter C). 181_. 1810s.

Rarity: —

$5 • W-MA-1010-005-G130

Left: 5 / MASSACHUSETTS / 5. ***Center:*** 5 / Shield bearing Indian surmounted by arm and shield / 5. ***Bottom center:*** FIVE. ***Right:*** FIVE / 5 / FIVE. ***Engraver:*** Reed & Stiles. ***Comments:*** H-MA-385-G110. 18__. 1820s.

Rarity: —

$5 • W-MA-1010-005-G140

Left: Lathework chain bearing MASSACHUSETTS / 5 / 5. ***Center:*** Alternating flower garlands and gridwork segments. ***Right:*** 5 / 5. ***Engraver:*** PSSP. ***Comments:*** H-MA-385-G112. 18__. 1820s.

Rarity: —

$5 • W-MA-1010-005-G140a

Center: White boxes flanking FIVE DOLLARS with zigzag ruled lines. ***Engraver:*** PSSP. ***Comments:*** H-MA-385-G114. Similar to W-MA-1010-005-G140. 18__. 1820s–1830s.

Rarity: —

$5 • W-MA-1010-005-G140b

Engraver: PSSP. ***Comments:*** H-MA-385-G116. Similar to W-MA-1010-005-G140 but with spiral lathework lines. 18__. 1830s.

Rarity: —

$5 • W-MA-1010-005-G150

Left: 5 / Portrait of George Washington. ***Center:*** Three women seated with shield / Lazy 5. ***Right:*** 5. ***Engraver:*** Draper, Toppan & Co. ***Comments:*** H-MA-385-G120. The spurious W-MA-1010-005-S050 is a close imitation, except for wrong center vignette and lack of medallion engraving on lazy 5. 18__. 1840s–1850s.

Rarity: —

$5 • W-MA-1010-005-G150a

Engraver: Draper, Toppan & Co. / ABNCo. monogram. ***Comments:*** H-MA-385-G120a. Similar to W-MA-1010-005-G150 but with additional engraver imprint. 18__. 1850s–1860s.

Rarity: URS-6
VF $450

$10 • W-MA-1010-010-G160

Left: Ship / TEN / Plow. ***Center:*** State arms / 10. ***Right:*** Text / 10. ***Comments:*** H-MA-385-G140. 18__. 1700s.

Rarity: —
F $50

$10 • W-MA-1010-010-G160a

SBG

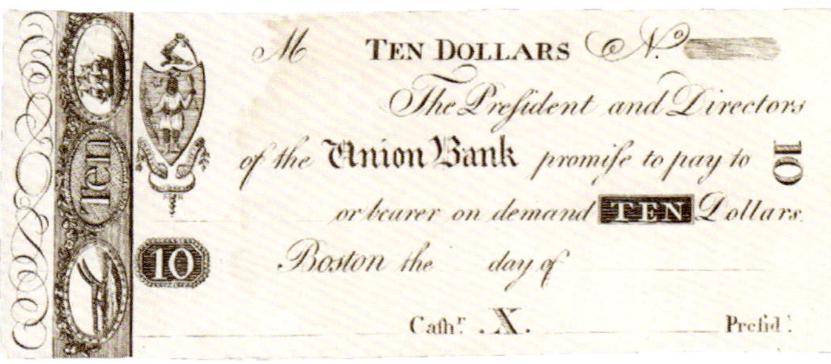

Comments: H-MA-385-G140a. Similar to W-MA-1010-010-G160 but with different date and style of legend. Proof. Reprint. 1800s.

Rarity: URS-3
CU $100; **Unc-Rem** $400; **Proof** $300

$10 • W-MA-1010-010-G170

Left: TEN. ***Center:*** 10 / Ship, Shield bearing Indian surmounted by arm and sword / 10. ***Bottom center:*** X. ***Right:*** X / MASSACHUSETTS / X. ***Engraver:*** A. Reed / Reed. ***Comments:*** H-MA-385-G147. 18__. 1810s.

Rarity: URS-4
Proof $500

$10 • W-MA-1010-010-G180

QDB

Engraver: Reed. ***Comments:*** H-MA-385-G148. Proof. 181_. 1810s.

Rarity: URS-4
Proof $500

$10 • W-MA-1010-010-G180a

Left: 10 / 10. ***Bottom center:*** 10. ***Right:*** Lathework dies. ***Engraver:*** Reed & Stiles. ***Comments:*** H-MA-385-G154. Similar to W-MA-1010-010-G180. 18__. 1820s.

Rarity: URS-3
Proof $500

$10 • W-MA-1010-010-G190

Left: Lathework chain bearing MASSACHUSETTS / 10 / 10 vertically. ***Center:*** Alternating flower garlands and gridwork segments. ***Right:*** 10 / 10 vertically. ***Engraver:*** Perkins. ***Comments:*** H-MA-385-G156. 18__. 1820s.

Rarity: —

$10 • W-MA-1010-010-G190a

Center: White boxes flanking TEN DOLLARS with zigzag ruled lines. ***Engraver:*** PSSP. ***Comments:*** H-MA-385-G158. Similar to W-MA-1010-010-G190. 18__. 1820s–1830s.

Rarity: —

$10 • W-MA-1010-010-G190b

Engraver: PSSP. ***Comments:*** H-MA-385-G160. Similar to W-MA-1010-010-G190 but with spiral lathework lines. 18__. 1830s.

Rarity: —

$10 • W-MA-1010-010-G200

HA

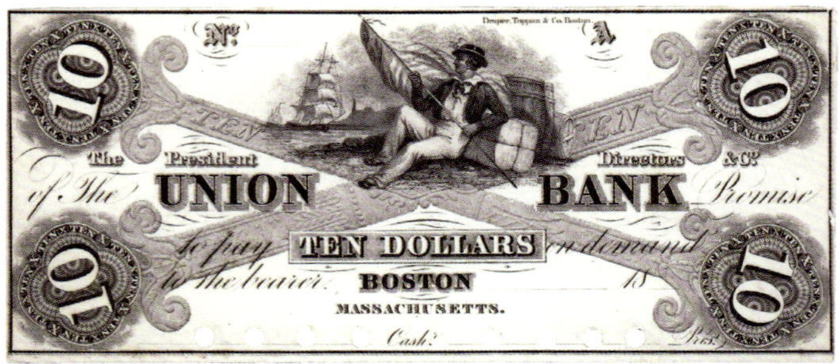

Engraver: Draper, Toppan & Co. ***Comments:*** H-MA-385-G164. 18__. 1840s–1860s.

Rarity: URS-3
VF $600; **Proof** $750

$10 • W-MA-1010-010-G200a

Engraver: Draper, Toppan & Co. / ABNCo. monogram. ***Comments:*** H-MA-385-G164a. Similar to W-MA-1010-010-G200 but with additional engraver imprint. 18__. 1850s–1860s.

Rarity: —

$20 • W-MA-1010-020-G210

Left: Plow / XX / Ship. ***Center:*** State arms / 20. ***Right:*** Text / 20. ***Comments:*** H-MA-385-G172. 18__. 1790s.

Rarity: —

$20 • W-MA-1010-020-G210a

Comments: H-MA-385-G172a. Similar to W-MA-1010-020-G210 but with different style of legend. 18__. 1800s.

Rarity: URS-4
VF $90

$20 • **W-MA-1010-020-G220**

CJF

Engraver: Reed. ***Comments:*** H-MA-385-G180. 18__. 1810s.

Rarity: URS-4

Proof $500

$20 • **W-MA-1010-020-G230**

Left: XX / 20 / XX. ***Center:*** 20 / Shield bearing Indian surmounted by arm and sword / 20. ***Bottom center:*** Ships. ***Right:*** 20 / MASSACHUSETTS / 20. ***Engraver:*** Reed & Stiles. ***Comments:*** H-MA-385-G188. 18__. 1820s.

Rarity: URS-3

Proof $500

$20 • **W-MA-1010-020-G240**

Left: Lathework chain bearing MASSACHUSETTS / 20 / 20 vertically. ***Center:*** Alternating flower garlands and gridwork segments with XX. ***Right:*** 20 / 20 vertically. ***Engraver:*** PSSP. ***Comments:*** H-MA-385-G190. 18__. 1820s–1840s.

Rarity: —

$20 • **W-MA-1010-020-G250**

Left: XX / Shield bearing Indian. ***Center:*** 20 / Woman, Eagle, Shield / 20. ***Bottom center:*** Ship. ***Right:*** XX / Portrait of John Jay / XX. ***Engraver:*** Rawdon, Wright & Hatch. ***Comments:*** H-MA-385-G196. 18__. 1840s–1850s.

Rarity: URS-4

VF $500; **Proof** $800

$30 • **W-MA-1010-030-G260**

Left: Plow / Ship. ***Center:*** State arms / 30. ***Right:*** Text / 30. ***Comments:*** H-MA-385-G204. 17__. 1700s.

Rarity: —

$30 • **W-MA-1010-030-G260a**

Comments: H-MA-385-G204a. Similar to W-MA-1010-030-G260 but with different style of legend. 18__. 1800s.

Rarity: URS-3

Unc-Rem $900

$50 • **W-MA-1010-050-G270**

Left: Plow / Ship. ***Center:*** State arms / 50. ***Right:*** Text / 50. ***Comments:*** H-MA-385-G212. 17__. 1790s.

Rarity: —

$50 • **W-MA-1010-050-G270a**

Comments: H-MA-385-G212a. Similar to W-MA-1010-050-G270 but with different style of legend. 18__. 1800s.

Rarity: —

$50 • **W-MA-1010-050-G280**

CJF

Engraver: Reed. ***Comments:*** H-MA-385-G220. 18__. 1810s.

Rarity: URS-4

Proof $750

$50 • **W-MA-1010-050-G290**

Left: 50 on lathework / L / 50 on lathework. ***Center:*** 50 / Shield bearing Indian surmounted by arm and sword / 50 / 50. ***Right:*** 50 / MASSACHUSETTS / 50. ***Engraver:*** Reed & Stiles. ***Comments:*** H-MA-385-G228. 18__. 1820s.

Rarity: URS-3

Proof $550

$50 • **W-MA-1010-050-G300**

Left: Lathework chain bearing MASSACHUSETTS / 50 / 50 vertically. ***Center:*** Alternating flower garlands and gridwork segments. ***Right:*** 50 / 50 vertically. ***Engraver:*** PSSP. ***Comments:*** H-MA-385-G230. 18__. 1820s–1840s.

Rarity: —

$50 • **W-MA-1010-050-G310**

CC

Engraver: Rawdon, Wright & Hatch. ***Comments:*** H-MA-385-G234. Proof. 18__. 1840s–1850s.

Rarity: URS-3

F $600; **Proof** $1,250

$100 • **W-MA-1010-100-G320**

Left: Plow / Ship. ***Center:*** State arms / 100. ***Right:*** Text / 100. ***Comments:*** H-MA-385-G240. 17__. 1790s.

Rarity: —

$100 • **W-MA-1010-100-G320a**

Comments: H-MA-385-G240a. Similar to W-MA-1010-100-G320 but with different style of legend. 18__. 1800s.

Rarity: URS-4

Unc-Rem $250

$100 • **W-MA-1010-100-G330**

Left: ONE HUNDRED. ***Center:*** 100 / Shield bearing Indian surmounted by arm and sword / 100. ***Bottom center:*** C. ***Right:*** 100 / MASSACHUSETTS / 100. ***Engraver:*** A. Reed / Reed. ***Comments:*** H-MA-385-G246. 18__. 1810s.

Rarity: URS-5

Proof $500

$100 • W-MA-1010-100-G340

Left: Panel with 100 / MASSACHUSETTS / 100 vertically. ***Center:*** 100 / State arms surmounted by arm and sword and draped with banner bearing motto / 100. ***Right:*** Panel with 100 / 100. ***Engraver:*** Reed & Stiles. ***Comments:*** H-MA-385-G248. 18__. 1820s.

Rarity: —

$100 • W-MA-1010-100-G350

Left: Lathework chain bearing MASSACHUSETTS / 100 / 100 vertically. ***Center:*** Alternating flower garlands and gridwork segments. ***Right:*** 100 / 100 vertically. ***Engraver:*** Perkins. ***Comments:*** H-MA-385-G250. 18__. 1820s–1840s.

Rarity: —

$100 • W-MA-1010-100-G360 CC

Engraver: Rawdon, Wright & Hatch. ***Comments:*** H-MA-385-G254. 18__. 1840s–1860s.

Rarity: URS-3
VF $600

$500 • W-MA-1010-500-G370

Left: Plow / Ship. ***Center:*** State arms / 500. ***Right:*** Text / 500. ***Comments:*** H-MA-385-G260. 18__. 1800s.

Rarity: —

$500 • W-MA-1010-500-G370a

Comments: H-MA-385-G260a. Similar to W-MA-1010-500-G370 but with different style of legend. 18__. 1800s.

Rarity: —

$500 • W-MA-1010-500-G380

Left: MASSACHUSETTS over lathework. ***Center:*** 500 / Text. ***Right:*** 500. ***Engraver:*** PSSP. ***Comments:*** H-MA-385-G264. 18__. 1820s–1850s.

Rarity: —

$500 • W-MA-1010-500-G380a

Engraver: PSSP / ABNCo. monogram. ***Comments:*** H-MA-385-G264a. Similar to W-MA-1010-500-G380 but with additional engraver imprint. 18__. 1860s.

Rarity: URS-4
Proof $2,250

$500 • W-MA-1010-500-G390 JF

Engraver: American Bank Note Co. ***Comments:*** H-MA-385-G268. Proof. 186_. 1860s.

Rarity: URS-2
Proof $4,500

Uncut Sheets

$1-$3-$2 • W-MA-900-001.003.002-US010 CJF

Comments: H-MA-385-G20, G72, G48. Reprint. 1800s.

Rarity: URS-3
Proof $1,500

$__-$50-$20-$10 • W-MA-900-__.050.020.010-US020

CJF

Comments: H-MA-385-__-G220, G180, G148. Top note missing. 1810s.

Rarity: URS-2
Proof $2,500

NON-VALID ISSUES

$1 • W-MA-1010-001-C010

SI

Comments: H-MA-385-C20. Counterfeit of W-MA-1010-001-G010. 18?0s.

Rarity: URS-4
VG $100

$1 • W-MA-1010-001-S010

SI

Engraver: New England Bank Note Co. ***Comments:*** H-MA-385-S5. 18__. 1850s.

Rarity: URS-8
VG $60; **VF** $75

$2 • W-MA-1010-002-C040

Comments: H-MA-385-C48. Counterfeit of W-MA-1010-002-G040. 18__. 1800s.

Rarity: URS-4
VF $150

$2 • W-MA-1010-002-S020

Left: 2 / TWO / 2. ***Center:*** Portrait of George Washington. ***Right:*** Eagle / 2. ***Comments:*** H-MA-385-S10.

Rarity: URS-7
F $75

$2 • W-MA-1010-002-N010

Center: Woman / 2 / Woman. ***Comments:*** H-MA-385-N5.

Rarity: —

$2 • W-MA-1010-002-A010

Left: TWO / Justice seated / TWO. ***Center:*** TWO / TWO on medallion head / Train, Hill and steamship / TWO / TWO. ***Right:*** TWO / Woman standing with pole and cap, Cornucopia and sheaf. ***Engraver:*** W.L. Ormsby. ***Comments:*** H-MA-385-A5. Altered from $2 Potomac River Bank, Georgetown, D.C. 18__. 1850s.

Rarity: —

$2 • W-MA-1010-002-A020

CC

Overprint: Red TWO. ***Engraver:*** Bald, Cousland & Co. / Baldwin, Bald & Cousland. ***Comments:*** H-MA-385-A10. 18__. 1850s.

Rarity: URS-7
F $100

$2 • W-MA-1010-002-A030

Left: 2 / Farmer plowing with black and white horses. ***Center:*** Two men loading wagon with sheaves, Three men cradling and binding. ***Right:*** 2 / Two floating cherubs with caduceus and sheaf. ***Tint:*** Red-brown 2s and TWO DOLLARS. ***Engraver:*** Danforth, Wright & Co. ***Comments:*** H-MA-385-A15. Altered from $2 Southern Bank of Georgia, Bainbridge, Georgia. March 1, 1858.

Rarity: URS-7
F $100

$2 • W-MA-1010-002-A040

Left: Portrait of Thomas Jefferson. ***Center:*** Ship, Factory scene, Horse-drawn wagons. ***Right:*** Portrait of Marquis de Lafayette. ***Engraver:*** New England Bank Note Co. ***Comments:*** H-MA-385-A20. Altered from W-MA-680-002-G070. 18__. 1830s.

Rarity: —

$2 • W-MA-1010-002-A050

Left: 2 / Blacksmith standing with forge and tools. ***Center:*** Farmer feeding hogs from basket. ***Bottom center:*** 2 on die. ***Right:*** 2 / Farmer carrying cornstalks. ***Overprint:*** Red 2 2. ***Engraver:*** Toppan, Carpenter & Co. ***Comments:*** H-MA-385-A25. Altered from $2 Farmers Bank, Wickford, Rhode Island. Aug. 6, 1855.

Rarity: —

$3 • W-MA-1010-003-C070

MR

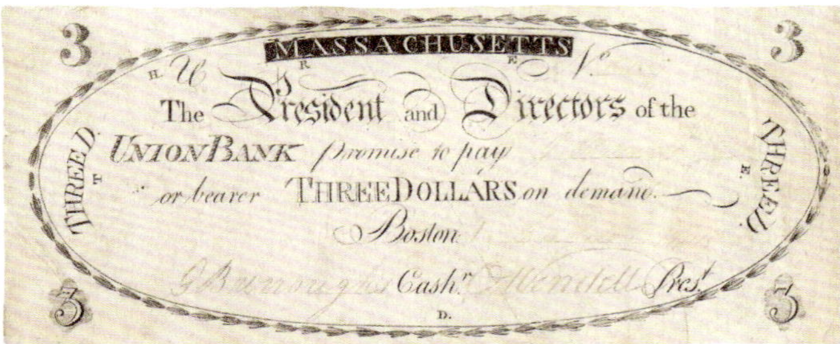

Comments: H-MA-385-C72. Counterfeit of W-MA-1010-003-G070. 1800s.

Rarity: URS-6
VF $150

$3 • W-MA-1010-003-S030

Center: Mechanic seated, Train. ***Comments:*** H-MA-385-S15.

Rarity: —

$3 • W-MA-1010-003-S040

CC

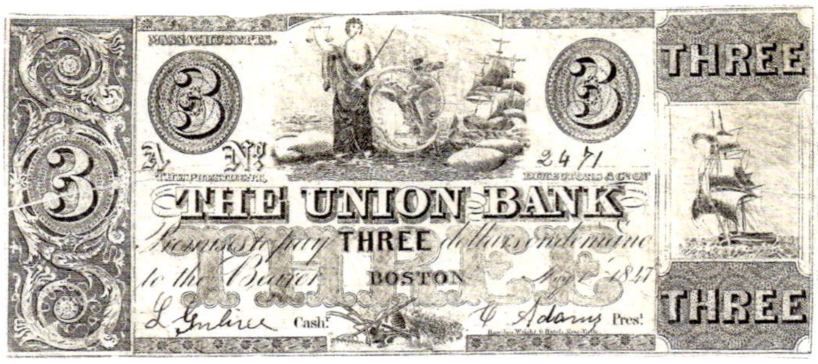

Engraver: Rawdon, Wright & Hatch. ***Comments:*** H-MA-385-S20. May 1, 1847.

Rarity: URS-7
F $125

$3 • W-MA-1010-003-N020

Left: 3. ***Center:*** 3 / Justice resting arm on shield surmounted by eagle on globe / 3. ***Right:*** THREE / Schooner / THREE. ***Comments:*** H-MA-385-N10.

Rarity: —

$3 • W-MA-1010-003-N030

Center: Two women and spread eagle. ***Comments:*** H-MA-385-N15.

Rarity: —

$3 • W-MA-1010-003-A060

Left: 3 / Country scene with trees, river, mountains. ***Center:*** Female portrait / Axe, Woodsman seated on log petting dog / Portrait of Rachel Jackson. ***Right:*** 3 / Woman. ***Overprint:*** Red. ***Engraver:*** Danforth, Bald & Co. ***Comments:*** H-MA-385-A30. Altered from $3 Eastern Bank, West Killingly, Connecticut series. 185_. 1850s.

Rarity: —

$5 • W-MA-1010-005-C110a

QDB

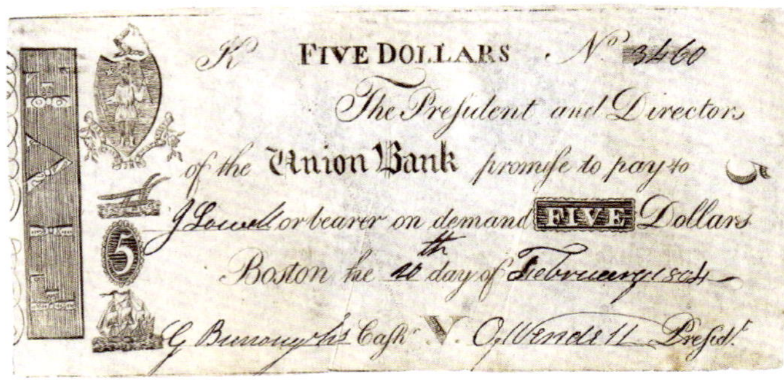

Comments: H-MA-385-C96a. Counterfeit of W-MA-1010-005-G110a. 1800s.

Rarity: URS-7
F $75

$5 • W-MA-1010-005-C120b

Engraver: A. Reed / Reed. ***Comments:*** H-MA-385-C104b. Counterfeit of W-MA-1010-005-G120b. 181_. 1810s.

Rarity: —

$5 • W-MA-1010-005-C130

SI

Engraver: Reed & Stiles. ***Comments:*** H-MA-385-C110. Counterfeit of W-MA-1010-005-G130. 18__. 1820s.

Rarity: URS-8
F $100; **VF** $150

$5 • W-MA-1010-005-S050

Left: 5 / State arms of Rhode Island. ***Center:*** 5 / V bearing portraits of five U.S. presidents, Flags, eagle / 5. ***Right:*** 5 / Steamboat. ***Engraver:*** Toppan, Carpenter & Co. ***Comments:*** H-MA-385-S25. From a modified, fraudulent plate originally for a counterfeit $5 of the National Bank, Providence, Rhode Island. 185_. 1850s.

Rarity: URS-7
F $100

Collectors and Researchers:

If you have new information about any banks or notes listed in this volume, contact Whitman Publishing, Attn: Obsolete Paper Money, 3101 Clairmont Road, Suite G, Atlanta, GA 30329.

$5 • W-MA-1010-005-S050a

CC

Overprint: Red 5 / 5 in dies. ***Engraver:*** Toppan, Carpenter & Co. ***Comments:*** H-Unlisted. Similar to W-MA-1010-005-S050. 185_. 1850s.

Rarity: URS-6
F $125; **VF** $200

$5 • W-MA-1010-005-S060

JF

Engraver: Draper, Toppan & Co. ***Comments:*** H-MA-385-S30. 18__. 1860s.

Rarity: URS-8
VF $100

$5 • W-MA-1010-005-S070

Center: Mechanic seated, Train. ***Comments:*** H-MA-385-S35.

Rarity: —

$5 • W-MA-1010-005-N040

Left: Man. ***Right:*** Male portrait. ***Comments:*** H-MA-385-N20.

Rarity: —

$5 • W-MA-1010-005-N050

Center: Two women and spread eagle. ***Comments:*** H-MA-385-N25.

Rarity: —

$5 • W-MA-1010-005-A070

Left: 5 / Portrait / FIVE. ***Center:*** Ship, Factory scene, Horse-drawn wagons. ***Right:*** 5 / Portrait / FIVE. ***Engraver:*** New England Bank Note Co. ***Comments:*** H-MA-385-A35. Altered from W-MA-680-005-G110. 18__. 1830s.

Rarity: —

$10 • W-MA-1010-010-C200

Left: 10 / 10. ***Center:*** Man seated with flag and parcels / Lazy X. ***Right:*** 10 / 10. ***Comments:*** H-Unlisted. Counterfeit of W-MA-1010-010-G200. Proof. 18__. 1840s–1860s.

Rarity: URS-7

$10 • W-MA-1010-010-S080

Center: Mechanic seated, Train. ***Comments:*** H-MA-385-S40.

Rarity: —

$10 • W-MA-1010-010-N060

Left: Woman with barrels and bales. ***Right:*** Woman and man. ***Comments:*** H-MA-385-N30.

Rarity: —

$10 • W-MA-1010-010-A080

Left: X / TEN vertically. ***Center:*** Man on horse under tree, Two men loading hay wagon, Three men reaping. ***Right:*** 10 / Woman seated with U.S. shield. ***Overprint:*** Red. ***Engraver:*** Danforth, Wright & Co. ***Comments:*** H-MA-385-A40. Altered from $10 Brownville Bank and Land Co., Omaha City, Nebraska series. Aug. 12, 1850.

Rarity: —

$20 • W-MA-1010-020-C210a

CC

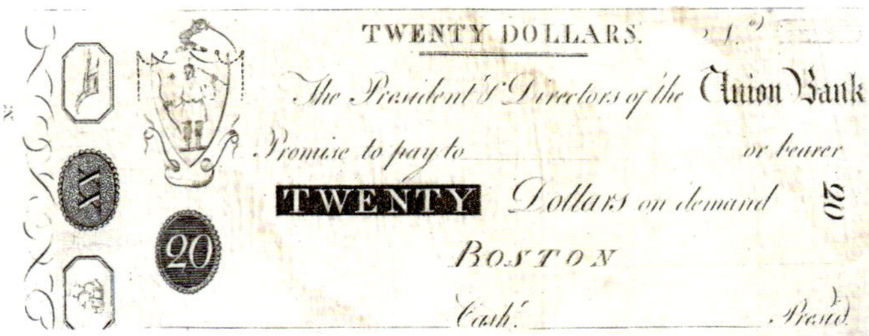

Comments: H-MA-385-C172a. Counterfeit of W-MA-1010-020-G210a. Remainder. 1800s.

Rarity: URS-6
Unc-Rem $450

$20 • W-MA-1010-020-A090

Left: Woman floating in clouds holding U.S. shield and flowers / XX. ***Center:*** XX / Slain deer, Indian man with headdress reclining. ***Right:*** 20 / Portrait of George Washington. ***Engraver:*** Rawdon, Wright, Hatch & Edson. ***Comments:*** H-MA-385-A45. Altered from $20 New England Bank, Fairmount, Maine. Oct. 1, 1857.

Rarity: —

$100 • W-MA-1010-100-C320

Comments: H-MA-385-C240. Counterfeit of W-MA-1010-100-G320. 18__. 1790s.

Rarity: —

$500 • W-MA-1010-500-R010

Comments: H-MA-385-R10. Raised from W-MA-1010-002-G060. 18__. 1850s.

Rarity: —

Warren Bank
1836 and 1837
W-MA-1020

History: The Warren Bank was chartered on April 9, 1836, with a starting capital of $500,000. The bank took its name from Dr. Joseph Warren, a leading patriot and physician who was killed by the British on June 17, 1775, at the battle on Breed's (Bunker) Hill. Its office was established at 72 State Street in Boston. The first president was B.T. Reed, and the first cashier was Thomas Drown. The first directors were B.T. Reed, William Bramhall, Gardner Brewer, Nathaniel Dana, John L. Dimmock, Albert Fearing, John Gardner, Jarius B. Lincoln, Josiah Reed, Aaron Rice, and Horace Scudder.

On April 20, 1837, the Warren Bank changed its name to the Shawmut Bank, W-MA-910.

Numismatic Commentary: Due to the swift name change of the Warren Bank, issues with the original title are extremely hard to locate. Rare notes with this name and address will likely show a vignette of a business block in Boston housing the bank itself.

VALID ISSUES

$1 • W-MA-1020-001-G010

Engraver: Unverified, but likely Terry, Pelton & Co. ***Comments:*** H-MA-390-G2. No description available. 18__. 1836 and 1837.

Rarity: *None known*

$2 • W-MA-1020-002-G020

Engraver: Unverified, but likely Terry, Pelton & Co. ***Comments:*** H-MA-390-G4. No description available. 18__. 1836 and 1837.

Rarity: *None known*

$3 • W-MA-1020-003-G030

Left: Portrait of General Joseph Warren. ***Center:*** View of Merchants Row in Boston, Offices of Eastern Rail Road, Warren Ins. Co., and Warren Bank. ***Right:*** Bunker Hill Monument. ***Engraver:*** Terry, Pelton & Co. ***Comments:*** H-MA-390-G6. 18__. 1836 and 1837.

Rarity: URS-4
Proof $1,500

$5 • W-MA-1020-005-G040

Engraver: Unverified, but likely Terry, Pelton & Co. ***Comments:*** H-MA-390-G8. No description available. 18__. 1836 and 1837.

Rarity: *None known*

$10 • W-MA-1020-010-G050

Engraver: Unverified, but likely Terry, Pelton & Co. ***Comments:*** H-MA-390-G10. No description available. 18__. 1836 and 1837.

Rarity: *None known*

$20 • W-MA-1020-020-G060

Engraver: Unverified, but likely Terry, Pelton & Co. ***Comments:*** H-MA-390-G12. No description available. 18__. 1836 and 1837.

Rarity: *None known*

$50 • W-MA-1020-050-G070

Engraver: Unverified, but likely Terry, Pelton & Co. ***Comments:*** H-MA-390-G14. No description available. 18__. 1836 and 1837.

Rarity: *None known*

$100 • W-MA-1020-100-G080

Engraver: Unverified, but likely Terry, Pelton & Co. ***Comments:*** H-MA-390-G16. No description available. 18__. 1836 and 1837.

Rarity: *None known*

$500 • W-MA-1020-500-G090

Engraver: Unverified, but likely Terry, Pelton & Co. ***Comments:*** H-MA-390-G18. No description available. 18__. 1836 and 1837.

Rarity: *None known*

$1,000 • W-MA-1020-1000-G100

Engraver: Unverified, but likely Terry, Pelton & Co. ***Comments:*** H-MA-390-G20. No description available. 18__. 1836 and 1837.

Rarity: *None known*

Washington Bank
1825–1865
W-MA-1030

History: The Washington Bank was chartered in February 1825 with an authorized capital of $500,000. It was increased to $750,000 in 1855 and limited to $1,500,000.

The bank was located at the corner of Washington and Beach streets. Circulation was at $19,021 in 1838, $82,137 in 1839, and reached a high of $201,335 in 1845, to cite some selected figures. An accounting of 1838 showed: net profits on hand $17,317.90; cash deposited $124,700.41; total amount due from banks $661,039.31; gold, silver, and other coined metals in the banking house $11,169.76; bills of other banks incorporated in this state $15,979; bills of other banks incorporated elsewhere $2,147; balance due from other banks $10,469.62; amount of all debts due $621,273.93; total amount of resources of the bank $661,009.31.

The business of the Washington Bank was succeeded by the Washington National Bank, chartered on December 3, 1864.

Numismatic Commentary: All issues are hard to find, but PSSP style notes are available more often than later vignetted notes.

VALID ISSUES

$1 • W-MA-1030-001-G010

Left: Narrow panel of lathework circle segments. ***Center:*** 1 / 1 / Flower garlands and gridwork segments / 1 / 1. ***Right:*** Narrow panel of lathework circle segments. ***Engraver:*** PSSP. ***Comments:*** H-MA-395-G2. 18__. 1820s–1830s.

Rarity: URS-5
VF $400

$1 • W-MA-1030-001-G010a

Left: ONE / D / ONE vertically. ***Right:*** ONE / D / ONE vertically. ***Engraver:*** PSSP. ***Comments:*** H-MA-395-G4. Similar to W-MA-1030-001-G010. 18__. 1830s.

Rarity: —

$1 • W-MA-1030-001-G010b

Left: ONE / D / ONE vertically. ***Right:*** ONE / D / ONE vertically. ***Engraver:*** PSSP. ***Comments:*** H-MA-395-G6. Similar to W-MA-1030-001-G010. 18__. 1830s–1840s.

Rarity: —

$1 • W-MA-1030-001-G020

HA

Engraver: New England Bank Note Co. ***Comments:*** H-MA-395-G8. 18__. 1840s.

Rarity: URS-3
F $1,000

$1 • W-MA-1030-001-G030

Left: 1 / Portrait of George Washington. ***Center:*** Eagle / Steamboat / U.S. Capitol. ***Right:*** Merchandise / 1 / Train. ***Engraver:*** Rawdon, Wright, Hatch & Edson / New England Bank Note Co. ***Comments:*** H-MA-395-G10. 18__. 1850s.

Rarity: —

$1 • W-MA-1030-001-G030a

CC

Overprint: Red ONE. ***Engraver:*** Rawdon, Wright, Hatch & Edson / New England Bank Note Co. ***Comments:*** H-Unlisted. Similar to W-MA-1030-001-G030. 18__. 1850s.

Rarity: URS-1
F $1,400

$1 • W-MA-1030-001-G040

JF

Tint: Orange. ***Engraver:*** American Bank Note Co. ***Comments:*** H-MA-395-G12a. 18__. 1850s–1860s.

Rarity: URS-4
VF $2,500

$2 • W-MA-1030-002-G050

Left: Narrow panel of lathework circle segments. ***Center:*** 2 / 2 / Flower garlands and gridwork segments / 2 / 2. ***Right:*** Narrow panel of lathework circle segments. ***Engraver:*** PSSP. ***Comments:*** H-MA-395-G16. 18__. 1820s–1830s.

Rarity: —

$2 • W-MA-1030-002-G050a

Left: Five TWOs vertically. ***Right:*** Five TWOs vertically. ***Engraver:*** PSSP. ***Comments:*** H-MA-395-G18. Similar to W-MA-1030-002-G050. 18__. 1830s.

Rarity: —

$2 • W-MA-1030-002-G050b

Left: Five TWOs vertically. ***Right:*** Five TWOs vertically. ***Engraver:*** PSSP. ***Comments:*** H-MA-395-G20. Similar to W-MA-1030-002-G050. 18__. 1830s–1840s.

Rarity: —

$2 • W-MA-1030-002-G060

Left: TWO / TWO. ***Center:*** 2 / Shipping. ***Right:*** TWO / George Washington standing by horse / TWO. ***Engraver:*** New England Bank Note Co. ***Comments:*** H-MA-395-G22. 18__. 1840s.

Rarity: —

$2 • W-MA-1030-002-G070

Left: 2 / Portrait of George Washington. ***Center:*** View of State House. ***Right:*** 2 / State arms. ***Engraver:*** Rawdon, Wright, Hatch & Edson / New England Bank Note Co. ***Comments:*** H-MA-395-G24. 18__. 1850s.

Rarity: —

$2 • W-MA-1030-002-G080

Left: Cherub / TWO. ***Center:*** TWO / Soldier, Shield bearing bust of George Washington, Two Indians, Woman / TWO. ***Right:*** Cherub / TWO. ***Tint:*** Orange 2s. ***Engraver:*** American Bank Note Co. ***Comments:*** H-MA-395-G26a. 18__. 1850s–1860s.

Rarity: —

$3 • W-MA-1030-003-G090

Left: Narrow panel of lathework circle segments. ***Center:*** 3 / 3 / Flower garlands and gridwork segments / 3 / 3. ***Right:*** Narrow panel of lathework circle segments. ***Engraver:*** PSSP. ***Comments:*** H-MA-395-G28. 18__. 1820s–1830s.

Rarity: —

$3 • W-MA-1030-003-G090a

Left: THREE vertically. ***Right:*** THREE vertically. ***Engraver:*** PSSP. ***Comments:*** H-MA-395-G30. Similar to W-MA-1030-003-G090. 18__. 1830s.

Rarity: —

$3 • W-MA-1030-003-G090b

Engraver: PSSP. ***Comments:*** H-MA-395-G32. Similar to W-MA-1030-003-G090. 18__. 1830s–1840s.

Rarity: —

$3 • W-MA-1030-003-G100

Left: Woman seated on rock / THREE. ***Center:*** Steamship and sail ships at sea. ***Bottom center:*** Portrait of George Washington. ***Right:*** 3 / Sailor standing with hand on capstan. ***Engraver:*** Rawdon, Wright, Hatch & Edson / New England Bank Note Co. ***Comments:*** H-MA-395-G34. 18__. 1850s.

Rarity: —

$3 • W-MA-1030-003-G110

Left: 3. ***Center:*** George Washington on horseback, Officer submitting plans, Officers, tents, cannon, and horses. ***Right:*** 3 / Portrait of George Washington. ***Tint:*** Orange. ***Engraver:*** American Bank Note Co. ***Comments:*** H-MA-395-G36a. 18__. 1850s–1860s.

Rarity: —

$5 • W-MA-1030-005-G120

Left: Lathework chain bearing MASSACHUSETTS / 5 / 5. ***Center:*** Alternating flower garlands and gridwork segments. ***Right:*** 5 / 5. ***Engraver:*** PSSP. ***Comments:*** H-MA-395-G38. 18__. 1820s.

Rarity: —

$5 • W-MA-1030-005-G120a

Engraver: PSSP. ***Comments:*** H-MA-395-G40. Similar to W-MA-1030-005-G120 but with zigzag ruled lines. 18__. 1820s–1830s.

Rarity: —

$5 • **W-MA-1030-005-G120b**

Engraver: PSSP. ***Comments:*** H-MA-395-G42. Similar to W-MA-1030-005-G120 but with spiral lathework lines. 18__. 1830s.

Rarity: —

$5 • **W-MA-1030-005-G130**

Left: 5 / George Washington standing by horse. ***Center:*** View of State House. ***Right:*** 5 / Woman standing, Basket of fruit, Anchor. ***Engraver:*** Rawdon, Wright, Hatch & Edson / New England Bank Note Co. ***Comments:*** H-MA-395-G46. 18__. 1850s.

Rarity: —

$5 • **W-MA-1030-005-G130a**

Engraver: Rawdon, Wright, Hatch & Edson / New England Bank Note Co. / ABNCo. monogram. ***Comments:*** H-MA-395-G46b. Similar to W-MA-1030-005-G130 but with additional engraver imprint. Possible tint. 18__. 1850s–1860s.

Rarity: —

$10 • **W-MA-1030-010-G140**

Left: Lathework chain bearing MASSACHUSETTS / 10 / 10 vertically. ***Center:*** Alternating flower garlands and gridwork segments. ***Right:*** 10 / 10 vertically. ***Engraver:*** Perkins. ***Comments:*** H-MA-395-G50. 18__. 1820s.

Rarity: —

$10 • **W-MA-1030-010-G140a**

Engraver: PSSP. ***Comments:*** H-MA-395-G52. Similar to W-MA-1030-010-G140 but with zigzag ruled lines. 18__. 1820s–1830s.

Rarity: —

$10 • **W-MA-1030-010-G140b**

Engraver: PSSP. ***Comments:*** H-MA-395-G54. Similar to W-MA-1030-010-G140 but with spiral lathework lines. 18__. 1830s.

Rarity: —

$10 • **W-MA-1030-010-G150**

Left: TEN / George Washington standing by horse. ***Center:*** Train. ***Bottom center:*** State arms. ***Right:*** 10 / Steamship / TEN. ***Engraver:*** Rawdon, Wright, Hatch & Edson / New England Bank Note Co. ***Comments:*** H-MA-395-G58. 18__. 1850s.

Rarity: —

$10 • **W-MA-1030-010-G150a**

Engraver: Rawdon, Wright, Hatch & Edson / New England Bank Note Co. / ABNCo. monogram. ***Comments:*** H-MA-395-G58b. Similar to W-MA-1030-010-G150 but with additional engraver imprint. Possible tint. 18__. 1850s–1860s.

Rarity: —

$20 • **W-MA-1030-020-G160**

Left: Lathework chain bearing MASSACHUSETTS / 20 / 20 vertically. ***Center:*** Alternating flower garlands and gridwork segments. ***Right:*** 20 / 20 vertically. ***Engraver:*** PSSP. ***Comments:*** H-MA-395-G62. 18__. 1820s–1830s.

Rarity: —

$20 • **W-MA-1030-020-G170**

Left: TWENTY / Indian woman with bow and arrow. ***Center:*** XX / Steamboat, Eagle standing on shield, U.S. Capitol. ***Bottom center:*** Portrait of George Washington. ***Right:*** 20. ***Engraver:*** Rawdon, Wright, Hatch & Edson / New England Bank Note Co. ***Comments:*** H-MA-395-G66. 18__. 1850s.

Rarity: —

$20 • **W-MA-1030-020-G170a**

Engraver: Rawdon, Wright, Hatch & Edson / New England Bank Note Co. / ABNCo. monogram. ***Comments:*** H-MA-395-G66b. Similar to W-MA-1030-020-G170 but with additional engraver imprint. Possible tint. 18__. 1850s–1860s.

Rarity: —

$50 • **W-MA-1030-050-G180**

Left: Lathework chain bearing MASSACHUSETTS / 50 / 50 vertically. ***Center:*** Alternating flower garlands and gridwork segments. ***Right:*** 50 / 50 vertically. ***Engraver:*** PSSP. ***Comments:*** H-MA-395-G70. 18__. 1820s–1830s.

Rarity: —

$50 • **W-MA-1030-050-G190**

Left: 50 / Portrait of George Washington. ***Center:*** Woman reclining with bale, Train and canal, Ships. ***Bottom center:*** Shell. ***Right:*** 50 / 50. ***Engraver:*** Rawdon, Wright, Hatch & Edson / New England Bank Note Co. ***Comments:*** H-MA-395-G74. 18__. 1850s.

Rarity: —

$50 • **W-MA-1030-050-G190a**

Engraver: Rawdon, Wright, Hatch & Edson / New England Bank Note Co. / ABNCo. monogram. ***Comments:*** H-MA-395-G74b. Similar to W-MA-1030-050-G190 but with additional engraver imprint. Possible tint. 18__. 1850s–1860s.

Rarity: —

$100 • **W-MA-1030-100-G200**

Left: Lathework chain bearing MASSACHUSETTS / 100 / 100 vertically. ***Center:*** Alternating flower garlands and gridwork segments. ***Right:*** 100 / 100 vertically. ***Engraver:*** Perkins. ***Comments:*** H-MA-395-G78. 18__. 1820s–1830s.

Rarity: —

$100 • **W-MA-1030-100-G210**

Left: 100 / George Washington standing by horse. ***Center:*** 100 / Sailor reclining. ***Right:*** 100 / 100. ***Engraver:*** Rawdon, Wright, Hatch & Edson / New England Bank Note Co. ***Comments:*** H-MA-395-G82. 18__. 1850s.

Rarity: —

$100 • **W-MA-1030-100-G210a**

Engraver: Rawdon, Wright, Hatch & Edson / New England Bank Note Co. / ABNCo. monogram. ***Comments:*** H-MA-395-G82b. Similar to W-MA-1030-100-G210 but with additional engraver imprint. Possible tint. 18__. 1850s–1860s.

Rarity: —

$1,000 • **W-MA-1030-1000-G220**

Left: M. ***Center:*** Two women flanking shield, Ships and train / Bust of George Washington. ***Right:*** 1000 / George Washington standing by horse. ***Engraver:*** American Bank Note Co. ***Comments:*** H-MA-395-G86a. 18__. 1850s–1860s.

Rarity: —

NON-VALID ISSUES

$1 • W-MA-1030-001-C010b

SI

Engraver: PSSP. ***Comments:*** H-MA-395-C6. Counterfeit of W-MA-1030-001-G010b. Edges cut off in image. 18__. 1840s.

Rarity: URS-6
VF $90

$2 • W-MA-1030-002-C050b

CC

Engraver: PSSP. ***Comments:*** H-MA-395-C20. Counterfeit of W-MA-1030-002-G050b. 18__. 1840s.

Rarity: URS-6
F $75; **VF** $100

$2 • W-MA-1030-002-S010

CC

Engraver: Underwood, Bald, Spencer & Hufty. ***Comments:*** H-MA-395-S5. From a modified plate originally for W-MA-710-002-C120. 18__. 1840s.

Rarity: URS-5
F $75; **VF** $125

$3 • W-MA-1030-003-C090b

Engraver: PSSP. ***Comments:*** H-MA-395-C32. Counterfeit of W-MA-1030-003-G090b. 18__. 1841.

Rarity: URS-6
F $65; **VF** $90

$5 • W-MA-1030-005-C120b

Engraver: PSSP. ***Comments:*** H-MA-395-C42. Counterfeit of W-MA-1030-005-G120b. 18__. 1830s.

Rarity: —

$5 • W-MA-1030-005-R010

Engraver: Rawdon, Wright, Hatch & Edson / New England Bank Note Co. ***Comments:*** H-MA-395-R5. Raised from W-MA-1030-001-G030. 18__. 1850s.

Rarity: —

$5 • W-MA-1030-005-R020

Engraver: American Bank Note Co. ***Comments:*** H-MA-395-R10. Raised from W-MA-1030-001-G040. 18__. 1850s–1860s.

Rarity: —

$5 • W-MA-1030-005-A010

Left: FIVE / Ships. ***Center:*** FIVE / 5 / Ships / 5. ***Right:*** FIVE / Portrait of George Washington. ***Engraver:*** Rawdon, Wright, Hatch & Edson. ***Comments:*** H-MA-395-A5. Altered from $5 Washington Bank, Washington, D.C. 185_. 1850s.

Rarity: URS-5
VG $75

$10 • W-MA-1030-010-C140a

Engraver: PSSP. ***Comments:*** H-MA-395-C52. Counterfeit of W-MA-1030-010-G140a. 18__. 1820s–1830s.

Rarity: —

$10 • W-MA-1030-010-R030

Engraver: Rawdon, Wright, Hatch & Edson / New England Bank Note Co. ***Comments:*** H-MA-395-R15. Raised from W-MA-1030-001-G030. 18__. 1850s.

Rarity: —

$10 • W-MA-1030-010-A020

Left: 10 / Portrait of George Washington held by cherub / 10. ***Center:*** X / Spread eagle with shield and arrows, E PLURIBUS UNUM / X. ***Bottom center:*** Ship. ***Right:*** 10 / Indian man / 10. ***Engraver:*** Terry, Pelton & Co. ***Comments:*** H-MA-395-A10. Altered from $10 Citizens Bank, Augusta, Maine, or from notes of other failed banks using the same plate. 18__. 1840s.

Rarity: —

$20 • W-MA-1030-020-R040

Engraver: Rawdon, Wright, Hatch & Edson / New England Bank Note Co. ***Comments:*** H-MA-395-R20. Raised from W-MA-1030-001-G030. 18__. 1850s.

Rarity: —

Webster Bank

1853–1865

W-MA-1050

History: The Webster Bank was chartered on April 28, 1853, with an authorized capital of $1,500,000, a figure soon increased to $2,000,000. Its namesake was Daniel Webster, a native of New Hampshire who moved to Massachusetts and gained great fame in various federal positions. He was particularly known as an outstanding orator. His portrait was used on certain notes.

The bank opened its doors for business at 75 State Street on August 17, 1853. Circulation ranged from $274,222 in 1858 to $308,190 in 1860. Specie averaged at a value of $153,000.

The business of the Webster Bank was succeeded by the National Webster Bank of Boston, chartered on August 14, 1865.

Numismatic Commentary: This bank's lower denomination notes are notable for their large portrait of Daniel Webster and the Bunker Hill Monument. They are scarce but not unobtainable.

Valid Issues

$1 • W-MA-1050-001-G010

Left: Bunker Hill Monument, ONE. ***Center:*** Portrait of Daniel Webster, ONE DOLLAR. ***Right:*** 1. ***Engraver:*** Rawdon, Wright, Hatch & Edson / New England Bank Note Co. ***Comments:*** H-MA-400-G2. 18__. 1850s.

Rarity: URS-5
VF $750

$1 • W-MA-1050-001-G010a

JF

Engraver: Rawdon, Wright, Hatch & Edson / New England Bank Note Co. / ABNCo. monogram. ***Comments:*** H-MA-400-G2a. Similar to W-MA-1050-001-G010 but with additional engraver imprint. 18__. 1850s–1860s.

Rarity: URS-5
Proof $750

$2 • W-MA-1050-002-G020

Left: Bunker Hill Monument / TWO. ***Center:*** Portrait of Daniel Webster. ***Right:*** 2. ***Engraver:*** Rawdon, Wright, Hatch & Edson / New England Bank Note Co. ***Comments:*** H-MA-400-G4. 18__. 1850s.

Rarity: —

$2 • W-MA-1050-002-G020a

Engraver: Rawdon, Wright, Hatch & Edson / New England Bank Note Co. / ABNCo. monogram. ***Comments:*** H-MA-400-G4a. Similar to W-MA-1050-002-G020 but with additional engraver imprint. 18__. 1850s–1860s.

Rarity: —

$3 • W-MA-1050-003-G030

JF

Engraver: Rawdon, Wright, Hatch & Edson / New England Bank Note Co. ***Comments:*** H-MA-400-G6. 18__. 1850s.

Rarity: URS-3
VG $500

$3 • W-MA-1050-003-G030a

Left: Bunker Hill Monument / THREE. ***Center:*** Portrait of Daniel Webster. ***Right:*** 3. ***Engraver:*** Rawdon, Wright, Hatch & Edson / New England Bank Note Co. / ABNCo. monogram. ***Comments:*** H-MA-400-G6a. Similar to W-MA-1050-003-G030 but with additional engraver imprint. 18__. 1850s–1860s.

Rarity: —

$5 • W-MA-1050-005-G040

Left: Bunker Hill Monument. ***Center:*** Portrait of Daniel Webster. ***Right:*** FIVE. ***Overprint:*** 5. ***Engraver:*** Rawdon, Wright, Hatch & Edson / New England Bank Note Co. ***Comments:*** H-MA-400-G8. 18__. 1850s.

Rarity: URS-3
Proof $1,200

$5 • W-MA-1050-005-G050

Left: 5. ***Center:*** 5 / Portrait of Daniel Webster / 5. ***Right:*** 5. ***Engraver:*** Toppan, Carpenter & Co. ***Comments:*** H-MA-400-G10. 18__. 1850s–1860s.

Rarity: —

Selected auction price: Stack's Bowers Galleries, March 2013, Lot 5153, Unc $3,290

$5 • W-MA-1050-005-G050a

CJF

Overprint: Red 5 / 5. ***Engraver:*** Toppan, Carpenter & Co. ***Comments:*** H-Unlisted. Similar to W-MA-1050-005-G050. Proof. June 17, 1856. 1850s–1860s.

Rarity: URS-3
Proof $3,500

$10 • W-MA-1050-010-G060

Left: Bunker Hill Monument / TEN. ***Center:*** Portrait of Daniel Webster. ***Right:*** X. ***Engraver:*** Rawdon, Wright, Hatch & Edson / New England Bank Note Co. ***Comments:*** H-MA-400-G12. 18__. 1850s.

Rarity: —

$10 • W-MA-1050-010-G060a

Engraver: Rawdon, Wright, Hatch & Edson / New England Bank Note Co. / ABNCo. monogram. ***Comments:*** H-MA-400-G12a. Similar to W-MA-1050-010-G060 but with additional engraver imprint. 18__. 1850s–1860s.

Rarity: —

$20 • W-MA-1050-020-G070

Left: XX / TWENTY across XX. ***Center:*** Portrait of Daniel Webster. ***Right:*** 20 / View of Faneuil Hall. ***Engraver:*** Rawdon, Wright, Hatch & Edson / New England Bank Note Co. ***Comments:*** H-MA-400-G14. 18__. 1850s.

Rarity: —

$20 • W-MA-1050-020-G070a

Engraver: Rawdon, Wright, Hatch & Edson / New England Bank Note Co. / ABNCo. monogram. ***Comments:*** H-MA-400-G14a. Similar to W-MA-1050-020-G070 but with additional engraver imprint. 18__. 1850s–1860s.

Rarity: —

$50 • W-MA-1050-050-G080

JF

Engraver: Rawdon, Wright, Hatch & Edson / New England Bank Note Co. ***Comments:*** H-MA-400-G16. 18__. 1850s.

Rarity: URS-1
F $4,000

$50 • W-MA-1050-050-G080a

Left: 50 / FIFTY. ***Center:*** Portrait of Daniel Webster. ***Right:*** 50 / View of Faneuil Hall. ***Engraver:*** Rawdon, Wright, Hatch & Edson / New England Bank Note Co. / ABNCo. monogram. ***Comments:*** H-MA-400-G16a. Similar to W-MA-1050-050-G080 but with additional engraver imprint. 18__. 1850s–1860s.

Rarity: —

$100 • W-MA-1050-100-G090

Left: 100 / 100. ***Center:*** Portrait of Daniel Webster. ***Right:*** C / View of Faneuil Hall. ***Engraver:*** Rawdon, Wright, Hatch & Edson / New England Bank Note Co. ***Comments:*** H-MA-400-G18. 18__. 1850s.

Rarity: —

$100 • W-MA-1050-100-G090a

Engraver: Rawdon, Wright, Hatch & Edson / New England Bank Note Co. / ABNCo. monogram. ***Comments:*** H-MA-400-G18a. Similar to W-MA-1050-100-G090 but with additional engraver imprint. 18__. 1850s–1860s.

Rarity: —

$500 • W-MA-1050-500-G100

JF

Engraver: Rawdon, Wright, Hatch & Edson / New England Bank Note Co. / ABNCo. monogram. ***Comments:*** H-Unlisted. 18__. 1850s–1860s.

Rarity: URS-1
F $5,000

$500 • W-MA-1050-500-G100a

Left: 500 / 500. ***Center:*** Portrait of Daniel Webster. ***Right:*** 500 / View of Faneuil Hall. ***Engraver:*** American Bank Note Co. ***Comments:*** H-MA-400-G20. Similar to W-MA-1050-500-G100. 18__. 1850s–1860s.

Rarity: —

$1,000 • W-MA-1050-1000-G110

Left: M / 1000. ***Center:*** Portrait of Daniel Webster. ***Right:*** 1000 / View of Faneuil Hall. ***Engraver:*** American Bank Note Co. ***Comments:*** H-MA-400-G22. 18__. 1850s–1860s.

Rarity: —

Non-Valid Issues

$3 • W-MA-1050-003-C030

Engraver: Rawdon, Wright, Hatch & Edson / New England Bank Note Co. ***Comments:*** H-MA-400-C6. Counterfeit of W-MA-1050-003-G030. 18__. 1850s

Rarity: —
VG $300

$5 • W-MA-1050-005-C040

CC

Engraver: Rawdon, Wright, Hatch & Edson / New England Bank Note Co. ***Comments:*** H-MA-400-C8. Counterfeit of W-MA-1050-005-G040. 18__. 1850s.

Rarity: URS-7
F $100; **VF** $150

$10 • W-MA-1050-010-C060

Engraver: Rawdon, Wright, Hatch & Edson / New England Bank Note Co. ***Comments:*** H-MA-400-C12. Counterfeit of W-MA-1050-010-G060. 18__. 1850s.

Rarity: —

Winnisimmet Bank

1833–1835

W-MA-1070

History: The Winnisimmet Bank was chartered on March 27, 1833, and was located near the Winnisimmet Ferry in Boston. By an act of the legislature its name was changed to the Fulton Bank, W-MA-550, on March 6, 1835.

Numismatic Commentary: Although most images are unconfirmed today, at least one issue will show the Evacuation of Boston, a fine historical scene imaging George Washington and a couple of aides on horseback watching the British Fleet leave the city.

Valid Issues

$1 • W-MA-1070-001-G010

CJF

Engraver: Unverified, but likely New England Bank Note Co. / PSSP. ***Comments:*** H-MA-405-G2. 18__. 1833–1835.

Rarity: URS-2
G $750

$2 • W-MA-1070-002-G020

Engraver: Unverified, but likely New England Bank Note Co. / PSSP. ***Comments:*** H-MA-405-G4. No description available. 18__. 1833–1835.

Rarity: *None known*

$3 • W-MA-1070-003-G030

Engraver: Unverified, but likely New England Bank Note Co. / PSSP. ***Comments:*** H-MA-405-G6. No description available. 18__. 1833–1835.

Rarity: *None known*

$5 • W-MA-1070-005-G040

Engraver: Unverified, but likely New England Bank Note Co. / PSSP. ***Comments:*** H-MA-405-G8. No description available. 18__. 1833–1835.

Rarity: *None known*

$10 • W-MA-1070-010-G050

Engraver: Unverified, but likely New England Bank Note Co. / PSSP. ***Comments:*** H-MA-405-G10. No description available. 18__. 1833–1835.

Rarity: *None known*

$20 • W-MA-1070-020-G060

Engraver: Unverified, but likely New England Bank Note Co. / PSSP. ***Comments:*** H-MA-405-G12. No description available. 18__. 1833–1835.

Rarity: *None known*

$50 • W-MA-1070-050-G070

Engraver: Unverified, but likely New England Bank Note Co. / PSSP. ***Comments:*** H-MA-405-G14. No description available. 18__. 1833–1835.

Rarity: *None known*

$100 • W-MA-1070-100-G080

Engraver: Unverified, but likely New England Bank Note Co. / PSSP. ***Comments:*** H-MA-405-G16. No description available. 18__. 1833–1835.

Rarity: *None known*

$500 • W-MA-1070-500-G090

Engraver: Unverified, but likely New England Bank Note Co. / PSSP. ***Comments:*** H-MA-405-G18. No description available. 18__. 1833–1835.

Rarity: *None known*

$1,000 • W-MA-1070-1000-G100

Engraver: Unverified, but likely New England Bank Note Co. / PSSP. ***Comments:*** H-MA-405-G20. No description available. 18__. 1833–1835.

Rarity: *None known*

Braintree, Massachusetts

The land upon which Braintree was later founded was colonized by Captain Wollaston in 1625. It was initially named Mount Wollaston, but under Thomas Morton it was renamed Merry Mount. The town of Braintree was incorporated in 1640 and named after the town of Braintree, England. Later it was split into Randolph, Holbrook, and Quincy, as well as part of Milton. John Adams and John Quincy Adams were both born in the northern precinct of Braintree, which is now the city of Quincy. Braintree is divided into the neighborhoods of East Braintree, South Braintree, North Braintree, and Braintree Highlands.

Union Bank of Weymouth and Braintree

1832–1864

W-MA-1090

History: The Union Bank of Weymouth and Braintree was chartered on March 17, 1832, with an authorized capital of $100,000. Bills in circulation totaled $37,379 in 1839. The capital was raised to $150,000 by 1854. The circulation was $92,032 in 1863.

The interests of the bank were succeeded by the Union National Bank of Weymouth, chartered September 6, 1864.

See also listing under Weymouth, W-MA-3320.

Bridgewater, Massachusetts

Originally a plantation granted to Duxbury, the area of Bridgewater was incorporated as a town in 1656. The first mill was erected on Town River, a body of water that issues from a pond known as Nippenicket. Iron manufacturing in multiple forms took place here, and the making of small arms in New England had its birth in Bridgewater. Cannons, edged tools, nails, bar irons, anchors, cotton gins, sugar mills, shovels, hoops, tacks, and castings were sold extensively. Other mills included paper, cotton, and various other manufacturing establishments. Chaise making and shoemaking were also substantial businesses. In 1794 the population was 3,990; in 1800 it was 5,200; in 1830 it was 6,503.

See also East Bridgewater and North Bridgewater, Massachusetts.

North Bridgewater Bank

1854–1860s

W-MA-1110

History: The North Bridgewater Bank was chartered on March 28, 1854, with an authorized capital of $100,000. The first president was Martin Wales, and the first cashier was Rufus P. Kingman. The banking rooms were in the Brett & Kingman Block. The first bills were issued on September 4, 1854. President Wales was pictured on certain of the smaller-denomination notes.

Circulation ranged from $72,464 in 1853 to $87,529 in 1858. Specie ranged from $4,734 to $6,837.35 during the same time.

In September 1866, the North Bridgewater Bank was the last of the state-chartered banks in operation. It declared a final dividend and asked the shareholders to surrender their stock.

See also listing under North Bridgewater, W-MA-2530.

Brighton, Massachusetts

Named after the English city of Brighton and Hove, for the first 160 years of its existence Brighton was a part of Cambridge and was also known as "Little Cambridge." Prior to the American Revolution, Little Cambridge was a prosperous farming community comprised of fewer than 300 occupants. Wealthy Boston merchants such as Benjamin Faneuil resided here. The residents seceded from Cambridge when the cattle industry was impacted by governmental decisions, and in 1807 permission to separate was obtained. The land was renamed Brighton.

The Massachusetts Society for Promoting Agriculture established an exhibition hall and fair grounds in Brighton Center, thus making Brighton the home of the largest agricultural fair and cattle show in Massachusetts. By 1820 horticulture became an important part of Brighton commerce, and two decades later the town was one of the most influential horticultural centers in the area.

Stockyard facilities and a hotel called the Cattle Fair were constructed in 1832 on the north side of Brighton Center. The building of a railroad through town in 1834 solidified the importance of the cattle trade, and by 1866 the town contained 42 slaughterhouses.

Bank of Brighton

1831–1860s

W-MA-1125

History: The Bank of Brighton was chartered on March 9, 1831, with an authorized capital of $150,000. In 1837 its capital had increased to $200,000. Between 1849 and 1857 it was $250,000, but later in 1862 it was again reduced to $200,000. In 1837 its charter was renewed to last until 1870. In 1853 the president of the bank and certain others left to form the Brighton Market Bank, W-MA-1160, chartered in 1854. Circulation of the Bank of Brighton ranged from $101,318 in 1861 to $249,345 in 1849. Real estate was valued at $5,000 in 1861 and specie was $21,073.23.

In May 1865, the interests of the bank were succeeded by the National Bank of Brighton, Boston, which was given a capital of $200,000 and carried the same officers forward.

Numismatic Commentary: Notes of this bank are still plentiful, and many will show various scenes of the center of town with livestock parading about.

Valid Issues

$1 • W-MA-1125-001-G010

Left: Lathework panel bearing MASSACHUSETTS vertically. ***Center:*** 1 / 1 / Alternating flower garlands and gridwork segments / ONE / 1 / 1. ***Right:*** Lathework panel bearing ONE / D / ONE vertically. ***Engraver:*** PSSP. ***Comments:*** H-MA-410-G2. 18__. 1830s.

Rarity: —

$1 • W-MA-1125-001-G020

SI

Engraver: New England Bank Note Co. ***Comments:*** H-MA-410-G4. 18__. 1830s–1850s.

Rarity: URS-5

F $500; **VF** $750

$1 • W-MA-1125-001-G030

CJF

Engraver: Danforth, Wright & Co. ***Comments:*** H-Unlisted. Proof. 18__. 1850s.

Rarity: URS-1

Proof $5,000

$1 • W-MA-1125-001-G030a

CJF

Overprint: Red 1 / 1. ***Engraver:*** Danforth, Wright & Co. ***Comments:*** H-MA-410-G8a. Similar to W-MA-1125-001-G030. 18__. 1850s.

Rarity: URS-4

VG $500; **F** $850; **Proof** $5,500

$1 • W-MA-1125-001-G030b

Left: 1 / ONE / 1 with ONE DOLLAR. ***Center:*** View of Brighton / 1, ONE, 1. ***Right:*** 1 / Bull's head / ONE. ***Overprint:*** Red 1 1. ***Engraver:*** Danforth, Wright & Co. / ABNCo. monogram. ***Comments:*** H-MA-410-G8b. Similar to W-MA-1125-001-G030 but with additional engraver imprint. 18__. 1850s–1860s.

Rarity: —

$2 • W-MA-1125-002-G040

Left: Lathework panel bearing MASSACHUSETTS vertically. ***Center:*** 2 / 2 / Alternating flower garlands and gridwork segments / TWO / 2 / 2. ***Right:*** Lathework panel bearing five TWOs vertically. ***Engraver:*** PSSP. ***Comments:*** H-MA-410-G10. 18__. 1830s.

Rarity: —

$2 • W-MA-1125-002-G050

Left: TWO / Woman / 2. ***Center:*** View of Brighton. ***Right:*** 2 / TWO. ***Engraver:*** New England Bank Note Co. ***Comments:*** H-MA-410-G12. 18__. 1830s–1850s.

Rarity: URS-7
F $100

$2 • W-MA-1125-002-G060

CJF

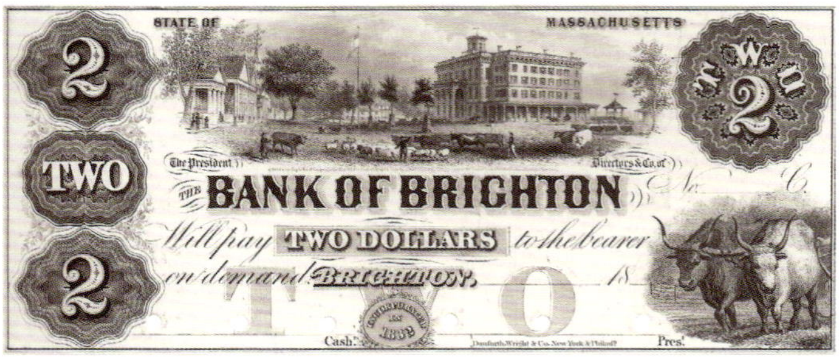

Engraver: Danforth, Wright & Co. ***Comments:*** H-Unlisted. Proof. 18__. 1850s.

Rarity: URS-2
Proof $3,000

$2 • W-MA-1125-002-G060a

CC

Tint: Red. ***Engraver:*** Danforth, Wright & Co. ***Comments:*** H-MA-410-G16a. Similar to W-MA-1125-002-G060. 18__. 1850s.

Rarity: URS-1
Proof $6,000

$2 • W-MA-1125-002-G060b

Left: 2 / TWO / 2. ***Center:*** View of Brighton. ***Right:*** TWO over 2 / Oxen. ***Overprint:*** Red. ***Engraver:*** Danforth, Wright & Co. / ABNCo. monogram. ***Comments:*** H-MA-410-G16b. Similar to W-MA-1125-002-G060 but with additional engraver imprint. 18__. 1850s–1860s.

Rarity: —

$3 • W-MA-1125-003-G070

Left: Lathework panel bearing MASSACHUSETTS vertically. ***Center:*** 3 / 3 / Alternating flower garlands and gridwork segments / THREE / 3 / 3. ***Right:*** Lathework panel bearing THREE vertically. ***Engraver:*** PSSP. ***Comments:*** H-MA-410-G18. 18__. 1830s.

Rarity: —

$3 • W-MA-1125-003-G080

Left: 3 / Portrait / 3. ***Center:*** View of Brighton. ***Right:*** 3 / Cattle / THREE. ***Engraver:*** New England Bank Note Co. ***Comments:*** H-MA-410-G20. 18__. 1830s–1850s.

Rarity: —

$3 • W-MA-1125-003-G090

CJF

Engraver: Danforth, Wright & Co. ***Comments:*** H-Unlisted. Proof. 18__. 1850s.

Rarity: URS-2
Proof $3,500

$3 • W-MA-1125-003-G090a

CC

Tint: Red. ***Engraver:*** Danforth, Wright & Co. ***Comments:*** H-MA-410-G24a. Similar to W-MA-1125-003-G090. 18__. 1850s.

Rarity: URS-1
Proof $6,000

$3 • W-MA-1125-003-G090b

Overprint: Red. ***Engraver:*** Danforth, Wright & Co. / ABNCo. monogram. ***Comments:*** H-MA-410-G24b. Similar to W-MA-1125-003-G090 but with additional engraver imprint. 18__. 1850s–1860s.

Rarity: —

$5 • W-MA-1125-005-G100

Left: Lathework chain bearing MASSACHUSETTS vertically / 5 / 5. ***Center:*** Alternating flower garlands and gridwork segments / FIVE. ***Right:*** 5 / 5. ***Engraver:*** PSSP. ***Comments:*** H-MA-410-G26. 18__. 1830s.

Rarity: —

$5 • W-MA-1125-005-G110

Left: 5 / Portrait of Benjamin Franklin / 5. ***Center:*** View of Brighton. ***Right:*** 5 / Woman / V. ***Engraver:*** New England Bank Note Co. ***Comments:*** H-MA-410-G28. 18__. 1830s–1850s.

Rarity: —

$5 • W-MA-1125-005-G120

CJF

Engraver: Danforth, Wright & Co. ***Comments:*** H-Unlisted. Proof. 18__. 1850s.

Rarity: URS-3
Proof $2,500

$5 • W-MA-1125-005-G120a

CC

Tint: Red. ***Engraver:*** Danforth, Wright & Co. ***Comments:*** H-MA-410-G32a. Similar to W-MA-1125-005-G120. 18__. 1850s.

Rarity: URS-1
Proof $6,000

$5 • W-MA-1125-005-G120b

CC

Tint: Red. ***Engraver:*** Danforth, Wright & Co. ***Comments:*** H-Unlisted. Similar to W-MA-1125-005-G120. Proof. 18__. 1850s.

Rarity: URS-3
Proof $6,000

$5 • W-MA-1125-005-G120c

Left: 5 / V in FIVE / 5. ***Center:*** View of Brighton. ***Right:*** 5 and FIVE across V / Cattle and sheep. ***Overprint:*** Red. ***Engraver:*** Danforth, Wright & Co. / ABNCo. monogram. ***Comments:*** H-MA-410-G32b. Similar to W-MA-1125-005-G120 but with additional engraver imprint. 18__. 1850s–1860s.

Rarity: —

$10 • W-MA-1125-010-G130

Left: Lathework chain bearing MASSACHUSETTS / 10 / 10 vertically. ***Center:*** Alternating flower garlands and gridwork segments / TEN. ***Right:*** 10 / 10. ***Engraver:*** PSSP. ***Comments:*** H-MA-410-G34. 18__. 1830s.

Rarity: —

$10 • W-MA-1125-010-G140

Left: 10 / Portrait of George Washington / 10. ***Center:*** View of Brighton. ***Right:*** 10 / Woman / TEN. ***Engraver:*** New England Bank Note Co. ***Comments:*** H-MA-410-G36. 18__. 1830s–1850s.

Rarity: —

$10 • W-MA-1125-010-G150

QDB

Engraver: Danforth, Wright & Co. ***Comments:*** H-Unlisted. Proof. 18__. 1850s.

Rarity: URS-2
Proof $300

$10 • W-MA-1125-010-G150a

Left: X / Portrait of Daniel Webster / TEN. ***Center:*** View of Brighton. ***Right:*** 10 / Train. ***Overprint:*** Red. ***Engraver:*** Danforth, Wright & Co. ***Comments:*** H-MA-410-G40a. Similar to W-MA-1125-010-G150. 18__. 1850s.

Rarity: —

How to Read the Whitman Numbering System

$1 • W-MA-010-001-G010a

Denomination: Value of the note shown.

W: Whitman number. This number is a sortable code unique to each bank and note.

MA: Abbreviation for the state under study.

010: Numerical designation specific to each bank.

001: The denomination in dollars.

G010a: G indicates a good or valid note. Other categories are indicated thus: C (counterfeit); R (raised); S (spurious); N (not-attributed); A (altered). Numbers are assigned starting with 010, 020, et seq. Terminal letters following the number indicate variations of a note: a series of different colored overprints, tints, payees, etc., all on the same design of note. For more information, see the “How to Use This Book” section at the front of the volume, page xiv.

$10 • W-MA-1125-010-G150b

CC

Tint: Red. ***Engraver:*** Danforth, Wright & Co. ***Comments:*** H-Unlisted. Similar to W-MA-1125-010-G150. Proof. 18__. 1850s.

Rarity: URS-1
Proof $6,000

$10 • W-MA-1125-010-G150c

Overprint: Red. ***Engraver:*** Danforth, Wright & Co. / ABNCo. monogram. ***Comments:*** H-MA-410-G40b. Similar to W-MA-1125-010-G150 but with additional engraver imprint. 18__. 1850s–1860s.

Rarity: —

$20 • W-MA-1125-020-G160

Left: Lathework chain bearing MASSACHUSETTS / 20 / 20. ***Center:*** Alternating flower garlands and gridwork segments / TWENTY. ***Right:*** 20 / 20 vertically. ***Engraver:*** PSSP. ***Comments:*** H-MA-410-G42. 18__. 1830s.

Rarity: —

$20 • W-MA-1125-020-G170

SI

Engraver: New England Bank Note Co. ***Comments:*** H-MA-410-G44. 18__. 1830s–1850s.

Rarity: URS-8
F $65; **VF** $100

$20 • W-MA-1125-020-G180

Left: XX / Portrait of George Washington. ***Center:*** View of Brighton. ***Right:*** 20 / Woman seated by column with shield and wheel. ***Overprint:*** Red. ***Engraver:*** Danforth, Wright & Co. ***Comments:*** H-MA-410-G48a. 18__. 1850s.

Rarity: —

$20 • W-MA-1125-020-G180a

Overprint: Red. ***Engraver:*** Danforth, Wright & Co. / ABNCo. monogram. ***Comments:*** H-MA-410-G48b. Similar to W-MA-1125-020-G180 but with additional engraver imprint. 18__. 1850s–1860s.

Rarity: URS-3

$20 • W-MA-1125-020-G180b

CC

Tint: Red. ***Engraver:*** Danforth, Wright & Co. / ABNCo. monogram. ***Comments:*** H-Unlisted. Similar to W-MA-1125-020-G180 but with additional engraver imprint. Proof. 18__. 1850s.

Rarity: URS-1
Proof $6,500

$50 • W-MA-1125-050-G190

Engraver: PSSP. ***Comments:*** H-MA-410-G50. 18__. 1830s.

Rarity: URS-3
F $750

$50 • W-MA-1125-050-G200

Comments: H-MA-410-G52. No description available. 18__. 1830s–1840s.

Rarity: *None known*

$50 • W-MA-1125-050-G210

CJF

Comments: H-Unlisted. 18__. 1830s–1840s.

Rarity: URS-4
VF $500

$50 • W-MA-1125-050-G220

RMS

Engraver: Toppan, Carpenter, Casilear & Co. ***Comments:*** H-MA-410-G56. 18__. 1850s.

Rarity: URS-8
F $75; **VF** $90

$50 • W-MA-1125-050-G230

Left: Woman with fruit / 50. ***Center:*** Horses jumping fence pursued by boy. ***Right:*** 50 / Street scene. ***Engraver:*** American Bank Note Co. ***Comments:*** H-MA-410-G58. 1850s–1860s.

Rarity: URS-3
Proof $3,000

$50 • **W-MA-1125-050-G230a**

CC

Tint: Red. ***Engraver:*** Danforth, Wright & Co. / ABNCo. monogram. ***Comments:*** H-Unlisted. Similar to W-MA-1125-050-G230 but with different engraver imprint. Proof. January 1, 18__. 1850s–1860s.

Rarity: URS-1
Proof $6,500

$100 • **W-MA-1125-100-G240**

Left: Lathework chain bearing MASSACHUSETTS / 100 / 100 vertically. ***Center:*** Alternating flower garlands and gridwork segments / HUNDRED. ***Right:*** 100 / 100 vertically. ***Engraver:*** PSSP. ***Comments:*** H-MA-410-G60. 18__. 1830s.

Rarity: URS-2
Proof $3,000

$100 • **W-MA-1125-100-G250**

CJF

Engraver: Toppan, Carpenter, Casilear & Co. ***Comments:*** H-MA-410-G64. 18__. 1850s.

Rarity: URS-7
VG $75; **VF** $150

$100 • **W-MA-1125-100-G260**

Left: 100 / Street scene. ***Center:*** Cattle drinking, Drover on horse, Two boys. ***Right:*** 100 / Men dressing leather. ***Engraver:*** American Bank Note Co. ***Comments:*** H-MA-410-G66. 1850s–1860s.

Rarity: URS-2
Proof $5,000

$100 • **W-MA-1125-100-G260a**

CC

Tint: Red. ***Engraver:*** Danforth, Wright & Co. / ABNCo. monogram. ***Comments:*** H-Unlisted. Similar to W-MA-1125-100-G260 but with different engraver imprint. Proof. January 1, 18__. 1850s–1860s.

Rarity: URS-1
Proof $6,750

$100 • **W-MA-1125-100-G270**

TD

Engraver: New England Bank Note Co. ***Comments:*** H-Unlisted. 18__. 1840s.

Rarity: URS-4
F $500

$500 • **W-MA-1125-500-G280**

Left: Liberty standing with shield bearing 500. ***Center:*** Building, Black horse and white horse flanking shield bearing state arms surmounted by eagle, Train. ***Right:*** 500 / Hotel. ***Engraver:*** American Bank Note Co. ***Comments:*** H-MA-410-G70. 1850s–1860s.

Rarity: —

$500 • **W-MA-1125-500-G280a**

CC

Tint: Red. ***Engraver:*** Danforth, Wright & Co. / ABNCo. monogram. ***Comments:*** H-Unlisted. Similar to W-MA-1125-500-G280 but with different engraver imprint. January 1, 18__. 1850s–1860s.

Rarity: URS-1
Proof $8,500

Uncut Sheets

$1-$2-$3-$5 • **W-MA-1125-001.002.003.005-US010**

Vignette(s): ***($1)*** View of Brighton / Bull's head. ***($2)*** View of Brighton / Oxen. ***($3)*** View of Brighton / Three cows. ***($5)*** View of Brighton / Cattle and sheep. ***Overprint(s):*** None. ***Comments:*** All unlisted in Haxby. Proof.

Rarity: URS-3
Proof $500

$1-$2-$3-$5 • **W-MA-1125-001.002.003.005-US010a**

Overprint(s): Red. ***Comments:*** H-MA-410-G8a, G16a, G24a, G32a. Similar to W-MA-1125-001.002.003.005-US010.

Rarity: —

$1-$2-$3-$5 • W-MA-1125-001.002.003.005-US010b

Vignette(s): ($1) View of Brighton / Bull's head. ***($2)*** View of Brighton / Oxen. ***($3)*** View of Brighton / Three cows. ***($5)*** View of Brighton / Cattle and sheep. ***Tint(s):*** Ochre. ***Comments:*** All unlisted in Haxby. Similar to W-MA-1125-001.002.003.005-US010.

Rarity: —

$10-$20 • W-MA-1125-010.020-US020

Vignette(s): ($10) No description available. ***($20)*** Portrait of George Washington / View of Brighton / Woman seated by column with shield and wheel. ***Tint(s):*** Ochre. ***Comments:*** All unlisted in Haxby.

Rarity: —

$50-$100 • W-MA-1125-050.100-US030

Vignette(s): ($50) Women with fruit / Horses jumping fence pursued by boy / Street scene. ***($100)*** Street scene / Cattle drinking, Drover on horse, Two boys / Men dressing leather. ***Engraver:*** Danforth, Wright & Co. ***Comments:*** All unlisted in Haxby. January 1, 18__. 1850s–1860s.

Rarity: —

$50-$100 • W-MA-1125-050.100-US030a

Tint(s): Red. ***Comments:*** All unlisted in Haxby. Similar to W-MA-1125-050.100-US030. January 1, 18__. 1850s–1860s.

Rarity: —

Non-Valid Issues

$1 • W-MA-1125-001-N010

Left: Woman with flag. ***Center:*** Farmer reclining on sheaf, Reapers. ***Comments:*** H-MA-410-N5.

Rarity: —

$2 • W-MA-1125-002-N020

Center: Train / Woman / Portrait of George Washington. ***Comments:*** H-MA-410-N10.

Rarity: —

$3 • W-MA-1125-003-A010

Left: Portrait of George Washington / 3. ***Center:*** Building, Herd of cattle standing and lying down, Two men. ***Right:*** 3 / Bust of woman with flower. ***Engraver:*** National Bank Note Co. ***Comments:*** H-MA-410-AR15. Altered and lowered from $5 North Western Bank, Warren, Pennsylvania. July 7, 1861.

Rarity: —

$5 • W-MA-1125-005-R010

Engraver: Danforth, Wright & Co. ***Comments:*** H-MA-410-R5. Raised from W-MA-1125-001-G030a. 18__. 1850s.

Rarity: —

$5 • W-MA-1125-005-A020

Left: Men driving cattle into stream / 5. ***Center:*** Five men haying, Wagon and two oxen. ***Right:*** 5. ***Tint:*** Brown-orange lathework outlining white 5. ***Engraver:*** Bald, Cousland & Co. ***Comments:*** H-MA-410-A20. Altered from $5 Pioneer Association, Lafayette, Indiana. 18__. 1850s.

Rarity: —

$10 • W-MA-1125-010-N030

Left: Woman. ***Center:*** Two sailing ships. ***Right:*** Steamboat. ***Engraver:*** New England Bank Note Co. ***Comments:*** H-MA-410-N15. 18__. 1840s.

Rarity: —

$10 • W-MA-1125-010-N040

Left: X / X. ***Center:*** Woman seated. ***Right:*** TEN. ***Comments:*** H-MA-410-N20.

Rarity: —

$10 • W-MA-1125-010-AR010

Left: Portrait of George Washington / X. ***Center:*** Cattle and horses. ***Right:*** X / Girl. ***Engraver:*** National Bank Note Co. ***Comments:*** H-MA-410-AR30. Altered and raised from $5 North Western Bank, Warren, Pennsylvania. July 7, 186_. 1860s.

Rarity: URS-4
VG $100

$10 • W-MA-1125-010-A030

CJF

Tint: Red-brown lathework outlining white TEN. ***Engraver:*** Bald, Cousland & Co. / Baldwin, Bald & Cousland. ***Comments:*** H-MA-410-A25. Altered from $10 Southern Bank of Georgia, Bainbridge, Georgia. Nov. 5, 1860.

Rarity: URS-7
F $150

$20 • W-MA-1125-020-N050

Center: Beehive / Blacksmith shoeing horse / Man on horse. ***Comments:*** H-MA-410-N25.

Rarity: —

Bank of Brighton of Brighton

1850s

W-MA-1140

History: A non-existent bank represented only by notes altered from those of other banks. The notes were intended to pass for those of the Bank of Brighton, W-MA-1125.

Issues

$1 • W-MA-1140-001-A010

SI

Tint: Red-brown dies outlining white 1s and panel outlining white ONE DOLLAR. ***Engraver:*** Danforth, Wright & Co. ***Comments:*** H-MA-411-A5. Altered from $10 Southern Bank of Georgia, Bainbridge, Georgia. March 1, 18__. 1850s–1860s.

Rarity: URS-9
VG $75

$2 • **W-MA-1140-002-A020** CC

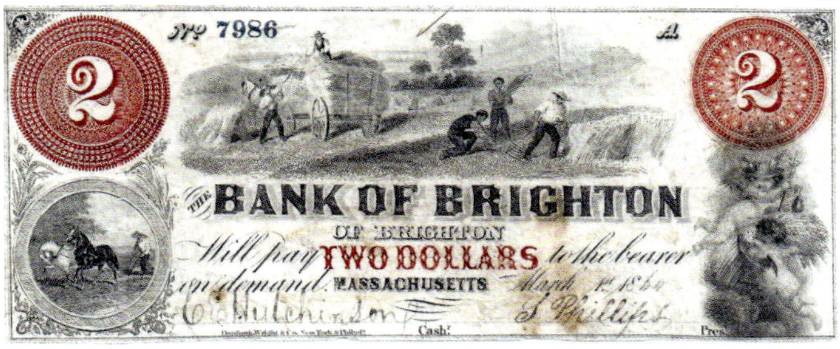

Tint: Red-brown dies outlining white 2s and TWO DOLLARS. ***Engraver:*** Danforth, Wright & Co. ***Comments:*** H-MA-411-A10. Altered from $2 Southern Bank of Georgia, Bainbridge, Georgia. March 1, 18__. 1860s.

Rarity: URS-9
VG $75

Brighton Bank
1828–1830
W-MA-1150

History: The Brighton Bank was chartered on March 7, 1828, with an authorized capital of $150,000. By early 1830 rumors of problems and poor management resulted in the state launching an investigation. The report was presented on February 22 and revealed that two stockholders owed more money to the bank than the bank's authorized capital—Sherman Leland owed the amount of 68,350 and Ralph Huntington, the bank's president, the amount of $123,024.28. The investigators reported that no money at all had ever been paid in, that the bank had no cash, and that the requirements of its charter had been grossly violated. In spite of this, the bank had issued a large number of bank notes that were given out as "loans," including to Leland and Huntington. About the same time an advertisement stated that the bank had over $19,000 in specie in its vaults. Acting on the report of the investigators, the Legislature voided the bank's charter on March 28, 1830.

In the meantime the bank issued many statements affirming that it was soundly operated, had large cash reserves, had funds settled with the Suffolk Bank, and that the investigation was unfair. Matters were confused, to say the least. The bank's bills continued to have market value, albeit at a discount. In March 1833, the bank announced that its liquidation was in progress but that affairs were secure, and the stockholders had been paid dividends totaling $10,875, with more to come. Many comments concerning the legislative investigation and the bank appeared in newspapers for years afterward. Finally, in 1837 it was generally listed as a failed bank. The full story of the Brighton Bank would furnish a fertile fielvd for research.

Brighton Market Bank
1854–1865
W-MA-1160

History: The Brighton Market Bank was organized in May 1854 when individuals associated with the Bank of Brighton, W-MA-1125, left to form their own entity. This included the president of the Bank of Brighton, Life Baldwin. The bank began business on September 18 of the same year. The starting authorized capital was $100,000.

The bank's capital was increased to $250,000 by 1857. It fluctuated between $200,000 and $250,000 for the remainder of the corporation's existence.

Circulation ranged from a low of $203,264 in 1861 to a high of $249,248 in 1863. Selected figures for 1857 were: bills of this bank and other New England states $7,797.01; specie $18,962.77; real estate $8,240.28.

On February 14, 1865, the business of the Brighton Market Bank was succeeded by the National Market Bank of Brighton.

Numismatic Commentary: Some of the notes of this bank show a similar livestock scene as imaged on notes of the Bank of Brighton, W-MA-1125, but these are much harder to locate.

Valid Issues

$1 • **W-MA-1160-001-G010**

Left: 1 / Woman standing with staff, Shield / ONE. ***Center:*** View of livestock market in Brighton / ONE. ***Right:*** 1 / Woman holding 1 bearing ONE. ***Overprint:*** Red ONE. ***Engraver:*** Rawdon, Wright, Hatch & Edson / New England Bank Note Co. ***Comments:*** H-MA-415-G2a. Sept. 4, 18__. 1850s–1860s.

Rarity: —

$1 • **W-MA-1160-001-G010a** CJF

Overprint: Red ONE. ***Engraver:*** Rawdon, Wright, Hatch & Edson / New England Bank Note Co. / ABNCo. monogram. ***Comments:*** H-MA-415-G2b. Similar to W-MA-1160-001-G010 but with additional engraver imprint. Sept. 4, 18__. 1850s–1860s.

Rarity: URS-4
VF $1,500

$2 • **W-MA-1160-002-G020**

Left: Two women standing with sword and balance / 2. ***Center:*** View of livestock market in Brighton. ***Right:*** 2 / Sailor and Indian man flanking shield bearing TWO. ***Overprint:*** Red TWO. ***Engraver:*** Rawdon, Wright, Hatch & Edson / New England Bank Note Co. ***Comments:*** H-MA-415-G4a. Sept. 4, 18__. 1850s.

Rarity: —

$2 • **W-MA-1160-002-G020a**

Overprint: Red TWO. ***Engraver:*** Rawdon, Wright, Hatch & Edson / New England Bank Note Co. / ABNCo. monogram. ***Comments:*** H-MA-415-G4b. Similar to W-MA-1160-002-G020 but with additional engraver imprint. Sept. 4, 18__. 1850s–1860s.

Rarity: —

$3 • **W-MA-1160-003-G030**

Left: 3 / Cattle / THREE. ***Center:*** View of livestock market in Brighton. ***Bottom center:*** Man plowing. ***Right:*** 3 / Mechanic, sailor, and farmer standing with 3. ***Overprint:*** Red THREE. ***Engraver:*** Rawdon, Wright, Hatch & Edson / New England Bank Note Co. ***Comments:*** H-MA-415-G6a. Sept. 4, 18__. 1850s–1860s.

Rarity: —

$3 • **W-MA-1160-003-G030a**

Overprint: Red THREE. ***Engraver:*** Rawdon, Wright, Hatch & Edson / New England Bank Note Co. / ABNCo. monogram. ***Comments:*** H-MA-415-G6b. Similar to W-MA-1160-003-G030 but with additional engraver imprint. Sept. 4, 18__. 1850s–1860s.

Rarity: —

$5 • **W-MA-1160-005-G040**

Left: 5 / Female portrait / 5. ***Center:*** View of livestock market in Brighton. ***Right:*** 5 / Liberty seated with shield and globe. ***Overprint:*** Red FIVE. ***Engraver:*** Rawdon, Wright, Hatch & Edson / New England Bank Note Co. ***Comments:*** H-MA-415-G8a. Sept. 4, 18__. 1850s.

Rarity: —

$5 • **W-MA-1160-005-G040a**

Overprint: Red FIVE. ***Engraver:*** Rawdon, Wright, Hatch & Edson / New England Bank Note Co. / ABNCo. monogram. ***Comments:*** H-MA-415-G8b. Similar to W-MA-1160-005-G040 but with additional engraver imprint. Sept. 4, 18__. 1850s–1860s.

Rarity: —

$10 • **W-MA-1160-010-G050**

Left: Man and boy washing sheep / X. ***Center:*** Farm scene, Woman and man seated, Three men with sickle and scythe. ***Bottom center:*** Hay wagon. ***Right:*** 10 / Train, Cattle. ***Overprint:*** Red. ***Engraver:*** Rawdon, Wright, Hatch & Edson / New England Bank Note Co. ***Comments:*** H-MA-415-G10a. Sept. 4, 18__. 1850s–1860s.

Rarity: —

$10 • **W-MA-1160-010-G050a**

Overprint: Red. ***Engraver:*** Rawdon, Wright, Hatch & Edson / New England Bank Note Co. / ABNCo. monogram. ***Comments:*** H-MA-415-G10b. Similar to W-MA-1160-010-G050 but with additional engraver imprint. Sept. 4, 18__. 1850s–1860s.

Rarity: —

$20 • **W-MA-1160-020-G060**

Left: Woman seated with sheaf and balance / 20. ***Center:*** Two farmers seated at lunch, Two boys lying down, Woman and two children. ***Bottom center:*** Farmer cradling grain. ***Right:*** 20 / Cattle and pigs. ***Overprint:*** Red. ***Engraver:*** Rawdon, Wright, Hatch & Edson / New England Bank Note Co. ***Comments:*** H-MA-415-G12a. Sept. 4, 18__. 1850s–1860s.

Rarity: —

$20 • **W-MA-1160-020-G060a**

Overprint: Red. ***Engraver:*** Rawdon, Wright, Hatch & Edson / New England Bank Note Co. / ABNCo. monogram. ***Comments:*** H-MA-415-G12b. Similar to W-MA-1160-020-G060 but with additional engraver imprint. Sept. 4, 18__. 1850s–1860s.

Rarity: —

$50 • **W-MA-1160-050-G070**

Left: Woman with rake / 50. ***Center:*** Cattle. ***Bottom center:*** Farm tools and produce. ***Right:*** 50 / Woman churning. ***Overprint:*** Red FIFTY. ***Engraver:*** Rawdon, Wright, Hatch & Edson / New England Bank Note Co. / ABNCo. monogram. ***Comments:*** H-MA-415-G14a. Sept. 4, 18__. 1850s–1860s.

Rarity: —

$50 • **W-MA-1160-050-G080**

Left: Woman seated on bale holding die bearing 50 / FIFTY. ***Center:*** Three boys catching runaway horse, Horse and colt. ***Right:*** Woman seated on bale holding die bearing 50 / FIFTY. ***Engraver:*** Rawdon, Wright, Hatch & Edson / New England Bank Note Co. / ABNCo. monogram. ***Comments:*** H-MA-415-G16. Sept. 4, 18__. 1850s–1860s.

Rarity: —

$100 • **W-MA-1160-100-G090**

CJF

Overprint: Red HUNDRED. ***Engraver:*** Rawdon, Wright, Hatch & Edson / New England Bank Note Co. ***Comments:*** H-Unlisted. Sept. 4, 18__. 1850s–1860s.

Rarity: URS-7
VG $150; **VF** $300

$100 • **W-MA-1160-100-G090a**

Left: C / C. ***Center:*** Woman reclining / C. ***Right:*** 100 / Portrait of Daniel Webster / 100. ***Overprint:*** Red HUNDRED. ***Engraver:*** Rawdon, Wright, Hatch & Edson / New England Bank Note Co. / ABNCo. monogram. ***Comments:*** H-MA-415-G18a. Similar to W-MA-1160-100-G090 but with additional engraver imprint. Sept. 4, 18__. 1850s–1860s.

Rarity: URS-7
VG $175; **F** $250; **VF** $300

$100 • **W-MA-1160-100-G100**

Left: C / 100. ***Center:*** Woman standing with pitcher, Man watering two horses at trough / Portrait of boy with cap. ***Right:*** 100 / Milkmaid driving cow and calf. ***Engraver:*** Rawdon, Wright, Hatch & Edson / New England Bank Note Co. / ABNCo. monogram. ***Comments:*** H-MA-415-G20. Sept. 4, 18__. 1850s–1860s.

Rarity: —

$500 • **W-MA-1160-500-G110**

Left: Portrait of boy / 500. ***Center:*** 500. ***Right:*** 500 / Woman and cherub flanking portrait of George Washington. ***Engraver:*** Rawdon, Wright, Hatch & Edson / New England Bank Note Co. / ABNCo. monogram. ***Comments:*** H-MA-415-G22. Sept. 4, 18__. 1850s–1860s.

Rarity: —

NON-VALID ISSUES

$5 • W-MA-1160-005-A010

Left: Horses running / V. ***Center:*** Liberty and Ceres flanking shield surmounted by horse's head. ***Bottom center:*** Sleeping dog. ***Right:*** 5 / Portrait of girl shading eyes. ***Overprint:*** Red FIVE. ***Engraver:*** Bald, Cousland & Co. / Baldwin, Bald & Cousland. ***Comments:*** H-MA-415-A10. Altered from $5 Bank of Morgan, Morgan, Georgia. 18__. 1850s.

Rarity: —

$5 • W-MA-1160-005-A020

Left: Man driving cattle / 5. ***Center:*** 5. ***Right:*** 5 / Man farming, Cattle. ***Tint:*** Red-brown lathework outlining white 5. ***Engraver:*** Bald, Cousland & Co. ***Comments:*** H-MA-415-A15. Altered from $5 Pioneer Association, Lafayette, Indiana. 1850s–1860s.

Rarity: URS-7
VG $90

$10 • W-MA-1160-010-C050

Engraver: Rawdon, Wright, Hatch & Edson / New England Bank Note Co. / ABNCo. monogram. ***Comments:*** H-MA-415-C10a. Counterfeit of W-MA-1160-010-G050 or G050a. Sept. 4, 18__. 1850s–1860s.

Rarity: —

$10 • W-MA-1160-010-A030

CJF

Tint: Red-brown lathework outlining white TEN. ***Engraver:*** Bald, Cousland & Co. / Baldwin, Bald & Cousland. ***Comments:*** H-MA-415-A20. Altered from $10 Southern Bank of Georgia, Bainbridge, Georgia. Nov. 5, 1860.

Rarity: URS-7
VG $100

$100 • W-MA-1160-100-C090a

Engraver: Rawdon, Wright, Hatch & Edson / New England Bank Note Co. / ABNCo. monogram. ***Comments:*** H-MA-415-C18a. Counterfeit of W-MA-1160-100-G090a. Sept. 4, 18__. 1850s–1860s.

Rarity: URS-6
F $140

Brighton Market Bank of Brighton

1860s

W-MA-1165

History: A non-existent bank represented only by notes altered from other banks.

ISSUES

$1 • W-MA-1165-001-A010

SI

Tint: Red-brown dies outlining white 1s and panel outlining white ONE DOLLAR. ***Engraver:*** Danforth, Wright & Co. ***Comments:*** H-MA-415-A5. Altered from $1 Southern Bank of Georgia, Bainbridge, Georgia. March 1, 18__. 1860s.

Rarity: URS-7
VG $75

BUCKSTOWN, MASSACHUSETTS

Buckstown, incorporated in 1792, was the first name for what in 1817 became Bucksport. Members of the Buck family were among the first settlers. See also Buckstown and Bucksport, Maine.

Penobscot Bank

1806–1811

W-MA-1170 • W-ME-580

History: The Penobscot Bank was authorized on March 20, 1806, and went into business in June. Unfortunately, the bank was launched at an inopportune time, as the Embargo Act of 1807 and the Non-Intercourse Act of 1808 restricted shipping and caused a general economic depression in New England. This eventually led to the War of 1812. The Penobscot Bank failed in 1811 and went into liquidation, becoming the first institution in the Maine District of Massachusetts to do so. The bills became worthless, although for some months afterwards they continued to circulate at a discount in places distant from Buckstown and among people who were not aware that the bank had failed.

Numismatic Commentary: The Penobscot Bank ordered all of its notes from Jacob Perkins in Newburyport, Massachusetts. In the short period of activity beginning in 1806, three styles of Perkins notes were ordered, as described below. Much concerning the notes is assumptive: denominations of $1, $2, $3, $5, and $10 notes were made in at least two styles, likely three for some. In addition, a $20 was mentioned in contemporary print. Not all are known today, and whether all of the varieties listed below were actually produced is unknown. Issued notes are generally unverified.

Valid Issues

$1 • W-MA-1170-001-G010

QDB

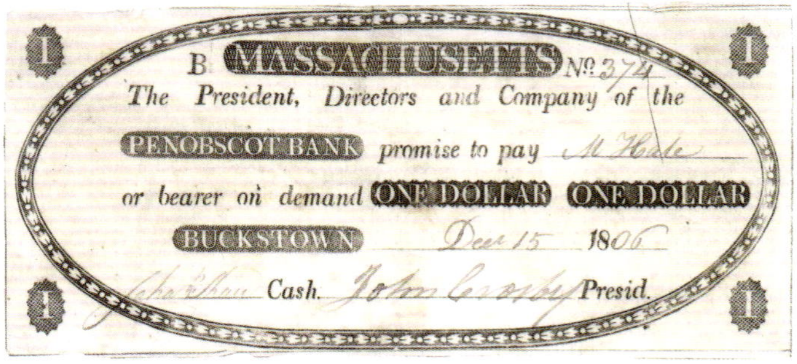

Engraver: PSSP. ***Comments:*** H-MA-420-G4, Wait-Unlisted. 18__. 1800s.

Rarity: URS-3
VF $750

$1 • W-MA-1170-001-G020

Left: 1 / 1. ***Center:*** Flower garlands, ONE. ***Right:*** 1 / 1. ***Engraver:*** PSSP. ***Comments:*** H-MA-420-G6, Wait-Unlisted. 1807–1809.

Rarity: —

$1 • W-MA-1170-001-G030

Left: 1 / 1. ***Center:*** PENOBSCOT BANK, Text. ***Right:*** 1 / 1. ***Engraver:*** PSSP. ***Comments:*** H-MA-420-G8, Wait-Unlisted. 1810.

Rarity: —

$2 • W-MA-1170-002-G040

Engraver: PSSP. ***Comments:*** H-MA-420-G12, Wait-1. Similar to W-MA-1170-001-G010 but with different denomination. 1806.

Rarity: —

$2 • W-MA-1170-002-G050

CC

Engraver: PSSP. ***Comments:*** H-MA-420-G14, Wait-Unlisted. Similar to W-MA-1170-001-G020 but with different denomination. 18__. 1807–1809.

Rarity: URS-6
VF $250

$2 • W-MA-1170-002-G060

Engraver: PSSP. ***Comments:*** H-MA-420-G16, Wait-Unlisted. Similar to W-MA-1170-001-G030 but with different denomination. 1810.

Rarity: —

$3 • W-MA-1170-003-G070

Left: 3 / 3. ***Center:*** Flower garlands, THREE. ***Right:*** 3 / 3. ***Engraver:*** PSSP. ***Comments:*** H-MA-420-G20, Wait-2. 1806.

Rarity: —

$3 • W-MA-1170-003-G080

Engraver: PSSP. ***Comments:*** H-MA-420-G22, Wait-Unlisted. Similar to W-MA-1170-001-G020 but with different denomination. 1807–1809.

Rarity: —

$3 • W-MA-1170-003-G090

QDB

Engraver: PSSP. ***Comments:*** H-MA-420-G24, Wait-Unlisted. Similar to W-MA-1170-001-G030 but with different denomination. 18__. 1800s.

Rarity: URS-3
VF $750

$5 • W-MA-1170-005-G100

QDB

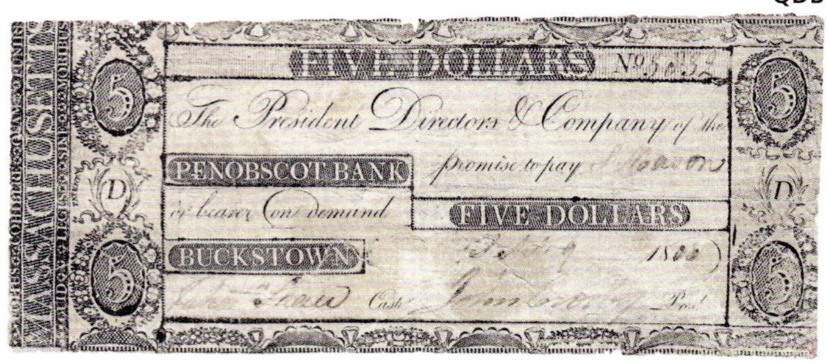

Engraver: PSSP. ***Comments:*** H-MA-420-G28, Wait-3. 18__. 1800s.

Rarity: URS-5
F $400

$5 • W-MA-1170-005-G110

Engraver: PSSP. ***Comments:*** H-MA-420-G30, Wait-Unlisted. Similar to W-MA-1170-005-G100 but with rose-covered FIVE. 1808.

Rarity: —

$10 • W-MA-1170-010-G120

CJF

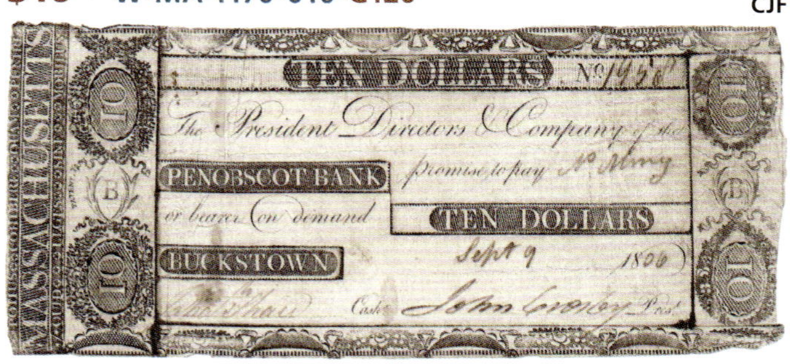

Engraver: PSSP. ***Comments:*** H-MA-420-G34, Wait-4. 18__. 1800s.

Rarity: URS-5
F $420

$10 • W-MA-1170-010-G130

Engraver: PSSP. ***Comments:*** H-MA-420-G36, Wait-4. Similar to W-MA-1170-010-G120 but with rose-covered TEN. 1808.

Rarity: —

$20 • W-MA-1170-020-G140
Left: MASSACHUSETTS / 20, Plate letter, 20. ***Center:*** Flower garlands, TWENTY. ***Right:*** 20, Plate letter, 20. ***Engraver:*** PSSP. ***Comments:*** H-MA-420-G40, Wait-Unlisted. 1806–1809.

Rarity: —

Cabotville, Massachusetts

Now known as Chicopee, the area called Cabotville was petitioned to be split from Springfield in January 1844. The request was met with tough opposition and delayed. In 1791 the Cabotville population was 1,594, which grew to 10,985 by 1840. A large increase occurred when railroad service was instituted in the district in 1845, and the population was counted at 19,189 by 1848. The same year another petition was sent to the Legislature requesting the town of Springfield to be incorporated as a city. This act was also strongly opposed, and so the northern residents resumed their efforts to obtain an act of incorporation as a new town. After a visit in-person from a committee of the Legislature and a hearing, the town was divided. In 1848 the town of Cabotville was incorporated into Chicopee.

Cabot Bank

1845–1865

W-MA-1180

History: The Cabot Bank was chartered on January 24, 1845, with an authorized capital of $150,000. Principals included N.P. Ames, John Chase, D.M. Bryant, and Robert Bemis. The president in 1847 was J. Chase, and G. Walker was cashier. In 1851 John Wells became president, and J.L. Warriner became cashier. Circulation in 1849 was $95,935. By 1863 it was $136,133.

On April 26, 1865, the First National Bank of Chicopee was chartered and succeeded the business of the Cabot Bank.

See also listings under Chicopee, W-MA-1360, and Springfield, W-MA-3110.

Numismatic Commentary: Genuine notes issued at the Cabotville location are harder to find than those issued at the Chicopee location. However, all notes regardless of location are hard to come by.

Valid Issues

$1 • W-MA-1180-001-G010

CJF

Engraver: New England Bank Note Co. ***Comments:*** H-MA-425-G2. 18__. 1840s–1850s.

Rarity: URS-4
F $750

$2 • W-MA-1180-002-G020
Left: Woman with sheaf leaning on 2. ***Center:*** 2 / Shepherd seated, Dog tending flock of sheep. ***Right:*** 2 / Beehive and flowers. ***Engraver:*** New England Bank Note Co. ***Comments:*** H-MA-425-G4. 18__. 1840s–1850s.

Rarity: —

$3 • W-MA-1180-003-G030
Left: THREE / Man with sheaf and sickle. ***Center:*** Eagle on rock, Ship / 3. ***Right:*** 3 / State arms. ***Engraver:*** New England Bank Note Co. ***Comments:*** H-MA-425-G6. 18__. 1840s–1850s.

Rarity: —

$5 • W-MA-1180-005-G040
Left: FIVE / 5. ***Center:*** Train / V. ***Right:*** FIVE / Blacksmith standing with hammer, 5 / FIVE. ***Engraver:*** New England Bank Note Co. ***Comments:*** H-MA-425-G8. 18__. 1840s–1850s.

Rarity: —

$10 • W-MA-1180-010-G050
Left: Eagle on branch, Canal scene and train / 10. ***Center:*** X. ***Right:*** TEN / Train / TEN. ***Engraver:*** New England Bank Note Co. ***Comments:*** H-MA-425-G10. 18__. 1840s–1850s.

Rarity: —

$20 • W-MA-1180-020-G060
Left: 20 / Woman seated with book on lap and opening chest. ***Center:*** XX / Eagle on rock / XX. ***Right:*** 20 / Ship in harbor. ***Engraver:*** New England Bank Note Co. ***Comments:*** H-MA-425-G12. 18__. 1840s–1850s.

Rarity: —

$50 • W-MA-1180-050-G070
Left: FIFTY / Woman standing with wreath and flowers / FIFTY. ***Center:*** 50 / Man restraining prancing horse / 50. ***Right:*** FIFTY / Woman standing with cornucopia / FIFTY. ***Engraver:*** New England Bank Note Co. ***Comments:*** H-MA-425-G14. 18__. 1840s–1850s.

Rarity: —

$100 • W-MA-1180-100-G080
Left: ONE HUNDRED on 100 / Portrait of William Henry Harrison. ***Center:*** Wharf scene, Men loading wagon with barrels. ***Right:*** ONE HUNDRED on 100 / Portrait of Christopher Columbus. ***Engraver:*** New England Bank Note Co. ***Comments:*** H-MA-425-G16. 18__. 1840s–1850s.

Rarity: —

Non-Valid Issues

$3 • W-MA-1180-003-S010

CJF

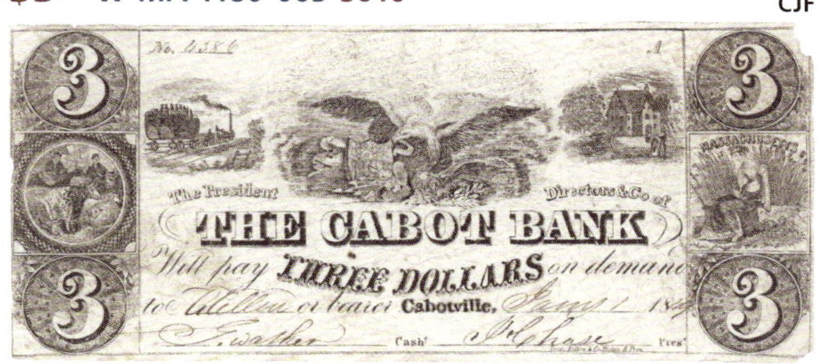

Engraver: Terry, Pelton & Co. ***Comments:*** H-MA-425-S5. 18__. 1840s.

Rarity: URS-7
VG $75

$5 • W-MA-1180-005-S020 ANS

Comments: H-MA-425-S10. 184_. 1840s.

Rarity: URS-7

VG $90; **F** $100; **VF** $150

$10 • W-MA-1180-010-N010

Left: Woman. ***Center:*** Blacksmith shoeing horse, Child seated on horse, Man leaning on wheel and holding horse. ***Right:*** TEN vertically. ***Comments:*** H-MA-425-N10. 18__. 1840s.

Rarity: —

CAMBRIDGE, MASSACHUSETTS

In May 1638, a settlement on the Charles River was named Cambridge after the University of Cambridge in England. Located upriver from the Boston Harbor, Cambridge contained a spring which locals believed had medicinal properties. The settlement was at first called "the newe towne" and thus was sometimes known as Newe Towne. It was one of several towns founded by the Puritans of the Massachusetts Bay Colony. Harvard College was established there.

In 1775 George Washington took command of volunteer American soldiers camped on the Cambridge Common, which is now called the birthplace of the U.S. Army. Between 1790 and mid-1840, Cambridge expanded due to the construction of the West Boston Bridge, which connected Cambridge and Boston directly. A second bridge opened in 1809 and furthered such growth. In the mid-19th century, Cambridge was home to several famous poets, including Henry Wadsworth Longfellow and Oliver Wendell Holmes.

In 1846 Cambridge was incorporated as a city. The city's largest employer was the New England Glass Company, which was founded in 1818 and became the largest glassworks in the world. Cambridge also became a haven for fleeing Irish immigrants after the potato famine of 1845, and thousands settled in Boston and Cambridge to work in clay pits and brickyards.

See also Cambridgeport and East Cambridge, Massachusetts.

Cambridge Bank

1826–1865

W-MA-1190

History: The Cambridge Bank was chartered on March 4, 1826, with a capital of $150,000. In 1837 an act was passed by the legislature to reduce this amount to $100,000. At the time, the institution was suffering from the effects of the financial panic. Problems increased with mismanagement. In 1840 changes were made in the officers and directors, after which the bank built up to a firm footing and fine reputation. Circulation ranged from a low of $49,855 in 1839 to a high of $96,952 in 1863.

Figures for 1857 included: bills of this bank and other New England states $2,926.05; specie $11,740.23; real estate $6,000.

The business of the Cambridge Bank was succeeded by the Cambridge National Bank, chartered on June 6, 1865.

Numismatic Commentary: A few vignetted issues will show a street scene in Cambridge, including the business block housing the bank with a horse-drawn street car nearby.

VALID ISSUES

$1 • W-MA-1190-001-G010

Left: Narrow panel of lathework circle segments. ***Center:*** 1 / 1 / Flower garlands and gridwork segments / 1 / 1. ***Right:*** Narrow panel of lathework circle segments. ***Engraver:*** PSSP. ***Comments:*** H-MA-430-G2. 18__. 1820s–1830s.

Rarity: —

$1 • W-MA-1190-001-G010a

Left: ONE / D / ONE vertically. ***Right:*** ONE / D / ONE vertically. ***Engraver:*** PSSP. ***Comments:*** H-MA-430-G4. Similar to W-MA-1190-001-G010. 18__. 1830s.

Rarity: —

$1 • W-MA-1190-001-G010b

Left: ONE / D / ONE vertically. ***Right:*** ONE / D / ONE vertically. ***Engraver:*** PSSP. ***Comments:*** H-MA-430-G6. Similar to W-MA-1190-001-G010. 18__. 1830s–1840s.

Rarity: —

$1 • W-MA-1190-001-G020

Left: ONE / Blacksmith with sledge. ***Center:*** Street scene in Cambridge. ***Right:*** 1 / Portrait of child. ***Engraver:*** Rawdon, Wright, Hatch & Edson / New England Bank Note Co. ***Comments:*** H-MA-430-G10. 18__. 1850s.

Rarity: —

$1 • W-MA-1190-001-G020a

Overprint: Green panel outlining white ONE. ***Engraver:*** Rawdon, Wright, Hatch & Edson / New England Bank Note Co. / ABNCo. monogram. ***Comments:*** H-MA-430-G10c. Similar to W-MA-1190-001-G020 but with additional engraver imprint. 18__. 1860s.

Rarity: URS-5

F $300; **VF** $650

$1 • W-MA-1190-001-G020b CJF

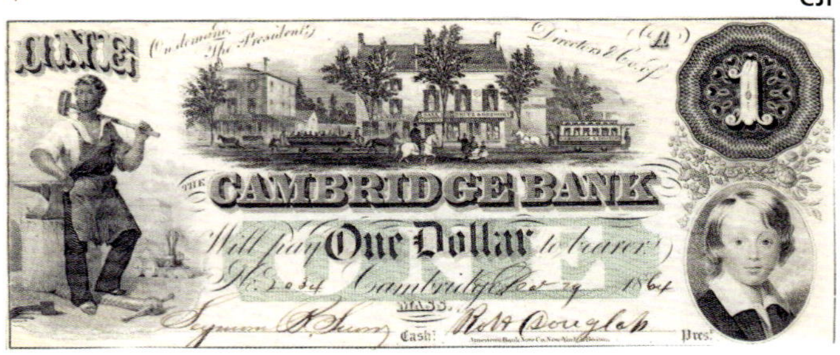

Overprint: Green panel outlining white ONE. ***Engraver:*** American Bank Note Co. ***Comments:*** H-MA-430-G10d. Similar to W-MA-1190-001-G020 but with different engraver imprint. 18__. 1860s.

Rarity: URS-3

VF $700; **EF** $1,000

$2 • **W-MA-1190-002-G030**

Left: Narrow panel of lathework circle segments. ***Center:*** 2 / 2 / Flower garlands and gridwork segments / 2 / 2. ***Right:*** Narrow panel of lathework circle segments. ***Engraver:*** PSSP. ***Comments:*** H-MA-430-G12. 18__. 1820s–1830s.

Rarity: —

$2 • **W-MA-1190-002-G030a**

Left: Five TWOs vertically. ***Right:*** Five TWOs vertically. ***Engraver:*** PSSP. ***Comments:*** H-MA-430-G14. Similar to W-MA-1190-002-G030. 18__. 1830s.

Rarity: —

$2 • **W-MA-1190-002-G030b**

Left: Five TWOs vertically. ***Right:*** Five TWOs vertically. ***Engraver:*** PSSP. ***Comments:*** H-MA-430-G16. Similar to W-MA-1190-002-G030. 18__. 1830s–1840s.

Rarity: —

$2 • **W-MA-1190-002-G040**

Left: Justice / 2. ***Center:*** Street scene in Cambridge. ***Right:*** 2 / Cattle, Train on bridge. ***Engraver:*** Rawdon, Wright, Hatch & Edson / New England Bank Note Co. ***Comments:*** H-MA-430-G20. 18__. 1850s.

Rarity: —

$2 • **W-MA-1190-002-G040a**

Overprint: Green outlining white TWO. ***Engraver:*** Rawdon, Wright, Hatch & Edson / New England Bank Note Co. / ABNCo. monogram. ***Comments:*** H-MA-430-G20c. Similar to W-MA-1190-002-G040 but with additional engraver imprint. 18__. 1860s.

Rarity: —

$2 • **W-MA-1190-002-G040b**

Overprint: Green outlining white TWO. ***Engraver:*** American Bank Note Co. ***Comments:*** H-MA-430-G20d. Similar to W-MA-1190-002-G040 but with different engraver imprint. 18__. 1860s.

Rarity: —

$3 • **W-MA-1190-003-G050**

Left: Narrow panel of lathework circle segments. ***Center:*** 3 / 3 / Flower garlands and gridwork segments / 3 / 3. ***Right:*** Narrow panel of lathework circle segments. ***Engraver:*** PSSP. ***Comments:*** H-MA-430-G22. 18__. 1820s–1830s.

Rarity: —

$3 • **W-MA-1190-003-G050a**

Left: THREE vertically. ***Right:*** THREE vertically. ***Engraver:*** PSSP. ***Comments:*** H-MA-430-G24. Similar to W-MA-1190-003-G050. 18__. 1830s.

Rarity: —

$3 • **W-MA-1190-003-G050b**

Left: THREE vertically. ***Right:*** THREE vertically. ***Engraver:*** PSSP. ***Comments:*** H-MA-430-G26. Similar to W-MA-1190-003-G050. 18__. 1830s.

Rarity: URS-4
F $250

Collectors and Researchers:

If you have new information about any banks or notes listed in this volume, contact Whitman Publishing, Attn: Obsolete Paper Money, 3101 Clairmont Road, Suite G, Atlanta, GA 30329.

$3 • **W-MA-1190-003-G060**

Left: 3 / Two women standing. ***Center:*** View of Cambridge / THREE. ***Right:*** 3 / Woman seated with shield, pole and cap. ***Engraver:*** Rawdon, Wright, Hatch & Edson / New England Bank Note Co. ***Comments:*** H-MA-430-G30. 18__. 1850s.

Rarity: —

$3 • **W-MA-1190-003-G060a** SI

Overprint: Green panel outlining white THREE. ***Engraver:*** Rawdon, Wright, Hatch & Edson / New England Bank Note Co. / ABNCo. monogram. ***Comments:*** H-MA-430-G30c. Similar to W-MA-1190-003-G060 but with additional engraver imprint. 18__. 1860s.

Rarity: URS-3
G $750; **VF** $2,000

$3 • **W-MA-1190-003-G060b**

Overprint: Green panel outlining white THREE. ***Engraver:*** American Bank Note Co. ***Comments:*** H-MA-430-G30d. Similar to W-MA-1190-003-G060 but with different engraver imprint. 18__. 1860s.

Rarity: —

$5 • **W-MA-1190-005-G070**

Left: Lathework chain bearing MASSACHUSETTS / 5 / 5. ***Center:*** Alternating flower garlands and gridwork segments. ***Right:*** 5 / 5. ***Engraver:*** PSSP. ***Comments:*** H-MA-430-G32. 18__. 1820s.

Rarity: —

$5 • **W-MA-1190-005-G070a**

Engraver: PSSP. ***Comments:*** H-MA-430-G34. Similar to W-MA-1190-005-G070 but with zigzag ruled lines. 18__. 1820s–1830s.

Rarity: —

$5 • **W-MA-1190-005-G070b**

Engraver: PSSP. ***Comments:*** H-MA-430-G36. Similar to W-MA-1190-005-G070 but with spiral lathework lines. 18__. 1830s.

Rarity: —

$5 • **W-MA-1190-005-G080**

Left: 5 / Female portrait. ***Center:*** Street scene in Cambridge. ***Right:*** 5 / Portrait of Benjamin Franklin. ***Engraver:*** Rawdon, Wright, Hatch & Edson / New England Bank Note Co. ***Comments:*** H-MA-430-G40. 18__. 1850s.

Rarity: —

$5 • **W-MA-1190-005-G080a**

Overprint: Green panel outlining white FIVE. ***Engraver:*** Rawdon, Wright, Hatch & Edson / New England Bank Note Co. / ABNCo. monogram. ***Comments:*** H-MA-430-G40c. Similar to W-MA-1190-005-G080 but with additional engraver imprint. 18__. 1860s.

Rarity: —

$5 • **W-MA-1190-005-G080b**

Overprint: Green panel outlining white FIVE. ***Engraver:*** American Bank Note Co. ***Comments:*** H-MA-430-G40d. Similar to W-MA-1190-005-G080 but with different engraver imprint. 18__. 1860s.

Rarity: —

$10 • **W-MA-1190-010-G090**

Left: Lathework chain bearing MASSACHUSETTS / 10 / 10 vertically. ***Center:*** Alternating flower garlands and gridwork segments. ***Right:*** 10 / 10 vertically. ***Engraver:*** Perkins. ***Comments:*** H-MA-430-G42. 18__. 1820s.

Rarity: —

$10 • **W-MA-1190-010-G090a**

Engraver: PSSP. ***Comments:*** H-MA-430-G44. Similar to W-MA-1190-010-G090 but with zigzag ruled lines. 18__. 1820s–1830s.

Rarity: —

$10 • **W-MA-1190-010-G090b**

Engraver: PSSP. ***Comments:*** H-MA-430-G46. Similar to W-MA-1190-010-G090 but with spiral lathework lines. 18__. 1830s.

Rarity: —

$10 • **W-MA-1190-010-G100**

Left: TEN / Portrait of George Washington. ***Center:*** Street scene in Cambridge. ***Right:*** 10 / Blacksmith at forge. ***Engraver:*** Rawdon, Wright, Hatch & Edson / New England Bank Note Co. ***Comments:*** H-MA-430-G50. 18__. 1850s.

Rarity: —

$10 • **W-MA-1190-010-G100a**

Overprint: Green panel outlining white TEN. ***Engraver:*** Rawdon, Wright, Hatch & Edson / New England Bank Note Co. / ABNCo. monogram. ***Comments:*** H-MA-430-G50c. Similar to W-MA-1190-010-G100 but with additional engraver imprint. 18__. 1860s.

Rarity: —

$10 • **W-MA-1190-010-G100b**

Overprint: Green panel outlining white TEN. ***Engraver:*** American Bank Note Co. ***Comments:*** H-MA-430-G50d. Similar to W-MA-1190-010-G100 but with different engraver imprint. 18__. 1860s.

Rarity: —

$20 • **W-MA-1190-020-G110**

Left: Lathework chain bearing MASSACHUSETTS / 20 / 20 vertically. ***Center:*** Alternating flower garlands and gridwork segments. ***Right:*** 20 / 20 vertically. ***Engraver:*** PSSP. ***Comments:*** H-MA-430-G52. 18__. 1820s–1830s.

Rarity: —

$20 • **W-MA-1190-020-G120**

Left: TWENTY / Woman feeding fowl. ***Center:*** Street scene in Cambridge. ***Right:*** 20 / XX. ***Engraver:*** Rawdon, Wright, Hatch & Edson / New England Bank Note Co. ***Comments:*** H-MA-430-G56. 18__. 1850s.

Rarity: —

$20 • **W-MA-1190-020-G120a**

Overprint: Green. ***Engraver:*** Rawdon, Wright, Hatch & Edson / New England Bank Note Co. / ABNCo. monogram. ***Comments:*** H-MA-430-G56c. Similar to W-MA-1190-020-G120 but with additional engraver imprint. 18__. 1860s.

Rarity: —

$50 • **W-MA-1190-050-G130**

Left: Lathework chain bearing MASSACHUSETTS / 50 / 50 vertically. ***Center:*** Alternating flower garlands and gridwork segments. ***Right:*** 50 / 50 vertically. ***Engraver:*** PSSP. ***Comments:*** H-MA-430-G60. 18__. 1820s–1830s.

Rarity: —

$50 • **W-MA-1190-050-G140**

Left: 50 / 50. ***Center:*** Street scene in Cambridge. ***Right:*** 50 / Portrait of Daniel Webster. ***Engraver:*** Rawdon, Wright, Hatch & Edson / New England Bank Note Co. ***Comments:*** H-MA-430-G64. 18__. 1850s.

Rarity: —

$50 • **W-MA-1190-050-G140a**

Overprint: Green. ***Engraver:*** Rawdon, Wright, Hatch & Edson / New England Bank Note Co. / ABNCo. monogram. ***Comments:*** H-MA-430-G64c. Similar to W-MA-1190-050-G140 but with additional engraver imprint. 18__. 1860s.

Rarity: —

$100 • **W-MA-1190-100-G150**

Left: Lathework chain bearing MASSACHUSETTS / 100 / 100 vertically. ***Center:*** Alternating flower garlands and gridwork segments. ***Right:*** 100 / 100 vertically. ***Engraver:*** Perkins. ***Comments:*** H-MA-430-G68. 18__. 1820s–1830s.

Rarity: —

$100 • **W-MA-1190-100-G160**

Left: 100 / Sailor and barrels / C on 100. ***Center:*** Street scene in Cambridge. ***Right:*** 100 / Female portrait. ***Engraver:*** Rawdon, Wright, Hatch & Edson / New England Bank Note Co. ***Comments:*** H-MA-430-G72. 18__. 1850s.

Rarity: —

$100 • **W-MA-1190-100-G160a**

Overprint: Green. ***Engraver:*** Rawdon, Wright, Hatch & Edson / New England Bank Note Co. / ABNCo. monogram. ***Comments:*** H-MA-430-G72c. Similar to W-MA-1190-100-G160 but with additional engraver imprint. 18__. 1860s.

Rarity: —

$500 • **W-MA-1190-500-G170**

Left: Lathework chain bearing MASSACHUSETTS / 500 / 500 vertically. ***Center:*** Alternating flower garlands and gridwork segments. ***Right:*** 500 / 500 vertically. ***Engraver:*** PSSP. ***Comments:*** H-MA-430-G76. 18__. 1820s–1830s.

Rarity: —

$500 • **W-MA-1190-500-G180**

Left: 500 / D / 500. ***Center:*** Street scene in Cambridge. ***Right:*** 500 / 500 / 500. ***Engraver:*** Rawdon, Wright, Hatch & Edson / New England Bank Note Co. ***Comments:*** H-MA-430-G80. 18__. 1850s.

Rarity: —

Non-Valid Issues

$1 • **W-MA-1190-001-C020**

Engraver: Rawdon, Wright, Hatch & Edson / New England Bank Note Co. ***Comments:*** H-MA-430-C10. Counterfeit of W-MA-1190-001-G020 or variety. 18__. 1850s.

Rarity: —

$3 • W-MA-1190-003-C060
Engraver: Rawdon, Wright, Hatch & Edson / New England Bank Note Co. ***Comments:*** H-MA-430-C30. Counterfeit of W-MA-1190-003-G060 or variety. 18__. 1850s.
Rarity: —

$3 • W-MA-1190-003-N010
Center: Two women flanking shield surmounted by eagle. ***Right:*** Male portrait. ***Comments:*** H-MA-430-N5. 1850s.
Rarity: —

$5 • W-MA-1190-005-N020
Left: Male reaper. ***Center:*** Train. ***Right:*** Woman seated with sheaves. ***Comments:*** H-MA-430-N10.
Rarity: —

$5 • W-MA-1190-005-A010
Left: Man seated on ground shearing sheep, Man holding sheep, Boy. ***Center:*** Three men rolling log in forest, Two men with baskets harvesting corn. ***Comments:*** H-MA-430-A5. Altered from $5 Bank of Greensborough, Greensborough, Georgia series. Whole-note vignette. 1850s.
Rarity: —

$10 • W-MA-1190-010-R010
Engraver: Rawdon, Wright, Hatch & Edson / New England Bank Note Co. ***Comments:*** H-MA-430-R5. Raised from W-MA-1190-001-G020. 18__. 1850s.
Rarity: —

Cambridge City Bank
1853–1865
W-MA-1200

History: The Cambridge City Bank was chartered on April 18, 1853, with an authorized capital of $100,000. The bank's president was John Livermore, and the cashier was Edward Richardson. The directors were John Livermore, S.P. Heywood, W.P. Fiske, Eliphalet Davis, H.M. Chamberlain, George S. Gale, and George W. Whittemore.

Specie in 1854 was listed at $5,998. Circulation from 1857 to 1860 was listed at $44,768. In 1861 it was $57,041, and in 1863 it was $73,091. Selected figures for 1857 included: bills of this bank and other New England states $2,009; specie $14,937.75. In 1861 specie was valued at $12,733.34.

The business of this bank was assumed by the National City Bank, chartered on January 31, 1865.

See also listing under Cambridgeport, W-MA-1260.

Cambridge Market Bank
1851–1866
W-MA-1210

History: The Cambridge Market Bank was chartered on October 1, 1851, with an authorized capital of $150,000. The capital fluctuated between $100,000 and $150,000 during the first few years of the bank's existence and then settled at $150,000 from 1855 onward.

Some bank values included: circulation $163,053; real estate $4,818.02; specie $5,604.82. In 1854 circulation was $157,715; profits were $4,758. By 1857 circulation had reached a low of $85,465, but it was back up to $145,648 by 1863.

In September 1865, the Cambridge Market Bank was one of only a few state banks remaining. It closed in 1866 after a profitable run.

Numismatic Commentary: The notes collectors are likely to encounter will show a healthy steer, ready for market. Issues with other motifs rarely show up in the marketplace.

Valid Issues

$1 • W-MA-1210-001-G010

CC

Overprint: Red ONE. ***Engraver:*** Rawdon, Wright, Hatch & Edson / New England Bank Note Co. ***Comments:*** H-MA-435-G2a. 18__. 1850s.
Rarity: URS-5
VG $150; **VF** $375

$1 • W-MA-1210-001-G010a
Left: ONE on 1 / Steer. ***Center:*** Steer. ***Right:*** ONE / Woman holding 1 with cherub. ***Overprint:*** Red ONE. ***Engraver:*** Rawdon, Wright, Hatch & Edson / New England Bank Note Co. / ABNCo. monogram. ***Comments:*** H-MA-435-G2b. Similar to W-MA-1210-001-G010 but with additional engraver imprint. 18__. Circa 1860.
Rarity: URS-5
VG $150; **VF** $350

$1 • W-MA-1210-001-G010b

CJF

Overprint: Green panel outlining white ONE. ***Engraver:*** Rawdon, Wright, Hatch & Edson / New England Bank Note Co. / ABNCo. monogram. ***Comments:*** H-MA-435-G2c. Similar to W-MA-1210-001-G010 but with additional engraver imprint. 18__. 1860s.
Rarity: URS-3
VF $750

$2 • W-MA-1210-002-G020
Left: TWO / Woman seated on bale. ***Center:*** 2 with cherub / Cow. ***Right:*** 2 / Livestock. ***Overprint:*** Red TWO. ***Engraver:*** Rawdon, Wright, Hatch & Edson / New England Bank Note Co. ***Comments:*** H-MA-435-G4a. 18__. 1850s.
Rarity: —

$2 • W-MA-1210-002-G020a

Overprint: Red TWO. ***Engraver:*** Rawdon, Wright, Hatch & Edson / New England Bank Note Co. / ABNCo. monogram. ***Comments:*** H-MA-435-G4b. Similar to W-MA-1210-002-G020 but with additional engraver imprint. 18__. Circa 1860.

Rarity: URS-3
VF $1,000

$2 • W-MA-1210-002-G020b

CJF

Overprint: Green panel outlining white TWO. ***Engraver:*** Rawdon, Wright, Hatch & Edson / New England Bank Note Co. / ABNCo. monogram. ***Comments:*** H-MA-435-G4c. Similar to W-MA-1210-002-G020 but with additional engraver imprint. 18__. 1860s.

Rarity: URS-5
VG $350; **VF** $750

$3 • W-MA-1210-003-G030

Left: Woman / THREE. ***Center:*** Drove of cattle and sheep, Man on horse. ***Right:*** 3 / Farmer, sailor, and mechanic standing with 3. ***Overprint:*** Red THREE. ***Engraver:*** Rawdon, Wright, Hatch & Edson / New England Bank Note Co. ***Comments:*** H-MA-435-G6a. 18__. 1850s.

Rarity: —

$3 • W-MA-1210-003-G030a

Overprint: Red THREE. ***Engraver:*** Rawdon, Wright, Hatch & Edson / New England Bank Note Co. / ABNCo. monogram. ***Comments:*** H-MA-435-G6b. Similar to W-MA-1210-003-G030 but with additional engraver imprint. 18__. Circa 1860.

Rarity: —

$3 • W-MA-1210-003-G030b

Overprint: Green panel outlining white THREE. ***Engraver:*** Rawdon, Wright, Hatch & Edson / New England Bank Note Co. / ABNCo. monogram. ***Comments:*** H-MA-435-G6c. Similar to W-MA-1210-003-G030 but with additional engraver imprint. 18__. 1860s.

Rarity: —

$5 • W-MA-1210-005-G040

Left: Eagle / Liberty / FIVE. ***Center:*** Drove of cattle and sheep, Man on horse. ***Right:*** 5 / Eagle and shield / FIVE. ***Overprint:*** Red FIVE. ***Engraver:*** Rawdon, Wright, Hatch & Edson / New England Bank Note Co. ***Comments:*** H-MA-435-G8a. 18__. 1850s.

Rarity: —

$5 • W-MA-1210-005-G040a

Overprint: Likely red FIVE. ***Engraver:*** Rawdon, Wright, Hatch & Edson / New England Bank Note Co. / ABNCo. monogram. ***Comments:*** H-MA-435-G8b. Similar to W-MA-1210-005-G040 but with additional engraver imprint. 18__. Circa 1860.

Rarity: —

$10 • W-MA-1210-010-G050

Left: Man plowing with black horse and white horse / X. ***Center:*** 10. ***Right:*** TEN / Justice standing. ***Overprint:*** Red TEN. ***Engraver:*** Rawdon, Wright, Hatch & Edson / New England Bank Note Co. ***Comments:*** H-MA-435-G10a. 18__. 1850s.

Rarity: —

$10 • W-MA-1210-010-G050a

Overprint: Likely red TEN. ***Engraver:*** Rawdon, Wright, Hatch & Edson / New England Bank Note Co. / ABNCo. monogram. ***Comments:*** H-MA-435-G10b. Similar to W-MA-1210-010-G050 but with additional engraver imprint. 18__. Circa 1860.

Rarity: —

$20 • W-MA-1210-020-G060

Left: 20 / Cattle. ***Center:*** Train. ***Right:*** 20 / Woman seated between 2 and 0. ***Overprint:*** Red. ***Engraver:*** Rawdon, Wright, Hatch & Edson / New England Bank Note Co. ***Comments:*** H-MA-435-G12a. 18__. 1850s.

Rarity: —

$20 • W-MA-1210-020-G060a

Overprint: Likely red. ***Engraver:*** Rawdon, Wright, Hatch & Edson / New England Bank Note Co. / ABNCo. monogram. ***Comments:*** H-MA-435-G12b. Similar to W-MA-1210-020-G060 but with additional engraver imprint. 18__. Circa 1860.

Rarity: —

$50 • W-MA-1210-050-G070

Left: 50 / Woman. ***Center:*** Cattle, Houses. ***Right:*** 50. ***Overprint:*** Red. ***Engraver:*** Rawdon, Wright, Hatch & Edson / New England Bank Note Co. ***Comments:*** H-MA-435-G14a. 18__. 1850s.

Rarity: —

$50 • W-MA-1210-050-G070a

Overprint: Likely red. ***Engraver:*** Rawdon, Wright, Hatch & Edson / New England Bank Note Co. / ABNCo. monogram. ***Comments:*** H-MA-435-G14b. Similar to W-MA-1210-050-G070 but with additional engraver imprint. 18__. Circa 1860.

Rarity: —

$100 • W-MA-1210-100-G080

Left: 100 / Cattle. ***Center:*** Eagle on shield. ***Right:*** 100 / Bull's head. ***Overprint:*** Red. ***Engraver:*** Rawdon, Wright, Hatch & Edson / New England Bank Note Co. ***Comments:*** H-MA-435-G16a. 18__. 1850s.

Rarity: —

$100 • W-MA-1210-100-G080a

Overprint: Likely red. ***Engraver:*** Rawdon, Wright, Hatch & Edson / New England Bank Note Co. / ABNCo. monogram. ***Comments:*** H-MA-435-G16b. Similar to W-MA-1210-100-G080 but with additional engraver imprint. 18__. Circa 1860.

Rarity: —

$500 • W-MA-1210-500-G090

Center: Scene in woods, Oxen drawing sled loaded with wood. ***Tint:*** Green 500 / D / 500 / 500. ***Engraver:*** American Bank Note Co. ***Comments:*** H-MA-435-G18. 1860s.

Rarity: —

Non-Valid Issues

$5 • W-MA-1210-005-N010

Left: Male reaper. ***Center:*** Train. ***Right:*** Woman seated with sheaf. ***Comments:*** H-MA-435-N5. 1850s.

Rarity: —

$5 • W-MA-1210-005-A010

Left: Man seated on ground shearing sheep, Man holding sheep, Boy / 5. ***Center:*** Three men rolling log in forest. ***Right:*** Two men with baskets harvesting corn / 5. ***Comments:*** H-MA-435-A5. Altered from $5 Bank of Greensborough, Georgia series. Whole-note vignette. 1850s.

Rarity: —

$5 • W-MA-1210-005-A020

Center: Indian woman and hunter flanking five gold dollars, Three cherubs. ***Comments:*** H-MA-435-A10. 1850s.

Rarity: —

Charles River Bank

1832–1865

W-MA-1220

History: The Charles River Bank was chartered on February 29, 1832, with $100,000 in authorized capital. In 1834 a new charter was granted, and in 1837 it was extended to last until 1875.

In 1834 quantities of counterfeit $2 bills of the PSSP style were in circulation. Many warnings were issued throughout 1836. The Cleveland *Plain Dealer* reported in 1836 that a "Wholesale counterfeiter was arrested on Saturday last, at Burlington. He had in his possession $2s of the Charles River Bank, among others."

Circulation ranged from a low of $45,558 in 1839 to a high of $81,774 in 1863. Specie was $12,669.34 in 1857 and increased to $20,014.10 by the next year. It was back down to $10,966.76 in 1861.

The business of the Charles River Bank was succeeded by the Charles River National Bank of Cambridge, chartered on January 19, 1865.

Numismatic Commentary: Most issues of the Charles River Bank are very hard to locate. Counterfeit PSSP notes show up from time to time. If collectors are lucky, a note with a vignette of the Harvard campus might be located.

As of 2003 there was a $20-$50 face plate remaining at the American Bank Note Co. archives.

Valid Issues

$1 • W-MA-1220-001-G010

Left: Lathework panel bearing MASSACHUSETTS vertically. ***Center:*** 1 / 1 / Alternating flower garlands and gridwork segments / ONE / 1 / 1. ***Right:*** Lathework panel bearing ONE / D / ONE vertically. ***Engraver:*** PSSP. ***Comments:*** H-MA-440-G2. 18__. 1830s.

Rarity: —

$1 • W-MA-1220-001-G020

JF

Engraver: New England Bank Note Co. ***Comments:*** H-MA-440-G4. 18__. 1830s–1840s.

Rarity: URS-1

F $5,000; **VF** $6,000

$1 • W-MA-1220-001-G020a

Left: 1 / Women and cherub with globe / ONE. ***Center:*** View of Harvard College, Omnibus and four horses, Church. ***Bottom center:*** Dog with key and strongbox. ***Right:*** 1 / Portrait of Judge Storey. ***Overprint:*** Red. ***Engraver:*** New England Bank Note Co. ***Comments:*** H-MA-440-G4a. Similar to W-MA-1220-001-G020. 18__. 1850s.

Rarity: —

$1 • W-MA-1220-001-G020b

Overprint: Red. ***Engraver:*** New England Bank Note Co. / ABNCo. monogram. ***Comments:*** H-MA-440-G4b. Similar to W-MA-1220-001-G020 but with additional engraver imprint. 18__. 1850s–1860s.

Rarity: —

$2 • W-MA-1220-002-G030

Center: 2 / 2 / Alternating flower garlands and gridwork segments / 2 / 2. ***Engraver:*** PSSP. ***Comments:*** H-MA-440-G6. 18__. 1830s.

Rarity: —

$2 • W-MA-1220-002-G040

Left: 2 / George Washington standing by horse / TWO. ***Center:*** View of Harvard College. ***Right:*** 2 / Portrait of Judge Storey / TWO. ***Engraver:*** New England Bank Note Co. ***Comments:*** H-MA-440-G8. 18__. 1830s–1840s.

Rarity: —

$2 • W-MA-1220-002-G040a

Overprint: Red. ***Engraver:*** New England Bank Note Co. ***Comments:*** H-MA-440-G8a. Similar to W-MA-1220-002-G040. 18__. 1850s.

Rarity: —

$2 • W-MA-1220-002-G040b

Overprint: Likely red. ***Engraver:*** New England Bank Note Co. / ABNCo. monogram. ***Comments:*** H-MA-440-G8b. Similar to W-MA-1220-002-G040 but with additional engraver imprint. 18__. 1850s–1860s.

Rarity: —

$3 • W-MA-1220-003-G050

Left: Lathework panel bearing MASSACHUSETTS vertically. ***Center:*** 3 / 3 / Alternating flower garlands and gridwork segments / THREE / 3 / 3. ***Right:*** Lathework panel bearing THREE vertically. ***Engraver:*** PSSP. ***Comments:*** H-MA-440-G10. 18__. 1830s–1840s.

Rarity: —

$3 • W-MA-1220-003-G060

Left: 3 / Justice kneeling / THREE. ***Center:*** View of Harvard College. ***Right:*** 3 / Portrait of Judge Storey / THREE. ***Engraver:*** New England Bank Note Co. ***Comments:*** H-MA-440-G12. 18__. 1830s–1840s.

Rarity: —

$3 • W-MA-1220-003-G060a

Overprint: Red THREE. ***Engraver:*** New England Bank Note Co. ***Comments:*** H-MA-440-G12a. Similar to W-MA-1220-003-G060. 18__. 1850s.

Rarity: —

$3 • W-MA-1220-003-G060b

Overprint: Red THREE. ***Engraver:*** New England Bank Note Co. / ABNCo. monogram. ***Comments:*** H-MA-440-G12b. Similar to W-MA-1220-003-G060 but with additional engraver imprint. 18__. 1850s–1860s.

Rarity: URS-3
VF $750

$5 • W-MA-1220-005-G070

Left: Lathework chain bearing MASSACHUSETTS / 5 / 5. ***Center:*** Alternating flower garlands and gridwork segments / FIVE. ***Right:*** 5 / 5. ***Engraver:*** PSSP. ***Comments:*** H-MA-440-G14. 18__. 1830s.

Rarity: —

$5 • W-MA-1220-005-G080

Left: Justice standing / FIVE. ***Center:*** View of Harvard College. ***Right:*** 5 / Portrait of Judge Storey / FIVE. ***Engraver:*** New England Bank Note Co. ***Comments:*** H-MA-440-G16. 18__. 1830s–1840s.

Rarity: —

$5 • W-MA-1220-005-G080a

Overprint: Red. ***Engraver:*** New England Bank Note Co. ***Comments:*** H-MA-440-G16a. Similar to W-MA-1220-005-G080. 18__. 1850s.

Rarity: —

$5 • W-MA-1220-005-G080b

Overprint: Red. ***Engraver:*** New England Bank Note Co. / ABNCo. monogram. ***Comments:*** H-MA-440-G16b. Similar to W-MA-1220-005-G080 but with additional engraver imprint. 18__. 1850s–1860s.

Rarity: —

$10 • W-MA-1220-010-G090

Left: Lathework chain bearing MASSACHUSETTS / 10 / 10. ***Center:*** Alternating flower garlands and gridwork segments / TEN. ***Right:*** 10 / 10. ***Engraver:*** PSSP. ***Comments:*** H-MA-440-G18. 18__. 1830s.

Rarity: —

$10 • W-MA-1220-010-G100

Left: 10 / Portrait of Benjamin Franklin / TEN. ***Center:*** View of Harvard College. ***Right:*** 10 / Portrait of Judge Storey / TEN. ***Engraver:*** New England Bank Note Co. ***Comments:*** H-MA-440-G20. 18__. 1830s–1840s.

Rarity: —

$10 • W-MA-1220-010-G100a

Overprint: Red. ***Engraver:*** New England Bank Note Co. ***Comments:*** H-MA-440-G20a. Similar to W-MA-1220-010-G100. 18__. 1850s.

Rarity: —

$10 • W-MA-1220-010-G100b

Overprint: Red. ***Engraver:*** New England Bank Note Co. / ABNCo. monogram. ***Comments:*** H-MA-440-G20b. Similar to W-MA-1220-010-G100 but with additional engraver imprint. 18__. 1850s–1860s.

Rarity: —

$20 • W-MA-1220-020-G110

Left: Lathework chain bearing MASSACHUSETTS / 20 / 20. ***Center:*** Alternating flower garlands and gridwork segments / TWENTY. ***Right:*** 20 / 20. ***Engraver:*** PSSP. ***Comments:*** H-MA-440-G22. 18__. 1830s.

Rarity: —

$20 • W-MA-1220-020-G120

Left: 20 / Liberty seated with hands on shield. ***Center:*** Eagle on shield, Train and ship. ***Right:*** Woman with sheaf under her arm / 20. ***Engraver:*** Toppan, Carpenter & Co. ***Comments:*** H-MA-440-G24. 18__. 1840s–1850s.

Rarity: —

$50 • W-MA-1220-050-G130

Left: Bust of George Washington / 50. ***Center:*** Women flanking shield bearing Indian surmounted by eagle / FIFTY. ***Right:*** 50 / Helmeted medallion head. ***Engraver:*** Toppan, Carpenter & Co. ***Comments:*** H-MA-440-G28. 18__. 1840s–1850s.

Rarity: URS-3
Proof $1,250

$100 • W-MA-1220-100-G140

CC

Engraver: Toppan, Carpenter & Co. ***Comments:*** H-MA-440-G32. 18__. 1840s–1850s.

Rarity: URS-3
Proof $3,000

Non-Valid Issues

$1 • W-MA-1220-001-A010

Left: ONE / Two Indians reclining and smoking. ***Center:*** 1 / Three allegorical women with eagle, pole and cap, shield, balance, and book / 1. ***Bottom center:*** Cattle. ***Right:*** 1 / Portrait of George Washington / ONE. ***Engraver:*** Terry, Pelton & Co. ***Comments:*** H-MA-440-A5. Altered from $1 Citizens Bank, Augusta, Maine, or from notes of other failed banks using the same plate. 18__. 1840s.

Rarity: —

$2 • W-MA-1220-002-C030

CJF

Engraver: PSSP. ***Comments:*** H-MA-440-C6. Counterfeit of W-MA-1220-002-G030. 18__. 1830s.

Rarity: URS-8

VG $75

$2 • W-MA-1220-002-C040

Engraver: New England Bank Note Co. ***Comments:*** H-MA-440-C8. Counterfeit of W-MA-1220-002-G040. 18__. 1830s.

Rarity: —

$2 • W-MA-1220-002-A020

Left: TWO / Portrait of cherub / 2. ***Center:*** 2 / Ceres giving grain to seated Liberty / 2. ***Bottom center:*** Anchor and implements. ***Right:*** 2 / Female portrait / TWO. ***Engraver:*** Terry, Pelton & Co. ***Comments:*** H-MA-440-A10. Altered from $2 Citizens Bank, Augusta, Maine, or from notes of other failed banks using the same plate. 18__. 1840s.

Rarity: —

$3 • W-MA-1220-003-A030

Left: 3 / Woman standing with branch, trident, and THREE / THREE. ***Center:*** Female portrait / Ceres and Justice flanking shield bearing anchor and surmounted by eagle / Portrait of cherub. ***Bottom center:*** Anchor and implements. ***Right:*** 3 / Ceres seated in grain field / THREE. ***Engraver:*** Terry, Pelton & Co. ***Comments:*** H-MA-440-A15. Altered from $3 Citizens Bank, Augusta, Maine, or from notes of other failed banks using the same plate. 18__. 1840s.

Rarity: —

$5 • W-MA-1220-005-A040

Left: FIVE / Portrait of Marquis de Lafayette / FIVE. ***Center:*** 5 / Agricultural items, Two allegorical women standing and one seated / Ship. ***Bottom center:*** Anchor and implements. ***Right:*** V / Portrait of Marquis de Lafayette / FIVE. ***Engraver:*** Terry, Pelton & Co. ***Comments:*** H-MA-440-A20. Altered from $5 Citizens Bank, Augusta, Maine, or from notes of other failed banks using the same plate. 18__. 1840s.

Rarity: —

$10 • W-MA-1220-010-R010

Engraver: New England Bank Note Co. ***Comments:*** H-MA-440-R5. Raised from W-MA-1220-001-G020. 18__. 1840s.

Rarity: —

$10 • W-MA-1220-010-A050

Left: 10 / Portrait of George Washington held by cherub / 10. ***Center:*** X / Spread eagle with shield and arrows, E PLURIBUS UNUM / X. ***Bottom center:*** Ship. ***Right:*** 10 / Indian man / 10. ***Engraver:*** Terry, Pelton & Co. ***Comments:*** H-MA-440-A25. Altered from $10 Citizens Bank, Augusta, Maine, or from notes of other failed banks using the same plate. 18__. 1840s.

Rarity: —

$20 • W-MA-1220-020-R020

Engraver: New England Bank Note Co. ***Comments:*** H-MA-440-R10. Raised from W-MA-1220-003-G060. 18__. 1840s.

Rarity: —

$50 • W-MA-1220-050-R030

Engraver: New England Bank Note Co. ***Comments:*** H-MA-440-R15. Raised from W-MA-1220-001-G020. 18__. 1840s.

Rarity: —

$50 • W-MA-1220-050-R040

Engraver: New England Bank Note Co. ***Comments:*** H-MA-440-R20. Raised from W-MA-1220-002-G040. 18__. 1840s.

Rarity: —

$50 • W-MA-1220-050-R050

Engraver: New England Bank Note Co. ***Comments:*** H-MA-440-R25. Raised from W-MA-1220-003-G060. 18__. 1840s.

Rarity: —

Harvard Bank

1861–1864

W-MA-1230

History: The Harvard Bank went into operation in April 1861 with a capital of $200,000. Harvard College held 50 shares valued at $5,000 par. The bank's circulation was $59,521 in 1862, real estate was $2,280.86, and specie totaled $5,271.61.[75] In 1863 the circulation was $126,461.

The business of the bank was succeeded by the First National Bank of Cambridge, chartered on May 21, 1864. It was located at the corner of Main and Prospect streets.

See also listing under Cambridgeport, W-MA-1270.

How to Read the Whitman Numbering System

$1 • W-MA-010-001-G010a

Denomination: Value of the note shown.

W: Whitman number. This number is a sortable code unique to each bank and note.

MA: Abbreviation for the state under study.

010: Numerical designation specific to each bank.

001: The denomination in dollars.

G010a: G indicates a good or valid note. Other categories are indicated thus: C (counterfeit); R (raised); S (spurious); N (not-attributed); A (altered). Numbers are assigned starting with 010, 020, et seq. Terminal letters following the number indicate variations of a note: a series of different colored overprints, tints, payees, etc., all on the same design of note. For more information, see the "How to Use This Book" section at the front of the volume, page xiv.

Numismatic Commentary: Notes of the Harvard Bank are very hard to locate, with those bearing the college scenery being the most coveted. The oval portrait is that of Thomas Dowse, a self-educated man who put together a superb library of important books and donated it to the Massachusetts Historical Society. The library remains intact in that institution today.

Valid Issues

$1 • W-MA-1230-001-G010

CC

Tint: Green die bearing ONEs, 1s, and border. ***Engraver:*** American Bank Note Co. ***Comments:*** H-MA-445-G2a. March 5, 1861.

Rarity: URS-2
F $6,500

$2 • W-MA-1230-002-G020

CJF

Tint: Green die bearing TWO, 2, and panel of microlettering. ***Engraver:*** American Bank Note Co. ***Comments:*** H-MA-445-G4a. March 5, 1861.

Rarity: URS-3
VF $4,750

$5 • W-MA-1230-005-G030

CC

Tint: Green die bearing FIVE, FI5VE, and panel of microlettering. ***Engraver:*** American Bank Note Co. ***Comments:*** H-MA-445-G6a. March 5, 1861.

Rarity: URS-4
F $5,000

$10 • W-MA-1230-010-G040

Left: 10 / State arms. ***Center:*** Portrait of Thomas Dowse. ***Right:*** 10 / Woman with shield bearing state arms. ***Engraver:*** American Bank Note Co. ***Comments:*** H-MA-445-G8a. Mar. 5, 1861.

Rarity: URS-5
F $1,000; **VF** $1,750

$20 • W-MA-1230-020-G050

Left: 20 / State arms. ***Center:*** View of Harvard College. ***Right:*** 20 / TWENTY / 20. ***Tint:*** Green. ***Engraver:*** American Bank Note Co. ***Comments:*** H-MA-445-G10a. Mar. 5, 1861.

Rarity: —

$50 • W-MA-1230-050-G060

Left: 50 / State arms. ***Center:*** State arms / Portrait of Thomas Dowse. ***Right:*** 50 / 50. ***Tint:*** Green. ***Engraver:*** American Bank Note Co. ***Comments:*** H-MA-445-G12a. Mar. 5, 1861.

Rarity: —

Non-Valid Issues

$5 • W-MA-1230-005-N010

Left: 5 / Man. ***Center:*** Santa Claus. ***Right:*** 5 / Woman. ***Comments:*** H-MA-445-N5. A popular "Santa Claus" note.

Rarity: *None known*

$10 • W-MA-1230-010-R010

CC

Tint: Green die bearing TENs and border. ***Engraver:*** American Bank Note Co. ***Comments:*** H-MA-445-R5. Raised from W-MA-1230-001-G010. March 5, 1861.

Rarity: URS-3
VF $450

Lechmere Bank

1853–1865

W-MA-1240

History: The Lechmere Bank was incorporated on April 28, 1853, with $100,000 in authorized capital, "to be established in that part of Cambridge known as East Cambridge." Business began as soon as half of the capital amount was paid in. The capital was raised to $150,000 by 1858.

The bank's first president was Edmund Boynton, and John Savage Jr. was its first cashier. The bank's circulation was $68,207 in 1857, $89,507 in 1858, and $68,207 in 1860. Selected figures for 1857 included: bills of this bank and other New England states $5,358.95; specie $24,285.70.

The business of the Lechmere Bank was succeeded by the Lechmere National Bank of East Cambridge, chartered in December 1864. The state bank wound down its business starting in 1865.

See also listing under East Cambridge, W-MA-1510.

Numismatic Commentary: The Lechmere Bank issued bills in denominations of $1, $2, $5, $10, $50, $100, and $500. Imaged on the bills are a view of East Cambridge and a portrait of Edmund Winchester, which are used exclusively on the currency of this bank.[76]

Middlesex Bank
1831–1838
W-MA-1250

History: The Middlesex Bank was incorporated on March 19, 1831, with $100,000 capital. This amount was said to have been paid in by July 1831. However, nearly all of the funds were loaned to the stockholders in that month, and by September additional loans far exceeding the bank's capital were made. An audit revealed that the bank had far more debts than could be paid. The situation improved, and for most of the rest of the decade the bank operated without incident. Its bills were exchanged by the Suffolk Bank at only a slight discount. By 1837 matters took a turn for the worse. On January 12, 1838, the bank closed its doors.[77]

Numismatic Commentary: All issues from this bank are hard to locate. At least one variety has a pleasant scene of the Cambridge shoreline on the Charles River.

Valid Issues

$1 • W-MA-1250-001-G010

Left: Lathework panel bearing MASSACHUSETTS vertically. ***Center:*** 1 / 1 / Alternating flower garlands and gridwork segments / ONE / 1 / 1. ***Right:*** Lathework panel bearing ONE / D / ONE vertically. ***Engraver:*** PSSP. ***Comments:*** H-MA-450-G2. 18__. 1830s.

Rarity: URS-6
VG $750; **F** $1,250

$1 • W-MA-1250-001-G020

QDB

Engraver: New England Bank Note Co. / PSSP. ***Comments:*** H-MA-450-G4. 18__. 1830s.

Rarity: URS-3
VG $750; **F** $1,200; **VF** $1,500

$2 • W-MA-1250-002-G030

Left: Lathework panel bearing MASSACHUSETTS vertically. ***Center:*** 2 / 2 / Alternating flower garlands and gridwork segments / TWO / 2 / 2. ***Right:*** Lathework panel bearing five TWOs vertically. ***Engraver:*** PSSP. ***Comments:*** H-MA-450-G6. 18__. 1830s.

Rarity: —

$2 • W-MA-1250-002-G040

CJF

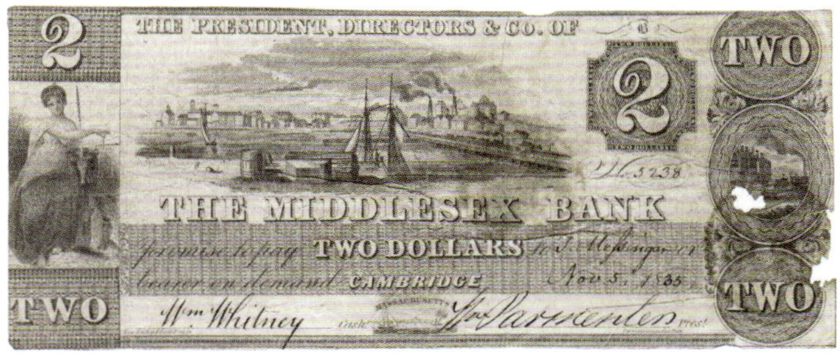

Engraver: New England Bank Note Co. / PSSP. ***Comments:*** H-MA-450-G8. The bridge pictured joined Cambridge to Boston. 18__. 1830s.

Rarity: URS-4
VG $400

$3 • W-MA-1250-003-G050

Left: Lathework panel bearing MASSACHUSETTS vertically. ***Center:*** 3 / 3 / Alternating flower garlands and gridwork segments / THREE / 3 / 3. ***Right:*** Lathework panel bearing THREE vertically. ***Engraver:*** PSSP. ***Comments:*** H-MA-450-G10. 18__. 1830s.

Rarity: —

$5 • W-MA-1250-005-G060

Left: Narrow chain bearing MASSACHUSETTS / 5 / 5. ***Center:*** Alternating flower garlands and gridwork segments / FIVE. ***Right:*** 5 / 5. ***Engraver:*** PSSP. ***Comments:*** H-MA-450-G14. 18__. 1830s.

Rarity: —

$10 • W-MA-1250-010-G070

Left: Narrow chain bearing MASSACHUSETTS / 10 / 10. ***Center:*** Alternating flower garlands and gridwork segments / TEN. ***Right:*** 10 / 10. ***Engraver:*** PSSP. ***Comments:*** H-MA-450-G18. 18__. 1830s.

Rarity: —

$20 • W-MA-1250-020-G080

Left: Narrow chain bearing MASSACHUSETTS / 20 / 20. ***Center:*** Alternating flower garlands and gridwork segments / TWENTY. ***Right:*** 20 / 20. ***Engraver:*** PSSP. ***Comments:*** H-MA-450-G20. 18__. 1830s.

Rarity: —

Uncut Sheets

$1-$1-$2-$3 • W-MA-1250-001.001.002.003-US010

Engraver: Danforth, Underwood, Bald & Spencer. ***Comments:*** All unlisted in Haxby. Vignettes for designs never issued. 1830s.

Rarity: —

Cambridgeport, Massachusetts

Cambridgeport, a district of Cambridge, was bounded by the Charles River and the Grand Junction Railroad in the mid-19th century. It was home to several factories.

See also Cambridge and East Cambridge, Massachusetts.

Cambridge City Bank
1853–1865
W-MA-1260

History: The Cambridge City Bank was chartered on April 18, 1853, with an authorized capital of $100,000. The bank's president was John Livermore, and the cashier was Edward Richardson. The directors were John Livermore, S.P. Heywood, W.P. Fiske, Eliphalet Davis, H.M. Chamberlain, George S. Gale, and George W. Whittemore.

Specie in 1854 was listed at $5,998. Circulation from 1857 to 1860 was listed at $44,768. In 1861 it was $57,041, and in 1863 it was $73,091. Selected figures for 1857 included: bills of this bank and other New England states $2,009; specie $14,937.75. In 1861 specie was valued at $12,733.34.

The business of this bank was assumed by the National City Bank, chartered on January 31, 1865.

See also listing under Cambridge, W-MA-1200.

Numismatic Commentary: Notes from this bank are hard to locate. Many have vignettes showing gold coins, a bonus for collectors of coins on paper money.

Valid Issues

$1 • W-MA-1260-001-G010

JF

Overprint: Red ONE. ***Engraver:*** Rawdon, Wright, Hatch & Edson / New England Bank Note Co. ***Comments:*** H-MA-455-G2a. 18__. 1850s.

Rarity: URS-3
F $2,000; **CU** $5,000

$1 • W-MA-1260-001-G010a

CJF

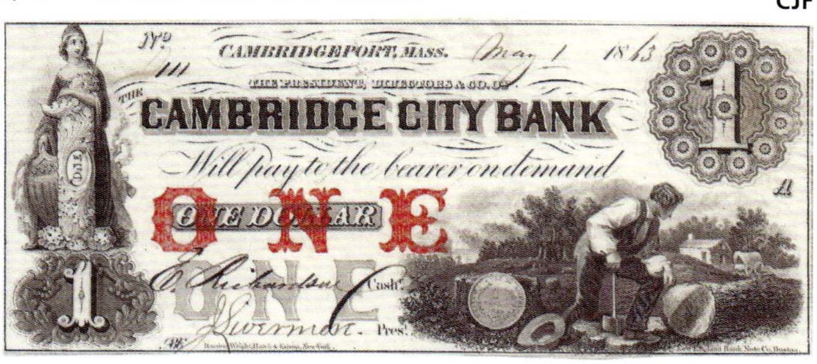

Overprint: Red ONE. ***Engraver:*** Rawdon, Wright, Hatch & Edson / New England Bank Note Co. / ABNCo. monogram. ***Comments:*** H-MA-455-G2b. Similar to W-MA-1260-001-G010 but with additional engraver imprint. 18__. 1850s–1860s.

Rarity: URS-4
VF $1,000

$2 • W-MA-1260-002-G020

Left: Liberty seated feeding eagle / 2. ***Center:*** Milkmaid seated with pail, Men reclining, Cows, Two gold dollars. ***Right:*** 2 / TWO DOLLARS / Train. ***Overprint:*** Red TWO. ***Engraver:*** Rawdon, Wright, Hatch & Edson / New England Bank Note Co. ***Comments:*** H-MA-455-G4a. 18__. 1850s.

Rarity: —

$2 • W-MA-1260-002-G020a

Overprint: Red TWO. ***Engraver:*** Rawdon, Wright, Hatch & Edson / New England Bank Note Co. / ABNCo. monogram. ***Comments:*** H-MA-455-G4b. Similar to W-MA-1260-002-G020 but with additional engraver imprint. 18__. 1850s–1860s.

Rarity: —

$3 • W-MA-1260-003-G030

Left: 3. ***Center:*** Farmer, sailor, and blacksmith with three gold dollars, Woman. ***Right:*** 3 / Farmer, sailor, and blacksmith standing with 3. ***Overprint:*** Red THREE. ***Engraver:*** Rawdon, Wright, Hatch & Edson / New England Bank Note Co. ***Comments:*** H-MA-455-G6a. 18__. 1850s.

Rarity: —

$3 • W-MA-1260-003-G030a

Overprint: Red THREE. ***Engraver:*** Rawdon, Wright, Hatch & Edson / New England Bank Note Co. / ABNCo. monogram. ***Comments:*** H-MA-455-G6b. Similar to W-MA-1260-003-G030 but with additional engraver imprint. 18__. 1850s–1860s.

Rarity: —

$5 • W-MA-1260-005-G040

Left: Man and woman with three cherubs and five coins / 5. ***Center:*** Scene with ships / FIVE. ***Right:*** 5 / 5 with five women. ***Engraver:*** Rawdon, Wright, Hatch & Edson / New England Bank Note Co. ***Comments:*** H-MA-455-G8a. 18__. 1850s.

Rarity: —

$5 • W-MA-1260-005-G040a

Engraver: Rawdon, Wright, Hatch & Edson / New England Bank Note Co. / ABNCo. monogram. ***Comments:*** H-MA-455-G8b. Similar to W-MA-1260-005-G040 but with additional engraver imprint. 18__. 1850s–1860s.

Rarity: —

$10 • W-MA-1260-010-G050

CC

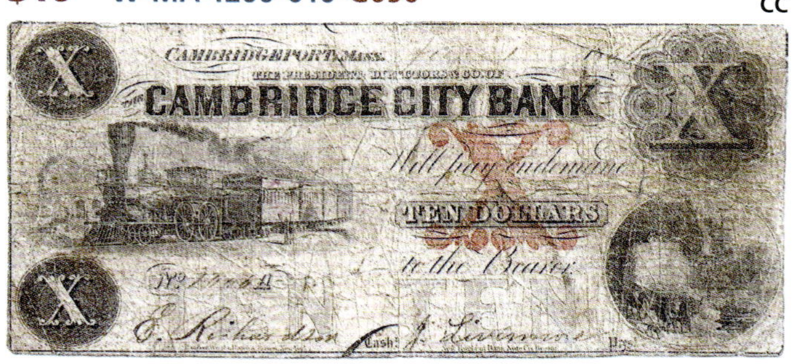

Overprint: Red X. ***Engraver:*** Rawdon, Wright, Hatch & Edson / New England Bank Note Co. ***Comments:*** H-MA-455-G10a. 18__. 1850s.

Rarity: URS-5
VG $300; **VF** $500

$10 • W-MA-1260-010-G050a

Left: X / X. ***Center:*** Train. ***Right:*** X / Load of hay, Man on horse, Dog. ***Overprint:*** Red. ***Engraver:*** Rawdon, Wright, Hatch & Edson / New England Bank Note Co. / ABNCo. monogram. ***Comments:*** H-MA-455-G10b. Similar to W-MA-1260-010-G050 but with additional engraver imprint. 18__. 1850s–1860s.

Rarity: —

$20 • W-MA-1260-020-G060

Left: XX / Mercury seated between 2 and 0. ***Center:*** Woman seated with balance / Shield and strongbox / Train and steamboat. ***Right:*** 20. ***Overprint:*** Red. ***Engraver:*** Rawdon, Wright, Hatch & Edson / New England Bank Note Co. ***Comments:*** H-MA-455-G12a. 18__. 1850s.

Rarity: —

$20 • W-MA-1260-020-G060a

Overprint: Red. ***Engraver:*** Rawdon, Wright, Hatch & Edson / New England Bank Note Co. / ABNCo. monogram. ***Comments:*** H-MA-455-G12b. Similar to W-MA-1260-020-G060 but with additional engraver imprint. 18__. 1850s–1860s.

Rarity: —

$50 • W-MA-1260-050-G070

Left: 50 / Woman. ***Center:*** Spread eagle / U.S. Capitol and steamship. ***Right:*** 50. ***Overprint:*** Red. ***Engraver:*** Rawdon, Wright, Hatch & Edson / New England Bank Note Co. ***Comments:*** H-MA-455-G14a. 18__. 1850s.

Rarity: —

$50 • W-MA-1260-050-G070a

Overprint: Red. ***Engraver:*** Rawdon, Wright, Hatch & Edson / New England Bank Note Co. / ABNCo. monogram. ***Comments:*** H-MA-455-G14b. Similar to W-MA-1260-050-G070 but with additional engraver imprint. 18__. 1850s–1860s.

Rarity: —

$100 • W-MA-1260-100-G080

Left: Woman with spear and shield / HUNDRED. ***Center:*** Woman, Eagle and globe, Ships. ***Right:*** 100 / Hunter. ***Overprint:*** Red. ***Engraver:*** Rawdon, Wright, Hatch & Edson / New England Bank Note Co. ***Comments:*** H-MA-455-G16a. 18__. 1850s.

Rarity: —

$100 • W-MA-1260-100-G080a

Overprint: Red. ***Engraver:*** Rawdon, Wright, Hatch & Edson / New England Bank Note Co. / ABNCo. monogram. ***Comments:*** H-MA-455-G16b. Similar to W-MA-1260-100-G080 but with additional engraver imprint. 18__. 1850s–1860s.

Rarity: —

Non-Valid Issues

$1 • W-MA-1260-001-A010

Left: ONE / Man riding horse hitched to cart, Two people standing. ***Center:*** Train at country depot. ***Right:*** 1 / Woman shading eyes with left hand. ***Comments:*** H-MA-455-A5. Altered from $1 Bank of Greensborough, Greensborough, Georgia series. 1850s.

Rarity: —

$2 • W-MA-1260-002-C020

Engraver: Rawdon, Wright, Hatch & Edson / New England Bank Note Co. ***Comments:*** H-MA-455-C4a. Counterfeit of W-MA-1260-002-G020 but without overprint. 18__. 1850s.

Rarity: —

$2 • W-MA-1260-002-A020

Left: 2 / Man carrying basket of cotton. ***Center:*** TWO on die. ***Right:*** 2 / Woman reclining with cornucopia. ***Comments:*** H-MA-455-A10. Altered from $2 Bank of Greensborough, Greensborough, Georgia series. 1850s.

Rarity: —

$5 • W-MA-1260-005-C040

CJF

Overprint: Red FIVE. ***Engraver:*** Rawdon, Wright, Hatch & Edson / New England Bank Note Co. ***Comments:*** H-MA-455-C8a. Counterfeit of W-MA-1260-005-G040. 18__. 1850s.

Rarity: URS-7
F $100; **VF** $150

$5 • W-MA-1260-005-R010

Engraver: Rawdon, Wright, Hatch & Edson / New England Bank Note Co. ***Comments:*** H-MA-455-R5. Raised from W-MA-1260-002-G020. 18__. 1850s.

Rarity: —

$5 • W-MA-1260-005-A030

Left: 5 / Man and woman seated with child. ***Center:*** FIVE / Three men. ***Right:*** 5 / Men with baskets harvesting corn. ***Comments:*** H-MA-455-A15. Altered from $5 Bank of Greensborough, Greensborough, Georgia series. 1850s.

Rarity: —

$10 • W-MA-1260-010-R020

Engraver: Rawdon, Wright, Hatch & Edson / New England Bank Note Co. ***Comments:*** H-MA-455-R10. Raised from W-MA-1260-002-G020. 18__. 1850s.

Rarity: —

$10 • W-MA-1260-010-A040

Left: 10 / Woman seated on ground under palm tree, head resting on hand, Shovel and sickle. ***Center:*** Woman reclining with shield bearing scroll, Pole and cap. ***Right:*** 10. ***Comments:*** H-MA-455-A20. Altered from $10 Bank of Greensborough, Georgia series. 1850s.

Rarity: —

$20 • W-MA-1260-020-R030

Engraver: Rawdon, Wright, Hatch & Edson / New England Bank Note Co. ***Comments:*** H-MA-455-R15. Raised from W-MA-1260-002-G020. 18__. 1850s.

Rarity: —

Harvard Bank

1861–1864

W-MA-1270

History: The Harvard Bank went into operation in April 1861 with a capital of $200,000. Harvard College held 50 shares valued at $5,000 par. The bank's circulation was $59,521 in 1862, real estate was $2,280.86, and specie totaled $5,271.61.[78] In 1863 the circulation was $126,461.

The business of the bank was succeeded by the First National Bank of Cambridge, chartered on May 21, 1864. It was located at the corner of Main and Prospect streets.

See also listing under Cambridge, W-MA-1230.

Canton, Massachusetts

Originally a part of Dorchester, Canton was settled in 1630 and separated from Dorchester in 1727 under the name of Stoughton. It was officially incorporated as Canton on February 23, 1797. The nation's first copper rolling mill was built here by Paul Revere, and the Canton Viaduct, built in 1835, is the oldest railroad bridge of that design in the world.

Neponset Bank

1836–1864

W-MA-1280

History: The Neponset Bank was chartered on March 1, 1836, with an authorized capital of $100,000. Frederick W. Lincoln was the first president, and James Dunbar was the first cashier. In 1839 the circulation was $30,967. By 1845 it had increased to $70,401. By 1849 it was down again to $35,365, and it fluctuated between $77,441 in 1857 and $97,842 in 1863.

Selected figures for 1857 included: bills of this bank and other New England states $3,757.16; specie $6,055.02. Specie was listed at $5,666.19 in 1861.

In 1864 the business of the Neponset Bank was succeeded by the Neponset National Bank of Canton.

Numismatic Commentary: Notes from this bank will prove hard to find. At least two of the denominations will show vignettes with a local flavor: a scene of the railroad viaduct passing over a river and through the town.

Valid Issues

$1 • W-MA-1280-001-G010

Left: 1 / Woman wearing bonnet with pail / ONE. ***Center:*** Machinery and merchandise flanking Ceres seated holding sickle and rake, Factories and harbor / ONE / Panel outlining white ONE. ***Right:*** 1 / Ship / ONE. ***Engraver:*** PSSP / New England Bank Note Co. ***Comments:*** H-MA-460-G2. 18__. 1830s.

Rarity: —

$1 • W-MA-1280-001-G020

Left: ONE / Bust of George Washington / ONE. ***Center:*** 1 / Two blacksmiths at anvil in front of forge / 1 / Panel outlining white ONE. ***Right:*** ONE / Woman / ONE. ***Engraver:*** New England Bank Note Co. ***Comments:*** H-MA-460-G4. 18__. 1840s–1850s.

Rarity: —

$1 • W-MA-1280-001-G030

Left: ONE / Woman leaning on 1. ***Center:*** Man and woman, Haying scene. ***Right:*** 1 / Eagle with wings spread / ONE. ***Back:*** Brown lathework with bank title. ***Engraver:*** Rawdon, Wright, Hatch & Edson / New England Bank Note Co. ***Comments:*** H-MA-460-G6. 18__. 1850s.

Rarity: —

$1 • W-MA-1280-001-G030a

Overprint: Red ONE. ***Engraver:*** Rawdon, Wright, Hatch & Edson / New England Bank Note Co. ***Comments:*** H-MA-460-G6a. Similar to W-MA-1280-001-G030. 18__. 1850s.

Rarity: —

$1 • W-MA-1280-001-G030b

TD

Overprint: Red ONE. ***Back:*** Brown. ***Engraver:*** Rawdon, Wright, Hatch & Edson / New England Bank Note Co. / ABNCo. monogram. ***Comments:*** H-MA-460-G6b. Similar to W-MA-1280-001-G030 but with additional engraver imprint. 18__. 1850s–1860s.

Rarity: URS-3

F $750

$2 • W-MA-1280-002-G040

Left: 2 / Woman standing with staff and cornucopia / TWO. ***Center:*** TWO / Machinery and merchandise flanking Ceres seated holding sickle and rake, Factories and harbor / Panel outlining white TWO. ***Right:*** 2 / Woman wearing hat, Trees / TWO. ***Engraver:*** New England Bank Note Co. / PSSP. ***Comments:*** H-MA-460-G8. 18__. 1830s.

Rarity: —

$2 • W-MA-1280-002-G050

TD

Engraver: New England Bank Note Co. ***Comments:*** H-MA-460-G10. 18__. 1840s–1850s.

Rarity: URS-3

F $500

$2 • W-MA-1280-002-G060

Left: Woman with shield / TWO. ***Center:*** Justice seated with shield, Train and steamship. ***Right:*** 2 / Women embracing. ***Back:*** Brown lathework with bank title. ***Engraver:*** Rawdon, Wright, Hatch & Edson / New England Bank Note Co. ***Comments:*** H-MA-460-G12. 18__. 1850s.

Rarity: —

$2 • W-MA-1280-002-G060a

Overprint: Red TWO. ***Engraver:*** Rawdon, Wright, Hatch & Edson / New England Bank Note Co. ***Comments:*** H-MA-460-G12a. Similar to W-MA-1280-002-G060. 18__. 1850s.

Rarity: —

$2 • W-MA-1280-002-G060b

TD, TD

Overprint: Red TWO. ***Engraver:*** Rawdon, Wright, Hatch & Edson / New England Bank Note Co. / ABNCo. monogram. ***Comments:*** H-MA-460-G12b. Similar to W-MA-1280-002-G060 but with additional engraver imprint. 18__. 1850s–1860s.

Rarity: URS-4
F $1,000; **VF** $1,100; **Proof** $2,000

$3 • W-MA-1280-003-G070

Left: THREE / Beehive and foliage / THREE. ***Center:*** Machinery and merchandise flanking Ceres seated holding sickle and rake, Factories and harbor / THREE / Panel outlining white THREE. ***Right:*** 3 on THREE / Two reapers / 3 on THREE. ***Engraver:*** New England Bank Note Co. / PSSP. ***Comments:*** H-MA-460-G14. 18__. 1830s.

Rarity: —

$3 • W-MA-1280-003-G080

Left: THREE / Farmer sharpening scythe / 3 across THREE. ***Center:*** 3 / Beehive and cornucopia, Woman placing garland on eagle / 3 / Panel outlining white THREE. ***Right:*** THREE / Sailor standing on wharf with hat / 3 across THREE. ***Engraver:*** New England Bank Note Co. ***Comments:*** H-MA-460-G16. 18__. 1840s.

Rarity: —

$3 • W-MA-1280-003-G090

Left: 3 / Female portrait / THREE. ***Center:*** Drove of cattle and sheep, Man on horseback. ***Right:*** 3 / Blacksmith, farmer, and sailor in and around 3 / THREE. ***Back:*** Brown lathework with bank title. ***Engraver:*** Rawdon, Wright, Hatch & Edson / New England Bank Note Co. ***Comments:*** H-MA-460-G18. 18__. 1850s.

Rarity: —

$3 • W-MA-1280-003-G090a

Overprint: Red THREE. ***Engraver:*** Rawdon, Wright, Hatch & Edson / New England Bank Note Co. ***Comments:*** H-MA-460-G18a. Similar to W-MA-1280-003-G090. 18__. 1850s.

Rarity: —

$3 • W-MA-1280-003-G090b

TD

Overprint: Red THREE. ***Engraver:*** Rawdon, Wright, Hatch & Edson / New England Bank Note Co. / ABNCo. monogram. ***Comments:*** H-MA-460-G18b. Similar to W-MA-1280-003-G090 but with additional engraver imprint. 18__. 1850s–1860s.

Rarity: URS-3
F $2,000

$5 • W-MA-1280-005-G100

Left: 5 / Blacksmith at anvil / FIVE. ***Center:*** Mercury standing with 5, Cornucopia and merchandise, Factories and ship / V / Panel outlining white FIVE. ***Right:*** 5 / Ceres kneeling / FIVE. ***Engraver:*** New England Bank Note Co. / PSSP. ***Comments:*** H-MA-460-G20. 18__. 1830s.

Rarity: —

$5 • W-MA-1280-005-G110

Left: FIVE / Carpenter at work / 5. ***Center:*** Viaduct of the Boston and Providence Railroad. ***Right:*** 5 / Indian man standing with bow / FIVE. ***Engraver:*** New England Bank Note Co. ***Comments:*** H-MA-460-G24. 18__. 1830s–1850s.

Rarity: —

$5 • W-MA-1280-005-G110a

Overprint: Red FIVE. ***Engraver:*** New England Bank Note Co. ***Comments:*** H-MA-460-G24a. Similar to W-MA-1280-005-G110. 18__. 1850s.

Rarity: —

$5 • **W-MA-1280-005-G110b**

TD

Overprint: Red FIVE. ***Back:*** Likely green. ***Engraver:*** Rawdon, Wright, Hatch & Edson / New England Bank Note Co. / ABNCo. monogram. ***Comments:*** H-MA-460-G24b. Similar to W-MA-1280-005-G110 but with additional engraver imprint. 18__. 1850s–1860s.

Rarity: URS-3
F $1,500; **VF** $2,000

$10 • **W-MA-1280-010-G120**

Engraver: Unverified, but likely New England Bank Note Co. ***Comments:*** H-MA-460-G26. No description available. 18__. 1830s.

Rarity: *None known*

$10 • **W-MA-1280-010-G130**

Left: 10 / Portrait of George Washington / X. ***Center:*** Viaduct of Boston and Providence Railroad / TEN. ***Right:*** 10 / Portrait of Paul Revere / TEN. ***Back:*** Lathework with bank title. ***Engraver:*** New England Bank Note Co. ***Comments:*** H-MA-460-G28. 18__. 1830s–1850s.

Rarity: —

$10 • **W-MA-1280-010-G130a**

Overprint: Red TEN. ***Engraver:*** New England Bank Note Co. ***Comments:*** H-MA-460-G28a. Similar to W-MA-1280-010-G130. 18__. 1850s.

Rarity: —

$10 • **W-MA-1280-010-G130b**

TD

Overprint: Red TEN. ***Back:*** Green. ***Engraver:*** Rawdon, Wright, Hatch & Edson / New England Bank Note Co. / ABNCo. monogram. ***Comments:*** H-MA-460-G28b. Similar to W-MA-1280-010-G130 but with additional engraver imprint. 18__. 1850s–1860s.

Rarity: URS-3
VF $1,500

$20 • **W-MA-1280-020-G140**

Left: 20 / XX / 20. ***Center:*** 20 / Men plowing, Woman seated with scales, Sheaf and bales, Ship / 20. ***Right:*** TWENTY vertically. ***Engraver:*** New England Bank Note Co. ***Comments:*** H-MA-460-G30. 18__. 1830s.

Rarity: —

$20 • **W-MA-1280-020-G150**

Left: 20 / Woman seated with book, opening chest. ***Center:*** XX / Eagle on rock / XX. ***Right:*** 20 / Ship in harbor. ***Engraver:*** New England Bank Note Co. ***Comments:*** H-MA-460-G32. 18__. 1840s–1850s.

Rarity: —

$20 • **W-MA-1280-020-G160**

JF

Tint: Orange. ***Engraver:*** American Bank Note Co. ***Comments:*** H-MA-460-G34a. February 1, 186_. 1860s.

Rarity: URS-2
Proof $3,000

$50 • **W-MA-1280-050-G170**

Left: FIFTY / Woman standing with wreath and flowers / FIFTY. ***Center:*** FIFTY DOLLARS / 50. ***Right:*** FIFTY vertically. ***Engraver:*** New England Bank Note Co. / PSSP. ***Comments:*** H-MA-460-G36. 18__. 1830s.

Rarity: —

$50 • **W-MA-1280-050-G180**

Left: FIFTY / Woman standing with wreath and flowers / FIFTY. ***Center:*** 50 / Man restraining prancing horse / 50. ***Right:*** FIFTY / Woman standing with cornucopia / FIFTY. ***Engraver:*** New England Bank Note Co. ***Comments:*** H-MA-460-G38. 18__. 1840s–1850s.

Rarity: —

$50 • **W-MA-1280-050-G190**

Left: 50 / Woman with pail and pitcher, Ducks. ***Center:*** FIFTY DOLLARS. ***Right:*** 50 / Dog and strongbox. ***Tint:*** Orange. ***Engraver:*** American Bank Note Co. ***Comments:*** H-MA-460-G40a. Feb. 1, 186_. 1860s.

Rarity: —

$100 • **W-MA-1280-100-G200**

Left: Lathework panel bearing C / Portrait of George Washington / C. ***Center:*** 100 / Manhattan reclining, pouring water, Ship / 100. ***Right:*** Lathework panel bearing ONE HUNDRED vertically. ***Engraver:*** New England Bank Note Co. / PSSP. ***Comments:*** H-MA-460-G42. 18__. 1830s.

Rarity: —

$100 • **W-MA-1280-100-G210**

Left: ONE HUNDRED on 100 / Portrait of William Henry Harrison. ***Center:*** Wharf scene, Men loading wagon with barrels. ***Right:*** ONE HUNDRED on 100 / Portrait of Christopher Columbus. ***Engraver:*** New England Bank Note Co. ***Comments:*** H-MA-460-G44. 18__. 1840s–1850s.

Rarity: —

$100 • W-MA-1280-100-G220

Left: C / Portrait of girl. ***Center:*** Die bearing ONE HUNDRED DOLLARS. ***Right:*** 100 / State arms. ***Tint:*** Orange. ***Engraver:*** American Bank Note Co. ***Comments:*** H-MA-460-G46a. Feb. 1, 186_. 1860s.

Rarity: URS-3
Proof $3,000

$100 • W-MA-1280-100-G220a

HA

Tint: Green. ***Engraver:*** American Bank Note Co. ***Comments:*** H-Unlisted. Similar to W-MA-1280-100-G220. February 1, 186_. 1860s.

Rarity: URS-3
Proof $3,000
Selected auction price: Heritage, April–May 2009, Lot 12320, Unc $2,530

$500 • W-MA-1280-500-G230

Left: 500 / 500 / 500. ***Center:*** 500 / Woman seated with shield bearing D, Fasces, cornucopia, lyre, and sheaf / 500. ***Right:*** 500 / D / 500. ***Engraver:*** PSSP / New England Bank Note Co. ***Comments:*** H-MA-460-G48. 18__. 1830s–1840s.

Rarity: —

Non-Valid Issues

$3 • W-MA-1280-003-N010

Center: Train. ***Right:*** Justice. ***Comments:*** H-MA-460-N5.

Rarity: —

$5 • W-MA-1280-005-A010

Left: FIVE / Minerva standing with spear, helmet, and shield / FIVE. ***Center:*** Three allegorical women reclining with sheaf, pole and cap, globe, and quadrant / FIVE. ***Right:*** 5 / Portrait of George Washington. ***Engraver:*** Danforth, Bald & Co. ***Comments:*** H-MA-460-A5. Altered from $5 Columbia Bank, Washington, D.C. 18__. 1850s.

Rarity: —

$10 • W-MA-1280-010-A020

Left: 10 / Woman with scroll seated on chest. ***Center:*** X on medallion U.S. shield / Three women seated on shore, one pointing to ship. ***Right:*** 10 / Cattle and telegraph poles, Train on bridge ***Overprint:*** Red TEN. ***Engraver:*** Danforth, Bald & Co. ***Comments:*** H-MA-460-A10. Altered from $10 Columbia Bank, Washington, D.C. 18__. 1850s.

Rarity: —

Castine, Massachusetts

Castine, in Hancock County, is located on a peninsula at the Bagaduce River (sometimes spelled as Bigaduce) on the Eastern side of Penobscot Bay near the Penobscot River. Earlier known as Pentagoet, it was an important trading station. Ownership changed hands several times, and the French, Dutch, and English each flew their flags over it at one time or another. In 1796 Castine was incorporated as a village, becoming the shire town for Hancock County. At the time, Castine was located in the Maine District of Massachusetts. In March 1820, it became part of the new state of Maine.

In the 1850s Castine was considered the wealthiest town in its district as well as a center for shipbuilding and ownership of ships engaged in Atlantic trade. Cordage and iron chains were manufactured there, but the main business lay in the fisheries. In 1850 the population was 1,260.

Castine Bank

1815–1820 • 1820 and 1821

W-MA-1290 • W-ME-640

History: The Castine Bank was authorized on February 16, 1816, in the Maine District of Massachusetts. The authorized capital was $100,000, divided into shares of $100 each. The bank was permitted to commence operations once $25,000 had been paid in. Its capital was $100,000 in 1819. However, all was not well, and rumors circulated concerning the bank's stability.

After Maine became a state on March 15, 1820, the Castine Bank was in precarious condition and only continued business until May 18, 1820, when it stopped redeeming its notes. On June 15, 1820, the new legislature mounted an investigation and found that as of January 1, 1820, it had $170,709 of currency in circulation, $20,709 more than permitted under its Massachusetts charter.[79] The charter was repealed March 20, 1821.

Numismatic Commentary: PSSP notes were issued first and are dated beginning in 1816. The $5, $10, and $20 denominations have a Stereotype Steel Check Plate reverse (except for Proofs which are plain). Signed Abner Reed notes are typically dated 1818 or 1819. As Massachusetts law mandated the use of Perkins plates at the time, it is unclear as to the genesis of the Reed notes, most of which were signed and issued. The Reed notes are very attractive, each with a scenic vignette at the center top. All Castine Bank notes became worthless in 1820, with the result that examples are easily enough found in the marketplace, although certain varieties are scarce. All have the Massachusetts imprint.

Valid Issues

Notes With Massachusetts Address: Demand Notes

$1 • W-MA-1290-001-G010

CJF

Engraver: PSSP. ***Comments:*** H-MA-465-G20, Wait-1. 18__. 1810s.

Rarity: URS-6
F $250

$1 • W-MA-1290-001-G020

QDB

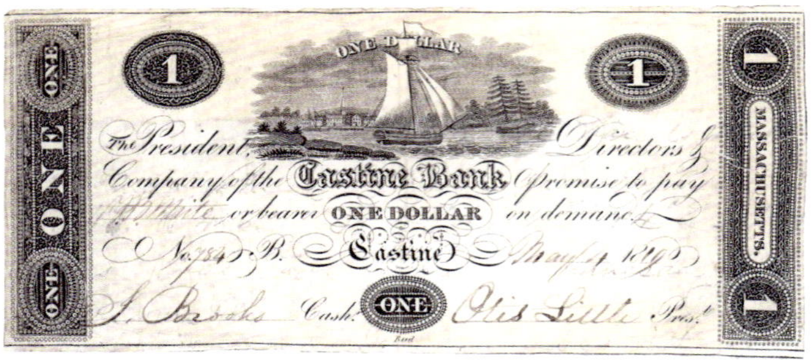

Engraver: Abner Reed. ***Comments:*** H-MA-465-G24, Wait-2. 18__. 1810s.

Rarity: URS-7
F $200; **Proof** $2,200

$2 • W-MA-1290-002-G030

Engraver: PSSP. ***Comments:*** H-MA-465-G28, Wait-3. Similar to W-MA-1290-001-G010 but with different denomination. Issued note unverified. 1810s.

Rarity: *None known*

$2 • W-MA-1290-002-G040

CJF

Engraver: Abner Reed. ***Comments:*** H-MA-465-G32, Wait-4. 18__. 1810s.

Rarity: URS-7
F $300; **Proof** $1,000

$3 • W-MA-1290-003-G050

Engraver: PSSP. ***Comments:*** H-MA-465-G36, Wait-5. Similar to W-MA-1290-001-G010 but with different denomination. Issued note unverified. 1810s.

Rarity: *None known*

$3 • W-MA-1290-003-G060

CJF

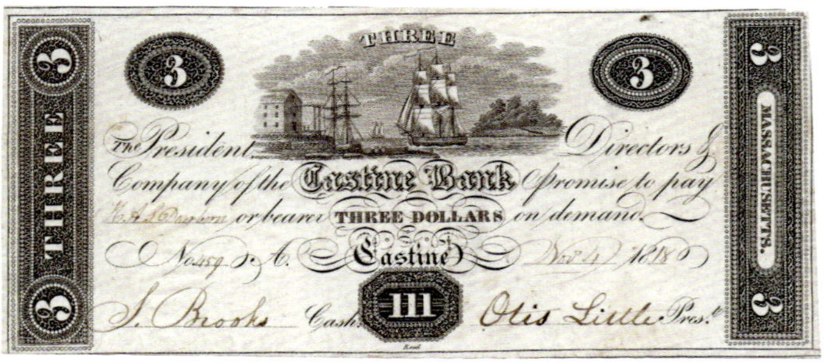

Engraver: Abner Reed. ***Comments:*** H-MA-465-G40, Wait-6. 18__. 1810s.

Rarity: URS-7
Proof $1,000

$5 • W-MA-1290-005-G070

CJF, CJF

Engraver: PSSP. ***Comments:*** H-MA-465-G44, Wait-7. 18__. 1810s.

Rarity: URS-6
F $150

$5 • W-MA-1290-005-G080

CJF

Engraver: Abner Reed. ***Comments:*** H-MA-465-G48, Wait-8. 18__. 1810s.

Rarity: URS-7
Proof $1,000

$10 • W-MA-1290-010-G090

QDB, QDB

Engraver: PSSP. ***Comments:*** H-MA-465-G52, Wait-9. 18__. 1810s.

Rarity: URS-6
F $150

$10 • W-MA-1290-010-G100

CJF

Engraver: Abner Reed. ***Comments:*** H-MA-465-G56, Wait-10. 18__. 1810s.

Rarity: URS-7
VF $350

$20 • W-MA-1290-020-G120

Left: State arms / 20, Plate letter, 20. ***Center:*** Flower garlands, TWENTY. ***Right:*** 20, Plate letter, 20. ***Engraver:*** PSSP. ***Comments:*** H-MA-465-G60, Wait-Unlisted. Issued note unverified. 1810s.

Rarity: *None known*

Post Note

$__ • W-MA-1290-__-G130

CJF

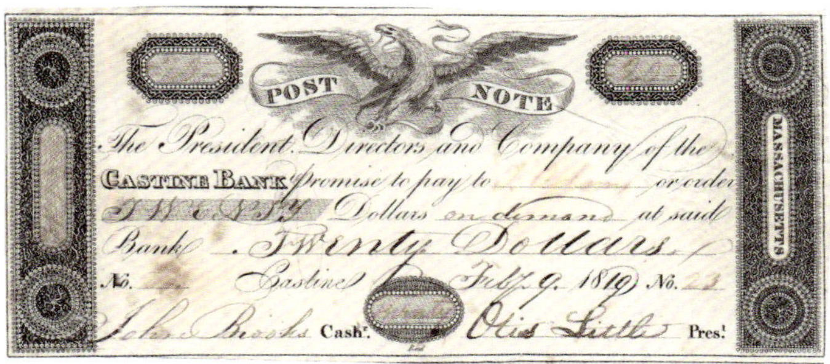

Comments: H-MA-465-G72, Wait-Unlisted. Denomination filled in by hand. 18__. 1810s.

Rarity: URS-2
VF $600

Charlestown, Massachusetts

A neighborhood of Boston, Charlestown was a Puritan city during the colonial era. It was founded in 1628 and became a city in 1847. It was annexed by Boston in 1874.

The greater Charlestown territory originally encompassed Melrose, Malden, Stoneham, Somerville, Medford, Everett, Woburn, Burlington, Arlington, and Cambridge. Part of the settlement was destroyed by fire during the Battle of Bunker Hill in 1775. A decade later, 13 new wharves lined the harbor, and new bridges increased trade. The Middlesex Canal opened to Charlestown in 1803, and around 1825 the first toll-free bridge was built connecting Charlestown to Boston. This was another city to witness a rush of Irish immigrants in the 1860s, and between 1830 and 1870 the population rose to more than 28,000.

Bunker Hill Bank

1825–1864

W-MA-1300

History: The Bunker Hill Bank was chartered on June 28, 1825, with an authorized capital of $150,000. The charter was renewed in 1837 to last until January 1, 1875. In 1839 the bank had $150,000 in capital, which was increased to $200,000 in 1848. In 1839 the bank had a circulation of $71,185. It was increased to $129,529 by 1845, and in 1849 it was $141,420. In 1855 capital was $300,000. Selected figures for 1857 included: bills of this bank and other New England states $9,190; specie $75,334.76; real estate $24,000.

The business of the Bunker Hill Bank was succeeded by the Bunker Hill National Bank of Charlestown, chartered on December 20, 1864.

Numismatic Commentary: Some bills of the Bunker Hill Bank, not to be confused with the Monument Bank of Charleston, depict the Bunker Hill Monument, a familiar icon which is also memorialized on Civil War tokens. Others will show historical vignettes. The notes from this bank are colorful and distinctive.

Valid Issues

$1 • W-MA-1300-001-G010

Left: Narrow panel of lathework circle segments. ***Center:*** 1 / 1 / Flower garlands and gridwork segments / 1 / 1. ***Right:*** Narrow panel of lathework circle segments. ***Engraver:*** PSSP. ***Comments:*** H-MA-470-G2. 18__. 1820s–1830s.

Rarity: —

$1 • W-MA-1300-001-G010a

Left: ONE / D / ONE vertically. ***Right:*** ONE / D / ONE vertically. ***Engraver:*** PSSP. ***Comments:*** H-MA-470-G4. Similar to W-MA-1300-001-G010. 18__. 1830s.

Rarity: —

$1 • W-MA-1300-001-G020

CJF

Engraver: New England Bank Note Co. / PSSP. ***Comments:*** H-MA-470-G8. 18__.

Rarity: URS-3
VF $800; **Proof** $2,500

$1 • W-MA-1300-001-G020a

HA

Overprint: Red bank title. ***Engraver:*** New England Bank Note Co. / PSSP. ***Comments:*** H-MA-470-G8a. Similar to W-MA-1300-001-G020. 18__. 1830s–1840s.

Rarity: URS-3
F $700; **VF** $900; **Proof** $2,500

$1 • W-MA-1300-001-G020b

Left: 1 / Justice reclining on pot / ONE. ***Center:*** Bunker Hill Monument / Gray 1 / 1. ***Right:*** 1 / Portrait of George Washington at Dorchester Heights, 1775 / ONE. ***Engraver:*** New England Bank Note Co. / PSSP. ***Comments:*** H-MA-470-G8c. Similar to W-MA-1300-001-G020. 18__.

Rarity: —

$1 • W-MA-1300-001-G020c

Center: Gray 1 / 1. ***Overprint:*** Red. ***Engraver:*** New England Bank Note Co. / PSSP. ***Comments:*** H-MA-470-G8d. Similar to W-MA-1300-001-G020. 18__. 1840s–1850s.

Rarity: URS-5
VF $450
Selected auction price: Heritage, January 2010, Lot 12825, VF $1,725

$1 • W-MA-1300-001-G030

Left: 1. ***Center:*** "Presentation of the Declaration of Independence". ***Right:*** 1 / Woman with calf. ***Tint:*** Red die bearing 1. ***Engraver:*** Toppan, Carpenter & Co. / American Bank Note Co. ***Comments:*** H-MA-470-G10a. June 17, 1858.

Rarity: URS-5
VF $500

$1 • W-MA-1300-001-G030a

CJF

Overprint: Green 1 / 1 / ONE, Red bank title, panel outlining ONE DOLLAR, and die outlining white 1. ***Engraver:*** Toppan, Carpenter & Co. / American Bank Note Co. ***Comments:*** H-MA-470-G10b. Similar to W-MA-1300-001-G030. June 17, 1858.

Rarity: URS-5
VF $5,000
Selected auction price: Stack's Bowers Galleries, 2013, Lot 24310, VF $5,405

$2 • W-MA-1300-002-G040

Left: Narrow panel of lathework circle segments. ***Center:*** 2 / 2 / Flower garlands and gridwork segments / 2 / 2. ***Right:*** Narrow panel of lathework circle segments. ***Engraver:*** PSSP. ***Comments:*** H-MA-470-G12. 18__. 1820s–1830s.

Rarity: —

$2 • W-MA-1300-002-G040a

Left: Five TWOs vertically. ***Right:*** Five TWOs vertically. ***Engraver:*** PSSP. ***Comments:*** H-MA-470-G14. Similar to W-MA-1300-002-G040. 18__. 1830s.

Rarity: —

$2 • W-MA-1300-002-G050

Left: 2 / Justice / TWO. ***Center:*** Bunker Hill Monument. ***Right:*** 2 / Portrait of General Joseph Warren / TWO. ***Engraver:*** New England Bank Note Co. / PSSP. ***Comments:*** H-MA-470-G18. 18__.

Rarity: URS-3
Proof $1,400

$2 • W-MA-1300-002-G050a

QDB

Overprint: Red bank title. ***Engraver:*** New England Bank Note Co. / PSSP. ***Comments:*** H-MA-470-G18a. Similar to W-MA-1300-002-G050. 18__. 1830s–1840s.

Rarity: URS-2
Proof $2,000

$2 • W-MA-1300-002-G050b

Center: Gray 2 / 2. ***Engraver:*** New England Bank Note Co. / PSSP. ***Comments:*** H-MA-470-G18c. Similar to W-MA-1300-002-G050. 18__.

Rarity: —

$2 • W-MA-1300-002-G050c

CC

Overprint: Red bank title. ***Engraver:*** New England Bank Note Co. / PSSP. ***Comments:*** H-MA-470-G18d. Similar to W-MA-1300-002-G050. 18__. 1830s–1840s.

Rarity: URS-3
F $900; **VF** $1,500; **Proof** $5,000
Selected auction price: Heritage, January 2010, Lot 12826, VF $1,380

$2 • W-MA-1300-002-G060

CJF

Tint: Red bank title, shield outlining white 2, die outlining white 2, and panel outlining white TWO DOLLARS. ***Engraver:*** Toppan, Carpenter & Co. / American Bank Note Co. ***Comments:*** H-MA-470-G20a. June 17, 1858.

Rarity: URS-5
VF $500; **AU** $900
Selected auction price: Stack's Bowers Galleries, August 2012, Lot 3242, AU $862

$2 • W-MA-1300-002-G060a

Left: 2. ***Center:*** Indian and sailor flanking shield bearing 2 surmounted by eagle / Woman with pedestal. ***Right:*** 2 / Portrait of girl. ***Overprint:*** Green. ***Engraver:*** Toppan, Carpenter & Co. / American Bank Note Co. ***Comments:*** H-MA-470-G20b. Similar to W-MA-1300-002-G060. June 17, 1858.

Rarity: —

$3 • W-MA-1300-003-G070

Comments: H-Unlisted. June 17, 1858.

Rarity: —
Selected auction price: Stack's Bowers Galleries, November 2013, Lot 1052, EF $1,645

$3 • W-MA-1300-003-G080

Left: Narrow panel of lathework circle segments. ***Center:*** 3 / 3 / Flower garlands and gridwork segments / 3 / 3. ***Right:*** Narrow panel of lathework circle segments. ***Engraver:*** PSSP. ***Comments:*** H-MA-470-G22. 18__. 1820s–1830s.

Rarity: —

$3 • W-MA-1300-003-G080a

Left: THREE vertically. ***Right:*** THREE vertically. ***Engraver:*** PSSP. ***Comments:*** H-MA-470-G24. Similar to W-MA-1300-003-G080. 18__. 1830s.

Rarity: —

$3 • W-MA-1300-003-G090

Left: 3 / Portrait of General Joseph Warren / THREE. ***Center:*** 3 / Bunker Hill Monument / 3. ***Right:*** 3 / Eagle and shield / 3. ***Engraver:*** New England Bank Note Co. / PSSP. ***Comments:*** H-MA-470-G28. 18__.

Rarity: —

$3 • W-MA-1300-003-G090a

Overprint: Red. ***Engraver:*** New England Bank Note Co. / PSSP. ***Comments:*** H-MA-470-G28a. Similar to W-MA-1300-003-G090. 18__. 1830s–1840s.

Rarity: —

$3 • W-MA-1300-003-G090b

Center: Gray 3 / 3. ***Engraver:*** New England Bank Note Co. / PSSP. ***Comments:*** H-MA-470-G28c. Similar to W-MA-1300-003-G090. 18__.

Rarity: —

$3 • W-MA-1300-003-G090c

Center: Gray 3 / 3. ***Overprint:*** Red. ***Engraver:*** New England Bank Note Co. / PSSP. ***Comments:*** H-MA-470-G28d. Similar to W-MA-1300-003-G090. 18__. 1840s–1850s.

Rarity: URS-4
VF $550

$3 • W-MA-1300-003-G100

CJF

Tint: Red bank title, die outlining white 3, and panel outlining white THREE DOLLARS. ***Engraver:*** Toppan, Carpenter & Co. / American Bank Note Co. ***Comments:*** H-MA-470-G30. June 17, 1858.

Rarity: URS-3
F $2,000

$5 • W-MA-1300-005-G110

Left: Lathework chain bearing MASSACHUSETTS / 5 / 5. ***Center:*** Alternating flower garlands and gridwork segments. ***Right:*** 5 / 5. ***Engraver:*** PSSP. ***Comments:*** H-MA-470-G32. 18__. 1820s.

Rarity: —

$5 • W-MA-1300-005-G110a

Engraver: PSSP. ***Comments:*** H-MA-470-G34. Similar to W-MA-1300-005-G110 but with zigzag ruled lines. 18__. 1820s–1830s.

Rarity: —

$5 • W-MA-1300-005-G110b

Engraver: PSSP. ***Comments:*** H-MA-470-G36. Similar to W-MA-1300-005-G110 but with spiral lathework lines. 18__. 1830s.

Rarity: —

$5 • W-MA-1300-005-G120

CJF

Overprint: Red bank title. ***Engraver:*** New England Bank Note Co. / PSSP. ***Comments:*** H-MA-470-G38a. 18__. 1830s–1850s.

Rarity: URS-4
VF $1,000

$5 • W-MA-1300-005-G130

CC

Overprint: Red-brown bank title, die outlining white V, and die outlining white 5. ***Engraver:*** Toppan, Carpenter & Co. / American Bank Note Co. ***Comments:*** H-MA-470-G40a. June 17, 1858.

Rarity: URS-4
VF $4,500

$5 • W-MA-1300-005-G130a

CJF

Overprint: Red-brown bank title, die outlining white V, die outlining white 5, and panel outlining white FIVE DOLLARS. ***Engraver:*** Toppan, Carpenter & Co. / American Bank Note Co. ***Comments:*** H-MA-470-G42a. Similar to W-MA-1300-005-G130 but with different female portrait and modified microlettering. June 17, 1858.

Rarity: URS-4
VF $3,000
Selected auction price: Heritage, January 2013, Lot 15819, VF $2,350

$10 • W-MA-1300-010-G140

Left: Lathework chain bearing MASSACHUSETTS / 10 / 10 vertically. ***Center:*** Alternating flower garlands and gridwork segments. ***Right:*** 10 / 10 vertically. ***Engraver:*** PSSP. ***Comments:*** H-MA-470-G44. 18__. 1820s.

Rarity: —

$10 • W-MA-1300-010-G140a

Engraver: PSSP. ***Comments:*** H-MA-470-G46. Similar to W-MA-1300-010-G140 but with zigzag ruled lines. 18__. 1820s–1830s.

Rarity: —

$10 • W-MA-1300-010-G140b

Engraver: PSSP. ***Comments:*** H-MA-470-G48. Similar to W-MA-1300-010-G140 but with spiral lathework lines. 18__. 1830s.

Rarity: —

Collectors and Researchers:

If you have new information about any banks or notes listed in this volume, contact Whitman Publishing, Attn: Obsolete Paper Money, 3101 Clairmont Road, Suite G, Atlanta, GA 30329.

$10 • W-MA-1300-010-G150

CJF

Overprint: Red bank title. ***Engraver:*** New England Bank Note Co. / PSSP. ***Comments:*** H-MA-470-G50a. 18__. 1830s–1850s.

Rarity: URS-3
VF $100; **Proof** $4,000

$10 • W-MA-1300-010-G160

Left: Female portrait / 10. ***Center:*** U.S. Capitol. ***Right:*** 10 / Woman seated. ***Tint:*** Red-brown bank name and 10. ***Engraver:*** Toppan, Carpenter & Co. / American Bank Note Co. ***Comments:*** H-MA-470-G52a. June 17, 1858.

Rarity: URS-3
VF $750

$20 • W-MA-1300-020-G170

Left: Lathework chain bearing MASSACHUSETTS / 20 / 20 vertically. ***Center:*** Alternating flower garlands and gridwork segments. ***Right:*** 20 / 20 vertically. ***Engraver:*** PSSP. ***Comments:*** H-MA-470-G54. 18__. 1820s–1830s.

Rarity: —

$20 • W-MA-1300-020-G180

JF

Overprint: Red bank title. ***Engraver:*** New England Bank Note Co. ***Comments:*** H-MA-470-G58. Remainder. 18__. 1840s–1850s.

Rarity: URS-2
Proof $2,500

$20 • W-MA-1300-020-G190

Left: 20 / Man with spyglass. ***Center:*** 20 / Man and woman flanking bust / 20. ***Right:*** 20 / Portrait of Thomas Jefferson. ***Tint:*** Red-brown 20 / 20. ***Engraver:*** Toppan, Carpenter & Co. ***Comments:*** H-MA-470-G60a. June 17, 1856.

Rarity: —

$20 • W-MA-1300-020-G190a

Tint: Red-brown 20 / 20. ***Engraver:*** Toppan, Carpenter & Co. / ABNCo. monogram. ***Comments:*** H-MA-470-G60b. Similar to W-MA-1300-020-G190 but with additional engraver imprint. June 17, 1856.

Rarity: URS-3
VF $750

$50 • W-MA-1300-050-G200

Left: Lathework chain bearing MASSACHUSETTS / 50 / 50 vertically. ***Center:*** Alternating flower garlands and gridwork segments ***Right:*** 50 / 50 vertically. ***Engraver:*** PSSP. ***Comments:*** H-MA-470-G62. 18__. 1820s–1830s.

Rarity: —

$50 • W-MA-1300-050-G210

Left: FIFTY / Woman standing with wreath and flowers / FIFTY. ***Center:*** 50 / Man restraining prancing horse / 50. ***Right:*** FIFTY / Woman standing with cornucopia / FIFTY. ***Engraver:*** New England Bank Note Co. ***Comments:*** H-MA-470-G66. Beware of altered notes from the same plate as the genuine. 18__. 1840s–1850s.

Rarity: —

$50 • W-MA-1300-050-G220

Left: 50 / Female portrait. ***Center:*** Old man with musket, Woman loading musket. ***Right:*** 50 / Portrait of John Quincy Adams. ***Tint:*** Red-brown. ***Engraver:*** Toppan, Carpenter & Co. ***Comments:*** H-MA-470-G68a. June 17, 1856.

Rarity: —

$50 • W-MA-1300-050-G220a

Tint: Red-brown. ***Engraver:*** Toppan, Carpenter & Co. / ABNCo. monogram. ***Comments:*** H-MA-470-G68b. Similar to W-MA-1300-050-G220 but with additional engraver imprint. June 17, 1856.

Rarity: —

$100 • W-MA-1300-100-G230

Left: Lathework chain bearing MASSACHUSETTS / 100 / 100 vertically. ***Center:*** Alternating flower garlands and gridwork segments. ***Right:*** 100 / 100 vertically. ***Engraver:*** Perkins. ***Comments:*** H-MA-470-G70. 18__. 1820s–1830s.

Rarity: —

$100 • W-MA-1300-100-G240

Left: ONE HUNDRED on 100 / Portrait of William Henry Harrison. ***Center:*** Wharf scene, Men loading wagon with barrels. ***Right:*** ONE HUNDRED on 100 / Portrait of Christopher Columbus. ***Engraver:*** New England Bank Note Co. ***Comments:*** H-MA-470-G74. 18__. 1840s–1850s.

Rarity: —

$100 • W-MA-1300-100-G250

Left: C / Portrait of boy. ***Center:*** C, Angel blowing trumpet, Globe and eagle. ***Right:*** 100 / Indian in shield. ***Tint:*** Red-brown bank title and C. ***Engraver:*** Toppan, Carpenter & Co. ***Comments:*** H-MA-470-G76a. June 17, 1856.

Rarity: URS-3
VF $750

$100 • W-MA-1300-100-G250a

Tint: Red-brown bank title and C. ***Engraver:*** Toppan, Carpenter & Co. / ABNCo. monogram. ***Comments:*** H-MA-470-G76b. Similar to W-MA-1300-100-G250 but with additional engraver imprint. June 17, 1856.

Rarity: —

$500 • W-MA-1300-500-G260

Left: D / Soldier with drum. ***Center:*** "Landing of the Pilgrims". ***Right:*** 500 / Female portrait. ***Tint:*** Red-brown. ***Engraver:*** Toppan, Carpenter & Co. ***Comments:*** H-MA-470-G80a. June 17, 1856.

Rarity: —

$500 • W-MA-1300-500-G270

Left: D / Portrait of George Washington. ***Center:*** Marine view. ***Bottom center:*** 500. ***Right:*** 500 / Portrait of Benjamin Franklin. ***Tint:*** Red-brown. ***Engraver:*** Toppan, Carpenter & Co. ***Comments:*** H-MA-470-G84a. June 17, 1856.

Rarity: —

$1,000 • W-MA-1300-1000-G280

JF

Overprint: Red-brown bank title. ***Engraver:*** New England Bank Note Co. ***Comments:*** H-Unlisted. Remainder. 18__.

Rarity: URS-1
Proof $7,500

Uncut Sheets

$1-$2-$3 • W-MA-1300-001.002.003-US010

Vignette(s): ***($1)*** "Presentation of the Declaration of Independence" / Woman with calf. ***($2)*** Indian and sailor flanking shield bearing 2 surmounted by eagle / Woman with pedestal / Portrait of girl. ***($3)*** Launch of the Adriatic / Eagle and shield. ***Comments:*** All unlisted in Haxby. Similar to H-MA-470-G10a, G20a, G30. Partially completed Proof. June 17, 1858.

Rarity: —
Selected auction price: Heritage, April 2012, Lot 15241, AU $920

Non-Valid Issues

$3 • W-MA-1300-003-R010

Engraver: New England Bank Note Co. / PSSP. ***Comments:*** H-MA-470-R5. Raised from W-MA-1300-001-G020a. 18__. 1840s.

Rarity: —

$3 • W-MA-1300-003-R020

Engraver: Toppan, Carpenter & Co. / American Bank Note Co. ***Comments:*** H-MA-470-R10. Raised from W-MA-1300-001-G030. June 17, 1858.

Rarity: —

$10 • W-MA-1300-010-R030

Engraver: Toppan, Carpenter & Co. / American Bank Note Co. ***Comments:*** H-MA-470-R15. Raised from W-MA-1300-001-G030. June 17, 1858.

Rarity: —

$10 • W-MA-1300-010-R040

Engraver: Toppan, Carpenter & Co. / American Bank Note Co. ***Comments:*** H-MA-470-R20. Raised from W-MA-1300-001-G030. June 17, 1858.

Rarity: —

$50 • W-MA-1300-050-A010

Left: FIFTY / Woman standing with wreath and flowers / FIFTY. ***Center:*** 50 / Man restraining prancing horse / 50. ***Right:*** FIFTY / Woman standing with cornucopia / FIFTY. ***Engraver:*** New England Bank Note Co. ***Comments:*** H-MA-470-A10. Altered from unknown source. Genuine notes of this design were issued. 18__. 1840s–1850s.

Rarity: —

Charlestown Bank

1832–1850

W-MA-1310

History: The Charlestown Bank was chartered on March 13, 1832, with an authorized capital of $150,000. The original founders of the Charlestown Bank were Hamilton Davidson, John M. Fiske, Abijah Goodridge, Paul Willard, Nathan Lynde, Arthur W. Austin, John Cheever, Samuel Poor, and Edward Hearsey. Edward D. Clark was president and Paul Willard cashier in 1835.

The capital of the bank was $150,000 in 1838. Its circulation was $27,120 in 1839. In 1850 it surrendered its charter, and its remaining notes were redeemed by the Suffolk Bank.

Numismatic Commentary: All issues of the Charlestown Bank are especially hard to locate. Of these, at least one issue has perhaps the most historical vignette on any obsolete bank note. On this note collectors will find a panoramic view of the Battle of Bunker Hill, also known as Breed's Hill, as seen from the British position on the battlefield. Collectors may observe the columns of British soldiers marching to the right in an effort to engage General Putnam's Colonials along the Mystic River's edge. Other troops can be seen attacking the trench line at the top of the hill, and in the background, the fires and smoke from the burning of Charlestown can plainly be seen.

Valid Issues

$1 • W-MA-1310-001-G010

Left: Lathework panel bearing MASSACHUSETTS vertically. ***Center:*** 1 / 1 / Alternating flower garlands and gridwork segments / ONE / 1 / 1. ***Right:*** Lathework panel bearing ONE / D / ONE vertically. ***Engraver:*** PSSP. ***Comments:*** H-MA-473-G2. 18__. 1830s.

Rarity: —

$1 • W-MA-1310-001-G020

Engraver: Unverified, but likely New England Bank Note Co. ***Comments:*** H-MA-473-G4. No description available. 18__. 1830s–1840s.

Rarity: *None known*

$2 • W-MA-1310-002-G030

Left: Lathework panel bearing five TWOs vertically. ***Center:*** 2 / 2 / Alternating flower garlands and gridwork segments / TWO / 2 / 2. ***Right:*** Lathework panel bearing five TWOs vertically. ***Engraver:*** PSSP. ***Comments:*** H-MA-473-G8. 18__. 1830s.

Rarity: —

$2 • W-MA-1310-002-G040

Engraver: Unverified, but likely New England Bank Note Co. ***Comments:*** H-MA-473-G10. No description available. 18__. 1830s–1840s.

Rarity: *None known*

$3 • W-MA-1310-003-G050

MHS

Engraver: PSSP / New England Bank Note Co. ***Comments:*** H-Unlisted. 18__. 1830s.[80] Courtesy of the Massachusetts Historical Society.

Rarity: URS-1

$3 • W-MA-1310-003-G060

Left: Lathework panel bearing MASSACHUSETTS vertically. ***Center:*** 3 / 3 / Alternating flower garlands and gridwork segments / THREE / 3 / 3. ***Right:*** Lathework panel bearing THREE vertically. ***Engraver:*** PSSP. ***Comments:*** H-MA-473-G14. 18__. 1830s.

Rarity: —

$3 • W-MA-1310-003-G070

Engraver: Unverified, but likely New England Bank Note Co. ***Comments:*** H-MA-473-G16. 18__. 1830s–1840s.

Rarity: URS-1
VF $5,000

$5 • W-MA-1310-005-G080

Left: Lathework chain bearing MASSACHUSETTS / 5 / 5. ***Center:*** Alternating flower garlands and gridwork segments / FIVE. ***Right:*** 5 / 5. ***Engraver:*** PSSP. ***Comments:*** H-MA-473-G20. 18__. 1830s.

Rarity: —

$5 • W-MA-1310-005-G090

Engraver: Unverified, but likely New England Bank Note Co. ***Comments:*** H-MA-473-G22. No description available. 18__. 1830s–1840s.

Rarity: *None known*

$10 • W-MA-1310-010-G100

Left: Lathework chain bearing MASSACHUSETTS / 10 / 10. ***Center:*** Alternating flower garlands and gridwork segments / TEN. ***Right:*** 10 / 10. ***Engraver:*** PSSP. ***Comments:*** H-MA-473-G26. 18__. 1830s.

Rarity: —

$10 • W-MA-1310-010-G110

Engraver: Unverified, but likely New England Bank Note Co. ***Comments:*** H-MA-473-G28. No description available. 18__. 1830s–1840s.

Rarity: *None known*

$20 • W-MA-1310-020-G120

Engraver: Unverified, but likely New England Bank Note Co. ***Comments:*** H-MA-473-G32. No description available. 18__. 1830s–1840s.

Rarity: *None known*

$50 • W-MA-1310-050-G130

Engraver: Unverified, but likely New England Bank Note Co. ***Comments:*** H-MA-473-G36. No description available. 18__. 1830s–1840s.

Rarity: *None known*

$100 • W-MA-1310-100-G140

Engraver: Unverified, but likely New England Bank Note Co. ***Comments:*** H-MA-473-G40. No description available. 18__. 1830s–1840s.

Rarity: *None known*

$500 • W-MA-1310-500-G150

Engraver: Unverified, but likely New England Bank Note Co. ***Comments:*** H-MA-473-G42. No description available. 18__. 1830s–1840s.

Rarity: *None known*

Non-Valid Issues

$3 • W-MA-1310-003-S010

Left: 3 / Cattle and drover / 3. ***Center:*** Train, Eagle with arrows in talons, House and trees. ***Right:*** 3 / Ceres seated / 3. ***Engraver:*** Terry, Pelton & Co. ***Comments:*** H-MA-473-S5. 18__. 1840s.

Rarity: —

Monument Bank

1855–1865

W-MA-1320

History: The Monument Bank was chartered on March 28, 1854, with an authorized capital of $150,000.

Selected figures for 1857 included: bills of this bank and other New England states $4,825; specie $13,429.88; real estate $7,500. A report in 1860 stated that bills in circulation of $5 and more in value totaled $102,035, and bills of denominations lower than $5 totaled $33,811. In 1861 total circulation was $130,963, and in 1863 it was $148,514.

The business of the Monument Bank was succeeded by the Monument National Bank of Charlestown, chartered on April 12, 1865.

Numismatic Commentary: Many of the issues from this bank will have a vignette of "Death of General Warren at the Battle of Bunker Hill." Many others will show the Bunker Hill Monument. These notes are historical in nature and are in demand by most collectors.

Valid Issues

$1 • W-MA-1320-001-G010

CJF

Engraver: Toppan, Carpenter & Co. ***Comments:*** H-Unlisted. Proof. March 12, 1855.

Rarity: URS-1
Proof $3,200

$1 • W-MA-1320-001-G010a

Left: 1 / Drummer boy and two soldiers. ***Center:*** Death of General Joseph Warren at Battle of Bunker Hill. ***Right:*** 1 / Bunker Hill Monument. ***Overprint:*** Red. ***Engraver:*** Toppan, Carpenter & Co. ***Comments:*** H-MA-475-G2a. Similar to W-MA-1320-001-G010. 1850s.

Rarity: —

$1 • W-MA-1320-001-G010b

CJF

Overprint: Red panel outlining white ONE. ***Engraver:*** American Bank Note Co. ***Comments:*** H-MA-475-G2d. Similar to W-MA-1320-001-G010. March 12, 186_. 1860s.

Rarity: URS-2
F $1,500; **VF** $5,000; **AU** $3,500

$2 • W-MA-1320-002-G020

Left: 2 / Portrait of General Joseph Warren. ***Center:*** Death of General Joseph Warren at Battle of Bunker Hill. ***Right:*** TWO / Bunker Hill Monument. ***Engraver:*** American Bank Note Co. ***Comments:*** H-Unlisted.

Rarity: URS-1
Proof $5,000

$2 • W-MA-1320-002-G020a

Overprint: Red. ***Engraver:*** Toppan, Carpenter & Co. ***Comments:*** H-MA-475-G4a. Similar to W-MA-1320-002-G020 but with different engraver imprint. 1850s.

Rarity: —

$2 • W-MA-1320-002-G020b

Overprint: Red panel outlining white TWO. ***Comments:*** H-MA-475-G4d. Similar to W-MA-1320-002-G020. 1860s.

Rarity: —

$3 • W-MA-1320-003-G030

Left: THREE / Bunker Hill Monument. ***Center:*** 3 / Death of General Joseph Warren at Battle of Bunker Hill. ***Right:*** 3. ***Overprint:*** Red. ***Engraver:*** Toppan, Carpenter & Co. ***Comments:*** H-MA-475-G6a. 1850s.

Rarity: —

$3 • W-MA-1320-003-G030a

Overprint: Red panel outlining white THREE. ***Comments:*** H-MA-475-G6d. Similar to W-MA-1320-003-G030. 1860s.

Rarity: —

$5 • **W-MA-1320-005-G040**

QDB

Engraver: Toppan, Carpenter & Co. ***Comments:*** H-Unlisted. Proof. 185_. 1850s.

Rarity: URS-3
Proof $3,500

$5 • **W-MA-1320-005-G040a**

Left: 5 / 5. ***Center:*** Death of General Joseph Warren at Battle of Bunker Hill. ***Right:*** 5 / Bunker Hill Monument. ***Overprint:*** Red. ***Engraver:*** Toppan, Carpenter & Co. ***Comments:*** H-MA-475-G8a. Similar to W-MA-1320-005-G040. 1850s.

Rarity: URS-3
Proof $1,750

$5 • **W-MA-1320-005-G040b**

Overprint: Red panel outlining white FIVE. ***Comments:*** H-MA-475-G8d. Similar to W-MA-1320-005-G040. 1860s.

Rarity: —

$10 • **W-MA-1320-010-G050**

Left: 10 / Men mining. ***Center:*** X / Portrait of George Washington / X. ***Right:*** TEN / Bunker Hill Monument. ***Overprint:*** Red X X. ***Engraver:*** Toppan, Carpenter & Co. ***Comments:*** H-MA-475-G10a. 1850s.

Rarity: —

$10 • **W-MA-1320-010-G050a**

JF

Overprint: Red X / X. ***Engraver:*** Toppan, Carpenter & Co. / ABNCo. monogram. ***Comments:*** H-MA-475-G10c. Similar to W-MA-1320-010-G050 but with additional engraver imprint. March 12, 1857.

Rarity: URS-2
VF $2,500

$50 • **W-MA-1320-050-G060**

Left: L / Bunker Hill Monument / FIFTY. ***Center:*** 50 / Surrender of Cornwallis at Yorktown. ***Right:*** 50. ***Engraver:*** Toppan, Carpenter & Co. ***Comments:*** H-MA-475-G12. 1850s.

Rarity: —

$100 • **W-MA-1320-100-G070**

Left: C / Bunker Hill Monument. ***Center:*** Eagle on shield / View of Charlestown and Bunker Hill Monument / Schooners / Train. ***Right:*** 100 / Portrait of Daniel Webster. ***Engraver:*** Toppan, Carpenter & Co. ***Comments:*** H-MA-475-G14. 1850s.

Rarity: —

$500 • **W-MA-1320-500-G080**

Left: FIVE HUNDRED vertically. ***Center:*** Woman / Two angels and cherub scattering gold coin on city. ***Right:*** 500 / Bunker Hill Monument. ***Engraver:*** Toppan, Carpenter & Co. ***Comments:*** H-MA-475-G16. 1850s.

Rarity: —

Non-Valid Issues

$5 • **W-MA-1320-005-R010**

Comments: H-MA-475-R5. Raised from W-MA-1320-001-G010 series. 1850s–1860s.

Rarity: —

$20 • **W-MA-1320-020-R020**

Engraver: Toppan, Carpenter & Co. ***Comments:*** H-MA-475-R10. Raised from W-MA-1320-002-G020 series. The bank issued no $20 notes. 1850s.

Rarity: —

Phoenix Bank

1832–1842

W-MA-1330

History: The Phoenix Bank was chartered on March 13, 1832, with an authorized capital of $150,000. In 1833 Mr. Delafield was the president. In 1836 the bank's capital had increased to $300,000. In 1837, the year of the panic, it was reduced to $150,000. By 1839 it was back up to $300,000. Circulation was $102,344 in 1836 and $84,266 in 1839.

In an examination of December 1841, the investigating commissioner was deceived and his examination proved unsuccessful in discovering a fraud which had destroyed nearly the entire capital of the bank. The peculation was discovered later in the year and proved to be the doing of bank president William Wyman, who was also the primary manager of the bank's assets. His good nature and seeming high level of integrity made his deception foolproof until the end. An injunction was applied at the discovery of this fraud, and on October 18 it was made permanent. Receivers were appointed and the affairs of the bank were shut down.[81] The bank's notes became worthless.

There was a bank of similar name but a different time and unrelated charter in Nantucket, W-MA-2320.

Numismatic Commentary: Notes from this bank are available in the marketplace, but VF or better specimens are very hard to find. Most will carry a view of the Boston Harbor.

Valid Issues

$1 • **W-MA-1330-001-G010**

Left: Lathework panel bearing MASSACHUSETTS vertically. ***Center:*** 1 / 1 / Alternating flower garlands and gridwork segments / ONE / 1 / 1. ***Right:*** Lathework panel bearing ONE / D / ONE vertically. ***Engraver:*** PSSP. ***Comments:*** H-MA-480-G2. 18__. 1830s.

Rarity: —

$1 • **W-MA-1330-001-G020**

CJF

Engraver: New England Bank Note Co. ***Comments:*** H-MA-480-G4. 18__. 1830s.

Rarity: URS-8
VG $75

$2 • **W-MA-1330-002-G030**

Left: Lathework panel bearing MASSACHUSETTS vertically. ***Center:*** 2 / 2 / Alternating flower garlands and gridwork segments / TWO / 2 / 2. ***Right:*** Lathework panel bearing five TWOs vertically. ***Engraver:*** PSSP. ***Comments:*** H-MA-480-G6. 18__. 1830s.

Rarity: —

$2 • **W-MA-1330-002-G040**

CC

Engraver: New England Bank Note Co. ***Comments:*** H-MA-480-G8. 18__. 1830s.

Rarity: URS-6
VG $175

$3 • **W-MA-1330-003-G050**

Left: Lathework panel bearing MASSACHUSETTS vertically. ***Center:*** 3 / 3 / Alternating flower garlands and gridwork segments / THREE / 3 / 3. ***Right:*** Lathework panel bearing THREE vertically. ***Engraver:*** PSSP. ***Comments:*** H-MA-480-G10. 18__. 1830s.

Rarity: —
VG $70

$3 • **W-MA-1330-003-G060**

CJF

Engraver: New England Bank Note Co. ***Comments:*** H-MA-480-G12. 18__. 1830s.

Rarity: URS-6
VG $125; **F** $175

$5 • **W-MA-1330-005-G070**

Left: Lathework chain bearing MASSACHUSETTS / 5 / 5. ***Center:*** Alternating flower garlands and gridwork segments / FIVE. ***Right:*** 5 / 5. ***Engraver:*** PSSP. ***Comments:*** H-MA-480-G14. 18__. 1830s.

Rarity: —

$5 • **W-MA-1330-005-G080**

CJF

Engraver: New England Bank Note Co. ***Comments:*** H-MA-480-G16. 18__. 1830s.

Rarity: URS-6
VG $150; **VF** $200

$10 • **W-MA-1330-010-G090**

Left: Lathework chain bearing MASSACHUSETTS / 10 / 10 vertically. ***Center:*** Alternating flower garlands and gridwork segments / TEN. ***Right:*** 10 / 10 vertically. ***Engraver:*** PSSP. ***Comments:*** H-MA-480-G18. 18__. 1830s.

Rarity: —

How to Read the Whitman Numbering System

$1 • **W-MA-010-001-G010a**

Denomination: Value of the note shown.

W: Whitman number. This number is a sortable code unique to each bank and note.

MA: Abbreviation for the state under study.

010: Numerical designation specific to each bank.

001: The denomination in dollars.

G010a: G indicates a good or valid note. Other categories are indicated thus: C (counterfeit); R (raised); S (spurious); N (not-attributed); A (altered). Numbers are assigned starting with 010, 020, et seq. Terminal letters following the number indicate variations of a note: a series of different colored overprints, tints, payees, etc., all on the same design of note. For more information, see the "How to Use This Book" section at the front of the volume, page xiv.

$10 • W-MA-1330-010-G100

CC

Engraver: New England Bank Note Co. ***Comments:*** H-MA-480-G20. 18__. 1830s.

Rarity: URS-6
VG $125; **F** $200

$20 • W-MA-1330-020-G110

Left: Lathework chain bearing MASSACHUSETTS / 20 / 20 vertically. ***Center:*** Alternating flower garlands and gridwork segments / TWENTY. ***Right:*** 20 / 20 vertically. ***Engraver:*** PSSP. ***Comments:*** H-MA-480-G22. 18__. 1830s.

Rarity: —

$20 • W-MA-1330-020-G120

SI

Engraver: New England Bank Note Co. ***Comments:*** H-Unlisted. 18__. 1830s.

Rarity: —

$20 • W-MA-1330-020-G130

Engraver: Unverified, but likely New England Bank Note Co. / PSSP. ***Comments:*** H-MA-480-G24. No description available. 18__. 1830s.

Rarity: *None known*

$50 • W-MA-1330-050-G140

Left: Lathework chain bearing MASSACHUSETTS / 50 / 50 vertically. ***Center:*** Alternating flower garlands and gridwork segments / FIFTY. ***Right:*** 50 / 50 vertically. ***Engraver:*** PSSP. ***Comments:*** H-MA-480-G26. 18__. 1830s.

Rarity: —

$50 • W-MA-1330-050-G150

Engraver: Unverified, but likely New England Bank Note Co. / PSSP. ***Comments:*** H-MA-480-G28. No description available. 18__. 1830s.

Rarity: *None known*

$100 • W-MA-1330-100-G160

Left: Lathework chain bearing MASSACHUSETTS / 100 vertically. ***Center:*** Alternating flower garlands and gridwork segments / HUNDRED. ***Right:*** 100 / 100 vertically. ***Engraver:*** PSSP. ***Comments:*** H-MA-480-G30. 18__. 1830s.

Rarity: —

$100 • W-MA-1330-100-G170

Engraver: Unverified, but likely New England Bank Note Co. / PSSP. ***Comments:*** H-MA-480-G32. No description available. 18__. 1830s.

Rarity: *None known*

$500 • W-MA-1330-500-G180

Engraver: Unverified, but likely New England Bank Note Co. / PSSP. ***Comments:*** H-MA-480-G36. 18__. 1830s.

Rarity: URS-5
VG $500; **VF** $1,000

$500 • W-MA-1330-500-G190

CC

Engraver: PSSP. ***Comments:*** H-Unlisted. 18__. 1840s.

Rarity: URS-4
VG $500; **F** $850; **VF** $1,000

Chelsea, Massachusetts

Located across the Mystic River from Boston, Chelsea was originally known as Winnisimmet, which means "good spring nearby" in the native tongue of the tribe that once lived there. Settled by Samuel Maverick in 1624, the land was sold to Richard Bellingham in 1635. It was incorporated and separated from Boston in 1739 when it was named Chelsea after a neighborhood in London.

The second battle of the Revolutionary War, the Battle of Chelsea Creek, was fought in 1775 and witnessed the first capture of a British ship by American revolutionaries. The area of Chelsea once included Revere, Winthrop, Saugus, and North Chelsea, which separated in 1846. It was reincorporated as a city in 1857 and became an industrial center for the production of rubber, elastic, boots, shoes, stoves, and adhesives.

Chelsea Bank

1836 and 1837

W-MA-1340

History: The Chelsea Bank was incorporated on April 16, 1836, with an authorized capital of $100,000. The officers were fraudsters and circulated notes far in excess of legal limits. A committee investigated the bank in 1837 and shut it down.

Numismatic Commentary: These notes can be found in limited quantities in the marketplace.

Valid Issues

$1 • W-MA-1340-001-G010

CJF

Engraver: PSSP / New England Bank Note Co. ***Comments:*** H-MA-485-G2. 18__. 1836 and 1837.

Rarity: URS-7
VG $100; **F** $140; **VF** $175

$2 • W-MA-1340-002-G020

Left: 2 / Woman standing with staff / TWO. ***Center:*** TWO / Machinery and merchandise flanking Ceres seated holding sickle and rake, Factories and harbor / TWO. ***Right:*** 2 / Woman / TWO. ***Engraver:*** PSSP / New England Bank Note Co. ***Comments:*** H-MA-485-G4. 18__. 1836.

Rarity: URS-8
F $150

$3 • W-MA-1340-003-G030

Engraver: Unverified, but likely PSSP / New England Bank Note Co. ***Comments:*** H-MA-485-G6. 18__. 1836.

Rarity: URS-8
F $200

$3 • W-MA-1340-003-G040

CJF

Engraver: PSSP / New England Bank Note Co. ***Comments:*** H-Unlisted. 18__. 1830s.

Rarity: URS-5
F $200; **VF** $300

$5 • W-MA-1340-005-G050

Engraver: Unverified, but likely New England Bank Note Co. ***Comments:*** H-MA-485-G8. No description available. 18__. 1836.

Rarity: *None known*

$10 • W-MA-1340-010-G060

Engraver: Unverified, but likely New England Bank Note Co. ***Comments:*** H-MA-485-G10. No description available. 18__. 1836.

Rarity: *None known*

$20 • W-MA-1340-020-G070

Engraver: Unverified, but likely New England Bank Note Co. ***Comments:*** H-MA-485-G12. No description available. 18__. 1836.

Rarity: *None known*

$50 • W-MA-1340-050-G080

Engraver: Unverified, but likely New England Bank Note Co. ***Comments:*** H-MA-485-G14. No description available. 18__. 1836.

Rarity: *None known*

$100 • W-MA-1340-100-G090

Engraver: Unverified, but likely New England Bank Note Co. ***Comments:*** H-MA-485-G16. No description available. 18__. 1836.

Rarity: *None known*

$500 • W-MA-1340-500-G100

Engraver: Unverified, but likely New England Bank Note Co. ***Comments:*** H-MA-485-G18. No description available. 18__. 1836.

Rarity: *None known*

$1,000 • W-MA-1340-1000-G110

Engraver: Unverified, but likely New England Bank Note Co. ***Comments:*** H-MA-485-G20. No description available. 18__. 1836.

Rarity: *None known*

Tradesmans Bank

1850–1864

W-MA-1350

History: The Tradesmans Bank was incorporated in 1850 with an authorized capital of $150,000. In 1851 it had an incompletely paid-in capital of $72,750, a circulation of $78,879, and specie amounting to $1,647.32. By the end of that year its capital had nearly doubled to $150,000, where it remained for the duration of the bank's existence. Its specie also increased by more than twice its original amount, and circulation was at $133,032. In 1863 circulation was up to $164,020.

Selected figures for 1857 included: bills of this bank and other New England states $9,060.63; specie $9,966.95.

The business of the Tradesmans Bank was succeeded by the First National Bank of Chelsea, chartered on October 14, 1864.

Numismatic Commentary: Notes from this bank will be hard to find. Many will show a view of the harbor with a ferry slip as seen from the confluence of the Mystic River and Chelsea Creek.

Valid Issues

$1 • W-MA-1350-001-G010

Left: Woman holding 1 / ONE. ***Center:*** View of Chelsea and harbor / ONE. ***Right:*** 1 / State arms. ***Engraver:*** Rawdon, Wright, Hatch & Edson / New England Bank Note Co. ***Comments:*** H-MA-490-G2. Sept. 2, 185_. 1850s.

Rarity: URS-4
VF $450

$1 • W-MA-1350-001-G010a

CJF

Overprint: Red ONE. ***Engraver:*** Rawdon, Wright, Hatch & Edson / New England Bank Note Co. ***Comments:*** H-MA-490-G2a. Similar to W-MA-1350-001-G010. Sept. 2, 185_. 1850s.

Rarity: URS-4
F $500; **VF** $750

$1 • W-MA-1350-001-G010b

Overprint: Red ONE. ***Engraver:*** Rawdon, Wright, Hatch & Edson / New England Bank Note Co. / ABNCo. monogram. ***Comments:*** H-MA-490-G2b. Similar to W-MA-1350-001-G010 but with additional engraver imprint. Sept. 2, 185_. 1850s.

Rarity: —

$2 • W-MA-1350-002-G020

CC

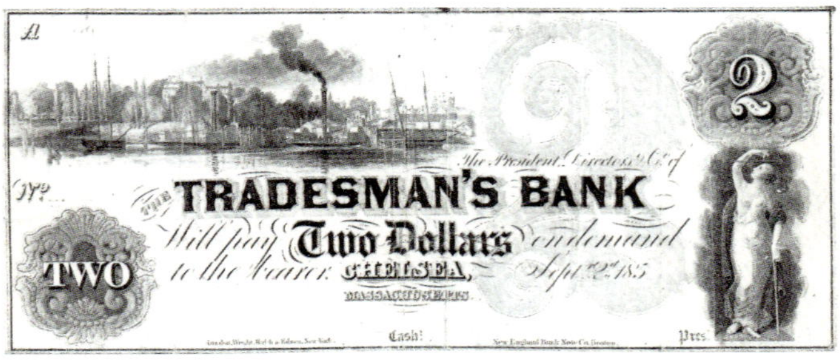

Engraver: Rawdon, Wright, Hatch & Edson / New England Bank Note Co. ***Comments:*** H-MA-490-G4. Sept. 2, 185_. 1850s.

Rarity: URS-4
VF $500

$2 • W-MA-1350-002-G020a

Left: View of Chelsea and harbor / TWO over 2. ***Center:*** 2. ***Right:*** 2 / Woman standing. ***Overprint:*** Red TWO. ***Engraver:*** Rawdon, Wright, Hatch & Edson / New England Bank Note Co. ***Comments:*** H-MA-490-G4a. Similar to W-MA-1350-002-G020. Sept. 2, 185_. 1850s.

Rarity: —

$2 • W-MA-1350-002-G020b

Overprint: Red TWO. ***Engraver:*** Rawdon, Wright, Hatch & Edson / New England Bank Note Co. / ABNCo. monogram. ***Comments:*** H-MA-490-G4b. Similar to W-MA-1350-002-G020 but with additional engraver imprint. Sept. 2, 185_. 1850s.

Rarity: URS-4
F $600; **VF** $800

$3 • W-MA-1350-003-G030

Left: View of Chelsea and harbor / THREE. ***Center:*** 3. ***Right:*** 3 / Blacksmith and anvil. ***Engraver:*** Rawdon, Wright, Hatch & Edson / New England Bank Note Co. ***Comments:*** H-MA-490-G6. Sept. 2, 185_. 1850s.

Rarity: —

$3 • W-MA-1350-003-G030a

Overprint: Red THREE. ***Engraver:*** Rawdon, Wright, Hatch & Edson / New England Bank Note Co. ***Comments:*** H-MA-490-G6a. Similar to W-MA-1350-003-G030. Sept. 2, 185_. 1850s.

Rarity: —

$3 • W-MA-1350-003-G030b

CJF

Overprint: Red THREE. ***Engraver:*** Rawdon, Wright, Hatch & Edson / New England Bank Note Co. / ABNCo. monogram. ***Comments:*** H-MA-490-G6b. Similar to W-MA-1350-003-G030 but with additional engraver imprint. Sept. 2, 185_. 1850s.

Rarity: URS-3
VF $1,000

$5 • W-MA-1350-005-G040

JF

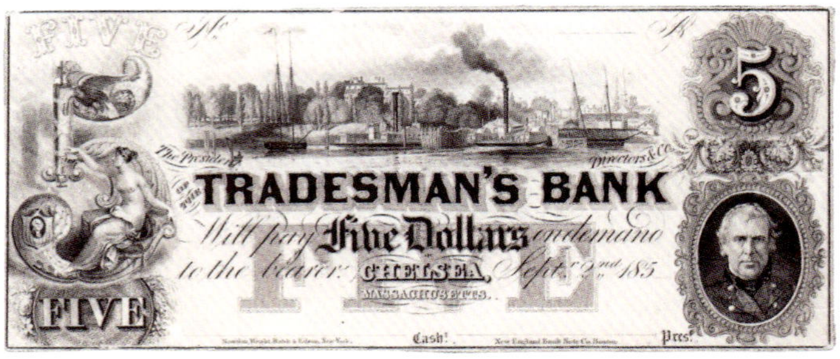

Engraver: Rawdon, Wright, Hatch & Edson / New England Bank Note Co. ***Comments:*** H-MA-490-G8. Sept. 2, 185_. 1850s.

Rarity: URS-2
Proof $1,000

$5 • W-MA-1350-005-G040a

Left: FIVE / Woman seated in 5 / FIVE. ***Center:*** View of Chelsea and harbor / FIVE. ***Right:*** 5 / Portrait of Zachary Taylor. ***Overprint:*** Red FIVE. ***Engraver:*** Rawdon, Wright, Hatch & Edson / New England Bank Note Co. ***Comments:*** H-MA-490-G8a. Similar to W-MA-1350-005-G040. Sept. 2, 185_. 1850s.

Rarity: —

$5 • W-MA-1350-005-G040b

Overprint: Red FIVE. ***Engraver:*** Rawdon, Wright, Hatch & Edson / New England Bank Note Co. / ABNCo. monogram. ***Comments:*** H-MA-490-G8b. Similar to W-MA-1350-005-G040 but with additional engraver imprint. Sept. 2, 185_. 1850s.

Rarity: —

$10 • W-MA-1350-010-G050

Left: View of Chelsea and harbor / TEN. ***Center:*** Medallion X / TEN. ***Right:*** 10 / Woman standing with cornucopia and anchor. ***Engraver:*** Rawdon, Wright, Hatch & Edson / New England Bank Note Co. ***Comments:*** H-MA-490-G10. Sept. 2, 185_. 1850s.

Rarity: —

$10 • W-MA-1350-010-G050a

CJF

Overprint: Red TEN. ***Engraver:*** Rawdon, Wright, Hatch & Edson / New England Bank Note Co. ***Comments:*** H-MA-490-G10a. Similar to W-MA-1350-010-G050. Sept. 2, 185_. 1850s.

Rarity: URS-3
VF $750

$10 • W-MA-1350-010-G050b

Overprint: Red TEN. ***Engraver:*** Rawdon, Wright, Hatch & Edson / New England Bank Note Co. / ABNCo. monogram. ***Comments:*** H-MA-490-G10b. Similar to W-MA-1350-010-G050 but with additional engraver imprint. Sept. 2, 185_. 1850s.

Rarity: —

$20 • W-MA-1350-020-G060

Left: 20 / Indian woman with bow and arrows. ***Center:*** View of Chelsea and harbor. ***Bottom center:*** Machinery. ***Right:*** 20 / Woman seated with 2 and 0. ***Engraver:*** Rawdon, Wright, Hatch & Edson / New England Bank Note Co. ***Comments:*** H-MA-490-G12. Sept. 2, 185_. 1850s.

Rarity: —

$20 • W-MA-1350-020-G060a

CJF

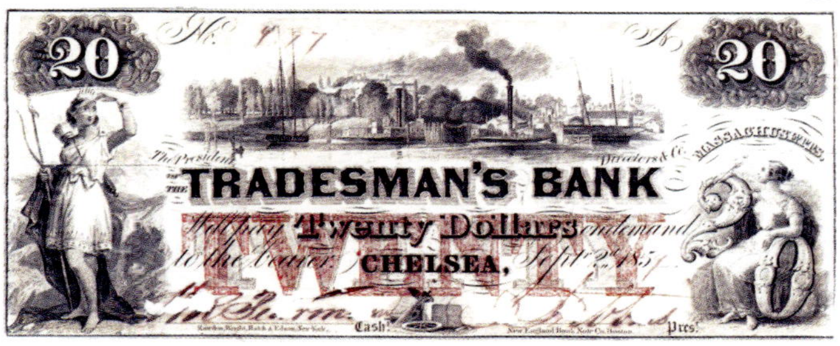

Overprint: Red TWENTY. ***Engraver:*** Rawdon, Wright, Hatch & Edson / New England Bank Note Co. ***Comments:*** H-MA-490-G12a. Similar to W-MA-1350-020-G060. Sept. 2, 185_. 1850s.

Rarity: URS-3
VF $1,250

$20 • W-MA-1350-020-G060b

Overprint: Red TWENTY. ***Engraver:*** Rawdon, Wright, Hatch & Edson / New England Bank Note Co. / ABNCo. monogram. ***Comments:*** H-MA-490-G12b. Similar to W-MA-1350-020-G060 but with additional engraver imprint. Sept. 2, 185_. 1850s–1860s.

Rarity: —

$50 • W-MA-1350-050-G070

Left: 50 / Woman standing. ***Center:*** View of Chelsea and harbor. ***Right:*** 50 / Woman with flag and three cherubs. ***Engraver:*** Rawdon, Wright, Hatch & Edson / New England Bank Note Co. ***Comments:*** H-MA-490-G14. Sept. 2, 18__. 1850s.

Rarity: —

$50 • W-MA-1350-050-G070a

Overprint: Red FIFTY. ***Engraver:*** Rawdon, Wright, Hatch & Edson / New England Bank Note Co. ***Comments:*** H-MA-490-G14a. Similar to W-MA-1350-050-G070. Sept. 2, 18__. 1850s.

Rarity: —

$50 • W-MA-1350-050-G070b

CJF

Tint: Red-brown. ***Engraver:*** Rawdon, Wright, Hatch & Edson / New England Bank Note Co. / ABNCo. monogram. ***Comments:*** H-MA-490-G14b. Similar to W-MA-1350-050-G070 but with additional engraver imprint. Sept. 2, 18__. 1850s–1860s.

Rarity: URS-3
VF $1,500

$100 • W-MA-1350-100-G080

Left: 100 / Sailor, Ship. ***Center:*** View of Chelsea and harbor / 100. ***Right:*** 100 / Stonecutter at work. ***Engraver:*** Rawdon, Wright, Hatch & Edson / New England Bank Note Co. ***Comments:*** H-MA-490-G16. Sept. 2, 18__. 1850s.

Rarity: —

$100 • W-MA-1350-100-G080a

CJF

Tint: Red-brown. ***Engraver:*** Rawdon, Wright, Hatch & Edson / New England Bank Note Co. / ABNCo. monogram. ***Comments:*** H-MA-490-G16b. Similar to W-MA-1350-100-G080 but with additional engraver imprint. Sept. 2, 18__. 1850s–1860s.

Rarity: URS-3
VF $1,500

$500 • W-MA-1350-500-G090

Left: 500 / Ship on stocks / 500. ***Center:*** View of Chelsea and harbor / 500. ***Bottom center:*** State arms. ***Right:*** 500 / Steamboat / 500. ***Engraver:*** Rawdon, Wright, Hatch & Edson / New England Bank Note Co. ***Comments:*** H-MA-490-G18. Sept. 2, 185_. 1850s.

Rarity: —

$500 • W-MA-1350-500-G090a

Tint: Red-brown. ***Engraver:*** Rawdon, Wright, Hatch & Edson / New England Bank Note Co. / ABNCo. monogram. ***Comments:*** H-MA-490-G18b. Similar to W-MA-1350-500-G090 but with additional engraver imprint. Sept. 2, 185_. 1850s–1860s.

Rarity: —

NON-VALID ISSUES

$3 • W-MA-1350-003-S010

CJF

Engraver: New England Bank Note Co. ***Comments:*** H-MA-490-S5. Sept. 2, 185_. 1850s.

Rarity: URS-7
VG $75; **F** $125; **VF** $175

$5 • W-MA-1350-005-R010

Engraver: Rawdon, Wright, Hatch & Edson / New England Bank Note Co. ***Comments:*** H-MA-490-R5. Raised from W-MA-1350-001-G010 or G010a. Sept. 2, 185_. 1850s.

Rarity: —

$5 • W-MA-1350-005-N010

CJF

Comments: H-MA-490-N5. 18__. 1850s.

Rarity: URS-7
VG $50

$5 • W-MA-1350-005-N020

Center: Woman and man seated, Gun, Animals. ***Right:*** Female portrait. ***Comments:*** H-MA-490-N10.

Rarity: —

$10 • W-MA-1350-010-R020

Engraver: Rawdon, Wright, Hatch & Edson / New England Bank Note Co. ***Comments:*** H-MA-490-R10. Raised from W-MA-1350-001-G010 or G010a. Sept. 2, 185_. 1850s.

Rarity: —

$10 • W-MA-1350-010-R030

Engraver: Rawdon, Wright, Hatch & Edson / New England Bank Note Co. ***Comments:*** H-MA-490-R15. Raised from W-MA-1350-002-G020 or G020a. Sept. 2, 185_. 1850s.

Rarity: —

$20 • W-MA-1350-020-R040

Engraver: Rawdon, Wright, Hatch & Edson / New England Bank Note Co. ***Comments:*** H-MA-490-R20. Raised from W-MA-1350-001-G010 or G010a. Sept. 2, 185_. 1850s.

Rarity: —

$100 • W-MA-1350-100-R050

Center: View of Chelsea and harbor. ***Engraver:*** Rawdon, Wright, Hatch & Edson / New England Bank Note Co. ***Comments:*** H-MA-490-R25. Raised from a note of unknown denomination. Sept. 2, 185_. 1850s.

Rarity: —

CHICOPEE, MASSACHUSETTS

Named after a waterway that empties into the Connecticut River, Chicopee was first settled in 1640. The name is of Cherokee origin and has a variety of possible meanings, including "violent," "water," "cedar," and "river of elms."

Chicopee was a part of Springfield until it became a separate town in 1848. It was granted a charter on April 18, 1890, when it became an official city (this being after the era studied here). Iron ore was mined and used to create hollow ironware such as pots and kettles. Paper, leather, matches, and shoes were also produced here. Brick-making is one of the oldest industries for the area. Cotton also was once a leading industry beginning in 1824, when yarn was sent out to be woven on household looms.

The Ames Manufacturing Company was founded in 1834 and provided many implements of war, including swords, bayonets, cannons, and projectiles. In contrast to this industry, horticulture came to Chicopee when Dexter Snow, the second florist in all of western Massachusetts, cultivated the Verbena in 1855.

Cabot Bank

1845–1865

W-MA-1360

History: The Cabot Bank was chartered on January 24, 1845, with an authorized capital of $150,000. Principals included N.P. Ames, John Chase, D.M. Bryant, and Robert Bemis. The president in 1847 was J. Chase, and G. Walker was cashier. In 1851 John Wells became president, and J.L. Warriner became cashier. Circulation in 1849 was $95,935. By 1863 it was $136,133.

On April 26, 1865, the First National Bank of Chicopee was chartered and succeeded the business of the Cabot Bank.

See also listings under Cabotville, W-MA-1180, and Springfield, W-MA-3110.

Numismatic Commentary: Collectors may be able to find notes similar in design but with the two different bank locations: one with the Cabotville town name and others with the Chicopee name. All are hard to locate.

VALID ISSUES

$1 • W-MA-1360-001-G010

Left: ONE / Man and boy driving sheep. ***Center:*** Men working in blacksmith's shop / 1. ***Right:*** 1 / Man with scythe. ***Overprint:*** Red ONE. ***Engraver:*** New England Bank Note Co. ***Comments:*** H-MA-425-G20a. Similar to 425-G2 but with different location. 18__. 1850s.

Rarity: URS-4
F $350

$1 • **W-MA-1360-001-G010a**

CC

Overprint: Red ONE. ***Engraver:*** New England Bank Note Co. / ABNCo. monogram. ***Comments:*** H-Unlisted. Similar to W-MA-1360-001-G010 but with different date and additional engraver imprint. Nov. 1, 18__. 1850s–1860s.

Rarity: URS-4
F $400

$1 • **W-MA-1360-001-G010b**

CJF

Overprint: Red ONE. ***Engraver:*** New England Bank Note Co. / ABNCo. monogram. ***Comments:*** H-MA-425-G20b. Similar to W-MA-1360-001-G010 but with different date and additional engraver imprint. Nov. 1, 18__. 1850s–1860s.

Rarity: URS-3
F $500; **VF** $750

$2 • **W-MA-1360-002-G020**

Left: Woman with sheaf leaning on 2. ***Center:*** 2 / Shepherd seated, Dog tending flock of sheep. ***Right:*** 2 / Beehive and flowers. ***Overprint:*** Red TWO. ***Engraver:*** New England Bank Note Co. ***Comments:*** H-MA-425-G22a. Similar to W-MA-1180-002-G020 but with different location. 18__. 1850s.

Rarity: —

$2 • **W-MA-1360-002-G020a**

Overprint: Red TWO. ***Engraver:*** New England Bank Note Co. / ABNCo. monogram. ***Comments:*** H-MA-425-G22b. Similar to W-MA-1360-002-G020 but with different date and additional engraver imprint. Nov. 1, 18__. 1850s–1860s.

Rarity: —

$3 • **W-MA-1360-003-G030**

Left: THREE / Man with sheaf and sickle. ***Center:*** Eagle on rock, Ship / 3. ***Right:*** 3 / State arms. ***Overprint:*** Red THREE. ***Engraver:*** New England Bank Note Co. ***Comments:*** H-MA-425-G24a. Similar to W-MA-1180-003-G030 but with different location. 18__. 1850s.

Rarity: —

$3 • **W-MA-1360-003-G030a**

Overprint: Red THREE. ***Engraver:*** New England Bank Note Co. / ABNCo. monogram. ***Comments:*** H-MA-425-G24b. Similar to W-MA-1360-003-G030 but with different date and additional engraver imprint. Nov. 1, 18__. 1850s–1860s.

Rarity: —

$5 • **W-MA-1360-005-G040**

Left: FIVE / 5. ***Center:*** Train / V. ***Right:*** FIVE / Blacksmith standing with hammer, 5 / FIVE. ***Overprint:*** Red. ***Engraver:*** New England Bank Note Co. ***Comments:*** H-MA-425-G26a. Similar to W-MA-1180-005-G040 but with different location. 18__. 1850s.

Rarity: —

$5 • **W-MA-1360-005-G040a**

Overprint: Red. ***Engraver:*** New England Bank Note Co. / ABNCo. monogram. ***Comments:*** H-MA-425-G26b. Similar to W-MA-1360-005-G040 but with different date and additional engraver imprint. Nov. 1, 18__. 1850s–1860s.

Rarity: —

$10 • **W-MA-1360-010-G050**

Left: Eagle on branch, Canal scene and train / 10. ***Center:*** X. ***Right:*** TEN / Train / TEN. ***Overprint:*** Red. ***Engraver:*** New England Bank Note Co. ***Comments:*** H-MA-425-G28a. Similar to W-MA-1180-010-G050 but with different location. 18__. 1850s.

Rarity: —

$10 • **W-MA-1360-010-G050a**

Overprint: Red. ***Engraver:*** New England Bank Note Co. / ABNCo. monogram. ***Comments:*** H-MA-425-G28b. Similar to W-MA-1360-010-G050 but with different date and additional engraver imprint. Nov. 1, 18__. 1850s–1860s.

Rarity: —

$20 • **W-MA-1360-020-G060**

Left: 20 / Woman seated with book on lap and opening chest. ***Center:*** XX / Eagle on rock / XX. ***Right:*** 20 / Ship in harbor. ***Overprint:*** Likely red. ***Engraver:*** New England Bank Note Co. ***Comments:*** H-MA-425-G30a. Similar to W-MA-1180-020-G060 but with different location. 18__. 1850s.

Rarity: —

$20 • **W-MA-1360-020-G070**

Left: 20 / 20. ***Center:*** 20 and TWENTY DOLLARS / Male portrait surrounded by flags and drum / 20 and TWENTY DOLLARS. ***Right:*** 20 / 20. ***Engraver:*** American Bank Note Co. ***Comments:*** H-MA-425-G32a. 1860s.

Rarity: —

$50 • **W-MA-1360-050-G080**

Left: FIFTY / Woman standing with wreath and flowers / FIFTY. ***Center:*** 50 / Man restraining prancing horse / 50. ***Right:*** FIFTY / Woman standing with cornucopia / FIFTY. ***Overprint:*** Likely red. ***Engraver:*** New England Bank Note Co. ***Comments:*** H-MA-425-G34. Similar to W-MA-1180-050-G070 but with different location. 18__. 1850s.

Rarity: —

$50 • **W-MA-1360-050-G090**

Left: 50 / Justice leaning on pedestal. ***Center:*** Portrait of General George B. McClellan. ***Right:*** 50 / State arms. ***Tint:*** Green dies bearing white 50 / FIFTY / 50. ***Engraver:*** American Bank Note Co. ***Comments:*** H-MA-425-G36a. 1860s.

Rarity: —

$100 • W-MA-1360-100-G100

Left: ONE HUNDRED on 100 / Portrait of William Henry Harrison. ***Center:*** Wharf scene, Men loading wagon with barrels. ***Right:*** ONE HUNDRED on 100 / Portrait of Christopher Columbus. ***Overprint:*** Likely red. ***Engraver:*** New England Bank Note Co. ***Comments:*** H-MA-425-G38. Similar to W-MA-1180-100-G080 but with different location. 18__. 1850s.

Rarity: —

$100 • W-MA-1360-100-G110

Left: C / Woman with lamp and flowers, Wheel. ***Center:*** Portrait of Secretary Salmon P. Chase. ***Right:*** 100 / Battle scene, Soldier with bayonet, Drum. ***Tint:*** Green 100 / 100. ***Engraver:*** American Bank Note Co. ***Comments:*** H-MA-425-G40a. 1860s.

Rarity: —

Concord, Massachusetts

Originally known as "Musketaquid," Concord lies at the joining of two rivers. In 1635 British settlers acquired the land from a local tribe, and it was called Concord after the nonviolent nature of the purchase. Later, sections of Bedford and Lincoln would separate from Concord, followed by the splitting off of Carlisle in the mid-19th century.

The initial skirmish in the Revolutionary War occurred here with the Battle of Lexington and Concord. On April 19, 1775, the British Army attempted to move in from Boston, only to be repulsed by the colonists of Concord and surrounding towns. The town is also well-known for its literary legacy in the persons of Ralph Waldo Emerson, Nathaniel Hawthorne, Louisa May Alcott, and Henry David Thoreau. It was while imprisoned in Concord that Thoreau wrote his popular "Civil Disobedience," also known as "Resistance to Civil Government." Thoreau, a passionate abolitionist, was jailed for refusing to pay his poll tax. He declined to acknowledge a government that was also a slave's government. The next morning he was released after learning that someone had paid the tax for him.

Concord Bank

1832–1865

W-MA-1370

History: The Concord Bank was incorporated on March 3, 1832, with an authorized capital of $100,000. This figure was maintained throughout the bank's existence.

Circulation was $68,881 in 1839. In 1840 there was unfavorable publicity when the bank stopped redeeming its own notes and the Suffolk Bank stopped acting as a clearing house for the bills. In time, the situation was resolved, and normal business continued. Circulation fluctuated between $80,623 in 1845 and $95,858 in 1863. Selected figures for 1857 included: bills of this bank and other New England states $437.30; specie $13,376; real estate $2,400.

The business of the Concord Bank was succeeded by the Concord National Bank, chartered on February 23, 1865.

Numismatic Commentary: Genuine notes on this bank are hard to locate, with the PSSP style being the type most often encountered. Collectors should note the ABNCo. monogram that appears on some of these PSSP style issues. This happened only when the original PSSP plate was brought back into use after the American Bank Note Co. took over operations in 1858, 20 or more years after the original use of the PSSP plate.

Valid Issues

$1 • W-MA-1370-001-G010

Center: 1 / 1 / Alternating flower garlands and gridwork segments / 1 / 1. ***Engraver:*** PSSP. ***Comments:*** H-MA-495-G2. 18__. 1830s–1850s.

Rarity: —

$1 • W-MA-1370-001-G010a

Engraver: PSSP / ABNCo. monogram. ***Comments:*** H-MA-495-G2a. Similar to W-MA-1370-001-G010 but with additional engraver imprint. 18__. 1850s–1860s.

Rarity: URS-4
Proof $1,000

$1 • W-MA-1370-001-G010b

QDB

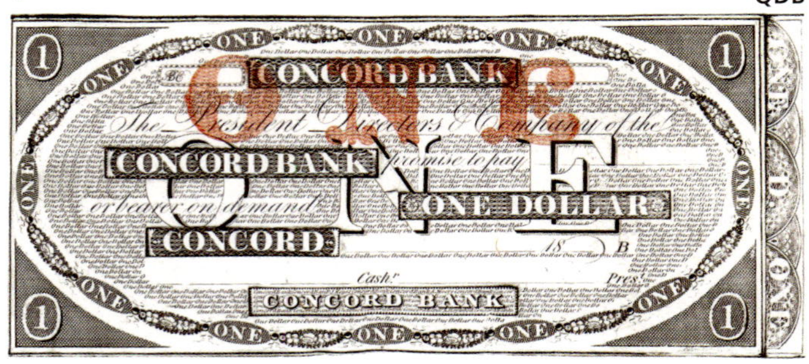

Overprint: Red ONE. ***Engraver:*** PSSP. ***Comments:*** H-Unlisted. Similar to W-MA-1370-001-G010 but with additional engraver imprint. 18__.

Rarity: URS-2
Proof $2,000

$1 • W-MA-1370-001-G020

Engraver: Unverified, but likely New England Bank Note Co. ***Comments:*** H-MA-495-G4. No description available. 18__. 1830s.

Rarity: *None known*

$2 • W-MA-1370-002-G030

Center: 2 / 2 / Alternating flower garlands and gridwork segments / 2 / 2. ***Engraver:*** PSSP. ***Comments:*** H-MA-495-G6. 18__. 1840s–1850s.

Rarity: —

$2 • W-MA-1370-002-G030a

CC

Engraver: PSSP / ABNCo. monogram. ***Comments:*** H-MA-495-G6a. Similar to W-MA-1370-002-G030 but with additional engraver imprint. 18__. 1850s–1860s.

Rarity: URS-3
Proof $1,500

$3 • W-MA-1370-003-G040

Center: 3 / 3 / Alternating flower garlands and gridwork segments / 3 / 3. *Engraver:* PSSP. *Comments:* H-MA-495-G10. 18__. 1840s–1850s.

Rarity: —

$3 • W-MA-1370-003-G040a

CJF

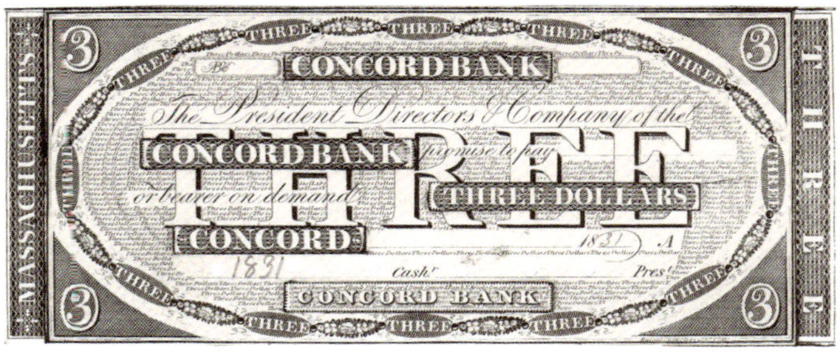

Engraver: PSSP / ABNCo. monogram. *Comments:* H-MA-495-G10a. Similar to W-MA-1370-003-G040 but with additional engraver imprint. Remainder. 18__. 1850s–1860s.

Rarity: URS-2
Proof $1,000

$5 • W-MA-1370-005-G050

Left: Lathework chain bearing MASSACHUSETTS / 5 / 5. *Center:* Alternating flower garlands and gridwork segments / FIVE. *Right:* 5 / 5. *Engraver:* PSSP. *Comments:* H-MA-495-G14. 18__. 1830s.

Rarity: —

$5 • W-MA-1370-005-G050a

Engraver: PSSP / ABNCo. monogram. *Comments:* H-MA-495-G14a. Similar to W-MA-1370-005-G050 but with additional engraver imprint. 18__. 1850s–1860s.

Rarity: —

$5 • W-MA-1370-005-G060

HA

Engraver: PSSP. *Comments:* H-Unlisted. 18__. 1840s.

Rarity: URS-5
F $250

$10 • W-MA-1370-010-G070

Left: Lathework chain bearing MASSACHUSETTS / 10 / Allegorical woman / 10 vertically. *Center:* Text / TEN. *Right:* 10 / Indian / 10 vertically. *Engraver:* PSSP. *Comments:* H-MA-495-G18. 18__. 1830s.

Rarity: —

$10 • W-MA-1370-010-G070a

JF

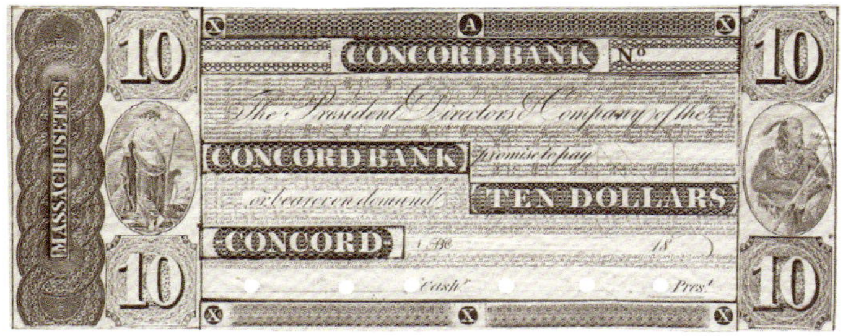

Engraver: PSSP / ABNCo. monogram. *Comments:* H-MA-495-G18a. Similar to W-MA-1370-010-G070 but with additional engraver imprint. Remainder. 18__. 1850s–1860s.

Rarity: URS-2
Proof $2,000

$20 • W-MA-1370-020-G080

Left: Lathework chain bearing MASSACHUSETTS / 20 / Ceres / 20 vertically. *Center:* Text. *Right:* 20 / State arms / 20 vertically. *Engraver:* PSSP. *Comments:* H-MA-495-G20. 18__. 1830s.

Rarity: —

$20 • W-MA-1370-020-G080a

JF

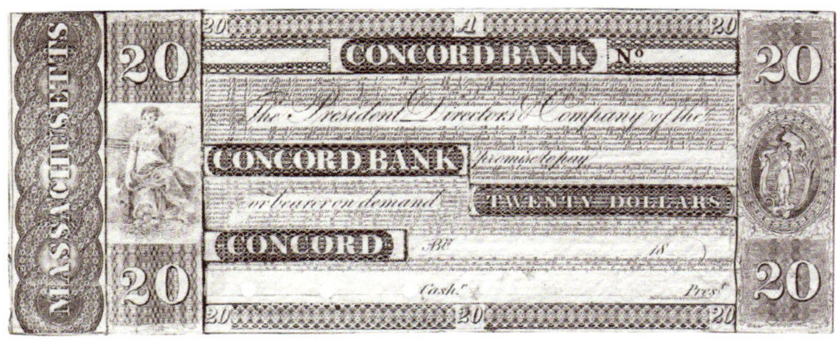

Engraver: PSSP / ABNCo. monogram. *Comments:* H-MA-495-G20a. Similar to W-MA-1370-020-G080 but with additional engraver imprint. 18__. 1850s–1860s.

Rarity: URS-2
Proof $2,000

$50 • W-MA-1370-050-G090

Left: Lathework chain bearing MASSACHUSETTS / 50 / Ceres / 50 vertically. *Center:* Text. *Right:* 50 / State arms / 50 vertically. *Engraver:* PSSP. *Comments:* H-MA-495-G22. 18__. 1830s.

Rarity: URS-3
Proof $2,500

$50 • W-MA-1370-050-G090a

QDB

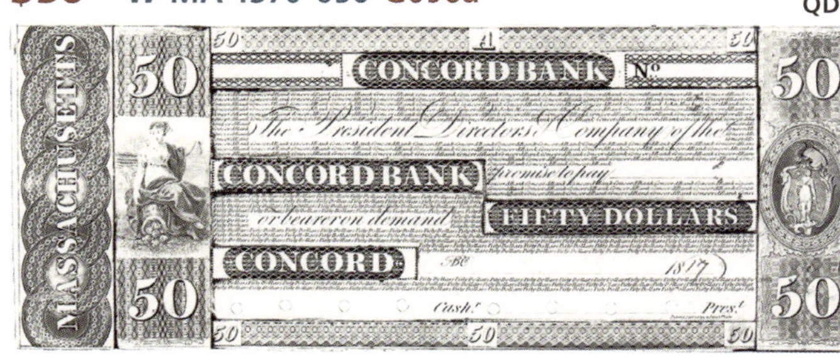

Engraver: PSSP / ABNCo. monogram. *Comments:* H-Unlisted. Similar to W-MA-1370-050-G090 but with additional engraver imprint. Remainder. 18__.

Rarity: URS-3
Proof $1,800

$100 • **W-MA-1370-100-G100**

Left: Lathework chain bearing MASSACHUSETTS / 100 / 100 vertically. ***Center:*** Alternating flower garlands and gridwork segments / HUNDRED. ***Right:*** 100 / 100 vertically. ***Engraver:*** PSSP. ***Comments:*** H-MA-495-G26. 18__. 1830s.

Rarity: —

$500 • **W-MA-1370-500-G110**

SI

Engraver: PSSP / ABNCo. monogram. ***Comments:*** H-Unlisted. Remainder. 18__.

Rarity: URS-2
Proof $5,000

Non-Valid Issues

$1 • **W-MA-1370-001-A010**

CJF

Engraver: New England Bank Note Co. ***Comments:*** H-MA-495-A5. Altered from $1 Washington County Bank, Calais, Maine, or from notes of other failed banks using the same plate. 18__. 1830s.

Rarity: URS-8
F $100

$3 • **W-MA-1370-003-A020**

Left: THREE / Beehive and foliage / THREE. ***Center:*** Ceres seated holding sickle and rake, Factories and harbor / THREE. ***Right:*** 3 on THREE / Two reapers / 3 on THREE. ***Engraver:*** New England Bank Note Co. ***Comments:*** H-MA-495-A10. Altered from $3 Washington County Bank, Calais, Maine, or from notes of other failed banks using the same plate. 18__. 1830s.

Rarity: —

$5 • **W-MA-1370-005-A030**

Left: 5 / Blacksmith with anvil / FIVE. ***Center:*** Man with wreath holding shield bearing 5 / Sailing ship / V on die. ***Bottom center:*** FIVE. ***Right:*** 5 / Woman seated / FIVE. ***Engraver:*** New England Bank Note Co. ***Comments:*** H-MA-495-A15. Altered from $5 Washington County Bank, Calais, Maine, or from notes of other failed banks using the same plate. 18__. 1830s.

Rarity: URS-8
F $100

$5 • **W-MA-1370-005-A040**

Left: 5 / FIVE / FIVE. ***Center:*** Reclining Indian woman and seated frontiersman flanking five silver dollars, Three cherubs. ***Right:*** 5 / Female portrait / FIVE. ***Overprint:*** FIVE. ***Engraver:*** Danforth, Wright & Co. ***Comments:*** H-MA-495-A20. Altered from $5 Farmers and Merchants Bank of Memphis, Memphis, Tennessee. 1850s.

Rarity: —

$5 • **W-MA-1370-005-A050**

Left: FIVE / Portrait of Benjamin Franklin / FIVE. ***Center:*** Portrait of George Washington flanked by five allegorical women. ***Right:*** 5 / Portrait of Andrew Jackson / 5. ***Engraver:*** Danforth, Wright & Co. ***Comments:*** H-MA-495-A25. Altered from $5 Mechanics Bank of Memphis, Memphis, Tennessee series. 1850s.

Rarity: —

$10 • **W-MA-1370-010-A060**

Left: 10 / Farmer sowing / TEN. ***Center:*** Mercury standing with 10 / Merchandise, factories, and ship / Canal scene. ***Right:*** 10 / Ship / TEN. ***Engraver:*** New England Bank Note Co. ***Comments:*** H-MA-495-A30. Altered from $10 Washington County Bank, Calais, Maine, or from notes of other failed banks using the same plate. 18__. 1830s.

Rarity: —

$10 • **W-MA-1370-010-A070**

Left: X / Man with sickle. ***Center:*** Ships in harbor / X on die. ***Right:*** 10 / Woman carrying hat and sheaf. ***Engraver:*** New England Bank Note Co. ***Comments:*** H-MA-495-A35. Altered from $10 Hamilton Bank, Scituate, Rhode Island, or from notes of other failed banks using the same plate. 18__. 1830s.

Rarity: URS-6
F $125

$20 • **W-MA-1370-020-A080**

CJF

Engraver: New England Bank Note Co. ***Comments:*** H-MA-495-A40. Altered from $20 Hamilton Bank, Scituate, Rhode Island, or from notes of other failed banks using the same plate. 18__. 1840s.

Rarity: URS-6
F $125

Conway, Massachusetts

In 1762 Conway was established as part of Deerfield. It separated in 1775 and was incorporated bearing the surname of General Henry Seymour Conway. The town was known mostly for sheep herding and industries along the river but remained predominantly a farming community. Water power provided for all of the town's manufactories, including cotton and yarn. There was also a saw mill and a manufactory for hand rakes. Fruit, tobacco, and dairy products were also important in commerce.

Conway Bank

1854–1864

W-MA-1380

History: The Conway Bank was incorporated on March 28, 1854, with $100,000 in authorized capital. Business commenced in September of that year.

The capital was raised to $150,000 in 1857. Selected figures for 1857 included: bills of this bank and other New England states $2,245.92; specie $7,390.53. Later, circulation ranged from a low of $72,183 in 1862 to a high of $148,491 in 1863.

The business of the Conway Bank was succeeded by the Conway National Bank, chartered on March 15, 1865.

Numismatic Commentary: Genuine notes from the Conway Bank are hard to locate, although plenty of non-valid notes are still in the marketplace.

As of 2003 there was a $1-$1-$2-$5 tint plate remaining at the American Bank Note Co. archives.

Valid Issues

$1 • W-MA-1380-001-G010

JF

Engraver: Bald, Cousland & Co. / Bald, Adams & Co. ***Comments:*** H-Unlisted. Proof. Sept. 12, 1854. 1850s–1860s.

Rarity: URS-9

Proof $500

$1 • W-MA-1380-001-G010a

CJF

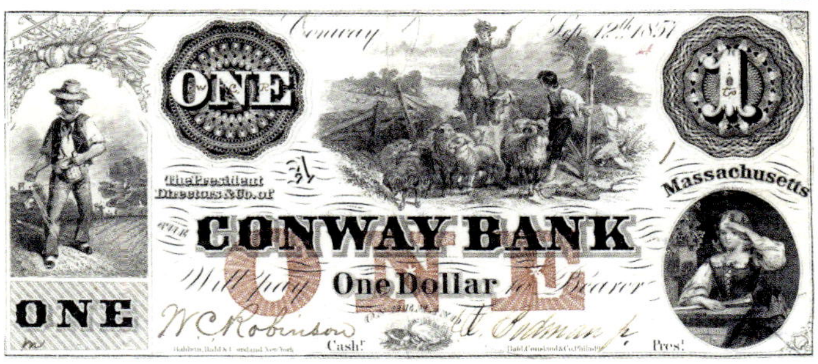

Overprint: Red ONE. ***Engraver:*** Bald, Cousland & Co. / Baldwin, Bald & Cousland. ***Comments:*** H-MA-500-G2a. Similar to W-MA-1380-001-G010 but with different engraver imprint. Sept. 12, 1857. 1850s–1860s.

Rarity: URS-4

F $350; **Unc-S&D** $1,000

$1 • W-MA-1380-001-G010b

Left: Farmer sowing grain / ONE. ***Center:*** ONE / Boy on horse driving cow and sheep, Boy holding gate. ***Bottom center:*** Ducks. ***Right:*** 1 / Girl shading eyes with hand. ***Overprint:*** Red. ***Engraver:*** Bald, Cousland & Co. / ABNCo. monogram. ***Comments:*** H-MA-500-G2b. Similar to W-MA-1380-001-G010 but with additional engraver imprint. 18__. 1850s–1860s.

Rarity: URS-3

VF $500

$2 • W-MA-1380-002-G020

JF

Engraver: Bald, Cousland & Co. / Bald, Adams & Co. ***Comments:*** H-Unlisted. Proof. Sept. 12, 1854. 1850s.

Rarity: URS-5

Proof $750

$2 • W-MA-1380-002-G020a

CC

Overprint: Red 2 / 2. ***Engraver:*** Bald, Cousland & Co. / Bald, Adams & Co. ***Comments:*** H-MA-500-G4a. Similar to W-MA-1380-002-G020. Sept. 12, 1854. 1850s.

Rarity: URS-4

CU $425; **Proof** $1,500

$2 • W-MA-1380-002-G020b

Overprint: Red. ***Engraver:*** Bald, Cousland & Co. / ABNCo. monogram. ***Comments:*** H-MA-500-G4b. Similar to W-MA-1380-002-G020 but with additional engraver imprint. 18__. 1850s–1860s.

Rarity: —

$2 • W-MA-1380-002-G030

Left: 2 / Reverses of U.S. and Spanish-American silver dollars. ***Center:*** Woman and man at trough. ***Bottom center:*** Steer. ***Right:*** 2 / Woman seated with 2. ***Overprint:*** Red TWO. ***Engraver:*** Wellstood, Hay & Whiting. ***Comments:*** H-Unlisted. August 12, 1856. 1850s.

Rarity: URS-5

F $250

$3 • W-MA-1380-003-G040

JF

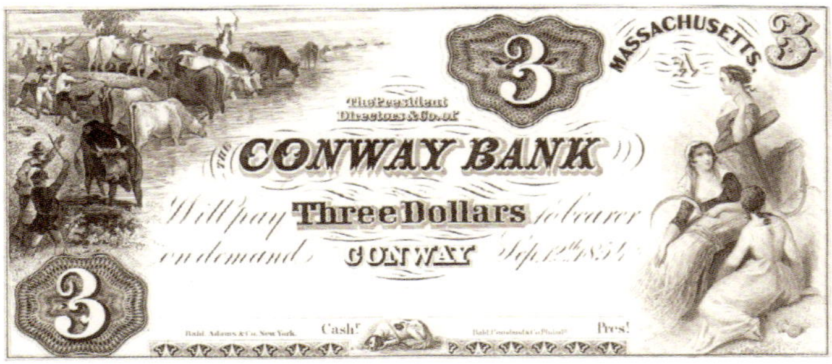

Engraver: Bald, Cousland & Co. / Bald, Adams & Co. ***Comments:*** H-Unlisted. Proof. Sept. 12, 1854. 1850s.

Rarity: URS-5
Proof $650

$3 • W-MA-1380-003-G040a

Left: Drover with cattle / 3. ***Center:*** 3 / 3. ***Bottom center:*** Dog. ***Right:*** 3 / Three women. ***Overprint:*** Red 3. ***Engraver:*** Bald, Cousland & Co. ***Comments:*** H-MA-500-G6a. Similar to W-MA-1380-003-G040 but with different engraver imprint. 18__. 1850s.

Rarity: URS-4
Proof $1,250

$3 • W-MA-1380-003-G040b

CJF

Overprint: Red 3. ***Engraver:*** Bald, Cousland & Co. / ABNCo. monogram. ***Comments:*** H-MA-500-G6b. Similar to W-MA-1380-003-G040 but with additional engraver imprint. 18__. 1850s–1860s.

Rarity: URS-5
Proof $1,500

$5 • W-MA-1380-005-G050

CC

Engraver: Bald, Cousland & Co. / Bald, Adams & Co. ***Comments:*** H-Unlisted. Proof. September 12, 1854. 1850s.

Rarity: URS-3
Proof $1,000

$5 • W-MA-1380-005-G050a

CC

Overprint: Red FIVE. ***Engraver:*** Bald, Cousland & Co. / Bald, Adams & Co. ***Comments:*** H-MA-500-G8a. Similar to W-MA-1380-005-G050. Proof. September 12, 1854. 1850s.

Rarity: URS-3
Proof $1,500

$5 • W-MA-1380-005-G050b

Left: V / Man carrying basket of cotton. ***Center:*** Four women tending looms. ***Right:*** 5 / Male portrait. ***Overprint:*** Red. ***Engraver:*** Bald, Cousland & Co. / ABNCo. monogram. ***Comments:*** H-MA-500-G8b. Similar to W-MA-1380-005-G050 but with additional engraver imprint. 18__. 1850s–1860s.

Rarity: —

$10 • W-MA-1380-010-G060

CC

Engraver: Bald, Cousland & Co. / Bald, Adams & Co. ***Comments:*** H-Unlisted. Proof. Sept. 12, 1854. 1850s.

Rarity: URS-3
Proof $700

$10 • W-MA-1380-010-G060a

CC

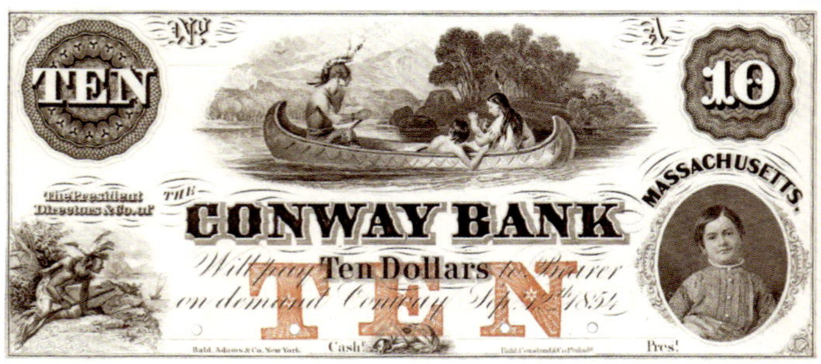

Overprint: Red TEN. ***Engraver:*** Bald, Cousland & Co. / Bald, Adams & Co. ***Comments:*** H-MA-500-G10a. Similar to W-MA-1380-010-G060. Sept. 12, 1854. 1850s.

Rarity: URS-3
Proof $1,000

$10 • W-MA-1380-010-G060b

Overprint: Red. ***Engraver:*** Bald, Cousland & Co. / ABNCo. monogram. ***Comments:*** H-MA-500-G10b. Similar to W-MA-1380-010-G060 but with additional engraver imprint. 18__. 1850s–1860s.

Rarity: URS-4
F $450; **EF** $750

$20 • W-MA-1380-020-G070

JF

Engraver: Bald, Cousland & Co. / Bald, Adams & Co. ***Comments:*** H-Unlisted. A popular "Santa Claus" note. Proof. Sept. 12, 1854. 1850s.

Rarity: URS-4
Proof $750

$20 • W-MA-1380-020-G070a

Left: XX / Indian man drawing arrow from quiver. ***Center:*** Santa Claus in sleigh drawn by reindeer over rooftops. ***Right:*** 20 / Trees, arch, and stream. ***Overprint:*** Red. ***Engraver:*** Bald, Cousland & Co. / Bald, Adams & Co. ***Comments:*** H-MA-500-G12a. Similar to W-MA-1380-020-G070. A popular "Santa Claus" note. 18__. 1850s.

Rarity: URS-4
Proof $10,000

$20 • W-MA-1380-020-G070b

Overprint: Red. ***Engraver:*** Bald, Cousland & Co. / ABNCo. monogram. ***Comments:*** H-MA-500-G12b. Similar to W-MA-1380-020-G070 but with additional engraver imprint. A popular "Santa Claus" note. 18__. 1850s–1860s.

Rarity: —

$50 • W-MA-1380-050-G080

CC

Engraver: Bald, Cousland & Co. / Bald, Adams & Co. ***Comments:*** H-Unlisted. Proof. Sept. 12, 1854. 1850s.

Rarity: URS-4
Proof $750

$50 • W-MA-1380-050-G080a

Left: L / Hunter warming hands by fire, Dog, gun, and trees. ***Center:*** Justice seated in clouds with sword, balance, and eagle. ***Right:*** 50 / Woman binding shoes, Child. ***Overprint:*** Red. ***Engraver:*** Bald, Cousland & Co. / Bald, Adams & Co. ***Comments:*** H-MA-500-G14a. Similar to W-MA-1380-050-G080. 18__. 1850s.

Rarity: URS-4
Proof $1,000

$50 • W-MA-1380-050-G080b

Overprint: Red. ***Engraver:*** Bald, Cousland & Co. / ABNCo. monogram. ***Comments:*** H-MA-500-G14b. Similar to W-MA-1380-050-G080 but with additional engraver imprint. 18__. 1850s–1860s.

Rarity: —

$100 • W-MA-1380-100-G090

CC

Engraver: Bald, Adams & Co. / Bald, Cousland & Co. ***Comments:*** H-Unlisted. Proof. Sept. 12, 1854. 1850s.

Rarity: URS-4
Proof $1,200

$100 • W-MA-1380-100-G090a

Left: C / Male portrait. ***Center:*** Wood-cutting scene, Three men placing chain under log, Oxen, Trees. ***Right:*** 100 / Old man smoking pipe. ***Engraver:*** Bald, Adams & Co. / Bald, Cousland & Co. ***Comments:*** H-MA-500-G16a. Similar to W-MA-1380-100-G090. 18__. 1850s.

Rarity: URS-5
AU $325; **Proof** $1,500

$100 • W-MA-1380-100-G090b

Engraver: Bald, Cousland & Co. / ABNCo. monogram. ***Comments:*** H-MA-500-G16b. Similar to W-MA-1380-100-G090 but with additional engraver imprint. 18__. 1850s–1860s.

Rarity: —

Uncut Sheets

$1-$1-$2-$5 •

W-MA-1380-001.001.002.005-US010

SBG

Overprint(s): None. ***Comments:*** All unlisted in Haxby. September 12, 1854. 1850s.

Rarity: URS-3
Proof $1,500

$1-$1-$2-$5 • W-MA-1380-001.001.002.005-US010a

Vignette(s): ($1) Farmer sowing grain / Boy on horse driving cow and sheep, Boy holding gate / Ducks / Girl shading eyes with hand. ***($1)*** Farmer sowing grain / Boy on horse driving cow and sheep, Boy holding gate / Ducks / Girl shading eyes with hand. ***($2)*** Mechanic seated and sailor standing with flag / Two girls carrying sheaf. ***($5)*** Man carrying basket of cotton / Four women tending looms / Male portrait. ***Overprint(s):*** Red. ***Comments:*** H-MA-500-G2a, G2a, G4a, G8a. Similar to W-MA-1380-001.001.002.005-US010. September 12, 1854.

Rarity: URS-4
Proof $5,000

$3-$5-$10-$20 •

W-MA-1380-003.005.010.020-US020

SBG

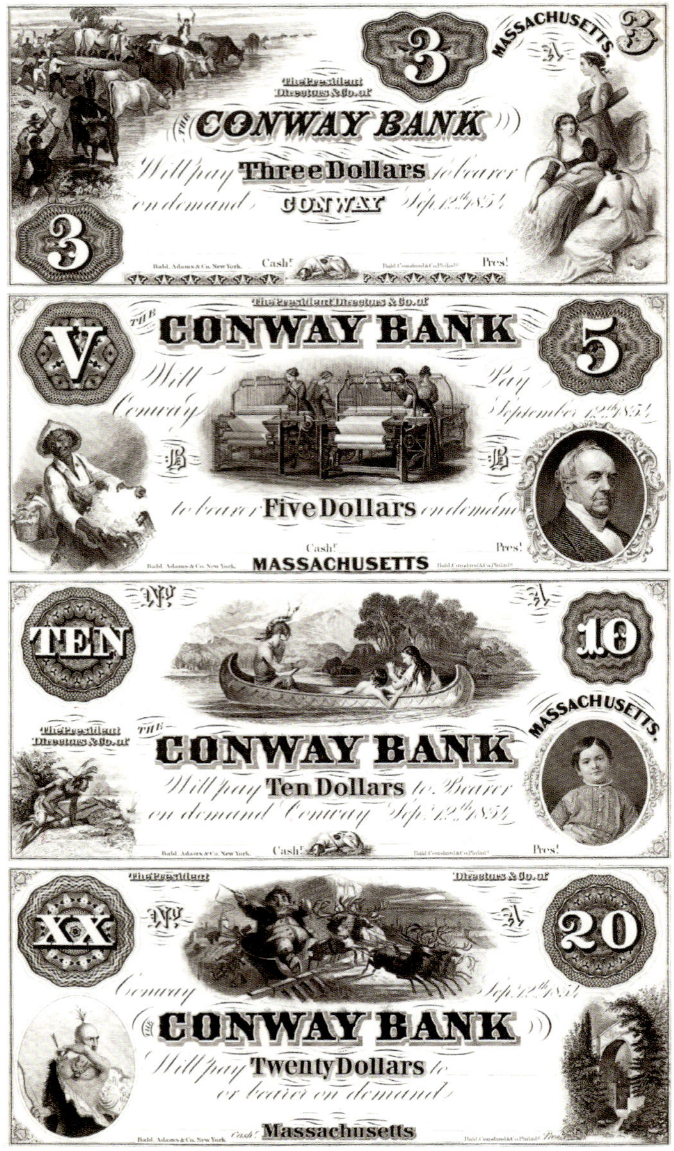

Comments: All unlisted in Haxby. September 12, 1854. 1850s.

Rarity: URS-4
Proof $14,000

$3-$5-$10-$20 • W-MA-1380-003.005.010.020-US020a

SBG

Overprint(s): Red. ***Comments:*** H-MA-500-G6a, G8a, G10a, G12a. Similar to W-MA-1380-003.005.010.020-US020. Sept. 12, 1854. 1850s.

Rarity: URS-4
Proof $15,000

$50-$100 • W-MA-1380-050.100-US030

SBG

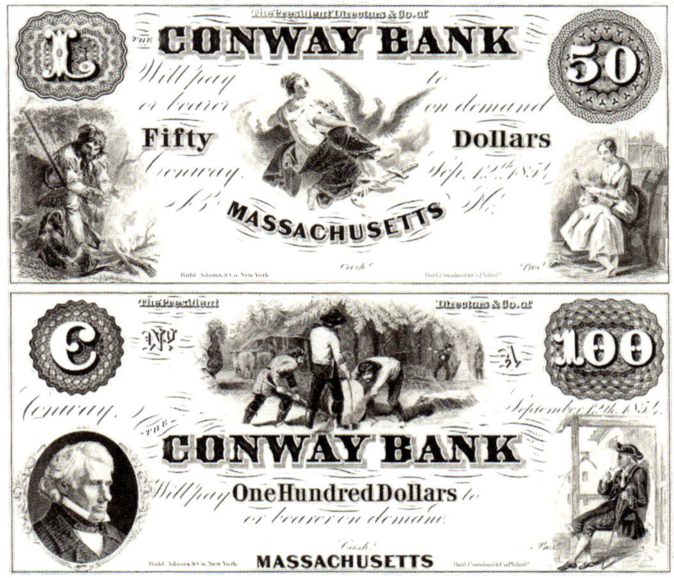

Overprint(s): None. ***Comments:*** All unlisted in Haxby. Partial sheet. Proof. September 12, 1854. 1850s.

Rarity: URS-3
Proof $2,000

Non-Valid Issues

$2 • W-MA-1380-002-C020a

Engraver: Bald, Cousland & Co. ***Comments:*** H-MA-500-C4a. Counterfeit of W-MA-1380-002-G020a. 18__. 1850s.

Rarity: —

$2 • W-MA-1380-002-A010

CJF

Overprint: Red TWO. ***Engraver:*** Wellstood, Hay & Whiting. ***Comments:*** H-MA-500-A5. Altered from $2 Thames Bank, Laurel, Indiana. August 12, 1856. 1850s.

Rarity: URS-5
VG $100; **F** $250

$3 • W-MA-1380-003-R010

Engraver: Bald, Cousland & Co. ***Comments:*** H-MA-500-R5. Raised from W-MA-1380-001-G010a. 18__. 1850s.

Rarity: —

Collectors and Researchers:

If you have new information about any banks or notes listed in this volume, contact Whitman Publishing, Attn: Obsolete Paper Money, 3101 Clairmont Road, Suite G, Atlanta, GA 30329.

$3 • W-MA-1380-003-A020
Left: THREE / Beehive and foliage / THREE. ***Center:*** Machinery and merchandise flanking Ceres seated holding sickle and rake, Factories and harbor / THREE. ***Right:*** 3 on THREE / Two reapers / 3 on THREE. ***Engraver:*** New England Bank Note Co. ***Comments:*** H-MA-500-A10. Altered from $3 Washington County Bank, Calais, Maine, or from notes of other failed banks using the same plate. 18__. 1850s.

Rarity: —

$5 • W-MA-1380-005-R020
Engraver: Bald, Cousland & Co. ***Comments:*** H-MA-500-R10. Raised from W-MA-1380-001-G010a. 18__. 1850s.

Rarity: —

$5 • W-MA-1380-005-N010
Center: Woman watering eagle. ***Comments:*** H-MA-500-N5. 1850s.

Rarity: —

$5 • W-MA-1380-005-A030
Left: 5 / Blacksmith at anvil / FIVE. ***Center:*** Mercury standing with 5, Cornucopia and merchandise, Factories and ship. ***Right:*** 5 / Ceres kneeling / FIVE. ***Engraver:*** New England Bank Note Co. ***Comments:*** H-MA-500-A15. Altered from $5 Washington County Bank, Calais, Maine, or from notes of other failed banks using the same plate. 18__. 1850s.

Rarity: —

$10 • W-MA-1380-010-S010
CC

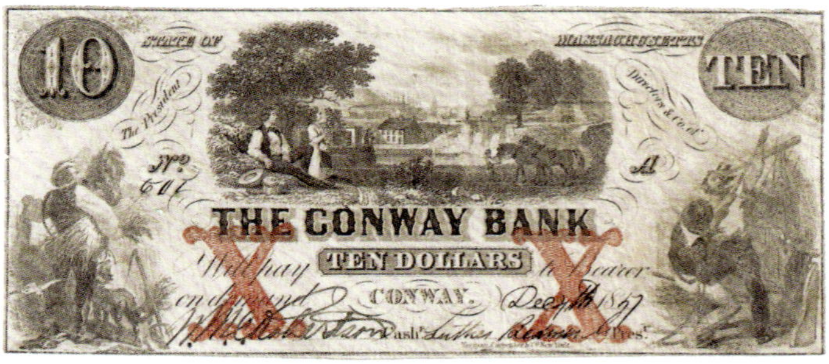

Overprint: Red X / X. ***Engraver:*** Toppan, Carpenter & Co. ***Comments:*** H-MA-500-S5. 18__. 1850s.

Rarity: URS-7
VG $90; **F** $100

$10 • W-MA-1380-010-A040
Left: 10 / Farmer sowing / TEN. ***Center:*** Mercury standing with 10 / Merchandise, Factories and ship / Canal scene. ***Right:*** 10 / Ship / TEN. ***Engraver:*** New England Bank Note Co. ***Comments:*** H-MA-500-A20. Altered from $10 Washington County Bank, Calais, Maine, or from notes of other failed banks using the same plate. 18__. 1850s.

Rarity: —

DANVERS, MASSACHUSETTS

The Naumkeag branch of the Massachusetts natives controlled the land that is now Danvers until 1630, when settlers arrived to the area. It was officially settled in 1636 and incorporated in 1757. Witch hunts in 1692 remain a sorry chapter in the area's history.

A section of Danvers broke away in 1855 to become the town of South Danvers, which later became Peabody. Danvers was originally an agricultural town and developed two types of vegetables, including the Danvers onion and the Danvers half-long carrot.

See also North Danvers and South Danvers, Massachusetts.

Danvers Bank
1825–1855
W-MA-1390

History: The Danvers Bank was incorporated on February 26, 1825, with an authorized capital of $120,000. This amount was raised to $150,000 in 1839. Circulation was at a low of $40,578 in 1839 but peaked at a high of $96,418 in 1863.

After 1855 notes bearing the imprint of South Danvers began circulating.

See also listing under South Danvers, W-MA-3050.

Numismatic Commentary: Notes from this bank are hard to locate.

VALID ISSUES

$1 • W-MA-1390-001-G010
Left: Panel of lathework circle segments. ***Center:*** 1 / 1 / Flower garlands and gridwork segments / 1 / 1. ***Right:*** Panel of lathework circle segments. ***Engraver:*** PSSP. ***Comments:*** H-MA-505-G2. 18__. 1820s–1830s.

Rarity: —

$1 • W-MA-1390-001-G010a
Left: ONE / D / ONE vertically. ***Right:*** ONE / D / ONE vertically. ***Engraver:*** PSSP. ***Comments:*** H-MA-505-G4. Similar to W-MA-1390-001-G010. 18__. 1830s.

Rarity: —

$1 • W-MA-1390-001-G020
Left: 1 / Woman wearing bonnet with pail / ONE. ***Center:*** Machinery and merchandise flanking Ceres seated holding sickle and rake, Factories and harbor / Panel outlining white ONE. ***Right:*** 1 / Ship / ONE. ***Engraver:*** PSSP / New England Bank Note Co. ***Comments:*** H-MA-505-G8. 18__. 1830s–1840s.

Rarity: —

$1 • W-MA-1390-001-G030
Left: ONE / Bust of George Washington / ONE. ***Center:*** 1 / Two blacksmiths at anvil in front of forge / 1 / Panel outlining white ONE. ***Right:*** ONE / Woman / ONE. ***Engraver:*** New England Bank Note Co. ***Comments:*** H-MA-505-G10. 18__. 1840s–1850s.

Rarity: —

$1 • W-MA-1390-001-G040
Left: 1 / Male portrait. ***Center:*** Farmer seated with pitcher, Dog and sheaf. ***Right:*** 1 / Male portrait. ***Engraver:*** Rawdon, Wright, Hatch & Edson. ***Comments:*** H-MA-505-G12. 18__. 1850s–1860s.

Rarity: URS-5
Proof $1,500

$1 • W-MA-1390-001-G040a

JF

Overprint: Red ONE. ***Engraver:*** Rawdon, Wright, Hatch & Edson / New England Bank Note Co. ***Comments:*** H-Unlisted. Similar to W-MA-1390-001-G040 but with additional engraver imprint. Oct. __, 18__. 1850s–1860s.

Rarity: URS-3
VF $2,000

$2 • W-MA-1390-002-G050

Left: Panel of lathework circle segments. ***Center:*** 2 / 2 / Flower garlands and gridwork segments / 2 / 2. ***Right:*** Panel of lathework circle segments. ***Engraver:*** PSSP. ***Comments:*** H-MA-505-G14. 18__. 1820s–1830s.

Rarity: —

$2 • W-MA-1390-002-G050a

Left: Five TWOs vertically. ***Right:*** Five TWOs vertically. ***Engraver:*** PSSP. ***Comments:*** H-MA-505-G16. Similar to W-MA-1390-002-G050. 18__. 1830s.

Rarity: —

$2 • W-MA-1390-002-G060

Left: 2 / Woman standing with staff and cornucopia / TWO. ***Center:*** TWO / Machinery and merchandise flanking Ceres seated holding sickle and rake, Factories and harbor / Panel outlining white TWO. ***Right:*** 2 / Woman wearing hat, Trees / TWO. ***Engraver:*** PSSP / New England Bank Note Co. ***Comments:*** H-MA-505-G20. 18__. 1830s–1840s.

Rarity: —

$2 • W-MA-1390-002-G070

Left: TWO / Female portrait / 2. ***Center:*** 2 / Woman giving drink to one of two seated men / 2 / Panel outlining white TWO. ***Right:*** TWO / Bust of female reaper. ***Engraver:*** New England Bank Note Co. ***Comments:*** H-MA-505-G22. 18__. 1840s–1850s.

Rarity: —

$2 • W-MA-1390-002-G080

Left: 2 / Male portrait. ***Center:*** Cows, Milkmaid seated with pail on knee. ***Right:*** 2 / Male portrait. ***Engraver:*** Rawdon, Wright, Hatch & Edson. ***Comments:*** H-MA-505-G24. 18__. 1850s–1860s.

Rarity: —

$2 • W-MA-1390-002-G080a

CJF

Overprint: Red TWO. ***Engraver:*** Rawdon, Wright, Hatch & Edson / New England Bank Note Co. ***Comments:*** H-Unlisted. Similar to W-MA-1390-002-G080 but with additional engraver imprint. Oct. __, 18__. 1850s–1860s.

Rarity: URS-3
F $750; **VF** $2,500

$2 • W-MA-1390-002-G080b

Engraver: Rawdon, Wright, Hatch & Edson / New England Bank Note Co. ***Comments:*** H-Unlisted. Similar to W-MA-1390-002-G080 but with additional engraver imprint.

Rarity: URS-4
VG $350

$3 • W-MA-1390-003-G090

Left: Narrow panel of lathework circle segments. ***Center:*** 3 / 3 / Flower garlands and gridwork segments / 3 / 3. ***Right:*** Narrow panel of lathework circle segments. ***Engraver:*** PSSP. ***Comments:*** H-MA-505-G26. 18__. 1820s–1830s.

Rarity: —

$3 • W-MA-1390-003-G090a

Left: THREE vertically. ***Right:*** THREE vertically. ***Engraver:*** PSSP. ***Comments:*** H-MA-505-G28. Similar to W-MA-1390-003-G090. 18__. 1830s.

Rarity: —

$3 • W-MA-1390-003-G100

Left: THREE / Beehive and foliage / THREE. ***Center:*** Machinery and merchandise flanking Ceres seated holding sickle and rake, Factories and harbor / Panel outlining white THREE. ***Right:*** 3 on THREE / Two reapers / 3 on THREE. ***Engraver:*** PSSP / New England Bank Note Co. ***Comments:*** H-MA-505-G32. 18__. 1830s–1840s.

Rarity: —

$3 • W-MA-1390-003-G110

Left: THREE / Farmer standing sharpening scythe / 3 across THREE. ***Center:*** 3 / Beehive and cornucopia, Woman seated placing garland on eagle / 3 / Panel outlining white THREE. ***Right:*** THREE / Sailor standing on wharf with hat / 3 across THREE. ***Engraver:*** New England Bank Note Co. ***Comments:*** H-MA-505-G34. 18__. 1840s–1850s.

Rarity: —

$3 • W-MA-1390-003-G120

Left: 3 / Male portrait. ***Center:*** Woman reclining with bale, Spinning wheel, Factories and bridge. ***Right:*** 3 / Male portrait. ***Engraver:*** Rawdon, Wright, Hatch & Edson. ***Comments:*** H-MA-505-G36. 18__. 1850s–1860s.

Rarity: —

$3 • W-MA-1390-003-G120a

Engraver: Rawdon, Wright, Hatch & Edson / New England Bank Note Co. ***Comments:*** H-Unlisted. Similar to W-MA-1390-003-G120 but with additional engraver imprint.

Rarity: URS-3
VG $300

$5 • W-MA-1390-005-G130

Left: Lathework chain bearing MASSACHUSETTS / 5 / 5. ***Center:*** Alternating flower garlands and gridwork segments. ***Right:*** 5 / 5. ***Engraver:*** PSSP. ***Comments:*** H-MA-505-G38. 18__. 1820s.

Rarity: —

$5 • W-MA-1390-005-G130a

CJF

Engraver: PSSP. ***Comments:*** H-MA-505-G40. Similar to W-MA-1390-005-G130 but with spiral lathework lines. 18__. 1820s–1830s.

Rarity: URS-3
VG $300

$5 • W-MA-1390-005-G130b

Engraver: PSSP. ***Comments:*** H-MA-505-G42. Similar to W-MA-1390-005-G130 but with spiral lathework lines. 18__. 1830s.

Rarity: —

$5 • W-MA-1390-005-G140

Left: 5 / Blacksmith at anvil / FIVE. ***Center:*** Mercury standing with 5, Cornucopia and merchandise, Factories and ship / V / Panel outlining white FIVE. ***Right:*** 5 / Ceres kneeling / FIVE. ***Engraver:*** PSSP / New England Bank Note Co. ***Comments:*** H-MA-505-G46. 18__. 1830s–1840s.

Rarity: —

$5 • W-MA-1390-005-G150

Left: 5 / FIVE / 5. ***Center:*** V / Eagle / V. ***Right:*** 5 / FIVE / 5. ***Back:*** Sailing ships / Train and scrollwork. ***Engraver:*** New England Bank Note Co. ***Comments:*** H-MA-505-G48. 18__. 1840s–1850s.

Rarity: —

$5 • W-MA-1390-005-G160

Left: 5 / Male portrait. ***Center:*** Farmer plowing with two horses, Man harrowing, Train. ***Right:*** 5 / Male portrait. ***Engraver:*** Rawdon, Wright, Hatch & Edson. ***Comments:*** H-MA-505-G50. 18__. 1850s–1860s.

Rarity: —

$10 • W-MA-1390-010-G170

Left: Lathework chain bearing MASSACHUSETTS / 10 / 10 vertically. ***Center:*** Alternating flower garlands and gridwork segments. ***Right:*** 10 / 10 vertically. ***Engraver:*** Perkins. ***Comments:*** H-MA-505-G52. 18__. 1820s.

Rarity: —

$10 • W-MA-1390-010-G170a

Engraver: PSSP. ***Comments:*** H-MA-505-G54. Similar to W-MA-1390-010-G170 but with zigzag ruled lines. 18__. 1820s–1830s.

Rarity: —

$10 • W-MA-1390-010-G170b

Engraver: PSSP. ***Comments:*** H-MA-505-G56. Similar to W-MA-1390-010-G170 but with spiral lathework lines. 18__. 1830s.

Rarity: —

$10 • W-MA-1390-010-G180

Left: 10 / Farmer sowing / TEN. ***Center:*** Mercury standing with 10, Cornucopia and merchandise, Factories and ship, Canal scene / Panel outlining white TEN. ***Right:*** 10 / Ship / TEN. ***Engraver:*** PSSP / New England Bank Note Co. ***Comments:*** H-MA-505-G60. 18__. 1830s–1840s.

Rarity: —

$10 • W-MA-1390-010-G190

Left: 10 / Male portrait ***Center:*** Eagle / U.S. Capitol and steamship. ***Right:*** 10 / Male portrait. ***Engraver:*** Rawdon, Wright, Hatch & Edson. ***Comments:*** H-MA-505-G62. 18__. 1850s–1860s.

Rarity: —

$20 • W-MA-1390-020-G200

Left: Lathework chain bearing MASSACHUSETTS / 20 / 20 vertically. ***Center:*** Alternating flower garlands and gridwork segments. ***Right:*** 20 / 20 vertically. ***Engraver:*** PSSP. ***Comments:*** H-MA-505-G64. 18__. 1820s–1830s.

Rarity: —

$20 • W-MA-1390-020-G210

Left: 20 / Male portrait. ***Center:*** TWENTY / Two women flanking male portrait surmounted by eagle / TWENTY. ***Right:*** 20. ***Engraver:*** Rawdon, Wright, Hatch & Edson. ***Comments:*** H-MA-505-G68. 18__. 1850s–1860s.

Rarity: —

$50 • W-MA-1390-050-G220

Left: Lathework chain bearing MASSACHUSETTS / 50 / 50. ***Center:*** Alternating flower garlands and gridwork segments. ***Right:*** 50 / 50 vertically. ***Engraver:*** PSSP. ***Comments:*** H-MA-505-G70. 18__. 1820s–1830s.

Rarity: —

$50 • W-MA-1390-050-G230

Left: 50 / Steamboat and schooner. ***Center:*** Farmyard scene, Load of hay with two men on it, Man with rake and pail. ***Right:*** L / Justice kneeling. ***Engraver:*** New England Bank Note Co. ***Comments:*** H-MA-505-G74. 18__. 1830s–1840s.

Rarity: —

$50 • W-MA-1390-050-G240

Left: Male portrait / 50. ***Center:*** FIFTY / State arms / DOLLARS. ***Right:*** 50 / Male portrait. ***Engraver:*** Rawdon, Wright, Hatch & Edson. ***Comments:*** H-MA-505-G76. 18__. 1850s–1860s.

Rarity: —

$100 • W-MA-1390-100-G250

Left: Lathework chain bearing MASSACHUSETTS / 100 / 100 vertically. ***Center:*** Alternating flower garlands and gridwork segments. ***Right:*** 100 / 100 vertically. ***Engraver:*** Perkins. ***Comments:*** H-MA-505-G78. 18__. 1820s–1830s.

Rarity: —

$100 • W-MA-1390-100-G260

Engraver: Unverified, but likely New England Bank Note Co. ***Comments:*** H-MA-505-G80. No description available. 18__. 1830s–1840s.

Rarity: *None known*

$100 • W-MA-1390-100-G270

Left: 100 / Male portrait. ***Center:*** 100 / Three women / 100. ***Right:*** 100 / Portrait. ***Engraver:*** Rawdon, Wright, Hatch & Edson. ***Comments:*** H-MA-505-G82. 18__. 1850s–1860s.

Rarity: —

Non-Valid Issues

$1 • W-MA-1390-001-A010

Left: Woman with grain floating above harbor, Waterfall and farm. ***Center:*** Three men rolling log. ***Right:*** 1. ***Tint:*** Brown-orange lathework outlining white 1. ***Engraver:*** Bald, Cousland & Co. ***Comments:*** H-MA-505-A5. Altered from $1 Pioneer Association, Lafayette, Indiana. 18__. 1850s.

Rarity: —

$2 • W-MA-1390-002-A020

CC

Back: Red-brown. ***Engraver:*** W.L. Ormsby. ***Comments:*** H-MA-505-A10. Altered from $2 Farmers and Drovers Bank, Petersburg, Indiana. Oct. 4, 1858.

Rarity: URS-5
F $75; **VF** $175

$3 • W-MA-1390-003-A030

CC

Overprint: Red THREE. ***Engraver:*** New England Bank Note Co. / Rawdon, Wright, Hatch & Edson. ***Comments:*** H-MA-505-A15. Altered from $3 Waubeek Bank, De Soto, Nebraska. 1857.

Rarity: URS-4
VG $100; **VF** $175

$5 • W-MA-1390-005-C160

Engraver: Rawdon, Wright, Hatch & Edson. ***Comments:*** H-MA-505-C50. Counterfeit of W-MA-1390-005-G160. 18__. 1850s.

Rarity: —

$5 • W-MA-1390-005-R010

CJF

Overprint: Red FIVE. ***Engraver:*** Rawdon, Wright, Hatch & Edson / New England Bank Note Co. ***Comments:*** H-Unlisted. Raised from W-MA-1390-001-G040a. 18__. 1850s–1860s.

Rarity: URS-3
F $1,250

$5 • W-MA-1390-005-S010

CC

Engraver: New England Bank Note Co. ***Comments:*** H-Unlisted. 18__.

Rarity: —
VF $500

$5 • W-MA-1390-005-A040

Left: Several men with sticks driving herd of cattle into stream / 5. ***Center:*** Five men raking and loading hay, Ox wagon. ***Right:*** 5. ***Tint:*** Red-brown lathework outlining white 5. ***Engraver:*** Bald, Cousland & Co. ***Comments:*** H-MA-505-A20. Altered from $5 Pioneer Association, Lafayette, Indiana. 18__. 1850s.

Rarity: —

$5 • W-MA-1390-005-A050

Left: V / Portrait of Henry Clay. ***Center:*** Steamboat. ***Right:*** 5 / Portrait of George Washington. ***Overprint:*** Red FIVE. ***Engraver:*** New England Bank Note Co. / Rawdon, Wright, Hatch & Edson. ***Comments:*** H-MA-505-A25. Altered from $5 Waubeek Bank, De Soto, Nebraska. 1857.

Rarity: —

$10 • W-MA-1390-010-A060

Left: 10 / Woman seated on ground under palm tree, Shovel and sickle. ***Center:*** Woman reclining with shield bearing scroll, pole and cap. ***Right:*** 10. ***Comments:*** H-MA-505-A30. Altered from $10 Bank of Greensborough, Greensborough, Georgia series. 1850s.

Rarity: —

$10 • W-MA-1390-010-A070

Engraver: Rawdon, Wright, Hatch & Edson / New England Bank Note Co. ***Comments:*** H-Unlisted. Altered from W-MA-1390-001-G040 but with additional engraver imprint.

Rarity: URS-3
VG $175

$50 • W-MA-1390-050-A080

Left: 50 / Woman standing, Bowl of fruit above shield bearing anchor / 50. ***Center:*** L / Hebe watering eagle / L. ***Bottom center:*** Anchor and implements. ***Right:*** 50 / Farmer holding grain / 50. ***Engraver:*** Terry, Pelton & Co. ***Comments:*** H-MA-505-A35. Altered from $50 Citizens Bank, Augusta, Maine, or from notes of other failed banks using the same plate. 18__. 1840s.

Rarity: —

Village Bank

1836–1865

W-MA-1400

History: The Village Bank was chartered on March 1, 1836, with an authorized capital of $120,000, which was raised to $160,000 and then further to $200,000 in 1854. It dropped to $150,000 again in 1863 and 1864. Circulation ranged from a low of $30,392 in 1839 to a high of $84,930 in 1854. Selected figures for 1854 included: real estate $17,782.69; specie $5,058.30.

The business of the Village Bank was succeeded by the First National Bank of Danvers, organized in December 1864. The state bank began winding down its business in early 1865.

Numismatic Commentary: Genuine notes from this bank will appear in the marketplace a little more often than from the Danvers Bank preceding. Attractive vignettes showing beef cattle will usually be seen.

Valid Issues

$1 • W-MA-1400-001-G010

Comments: H-MA-510-G4. No description available. 18__. 1830s–1840s.

Rarity: *None known*

$1 • W-MA-1400-001-G020

CJF

Engraver: Toppan, Carpenter, Casilear & Co. ***Comments:*** H-MA-510-G8. 18__. 1850s.

Rarity: URS-4
VF $600

$1 • W-MA-1400-001-G020a

CJF

Tint: Red-orange panel of microlettering bearing ONE. ***Engraver:*** Toppan, Carpenter, Casilear & Co. ***Comments:*** H-MA-510-G8b. Similar to W-MA-1400-001-G020. October 1, 1857.

Rarity: URS-4
F $750

$2 • W-MA-1400-002-G030

Comments: H-MA-510-G12. No description available. 18__. 1830s–1840s.

Rarity: *None known*

$2 • W-MA-1400-002-G040

Left: 2 / Ship. ***Center:*** 2. ***Right:*** Woman holding shield bearing 2 / TWO. ***Engraver:*** Toppan, Carpenter, Casilear & Co. ***Comments:*** H-MA-510-G16. 18__. 1850s.

Rarity: URS-3
Proof $550

$2 • W-MA-1400-002-G040a

CJF

Tint: Red-orange panel of microlettering bearing TWO, TWO, and 2. ***Engraver:*** Toppan, Carpenter, Casilear & Co. ***Comments:*** H-MA-510-G16b. Similar to W-MA-1400-002-G040. October 1, 1857.

Rarity: URS-3
F $1,250

$3 • W-MA-1400-003-G050

Comments: H-MA-510-G20. No description available. 18__. 1830s–1840s.

Rarity: *None known*

$3 • W-MA-1400-003-G060

Left: 3 / Portrait of Millard Fillmore. ***Center:*** Train. ***Right:*** 3 / Liberty seated. ***Engraver:*** Toppan, Carpenter, Casilear & Co. ***Comments:*** H-MA-510-G24. 18__. 1850s.

Rarity: —

$3 • W-MA-1400-003-G060a

Tint: Red-orange panel of microlettering bearing THREE. ***Engraver:*** Toppan, Carpenter, Casilear & Co. ***Comments:*** H-MA-510-G24b. Similar to W-MA-1400-003-G060. Oct. 1, 1857.

Rarity: URS-3
VF $1,250

$5 • W-MA-1400-005-G070

Comments: H-MA-510-G28. No description available. 18__. 1830s–1840s.

Rarity: *None known*

$5 • W-MA-1400-005-G080

CJF

Engraver: Toppan, Carpenter, Casilear & Co. ***Comments:*** H-MA-510-G32. 18__. 1850s.

Rarity: URS-4
VF $600

$5 • W-MA-1400-005-G080a

TD

Tint: Red-orange panel of microlettering bearing FIVE / 5 / 5. ***Engraver:*** Toppan, Carpenter & Co. ***Comments:*** H-MA-510-G32b. Similar to W-MA-1400-005-G080 but with different date. October 1, 1857.

Rarity: URS-3
F $750

$10 • W-MA-1400-010-G090

Comments: H-MA-510-G36. No description available. 18__. 1830s–1840s.

Rarity: *None known*

$10 • W-MA-1400-010-G100

CJF

Engraver: Toppan, Carpenter, Casilear & Co. ***Comments:*** H-MA-510-G40. 18__. 1850s.

Rarity: URS-4
VF $500

$10 • W-MA-1400-010-G100a

Left: Woman carrying sheaf and shading eyes with hand / X. ***Center:*** Cattle and sheep, Drover on horses. ***Right:*** 10 / George Washington on horseback. ***Tint:*** Red-orange. ***Engraver:*** Toppan, Carpenter, Casilear & Co. ***Comments:*** H-MA-510-G40b. Similar to W-MA-1400-010-G100 but with different date. Oct. 1, 1857.

Rarity: —

$20 • W-MA-1400-020-G110

Comments: H-MA-510-G44. No description available. 18__. 1830s–1840s.

Rarity: *None known*

$20 • W-MA-1400-020-G120

Left: 20 / Justice seated, Eagle on strongbox. ***Center:*** Woman seated with arms extended holding balance, pole and cap, flanked by two cherubs. ***Right:*** 20 / Woman with sheaf on shoulder. ***Engraver:*** Toppan, Carpenter, Casilear & Co. ***Comments:*** H-MA-510-G48. 18__. 1850s.

Rarity: —

$20 • W-MA-1400-020-G130

Left: 20 / Woman holding grain. ***Right:*** 20 / Man plowing with two horses. ***Tint:*** Red 20 on XX and TWENTY on red die. ***Engraver:*** American Bank Note Co. ***Comments:*** H-MA-510-G50. 18__. 1850s–1860s.

Rarity: —

$50 • W-MA-1400-050-G140

Comments: H-MA-510-G54. No description available. 18__. 1830s–1840s.

Rarity: *None known*

$50 • W-MA-1400-050-G150

Left: 50 / Bust of woman with sickle / 50. ***Center:*** Factories and train, Two women seated, Ship. ***Right:*** 50 / Farmer picking corn. ***Engraver:*** Toppan, Carpenter, Casilear & Co. ***Comments:*** H-MA-510-G58. 18__. 1850s.

Rarity: —

$50 • W-MA-1400-050-G160

Left: 50 / Horses, Goat and kid drinking at trough, Man. ***Right:*** 50 / Male portrait. ***Tint:*** FIFTY on red background. ***Engraver:*** American Bank Note Co. ***Comments:*** H-MA-510-G60. 18__. 1850s–1860s.

Rarity: —

$100 • W-MA-1400-100-G170

Comments: H-MA-510-G64. No description available. 18__. 1830s–1840s.

Rarity: *None known*

$100 • W-MA-1400-100-G180

Left: 100 / Sailor seated with hat and flag. ***Center:*** Woman and cherubs scattering flowers in clouds above city, Ships. ***Right:*** 100 / Female portrait / 100. ***Engraver:*** Toppan, Carpenter, Casilear & Co. ***Comments:*** H-MA-510-G68. 18__. 1850s.

Rarity: —

$100 • W-MA-1400-100-G190

Left: 100 / Female portrait. ***Right:*** 100 / Two mechanics. ***Tint:*** 100 on C on red die. ***Engraver:*** American Bank Note Co. ***Comments:*** H-MA-510-G70. 18__. 1850s–1860s.

Rarity: —

$500 • W-MA-1400-500-G200

Left: D / Three women, two seated and one standing with open book. ***Right:*** 500 / Woman with cornucopia and flowers. ***Tint:*** Red die bearing 500 and words FIVE HUNDRED. ***Engraver:*** American Bank Note Co. ***Comments:*** H-MA-510-G80. 18__. 1850s–1860s.

Rarity: —

Uncut Sheets

$20-$50-$100-$500 • W-MA-1400-020.050.100.500-US010

Vignette(s): ***($20)*** Woman holding grain / Man plowing with two horses. ***($50)*** Horses, Goat and kid drinking at trough, Man / Male portrait. ***($100)*** Female portrait / Two mechanics. ***($500)*** Three women, two seated and one standing with open book / Woman with cornucopia and flowers. ***Tint(s):*** Red. ***Comments:*** All unlisted in Haxby. Similar to H-MA-510-G50, G60, G70, G80 but with different engraver imprint. October 1, 1857.

Rarity: —

Non-Valid Issues

$2 • W-MA-1400-002-A010

Left: TWO / Justice seated / TWO. ***Center:*** TWO / TWO on medallion head / Train, hill, and steamship / TWO / TWO. ***Right:*** TWO / Woman standing with pole and cap, Cornucopia and sheaf. ***Engraver:*** W.L. Ormsby. ***Comments:*** H-MA-510-A5. Altered from $2 Potomac River Bank, Georgetown, D.C. 18__. 1850s.

Rarity: URS-5
VG $75

$2 • W-MA-1400-002-A020

Left: TWO and 2 on die / State arms vertically. ***Center:*** Three woodsmen feeling and cutting trees. ***Right:*** 2 / Ceres with sheaf. ***Engraver:*** Danforth, Wright & Co. ***Comments:*** H-MA-510-A10. Altered from $2 Bank of Washtenaw, Washtenaw, Michigan. 1850s.

Rarity: —

$3 • W-MA-1400-003-A030

Left: 3 / Portrait of Benjamin Franklin. ***Center:*** Woman reclining on strongbox / 3 on shield, Produce. ***Right:*** 3 / Indian woman seated under tree. ***Engraver:*** Danforth, Bald & Co. ***Comments:*** H-MA-510-A15. Altered from $3 Columbia Bank, Washington, D.C. 18__. 1850s.

Rarity: —

$5 • W-MA-1400-005-SA010

SI

Comments: H-MA-510-SA10. Spurious and altered. 18__. 1840s.

Rarity: URS-7
VG $75

$5 • W-MA-1400-005-A040

Left: Portrait of Henry Clay / V. ***Center:*** Farmer feeding hogs. ***Bottom center:*** Dog lying down. ***Right:*** 5 / Farmer carrying basket of corn. ***Overprint:*** Red FIVE. ***Engraver:*** Wellstood, Hay & Whiting. ***Comments:*** H-MA-510-A20. Altered from $5 Thames Bank, Laurel, Indiana. 1850s.

Rarity: —

$5 • W-MA-1400-005-A050

CJF

Back: Five portraits of George Washington, each surrounded by 5s. ***Engraver:*** W.L. Ormsby. ***Comments:*** H-MA-510-A25. Altered from $5 Crawfordsville, Logansport and Northern Indian R.R. Co. Logansport, Indiana. 185_. 1850s.

Rarity: URS-5
VG $100

$10 • W-MA-1400-010-R010

Comments: H-MA-510-R5. Raised from W-MA-1400-001-G010. 18__. 1840s.

Rarity: —

Village Bank of Danvers

1850s

W-MA-1410

History: A non-existent bank represented only by notes altered from those of other banks. The notes were intended to pass for those of the Village Bank, W-MA-1400.

Issues

$5 • W-MA-1410-005-A010

Left: FIVE vertically. ***Center:*** Farming scene / 5 on die / Two men with horse. ***Right:*** V / 5 on die / V. ***Engraver:*** Rawdon, Wright, Hatch & Edson. ***Comments:*** H-MA-511-A5. Altered from $5 Farmers and Mechanics Bank at Pontiac, Pontiac, Michigan. 18__. 1840s.

Rarity: —

Warren Bank

1832–1864

W-MA-1420

History: The Warren Bank was chartered on March 3, 1832, with an authorized capital of $120,000. In 1839 its capital was $150,000. Later, capital ranged from a low of $120,000 in 1845 to a high of $250,000 in 1857. Circulation was listed at $39,290 in 1839. In 1849 it was $60,840, and in 1857 it was $120,265. Selected figures for 1857 included: bills of this bank and other New England states $3,182.54; specie $11,280.79; real estate $6,000.

The business of the Warren Bank was succeeded by the Warren National Bank of Danvers, chartered on November 18, 1864.

See also listing under South Danvers, W-MA-3060.

Numismatic Commentary: Many issues from this bank show portraits of the philanthropist George Peabody at multiple ages during his life. These notes are hard to find.

VALID ISSUES

$1 • W-MA-1420-001-G010

Left: Lathework panel bearing MASSACHUSETTS vertically. ***Center:*** 1 / 1 / Alternating flower garlands and gridwork segments / ONE / 1 / 1. ***Right:*** Lathework panel bearing ONE / D / ONE vertically. ***Engraver:*** PSSP. ***Comments:*** H-MA-515-G2. 18__. 1830s.

Rarity: —

$1 • W-MA-1420-001-G020

Left: 1 / Woman wearing bonnet with pail / ONE. ***Center:*** Machinery and merchandise flanking Ceres seated holding sickle and rake, Factories and harbor / Panel outlining white ONE. ***Right:*** 1 / Ship / ONE. ***Engraver:*** PSSP / New England Bank Note Co. ***Comments:*** H-MA-515-G4. 18__. 1830s–1840s.

Rarity: —

$1 • W-MA-1420-001-G030

Left: Commerce seated with rudder and barrel / 1. ***Center:*** 1 bearing "Presentation of the Declaration of Independence". ***Right:*** 1 / Woman standing with apron full of grain. ***Engraver:*** New England Bank Note Co. ***Comments:*** H-MA-515-G6. 18__. 1840s–1850s.

Rarity: —

$1 • W-MA-1420-001-G040

CC, CC

Back: View of street in Danvers, Church and Warren Bank. ***Engraver:*** Rawdon, Wright, Hatch & Edson / New England Bank Note Co. ***Comments:*** H-MA-515-G8a. 1 Jan. 18__. 1850s.

Rarity: URS-3
F $500; **VF** $1,250

$1.25 • W-MA-1420-001.25-G050

Left: 1 / 25/100 / Train / 1 25/100. ***Center:*** Sloop and other ships at sea / $1.25 cts. ***Right:*** 1 25/100 / Eagle. ***Engraver:*** New England Bank Note Co. ***Comments:*** H-MA-515-G10. 18__. 1830s.

Rarity: —

$1.50 • W-MA-1420-001.50-G060

Left: 1 Doll 50 Cts. vertically. ***Center:*** Eagle on rock in ocean / $1 50/100. ***Right:*** 1 50/100 / Justice. ***Engraver:*** New England Bank Note Co. ***Comments:*** H-MA-515-G12. 18__. 1830s.

Rarity: —

$1.75 • W-MA-1420-001.75-G070

Left: $1.75 Cts / Woman watering eagle / 1 75/100. ***Center:*** Three sloops at sea. ***Right:*** $1.75 Cts. / Dog, Woman seated with grain / 1 75/100. ***Engraver:*** New England Bank Note Co. ***Comments:*** H-MA-515-G14. 18__. 1830s.

Rarity: —

$2 • W-MA-1420-002-G080

CC

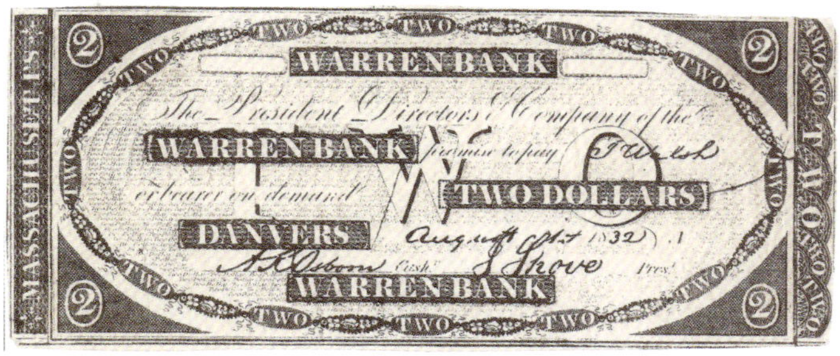

Engraver: PSSP. ***Comments:*** H-MA-515-G16. 18__. 1830s.

Rarity: —

$2 • W-MA-1420-002-G090

Left: 2 / Cornucopia, Woman standing with staff / TWO. ***Center:*** TWO / Machinery and merchandise flanking Ceres seated holding sickle and rake, Factories and harbor / Panel outlining white TWO. ***Right:*** 2 / Woman wearing hat, Trees / TWO. ***Engraver:*** New England Bank Note Co. / PSSP. ***Comments:*** H-MA-515-G18. 18__. 1830s–1840s.

Rarity: —

$2 • W-MA-1420-002-G100

Left: Men driving sheep into stream. ***Center:*** 2 bearing "Presentation of the Declaration of Independence". ***Right:*** TWO / Woman seated with wreath of flowers / TWO. ***Engraver:*** New England Bank Note Co. ***Comments:*** H-MA-515-G20. 18__. 1840s–1850s.

Rarity: —

$2 • W-MA-1420-002-G110

CC

Engraver: Rawdon, Wright, Hatch & Edson / New England Bank Note Co. ***Comments:*** H-MA-515-G22a. 1 Jan. 18__. 1850s.

Rarity: URS-3
F $1,600

$3 • W-MA-1420-003-G120

Left: Lathework panel bearing MASSACHUSETTS. ***Center:*** 3 / 3 / Alternating flower garlands and gridwork segments / THREE / 3 / 3. ***Right:*** Lathework panel bearing THREE vertically. ***Engraver:*** PSSP. ***Comments:*** H-MA-515-G24. 18__. 1830s.

Rarity: —

$3 • W-MA-1420-003-G130
Left: THREE / Beehive and foliage / THREE. ***Center:*** Machinery and merchandise flanking Ceres seated holding sickle and rake, Factories and harbor / Panel outlining white THREE. ***Right:*** 3 on THREE / Two reapers / 3 on THREE. ***Engraver:*** New England Bank Note Co. / PSSP. ***Comments:*** H-MA-515-G26. 18__. 1830s–1840s.
Rarity: —

$3 • W-MA-1420-003-G140
Left: Barnyard scene, Man on horse, Boy and cattle / 3. ***Center:*** 3. ***Right:*** 3 on THREE / Woman with flowers / THREE. ***Engraver:*** New England Bank Note Co. ***Comments:*** H-MA-515-G28. 18__. 1840s–1850s.
Rarity: —

$3 • W-MA-1420-003-G150
Left: Woman seated against bale holding balance / 3. ***Center:*** Portrait of George Peabody. ***Right:*** 3 / Indian woman seated. ***Engraver:*** Rawdon, Wright, Hatch & Edson / New England Bank Note Co. ***Comments:*** H-MA-515-G30a. Jan. 1, 18__. 1850s.
Rarity: —

$5 • W-MA-1420-005-G160
Left: Lathework chain bearing MASSACHUSETTS / 5 / 5. ***Center:*** Alternating flower garlands and gridwork segments / FIVE. ***Right:*** 5 / 5. ***Engraver:*** PSSP. ***Comments:*** H-MA-515-G32. 18__. 1830s.
Rarity: —

$5 • W-MA-1420-005-G170
Left: 5 / Blacksmith at anvil. ***Center:*** Mercury standing with 5, Cornucopia and merchandise, Factories and ship / V / Panel outlining white FIVE. ***Right:*** 5 / Ceres kneeling / FIVE. ***Engraver:*** New England Bank Note Co. / PSSP. ***Comments:*** H-MA-515-G34. 18__. 1830s–1840s.
Rarity: —

$5 • W-MA-1420-005-G180
Left: Eagle, shield, and anchor, Factories and ships / FIVE. ***Center:*** V with woman, cornucopia, and cherub. ***Right:*** 5 / Girl with ringlets holding basket. ***Engraver:*** New England Bank Note Co. ***Comments:*** H-MA-515-G36. Beware of spurious W-MA-1420-005-S020 closely resembling the genuine. 18__. 1840s–1850s.
Rarity: —

$5 • W-MA-1420-005-G190
Left: 5 / Two women. ***Center:*** Portrait of George Peabody. ***Right:*** 5 / Portrait. ***Engraver:*** Rawdon, Wright, Hatch & Edson / New England Bank Note Co. ***Comments:*** H-MA-515-G38. Jan. 1, 18__. 1850s.
Rarity: —

$10 • W-MA-1420-010-G200
Left: Lathework chain bearing MASSACHUSETTS / 10 / 10 vertically. ***Center:*** Alternating flower garlands and gridwork segments / TEN. ***Right:*** 10 / 10 vertically. ***Engraver:*** PSSP. ***Comments:*** H-MA-515-G40. 18__. 1830s.
Rarity: —

$10 • W-MA-1420-010-G210
Engraver: Unverified, but likely New England Bank Note Co. ***Comments:*** H-MA-515-G42. No description available. 18__. 1830s–1840s.
Rarity: *None known*

$10 • W-MA-1420-010-G220
Left: Train, Mechanic seated with tools, Building / TEN. ***Center:*** X. ***Right:*** 10 / Male reaper standing with sheaf on knee. ***Engraver:*** New England Bank Note Co. ***Comments:*** H-MA-515-G44. 18__. 1840s–1850s.
Rarity: —

$10 • W-MA-1420-010-G230
Left: 10 / Indian woman. ***Center:*** Portrait of George Peabody. ***Right:*** 10 / Woman. ***Engraver:*** Rawdon, Wright, Hatch & Edson / New England Bank Note Co. ***Comments:*** H-MA-515-G46. Jan. 1, 18__. 1850s.
Rarity: —

$20 • W-MA-1420-020-G240
Left: Lathework chain bearing MASSACHUSETTS / 20 / 20 vertically. ***Center:*** Alternating flower garlands and gridwork segments / TWENTY. ***Right:*** 20 / 20 vertically. ***Engraver:*** PSSP. ***Comments:*** H-MA-515-G48. 18__. 1830s.
Rarity: —

$20 • W-MA-1420-020-G250
Left: Steamboat / XX / Train. ***Center:*** Three women seated with eagle, pole and cap, shield, scales, and book / 20 / Panel outlining white TWENTY. ***Right:*** XX / Milkmaid standing with pail. ***Engraver:*** New England Bank Note Co. ***Comments:*** H-MA-515-G50. 18__. 1830s–1840s.
Rarity: —

$20 • W-MA-1420-020-G260
Left: 20 / Minerva standing with spear. ***Center:*** Woman seated between 2 and 0. ***Right:*** 20 / Woman reclining on cornucopia / 20. ***Engraver:*** Rawdon, Wright, Hatch & Edson. ***Comments:*** H-MA-515-G52. 18__. 1850s.
Rarity: —

$50 • W-MA-1420-050-G270
Left: 50 / Steamboat and schooner. ***Center:*** Farmyard scene, Load of hay with two men on it, Man with rake and pail. ***Right:*** L / Justice kneeling. ***Engraver:*** New England Bank Note Co. ***Comments:*** H-MA-515-G56. 18__. 1830s–1840s.
Rarity: —

$50 • W-MA-1420-050-G280
Left: 50 / Minerva standing by column. ***Center:*** Ceres and Vulcan flanking cornucopia. ***Right:*** 50 / Cherub in sailboat / 50. ***Engraver:*** Rawdon, Wright, Hatch & Edson. ***Comments:*** H-MA-515-G60. 18__. 1850s.
Rarity: —

$100 • W-MA-1420-100-G290
Engraver: Unverified, but likely New England Bank Note Co. ***Comments:*** H-MA-515-G64. No description available. 18__. 1830s–1840s.
Rarity: *None known*

$100 • W-MA-1420-100-G300
Left: 100 / Vulcan seated with sledge and anchor. ***Center:*** Train on bridge, Eagle on limb, Canal locks / C. ***Bottom center:*** 100. ***Right:*** 100 / Ceres seated, Cornucopia. ***Engraver:*** Rawdon, Wright, Hatch & Edson. ***Comments:*** H-MA-515-G68. 18__. 1850s.
Rarity: —

Non-Valid Issues

$1 • W-MA-1420-001-N010

Left: Children. ***Center:*** Farmer seated on sheaf. ***Right:*** Women. ***Comments:*** H-MA-515-N5.

Rarity: —

$5 • W-MA-1420-005-S010

CJF

Engraver: New England Bank Note Co. ***Comments:*** H-MA-515-S5. 18__. Circa 1840s.

Rarity: URS-7
VG $75

$5 • W-MA-1420-005-S020

CJF

Tint: Orange FIVE. ***Engraver:*** New England Bank Note Co. / ABNCo. monogram. ***Comments:*** H-MA-515-S10. Spurious design imitating a rough verbal description of W-MA-1420-005-G180. Aug. 1, 1860.

Rarity: URS-9
VG $65

$5 • W-MA-1420-005-S030

Left: V / Ox / V. ***Center:*** 5 / Train on bridge, Ceres seated, Sheaf and canal lock. ***Bottom center:*** Sheaf, Plow. ***Right:*** Lathework panel bearing FIVE vertically. ***Comments:*** H-MA-515-S15. 184_. 1840s.

Rarity: —

$10 • W-MA-1420-010-R010

Engraver: Rawdon, Wright, Hatch & Edson / New England Bank Note Co. ***Comments:*** H-MA-515-R5. Raised from W-MA-1420-001-G040. Jan. 1, 18__. 1850s.

Rarity: —

Dedham, Massachusetts

Colonists from Roxbury and Watertown settled Dedham in 1635. The town was incorporated in 1636. It soon became the county seat of Norfolk County. Originally the residents wanted to name the town Contentment, but the Massachusetts General Court overruled and named the town after Dedham in England. The first man-made canal of North America was built in Dedham in 1639, linking the Charles River and the Neponset River and giving power to several mills. The first tax-funded and public school was also authorized in Dedham and became known as "the seed of American education."

Dedham is also well-known for its pottery, which is recognized by its blue and white colors, crackle glaze, and motifs of rabbits and various other animals.

Dedham Bank

1814–1864

W-MA-1430

History: The Dedham Bank was chartered on February 26, 1814, with $100,000 authorized capital. In 1816 the Legislature censured and fined the bank for circulating notes that were payable at the Middletown Bank in Connecticut—making redemption difficult. The capital was increased to $150,000 in 1839. In 1849 it jumped again to $200,000, and by 1857 it was as high as $300,000. Selected figures for 1857 included: bills of this bank and other New England states $3,568; specie $20,142.49.

In 1864 the bank's business was succeeded by the Dedham National Bank.

Numismatic Commentary: Genuine notes are very hard to locate. Some of the earlier issues bear a portrait of Fisher Ames, a congressional representative during the last decade of the 1700s and a native of Dedham.

Valid Issues

$1 • W-MA-1430-001-G010

Center: 1 / 1 / Flower garlands and gridwork segments / ONE / 1 / 1. ***Engraver:*** PSSP. ***Comments:*** H-MA-520-G20. 18__. 1810s–1820s.

Rarity: —

$1 • W-MA-1430-001-G010a

Left: Panel of lathework circle segments. ***Right:*** Panel of lathework circle segments. ***Engraver:*** PSSP. ***Comments:*** H-MA-520-G22. Similar to W-MA-1430-001-G010. 18__. 1820s.

Rarity: —

$1 • W-MA-1430-001-G010b

Left: Panel of lathework circle segments. ***Right:*** Panel of lathework circle segments. ***Engraver:*** PSSP. ***Comments:*** H-MA-520-G24. Similar to W-MA-1430-001-G010. 18__. 1820s–1830s.

Rarity: —

$1 • W-MA-1430-001-G010c

Left: ONE / D / ONE vertically. ***Right:*** ONE / D / ONE vertically. ***Engraver:*** PSSP. ***Comments:*** H-MA-520-G26. Similar to W-MA-1430-001-G010. 18__. 1830s.

Rarity: —

$1 • W-MA-1430-001-G020 TD

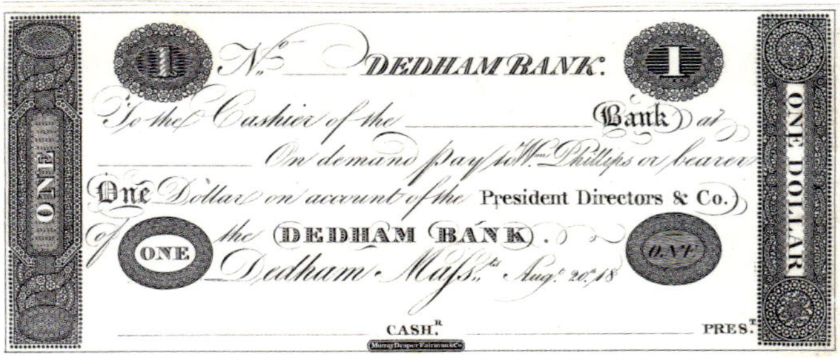

Engraver: Murray, Draper, Fairman & Co. ***Comments:*** H-Unlisted. Proof. Aug. 20, 18__.

Rarity: URS-2

Proof $750

$1 • W-MA-1430-001-G030

Left: 1 / Portrait of Fisher Adams / ONE. ***Center:*** ONE / Two men in blacksmith shop / ONE. ***Right:*** 1 / Portrait of George Washington / ONE. ***Back:*** Plain. ***Engraver:*** New England Bank Note Co. / PSSP. ***Comments:*** H-MA-520-G28. 18__. 1830s–1850s.

Rarity: —

$1 • W-MA-1430-001-G030a TD, TD

Back: Check Plate. ***Engraver:*** New England Bank Note Co. / PSSP. ***Comments:*** H-MA-520-G28a. Similar to W-MA-1430-001-G030. 18__. 1830s–1840s.

Rarity: URS-3

VF $1,000

$1 • W-MA-1430-001-G030b CJF, CJF

Overprint: Red ONE. ***Engraver:*** New England Bank Note Co. / PSSP. ***Comments:*** H-MA-520-G28b. Similar to W-MA-1430-001-G030. 18__. 1850s–1860s.

Rarity: URS-5

F $325; **EF** $700

$1 • W-MA-1430-001-G030c

Overprint: Red ONE. ***Engraver:*** New England Bank Note Co. / PSSP / ABNCo. monogram. ***Comments:*** H-MA-520-G28c. Similar to W-MA-1430-001-G030 but with additional engraver imprint. 18__. 1850s–1860s.

Rarity: URS-5

VG $400; **VF** $550; **EF** $750

$1 • W-MA-1430-001-G040 TD

Engraver: PSSP. ***Comments:*** H-Unlisted. 18__. 1830s.

Rarity: URS-3

VF $1,000

How to Read the Whitman Numbering System

$1 • W-MA-010-001-G010a

Denomination: Value of the note shown.

W: Whitman number. This number is a sortable code unique to each bank and note.

MA: Abbreviation for the state under study.

010: Numerical designation specific to each bank.

001: The denomination in dollars.

G010a: G indicates a good or valid note. Other categories are indicated thus: C (counterfeit); R (raised); S (spurious); N (not-attributed); A (altered). Numbers are assigned starting with 010, 020, et seq. Terminal letters following the number indicate variations of a note: a series of different colored overprints, tints, payees, etc., all on the same design of note. For more information, see the “How to Use This Book” section at the front of the volume, page xiv.

$2 • W-MA-1430-002-G050

Center: 2 / 2 / Flower garlands and gridwork segments / TWO / 2 / 2. ***Engraver:*** PSSP. ***Comments:*** H-MA-520-G32. 18__. 1810s–1820s.

Rarity: —

$2 • W-MA-1430-002-G050a

Left: Panel of lathework circle segments. ***Right:*** Panel of lathework circle segments. ***Engraver:*** PSSP. ***Comments:*** H-MA-520-G34. Similar to W-MA-1430-002-G050. 18__. 1820s.

Rarity: —

$2 • W-MA-1430-002-G050b

Left: Panel of lathework circle segments. ***Right:*** Panel of lathework circle segments. ***Engraver:*** PSSP. ***Comments:*** H-MA-520-G36. Similar to W-MA-1430-002-G050. 18__. 1820s–1830s.

Rarity: —

$2 • W-MA-1430-002-G050c

TD

Engraver: PSSP. ***Comments:*** H-MA-520-G38. Similar to W-MA-1430-002-G050. 18__. 1830s–1840s.

Rarity: URS-3
VF $1,000

$2 • W-MA-1430-002-G060

Left: 2 / Portrait of Fisher Ames / TWO. ***Center:*** TWO / Spread eagle perched on globe / TWO. ***Right:*** 2 / Portrait of George Washington / TWO. ***Engraver:*** New England Bank Note Co. / PSSP. ***Comments:*** H-MA-520-G40. 18__. 1830s–1850s.

Rarity: —

$2 • W-MA-1430-002-G060a

Back: Check Plate. ***Engraver:*** New England Bank Note Co. / PSSP. ***Comments:*** H-MA-520-G40a. Similar to W-MA-1430-002-G060. 18__. 1830s–1840s.

Rarity: —

$2 • W-MA-1430-002-G060b

Overprint: Red TWO. ***Engraver:*** New England Bank Note Co. / PSSP. ***Comments:*** H-MA-520-G40b. Similar to W-MA-1430-002-G060. 18__. 1850s.

Rarity: —

$2 • W-MA-1430-002-G060c

Overprint: Red TWO. ***Engraver:*** New England Bank Note Co. / PSSP / ABNCo. monogram. ***Comments:*** H-MA-520-G40c. Similar to W-MA-1430-002-G060 but with additional engraver imprint. 18__. 1850s–1860s.

Rarity: —

$3 • W-MA-1430-003-G070

Center: 3 / 3 / Oval of flower garlands and gridwork segments / 3 / 3. ***Engraver:*** PSSP. ***Comments:*** H-MA-520-G42. 18__. 1810s–1820s.

Rarity: —

$3 • W-MA-1430-003-G070a

Left: Panel of lathework circle segments. ***Right:*** Panel of lathework circle segments. ***Engraver:*** PSSP. ***Comments:*** H-MA-520-G44. Similar to W-MA-1430-003-G070. 18__. 1820s.

Rarity: —

$3 • W-MA-1430-003-G070b

Left: Panel of lathework circle segments. ***Right:*** Panel of lathework circle segments. ***Engraver:*** PSSP. ***Comments:*** H-MA-520-G46. Similar to W-MA-1430-003-G070. 18__. 1820s–1830s.

Rarity: —

$3 • W-MA-1430-003-G080

Left: Lathework. ***Center:*** Ceres. ***Right:*** Lathework. ***Engraver:*** PSSP. ***Comments:*** H-MA-520-G48. 18__. 1830s.

Rarity: —

$3 • W-MA-1430-003-G090

Left: 3 / Portrait of Fisher Ames / THREE. ***Center:*** Woman pointing, Reapers / Printing press. ***Right:*** 3 / Portrait of George Washington / THREE. ***Back:*** Plain. ***Engraver:*** New England Bank Note Co. / PSSP. ***Comments:*** H-MA-520-G52. 18__. 1830s–1850s.

Rarity: —

$3 • W-MA-1430-003-G090a

JF

Back: Check Plate. ***Engraver:*** New England Bank Note Co. / PSSP. ***Comments:*** H-MA-520-G52a. Similar to W-MA-1430-003-G090. 18__. 1830s–1840s.

Rarity: URS-3
VF $1,250

$3 • W-MA-1430-003-G090b

Overprint: Red THREE. ***Engraver:*** New England Bank Note Co. / PSSP. ***Comments:*** H-MA-520-G52b. Similar to W-MA-1430-003-G090. 18__. 1850s.

Rarity: —

$3 • W-MA-1430-003-G090c

Overprint: Red THREE. ***Engraver:*** New England Bank Note Co. / PSSP / ABNCo. monogram. ***Comments:*** H-MA-520-G52c. Similar to W-MA-1430-003-G090 but with additional engraver imprint. 18__. 1850s–1860s.

Rarity: —

$5 • **W-MA-1430-005-G100**

Left: Panel bearing state arms / 5 / 5. ***Center:*** Alternating flower garlands and gridwork segments. ***Right:*** 5 / 5. ***Engraver:*** PSSP. ***Comments:*** H-MA-520-G54. 18__. 1810s–1820s.

Rarity: —

$5 • **W-MA-1430-005-G100a**

Left: Lathework chain bearing MASSACHUSETTS vertically. ***Right:*** Panel of lathework circle segments. ***Engraver:*** PSSP. ***Comments:*** H-MA-520-G56. Similar to W-MA-1430-005-G100. 18__. 1820s.

Rarity: —

$5 • **W-MA-1430-005-G100b**

Left: Lathework chain bearing MASSACHUSETTS vertically. ***Right:*** Panel of lathework circle segments. ***Engraver:*** PSSP. ***Comments:*** H-MA-520-G58. Similar to W-MA-1430-005-G100. 18__. 1820s.

Rarity: —

$5 • **W-MA-1430-005-G100c**

Engraver: PSSP. ***Comments:*** H-MA-520-G60. Similar to W-MA-1430-005-G100 but with zigzag ruled lines. 18__. 1820s–1830s.

Rarity: —

$5 • **W-MA-1430-005-G100d**

Engraver: PSSP. ***Comments:*** H-MA-520-G62. Similar to W-MA-1430-005-G100 but with spiral lathework lines. 18__. 1830s.

Rarity: —

$5 • **W-MA-1430-005-G110** TD

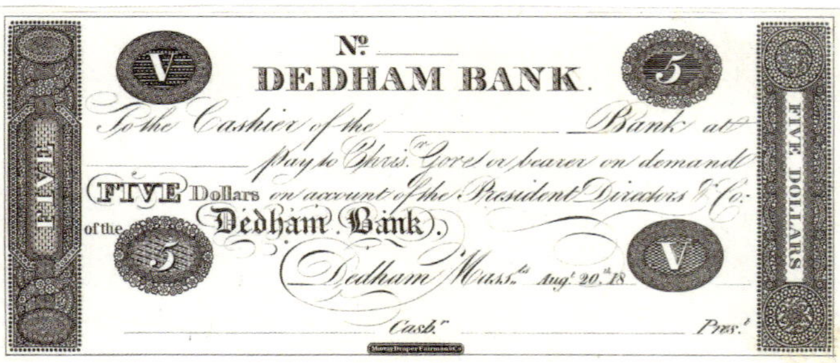

Engraver: Murray, Draper, Fairman & Co. ***Comments:*** H-Unlisted. Proof. Aug. 20, 18__.

Rarity: URS-2
Proof $1,000

$5 • **W-MA-1430-005-G120**

Left: 5 / Portrait of Fisher Ames / FIVE. ***Center:*** Man on horse, Dog and sheep / Train, Three men working / Cattle. ***Bottom center:*** Dog, key, and strongbox. ***Right:*** 5 / Portrait of George Washington / FIVE. ***Back:*** Plain. ***Engraver:*** New England Bank Note Co. / PSSP. ***Comments:*** H-MA-520-G64. 18__. 1830s–1850s.

Rarity: —

$5 • **W-MA-1430-005-G120a** TD

Back: Check Plate. ***Engraver:*** New England Bank Note Co. / PSSP. ***Comments:*** H-MA-520-G64a. Similar to W-MA-1430-005-G120. 18__. 1830s–1840s.

Rarity: URS-3
G $500

$5 • **W-MA-1430-005-G120b**

Overprint: Red FIVE. ***Engraver:*** New England Bank Note Co. / PSSP. ***Comments:*** H-MA-520-G64b. Similar to W-MA-1430-005-G120. 18__. 1850s.

Rarity: —

$5 • **W-MA-1430-005-G120c**

Overprint: Red FIVE. ***Engraver:*** New England Bank Note Co. / PSSP / ABNCo. monogram. ***Comments:*** H-MA-520-G64c. Similar to W-MA-1430-005-G120 but with additional engraver imprint. 18__. 1850s–1860s.

Rarity: —

$10 • **W-MA-1430-010-G130**

Left: Lathework panel bearing MASSACHUSETTS / 10 / 10 vertically. ***Center:*** Alternating flower garlands and gridwork segments / TEN. ***Right:*** 10 / 10 vertically. ***Engraver:*** Perkins. ***Comments:*** H-MA-520-G66. 18__. 1810s–1820s.

Rarity: —

$10 • **W-MA-1430-010-G130a**

Left: Lathework chain bearing MASSACHUSETTS vertically. ***Right:*** Panel of lathework circle segments. ***Engraver:*** Perkins. ***Comments:*** H-MA-520-G68. Similar to W-MA-1430-010-G130. 18__. 1820s.

Rarity: —

$10 • **W-MA-1430-010-G130b**

Left: Lathework chain bearing MASSACHUSETTS vertically. ***Right:*** Panel of lathework circle segments. ***Engraver:*** Perkins. ***Comments:*** H-MA-520-G70. Similar to W-MA-1430-010-G130. 18__. 1820s.

Rarity: —

$10 • **W-MA-1430-010-G130c**

Engraver: PSSP. ***Comments:*** H-MA-520-G72. Similar to W-MA-1430-010-G130 but with zigzag ruled lines. 18__. 1820s–1830s.

Rarity: —

$10 • **W-MA-1430-010-G130d**

Engraver: PSSP. ***Comments:*** H-MA-520-G74. Similar to W-MA-1430-010-G130 but with spiral lathework lines. 18__. 1830s.

Rarity: —

$10 • **W-MA-1430-010-G140** TD

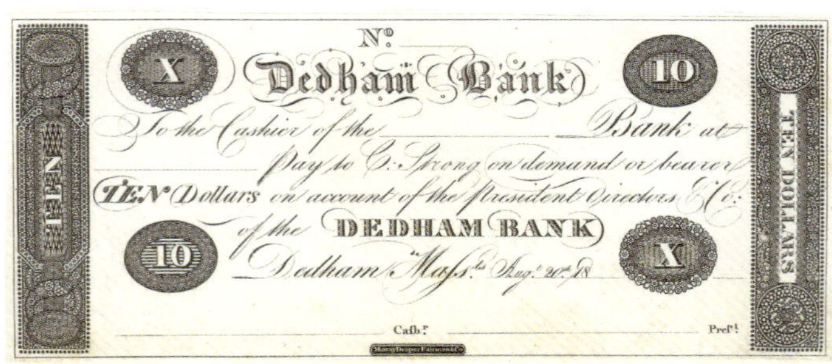

Engraver: Murray, Draper, Fairman & Co. ***Comments:*** H-Unlisted. Proof. Aug. 20, 18__.

Rarity: URS-2
Proof $1,000

$10 • W-MA-1430-010-G150

Left: 10 / Portrait of Fisher Ames / TEN. ***Center:*** Train passing cliffs, Three workmen with wheelbarrow / Woman seated with die bearing X. ***Bottom center:*** Dog, key, and strongbox. ***Right:*** 10 / Portrait of George Washington / TEN. ***Back:*** Plain. ***Engraver:*** New England Bank Note Co. / PSSP. ***Comments:*** H-MA-520-G76. 18__. 1830s–1850s.

Rarity: —

$10 • W-MA-1430-010-G150a

Back: Check Plate. ***Engraver:*** New England Bank Note Co. / PSSP. ***Comments:*** H-MA-520-G76a. Similar to W-MA-1430-010-G150. 18__. 1830s–1840s.

Rarity: —

$10 • W-MA-1430-010-G150b

CC

Overprint: Red TEN. ***Engraver:*** New England Bank Note Co. / PSSP. ***Comments:*** H-MA-520-G76b. Similar to W-MA-1430-010-G150. 18__. 1850s.

Rarity: URS-3
Proof $2,750

$10 • W-MA-1430-010-G150c

Overprint: Red TEN. ***Engraver:*** New England Bank Note Co. / PSSP / ABNCo. monogram. ***Comments:*** H-MA-520-G76c. Similar to W-MA-1430-010-G150 but with additional engraver imprint. 18__. 1850s–1860s.

Rarity: —

$20 • W-MA-1430-020-G160

Left: Panel bearing state arms / 20 / 20 vertically. ***Center:*** Alternating flower garlands and gridwork segments. ***Right:*** 20 / 20 vertically. ***Engraver:*** Perkins. ***Comments:*** H-MA-520-G78. 18__. 1810s–1820s.

Rarity: —

$20 • W-MA-1430-020-G160a

Left: Lathework chain bearing MASSACHUSETTS vertically. ***Engraver:*** PSSP. ***Comments:*** H-MA-520-G80. Similar to W-MA-1430-020-G160. 18__. 1820s–1830s.

Rarity: —

$20 • W-MA-1430-020-G170

Engraver: Unverified, but likely PSSP / New England Bank Note Co. ***Comments:*** H-MA-520-G82. No description available. 18__. 1830s.

Rarity: *None known*

$20 • W-MA-1430-020-G180

Left: 20 / Woman seated with book on lap opening chest. ***Center:*** XX / Eagle on rock / XX. ***Right:*** 20 / Ship in harbor. ***Engraver:*** New England Bank Note Co. ***Comments:*** H-MA-520-G86. 18__. 1840s–1850s.

Rarity: —

$20 • W-MA-1430-020-G190

TD

Tint: Green. ***Engraver:*** American Bank Note Co. ***Comments:*** H-MA-520-G88a. Proof. 18__. 1860s.

Rarity: URS-3
Proof $3,000

$50 • W-MA-1430-050-G200

Left: Panel bearing state arms / 50 / 50 vertically. ***Center:*** Alternating flower garlands and gridwork segments. ***Right:*** 50 / 50 vertically. ***Engraver:*** Perkins. ***Comments:*** H-MA-520-G90. 18__. 1810s–1820s.

Rarity: —

$50 • W-MA-1430-050-G200a

Left: Lathework chain bearing MASSACHUSETTS vertically. ***Engraver:*** PSSP. ***Comments:*** H-MA-520-G92. Similar to W-MA-1430-050-G200. 18__. 1820s–1830s.

Rarity: —

$50 • W-MA-1430-050-G210

Engraver: Unverified, but likely PSSP / New England Bank Note Co. ***Comments:*** H-MA-520-G94. No description available. 18__. 1830s.

Rarity: *None known*

$50 • W-MA-1430-050-G220

CC

Overprint: Red FIFTY. ***Engraver:*** New England Bank Note Co. ***Comments:*** H-MA-520-G98. 18__. 1840s–1850s.

Rarity: URS-1
Proof $4,250

$50 • W-MA-1430-050-G230

Left: 50 / Woman seated with book and shield. ***Center:*** Eagle and woman flanking shield. ***Right:*** 50 / Eagle. ***Tint:*** Green. ***Engraver:*** American Bank Note Co. ***Comments:*** H-MA-520-G100a. 18__. 1860s.

Rarity: —

$100 • W-MA-1430-100-G240

Left: Panel bearing state arms / 100 / 100 vertically. ***Center:*** Alternating flower garlands and gridwork segments. ***Right:*** 100 / 100 vertically. ***Engraver:*** Perkins. ***Comments:*** H-MA-520-G102. 18__. 1810s–1820s.

Rarity: —

$100 • W-MA-1430-100-G240a

Left: Lathework chain bearing MASSACHUSETTS vertically. ***Engraver:*** Perkins. ***Comments:*** H-MA-520-G104. Similar to W-MA-1430-100-G240. 18__. 1820s–1830s.

Rarity: —

$100 • W-MA-1430-100-G250

Engraver: Unverified, but likely PSSP / New England Bank Note Co. ***Comments:*** H-MA-520-G108. No description available. 18__. 1830s.

Rarity: *None known*

$100 • W-MA-1430-100-G260

Left: ONE HUNDRED on 100 / Portrait of William Henry Harrison. ***Center:*** Wharf scene, Men loading wagon with barrels. ***Right:*** ONE HUNDRED on 100 / Portrait of Christopher Columbus. ***Engraver:*** New England Bank Note Co. ***Comments:*** H-MA-520-G110. 18__. 1840s–1850s.

Rarity: —

$100 • W-MA-1430-100-G270

JF

Tint: Green. ***Engraver:*** American Bank Note Co. ***Comments:*** H-MA-520-G112a. Proof. 18__. 1860s.

Rarity: URS-3
Proof $6,500

$500 • W-MA-1430-500-G280

Left: Indian paddling canoe, Forest and mountains / 500 / D D. ***Bottom center:*** D / 500. ***Right:*** 500 / Justice. ***Engraver:*** New England Bank Note Co. ***Comments:*** H-MA-520-G116. 18__. 1840s–1850s.

Rarity: —

$500 • W-MA-1430-500-G290

CC

Tint: Green. ***Engraver:*** American Bank Note Co. ***Comments:*** H-MA-520-G118a. Proof. 18__. 1860s.

Rarity: URS-1
Proof $10,000

$500 • W-MA-1430-500-G300

TD

Engraver: New England Bank Note Co. ***Comments:*** H-Unlisted. Remainder. 18__.

Rarity: URS-1
Proof $5,000

Non-Valid Issues

$1 • W-MA-1430-001-A010

Left: Woman with grain floating above harbor, Waterfall and farm. ***Center:*** 1 / Three men rolling log. ***Right:*** 1. ***Tint:*** Brown-orange lathework outlining white 1. ***Engraver:*** Bald, Cousland & Co. ***Comments:*** H-MA-520-A5. Altered from $1 Pioneer Association, Lafayette, Indiana. 18__. 1850s.

Rarity: —

$5 • W-MA-1430-005-N010

Left: Steamboat / Eagle. ***Center:*** Woman with scroll / Train. ***Right:*** Steamboat / Eagle. ***Engraver:*** Toppan, Carpenter & Co. ***Comments:*** H-MA-520-N5. 18__. 1840s.

Rarity: —

Dorchester, Massachusetts

Named after the town of Dorchester in Dorset county, England, Dorchester was incorporated in 1630 by the Puritans. The first town meeting in America was held in Dorchester on October 8, 1633. In 1639 the town established the first elementary school in America. The first powder mill, paper mill, cracker manufactory, chocolate mill, and playing-card manufactory in the country were located in Dorchester, and the first grist mill was started beside the Neponset River on the Dorchester bank. The shipbuilding industry began early in 1640, followed by whale and cod fishing in the 1830s and horseshoe nail making in the 1860s. Most popular 19th centur y fruits were grown in the agricultural center of Dorchester.

Over time, parts of Dorchester was ceded to other towns, including Quincy, Hyde Park, Milton, Stoughton, and Boston.

Blue Hill Bank

1851–1864

W-MA-1445

History: On February 26, 1851, the name of the Dorchester and Milton Bank, W-MA-1460, was changed to the Blue Hill Bank, effective as of that date. The capital was $100,000. By 1857 it had increased to $150,000. Circulation was listed at $79,668 in 1854; its low was $68,116 in 1862. Selected figures for 1857 included: bills of this bank and other New England states $1,587; specie $20,908.52; real estate $6,000.

In 1865 the interests of the bank were succeeded by the Blue Hill National Bank of Dorchester, which again changed its name in 1881 to the Blue Hill National Bank of Milton.

Numismatic Commentary: Although hard to find, notes from the Blue Hill Bank turn up from time to time. Some have a vignette of the village center with horse-drawn carts passing by.

Valid Issues

$1 • W-MA-1445-001-G010

TD

Engraver: New England Bank Note Co. ***Comments:*** H-MA-525-G2. 18__. 1850s.

Rarity: URS-4

F $500

$1 • W-MA-1445-001-G020

Left: 1 / Female portrait. ***Center:*** Street scene, Bank and other buildings. ***Right:*** 1 / Cattle. ***Engraver:*** American Bank Note Co. ***Comments:*** H-MA-525-G4a. 1850s–1860s.

Rarity: —

F $1,175

$1 • W-MA-1445-001-G020a

TD

Overprint: Red ONE. ***Engraver:*** Rawdon, Wright, Hatch & Edson / New England Bank Note Co. ***Comments:*** H-Unlisted. Similar to W-MA-1445-001-G020 but with different engraver imprint. Jan. 1, 18__. 1850s.

Rarity: URS-3

F $1,200

$1 • W-MA-1445-001-G020b

TD

Overprint: Green panel outlining white ONE. ***Engraver:*** Rawdon, Wright, Hatch & Edson / New England Bank Note Co. ***Comments:*** H-Unlisted. Similar to W-MA-1445-001-G020 but with different engraver imprint. Jan. 1, 18__. 1860s.

Rarity: URS-3

VF $1,500

$2 • W-MA-1445-002-G030

TD

Engraver: New England Bank Note Co. ***Comments:*** H-MA-525-G6. 18__. 1850s.

Rarity: —

$2 • W-MA-1445-002-G030a

SI

Engraver: New England Bank Note Co. / ABNCo. monogram. ***Comments:*** H-Unlisted. Similar to W-MA-1445-002-G030 but with additional engraver imprint. Proof. 18__.

Rarity: URS-2

Proof $1,500

$2 • W-MA-1445-002-G040

Left: 2 / Female portrait. ***Center:*** Street scene, Bank and other buildings. ***Bottom center:*** Horses. ***Right:*** 2 / Woman. ***Engraver:*** American Bank Note Co. ***Comments:*** H-MA-525-G8. 1850s–1860s.

Rarity: —

$2 • W-MA-1445-002-G040a

TD

Overprint: Red TWO. ***Engraver:*** Rawdon, Wright, Hatch & Edson / New England Bank Note Co. ***Comments:*** H-Unlisted. Similar to W-MA-1445-002-G040 but with different engraver imprint. Jan. 1, 18__. 1860s.

Rarity: URS-3

VF $1,750

$2 • W-MA-1445-002-G040b

TD

Overprint: Green panel outlining white TWO. ***Engraver:*** Rawdon, Wright, Hatch & Edson / New England Bank Note Co. / ABNCo. monogram. ***Comments:*** H-Unlisted. Similar to W-MA-1445-002-G040 but with additional engraver imprint. Jan. 1, 18__. 1860s.

Rarity: URS-3
VF $1,750

$3 • W-MA-1445-003-G050

Left: THREE / 3. ***Center:*** Bales, Sailor standing with hat, Harbor / 3. ***Right:*** 3 / THREE / Train. ***Engraver:*** New England Bank Note Co. ***Comments:*** H-MA-525-G10. 18__. 1850s.

Rarity: —

$3 • W-MA-1445-003-G060

Left: 3 / Stone cutter. ***Center:*** Street scene, Bank and other buildings. ***Right:*** 3 / Woman. ***Engraver:*** American Bank Note Co. ***Comments:*** H-MA-525-G12a. 1850s–1860s.

Rarity: URS-3
F $1,250; **VF** $1,750

$3 • W-MA-1445-003-G060a

TD

Overprint: Red THREE. ***Engraver:*** Rawdon, Wright, Hatch & Edson / New England Bank Note Co. ***Comments:*** H-Unlisted. Similar to W-MA-1445-003-G060 but with different engraver imprint. Jan. 1, 18__. 1860s.

Rarity: URS-3
VF $1,100

$5 • W-MA-1445-005-G070

Left: Eagle on shield and anchor, Factories and ships / FIVE. ***Center:*** V with woman, cornucopia, and cherub. ***Right:*** 5 / Girl with ringlets holding basket. ***Engraver:*** New England Bank Note Co. ***Comments:*** H-MA-525-G14. 18__. 1850s.

Rarity: —

$5 • W-MA-1445-005-G070a

Tint: Green. ***Engraver:*** New England Bank Note Co. / ABNCo. monogram. ***Comments:*** H-MA-525-G14b. Similar to W-MA-1445-005-G070 but with additional engraver imprint. Beware of spurious W-MA-1445-005-S010. 1850s.

Rarity: —

$5 • W-MA-1445-005-G080

Left: 5 / Liberty standing by pedestal / FIVE. ***Center:*** Street scene, Bank and other buildings. ***Right:*** 5 / Ceres seated on plow. ***Engraver:*** American Bank Note Co. ***Comments:*** H-MA-525-G16. 1850s–1860s.

Rarity: —

$5 • W-MA-1445-005-G080a

TD

Overprint: Red FIVE. ***Engraver:*** Rawdon, Wright, Hatch & Edson / New England Bank Note Co. ***Comments:*** H-Unlisted. Similar to W-MA-1445-005-G080 but with different engraver imprint. Jan. 1, 18__. 1860s.

Rarity: URS-4
F $1,000; **VF** $1,250

$5 • W-MA-1445-005-G080b

TD

Overprint: Green panel outlining white FIVE. ***Engraver:*** Rawdon, Wright, Hatch & Edson / New England Bank Note Co. / ABNCo. monogram. ***Comments:*** H-Unlisted. Similar to W-MA-1445-005-G080 but with additional engraver imprint. Jan. 1, 18__. 1860s.

Rarity: URS-3
VF $1,750

$10 • W-MA-1445-010-G090

Left: Train, Mechanic seated with tools, Building / TEN. ***Center:*** X. ***Right:*** 10 / Reaper standing with sheaf. ***Engraver:*** New England Bank Note Co. ***Comments:*** H-MA-525-G18a. 18__. 1850s.

Rarity: —

$10 • W-MA-1445-010-G090a

SI

Engraver: New England Bank Note Co. / ABNCo. monogram. ***Comments:*** H-Unlisted. Similar to W-MA-1445-010-G090 but with additional engraver imprint. Proof. 18__.

Rarity: URS-2
Proof $1,000

$10 • W-MA-1445-010-G090b

Tint: Green. ***Engraver:*** New England Bank Note Co. / ABNCo. monogram. ***Comments:*** H-MA-525-G18b. Similar to W-MA-1445-010-G090 but with additional engraver imprint. 1850s–1860s.

Rarity: —

$10 • W-MA-1445-010-G100

Left: X / Farmer with scythe. ***Center:*** Street scene, Bank and other buildings. ***Right:*** 10 / Two women. ***Engraver:*** American Bank Note Co. ***Comments:*** H-MA-525-G20a. 1850s–1860s.

Rarity: —

$10 • W-MA-1445-010-G100a

Engraver: Rawdon, Wright, Hatch & Edson / New England Bank Note Co. / ABNCo. monogram ***Comments:*** H-Unlisted. Similar to W-MA-1445-010-G100 but with additional engraver imprint.

Rarity: URS-3

VF $1,750

$10 • W-MA-1445-010-G100b

TD

Overprint: Red TEN. ***Engraver:*** Rawdon, Wright, Hatch & Edson / New England Bank Note Co. ***Comments:*** H-Unlisted. Similar to W-MA-1445-010-G100 but with different engraver imprint. Jan. 1, 18__. 1850s.

Rarity: URS-3

F $100; **VF** $1,500

$10 • W-MA-1445-010-G100c

TD

Overprint: Green panel outlining white TEN. ***Engraver:*** Rawdon, Wright, Hatch & Edson / New England Bank Note Co. / ABNCo. monogram. ***Comments:*** H-Unlisted. Similar to W-MA-1445-010-G100 but with additional engraver imprint. Jan. 1, 18__. 1860s.

Rarity: URS-3

VF $1,600

$20 • W-MA-1445-020-G110

Left: 20 / Minerva standing with spear. ***Center:*** Women seated between 2 and 0. ***Bottom center:*** XX. ***Right:*** 20 / Woman reclining on cornucopia / 20. ***Engraver:*** New England Bank Note Co. ***Comments:*** H-MA-525-G22. 18__. 1850s.

Rarity: —

$20 • W-MA-1445-020-G120

TD

Tint: Green. ***Engraver:*** American Bank Note Co. ***Comments:*** H-MA-525-G24a. Proof. 186_. 1860s.

Rarity: URS-2

Proof $3,500

$50 • W-MA-1445-050-G130

Left: 50 / Steamboat and schooner. ***Center:*** Farmyard scene, Load of hay with two men on it, Man with rake and pail. ***Right:*** L / Justice kneeling. ***Engraver:*** New England Bank Note Co. ***Comments:*** H-MA-525-G26. 18__. 1850s.

Rarity: —

$50 • W-MA-1445-050-G140

TD

Tint: Green. ***Engraver:*** American Bank Note Co. ***Comments:*** H-MA-525-G28a. Bottom corner cut off. 1860s.

Rarity: URS-2

Proof $5,000

$100 • W-MA-1445-100-G150

TD

Engraver: New England Bank Note Co. ***Comments:*** H-MA-525-G30. 18__. 1850s.

Rarity: URS-2

F $3,250

$100 • W-MA-1445-100-G160 TD

Tint: Green. ***Engraver:*** American Bank Note Co. ***Comments:*** H-MA-525-G32a. Bottom corner cut off. 186_. 1860s

Rarity: URS-2
Proof $7,500

$500 • W-MA-1445-500-G170 TD

Tint: Green. ***Engraver:*** American Bank Note Co. ***Comments:*** H-MA-525-G34a. 186_. 1860s.

Rarity: URS-2
Proof $2,000

Non-Valid Issues

$5 • W-MA-1445-005-R010 TD

Overprint: Red FIVE. ***Engraver:*** Rawdon, Wright, Hatch & Edson / New England Bank Note Co. ***Comments:*** H-Unlisted. Raised from W-MA-1445-001-G020a. Jan. 1, 18__. June handwritten over Jan. in date.

Rarity: —

$5 • W-MA-1445-005-S010 CJF

Overprint: Red FIVE. ***Engraver:*** New England Bank Note Co. / ABNCo. monogram. ***Comments:*** H-MA-525-S5a. Spurious design imitating a rough verbal description of W-MA-1445-005-G070a. Aug. 1, 1860.

Rarity: URS-8
F $75

$10 • W-MA-1445-010-C090b TD

Tint: Green panel of microlettering. ***Engraver:*** New England Bank Note Co. / ABNCo. monogram. ***Comments:*** H-MA-525-C18b. Counterfeit of W-MA-1445-010-G090b. 18__. 1860s.

Rarity: URS-9
F $85; **VF** $150

$20 • W-MA-1445-020-R020

Engraver: American Bank Note Co. ***Comments:*** H-MA-525-R5. Raised from W-MA-1445-001-G020. 1860s.

Rarity: —

$100 • W-MA-1445-100-C150

Engraver: New England Bank Note Co. ***Comments:*** H-MA-525-C30. Counterfeit of W-MA-1445-100-G150. 18__. 1850s.

Rarity: —

Dorchester and Milton Bank
1832–1851
W-MA-1460

History: The Dorchester and Milton Bank was chartered on March 12, 1832, with an authorized capital of $100,000. Its location was in Lower Mills, a village within Dorchester. Circulation in 1839 was $33,373, and in 1845 it was $62,655. By 1849 it was down to $45,860. In 1851 the bank was entered at night and about $30,000 of its bills were stolen.

On February 26, 1851, the Legislature changed the name of the Dorchester and Milton Bank to the Blue Hill Bank, W-MA-1445, effective as of that date. Later newspapers and other accounts sometimes used the old name.

Numismatic Commentary: Notes from this bank are occasionally available in the marketplace.

Valid Issues

$1 • W-MA-1460-001-G010

Left: Lathework panel bearing MASSACHUSETTS vertically. ***Center:*** 1 / 1 / Alternating flower garlands and gridwork segments / ONE / 1 / 1. ***Right:*** Lathework panel bearing ONE / D / ONE vertically. ***Engraver:*** PSSP. ***Comments:*** H-MA-530-G2. 18__. 1830s.

Rarity: —

$1 • W-MA-1460-001-G020

TD

Comments: H-Unlisted. Mock-up note. 18__.

Rarity: URS-1

Proof $500

$1 • W-MA-1460-001-G030

TD

Engraver: New England Bank Note Co. ***Comments:*** H-MA-530-G4. 18__. 1830s–1840s.

Rarity: URS-4

VF $350

$1 • W-MA-1460-001-G040

JF

Engraver: New England Bank Note Co. ***Comments:*** H-MA-530-G6. 18__. 1840s–1850s.

Rarity: URS-4

VF $350

$2 • W-MA-1460-002-G050

Left: Lathework panel bearing MASSACHUSETTS vertically. ***Center:*** 2 / 2 / Alternating flower garlands and gridwork segments / TWO / 2 / 2. ***Right:*** Five TWOs vertically. ***Engraver:*** PSSP. ***Comments:*** H-MA-530-G8. 18__. 1830s.

Rarity: —

$2 • W-MA-1460-002-G060

Engraver: Unverified, but likely New England Bank Note Co. ***Comments:*** H-MA-530-G10. No description available. 18__. 1830s–1840s.

Rarity: *None known*

$2 • W-MA-1460-002-G070

TD

Engraver: New England Bank Note Co. ***Comments:*** H-MA-530-G12. 18__. 1840s–1850s.

Rarity: URS-3

VF $750

$3 • W-MA-1460-003-G080

Left: Lathework panel bearing MASSACHUSETTS vertically. ***Center:*** 3 / 3 / Alternating flower garlands and gridwork segments / THREE / 3 / 3. ***Right:*** Lathework panel bearing THREE vertically. ***Engraver:*** PSSP. ***Comments:*** H-MA-530-G14. 18__. 1830s.

Rarity: —

$3 • W-MA-1460-003-G090

Engraver: Unverified, but likely New England Bank Note Co. ***Comments:*** H-MA-530-G16. No description available. 18__. 1830s–1840s.

Rarity: *None known*

$3 • W-MA-1460-003-G100

TD

Engraver: New England Bank Note Co. ***Comments:*** H-MA-530-G18. 18__. 1840s–1850s.

Rarity: —

$3 • W-MA-1460-003-G110

TD

Engraver: New England Bank Note Co. ***Comments:*** H-Unlisted. 18__. 1840s.

Rarity: URS-3

VF $1,000

$5 • W-MA-1460-005-G120 TD

Engraver: PSSP. ***Comments:*** H-MA-530-G20. 18__. 1830s.

Rarity: URS-4

VF $350

$5 • W-MA-1460-005-G130 TD

Engraver: PSSP. ***Comments:*** H-Unlisted. 18__. 1840s.

Rarity: URS-3

F $800

$5 • W-MA-1460-005-G140

Left: Eagle on shield and anchor, Factories and ships / FIVE. ***Center:*** V with woman, cornucopia, and cherub. ***Right:*** 5 / Girl with ringlets holding basket. ***Engraver:*** New England Bank Note Co. ***Comments:*** H-MA-530-G22. 18__. 1840s–1850s.

Rarity: —

$10 • W-MA-1460-010-G150

Left: Lathework chain bearing MASSACHUSETTS / 10 / 10 vertically. ***Center:*** Alternating flower garlands and gridwork segments / TEN. ***Right:*** 10 / 10 vertically. ***Engraver:*** PSSP. ***Comments:*** H-MA-530-G24. 18__. 1830s.

Rarity: —

$10 • W-MA-1460-010-G160 TD

Engraver: PSSP. ***Comments:*** H-MA-530-G26. 18__. 1840s.

Rarity: URS-4

VF $350

$10 • W-MA-1460-010-G170

Left: Train, Mechanic seated with tools, Building / TEN. ***Center:*** X. ***Right:*** 10 / Reaper standing with sheaf. ***Engraver:*** New England Bank Note Co. ***Comments:*** H-MA-530-G28. 18__. 1840s–1850s.

Rarity: —

$20 • W-MA-1460-020-G180

Left: Lathework chain bearing MASSACHUSETTS / 20 / 20 vertically. ***Center:*** Alternating flower garlands and gridwork segments / TWENTY. ***Right:*** 20 / 20 vertically. ***Engraver:*** PSSP. ***Comments:*** H-MA-530-G30. 18__. 1830s.

Rarity: —

$20 • W-MA-1460-020-G190 TD

Engraver: Underwood, Bald & Spencer. ***Comments:*** H-Unlisted. 18__.

Rarity: URS-2

Proof $1,500

$50 • W-MA-1460-050-G200

Left: Lathework chain bearing MASSACHUSETTS / 50 / 50 vertically. ***Center:*** Alternating flower garlands and gridwork segments / FIFTY. ***Right:*** 50 / 50 vertically. ***Engraver:*** PSSP. ***Comments:*** H-MA-530-G32. 18__. 1830s.

Rarity: —

Non-Valid Issues

$2 • W-MA-1460-002-C050 CC

Engraver: PSSP. ***Comments:*** H-MA-530-C8. Counterfeit of W-MA-1460-002-G050. 18__. Circa 1832.

Rarity: URS-8

VG $75; **VF** $175

Mattapan Bank

1849–1864

W-MA-1470

History: The Mattapan Bank was chartered in 1849 with an authorized capital of $100,000. The bank commenced operations in Dorchester in an office on Harrison Square. Beginning in early 1850, many counterfeit $3 bills of the bank appeared in circulation. Warnings about these continued to be printed into 1851. In June of that year, the bank announced that there were no genuine $3 notes in circulation, as "they have all been called in."

Circulation ranged from a low of $33,299 in 1857 to a high of $81,523 in 1863. Real estate was valued at $6,000. Specie was counted to be worth $5,161.34 in 1854 and $9,514.05 in 1862.

The First National Bank of Dorchester, chartered on December 14, 1863, succeeded the interests of the state bank, which wound down its operations in 1864.

Numismatic Commentary: All genuine notes of the Mattapan Bank are hard to find.

Valid Issues

$1 • W-MA-1470-001-G010

TD

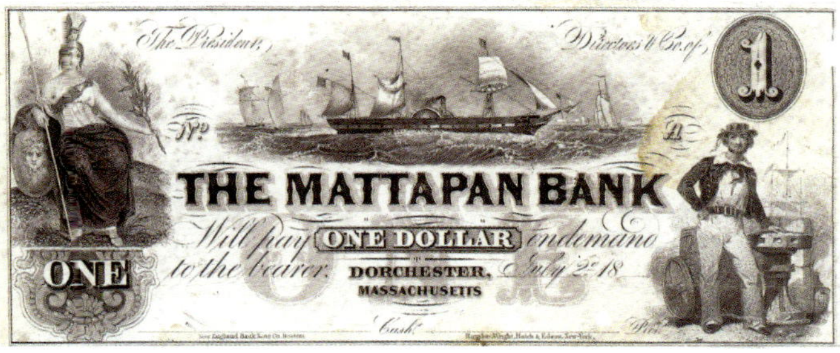

Engraver: New England Bank Note Co. / Rawdon, Wright, Hatch & Edson. ***Comments:*** H-MA-535-G2. Remainder. July 2, 18__. 1849–1850s.

Rarity: URS-3
Proof $750

$1 • W-MA-1470-001-G010a

TD

Overprint: Red ONE. ***Engraver:*** New England Bank Note Co. / Rawdon, Wright, Hatch & Edson / ABNCo. monogram. ***Comments:*** H-Unlisted. Similar to W-MA-1470-001-G010 but with additional engraver imprint. 18__. 1860s.

Rarity: URS-3
VF $1,250

$2 • W-MA-1470-002-G020

CJF

Engraver: New England Bank Note Co. / Rawdon, Wright, Hatch & Edson. ***Comments:*** H-MA-535-G4. July 2, 18__. 1849–1850s.

Rarity: URS-3
VF $650

$2 • W-MA-1470-002-G020a

TD

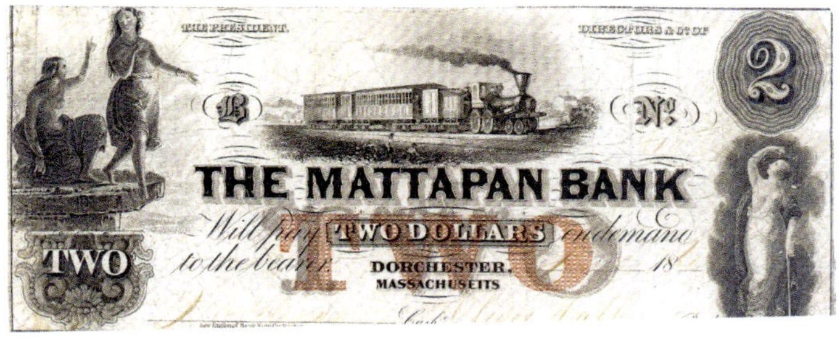

Overprint: Red TWO. ***Engraver:*** New England Bank Note Co. / Rawdon, Wright, Hatch & Edson / ABNCo. monogram. ***Comments:*** H-Unlisted. Similar to W-MA-1470-002-G020 but with additional engraver imprint. Bottom of note cut off. 18__.

Rarity: URS-3
F $300

$3 • W-MA-1470-003-G030

Left: 3 / Cattle. ***Center:*** Woman seated with cornucopia, Factories, bridge, canal, and train. ***Right:*** 3 / Ship. ***Engraver:*** New England Bank Note Co. / Rawdon, Wright, Hatch & Edson. ***Comments:*** H-MA-535-G6. July 2, 18__. 1849–1850s.

Rarity: —

$3 • W-MA-1470-003-G040

Left: 3 / Sailor, mechanic, and farmer standing with 3. ***Center:*** Mechanic reclining with hammer on shoulder, Train and factory. ***Right:*** 3 / Woman. ***Engraver:*** New England Bank Note Co. / Rawdon, Wright, Hatch & Edson. ***Comments:*** H-MA-535-G8. 1850s.

Rarity: —

$5 • W-MA-1470-005-G050

Left: Indian man with wampum belt, bow, and arrows / FIVE. ***Center:*** Steamship and ships. ***Right:*** 5 / Two women, one with sword and shield, one seated with arm on 5. ***Engraver:*** New England Bank Note Co. / Rawdon, Wright, Hatch & Edson. ***Comments:*** H-MA-535-G10. 18__. 1849–1850s.

Rarity: —

$5 • W-MA-1470-005-G050a

TD

Overprint: Red FIVE. ***Engraver:*** New England Bank Note Co. / Rawdon, Wright, Hatch & Edson / ABNCo. monogram. ***Comments:*** H-Unlisted. Similar to W-MA-1470-005-G050 but with additional engraver imprint. 18__. 1860s.

Rarity: URS-3
VF $750

$10 • W-MA-1470-010-G060

Left: 10 / Stonecutter at work. ***Center:*** Eagle on shield, Ship and steamship. ***Right:*** 10 / Indian woman holding ear of corn and X. ***Engraver:*** New England Bank Note Co. / Rawdon, Wright, Hatch & Edson. ***Comments:*** H-MA-535-G12. 18__. 1849–1850s.

Rarity: —

$10 • W-MA-1470-010-G060a

TD

Overprint: Red TEN. ***Engraver:*** New England Bank Note Co. / Rawdon, Wright, Hatch & Edson. ***Comments:*** H-Unlisted. Similar to W-MA-1470-010-G060. 18__. 1850s.

Rarity: URS-3
VF $800

$20 • W-MA-1470-020-G070

Left: 20 / Minerva standing with spear. ***Center:*** Woman seated between 2 and 0. ***Right:*** 20 / Woman reclining on cornucopia / 20. ***Engraver:*** Rawdon, Wright, Hatch & Edson. ***Comments:*** H-MA-535-G14. 18__. 1850s.

Rarity: —

$20 • W-MA-1470-020-G080

TD

Tint: Green. ***Engraver:*** American Bank Note Co. ***Comments:*** H-MA-535-G16a. 18__. 1860s.

Rarity: URS-3
VF $2,000

$50 • W-MA-1470-050-G090

Left: 50 / Minerva standing by column. ***Center:*** Ceres and Vulcan flanking cornucopia. ***Right:*** 50 / Cherub in sailboat / 50. ***Engraver:*** Rawdon, Wright, Hatch & Edson. ***Comments:*** H-MA-535-G18. 18__. 1850s.

Rarity: —

$50 • W-MA-1470-050-G100

Left: Woman seated holding sheaf, Bale and shield bearing 50 DOLLARS, Ships. ***Center:*** 50 / 50. ***Right:*** 50 / State arms. ***Tint:*** Green. ***Engraver:*** American Bank Note Co. ***Comments:*** H-MA-535-G20a. 18__. 1860s.

Rarity: —

$100 • W-MA-1470-100-G110

Left: 100 / Vulcan seated with sledge and anchor. ***Center:*** Train on bridge, Eagle on limb, Canal locks / C. ***Bottom center:*** 100. ***Right:*** 100 / Ceres seated, Cornucopia. ***Engraver:*** Rawdon, Wright, Hatch & Edson. ***Comments:*** H-MA-535-G22. 18__. 1850s.

Rarity: —

$100 • W-MA-1470-100-G120

Left: 100 / Ship carpenter holding axe. ***Center:*** Three sailors on beach, one using spyglass / C. ***Bottom center:*** C. ***Right:*** 100 / Woman feeding chickens. ***Tint:*** Green. ***Engraver:*** American Bank Note Co. ***Comments:*** H-MA-535-G24a. 18__. 1860s.

Rarity: —

Non-Valid Issues

$3 • W-MA-1470-003-C030

NJW

Engraver: New England Bank Note Co. / Rawdon, Wright, Hatch & Edson. ***Comments:*** H-MA-535-C6. Counterfeit of W-MA-1470-003-G030. July 2, 18__. 1849.

Rarity: URS-6
VG $65; **VF** $150

$5 • W-MA-1470-005-C050

Engraver: New England Bank Note Co. / Rawdon, Wright, Hatch & Edson. ***Comments:*** H-MA-535-C10. Counterfeit of W-MA-1470-005-G050. 18__. 1850s.

Rarity: —

$10 • W-MA-1470-010-R010

Engraver: New England Bank Note Co. / Rawdon, Wright, Hatch & Edson. ***Comments:*** H-MA-535-R5. Raised from W-MA-1470-003-G030 or C030. 18__. Circa 1850.

Rarity: —

$10 • W-MA-1470-010-S010

TD

Engraver: Rawdon, Wright, Hatch & Edson. ***Comments:*** H-Unlisted. July 2, 18__. 1850s.

Rarity: URS-3
VF $850

$20 • **W-MA-1470-020-R020**

Engraver: New England Bank Note Co. / Rawdon, Wright, Hatch & Edson. ***Comments:*** H-MA-535-R10. Raised from W-MA-1470-003-G030 or C030. 18__. Circa 1850.

Rarity: —

Duxbury, Massachusetts

Originally inhabited by the Wampanoags, who called the area Mattakeesett or "place of many fish," the district that became Duxbury was officially incorporated in 1637. It was a farming community during the 17th and 18th centuries, but shipbuilding began in the community after the end of the American Revolution. When the Treaty of Paris reestablished fishing rights, a sudden call for ships was answered by the building of large fishing schooners, which expanded into ever-larger shipbuilding for the town. By the 1840s, the town of Duxbury had 20 shipyards and built about 10 large ships every year.

Ezra Weston, the owner of the largest industry in Duxbury, was famous for his merchant fleet. In 1841 his son constructed the largest ship ever built in New England up to that time, weighing 880 tons. The shipbuilding era for Duxbury ended in the 1850s as steamships and railways became the more efficient means of transportation. This marked the decline for the economic prominence that had heretofore been enjoyed by the area.

Duxbury Bank

1833–1842

W-MA-1480

History: The Duxbury Bank was chartered on March 25, 1833, with an authorized capital of $100,000. Business commenced on October 1 of that year. The bank was located at the junction of Washington Street and Powder Point. Loans included arrangements with maritime interests. The bank's circulation in 1839 was $52,398.

In November 1842, the stockholders voted unanimously to wind up the bank's affairs and close down. The bank redeemed its notes for several years, after which any bills remaining in circulation became worthless.

Numismatic Commentary: Genuine notes of the Duxbury Bank are very rare. Many show the anti-counterfeiting device on the back called a "Check Plate," printed in the Congreve style by Abel Bowen of Boston.

Valid Issues

$1 • **W-MA-1480-001-G010**

Left: 1 / Ship on stocks / 1. ***Center:*** ONE / Woman with sheaf pointing to ship / ONE. ***Right:*** 1 / Beehive / 1. ***Back:*** Blue and brown Congreve. ***Engraver:*** New England Bank Note Co. / PSSP. ***Comments:*** H-MA-540-G2. 18__. 1850s.

Rarity: —

$1 • **W-MA-1480-001-G010a**

TD

Back: Plain. ***Engraver:*** New England Bank Note Co. / PSSP. ***Comments:*** H-MA-540-G2a. Similar to W-MA-1480-001-G010. 18__. 1840s.

Rarity: URS-3

VF $1,000

$2 • **W-MA-1480-002-G020**

Left: 2 / Woman with cornucopia and staff / TWO. ***Center:*** TWO / Ceres seated with machinery and merchandise, Factories and ships. ***Right:*** 2 / Female portrait / TWO. ***Back:*** Blue and brown Congreve. ***Engraver:*** New England Bank Note Co. / PSSP. ***Comments:*** H-MA-540-G4. 18__. 1830s.

Rarity: URS-7

VG $100; **VF** $175

$2 • **W-MA-1480-002-G020a**

TD

Back: Plain. ***Engraver:*** New England Bank Note Co. / PSSP. ***Comments:*** H-MA-540-G4a. Similar to W-MA-1480-002-G020. 18__. 1850s.

Rarity: URS-3

F $500

$2 • **W-MA-1480-002-G030**

TD

Engraver: New England Bank Note Co. / PSSP. ***Comments:*** H-Unlisted. 18__. 1840s.

Rarity: URS-3

VG $200

$3 • W-MA-1480-003-G040

CJF, CJF

Back: Blue and brown Congreve bearing CHECK. ***Engraver:*** New England Bank Note Co. / PSSP. ***Comments:*** H-MA-540-G6. Remainder. 18__. 1830s.

Rarity: URS-2
Unc-Rem $1,200

$3 • W-MA-1480-003-G040a

Back: Plain. ***Engraver:*** New England Bank Note Co. / PSSP. ***Comments:*** H-MA-540-G6a. Similar to W-MA-1480-003-G040. 18__. 1840s.

Rarity: —

$5 • W-MA-1480-005-G050

Back: Blue and brown Congreve. ***Engraver:*** New England Bank Note Co. / PSSP. ***Comments:*** H-MA-540-G8. 18__. 1830s.

Rarity: —

$5 • W-MA-1480-005-G050a

Back: Plain. ***Engraver:*** New England Bank Note Co. / PSSP. ***Comments:*** H-MA-540-G8a. Similar to W-MA-1480-005-G050. 18__. 1840s.

Rarity: —

$10 • W-MA-1480-010-G060

Back: Blue and brown Congreve. ***Engraver:*** New England Bank Note Co. / PSSP. ***Comments:*** H-MA-540-G10. 18__. 1830s.

Rarity: —

$10 • W-MA-1480-010-G060a

Back: Plain. ***Engraver:*** New England Bank Note Co. / PSSP. ***Comments:*** H-MA-540-G10a. Similar to W-MA-1480-010-G060. 18__. 1840s.

Rarity: —

$20 • W-MA-1480-020-G070

Back: Blue and brown Congreve. ***Engraver:*** New England Bank Note Co. / PSSP. ***Comments:*** H-MA-540-G12. 18__. 1830s.

Rarity: —

$20 • W-MA-1480-020-G070a

Back: Plain. ***Engraver:*** New England Bank Note Co. / PSSP. ***Comments:*** H-MA-540-G12a. Similar to W-MA-1480-020-G070. 18__. 1830s.

Rarity: —

$50 • W-MA-1480-050-G080

Back: Blue and brown Congreve. ***Engraver:*** New England Bank Note Co. / PSSP. ***Comments:*** H-MA-540-G14. 18__. 1830s.

Rarity: —

$50 • W-MA-1480-050-G080a

Back: Plain. ***Engraver:*** New England Bank Note Co. / PSSP. ***Comments:*** H-MA-540-G14a. Similar to W-MA-1480-050-G080. 18__. 1840s.

Rarity: —

$100 • W-MA-1480-100-G090

Back: Blue and brown Congreve. ***Engraver:*** New England Bank Note Co. / PSSP. ***Comments:*** H-MA-540-G16. 18__. 1830s.

Rarity: —

$100 • W-MA-1480-100-G090a

Back: Plain. ***Engraver:*** New England Bank Note Co. / PSSP. ***Comments:*** H-MA-540-G16a. Similar to W-MA-1480-100-G090. 18__. 1840s.

Rarity: —

Non-Valid Issues

$1 • W-MA-1480-001-A010

Left: ONE / Two Indians reclining and smoking. ***Center:*** 1 / Three allegorical women with eagle, pole and cap, shield, balance, and book / 1. ***Bottom center:*** Cattle. ***Right:*** 1 / Portrait of George Washington / ONE. ***Engraver:*** Terry, Pelton & Co. ***Comments:*** H-MA-540-A5. Altered from W-MA-2860-001-G020. 18__. Circa 1840.

Rarity: —

$2 • W-MA-1480-002-A020

Left: TWO / Portrait of cherub / 2. ***Center:*** 2 / Ceres giving grain to seated Liberty / 2. ***Bottom center:*** Anchor and implements. ***Right:*** 2 / Female portrait / TWO. ***Engraver:*** New England Bank Note Co. / Rawdon, Wright, Hatch & Edson. ***Comments:*** H-MA-540-A10. Altered from W-MA-2860-002-G070. 18__. Circa 1840.

Rarity: —

$3 • W-MA-1480-003-A030

Left: 3 / Woman standing with branch, trident, and THREE / THREE. ***Center:*** Female portrait / Ceres and Justice flanking shield bearing anchor surmounted by eagle / Portrait of cherub. ***Bottom center:*** Anchor and implements. ***Right:*** 3 / Ceres seated in grain field / THREE. ***Engraver:*** Terry, Pelton & Co. ***Comments:*** H-MA-540-A15. Altered from W-MA-2860-003-G090. 18__. Circa 1840.

Rarity: —

$5 • W-MA-1480-005-A040

Left: FIVE / Portrait of Benjamin Franklin / V. ***Center:*** 5 / Agricultural items, Two allegorical women standing and one seated, Ship. ***Bottom center:*** Anchor and implements. ***Right:*** V / Portrait of Marquis de Lafayette / FIVE. ***Engraver:*** Terry, Pelton & Co. ***Comments:*** H-MA-540-A20. Altered from W-MA-2860-005-G110. 18__. Circa 1840.

Rarity: —

$10 • W-MA-1480-010-A050

Left: 10 / Portrait of George Washington held by cherub / 10. ***Center:*** X / Spread eagle with shield and arrows, E PLURIBUS UNUM / X. ***Bottom center:*** Ship. ***Right:*** 10 / Indian man / 10. ***Engraver:*** Terry, Pelton & Co. ***Comments:*** H-MA-540-A25. Altered from W-MA-2860-010-A010. 18__. Circa 1840.

Rarity: —

East Boston, Massachusetts

East Boston, a neighborhood of Boston, was originally six islands that were later connected via landfill: Noddle, Hog, Breed's, Governor's, Bird, and Apple. Noddle Island once served as grazing land for cattle. In 1836 the neighborhood was annexed to Boston.

At the turn of the 19th century, William H. Sumner desired to construct a turnpike which would connect Salem and Boston by going through Noddle Island. However, due to plans for a future naval yard and the concerns of the War of 1812, the turnpike was rerouted through Chelsea. As a result, Sumner spent the next decades forming the East Boston Company in order to purchase the whole land of Noddle Island. A paddle boat system was devised as transportation between the island and the mainland.

During the 1830s the East Boston Company continued to promote and enhance East Boston by expanding railroads, ferries, and bridges. The East Boston Lumber Company and the Boston Sugar Refinery were also located here.

In 1833 the population of East Boston was eight. A mere five years later it had increased to 1,000, and then to 6,500 in 1847, and again to 30,000 in 1880.

See also Boston and South Boston, Massachusetts.

Maverick Bank

1854–1864

W-MA-1490

History: The Maverick Bank was conceived in 1849, but it was not chartered until March 28, 1854. The institution had an authorized capital of $400,000, a figure that the bank maintained throughout its existence. Business commenced on August 1.

In June 1856, the bank moved from East Boston to 75 State Street in the heart of Boston's financial district. Circulation in 1857 was $100,766. In 1860 it was $100,676. Specie amounted to $47,104.81.

On December 31, 1864, the Maverick National Bank of Boston was chartered to succeed the interests of the Maverick Bank. There had been some delays in the application due to the fact that certain British stockholders had objected to the idea.

See also listing under Boston, W-MA-720.

East Bridgewater, Massachusetts

Originally a part of Plymouth and Duxbury, the district that became East Bridgewater separated from Bridgewater and was incorporated in June 1823. The town is north of the Taunton River and was economically provided for by agricultural pursuits during the 19th century. Boot and shoe manufacturing was important, as were textile mills.

See also Bridgewater and North Bridgewater, Massachusetts.

East Bridgewater Bank

1828–1847

W-MA-1500

History: The East Bridgewater Bank was chartered on March 8, 1828, with an authorized capital of $100,000 "in gold and silver." The founders were Isaac Whitman, Levi Keith, Nahum Mitchell, Ephraim Hyde, Aaron Hobart, John E. Howard, Nathan Lazell Jr., and Nathaniel Cross.

The bank surrendered its charter in March 1840 and, through the Suffolk Bank, redeemed all of its bills that were presented.

Numismatic Commentary: All known issues are engraved by Terry, Pelton & Co. and are hard to find, all except for the $1.25 and $1.50 issues. These two notes may also be found as an uncut sheet.

Valid Issues

$1 • W-MA-1500-001-G010

CJF

Engraver: Terry, Pelton & Co. ***Comments:*** H-MA-545-G2. Proof. 18__. 1830s–1840s.

Rarity: URS-2
Proof $1,000

$1.25 • W-MA-1500-001.25-G020

CJF

Engraver: Terry, Pelton & Co. ***Comments:*** H-MA-545-G4. 18__. 1830s–1840s.

Rarity: URS-5
Unc-Rem $300

$1.50 • W-MA-1500-001.50-G030

CJF

Engraver: Terry, Pelton & Co. ***Comments:*** H-MA-545-G6. 18__. 1830s–1840s.

Rarity: URS-5
Unc-Rem $300

$1.75 • W-MA-1500-001.75-G040

Left: 1 Doll. 75 Cts. vertically. ***Center:*** Female portrait / Sailor with hat and pipe leaning on anchor, arms and legs crossed / $1 75/100. ***Bottom center:*** Ship. ***Right:*** $1 75/100 / Two reapers, one bending over / $1 75/100. ***Engraver:*** Terry, Pelton & Co. ***Comments:*** H-MA-545-G8. 18__. 1830s–1840s.

Rarity: —

$2 • W-MA-1500-002-G050

TD

Engraver: Terry, Pelton & Co. ***Comments:*** H-MA-545-G10. 18__. 1830s–1840s.

Rarity: URS-3
F $100; **VF** $800; **Proof** $2,250

$3 • W-MA-1500-003-G060

Left: THREE vertically. ***Center:*** 3 / Barn with horse / Man. ***Right:*** 3 / Portrait of Benjamin Franklin. ***Engraver:*** Terry, Pelton & Co. ***Comments:*** H-MA-545-G12. 18__. 1830s–1840s.

Rarity: URS-3
Proof $1,100

$5 • W-MA-1500-005-G070

CJF

Engraver: Terry, Pelton & Co. ***Comments:*** H-MA-545-G14. Proof. 18__. 1830s–1840s.

Rarity: —

$10 • W-MA-1500-010-G080

TD

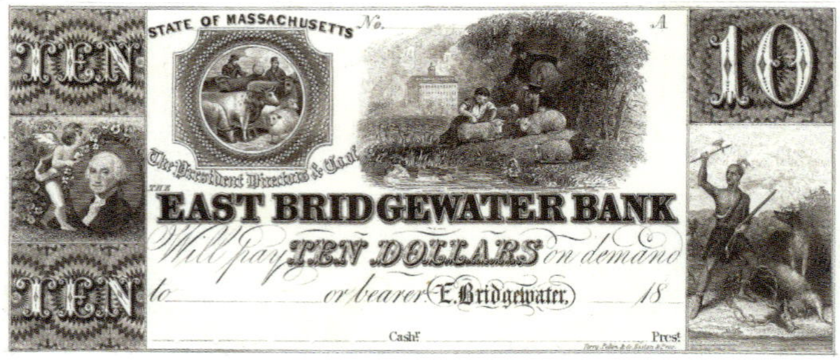

Engraver: Terry, Pelton & Co. ***Comments:*** H-MA-545-G16. Proof. 18__. 1830s–1840s.

Rarity: URS-2
Proof $2,000

$20 • W-MA-1500-020-G090

Left: XX / River scene / XX. ***Center:*** Indian with rifle and tomahawk. ***Right:*** 20 / Man standing / 20. ***Engraver:*** Terry, Pelton & Co. ***Comments:*** H-MA-545-G18. 18__. 1830s–1840s.

Rarity: URS-3
Proof $1,100

Uncut Sheets

$1.50-$1.25 • W-MA-1500-001.50.001.25-US010

CJF

Comments: H-MA-545-G6, G4. 18__. 1830s–1840s.

Rarity: URS-4
Unc-Rem $800

East Cambridge, Massachusetts

One of the neighborhoods of Cambridge, East Cambridge is bounded on the east by the Charles River.

See also Cambridge and Cambridgeport, Massachusetts.

Lechmere Bank
1854–1865
W-MA-1510

History: The Lechmere Bank was incorporated on April 28, 1853, with $100,000 in authorized capital, "to be established in that part of Cambridge known as East Cambridge." Business began as soon as half of the capital amount was paid in. The capital was raised to $150,000 by 1858.

The bank's first president was Edmund Boynton, and John Savage Jr. was its first cashier. The bank's circulation was $68,207 in 1857, $89,507 in 1858, and $68,207 in 1860. Selected figures for 1857 included: bills of this bank and other New England states $5,358.95; specie $24,285.70.

The business of the Lechmere Bank was succeeded by the Lechmere National Bank of East Cambridge, chartered in December 1864. The state bank wound down its business starting in 1865.

See also listing under Cambridge, W-MA-1240.

Numismatic Commentary: All genuine notes from this bank are especially hard to locate.

Valid Issues

$1 • W-MA-1510-001-G010
Left: ONE / Woman seated with shield. ***Center:*** Train on Cambridge Bridge, Wharf, View of East Cambridge. ***Right:*** 1 / Portrait of Edmund Winchester. ***Engraver:*** Rawdon, Wright, Hatch & Edson. ***Comments:*** H-MA-550-G2. 18__. 1850s.

Rarity: —

$1 • W-MA-1510-001-G010a
Overprint: Likely red. ***Engraver:*** Rawdon, Wright, Hatch & Edson. ***Comments:*** H-MA-550-G2a. Similar to W-MA-1510-001-G010. 18__. 1850s.

Rarity: URS-5
Proof $2,250

$1 • W-MA-1510-001-G010b
CC

Overprint: Red ONE. ***Engraver:*** Toppan, Carpenter, Casilear & Co. ***Comments:*** H-Unlisted. Similar to W-MA-1510-001-G010 but with different engraver imprint. 185_. 1850s.

Rarity: URS-2
VF $1,700

$2 • W-MA-1510-002-G020
Left: 2 / Female portrait. ***Center:*** Train on Cambridge Bridge. ***Right:*** 2 / Portrait of Edmund Winchester. ***Engraver:*** Rawdon, Wright, Hatch & Edson. ***Comments:*** H-MA-550-G4. 18__. 1850s.

Rarity: —

$2 • W-MA-1510-002-G020a
Overprint: Likely red. ***Engraver:*** Rawdon, Wright, Hatch & Edson. ***Comments:*** H-MA-550-G4a. Similar to W-MA-1510-002-G020. 18__. 1850s.

Rarity: —

$3 • W-MA-1510-003-G030
Center: 3 / Train on Cambridge Bridge, East Cambridge. ***Right:*** 3 / Portrait of Edmund Winchester. ***Engraver:*** Rawdon, Wright, Hatch & Edson. ***Comments:*** H-MA-550-G6. 18__. 1850s.

Rarity: —

$3 • W-MA-1510-003-G030a
Overprint: Red 3. ***Engraver:*** Rawdon, Wright, Hatch & Edson. ***Comments:*** H-MA-550-G6a. Similar to W-MA-1510-003-G030. 18__. 1850s.

Rarity: —

$5 • W-MA-1510-005-G040
Left: FIVE / Woman seated with shield. ***Center:*** Train on Cambridge Bridge, East Cambridge / 5. ***Right:*** 5 / Portrait of Edmund Winchester. ***Engraver:*** Rawdon, Wright, Hatch & Edson. ***Comments:*** H-MA-550-G8. 18__. 1850s.

Rarity: —

$5 • W-MA-1510-005-G040a
Overprint: Likely red. ***Engraver:*** Rawdon, Wright, Hatch & Edson. ***Comments:*** H-MA-550-G8a. Similar to W-MA-1510-005-G040. 18__. 1850s.

Rarity: —

$10 • W-MA-1510-010-G050
Left: Woman holding die bearing 10 / TEN. ***Center:*** Portrait of Edmund Winchester. ***Right:*** Woman holding die bearing 10 / TEN. ***Engraver:*** Rawdon, Wright, Hatch & Edson. ***Comments:*** H-MA-550-G10. 18__. 1850s.

Rarity: —

$20 • W-MA-1510-020-G060
Left: 20 / Sailor leaning on capstan. ***Center:*** Blacksmith shoeing horse. ***Right:*** 20 / Portrait of Edmund Winchester. ***Engraver:*** Rawdon, Wright, Hatch & Edson. ***Comments:*** H-MA-550-G12. 18__. 1850s.

Rarity: —

$50 • W-MA-1510-050-G070
Left: 50 / State arms. ***Center:*** Woman with shield, View of U.S. Capitol. ***Right:*** 50 / Portrait of John Hancock. ***Engraver:*** Rawdon, Wright, Hatch & Edson. ***Comments:*** H-MA-550-G14. 18__. 1850s.

Rarity: —

$100 • W-MA-1510-100-G080
Left: 100 / Female portrait. ***Center:*** Three women. ***Right:*** 100 / Portrait of Edmund Winchester. ***Engraver:*** Rawdon, Wright, Hatch & Edson. ***Comments:*** H-MA-550-G16. 18__. 1850s.

Rarity: —

$500 • W-MA-1510-500-G090
Left: D / Portrait of George Washington. ***Center:*** View of U.S. Capitol. ***Bottom center:*** Eagle. ***Right:*** 500 / Male portrait. ***Engraver:*** Rawdon, Wright, Hatch & Edson. ***Comments:*** H-MA-550-G18. 18__. 1850s.

Rarity: —

Non-Valid Issues

$5 • W-MA-1510-005-R010 JF

Overprint: Red FIVE. ***Engraver:*** Toppan, Carpenter, Casilear & Co. ***Comments:*** H-Unlisted. Raised from W-MA-1510-001-G010b. January 16, 185_. 1850s.

Rarity: URS-2
VF $1,700

$10 • W-MA-1510-010-R020

Engraver: Rawdon, Wright, Hatch & Edson. ***Comments:*** H-MA-550-R5. Raised from W-MA-1510-001-G010. 18__. 1850s.

Rarity: —

Eastport, Massachusetts

On February 24, 1798, the name of this settlement was officially changed from Moose Island to Eastport, because it is the most easterly situated port in the United States. During the War of 1812 it was staunchly defended against the British until July 11, 1814, when the American flag was lowered. Islanders were forced to take an oath of allegiance to the British, and about two-thirds of the residents did so. After the war ended, British troops remained for three years, claiming the island was within the original limits of New Brunswick. In 1839 the main business district of Eastport was burned. The village was engaged in shipbuilding, fisheries, and the maritime trade, the harbor being excellent and open year round. Steamers connected to many different places. In 1850 the population was 4,125.

See also Eastport, Maine.

Passamaquoddy Bank

1819 and 1820 • 1820–1826

W-MA-1520 • W-ME-730

History: The Passamaquoddy Bank was chartered by the General Court of Massachusetts in 1819 with an authorized capital of $50,000, the smallest amount of any bank in the Maine District up to that time. All others were for $100,000 or more. In January 1820, the capital was reported as paid in full, and bills in circulation amounted to $68,978.[82] After Maine became a state on March 15, 1820, the bank issued paper money with that address. On April 8, 1826, there was a "run" on the bank when holders of paper money rushed to exchange it for coins or for good notes of other banks. They were turned away as there was no cash on hand. In the meantime the bank dishonored two drafts for about $11,000 sent to its redemption agent in Boston, as it had no way to pay. The charter of the bank was revoked in 1827. The bank had neglected or refused to present its books to the investigating committee.[83] Liquidation of the bank continued into 1829. See also listing under Maine.

Numismatic Commentary: With its thoroughly Indian name, the Passamaquoddy Bank issued notes that are moderately available in the marketplace today.

Valid Issues

Notes With Massachusetts Address

$1 • W-MA-1520-001-G010

Left: 1 / 1. ***Center:*** ONE DOLLAR, Text. ***Right:*** 1 / 1. ***Engraver:*** PSSP. ***Comments:*** H-MA-555-G2, Wait-Unlisted. 1810s.

Rarity: —

$1 • W-MA-1520-001-G010a

Left: 1 / 1. ***Center:*** ONE DOLLAR, Text. ***Right:*** 1 / 1. ***Engraver:*** PSSP-Variety. ***Comments:*** H-Unlisted, Wait-Unlisted. Similar to W-MA-1520-001-G010. 1810s.

Rarity: —

$2 • W-MA-1520-002-G020

Left: 2 / TWO vertically / 2. ***Center:*** TWOs. ***Right:*** 2 / TWO vertically / 2. ***Engraver:*** PSSP. ***Comments:*** H-MA-555-G6, Wait-Unlisted. 18__. 1810s.

Rarity: —

$2 • W-MA-1520-002-G020a HA

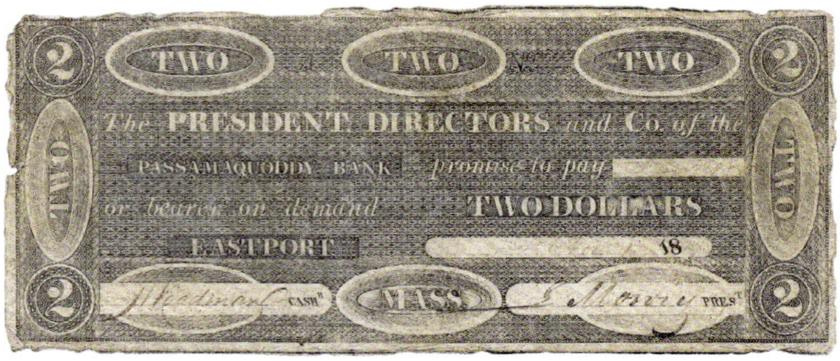

Engraver: PSSP-Variety. ***Comments:*** H-Unlisted, Wait-Unlisted. Similar to W-MA-1520-002-G020. 18__. 1810s.

Rarity: URS-4
VG $250

$3 • W-MA-1520-003-G030

Left: 3 / THREE vertically / 3. ***Center:*** THREEs. ***Right:*** 3 / THREE vertically / 3. ***Engraver:*** PSSP. ***Comments:*** H-MA-555-G10, Wait-Unlisted. 18__. 1810s.

Rarity: —

$3 • W-MA-1520-003-G030a HA

Engraver: PSSP-Variety. ***Comments:*** H-Unlisted, Wait-Unlisted. Similar to W-MA-1520-003-G030. 18__. 1810s.

Rarity: URS-4
VG $250

$5 • W-MA-1520-005-G040

CJF

Engraver: PSSP. ***Comments:*** H-MA-555-G16, Wait-Unlisted. 18__. 1810s.

Rarity: URS-6
F $200

$10 • W-MA-1520-010-G050

HA

Engraver: PSSP. ***Comments:*** H-MA-555-G20, Wait-Unlisted. 18__. 1810s.

Rarity: URS-5
F $400; **VF** $650

$50 • W-MA-1520-050-G060

QDB

Engraver: Perkins. ***Comments:*** H-Unlisted, Wait-Unlisted. 18__. 1819 and 1820.

Rarity: URS-2
EF $4,500

Notes With Maine Address

$1 • W-ME-730-001-G010

CJF

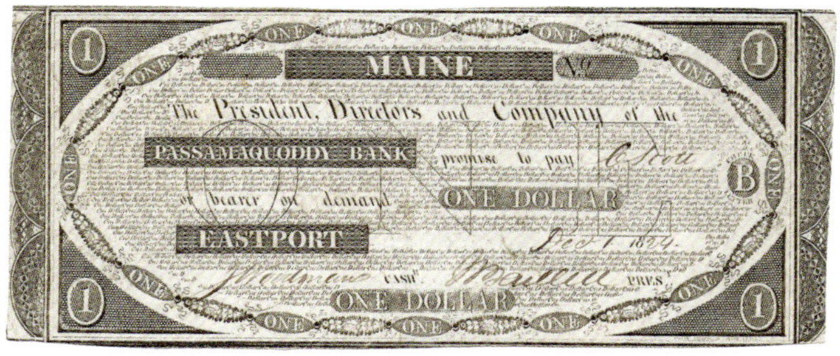

Engraver: PSSP. ***Comments:*** H-ME-285-G4, Wait-15. 18__. 1820s.

Rarity: URS-5
F $400

$1 • W-ME-730-001-G020

Left: 1 / 1. ***Center:*** Watermelon. ***Right:*** 1 / 1. ***Engraver:*** PSSP. ***Comments:*** H-ME-285-G8, Wait-14. Similar to W-ME-730-001-G010 but with different denomination. 1820s.

Rarity: —

$2 • W-ME-730-002-G030

QDB

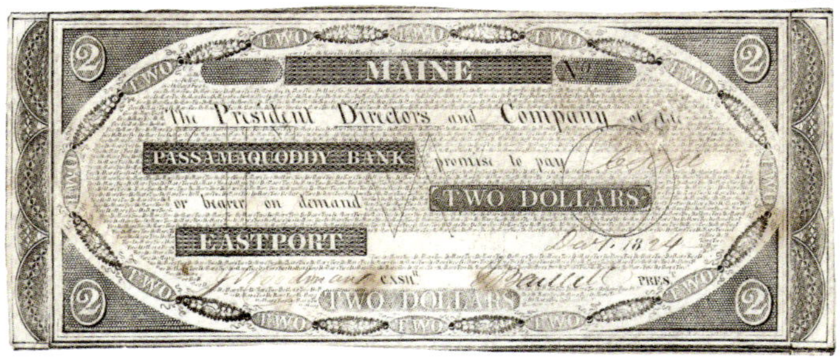

Engraver: PSSP. ***Comments:*** H-ME-285-G12, Wait-17. 18__. 1820s.

Rarity: URS-5
VF $500

$2 • W-ME-730-002-G040

Left: 2 / 2. ***Center:*** Watermelon. ***Right:*** 2 / 2. ***Engraver:*** PSSP. ***Comments:*** H-ME-285-G16, Wait-16. Similar to W-ME-730-002-G030 but with different denomination. 1820s.

Rarity: —

$3 • W-ME-730-003-G050

Engraver: PSSP. ***Comments:*** H-ME-285-G20, Wait-19. 1820s.

Rarity: —

How to Read the Whitman Numbering System

$1 • W-MA-010-001-G010a

Denomination: Value of the note shown.

W: Whitman number. This number is a sortable code unique to each bank and note.

MA: Abbreviation for the state under study.

010: Numerical designation specific to each bank.

001: The denomination in dollars.

G010a: G indicates a good or valid note. Other categories are indicated thus: C (counterfeit); R (raised); S (spurious); N (not-attributed); A (altered). Numbers are assigned starting with 010, 020, et seq. Terminal letters following the number indicate variations of a note: a series of different colored overprints, tints, payees, etc., all on the same design of note. For more information, see the "How to Use This Book" section at the front of the volume, page xiv.

$3 • W-ME-730-003-G060

CJF

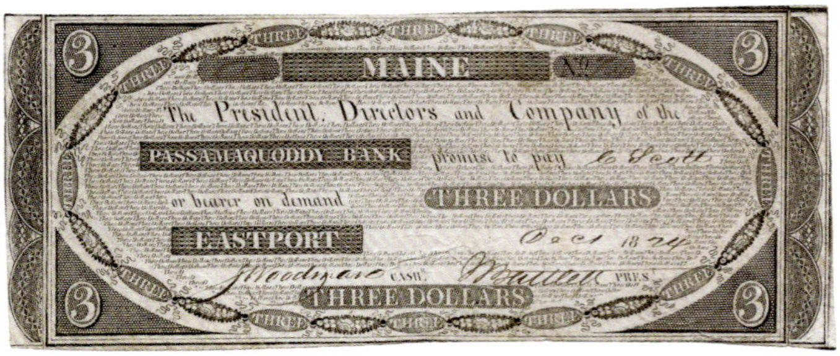

Engraver: PSSP. ***Comments:*** H-ME-285-G24, Wait-18. 18__. 1820s.

Rarity: URS-5
F $200

$5 • W-ME-730-005-G070

Left: FIVE vertically. ***Center:*** 5 / Farming scene and buildings, Four women, Anchor, sheaf, and plow, Churches, cart, and ships / 5. ***Right:*** FIVE vertically. ***Engraver:*** PSSP. ***Comments:*** H-Unlisted, Wait-20.

Rarity: —

$5 • W-ME-730-005-G080

CJF

Engraver: PSSP. ***Comments:*** H-ME-285-G32, Wait-21. 18__. 1820s.

Rarity: URS-5
F $250

$10 • W-ME-730-010-G090

CJF

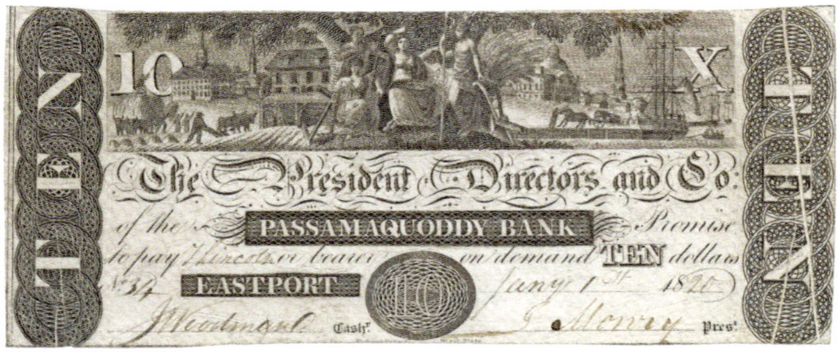

Engraver: PSSP. ***Comments:*** H-Unlisted, Wait-22. 18__. 1820s.

Rarity: URS-5
F $250

$10 • W-ME-730-010-G100

Left: 10 / TEN vertically / 10. ***Center:*** TENs. ***Right:*** 10 / TEN vertically / 10. ***Engraver:*** PSSP. ***Comments:*** H-ME-285-G40, Wait-Unlisted. 1820s.

Rarity: —

Non-Valid Issues

$1 • W-ME-730-001-C010

Comments: H-ME-285-C4, Wait-Unlisted. Counterfeit of W-ME-730-001-G010. 1820s.

Rarity: —

$2 • W-ME-730-002-C030

Comments: H-ME-285-C12, Wait-Unlisted. Counterfeit of W-ME-730-002-G030. 1820s.

Rarity: —

$3 • W-ME-730-003-C050

Comments: H-ME-285-C20, Wait-Unlisted. Counterfeit of W-ME-730-003-G050. 1820s.

Rarity: —

Edgartown, Massachusetts

One of the primary locations for the whaling industry in the 1800s, Edgartown was established when a group of families started a colony on the island of Martha's Vineyard in 1642. It was incorporated in 1671 and originally called Great Harbor. It was named Edgartown after the young son of James II of England.

Marthas Vineyard Bank
1854–1865
W-MA-1530

History: The Vineyard Bank was chartered on April 12, 1854, with an authorized capital of $100,000. By September 1855, there were notes issued bearing the name of Marthas Vineyard Bank, the title the bank also used in news items and statements. In 1861 an act of the State Legislature made it official.

Circulation in 1857 amounted to $71,486. In 1858 it was $81,440, and in 1863 it was $100,829. Other figures for 1857 included: bills of this bank and other New England states $374; specie $5,573.98; real estate $5,000.

The business of the Marthas Vineyard Bank was succeeded by the Marthas Vineyard National Bank of Edgartown, chartered in 1865.

Numismatic Commentary: Obsolete notes, like National Bank Notes, from the Massachusetts islands are highly sought after due to their relative scarcity and the history of the offshore locations. While not impossible to obtain, the collector will probably breathe a sigh of relief after finding an example.

Valid Issues

$1 • W-MA-1530-001-G010

Left: Steamboat and other ships / 1. ***Center:*** Steamship. ***Right:*** 1 / Liberty seated between globe and shield. ***Engraver:*** Rawdon, Wright, Hatch & Edson / New England Bank Note Co. ***Comments:*** H-MA-560-G2. 18__. 1850s.

Rarity: —

$1 • W-MA-1530-001-G010a

Engraver: Rawdon, Wright, Hatch & Edson / New England Bank Note Co. / ABNCo. monogram. ***Comments:*** H-MA-560-G2c. Similar to W-MA-1530-001-G010 but with additional engraver imprint. 18__. 1860s.

Rarity: URS-3
VF $750

$1 • W-MA-1530-001-G010b

CJF

Overprint: Red ONE. ***Engraver:*** Rawdon, Wright, Hatch & Edson / New England Bank Note Co. / ABNCo. monogram. ***Comments:*** H-Unlisted. Similar to W-MA-1530-001-G010 but with additional engraver imprint. 18__. 1850s.

Rarity: URS-2
F $1,750; **VF** $4,000

$2 • W-MA-1530-002-G020

Left: 2 / Farmer walking with fork, rake, and jug. ***Center:*** Hay wagon, train, and village. ***Right:*** Woman standing with dinner horn, Woman at table. ***Engraver:*** Rawdon, Wright, Hatch & Edson / New England Bank Note Co. ***Comments:*** H-MA-560-G4. Whole-note vignette. 18__. 1850s.

Rarity: —

$2 • W-MA-1530-002-G020a

Tint: Red-brown. ***Engraver:*** New England Bank Note Co. / ABNCo. monogram. ***Comments:*** H-MA-560-G4c. Similar to W-MA-1530-002-G020 but with additional engraver imprint. 18__. 1860s.

Rarity: —

$3 • W-MA-1530-003-G030

Left: Slain deer hanging on tree limb, Dog / THREE. ***Center:*** Farmer seated with scythe, Sailor reclining on bale, Blacksmith seated, Three gold dollars. ***Engraver:*** Rawdon, Wright, Hatch & Edson / New England Bank Note Co. ***Comments:*** H-MA-560-G6. 18__. 1850s.

Rarity: —

$3 • W-MA-1530-003-G030a

Tint: Red-brown. ***Engraver:*** New England Bank Note Co. / ABNCo monogram. ***Comments:*** H-MA-560-G6c. Similar to W-MA-1530-003-G030 but with additional engraver imprint. 18__. 1850s.

Rarity: —

$5 • W-MA-1530-005-G040

Left: Portrait of sailor boy / V. ***Center:*** Indian woman and hunter flanking five gold dollars and three cherubs. ***Right:*** 5 / Woman reclining with 5 / Ship. ***Engraver:*** Rawdon, Wright, Hatch & Edson / New England Bank Note Co. ***Comments:*** H-MA-560-G8. 18__. 1850s.

Rarity: —

$5 • W-MA-1530-005-G040a

Tint: Red-brown. ***Engraver:*** New England Bank Note Co. / ABNCo. monogram. ***Comments:*** H-MA-560-G8c. Similar to W-MA-1530-005-G040 but with additional engraver imprint. 18__. 1860s.

Rarity: URS-1
F $7,500

$10 • W-MA-1530-010-G050

Left: Female portrait / 10. ***Center:*** Nine cherubs, Woman reclining, Cornucopia and ten gold dollars. ***Right:*** 10 / Ship under sail. ***Engraver:*** Rawdon, Wright, Hatch & Edson / New England Bank Note Co. ***Comments:*** H-MA-560-G10. 18__. 1850s.

Rarity: —

$10 • W-MA-1530-010-G050a

Tint: Red-brown. ***Engraver:*** New England Bank Note Co. / American Bank Note Co. ***Comments:*** H-MA-560-G10c. Similar to W-MA-1530-010-G050 but with additional engraver imprint. 18__. 1860s.

Rarity: —

$20 • W-MA-1530-020-G060

Left: Woman / XX. ***Center:*** Stonecutters and architect. ***Right:*** 20 / Sailor. ***Engraver:*** Rawdon, Wright, Hatch & Edson / New England Bank Note Co. ***Comments:*** H-MA-560-G12. 18__. 1850s.

Rarity: —

$50 • W-MA-1530-050-G070

Left: Sailor / 50. ***Center:*** Indian man with bow and arrow, Eagle flying, Indians in canoe, Deer. ***Right:*** 50 / Two women. ***Engraver:*** Rawdon, Wright, Hatch & Edson / New England Bank Note Co. ***Comments:*** H-MA-560-G14. 18__. 1850s.

Rarity: —

$100 • W-MA-1530-100-G080

Left: C / Justice standing. ***Center:*** Two women flanking shield bearing state arms surmounted by eagle. ***Right:*** 100 / Eagle on shield / 100. ***Engraver:*** Rawdon, Wright, Hatch & Edson / New England Bank Note Co. ***Comments:*** H-MA-560-G16. 18__. 1850s.

Rarity: —

Non-Valid Issues

$1 • W-MA-1530-001-A010

Left: ONE / Woman seated on sheaf watering eagle perched on shoulder / ONE. ***Center:*** Ships, Eagle on shield. ***Right:*** 1 / Ceres kneeling with sheaf, Farm. ***Engraver:*** Danforth, Bald & Co. ***Comments:*** H-MA-560-A5. Altered from $1 Columbia Bank, Washington, D.C. 18__. 1850s.

Rarity: —

$2 • W-MA-1530-002-A020

JF

Tint: Red-brown dies outlining white 2s and TWO DOLLARS. ***Engraver:*** Danforth, Wright & Co. ***Comments:*** H-MA-560-A10. Altered from $2 Southern Bank of Georgia, Bainbridge, Georgia. March 1, 1858.

Rarity: URS-5
F $500

$2 • W-MA-1530-002-A030

Left: 2 / Portrait of Benjamin Franklin / TWO. ***Center:*** Train, Station. ***Bottom center:*** U.S. shield. ***Right:*** 2 / Minerva seated, 2 / TWO. ***Overprint:*** TWO. ***Engraver:*** Rawdon, Wright, Hatch & Edson. ***Comments:*** H-MA-560-A15. Altered from $2 Farmers and Merchants Bank of Memphis, Tennessee series. 1850s.

Rarity: —

$2 • W-MA-1530-002-N010

Center: Indian man in canoe. ***Right:*** Woman. ***Comments:*** H-MA-560-N5.

Rarity: —

$3 • W-MA-1530-003-A040

TD

Engraver: Danforth, Bald & Co. ***Comments:*** H-MA-560-A20. Altered from $3 Columbia Bank, Washington, D.C. 18__. 1860.

Rarity: URS-8
VG $125; **F** $350

$3 • W-MA-1530-003-A050

Left: 3 / Portrait of George Washington / THREE. ***Center:*** Woman seated on wharf with caduceus, Ship. ***Bottom center:*** Strongbox and cornucopia with coins. ***Right:*** 3 / Mechanic, sailor, and farmer standing with 3. ***Overprint:*** THREE. ***Engraver:*** Rawdon, Wright, Hatch & Edson. ***Comments:*** H-MA-560-A25. Altered from $3 Farmers and Merchants Bank of Memphis, Memphis, Tennessee series. 1850s.

Rarity: —

$5 • W-MA-1530-005-A060

TD

Tint: Red-brown lathework outlining white 5. ***Engraver:*** Bald, Cousland & Co. ***Comments:*** H-MA-560-A30. Altered from $5 Pioneer Association, Lafayette, Indiana. 18__. 1850s–1860s.

Rarity: URS-6
VF $750

$5 • W-MA-1530-005-A070

CJF

Overprint: Blue FIVE. ***Engraver:*** Rawdon, Wright, Hatch & Edson. ***Comments:*** H-MA-560-A35. Altered from $5 Farmers and Merchants Bank of Memphis, Memphis, Tennessee series. 18__. 1850s.

Rarity: URS-8
VG $125

$5 • W-MA-1530-005-A080

Left: FIVE / Woman standing / FIVE. ***Center:*** Two women seated, one reclining. ***Right:*** 5 / Portrait of George Washington. ***Engraver:*** Danforth, Bald & Co. ***Comments:*** H-MA-560-A40. Altered from $5 Columbia Bank, Washington, D.C. 18__. 1860s.

Rarity: URS-5
VG $90

$10 • W-MA-1530-010-A090

Left: Diagonal X / TEN. ***Center:*** Woman leaning on rock, Train / Ceres with sheaf on back. ***Right:*** 10 / Portrait of George Washington. ***Overprint:*** Red TEN. ***Engraver:*** Bald, Cousland & Co. / Baldwin, Bald & Cousland. ***Comments:*** H-MA-560-A45. Altered from $10 Southern Bank of Georgia, Bainbridge, Georgia. 18__. 1860s.

Rarity: —

Fairhaven, Massachusetts

Located on the southern coast of Massachusetts, Fairhaven was originally settled in 1670 under the name of Cushnea as the eastern part of Dartmouth. In 1787 it separated from Dartmouth and formed New Bedford, which included the towns of Fairhaven, Acushnet, and New Bedford. Eventually Fairhaven separated from New Bedford and was incorporated in 1812. Later, in 1815 and 1836, respectively, the areas of Freetown and Rochester were annexed.

The first naval battle of the Revolutionary War was fought at the mouth of the Acushnet River on May 14, 1775, within sight of Fairhaven's Fort Phoenix. A direct attack on Fairhaven was repulsed by the militia and their commander, Major Israel Fearing. The Fort was repaired and enlarged before the War of 1812, when it yet again repelled an attack by British forces.

Whaling and whale oil were the economic heart for Fairhaven. In 1838 the town was considered the second-largest whaling port in the country. The town was mainly populated by shipwrights, chandlers, ropemakers, coopers, and sailmakers, supplementing the whaling industry of New Bedford.

Fairhaven Bank
1831–1864
W-MA-1540

History: The Fairhaven Bank was incorporated on April 19, 1831, with an authorized capital of $100,000. This was increased to $200,000 in 1839. By 1857 it was $300,000, and by 1864 it was down to $240,000.

Circulation ranged from a low of $49,749 in 1857 to a high of $224,821 in 1863. Selected figures for 1857 included: bills of this bank and other New England states $1,770; specie $17,701.47; real estate $3,000.

The business of the Fairhaven Bank was succeeded by the Fairhaven National Bank in 1864.

Numismatic Commentary: Like the banks from the somewhat nearby islands of Martha's Vineyard and Nantucket, the Fairhaven Bank's notes are also hard to locate. Even though Fairhaven lies on the mainland, it is a shoreline town on Buzzard's Bay, and its notes carry some of the same cachet as the island banks. Whaling scenes, always a popular topic, are found on some of its notes.

Valid Issues

$1 • W-MA-1540-001-G010
Left: Lathework panel bearing MASSACHUSETTS vertically. ***Center:*** 1 / 1 / Alternating flower garlands and gridwork segments / ONE / 1 / 1. ***Right:*** Lathework panel bearing ONE / D / ONE vertically. ***Engraver:*** PSSP. ***Comments:*** H-MA-565-G2. 18__. 1830s.

Rarity: —

$1 • W-MA-1540-001-G020
Left: 1 / Woman wearing bonnet with pail / ONE. ***Center:*** Machinery and merchandise flanking Ceres seated holding sickle and rake, Factories and harbor / Panel outlining white ONE. ***Right:*** 1 / Ship / ONE. ***Engraver:*** PSSP / New England Bank Note Co. ***Comments:*** H-MA-565-G6. 18__. 1830s.

Rarity: —

$1 • W-MA-1540-001-G030
Left: Woman standing / ONE. ***Center:*** Steamboat and two ships. ***Right:*** Justice standing / ONE. ***Engraver:*** Rawdon, Wright, Hatch & Edson. ***Comments:*** H-MA-565-G10. 18__. 1850s.

Rarity: —

$1.25 • W-MA-1540-001.25-G040
Left: 1 25/100 / Train / 1 25/100. ***Center:*** Sloop and other ships at sea / $1.25 cts. ***Right:*** 1 25/100 / Eagle. ***Engraver:*** New England Bank Note Co. ***Comments:*** H-MA-565-G14. 18__. 1830s.

Rarity: —

$1.50 • W-MA-1540-001.50-G050
Left: 1 Doll. 50 Cents vertically. ***Center:*** Eagle on rock in ocean / $1 50/100. ***Right:*** 1 50/100 / Justice. ***Engraver:*** New England Bank Note Co. ***Comments:*** H-MA-565-G16. 18__. 1830s.

Rarity: —

$1.75 • W-MA-1540-001.75-G060
Left: $1.75 Cts. / Woman watering eagle / 1 75/100. ***Center:*** Three sloops at sea. ***Right:*** $1.75 Cts. / Woman seated with grain, Dog / 1 75/100. ***Engraver:*** New England Bank Note Co. ***Comments:*** H-MA-565-G18. 18__. 1830s.

Rarity: —

$2 • W-MA-1540-002-G070
Left: Lathework panel bearing MASSACHUSETTS vertically. ***Center:*** 2 / 2 / Alternating flower garlands and gridwork segments / TWO / 2 / 2. ***Right:*** Lathework panel bearing five TWOs vertically. ***Engraver:*** PSSP. ***Comments:*** H-MA-565-G20. 18__. 1830s.

Rarity: —

$2 • W-MA-1540-002-G080
Left: 2 / Woman standing with staff, Cornucopia / TWO. ***Center:*** TWO / Machinery and merchandise flanking Ceres seated holding sickle and rake, Factories and harbor / Panel outlining white TWO. ***Right:*** 2 / Woman wearing hat, Trees / TWO. ***Engraver:*** New England Bank Note Co. / PSSP. ***Comments:*** H-MA-565-G24. 18__. 1830s.

Rarity: —

$2 • W-MA-1540-002-G090

CC

Engraver: New England Bank Note Co. ***Comments:*** H-MA-565-G28. 18__. 1850s.

Rarity: URS-1
VG $3,500

$2 • W-MA-1540-002-G090a
Left: 2 bearing female portrait / TWO. ***Center:*** Whaling scene. ***Right:*** 2 bearing female portrait / TWO. ***Overprint:*** Green panel outlining white TWO. ***Engraver:*** New England Bank Note Co. / ABNCo. monogram. ***Comments:*** H-Unlisted. Similar to W-MA-1540-002-G090 but with additional engraver imprint.

Rarity: URS-3
F $2,000

$3 • W-MA-1540-003-G100
Left: Lathework panel bearing MASSACHUSETTS vertically. ***Center:*** 3 / 3 / Alternating flower garlands and gridwork segments / THREE / 3 / 3. ***Right:*** Lathework panel bearing THREE vertically. ***Engraver:*** PSSP. ***Comments:*** H-MA-565-G30. 18__. 1830s.

Rarity: —

$3 • W-MA-1540-003-G110

CC

Engraver: PSSP / New England Bank Note Co. ***Comments:*** H-MA-565-G34. 18__. 1830s.

Rarity: URS-3
VF $600

$3 • W-MA-1540-003-G120

Left: 3 / Sailor standing by capstan. ***Center:*** Woman and Enterprise, Steamship and train on bridge. ***Right:*** 3 / Farmer, sailor, and mechanic standing with 3. ***Engraver:*** Rawdon, Wright, Hatch & Edson. ***Comments:*** H-MA-565-G38. 18__. 1850s.

Rarity: —

$5 • W-MA-1540-005-G130

Left: Lathework chain bearing MASSACHUSETTS / 5 / 5. ***Center:*** Alternating flower garlands and gridwork segments / FIVE DOLLARS with spiral lathework lines. ***Right:*** 5 / 5. ***Engraver:*** PSSP. ***Comments:*** H-MA-565-G40. 18__. 1830s.

Rarity: —

$5 • W-MA-1540-005-G140

Left: 5 / Blacksmith at anvil / FIVE. ***Center:*** Mercury standing with 5, Cornucopia and merchandise, Factories and ship / V / Panel outlining white FIVE. ***Right:*** 5 / Ceres kneeling / FIVE. ***Engraver:*** PSSP / New England Bank Note Co. ***Comments:*** H-MA-565-G44. 18__. 1830s.

Rarity: —

$5 • W-MA-1540-005-G150

CC

Overprint: Green panel outlining white FIVE. ***Engraver:*** New England Bank Note Co. / ABNCo. monogram. ***Comments:*** H-MA-565-G48. 18__. 1850s–1860s.

Rarity: URS-4
F $1,250

$10 • W-MA-1540-010-G160

Left: Lathework chain bearing MASSACHUSETTS / 10 / 10 vertically. ***Center:*** Alternating flower garlands and gridwork segments / TEN DOLLARS with spiral lathework lines. ***Right:*** 10 / 10 vertically. ***Engraver:*** PSSP. ***Comments:*** H-MA-565-G50. 18__. 1830s.

Rarity: —

$10 • W-MA-1540-010-G170

Left: TEN / Farmer sowing / TEN. ***Center:*** Mercury standing with 10, Cornucopia and merchandise, Factories and ship, Canal scene / Panel outlining white TEN. ***Right:*** 10 / Ship / TEN. ***Engraver:*** PSSP / New England Bank Note Co. ***Comments:*** H-MA-565-G54. 18__. 1830s.

Rarity: —

$10 • W-MA-1540-010-G180

Left: Ceres, Train and canal / X. ***Center:*** 10. ***Right:*** TEN / Medallion head / 10. ***Engraver:*** Rawdon, Wright, Hatch & Edson. ***Comments:*** H-MA-565-G58. 18__. 1850s.

Rarity: —

$20 • W-MA-1540-020-G190

Left: Lathework chain bearing MASSACHUSETTS / 20 / 20 vertically. ***Center:*** Alternating flower garlands and gridwork segments. ***Right:*** 20 / 20 vertically. ***Engraver:*** PSSP. ***Comments:*** H-MA-565-G60. 18__. 1830s.

Rarity: —

$20 • W-MA-1540-020-G200

Engraver: Unverified, but likely New England Bank Note Co. ***Comments:*** H-MA-565-G64. No description available. 18__. 1840s.

Rarity: *None known*

$20 • W-MA-1540-020-G210

Left: 20 / Minerva standing with spear. ***Center:*** Woman seated with 2 and 0. ***Bottom center:*** XX. ***Right:*** 20 / Woman reclining on cornucopia / 20. ***Engraver:*** Rawdon, Wright, Hatch & Edson. ***Comments:*** H-MA-565-G68. 18__. 1850s.

Rarity: —

$20 • W-MA-1540-020-G220

Left: Woman standing with eagle / 20. ***Center:*** TWENTY, 20 / Female portrait. ***Right:*** 20 / Portrait of Benjamin Franklin. ***Engraver:*** New England Bank Note Co. ***Comments:*** H-MA-565-G70. 18__. 1850s.

Rarity: —

$20 • W-MA-1540-020-G230

JF

Tint: Green. ***Engraver:*** American Bank Note Co. ***Comments:*** H-MA-565-G72a. Proof. 186_. 1860s.

Rarity: URS-2
Proof $1,600

$50 • W-MA-1540-050-G240

Engraver: Unverified, but likely New England Bank Note Co. ***Comments:*** H-MA-565-G76. No description available. 18__. 1840s.

Rarity: *None known*

$50 • W-MA-1540-050-G250

Left: 50 / Minerva standing by column. ***Center:*** Ceres and Vulcan flanking cornucopia. ***Right:*** 50 / Cherub in sailboat / 50. ***Engraver:*** Rawdon, Wright, Hatch & Edson. ***Comments:*** H-MA-565-G80. 18__. 1850s.

Rarity: —

$50 • W-MA-1540-050-G260

Left: FIFTY / Sheaves and fruit / 50. ***Center:*** 50 / Three women seated with eagle, pole and cap, shield, scales, and book. ***Right:*** FIFTY across 50 / Vulcan seated with tools, Train. ***Engraver:*** New England Bank Note Co. ***Comments:*** H-MA-565-G82. 18__. 1850s.

Rarity: —

$50 • W-MA-1540-050-G270

Left: 50 / Men with horse. ***Center:*** Bust of George Washington / Cattle. ***Right:*** 50 / Woman standing. ***Tint:*** Green. ***Engraver:*** American Bank Note Co. ***Comments:*** H-MA-565-G84a. 186_. 1860s.

Rarity: URS-2
Proof $5,000

$100 • W-MA-1540-100-G280

Engraver: Unverified, but likely New England Bank Note Co. ***Comments:*** H-MA-565-G88. No description available. 18__. 1840s.

Rarity: *None known*

$100 • W-MA-1540-100-G290

Left: 100 / Vulcan seated with sledge and anchor. ***Center:*** Train on bridge, Eagle on limb, Canal locks / C. ***Bottom center:*** 100. ***Right:*** 100 / Ceres seated, Cornucopia. ***Engraver:*** Rawdon, Wright, Hatch & Edson. ***Comments:*** H-MA-565-G92. 18__. 1850s.

Rarity: —

$100 • W-MA-1540-100-G300

Left: C / Men with fishing boat at shore / 100. ***Center:*** Cornucopia, Eagle perched on bale, Sheaf / 100. ***Right:*** 100 / Ceres / 100. ***Engraver:*** New England Bank Note Co. ***Comments:*** H-MA-565-G94. 18__. 1850s.

Rarity: —

$100 • W-MA-1540-100-G310

Left: C / 100. ***Center:*** Farmer seated, Boy, Sailor leaning on capstan. ***Right:*** 100 / Dog and strongbox. ***Tint:*** Green. ***Engraver:*** American Bank Note Co. ***Comments:*** H-MA-565-G96a. 18__. 1860s.

Rarity: —

$500 • W-MA-1540-500-G320

Left: Woman seated on sheaves, Men reaping, Man on horse / 500. ***Center:*** 500 / D. ***Right:*** 500 vertically. ***Engraver:*** Rawdon, Wright, Hatch & Co. ***Comments:*** H-MA-565-G100. 18__. 1850s.

Rarity: —

Non-Valid Issues

$1 • W-MA-1540-001-A010

Comments: H-MA-565-A5. No description available. Altered from unknown source. 18__. 1840s.

Rarity: *None known*

$2 • W-MA-1540-002-A020

Comments: H-MA-565-A10. No description available. Altered from unknown source. 18__. 1840s.

Rarity: *None known*

$3 • W-MA-1540-003-A030

Comments: H-MA-565-A15. No description available. Altered from unknown source. 18__. 1840s.

Rarity: *None known*

$3 • W-MA-1540-003-A040

CC

Comments: H-Unlisted. Altered from unknown source. 18__. 1840s.

Rarity: URS-5
VF $250

$5 • W-MA-1540-005-R010

Engraver: Rawdon, Wright, Hatch & Edson. ***Comments:*** H-MA-565-R5. Raised from W-MA-1540-001-G030. 18__. 1850s.

Rarity: —

$5 • W-MA-1540-005-A050

Comments: H-MA-565-A20. No description available. Altered from unknown source. 18__. 1840s.

Rarity: *None known*

$10 • W-MA-1540-010-R020

Engraver: Rawdon, Wright, Hatch & Edson. ***Comments:*** H-MA-565-R10. Raised from W-MA-1540-001-G030. 18__. 1850s.

Rarity: —

$10 • W-MA-1540-010-A060

Comments: H-MA-565-A25. No description available. Altered from unknown source. 18__. 1840s.

Rarity: *None known*

$20 • W-MA-1540-020-R030

Engraver: Rawdon, Wright, Hatch & Edson. ***Comments:*** H-MA-565-R15. Raised from W-MA-1540-001-G030. 18__. 1850s.

Rarity: —

Fall River, Massachusetts

Named after the cascades in the Quequechan River, which has eight waterfalls, the area that is known as Fall River was once inhabited by the Pokanoket Wampanoag tribe. Quequechan is believed to mean "falling river." It was originally located entirely in Rhode Island.

In early times Fall River was made up of Freetown, to the north, and Tiverton, Rhode Island, in the south, until on February 26, 1803, it was incorporated as a town on its own. A year later it changed its name to Troy, which continued for 30 years until it changed back to Fall River on February 12, 1834. In 1856 the town of Tiverton decided to split from Fall River, and in 1861 the U.S. Supreme Court moved the boundary of the state line, placing Fall River entirely within Massachusetts.

Saw mills, grist mills, and fulling mills were the early forms of industry in Fall River. On July 2, 1843, a massive fire destroyed 291 buildings across the center of town, leaving 200 families homeless and destroying shops, the custom house, post office, hotels, churches, and banks. A fund of $50,000 for the aid of the struggling victims was donated by people in towns including Boston, Cambridge, Providence, and New Bedford. Textiles were a major industry under the influence of nearby Rhode Island developments. The Fall River Iron Works, as well as spinning mills, cotton manufactories, woolen manufactories, thread mills, a twine mill, a loom-making firm, and a linen manufactory were also located here. As early as 1837 the port of Fall River was designated by the federal government from its original port of entry in Dighton. Coal and iron from Europe were also imported in Fall River.

See also Troy, Massachusetts, and Fall River, Rhode Island.

Fall River Bank

1834–1865

W-MA-1550

History: The Fall River Bank of Troy, Massachusetts, was chartered on February 26, 1825, with an authorized capital of $100,000. Bank notes were issued with the Troy address.

In 1834 the charter of the Fall River Bank was modified to change its location and reflect the renaming of the city of Troy to Fall River. From then on the bank was located in Fall River, giving it two locations without actually moving.

Circulation ranged from a low of $58,636 in 1839 to a high of $142,064 in 1863.

Selected figures for 1857 included: bills of this bank and other New England states $1,099.54; specie $11,223.36; real estate $8,000.

The business of the Fall River Bank was succeeded by the Fall River National Bank, chartered in November 1864. The state bank continued its operations into early 1865.

See also listing under Troy, W-MA-3230.

Numismatic Commentary: Genuine notes are hard to locate. Some Proof issues appear occasionally in the marketplace. Collectors may have to settle for some of the abundant counterfeit issues, including a curious $10 note dated 1854 but also carrying the ABNCo. monogram, an addition to the plate that would not have occurred until 1858.

Valid Issues

$1 • W-MA-1550-001-G010

Left: 1 / ONE / 1. ***Center:*** Steamboat / Steamboat. ***Right:*** 1 / Beehive / ONE. ***Engraver:*** New England Bank Note Co. / PSSP. ***Comments:*** H-MA-1230-G64. 18__. 1830s–1850s.

Rarity: —

$1 • W-MA-1550-001-G020

Left: 1 / Woman seated in shell, Ship. ***Center:*** Women tending looms. ***Bottom center:*** Indian. ***Right:*** 1 / Female portrait. ***Overprint:*** Red ONE. ***Engraver:*** Toppan, Carpenter, Casilear & Co. ***Comments:*** H-MA-1230-G68a. Mar. 1, 1854.

Rarity: —

$1 • W-MA-1550-001-G020a

Overprint: Red ONE. ***Engraver:*** Toppan, Carpenter, Casilear & Co. / ABNCo. monogram. ***Comments:*** H-MA-1230-G68b. Similar to W-MA-1550-001-G020 but with additional engraver imprint. Mar. 1, 1854.

Rarity: —

$2 • W-MA-1550-002-G030

Left: TWO / Woman standing with rake / TWO. ***Center:*** 2 / Steamboat / 2. ***Right:*** TWO / Justice / TWO. ***Engraver:*** New England Bank Note Co. / PSSP. ***Comments:*** H-MA-1230-G72. 18__. 1830s–1850s.

Rarity: —

$2 • W-MA-1550-002-G040

Left: 2 / Scene on plank road, Men, Cattle and load of hay. ***Center:*** Woman reclining on bale, Ships. ***Right:*** 2 / Train, Houses. ***Overprint:*** Red TWO. ***Engraver:*** Toppan, Carpenter, Casilear & Co. ***Comments:*** H-MA-1230-G76a. Mar. 1, 1854.

Rarity: —

$2 • W-MA-1550-002-G040a

Overprint: Red TWO. ***Engraver:*** Toppan, Carpenter, Casilear & Co. / ABNCo. monogram. ***Comments:*** H-MA-1230-G76b. Similar to W-MA-1550-002-G040 but with additional engraver imprint. Mar. 1, 1854.

Rarity: —

$3 • W-MA-1550-003-G050

Left: THREE / Portrait of George Washington / THREE. ***Center:*** Factories and machinery / Farming scene / Steamboat. ***Right:*** 3 / Eagle / 3. ***Engraver:*** New England Bank Note Co. / PSSP. ***Comments:*** H-MA-1230-G80. 18__. 1830s–1850s.

Rarity: —

$3 • W-MA-1550-003-G060

Left: 3 / Anchor. ***Center:*** Sailor with sextant, Ships. ***Right:*** 3 / Female portrait. ***Overprint:*** Red THREE. ***Engraver:*** Toppan, Carpenter, Casilear & Co. ***Comments:*** H-MA-1230-G84a. Mar. 1, 1854.

Rarity: —

$3 • W-MA-1550-003-G060a

Overprint: Red THREE. ***Engraver:*** Toppan, Carpenter, Casilear & Co. / ABNCo. monogram. ***Comments:*** H-MA-1230-G84b. Similar to W-MA-1550-003-G060 but with additional engraver imprint. Mar. 1, 1854.

Rarity: —

$5 • W-MA-1550-005-G070

CC

Engraver: New England Bank Note Co. / PSSP. ***Comments:*** H-MA-1230-G88. 18__. 1830s–1850s.

Rarity: URS-5

F $350

$5 • W-MA-1550-005-G080

Left: 5 / Blacksmith with anvil. ***Center:*** Warship and merchant ship, Steamer. ***Right:*** 5 / Female portrait. ***Overprint:*** Red FIVE. ***Engraver:*** Toppan, Carpenter, Casilear & Co. ***Comments:*** H-MA-1230-G92a. Mar. 1, 1854.

Rarity: —

$5 • W-MA-1550-005-G080a

Overprint: Red FIVE. ***Engraver:*** Toppan, Carpenter, Casilear & Co. / ABNCo. monogram. ***Comments:*** H-MA-1230-G92b. Similar to W-MA-1550-005-G080 but with additional engraver imprint. Mar. 1, 1854.

Rarity: —

$10 • W-MA-1550-010-G090

Left: TEN / Woman. ***Center:*** Shipping scene / Farm scene. ***Right:*** 10 / Woman. ***Engraver:*** New England Bank Note Co. / PSSP. ***Comments:*** H-MA-1230-G96. 18__. 1830s–1850s.

Rarity: —

$10 • W-MA-1550-010-G090a

Left: 10 / Man leaning on pedestal. ***Center:*** Two ships / TEN. ***Right:*** 10 / Woman writing on tablet above pedestal. ***Overprint:*** Red TEN. ***Engraver:*** Toppan, Carpenter, Casilear & Co. ***Comments:*** H-MA-1230-G100a. Mar. 1, 1854.

Rarity: —

$10 • W-MA-1550-010-G090b

Overprint: Red TEN. ***Engraver:*** Toppan, Carpenter, Casilear & Co. / ABNCo. monogram. ***Comments:*** H-MA-1230-G100b. Similar to W-MA-1550-010-G090a but with additional engraver imprint. Mar. 1, 1854.

Rarity: —

$20 • W-MA-1550-020-G100

Left: 20 / Minerva standing with spear. ***Center:*** Woman seated between 2 and 0. ***Bottom center:*** XX. ***Right:*** 20 / Woman reclining on cornucopia / 20. ***Engraver:*** Rawdon, Wright, Hatch & Edson. ***Comments:*** H-MA-1230-G104. 18__. 1850s.

Rarity: —

$20 • W-MA-1550-020-G110

CJF

Engraver: American Bank Note Co. ***Comments:*** H-MA-1230-G108. Proof. June 2, 18__. 1860s.

Rarity: URS-2

Proof $2,000

$50 • W-MA-1550-050-G120

JF

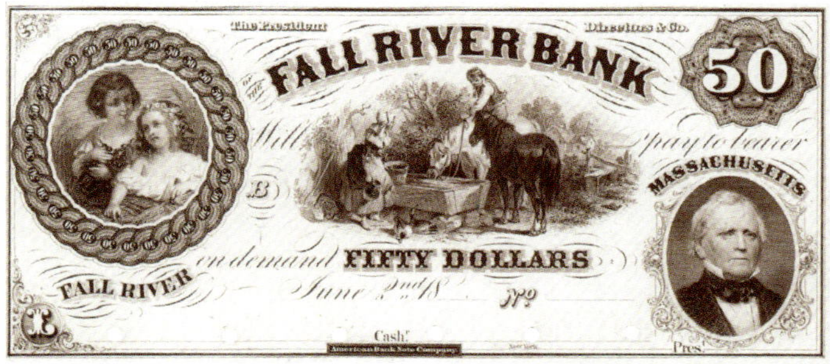

Engraver: American Bank Note Co. ***Comments:*** H-MA-1230-G112. Proof. June 2, 18__. 1860s.

Rarity: URS-2

Proof $4,000

$100 • W-MA-1550-100-G130

Left: 100 / Vulcan seated with sledge and anchor. ***Center:*** Train on bridge, Eagle on limb, Canal locks / C. ***Bottom center:*** 100. ***Right:*** 100 / Ceres seated, Cornucopia. ***Engraver:*** Rawdon, Wright, Hatch & Edson. ***Comments:*** H-MA-1230-G116. 18__. 1850s.

Rarity: —

$100 • W-MA-1550-100-G140

Left: C / Portrait of girl. ***Center:*** Steamship. ***Right:*** 100 / Male portrait. ***Engraver:*** American Bank Note Co. ***Comments:*** H-MA-1230-G120. June 2, 18__. 1860s.

Rarity: —

$500 • W-MA-1550-500-G150

Left: 500 / Indian woman seated with bow. ***Bottom center:*** Eagle. ***Right:*** 500 / Three allegorical women on wharf, one reclining with lyre, one seated with staff, one kneeling with sheaf / 500. ***Engraver:*** Toppan, Carpenter, Casilear & Co. ***Comments:*** H-MA-1230-G124. 18__. 1850s.

Rarity: —

Non-Valid Issues

$1 • W-MA-1550-001-S010

CJF

Engraver: Draper, Toppan & Co. ***Comments:*** H-MA-1230-S5. July 1, 1850. 1850s.

Rarity: URS-7

VG $75

$2 • **W-MA-1550-002-A010** CJF

Comments: H-MA-1230-A5. 18__. 1840s.

Rarity: URS-6

F $75

$5 • **W-MA-1550-005-C070** MK

Engraver: New England Bank Note Co. ***Comments:*** H-MA-1230-C88. Counterfeit of W-MA-1550-005-G070. Poorly engraved. 18__. 1830s–1850s.

Rarity: URS-7

VG $75

$10 • **W-MA-1550-010-C090b** MK

Overprint: Red TEN. ***Engraver:*** Toppan, Carpenter, Casilear & Co. / ABNCo. monogram. ***Comments:*** H-MA-1230-C100b. Counterfeit of W-MA-1550-010-G090b. March 1, 1854.

Rarity: URS-8

F $75

$10 • **W-MA-1550-010-R010** CJF

Overprint: Red TEN. ***Engraver:*** Toppan, Carpenter, Casilear & Co. ***Comments:*** H-Unlisted. Sept. 1, 185_. 1850s.

Rarity: —

$10 • **W-MA-1550-010-R020**

Engraver: Toppan, Carpenter, Casilear & Co. ***Comments:*** H-MA-1230-R5. Raised from W-MA-1550-001-G020. Mar. 1, 1854.

Rarity: —

Fall River Union Bank

1823–1860 • 1860–1864

W-RI-370 • W-MA-1560

History: The Fall River Union Bank was incorporated as the Bristol Union Bank, Bristol, Rhode Island, in 1823 with a nominal capital of $200,000. The location of the bank was changed to Tiverton, Rhode Island, in 1830, and the title was changed to the Fall River Union Bank in 1831.

The bank's capital was $199,512 in 1848, divided into 2,000 shares valued at $100 each. Bills in circulation totaled $68,128 in 1849. By 1857 capital had been decreased to $99,500. The bank was located in a building on the corner of South Main and Rodman streets.

The Fall River Union Bank became a Massachusetts bank in 1860 as a result of the boundary change which took place at the January session of the legislatures of the two states involved. A portion of Tiverton, Rhode Island, became part of Fall River, and all of Fall River, Rhode Island, became part of Massachusetts. Notes are imprinted at Fall River, Massachusetts, beginning in 1860.

In January 1863, the bank's circulation was $42,666. The business of the Fall River Union Bank was succeeded by the First National Bank of Fall River, chartered in February 1864.

See also listings under Rhode Island.

Numismatic Commentary: All issues bearing the imprint of Fall River in Massachusetts are relatively unknown. Any example is a rare prize.

Valid Issues

Notes With Rhode Island Address

$50 • **W-RI-370-050-G010**

Left: FIFTY / Grain, fruit, and flowers / 50. ***Center:*** 50 / Three allegorical women, Eagle and ship. ***Right:*** FIFTY on 50 / Blacksmith. ***Engraver:*** New England Bank Note Co. / ABNCo. monogram. ***Comments:*** H-RI-495-G70, Durand-2229. 18__. 1858–1860s.

Rarity: —

$100 • **W-RI-370-100-G020**

Left: C / Men and fishing boats / 100. ***Center:*** Eagle on bale, Cornucopia, Flowers, Fruit / 100. ***Right:*** 100 / Ceres / 100. ***Engraver:*** New England Bank Note Co. / ABNCo. monogram. ***Comments:*** H-RI-495-G72, Durand-2231. 18__. 1858–1860s.

Rarity: —

$500 • **W-RI-370-500-G030**

Left: Indian in canoe / 500. ***Center:*** 500. ***Right:*** 500 / Justice. ***Engraver:*** New England Bank Note Co. / ABNCo. monogram. ***Comments:*** H-RI-495-G74, Durand-2233. 18__. 1858–1860s.

Rarity: —

Notes With Massachusetts Address

$1 • **W-MA-1560-001-G010**

Left: Man on horse, Boy with hand on one of four cows, Houses / 1. ***Center:*** 1 / Dolphin. ***Right:*** ONE / Indian man with bow and arrow / 1. ***Engraver:*** American Bank Note Co. ***Comments:*** H-MA-570-G2. Similar to $1 Fall River Union Bank, Rhode Island, but with different state. 1862–1864.

Rarity: —

$2 • **W-MA-1560-002-G020**

Left: Train, dock, and ships, Depot and men / 2 bearing female portrait / 2. ***Center:*** 2 bearing female portrait. ***Right:*** 2 / Portrait of George Washington and horse / TWO. ***Engraver:*** American Bank Note Co. ***Comments:*** H-MA-570-G4. Similar to $2 Fall River Union Bank, Rhode Island, but with different state. 1862–1864.

Rarity: —

$5 • **W-MA-1560-005-G030**

Left: Indian man paddling canoe on river / V in FIVE. ***Center:*** V. ***Right:*** 5 / Spread eagle perched on shield bearing 5. ***Engraver:*** American Bank Note Co. ***Comments:*** H-MA-570-G6. 1862–1864.

Rarity: URS-5
F $300

$10 • **W-MA-1560-010-G040**

Left: Mechanic seated on boiler working bellows / X. ***Center:*** X. ***Right:*** TEN / Portrait of George Washington / TEN. ***Engraver:*** American Bank Note Co. ***Comments:*** H-MA-570-G8. Similar to $10 Fall River Union Bank, Rhode Island, but with different state. 1862–1864.

Rarity: —

$20 • **W-MA-1560-020-G050**

Left: Woman reclining on rock with eagle and sheaf / 20. ***Center:*** TWENTY and 20 / Female portrait. ***Right:*** 20 / Portrait of Benjamin Franklin. ***Engraver:*** American Bank Note Co. ***Comments:*** H-MA-570-G10. 1862–1864.

Rarity: —

$50 • **W-MA-1560-050-G060**

Left: FIFTY / Sheaves and fruit / 50. ***Center:*** 50 / Three women seated with eagle, pole and cap, shield, scales, and book. ***Right:*** FIFTY across 50 / Train, Vulcan seated with tools. ***Engraver:*** New England Bank Note Co. / American Bank Note Co. ***Comments:*** H-MA-570-G12. Similar to $50 Fall River Union Bank, Rhode Island, but with different state. 1862–1864.

Rarity: —

$100 • **W-MA-1560-100-G070**

Left: C / Men with fishing boat at shore / 100. ***Center:*** Cornucopia, Eagle perched on bale, Sheaf / 100. ***Right:*** 100 / Ceres / 100. ***Engraver:*** New England Bank Note Co. / American Bank Note Co. ***Comments:*** H-MA-570-G14. Similar to $100 Fall River Union Bank, Rhode Island, but with different state. 1862–1864.

Rarity: —

$500 • **W-MA-1560-500-G080**

Left: Indian paddling canoe, Forest and mountains / 500 / D D. ***Bottom center:*** 500. ***Right:*** 500 / Justice. ***Engraver:*** New England Bank Note Co. / American Bank Note Co. ***Comments:*** H-MA-570-G16. Similar to $500 Fall River Union Bank, Rhode Island, but with different state. 1862–1864.

Rarity: —

Massasoit Bank
1846–1865
W-MA-1570

History: The Massasoit Bank was chartered on April 15, 1846, with an authorized capital of $100,000, a figure that increased to $200,000 in 1855. Specie held in the vault averaged $10,000 over the years. Circulation ranged from a low of $49,000 in 1849 to a high of $101,470 in 1863. Selected figures for 1857 included: bills of this bank and other New England states $8,171.57; specie $8,861.56.

The interests of the Massasoit Bank were succeeded by the Massasoit National Bank, chartered on December 8, 1864. The state bank began to wind down its business in early 1865.

Numismatic Commentary: Genuine notes from this bank are hard to find. Some Proofs have emerged in recent years.

Valid Issues

$1 • **W-MA-1570-001-G010**

CJF

Engraver: New England Bank Note Co. ***Comments:*** H-MA-575-G2. 18__. 1840s–1850s.

Rarity: URS-3
F $800; **VF** $1,000

$1 • **W-MA-1570-001-G010a**

CC

Overprint: Red ONE. ***Engraver:*** New England Bank Note Co. ***Comments:*** H-Unlisted. Similar to W-MA-1570-001-G010. Jan. 1, 185_. 1840s–1850s.

Rarity: URS-2
VF $1,000; **EF** $1,100; **Unc-S&D** $2,000

$2 • **W-MA-1570-002-G020**

Left: 2 / Eagle in 2. ***Center:*** Steamboat / Portrait of Indian man / Train. ***Right:*** 2 / Eagle in 2. ***Engraver:*** Rawdon, Wright, Hatch & Edson / New England Bank Note Co. ***Comments:*** H-MA-575-G4. Jan. 1, 185_. 1850s.

Rarity: —

$3 • **W-MA-1570-003-G030**
Left: 3 / Farmer carrying rake, jug, and fork. ***Center:*** Hay, wagon, train, and village. ***Right:*** 3 / Woman standing with dinner horn, Woman at table. ***Engraver:*** Rawdon, Wright, Hatch & Edson / New England Bank Note Co. ***Comments:*** H-MA-575-G6. Whole-note vignette. Jan. 1, 185_. 1850s.

Rarity: —

$5 • **W-MA-1570-005-G040**
Left: Indian man standing with gun, slain deer on ground, Dog / 5. ***Center:*** Indian woman seated in V. ***Right:*** Eagle on shield / 5 / FIVE. ***Engraver:*** Rawdon, Wright, Hatch & Edson / New England Bank Note Co. ***Comments:*** H-MA-575-G8. Jan. 1, 185_. 1850s.

Rarity: —

$10 • **W-MA-1570-010-G050**
Left: X / Portrait of George Washington standing by horse. ***Center:*** Female portrait / X / Female portrait. ***Right:*** 10 / Indian man kneeling on rock, holding bow. ***Engraver:*** Rawdon, Wright, Hatch & Edson / New England Bank Note Co. ***Comments:*** H-MA-575-G10. 1850s.

Rarity: —

$20 • **W-MA-1570-020-G060**
Left: Two Indian men, one seated on rock, one standing with arms raised, Steamboat / 20. ***Center:*** 20. ***Right:*** XX / Woman with basket of fruit on head. ***Engraver:*** Rawdon, Wright, Hatch & Edson / New England Bank Note Co. ***Comments:*** H-MA-575-G12. 1850s.

Rarity: —

$50 • **W-MA-1570-050-G070**
Left: FIFTY / Woman standing with wreath and flowers / FIFTY. ***Center:*** 50 / Man restraining prancing horse / 50. ***Right:*** FIFTY / Woman standing with cornucopia / FIFTY. ***Engraver:*** New England Bank Note Co. ***Comments:*** H-MA-575-G14. 18__. 1850s.

Rarity: —

$50 • **W-MA-1570-050-G080**
Left: Man and woman in sea / 50. ***Center:*** Portrait of girl. ***Right:*** 50 / Female portrait. ***Tint:*** Green. ***Engraver:*** American Bank Note Co. ***Comments:*** H-MA-575-G16a. 186_. 1860s.

Rarity: —

$100 • **W-MA-1570-100-G090**
Left: ONE HUNDRED on 100 / Portrait of William Henry Harrison. ***Center:*** Wharf scene, Men loading wagon with barrels. ***Right:*** ONE HUNDRED on 100 / Portrait of Christopher Columbus. ***Engraver:*** New England Bank Note Co. ***Comments:*** H-MA-575-G18. 18__. 1850s.

Rarity: —

$100 • **W-MA-1570-100-G100**

JF

Tint: Green. ***Engraver:*** American Bank Note Co. ***Comments:*** H-MA-575-G20a. Proof. 186_. 1860s.

Rarity: URS-2
Proof $7,500

$500 • **W-MA-1570-500-G110**
Center: Indian paddling canoe, Forest and mountains / 500 / D D. ***Bottom center:*** 500. ***Right:*** 500 / Justice. ***Engraver:*** New England Bank Note Co. ***Comments:*** H-MA-575-G22. 18__. 1850s.

Rarity: —

Non-Valid Issues

$10 • **W-MA-1570-010-S010**

CJF

Engraver: Danforth, Wright & Co. ***Comments:*** H-MA-575-S5. 18__. 1850s.

Rarity: URS-6
F $200

$10 • **W-MA-1570-010-N010**
Left: Portrait of George Washington. ***Center:*** Female portrait / 10 / Female portrait. ***Right:*** Portrait of William Henry Harrison. ***Comments:*** H-MA-575-N5.

Rarity: —

Metacomet Bank
1853–1865
W-MA-1580

History: The Metacomet Bank was chartered on April 28, 1853, with an authorized capital of $400,000. December 5, 1853, was the first day of business. By 1855 the capital had been increased to $600,000. Circulation ranged from $132,216 to $210,327 throughout the existence of the bank.

Selected figures for 1857 included: bills of this bank and other New England states $7,205.09; specie $12,370.18. Specie had decreased to $8,901.36 by 1858.

The business of the Metacomet Bank was succeeded by the Metacomet National Bank, chartered in March 1865.

Numismatic Commentary: Genuine notes are hard but not impossible to locate. Some will show a vignette of King Philip and presumably his wife and son in a canoe hunting porpoises. His Indian name, "Metacom," is incorporated into the vignette near the rear of the canoe.

Valid Issues

$1 • W-MA-1580-001-G010

TD

Engraver: Baldwin, Adams & Co. ***Comments:*** H-Unlisted. Proof. November 15, 1853.

Rarity: URS-2
Proof $1,100

$1 • W-MA-1580-001-G010a

CJF

Overprint: Red lazy 1. ***Engraver:*** Baldwin, Adams & Co. ***Comments:*** H-MA-580-G2a. Similar to W-MA-1580-001-G010. November 15, 1853.

Rarity: URS-4
Proof $1,250

$2 • W-MA-1580-002-G020

CJF

Overprint: Red lazy 2. ***Engraver:*** Baldwin, Adams & Co. ***Comments:*** H-Unlisted. Proof. November 15, 1853.

Rarity: URS-4
Proof $750

$2 • W-MA-1580-002-G020a

JF

Overprint: Red lazy 2. ***Engraver:*** Baldwin, Adams & Co. ***Comments:*** H-MA-580-G4a. Similar to W-MA-1580-002-G020. November 15, 1853.

Rarity: URS-3
Proof $1,750

$3 • W-MA-1580-003-G030

Left: 3 / Male portrait. ***Center:*** Steamboat and sail ships. ***Right:*** 3 / Indian paddling in canoe, harpooning whale. ***Overprint:*** Red lazy 3. ***Engraver:*** Baldwin, Adams & Co. ***Comments:*** H-MA-580-G6a. Nov. 15, 1853.

Rarity: —

$5 • W-MA-1580-005-G040

CJF

Engraver: Baldwin, Adams & Co. ***Comments:*** H-MA-580-G8. Proof. November 15, 1853.

Rarity: URS-4
Proof $850

$5 • W-MA-1580-005-G040a

JF

Overprint: Red lazy 5. ***Engraver:*** Baldwin, Adams & Co. ***Comments:*** H-MA-580-G8a. Similar to W-MA-1580-005-G040. November 15, 1853.

Rarity: URS-3
Proof $1,250

$10 • **W-MA-1580-010-G050** CC

Engraver: Baldwin, Adams & Co. ***Comments:*** H-MA-580-G10. Proof. November 15, 1853.

Rarity: URS-3
Proof $1,250

$10 • **W-MA-1580-010-G050a** CJF

Overprint: Red TEN. ***Engraver:*** Baldwin, Adams & Co. ***Comments:*** H-MA-580-G10a. Similar to W-MA-1580-010-G050. November 15, 1853.

Rarity: URS-3
EF $750; **Proof** $1,500

$20 • **W-MA-1580-020-G060**

Left: XX / XX. ***Center:*** Steamboat and sail ships. ***Right:*** 20 / Indian paddling in canoe, harpooning whale. ***Overprint:*** Red. ***Engraver:*** Baldwin, Adams & Co. ***Comments:*** H-MA-580-G12a. Nov. 15, 1853.

Rarity: —

$50 • **W-MA-1580-050-G070** CJF

Engraver: Baldwin, Adams & Co. ***Comments:*** H-MA-580-G14. Proof. 18__. 1850s.

Rarity: URS-3
Proof $1,500

$100 • **W-MA-1580-100-G080** CJF

Engraver: Baldwin, Adams & Co. ***Comments:*** H-MA-580-G16. Proof. 18__. 1850s.

Rarity: URS-4
Proof $1,000

$500 • **W-MA-1580-500-G090** JF

Engraver: Baldwin, Adams & Co. ***Comments:*** H-MA-580-G18. Proof. 18__. 1850s.

Rarity: URS-3
Proof $2,500

$1,000 • **W-MA-1580-1000-G100** CJF

Engraver: Baldwin, Adams & Co. ***Comments:*** H-MA-580-G20. Proof. 18__. 1850s.

Rarity: URS-3
Proof $3,500

Uncut Sheets

$1-$1-$2-$5 • **W-MA-1580-001.001.002.005-US010**

Vignette(s): ***($1)*** Indian man / Indian paddling in canoe / Male portrait. ***($1)*** Indian man / Indian paddling in canoe / Male portrait. ***($2)*** Male portrait / Steamboat and sail ships / Indian man. ***($5)*** Woman paddling, child / Indian family in canoe / Man harpooning whale / Male portrait. ***Overprint(s):*** None. ***Comments:*** Similar to H-MA-580-G2a, G2a, G4a, G8a. November 15, 1853.

Rarity: —

$1-$1-$2-$5 • W-MA-1580-001.001.002.005-US010a JF

Overprint(s): Red. *Comments:* H-MA-580-G2a, G2a, G4a, G8a. Similar to W-MA-1580-001.001.002.005-US010. November 15, 1853.

Rarity: URS-3
Proof $5,000

$3-$10-$20 • W-MA-1580-003.010.020-US020

Vignette(s): ($3) Male portrait / Steamboat and sail ships / Indian man in canoe. *($10)* Indians paddling in canoe / Male portrait. *($20)* Steamboat and sail ships / Indian man in canoe. *Overprint(s):* None. *Comments:* Similar to H-MA-580-G6a, G10a, G12a. November 15, 1853.

Rarity: —

$50-$100-$500-$1,000 • W-MA-1580-050.100.500.1000-US030 CJF

Comments: H-MA-580-G14, G16, G18, G20. Proof. 18__. 1850s.

Rarity: URS-2
Proof $7,500

Non-Valid Issues

$1 • W-MA-1580-001-A010

Left: ONE / Woman seated on sheaf watering eagle perched on shoulder / ONE. *Center:* Eagle on shield, Ships. *Right:* 1 / Ceres kneeling with sheaf, Farm. *Engraver:* Danforth, Bald & Co. *Comments:* H-MA-580-A5. Altered from $1 Columbia Bank, Washington, D.C. 18__. 1850s.

Rarity: —

$1 • W-MA-1580-001-A020

Left: ONE on die vertically. ***Center:*** Man on horseback overseeing cotton harvest / Indian stalking two deer. ***Bottom center:*** Sleeping dog. ***Right:*** 1 / Female portrait. ***Overprint:*** Red ONE. ***Engraver:*** Bald, Cousland & Co. / Baldwin, Bald & Cousland. ***Comments:*** H-MA-580-A10. Altered from $1 Southern Bank of Georgia, Bainbridge, Georgia. 18__. 1860s.

Rarity: —

$1 • W-MA-1580-001-A030

Left: 1 / Cattle and telegraph poles, Train on bridge. ***Center:*** Young woman seated with two calves, Trees and river. ***Right:*** 1 / Female portrait. ***Tint:*** Red-brown 1s and panel outlining white ONE DOLLAR. ***Engraver:*** Danforth, Wright & Co. ***Comments:*** H-MA-580-A15. Altered from $1 Southern Bank of Georgia, Bainbridge, Georgia. March 1, 1858.

Rarity: —

$1 • W-MA-1580-001-A040 SBG

Overprint: Red ONE. ***Engraver:*** Wellstood, Hay & Whiting. ***Comments:*** H-MA-580-A20. Altered from $1 Thames Bank, Laurel, Indiana. August 2, 1856. 1850s.

Rarity: URS-7
VF $150

$1 • W-MA-1580-001-A050

Left: Woman standing with apron full of flowers / ONE vertically. ***Center:*** Reaper seated by cradle, Two reapers, Hay wagon / 1. ***Right:*** ONE / Indian standing on cliff. ***Overprint:*** Red ONE. ***Engraver:*** New England Bank Note Co. / Rawdon, Wright, Hatch & Edson. ***Comments:*** H-MA-580-A25. Altered from $1 Waubeek Bank, De Soto, Nebraska. 1857.

Rarity: —

$1 • W-MA-1580-001-A060 MK

Engraver: Danforth, Wright & Co. ***Comments:*** H-MA-580-A30. Altered from $1 Bank of Washtenaw, Washtenaw, Michigan. 185_. 1850s.

Rarity: URS-6
F $100

$1 • W-MA-1580-001-A070 SI

Overprint: Red ONE. ***Engraver:*** Rawdon, Wright, Hatch & Edson. ***Comments:*** H-MA-580-A35. Altered from $1 Farmers and Merchants Bank of Memphis, Memphis, Tennessee series. 1 August 1854. 1850s.

Rarity: —

$2 • W-MA-1580-002-N010

Center: Steamship. ***Right:*** Indian woman. ***Comments:*** H-MA-580-N5.

Rarity: —

$2 • W-MA-1580-002-A080

Left: TWO and 2 on die / State arms vertically. ***Center:*** Three woodsmen felling and cutting trees. ***Right:*** 2 / Ceres with sheaf. ***Engraver:*** Danforth, Wright & Co. ***Comments:*** H-MA-580-A40. Altered from $2 Bank of Washtenaw, Washtenaw, Michigan series. 1850s.

Rarity: —

$2 • W-MA-1580-002-A090 CJF

Overprint: Red TWO. ***Engraver:*** Danforth, Wright & Co. ***Comments:*** H-Unlisted. July 10, 1856.

Rarity: URS-7
VG $100

$2 • W-MA-1580-002-A100

Left: 2 / Portrait of Benjamin Franklin / TWO. ***Center:*** Train / TWO. ***Bottom center:*** Shield. ***Right:*** 2 / Medallion 2 / TWO. ***Overprint:*** TWO. ***Engraver:*** Rawdon, Wright, Hatch & Edson. ***Comments:*** H-MA-580-A45. Altered from $2 Farmers and Merchants Bank of Memphis, Tennessee series. 1850s.

Rarity: —

$3 • W-MA-1580-003-N020

Center: Three women with shield bearing 3. ***Comments:*** H-MA-580-N10. 1850s.

Rarity: —

$3 • W-MA-1580-003-A110

CJF

Overprint: Red THREE. ***Engraver:*** Rawdon, Wright, Hatch & Edson. ***Comments:*** H-MA-580-A55. Altered from $3 Farmers and Merchants Bank of Memphis, Tennessee series. 18__. 1850s.

Rarity: URS-5
F $150

$10 • W-MA-1580-010-R010

Engraver: Bald, Adams & Co. ***Comments:*** H-MA-580-R5. Raised from W-MA-1580-001-G010a. November 15, 1853.

Rarity: —

$20 • W-MA-1580-020-R020

Comments: H-MA-580-R15. Raised from W-MA-1580-002-G020a. November 15, 1853.

Rarity: —

Pocasset Bank

1854–1860 • 1860–1865

W-RI-380 • W-MA-1590

History: The Pocasset Bank was incorporated in May 1854 with an authorized capital of $200,000. The official address was Tiverton, Rhode Island, but "Main Street, Fall River" was given on some reports, that section being in Rhode Island at the time. After a boundary change between Tiverton and Fall River was put into effect in the 1860 January session of the two state legislatures involved, the institution became a Massachusetts bank when Fall River became a part of Massachusetts.

The bank's circulation was $67,033 in 1860 and $82,007 in 1863. Real estate was valued at $100, and specie was listed at $4,830.48.

The business of the bank was succeeded by the Pocasset National Bank, chartered on December 31, 1864. The state bank began winding up its affairs in early 1865.

See also listings under Rhode Island.

Numismatic Commentary: Genuine notes from this bi-state bank are hard to locate. Notes from the Rhode Island address are more plentiful. Some of the vignettes will show Weetamoe, an Indian queen, escaping on a raft of logs from English pursuers. She perished in the waters of the Narragansett Bay when the raft overturned.

As of 2003 there was a $1-$1-$2-$5 tint plate remaining at the American Bank Note Co. archives.

Valid Issues

Notes with Rhode Island Address

$1 • W-RI-380-001-G010

CC

Overprint: Red 1. ***Engraver:*** Wellstood, Hanks, Hay & Whiting / ABNCo. monogram. ***Comments:*** H-RI-500-G20a, Durand-433. 18__. 1850s.

Rarity: —

$1 • W-RI-380-001-G010a

Overprint: Blue 1. ***Engraver:*** Wellstood, Hanks, Hay & Whiting / ABNCo. monogram. ***Comments:*** H-RI-500-G20b, Durand-434. Similar to W-RI-380-001-G010. 18__. 1850s.

Rarity: —

$2 • W-RI-380-002-G020

RD

Engraver: Wellstood, Hanks, Hay & Whiting / ABNCo. monogram. ***Comments:*** H-Unlisted. 18__. 1850s.

Rarity: —

$2 • W-RI-380-002-G020a

CC

Overprint: Red 2. ***Engraver:*** Wellstood, Hanks, Hay & Whiting / ABNCo. monogram. ***Comments:*** H-RI-500-G22a, Durand-435. Similar to W-RI-380-002-G020. 18__. 1850s.

Rarity: —

$2 • **W-RI-380-002-G020b** MK

Overprint: Blue 2. ***Engraver:*** Wellstood, Hanks, Hay & Whiting / ABNCo. monogram. ***Comments:*** H-RI-500-G22b, Durand-436. Similar to W-RI-380-002-G020. 18__. 1850s.

Rarity: —

$2 • **W-RI-380-002-G030**

Left: TWO on 2 / Indian woman. ***Center:*** Cow and calf in stream, Sheep and house. ***Right:*** 2 / Portrait of two girls. ***Comments:*** H-RI-500-G24, Durand-437. 18__. 1860s.

Rarity: —

$5 • **W-RI-380-005-G040**

Left: FIVE / Reverses of three U.S. and two Spanish-American silver dollars. ***Center:*** 5 / Indian woman poling raft. ***Bottom center:*** Men loading wagon with hay. ***Right:*** FIVE across 5 / FIVE. ***Overprint:*** Red 5. ***Engraver:*** Wellstood, Hanks, Hay & Whiting / ABNCo. monogram. ***Comments:*** H-RI-500-G26a, Durand-440. 18__. 1850s.

Rarity: —

$5 • **W-RI-380-005-G040a**

Overprint: Blue 5. ***Engraver:*** Wellstood, Hanks, Hay & Whiting / ABNCo. monogram. ***Comments:*** H-RI-500-G26b, Durand-441. Similar to W-RI-380-005-G040. 18__. 1850s.

Rarity: —

$10 • **W-RI-380-010-G050**

Left: 10 / Stonecutter at work, Marble quarry. ***Right:*** 10 / Indian woman poling raft. ***Engraver:*** Wellstood, Hanks, Hay & Whiting. ***Comments:*** H-Unlisted, Durand-442.

Rarity: —

$20 • **W-RI-380-020-G060**

Left: 20 / Indian woman poling raft. ***Bottom center:*** Anchor on shield. ***Right:*** Justice in clouds / 20. ***Engraver:*** Wellstood, Hanks, Hay & Whiting. ***Comments:*** H-Unlisted, Durand-443.

Rarity: —

$50 • **W-RI-380-050-G070**

Left: 50 / Farm scene, Woman standing, Man seated at lunch. ***Bottom center:*** 50. ***Right:*** Indian woman poling raft / 50. ***Engraver:*** Wellstood, Hanks, Hay & Whiting. ***Comments:*** H-Unlisted, Durand-444.

Rarity: —

$100 • **W-RI-380-100-G080**

Left: 100 / Sailing ship. ***Center:*** C / Indian woman poling raft. ***Right:*** 100 / Farmer sharpening scythe. ***Engraver:*** Wellstood, Hanks, Hay & Whiting. ***Comments:*** H-Unlisted, Durand-445.

Rarity: —

$500 • **W-RI-380-500-G090**

Left: 500 / Warship under sail, Ship. ***Center:*** D. ***Right:*** 500 / Indian woman poling raft. ***Engraver:*** Wellstood, Hanks, Hay & Whiting. ***Comments:*** H-Unlisted, Durand-446.

Rarity: —

$1,000 • **W-RI-380-1000-G100**

Left: Indian woman poling raft / 1000. ***Center:*** M. ***Right:*** 1000 / Indian seated smoking pipe, Indian woman, Canoe and wigwam. ***Engraver:*** Wellstood, Hanks, Hay & Whiting. ***Comments:*** H-Unlisted, Durand-447.

Rarity: —

Notes with Massachusetts Address

$1 • **W-MA-1590-001-G010**

Engraver: American Bank Note Co. ***Comments:*** H-MA-585-G2a. Similar to W-RI-380-001-G010 but with different state and imprint. 18__. 1860s.

Rarity: —

$2 • **W-MA-1590-002-G020**

Engraver: American Bank Note Co. ***Comments:*** H-MA-585-G4a. Similar to W-RI-380-002-G020 but with different state and imprint. 18__. 1860s.

Rarity: —

$2 • **W-MA-1590-002-G030** CJF

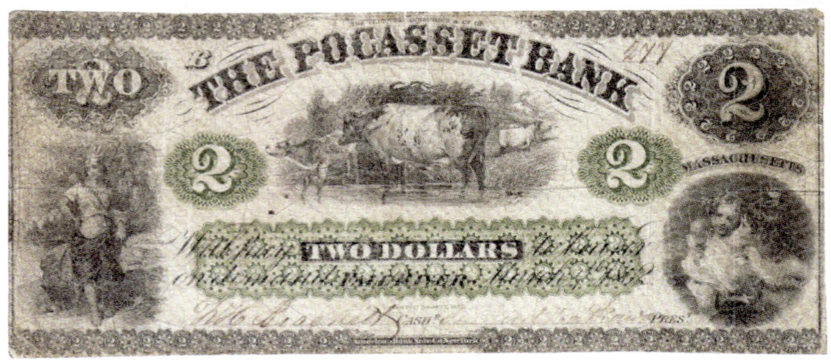

Tint: Green. ***Engraver:*** American Bank Note Co. ***Comments:*** H-MA-585-G6a. Similar to W-RI-380-002-G030 but with different state and imprint. March 4, 1862.

Rarity: URS-3

VF $1,500

$5 • **W-MA-1590-005-G040** CJF

Overprint: Green 5 / FIVE / 5. ***Engraver:*** Wellstood, Hanks, Hay & Whiting / ABNCo. monogram. ***Comments:*** H-MA-585-G8a. Similar to W-RI-380-005-G040 but with different state and imprint. March 4, 1862. 1860s.

Rarity: URS-2

VF $1,500

$10 • W-MA-1590-010-G050

Engraver: American Bank Note Co. ***Comments:*** H-MA-585-G10. Similar to W-RI-380-010-G050 but with different state and imprint. 18__. 1860s.

Rarity: —

$20 • W-MA-1590-020-G060

Engraver: American Bank Note Co. ***Comments:*** H-MA-585-G12a. Similar to W-RI-380-020-G060 but with different state and imprint. 18__. 1860s.

Rarity: —

$50 • W-MA-1590-050-G070

Engraver: American Bank Note Co. ***Comments:*** H-MA-585-G14a. Similar to W-RI-380-050-G070 but with different state and imprint. 18__. 1860s.

Rarity: —

$100 • W-MA-1590-100-G080

Engraver: American Bank Note Co. ***Comments:*** H-MA-585-G16a. Similar to W-RI-380-100-G080 but with different state and imprint. 18__. 1860s.

Rarity: —

$500 • W-MA-1590-500-G090

Engraver: American Bank Note Co. ***Comments:*** H-MA-585-G18a. Similar to W-RI-380-500-G090 but with different state and imprint. 18__. 1860s.

Rarity: —

$1,000 • W-MA-1590-1000-G100

Engraver: American Bank Note Co. ***Comments:*** H-MA-585-G20. Similar to W-RI-380-1000-G100 but with different state and imprint. 18__. 1860s.

Rarity: —

Non-Valid Issues

Notes with Massachusetts Address

$2 • W-MA-1590-002-C020

Engraver: American Bank Note Co. ***Comments:*** H-MA-585-C4a. Counterfeit of W-MA-1590-002-G020. 18__. 1860s.

Rarity: —

$5 • W-MA-1590-005-C040

Engraver: American Bank Note Co. ***Comments:*** H-MA-585-C8. Counterfeit of W-MA-1590-005-G040. 18__. 1860s.

Rarity: URS-7
VG $100; **VF** $175

$5 • W-MA-1590-005-A010

CJF

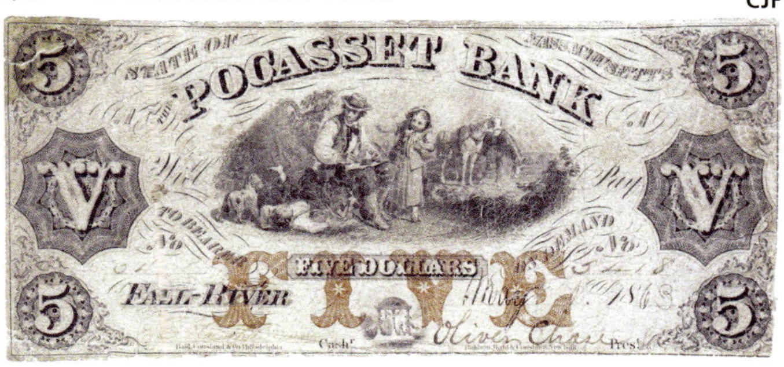

Overprint: Red FIVE. ***Engraver:*** Bald, Cousland & Co. / Baldwin, Bald & Cousland. ***Comments:*** H-MA-585-A5. 18__. 1860s.

Rarity: URS-7
VG $100; **VF** $225

Wamsutta Bank
1856–1864
W-MA-1600

History: The Wamsutta Bank was chartered on June 5, 1856, with an authorized capital of $100,000. It opened its doors for business in October. Selected figures for 1857 included: bills of this bank and other New England states $1,468.20; specie $6,033.26. Circulation was $43,408 in 1860 and $94,976 in 1863. By 1864 specie had decreased to $5,744.68.

The interests of the Wamsutta Bank were succeeded by the Second National Bank of Fall River, chartered on May 26, 1864.

Numismatic Commentary: Notes from this bank are extremely hard to find.

Valid Issues

$1 • W-MA-1600-001-G010

Left: ONE / Woman standing with 1. ***Center:*** Indian man seated with globe dollar, Slain deer. ***Right:*** 1 / Portrait of Red Jacket. ***Engraver:*** Rawdon, Wright, Hatch & Edson. ***Comments:*** H-MA-590-G2. 18__. 1850s.

Rarity: —

$1 • W-MA-1600-001-G010a

CJF

Overprint: Red ONE. ***Engraver:*** Rawdon, Wright, Hatch & Edson. ***Comments:*** H-Unlisted. Similar to W-MA-1600-001-G010. 18__. 1850s.

Rarity: URS-2
VG $750

$2 • W-MA-1600-002-G020

Left: TWO / Woman seated on plow holding sheaf. ***Center:*** Farmer reclining and milkmaid seated, Two gold dollars, Cattle and farm. ***Right:*** 2 / Indian woman seated. ***Engraver:*** Rawdon, Wright, Hatch & Edson. ***Comments:*** H-MA-590-G4. 18__. 1850s.

Rarity: —

$3 • W-MA-1600-003-G030

Left: 3 / Portrait. ***Center:*** Farmer, sailor, and mechanic seated with three gold dollars. ***Right:*** THREE / Liberty standing with flag and shield, Indian woman seated. ***Engraver:*** Rawdon, Wright, Hatch & Edson. ***Comments:*** H-MA-590-G6. 18__. 1850s.

Rarity: —

$5 • W-MA-1600-005-G040

Left: V / Farmer seated with scythe. ***Center:*** Indian woman and hunter flanking five gold dollars and three cherubs. ***Right:*** 5 / Portrait of Indian woman. ***Engraver:*** Rawdon, Wright, Hatch & Edson. ***Comments:*** H-MA-590-G8. 18__. 1850s.

Rarity: —

$10 • **W-MA-1600-010-G050**
Left: 10 / Portrait of Indian man. ***Center:*** Woman reclining with cornucopia and shield facing nine cherubs, Ten gold dollars. ***Bottom center:*** Mechanic. ***Right:*** X / Cherub holding shell and seated on dolphin. ***Engraver:*** Rawdon, Wright, Hatch & Edson. ***Comments:*** H-MA-590-G10. 18__. 1850s.

Rarity: —

$50 • **W-MA-1600-050-G060**
Left: FIFTY / Woman holding spear and leaning on shield. ***Center:*** Indian family seated on cliff overlooking city. ***Right:*** 50 / Female portrait. ***Engraver:*** Rawdon, Wright, Hatch & Edson. ***Comments:*** H-MA-590-G12. 18__. 1850s.

Rarity: —

$100 • **W-MA-1600-100-G070**
Left: Deer and dog / HUNDRED. ***Center:*** Woman seated on rock, Three cherubs and dolphin playing in water. ***Right:*** 100 / Portrait of Indian man. ***Engraver:*** Rawdon, Wright, Hatch & Edson. ***Comments:*** H-MA-590-G14. 18__. 1850s.

Rarity: —

$500 • **W-MA-1600-500-G080**
Left: 500. ***Center:*** Indian paddling canoe, Forest and mountains / 500 / D D. ***Right:*** 500 / Justice. ***Overprint:*** Red 500. ***Engraver:*** Rawdon, Wright, Hatch & Edson. ***Comments:*** H-MA-590-G16a. 18__. 1850s.

Rarity: —

Non-Valid Issues

$2 • **W-MA-1600-002-N010**
Center: Woman seated on shore with merchandise, Ships. ***Comments:*** H-MA-590-N5. 1850s.

Rarity: —

$2 • **W-MA-1600-002-N020**
Center: Indian family in canoe. ***Comments:*** H-MA-590-N10. 1850s.

Rarity: —

$3 • **W-MA-1600-003-A010**
Left: 3 / Female portrait. ***Center:*** Three cherubs playing with three silver dollars. ***Right:*** 3 / Country scene with men on horseback. ***Overprint:*** Red THREE. ***Engraver:*** Rawdon, Wright, Hatch & Edson / New England Bank Note Co. ***Comments:*** H-MA-590-A5. Altered from $3 Warwick Bank, Warwick, Rhode Island. 18__. 1850s.

Rarity: —

$5 • **W-MA-1600-005-N030**
Left: FIVE vertically. ***Center:*** Three children on seashore, Ship. ***Right:*** Bust of George Washington. ***Comments:*** H-MA-590-N15. 1850s.

Rarity: —

$5 • **W-MA-1600-005-A020**
Left: FIVE / State arms vertically. ***Center:*** Farmer, sailor, and mechanic. ***Right:*** 5 / Portrait of Franklin Pierce. ***Engraver:*** Danforth, Wright & Co. ***Comments:*** H-MA-590-A10. Altered from $5 Bank of Washtenaw, Washtenaw, Michigan. 1850s.

Rarity: URS-7
VG $100; **VF** $175

Wamsutta Bank of Fall River
1850s
W-MA-1620

History: A non-existent bank represented only by notes altered from those of other banks. The notes were intended to pass for those of the Wamsutta Bank, W-MA-1600.

Issues

$5 • **W-MA-1620-005-A010** CC

Overprint: Blue FIVE. ***Engraver:*** Rawdon, Wright, Hatch & Edson. ***Comments:*** H-MA-591-A5. Altered from $5 Farmers and Merchants Bank of Memphis, Memphis, Tennessee series. 1850s.

Rarity: URS-6
F $225

Wamsutta Bank of Massachusetts
1850s
W-MA-1640

History: A non-existent bank represented only by notes altered from those of other banks. The notes were intended to pass for those of the Wamsutta Bank, W-MA-1600.

Issues

$2 • **W-MA-1640-002-A010** HA

Tint: Red-brown dies outlining white 2s and TWO DOLLARS. ***Engraver:*** Danforth, Wright & Co. ***Comments:*** H-MA-592-A5. Altered from $2 Southern Bank of Georgia, Bainbridge, Georgia. March 1, 18__. 1860s.

Rarity: URS-8
VG $750

Falmouth, Massachusetts

The town later known as Falmouth was first settled by English colonists in 1660 and incorporated in 1686 under the name of Suckanessett. Later, Bartholomew Gosnold named Falmouth after his home port in Falmouth, Cornwall, England.

During the 19th century, Falmouth was a lively whaling port as well as an import-export center for packet ships. Sheep husbandry was also very popular after the introduction of the Merino sheep and the inception of water-powered mills to process the wool. Wool-carding mills in East Falmouth appeared by the early 19th century. Salt was mined in Falmouth, producing more than 35,000 bushels from seawater annually. Products shipped in quantity to Boston and New York included lumber, salt, glass, whale oil, and onions.

Falmouth Bank

1821–1865

W-MA-1650

History: The Falmouth Bank was chartered on February 14, 1821, with $100,000 authorized stock. John Jenkins was the first president, and S.B. Bourne was the founding cashier. The capital was increased to $250,000 in 1857 but was reduced to $100,000 by 1860.

Selected figures for 1857 included: bills of this bank and other New England states $1,988; specie $3,153.50; real estate $4,300. Circulation of the bank was at a low of $40,507 in 1857 and at a high of $62,440 in 1863.

The business of the Falmouth Bank was succeeded by the Falmouth National Bank, chartered in 1865.

Numismatic Commentary: A collector would be considered fortunate to find any note from this bank. Notes from Cape Cod and the islands are especially sought after.

As of 2003 there was a $5-$5 face plate remaining at the American Bank Note Co. archives.

Valid Issues

$1 • W-MA-1650-001-G010

Center: 1 / 1 / Flower garlands and gridwork segments / ONE / 1 / 1. ***Engraver:*** PSSP. ***Comments:*** H-MA-595-G2. 18__. 1820s.

Rarity: —

$1 • W-MA-1650-001-G010a

Left: Panel of lathework circle segments. ***Right:*** Panel of lathework circle segments. ***Engraver:*** PSSP. ***Comments:*** H-MA-595-G4. Similar to W-MA-1650-001-G010. 18__. 1820s.

Rarity: —

$1 • W-MA-1650-001-G010b

Left: Panel of lathework circle segments. ***Right:*** Panel of lathework circle segments. ***Engraver:*** PSSP. ***Comments:*** H-MA-595-G6. Similar to W-MA-1650-001-G010. 18__. 1820s–1830s.

Rarity: —

$1 • W-MA-1650-001-G010c

Left: ONE / D / ONE vertically. ***Right:*** ONE / D / ONE vertically. ***Engraver:*** PSSP. ***Comments:*** H-MA-595-G8. Similar to W-MA-1650-001-G010. 18__. 1830s.

Rarity: —

$1 • W-MA-1650-001-G020

Comments: H-MA-595-G10. No description available. 18__. 1830s–1840s.

Rarity: *None known*

$1 • W-MA-1650-001-G030

Left: 1 / Portrait of George Washington, ***Center:*** Woman seated with rudder / 1 / Woman seated. ***Right:*** 1 / Portrait of Benjamin Franklin. ***Engraver:*** New England Bank Note Co. ***Comments:*** H-MA-595-G12. 18__. 1840s–1850s.

Rarity: —

$1 • W-MA-1650-001-G040

CJF

Overprint: Red ONE. ***Engraver:*** New England Bank Note Co. ***Comments:*** H-MA-595-G16a. 18__. 1850s.

Rarity: URS-2

VF $1,500

$1 • W-MA-1650-001-G050

CC

Tint: Green. ***Engraver:*** American Bank Note Co. ***Comments:*** H-MA-595-G20a. Jan. 1, 1861.

Rarity: URS-1

Proof $7,000

$2 • W-MA-1650-002-G060

Center: 2 / 2 / Flower garlands and gridwork segments / TWO / 2 / 2. ***Engraver:*** PSSP. ***Comments:*** H-MA-595-G22. 18__. 1820s.

Rarity: —

$2 • W-MA-1650-002-G060a

Left: Panel of lathework circle segments. ***Right:*** Panel of lathework circle segments. ***Engraver:*** PSSP. ***Comments:*** H-MA-595-G24. Similar to W-MA-1650-002-G060. 18__. 1820s.

Rarity: —

$2 • W-MA-1650-002-G060b

Left: Panel of lathework circle segments. ***Right:*** Panel of lathework circle segments. ***Engraver:*** PSSP. ***Comments:*** H-MA-595-G26. Similar to W-MA-1650-002-G060. 18__. 1820s–1830s.

Rarity: —

$2 • W-MA-1650-002-G060c

Left: Five TWOs vertically. ***Right:*** Five TWOs vertically. ***Engraver:*** PSSP. ***Comments:*** H-MA-595-G28. Similar to W-MA-1650-002-G060. 18__. 1830s.

Rarity: —

$2 • W-MA-1650-002-G070

Comments: H-MA-595-G30. No description available. 18__. 1830s–1840s.

Rarity: *None known*

$2 • W-MA-1650-002-G080

Left: 2 / Portrait of Christopher Columbus. ***Center:*** Woman standing with cornucopia / 2 / Justice seated. ***Right:*** 2 / Male portrait. ***Engraver:*** New England Bank Note Co. ***Comments:*** H-MA-595-G32. 18__. 1840s–1850s.

Rarity: —

$2 • W-MA-1650-002-G090

Left: 2 / George Washington after crossing the Delaware in the Battle of Trenton, 1776 / 2. ***Center:*** 2 / Woman seated with shield bearing 2, Cornucopia / 2. ***Right:*** 2 / George Washington after crossing the Delaware in the Battle of Trenton, 1776 / 2. ***Overprint:*** Red TWO. ***Engraver:*** New England Bank Note Co. ***Comments:*** H-MA-595-G36a. 18__. 1850s.

Rarity: —

$2 • W-MA-1650-002-G100

Left: 2 / Two women. ***Center:*** 2 / Sailor reclining next to anchor, Ship / 2 / TWO. ***Right:*** 2 / Man picking corn. ***Tint:*** Green. ***Engraver:*** American Bank Note Co. ***Comments:*** H-MA-595-G40a. Jan. 1, 1861.

Rarity: —

$3 • W-MA-1650-003-G110

Center: 3 / 3 / Oval of flower garlands and gridwork segments / 3 / 3. ***Engraver:*** PSSP. ***Comments:*** H-MA-595-G42. 18__. 1820s.

Rarity: —

$3 • W-MA-1650-003-G110a

Left: Panel of lathework circle segments. ***Right:*** Panel of lathework circle segments. ***Engraver:*** PSSP. ***Comments:*** H-MA-595-G44. Similar to W-MA-1650-003-G110. 18__. 1820s.

Rarity: —

$3 • W-MA-1650-003-G110b

Left: Panel of lathework circle segments. ***Right:*** Panel of lathework circle segments. ***Engraver:*** PSSP. ***Comments:*** H-MA-595-G46. Similar to W-MA-1650-003-G110. 18__. 1820s–1830s.

Rarity: —

$3 • W-MA-1650-003-G110c

Left: THREE vertically. ***Right:*** THREE vertically. ***Engraver:*** PSSP. ***Comments:*** H-MA-595-G48. Similar to W-MA-1650-003-G110. 18__. 1830s.

Rarity: —

$3 • W-MA-1650-003-G120

Comments: H-MA-595-G50. No description available. 18__. 1830s–1840s.

Rarity: *None known*

$3 • W-MA-1650-003-G130

Left: 3 / George Washington standing by horse. ***Center:*** Female portrait / 3 / Portrait of girl with ringlets. ***Right:*** 3 / Vulcan standing with sledge. ***Engraver:*** New England Bank Note Co. ***Comments:*** H-MA-595-G52. Beware of W-MA-1650-003-S010. 18__. 1840s–1850s.

Rarity: —

$3 • W-MA-1650-003-G140

Left: 3 / Portrait of cherub / 3. ***Center:*** 3 / Woman seated with lyre and shield bearing 3 / 3. ***Right:*** 3 / Portrait of cherub / 3. ***Overprint:*** Red THREE. ***Engraver:*** PSSP. ***Comments:*** H-MA-595-G56a. 18__. 1820s.

Rarity: —

$3 • W-MA-1650-003-G150

Left: Three men in boat / 3. ***Center:*** Female portrait / 3. ***Right:*** 3 / Woman. ***Tint:*** Green. ***Engraver:*** American Bank Note Co. ***Comments:*** H-MA-595-G60a. Jan. 1, 1861.

Rarity: —

$5 • W-MA-1650-005-G160

Left: Lathework chain bearing MASSACHUSETTS / 5 / 5. ***Center:*** Alternating flower garlands and gridwork segments. ***Right:*** 5 / 5. ***Engraver:*** PSSP. ***Comments:*** H-MA-595-G62. 18__. 1820s.

Rarity: —

$5 • W-MA-1650-005-G160a

Center: Alternating flower garlands and gridwork segments / White boxes flanking FIVE DOLLARS. ***Engraver:*** PSSP. ***Comments:*** H-MA-595-G64. Similar to W-MA-1650-005-G160. 18__. 1820s.

Rarity: —

$5 • W-MA-1650-005-G160b

Engraver: PSSP. ***Comments:*** H-MA-595-G66. Similar to W-MA-1650-005-G160 but with zigzag ruled lines. 18__. 1820s–1830s.

Rarity: —

$5 • W-MA-1650-005-G160c

Engraver: PSSP. ***Comments:*** H-MA-595-G68. Similar to W-MA-1650-005-G160 but with spiral lathework lines. 18__. 1830s.

Rarity: —

$5 • W-MA-1650-005-G170

Comments: H-MA-595-G70. No description available. 18__. 1830s–1840s.

Rarity: *None known*

$5 • W-MA-1650-005-G180

Left: FIVE / Justice. ***Center:*** FIVE / Woman and four cherubs in 5. ***Right:*** 5 / Woman with basket of flowers. ***Comments:*** H-MA-595-G72. 18__. Circa 1850s.

Rarity: —

$10 • W-MA-1650-010-G190

Left: Lathework chain bearing MASSACHUSETTS / 10 / 10 vertically. ***Center:*** Alternating flower garlands and gridwork segments. ***Right:*** 10 / 10 vertically. ***Engraver:*** Perkins. ***Comments:*** H-MA-595-G74. 18__. 1820s.

Rarity: —

$10 • W-MA-1650-010-G190a

Left: Lathework chain bearing MASSACHUSETTS vertically. ***Right:*** Panel of lathework circle segments. ***Engraver:*** Perkins. ***Comments:*** H-MA-595-G76. Similar to W-MA-1650-010-G190. 18__. 1820s.

Rarity: —

$10 • W-MA-1650-010-G190b

Engraver: PSSP. ***Comments:*** H-MA-595-G78. Similar to W-MA-1650-010-G190 but with zigzag ruled lines. 18__. 1820s–1830s.

Rarity: —

$10 • W-MA-1650-010-G190c

Engraver: PSSP. ***Comments:*** H-MA-595-G80. Similar to W-MA-1650-010-G190 but with spiral lathework lines. 18__. 1830s.

Rarity: —

$10 • W-MA-1650-010-G200

Comments: H-MA-595-G82. No description available. 18__. 1830s–1840s.

Rarity: *None known*

$10 • W-MA-1650-010-G210

Left: 10 / Two women standing. ***Center:*** 1 and 0 flanking woman seated on chest holding key. ***Right:*** 10 / Two women standing. ***Comments:*** H-MA-595-G84. 18__. Circa 1850s.

Rarity: —

$20 • W-MA-1650-020-G220

Left: Panel bearing state arms / 20 / 20 vertically. ***Center:*** Alternating flower garlands and gridwork segments. ***Right:*** 20 / 20 vertically. ***Engraver:*** Perkins. ***Comments:*** H-MA-595-G86. 18__. 1820s.

Rarity: —

$20 • W-MA-1650-020-G220a

Left: Lathework chain bearing MASSACHUSETTS vertically. ***Engraver:*** PSSP. ***Comments:*** H-MA-595-G88. Similar to W-MA-1650-020-G220. 18__. 1820s–1830s.

Rarity: —

$20 • W-MA-1650-020-G230

Left: 20 / Woman seated. ***Center:*** Eagle on shield, Sheaf, Factories and falls. ***Right:*** 20 / Woman seated. ***Comments:*** H-MA-595-G92. 18__. Circa 1850s.

Rarity: —

$50 • W-MA-1650-050-G240

Left: Panel bearing state arms / 50 / 50 vertically. ***Center:*** Alternating flower garlands and gridwork segments. ***Right:*** 50 / 50 vertically. ***Engraver:*** Perkins. ***Comments:*** H-MA-595-G94. 18__. 1820s.

Rarity: —

$50 • W-MA-1650-050-G240a

Left: Lathework chain bearing MASSACHUSETTS vertically. ***Engraver:*** PSSP. ***Comments:*** H-MA-595-G96. Similar to W-MA-1650-050-G240. 18__. 1820s–1830s.

Rarity: —

$50 • W-MA-1650-050-G250

Left: 50 / Female portrait / 50. ***Center:*** Hunter with gun and woodsman with ax flanking bull. ***Right:*** 50 / Portrait. ***Comments:*** H-MA-595-G100. 18__. Circa 1850s.

Rarity: —

$100 • W-MA-1650-100-G260

Left: Panel bearing state arms / 100 / 100 vertically. ***Center:*** Alternating flower garlands and gridwork segments. ***Right:*** 100 / 100 vertically. ***Engraver:*** Perkins. ***Comments:*** H-MA-595-G102. 18__. 1820s.

Rarity: —

$100 • W-MA-1650-100-G260a

Left: Lathework chain bearing MASSACHUSETTS vertically. ***Engraver:*** Perkins. ***Comments:*** H-MA-595-G104. Similar to W-MA-1650-100-G260. 18__. 1820s–1830s.

Rarity: —

$100 • W-MA-1650-100-G270

Left: 100 / Female portrait / 100. ***Center:*** C / Ships of war / C. ***Right:*** 100 / Justice / 100. ***Comments:*** H-MA-595-G108. 18__. Circa 1850s.

Rarity: —

$100 • W-MA-1650-100-G280

Left: 100 / Sailor standing, Woman seated. ***Center:*** C / Three men with sheaf / C. ***Right:*** 100 / Man with barrel. ***Engraver:*** American Bank Note Co. ***Comments:*** H-MA-595-G110a. Jan. 1, 1861.

Rarity: —

Non-Valid Issues

$2 • W-MA-1650-002-A010

Left: 2 / Woman standing with staff, Cornucopia / TWO. ***Center:*** TWO / Machinery and merchandise flanking Ceres seated holding sickle and rake, Factories and harbor. ***Engraver:*** New England Bank Note Co. ***Comments:*** H-MA-595-A5. Altered from $2 Washington County Bank, Calais, Maine, or from notes of other failed banks using the same plate. 18__. 1840s.

Rarity: —

How to Read the Whitman Numbering System

$1 • W-MA-010-001-G010a

Denomination: Value of the note shown.

W: Whitman number. This number is a sortable code unique to each bank and note.

MA: Abbreviation for the state under study.

010: Numerical designation specific to each bank.

001: The denomination in dollars.

G010a: G indicates a good or valid note. Other categories are indicated thus: C (counterfeit); R (raised); S (spurious); N (not-attributed); A (altered). Numbers are assigned starting with 010, 020, et seq. Terminal letters following the number indicate variations of a note: a series of different colored overprints, tints, payees, etc., all on the same design of note. For more information, see the “How to Use This Book” section at the front of the volume, page xiv.

$3 • W-MA-1650-003-S010 TD

Comments: H-MA-595-S5. Spurious design imitating a rough verbal description of W-MA-1650-003-G130. Jan. __, 185_. 1850s.

Rarity: URS-6
F $200; **VF** $275

$3 • W-MA-1650-003-S010a SI

Overprint: Red 3 / 3. ***Comments:*** H-Unlisted. Similar to W-MA-1650-003-S010. Jan. __, 185_. 1850s.

Rarity: URS-7
VF $250

$3 • W-MA-1650-003-A020
Left: THREE / Beehive and foliage / THREE. ***Center:*** Machinery and merchandise flanking Ceres seated holding sickle and rake, Factories and harbor / THREE. ***Right:*** 3 on THREE / Two reapers / 3 on THREE. ***Engraver:*** New England Bank Note Co. ***Comments:*** H-MA-595-A10. Altered from $3 Washington County Bank, Calais, Maine, or from notes of other failed banks using the same plate. 18__. 1840s.

Rarity: —

$5 • W-MA-1650-005-R010
Engraver: New England Bank Note Co. ***Comments:*** H-MA-595-R5. Raised from W-MA-1650-001-G030. 18__. 1840s–1850s.

Rarity: —

$5 • W-MA-1650-005-S020
Left: Allegorical man seated with scroll, Ship / V. ***Center:*** 5. ***Right:*** Die bearing Portrait of George Washington and FIVE DOLLARS. ***Comments:*** H-MA-595-S10. 18__. 1850s.

Rarity: —

$5 • W-MA-1650-005-N010
Center: Marine view / 5. ***Comments:*** H-MA-595-N5.

Rarity: —

$10 • W-MA-1650-010-A030 CJF

Engraver: Terry, Pelton & Co. ***Comments:*** H-MA-595-A15. Altered from $10 Citizens Bank, Augusta, Maine, or from notes of other failed banks using the same plate. 18__. 1840s.

Rarity: URS-6
VG $200

Fitchburg, Massachusetts

Settled in 1730 and incorporated in 1764, Fitchburg was named after John Fitch, who was abducted along with his family to Canada in 1748. They were returned after a year. The town is located on the Nashua River. The Fitchburg Railroad once linked Boston and Albany, New York. The town was an industrial center in the 19th century, operated by water power that ran large mills in the production of machines, tools, clothing, paper, and firearms.

Fitchburg Bank
1832–1865
W-MA-1660

History: The Fitchburg Bank was chartered on February 28, 1832, and began operations in July of that year with a capital of $100,000. Capital had increased to $150,000 by 1847 and to $200,000 by 1849. In 1857 it was $250,000. Circulation ranged from $71,818 in 1839 to $247,833 in 1863. Selected figures for 1857 included: bills of this bank and other New England states $3,500; specie $37,178.20; real estate $3,000.

The business of the Fitchburg Bank was succeeded by the Fitchburg National Bank, chartered in 1865.

Numismatic Commentary: Genuine notes from this bank are hard to find, but spurious issues are relatively common.

Valid Issues

$1 • W-MA-1660-001-G010
Left: Lathework panel bearing MASSACHUSETTS vertically. ***Center:*** 1 / 1 / Alternating flower garlands and gridwork segments / ONE / 1 / 1. ***Right:*** Lathework panel bearing ONE / D / ONE vertically. ***Engraver:*** PSSP. ***Comments:*** H-MA-600-G2. 18__. 1830s.

Rarity: —

$1 • W-MA-1660-001-G020
Engraver: Unverified, but likely New England Bank Note Co. ***Comments:*** H-MA-600-G4. No description available. 18__. 1830s–1840s.

Rarity: *None known*

$1 • W-MA-1660-001-G030
Left: Train, Building / 1. ***Center:*** Medallion 1. ***Right:*** ONE / Medallion head / ONE. ***Engraver:*** New England Bank Note Co. ***Comments:*** H-MA-600-G8. 18__. 1850s.
Rarity: —

$1 • W-MA-1660-001-G030a
CJF

Overprint: Red ONE. ***Engraver:*** New England Bank Note Co. ***Comments:*** H-Unlisted. Similar to W-MA-1660-001-G030. 18__. 1850s.
Rarity: URS-3
VG $1,000; **VF** $1,250

$2 • W-MA-1660-002-G040
Left: Lathework panel bearing MASSACHUSETTS vertically. ***Center:*** 2 / 2 / Alternating flower garlands and gridwork segments / TWO / 2 / 2. ***Right:*** Lathework panel bearing five TWOs vertically. ***Engraver:*** PSSP. ***Comments:*** H-MA-600-G10. 18__. 1830s.
Rarity: —

$2 • W-MA-1660-002-G050
Engraver: Unverified, but likely New England Bank Note Co. ***Comments:*** H-MA-600-G12. No description available. 18__. 1830s.
Rarity: *None known*

$2 • W-MA-1660-002-G060
Left: Eagle on limb, Train and canal / 2. ***Center:*** Medallion 2. ***Bottom center:*** Road and fence. ***Right:*** TWO / Ceres / TWO. ***Comments:*** H-MA-600-G16. 18__. 1850s.
Rarity: —

$3 • W-MA-1660-003-G070
Left: Lathework panel bearing MASSACHUSETTS vertically. ***Center:*** 3 / 3 / Alternating flower garlands and gridwork segments / THREE / 3 / 3. ***Right:*** Lathework panel bearing THREE vertically. ***Engraver:*** PSSP. ***Comments:*** H-MA-600-G18. 18__. 1830s.
Rarity: —

$3 • W-MA-1660-003-G080
Engraver: Unverified, but likely New England Bank Note Co. ***Comments:*** H-MA-600-G20. No description available. 18__. 1830s–1840s.
Rarity: *None known*

$3 • W-MA-1660-003-G090
Left: Man on horseback driving cattle and sheep / 3. ***Center:*** Medallion 3. ***Right:*** 3 / Blacksmith by anvil and forge. ***Comments:*** H-MA-600-G24. 18__. 1850s.
Rarity: —

$5 • W-MA-1660-005-G100
Left: Lathework chain bearing MASSACHUSETTS / 5 / 5 vertically. ***Center:*** Alternating flower garlands and gridwork segments / FIVE. ***Right:*** 5 / 5. ***Engraver:*** PSSP. ***Comments:*** H-MA-600-G26. 18__. 1830s.
Rarity: —

$5 • W-MA-1660-005-G110
Engraver: Unverified, but likely New England Bank Note Co. ***Comments:*** H-MA-600-G28. No description available. 18__. 1830s–1840s.
Rarity: *None known*

$5 • W-MA-1660-005-G120
Left: Canal scene, Boat and inclined railway, Buildings / FIVE. ***Center:*** Train. ***Bottom center:*** Beehive and farm tools. ***Right:*** 5 / Portrait of Daniel Webster / FIVE. ***Comments:*** H-MA-600-G32. 18__. 1850s.
Rarity: —

$10 • W-MA-1660-010-G130
Left: Lathework chain bearing MASSACHUSETTS / 10 / 10 vertically. ***Center:*** TEN. ***Right:*** 10 / 10 vertically. ***Engraver:*** PSSP. ***Comments:*** H-MA-600-G34. 18__. 1830s.
Rarity: —

$10 • W-MA-1660-010-G140
Engraver: Unverified, but likely New England Bank Note Co. ***Comments:*** H-MA-600-G36. No description available. 18__. 1830s–1840s.
Rarity: *None known*

$10 • W-MA-1660-010-G150
Left: TEN / Portrait of Martin Van Buren / 10. ***Center:*** State arms, Wharf scene, Sailor, bale, and ships. ***Right:*** 10 / Milkmaid with pail and stool. ***Comments:*** H-MA-600-G40. 18__. 1850s.
Rarity: —

$20 • W-MA-1660-020-G160
Left: Lathework chain bearing MASSACHUSETTS / 20 / 20 vertically. ***Center:*** Alternating flower garlands and gridwork segments / TWENTY. ***Right:*** 20 / 20 vertically. ***Engraver:*** PSSP. ***Comments:*** H-MA-600-G42. 18__. 1830s.
Rarity: —

$20 • W-MA-1660-020-G170
Engraver: Unverified, but likely New England Bank Note Co. ***Comments:*** H-MA-600-G44. No description available. 18__. 1830s–1840s.
Rarity: *None known*

$20 • W-MA-1660-020-G180
Left: 20 / Woman seated with book on lap opening chest. ***Center:*** XX / Eagle on rock / XX. ***Right:*** 20 / Ship in harbor. ***Engraver:*** New England Bank Note Co. ***Comments:*** H-MA-600-G48. 18__. 1840s.
Rarity: —

$20 • W-MA-1660-020-G190
Left: 20 / Minerva standing with spear. ***Center:*** Woman seated between 2 and 0. ***Right:*** 20 / Woman reclining on cornucopia / 20. ***Engraver:*** Rawdon, Wright, Hatch & Edson. ***Comments:*** H-MA-600-G52. 18__. 1850s.
Rarity: —

$20 • W-MA-1660-020-G200
Left: Shell / XX. ***Center:*** Woman seated on bale with sheaf. ***Right:*** 20 / Woman seated with spindle and distaff, Merchandise. ***Comments:*** H-MA-600-G56. 18__. 1850s.
Rarity: —

$50 • **W-MA-1660-050-G210**
Left: Lathework chain bearing MASSACHUSETTS / 50 / 50 vertically. ***Center:*** Alternating flower garlands and gridwork segments / FIFTY. ***Right:*** 50 / 50 vertically. ***Engraver:*** PSSP. ***Comments:*** H-MA-600-G58. 18__. 1830s.
Rarity: —

$50 • **W-MA-1660-050-G220**
Left: FIFTY / Woman standing with wreath and flowers / FIFTY. ***Center:*** 50 / Man restraining prancing horse / 50. ***Right:*** FIFTY / Woman standing with cornucopia / FIFTY. ***Engraver:*** New England Bank Note Co. ***Comments:*** H-MA-600-G64. 18__. 1840s–1850s.
Rarity: —

$50 • **W-MA-1660-050-G230**
Left: FIFTY / Sheaves and fruit / 50. ***Center:*** 50 / Three women seated with eagle, pole and cap, shield, scales, and book. ***Right:*** FIFTY across 50 / Vulcan seated with tools, Train. ***Engraver:*** New England Bank Note Co. ***Comments:*** H-MA-600-G68. 18__. 1850s.
Rarity: —

$50 • **W-MA-1660-050-G240**
Left: 50 / Eagle on shield. ***Center:*** 50 / Male portrait / 50. ***Right:*** 50 / Dog lying by strongbox. ***Tint:*** Color unknown. ***Engraver:*** American Bank Note Co. ***Comments:*** H-MA-600-G72. 1860s.
Rarity: —

$100 • **W-MA-1660-100-G250**
Left: Lathework chain bearing MASSACHUSETTS / 100 / 100 vertically. ***Center:*** Alternating flower garlands and gridwork segments / HUNDRED. ***Right:*** 100 / 100 vertically. ***Engraver:*** PSSP. ***Comments:*** H-MA-600-G74. 18__. 1830s.
Rarity: —

$100 • **W-MA-1660-100-G260**
Engraver: Unverified, but likely New England Bank Note Co. ***Comments:*** H-MA-600-G76. No description available. 18__. 1830s–1840s.
Rarity: *None known*

$100 • **W-MA-1660-100-G270**
Left: 100 / Eagle / 100. ***Center:*** C / Phoebus in the Chariot of the Sun / 100. ***Right:*** C / Portrait of George Washington / C. ***Engraver:*** New England Bank Note Co. ***Comments:*** H-MA-600-G80. 18__. 1840s–1850s.
Rarity: —

$100 • **W-MA-1660-100-G280**
Left: ONE HUNDRED on 100 / Portrait of William Henry Harrison. ***Center:*** Wharf scene, Men loading wagon with barrels / ***Right:*** ONE HUNDRED on 100 / Portrait of Christopher Columbus. ***Engraver:*** New England Bank Note Co. ***Comments:*** H-MA-600-G84. 18__. 1840s–1850s.
Rarity: —

$100 • **W-MA-1660-100-G290**
Left: C / Men with fishing boat at shore / 100. ***Center:*** Eagle perched on bale, Cornucopia and sheaf / 100. ***Right:*** 100 / Ceres / 100. ***Engraver:*** Rawdon, Wright, Hatch & Co. ***Comments:*** H-MA-600-G88. 18__. 1850s.
Rarity: —

$100 • **W-MA-1660-100-G300**
Left: 100 / Ox and trees. ***Center:*** Male portrait. ***Right:*** 100 / State arms. ***Tint:*** Color unknown. ***Engraver:*** American Bank Note Co. ***Comments:*** H-MA-600-G92. 1860s.
Rarity: —

$500 • **W-MA-1660-500-G310**
Engraver: Unverified, but likely New England Bank Note Co. ***Comments:*** H-MA-600-G96. No description available. 18__. 1830s–1840s.
Rarity: *None known*

Non-Valid Issues

$5 • **W-MA-1660-005-A010**
Left: FIVE / Portrait of Benjamin Franklin / V. ***Center:*** 5 / Two allegorical women standing and one seated, Agricultural items and ship. ***Bottom center:*** Anchor and implements. ***Right:*** V / Portrait of Marquis de Lafayette / FIVE. ***Engraver:*** Terry, Pelton & Co. ***Comments:*** H-MA-600-A5. Altered from $5 Citizens Bank, Augusta, Maine, or from notes of other failed banks using the same plate. 18__.
Rarity: —

$5 • **W-MA-1660-005-A020**
Left: V / Portrait of Henry Clay. ***Center:*** Western river steamboat, Wharf. ***Right:*** 5 / Portrait of George Washington. ***Overprint:*** Red FIVE. ***Engraver:*** New England Bank Note Co. / Rawdon, Wright, Hatch & Edson. ***Comments:*** H-MA-600-A10. Altered from $5 Waubeek Bank, De Soto, Nebraska. 1857.
Rarity: —

$5 • **W-MA-1660-005-A030**
Left: 10 / Portrait of George Washington / 10. ***Center:*** X / Eagle with wings spread / X. ***Right:*** 10 / Woman seated, Indian man standing / 10. ***Engraver:*** Terry, Pelton & Co. ***Comments:*** H-MA-600-A15. 18__. 1830s.
Rarity: —

$20 • **W-MA-1660-020-C170**
Engraver: New England Bank Note Co. ***Comments:*** H-MA-600-C44. Counterfeit of W-MA-1660-020-G170. 18__. 1837.
Rarity: —

$50 • **W-MA-1660-050-R010**
Engraver: New England Bank Note Co. ***Comments:*** H-MA-600-R5. Raised from a note of unknown denomination. 18__. 1830s–1840s.
Rarity: —

Rollstone Bank
1849–1865
W-MA-1670

History: The Rollstone Bank was incorporated on May 1, 1849, with an authorized capital of $100,000. The capital was increased to $200,000 in 1852 and peaked at $250,000 in 1854. It was later reduced to $200,000 by 1857. Circulation was $148,058 in 1854, $136,942 in 1857, and $191,489 in 1863. Real estate was valued at $3,985.05, and specie was $10,200.72 per the 1854 *Annual Report*.

The business of the Rollstone Bank was succeeded by the Rollstone National Bank of Fitchburg, chartered on January 11, 1865.

Numismatic Commentary: Genuine issues are extremely hard to locate, and spurious or counterfeit examples are equally scarce.

Valid Issues

$1 • W-MA-1670-001-G010

Left: Woman reclining on bale with spinning wheel and barrels, City / ONE. ***Center:*** 1. ***Right:*** 1 / Woman and cherubs in clouds. ***Engraver:*** Rawdon, Wright, Hatch & Edson. ***Comments:*** H-MA-605-G2. 18__. 1849–1850s.

Rarity: —

$2 • W-MA-1670-002-G020

Left: Woman riding on deer / 2. ***Center:*** 2. ***Bottom center:*** Train. ***Right:*** TWO / Two women standing. ***Engraver:*** Rawdon, Wright, Hatch & Edson. ***Comments:*** H-MA-605-G4. 18__. 1849–1850s.

Rarity: —

$3 • W-MA-1670-003-G030

Left: Milkmaid seated with pail on knee, Cows / 3. ***Center:*** 3. ***Right:*** 3 / Female portrait / THREE. ***Engraver:*** Rawdon, Wright, Hatch & Edson. ***Comments:*** H-MA-605-G6. 18__. 1849–1850s.

Rarity: —

$5 • W-MA-1670-005-G040

Left: Train / 5. ***Center:*** Ceres seated in V. ***Right:*** 5 / Woman seated with 5 / Woman standing with sword and shield. ***Engraver:*** Rawdon, Wright, Hatch & Edson. ***Comments:*** H-MA-605-G8. 18__. 1850s.

Rarity: —

$10 • W-MA-1670-010-G050

Left: TEN. ***Center:*** Woman with bale holding sickle, Men loading train / X. ***Bottom center:*** Female portrait. ***Right:*** 10 / Justice. ***Engraver:*** Rawdon, Wright, Hatch & Edson. ***Comments:*** H-MA-605-G10. 18__. 1850s.

Rarity: —

$20 • W-MA-1670-020-G060

Left: 20 / Minerva standing with spear. ***Center:*** Woman seated between 2 and 0. ***Bottom center:*** XX. ***Right:*** 20 / Woman reclining on cornucopia / 20. ***Engraver:*** Rawdon, Wright, Hatch & Edson. ***Comments:*** H-MA-605-G12. 18__. 1850s.

Rarity: —

$50 • W-MA-1670-050-G070

Left: 50 / Minerva standing by column. ***Center:*** Ceres and Vulcan flanking cornucopia. ***Right:*** 50 / Cherub in sailboat / 50. ***Engraver:*** Rawdon, Wright, Hatch & Edson. ***Comments:*** H-MA-605-G14. 18__. 1850s.

Rarity: —

$100 • W-MA-1670-100-G080

Left: 100 / Vulcan seated with sledge and anchor. ***Center:*** Ceres and Vulcan flanking cornucopia. ***Bottom center:*** 100. ***Right:*** 100 / Ceres seated, Cornucopia. ***Engraver:*** Rawdon, Wright, Hatch & Edson. ***Comments:*** H-MA-605-G16. 18__. 1850s.

Rarity: —

$100 • W-MA-1670-100-G090

HA

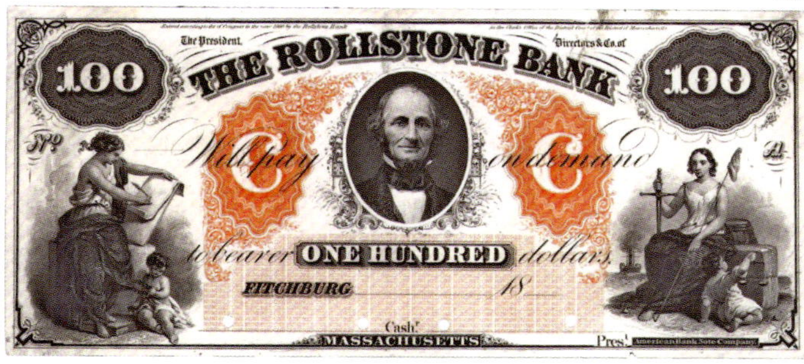

Tint: Orange. ***Engraver:*** American Bank Note Co. ***Comments:*** H-MA-605-G18a. 18__. 1860s.

Rarity: URS-2
Proof $7,500

Non-Valid Issues

$3 • W-MA-1670-003-C030

Comments: H-MA-605-C6. Counterfeit of W-MA-1670-003-G030. 18__. 1850s.

Rarity: URS-7
VG $100; **VF** $175

$3 • W-MA-1670-003-N010

SI

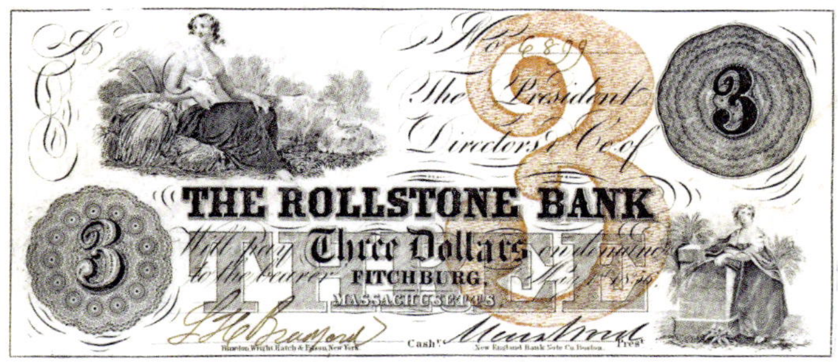

Overprint: Red 3. ***Engraver:*** New England Bank Note Co. / Rawdon, Wright, Hatch & Edson. ***Comments:*** H-MA-605-N5. May 1, 1856. 1850s.

Rarity: URS-6
F $75

$5 • W-MA-1670-005-S010

Left: Eagle with ribbon on shield / FIVE. ***Center:*** V. ***Right:*** 5 / Woman leaning on column. ***Engraver:*** Bald, Adams & Co. ***Comments:*** H-MA-605-S5. 185_. 1850s.

Rarity: —

$5 • W-MA-1670-005-A010

CJF

Overprint: Green 5 / 5 and red panel. ***Engraver:*** American Bank Note Co. ***Comments:*** H-MA-605-A5. Altered from $5 Egg Harbor Bank, Egg Harbor, New Jersey. 18__. 1850s–1860s.

Rarity: URS-6
F $125

$10 • W-MA-1670-010-R010
Engraver: Rawdon, Wright, Hatch & Edson. ***Comments:*** H-MA-605-R5. Raised from W-MA-1670-002-G020. 18__. 1850s.
Rarity: —

$20 • W-MA-1670-020-C060
Engraver: Rawdon, Wright, Hatch & Edson. ***Comments:*** H-MA-605-C12. Counterfeit of W-MA-1670-020-G060. 18__. 1850s.
Rarity: —

Framingham, Massachusetts

Framingham was incorporated in 1700 after the death of Thomas Danforth, who originally lived in Framingham, Suffolk, and strongly resisted the incorporation of the town during his life. It was first settled in 1647 by John Stone. Prior to the Civil War, Framingham was one of the hearts of the Abolitionist movement, hosting an annual rally and picnic with the Massachusetts Anti-Slavery Society. During the rally in 1854, William Lloyd Garrison burned pamphlets of the Fugitive Slave Law as well as copies of the Constitution. The Dennison Manufacturing Company, founded in 1844, was a jewelry and watch box company and grew to great fame nationwide for its products.

Framingham Bank
1833–1864
W-MA-1680

History: The Framingham Bank was chartered on March 25, 1833, with an authorized capital of $100,000. Founding cashier Rufus Brewer held the position for the entirety of the bank's existence, a remarkable tenure. The capital of the bank was $150,000 in 1847 and $200,000 in 1850. The figure was reduced to $100,000 by 1857 but rose back up to $200,000 in 1858. Its circulation ranged from $62,600 in 1839 to a high of $185,615 in 1863.

The business of the Framingham Bank was succeeded by the Framingham National Bank, chartered in 1864.

Valid Issues

$1 • W-MA-1680-001-G010
Left: 1 / Minerva standing with 1 / 1. ***Center:*** ONE / Plow, Commerce seated with caduceus and cornucopia, Ships / ONE. ***Right:*** 1 / Eagle / 1. ***Engraver:*** PSSP. ***Comments:*** H-MA-610-G4. 18__. 1830s–1850s.
Rarity: —

$1 • W-MA-1680-001-G020
JF

Engraver: New England Bank Note Co. / Rawdon, Wright, Hatch & Edson. ***Comments:*** H-Unlisted. 18__. 1850s.
Rarity: URS-3
VF $750

$1 • W-MA-1680-001-G020a
Left: ONE / Portrait of Daniel Webster. ***Center:*** Three cows, one lying down, Man plowing with oxen. ***Right:*** 1 / Two women. ***Overprint:*** Red. ***Engraver:*** New England Bank Note Co. / Rawdon, Wright, Hatch & Edson. ***Comments:*** H-MA-610-G8a. Similar to W-MA-1680-001-G020. 18__. 1850s.
Rarity: —

$1 • W-MA-1680-001-G020b
Overprint: Red. ***Engraver:*** New England Bank Note Co. / Rawdon, Wright, Hatch & Edson / ABNCo. monogram. ***Comments:*** H-MA-610-G8b. Similar to W-MA-1680-001-G020 but with additional engraver imprint. 18__. 1850s–1860s.
Rarity: —

$2 • W-MA-1680-002-G030
Left: 2 / Hebe watering eagle / 2. ***Center:*** 2 / Plow, Commerce seated on shore, Cornucopia / 2. ***Right:*** 2 / Justice standing / 2. ***Engraver:*** New England Bank Note Co. / Rawdon, Wright, Hatch & Edson. ***Comments:*** H-MA-610-G12. 18__. 1830s–1850s.
Rarity: —

$2 • W-MA-1680-002-G040
Left: Ceres seated on bale, Train and factory / TWO. ***Center:*** Cattle and hogs / 2. ***Right:*** 2 / Blacksmith by anvil and forge. ***Overprint:*** Red. ***Engraver:*** PSSP. ***Comments:*** H-MA-610-G16a. 18__. 1830s–1850s.
Rarity: —

$2 • W-MA-1680-002-G040a
Overprint: Red. ***Engraver:*** New England Bank Note Co. / Rawdon, Wright, Hatch & Edson. ***Comments:*** H-MA-610-G16b. Similar to W-MA-1680-002-G040 but with different engraver imprint. 18__. 1830s–1850s.
Rarity: —

$3 • W-MA-1680-003-G050
Left: 3 / Eagle on rock / 3. ***Center:*** 3 / Plow, Commerce seated with caduceus and cornucopia, Ships / 3 / Panel bearing THREE. ***Right:*** 3 / Woman standing with cornucopia / 3. ***Engraver:*** PSSP. ***Comments:*** H-MA-610-G20. 18__. 1830s–1850s.
Rarity: —

$3 • W-MA-1680-003-G060
Left: Woman and men, haying scene / 3. ***Center:*** 3 / THREE. ***Right:*** 3 / Portrait of George Washington. ***Overprint:*** Red THREE. ***Engraver:*** New England Bank Note Co. / Rawdon, Wright, Hatch & Edson. ***Comments:*** H-MA-610-G24a. 18__. 1850s.
Rarity: —

$3 • W-MA-1680-003-G060a

CJF

Overprint: Red THREE. ***Engraver:*** New England Bank Note Co. / Rawdon, Wright, Hatch & Edson / ABNCo. monogram. ***Comments:*** H-MA-610-G24b. Similar to W-MA-1680-003-G060 but with additional engraver imprint. 18__. 1850s–1860s.

Rarity: URS-2
F $1,250

$5 • W-MA-1680-005-G070

Left: Eagle. ***Right:*** Design. ***Engraver:*** PSSP. ***Comments:*** H-MA-610-G28. 18__. 1830s–1850s.

Rarity: —

$5 • W-MA-1680-005-G080

Left: Farmer seated on basket of corn, Men picking corn / 5. ***Center:*** 5. ***Right:*** FIVE / Two women, sailor, farmer, and mechanic surrounding V. ***Overprint:*** Red. ***Engraver:*** New England Bank Note Co. / Rawdon, Wright, Hatch & Edson. ***Comments:*** H-MA-610-G32a. 18__. 1850s.

Rarity: —

$5 • W-MA-1680-005-G080a

Engraver: New England Bank Note Co. / Rawdon, Wright, Hatch & Edson / ABNCo. monogram. ***Comments:*** H-MA-610-G32b. Similar to W-MA-1680-005-G080 but with additional engraver imprint. 18__. 1850s–1860s.

Rarity: —

$10 • W-MA-1680-010-G090

Back: Brown and blue Check Plate. ***Engraver:*** PSSP. ***Comments:*** H-MA-610-G40. 18__. 1830s–1850s.

Rarity: —

$10 • W-MA-1680-010-G100

Left: Cows, Milkmaid seated with pail on knee / X. ***Center:*** X. ***Right:*** 10 / Woman in clouds with flag and three cherubs. ***Engraver:*** New England Bank Note Co. / Rawdon, Wright, Hatch & Edson. ***Comments:*** H-MA-610-G44a. 18__. 1850s.

Rarity: —

$10 • W-MA-1680-010-G100a

Engraver: New England Bank Note Co. / Rawdon, Wright, Hatch & Edson / ABNCo. monogram. ***Comments:*** H-MA-610-G44b. Similar to W-MA-1680-010-G100 but with additional engraver imprint. 18__. 1850s–1860s.

Rarity: —

$20 • W-MA-1680-020-G110

Back: Brown and blue Check Plate. ***Engraver:*** PSSP. ***Comments:*** H-MA-610-G48. 18__. 1830s–1850s.

Rarity: —

$50 • W-MA-1680-050-G120

Back: Brown and blue Check Plate. ***Engraver:*** PSSP. ***Comments:*** H-MA-610-G52. 18__. 1830s–1850s.

Rarity: —

$50 • W-MA-1680-050-G130

Left: FIFTY / Woman standing with wreath and flowers. ***Center:*** 50 / Man restraining prancing horse / 50. ***Right:*** FIFTY / Woman standing with cornucopia / FIFTY. ***Engraver:*** New England Bank Note Co. ***Comments:*** H-MA-610-G56. 18__. 1850s.

Rarity: —

$100 • W-MA-1680-100-G140

Left: ONE HUNDRED on 100 / Portrait of William Henry Harrison. ***Center:*** Wharf scene, Men loading wagon with barrels. ***Right:*** ONE HUNDRED on 100 / Portrait of Christopher Columbus. ***Engraver:*** New England Bank Note Co. ***Comments:*** H-MA-610-G60. 18__. 1850s.

Rarity: —

$100 • W-MA-1680-100-G150

Back: Brown and blue Check Plate. ***Engraver:*** PSSP. ***Comments:*** H-MA-610-G64. 18__. 1830s–1850s.

Rarity: —

$500 • W-MA-1680-500-G160

Back: Brown and blue Check Plate. ***Engraver:*** PSSP. ***Comments:*** H-MA-610-G68. 18__. 1830s–1850s.

Rarity: —

Non-Valid Issues

$1 • W-MA-1680-001-A010

SI

Engraver: New England Bank Note Co. ***Comments:*** H-MA-610-A5. Altered from $1 Washington County Bank, Calais, Maine, or from notes of other failed banks using the same plate. 18__. 1840s.

Rarity: URS-5
VG $125

$2 • W-MA-1680-002-A020

Left: 2 / Woman standing with staff, Cornucopia / TWO. ***Center:*** TWO / Machinery and merchandise flanking Ceres seated holding sickle and rake, Factories and harbor. ***Engraver:*** New England Bank Note Co. ***Comments:*** H-MA-610-A10. Altered from $2 Washington County Bank, Calais, Maine, or from notes of other failed banks using the same plate. 18__. 1840s.

Rarity: —

$2 • W-MA-1680-002-A030

Left: 2 / Man on horseback / TWO. ***Center:*** Train. ***Right:*** 2 / Ship. ***Engraver:*** New England Bank Note Co. ***Comments:*** H-MA-610-A15. Altered from $2 Commercial Bank, Gratiot, Michigan. 18__. 1840s.

Rarity: —

$3 • W-MA-1680-003-A040

Left: THREE / Beehive and foliage / THREE. ***Center:*** Machinery and merchandise flanking Ceres seated holding sickle and rake, Factories and harbor / THREE. ***Right:*** 3 on THREE / Two reapers / 3 on THREE. ***Engraver:*** New England Bank Note Co. ***Comments:*** H-MA-610-A20. Altered from $3 Washington County Bank, Calais, Maine, or from notes of other failed banks using the same plate. 18__. 1840s.

Rarity: —

$5 • W-MA-1680-005-A050

Left: 5 / Blacksmith at anvil / FIVE. ***Center:*** Mercury standing with 5, Cornucopia and merchandise, Factories and ship, V. ***Right:*** 5 / Ceres kneeling / FIVE. ***Engraver:*** New England Bank Note Co. ***Comments:*** H-MA-610-A25. Altered from $5 Washington County Bank, Calais, Maine, or from notes of other failed banks using the same plate. 18__. 1840s.

Rarity: —

$10 • W-MA-1680-010-C100

Engraver: New England Bank Note Co. / Rawdon, Wright, Hatch & Edson. ***Comments:*** H-MA-610-C44a. Counterfeit of W-MA-1680-010-G100. 18__. 1850s.

Rarity: —

$10 • W-MA-1680-010-R010

Engraver: PSSP. ***Comments:*** H-MA-610-R5. Raised from W-MA-1680-001-G010. 18__. 1840s–1850s.

Rarity: —

$10 • W-MA-1680-010-R020

Engraver: New England Bank Note Co. / Rawdon, Wright, Hatch & Edson. ***Comments:*** H-MA-610-R10. Raised from W-MA-1680-001-G020a. 18__. 1850s.

Rarity: —

$10 • W-MA-1680-010-A060

JF

Engraver: New England Bank Note Co. ***Comments:*** H-MA-610-A30. Altered from $10 Commercial Bank, Gratiot, Michigan. 18__. 1840s.

Rarity: URS-6
F $125

$50 • W-MA-1680-050-C130

Engraver: New England Bank Note Co. ***Comments:*** H-MA-610-C56. Counterfeit of W-MA-1680-050-G130. 18__. 1850s.

Rarity: —

Gardiner, Massachusetts

Gardiner was originally a part of Pittston in the Maine District of Massachusetts and was called Cobbossee Contee. It was separated in 1803 and incorporated as Gardiner, named after the prominent landowning Gardiner family. In 1799 Gardiner had a population of 800 people, 150 of whom resided at Bowman's Point (then a part of Hallowell). On March 15, 1820, the state of Maine was formed, changing the address but not the location of Gardiner. The *Waterville*, a steamer, began its schedule on the Kennebec River in 1826 and served Gardiner. Stage travel was set up on a permanent basis in 1834. Gardiner was chartered as a city in 1849. By 1857 the community had saw mills, grist mills, hotels, and a woolen factory. It was at the head of summer navigation on the Kennebec River. The population in 1850 was 6,486, making it a very large community in its district.

Gardiner Bank

1814–1820 • 1820–1865

W-MA-1690 • W-ME-840

History: The Gardiner Bank was one of four banks chartered in the Maine District of Massachusetts in 1814, capitalized for $100,000. The charter was dated January 31, 1814, and was to expire by limitation on October 1, 1831. Circulation ranged from $52,110 in 1820 to $66,282 in October 1845. The bank continued in business and issued notes with the address of Maine after the district became a state on March 15, 1820. An act of April 1, 1831, allowed the bank to reduce its capital from $100,000 to $50,000, but this was not done. In 1865 the stockholders voted to reorganize as the Gardiner National Bank, charter 1174. It had an authorized capital of $100,000 but opened with $50,000. The records showed that since the bank's inception it had received $590,263. By 1867 only $1,433 remained in circulation or otherwise unaccounted for. The National Bank continued to redeem the notes. See also listing under Maine.

Numismatic Commentary: The Gardiner Bank is another very hard bank to collect. On occasion a counterfeit PSSP note will become available and be cherished by its new owner.

Valid Issues

Notes With Massachusetts Address

$1 • W-MA-1690-001-G010

Left: 1 / 1. ***Center:*** ONE DOLLAR, Text. ***Right:*** 1 / 1. ***Engraver:*** PSSP. ***Comments:*** H-MA-615-G10, Wait-Unlisted. 1810s.

Rarity: *None known*

$2 • W-MA-1690-002-G020

Engraver: PSSP. ***Comments:*** H-MA-615-G12, Wait-Unlisted. Similar to W-MA-1690-001-G010 but with different denomination. 1810s.

Rarity: *None known*

$3 • W-MA-1690-003-G030

Engraver: PSSP. ***Comments:*** H-MA-615-G14, Wait-Unlisted. Similar to W-MA-1690-001-G010 but with different denomination. 1810s.

Rarity: *None known*

$5 • W-MA-1690-005-G040

Left: State arms / 5, Plate letter, 5. ***Center:*** FIVE DOLLARS, Text. ***Right:*** 5, Plate letter, 5. ***Engraver:*** PSSP. ***Comments:*** H-MA-615-G16, Wait-Unlisted. 1810s.

Rarity: *None known*

$10 • W-MA-1690-010-G050

Engraver: PSSP. ***Comments:*** H-MA-615-G18, Wait-Unlisted. Similar to W-MA-1690-005-G040 but with different denomination. 1810s.

Rarity: *None known*

$20 • W-MA-1690-020-G060

Engraver: PSSP. ***Comments:*** H-MA-615-G20, Wait-Unlisted. Similar to W-MA-1690-005-G040 but with different denomination. 1810s.

Rarity: *None known*

$50 • W-MA-1690-050-G070

Engraver: PSSP. ***Comments:*** H-MA-615-G22, Wait-Unlisted. Similar to W-MA-1690-005-G040 but with different denomination. 1810s.

Rarity: *None known*

$100 • W-MA-1690-100-G080

Engraver: PSSP. ***Comments:*** H-MA-615-G24, Wait-Unlisted. Similar to W-MA-1690-005-G040 but with different denomination. 1810s.

Rarity: *None known*

Notes With Maine Address

$1 • W-ME-840-001-G010

Engraver: Unverified, but likely PSSP. ***Comments:*** H-Unlisted, Wait-3. No description available.

Rarity: *None known*

$1 • W-ME-840-001-G020

Left: 1 / 1. ***Center:*** Flower garlands bearing ONE, ONE. ***Right:*** 1 / 1. ***Engraver:*** PSSP. ***Comments:*** H-ME-330-G2, Wait-4. 1820s.

Rarity: —

$1 • W-ME-840-001-G030

Left: 1 / 1 / ONE, D, ONE vertically. ***Center:*** ONE DOLLAR, Text. ***Right:*** 1 / 1 / ONE, D, ONE vertically. ***Engraver:*** PSSP. ***Comments:*** H-ME-330-G6, Wait-4. 1830s–1840s.

Rarity: —

$1 • W-ME-840-001-G040

Left: 1. ***Center:*** Ships in harbor / 1. ***Right:*** 1 / Man leaning on rock, Lamb. ***Comments:*** H-ME-330-G8, Wait-4. 1840s–1850s.

Rarity: —

$1 • W-ME-840-001-G040a

CJF

Engraver: New England Bank Note Co. / ABNCo. monogram. ***Comments:*** H-Unlisted, Wait-Unlisted. 18__. 1850s–1864.

Rarity: URS-3
VF $750

$2 • W-ME-840-002-G050

Engraver: PSSP. ***Comments:*** H-ME-330-G10, Wait-5. Similar to W-ME-840-001-G010 but with different denomination. 1820s.

Rarity: —

$2 • W-ME-840-002-G060

QDB

Engraver: PSSP. ***Comments:*** H-ME-330-G14, Wait-5. 18__. 1840s.

Rarity: URS-3
F $350

$2 • W-ME-840-002-G070

Left: 2. ***Center:*** Cherub with scale, Shield, Woman seated, Ships and train / TWO. ***Right:*** 2 / Ship. ***Comments:*** H-ME-330-G16, Wait-6. 1840–1850s.

Rarity: —

$3 • W-ME-840-003-G080

Engraver: PSSP. ***Comments:*** H-ME-330-G18, Wait-9. Similar to W-ME-840-001-G010 but with different denomination. 1820s.

Rarity: —

$3 • W-ME-840-003-G090

Engraver: Unverified, but likely PSSP. ***Comments:*** H-Unlisted, Wait-8. No description available.

Rarity: *None known*

$3 • W-ME-840-003-G100

Engraver: PSSP. ***Comments:*** H-ME-330-G22, Wait-9. Similar to W-ME-840-002-G060 but with different denomination. 1830s–1840s.

Rarity: —

$3 • W-ME-840-003-G110

Left: 3. ***Center:*** Train, City / 3. ***Right:*** 3 / Female portrait / THREE. ***Comments:*** H-ME-330-G24, Wait-9. 1840s–1850s.

Rarity: —

$5 • W-ME-840-005-G120

CJF

Engraver: PSSP. ***Comments:*** H-ME-330-G26, Wait-11. 18__. 1860s.

Rarity: URS-3
VF $500

$10 • W-ME-840-010-G130

Engraver: PSSP. ***Comments:*** H-ME-330-G32, Wait-13. Similar to W-ME-840-005-G120 but with different denomination. 1820s.

Rarity: —

$20 • W-ME-840-020-G140

Engraver: PSSP. ***Comments:*** H-ME-30-G36, Wait-14. Similar to W-ME-840-005-G120 but with different denomination. 1820s–1830s.

Rarity: —

$20 • W-ME-840-020-G150

Left: 20 / Minerva. ***Center:*** Woman holding rake seated in 20. ***Right:*** 20 / Woman with cornucopia / 20. ***Comments:*** H-ME-330-G40, Wait-15. 1850s–1860s.

Rarity: —

$50 • W-ME-840-050-G160

Engraver: PSSP. ***Comments:*** H-ME-330-G42, Wait-16. Similar to W-ME-840-005-G120 but with different denomination. 1820s–1830s.

Rarity: —

$50 • W-ME-840-050-G170

Left: 50 / Minerva. ***Center:*** Man and woman seated with rake, hammer, and cornucopia. ***Right:*** 50 / Cherub steering sail boat / 50. ***Comments:*** H-ME-330-G46, Wait-17. 1850s–1860s.

Rarity: —

$100 • W-ME-840-100-G180

Engraver: PSSP. ***Comments:*** H-ME-330-G48, Wait-18. Similar to W-ME-840-005-G120 but with different denomination. 1820s–1830s.

Rarity: —

$100 • W-ME-840-100-G190

Left: 100 / Vulcan with hammer and anvil. ***Center:*** Eagle in tree, Train and canal boats. ***Right:*** 100 / Woman seated with rake. ***Comments:*** H-ME-330-G52, Wait-19. 1850s–1860s.

Rarity: —

$500 • W-ME-840-500-G200

Left: 500. ***Center:*** Indian paddling canoe, Trees and mountains. ***Right:*** 500 / Justice holding scales. ***Comments:*** H-ME-330-G56, Wait-20. 1840s–1850s.

Rarity: —

Non-Valid Issues

$2 • W-ME-840-002-N010

Center: Watermelon design. ***Engraver:*** PSSP. ***Comments:*** H-Unlisted, Wait-7.

Rarity: —

$3 • W-ME-840-003-C100

Comments: H-ME-330-C22, Wait-Unlisted. Counterfeit of W-ME-840-003-G100. 1840s.

Rarity: —

$3 • W-ME-840-003-N020

Right: 10 / Ships. ***Engraver:*** PSSP. ***Comments:*** H-Unlisted, Wait-10.

Rarity: —

Georgetown, Massachusetts

Georgetown was once a part of the Rowley plantation, purchased in 1639 by families from Yorkshire, England. It was incorporated as a town in 1838. There was a flax-breaking mill, a snuff mill, the production of watermelon and cornstalk molasses, nail forging, saddlebag making, harness and horse-collar making, and a dozen mills for making apple and pear cider. Rope making also took place here, as well as shipbuilding, which was unusual for the land-bound area. Teams of oxen would pull the ships down to the water in Rowley or Newbury. Timber for ships continued to be produced in Georgetown until the mid-1800s.

The most influential industry for the town, however, was shoemaking, which expanded throughout the 19th century. Tanning and currying leather, in relation to shoemaking, also cropped up, as well as the manufacturing of shoeboxes. The mass-production of shoe pegs was made possible through the invention of a machine by Paul Pillsbury in the early 1800s, which replaced the need to hand-sew soles and heels onto the rest of the shoe. Pillsbury also invented a machine for shelling corn and for stripping bark. Georgetown flourished throughout the latter 19th century, forming more industrial shops that manufactured clothing, cigars, soap, furniture, coffins, caskets, and lumber for wooden boxes and crates. In 1853 ice cutting had even begun, with four icehouses dedicated to local use and the shipment of ice to Boston and other markets.

Manufacturers Bank

1836–1855

W-MA-1700

History: On April 1, 1836, the Manufacturers Bank was chartered with an authorized capital of $100,000. In 1845 the Legislature passed an act that stated, in part, "The Manufacturers Bank, heretofore in Rowley, but to be called now in Georgetown, shall heareafter be known by the name of the Manufacturers Bank in Georgetown."[84]

Circulation was listed at $36,694 in 1845 and $21,495 in 1849. The bank's charter expired in 1851, but it took several years to wind up its affairs. In 1852 the shareholders received full reimbursement for their shares. Nearly all bills were redeemed at par. As of September 1, 1852, only $749 in notes remained outstanding. The Spicket Falls Bank in Methuen was the redemption agent.

See also listing under Rowley, W-MA-2820.

Numismatic Commentary: Issues from this bank that operated under two town locations are hard but not impossible to locate, given time. Extant issues more often are found bearing the Georgetown location.

Valid Issues

$1 • W-MA-1700-001-G010

Left: Panel bearing ONE vertically. ***Center:*** Sloop and other ships / 1. ***Right:*** ONE / Indian woman seated with bow and arrow / ONE. ***Engraver:*** New England Bank Note Co. ***Comments:*** H-MA-1045-G40. 18__. 1840s.

Rarity: —

$1 • **W-MA-1700-001-G020**

CJF

Engraver: New England Bank Note Co. ***Comments:*** H-MA-1045-G44. 18__. 1840s–1850s.

Rarity: URS-3
F $750

$1 • **W-MA-1700-001-G030**

JF

Comments: H-Unlisted. 18__. 1840s.

Rarity: URS-3
F $750

$2 • **W-MA-1700-002-G040**

Left: 2 / TWO / 2. ***Center:*** Sailing ship and ships / 2. ***Right:*** TWO / Woman drawing water from well / TWO. ***Engraver:*** New England Bank Note Co. ***Comments:*** H-MA-1045-G48. 18__. 1840s.

Rarity: —

$2 • **W-MA-1700-002-G050**

Left: Men driving sheep into stream / 2. ***Center:*** 2 bearing "Presentation of the Declaration of Independence". ***Right:*** TWO / Woman seated with wreath of flowers / TWO. ***Engraver:*** New England Bank Note Co. ***Comments:*** H-MA-1045-G52. 18__. 1840s–1850s.

Rarity: —

$3 • **W-MA-1700-003-G060**

Left: Panel bearing THREE vertically. ***Center:*** Man reaping with sickle, Woman standing with hat and sheaf / 3. ***Right:*** THREE / Steamship / 3 on THREE. ***Engraver:*** New England Bank Note Co. ***Comments:*** H-MA-1045-G56. 18__. 1840s.

Rarity: —

$3 • **W-MA-1700-003-G070**

Left: Barnyard scene, Man on horse, Boy and cattle. ***Center:*** 3. ***Right:*** 3 on THREE / Woman with flowers / THREE. ***Engraver:*** New England Bank Note Co. ***Comments:*** H-MA-1045-G60. 18__. 1840s–1850s.

Rarity: —

$5 • **W-MA-1700-005-G080**

CJF

Engraver: New England Bank Note Co. ***Comments:*** H-MA-1045-G64. 18__. 1840s.

Rarity: URS-4
VG $500; **F** $1,000

$5 • **W-MA-1700-005-G090**

Left: Eagle on shield and anchor, Factories and ships. ***Center:*** V with woman, cornucopia, and cherub. ***Right:*** 5 / Girl with ringlets holding basket. ***Engraver:*** New England Bank Note Co. ***Comments:*** H-MA-1045-G68. 18__. 1840s–1850s.

Rarity: —

$10 • **W-MA-1700-010-G100**

Engraver: Unverified, but likely New England Bank Note Co. ***Comments:*** H-MA-1045-G72. No description available. 18__. 1840s.

Rarity: *None known*

$20 • **W-MA-1700-020-G110**

Engraver: Unverified, but likely New England Bank Note Co. ***Comments:*** H-MA-1045-G76. No description available. 18__. 1840s.

Rarity: *None known*

$50 • **W-MA-1700-050-G120**

Engraver: Unverified, but likely New England Bank Note Co. ***Comments:*** H-MA-1045-G80. No description available. 18__. 1840s.

Rarity: *None known*

$100 • **W-MA-1700-100-G130**

Engraver: Unverified, but likely New England Bank Note Co. ***Comments:*** H-MA-1045-G84. No description available. 18__. 1840s.

Rarity: *None known*

Non-Valid Issues

$1 • **W-MA-1700-001-A010**

Left: 1 / Woman wearing bonnet with pail / ONE. ***Center:*** Merchandise and machinery flanking Ceres holding sickle and rake, Factories and harbor. ***Right:*** 1 / Ship / ONE. ***Engraver:*** New England Bank Note Co. ***Comments:*** H-MA-1045-A5. Altered from $1 Washington County Bank, Calais, Maine, or from notes of other failed banks using the same plate. 18__. 1840s.

Rarity: —

$2 • **W-MA-1700-002-A020**

Left: 2 / Woman standing / TWO. ***Center:*** TWO / Woman with rake and shield / TWO. ***Right:*** 2 / Woman / TWO. ***Engraver:*** New England Bank Note Co. ***Comments:*** H-MA-1045-A10. Altered from $2 Washington County Bank, Calais, Maine, or from notes of other failed banks using the same plate. 18__. 1840s.

Rarity: —

$3 • W-MA-1700-003-A030

Left: THREE / Beehive and foliage / THREE. ***Center:*** Machinery and merchandise flanking Ceres seated holding sickle and rake, Factories and harbor / THREE. ***Right:*** 3 on THREE / Two reapers / 3 on THREE. ***Engraver:*** New England Bank Note Co. ***Comments:*** H-MA-1045-A15. Altered from $3 Washington County Bank, Calais, Maine, or from notes of other failed banks using the same plate. 18__. 1840s.

Rarity: —

$5 • W-MA-1700-005-A040

Left: FIVE / Portrait of Benjamin Franklin / V. ***Center:*** 5 / Three women standing / 5. ***Right:*** V / Portrait of Marquis de Lafayette / FIVE. ***Engraver:*** Terry, Pelton & Co. ***Comments:*** H-MA-1045-A20. Altered from $5 Citizens Bank, Augusta, Maine, or from notes of other failed banks using the same plate. 18__. 1840s.

Rarity: —

$10 • W-MA-1700-010-A050

Left: 10 / Portrait of George Washington held by cherub / 10. ***Center:*** X / Spread eagle with shield and arrows, E PLURIBUS UNUM / X. ***Bottom center:*** Ship. ***Right:*** 10 / Indian man / 10. ***Engraver:*** Terry, Pelton & Co. ***Comments:*** H-MA-1045-A25. Altered from $10 Citizens Bank, Augusta, Maine, or from notes of other failed banks using the same plate. 18__. 1840s.

Rarity: —

GLOUCESTER, MASSACHUSETTS

In 1623 a group of men from Dorchester, England, founded the settlement of Gloucester on Cape Ann. Later the pioneers abandoned the land for richer soil in Salem, then known as Naumkeag. Slowly, settlers returned in the following years, and the town was incorporated in 1642. Gloucester is made up of the neighborhoods of Annisquam, Bay View, Lanesville, Folly Cove, Magnolia, Riverdale, East Gloucester, and West Gloucester. The town of Rockport was also once included in the boundaries of Gloucester, but the village separated in 1840. Gloucester was reincorporated in 1873.

Farming and logging made up the early industry of Gloucester, because the poor soil did little in the way of providing farmland for the settlers. Fishing was limited until the mid-18th century, when the Grand Banks became a prominent fishing ground. Granite also provided a plentiful industry for Gloucester. Shipbuilding was important in the town, and the first schooner is reported to have been built there in 1713. Located in both Rockport and Gloucester, an abandoned settlement known as Dogtown presents some intrigue to the location. It was settled in a haven protected from pirates and unfriendly natives, but it was abandoned after the War of 1812. The area received a bad reputation when the vacated buildings were inhabited by vagabonds and rogues.

Bank of Cape Ann
1856–1865
W-MA-1710

History: The Bank of Cape Ann was incorporated on May 21, 1856, with an authorized capital of $150,000. It opened for business in 1857.

Circulation in one report in 1857 was $120,707, in 1858 $107,515, and in 1860 $120,707.

The business of the Bank of Cape Ann was succeeded by the Cape Ann National Bank of Gloucester, chartered on March 1, 1865.

Numismatic Commentary: Issues from banks in seaside towns are usually hard to locate, but this bank may be the exception. While certainly not common, a patient collector should be able to eventually locate one or two issues.

VALID ISSUES

$1 • W-MA-1710-001-G010

CJF

Overprint: Red ONE. ***Engraver:*** American Bank Note Co. / Jocelyn, Draper, Welsh & Co. ***Comments:*** H-MA-620-G2a. 18__. 1850s.

Rarity: URS-3
Unc-S&D $2,000; **Proof** $1,500
Selected auction price: Heritage, April–May 2011, Lot 15228, Choice New $920

$1 • W-MA-1710-001-G010a

TD

Overprint: Red ONE. ***Engraver:*** American Bank Note Co. ***Comments:*** H-MA-620-G2b. Similar to W-MA-1710-001-G010 but with different engraver imprint. 18__. 1860s.

Rarity: URS-5
VG $500

$2 • W-MA-1710-002-G020

CJF

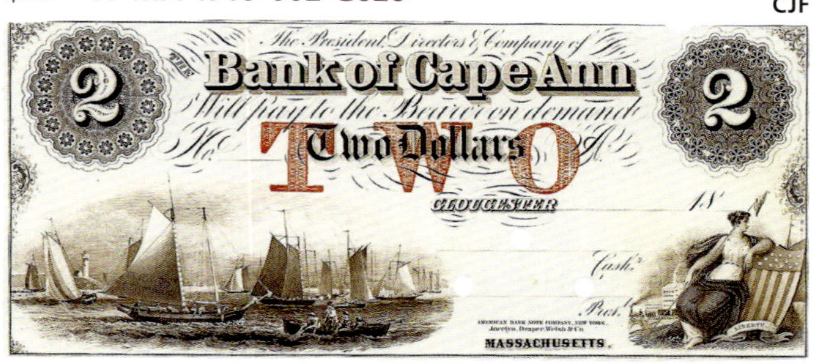

Overprint: Red TWO. ***Engraver:*** American Bank Note Co. / Jocelyn, Draper, Welsh & Co. ***Comments:*** H-MA-620-G4a. Proof. 18__. 1850s.

Rarity: URS-2
Proof $2,250

$2 • W-MA-1710-002-G020a

Left: 2 / Sailing ships. ***Center:*** TWO. ***Right:*** 2 / Woman seated with shield. ***Overprint:*** Red TWO. ***Engraver:*** American Bank Note Co. ***Comments:*** H-MA-620-G4b. Similar to W-MA-1710-002-G020 but with different engraver imprint. 18__. 1860s.

Rarity: —

$3 • W-MA-1710-003-G030

Left: Man standing with sickle / 3. ***Center:*** Woman with child and cow, Thatched hut / THREE. ***Right:*** 3 / Female portrait. ***Overprint:*** Red THREE. ***Engraver:*** American Bank Note Co. / Jocelyn, Draper, Welsh & Co. ***Comments:*** H-MA-620-G6a. 18__. 1850s.

Rarity: —

$3 • W-MA-1710-003-G030a

CJF

Overprint: Red THREE. ***Engraver:*** American Bank Note Co. ***Comments:*** H-MA-620-G6b. Similar to W-MA-1710-003-G030 but with different engraver imprint. 18__. 1860s.

Rarity: URS-3
VF $1,500

$5 • W-MA-1710-005-G040

CC

Overprint: Red FIVE. ***Engraver:*** American Bank Note Co. / Jocelyn, Draper, Welsh & Co. ***Comments:*** H-MA-620-G8a. Proof. 18__. 1850s.

Rarity: URS-3
Proof $4,000
Selected auction price: Stack's Bowers Galleries, January 2013, Lot 1053, Choice AU $3,818

$5 • W-MA-1710-005-G040a

Left: 5 / Girl with chickens. ***Center:*** Cod-fishing scene, Several schooners, Men in rowboat. ***Right:*** FIVE / 5 / FIVE / Indian woman resting on rock. ***Overprint:*** Red FIVE. ***Engraver:*** American Bank Note Co. ***Comments:*** H-MA-620-G8b. Similar to W-MA-1710-005-G040 but with different engraver imprint. 18__. 1860s.

Rarity: —

$10 • W-MA-1710-010-G050

JF

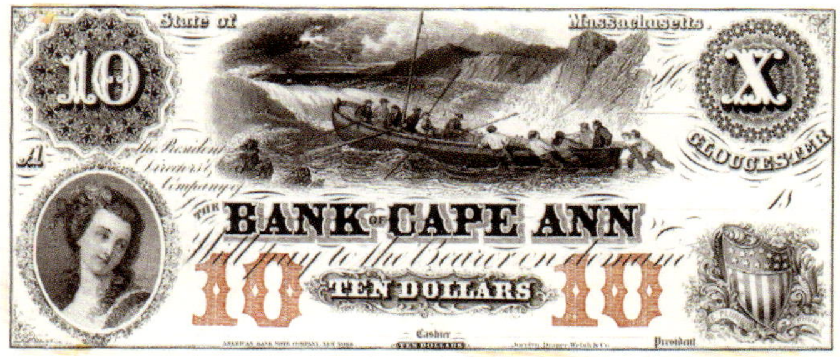

Overprint: Red 10 / 10. ***Engraver:*** American Bank Note Co. / Jocelyn, Draper, Welsh & Co. ***Comments:*** H-MA-620-G10a. Proof. 18__. 1850s.

Rarity: URS-3
Proof $4,000

$10 • W-MA-1710-010-G050a

CJF

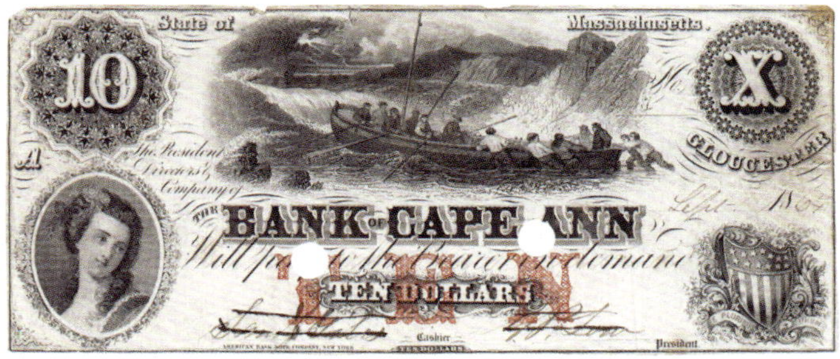

Overprint: Red TEN. ***Engraver:*** American Bank Note Co. ***Comments:*** H-MA-620-G10b. Similar to W-MA-1710-010-G050 but with different engraver imprint. 18__. 1860s.

Rarity: URS-3
VF $1,500

$20 • W-MA-1710-020-G060

Left: Eagle / 20. ***Center:*** Sailing ship. ***Right:*** 20 / Sailor seated. ***Engraver:*** American Bank Note Co. / Jocelyn, Draper, Welsh & Co. ***Comments:*** H-MA-620-G12a. 18__. 1850s.

Rarity: —

$20 • W-MA-1710-020-G060a

Engraver: American Bank Note Co. ***Comments:*** H-MA-620-G12b. Similar to W-MA-1710-020-G060 but with different engraver imprint. 18__. 1860s.

Rarity: —

$50 • W-MA-1710-050-G070

Left: Sailing ships / 50. ***Center:*** Woman. ***Right:*** 50 / Two men. ***Overprint:*** Red FIFTY. ***Engraver:*** American Bank Note Co. / Jocelyn, Draper, Welsh & Co. ***Comments:*** H-MA-620-G14a. 18__. 1850s.

Rarity: —

Collectors and Researchers:

If you have new information about any banks or notes listed in this volume, contact Whitman Publishing, Attn: Obsolete Paper Money, 3101 Clairmont Road, Suite G, Atlanta, GA 30329.

$50 • W-MA-1710-050-G070a
Overprint: Red FIFTY. ***Engraver:*** American Bank Note Co. ***Comments:*** H-MA-620-G14b. Similar to W-MA-1710-050-G070 but with different engraver imprint. 18__. 1860s.
Rarity: —

$100 • W-MA-1710-100-G080
Left: 100 / Women and Mercury in clouds. ***Right:*** C / Indian man with bow seated on rock. ***Overprint:*** Red. ***Engraver:*** American Bank Note Co. / Jocelyn, Draper, Welsh & Co. ***Comments:*** H-MA-620-G16a. 18__. 1850s.
Rarity: —

$100 • W-MA-1710-100-G080a
Overprint: Red. ***Engraver:*** American Bank Note Co. ***Comments:*** H-MA-620-G16b. Similar to W-MA-1710-100-G080 but with different engraver imprint. 18__. 1860s.
Rarity: —

Uncut Sheets

$1-$1-$2-$5 • W-MA-1710-001.001.002.005-US010
Vignette(s): ($1) Man standing / Sailing ships / Female portrait with flowers. ***($1)*** Man standing / Sailing ships / Female portrait with flowers. ***($2)*** Sailing ships / Woman seated with shield. ***($5)*** Woman with chickens / Cod-fishing scene, Several schooners, Men in rowboat / Indian woman resting on rock. ***Overprint(s):*** Red. ***Comments:*** H-MA-620-G2a, G2a, G4a, G8a. 18__. 1850s.
Rarity: —

$3-$10 • W-MA-1710-003.010-US020
Vignette(s): ($3) Man standing with sickle / Woman with child and cow, Thatched hut / Female portrait. ***($10)*** Female portrait / Boat with men rowing / Shield. ***Overprint(s):*** Red. ***Comments:*** H-MA-620-G6a, G10a. 18__. 1850s.
Rarity: —

Non-Valid Issues

$1 • W-MA-1710-001-N010
Left: Man harrowing. ***Center:*** Male portrait / Woman and eagle / Male portrait. ***Right:*** Man plowing. ***Comments:*** H-MA-620-N5. 1850s.
Rarity: —

$3 • W-MA-1710-003-N020
Left: Man harrowing. ***Center:*** Male portrait / Woman and eagle / Male portrait. ***Right:*** Man plowing. ***Comments:*** H-MA-620-N10. 1850s.
Rarity: —

$5 • W-MA-1710-005-N030
Center: Portrait of George Washington / Woman and eagle / Portrait of Benjamin Franklin. ***Comments:*** H-MA-620-N15. 1850s.
Rarity: URS-7
VG $100; **VF** $175

$5 • W-MA-1710-005-A010
Left: 5 / Sailing ship. ***Center:*** Whaling scene, Men in boat, Ship. ***Right:*** 5 / Sailor at ship's wheel. ***Engraver:*** Danforth, Wright & Co. ***Comments:*** H-MA-620-A5. Altered from $5 Commercial Bank of New Jersey, Perth Amboy, New Jersey, series. July 10, 1856.
Rarity: —

$5 • W-MA-1710-005-A020 CC

Engraver: Rawdon, Wright & Hatch. ***Comments:*** H-Unlisted. 18__. 1840s.
Rarity: URS-6
VG $150

$10 • W-MA-1710-010-N040
Left: Cattle. ***Center:*** Portrait of George Washington. ***Right:*** Agricultural implements. ***Comments:*** H-MA-620-N20. 1850s.
Rarity: —

$10 • W-MA-1710-010-N050
Center: Three ships, Steamship and ship. ***Right:*** Woman with spyglass. ***Comments:*** H-MA-620-N25. 1850s.
Rarity: —

Gloucester Bank {1st}
1800–1812
W-MA-1720

History: The Gloucester Bank was chartered on January 27, 1800, with an authorized capital of $40,000, "and no more," to be paid in specie.

In 1812 the bank's interests were succeeded by the second Gloucester Bank, W-MA-1730, of the same name.

Numismatic Commentary: In 1809 the Farmers Bank of Gloucester, *Rhode Island*, collapsed in a fraud perpetrated by Boston financier Andrew Dexter. Many contemporary accounts incorrectly gave the bank title as "Gloucester Bank," causing confusion. Notes from this bank will probably only be found in counterfeit examples.

Valid Issues

$1 • W-MA-1720-001-G010
Comments: H-MA-625-G20. Similar to W-MA-1720-005-G040 but with different denomination. 179_. 1790s.
Rarity: —

$1 • W-MA-1720-001-G010a
Comments: H-MA-625-G20a. Similar to W-MA-1720-001-G010 but with different date. 180_. 1800s.
Rarity: —

$2 • W-MA-1720-002-G020
Comments: H-MA-625-G24. Similar to W-MA-1720-005-G040 but with different denomination. 179_. 1790s.
Rarity: —

$2 • W-MA-1720-002-G020a
Comments: H-MA-625-G24a. Similar to W-MA-1720-002-G020 but with different date. 180_. 1800s.
Rarity: —

$3 • W-MA-1720-003-G030
Comments: H-MA-625-G28. Similar to W-MA-1720-005-G040 but with different denomination. 179_. 1790s.
Rarity: —

$3 • W-MA-1720-003-G030a
Comments: H-MA-625-G28a. Similar to W-MA-1720-003-G030 but with different date. 180_. 1800s.
Rarity: —

$5 • W-MA-1720-005-G040
Left: FIVE DOLLARS vertically. ***Center:*** Sailboat / 5. ***Comments:*** H-MA-625-G32. 179_. 1790s.
Rarity: —

$5 • W-MA-1720-005-G040a

CJF

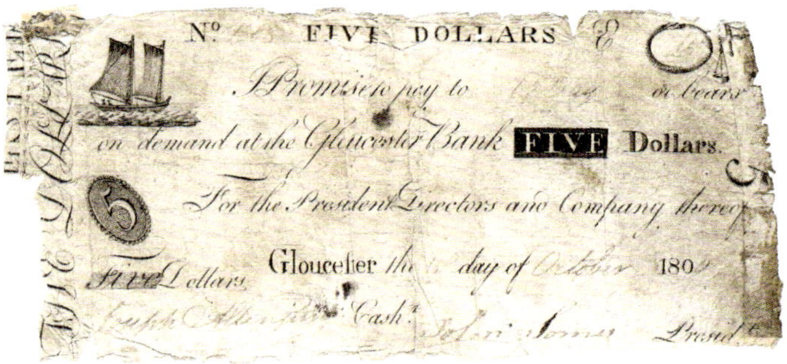

Comments: H-MA-625-G32a. Similar to W-MA-1720-005-G040 but with different date. 180_. 1800s.
Rarity: URS-4
VG $200

$10 • W-MA-1720-010-G050
Comments: H-MA-625-G62. Similar to W-MA-1720-005-G040 but with different denomination. 179_. 1790s.
Rarity: —

$10 • W-MA-1720-010-G050a
Comments: H-MA-625-G62a. Similar to W-MA-1720-010-G050 but with different date. 180_. 1800s.
Rarity: —

$20 • W-MA-1720-020-G060
Comments: H-MA-625-G66. Similar to W-MA-1720-005-G040 but with different denomination. 179_. 1790s.
Rarity: —

$20 • W-MA-1720-020-G060a
Comments: H-MA-625-G66a. Similar to W-MA-1720-020-G060 but with different date. 180_. 1800s.
Rarity: —

NON-VALID ISSUES

$10 • W-MA-1720-010-C050
Comments: H-MA-625-C62. Counterfeit of W-MA-1720-010-G050. 179_. 1790s.
Rarity: —

Gloucester Bank {2nd}
1812–1865
W-MA-1730

History: The second Gloucester Bank was incorporated on June 23, 1812. Its charter was renewed in 1827 with $120,000 capital.

In 1848 the president was Isaac Somes, and the cashier was John J. Babson. Capital was listed at $200,000 in 1839 and was increased to $300,000 in 1854. Circulation ranged from a low of $124,001 in 1839 to a high of $208,817 in 1845.

Selected figures for 1857 included: bills of this bank and other New England states $12,132.81; specie $9,355.13; real estate $8,500.

After May 1865, the business of the Gloucester Bank was succeeded by the first Gloucester National Bank.

Numismatic Commentary: Surviving notes from this bank are mostly of the PSSP design. Some of the later New England Bank Note Co. engraved notes show local seaside scenery with fishing boats being attended to.

VALID ISSUES

$1 • W-MA-1730-001-G010

CJF

Engraver: PSSP. ***Comments:*** H-MA-626-G10. 18__. 1812–1820s.
Rarity: URS-6
VG $200

$1 • W-MA-1730-001-G010a
Left: Panel of lathework circle segments. ***Right:*** Panel of lathework circle segments. ***Engraver:*** PSSP. ***Comments:*** H-MA-626-G12. Similar to W-MA-1730-001-G010. 18__. 1820s.
Rarity: —

$1 • W-MA-1730-001-G010b
Left: Panel of lathework circle segments. ***Right:*** Panel of lathework circle segments. ***Engraver:*** PSSP. ***Comments:*** H-MA-626-G14. Similar to W-MA-1730-001-G010. Printed in red ink. 18__. 1820s–1830s.
Rarity: —

$1 • W-MA-1730-001-G010c
Engraver: PSSP. ***Comments:*** H-MA-626-G14a. Similar to W-MA-1730-001-G010 but printed in black ink. 18__. 1830s.
Rarity: —

$1 • W-MA-1730-001-G010d
Left: ONE / D / ONE vertically. ***Right:*** ONE / D / ONE vertically. ***Engraver:*** PSSP. ***Comments:*** H-MA-626-G16. Similar to W-MA-1730-001-G010. 18__. 1830s.
Rarity: —

$1 • W-MA-1730-001-G020

Left: ONE vertically. ***Center:*** Wharf scene, Ship at dock, Schooner on side, Warehouses / ONE. ***Right:*** 1 / Sailing ship / ONE. ***Engraver:*** New England Bank Note Co. ***Comments:*** H-MA-626-G20. 18__. 1840s–1850s.

Rarity: —

$1 • W-MA-1730-001-G020a

CJF

Overprint: Red ONE. ***Engraver:*** New England Bank Note Co. ***Comments:*** H-MA-626-G20a. Similar to W-MA-1730-001-G020. 18__. 1850s.

Rarity: URS-4
VG $750

$1 • W-MA-1730-001-G020b

Overprint: Red ONE. ***Engraver:*** New England Bank Note Co. / ABNCo. monogram. ***Comments:*** H-MA-626-G20b. Similar to W-MA-1730-001-G020 but with additional engraver imprint. 18__. 1850s–1860s.

Rarity: —

$1.25 • W-MA-1730-001.25-G030

Left: 1 25/100 / Train / 1 25/100. ***Center:*** Sloop and other ships at sea / $1.25 cts. ***Right:*** 1 25/100 / Eagle. ***Engraver:*** New England Bank Note Co. ***Comments:*** H-MA-626-G22. 18__. 1830s.

Rarity: —

$1.50 • W-MA-1730-001.50-G040

Left: 1 Doll. 50 Cts vertically. ***Center:*** Eagle on rock in ocean / $1 50/100. ***Right:*** 1 50/100 / Justice. ***Engraver:*** New England Bank Note Co. ***Comments:*** H-MA-626-G23. 18__. 1830s.

Rarity: —

$1.75 • W-MA-1730-001.75-G050

Left: $1.75 Cts. / Woman watering eagle / 1 75/100. ***Center:*** Three sloops at sea. ***Right:*** $1.75 Cts. / Woman seated with grain, Dog / 1 75/100. ***Engraver:*** New England Bank Note Co. ***Comments:*** H-MA-626-G24. 18__. 1830s.

Rarity: —

$2 • W-MA-1730-002-G060

Center: 2 / 2 / Flower garlands and gridwork segments / TWO / 2 / 2. ***Engraver:*** PSSP. ***Comments:*** H-MA-626-G26. 18__. 1810s–1820s.

Rarity: URS-6
F $225; **VF** $325

$2 • W-MA-1730-002-G070

Left: Cattle. ***Center:*** Portrait. ***Right:*** Agricultural scene. ***Engraver:*** PSSP. ***Comments:*** H-MA-626-G28. 18__. 1820s.

Rarity: —

$2 • W-MA-1730-002-G080

Left: Panel of lathework circle segments. ***Right:*** Panel of lathework circle segments. ***Engraver:*** PSSP. ***Comments:*** H-MA-626-G30. Similar to W-MA-1730-002-G070. Printed in red ink. 18__. 1820s–1830s.

Rarity: —

$2 • W-MA-1730-002-G080a

Left: Five TWOs vertically. ***Right:*** Five TWOs vertically. ***Engraver:*** PSSP. ***Comments:*** H-MA-626-G32. Similar to W-MA-1730-002-G080. 18__. 1830s.

Rarity: —

$2 • W-MA-1730-002-G090

CC

Engraver: New England Bank Note Co. ***Comments:*** H-MA-626-G36. 18__. 1840s–1850s.

Rarity: URS-5
VG $400; **VF** $650

$2 • W-MA-1730-002-G090a

Left: 2 / TWO / 2. ***Center:*** Wharf scene, Ship at dock, Schooner on side, Warehouses / TWO. ***Bottom center:*** Ship, Barrels on wharf. ***Right:*** 2 / Horse, Wagon and men / 2. ***Overprint:*** Red. ***Engraver:*** New England Bank Note Co. ***Comments:*** H-MA-626-G36a. Similar to W-MA-1730-002-G090. 18__. 1850s.

Rarity: —

$2 • W-MA-1730-002-G090b

Overprint: Red. ***Engraver:*** New England Bank Note Co. / ABNCo. monogram. ***Comments:*** H-MA-626-G36b. Similar to W-MA-1730-002-G090 but with additional engraver imprint. 18__. 1850s–1860s.

Rarity: —

$3 • W-MA-1730-003-G100

CJF

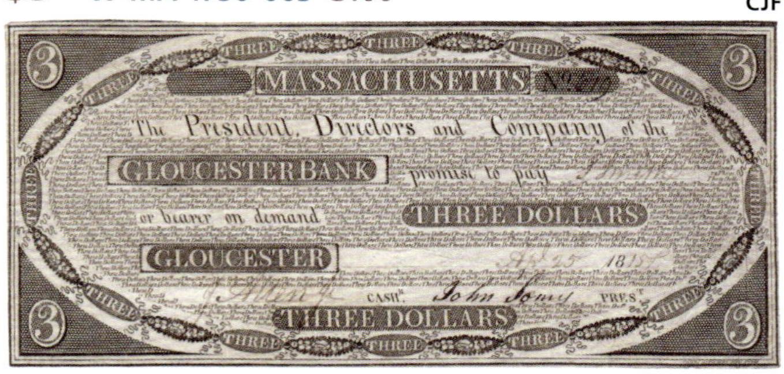

Engraver: PSSP. ***Comments:*** H-MA-626-G38. 18__. 1810s–1820s.

Rarity: URS-6
VF $250

$3 • W-MA-1730-003-G100a

Left: Panel of lathework circle segments. ***Center:*** 3 / 3 / Oval of flower garlands and gridwork segments / 3 / 3. ***Right:*** Panel of lathework circle segments. ***Engraver:*** PSSP. ***Comments:*** H-MA-626-G40. Similar to W-MA-1730-003-G100. 18__. 1820s.

Rarity: —

$3 • W-MA-1730-003-G100b

Left: Panel of lathework circle segments. ***Right:*** Panel of lathework circle segments. ***Engraver:*** PSSP. ***Comments:*** H-MA-626-G42. Similar to W-MA-1730-003-G100. Printed in red. 18__. 1820s–1830s.

Rarity: —

$3 • W-MA-1730-003-G100c

Engraver: PSSP. ***Comments:*** H-MA-626-G42a. Similar to W-MA-1730-003-G100 but printed in black ink. 18__. 1830s.

Rarity: —

$3 • W-MA-1730-003-G100d

Left: THREE vertically. ***Right:*** THREE vertically. ***Engraver:*** PSSP. ***Comments:*** H-MA-626-G44. Similar to W-MA-1730-003-G100. 18__. 1830s.

Rarity: —

$3 • W-MA-1730-003-G110

Left: Panel bearing THREE vertically. ***Center:*** Wharf scene, Ship at dock, Schooner on side, Warehouses. ***Right:*** 3 / Ships. ***Engraver:*** New England Bank Note Co. ***Comments:*** H-MA-626-G48. 18__. 1840s–1850s.

Rarity: —

$3 • W-MA-1730-003-G110a

Overprint: Red. ***Engraver:*** New England Bank Note Co. ***Comments:*** H-MA-626-G48a. Similar to W-MA-1730-003-G110. 18__. 1850s.

Rarity: —

$3 • W-MA-1730-003-G110b

Overprint: Red. ***Engraver:*** New England Bank Note Co. / ABNCo. monogram. ***Comments:*** H-MA-626-G48b. Similar to W-MA-1730-003-G110 but with additional engraver imprint. 18__. 1850s–1860s.

Rarity: —

$5 • W-MA-1730-005-G120

CJF

Engraver: PSSP. ***Comments:*** H-MA-626-G50. 18__. 1810s–1820s.

Rarity: URS-8
VF $200

$5 • W-MA-1730-005-G120a

Left: Lathework chain bearing MASSACHUSETTS vertically. ***Right:*** Panel of lathework circle segments. ***Engraver:*** PSSP. ***Comments:*** H-MA-626-G52. Similar to W-MA-1730-005-G120. 18__. 1820s.

Rarity: —

$5 • W-MA-1730-005-G120b

Left: Lathework chain bearing MASSACHUSETTS vertically. ***Right:*** Panel of lathework circle segments. ***Engraver:*** PSSP. ***Comments:*** H-MA-626-G54. Similar to W-MA-1730-005-G120. 18__. 1820s.

Rarity: URS-6
VG $250; **VF** $400

$5 • W-MA-1730-005-G120c

Engraver: PSSP. ***Comments:*** H-MA-626-G56. Similar to W-MA-1730-005-G120 but with zigzag ruled lines. 18__. 1820s–1830s.

Rarity: —

$5 • W-MA-1730-005-G120d

Engraver: PSSP. ***Comments:*** H-MA-626-G58. Similar to W-MA-1730-005-G120 but with spiral lathework lines. 18__. 1830s.

Rarity: —

$5 • W-MA-1730-005-G130

Left: FIVE vertically. ***Center:*** Buildings. ***Right:*** 5 / FIVE / People and building. ***Engraver:*** New England Bank Note Co. ***Comments:*** H-MA-626-G62. 18__. 1840s–1850s.

Rarity: —

$5 • W-MA-1730-005-G130a

Overprint: Red. ***Engraver:*** New England Bank Note Co. ***Comments:*** H-MA-626-G62a. Similar to W-MA-1730-005-G130. 18__. 1850s.

Rarity: —

$5 • W-MA-1730-005-G130b

Overprint: Red. ***Engraver:*** New England Bank Note Co. / ABNCo. monogram. ***Comments:*** H-MA-626-G62b. Similar to W-MA-1730-005-G130 but with additional engraver imprint. 18__. 1850s–1860s.

Rarity: —

$10 • W-MA-1730-010-G140

CJF

Engraver: Perkins. ***Comments:*** H-MA-626-G64. 18__. 1810s–1820s.

Rarity: URS-8
VF $200

$10 • W-MA-1730-010-G140a

Left: Lathework chain bearing MASSACHUSETTS vertically. ***Right:*** Panel of lathework circle segments. ***Engraver:*** Perkins. ***Comments:*** H-MA-626-G66. Similar to W-MA-1730-010-G140. 18__. 1820s.

Rarity: —

$10 • W-MA-1730-010-G140b

Left: Lathework chain bearing MASSACHUSETTS vertically. ***Right:*** Panel of lathework circle segments. ***Engraver:*** Perkins. ***Comments:*** H-MA-626-G68. Similar to W-MA-1730-010-G140. 18__. 1820s.

Rarity: —

$10 • W-MA-1730-010-G140c

Engraver: PSSP. ***Comments:*** H-MA-626-G70. Similar to W-MA-1730-010-G140 but with zigzag ruled lines. 18__. 1820s–1830s.

Rarity: —

$10 • W-MA-1730-010-G140d

Engraver: PSSP. ***Comments:*** H-MA-626-G72. Similar to W-MA-1730-010-G140 but with spiral lathework lines. 18__. 1830s.

Rarity: —

$10 • W-MA-1730-010-G150

Engraver: Unverified, but likely New England Bank Note Co. ***Comments:*** H-MA-626-G76. No description available. 18__. 1830s.

Rarity: *None known*

$10 • W-MA-1730-010-G160

Left: Panel bearing TEN vertically. ***Center:*** Wharf scene, Ship at dock, Schooner on side, Warehouses. ***Right:*** 10 / Sailboat / X. ***Engraver:*** New England Bank Note Co. ***Comments:*** H-MA-626-G80. Beware of W-MA-1730-010-S010. Bank title is center vignette on the genuine. 18__. 1840s–1850s.

Rarity: —

$10 • W-MA-1730-010-G160a

Overprint: Red. ***Engraver:*** New England Bank Note Co. ***Comments:*** H-MA-626-G80a. Similar to W-MA-1730-010-G160. 18__. 1850s.

Rarity: —

$10 • W-MA-1730-010-G160b

Overprint: Red. ***Engraver:*** New England Bank Note Co. / ABNCo. monogram. ***Comments:*** H-MA-626-G80b. Similar to W-MA-1730-010-G160 but with additional engraver imprint. 18__. 1850s–1860s.

Rarity: —

$20 • W-MA-1730-020-G170

CJF

Engraver: Perkins. ***Comments:*** H-MA-626-G82. 18__. 1810s–1820s.

Rarity: URS-5
F $300

$20 • W-MA-1730-020-G170a

Left: Lathework chain bearing MASSACHUSETTS vertically. ***Engraver:*** PSSP. ***Comments:*** H-MA-626-G84. Similar to W-MA-1730-020-G170. 18__. 1820s–1830s.

Rarity: —

$20 • W-MA-1730-020-G180

Left: 20 / Eagle. ***Center:*** Wharf scene, Ship at dock, Schooner on side, Warehouses / 20. ***Right:*** XX / Sailing ships / 20. ***Engraver:*** New England Bank Note Co. ***Comments:*** H-MA-626-G88. 18__. 1840s–1850s.

Rarity: —

$20 • W-MA-1730-020-G180a

Overprint: Red. ***Engraver:*** New England Bank Note Co. ***Comments:*** H-MA-626-G88a. Similar to W-MA-1730-020-G180. 18__. 1850s.

Rarity: —

$20 • W-MA-1730-020-G180b

Overprint: Red. ***Engraver:*** New England Bank Note Co. / ABNCo. monogram. ***Comments:*** H-MA-626-G88b. Similar to W-MA-1730-020-G180 but with additional engraver imprint. 18__. 1850s–1860s.

Rarity: —

$50 • W-MA-1730-050-G190

CJF

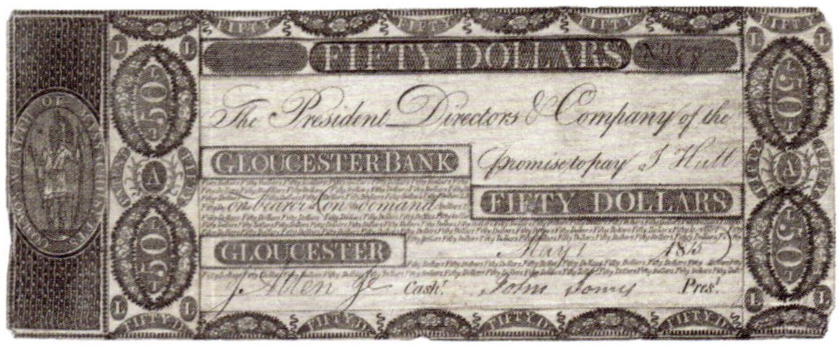

Engraver: Perkins. ***Comments:*** H-MA-626-G90. 18__. 1810s–1820s.

Rarity: URS-4
VG $400

$50 • W-MA-1730-050-G190a

Left: Lathework chain bearing MASSACHUSETTS vertically. ***Engraver:*** New England Bank Note Co. ***Comments:*** H-MA-626-G92. Similar to W-MA-1730-050-G190. 18__. 1820s–1830s.

Rarity: —

$50 • W-MA-1730-050-G200

Left: Wharf scene, Ship at dock, Schooner on side, Warehouses / 50. ***Center:*** 50. ***Right:*** 50 / Sailor, merchandise, and ships / FIFTY. ***Engraver:*** New England Bank Note Co. ***Comments:*** H-MA-626-G96. 18__. 1840s–1850s.

Rarity: —

$100 • W-MA-1730-100-G210

Left: Panel bearing state arms / 100 / 100 vertically. ***Center:*** Alternating flower garlands and gridwork segments. ***Right:*** 100 / 100 vertically. ***Engraver:*** Perkins. ***Comments:*** H-MA-626-G98. 18__. 1810s–1820s.

Rarity: —

$100 • W-MA-1730-100-G210a

Left: Lathework chain bearing MASSACHUSETTS vertically. ***Engraver:*** Perkins. ***Comments:*** H-MA-626-G100. Similar to W-MA-1730-100-G210. 18__. 1820s–1830s.

Rarity: —

$100 • W-MA-1730-100-G220

Left: Wharf scene, Ship at dock, Schooner on side, Warehouses / 100. ***Right:*** 100 / Sailing ships. ***Engraver:*** New England Bank Note Co. ***Comments:*** H-MA-626-G104. 18__. 1840s–1850s.

Rarity: —

Non-Valid Issues

$2 • W-MA-1730-002-C080

Engraver: PSSP. ***Comments:*** H-MA-626-C30. Counterfeit of W-MA-1730-002-G080. 18__. 1820s.

Rarity: —

$2 • **W-MA-1730-002-C095** SBG

Comments: H-Unlisted. 18__. 1820s.

Rarity: URS-6
VF $200

$2 • **W-MA-1730-002-A010**

Left: 2 / Farmer plowing with black and white horses. ***Center:*** Two men loading wagon with sheaves, Three people at right cradling and binding. ***Right:*** 2 / Two floating cherubs with caduceus and sheaf. ***Tint:*** Red-brown 2s and TWO DOLLARS. ***Comments:*** H-MA-626-A5. Altered from $2 Southern Bank of Georgia, Bainbridge, Georgia. March 1, 1858.

Rarity: —

$3 • **W-MA-1730-003-C100b**

Engraver: PSSP. ***Comments:*** H-MA-626-C42. Counterfeit of W-MA-1730-003-G100b. 18__. 1820s–1830s.

Rarity: —

$3 • **W-MA-1730-003-R010**

Engraver: PSSP. ***Comments:*** H-MA-626-R5. Raised from W-MA-1730-001-G010b. 18__. 1829.

Rarity: —

$5 • **W-MA-1730-005-R020**

Engraver: New England Bank Note Co. ***Comments:*** H-MA-626-R10. Raised from W-MA-1730-001-G020 series. 18__. 1850s.

Rarity: —

$10 • **W-MA-1730-010-R030**

Engraver: New England Bank Note Co. ***Comments:*** H-MA-626-R15. Raised from W-MA-1730-001-G020 series. 18__. 1850s.

Rarity: —

$10 • **W-MA-1730-010-S010** CC

Engraver: New England Bank Note Co. ***Comments:*** H-MA-626-S5. Spurious design imitating a rough verbal description of W-MA-1730-010-G160. Bank title is center vignette on genuine. April 1, 185_. 1850s.

Rarity: URS-7
F $300

Grafton, Massachusetts

In 1671 English missionary John Eliot built a church and a school on land which had originally been occupied by a tribe of Nipmuc Indians who called the area Hassanamisco, or "place of small stones." The town of Grafton was incorporated in 1735 and named after the Duke of Grafton, Charles Fitzroy.

Water power from the Blackstone and Quinsigamond rivers allowed for mills which produced cotton goods, woolen goods, boots, shoes, leather, scythes, chairs, tin, and other wooden wears, as well as shoe tools and bricks. Pear trees flourished in the soil. The population in 1830 was 1,889, and by 1837 it had increased to 2,910.

The town of Grafton is made up of six villages: Grafton, New England Village (also known as Upper and Lower Mills or North Grafton), Centerville, Farnumsville, Fisherville, and Saundersville. All of them, save for the central Grafton, are located next to a significant supply of water power.

Grafton Bank
1854–1864
W-MA-1745

History: The Grafton Bank was chartered on March 28, 1854, with an authorized capital of $100,000. By 1855 the bank was already on *Canfield's List of Altered, Counterfeit and Spurious Bank Notes*, reporting false $3s and $10s as having reached circulation.

Circulation in 1857 was listed at $50,772 and at $52,347 in 1860. By 1863 it was up to $81,344.

Selected figures for 1857 included: bills of this bank and other New England states $1,563; specie $4,542.03. Real estate was valued at $2,000 in 1860.

The business of the Grafton Bank was succeeded by the First National Bank of Grafton, chartered on January 7, 1864.

Numismatic Commentary: This bank was not a prolific issuer of notes, but examples do show up on occasion.

As of 2003 the American Bank Note Co. archive had a remaining $5 face plate.

Valid Issues

$1 • **W-MA-1745-001-G010** CC

Engraver: Bald, Adams & Co. ***Comments:*** H-Unlisted. Proof. Aug. 1, 1854.

Rarity: URS-3
Proof $750

$1 • W-MA-1745-001-G010a

Left: Farmer carrying pitchfork, walking beside ox-drawn hay wagon, Boy on hay / ONE. ***Center:*** Male portrait. ***Bottom center:*** Woman swimming. ***Right:*** 1 / Portrait of Henry Clay. ***Overprint:*** Red. ***Engraver:*** Bald, Adams & Co. ***Comments:*** H-MA-630-G2a. Similar to W-MA-1745-001-G010. Aug. 1, 1854.

Rarity: URS-3
Proof $750

$2 • W-MA-1745-002-G020 CC

Engraver: Bald, Adams & Co. / Bald, Cousland & Co. ***Comments:*** H-Unlisted. Proof. August 1, 1854.

Rarity: —
CU $525

$2 • W-MA-1745-002-G020a CJF

Overprint: Red 2 / 2. ***Engraver:*** Bald, Adams & Co. ***Comments:*** H-MA-630-G4a. Similar to W-MA-1745-002-G020 but with different engraver imprint. August 1, 1854.

Rarity: URS-3
EF $1,100

$3 • W-MA-1745-003-G030 CC

Engraver: Bald, Adams & Co. ***Comments:*** H-Unlisted. Proof. Aug. 1, 1854.

Rarity: URS-4
Proof $600

$3 • W-MA-1745-003-G030a

Left: Woman standing blowing dinner horn, Table and house, Men and hay wagon. ***Center:*** THREE. ***Right:*** 3 / Male portrait. ***Overprint:*** Red. ***Engraver:*** Bald, Adams & Co. ***Comments:*** H-MA-630-G6a. Similar to W-MA-1745-003-G030. August 1, 1854.

Rarity: URS-4
Proof $750

$5 • W-MA-1745-005-G040 QDB

Engraver: Bald, Adams & Co. ***Comments:*** H-Unlisted. Proof. Aug. 1, 1854.

Rarity: —

$5 • W-MA-1745-005-G040a

Left: V / Two shoemakers at work. ***Center:*** Portrait of John Quincy Adams / V / Male portrait. ***Right:*** 5 / Woman sewing boot, Child resting on her lap. ***Overprint:*** Red. ***Engraver:*** Bald, Adams & Co. ***Comments:*** H-MA-630-G8a. Similar to W-MA-1745-005-G040. Aug. 1, 1854.

Rarity: URS-4
Proof $750

$5 • W-MA-1745-005-G060

Left: V / Male portrait. ***Center:*** Shoemakers at work. ***Right:*** 5 / Male portrait. ***Engraver:*** Bald, Adams & Co. ***Comments:*** H-MA-630-G10. 1860s.

Rarity: —

$10 • W-MA-1745-010-G070 CC

Engraver: Bald, Adams & Co. ***Comments:*** H-Unlisted. Proof. Aug. 1, 1854.

Rarity: —

$10 • W-MA-1745-010-G070a

Left: X / Portrait of William Penn. ***Center:*** Horses running. ***Right:*** 10 / Male portrait. ***Overprint:*** Red. ***Engraver:*** Bald, Adams & Co. ***Comments:*** H-MA-630-G12a. Similar to W-MA-1745-010-G070. 1850s.

Rarity: URS-4
Proof $750

$20 • W-MA-1745-020-G080

CC

Engraver: Bald, Adams & Co. / Bald, Cousland & Co. ***Comments:*** H-Unlisted. Proof. Aug. 1, 1854. 1860s.

Rarity: —

$20 • W-MA-1745-020-G080a

Left: XX / Train. ***Center:*** Woman seated with arm on bale, Box and barrel. ***Right:*** 20 / Male portrait. ***Engraver:*** American Bank Note Co. ***Comments:*** H-MA-630-G14. Similar to W-MA-1745-020-G080 but with different engraver imprint. 1860s.

Rarity: URS-4
CU $525; **Proof** $750

$50 • W-MA-1745-050-G090

CC

Engraver: Bald, Adams & Co. ***Comments:*** H-Unlisted. Proof. Aug. 1, 1854.

Rarity: —
CU $595

$50 • W-MA-1745-050-G090a

Left: Farmer sowing grain / FIFTY. ***Center:*** L / Milkmaid and two cows, one lying down. ***Right:*** 50 / Male portrait. ***Overprint:*** Red. ***Engraver:*** Bald, Adams & Co. ***Comments:*** H-MA-630-G16a. Similar to W-MA-1745-050-G090. 1850s.

Rarity: URS-4
Proof $1,000

$100 • W-MA-1745-100-G100

CC

Engraver: Baldwin, Adams & Co. ***Comments:*** H-Unlisted. Proof. Aug. 1, 1854.

Rarity: URS-4
Proof $1,500

$100 • W-MA-1745-100-G100a

Left: Woman seated in clouds with eagle / 100. ***Center:*** Male portrait. ***Right:*** C / Woman seated sewing boot, Child leaning on her lap. ***Engraver:*** American Bank Note Co. ***Comments:*** H-MA-630-G18. Similar to W-MA-1745-100-G100 but with different engraver imprint. 1860s.

Rarity: URS-5
Proof $1,000

Uncut Sheets

$1-$3-$5-$10 • W-MA-1745-001.003.005.010-US010

SBG

Overprint(s): None. ***Comments:*** All unlisted in Haxby. Similar to H-MA-630-G2a, G6a, G8a, G12a. Aug. 1, 1854.

Rarity: URS-4
Proof $2,500

$1-$3-$5-$10 • W-MA-1745-001.003.005.010-US010a

Vignette(s): ***($1)*** Farmer carrying pitchfork, walking beside ox-drawn hay wagon, Boy on hay / Male portrait / Woman swimming / Portrait of Henry Clay. ***($3)*** Woman standing blowing dinner horn, Table and house, Men and hay wagon / Male portrait. ***($5)*** Two shoemakers at work / Portrait of John Quincy Adams / Male portrait / Woman sewing boot, Child resting on her lap. ***($10)*** Portrait of William Penn / Horses running / Male portrait. ***Overprint(s):*** Red. ***Comments:*** H-MA-630-G2a, G6a, G8a, G12a. Similar to W-MA-1745-001.003.005.010-US010. August 1, 1854.

Rarity: URS-3
Proof $2,000

$2-$20 • W-MA-1745-002.020-US020

SBG

Overprint(s): None. ***Comments:*** All unlisted in Haxby. Similar to H-MA-630-G4a, G14. Partial sheet. August 1, 1854.

Rarity: URS-4
Proof $1,500

$2-$20 • W-MA-1745-002.020-US020a

Vignette(s): ***($2)*** Portrait of Daniel Webster / Male portrait. ***($20)*** Train / Woman seated with arm on bale, Box and barrel. ***Overprint(s):*** Red. ***Comments:*** All unlisted in Haxby. Similar to W-MA-1745-002.020-US020. Partial sheet. August 1, 1854.

Rarity: URS-3
Proof $1,200

$50-$100 • W-MA-1745-050.100-US030

SBG

Overprint(s): None. ***Comments:*** All unlisted in Haxby. Similar to H-MA-630-G16a, G18. Partial sheet. Aug. 1, 1854.

Rarity: URS-4
Proof $2,800

$50-$100 • W-MA-1745-050.100-US030a

Vignette(s): ***($50)*** Farmer sowing grain / Milkmaid and two cows, one lying down / Male portrait. ***($100)*** Woman seated in clouds with eagle / Male portrait / Woman seated sewing boot, Child leaning on her lap. ***Overprint(s):*** Red. ***Comments:*** All unlisted in Haxby. Similar to W-MA-1745-050.100-US030. Partial sheet. August 1, 1854.

Rarity: —

Non-Valid Issues

$10 • W-MA-1745-010-N010

Left: Train. ***Center:*** Cherub with cornucopia. ***Bottom center:*** Bank building. ***Right:*** Female portrait. ***Comments:*** H-MA-630-N5. 1850s.

Rarity: —

Granville, Massachusetts

James Cornish bought the land that later became Granville from an Indian chief in 1686 for the price of a gun and 16 brass buttons. The township was settled in 1736. In January 1754, it was established as the district of Granville, and in 1775 it was incorporated as a town. It was named after the Earl of Granville, John Carteret. By 1810 a part of its territory was established as the

How to Read the Whitman Numbering System

$1 • W-MA-010-001-G010a

Denomination: Value of the note shown.

W: Whitman number. This number is a sortable code unique to each bank and note.

MA: Abbreviation for the state under study.

010: Numerical designation specific to each bank.

001: The denomination in dollars.

G010a: G indicates a good or valid note. Other categories are indicated thus: C (counterfeit); R (raised); S (spurious); N (not-attributed); A (altered). Numbers are assigned starting with 010, 020, et seq. Terminal letters following the number indicate variations of a note: a series of different colored overprints, tints, payees, etc., all on the same design of note. For more information, see the "How to Use This Book" section at the front of the volume, page xiv.

separate town of Tolland. The villages that make up the town are Granville, East Granville, South Granville, West Granville, and Granville Corner.

There were four saw mills and one grain mill in Granville, and timber as well as fruits, nuts, and berries were a large part of the economy. Children's toys and games, leather, whips, powder kegs, and machinery were also manufactured here during the era under study.

Bank of Sterling

19th Century

W-MA-1760

History: The Bank of Sterling seems to have been proposed at one time to the extent that the projectors contacted an antecedent of the American Bank Note Co. and ordered at least a $2-$5 face plate for its currency. No records have been found concerning any legislative action on such a proposal.

Numismatic Commentary: As of 2003 there was a $2-$5 face plate remaining at the American Bank Note Co. archives. Information of this proposed bank is included here in the event that Proof notes may someday be found.

Great Barrington, Massachusetts

The village of Great Barrington was established in 1726, and in 1761 it was incorporated as a town, named after the same in Gloucestershire, England. In the 1830s tanneries were a prominent industry, and there were a grist mill, a plaster mill, and other mechanic shops. A woolen factory and an iron ore furnace were also located there. Monument Mills was incorporated in 1850, and the Owen paper mill was started in 1856.

When the railroad furnished a convenient connection, Great Barrington became a resort occupied by wealthy families seeking respite from the cities. David Leavitt, a New York City banker, owned an intricate 300-acre estate here. He was one of the developers of the Housatonic Railroad.

Mahaiwe Bank

1847–1865

W-MA-1770

History: The Mahaiwe Bank was chartered on April 19, 1847, with an authorized capital of $100,000. Performance matched expectations, and the bank was profitable. The capital increased to $200,000 by 1854. Circulation in 1849 was $90,415, $195,682 in 1854, $139,426 in 1857, $139,426 in 1860, $100,308 in 1862, and $199,411 in 1863. Selected figures for 1854 included: real estate $2,733.92; specie $ 8,636. Figures for 1857 were: bills of this bank and other New England states $6,826.60; specie $6,958.62; real estate $2,733.92.

In 1865 the business of the Mahaiwe Bank was succeeded by the National Mahaiwe Bank of Great Barrington.

Numismatic Commentary: A collector should be able to secure a note or two from this bank without too much difficulty. Some of its issues show a vignette of an Indian maiden stepping from a precipice on Monument Mountain in defiance of the tribal law forbidding her from marrying a cousin with whom she had fallen in love.

Valid Issues

$1 • W-MA-1770-001-G010

Left: 1 / Female portrait. ***Center:*** Woman reclining holding 1 / ONE / 1 / ONE. ***Right:*** 1 / Cattle. ***Engraver:*** Rawdon, Wright, Hatch & Edson. ***Comments:*** H-MA-635-G2. 18__. 1847–1850s.

Rarity: —

$1 • W-MA-1770-001-G010a

Overprint: Red. ***Engraver:*** Rawdon, Wright, Hatch & Edson. ***Comments:*** H-MA-635-G2a. Similar to W-MA-1770-001-G010. 18__. 1850s.

Rarity: —

$1 • W-MA-1770-001-G010b

HA

Overprint: Red. ***Engraver:*** Rawdon, Wright, Hatch & Edson / ABNCo. monogram. ***Comments:*** H-MA-635-G2d. Similar to W-MA-1770-001-G010 but with additional engraver imprint. 18__. 1860s.

Rarity: URS-3
F $750

$2 • W-MA-1770-002-G020

Left: 2 / Portrait of girl. ***Center:*** Boy pushing sheep into stream, Man watching. ***Bottom center:*** State arms. ***Right:*** 2 / Stonecutter at work. ***Engraver:*** Rawdon, Wright, Hatch & Edson. ***Comments:*** H-MA-635-G4. 18__. 1847–1850s.

Rarity: —

$2 • W-MA-1770-002-G020a

Overprint: Red. ***Engraver:*** Rawdon, Wright, Hatch & Edson. ***Comments:*** H-MA-635-G4a. Similar to W-MA-1770-002-G020. 18__. 1850s.

Rarity: —

$2 • W-MA-1770-002-G020b

Tint: Green. ***Engraver:*** Rawdon, Wright, Hatch & Edson / ABNCo. monogram. ***Comments:*** H-MA-635-G4d. Similar to W-MA-1770-002-G020 but with additional engraver imprint. 18__. 1860s.

Rarity: —

$3 • W-MA-1770-003-G030

Left: Two men carrying a woman on their shoulders / THREE. ***Center:*** Train. ***Bottom center:*** State arms. ***Right:*** THREE / Woman standing with shield resting on pedestal / THREE. ***Engraver:*** Rawdon, Wright, Hatch & Edson. ***Comments:*** H-MA-635-G6. 18__. 1847–1850s.

Rarity: —

$3 • W-MA-1770-003-G030a

Overprint: Red. ***Engraver:*** Rawdon, Wright, Hatch & Edson. ***Comments:*** H-MA-635-G6a. Similar to W-MA-1770-003-G030. 18__. 1850s.

Rarity: —

$3 • W-MA-1770-003-G030b

Tint: Green. ***Engraver:*** Rawdon, Wright, Hatch & Edson / ABNCo. monogram. ***Comments:*** H-MA-635-G6d. Similar to W-MA-1770-003-G030 but with additional engraver imprint. 18__. 1860s.

Rarity: —

$5 • W-MA-1770-005-G040

CJF

Engraver: Rawdon, Wright, Hatch & Edson. ***Comments:*** H-MA-635-G8. Proof. 18__. 1847–1850s.

Rarity: URS-2
Proof $1,500

$5 • W-MA-1770-005-G040a

CJF

Overprint: Red FIVE. ***Engraver:*** Rawdon, Wright, Hatch & Edson. ***Comments:*** H-MA-635-G8a. Similar to W-MA-1770-005-G040. 18__. 1850s.

Rarity: URS-2
F $1,000

$5 • W-MA-1770-005-G040b

Left: Monument Mountain. ***Center:*** 5 on V on FIVE / Shield with Indian. ***Right:*** 5 / Three women with 5. ***Tint:*** Green. ***Engraver:*** Rawdon, Wright, Hatch & Edson. ***Comments:*** H-MA-635-G8b. Similar to W-MA-1770-005-G040. 18__. 1850s.

Rarity: —

$5 • W-MA-1770-005-G040c

Tint: Green. ***Engraver:*** Rawdon, Wright, Hatch & Edson / ABNCo. monogram. ***Comments:*** H-MA-635-G8d. Similar to W-MA-1770-005-G040 but with additional engraver imprint. 18__. 1860s.

Rarity: —

$10 • W-MA-1770-010-G050

Left: Deer / 10 / Farmer seated on plow. ***Center:*** Ceres seated on bale holding sickle and sheaf, Factory and train. ***Bottom center:*** State arms. ***Right:*** 10 / Indian woman holding ear of corn, hand on X. ***Engraver:*** Rawdon, Wright, Hatch & Edson. ***Comments:*** H-MA-635-G10. 18__. 1847–1850s.

Rarity: —

$10 • W-MA-1770-010-G050a

JF

Overprint: Red TEN. ***Engraver:*** Rawdon, Wright, Hatch & Edson. ***Comments:*** H-MA-635-G10a. Similar to W-MA-1770-010-G050. 18__. 1850s.

Rarity: URS-2
F $1,000

$10 • W-MA-1770-010-G050b

Tint: Green. ***Engraver:*** Rawdon, Wright, Hatch & Edson / ABNCo. monogram. ***Comments:*** H-MA-635-G10d. Similar to W-MA-1770-010-G050 but with additional engraver imprint. 18__. 1860s.

Rarity: —

$20 • W-MA-1770-020-G060

Left: 20 / Minerva standing with spear. ***Center:*** Woman seated between 2 and 0. ***Right:*** 20 / Woman reclining on cornucopia / 20. ***Engraver:*** Rawdon, Wright, Hatch & Edson. ***Comments:*** H-MA-635-G12. 18__. 1850s.

Rarity: —

$20 • W-MA-1770-020-G070

Left: 20 / Two women with sickle and sheaf. ***Center:*** State arms. ***Right:*** 20 / Woman standing with arm on pedestal holding torch. ***Tint:*** Green XX / XX. ***Engraver:*** American Bank Note Co. ***Comments:*** H-MA-635-G14. 18__. 1860s.

Rarity: —

$50 • W-MA-1770-050-G080

Left: 50 / Minerva standing by column. ***Center:*** Ceres and Vulcan flanking cornucopia. ***Right:*** 50 / Cherub in sailboat / 50. ***Engraver:*** Rawdon, Wright, Hatch & Edson. ***Comments:*** H-MA-635-G16. 18__. 1850s.

Rarity: —

$50 • W-MA-1770-050-G090

Left: L / Girl and boy feeding horse. ***Center:*** Man watering horses at trough, Livestock and barn. ***Right:*** 50 / Male portrait. ***Tint:*** Green. ***Engraver:*** American Bank Note Co. ***Comments:*** H-MA-635-G18. 1860s.

Rarity: —

$100 • W-MA-1770-100-G100

Left: 100 / Vulcan seated with sledge and anchor. ***Center:*** Train on bridge, Eagle on limb, Canal locks / C C. ***Bottom center:*** 100. ***Right:*** 100 / Ceres seated, Cornucopia. ***Engraver:*** Rawdon, Wright, Hatch & Edson. ***Comments:*** H-MA-635-G20. 18__. 1850s.

Rarity: —

Non-Valid Issues

$3 • W-MA-1770-003-S010

CC

Overprint: Red TEN. ***Engraver:*** Rawdon, Wright, Hatch & Edson / New England Bank Note Co. ***Comments:*** H-MA-635-S5. July 2, 18__. 1850s.

Rarity: URS-7
F $125; **EF** $175

$10 • W-MA-1770-010-C050a

CJF

Overprint: Red TEN. ***Engraver:*** Rawdon, Wright, Hatch & Edson. ***Comments:*** H-MA-635-C10a. Counterfeit of W-MA-1770-010-G050a. 18__. 1850s.

Rarity: URS-8
F $100

$10 • W-MA-1770-010-C050c

CJF

Overprint: Red X. ***Engraver:*** Rawdon, Wright, Hatch & Edson. ***Comments:*** H-Unlisted. Similar to W-MA-1770-010-C050a. 18__. 1850s.

Rarity: URS-6
F $150

$10 • W-MA-1770-010-R010

Engraver: Rawdon, Wright, Hatch & Edson. ***Comments:*** H-MA-635-R5. Raised from W-MA-1770-001-G010 or G010a. 18__. 1850s.

Rarity: —

Greenfield, Massachusetts

An Algonquian tribe first settled the land known as Greenfield, but they were killed off by an attack of Mohawk Indians in 1664. In 1686 the English arrived. Greenfield was separated from Deerfield in 1753 when it was incorporated as a town and named after the Green River. In 1795 the South Hadley Canal was opened, and Greenfield developed into a prosperous trade center. Waterfalls generated water power for mills. John Russell hired German workers in the country's first cutlery factory and established it as the Green River Works in 1834. The Connecticut River Railroad was the first railway to stop at the town, and the canal declined as a result.

Franklin Bank

1822–1831

W-MA-1780

History: The Franklin Bank was chartered in early 1822 with an authorized capital of $100,000. Samuel Willard was the main figure in organizing the institution. One of the bank's first activities was to place a large amount of paper money into circulation. This action attracted unfavorable notice, as did the news that quantities of bills had been discounted to a Boston speculator who was to distribute them as widely as possible. In June 1822, the *Boston Galaxy* published this satirical commentary:

> The Franklin bank is located at Greenfield, a small neat village, near the confluence of Deerfield and Connecticut rivers, and considerably celebrated for conference meeting, intellectual ladies, and hen-pecked husbands. We have not been so fortunate as to get a view of one of these bills; but the following device is respectfully offered to the directors to be engraved for a new emission, if they have not already adopted a similar one, viz: Let there be a representation of the inside of the bank, the president at his desk engaged in prayer,—the directors playing at all-fours,—the discount clerk keeping the game,—the cashier, (being also a member of the Temperate Society) mixing a pitcher of brandy toddy,—and the teller counting out religious tracts.—Over the whole group let there be a domestic hen, flapping her wings, and holding in her beak, a cock half-stripped of his feathers, his spurs broken off and his majestic comb dropping blood. If there be a vacancy in the background, it may be filled with a thin, weazle-laced, spindle shanked broker, a rusty jack knife in one hand, to denote his profession, Hopkins' Body of Divinity in the other, as emblematic of his religion and the noose of a bell rope round his neck, to designate how he made his money, and to what destination his love of money will bring him at last.—With this emaiematic engraving, the whole tribe of counterfeiters, past, present, and to come may be set at defiance.[85]

The bank's charter was renewed in 1831 with a capital of $100,000. On March 31, 1831, the Legislature authorized a name change to the Greenfield Bank, W-MA-1800.

Numismatic Commentary: All issues are hard to locate. Because of the time frame of the bank's existence, any issues found will be of the PSSP type.

Valid Issues

$1 • W-MA-1780-001-G010

Center: 1 / 1 / Flower garlands and gridwork segments / ONE / 1 / 1. ***Engraver:*** PSSP. ***Comments:*** H-MA-640-G2. 18__. 1820s.

Rarity: —

$1 • W-MA-1780-001-G010a

Left: Panel of lathework circle segments. ***Right:*** Panel of lathework circle segments. ***Engraver:*** PSSP. ***Comments:*** H-MA-640-G4. Similar to W-MA-1780-001-G010. 18__. 1820s.

Rarity: —

$1 • W-MA-1780-001-G010b

Left: Panel of lathework circle segments. ***Right:*** Panel of lathework circle segments. ***Engraver:*** PSSP. ***Comments:*** H-MA-640-G6. Similar to W-MA-1780-001-G010. 18__. 1820s–1830s.

Rarity: —

$2 • W-MA-1780-002-G020

Center: 2 / 2 / Flower garlands and gridwork segments / TWO / 2 / 2. ***Engraver:*** PSSP. ***Comments:*** H-MA-640-G8. 18__. 1820s.

Rarity: —

$2 • W-MA-1780-002-G020a

Left: Panel of lathework circle segments. ***Right:*** Panel of lathework circle segments. ***Engraver:*** PSSP. ***Comments:*** H-MA-640-G10. Similar to W-MA-1780-002-G020. 18__. 1820s.

Rarity: —

$2 • W-MA-1780-002-G020b

Left: Panel of lathework circle segments. ***Right:*** Panel of lathework circle segments. ***Engraver:*** PSSP. ***Comments:*** H-MA-640-G12. Similar to W-MA-1780-002-G020. 18__. 1820s–1830s.

Rarity: —

$3 • W-MA-1780-003-G030

CJF

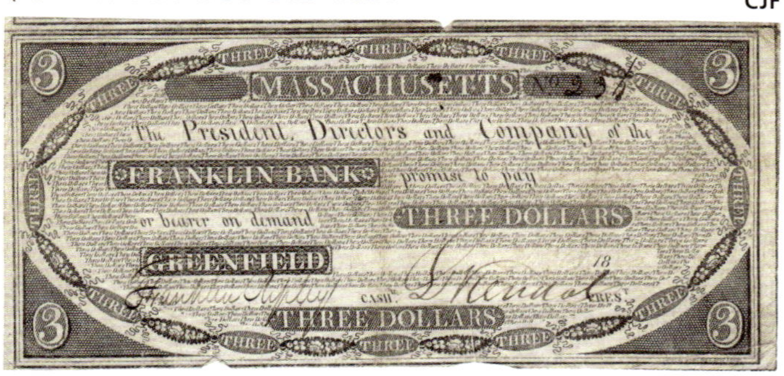

Engraver: PSSP. ***Comments:*** H-MA-640-G14. 18__. 1820s.

Rarity: URS-4
VF $400

$3 • W-MA-1780-003-G030a

Left: Panel of lathework circle segments. ***Center:*** 3 / 3 / Flower garlands and gridwork segments / 3 / 3. ***Right:*** Panel of lathework circle segments. ***Engraver:*** PSSP. ***Comments:*** H-MA-640-G16. Similar to W-MA-1780-003-G030. 18__. 1820s.

Rarity: —

$3 • W-MA-1780-003-G030b

Left: Panel of lathework circle segments. ***Right:*** Panel of lathework circle segments. ***Engraver:*** PSSP. ***Comments:*** H-MA-640-G18. Similar to W-MA-1780-003-G030. 18__. 1820s–1830s.

Rarity: —

$5 • W-MA-1780-005-G040

Left: Lathework chain bearing MASSACHUSETTS vertically / 5 / 5. ***Center:*** Alternating flower garlands and gridwork segments. ***Right:*** 5 / 5. ***Engraver:*** PSSP. ***Comments:*** H-MA-640-G20. 18__. 1820s.

Rarity: —

$5 • W-MA-1780-005-G040a

Left: Lathework chain bearing MASSACHUSETTS vertically. ***Right:*** Panel of lathework circle segments. ***Engraver:*** PSSP. ***Comments:*** H-MA-640-G22. Similar to W-MA-1780-005-G040. 18__. 1820s.

Rarity: —

$10 • W-MA-1780-010-G050

Left: Lathework chain bearing MASSACHUSETTS / 10 / 10 vertically. ***Center:*** Alternating flower garlands and gridwork segments. ***Right:*** 10 / 10 vertically. ***Engraver:*** Perkins. ***Comments:*** H-MA-640-G24. 18__. 1820s.

Rarity: —

$10 • W-MA-1780-010-G050a

Left: Lathework chain bearing MASSACHUSETTS vertically. ***Right:*** Panel of lathework circle segments. ***Engraver:*** Perkins. ***Comments:*** H-MA-640-G26. Similar to W-MA-1780-010-G050. 18__. 1820s.

Rarity: —

$20 • W-MA-1780-020-G060

Left: Panel bearing state arms / 20 / 20 vertically. ***Center:*** Alternating flower garlands and gridwork segments. ***Right:*** 20 / 20 vertically. ***Engraver:*** Perkins. ***Comments:*** H-MA-640-G28. 18__. 1820s.

Rarity: —

$50 • W-MA-1780-050-G070

Left: Panel bearing state arms / 50 / 50 vertically. ***Center:*** Alternating flower garlands and gridwork segments. ***Right:*** 50 / 50 vertically. ***Engraver:*** Perkins. ***Comments:*** H-MA-640-G30. 18__. 1820s.

Rarity: —

$100 • W-MA-1780-100-G080

Left: Panel bearing state arms / 100 vertically. ***Center:*** Alternating flower garlands and gridwork segments. ***Right:*** 100 / 100 vertically. ***Engraver:*** Perkins. ***Comments:*** H-MA-640-G32. 18__. 1820s.

Rarity: —

Franklin County Bank

1849–1865

W-MA-1790

History: The Franklin County Bank was chartered in May 1849 with an authorized capital of $200,000 and commenced operations on September 1. A.G. Hammond, Esquire, was appointed cashier. The capital of the Franklin County Bank was listed at $59,116 in 1849, $150,000 in 1851, and $200,000 in 1854. Circulation ranged from a low of $57,395 in October 1849 to a high of $196,899 in 1863. Selected figures for 1857 included:

bills of this bank and other New England states $1,889; specie $8 405.49; real estate $6,662.40.

The business of the Franklin County Bank was succeeded by the Franklin County National Bank of Greenfield, chartered on March 21, 1865.

Numismatic Commentary: Genuine issues from this bank are hard to locate. Few genuine notes have made an appearance in recent decades.

Valid Issues

$1 • W-MA-1790-001-G010

CJF

Engraver: Rawdon, Wright, Hatch & Edson / New England Bank Note Co. ***Comments:*** H-MA-645-G2. Proof. 18__. 1849–1850s.

Rarity: URS-3

Proof $750

$1 • W-MA-1790-001-G010a

CC

Overprint: Red ONE. ***Engraver:*** Rawdon, Wright, Hatch & Edson / New England Bank Note Co. ***Comments:*** H-Unlisted. Similar to W-MA-1790-001-G010. 18__. 1849–1850s.

Rarity: URS-3

AU $700

$1 • W-MA-1790-001-G010b

CJF

Tint: Red panel outlining white ONE. ***Engraver:*** Rawdon, Wright, Hatch & Edson / New England Bank Note Co. / ABNCo. monogram. ***Comments:*** H-Unlisted. Similar to W-MA-1790-001-G010 but with additional engraver imprint. 18__. 1849–1850s.

Rarity: URS-2

VF $1,000

$2 • W-MA-1790-002-G020

CJF

Engraver: Rawdon, Wright, Hatch & Edson / New England Bank Note Co. ***Comments:*** H-MA-645-G4. Proof. 18__. 1849–1850s.

Rarity: URS-2

Proof $1,000

$3 • W-MA-1790-003-G030

Left: Mechanic, sailor seated on bale, and farmer with scythe, Three gold dollars / 3. ***Center:*** 3. ***Right:*** 3 / Portrait of Daniel Webster. ***Engraver:*** Rawdon, Wright, Hatch & Edson / New England Bank Note Co. ***Comments:*** H-MA-645-G6. 18__. 1849–1850s.

Rarity: —

$5 • W-MA-1790-005-G040

CJF

Engraver: Rawdon, Wright, Hatch & Edson / New England Bank Note Co. ***Comments:*** H-MA-645-G8. Proof. 18__. 1849–1850s.

Rarity: URS-2

Proof $1,000

$10 • W-MA-1790-010-G050

CJF

Engraver: Rawdon, Wright, Hatch & Edson / New England Bank Note Co. ***Comments:*** H-MA-645-G10. Proof. 18__. 1849–1850s.

Rarity: URS-2

Proof $1,000

$20 • W-MA-1790-020-G060

Left: 20 / Minerva standing with spear. ***Center:*** Woman seated between 2 and 0 / TWENTY. ***Right:*** 20 / Woman reclining on cornucopia / 20. ***Engraver:*** Rawdon, Wright, Hatch & Edson / New England Bank Note Co. ***Comments:*** H-MA-645-G12. 18__. 1849–1850s.

Rarity: —

$20 • W-MA-1790-020-G070

Left: 20 / TWENTY / Male portrait. ***Right:*** 20 / Male portrait. ***Tint:*** Color unknown. ***Engraver:*** Rawdon, Wright, Hatch & Edson / New England Bank Note Co. ***Comments:*** H-MA-645-G14. 1850s–1860s.

Rarity: —

$50 • W-MA-1790-050-G080

Left: 50 / Minerva standing by column. ***Center:*** Ceres and Vulcan flanking cornucopia. ***Right:*** 50 / Cherub in sailboat / 50. ***Engraver:*** New England Bank Note Co. ***Comments:*** H-MA-645-G16. 18__. 1849–1850s.

Rarity: —

$50 • W-MA-1790-050-G090

Left: 50 / Woman with scroll bearing FIFTY DOLLARS, Child seated at her feet holding wreath. ***Right:*** 50 / FIFTY / Dog and strongbox. ***Tint:*** Color unknown. ***Comments:*** H-MA-645-G18. 1850s–1860s.

Rarity: —

$100 • W-MA-1790-100-G100

Left: 100 / Vulcan seated with sledge and anchor. ***Center:*** Train on bridge, Eagle on limb, Canal locks / C C. ***Bottom center:*** 100. ***Right:*** 100 / Ceres seated, Cornucopia. ***Engraver:*** Rawdon, Wright, Hatch & Edson. ***Comments:*** H-MA-645-G20. 18__. 1849–1850s.

Rarity: —

$100 • W-MA-1790-100-G110

Left: C / State arms. ***Center:*** C / Male portrait / C. ***Right:*** 100 / Eagle on rock. ***Tint:*** Color unknown. ***Comments:*** H-MA-645-G22. 1850s–1860s.

Rarity: —

Non-Valid Issues

$2 • W-MA-1790-002-R010

Engraver: Rawdon, Wright, Hatch & Edson / New England Bank Note Co. ***Comments:*** H-MA-645-R5. Raised from W-MA-1790-001-G010. 18__. 1850s.

Rarity: —

$3 • W-MA-1790-003-A010

HA

Engraver: Spencer, Hufty & Danforth. ***Comments:*** H-MA-645-A5. Altered from $3 Commercial Bank of Vermont, Poultney, Vermont. January 15, 1852.

Rarity: URS-7
VG $125

$5 • W-MA-1790-005-C040

Engraver: Rawdon, Wright, Hatch & Edson / New England Bank Note Co. ***Comments:*** H-MA-645-C8. Counterfeit of W-MA-1790-005-G040. 18__. 1850s.

Rarity: —

$5 • W-MA-1790-005-R020

Engraver: Rawdon, Wright, Hatch & Edson / New England Bank Note Co. ***Comments:*** H-MA-645-R10. Raised from W-MA-1790-001-G010. 18__. 1850s.

Rarity: —

$5 • W-MA-1790-005-S010

HA

Engraver: Bald, Adams & Co. ***Comments:*** H-Unlisted. Jan. __, 18__. 1860.

Rarity: URS-8
F $75

$5 • W-MA-1790-005-S010a

CJF

Overprint: Red FIVE. ***Engraver:*** Bald, Adams & Co. ***Comments:*** H-MA-645-S5a. Similar to W-MA-1790-005-S010. Jan. __, 18__. 1860.

Rarity: URS-8
F $75

$5 • W-MA-1790-005-N010

Bottom center: Arm and hammer. ***Comments:*** H-MA-645-N5.

Rarity: —

$10 • W-MA-1790-010-R030

Engraver: Rawdon, Wright, Hatch & Edson / New England Bank Note Co. ***Comments:*** H-MA-645-R15. Raised from W-MA-1790-001-G010. 18__. 1850s.

Rarity: —

$10 • W-MA-1790-010-S020

CC

Engraver: Durand, Perkins & Co. ***Comments:*** H-MA-645-S10. 18__. 1850s.

Rarity: URS-7
VG $125; **VF** $175

Greenfield Bank

1831–1864

W-MA-1800

History: The Greenfield Bank was formerly the Franklin Bank, W-MA-1780. The name was changed to the Greenfield Bank on March 31, 1831. At the time the capital was $100,000. The capital was $150,000 in 1839 and $200,000 in 1851. Circulation ranged from a low of $75,684 to a high of $199,484 in 1863.

Figures for 1854 included: specie $6,380; real estate $6,500; bank notes $8,701; money due by banks $68,955; loans $884,658. Selected figures for 1857 were: bills of this bank and other New England states $3,075; specie $11,900.59; real estate $7,500.

The Greenfield Bank relinquished its charter and was succeeded by the First National Bank of Greenfield in 1864.

Numismatic Commentary: This is another western Massachusetts bank for which notes are rare. At least one note shows local buildings in the center of town, one of which is the bank building.

Valid Issues

$1 • W-MA-1800-001-G010

Left: Lathework panel bearing MASSACHUSETTS vertically. ***Center:*** 1 / 1 / Alternating flower garlands and gridwork segments / ONE / 1 / 1. ***Right:*** Lathework panel bearing ONE / D / ONE vertically. ***Engraver:*** PSSP. ***Comments:*** H-MA-650-G2. 18__. 1830s.

Rarity: —

$1 • W-MA-1800-001-G020

Left: 1 / Minerva standing with 1 / 1. ***Center:*** ONE / Plow, Commerce seated with caduceus and cornucopia, Ships / ONE. ***Right:*** 1 / Eagle / 1. ***Engraver:*** PSSP. ***Comments:*** H-MA-650-G4. 18__. 1830s–1840s.

Rarity: —

$1 • W-MA-1800-001-G030

CC

Engraver: New England Bank Note Co. ***Comments:*** H-Unlisted. 18__. 1840s.

Rarity: URS-3
VF $750

$1 • W-MA-1800-001-G040

SBG

Engraver: New England Bank Note Co. / PSSP. ***Comments:*** H-Unlisted. 18__.

Rarity: URS-1
Proof $2,000

$1 • W-MA-1800-001-G050

Left: ONE / Justice in 1. ***Center:*** Man and boy driving sheep into stream, Houses. ***Right:*** ONE / Woman with harp on 1. ***Engraver:*** PSSP. ***Comments:*** H-MA-650-G6. 18__. 1830s–1840s.

Rarity: —

$2 • W-MA-1800-002-G060

Left: Lathework panel bearing MASSACHUSETTS vertically. ***Center:*** 2 / 2 / Alternating flower garlands and gridwork segments / TWO / 2 / 2. ***Right:*** Lathework panel bearing five TWOs vertically. ***Engraver:*** PSSP. ***Comments:*** H-MA-650-G8. 18__. 1830s.

Rarity: —

$2 • W-MA-1800-002-G070

Left: 2 / Hebe watering eagle / 2. ***Center:*** 2 / Plow, Commerce seated with caduceus and cornucopia, Ships / 2. ***Right:*** 2 / Justice standing / 2. ***Engraver:*** PSSP. ***Comments:*** H-MA-650-G10. 18__. 1830s.

Rarity: URS-5
Proof $1,750
Selected auction price: Stack's Bowers Galleries, August 2012, Lot 7131, Choice AU $1,610

$2 • W-MA-1800-002-G080

SI

Engraver: Rawdon, Wright, Hatch & Edson / New England Bank Note Co. / ABNCo. monogram. ***Comments:*** H-MA-650-G12. 18__. 1840s–1850s.

Rarity: URS-3
F $750

$2 • **W-MA-1800-002-G090**

SBG

Engraver: New England Bank Note Co. / PSSP. ***Comments:*** H-Unlisted. 18__.

Rarity: URS-3

Proof $1,800

$3 • **W-MA-1800-003-G100**

Left: Lathework panel bearing MASSACHUSETTS vertically. ***Center:*** 3 / 3 / Alternating flower garlands and gridwork segments / THREE / 3 / 3. ***Right:*** Lathework panel bearing THREE vertically. ***Engraver:*** PSSP. ***Comments:*** H-MA-650-G14. 18__. 1830s.

Rarity: —

$3 • **W-MA-1800-003-G110**

Left: 3 / Eagle on rock / 3. ***Center:*** 3 / Plow, Commerce seated with caduceus and cornucopia, Ships / 3 / Panel bearing THREE. ***Right:*** 3 / Woman standing with cornucopia / 3. ***Engraver:*** PSSP. ***Comments:*** H-MA-650-G16. 18__. 1830s.

Rarity: —

$3 • **W-MA-1800-003-G120**

Left: State arms / 3. ***Center:*** Train, depot, and steamboat. ***Right:*** THREE / Portrait of Zachary Taylor / THREE. ***Engraver:*** Rawdon, Wright, Hatch & Edson / New England Bank Note Co. ***Comments:*** H-MA-650-G18. 18__. 1840s–1850s.

Rarity: —

$5 • **W-MA-1800-005-G130**

Left: Lathework chain bearing MASSACHUSETTS / 5 / 5. ***Center:*** Alternating flower garlands and gridwork segments / FIVE DOLLARS lined by spiral lathework lines. ***Right:*** 5 / 5. ***Engraver:*** PSSP. ***Comments:*** H-MA-650-G20. 18__. 1830s.

Rarity: —

$5 • **W-MA-1800-005-G140**

CJF

Engraver: New England Bank Note Co. / PSSP / ABNCo. monogram. ***Comments:*** H-MA-650-G22. 18__. 1850s–1860s.

Rarity: URS-2

VF $1,500

$10 • **W-MA-1800-010-G150**

Left: Lathework chain bearing MASSACHUSETTS / 10 / 10 vertically. ***Center:*** Alternating flower garlands and gridwork segments / TEN DOLLARS lined by spiral lathework lines. ***Engraver:*** PSSP. ***Comments:*** H-MA-650-G24. 18__. 1830s.

Rarity: —

$10 • **W-MA-1800-010-G160**

Left: TEN / Cattle / TEN. ***Center:*** 10 / Three buildings / 10. ***Right:*** X / Woman with rake. ***Engraver:*** New England Bank Note Co. ***Comments:*** H-MA-650-G26. 18__. 1830s–1850s.

Rarity: —

$20 • **W-MA-1800-020-G170**

Left: Lathework chain bearing MASSACHUSETTS / 20 / 20 vertically. ***Center:*** Alternating flower garlands and gridwork segments. ***Right:*** 20 / 20 vertically. ***Engraver:*** PSSP. ***Comments:*** H-MA-650-G28. 18__. 1830s.

Rarity: —

$20 • **W-MA-1800-020-G180**

Left: 20 / XX / 20. ***Center:*** 20 / Men plowing, Woman seated with scales, Sheaf and bales, Ship / 20. ***Right:*** TWENTY vertically. ***Engraver:*** PSSP / New England Bank Note Co. ***Comments:*** H-MA-650-G30. 18__. 1830s.

Rarity: —

$20 • **W-MA-1800-020-G190**

Left: 20 / Minerva standing with spear. ***Center:*** Woman seated between 2 and 0. ***Right:*** 20 / Woman reclining on cornucopia / 20. ***Engraver:*** Rawdon, Wright, Hatch & Edson. ***Comments:*** H-MA-650-G32. 18__. 1850s.

Rarity: —

$20 • **W-MA-1800-020-G200**

Left: Two women with sickle and grain / 20. ***Center:*** 20 / Dog rescuing child from water / 20. ***Right:*** Indian woman beside rock / 20. ***Tint:*** Green. ***Engraver:*** American Bank Note Co. ***Comments:*** H-MA-650-G34a. 1860s.

Rarity: —

$50 • **W-MA-1800-050-G210**

Left: Lathework chain bearing MASSACHUSETTS / 50 / 50 vertically. ***Center:*** Alternating flower garlands and gridwork segments / FIFTY. ***Right:*** 50 / 50 vertically. ***Engraver:*** PSSP. ***Comments:*** H-MA-650-G36. 18__. 1830s.

Rarity: —

$50 • **W-MA-1800-050-G220**

Left: 50 / Cornucopia, Woman standing with ankles crossed, Staff, Anchor / 50. ***Center:*** FIFTY DOLLARS / 50. ***Right:*** FIFTY vertically. ***Engraver:*** New England Bank Note Co. / PSSP. ***Comments:*** H-MA-650-G38. 18__. 1830s.

Rarity: —

$50 • **W-MA-1800-050-G230**

Left: 50 / Minerva standing by column. ***Center:*** Ceres and Vulcan flanking cornucopia. ***Right:*** 50 / Cherub in sailboat / 50. ***Engraver:*** Rawdon, Wright, Hatch & Edson. ***Comments:*** H-MA-650-G40. 18__. 1850s.

Rarity: —

$50 • W-MA-1800-050-G240

Left: FIFTY / Woman seated with arm resting on wheel, Lamp, Flowers. ***Center:*** Eagle on shield. ***Right:*** 50 / Portrait of General George B. McClellan. ***Tint:*** Green L L. ***Engraver:*** American Bank Note Co. ***Comments:*** H-MA-650-G42a. 1860s.

Rarity: —

$100 • W-MA-1800-100-G250

Left: Lathework chain bearing MASSACHUSETTS / 100 / 100 vertically. ***Center:*** Alternating flower garlands and gridwork segments. ***Right:*** 100 / 100 vertically. ***Engraver:*** Perkins. ***Comments:*** H-MA-650-G44. 18__. 1830s.

Rarity: —

$100 • W-MA-1800-100-G260

Left: Lathework panel bearing C / Portrait of George Washington / C. ***Center:*** 100 / Manhattan reclining pouring water, Ship / 100. ***Right:*** Lathework panel bearing ONE HUNDRED vertically. ***Engraver:*** New England Bank Note Co. / PSSP. ***Comments:*** H-MA-650-G46. 18__. 1830s.

Rarity: —

$100 • W-MA-1800-100-G270

Left: 100 / Vulcan seated with sledge and anchor. ***Center:*** Train on bridge, Eagle on limb, Canal locks / C C. ***Bottom center:*** 100. ***Right:*** 100 / Ceres seated, Cornucopia. ***Engraver:*** Rawdon, Wright, Hatch & Edson. ***Comments:*** H-MA-650-G48. 18__. 1850s.

Rarity: —

$100 • W-MA-1800-100-G280

Left: Two children / 100. ***Center:*** State arms. ***Right:*** C / Blacksmith with foot on anvil. ***Tint:*** Likely green L. ***Engraver:*** American Bank Note Co. ***Comments:*** H-MA-650-G50a. 1860s.

Rarity: —

NON-VALID ISSUES

$2 • W-MA-1800-002-C080

Engraver: Rawdon, Wright, Hatch & Edson / New England Bank Note Co. ***Comments:*** H-MA-650-C12. Counterfeit of W-MA-1800-002-G080. 18__. 1840s.

Rarity: —

$5 • W-MA-1800-005-S010

CJF

Engraver: Murray, Draper, Fairman & Co. ***Comments:*** H-Unlisted. 18__. 1860s.

Rarity: URS-6

F $125

$5 • W-MA-1800-005-A010

CC

Tint: Red-brown lathework outlining white 5. ***Engraver:*** Bald, Cousland & Co. ***Comments:*** H-MA-650-A5. Altered from $5 Pioneer Association, Lafayette, Indiana. 18__. 1850s–1860s.

Rarity: URS-7

F $100

$10 • W-MA-1800-010-C160

Engraver: New England Bank Note Co. ***Comments:*** H-MA-650-C26. Counterfeit of W-MA-1800-010-G160. 18__. 1830s.

Rarity: —

$10 • W-MA-1800-010-N010

Center: Woman churning. ***Comments:*** H-MA-650-N5. 18__. 1830s.

Rarity: —

Endnotes

1. J. Hammond Trumbull, *The First Essays at Banking and the First Paper-Money in New England*, 1884, pp. 3–5, 23; Other sources.

2. Andrew McFarland Davis, "Papers Relating to the Land Bank of 1740," 1910.

3. The *Medley*, New Bedford, July 24, 1795.

4. Today a museum with Perkins memorabilia is located there.

5. Secretary of the Treasury William H. Crawford's report to the House of Representatives, February 24, 1820; Other sources.

6. Dudley P. Bailey Jr., "The History of Banking in Massachusetts, No. 2," *Banker's Magazine*, September 1876.

7. D.R. Whitney, *The Suffolk Bank*, 1878.

8. Such as the Farmers Exchange Bank, Gloucester, Rhode Island, and the Hillsborough Bank, Amherst, New Hampshire.

9. Dudley P. Bailey Jr., "The History of Banking in Massachusetts, No. 3," *Banker's Magazine*, October 1876.

10. *Niles' Weekly Register*, April 22, 1837.

11. The *Financial Register*, Volume 1, pp. 304–309.

12. *Niles' National Register*, January 20 and March 11, 1838.

13. Dudley P. Bailey Jr., "The History of Banking in Massachusetts," *Banker's Magazine*, September and October 1876.

14. *Ibid.*

15. *Banker's Magazine*, May 1855.

16. Reported in a letter from the secretary of the Treasury, March 28, 1860, in HR 36th Congress, 1st Sess. Ex. Doc. 49.

17. Dudley P. Bailey Jr., "The History of Banking in Massachusetts, No. 3," *Banker's Magazine*, October 1876.

18. *Congressional Serial Set*.

19. Edward W. Carpenter, *The History of the Town of Amherst, Massachusetts*. Press of Carpenter & Morehouse. 1896. pp. 1–2.

20. *From the Financial Register of the United States*, Volume 2, p. 271.

21. *Documents*, 1839, p. 26.

22. *Approved by the Governor*, March 25, 1845.

23. Some accounts state August 14, 1814.

24. James W. North, *History of Augusta*, Augusta, 1870.

25. *The Public and General Laws of the Commonwealth of Massachusetts from 1807 to 1816*; *Report of the Maine District Banks to the Commonwealth of Massachusetts*, 1820; *Niles' Register*, various; *Maine Resolves*, various; *An abstract of the returns of the directors of the several incorporated banks, within this State, made to the office of the Secretary of State*, January, 1824; *Report of the Commissioners Appointed by the Governor and Council to Examine Banks*, 1829; J.E. Godfrey, *Annals of Bangor*; *Sound Currency*, 1900; John Jay Knox, *A History of Banking in the United States*; Walter W. Chadbourne, *A History of Banking in Maine, 1799–1930*, 1936. Other sources.

26. *Banker's Magazine*, Volume 3, p. 523.

27. *American Masonic Register*, Volume 2, p. 31.

28. John Jay Knox, *The History of Banking*, 1900, p. 330.

29. John Jay Knox, *The History of Banking*, 1900.

30. *Report of the Maine District Banks to the Commonwealth of Massachusetts*.

31. John Jay Knox, *The History of Banking*, 1900, p. 330.

32. *Banker's Magazine*, March 1853.

33. *Banker's Magazine*, January 1857.

34. *Private and Special Statutes of the Commonwealth of Massachusetts*, 1837, p. 40.

35. The *Financial Register*, Volume 1, p. 286.

36. *Banker's Magazine*.

37. *Annual Report of the Secretary of the Treasury on the Condition of the Banks in the United States at the Commencement of the Year 1863*, pp. 41–43.

38. *Boston Directory*, 1856.

39. *Private and Special Statutes of the Commonwealth of Massachusetts*, Volume 9, 1860, p. 103.

40. *Banker's Magazine and Statistical Register*.

41. James A. Haxby.

42. *Banker's Magazine*.

43. *General Laws of Massachusetts*, p. 336.

44. *Niles' Weekly Register*, September 16, 1837.

45. The *Financial Register*, Volume 1, p. 240.

46. The *Financial Register*, Volume 1, p. 255.

47. *Public Documents of Massachusetts*, Issues 7–15, p. 74.

48. *Massachusetts Register*, Issue 86, p. 42.

49. *Niles' Weekly Register*, September 16, 1837.

50. The *Financial Register*, Volume 1, p. 286.

51. The *Financial Register*, Volume 1, p. 285.

52. *Register of Debates in Congress*, p. 34.

53. *Annual Report of the Board of Managers of the American Bible Society*, Volume 1, p. 648.

54. The *Financial Register*, Volume 1, p. 280.

55. *Laws of the Commonwealth of Massachusetts*, Volume 11, p. 578.

56. *Banker's Magazine and Statistical Register*, Volume 9, Part 1, p. 77.

57. *Banker's Magazine*, September 1853.

58. The *Financial Register*, Volume 1, p. 286.

59. The *Financial Register*, Volume 1, pp. 304–309.

60. James A. Haxby.

61. John Jay Knox, *History of Banking*, 1900.

62. *Private and Special Statutes of the Commonwealth of Massachusetts*, Volume 7, p. 41.

63. *Banker's Magazine.*

64. *Banker's Magazine.*

65. The *Financial Register.*

66. The *Financial Register*, Volume 1, p. 267.

67. *Financial Register of United States*, Volume 1, p. 314.

68. *Banker's Magazine*, Volume 14, 1860, p. 285.

69. *Public Documents of Massachusetts*, Issues 8–22, p. 109.

70. *Annual Report of the Commissioners of Savings Banks*, p. 31.

71. *Statement of Loans Made to the United States by Banks within the Same, Since March 1, 1812*, April 13, 1816.

72. William M. Gouge, *The Curse of Paper-Money and Banking*, 1833, pp. 117–119, from a report made to the State Senate, January 25, 1830.

73. William M. Gouge, *The Curse of Paper-Money and Banking*, 1833, pp. 117–119, from a report made to the State Senate, January 25, 1830.

74. Walter W. Chadbourne, *A History of Banking in Maine, 1799–1930*, 1936.

75. *Public Documents of Massachusetts*, Issues 7–15, pp. 15, 105.

76. *Banker's Magazine and Statistical Register*, Volume 8, Part 2, p. 681.

77. The *Financial Register*, Volume 1, p. 255.

78. *Public Documents of Massachusetts*, Issues 7–15, pp. 15, 105.

79. *Maine Resolves*, 1821, Chapter 84.

80. $3.00 banknote issued by the Charlestown Bank. Serial 1323, plate C. Ink on paper by New England Bank Note Co., [2 June 1830]. Original note from Paper Currency: Obsolete Bank Notes: Massachusetts: Charlestown. Massachusetts Historical Society.

81. *Precedents of Indictments and Pleas*, p. 291.

82. *Report of the Maine District Banks to the Commonwealth of Massachusetts*, 1821.

83. Walter W. Chadbourne, *A History of Banking in Maine, 1799–1930*, 1936.

84. *Acts and Resolves Passed by the General Court of Massachusetts*, p. 411.

85. *Niles' Weekly Register,* Volume 22, p. 245.

Glossary

back—the paper money equivalent of "reverse" used for coins. The front side of a note is called the face.

bank—in the present context, a business set up under a state or federal (e.g. Bank of the United States) charter to engage in the business of receiving and disbursing funds, making loans, issuing paper money, and engaging in related activities.

bank note—a small, rectangular piece of paper money $1 face value or higher issued by a state-chartered bank. Imprinted with a denomination or value and the name/location of the issuing bank. Intended for use in commercial transactions. *Synonyms*: bill, note, bank bill.

bank-note reporter—commercial booklet or publication sold at a premium to bankers, merchants, etc., listing whether banks were solvent or not, descriptions of their notes, and the discounts at which their paper currency traded with exchange brokers and in commerce. *Synonym*: counterfeit detector.

bill—see *bank note*.

blue pup—nickname for a bank that later became insolvent or a circulating note issued by a bank that would not redeem their bills at par. *Synonyms*: owl, red dog.

burin—small, sharp, steel tool, often with a wooden handle, used to carefully engrave on a copper or steel plate. A famous engraving tool.

Canada green—see *Patent green tint*.

capital of a bank—the amount of money authorized by a state charter to be paid in by shareholders and provide funds for a bank's operation.

cashier—in a small bank, the chief operating officer, sometimes the only employee, who opened and closed the bank, signed and supervised the issuance of currency, made loans (often subject to the approval of others), and conducted the business of the bank. The highest-salaried employee. In a large bank, the officer in charge of funds, receipts, and payments, the keeper of bank records.

certified note—a note graded and placed in a sealed holder by a commercial grading service.

charter—operating authorization given by a state legislature to permit a company to engage in banking.

charter expiration—charters were sometimes given to banks for a specific term, such as 20 years, after which a renewal could be applied for. In other instances, a corporation was dissolved and the same people obtained a new charter to continue in business.

circulation of a bank—the total face-value of a given bank's bills in commercial circulation (not including notes held in the bank's vault or not yet issued).

clearing house—a bank or organization that took in bills from various sources and sent them to member banks for exchange or redemption.

counter—technical name for the part of a note showing the denomination in a separate vignette, such as 5, 10, 20, etc., or as a Roman numeral, V, X, M, etc. Some counters are very ornate.

counterfeit—a bill in imitation of an original design but printed from false plates by someone not authorized to do so.

counterfeit detector—see *bank-note reporter*. Often spelled "detecter" in the mid-19th century.

country bank—a bank located in a town or village, not a city or metropolitan area. Sometimes bills of country banks traded at a discount in comparison to banks with large capital located in cities.

cycloidal configuration—latticework, usually printed in color, with arcs and inscriptions said to deter counterfeiting. Also referred to as the "cycloidal" or "kaleidograph counter". Term used by the National Bank Note Company, which utilized James McDonough's patent of March 23, 1860, in which an engraving combined the name of the issuer, the denomination, and geometric, cycloidal, rosette work into a product to prevent alteration or counterfeiting of bank notes.

cylinder die—see *transfer roll*.

date on a note—the time that a note or series of notes was issued. Sometimes a partial date such as 18__ was given, after which the year, month, and day would be added in ink. In other instances a full date was given, such as Jany. 1, 1853, representing the date of a certain series or design. Months were usually abbreviated. Notes with such a printed date could be used for a long time afterward.

denomination—the face or stated value printed on a bill, this being the amount for which the bill could be redeemed in specie or exchanged for other bills. Popular denominations of bills in use in commerce included $1, $2, $3, $5, $10, $20, $50, and $100. Other denominations were occasionally used.

deposit bank—a bank into which the Treasury Department placed federal funds. During the 1830s these were nicknamed "pet banks." Also spelled "deposite."

deuce—numismatic nickname for a $2 bill.

engraver—a skilled artist who, with a burin and other tools, hand-engraved lettering, motifs, and other elements into a printing plate or design element matrix. Various mechanical devices are sometimes used as well.

engraving—intaglio or recessed design elements and lettering engraved by hand or added by the siderographic process to a printing plate. A motif, print, or other reproduction on paper made from an engraved printing plate.

essay—an experimental impression of a partial or completed note printed to test the design or evaluate a concept. The paper money equivalent of a pattern or trial piece coin. French: *essai*.

exchange broker, broker—a person or business specializing in buying and selling current and obsolete paper money and gold and silver coins.

face—the paper money equivalent of "obverse" used for coins. The reverse side of a note is called the back.

free bank—a bank set up under one or another of the state laws enacted from the late 1830s onward whereby any group of people could form a bank providing that assurances were made that sufficient capital would be raised.

geometric lathe—machine that uses gears and linkages to create rosettes, spirals, and other decorative elements on a soft metal plate, which is then hardened and reproduced through siderography for use in creating bank-note printing plates.

grade—designation assigned by numismatists to signify the amount of wear or circulation a note has experienced and its condition today (see chapter 1 for more information). Grading can be expressed by adjectives such as Good, Extremely Fine, and Uncirculated or by abbreviations in combination with numbers from 1 to 70, such as EF-40 or Unc-63 (adapted from the ANA coin grading system).

green tint—see *Patent green tint.*

imprint—printed information added to a bank note, especially the name of an engraver or printer.

ink ball—a porous ball of cloth or other absorbent substance that was charged with ink and then wiped across the face of a printing plate. Superseded by the ink roller.

ink roller—a rubber roller that is partly immersed in a pan or other supply of ink then used to spread the ink across the face of a printing plate.

inked signature—the signature of a bank president or cashier on currency.

launder—often used in a derogatory sense, the cleaning of paper money to enhance its appearance. Careful cleaning, such as to remove grease or grime, can be beneficial but should be done only by experts. In the early 20th century the Treasury Department added several machines to launder soiled paper money, after which the reconditioned notes were again placed into circulation.

legal tender—a bank note that could be used to pay any and all debts except for custom duties. Most notes of state-chartered banks were accepted at par only within the region of issue.

margin—the blank area or white strip beyond the design or printed information at the border of a note. Wide margins are preferred to narrow ones. There are no general rules.

microprint, microprinting—nearly microscopic-size lettering added to a note, such as on Perkins Patent Stereotype Plate notes and related formats.

notaphily—originated by Kenneth R. Lake as a proposal to give a name to the study and appreciation of paper money. Originally found in Yasha Beresiner's "An Introduction to Paper Money," *The Numismatist*, March 1979.

note—see *bank note.*

obverse—see *face.*

overprint—color printing on a note; a design, grill, denomination, or other element intended to defer counterfeiting. Sometimes these were applied before the black section of the note was printed.

owl—nickname for a circulating note issued by a bank that would not redeem them at par or a bank that later became insolvent. Inspired by the worthless bills of the Owl Creek Bank of Mount Vernon, Ohio. *Synonyms*: blue pup, red dog.

panic—an excitement in financial circles caused by unfavorable economic or banking conditions in which holders of bank notes and securities became frightened and rushed to convert paper to gold and silver coins.

par—the value printed on a note.

Patent green tint, green tint, "Canada green"—green imprint, usually called "overprint," of lacy green said to be a deterrent against counterfeiting. Except for paper money sheets that required bronzing, the adding of a green tint was the first printing operation on a blank sheet as reported by S.M. Clark, *Report to the Secretary of the Treasury*, November 26, 1864. As to whether this priority was always followed is not known. The patent was held by Rawdon, Wright, Hatch & Edson, later the American Bank Note Co., having been acquired from a Canadian inventor.

payee—the first person to receive the note when it was issued. This became a nuisance, and many cashiers simply added a short name and used it over and over again. In other instances a name such as Benjamin Franklin or Henry Clay was added to the printing plate.

pet bank—popular nickname for a bank into which the Treasury Department placed federal funds during the second Andrew Jackson administration.

pinhole—in the 19th century it was common practice to stitch several notes together for safekeeping, hiding within a coat's lining, or storing in a small pile. Today, when certain notes are held to the light, tiny holes can be seen.

plate—a rectangle of copper or hardened steel with engraved or otherwise recessed lettering, motifs, and other elements used to print bank notes. Currency of the period under study was often printed four notes to a plate or, if higher denominations, two notes to a plate.

plate letter—a printed letter, often from A to D, signifying the note's position on a four-subject printing plate. In other instances, single plates with various letters were locked into a frame and plate letters were not in any order. If a plate was slightly altered, the plate letter might be given another letter to accompany it, such as Aa, aA, Ab. If a sheet had more than one denomination, each would start anew with A. As examples, a $1-$1-$1-$2 sheet might use A, B, C, A. A four subject sheet of $5 notes would use A, B, C, D.

plate position—the position of a note on a printing plate, sometimes determinable by the plate letter.

post note—a bill imprinted with a statement that it was redeemable at par only at a later specified date.

president—the chairman of the board of directors, presided over board meetings, signed currency. Often engaged in other activities, but visited a bank occasionally. Other times a local person who was on the premises often and made decisions beyond the duties of the cashier.

printer—an individual or firm that prints bank notes using a press, plates, paper, and ink. A printer may or may not have engraving skills. Most if not all printers of bank notes also produced other products such as book plates and decorative prints.

Progressive Proof note—a note printed from a plate which was not completely finished and was absent some lettering, ornaments, or other features. Used to inspect a design as it was being created.

Proof note—a Proof (capitalization optional) note is an impression from a complete or partially complete plate for testing or to illustrate its appearance such as showing to prospective bank clients. Proof notes are usually printed on only one side and show either the front or back. Such Proof notes are highly prized today. Specimen notes are related but were not issued for test purposes. Sometimes printed on ordinary bank-note paper, often on India paper, sometimes on light cardboard or mounted on a thin card. *Synonym*: Proof.

protector—a color overprint or underprint on a note; a design, grill, denomination, or other element intended to defer counterfeiting. *Synonym*: overprint.

rag—nickname for a circulating note that either had no value or was worn to the point of tattering.

ragpicker—nickname in the past for a collector of paper money.

red dog—nickname for a circulating note issued by a bank that would not redeem them at par or a bank that later became insolvent. *Synonyms*: blue pup, owl.

reenter, re-enter—engraving or transfer process whereby original information on a bank-note printing plate is removed and new information is entered in its place. This could permit an old plate to be used for a different bank.

reverse—see *back*.

roll, roller die—see *transfer roll*.

rose machine—a geometric lathe.

run on a bank—see *panic*. Sometimes engineered by profiteers who would encourage a run through rumors of insolvency (which would depreciate the value of a bank's bills), buy up discounted notes, and later redeem them at par as a form of speculation.

safety fund, safety fund bank—a bank chartered with the requirement that it deposit certain of its capital into approved bonds and other securities.

scrip, scrip note—a bill issued by an entity other than a chartered bank, such as a canal, railroad, factory, etc. A bill issued by a bank or other entity with a face value below $1.

security features—aspects of the design or printing of a note intended to deter copying and counterfeiting. In early times, this consisted of minute design elements expertly engraved, as well as printing on special paper. Chapter 7 of volume 1 in this series discusses various methods.

selvage—unused space on a sheet of paper money beyond the normal trim borders of the individual notes.

serial number—a number inked or printed by a numbering machine on a note prior to issuing it. Banks sometimes started serial numbers anew with each day or each month. Serial numbers were kept low by keying them to dates, making them faster to write. For this reason most serial numbers are in the hundreds or low thousands.

sheet of notes, uncut sheet—an uncut group of notes, as printed, usually four subjects with denominations from $1 to $20, usually with more than one denomination per sheet. $50, $100, and higher denominations were printed two to a sheet. Many notes were printed singly in earlier times.

shinplaster—derogatory nickname popular in the early 19th century to denote a scrip note or bank note that had no monetary value, such as an issue of the Hard Times era. Derived from the popular practice of mixing paper sheets and hardener to affix to a person's shins to relieve pain.

siderography, siderographic—the process of engraving a motif, lettering, or other elements on a soft steel plate, then hardening it, after which a cylinder die or transfer roll of soft steel is forcibly rolled into its surface under high pressure in a transfer press, picking up a relief image. The cylinder die is then hardened, placed into a transfer press, and rolled with pressure into a soft steel or copper plate. This transfers the design in recessed form. The plate is then hardened and used to print notes. Lettering, emblems, and other design elements can be added to plates in this manner.

signatures on notes—usually with the cashier's signature in ink at the lower left and the president's at the lower right. Legally a note had no value until signed by both officers.

specie—gold or silver coins.

specie payment—the payment of a gold or silver coin by a bank in exchange for a bank note presented for redemption.

specimen note—a Proof note for examination or display, a plate impression not intended for circulation.

spider press—a rectangular printing press used to make bank notes. The name derives from multiple thin arms extending from the press that are slowly turned by hand to press a sheet of dampened paper into the ink-filled recesses of a printing plate.

surcharge—extra printing or information added to a note after the main printing was finished. *Synonym*: overprint.

suspension, suspension of specie payments—when a bank refuses to redeem its notes in silver or gold coins. This usually happened when a bank had problems or in times of general financial distress. See *run on a bank*.

transfer roll—a hard steel cylinder with a hole at the center for a shaft, on the outside face of which is a raised design, vignette, counter, or other element used in bank-note printing. Transfer rolls are used to imprint a design into a printing plate by the siderographic process. *Synonyms*: cylinder die, roll, roller die.

Unc-Rem—grade designator signifying that an Uncirculated note is an unsigned, undated remainder.

Unc-S&D—grade designator signifying that an Uncirculated note was signed and dated, but never issued.

vignette—an ornamental or illustrative element of a bank note, such as a portrait, allegorical scene, or motif from history. Pronounced "vinn-yet."

wildcat bank—a bank with or without charter that issued paper money with little or no backing. Such banks were often set up in remote locations.

Bibliography

Bailey Jr., Dudley P. "The History of Banking in Massachusetts," *Banker's Magazine*, September and October 1876.

Baker, W.S. *American Engravers and Their Works*. Philadelphia: Gebbie & Barrie, 1875.

Ball, Douglas B. Historical information written for and included in the catalog of the *Abner Reed Sale of United States Paper Money*, NASCA, October 31 to November 2, 1983.

Bank Note Reporter. Iola, Wisconsin: 1990s to date.

Bathe, Greville and Dorothy. *Jacob Perkins: His Inventions, His Times & His Contemporaries*. The Historical Society of Philadelphia, Pennsylvania, 1943.

Berkey, William A. *The Money Question*. The Legal Tender Paper Monetary System of the United States. Grand Rapids, Michigan: Published by the author, 1876.

Blanchard, Julian. "Cycloidal Configurations," *Essay-Proof Journal*, Vol. 20, No. 2 (1963) through Vol. 21, No. 2 (1964). Reprint of Ormsby's circa 1862 pamphlet, with new introductory remarks.

Blanchard, Julian. "Waterman Lily Ormsby, 1809–1883, Bank Note Engraver," commencing in the *Essay-Proof Journal*, January 1957.

Bodenhorn, Howard. *State Banking in Early America: A New Economic History*. Oxford and New York: Oxford University Press, 2003.

Boggs, Winthrop S. *Ten Decades Ago 1840–1850: A Study of the Work of Rawdon, Wright, Hatch & Edson of New York City*. American Philatelic Society, 1949.

Bowers, Q. David and David M. Sundman. *The 100 Greatest American Currency Notes*. Atlanta, Georgia: Whitman Publishing LLC, 2005.

Bowers, Q. David. *Obsolete Paper Money Issued by Banks in the United States, 1782–1866*. Atlanta, Georgia: Whitman Publishing LLC, 2006.

Carpenter, Edward W. *The History of the Town of Amherst, Massachusetts*. Press of Carpenter & Morehouse, 1896.

Chaddock, Robert E. *The Safety Fund Banking System in New York 1829–1866*. Washington, D.C.: Government Printing Office, 1910, for the National Monetary Commission. 61st Congress, 2d Session, Senate, Document No. 581.

Cheap Money. New York City, New York: The Century Co., 1892.

Christie's. "Important Early American Bank Notes, 1810–1874" from the Archives of the American Bank Note Company, catalog of the auction sale held September 14 and 15, 1990.

Currier, John J. *History of Newburyport, Mass. 1764–1909*, Volume 2, 1909. Newburyport, Massachusetts: Published by the author, June 25, 1795.

Davis, Andrew McFarland (introduction by). *Colonial Currency Reprints*. 4 volumes. Boston, Massachusetts: The Prince Society, 1910 and 1911.

Davis, Andrew McFarland. "Papers Relating to the Land Bank of 1740." 1910.

Davis, Andrew McFarland. *Currency and Banking in the Province of the Massachusetts Bay*. New York City, New York: The Macmillan Company, 1901.

Dewey, Davis R. *State Banking Before the Civil War*. Washington, D.C.: Government Printing Office, 1910, for the National Monetary Commission. 61st Congress, 2d Session, Senate, Document No. 581.

Dillistin, William H. *Bank Note Reporters and Counterfeit Detectors, 1826–1866*. New York City, New York: American Numismatic Society, 1949. Numismatic Notes and Monographs No. 114.

Doty, Richard. *Pictures from a Distant Country: Seeing America Through Old Paper Money*. Atlanta, Georgia: Whitman Publishing LLC, 2013.

Dunbar, Charles F. *Chapters on the Theory and History of Banking*. New York and London: G.P. Putnam's Sons, 1892.

Dunbar, Seymour. *A History of Transportation in America*. 4 volumes. Indianapolis, Indiana: The Bobbs-Merrill Company, 1915.

Duncombe, Charles. *Duncombe's Free Banking: An Essay on Banking, Currency, Finance, Exchanges, and Political Economy*. Cleveland, Ohio: Sanford & Co., 1841.

Durand, Roger H. *Interesting Notes* series: *About Denominations* (1988), *About History* (1990), *About Indians* (1991), *About Territories* (1992), *About Christmas* (1993), *About Allegorical Representations* (1994), *About Vignettes* (1995), *About Portraits* (1996), *About Vignettes II* (1996), *About Portraits II* (1997), *About Vignettes III* (2001), *About Portraits III* (2004).

Essay-Proof Journal. New York City, New York: The Essay-Proof Society, 1944.

Financial Register of the United States, The. Vol. 1, July 1837 to July 1838. Philadelphia, Pennsylvania: Wirtz & Tatem, 1838.

Glaser, Lynn. *Counterfeiting in America*. New York City, New York: Clarkson N. Potter, Inc., 1968.

Golembe, Carter H. *State Banks and the Development of the West, 1830–1844*. New York City, New York: Arno Press, 1978. Originally presented as the author's thesis, Columbus University, 1952.

Gouge, William M. *The Curse of Paper-Money and Banking; or a Short History of Banking in the United States of America, with an Account of its Ruinous Effects on Landowners, Farmers, Trades, and on All the Illustrious Classes of the Community*. Philadelphia, Pennsylvania, 1833.

Griffiths, William H. *The Story of the American Bank Note Company*. New York City, New York: American Bank Note Company, 1959.

Harris, Elizabeth M. "Sir William Congreve and His Compound-Plate Printing," *United States National Museum Bulletin 252*, Paper 71 in *Contributions from The Museum of History and Technology*, Washington, D.C., Smithsonian Institution Press, 1967.

Haxby, James A. *Standard Catalog of United States Obsolete Bank Notes 1782–1866*. Krause Publications Inc., 1988.

Hessler, Gene. *The Engraver's Line*. Port Clinton, Ohio: BNR Press, 1993.

Hildreth, Richard. *The History of Banks, to Which is Added a Demonstration of the Advantages and Necessity of Free Competition in the World of Banking*. Boston, Massachusetts: Hilliard, Gray & Company, 1837.

Hunter, Dard. *Papermaking: The History and Technique of an Ancient Craft*. New York City, New York: Dover Publications, Inc., 1978. Reprint of 1943 edition by Alfred A. Knopf, Inc.

Kleeberg, John M. (editor). *Money of Pre-Federal America*. New York City, New York: American Numismatic Society, 1992 (programs presented at the Coinage of the Americas Conference, 1991).

Knapp, Samuel L. "Memoir of Jacob Perkins." Published in 1835 and 1836 in *Family Magazine*, New York. Reprinted with extensive added numismatic commentary in *The Colonial Newsletter*, Volume 27, No. 3, November 1987, Serial No. 77.

Knox, John Jay. *History of Banking*. New York City, New York: Bradford Rhodes & Company, 1900. Anthology of Knox's articles and speeches published posthumously.

Lewis, Lawrence Jr. *A History of the Bank of North America, the First Bank Chartered in the United States*. Philadelphia, Pennsylvania: J.B. Lippincott & Co., 1882.

McCabe, Robert. "Waterman Lilly Ormsby and the Continental Bank Note Co.," *Paper Money*, March–April 2001. Includes much information found in the National Archives by Wayne DeCesar, fully credited by McCabe.

McCulloch, Hugh. *Men and Measures of Half a Century*. New York City, New York: Charles Scribner's Sons, 1889.

McKay, George L. *Early American Currency*. New York City, New York: The Typophiles, 1944.

Mossman, Philip L. *Money of the American Colonies and Confederation: A Numismatic, Economic & Historical Correlation*. New York City, New York: American Numismatic Society, 1993. Magisterial study of early money in America, emphasizing coins, but with a chapter on paper money.

Newman, Eric P. *Early Paper Money of America*. 4th edition. Iola, Wisconsin: Krause Publications, 1997.

Niles' Register. Various issues of *Niles' Weekly Register* 1811 to 1837, title change to *Niles' National Register*, September 2, 1837, continuing to 1849. Baltimore, Maryland, briefly Washington, D.C.

Numismatic Scrapbook Magazine. Hewitt Brothers and Sidney Printing and Publishing Co., 1935–1966.

Numismatist, The. *Journal of the American Numismatic Association*; established by Dr. George F. Heath in 1888.

O'Brien, Donald C. "Abner Reed: A Connecticut Engraver." *The Connecticut Historical Society Bulletin*, Volume 44, No. 1. Hartford, Connecticut, January 1979.

Ormsby, W.L. *Bank Note Engraving*. New York City, New York: Published by the author, 1852.

Ormsby, W.L. *Cycloidal Configurations, or the Harvest of Counterfeiters, Containing Matter of the Highest Importance concerning Paper Money, also Explaining the Unit System of Bank Note Engraving*. New York City, New York: Published by the author, 1862.

Paper Money. *Journal of the Society of Paper Money Collectors*: 1960s to date.

Peyton, George. *How to Detect Counterfeit Bank Notes; or, an Illustrated Treatise on the Detection of Counterfeit, Altered, and Spurious Bank Notes, with Original Bank Note Plates and designs, by Rawdon, Wright, Hatch & Edson, Bank Note Engravers, of New-York, the Whole Forming an Unerring Guide, by which Every Person Can, on Examination, Detect Spurious Bank Notes of Every Description, No Matter How Well Executed They May Appear*. New York City, New York: Published by the author, 1856.

Raguet, Condy. *A Treatise on Currency & Banking*. 2nd edition. Philadelphia, Pennsylvania: Grigg & Elliot, 1840.

Rice, Foster Wild. "Antecedents of the American Bank Note Company of 1858," *The Essay-Proof Journal*, Fall 1961.

Scott, Kenneth. *Counterfeiting in Colonial America*. New York City, New York: Oxford University Press, 1957.

Sears, Louis Martin. *Jefferson and the Embargo*. Durham, North Carolina: Duke University Press, 1927.

Stauffer, David McNelly. *American Engravers Upon Copper and Steel*. New York City, New York: The Grolier Club of the City of New York, 1907.

The *Medley*. New Bedford, July 24, 1795.

Tomasko, Mark D. *The Feel of Steel: The Art and History of Bank-Note Engraving in the United States*. 2nd edition. New York City, New York: American Numismatic Society, 2012.

Trumbull, J. Hammond. *The first essays at banking and first paper-money in New-England: from the report of the council of the American Antiquarian society, presented at the annual meeting held in Worcester October 21, 1884*. Worcester: [s.n.]. 1864.

White, Horace. *Money and Banking*. Boston and London: Ginn & Company, 1896.

Whitney, D.R. *The Suffolk Bank*. 1878. Kessinger Publishing, 2010.

About the Author

Q. David Bowers became a professional numismatist as a teenager in 1953, later (1960) earning a B.A. in Finance from Pennsylvania State University, which in 1976 bestowed its Distinguished Alumnus Award on him. He served as president of the Professional Numismatists Guild from 1977 to 1979 and president of the American Numismatic Association from 1983 to 1985. He is a recipient of the Founders Award and Farran Zerbe Award, the highest honors of the PNG and the ANA. He is the author of more than 50 books, including many on paper money, and has received more honors from the Numismatic Literary Guild than has any other person. His column, "The Joys of Collecting," has been a feature of *Coin World* since 1961 and is the longest-running column by any author in the history of numismatics. He may be contacted at P.O. Box 539, Wolfeboro Falls, NH 03896 or by e-mail at qdbarchive@metrocast.net.

About the Foreword Writer

A graduate of Syracuse University, Anne E. Bentley has been with the Massachusetts Historical Society since 1973, first as conservator of manuscripts, then as curator of the art collection. Since 1984 she has been responsible for the Society's numismatic collection. Ms. Bentley has authored papers on the 1776 Massachusetts Pine Tree copper penny and a copper Columbia-Washington medal given to the MHS in 1791 by merchant Joseph Barrell. Along with John W. Adams, she co-wrote *Comitia Americana and Related Medals: Underappreciated Monuments to our Heritage*, and she also contributed to Adams's book, written with Fernando Chao (h), *Medallic Portraits of Admiral Vernon: Medals Sometimes Lie.*

About the State Editor

C. John Ferreri is one of America's most accomplished collectors and researchers in the field of obsolete paper money, having specialized in the series for more than 40 years. In addition he has presented many programs on currency, especially for New England clubs and other organizations. His research has been important in the creation of several specialized texts on the subject.

General Index

Index to Banks, by State

Massachusetts, Book 1

Abington through Greenfield

Found in Massachusetts, Book 2
Hallowell through Yarmouth

Haxby-to-Whitman Numbers
Cross-Reference and Index
Massachusetts, Book 1
Abington through Greenfield

Found in Massachusetts, Book 2
Hallowell through Yarmouth